The
Cartridge Collection

From The Pen Of Ken

By

Ken J. Rutterford

Published 2017 by arima publishing

www.arimapublishing.com

ISBN 978 1 84549 716 3

© Ken J Rutterford 2017

All rights reserved

This book is copyright. Subject to statutory exception and to provisions of relevant collective licensing agreements, no part of this publication may be reproduced, stored in a retrieval system, or transmitted in any form or by any means, without the prior written permission of the author.

Printed and bound in the United Kingdom

This book is sold subject to the conditions that it shall not, by way of trade or otherwise, be lent, re-sold, hired out, or otherwise circulated without the publisher's prior consent in any form of binding or cover other than that which it is published and without a similar condition including this condition being imposed on the subsequent purchaser.

arima publishing
ASK House, Northgate Avenue
Bury St Edmunds, Suffolk IP32 6BB
t: (+44) 01284 700321
www.arimapublishing.com

DEDICATION

This to our four children, Linda, Clifford, Robert (Bobby) and Alan. They lost their mother Daphne a few years back and they are now in the age group of between 50 and 60. When they were children, they often suffered from having to wait for long periods in strange places while their dad went off to visit gun shops and reference libraries while searching for old cartridges and the histories of the many firms that once loaded and sold their own cartridges. This was to become the fruits for this book.

INTRODUCTION

My main job in life had been working on over-head telephone plant, its construction and then its maintenance. At the ending of the year 1984 I had to take an early retirement due to my health. Now having over thirty years in retirement, arthritis has slowly crept up on me. There was the time when I could enjoy a walk-about with a gun, but not anymore. I have enjoyed two hobbies, well three if you count photography. My main two were old aircraft, especially those of deHavilland manufacture. The other one was collecting old shotgun cartridges and the histories of those firms that had made and marketed them. Now in my late eighties, I find that I can sit far better than what I can stand. This has also been true now for a good number of years. In order to keep my brain active, I have taken to producing art work. On considering my two hobbies, then the question came, what should I draw. As far too many people have drawn aircraft, I then decided on making my subject old shotgun cartridges. Many of these I already had in my collection. By drawing them I was also keeping a record of some of my own cartridge collection. That is how so many of the drawings in this book came in to being.

From then on I found that some of the more decorated cartridges would become a challenge for me to add to into my collection of cartridge drawings. Some of these then got me drawing a few of those that were more modern. As my drawings of cartridges increased in its numbers, it then became a collection in its own right. So now I was looking for ways in which to add additional rare cartridges into my drawing collection. I was then able to do this with thanks to so many other kind people, most of them being other cartridge collectors. Drawing of these cartridges has now been over a period in time which must well be over forty years. There has been so many of you kind people that have loaned me cartridges, or have let me take photographs from items in your collections, that I am not able to give any names. To do so, I know that I would leave a lot of names out. For this reason, I am not doing this in this book. All the same, if you are one of those persons that have helped me, then I here thank you very much. In so doing, you have contributed to the recording of the histories of shotgun cartridges. In order to be able to draw cartridges from photographs, I have had to stand a half a dozen cartridges in a row. I then had to take six or seven photographs of them by turning them around a little for each shot of the camera. I then took another shot of all the stampings and then another of the over-shot cards. Now some of you may have thought, I let him photograph my cartridges, but he has never drawn them. The reason for this is because not all of the photographs have come out clear enough for me to be able to use. I have to have a full set of drawings that are clear enough to be able to work from. If one of the photos fails in the set that were taken, then I am unable to use them. I remember going to one cartridge collectors meeting and taking many sets of photographs. Due to the poor conditions for photography, when I got home I then found out to my disappointment that I could not use any of them. Photographing sets of cartridges has generally worked out at about one or two photos for each cartridge drawn. I also needed the firms names and addresses to use for the headings.

Each drawing is an individual. Once made, I then stuck these drawings on to cards and filed them away so that I could add to them alphabetically. Each drawing I have given it a number starting with the letters DN. These letter just stood for, Drawing Number. They do not always run continuously, but rather in blocks of a numbering. This is due to several reasons. Wartime aircraft serial numbers to aircraft were a little bit like this. They would leave blocks of numbering out, but this was just to make the enemy think that we had more aircraft than what we had. In other words, it was propaganda. In my case, I started off my numbering with number one, but over a period of time things got a little out of hand. In order not to use a same number twice over, I have jumped on a bit and started renumbering a fresh. In a few rare cases I have accidentally drawn the same cartridge twice. I then have given it a new number, but once that I had discovered my mistake, that number was then cancelled out. I hope that I have not used a number twice over. If I have, then I expect that some person will find my mistake and pull me up over it.

Now I could not have made all of these drawings without the use of photo-copy machines. This being so, I must not knock them. At the beginning, I would go to a firm and use one of their machines. In those days they were far from being perfect. They would reduce down to their lowest at sixty-four percent. I was later to discover that some had reduced much lower and other much higher. The worst thing that I later discovered was that many of my drawings had been reduced and were way out of square. Place several of these drawings on a sheet of paper and they will not line up neatly. I found that the affect was like looking at a column of military all marching out of step. There was a time when I used a few of these drawings in pamphlets which I produced and sold around the cartridge clubs, but they looked awful. Due to this I felt that I could not use them altogether in a book.

My first drawings that I made I called them, Series One drawings. They were larger due to the cartridge tops and bottoms being drawn at double their size. This was because I could not get them reduced as low as fifty percent. This size of drawings I could only get four on to one normal sheet of paper. I then started producing my Series Two drawings. On these, the cartridge tops and bottoms I could then get reduced to their normal size. These drawings I could then get six of them on to a normal sheet of paper. Many of these Series Two drawings were converts off of my Series One drawings. This out of square situation worried me so much that I then started making my Series Three drawings. In these drawings I left out the boxed sections that I had placed in my Series Two. Due to my age and the time that it would take to bring all of my drawings up to the Series Three standard, I had to forget all about that. You will find that I have also made a few experimental drawings amongst them. Also the odd Provisional Drawing. Often these were made from old cartridge remains that have been found in the countryside. This just so that I can place those firms on record as no known cartridge has so far come to light by them.

I felt that when I leave this world that all of my efforts and drawings should not die along with me. What I needed to do was to get as many of them as what I could all placed together in to one book. I did not relish doing this with so many out of square drawings. I then hit on the idea of removing all of their outer frames and then placing all of the drawings in to ready printed boxes. This I have now done in the plates of this book. It is a compromise. I am far from happy with it, but it has given me the chance to let other people enjoy the fruits of my works and by placing many of these firms and their cartridges down in to history where they will not then be forgotten. Following on from this Introduction there are two pages. These pages are just to illustrate my Series One drawings and my Series Two and Three drawings.

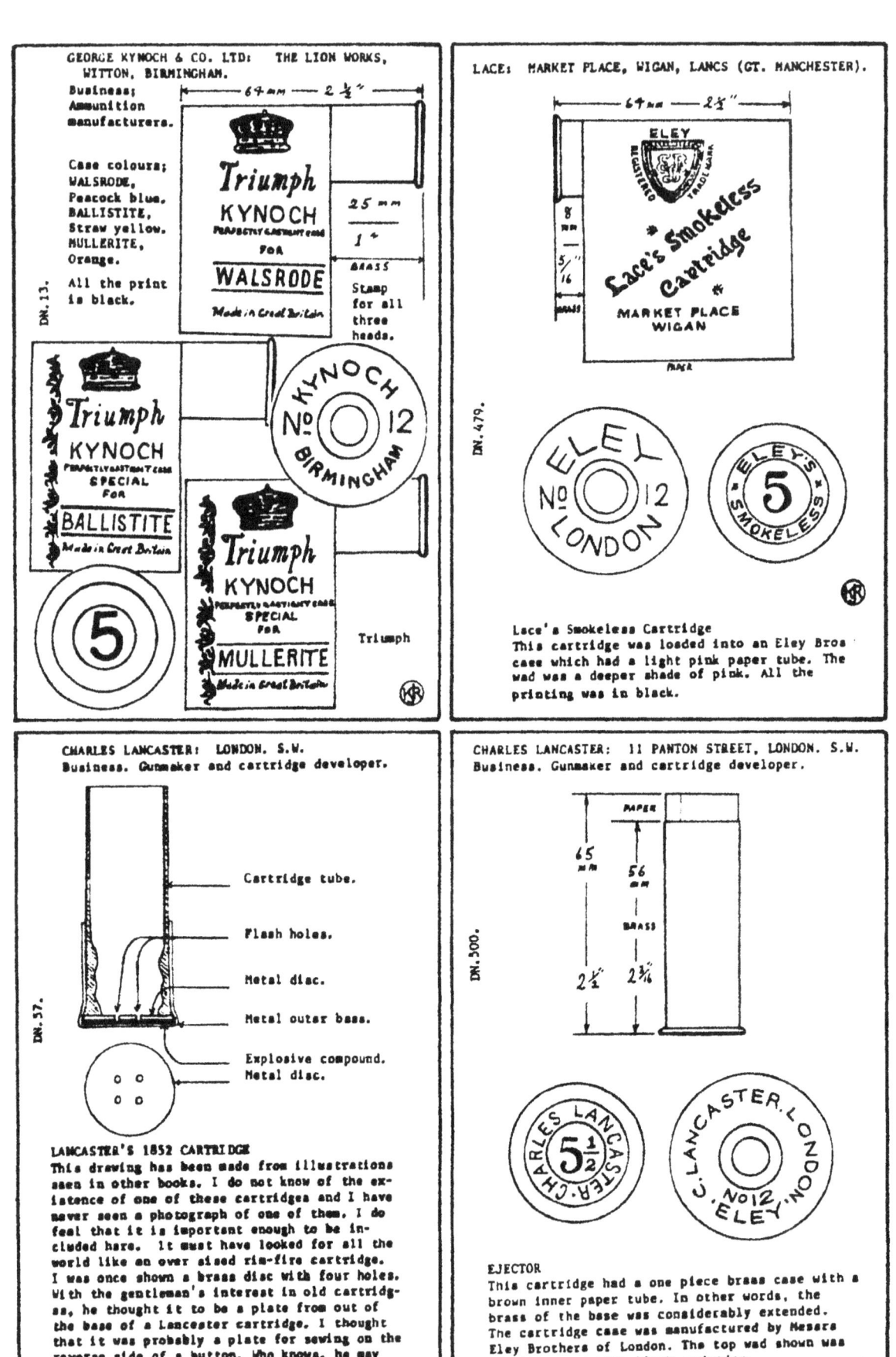

Drawing numbers. 13, 57, 479, 500.
A page of Series One drawings.

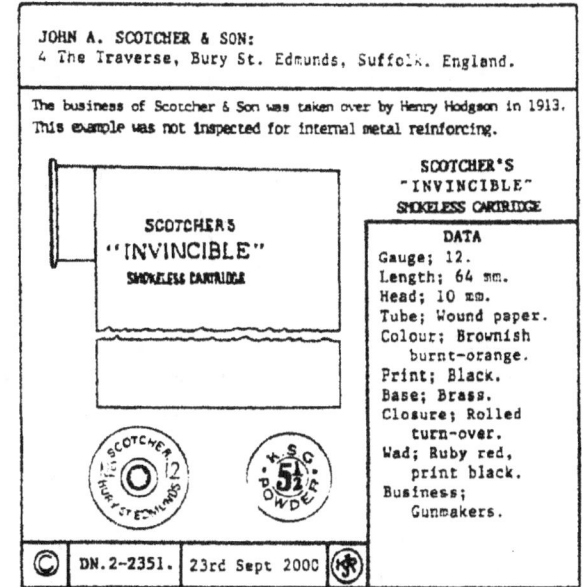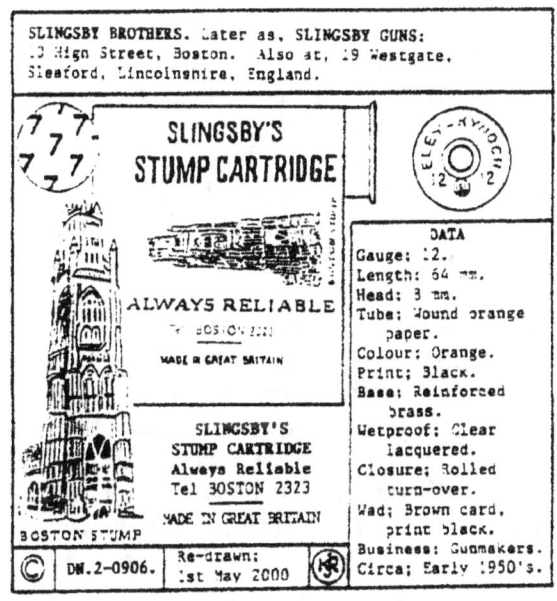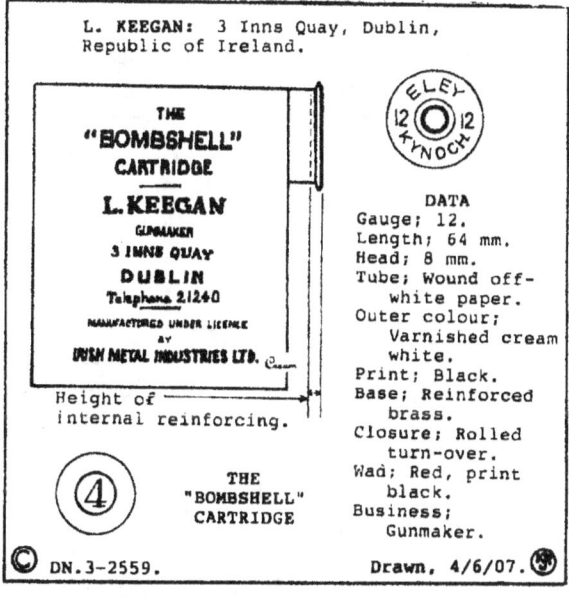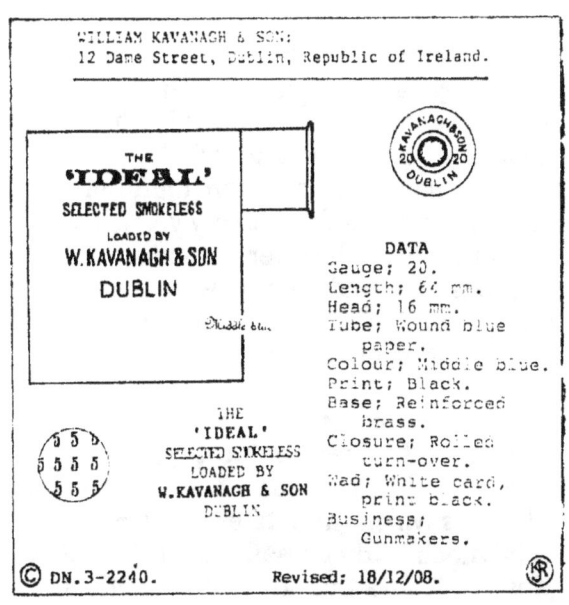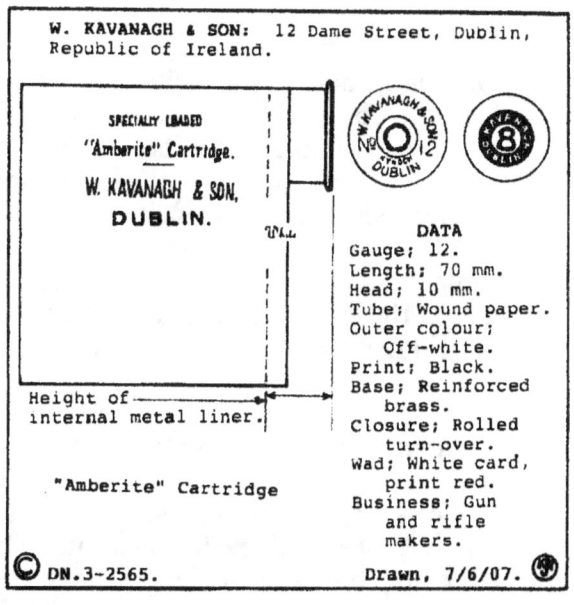

A page of Series Two and Series Three drawings.

THE WITTON FACTORY

Birmingham, England's Witton Factory during its lifetime produced more shotgun cartridges than any other factory in the British Isles. Over this long period of time it underwent several name changes as controlling interests changed hands. Within the plates of drawings in this book I have tried to show the names at the illustrated headings as to what they were at the times that a cartridge was produced. As some of their full titles were rather long, you will find that in some cases I have abbreviated them. Adjacent to each plate number I have given the first three letters to the start of each alphabetical name at the top and the bottom. As Imperial Chemical Industries and Imperial Metal Industries would have had the letters IMP so many times, for these I have shown them as ICI and IMI respectively. Due to the reasons that I have just mentioned, I have considered that a brief history of these cartridge works was needed. For those of you who would like to know more, then I can recommend two books that you should try to get and read. They are, ELEY CARTRIDGES by C. W. Harding and published by Quiller Press. The other is, KYNOCH by Dale J. Hedlund and published by Armory Publications.

This factory in open ground was started by Mr William Pursall around about the year 1862 to manufacture percussion caps and well away from other properties. The firm, Pursall, Phillips & Co had been manufacturing these caps and had had a disastrous explosion killing members of their staff. In order to continue with the making of these percussion caps, this new factory was needed. The manager was Mr George Kynoch. In a year or so hence, George Kynoch then became its owner. A few changes took place and then the firm became known as Kynoch & Co.

From the making of percussion caps, the factory then went on to making rifle ammunition for the military. From then on it started manufacturing shotgun cartridges which it continued to do through the years to come. Also from those early days it marketed cartridge cases for loading as well as ready loaded cartridges. An 1884 advertisement by the firm advertised Kynoch's Patent "Perfect" high brass twelve bore cartridges. By 1897, the firm were advertising paper tube wet-proof cartridges. A Kynoch brochure for 1898 advertised some other of their products, these were, soap, candles, cycles and their Patent Suction Gas Plant Engine. I am not sure as from when, but they also manufactured railway alarm signals that could be placed on the rails for an engine to run over and set off.

Kynoch's continued making shotgun cartridges, these their own brands and brands for other people in their Witton Factory in which they had now named, "The Lion Works". This up until 1914. Due to the Great War, or World War One, as it later became, the firm then went on to a wartime footing. They then made rifle ammunition and shells for the large guns. I do not know if any shotgun ammunition was made for the public during those wartime years. During those many years in which they were marketing their own shotgun ammunition they were in strong competition with other explosives firms. Eley Brothers Ltd of London were their largest rivals. This firm had several properties in the London area with their works in Angel Road, Edmonton, and an advertising address at 254 Gray's Inn Road.

Come the armistice, there was then not the need for so much explosives manufacturing in the country. In the November of 1918, several of the larger firms got together and formed a merger. Some of these, and just to name a few were, Nobel Explosives (not to be confused with Nobel Industries which was a later firm), E.C. Powder, Eley Brothers, Schultze and of course, Kynoch. Other smaller firms joined in later on. This new firm then called itself Explosives Trades Ltd. It used the initials

E.T.L. In two years time it then changed its name again to, Nobel Industries. The reasons that were given was that it had caused a confusion with other explosives firms. It then used the initials N.I. These letters can be seen on some of the head stampings of around that time. It was a bit of a mix-up, as Eley Brothers still continued trading for a while after the merger in their old name. Many of the names from some of the old larger firms were retained to honour them. Just to mention one or two, Bonax, Primax, Grand Prix, Westminster and Yeoman. Cartridge head stamps had the words ELEY NOBEL or KNYOCH NOBEL. As Nobel Indusries, the factory continued until around 1927. By then, all Eley shotgun cartridge manufacture had been long transferred to the Witton Factory.

In 1927, the firm Imperial Chemical Industries obtained the controlling interests. Shotgun cartridge manufacture continued and using many of the existing brand names. It became known as, Imperial Chemical Industries (I.C.I.) Metals Division, Eley-Kynoch Ltd. Or I have seen it displayed as Imperial Chemical Industries Sporting Ammunition, or just as Eley-Kynoch I.C.I. Under the I.C.I. banner, the factory continued producing their own brands of cartridges and selling new cases for loading and loading brands for other people. Like the years before them, they also exported overseas and had some branches in other parts of the British Empire which later became, The Commonwealth. It is worth knowing, not only did the United Kingdom export overseas, but our industries had to compete with many cartridge imports from abroad. Then in 1939 came the Second World War. This time it was not known as the war to end all wars. With this war starting, several brand names got dropped out, Bonax, just to mention one. Up until then, pinfire cartridges had still been made in 12 and 16 bore sizes, often for use in alarm guns. The factory then again went on a war time footing. Not so many shotgun cartridges were then produced, but some were made for military training and use by The Home Guard. After the war, shotgun production got under way again.

The ELEY-KYNOCH with the I.C.I circle stamping ceased in 1964 when Imperial Metal Industries obtained the controlling interests of the factory. Some brand names were retained such as, Grand Prix and Trapshooting. Other changes were star crimp closure and plastic tube cases. The head stamps were then ELEY-KYNOCH 12, or whatever the bore or gauge size was. It was then on the 14th of November 1973 that the firm had its big bang. It was an explosion that killed six of its staff in the loading area. A drill was being used to repair a broken guard on a machine and some loose powder got ignited. All cartridge loadings at the factory ceased until February of the following year. Production got away again, but the firm never fully recovered from the accident. Due to the explosion another firm set up business called, Hawk Best. All manufacturing at Witton then moved to Marchington. Head stampings then became HAWK BEST and later ELEY ELEY.

Stampings that may help you in dating cartridges

ELEY BROS. No 12 LONDON **1875**	E B No 12 LONDON **1885**	No 12 ELEY LONDON **1890**	ELEY No 12 LONDON **1895-1919**
ELEY No 12 GASTIGHT **1900**	ELEY LONDON No 12 GASTIGHT **1910**	KYNOCH No 12 BIRMINGHAM **1895-1919**	KYNOCH No 12 GASTIGHT **1895-1919**
NOBEL-GLASGOW 12 N 12 **1912-1919**	NOBEL No 12 GLASGOW **1910**	NOBEL'S No 12 BALLISTITE **1910**	KYNOCH E.T.L. 12 12 PRIMAX **1919-1920**
KYNOCH E.T.L. No 12 BIRMINGHAM **1919**	ELEY N.I. No 12 LONDON **1920**	NOBEL N.I. No 12 GLASGOW **1920**	ELEY 12 12 NOBEL **1925**
KYNOCH 12 12 NOBEL **1925**	ELEY-KYNOCH 12 ICI 12 **1927-1963**	ELEY-KYNOCH 12 **1963-1978**	ELEY-KYNOCH ICIANZ 12 12 MADE IN AUSTRALIA **1936-1949**
ELEY-KYNOCH 12 12 ICIANZ **1949-1956**	ICI 12 12 ICI **1965-1970**	IMI 12 12 IMI **1971-1978**	ELEY 12 12 ELEY **1979**

The years shown are only approximate of the times that these stampings were in circulation.

THE DRAWINGS EXPLAINED

In my book titled, "Cartridge Drawings Now And Then", I displayed over 50 plates of my drawings. I then gave some explanations to those plates of drawings. As in this book there are over 400 plates of drawings I feel that a few words about these drawings will not come amiss.

To start with, the details shown in a drawing of a cartridge is what was known to me at the time of making the drawing. You will see that in some of the drawings I may have shown positions of internal reinforcing. Much of this I have picked up by running a small magnet over the exterior of the cartridge to be drawn. There have been many times that I have not had that small magnet to hand. This being so, the drawn cartridge may have had internal metal reinforcing, but I have not been able to have shown it in the drawing. Likewise, any cartridges that were drawn from using sets of photographs may also have had internal metals that I have not been able to show. In some of my drawings I may have shown more than one head-stamping. This is because that I have seen that particular round with those stampings. There may have been other stampings used on that illustrated cartridge, but I can only show the items in these drawings that I know about.

Now for a few words on the colours of shotgun cartridges. The description in the drawings of the colours is as I have seen them or have had described to me. It is a known fact that different persons will not always describe a colour as being the same. Many paint manufacturing firms like to give a certain colour a name of their own. Cartridge manufacturers often describe their cartridge brands in the colour names which they have chosen in their price catalogues. Eley-Kynoch I.C.I., just to shorten their name, referred to their Gastight cartridges as being brick red. I cannot recall ever seeing any bricks of that colour. To me the colour was more like the fruits of the horsechestnut tree which as children, we then called conkers. Many of their other colours varied considerably. Their eau-de-nils and greys often went from being very light to being very dark in colour. You will find that in some of my drawings I have used the colours as what the manufacturers have described them as.

There was a time in the mid 1990.s, when I was a member of a United States of America's cartridge club. I was then persuaded to use the American firm, Pantone's Color Formula Guide 1000. This then described the colours more accurately. I obtained their permission and had to deal with a certain lady. This lady was then replaced by a gentleman who then told me I could not do some of the things that I had already done when I was dealing with that lady. I now cannot remember what they were. They were only trivial things, but due to them I stopped using the colours in their color-chart. It was just as well as those in the British Isles could not get any of their color-charts. Looking back to that time, I would have been better off if I had not used them. You may find a reference to the Pantone Color Formula in an odd drawing within this book.

Over the years the majority of printings on case walls had been in black. Occasionally this has been more of a blue-black. Prior to World War Two, some pink, dark green and eau-de-nil cases were printed in a dark or royal blue. This colour was also used on some sixteen gauge blue cases and some buff twenty gauge cases. On the sixteen's the printing had to be a darker colour than the paper tube colours. Back in the late 1920's and possibly in the early 1930's, the Witton Factory tried using silver printings on their sixteen blue cartridge cases, but this did not last for very long. Silver printings sometimes got used on twelve gauge purple paper tube cartridges.

Not all of the paper tubes had the outer colour all the way through them. With an empty case, this can be seen. To draw from a live cartridge and then its tube construction cannot be identified. To explain the colour of some greens I have given them as Spring Green, Summer Green and Winter Green. The Spring being a light green as what the Witton factory came out with in 1939. The Summer being more of a middle green and the Winter being a very dark green. Very early brown cartridges, both pin and centre-fire in the late 1800's had their tubes wound of a very rough textured paper. My description of this colour was cowpat brown as that is what they reminded me of. As some were lighter than others in colour, I could have gone for a wet cowpat, being darker in colour, or a dry cowpat being much lighter in colour. This I did not do, I just left it as Cowpat Brown and that was that.

Below is a sketch to illustrate the way that some of the cartridges have been drawn.

A. indicates that the case wall printings ran up the tube.

B. indicates that the case wall printings ran down the tube.

A. and B. Indicates that I have seen this cartridge that has had its printings by running in both directions. This may have also been true for many of the other drawings, if only I had known about it.

C. and D. This indicates that this cartridge has been seen by me produced in other chamber lengths.

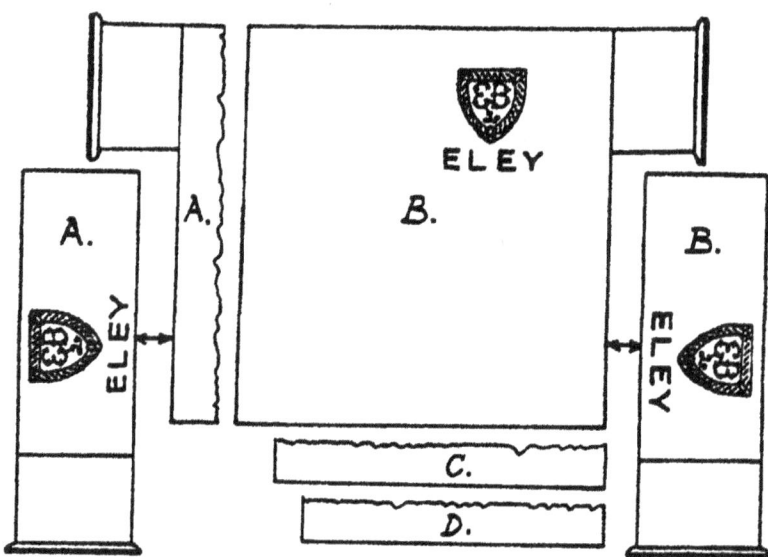

To use this book to satisfaction one should think alphabetically. The majority of the drawings are filed under their second names, the surnames, but not all of them. On following on from the plate numbers, you will find two lots of three letters. The first three letters are the starting of the word that the drawing was filed under. The first letters are for the top left hand drawing and the last are for the bottom right hand drawing. An exception to this ruling are the words, Imperial and Nobel. Imperial has the letters, ICI and IMI standing for, Imperial Chemical Industries and, Imperial Metal Industries. Nobel has the letters, N'EX and N'IN standing for Nobel Explosives Ltd and Nobel Industries. The last illustrated plates in this book are for cartridges where their firms and details are not known. All that it needs for me to say now is, Do please enjoy.

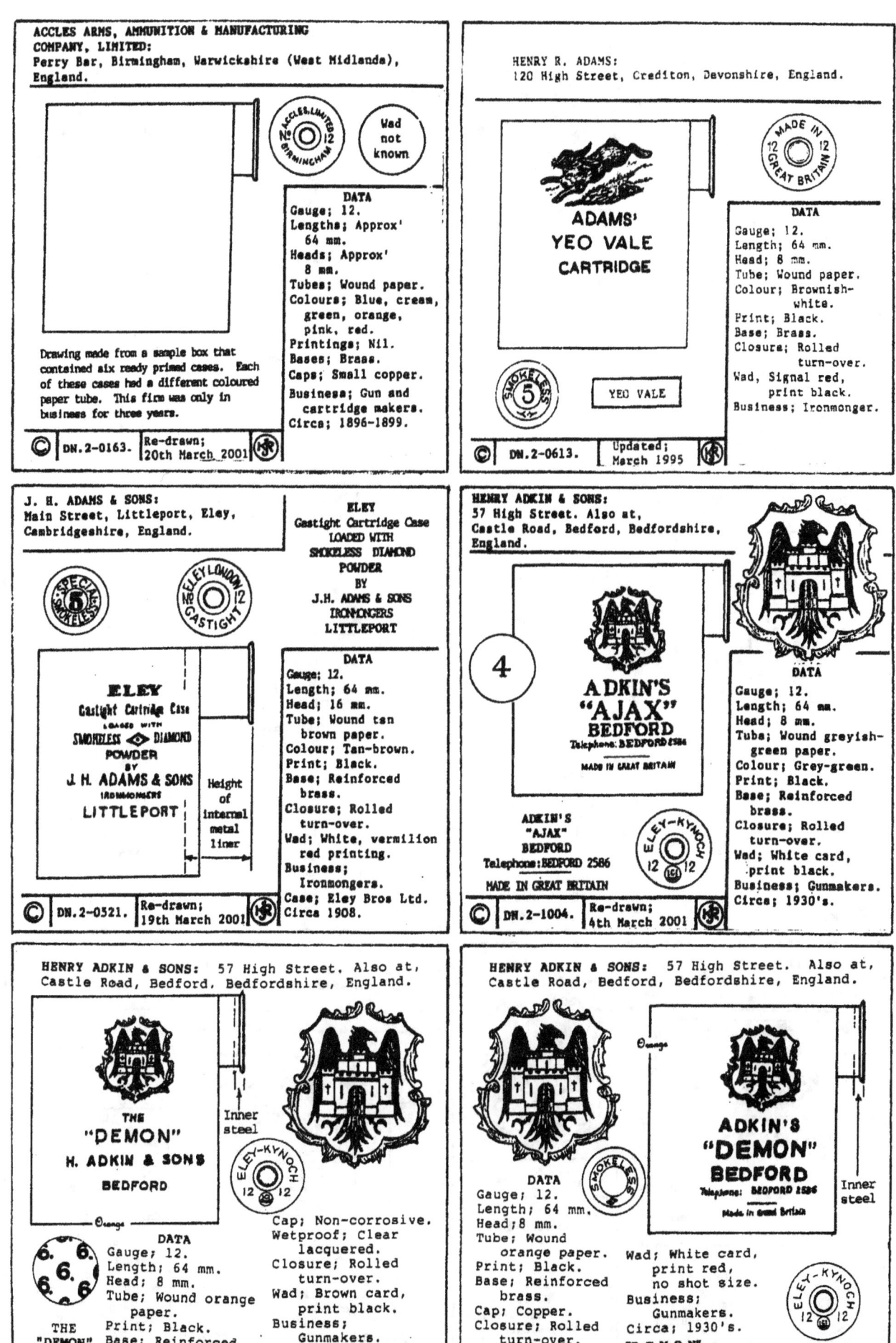

PLATE 1 [ACC - ADK]

HENRY ADKIN & SONS:
57 High Street. Also at, Castle Road, Bedford, Bedfordshire, England.

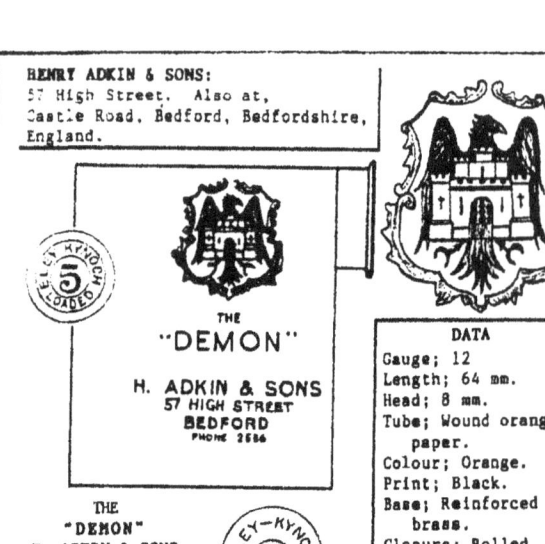

THE "DEMON"
H. ADKIN & SONS
57 HIGH STREET
BEDFORD
PHONE 2586

THE "DEMON"
H. ADKIN & SONS
57 HIGH STREET
BEDFORD
PHONE 2586

DATA
Gauge; 12
Length; 64 mm.
Head; 8 mm.
Tube; Wound orange paper.
Colour; Orange.
Print; Black.
Base; Reinforced brass.
Closure; Rolled turn-over.
Watproof; Lacquered.
Wad; Brown card, print black.
Business; Gunmakers.

© DN.2-1006. Re-drawn; 19th Jan 2001

HENRY ADKIN & SONS:
57 High Street. Also at, Castle Road, Bedford, Bedfordshire, England.

ADKIN & SONS
"DEMON"
BEDFORD.

ADKIN & SONS
"DEMON"
BEDFORD.

DATA
Gauge; 16.
Length; 64 mm.
Head; 7.5 mm.
Tube; Wound maroon paper.
Colour; Red wine maroon.
Print; Silver.
Base; Brass.
Closure; Rolled turn-over.
Wad; Buff, print black.
Business; Gunmakers.
Case; Nobel Explosives. Ltd.

© DN.2-2426. 18th June 2001

HENRY ADKIN & SONS: 57 High Street. Also at, Castle Road, Bedford, Bedfordshire, England.

ADKIN'S
"DEMON"
BEDFORD

ADKIN'S
"DEMOND"
BEDFORD

Both were used. Possibly also others.

DATA
Gauge; 12.
Length; 64 mm.
Head; 8 mm.
Tube; Wound orange paper.
Print; Black.
Head; Reinforced brass.
Cap; Copper.
Closure; Rolled turn-over.
Wad shown; Orange, print black.
Business; Gunmakers.
Circa; Prior 1930.

© DN.3-1003. Drawn, 20/6/08.

HENRY ADKIN & SONS: 57 High Street. Also at, Castle Road, Bedford, Bedfordshire, England.

ADKIN'S
Special Loading
BEDFORD
Telephone: BEDFORD 2586
Made in Great Britain

ADKIN'S
Special Loading
BEDFORD
Telephone: BEDFORD 2586
Made in Great Britain

Height of inner steel liner

DATA
Gauge; 12.
Length; 64 mm.
Head; 16 mm.
Tube; Wound light blue paper.
Print; Black or navy blue.
Base; Reinforced brass.
Cap; Copper.
Closure; Rolled turn-over.
Wad shown; Buff, print black.
Business; Gunmakers.
Circa; 1930's.

© DN.3-2832. Drawn, 20/6/08.

HENRY ADKIN & SONS:
57 High Street, And also at, Castle Road, Bedford, Bedfordshire, England.

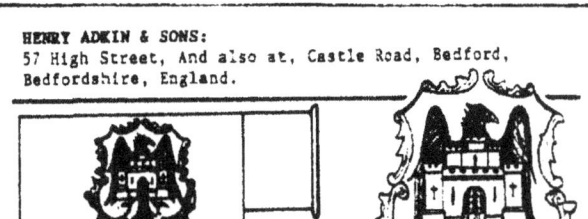

ADKIN'S
"RELIANCE"
BEDFORD
PHONE: BEDFORD 2586
MADE IN GREAT BRITAIN

ADKIN'S
"RELIANCE"
BEDFORD
PHONE: BEDFORD 2586
MADE IN GREAT BRITAIN

Cartridge was not examined for an internal liner.

DATA
Gauge; 12.
Length; 64 mm.
Head; 16 mm.
Tube; Wound red paper.
Colour; Crimson.
Print; Black.
Base; Brass.
Closure; Rolled turn-over.
Wad; Yellow card, print black.
Business; Gunmakers.
Circa; 1930's.

© DN.2-0266. Re-drawn; 12th Jan 2000.

ADLER MARKE: GERMANY:
Firm and address not known to me.

Jagdpatrone
Kornung 4. Adler-Marke,
W. Guttler,
Reichenstein Schlesien

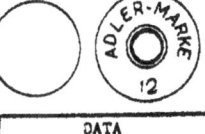

No iron or steel was used in the case construction. The example drawn was in a poor condition. Due to this, some of the case wall wording may be incorrect.
W. Guttler manufactured the gunpowder.

DATA
Gauge; 12.
Length; 65 mm.
Head; 7 mm.
Tube; Wound brown paper.
Colour; Light brown.
Print; Black
Base; Brass.
Closure; Rolled turn-over.
Wad; Off-white card, un-printed.
Origin; Germany.

© DN.2-2074. November 1998

PLATE 2 [ADK – ADL]

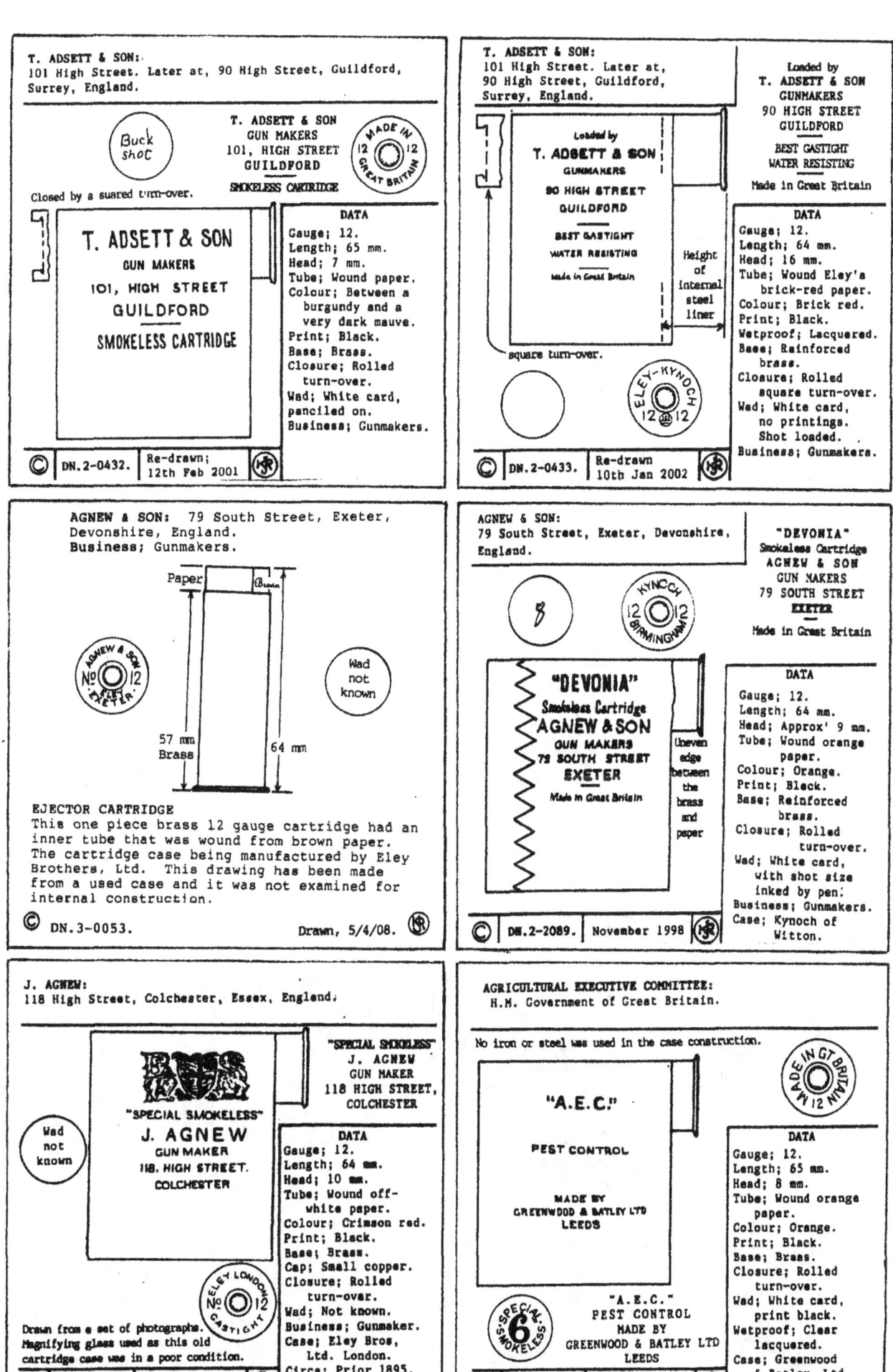

PLATE 3 [ADS - AGR]

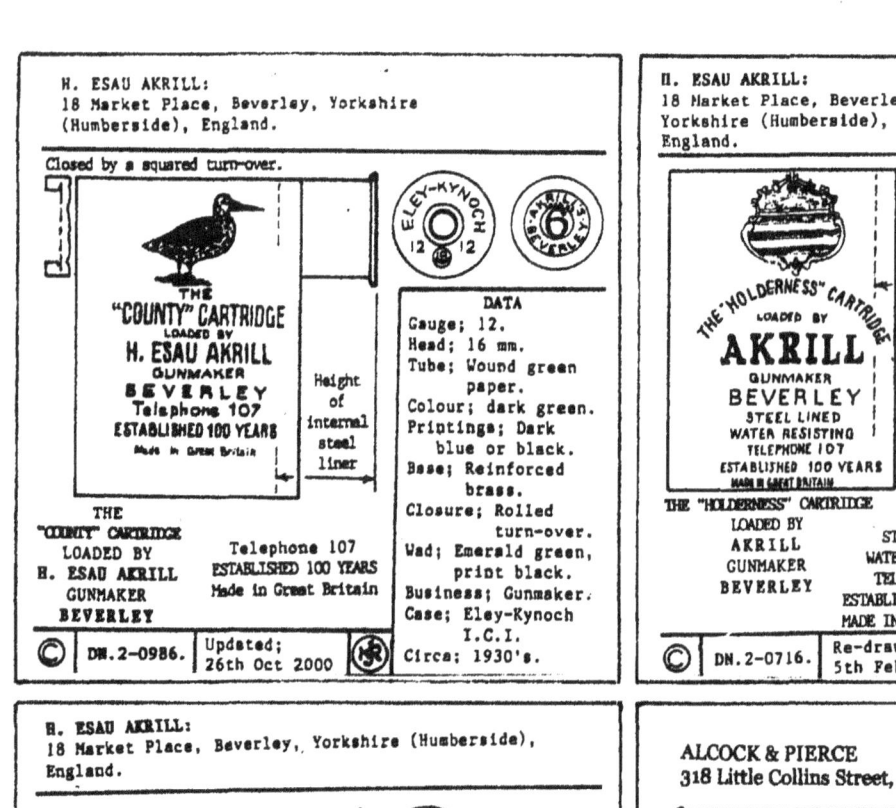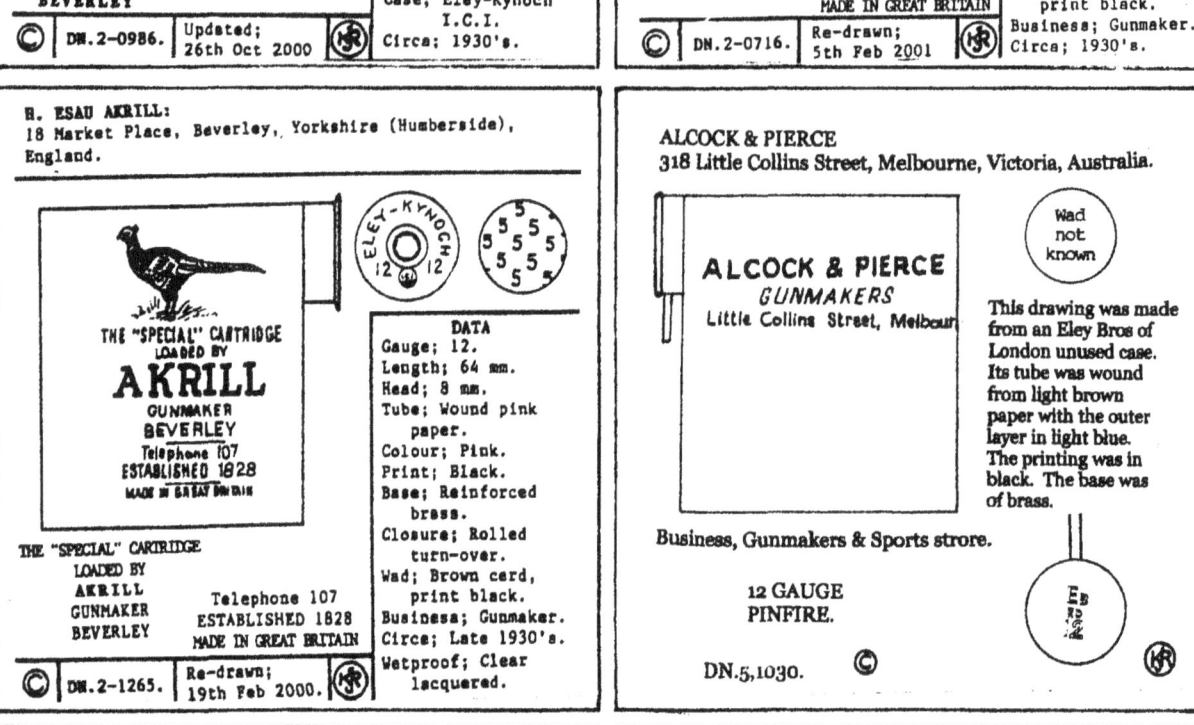

PLATE 4 [AKR - ALC]

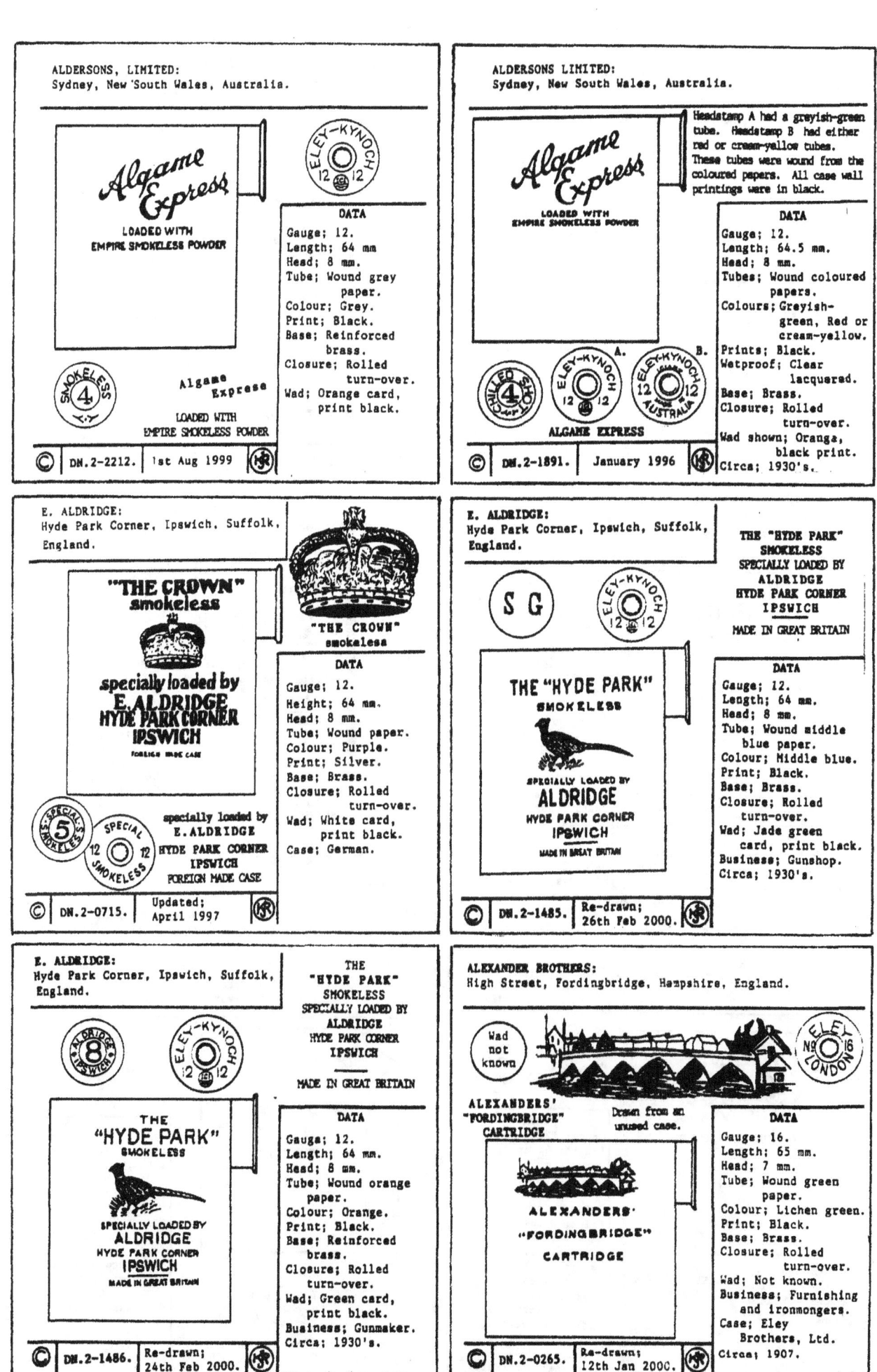

PLATE 5 [ALD - ALE]

W. F. ALEXANDER. Later, ALEXANDER BROTHERS:
High Street, Fordingbridge, Hampshire, England.

Drawing made from a used case.

Wad not known

ALEXANDER'S "FORDINGBRIDGE" CARTRIDGE

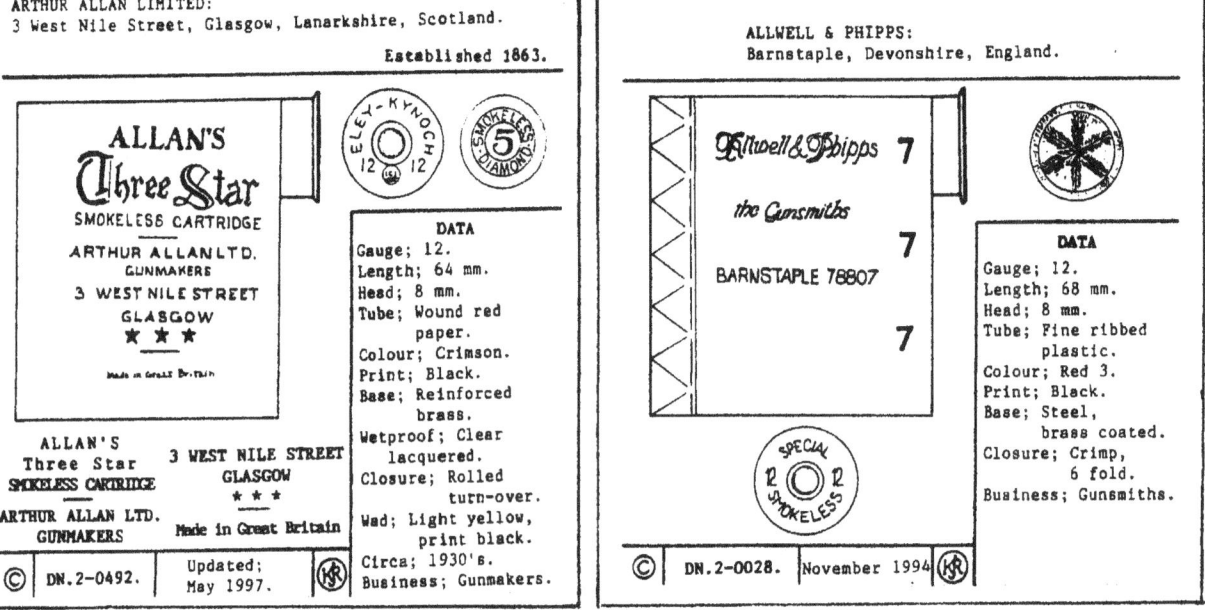

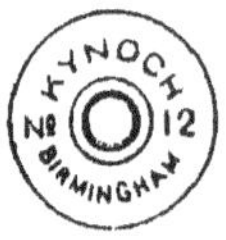

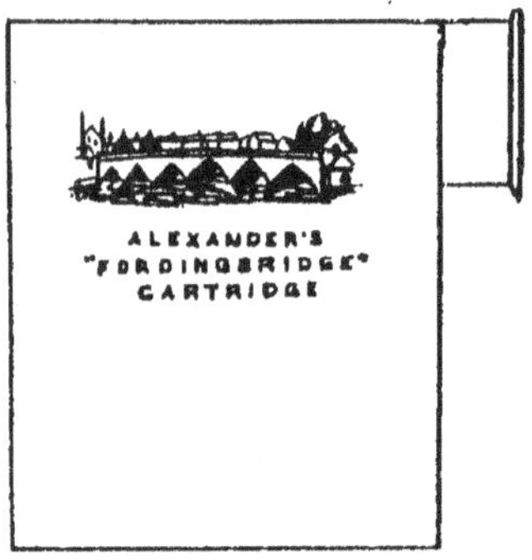

DATA

Gauge; 12.
Length; 64 mm.
Head; 11 mm.
Tube; Wound paper.
Colour; Dark red.
Base; Brass.
Wetproof; Wax impregnated.
Closure; Rolled turn-over.
Wad; Not known.
Business; Ironmongers etc.
Case; Kynoch.

© DN.2-0765. Re-drawn; 31st Jan 2001 KR

ALEXANDER & DUNCAN LIMITED:
Leominster. Also at, Hereford, Herefordshire (Hereford & Worcester), England.

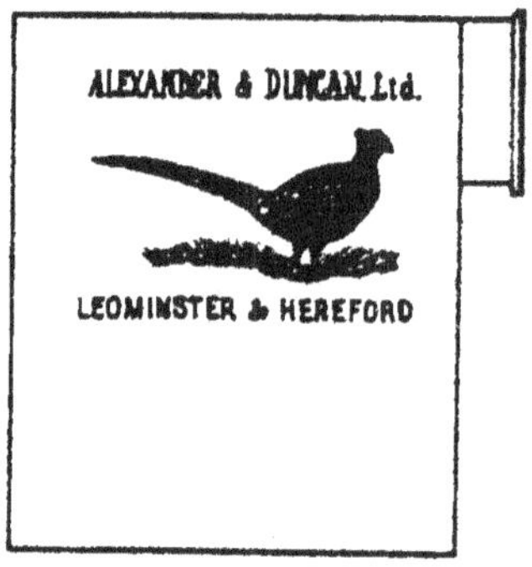

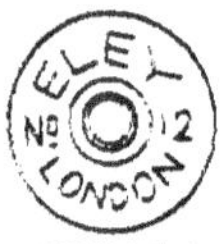

Wad not known

ALEXANDER & DUNCAN, Ltd.
LEOMINSTER & HEREFORD

DATA

Gauge; 12.
Length; 64 mm.
Head; 7.5 mm.
Tube; Wound red paper.
Colour; Red.
Print; Black.
Base; Brass with reinforcing.
Wetproof; Wax impregnated.
Closure; Rolled turn-over.
Case by; Eley Bros Ltd.
Business; Impliment dealers etc.

© DN.2-0431. Updated, February 1996 KR

ARTHUR ALLAN:
144 Trongate, Glasgow, Lanarkshire, Scotland.

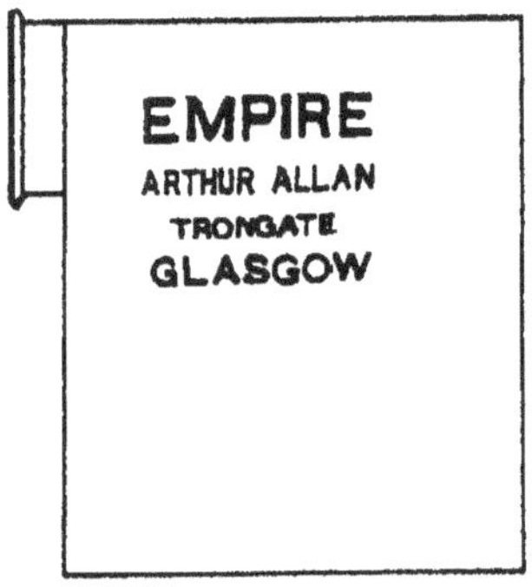

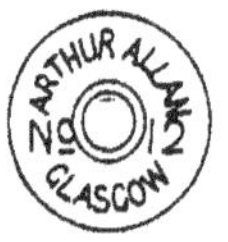

EMPIRE
ARTHUR ALLAN
TRONGATE
GLASGOW

DATA

Gauge; 12.
Length; 64.5 mm.
Head; 7 mm.
Tube; Wound paper.
Colour; Light blue.
PANTONE® 304 U.
Print; Dark blue.
Internal iner; Not known.
Base; Brass.
Closure; Rolled turn-over.
Wad; Not known.
Case; G. Kynoch & Co.
Business; Cutler, ironmonger and gunmaker.

Drawing made from photographs of an unused case.

Wad not known

Arthur ceased trading from Trongate in 1925.

© DN.2-1942. December 1996 KR

ARTHUR ALLAN, LTD: 3 West Nile Street,
Glasgow, Lanarkshire (Strathclyde), Scotland.

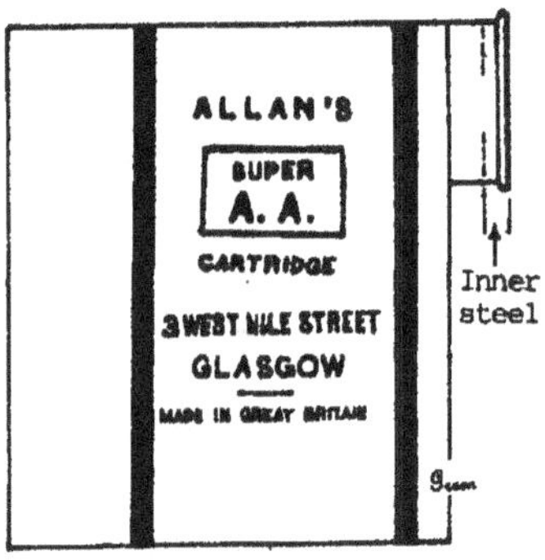

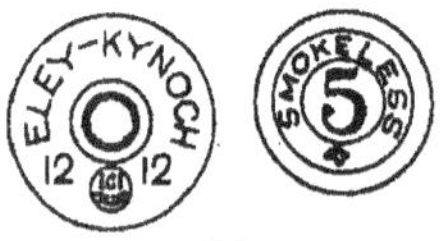

ALLAN'S
SUPER
A.A.
CARTRIDGE
3 WEST NILE STREET
GLASGOW
MADE IN GREAT BRITAIN

DATA

Gauge; 12.
Length; 64 mm.
Head; 8 mm.
Tube; Wound greyish-green paper.
Print; Black.
Base; Reinforced brass.
Cap; Copper.
Closure; Rolled turn-over.
Wad; White card, print red.
Business; Gunmaker.
Circa; 1930's.

© DN.3-2802. Drawn, 21/3/08. KR

ARTHUR ALLAN LIMITED:
3 West Nile Street, Glasgow, Lanarkshire, Scotland.
Established 1863.

DATA

Gauge; 12.
Length; 64 mm.
Head; 8 mm.
Tube; Wound red paper.
Colour; Crimson.
Print; Black.
Base; Reinforced brass.
Wetproof; Clear lacquered.
Closure; Rolled turn-over.
Wad; Light yellow, print black.
Circa; 1930's.
Business; Gunmakers.

ALLAN'S
Three Star
SMOKELESS CARTRIDGE
ARTHUR ALLAN LTD.
GUNMAKERS

3 WEST NILE STREET
GLASGOW
★ ★ ★
Made in Great Britain

© DN.2-0492. Updated; May 1997. KR

ALLWELL & PHIPPS:
Barnstaple, Devonshire, England.

DATA

Gauge; 12.
Length; 68 mm.
Head; 8 mm.
Tube; Fine ribbed plastic.
Colour; Red 3.
Print; Black.
Base; Steel, brass coated.
Closure; Crimp, 6 fold.
Business; Gunsmiths.

© DN.2-0028. November 1994 KR

PLATE 6 [ALE – ALL]

ALTHAM & SON:
Penrith, Cumberland (Cumbria), England.

Wad not known

REGISTERED EB TRADE MARK
ELEY
Patent Gas-Tight
WATER-PROOF
CARTRIDGE CASE
Made in Great Britain
FROM
"PEGAMOID"
BRAND PAPER

Drawing made from a used case.

DATA

Gauge; 12.
Length; 64 mm.
Head; 16 mm.
Tube; Wound brown Pegamoid brand paper.
Print; Black.
Base; Reinforced brass.
Closure; Rolled turn-over.
Wad; Not known.
Case; Eley Bros, Ltd. London.

© DN.2-0651. Re-drawn; 8th Oct 2000 KSR

ALTHAM & SON:
Penrith, Cumberland (Cumbria), England.

"SURE KILL"
SMOKELESS
ALTHAM'S
GUNSMITHS
PENRITH

DATA

Gauge; 12.
Length; 64 mm.
Head; 8 mm.
Tube; Wound paper.
Colour; Brownish buff.
Print; Navy blue.
Base; Brass.
Closure; Rolled turn-over.
Wad; White card, print black.
Case; Kynoch, Ltd. Birmingham.

© DN.2-2433. 21st June 2001 KSR

AMERICAN AMMUNITION COMPANY:
Oak Park & Chicago, Illinois. Also at,
Muscatine, Iowa, United States of America.

DATA

Gauge; 12.
Length; 64 mm.
Head; 8 mm.
Tube; Wound paper.
Colour; Eau-de-nil.
Print; Crimson.
Base; Brass.
Closure; Rolled turn-over.
Wad; White card with red wording and black shot size.
Business, Ammo manufacturers.

"A1"
SMOKELESS

The American Ammunition Company were active for about twelve years. This was somewhere between 1910 and 1922.

© DN.2-1670. Updated, March 1996 KSR

AMERICAN AMMUNITION COMPANY:
Oak Park, Illinois. Also at; Muscatine, Iowa, U.S.A.
Offices at; 40 Dearborn Street, Chicago, Illinois.
Later at, 180 Dearborn Street, Chicago, U.S.A.

Case originally for; CHARLES HELLIS & SONS;
119 Edgware Road, Hyde Park, London. W.2., England.

LOADED BY
CHARLESS HELLIS & SONS
CARTRIDGE LOADING EXPERTS
119 EDGWARE ROAD
Hyde Park, London

Closed by a squared turn-over

This cartridge was loaded in the U.S.A. by The American Ammunition Co.

Height of internal iron liner

DATA

Gauge; 12.
Length; 70 mm.
Head; 8 mm.
Tube; Wound paper.
Colour; Burgundy.
Print; White.
Base; Reinforced brass.
Closure; Rolled.
Wad; White card, printing red. shot size blue-black.
Business; Ammunition manufacturers.
Circa; 1910.

© DN.2-1976. May 1997. KSR

AMMUNITION (NOBEL) PTY, LTD:
Explosives Factory, West Footscray, Victoria, Australia.

DATA

Gauge; 12.
Length; 64 mm.
Head; 7 mm.
Tube; Wound grey paper.
Colour; Bluish-grey.
Print; Black.
Base; Brass (No iron used).
Closure; Rolled turn-over.
Wad shown; White card, print black.
Circa; 1924.
Business; Cartridge loading.

"TOP" BRAND

Imported from England and loaded by Nobel in the old Kynoch works at W. Footscray. This firm became I.C.I.A.N.Z. in 1928. Some cases were sold for home loaders.

© DN.2-1874. December 1995 KSR

F. A. ANDERSON:
49A High Street, East Grinstead, Sussex, England.

THE SACKVILLE CARTRIDGE
F.A.ANDERSON
Telephone 25604

British Loaded

Was also made in 16 and 20 gauge

DATA

Gauge; 12.
Length; 69 mm.
Head; 8 mm.
Tube; Wound brown paper.
Colour; Signal red.
Print; Black.
Base; Steel with brass coating.
Closure; Six fold crimp.
Business: Gunsmith, fishing tackle sports store.
Case; Fiocchi. Italy.

© DN.2-1319 Re-drawn Feb 19th 1999 KSR

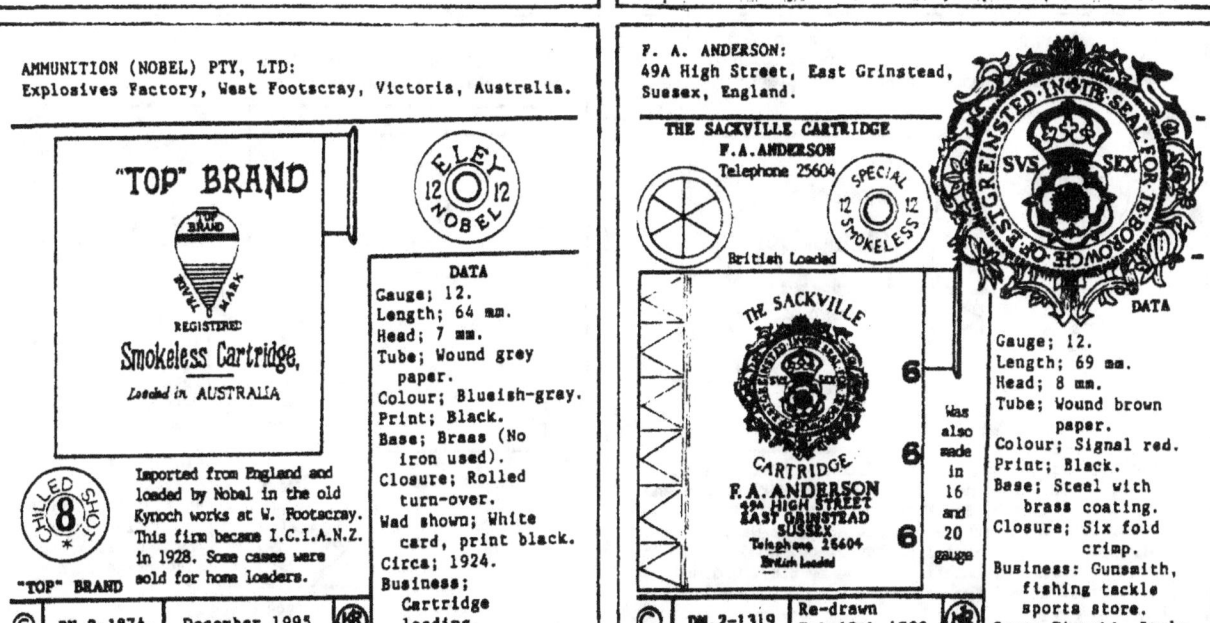

PLATE 7 [ALT - AND]

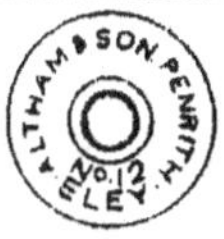

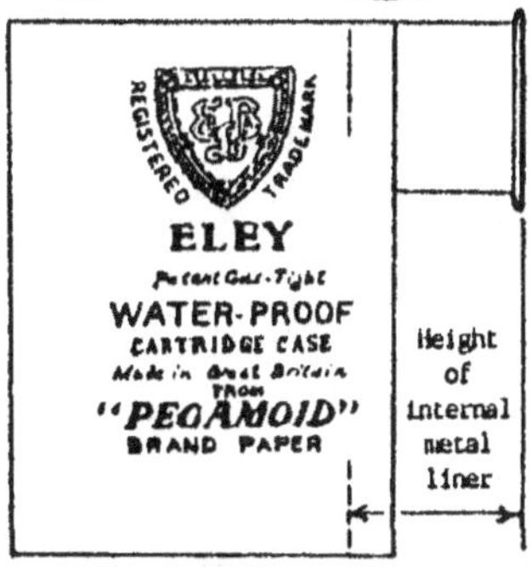

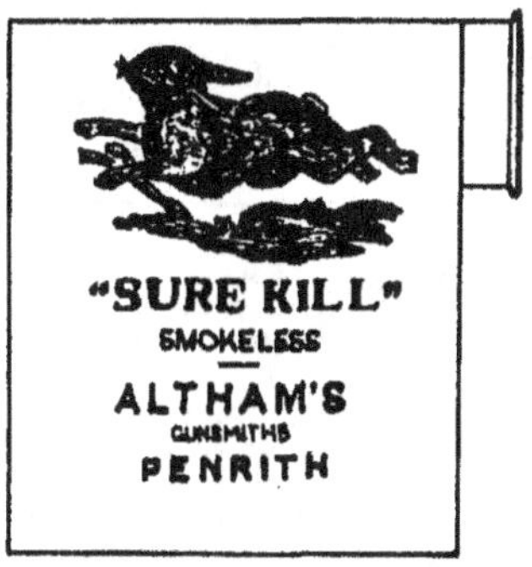

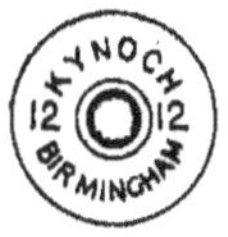

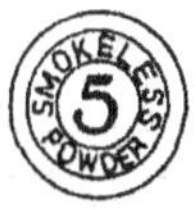

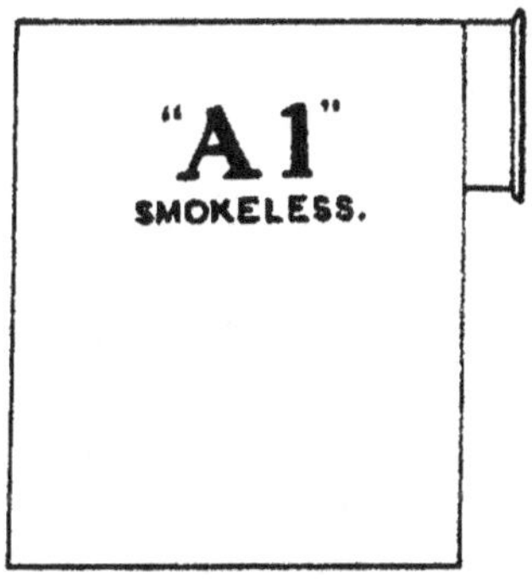

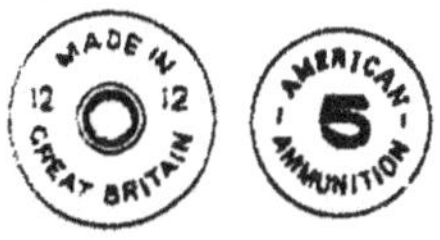

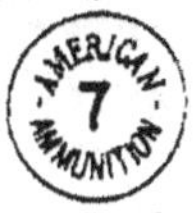

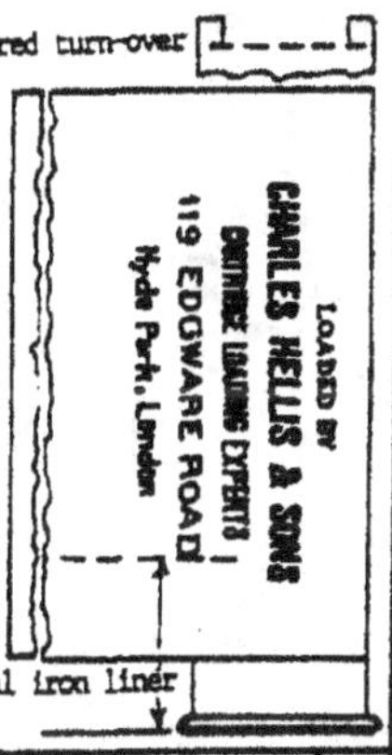

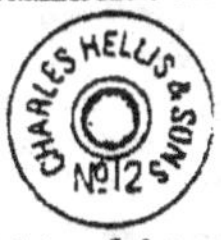

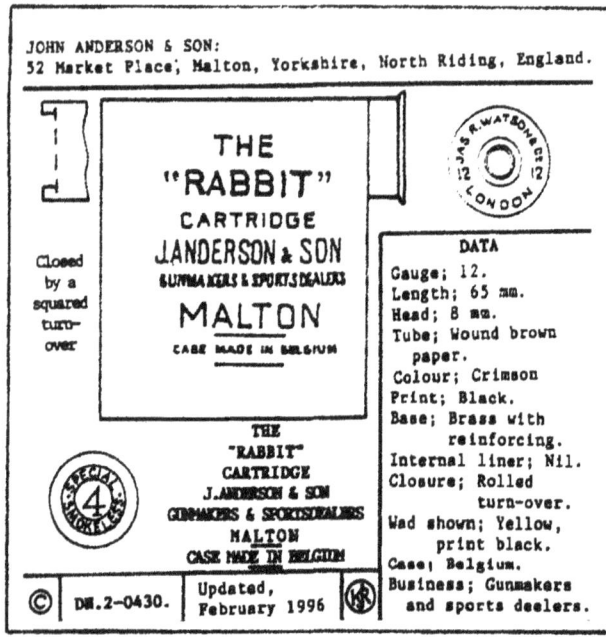
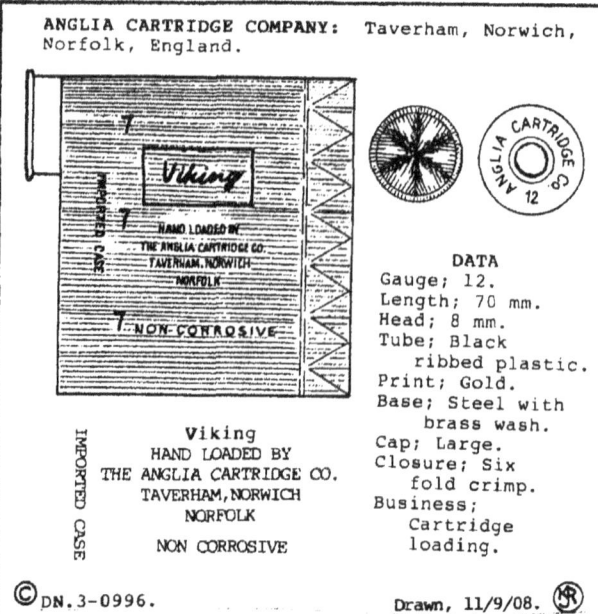
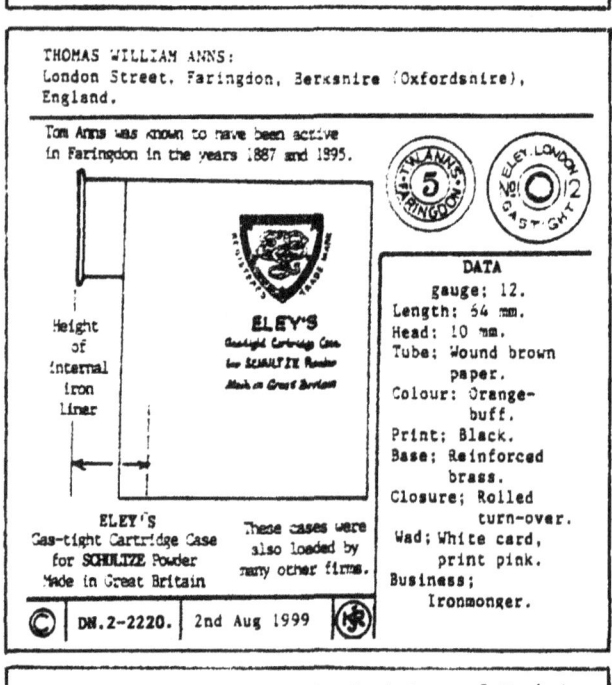
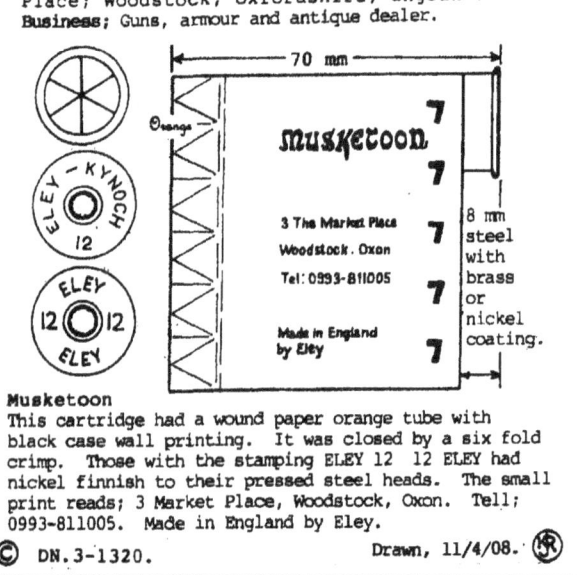
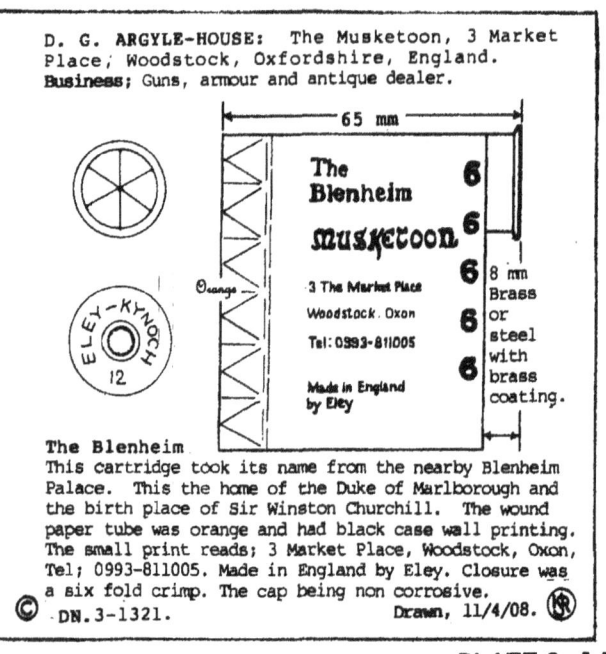
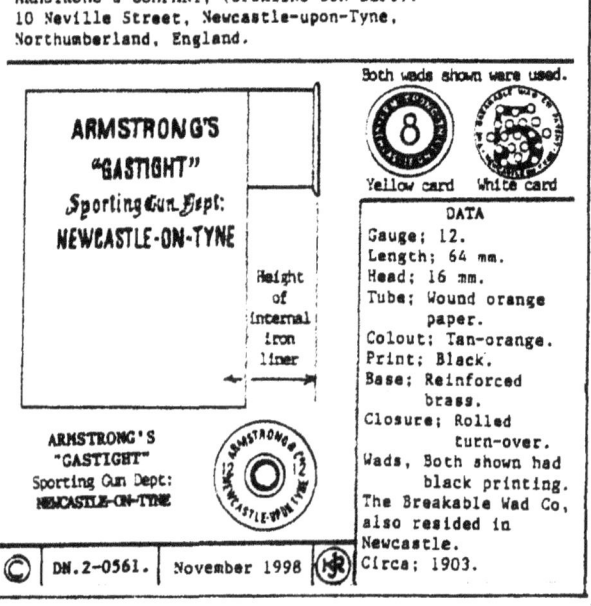

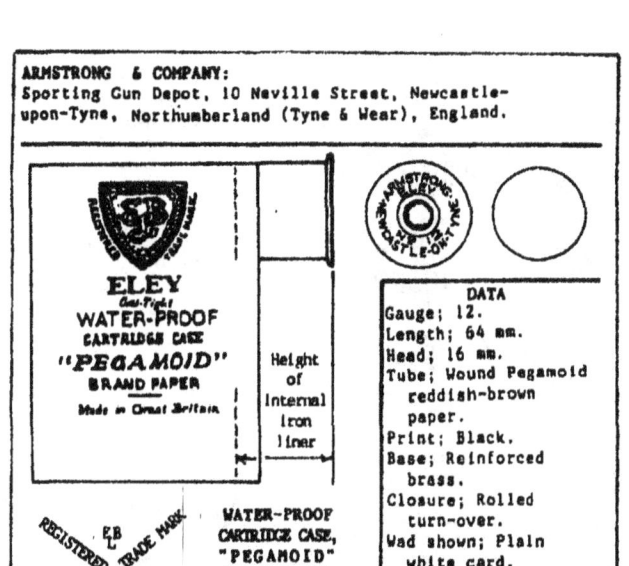
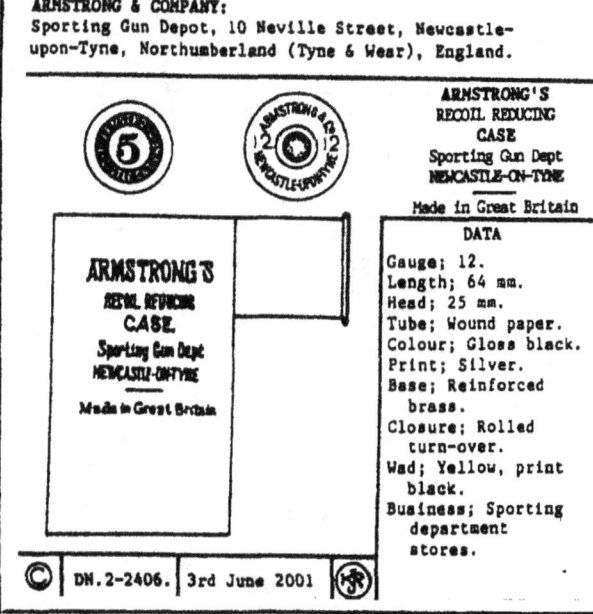
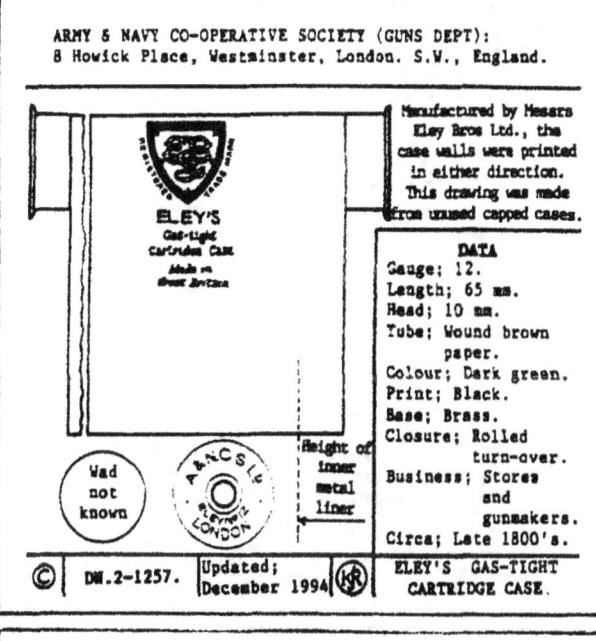
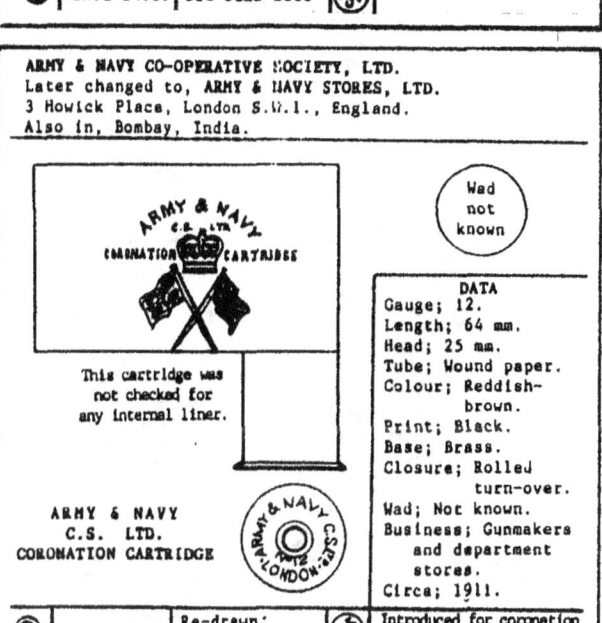
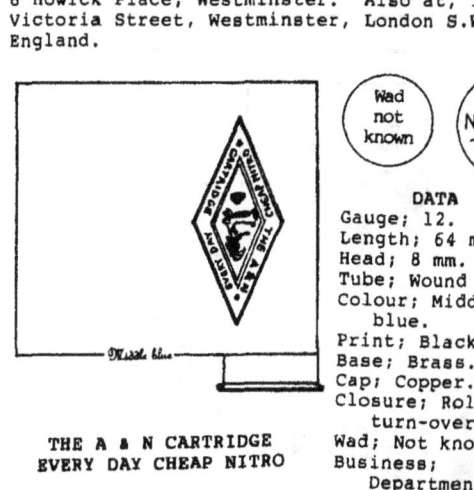

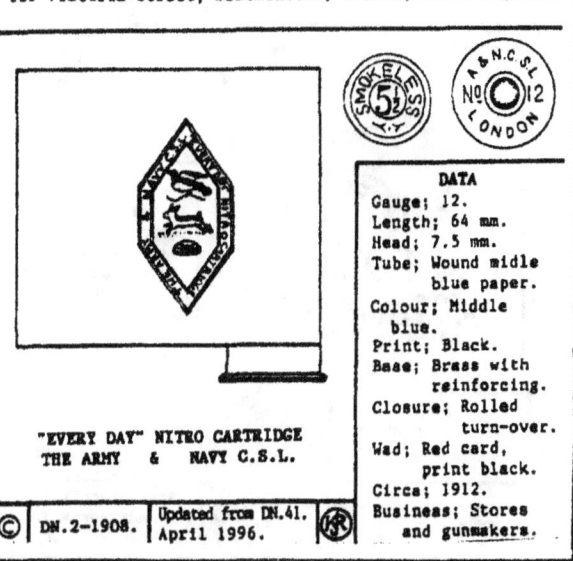

PLATE 9 [ARM – ARM]

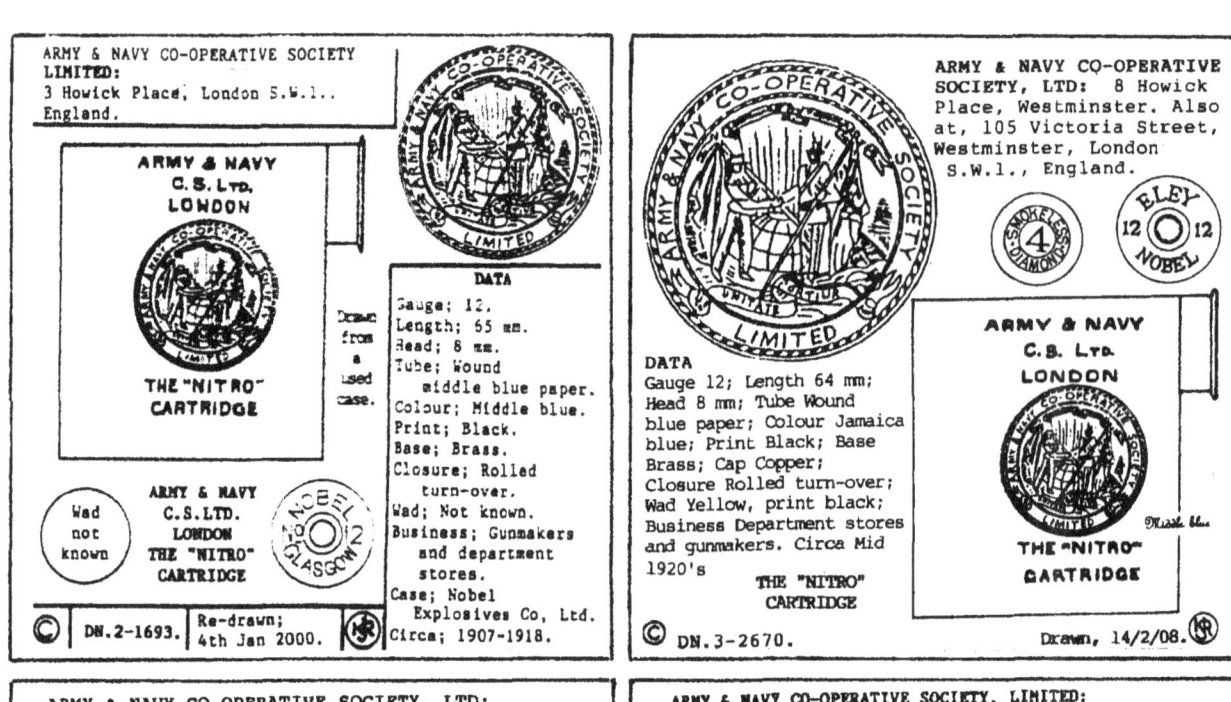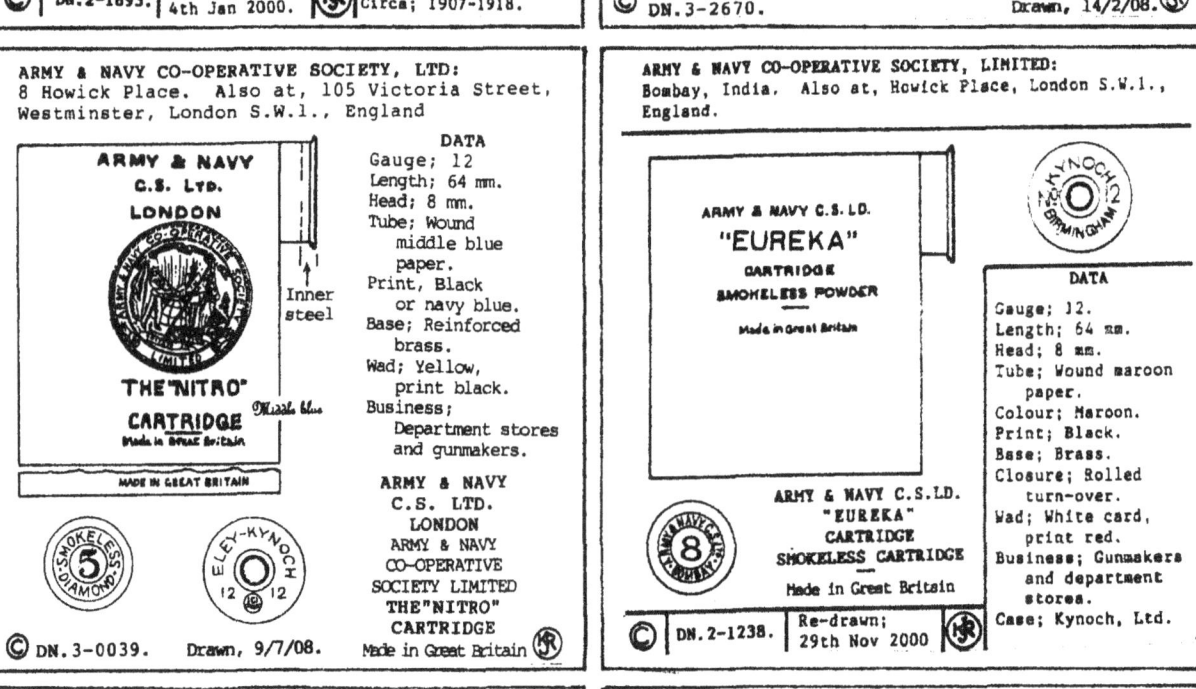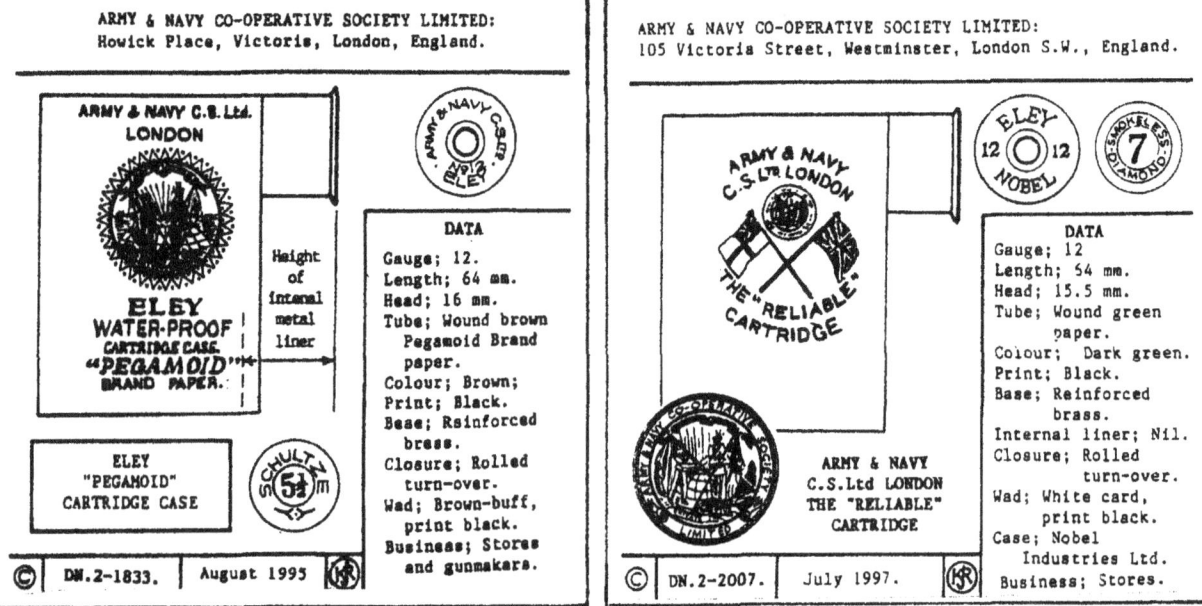

PLATE 10 [ARM – ARM]

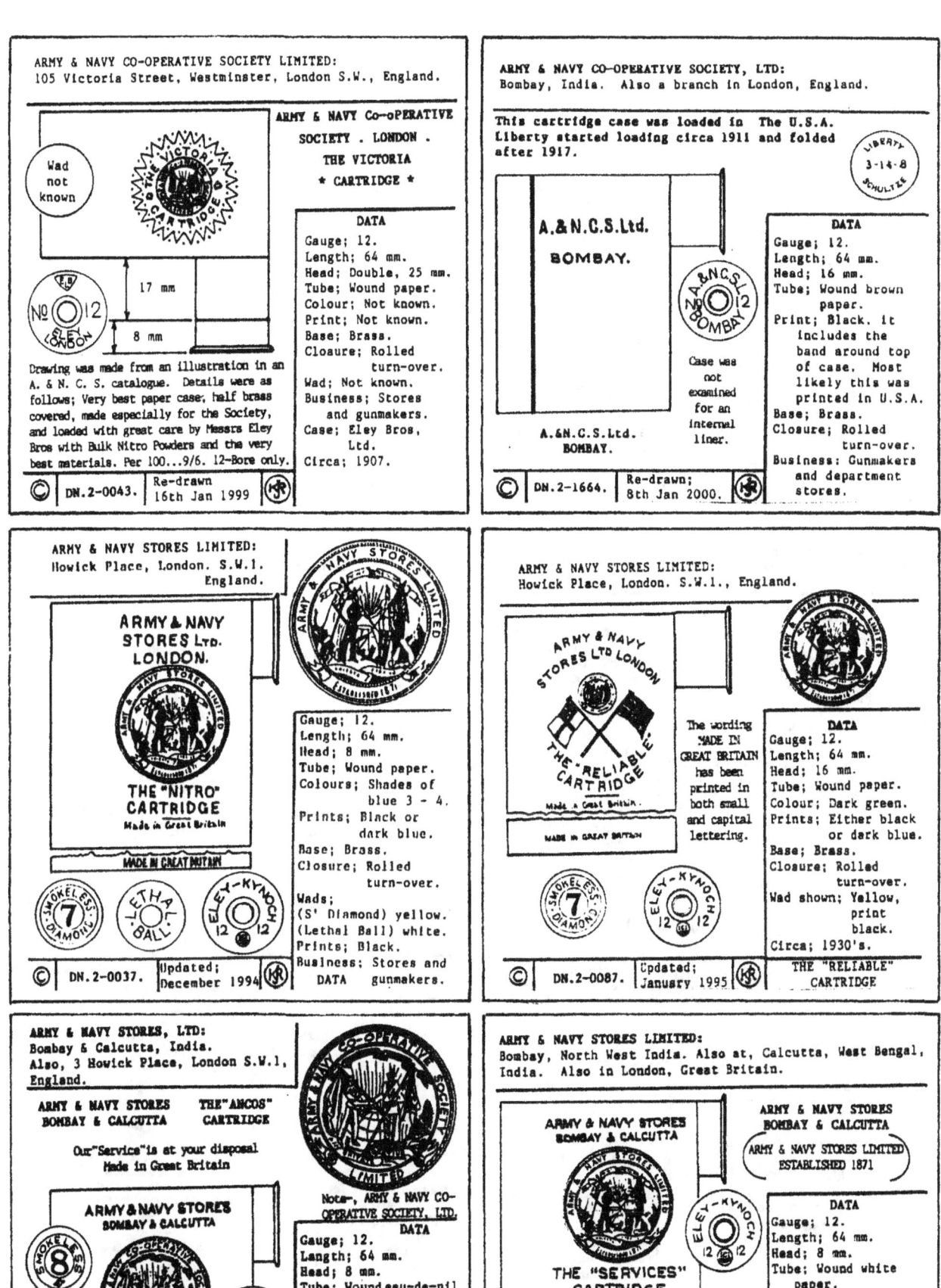

PLATE 11 [ARM - ARM]

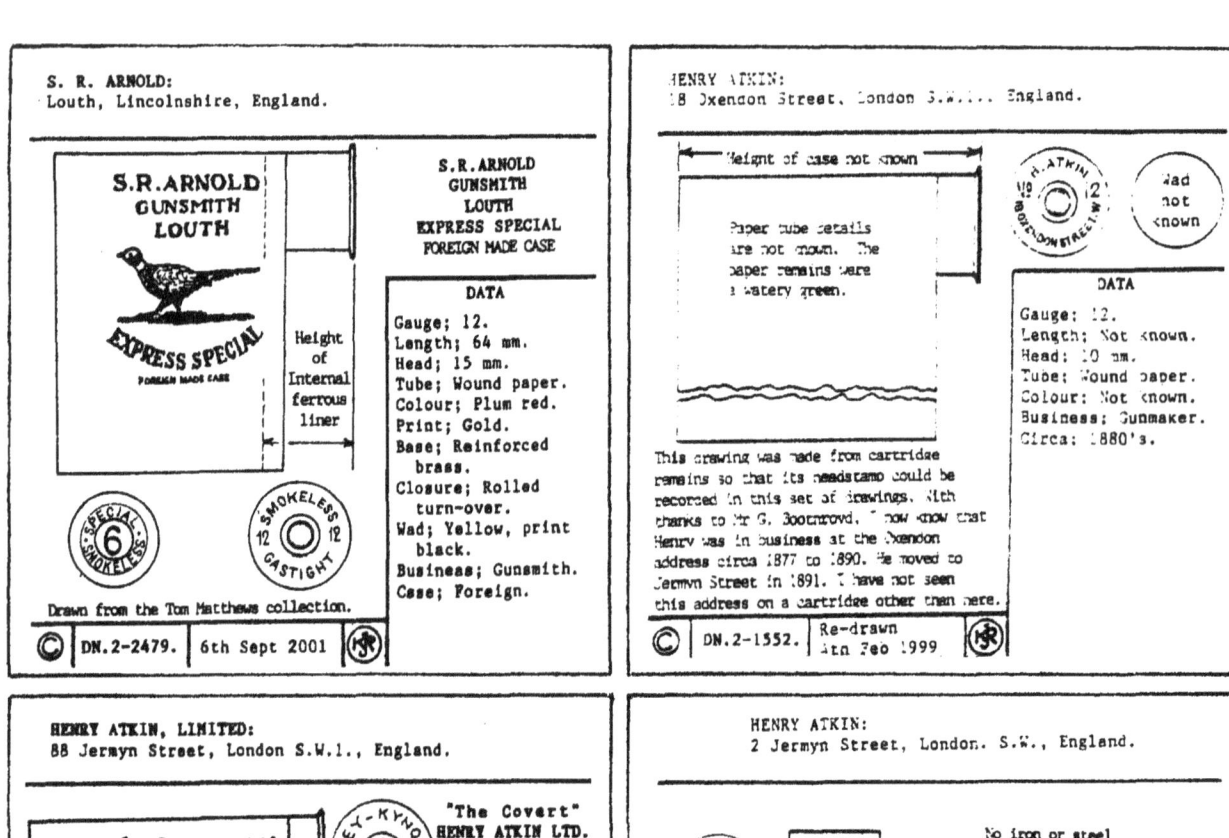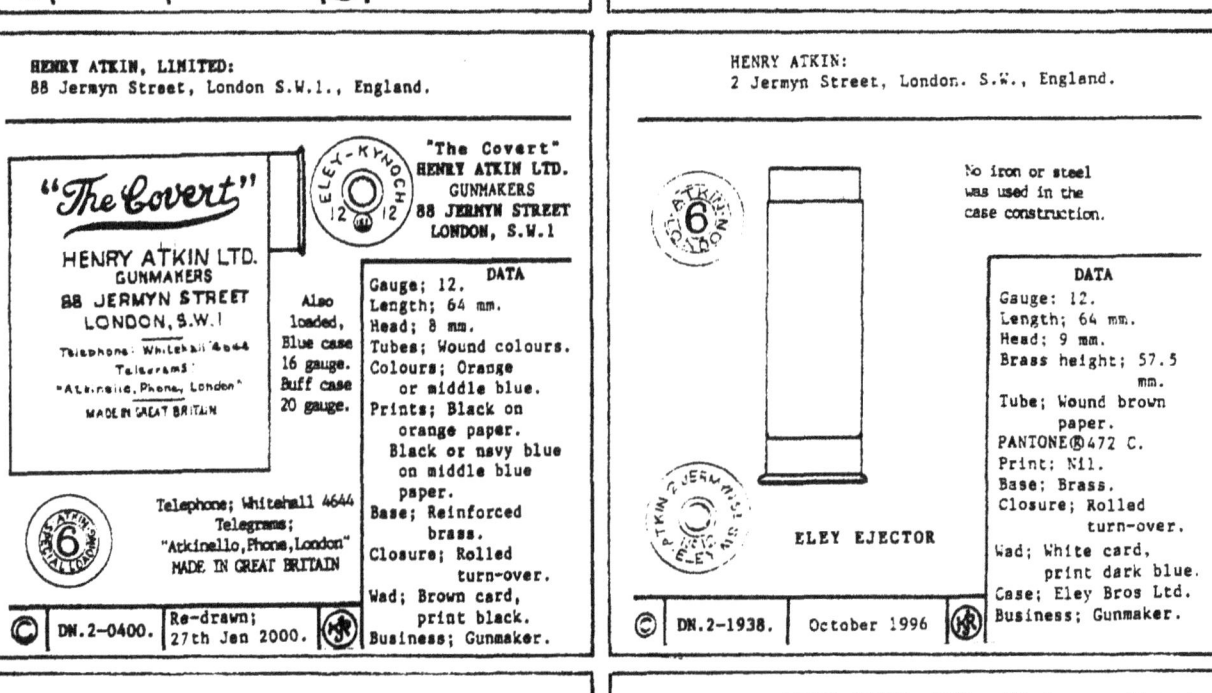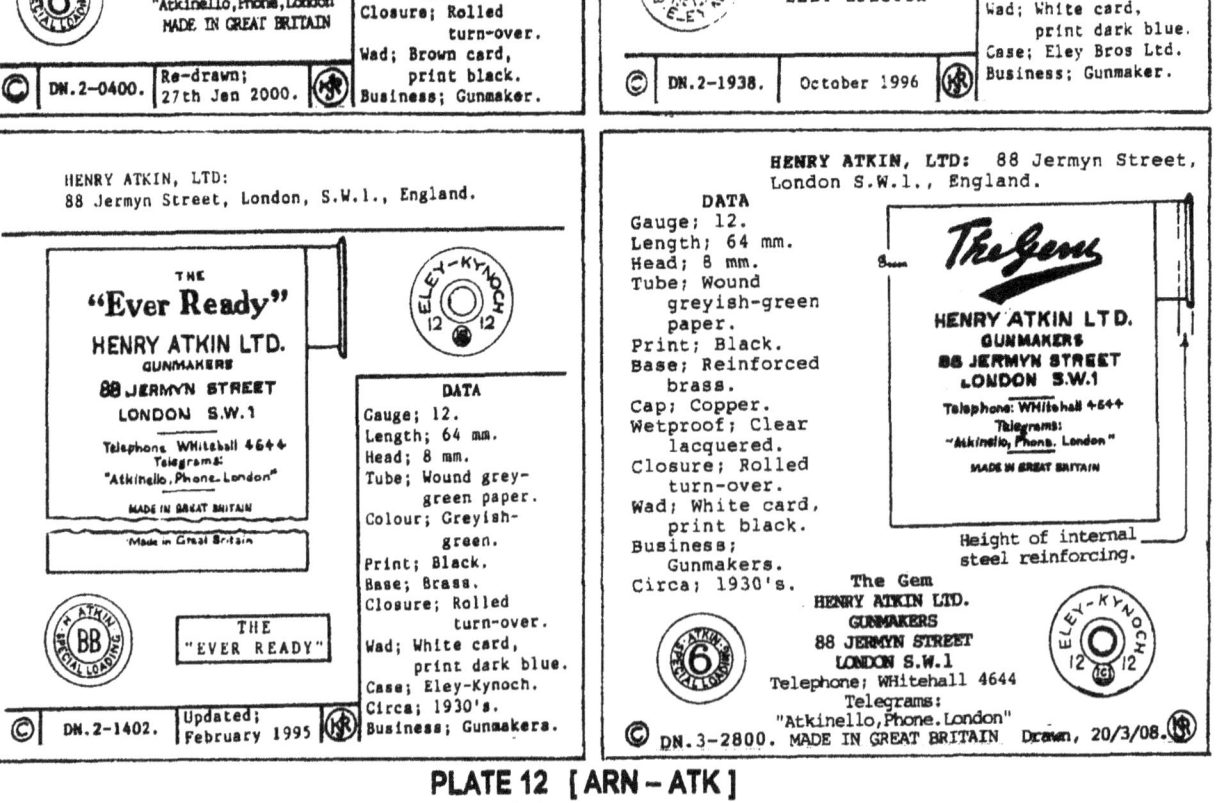

PLATE 12 [ARN – ATK]

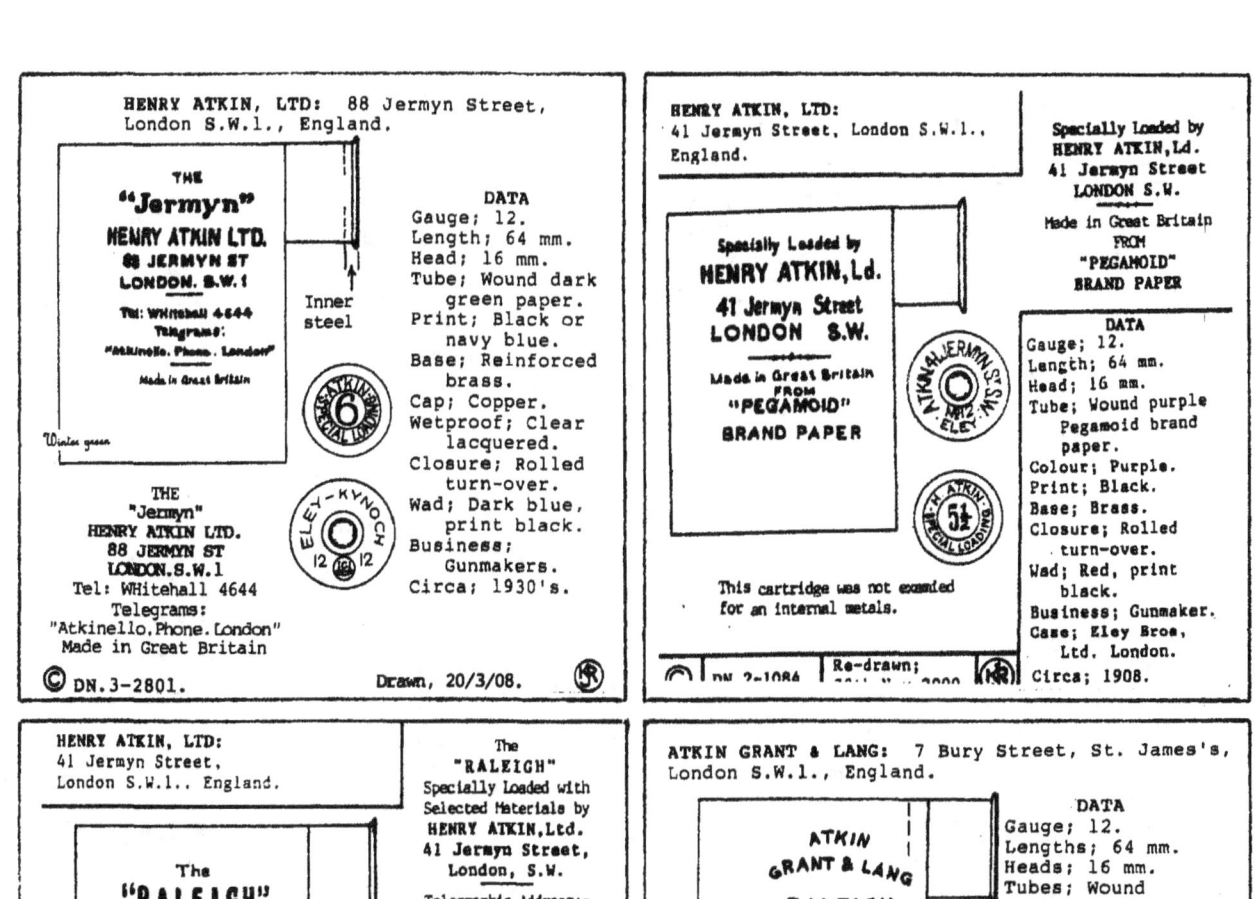
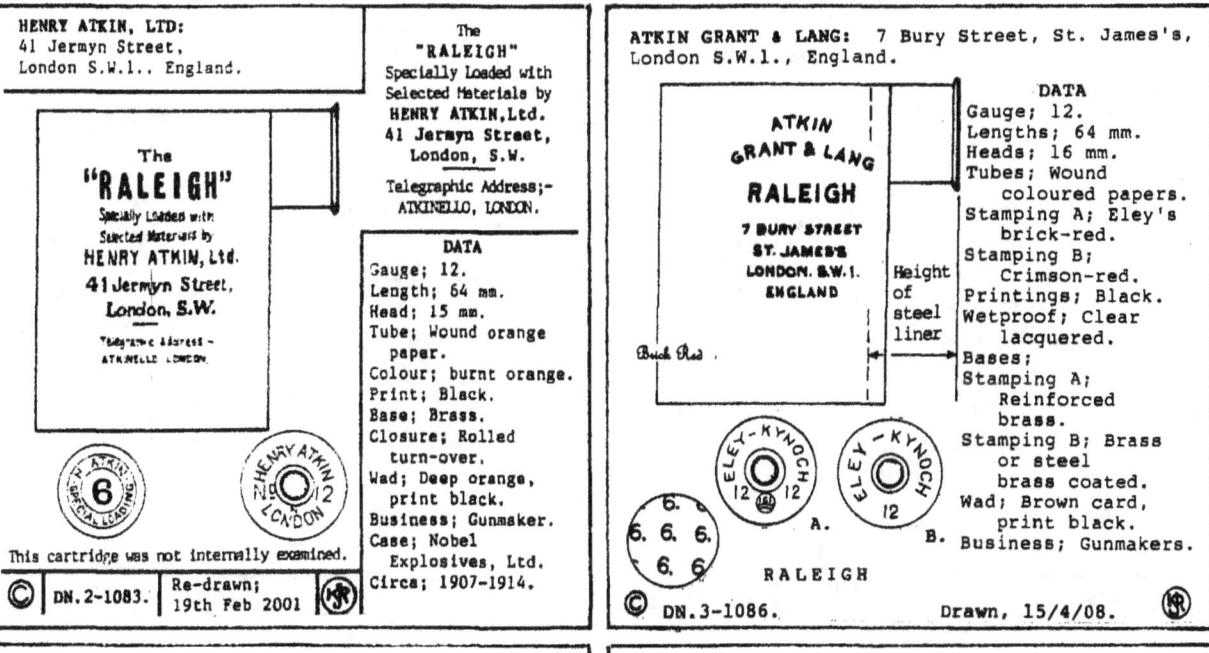
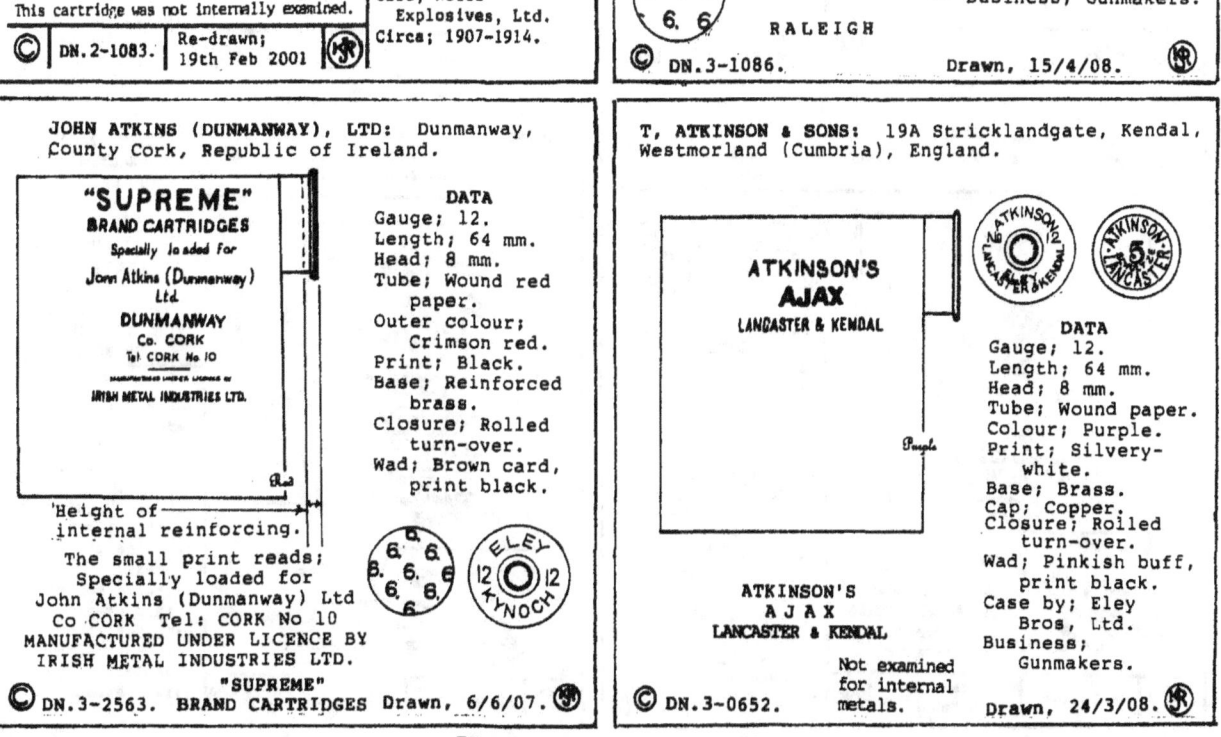

PLATE 13 [ATK-ATK]

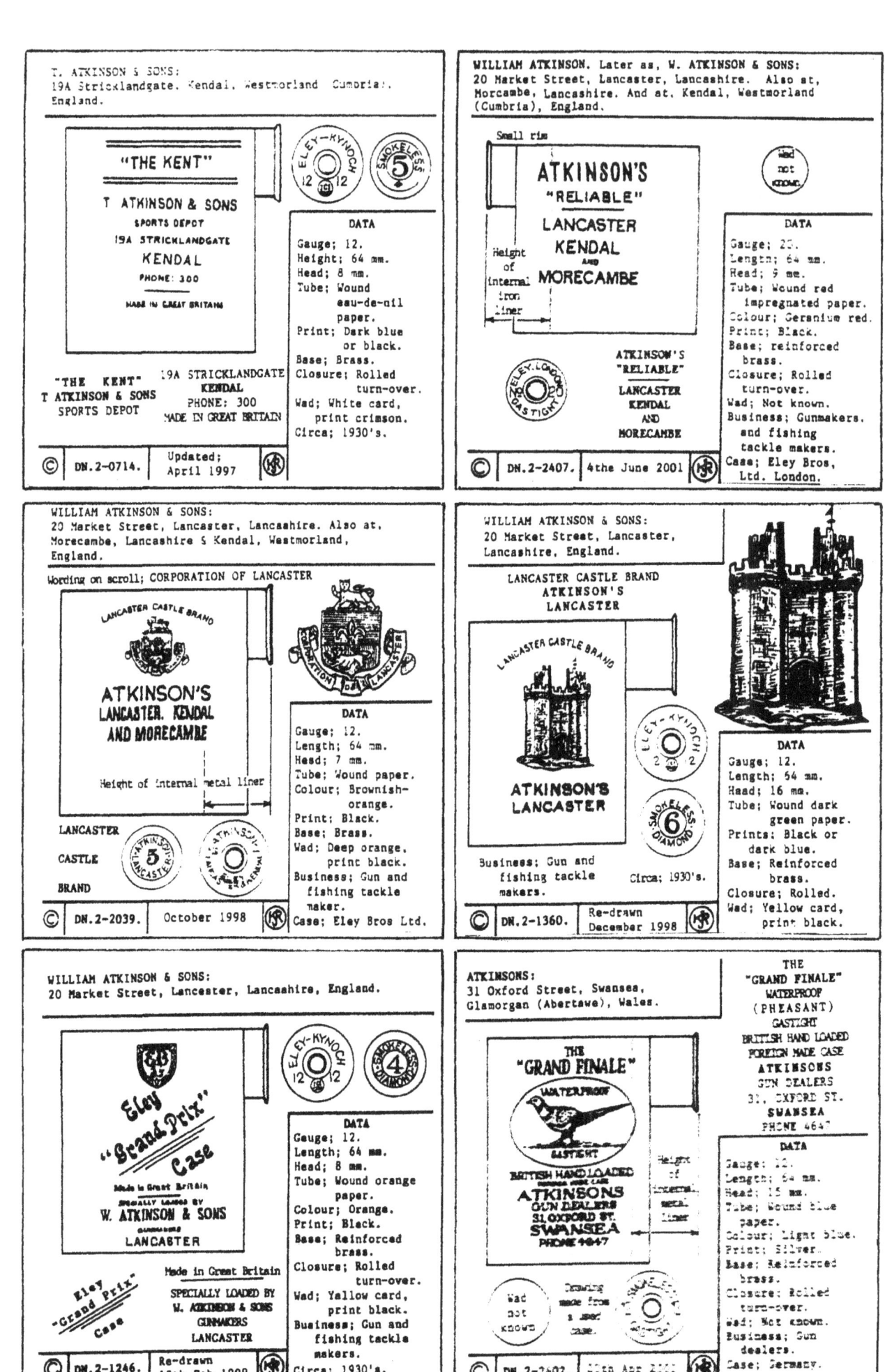

PLATE 14 [ATK-ATK]

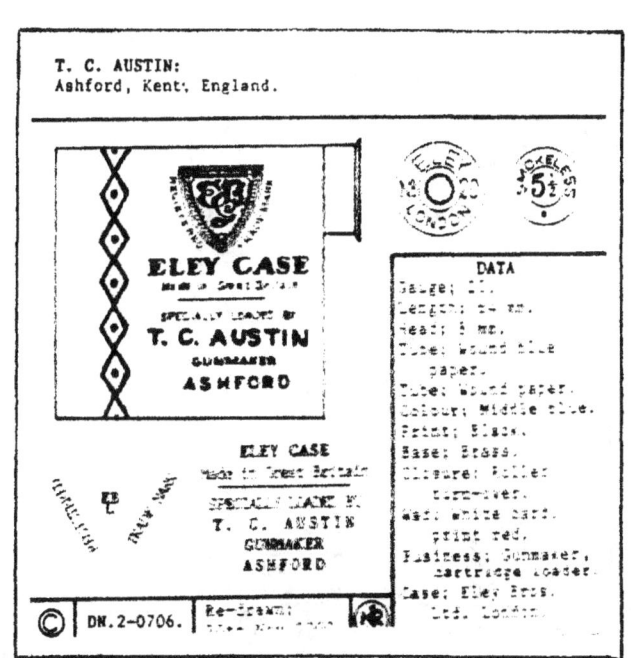
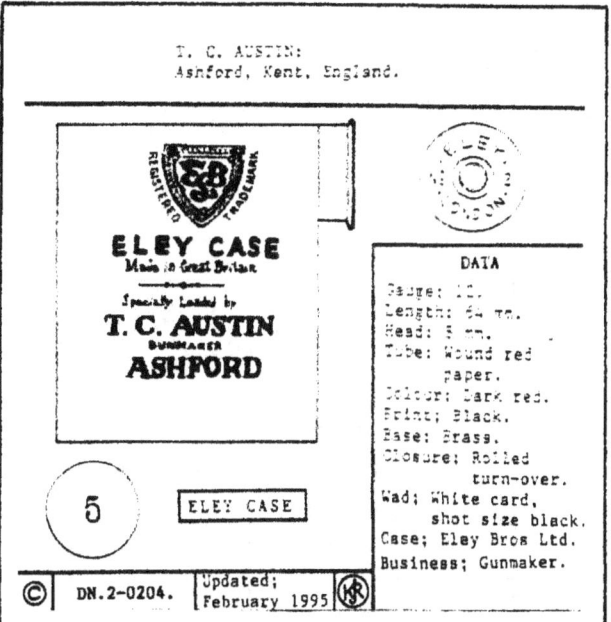

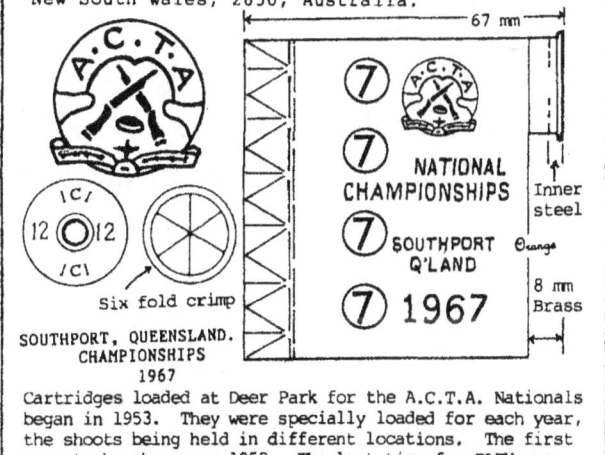

A.C.T.A. NATIONAL CHAMPIONSHIPS MELB. 1958
Cartridges loaded by I.C.I.A.N.Z. for these yearly shoots started in 1953. The first cartridge to show the year on it was as illustrated, 1958 and the shoot was held at Melbourne. The tube was wound from off-white paper and being varnished gave it an old straw or stone colour. The printing was in black. Closure was a six fold crimp and its base was brass or a brass finnish.
© DN.3-1111.   Drawn, 30/3/08.

SOUTHPORT, QUEENSLAND. CHAMPIONSHIPS 1967
Cartridges loaded at Deer Park for the A.C.T.A. Nationals began in 1953. They were specially loaded for each year, the shoots being held in different locations. The first year to be shown was 1958. The last time for ELEY was 1982. Shown here is 1967, it's tube was orange paper and the printing was in black. Wetproof by clear lacquer.
© DN.3-1515.   Drawn, 10/9/08.

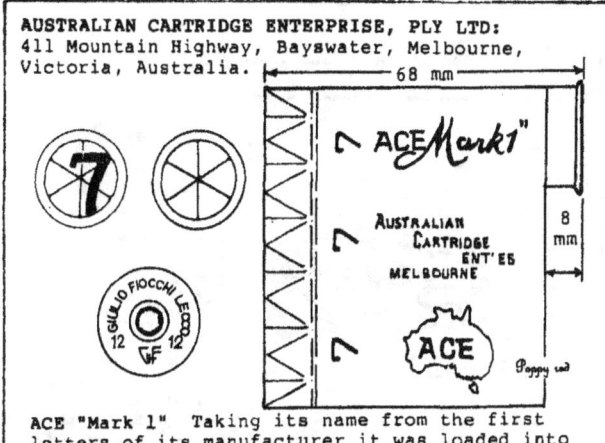

ACE "Mark 1" Taking its name from the first letters of its manufacturer it was loaded into an Italian Fiocchi case. The tube was of wound paper with the outer colour of poppy red. The case wall printings were in black. Shot sizes were either on the side or on the six fold crimp. The base was brass or a brass finnish. The cap was nickel. It was post World War Two and was not in business for many years.
DN.3-0544.   Drawn, 30/3/08.

PLATE 15 [AUS – AVE]

BACON & CURTIS, LTD:
44 & 180 The High Street, Poole, Dorsetshire, England.

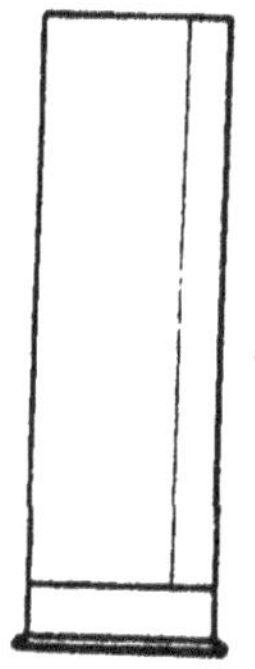

DATA
- Gauge; 12.
- Length; 64 mm.
- Head; 7 mm.
- Tube; Wound paper.
- Colour; Crimson.
- Print; Nil.
- Base; Brass.
- Closure; Rolled turn-over.
- Wad; White card, print crimson.
- Business; Ironmongers both wholesale and retail.

In 1889, Walter James Bacon was in business on his own in Poole. By 1911, his firm had become, Bacon & Curtis, Limited. They then had premises in Commercial Road, Parkstone and at Canford Cliffs. Also at 106 Old Christchurch Road, Bournemouth.

© DN.2-0454. Re-drawn; 28th Nov 2000

BAGNALL & KIRKWOOD:
31 Westgate Road, Newcastle-upon-Tyne, Northumberland (Tyne & Wear), England.

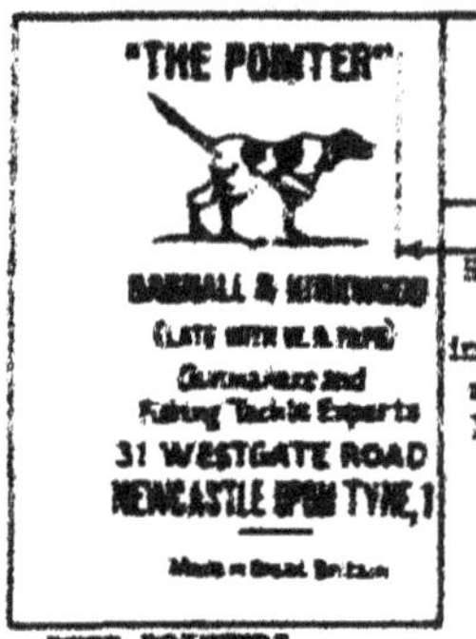

"THE POINTER"
BAGNALL & KIRKWOOD
(LATE WITH W.R.PAPE)
Gunmakers and Fishing Tackle Experts
31 WESTGATE ROAD
NEWCASTLE UPON TYNE, 1
Made in Great Britain

DATA
- Gauge; 12.
- Length; 64 mm.
- Head; 16 mm.
- Tube; Wound dark green paper.
- Colour; Dark green.
- Print; Black. or dark blue.
- Base; Brass with reinforcing.
- Wetproof; Clear lacquered.
- Closure; Rolled turn-over.
- Wad; White card, print pink.
- Circa; 1930's.

© DN.2-1614. Updated, March 1996

BAGNALL & KIRKWOOD:
31 Westgate Road, Newcastle upon Tyne, Northumberland (Tyne & Wear), England.

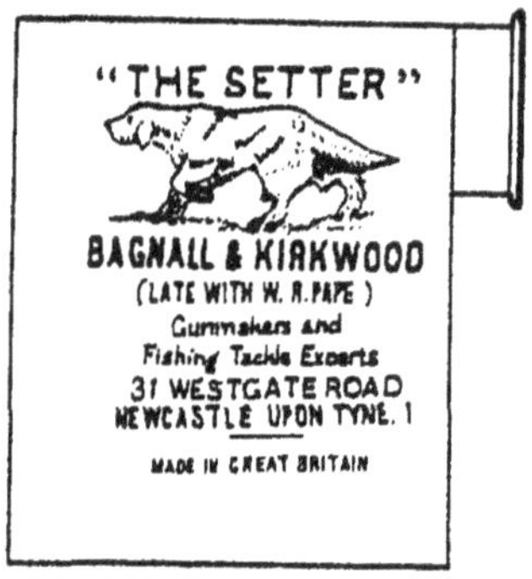

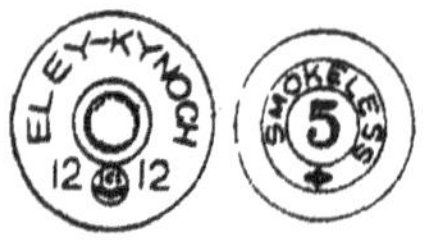

"THE SETTER"
BAGNALL & KIRKWOOD
(LATE WITH W.R.PAPE)
Gunmakers and Fishing Tackle Experts
31 WESTGATE ROAD
NEWCASTLE UPON TYNE. 1
MADE IN GREAT BRITAIN

DATA
- Gauge; 12.
- Length; 64 mm.
- Head; 8 mm.
- Tube; Wound pink paper.
- Colour; Pink.
- Print; Black.
- Base; Brass.
- Closure; Rolled turn-over.
- Wad; White card, print red.
- Business; Gunmakers and fishing tackle dealers.
- Circa; 1930's.

© DN.2-0209. Re-drawn November 1998

BAIKAL: Union of Soviet Socialist Republics.
(Business; Ammunition manufacturers).

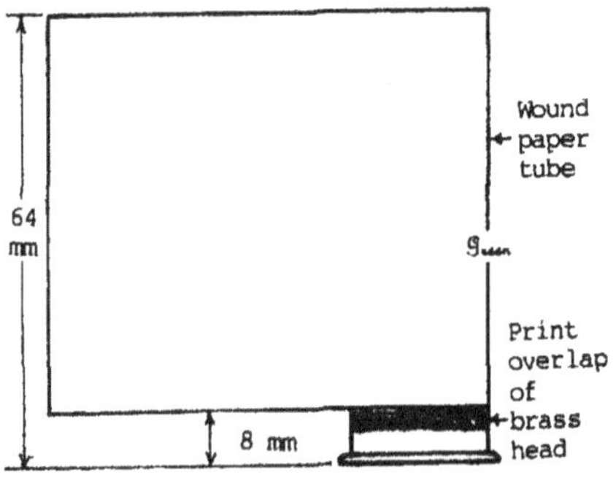

This was an early import of Baikal cartridges from Russia into Great Britain. The 60 on the headstamping refers to the year 1960. The external layer of the wound paper tube was printed overall in a dark gloss blueish green which usually overlapped on to the brass head. The top wad shown was middle-green with white lettering. The large flat bottom primer cap was brass.

© DN.3-1221. Revised, 3/2/09.

BAIKAL:
Baikal, Union of Soviet Socialist Republics.

These cartridges were imported into the UK. They came in 65mm and 70 mm case lengths with either deep red or light turquoise tube colours. There were several variations of the duck picture.

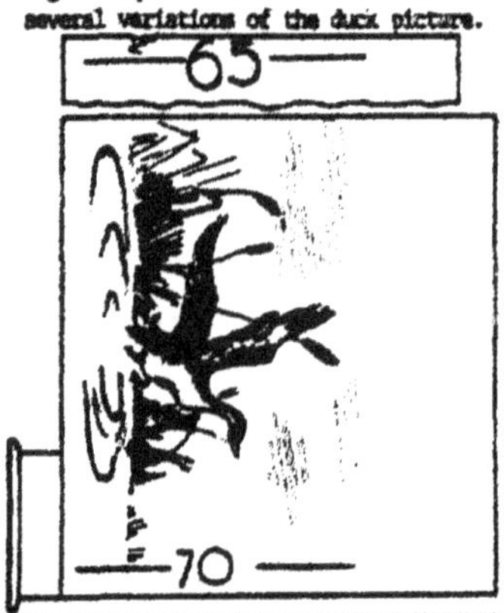

DATA
- Gauge; 12.
- Lengths; 65 mm and 70 mm.
- Heads; 8 mm and 9 mm.
- Tubes; Wound brown paper.
- Colours; Red or turquoise.
- Printings; black or dark blue.
- Heads; Steel with brass wash.
- Closures; Rolled turn-overs
- Wad shown; White card, print red.

© DN.2-0956. Updated; May 1995

BAIKAL:
Baikal, Union of Soviet Socialist Republics.

DATA
- Gauge; 12.
- Length; 64 mm.
- Head; 8 mm.
- Tube; Wound off-white paper.
- Colour; Off-white.
- Print; Black.
- Base; Steel with a brass coating.
- Closure; Rolled turn-over.
- Wad; Off-white card, print brown.
- Business; Ammunition manufacturers.
- Circa; 1970.

© DN.2-1179. Re-drawn; 16th Feb 2000.

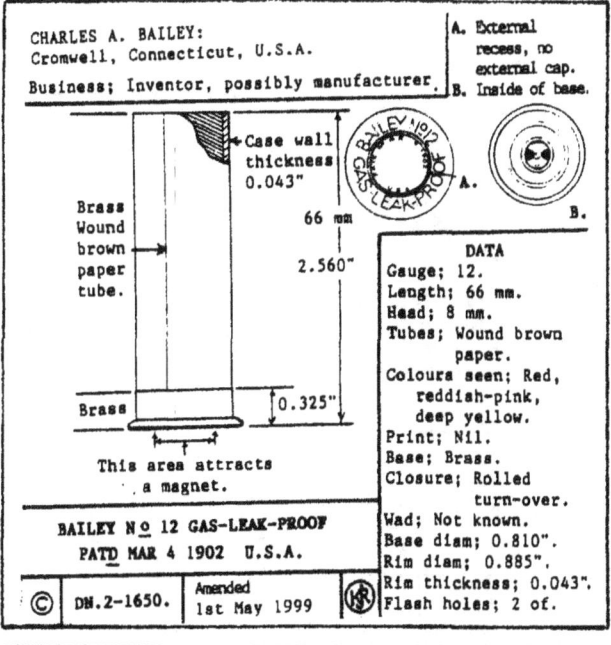

CHARLES A. BAILEY:
Cromwell, Connecticut, U.S.A.
Business; Inventor, possibly manufacturer.

A. External recess, no external cap.
B. Inside of base.

BAILEY No 12 GAS-LEAK-PROOF
PATD MAR 4 1902 U.S.A.

DN.2-1650.   Amended 1st May 1999

DATA
Gauge; 12.
Length; 66 mm.
Head; 8 mm.
Tubes; Wound brown paper.
Colours seen; Red, reddish-pink, deep yellow.
Print; Nil.
Base; Brass.
Closure; Rolled turn-over.
Wad; Not known.
Base diam; 0.810".
Rim diam; 0.885".
Rim thickness; 0.043".
Flash holes; 2 of.

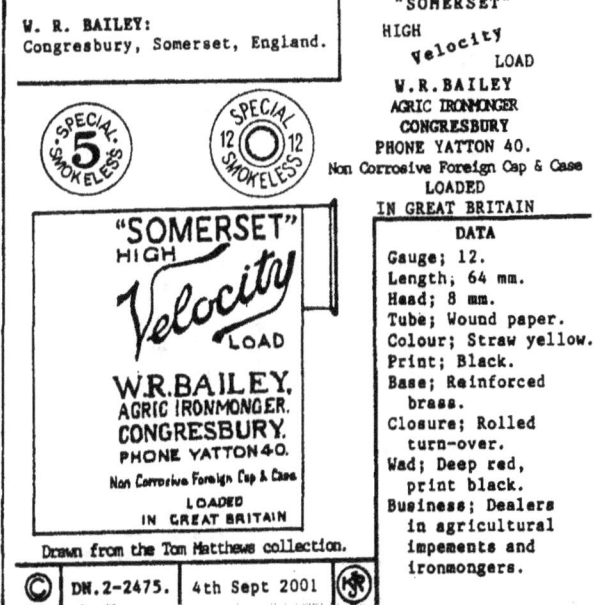

W. R. BAILEY:
Congresbury, Somerset, England.

DN.2-2475.   4th Sept 2001

DATA
Gauge; 12.
Length; 64 mm.
Head; 8 mm.
Tube; Wound paper.
Colour; Straw yellow.
Print; Black.
Base; Reinforced brass.
Closure; Rolled turn-over.
Wad; Deep red, print black.
Business; Dealers in agricultural impements and ironmongers.

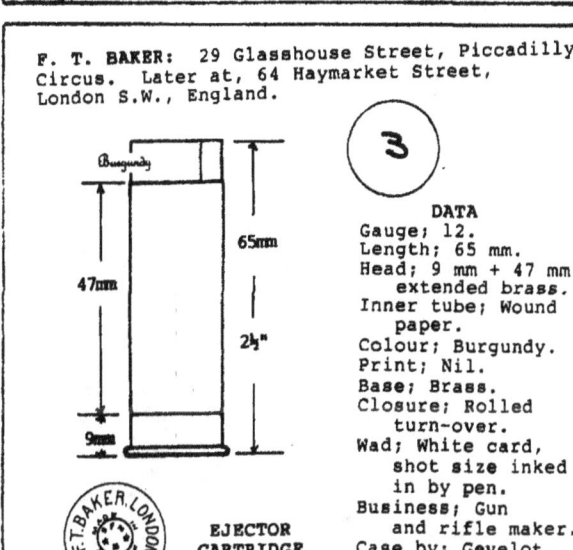

F. T. BAKER: 29 Glasshouse Street, Piccadilly Circus. Later at, 64 Haymarket Street, London S.W., England.

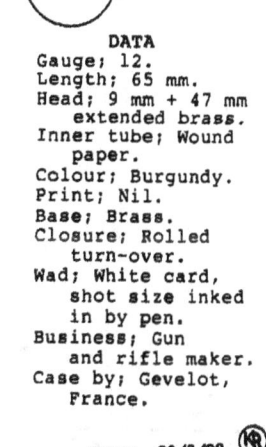

EJECTOR CARTRIDGE

DN.3-2798.   Drawn, 20/3/08.

DATA
Gauge; 12.
Length; 65 mm.
Head; 9 mm + 47 mm extended brass.
Inner tube; Wound paper.
Colour; Burgundy.
Print; Nil.
Base; Brass.
Closure; Rolled turn-over.
Wad; White card, shot size inked in by pen.
Business; Gun and rifle maker.
Case by; Gevelot, France.

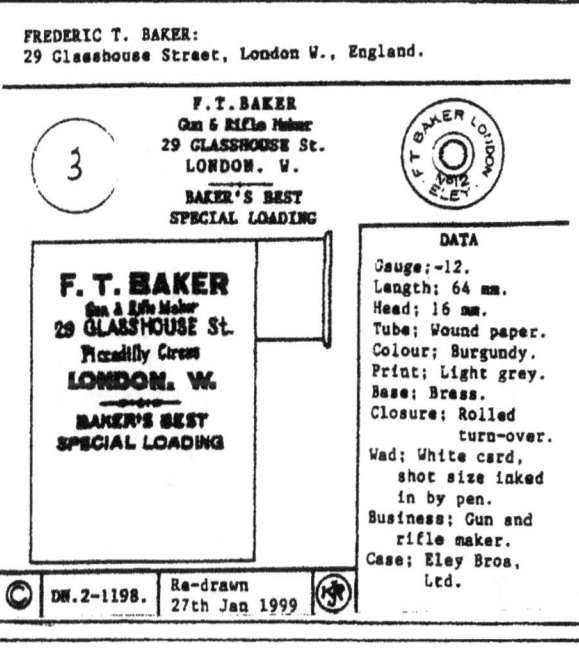

FREDERIC T. BAKER:
29 Glasshouse Street, London W., England.

DN.2-1198.   Re-drawn 27th Jan 1999

DATA
Gauge; -12.
Length; 64 mm.
Head; 16 mm.
Tube; Wound paper.
Colour; Burgundy.
Print; Light grey.
Base; Brass.
Closure; Rolled turn-over.
Wad; White card, shot size inked in by pen.
Business; Gun and rifle maker.
Case; Eley Bros, Ltd.

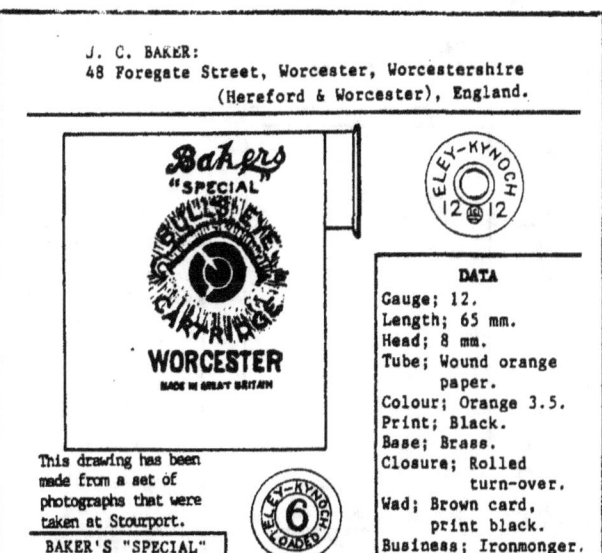

J. C. BAKER:
48 Foregate Street, Worcester, Worcestershire (Hereford & Worcester), England.

This drawing has been made from a set of photographs that were taken at Stourport.

BAKER'S "SPECIAL" BULL'S EYE CARTRIDGE

DN.2-0859.   Updated; January 1995.

DATA
Gauge; 12.
Length; 65 mm.
Head; 8 mm.
Tube; Wound orange paper.
Colour; Orange 3.5.
Print; Black.
Base; Brass.
Closure; Rolled turn-over.
Wad; Brown card, print black.
Business; Ironmonger.

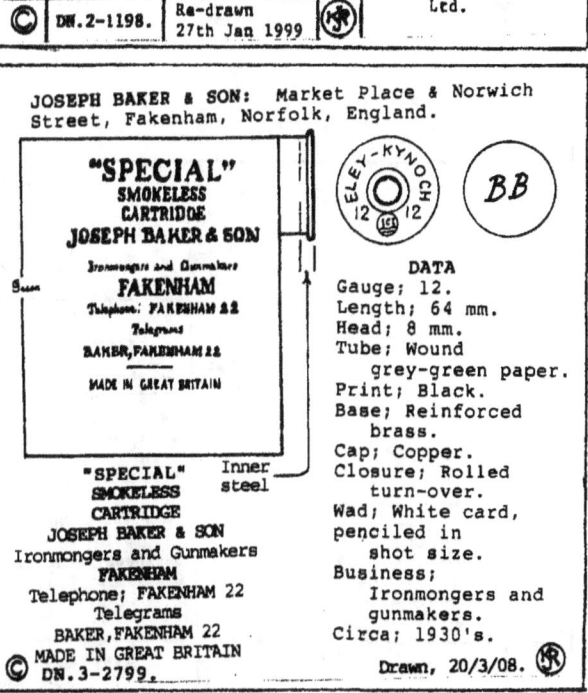

JOSEPH BAKER & SON: Market Place & Norwich Street, Fakenham, Norfolk, England.

DN.3-2799.   Drawn, 20/3/08.

DATA
Gauge; 12.
Length; 64 mm.
Head; 8 mm.
Tube; Wound grey-green paper.
Print; Black.
Base; Reinforced brass.
Cap; Copper.
Closure; Rolled turn-over.
Wad; White card, penciled in shot size.
Business; Ironmongers and gunmakers.
Circa; 1930's.

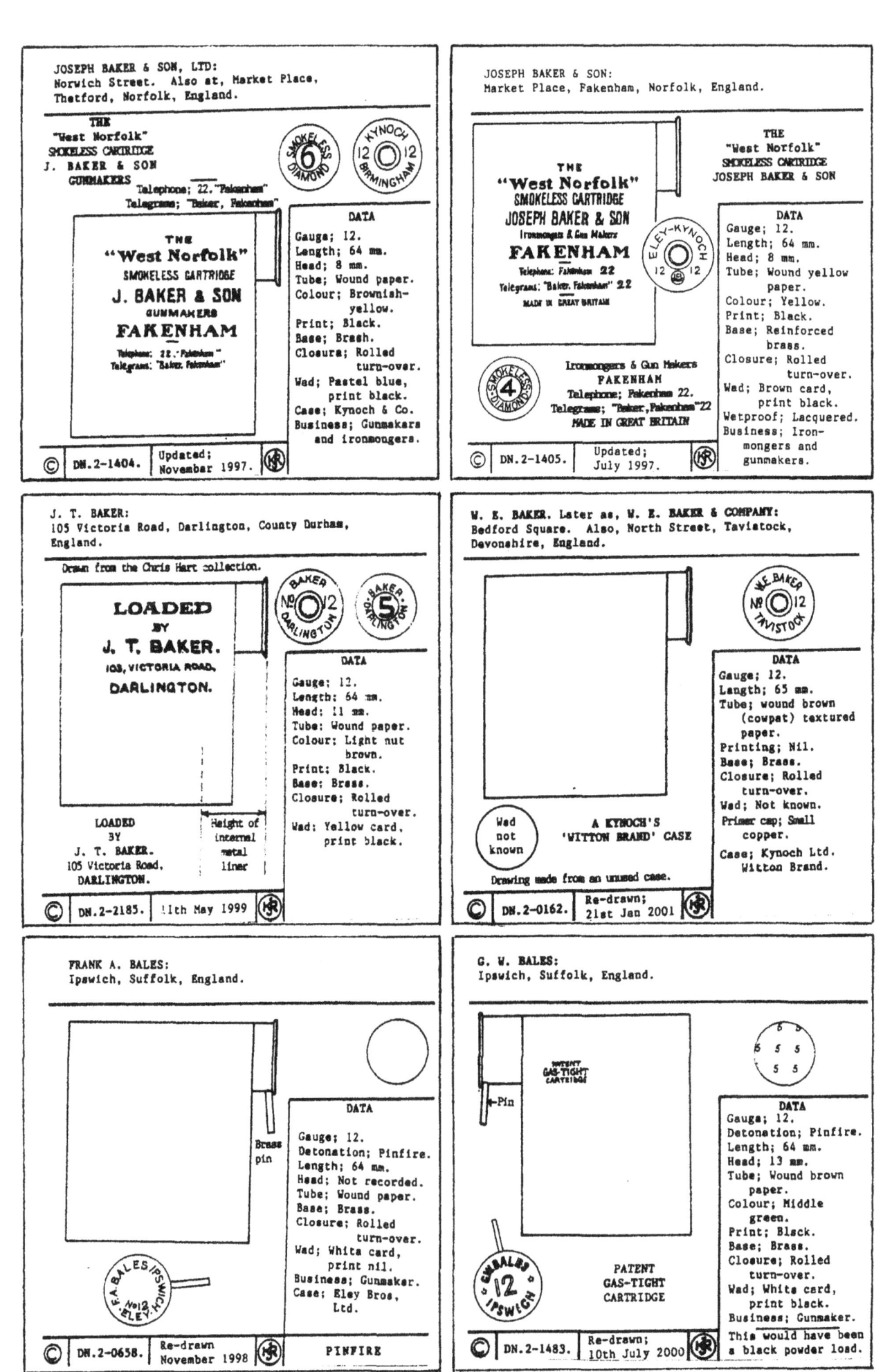

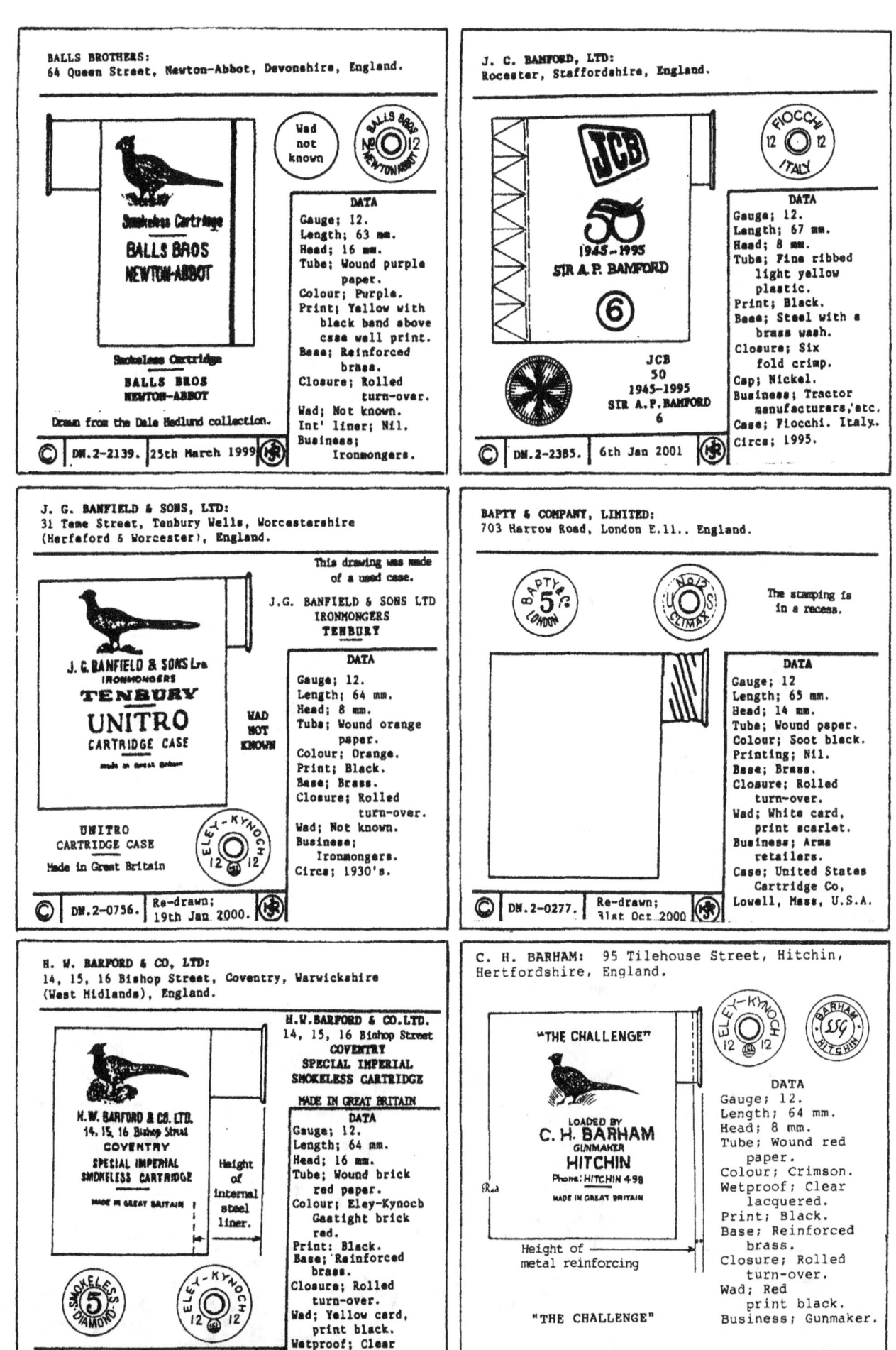

PLATE 19 [BAL – BAR]

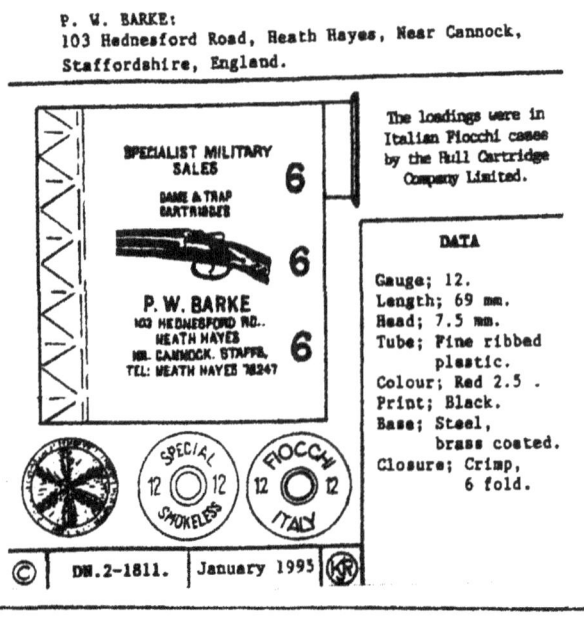
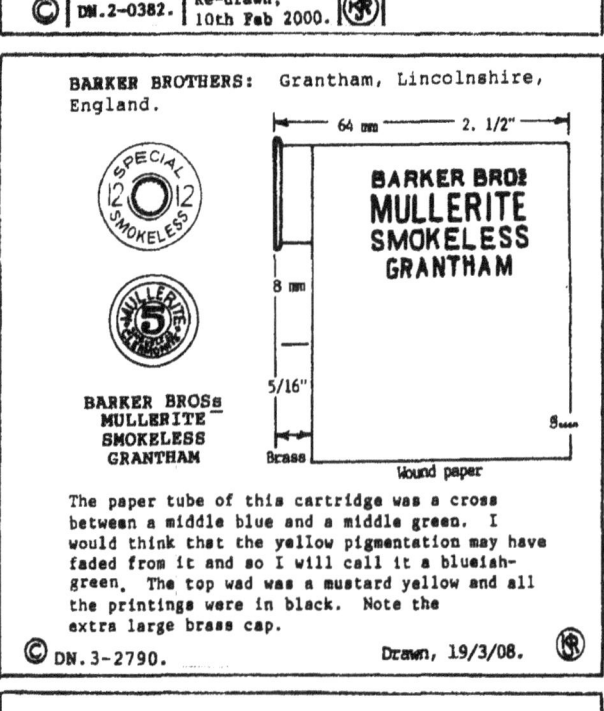

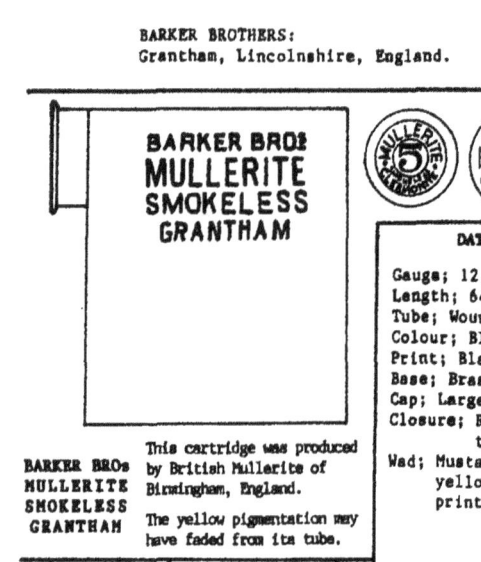
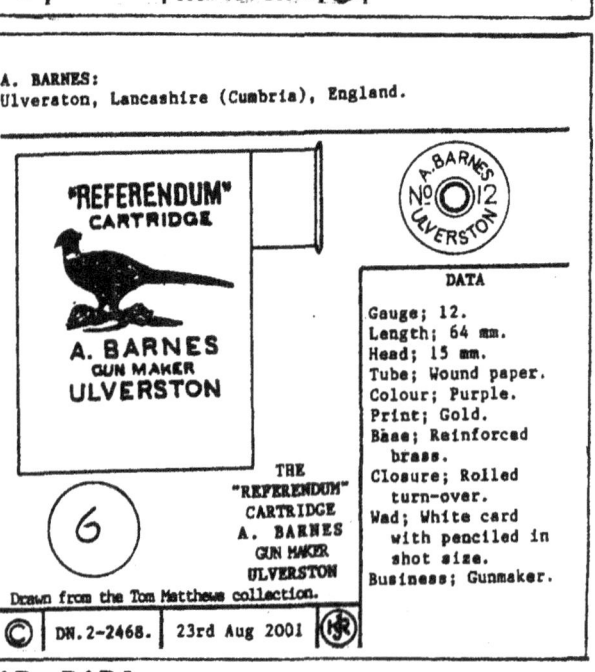

PLATE 20 [BAR - BAR]

GEORGE JAS. BARNES:
29 Church Street, Calne, Wiltshire, England.

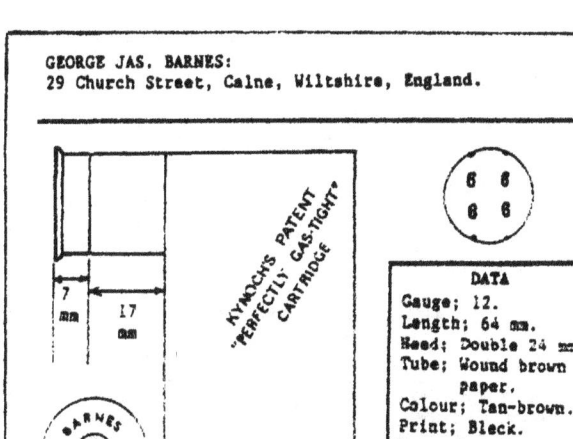

KYNOCH'S PATENT
"PERFECTLY GAS-TIGHT"
CARTRIDGE

DATA
Gauge; 12.
Length; 64 mm.
Head; Double 24 mm.
Tube; Wound brown paper.
Colour; Tan-brown.
Print; Black.
Base; Reinforced brass.
Closure; Rolled turn-over.
Wad; White card, print black.
Business; Ironmonger.
Case; Kynoch Works, Witton.

© DN.2-0346. Re-drawn November 1998

JOHN BARNES:
Burns Statue Square, Ayr, Ayrshire (South Clyde), Scotland.

"THE CHALLENGER"
SPECIALLY LOADED BY
JOHN BARNES
GUN MAKER
BURNS STATUE SQUARE
AYR
Made in Great Britain

DATA
Gauge; 12.
Length; 64 mm.
Head; 8 mm.
Tube; Wound orange paper.
Colour; Orange.
Print; Black.
Base; Reinforced brass.
Wetproof; Lacquered.
Closure; Rolled turn-over.
Wad; White card, print black.
Business; Gunmaker.
Circa; 1930's.

Drawn from the Tom Matthews collection.

© DN.2-2466. 22nd Aug 2001

W. BARNES:
Market Place, Ashbourne, Derbyshire, England.

W. BARNES
ASHBOURNE

DATA
Gauge; 20.
Length; 64 mm.
Head; 7 mm.
Tube; Wound paper.
Colour; Straw white.
Print; Black.
Base; Brass.
Closure; Rolled turn-over.
Wad; Brown card, print black.
Business; Ironmonger.
Case; Kynoch, Ltd.

W. BARNES
ASHBOURNE

Drawn from the Tom Matthews collection.

© DN.2-2484. 8th Sept 2001

BARNET & LEVET:
Bird Street, Lichfield, Staffordshire, England.

This drawing was made from two coloured photographs and rough sketches.

DATA
Gauge; 12.
Length; 64 mm.
Head; 16 mm.
Tube; Wound brown paper.
Colour; Middle brown.
Print; Black.
Base; Brass.
Closure; Rolled turn-over.
Wad; Coffee brown, print black.
Case; Cogswell & Harrison Limited.
Business; Ironmongers.

BARNARD & LEVET,
IRONMONGERS,
LICHFIELD.

Best CogSchultze Loading.

© DN.2-2015. July 1997. Provisional Drawing

BARNITTS' LIMITED: Colliergate, York,
Yorkshire, England.

BARNITTS'
"SPECIAL"
SOLD ONLY BY
BARNITTS' LIMITED
COLLIERGATE
YORK

DATA
Gauge; 12.
Length; 64 mm.
Head; 8 mm.
Tube; Wound blue paper.
Colour; Middle blue.
Print; Black.
Base; Brass.
Cap; Copper.
Closure; Rolled turn-over.
Wad; White card, print black.
Circa; Mid 1920's.

BARNITTS'
"SPECIAL"
SOLD ONLY BY
BARNITTS' LIMITED
COLLIERGATE
YORK

© DN.3-2791. Drawn, 19/3/08.

H. BARNWELL & SONS, LTD:
High Street, Hartley Wintney, Hampshire, England.

THE
"HARTLEY"
SPECIAL SMOKELESS

BRITISH HAND LOADED

H. BARNWELL & SONS
HARTLEY WINTNEY
HANTS
PHONE 45
FOREIGN MADE CASE

THE
"HARTLEY"
SPECIAL SMOKELESS

BRITISH HAND LOADED
H. BARNWELL & SONS
HARTLEY WINTNEY
HANTS
PHONE 45

DATA
Gauge; 12.
Length; 64 mm.
Head; 8 mm.
Tube; Wound paper.
Colour; Black.
Print; Silver.
Base; Brass.
Closure; Rolled turn-over.
Wad; White card, print black.
Business; Cycle manufacturer and garage. Also cartridge loading.
Case; possibly Germany.

They also made a cycle called, The Hartley.

© DN.2-0847. Re-drawn; 22nd Feb 2000.

GEORGE BARTRAM: 33-35 Bank Street, Braintree, Essex, England.

BARTRAM'S
"HARD HITTERS"
(SMOKELESS POWDER)
Made in Great Britain

DATA
Gauge; 12.
Length; 64 mm.
Head; 8 mm.
Tube; Wound paper.
Colour; Dull orange.
Print; Black.
Base; Brass.
Cap; Copper.
Closure; Rolled turn-over.
Wad; White card, print black.
Business; Gunmaker.
Case by; Eley Bros, Ltd.

DN.3-2792. Drawn, 19/3/08.

BASCHIERI & PELLAGRI. S.P.A.
Bologna, Italy.

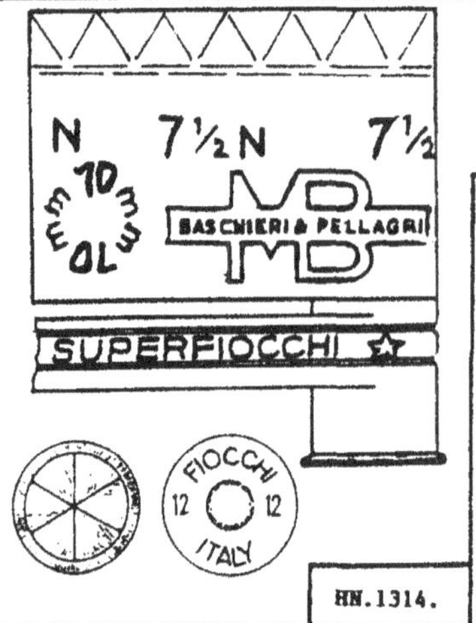

No iron or steel was used in the case construction.

DATA
Gauge; 12.
Length; 70 mm.
Head; 25 mm.
Tube; Fine ribbed plastic.
Colour; Yellow.
Print; Nut-brown.
Base; Brass.
Closure; Crimp, 6 fold.
Case; Fiocchi.

HN.1314.
DN.1945. February 1997

G. J. BASSETT:
4 Swan Street, Petersfield, Hampshire, England.

DATA
Gauge; 12.
Length; 65 mm.
Head; 8 mm.
Tube; Wound paper.
Colour; Dark mauve almost purple.
Print; Silver.
Base; Brass.
Closure; Rolled turn-over.
Wad; Yellow card, print black.
Business; Ironmongers.
Case; Germany.

DN.2-0749. Re-drawn; 18th Feb 2000.

A. BATES: 22 Sun Street, Canterbury.
Also at, Sturry & Whitstable, Kent, England.

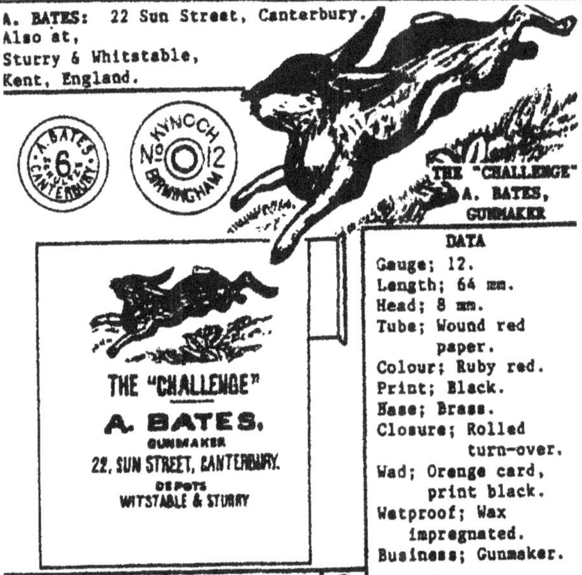

DATA
Gauge; 12.
Length; 64 mm.
Head; 8 mm.
Tube; Wound red paper.
Colour; Ruby red.
Print; Black.
Base; Brass.
Closure; Rolled turn-over.
Wad; Orange card, print black.
Wetproof; Wax impregnated.
Business; Gunmaker.

DN.2-0577. Re-drawn; 24th Jan 2000.

A. BATES:
22 Sun Street, & 1 Guildhall Street, Canterbury, Kent.
Also at, Sturry, Kent, England.

DATA
Gauge; 12.
Length; 64 mm.
Head; Duouble brass up to 25 mm.
Tube; Wound brown paper.
Colour; Brownish-orange.
Print; Black.
Base; Double brass.
Closure; Rolled turn-over.
Wad; Salmon, print black.
Internal liner; Nil.
Business; Gunmaker.
Case; Kynoch, Ltd.

Closed by a semi-squared turn-over.

DN.2-1862. November 1995

A. BATES:
22 Sun Street, & 1 Guildhall Street, Canterbury, Kent.
Also at, Whitstable & Sturry, Kent, England.

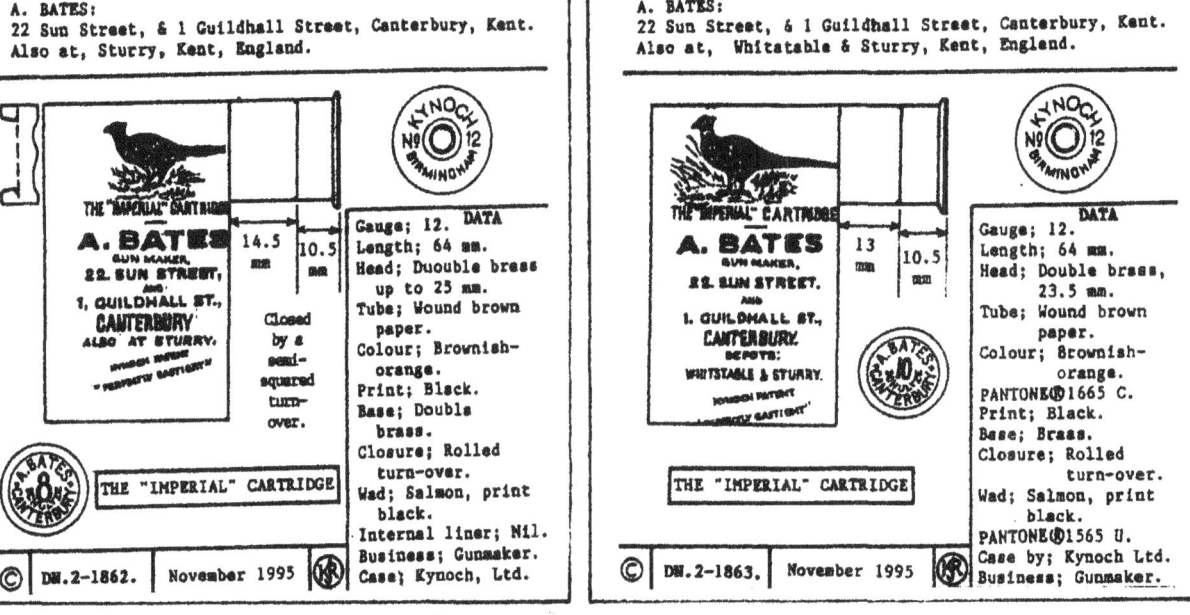

DATA
Gauge; 12.
Length; 64 mm.
Head; Double brass, 23.5 mm.
Tube; Wound brown paper.
Colour; Brownish-orange.
PANTONE® 1665 C.
Print; Black.
Base; Brass.
Closure; Rolled turn-over.
Wad; Salmon, print black.
PANTONE® 1565 U.
Case by; Kynoch Ltd.
Business; Gunmaker.

DN.2-1863. November 1995

PLATE 22 [BAR - BAT]

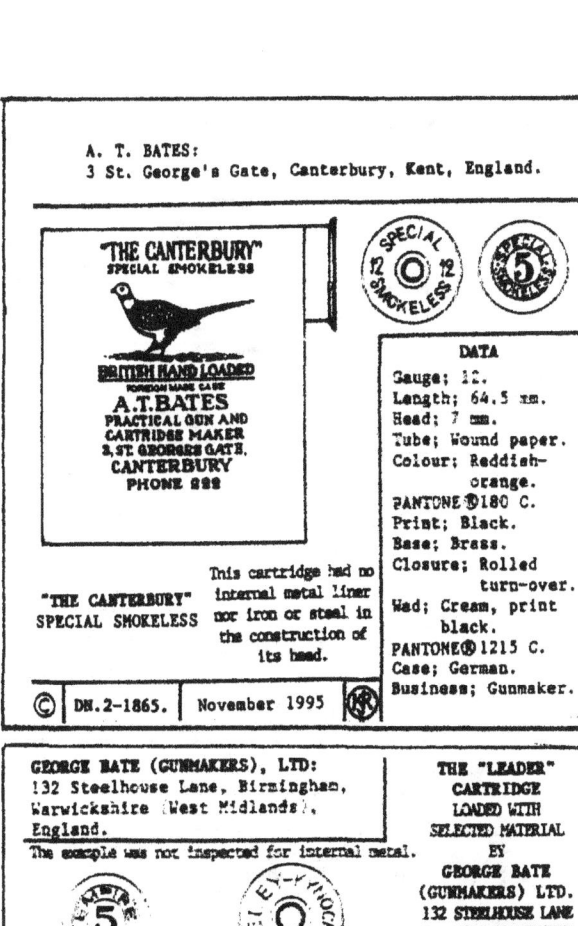
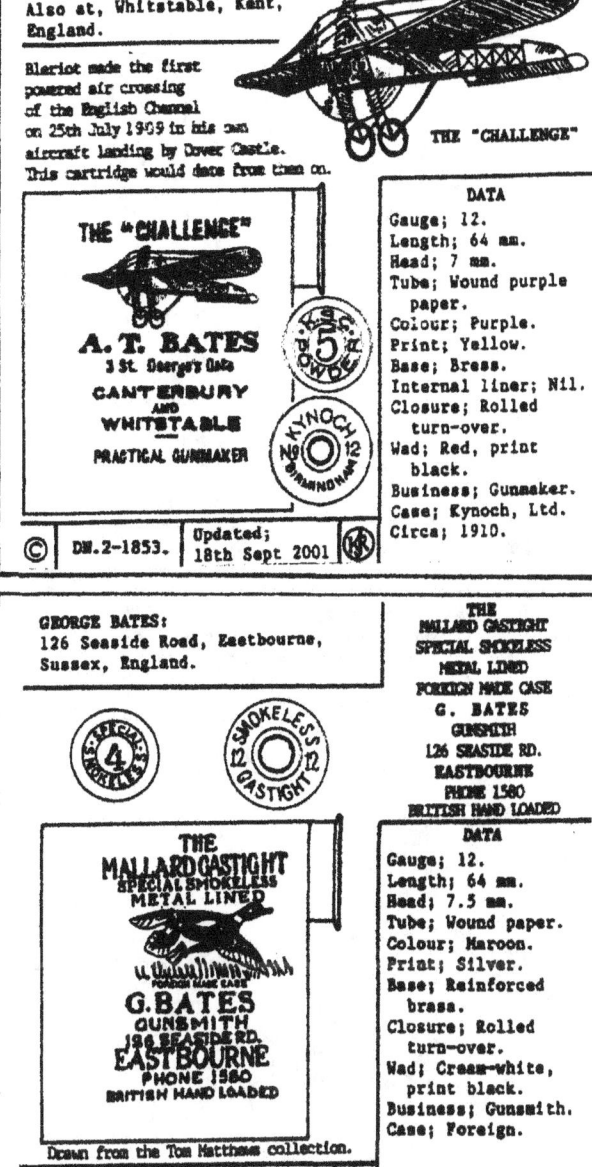
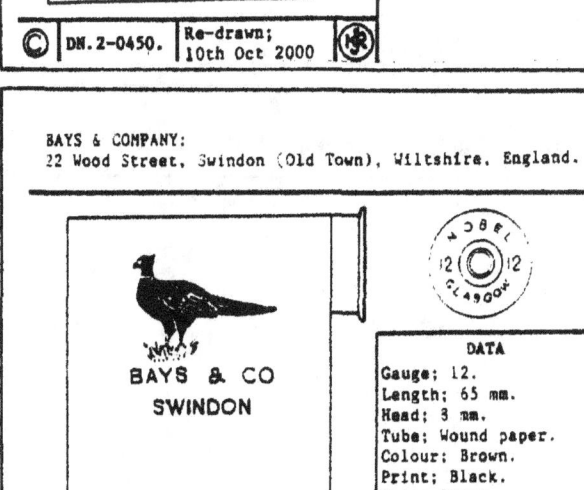
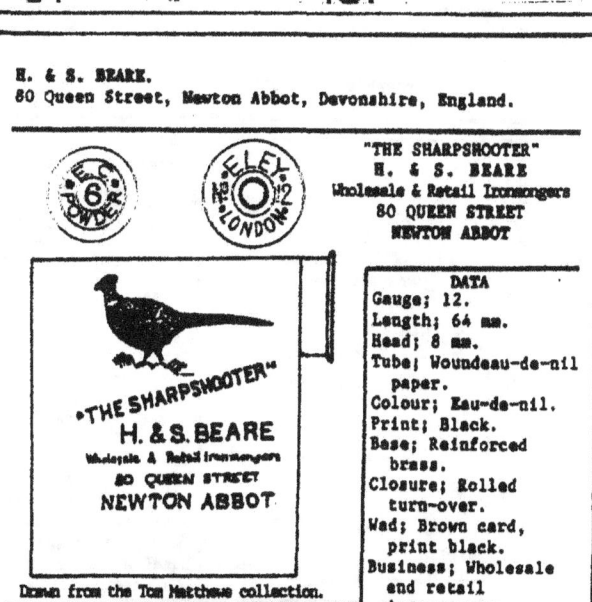

PLATE 23 [BAT – BEA]

F. BEESLEY:
2 St. James's Street, London S.W., England.

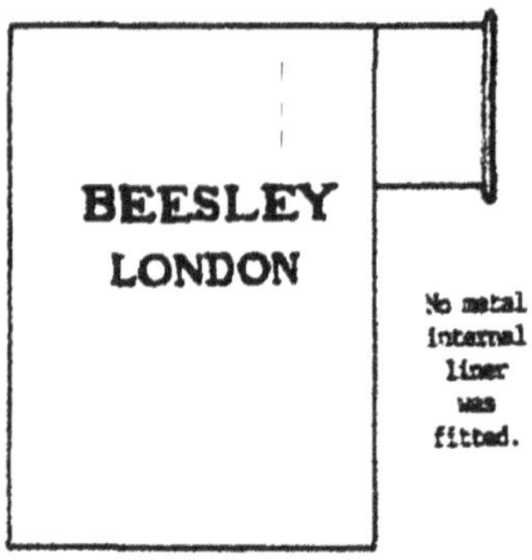

DATA
Gauge; 12.
Length; 64 mm.
Head; 16 mm.
Tube; Wound dark green paper.
Colour; Dark green.
Print; Black.
Base; Reinforced brass.
Closure; Rolled turn-over.
Wad; Not known.
Business; Gunmaker.
Case; Nobel Industries, Ltd
Circa; 1920's.

DN.2-2297. 16th May 2000

FREDERICK BEESLEY: 2 St. Jams's Street, London S.W.1., England.

DATA
Gauge; 12.
Length; 65mm.
Head; 20 mm.
Tube; Wound Pegamoid Eley's light maroon paper.
Print; Black.
Base; Brass (not examined for internal metals).
Cap; Copper.
Closure; Rolled turn-over.
Wad; Yellow, print black.
Case by; Nobel Industries, Ltd. (These cases were loaded by others).

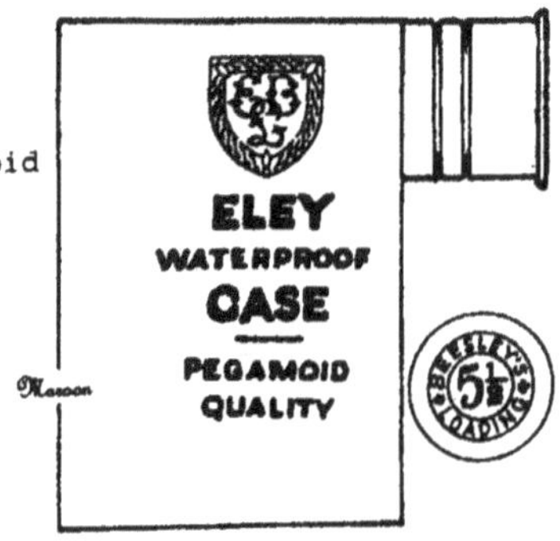

DN.3-0747. Drawn, 27/4/08.

BEAULIEU MANOR ESTATE:
Beaulieu, Hampshire, England.

DATA
Gauge; 12.
Lengths; 65 mm and 70 mm.
Heads; 8 mm.
Tubes; Wound off-white papers with outer layers in red. Later, red plastic.
Printings; Black.
Bases; Brass or steel with a brass wash.
Closures; Six fold crimps.
Cases by; Fiocchi.
Business; Private estate.
Loadings; Hull Cartridge Co.

DN.3-1096. Drawn, 2/3/08.

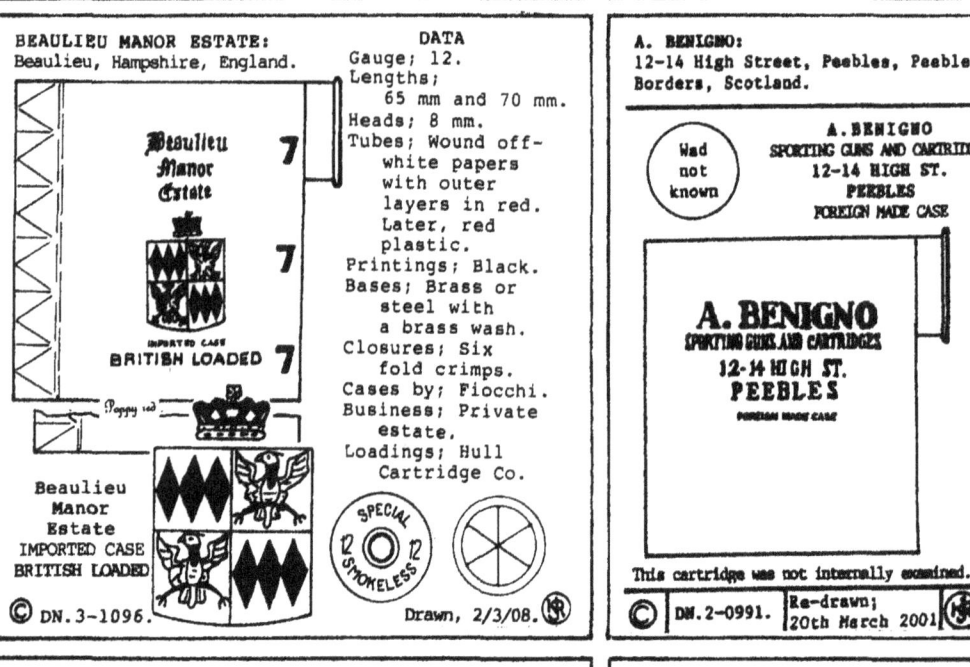

A. BENIGNO:
12-14 High Street, Peebles, Peebles-shire Borders, Scotland.

DATA
Gauge; 12.
Length; 65 mm.
Head; 7 mm.
Tube; Wound purple paper.
Colour; Purple.
Print; Silver.
Base; Brass.
Cap; Large copper.
Closure; Rolled turn-over.
Wad; Not known.
Business; Retailer in guns and cartridges.
Case; Foreign.

This cartridge was not internally examined.

DN.2-0991. Re-drawn; 20th March 2001

G. W. BENNETT:
Blackpool, Lancashire, England.

DATA
Gauge; 12.
Lengths; 64 mm.
Head; 8 mm.
Tube; Wound yellow paper.
Colour; Mustard yellow.
Print; Black.
Base; Brass.
Closure; Rolled turn-over.
Wad; Light yellow, print black.
Loading; Mullerite Cartridge Works.

DN.2-0398. Re-drawn 28th Jan 1999

JOSEPH BENTLEY:
309 Halifax Road, Liversedge, West Yorkshire, England.

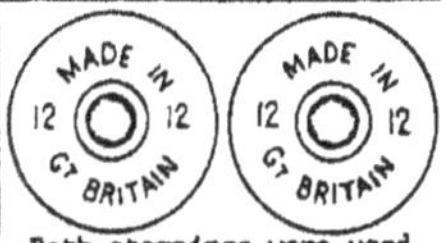

Both stampings were used.

DATA
Gauge; 12.
Lengths; 65 mm and 70 mm.
Head; 8 mm.
Tubes; Wound orange or crimson papers.
Colour; Orange or deep crimson.
Prints; Black.
Base; Brass.
Closure; Rolled turn-over.
Wad; Sky blue, print black.
Business; Cartridge loader.
Cases; Greenwood & Batley.

Various wads were used.

DN.2-0407. Re-drawn; 21st Jan 2000.

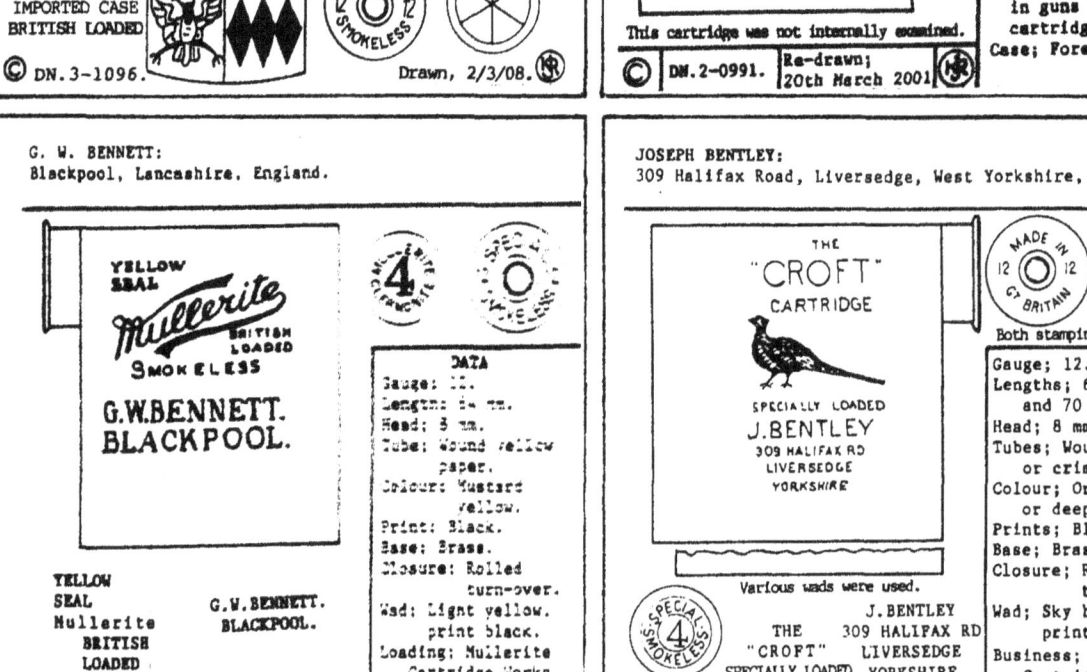

G & G. BISSET: London, England.
(Rest of address is not known).

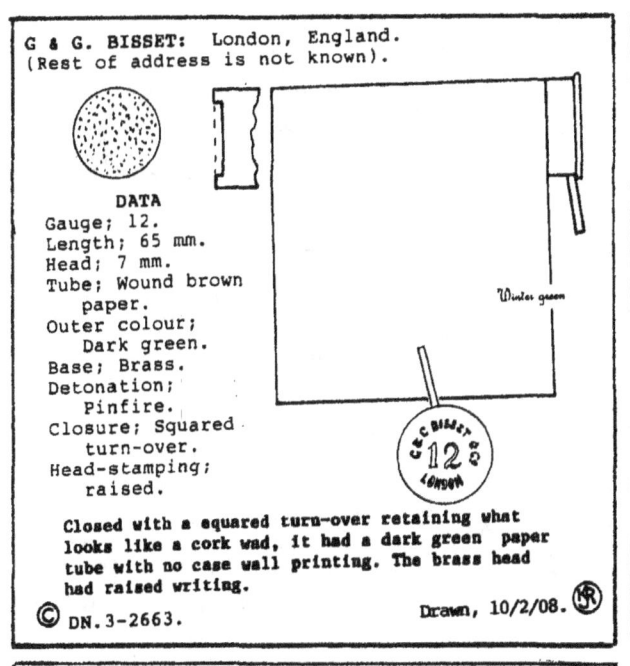

DATA
Gauge; 12.
Length; 65 mm.
Head; 7 mm.
Tube; Wound brown paper.
Outer colour; Dark green.
Base; Brass.
Detonation; Pinfire.
Closure; Squared turn-over.
Head-stamping; raised.

Closed with a squared turn-over retaining what looks like a cork wad, it had a dark green paper tube with no case wall printing. The brass head had raised writing.

© DN.3-2663.   Drawn, 10/2/08.

J. BLACK:
Bollington, Near Macclesfield, Cheshire, England.

Drawn from the Chris Hart collection.

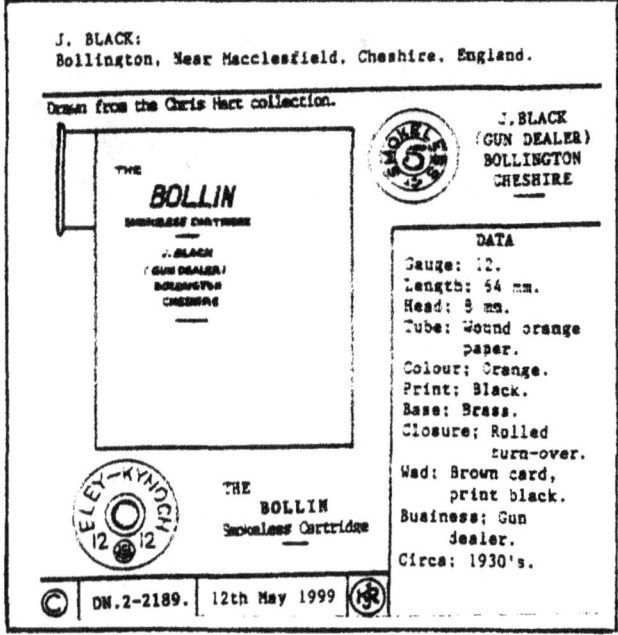

J. BLACK
(GUN DEALER)
BOLLINGTON
CHESHIRE

DATA
Gauge; 12.
Length; 64 mm.
Head; 8 mm.
Tube; Wound orange paper.
Colour; Orange.
Print; Black.
Base; Brass.
Closure; Rolled turn-over.
Wad; Brown card, print black.
Business; Gun dealer.
Circa; 1930's.

© DN.2-2189.   12th May 1999

C. G. BLACKADDER: Castle Douglas, Kirkcudbrightshire (Dumfries & Galloway), Scotland.

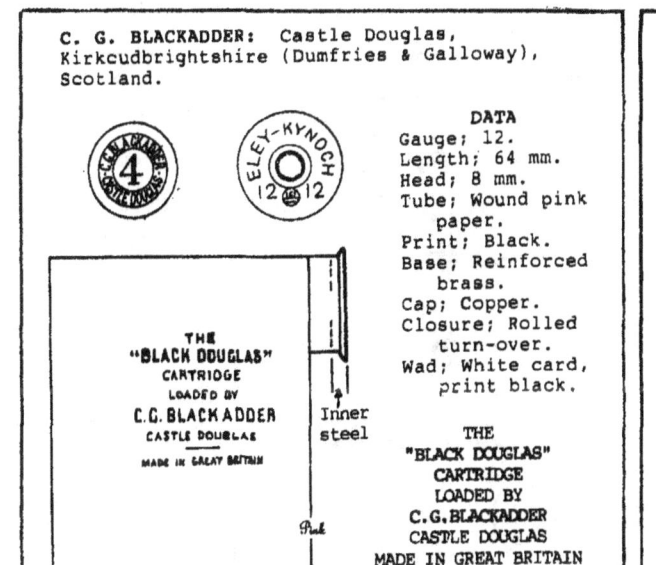

DATA
Gauge; 12.
Length; 64 mm.
Head; 8 mm.
Tube; Wound pink paper.
Print; Black.
Base; Reinforced brass.
Cap; Copper.
Closure; Rolled turn-over.
Wad; White card, print black.

THE
"BLACK DOUGLAS"
CARTRIDGE
LOADED BY
C.G. BLACKADDER
CASTLE DOUGLAS
MADE IN GREAT BRITAIN

© DN.3-0406.   Drawn, 1/4/08.

JAMES BLAKE:
12 The Square, Kelso, Roxburghshire (Borders), Scotland.

This drawing was made from a set of photographs.

DATA
Gauge; 12.
Length; 64 mm.
Head; 7 mm.
Tube; Wound orange paper.
Colour; Dull brownish-orange.
Print; Black.
Base; Brass.
Closure; Rolled turn-over.
Wad; Not known.
Business; Gunmaker.
Case; Eley Bros, Ltd.

© DN.2-1279.   Re-drawn; 25th Jan 2000.

JAMES BLAKE:
12 The Square, Kelso, Roxburghshire (Borders), Scotland.

THE
ROXBURGH
SMOKELESS CARTRIDGE
JAMES BLAKE
12 SQUARE
KELSO
Made in Great Britain

DATA
Gauge; 12.
Length; 64 mm.
Head; 8 mm.
Tube; Wound pink paper.
Colour; Shocking pink.
Print; Black.
Base; Brass.
Closure; Rolled turn-over.
Wad; White card, print black.
Case; Nobel Industries, Ltd.
Circa; 1920's.

© DN.2-2430.   20th June 2001

THOMAS BLAND & SONS:
King William Street, London.
Also in, Birmingham, England.

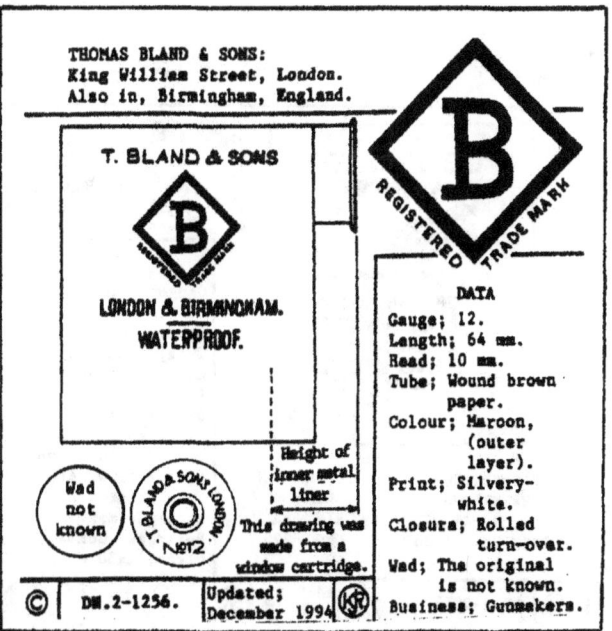

DATA
Gauge; 12.
Length; 64 mm.
Head; 10 mm.
Tube; Wound brown paper.
Colour; Maroon, (outer layer).
Print; Silvery-white.
Closure; Rolled turn-over.
Wad; The original is not known.
Business; Gunmakers.

© DN.2-1256.   Updated; December 1994

PLATE 25 [BIS - BLA]

THOMAS BLAND & SONS:
430 West Strand, London. Later at, King William Street, London. Also at, 41-43 Whitall Street, Birmingham, England.

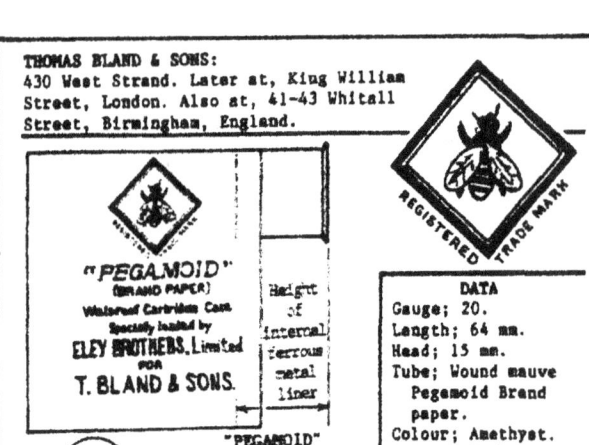
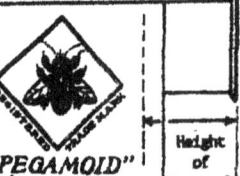

DATA
Gauge; 20.
Length; 64 mm.
Head; 15 mm.
Tube; Wound mauve Pegamoid Brand paper.
Colour; Amethyst.
Print; Black.
Base; Reinforced brass.
Closure; Rolled turn-over.
Wad; Not known.
Business; Gunmakers.
Case; Eley Bros, Ltd. London.

By courtesy of T. Matthews.

© DN.2-2485. 8th Sept 2001

THOMAS BLAND & SONS:
430 West Strand, London, W.C. Later at, 2 King William Street, Strand, London. Also at, 41-43 Whittall Street, Birmingham, Warwickshire (W. Midlands), England.

DATA
Gauge; 16.
Length; 64.5 mm.
Head; 15 mm.
Tube; Wound Pegamoid Brand paper.
Colour; Brown.
Print; Black.
Base; Reinforced brass.
Closure; Rolled turn-over.
Wad shown; White card, print red.
Business; Gun and rifle makers.
Circa; 1897-1900.

The example drawn may have been a reload.

© DN.2-1542. Updated, March 1996

RICHARD BLANTON: Market Place, Ringwood, Hampshire, England.

DATA
Gauge; 16.
Length; 64 mm.
Head; 7.5 mm.
Tube; Wound paper.
Outer colour; Dark-blue.
Print; Silver.
Base; Brass.
Cap; Copper.
Closure; Rolled turn-over.
Wad; White card, print pink.
Business; Gunmaker.
Case; Imported.

"COMPETITOR"

Drawn from a set of photographs.

© DN.3-2618. Drawn, 16/11/07.

RICHARD BLANTON:
Market Place, Ringwood, Hampshire, England.

"COMPETITOR" SPECIAL SMOKELESS FOREIGN MADE CASE BRITISH LOADED R. BLANTON GUNMAKER RINGWOOD PHONE 223

DATA
Gauge; 16.
Length; 64 mm.
Head; 7 mm.
Tube; Wound brown paper.
Colour; Yellow.
Print; Black.
Base; Reinforced brass.
Closure; Rolled turn-over.
Wad; yellow card, print black.
Business; Gunmaker.
Case; Germany.

Drawn from the Chris Hart collection.

© DN.2-2285. 19th April 2000

R. BLANTON:
Market Place, Ringwood, Hampshire, England.

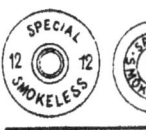

DATA
Gauge; 12.
Length; 65 mm.
Head; 8 mm.
Tube; Wound paper.
Colour; Lilac mauve.
Print; Silver.
Base; Brass.
Closure; Rolled turn-over.
Wad; Yellow card, print black.
Case; Garman.
Business; Gunmaker.
Circa; 1930's.

"COMPETITOR" WATERPROOF FOREIGN MADE CASE BRITISH LOADED

R. BLANTON GUNMAKER RINGWOOD PHONE 223

© DN.2-0853. Updated; April 1997

RICHARD BLANTON:
Market Place, Ringwood, Hampshire, England.

R. BLANTON GUNMAKER RINGWOOD

"THE IMPERIAL" SPECIAL SMOKELESS BRITISH LOADED FOREIGN MADE CASE

DATA
Gauge; 12.
Length; 65 mm.
Head; 15 mm.
Tube; Wound brown paper.
Colour; Maroon.
Print; Silver.
Base; Reinforced brass.
Closure; Rolled turn-over.
Wad; Yellow card, print black.
Business; Gunmaker.
Case; Germany.
Circa; Early 1930's.

Drawn from the Chris Hart collection.

© DN.2-2284. 18th April 2000

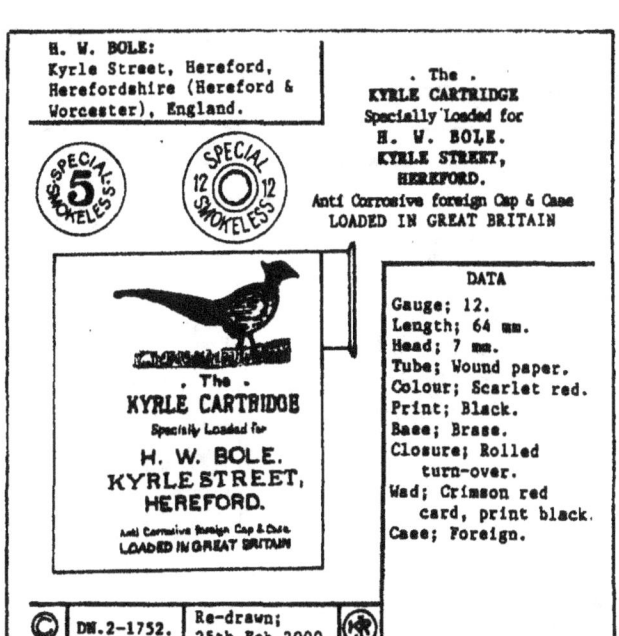
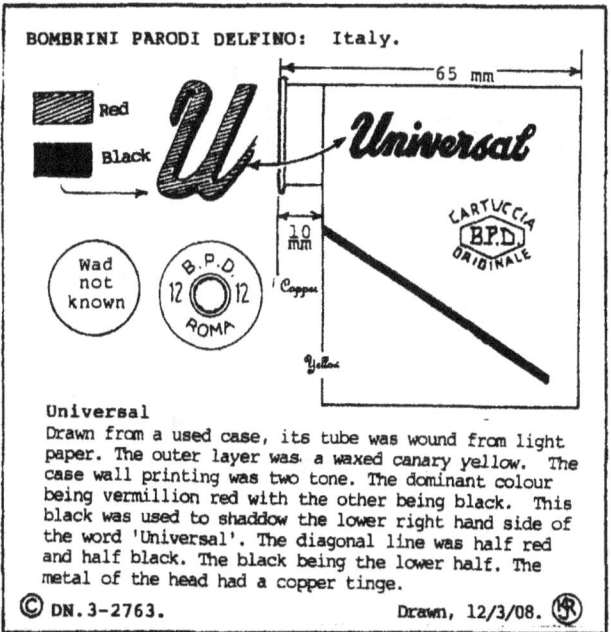
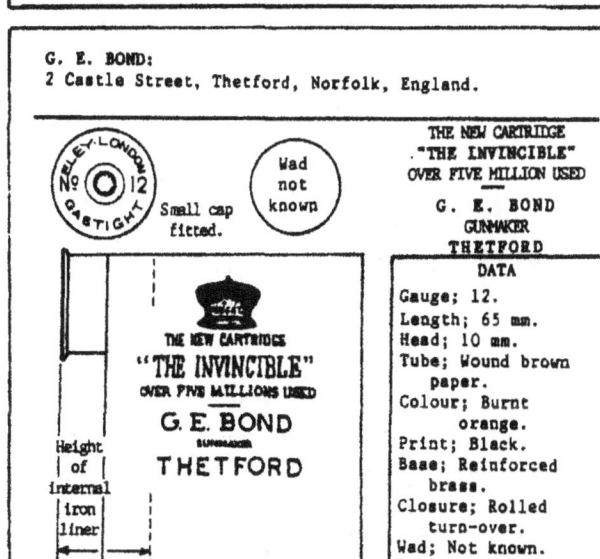
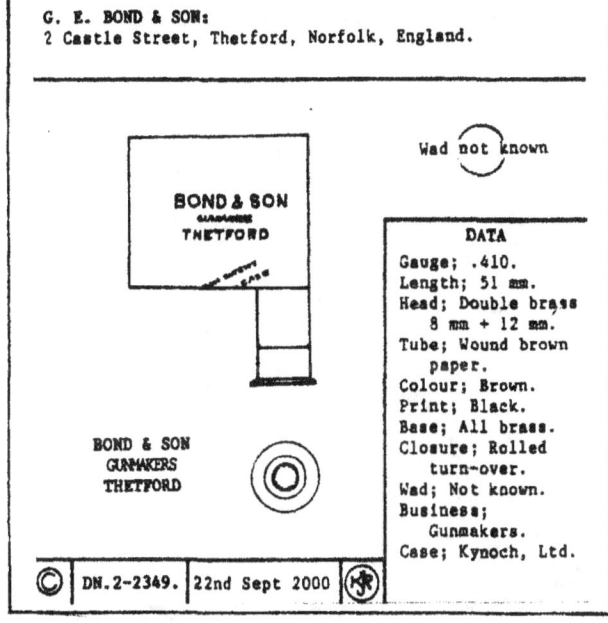
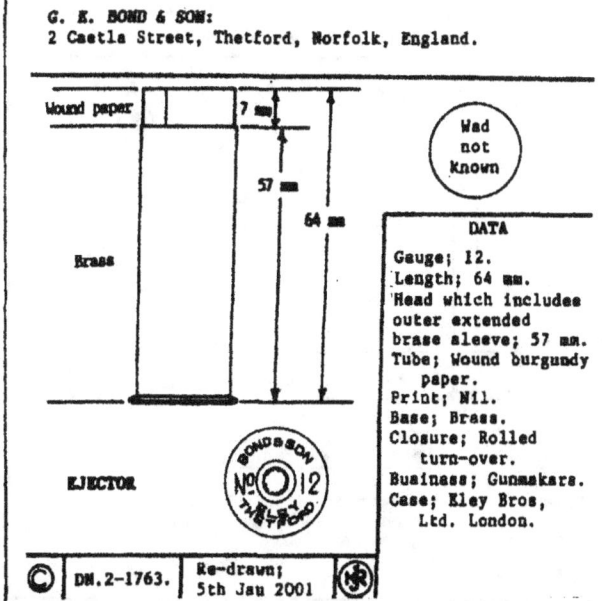
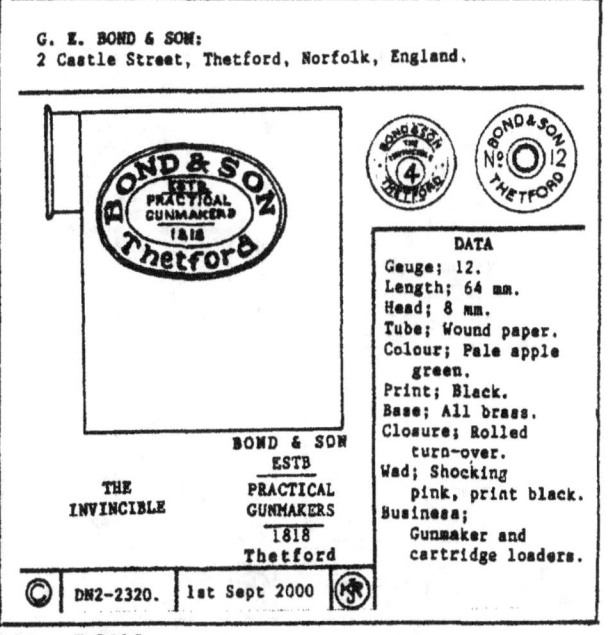

PLATE 27 [BOL – BON]

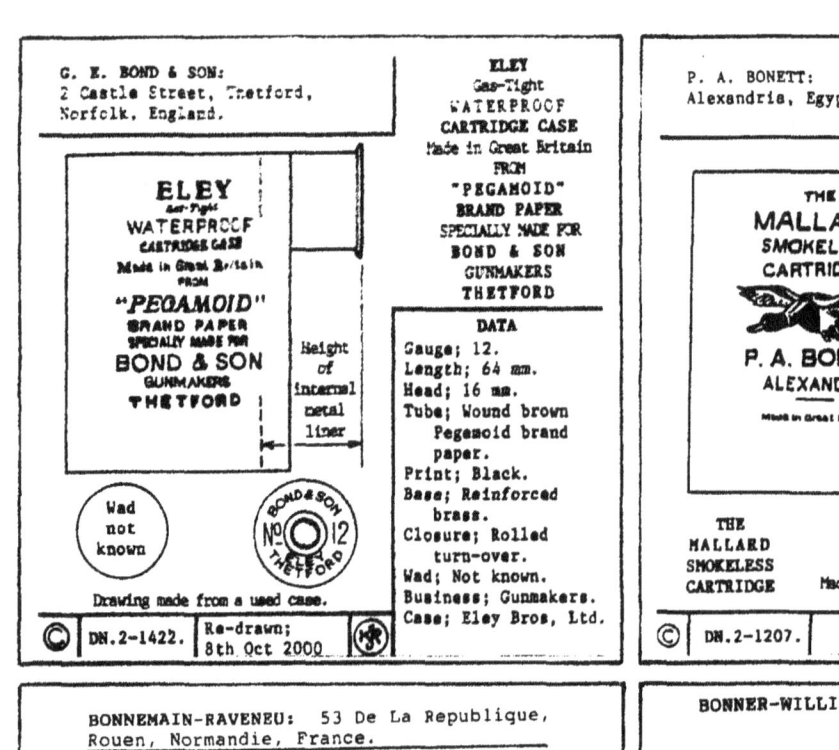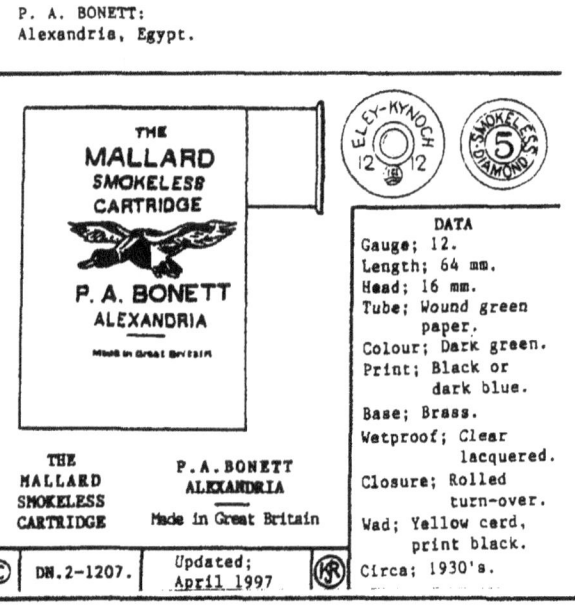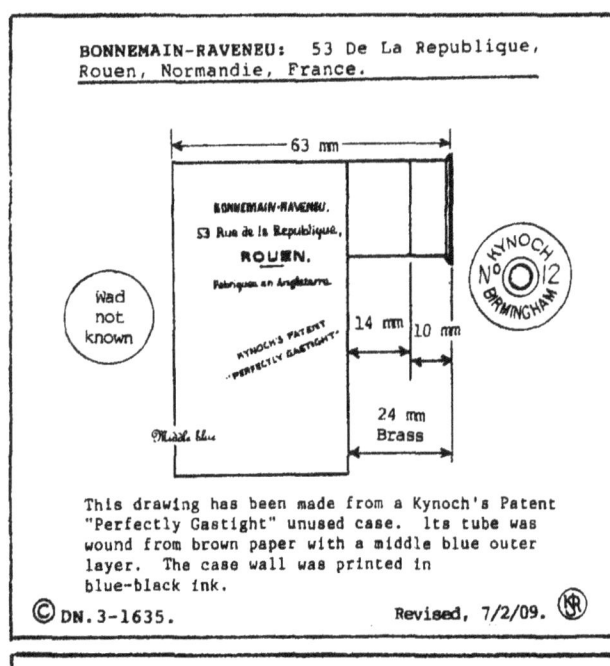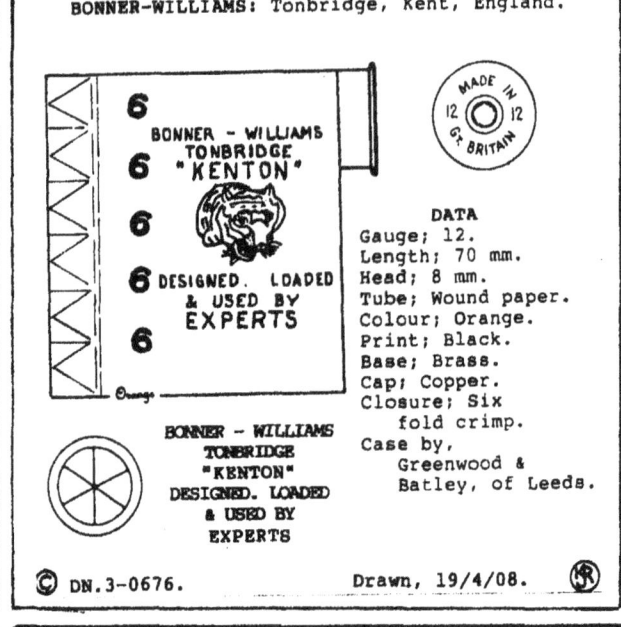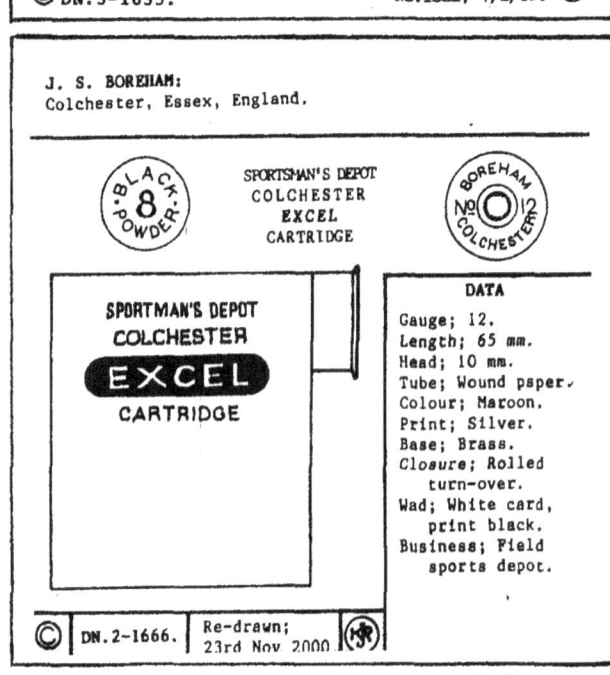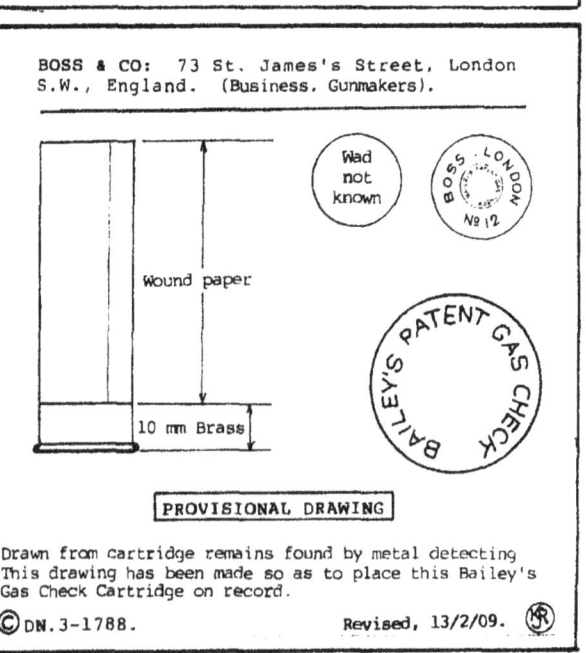

PLATE 28 [BON - BOS]

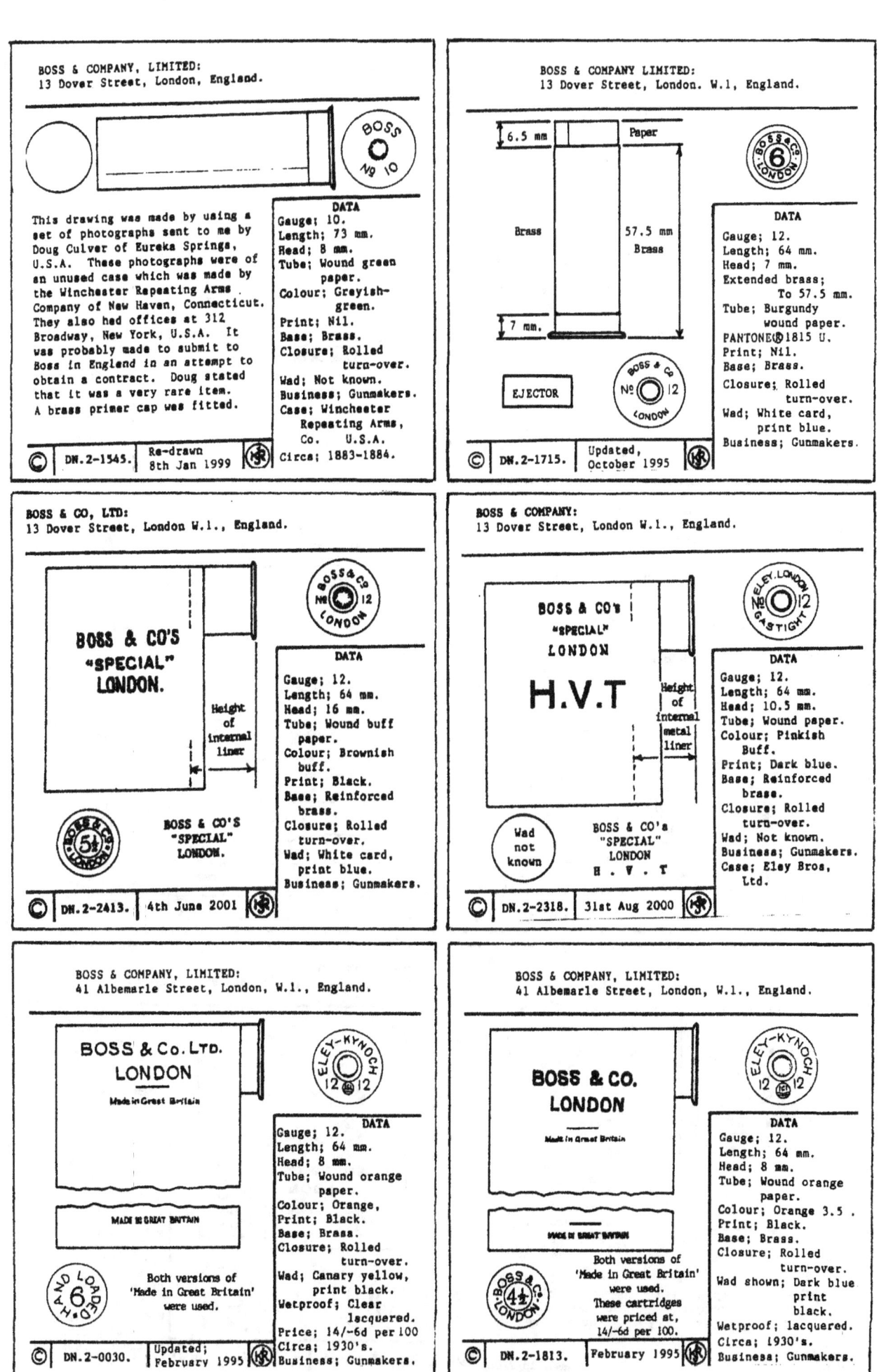

PLATE 29 [BOS-BOS]

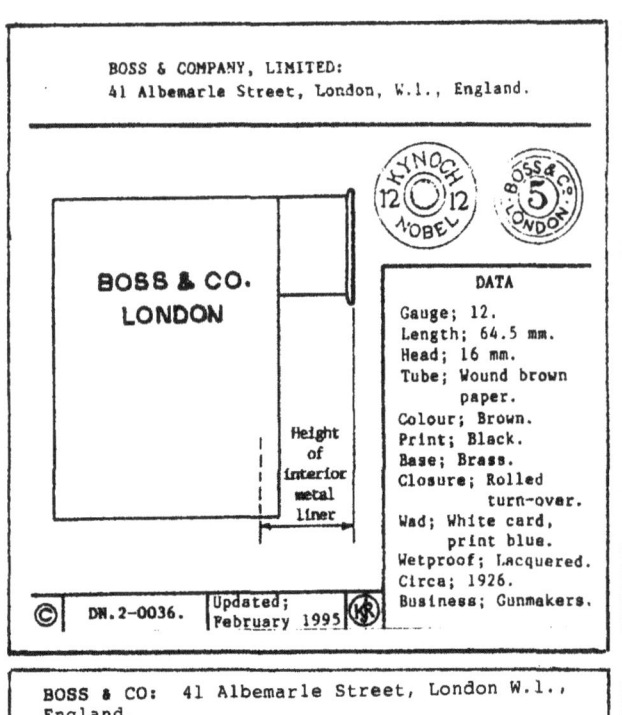
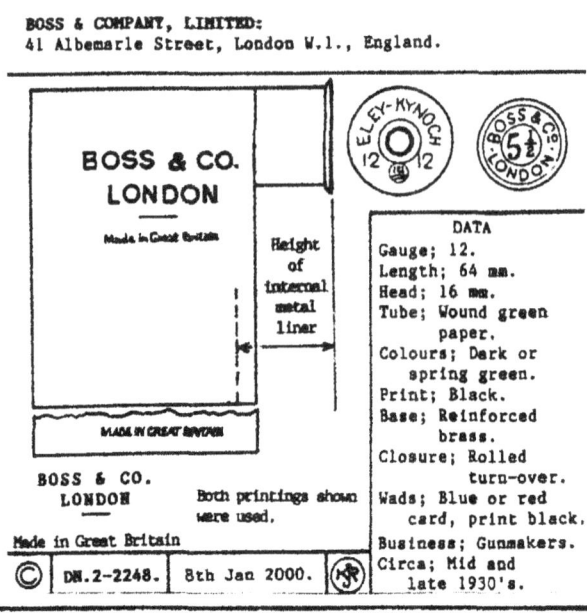
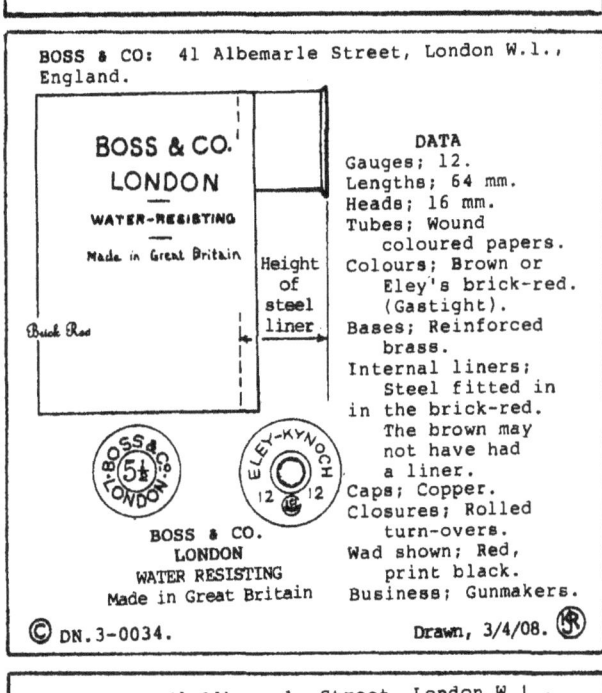
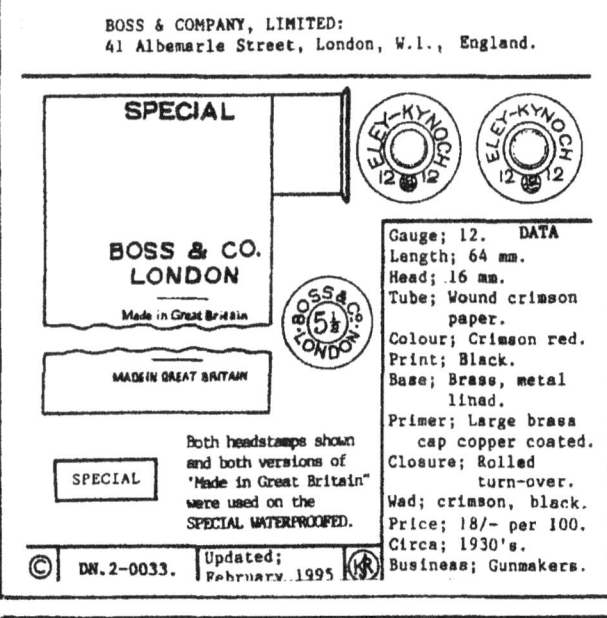

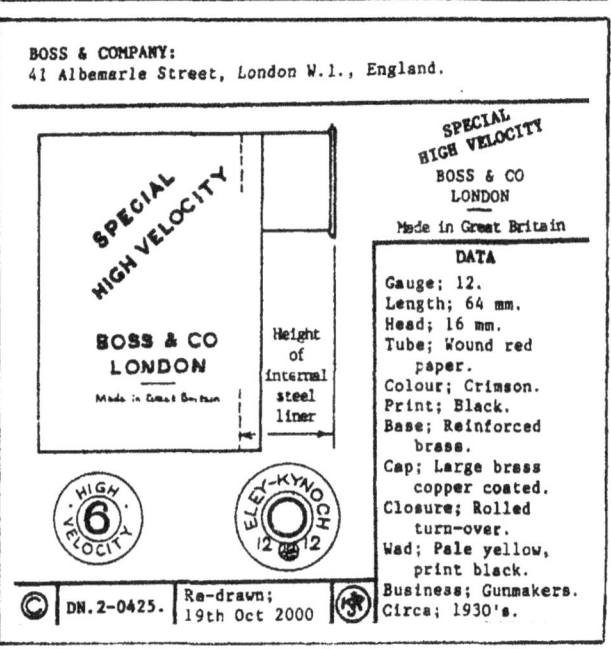

PLATE 30 [BOS – BOS]

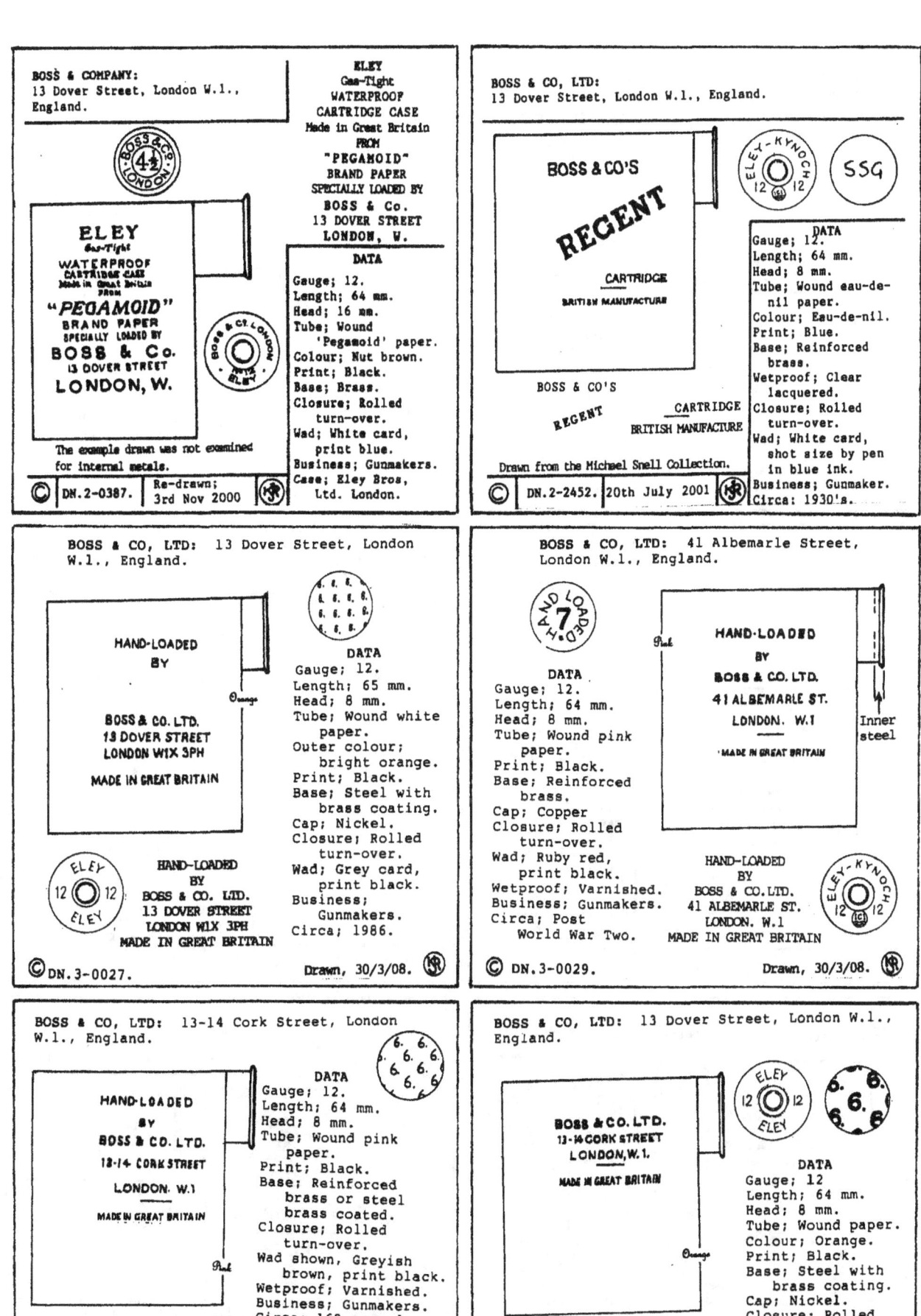

PLATE 31 [BOS - BOS]

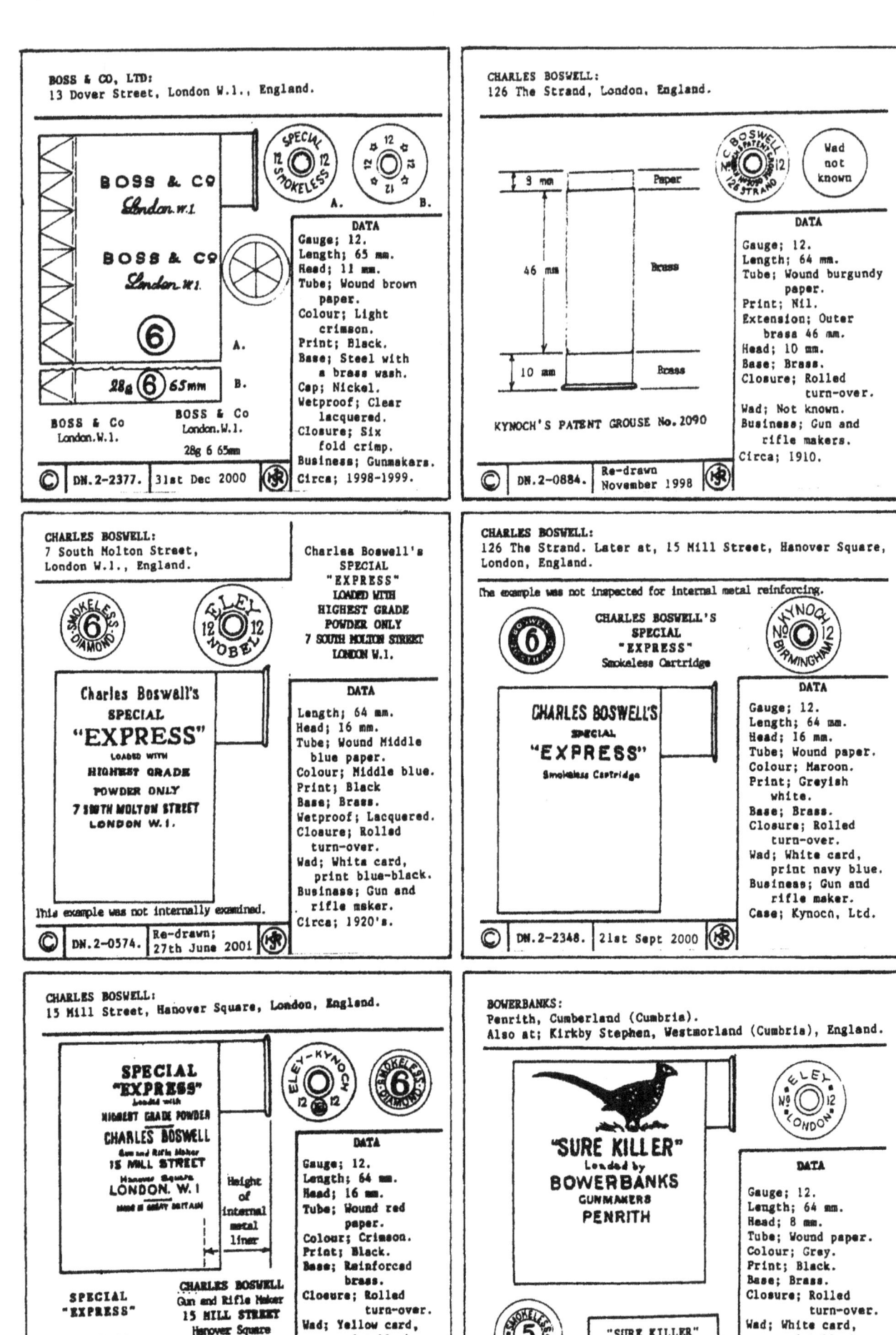

PLATE 32 [BOS - BOW]

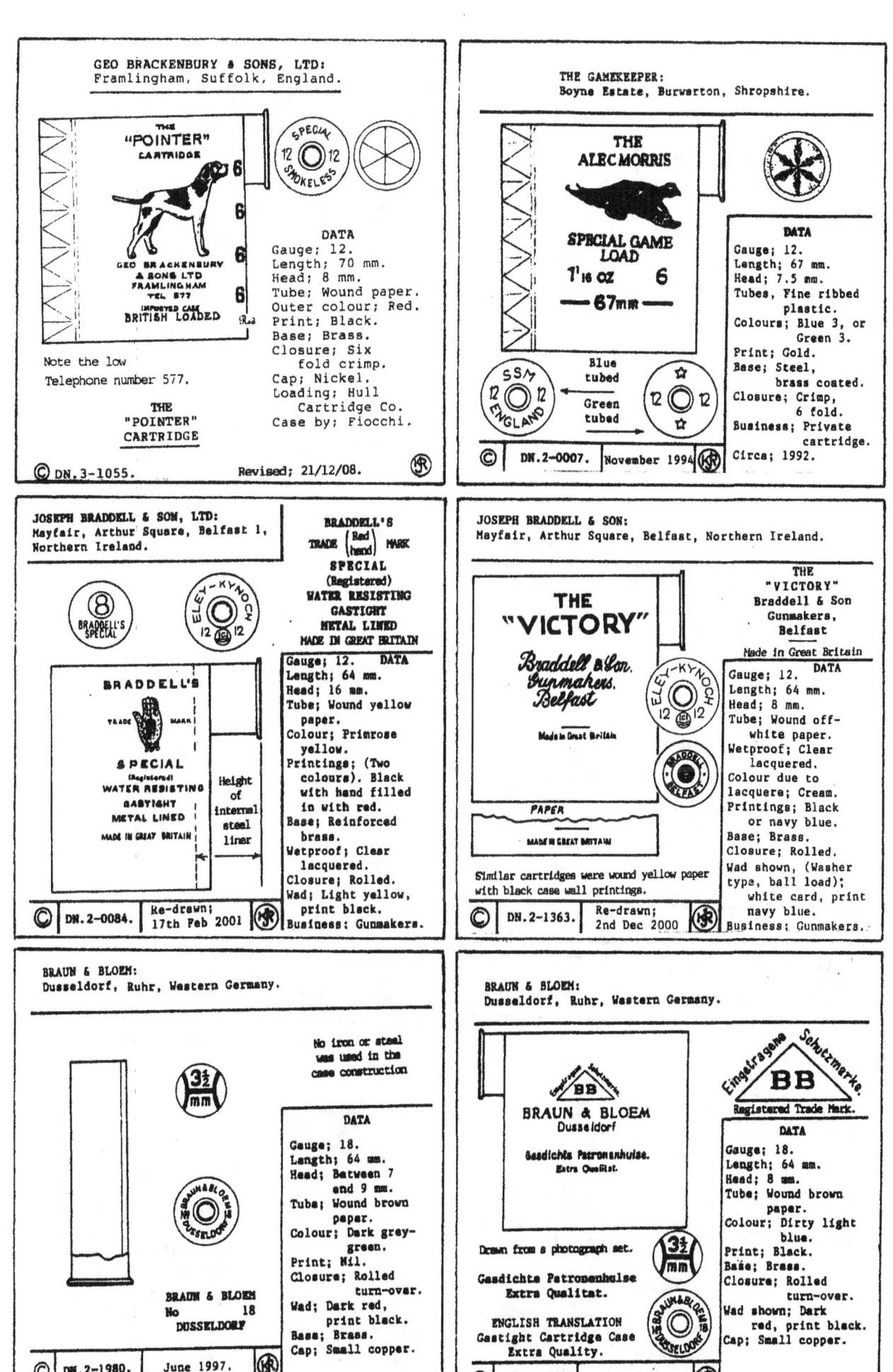

BRAXTED PARK ESTATE: Braxted Park, Witham, Essex, CM8 3EW, England.

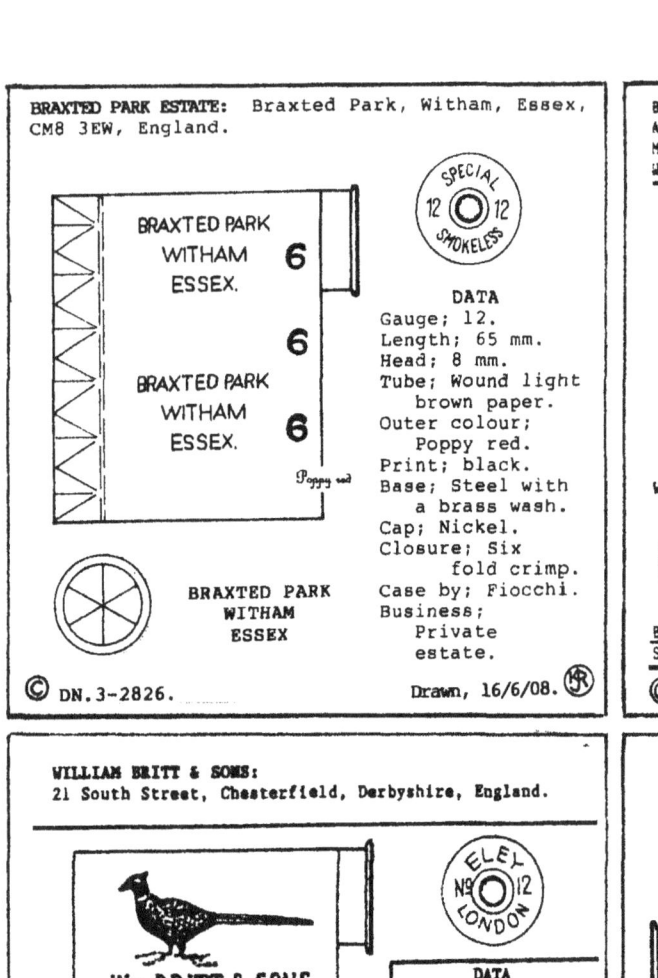

DATA
Gauge; 12.
Length; 65 mm.
Head; 8 mm.
Tube; Wound light brown paper.
Outer colour; Poppy red.
Print; black.
Base; Steel with a brass wash.
Cap; Nickel.
Closure; Six fold crimp.
Case by; Fiocchi.
Business; Private estate.

© DN.3-2826. Drawn, 16/6/08.

BRITISH ASSOCIATION FOR SHOOTING AND CONSERVATION:
Marford Mill, Chester Road, Rossett, Wrexham, Clwyd LL12 0HL, Wales.

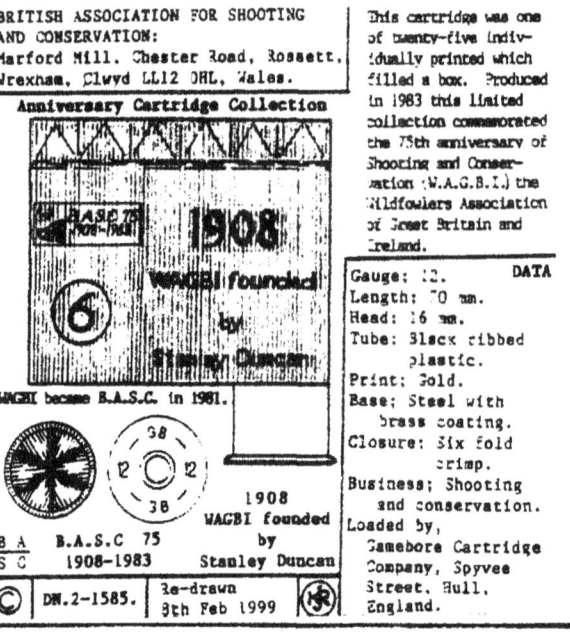

This cartridge was one of twenty-five individually printed which filled a box. Produced in 1983 this limited collection commemorated the 75th anniversary of Shooting and Conservation (W.A.G.B.I.) the Wildfowlers Association of Great Britain and Ireland.

DATA
Gauge; 12.
Length; 70 mm.
Head; 16 mm.
Tube; Black ribbed plastic.
Print; Gold.
Base; Steel with brass coating.
Closure; Six fold crimp.
Business; Shooting and conservation.
Loaded by, Gamebore Cartridge Company, Spyvee Street, Hull, England.

© DN.2-1585. Re-drawn 9th Feb 1999.

WILLIAM BRITT & SONS:
21 South Street, Chesterfield, Derbyshire, England.

DATA
Gauge; 12.
Length; 64 mm.
Head 8 mm.
Tube; Wound paper.
Colour; Tan brown.
Print; Black.
Base; Brass.
Closure; Rolled turn-over.
Wad; White card, print pink.
Business; Ironmongers.
Case; Eley Bros, Ltd. London.

© DN.2-0675. Re-drawn; 17th Feb 2000.

BROCK'S EXPLOSIVES, LTD: Sanquhar, Dumfriesshire (Dumfries & Galloway), Scotland.

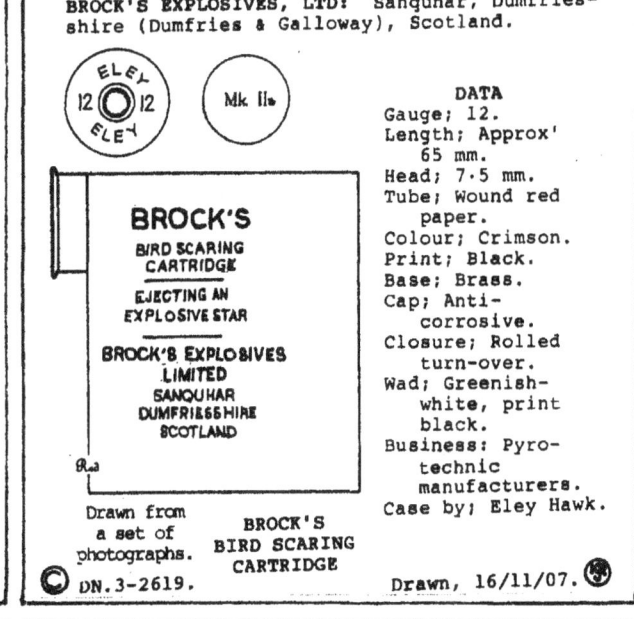

DATA
Gauge; 12.
Length; Approx' 65 mm.
Head; 7.5 mm.
Tube; Wound red paper.
Colour; Crimson.
Print; Black.
Base; Brass.
Cap; Anti-corrosive.
Closure; Rolled turn-over.
Wad; Greenish-white, print black.
Business; Pyrotechnic manufacturers.
Case by; Eley Hawk.

© DN.3-2619. Drawn, 16/11/07.

BROOKER:
Hitchin, Hertfordshire, England.

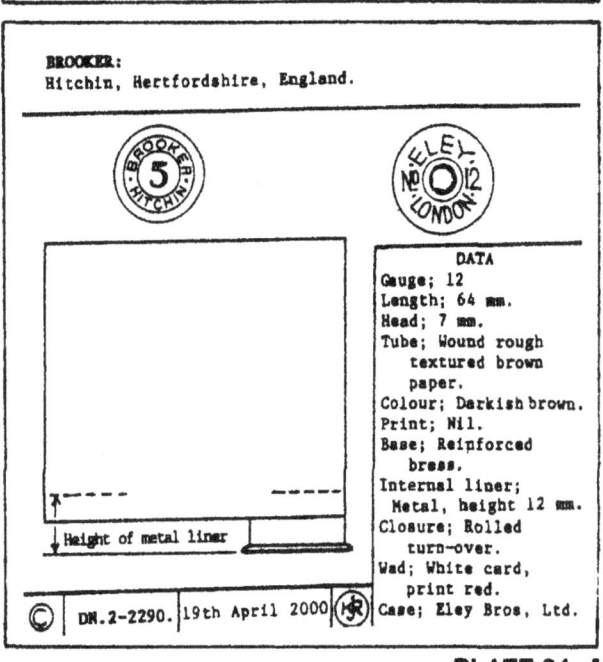

DATA
Gauge; 12
Length; 64 mm.
Head; 7 mm.
Tube; Wound rough textured brown paper.
Colour; Darkish brown.
Print; Nil.
Base; Reinforced brass.
Internal liner; Metal, height 12 mm.
Closure; Rolled turn-over.
Wad; White card, print red.
Case; Eley Bros, Ltd.

© DN.2-2290. 19th April 2000.

BROWN:
Morpeth, Northumberland, England.

DATA
Gauge; 12.
Length; 64 mm.
Head; 8 mm.
Tube; Rough brown paper.
Colour; Middle brown.
Print; Black.
Base; Brass.
Closure; Rolled turn-over.
Wad; Brown card, print purple.

© DN.2-2226. 17th Aug 1999.

PLATE 34 [BRA - BRO]

J. BROWN:
Morpeth, Northumberland, England.

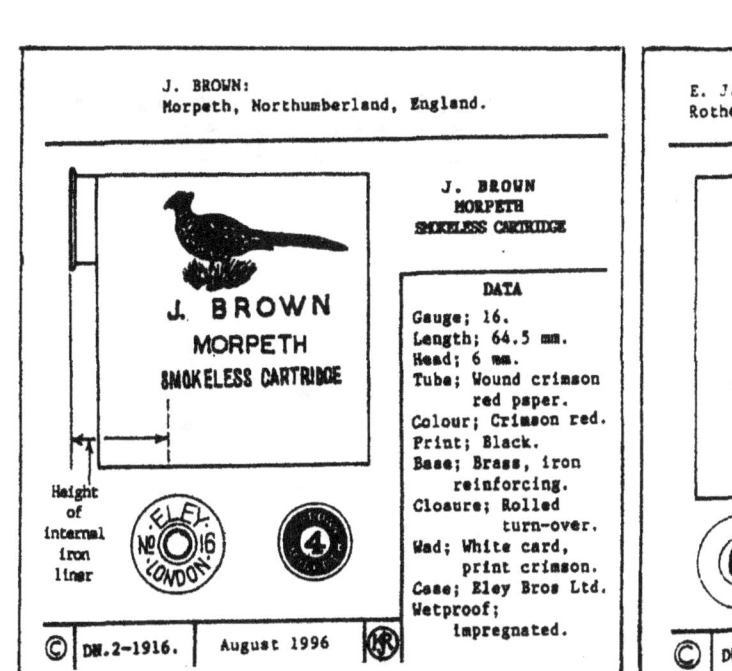

J. BROWN MORPETH SMOKELESS CARTRIDGE

DATA
Gauge; 16.
Length; 64.5 mm.
Head; 6 mm.
Tube; Wound crimson red paper.
Colour; Crimson red.
Print; Black.
Base; Brass, iron reinforcing.
Closure; Rolled turn-over.
Wad; White card, print crimson.
Case; Eley Bros Ltd.
Wetproof; impregnated.

DN.2-1916. August 1996

E. J. BROWN & COMPANY:
Rotherham, Yorkshire, England.

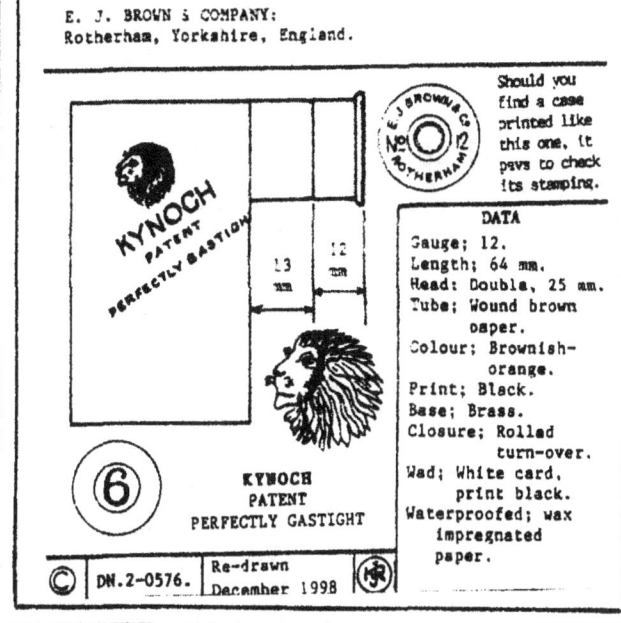

Should you find a case printed like this one, it pays to check its stamping.

DATA
Gauge; 12.
Length; 64 mm.
Head; Double, 25 mm.
Tube; Wound brown paper.
Colour; Brownish-orange.
Print; Black.
Base; Brass.
Closure; Rolled turn-over.
Wad; White card, print black.
Waterproofed; wax impregnated paper.

DN.2-0576. Re-drawn December 1998

BSA GUNS UK, LTD: (Birmingham Small Arms)
Armoury Road, Birmingham, B11, West Midlands, England.

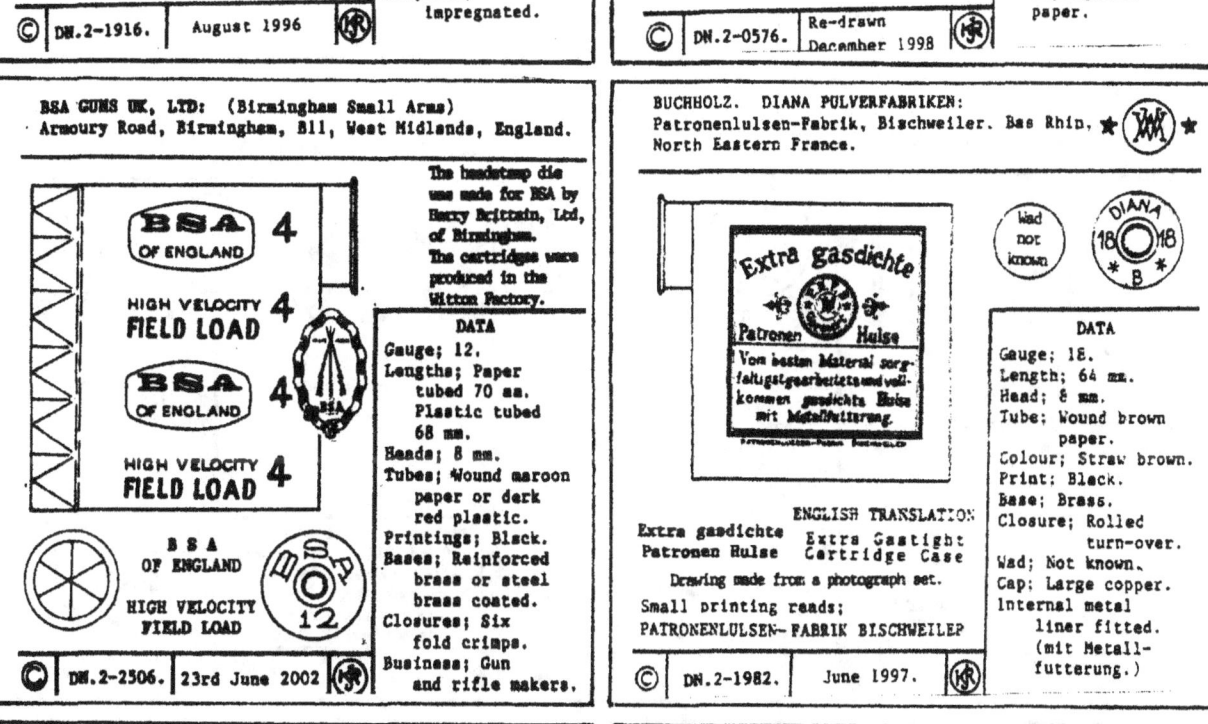

The headstamp die was made for BSA by Harry Brittain, Ltd, of Birmingham. The cartridges were produced in the Witton Factory.

DATA
Gauge; 12.
Lengths; Paper tubed 70 mm. Plastic tubed 68 mm.
Heads; 8 mm.
Tubes; Wound maroon paper or dark red plastic.
Printings; Black.
Bases; Reinforced brass or steel brass coated.
Closures; Six fold crimps.
Business; Gun and rifle makers.

DN.2-2506. 23rd June 2002

BUCHHOLZ. DIANA PULVERFABRIKEN:
Patronenhulsen-Fabrik, Bischweiler, Bas Rhin, North Eastern France.

ENGLISH TRANSLATION
Extra gasdichte = Extra Gastight
Patronen Hulse = Cartridge Case
Drawing made from a photograph set.
Small printing reads:
PATRONENHULSEN- FABRIK BISCHWEILER

DATA
Gauge; 18.
Length; 64 mm.
Head; 8 mm.
Tube; Wound brown paper.
Colour; Straw brown.
Print; Black.
Base; Brass.
Closure; Rolled turn-over.
Wad; Not known.
Cap; Large copper.
Internal metal liner fitted. (mit Metall-futterung.)

DN.2-1982. June 1997.

BUCK & COMPANY:
11 - 12 St. Andrew's Hill, London E.C., England.

Information was gleaned from an old advertisement.

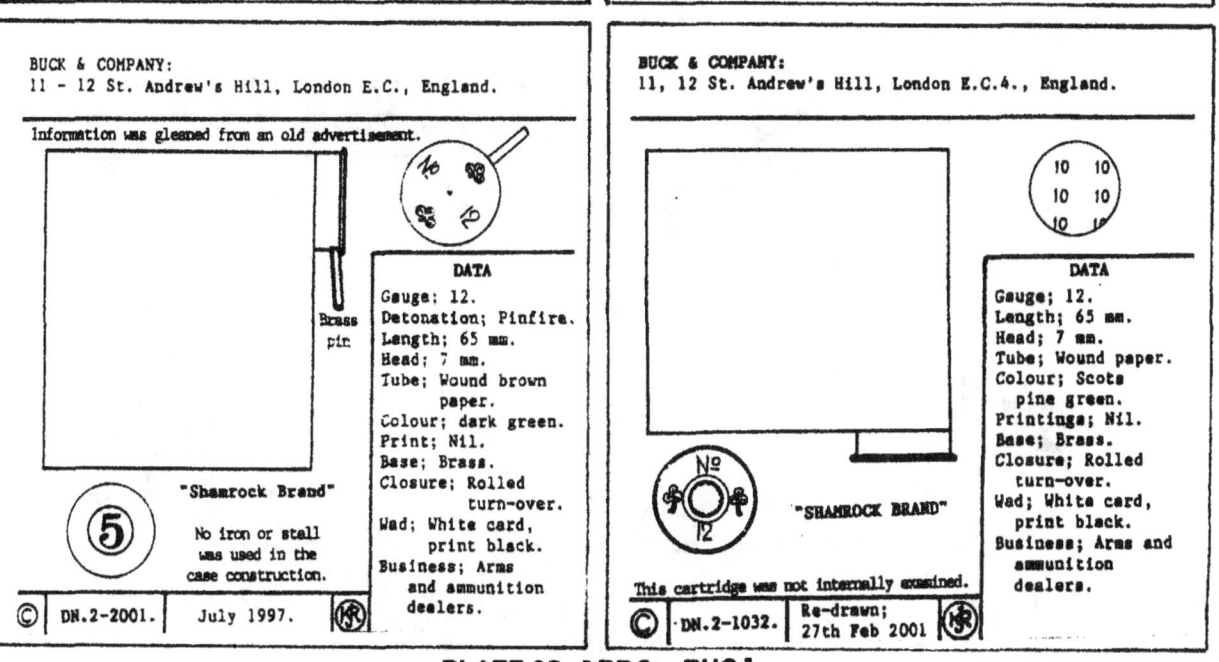

"Shamrock Brand"

No iron or stall was used in the case construction.

DATA
Gauge; 12.
Detonation; Pinfire.
Length; 65 mm.
Head; 7 mm.
Tube; Wound brown paper.
Colour; dark green.
Print; Nil.
Base; Brass.
Closure; Rolled turn-over.
Wad; White card, print black.
Business; Arms and ammunition dealers.

DN.2-2001. July 1997.

BUCK & COMPANY:
11, 12 St. Andrew's Hill, London E.C.4., England.

"SHAMROCK BRAND"

This cartridge was not internally examined.

DATA
Gauge; 12.
Length; 65 mm.
Head; 7 mm.
Tube; Wound paper.
Colour; Scots pine green.
Printings; Nil.
Base; Brass.
Closure; Rolled turn-over.
Wad; White card, print black.
Business; Arms and ammunition dealers.

DN.2-1032. Re-drawn; 27th Feb 2001

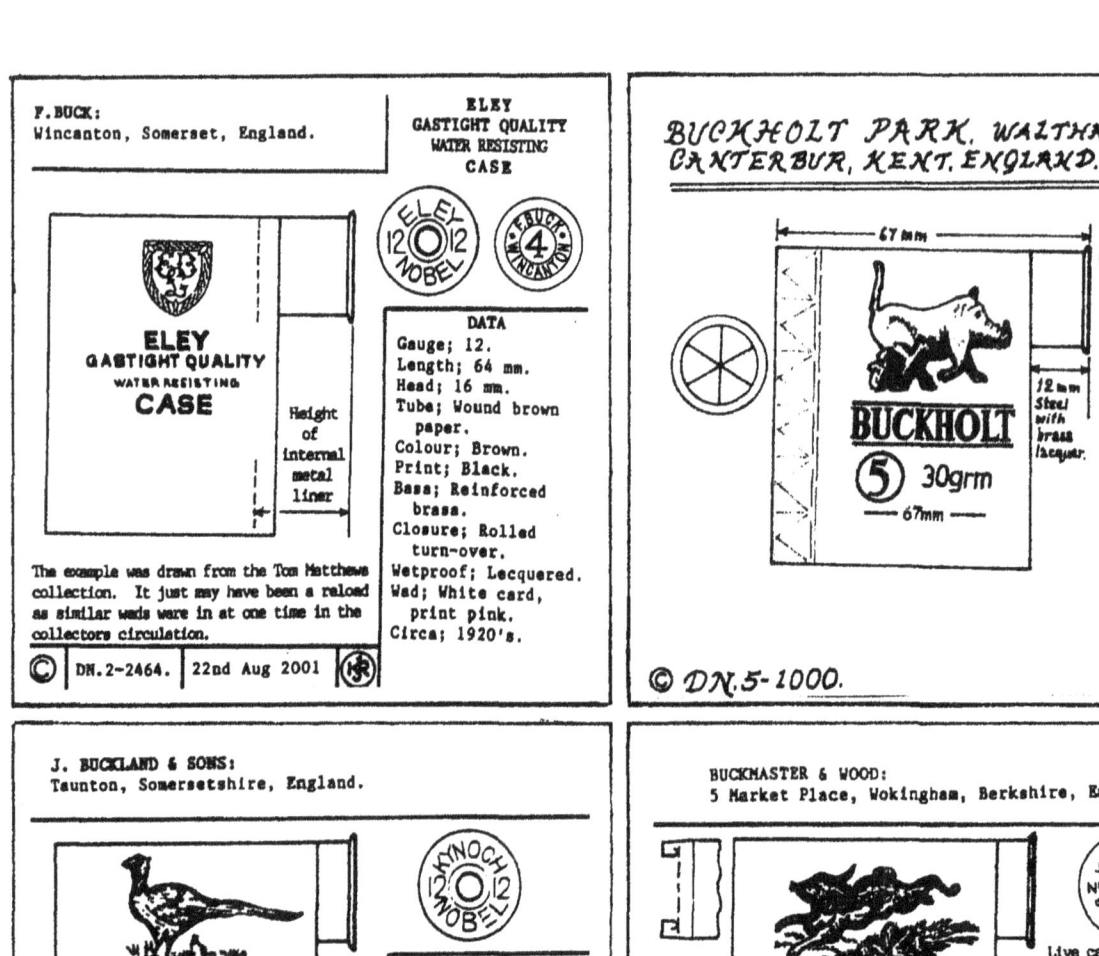
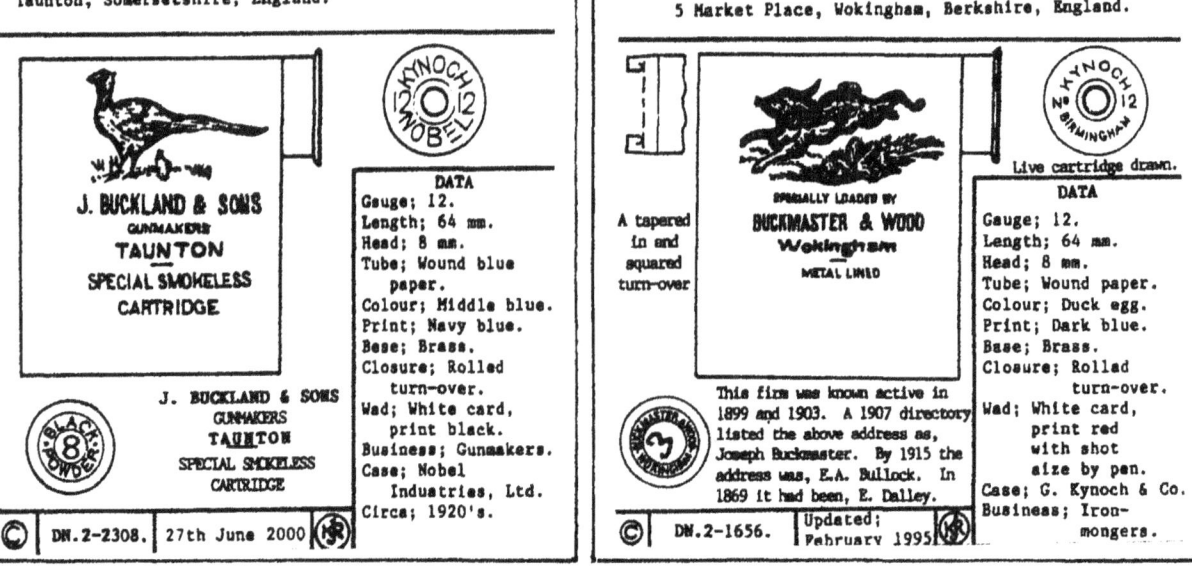
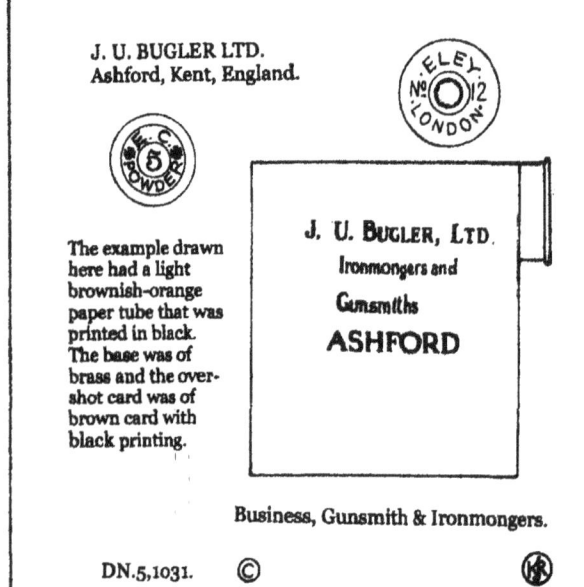
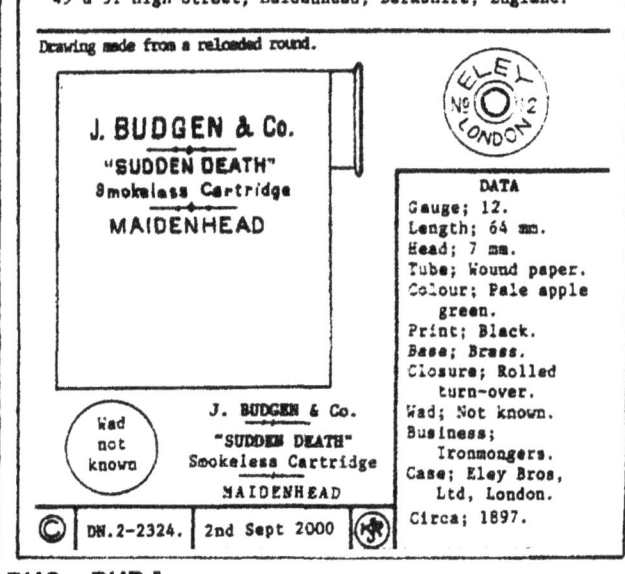

PLATE 36 [BUC – BUD]

GEORGE G. BULLMORE:
1 St. George Road, Newquay. Also at,
St. Columb, Cornwall, England.

GEORGE G. BULLMORE
NEWQUAY
AND
ST. COLUMB

Wad not known

GEORGE G. BULLMORE
NEWQUAY
AND
ST. COLUMB

This drawing was made from a used case.

(KYNOCH No 12 BIRMINGHAM)

DATA
Gauge; 12.
Length; 64 mm.
Head; 8 mm.
Tube; Wound paper.
Colour; Dull red.
Print; Black.
Base; Brass.
Closure; Rolled
 turn-over.
Wad; Not known.
Business;
 Ironmonger and
 agricultural
 merchant.

© DN.2-0457. Re-drawn; 14th Nov 2000

A. C. BULPIN:
Newton Abbot, Devonshire, England.

BULPIN'S
STRAIGHT SHOT

CARTRIDGE
NEWTON ABBOT

Wad not known

BULPIN'S
STRAIGHT SHOT
CARTRIDGE
NEWTON ABBOT

Drawing made from a used case.

(ELEY 12 12 NOBEL)

DATA
Gauge; 12.
Length; 64 mm.
Head; 8 mm.
Tube; Wound orange
 paper.
Colour; Orange.
Print; Black.
Base; Brass.
Closure; Rolled
 turn-over.
Wad; Not known.
Case; Nobel
 Industries, Ltd.
Circa; 1920's.

© DN.2-2305. 27th June 2000

W. BUNTING:
Cromford, Nr Wirksworth, Derbyshire, England.

YELLOW
SEAL
Mullerite
BRITISH
LOADED

SMOKELESS
W. BUNTING
CROMFORD

YELLOW
SEAL
Mullerite
BRITISH LOADED
SMOKELESS
W. BUNTING
CROMFORD

(SPECIAL 12 12 SMOKELESS)   (MULLERITE 5 CARTRIDGE)

DATA
Gauge; 12.
Length; 65 mm.
Head; 8 mm.
Tube; Wound brown
 paper.
Colour; Mustard
 yellow.
Print; Black.
Base; Reinforced
 brass.
Closure; Rolled
 turn-over.
Wad; Light yellow,
 print black.

© DN.2-0211. Re-drawn; 9th Jan 2002

FREDERICK H. BURGESS, LIMITED:
Premises at; Stafford, Eccleshall, Newcastle
& Wolverhampton, Staffordshire. Also at,
Newport & Shrewsbury, Shropshire, England.

FREDK. H. BURGESS LTD. | WOLVERHAMPTON. NEWCASTLE
"CHAMPION" | (STAFFS) NEWPORT (SALOP)
Branches at | SHREWSBURY.
STAFFORD (Head Office) |
ECCLESHALL. LICHFIELD. | MADE IN GREAT BRITAIN

FREDK. H. BURGESS LTD
"CHAMPION"

Branches at:
STAFFORD (Head Office)
ECCLESHALL. LICHFIELD.
WOLVERHAMPTON. NEWCASTLE
(STAFFS) NEWPORT (SALOP)
SHREWSBURY.

MADE IN GREAT BRITAIN

Drawn from a set of photographs

(SMOKELESS DIAMOND 5)   (ELEY-KYNOCH 12 4ch 12)

DATA
Gauge; 12.
Length; 64 mm.
Head; 8 mm.
Tube; Wound dark
 orange paper.
Colour; Orange.
Print; Black.
Base; Brass.
Closure; Rolled
 turn-over.
Wad; Yellow,
 print black.
Case; Eley-Kynoch
 I.C.I.

© DN.2-2033. October 1998

JAMES BURROW:
116 Fishergate, Preston, Lancashire, England.

THE
CHALLENGE
CARTRIDGE
LOADED BY
J. BURROW
GUNMAKER
116 FISHERGATE PRESTON

THE
CHALLENGE
CARTRIDGE
LOADED BY
J. BURROW
GUNMAKER
116 FISHERGATE PRESTON

(SMOKELESS 5)   (J.BURROW No 16 PRESTON)

DATA
Gauge; 16.
Length; 65 mm.
Head; 8 mm.
Tube; Wound orange
 paper.
Colour; Orange.
Print; Black.
Base; Brass.
Closure; Rolled
 turn-over.
Wad; White card,
 print pink.
Business; Gunmaker.

© DN.2-1917. August 1996

JAMES BURROW: 16 Fishergate, Preston,
Lancashire. Also at, 46 Lowther Street,
Carlisle, Cumberland (Cumbria), England.

THE
FIELD
CARTRIDGE
LOADED BY
J. BURROW
GUNMAKER
16 FISHERGATE, PRESTON
46 LOWTHER St, CARLISLE

Crimson end

THE
FIELD
CARTRIDGE
LOADED BY
J. BURROW
GUNMAKER
16 FISHERGATE, PRESTON
46 LOWTHER St, CARLISLE

(ELEY No 16 LONDON)   (SMOKELESS 5)

DATA
Gauge; 16.
Length; 64 mm.
Head; 15 mm.
Tube; Wound paper.
Colour; Crimson.
Print; Black.
Wetproof; Waxed.
Base; Brass.
Cap; Copper.
Closure; Rolled
 turn-over.
Wad; White card,
 print black.
Business;
 Gunmaker.
Case by; Eley
 Bros, Ltd.

© DN.3-2793. Drawn, 19/3/08.

PLATE 37 [BUL - BUR]

J. BURROW:
116 Fishergate, Preston, Lancashire. Also at,
46 Lowther Street, Carlisle, Cumberland (Cumbria),
England.

Closed by a squared type turn-over.

THE
"PARAGON"
CARTRIDGE

DATA

Gauge; 12.
Length; 64 mm.
Head; 8 mm.
Tube; Wound green paper.
Colour; Apple green.
Print; Black.
Base; Brass.
Internal liner; Nil.
Closure; Rolled turn-over.
Wad; White card, print pink.
Business; Gunmaker.
Case; Nobel Explosives, Ltd.

© | DN.2-1859. | November 1995 | KR

BUSSEMS & PARKING, LIMITED:
Mildenhall, Suffolk, England.

Drawn from the Chris Hart collection.

B&P
LTD
SPECIALLY LOADED FOR
BUSSEMS & PARKIN Ltd
MILDENHALL
PHONE 58

DATA

Gauge; 12.
Length; 64 mm.
Head; 8.5 mm.
Tube; Wound paper.
Colour; Yellow.
Print; Black.
Base; Brass.
Closure; Rolled turn-over.
Wad; Red card, print black.
Business; Ironmongers.

© | DN.2-2184. | 11th May 1999 | KR

GEORGE G. BUSSEY & CO:
London, England.

Wad not known

ONE PIECE ALL BRASS EJECTOR

DATA

Gauge; 14.
Length; 65 mm.
Head; Continuous of case.
Construction; Solid drawn brass.
Type; Ejector.
Closure; Not known.
Case manufacturer, not known.

© | DN.2-0119. | Updated: March 1995 | KR

GEORGE G. BUSSEY & COMPANY:
London, England.

ALL BRASS
EJECTOR TYPE
CARTRIDGE

DATA

Gauge: 12.
Length: 54 mm.
Tube: All brass.
Base: Brass.
Closure: Six fold brass crimp.

© | DN.2-0806. | Re-drawn 3rd Feb 1999 | KR

CALEDONIAN CARTRIDGE CO, LTD:
Arrat Works, Brechin, Angus (Tayside), Scotland.

BRIT CPX
THE OUNCE

DATA

Gauge; 12.
Length; 67 mm.
Head; 7 mm.
Tube; Fine ribbed plastic.
Colour; Flame red 2.5 .
Print, Old gold.
Base; Steel, brass coated.
Closure; Crimp, 6 fold.
Business; Manufacturers.

© | DN.2-1805. | January 1995 | KR

CALEDONIAN CARTRIDGE CO, LTD:
Arrat Works, Brechin, Angus (Tayside), Scotland.

BRIT CPX
B32

DATA

Gauge; 12.
Length; 68.5 mm.
Head; 7.5 mm.
Tube; Fine ribbed plastic.
Colour; Flame red 2.5 .
Print; Black.
Base; Steel, brass coated.
Closure; Crimp, 6 fold.
Business; Manufacturers.

© | DN.2-1804. | January 1995 | KR

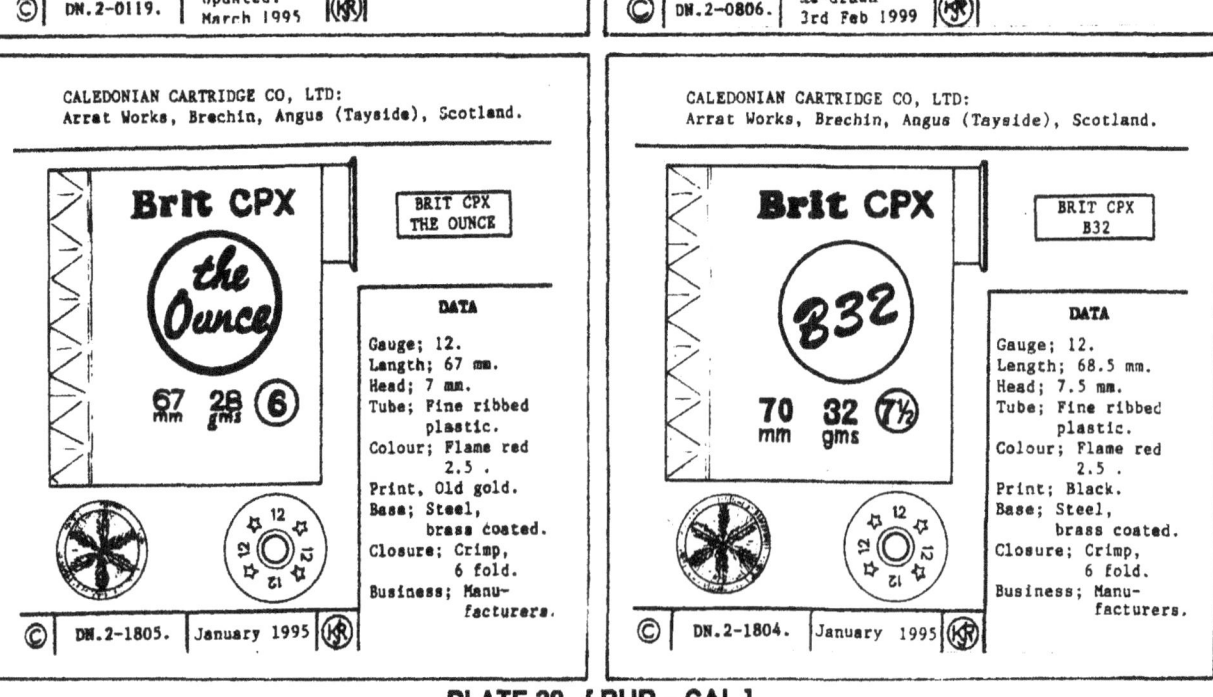

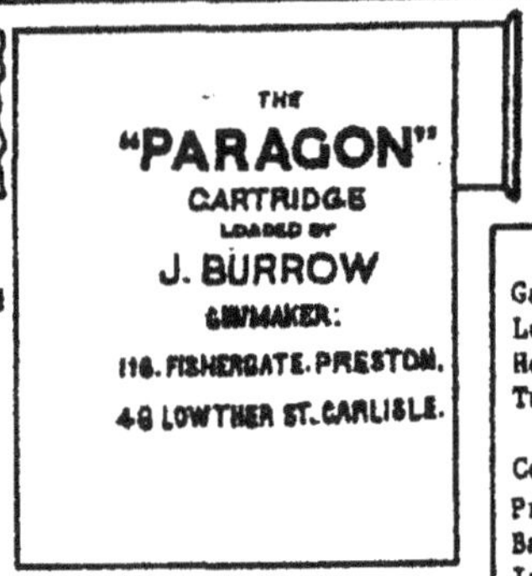

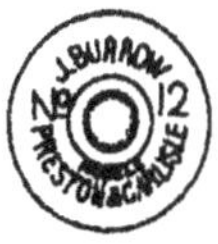

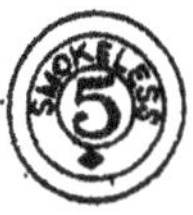

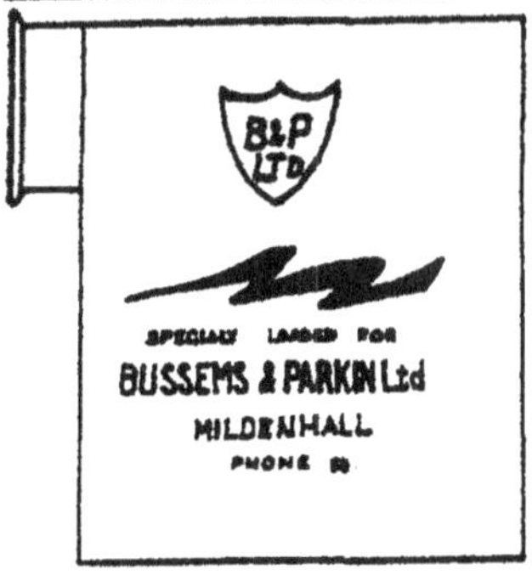

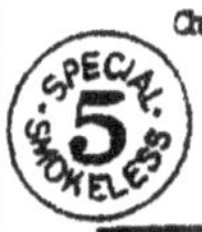

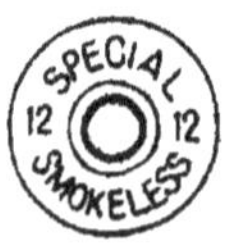

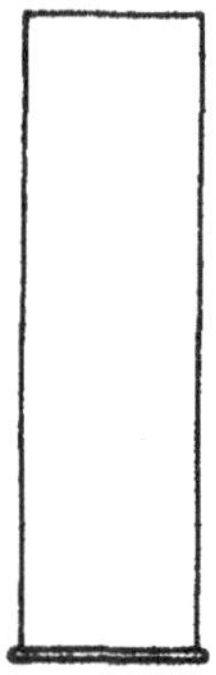

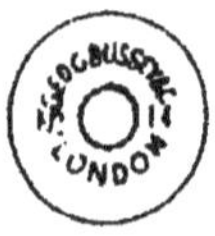

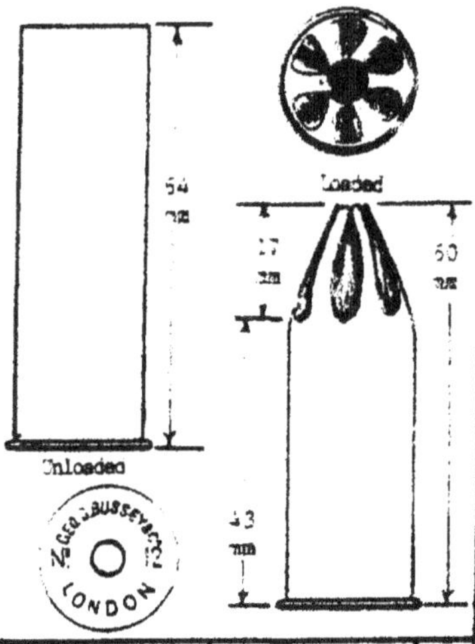

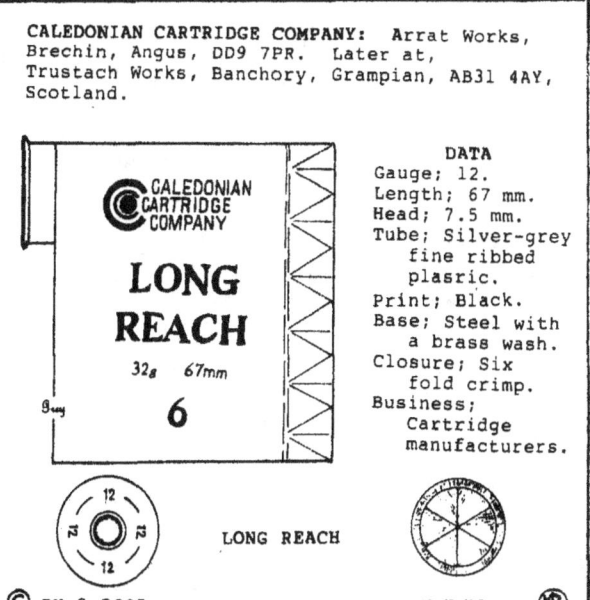

CALEDONIAN CARTRIDGE COMPANY: Arrat Works, Brechin, Angus, DD9 7PR. Later at, Trustach Works, Banchory, Grampian, AB31 4AY, Scotland.

DATA
Gauge; 12.
Length; 67 mm.
Head; 7.5 mm.
Tube; Silver-grey fine ribbed plastic.
Print; Black.
Base; Steel with a brass wash.
Closure; Six fold crimp.
Business; Cartridge manufacturers.

© DN.3-2835. Drawn, 21/8/08. LONG REACH

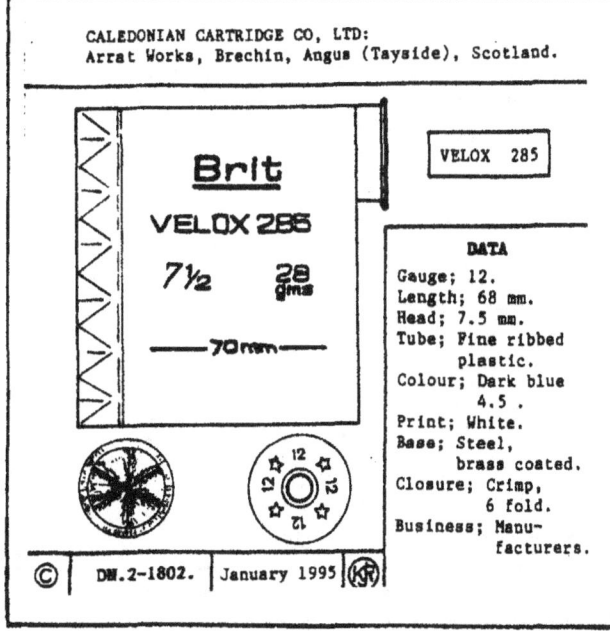

CALEDONIAN CARTRIDGE CO, LTD: Arrat Works, Brechin, Angus (Tayside), Scotland.

DATA
Gauge; 12.
Length; 68 mm.
Head; 7.5 mm.
Tube; Fine ribbed plastic.
Colour; Dark blue 4.5.
Print; White.
Base; Steel, brass coated.
Closure; Crimp, 6 fold.
Business; Manufacturers.

© DN.2-1802. January 1995

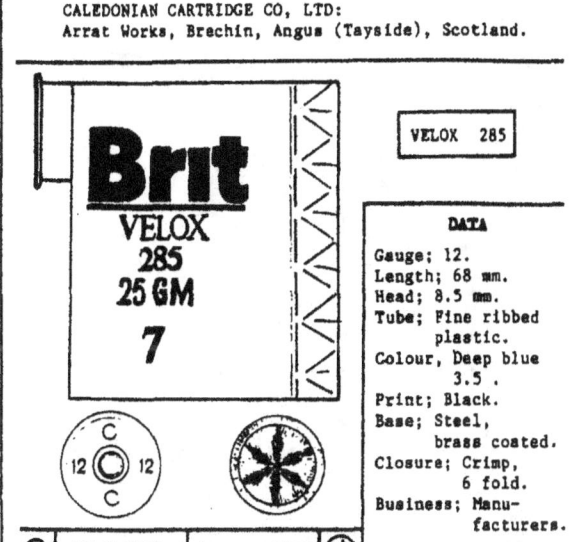

CALEDONIAN CARTRIDGE CO, LTD: Arrat Works, Brechin, Angus (Tayside), Scotland.

DATA
Gauge; 12.
Length; 68 mm.
Head; 8.5 mm.
Tube; Fine ribbed plastic.
Colour, Deep blue 3.5.
Print; Black.
Base; Steel, brass coated.
Closure; Crimp, 6 fold.
Business; Manufacturers.

© DN.2-1803. January 1995

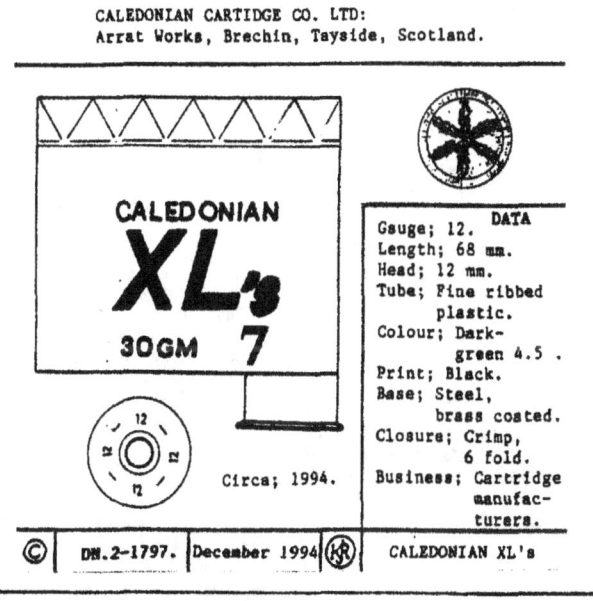

CALEDONIAN CARTRIDGE CO. LTD: Arrat Works, Brechin, Tayside, Scotland.

DATA
Gauge; 12.
Length; 68 mm.
Head; 12 mm.
Tube; Fine ribbed plastic.
Colour; Dark-green 4.5.
Print; Black.
Base; Steel, brass coated.
Closure; Crimp, 6 fold.
Business; Cartridge manufacturers.

© DN.2-1797. December 1994. CALEDONIAN XL's

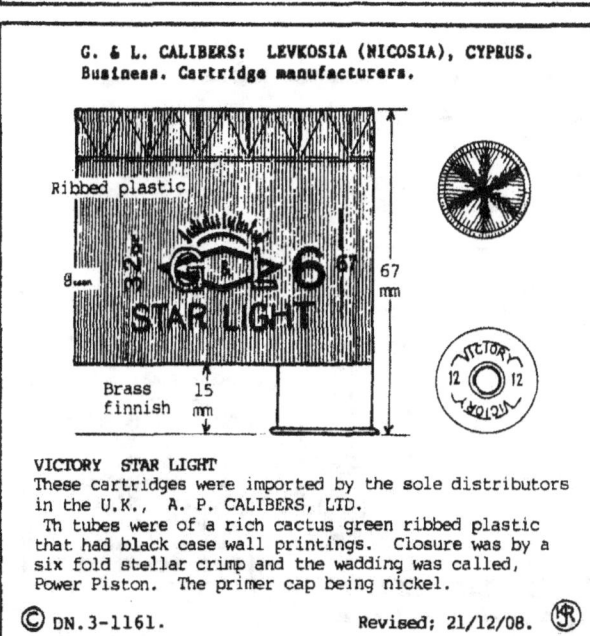

G. & L. CALIBERS: LEVKOSIA (NICOSIA), CYPRUS.
Business. Cartridge manufacturers.

VICTORY STAR LIGHT
These cartridges were imported by the sole distributors in the U.K., A. P. CALIBERS, LTD.
Th tubes were of a rich cactus green ribbed plastic that had black case wall printings. Closure was by a six fold stellar crimp and the wadding was called, Power Piston. The primer cap being nickel.

© DN.3-1161. Revised; 21/12/08.

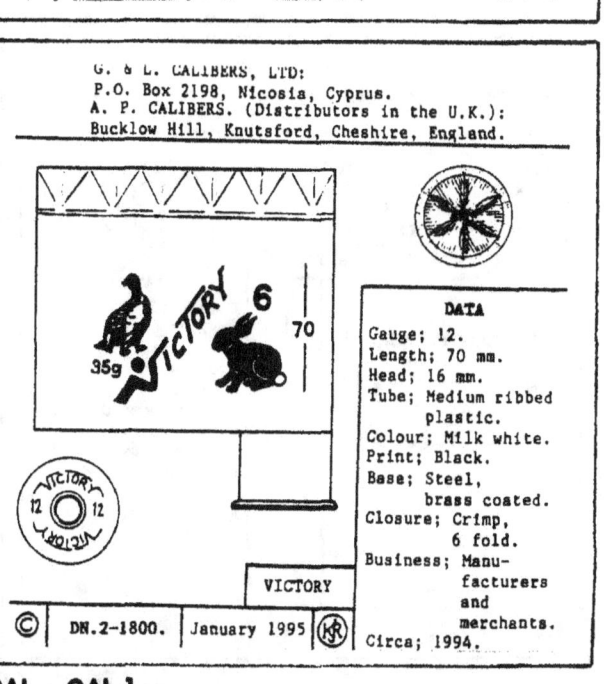

G. & L. CALIBERS, LTD:
P.O. Box 2198, Nicosia, Cyprus.
A. P. CALIBERS. (Distributors in the U.K.): Bucklow Hill, Knutsford, Cheshire, England.

DATA
Gauge; 12.
Length; 70 mm.
Head; 16 mm.
Tube; Medium ribbed plastic.
Colour; Milk white.
Print; Black.
Base; Steel, brass coated.
Closure; Crimp, 6 fold.
Business; Manufacturers and merchants.

© DN.2-1800. January 1995 Circa; 1994.

PLATE 39 [CAL – CAL]

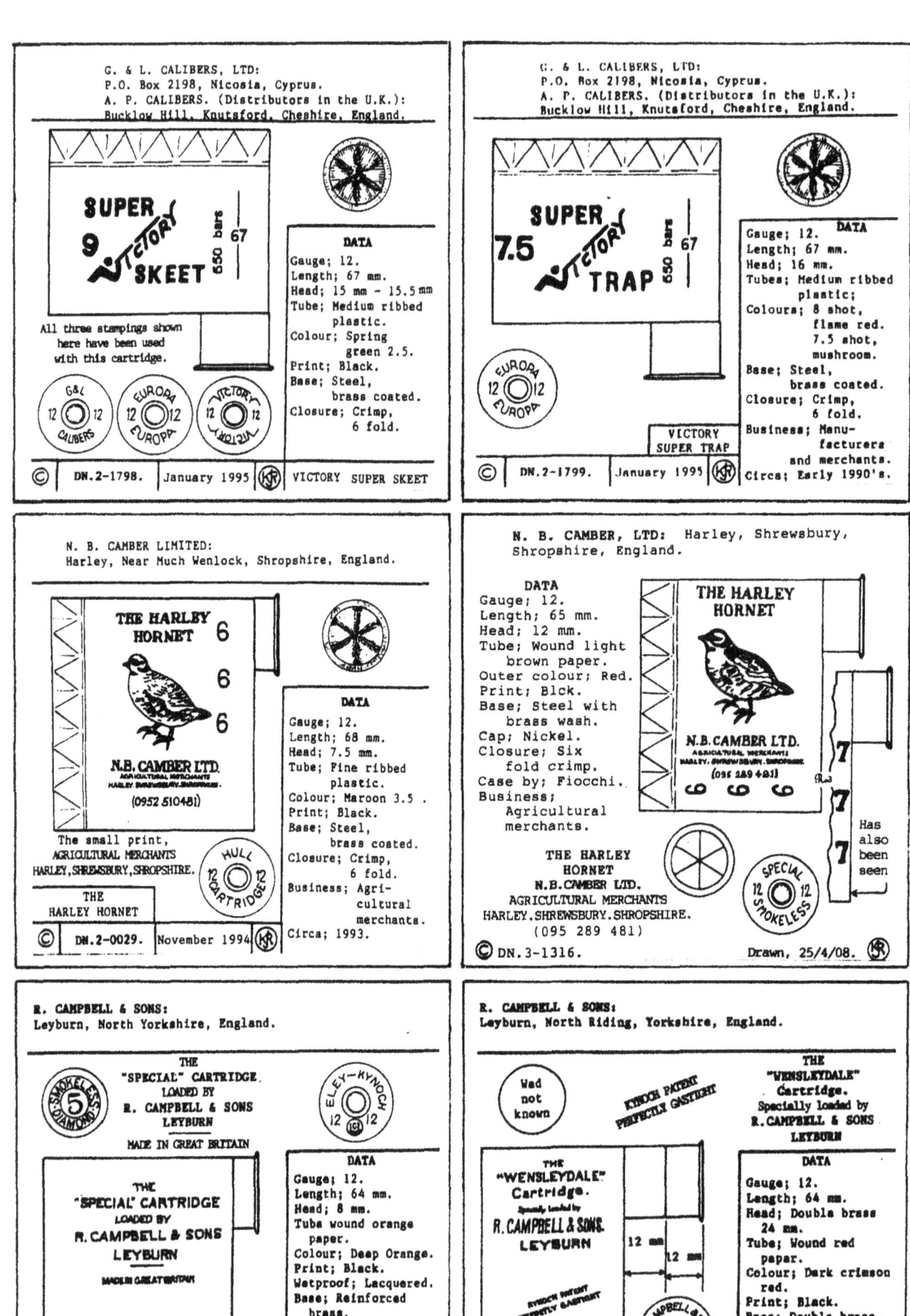

PLATE 40 [CAL - CAM]

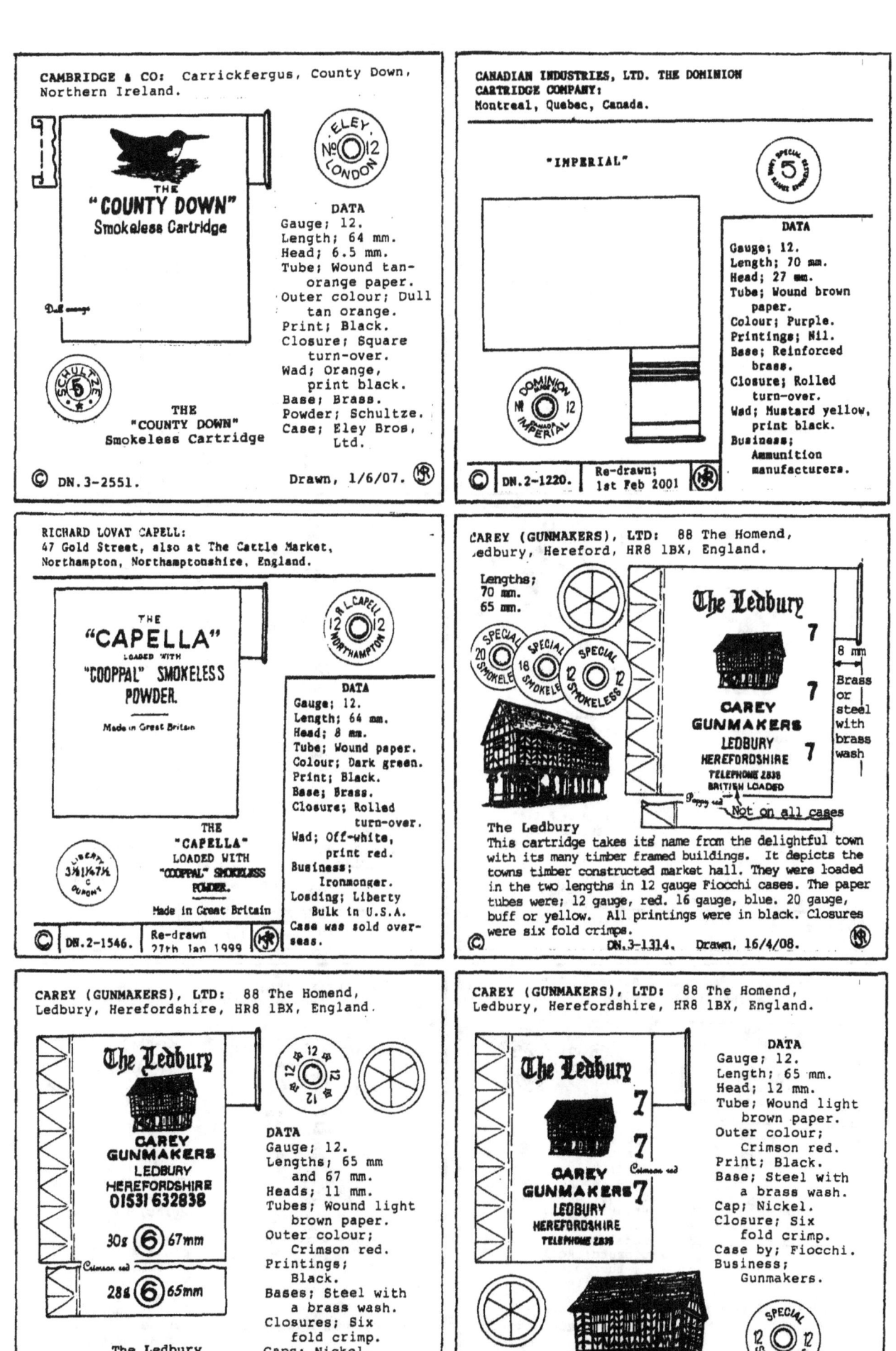

EARL OF CARNARVON:
Highclere Estate, Highclere, North Hampshire, England.

HIGHCLERE (shot size 6)

A — ELEY KYNOCH 12
B — MARTIGNONI 12 GENOVA

DATA
Gauge; 12.
Length; 65 mm.
Head; 8 mm.
Tube; Wound orange paper.
Colour; Orange.
Print; Black.
Wetproof; Clear lacquered.
Base; Steel with a nickel wash. Stamping 'A'.
Closure; Six fold crimp.
Business; Private cartridge.

Also loaded into an Italian case with the headstamp 'B'. This had a steel base with a brass wash. Its tube was made of fine ribbed red plastic, but no shot size was shown. Closure was a six fold crimp.

© DN.2-0778. Re-drawn; 22nd Apr 2001

CARR BROTHERS:
Cloth Hall Street, Huddersfield, Yorkshire West Riding, England.

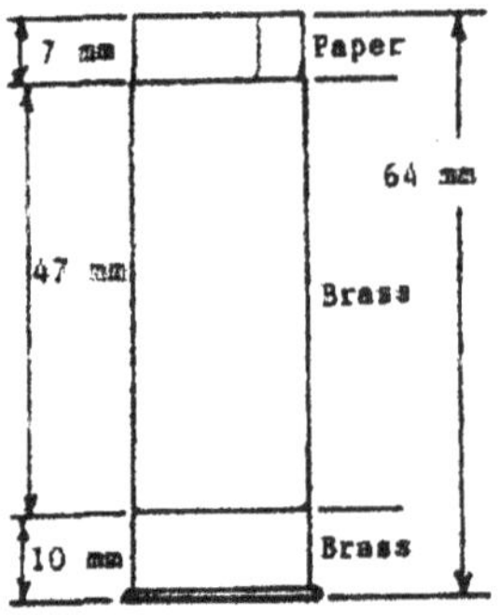

7 mm — Paper
47 mm — Brass
10 mm — Brass
Total 64 mm

Wad not known

CARR BROS No 12 HUDDERSFIELD — ELEY

ELEY'S EJECTOR

DATA
Gauge; 12.
Length; 64 mm.
Head; 10 mm with extended brass to 57 mm.
Tube; Wound brownish-buff paper.
Base; Brass.
Closure; Rolled turn-over.
Wad; Not known.
Business; Gunmakers.
Case; Eley Bros, Ltd.
The example was not examined for internal metals.

© DN.2-0543. Re-drawn; 11th Jan 2002

CARR & COMPANY:
Lower Parliament Street, Nottingham, Nottinghamshire, England.

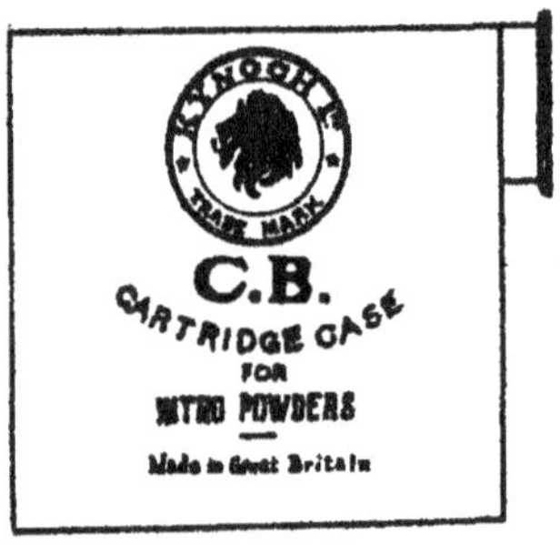

KYNOCH Ld TRADE MARK

C.B. CARTRIDGE CASE FOR NITRO POWDERS
Made in Great Britain

5 LONG CARR NOTTINGHAM — 20 KYNOCH BIRMINGHAM

C.B. CARTRIDGE CASE FOR NITRO POWDERS
Made in Great Britain

DATA
Gauge; 20.
Length; 64 mm.
Head; 6 mm.
Tube; Wound red paper.
Colour; Geranium red.
Print; Black.
Base; Brass.
Closure; Rolled turn-over.
Wad; White, print red.
Business; Ironmongers.
Case; Kynoch, Ltd.
Circa; 1912.

© DN.2-1442. Re-drawn; 17th Apr 2001

CARR & COMPANY:
4 Lower Parliament Street, Nottingham, Nottinghamshire, England.

CARR & CO. DEALERS IN GUNS, REVOLVERS, AND AMMUNITION ESTABLISHED 1828
4 LOWER PARLIAMENT STREET NOTTINGHAM

CARR & Co No 12 NOTTINGHAM — CARR 5 NOTTINGHAM

CARR & CO. DEALERS IN GUNS, REVOLVERS, AND AMMUNITION ESTABLISHED 1828
4 LOWER PARLIAMENT STREET NOTTINGHAM

DATA
Gauge; 12.
Length; 64 mm.
Head; 8 mm.
Tube; Wound paper.
Colour; Brownish-orange.
Print; Black.
Base; Brass.
Closure; Rolled turn-over.
Wad; White card, print red.
Case; G. Kynoch & Co.
Business; Gun and ammunition dealers.

© DN.2-0708. Updated; November 1997.

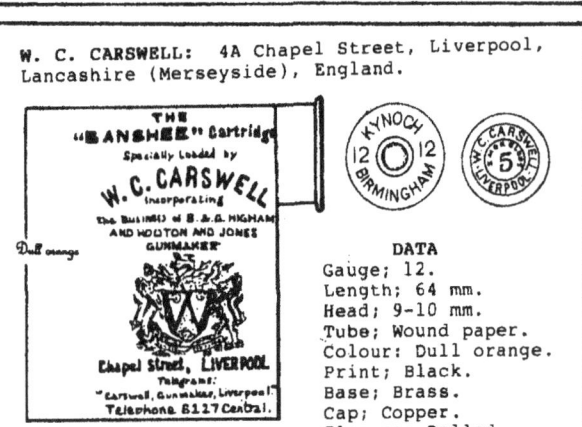

W. C. CARSWELL: 4A Chapel Street, Liverpool, Lancashire (Merseyside), England.

THE "BANSHEE" Cartridge
Specially Loaded by
W. C. CARSWELL
Incorporating
The Business of E. & G. HIGHAM AND HOOTON AND JONES GUNMAKERS
Chapel Street, LIVERPOOL
Telegrams: "CARSWELL, Gunmaker, Liverpool"
Telephone 6127 Central.

Dull orange

KYNOCH 12 12 BIRMINGHAM — W.C.CARSWELL 5 LIVERPOOL

THE "BANSHEE" CARTRIDGE

DATA
Gauge; 12.
Length; 64 mm.
Head; 9-10 mm.
Tube; Wound paper.
Colour; Dull orange.
Print; Black.
Base; Brass.
Cap; Copper.
Closure; Rolled turn-over.
Wad; White card, print black.
Case by; Kynoch.
Business; Gunmaker.

© DN.3-2665. Drawn, 11/2/08.

W. C. CARSWELL, LTD: 4A Chapel Street, Liverpool, Lancashire (Merseyside), England.

THE "BANSHEE" CARTRIDGE
Specially Loaded by
W. C. CARSWELL LTD.
Incorporating
the Business of E. & G. HIGHAM AND HOOTON AND JONES GUNMAKERS

4A CHAPEL ST., LIVERPOOL
Telegrams: "CARSWELL, GUNMAKER, LIVERPOOL"
Telephone: 2078 Central
MADE IN GREAT BRITAIN

Pink

ELEY-KYNOCH 12 12 — W.C.CARSWELL 4 LIVERPOOL

THE "BANSHEE" CARTRIDGE

DATA
Gauge; 12.
Length; 64 mm.
Head; 8 mm.
Tube; Wound pink paper.
Print; Black or navy-blue.
Base; Brass.
Closure; Rolled turn-over.
Wad; Rich green, print black.
Cap; Copper.
Business; Gunmaker.
Circa; 1930's.

© DN.3-2664. Drawn, 11/2/08.

PLATE 42 [CAR – CAR]

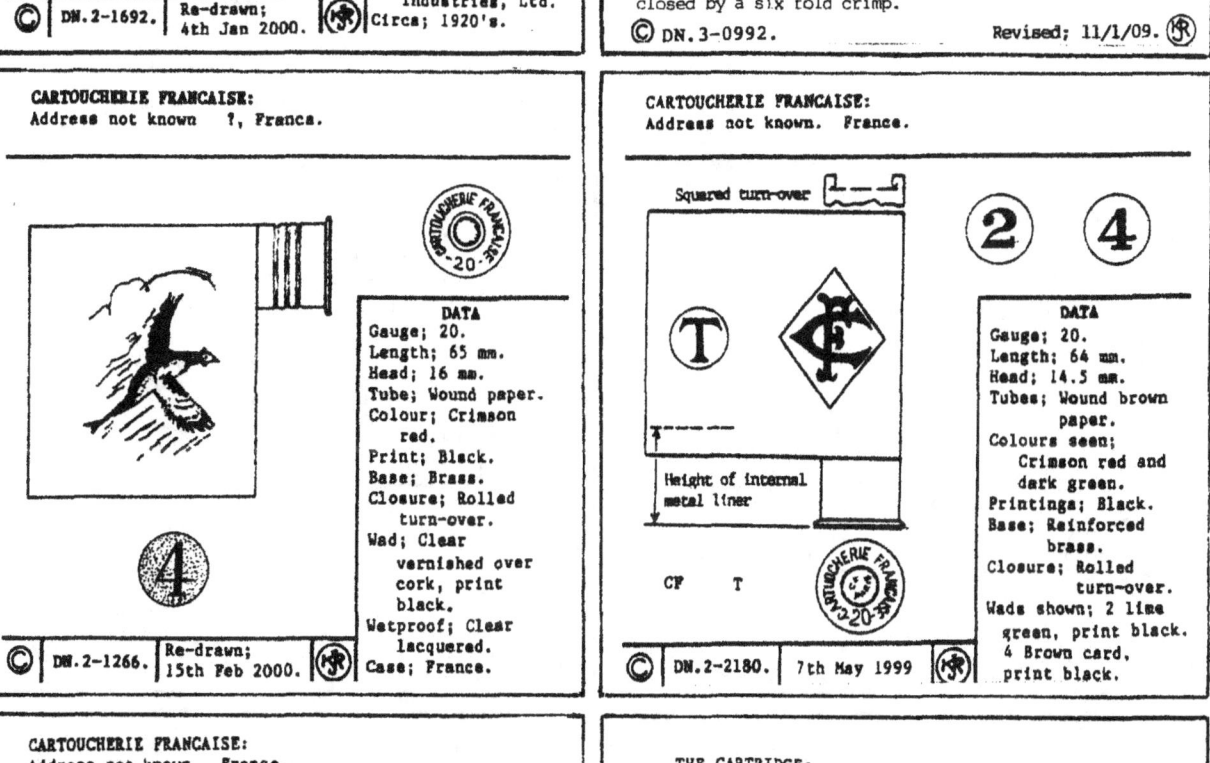
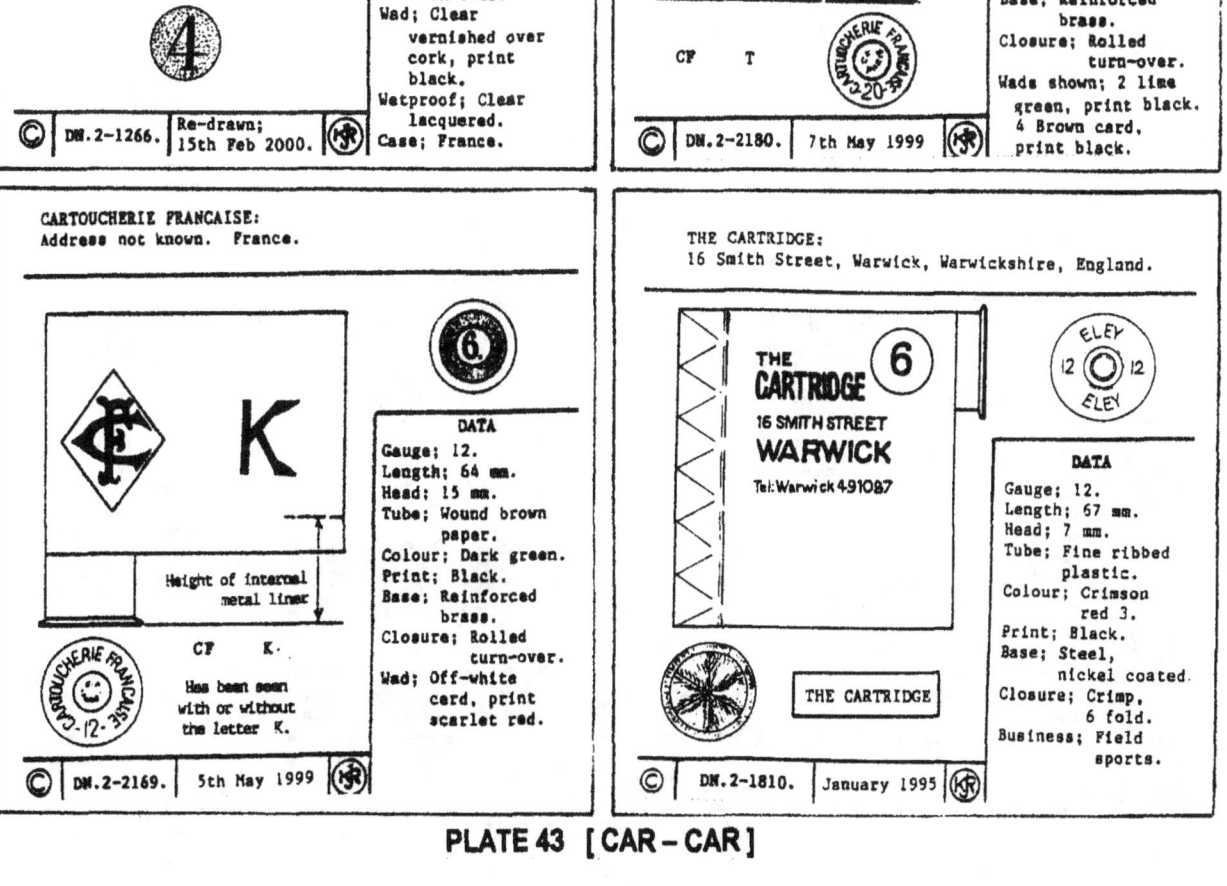

PLATE 43 [CAR – CAR]

CARTRIDGE SYNDICATE:
20-23 Holborn, London, England.

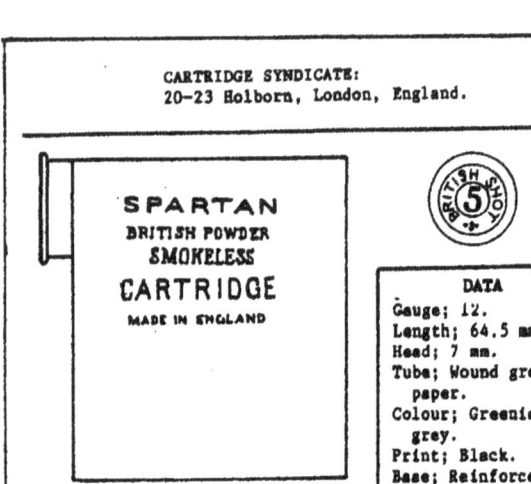

DATA
Gauge; 12.
Length; 64.5 mm.
Head; 7 mm.
Tube; Wound grey paper.
Colour; Greenish-grey.
Print; Black.
Base; Reinforced brass.
Closure; Rolled turn-over.
Wad; Dark red card, print black.
Produced by; Trent Gun & Cartridge.

© DN.2-0467. Updated, February 1996

CARTRIDGE SYNDICATE:
20/23 Holborn, London E.C.1., England.

DATA
Gauge; 12.
Length; 64 mm.
Head; 17 mm.
Tube; Wound paper.
Colour; Greenish-grey.
Print; Black.
Base; Brass.
Closure; Rolled turn-over.
Wad; Dark red, print black.
Case and loading; Trent Gun & Cartridge.

© DN.2-0465. Re-drawn; 11th Feb 2001

CARTRIDGE CYNDICATE: 20/23 Holborn, London E.C.1., England.

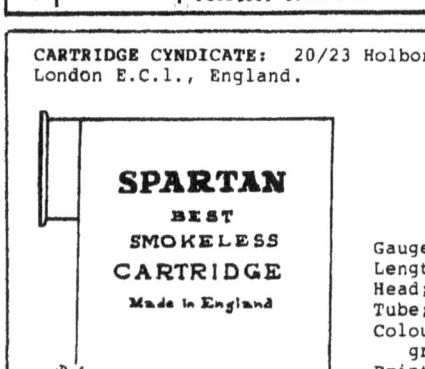

DATA
Gauge; 12.
Length; 65 mm.
Head; 9 mm.
Tube; Wound paper.
Colour; Deep greenish-grey.
Print; Black.
Base; Brass.
Cap; Large copper.
Closure; Rolled turn-over.
Wad; Dark red, print black.
Manufactured by; Trent Guns & Cartridges.

© DN.3-2667. Drawn, 12/2/08.

CARTRIDGE SYNDICATE: 20/23 Holborn, London E.C.1., England.

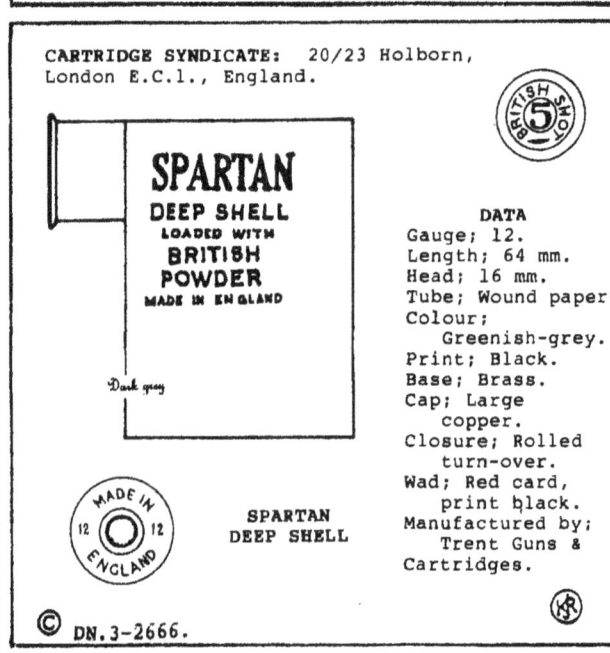

DATA
Gauge; 12.
Length; 64 mm.
Head; 16 mm.
Tube; Wound paper
Colour; Greenish-grey.
Print; Black.
Base; Brass.
Cap; Large copper.
Closure; Rolled turn-over.
Wad; Red card, print black.
Manufactured by; Trent Guns & Cartridges.

© DN.3-2666.

CARTUCHOS DEPOTIVOS DE MEXICO: Cuernavaca, Morelos, Mexico.
(Business; Ammunition manufacturers).

AGUILA
I have seen this cartridge in two different coloured cases. Both had tubes wound from brown paper with outer layers of ribbed waterproof coloured papers. One was a dark orange tan and the other was yellow. Both had black printings. They were fitted with a nickel cap and were closed by a six fold crimp.

© DN.3-0959. Revised; 12/1/09.

CARVER (WOLVERHAMPTON) LTD: Little's Lane, Wolverhampton, West Midlands, England.

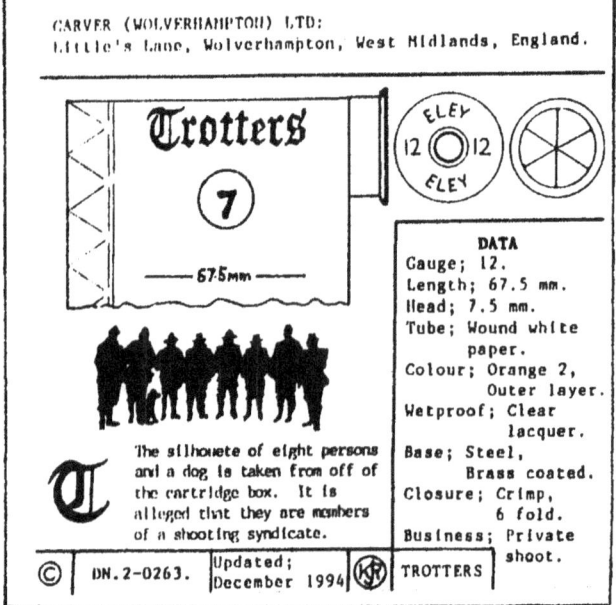

The silhouete of eight persons and a dog is taken from off of the cartridge box. It is alleged that they are members of a shooting syndicate.

DATA
Gauge; 12.
Length; 67.5 mm.
Head; 7.5 mm.
Tube; Wound white paper.
Colour; Orange 2, Outer layer.
Wetproof; Clear lacquer.
Base; Steel, Brass coated.
Closure; Crimp, 6 fold.
Business; Private shoot.

© DN.2-0263. Updated; December 1994 TROTTERS

PLATE 44 [CAR – CAR]

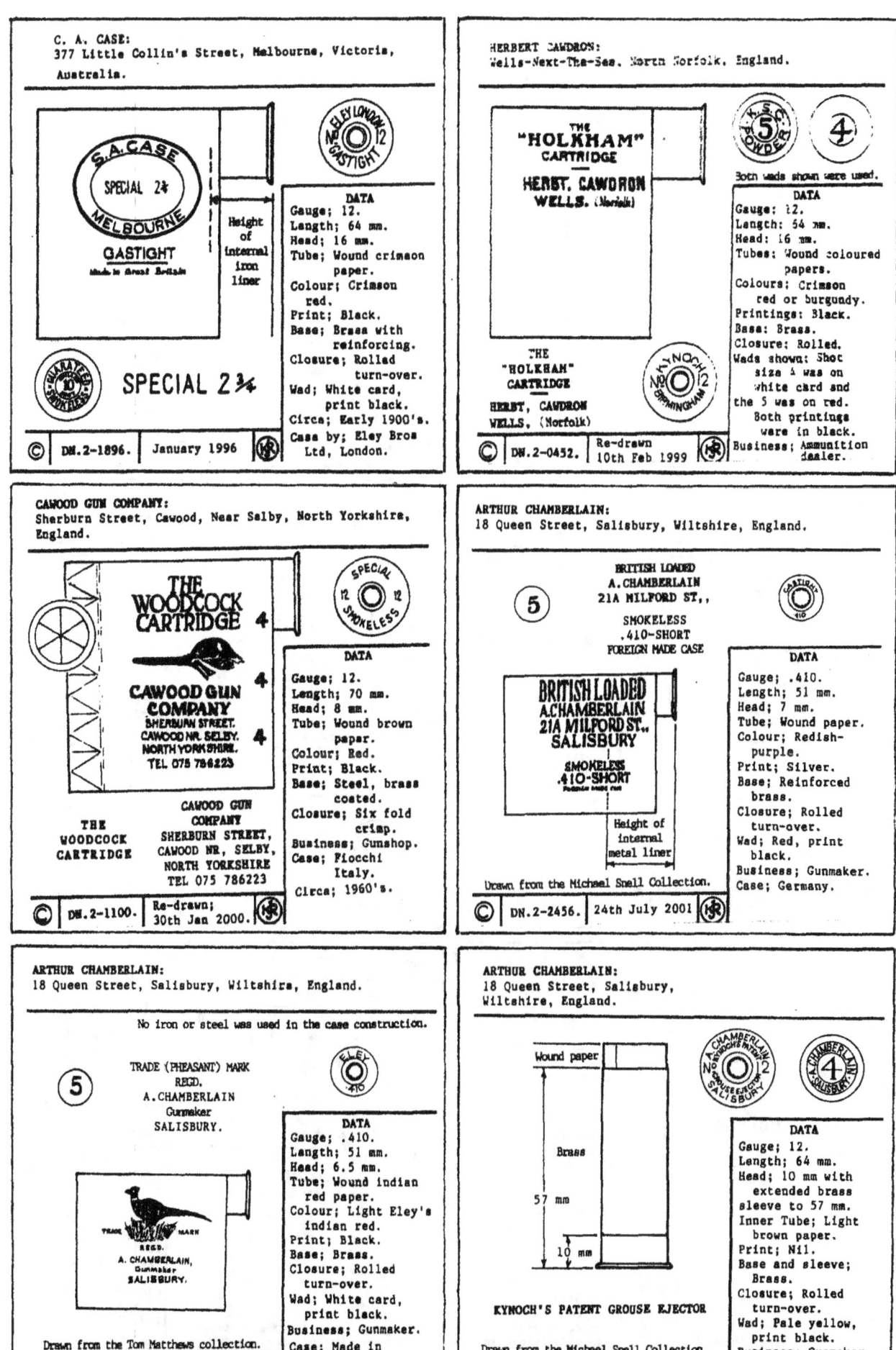

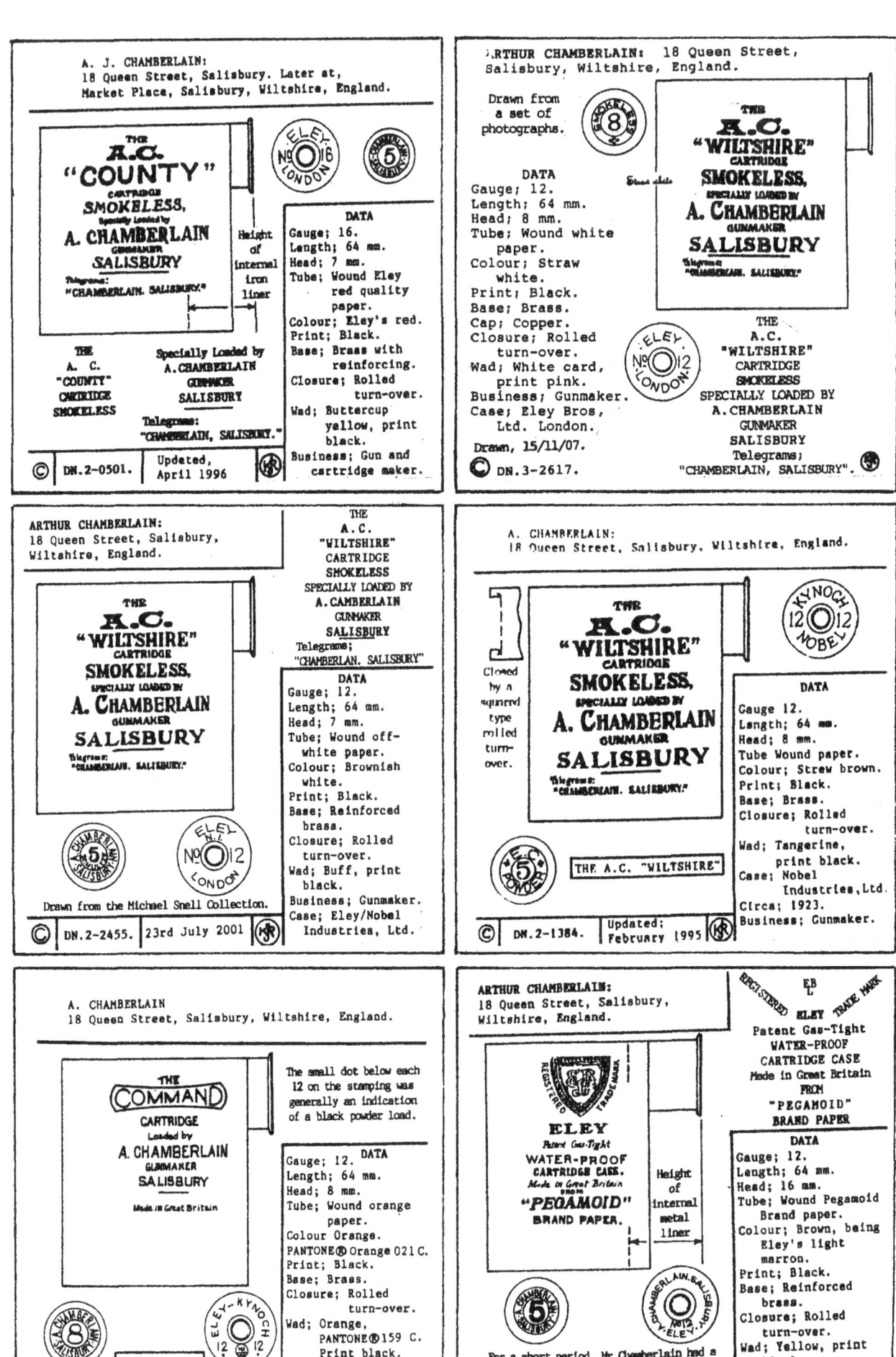

PLATE 46 [CHA - CHA]

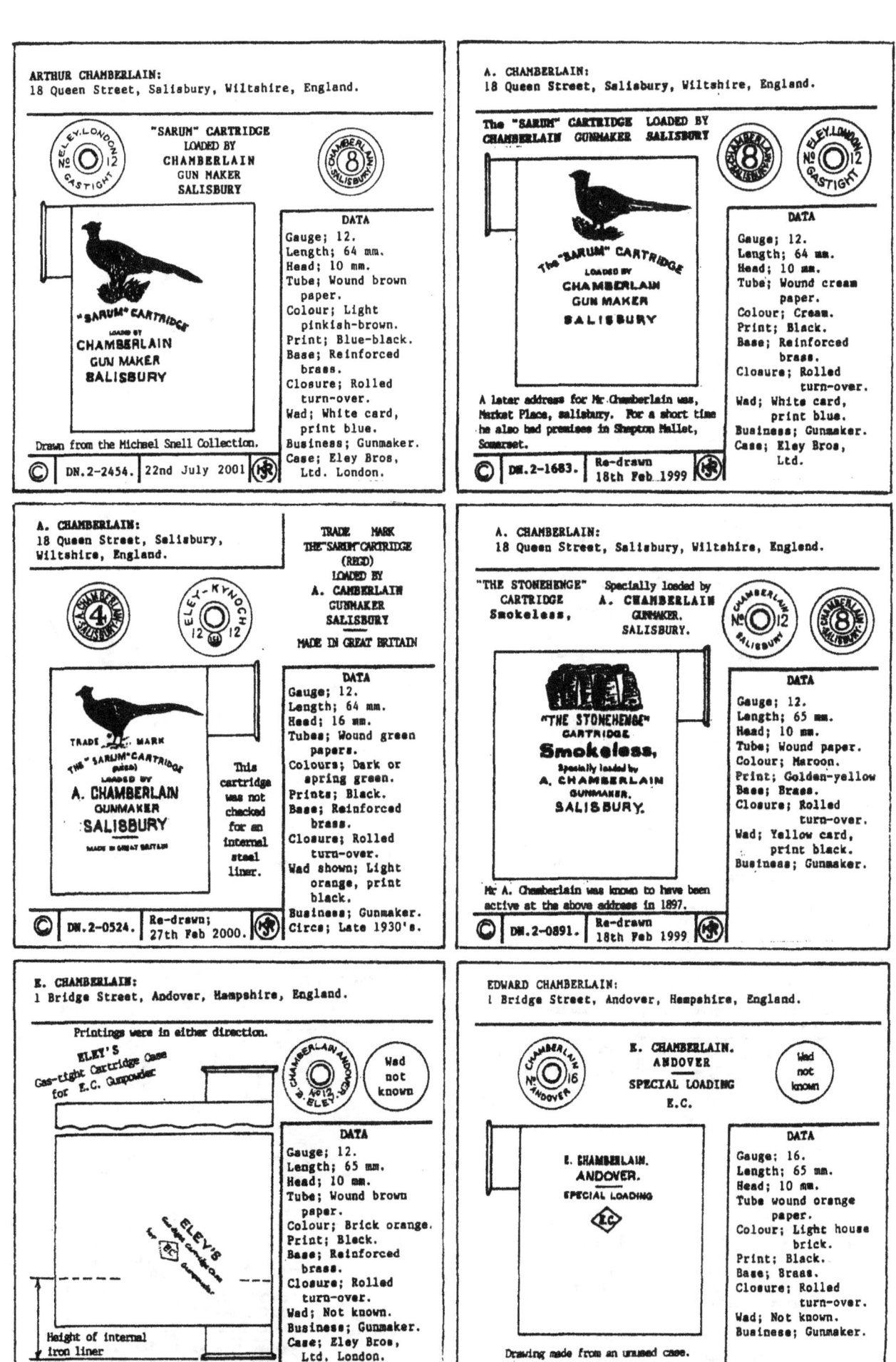

PLATE 47 [CHA – CHA]

EDWARD CHAMBERLAIN:
1 Bridge Street, Andover, Hampshire. Also at,
35 Wote Street, Basingstoke, Hampshire, England.

Wad not known

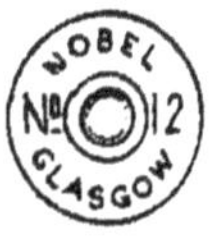

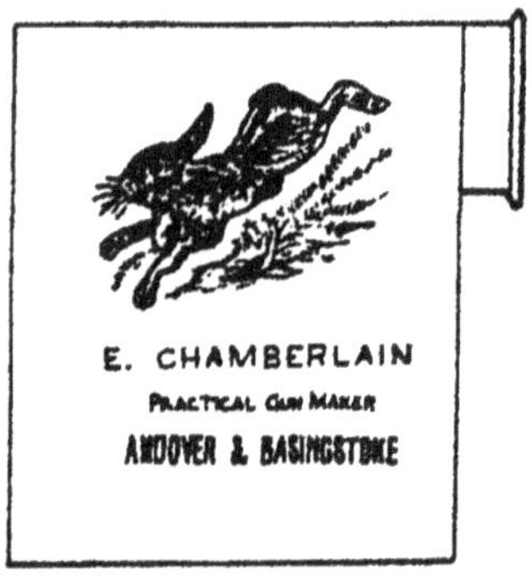

DATA
Gauge; 12.
Length; 64 mm.
Head; 8 mm.
Tube; Wound orange paper.
Colour; Brownish-orange.
PANTONE® 180 U.
Print; Black.
Base; Brass.
Closure; Rolled turn-over.
Wad; Not known.
Business; Gunmaker.
Case by; Nobel Explosives Company

© DN.2-0860. Updated, October 1995

EDWIN CHAMBERLAIN. 1 BRIDGE STREET, ANDOVER, Also at, 35 WOTE STREET, BASINGSTOKE, HAMPSHIRE, ENGLAND.

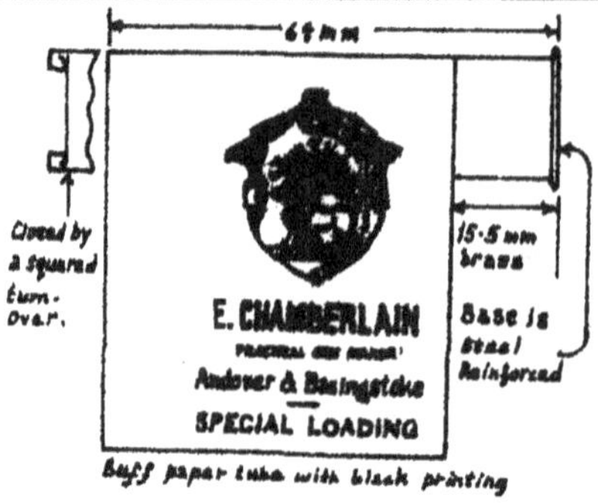

Buff paper tube with black printing

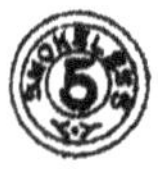

Jade green wad with black printing

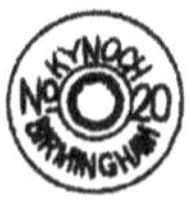

Gunmaker
Circa 1905.

© DN.5-1001.

EDWARD CHAMBERLAIN:
1 Bridge Street, Andover,
Hampshire, England.

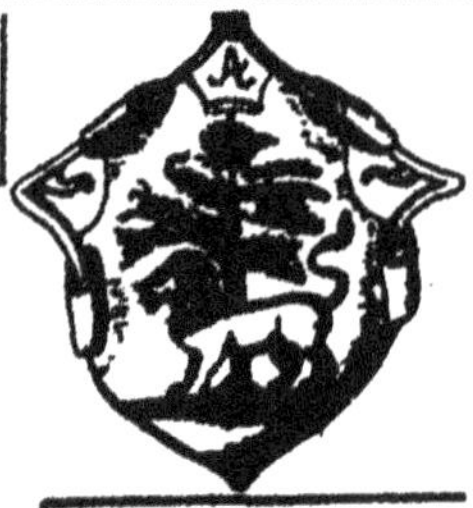

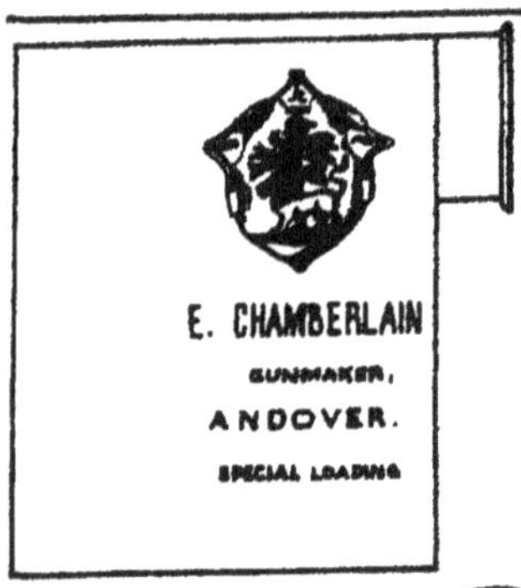

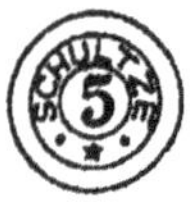

E. CHAMBERLAIN
GUNMAKER,
ANDOVER.
SPECIAL LOADING

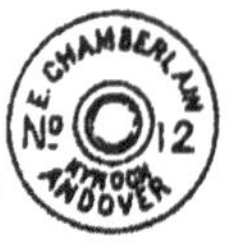

DATA
Gauge; 12.
Length; 64 mm.
Head; 10 mm.
Tube; Wound paper.
Colour; Deep orange.
Print; Black.
Base; Brass.
Closure; Rolled turn-over.
Wad; Dull orange, print black.
Business; Gunmaker and cartridge loader.

© DN.2-1042. Updated, March 1996

EDWARD CHAMBERLAIN:
1 Bridge street, Andover. Also,
35 Wote Street, Basingstoke,
Hampshire, England.

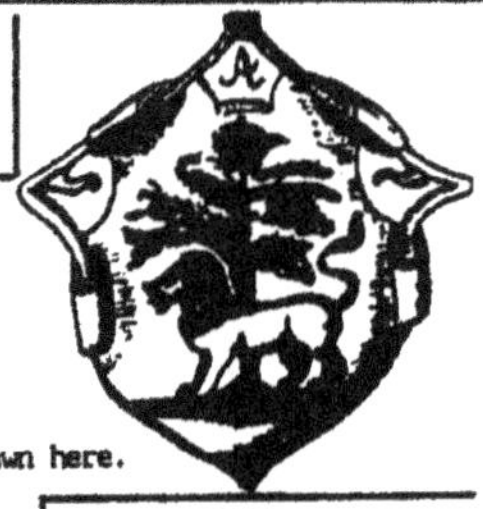

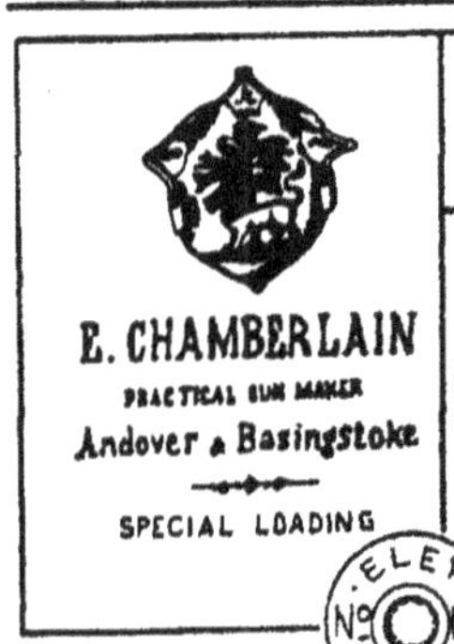

12 gauge drawn here.

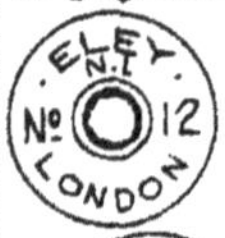

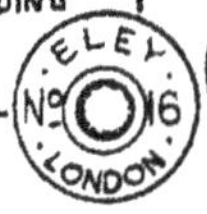

Wads not known

Was also made in 16 gauge with similar headstamping. Tube was pinkish-buff paper with black printing.

E. CHAMBERLAIN
PACTICAL GUN MAKER
Andover & Basingstoke
SPECIAL LOADING

DATA
Gauge; 12.
Length; 64 mm.
Head; 16 mm.
Tube; Wound green paper.
Colour; Olive green.
Print; Black.
Base; Reinforced brass.
Closure; Rolled turn-over.
Wad; Not known.
Business; Gunmaker.
Case; Nobel Industries, Ltd.
Circa; 1920.

© DN.2-0861. Re-drawn 31st Oct 2000

E. CHAMBERLAIN:
1 Bridge Street, Andover. Also at,
35 Wote Street, Basingstoke, Hampshire, England.

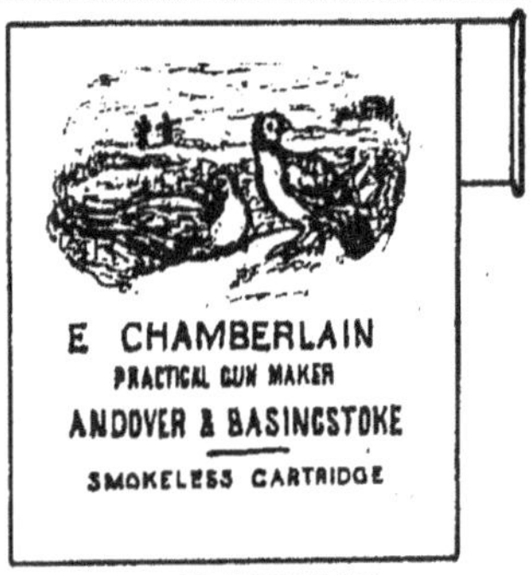

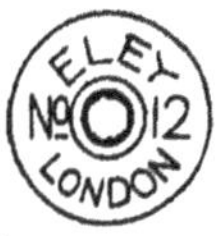

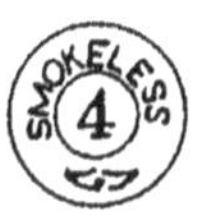

E CHAMBERLAN
PRACTICAL GUN MAKER
ANDOVER & BASINGSTOKE
SMOKELESS CARTRIDGE

Drawn from the Michael Snell Collection.

DATA
Gauge; 12.
Length; 64 mm.
Head; 8 mm.
Tube; Wound red paper.
Colour; Crimson red.
Print; Black.
Base; Brass.
Closure; Rolled turn-over.
Wad; White card, print black.
Business; Gunmaker.
Case; Eley Bros, Ltd. London.

© DN.2-2453. 21st July 2001

EDWARD CHAMBERLAIN:
1 Bridge Street, Andover, Hampshire.
Also at, 35 Wote Street, Basingstoke, Hampshire, England.

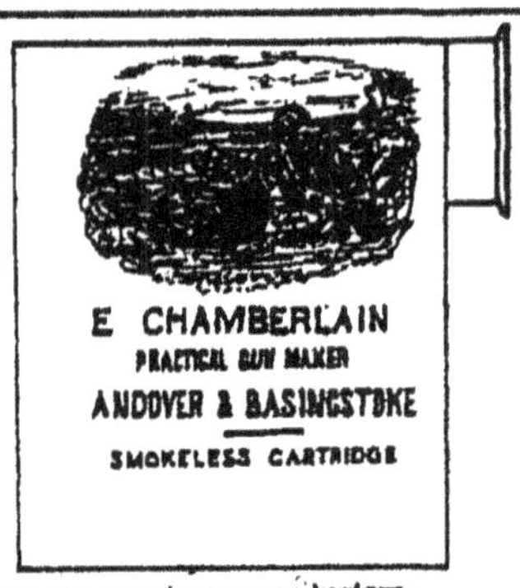

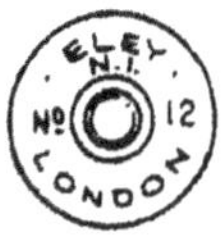

Wad not known

Note the two shooters on horizon.

Drawn from a used case.

E CHAMBERLAIN
PRACTICAL GUN MAKER
ANDOVER & BASINGSTOKE
SMOKELESS CARTRIDGE

DATA
Gauge; 12.
Length; 64 mm.
Head; 8.5 mm.
Tube; Wound orange paper.
Colour; Brownish orange.
Print; Black.
Base; Brass.
Closure; Rolled turn-over.
Wad; Not known.
Business; Gunmaker.
Circa; 1920-1924.
Case; Nobel Industries Ltd.

© DN.2-0495. Updated; April 1997

PLATE 48 [CHA – CHA]

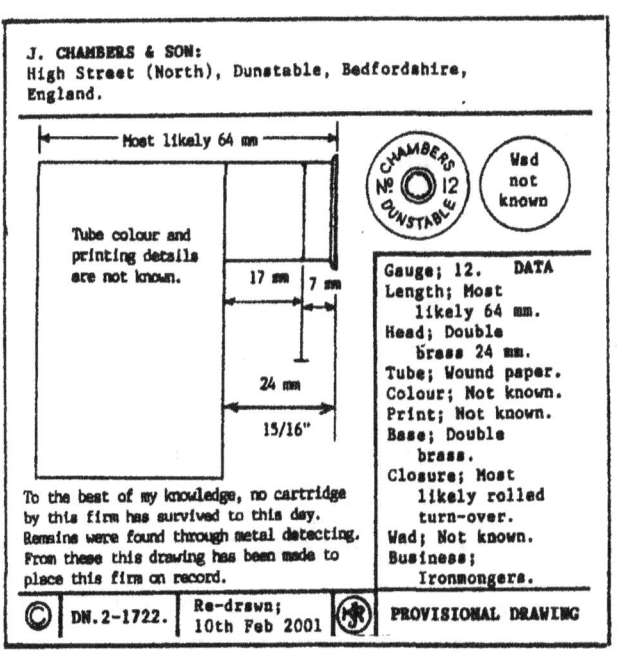
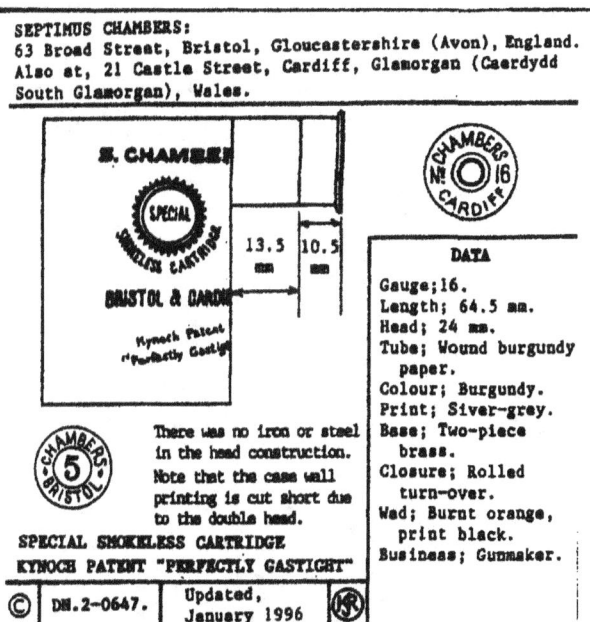
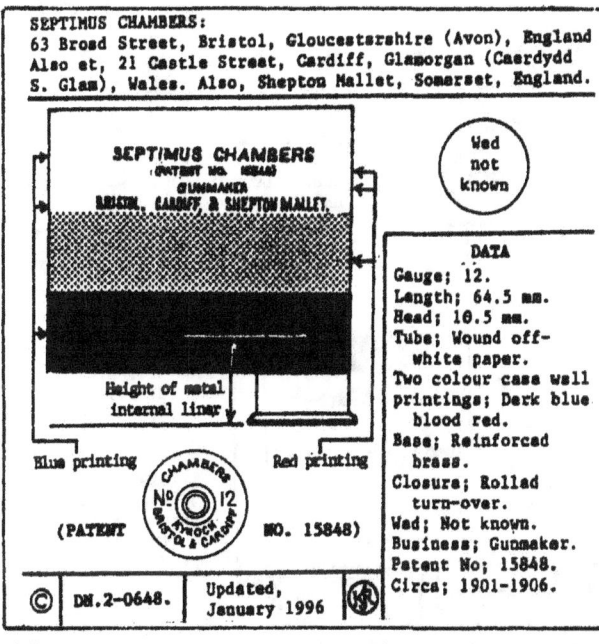
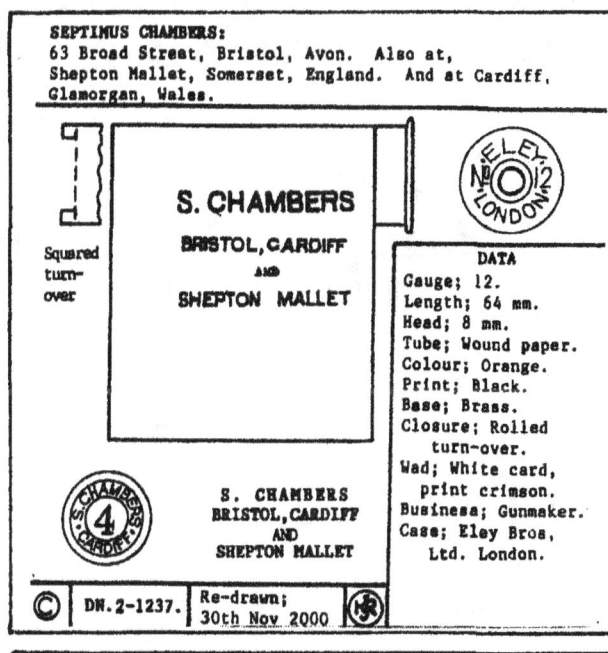
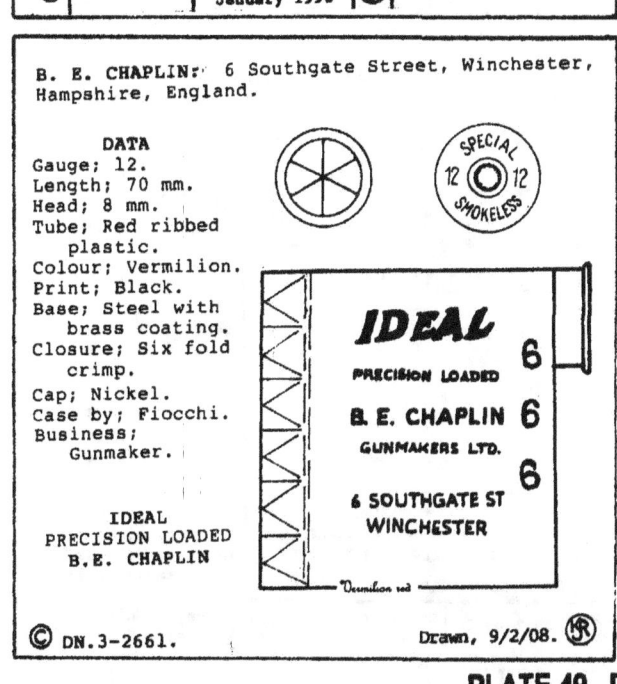
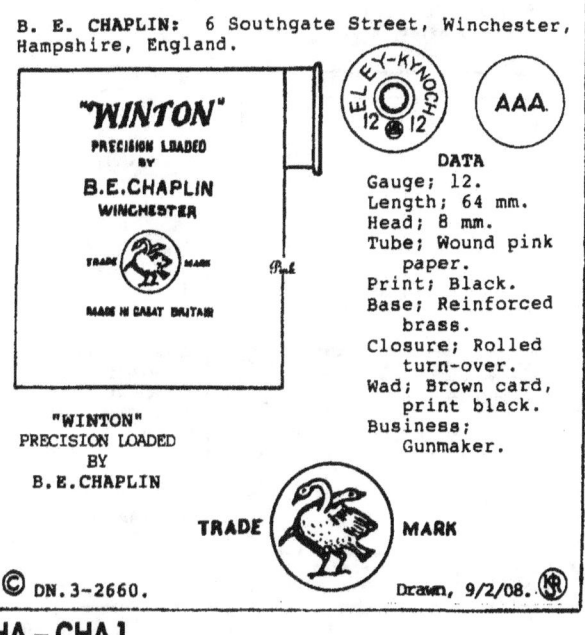

PLATE 49 [CHA – CHA]

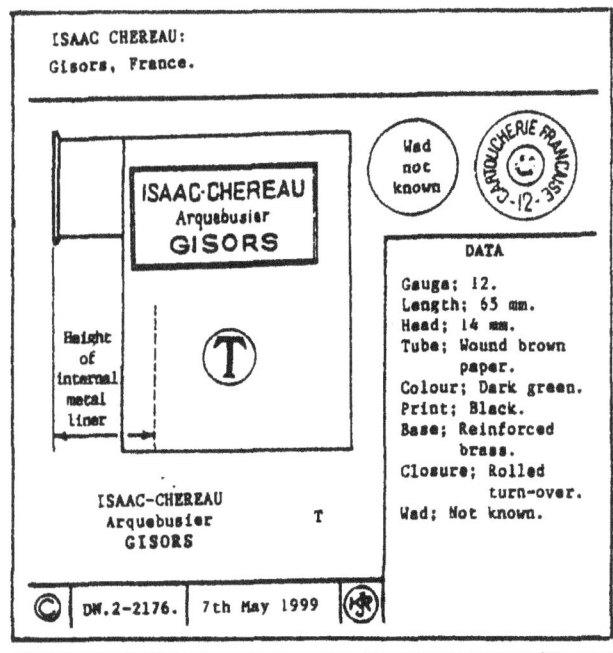

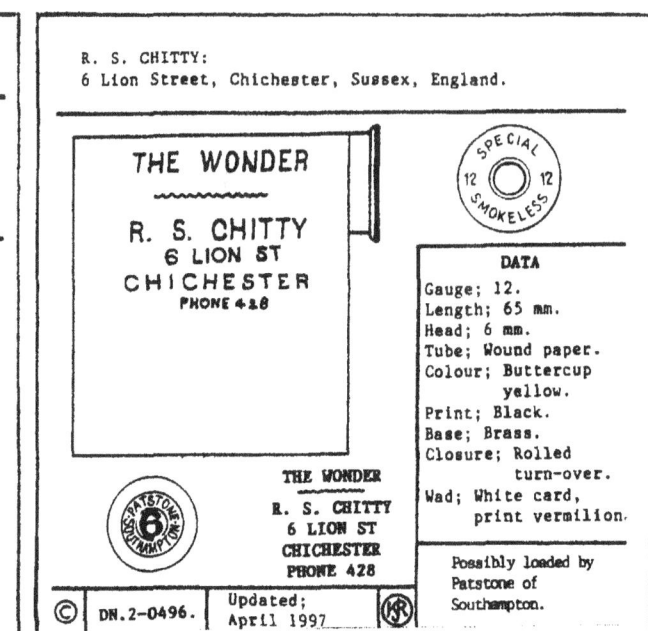

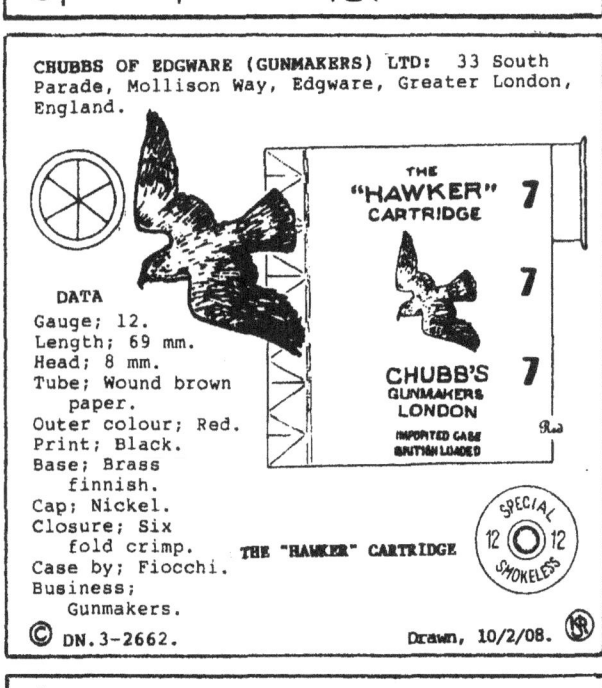

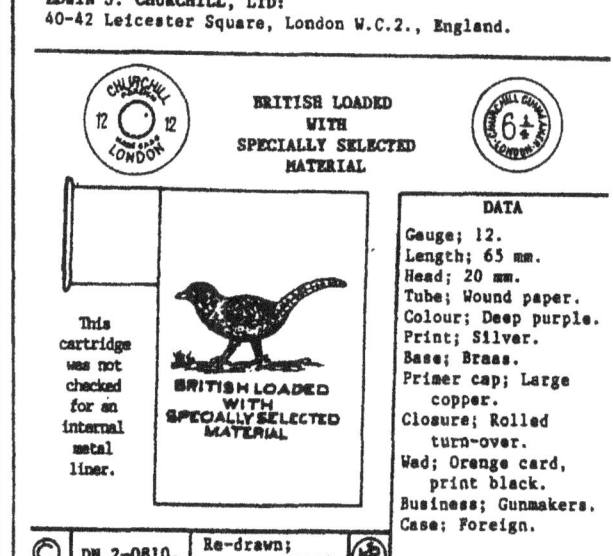

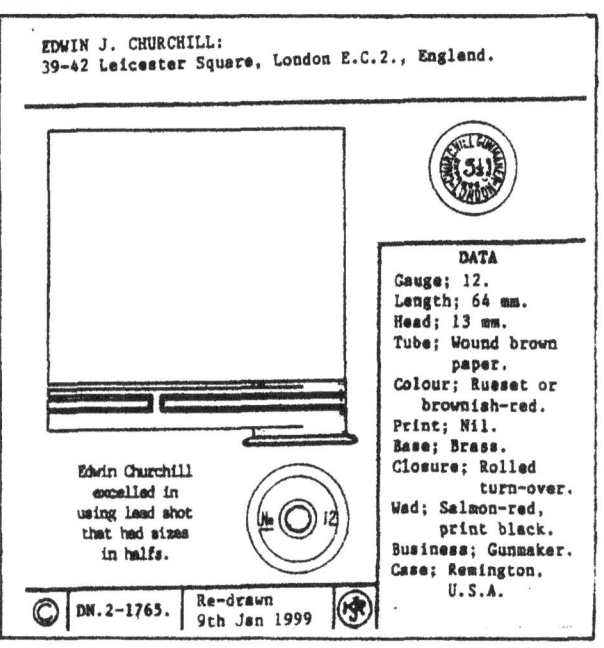

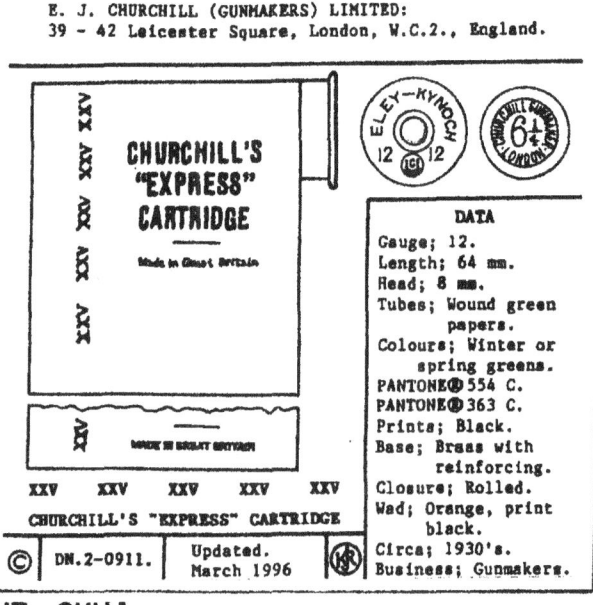

PLATE 50 [CHE – CHU]

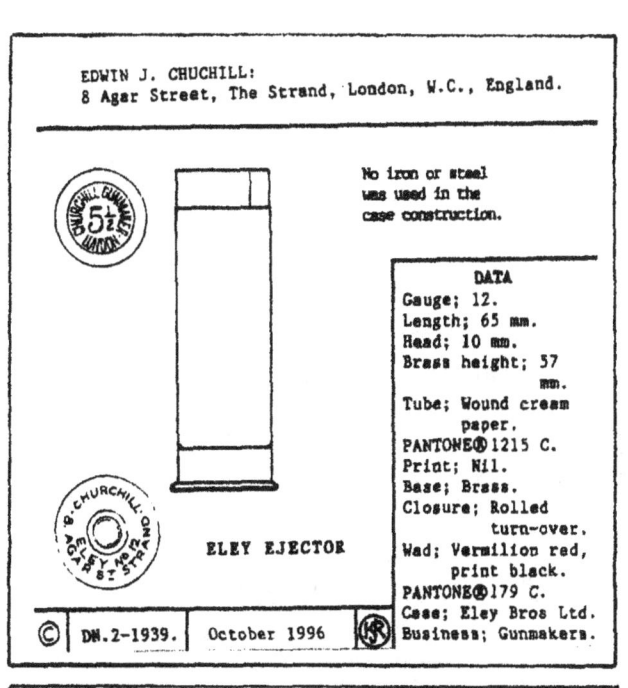

EDWIN J. CHURCHILL:
8 Agar Street, The Strand, London, W.C., England.

No iron or steel was used in the case construction.

DATA
Gauge; 12.
Length; 65 mm.
Head; 10 mm.
Brass height; 57 mm.
Tube; Wound cream paper.
PANTONE® 1215 C.
Print; Nil.
Base; Brass.
Closure; Rolled turn-over.
Wad; Vermilion red, print black.
PANTONE® 179 C.
Case; Eley Bros Ltd.
Business; Gunmakers.

ELEY EJECTOR

© DN.2-1939.   October 1996

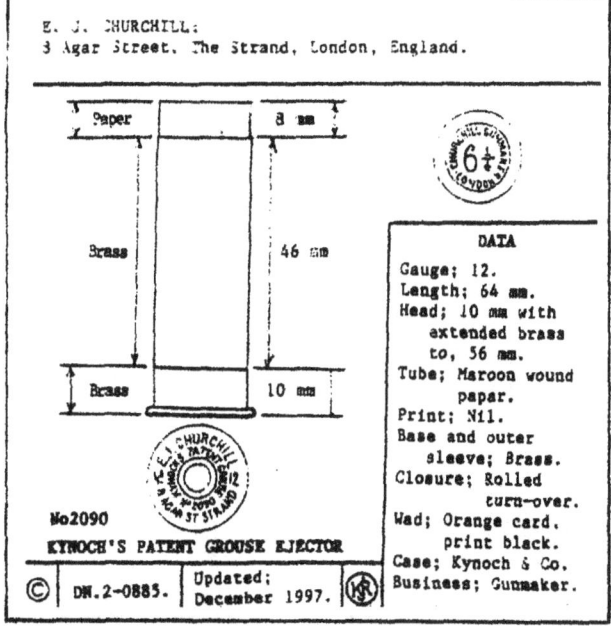

E. J. CHURCHILL:
3 Agar Street, The Strand, London, England.

DATA
Gauge; 12.
Length; 64 mm.
Head; 10 mm with extended brass to, 56 mm.
Tube; Maroon wound paper.
Print; Nil.
Base and outer sleeve; Brass.
Closure; Rolled turn-over.
Wad; Orange card, print black.
Case; Kynoch & Co.
Business; Gunmaker.

No2090
KYNOCH'S PATENT GROUSE EJECTOR

© DN.2-0885.   Updated; December 1997.

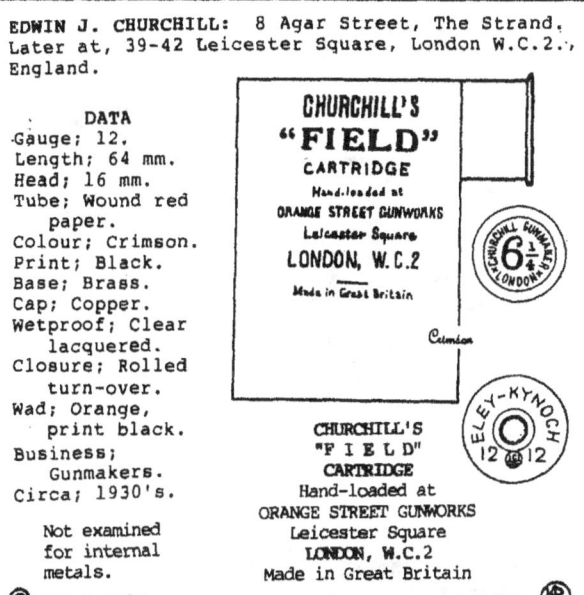

EDWIN J. CHURCHILL: 8 Agar Street, The Strand.
Later at, 39-42 Leicester Square, London W.C.2., England.

DATA
Gauge; 12.
Length; 64 mm.
Head; 16 mm.
Tube; Wound red paper.
Colour; Crimson.
Print; Black.
Base; Brass.
Cap; Copper.
Wetproof; Clear lacquered.
Closure; Rolled turn-over.
Wad; Orange, print black.
Business; Gunmakers.
Circa; 1930's.

Not examined for internal metals.

CHURCHILL'S "FIELD" CARTRIDGE
Hand-loaded at
ORANGE STREET GUNWORKS
Leicester Square
LONDON, W.C.2
Made in Great Britain

© DN.3-0913.   Drawn, 5/5/08.

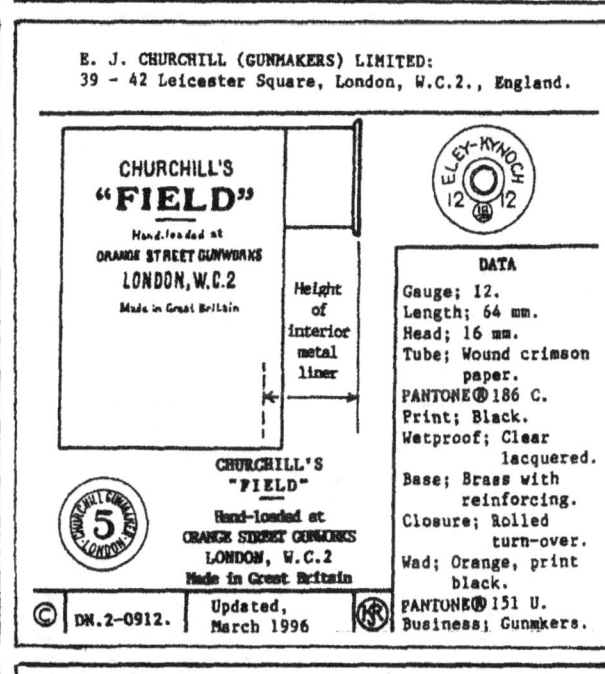

E. J. CHURCHILL (GUNMAKERS) LIMITED:
39 - 42 Leicester Square, London, W.C.2., England.

CHURCHILL'S "FIELD" CARTRIDGE
Hand-loaded at
ORANGE STREET GUNWORKS
LONDON, W.C.2
Made in Great Britain

Height of interior metal liner

DATA
Gauge; 12.
Length; 64 mm.
Head; 16 mm.
Tube; Wound crimson paper.
PANTONE® 186 C.
Print; Black.
Wetproof; Clear lacquered.
Base; Brass with reinforcing.
Closure; Rolled turn-over.
Wad; Orange, print black.
PANTONE® 151 U.
Business; Gunmakers.

© DN.2-0912.   Updated, March 1996

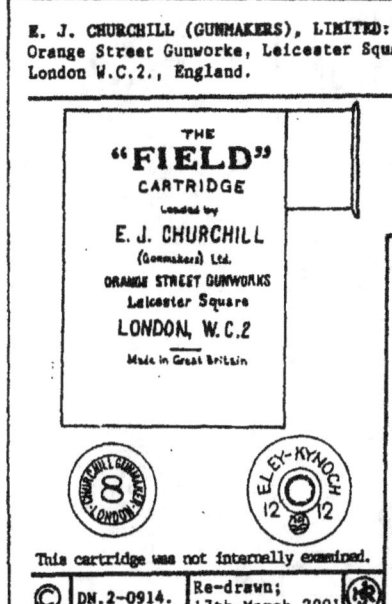

E. J. CHURCHILL (GUNMAKERS), LIMITED:
Orange Street Gunworks, Leicester Square, London W.C.2., England.

THE "FIELD" CARTRIDGE
Loaded by
E. J. CHURCHILL
(Gunmakers) Ltd.
ORANGE STREET GUNWORKS
Leicester Square
LONDON, W.C.2
Made in Great Britain

DATA
Gauge; 12.
Length; 64 mm.
Head; 16 mm.
Tube; Wound red paper.
Colour; Crimson.
Print; Black.
Base; Brass.
Closure; Rolled turn-over.
Wad; Orange, print black.
Business; Gunmakers.
Circa; 1930's.

This cartridge was not internally examined.

© DN.2-0914.   Re-drawn; 17th March 2001

EDWIN J. CHURCHILL:
39-42 Leicester Square, London W.C.2., England.

THE IMPERIAL CARTRIDGE
Hand loaded by
CHURCHILL
GUNMAKER
LONDON
Made in Great Britain

DATA
Gauge; 12
Length; 64 mm.
Head; 16 mm.
Tube; Wound crimson red paper.
Colour; Crimson red.
Print; Black.
Wetproof; Lacquered.
Base; Reinforced brass.
Closure; Rolled turn-over.
Wad; Orange, print black.
Business; Gunmaker and cartridge loader.

Case was not examined for an internal liner.

© DN.2-0319.   Re-drawn; 17th Jan 2002

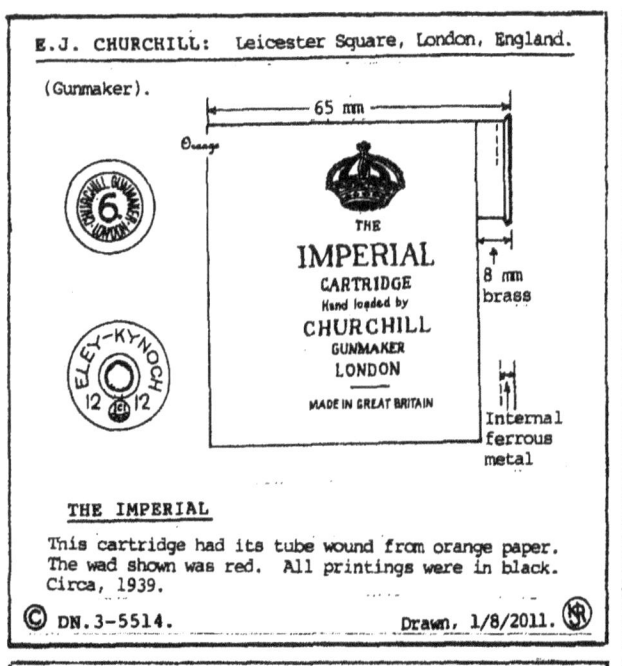
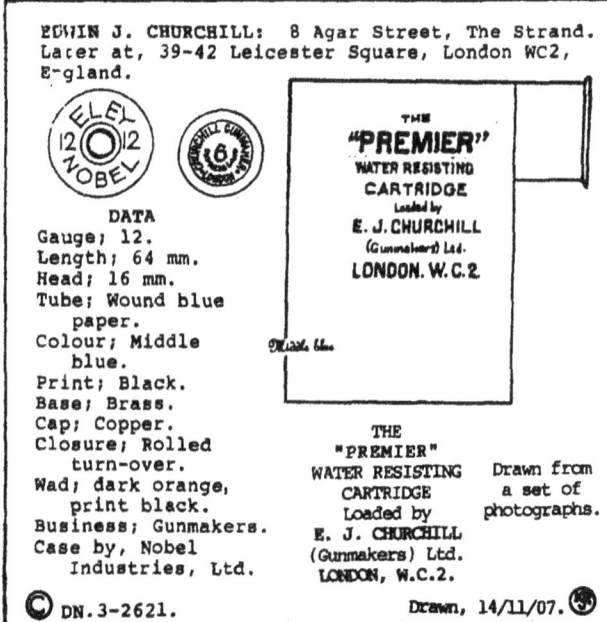
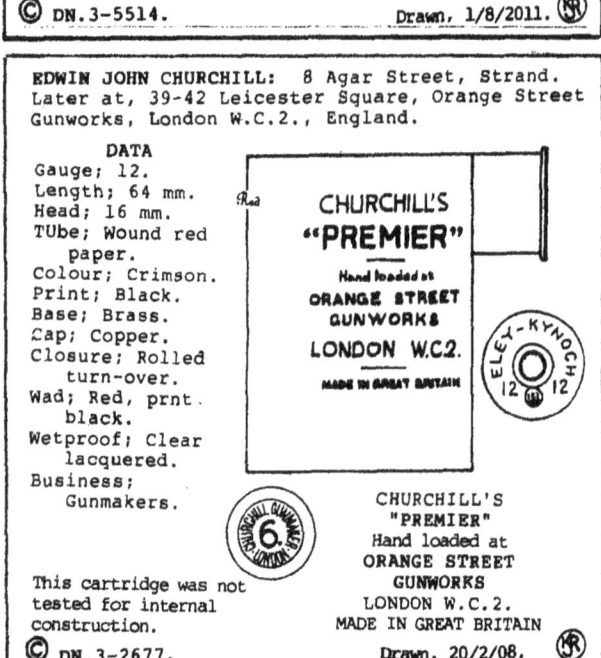
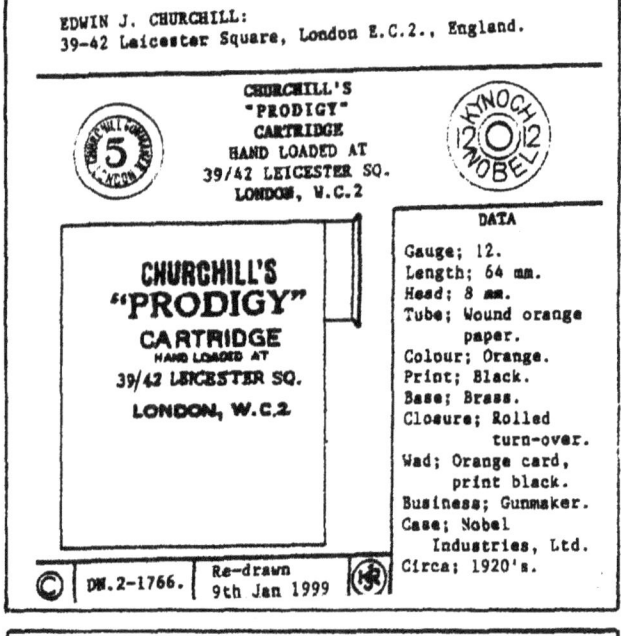
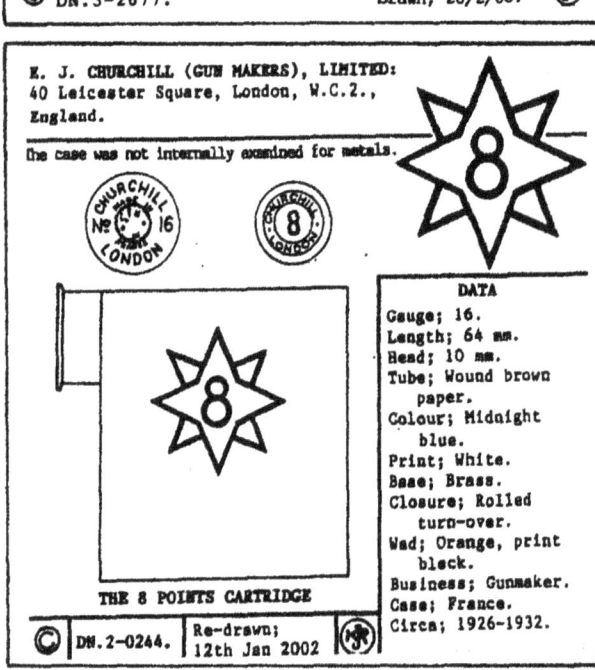
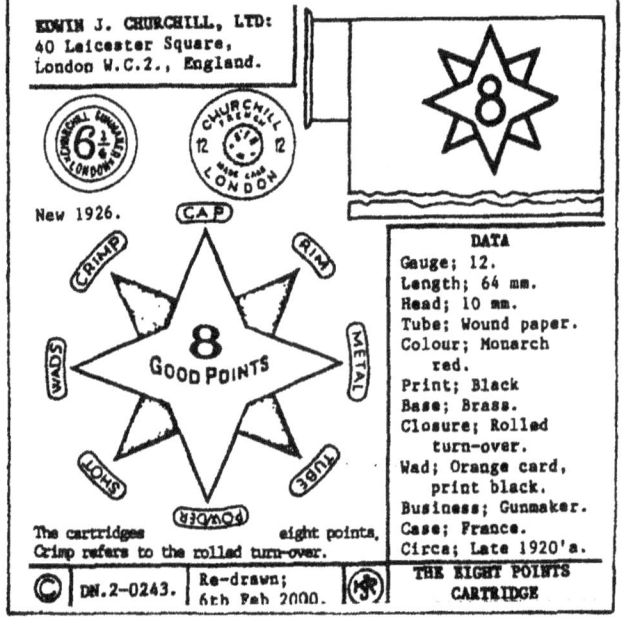

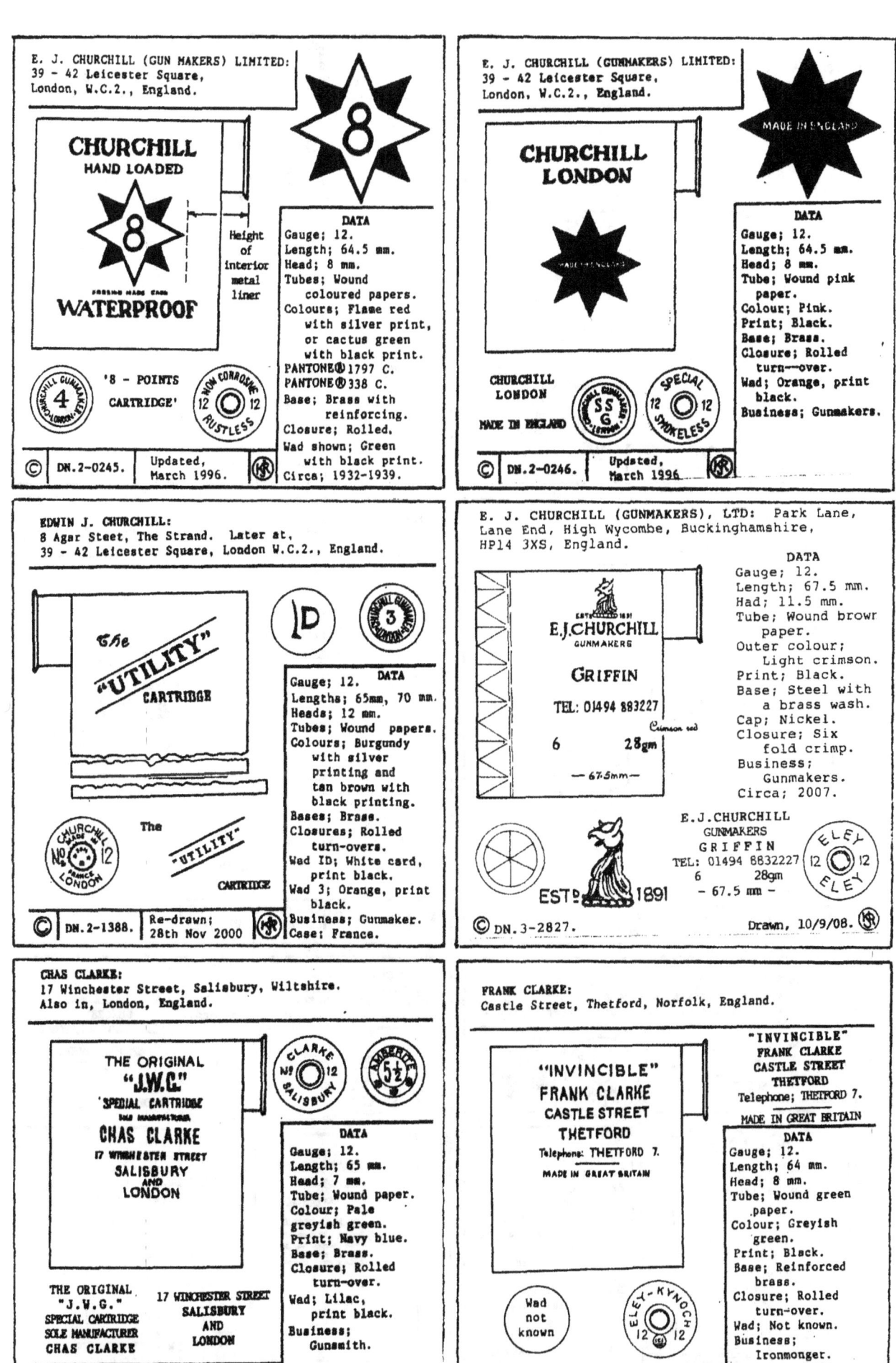

PLATE 53 [CHU - CLA]

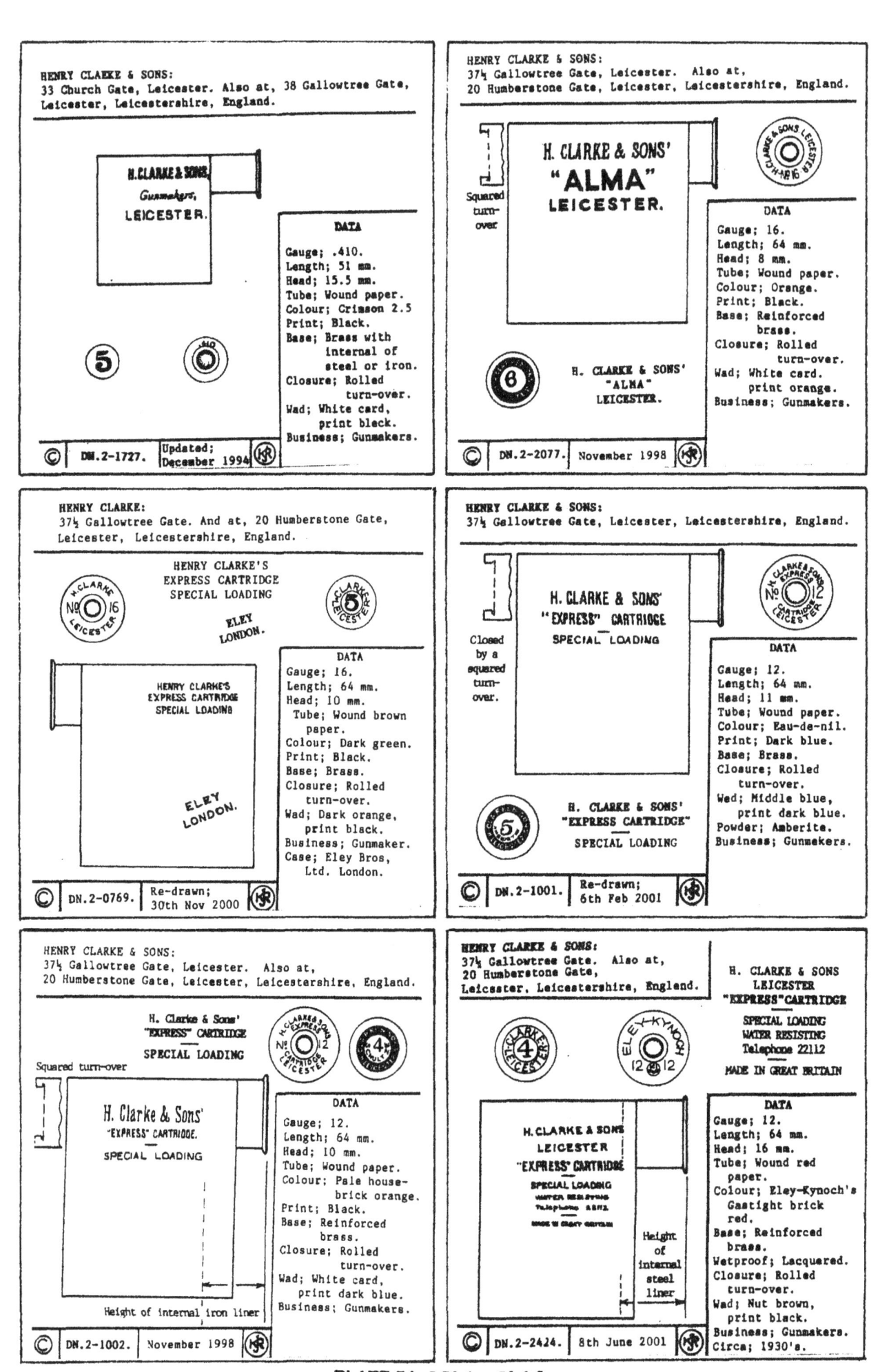

PLATE 54 [CLA - CLA]

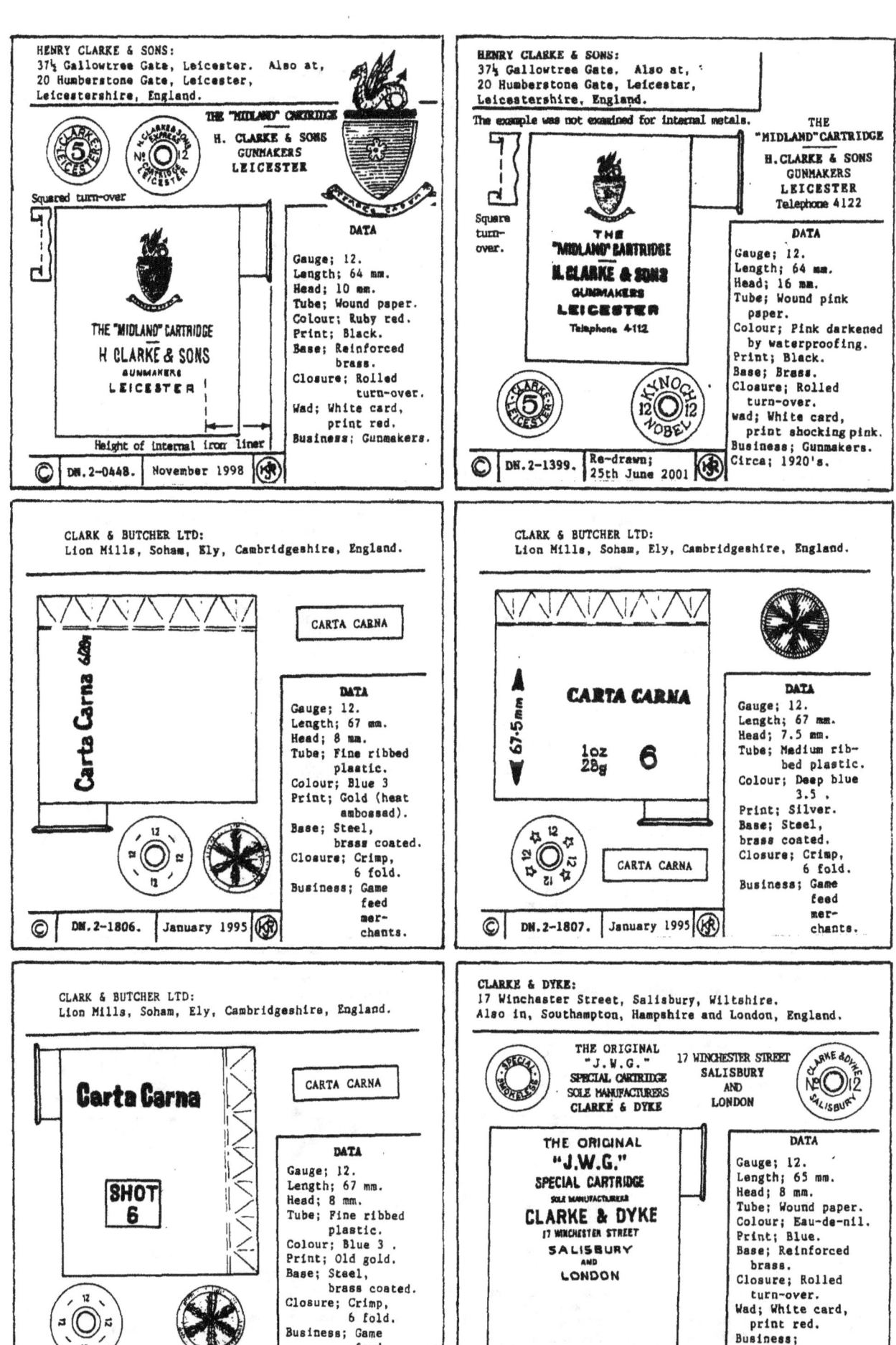

PLATE 55 [CLA - CLA]

CLARKE & DYKE:
17 Winchester Street, Salisbury, Wiltshire.
Also in, Southampton, Hampshire and London, England.

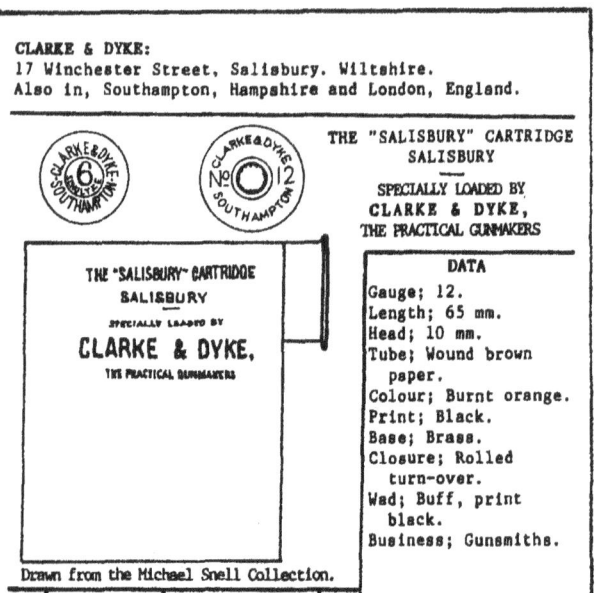

THE "SALISBURY" CARTRIDGE
SALISBURY

SPECIALLY LOADED BY
CLARKE & DYKE,
THE PRACTICAL GUNMAKERS

DATA
Gauge; 12.
Length; 65 mm.
Head; 10 mm.
Tube; Wound brown paper.
Colour; Burnt orange.
Print; Black.
Base; Brass.
Closure; Rolled turn-over.
Wad; Buff, print black.
Business; Gunsmiths.

Drawn from the Michael Snell Collection.

© DN.2-2448. 29th July 2001

CLATWORTHY COOKE & CO, LTD:
Taunton, Somerset, England.

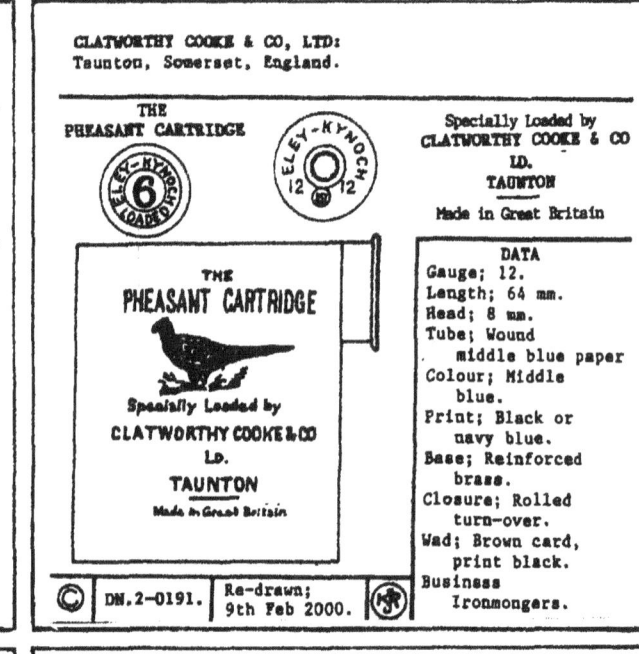

THE PHEASANT CARTRIDGE

Specially Loaded by
CLATWORTHY COOKE & CO
LD.
TAUNTON

Made in Great Britain

DATA
Gauge; 12.
Length; 64 mm.
Head; 8 mm.
Tube; Wound middle blue paper.
Colour; Middle blue.
Print; Black or navy blue.
Base; Reinforced brass.
Closure; Rolled turn-over.
Wad; Brown card, print black.
Business; Ironmongers.

© DN.2-0191. Re-drawn; 9th Feb 2000.

CLAYTON & SON:
Huntingdon & St. Neots, Huntingdonshire
Cambridgeshire, England.

Drawn from photographs taken from the Chris Hart collection.

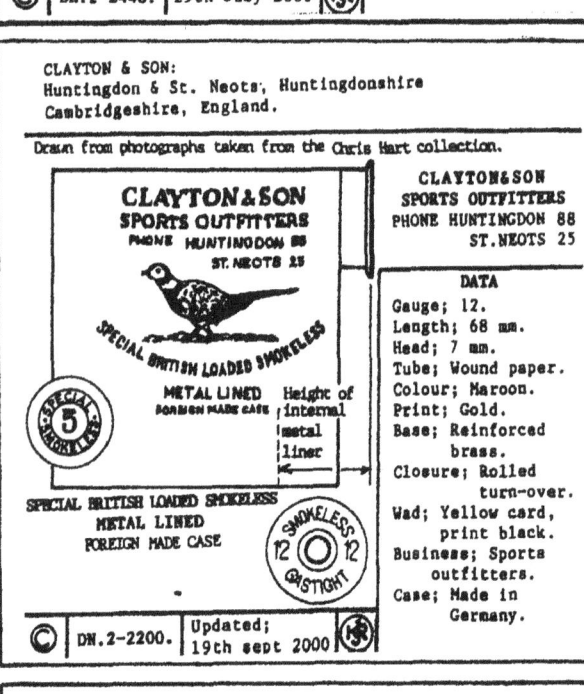

CLAYTON & SON
SPORTS OUTFITTERS
PHONE HUNTINGDON 88
ST. NEOTS 25

DATA
Gauge; 12.
Length; 68 mm.
Head; 7 mm.
Tube; Wound paper.
Colour; Maroon.
Print; Gold.
Base; Reinforced brass.
Closure; Rolled turn-over.
Wad; Yellow card, print black.
Business; Sports outfitters.
Case; Made in Germany.

© DN.2-2200. Updated; 19th Sept 2000.

R. & D. CLAYTON: The Traverse,
Bury St Edmunds, Suffolk, England.

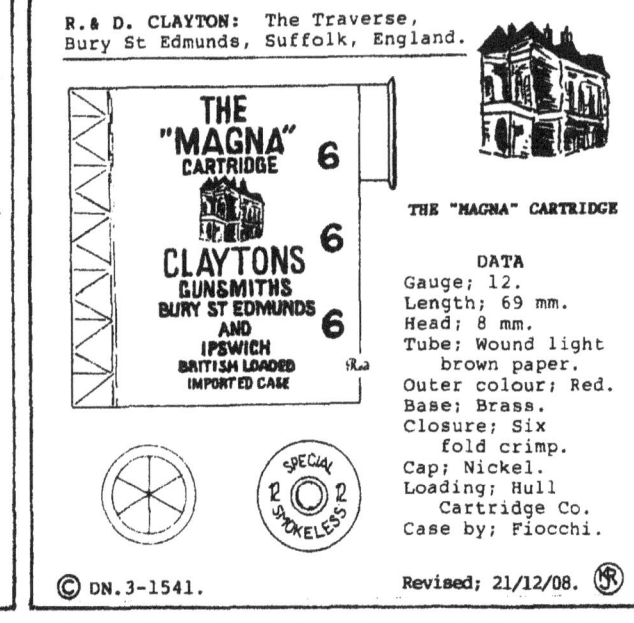

THE "MAGNA" CARTRIDGE

DATA
Gauge; 12.
Length; 69 mm.
Head; 8 mm.
Tube; Wound light brown paper.
Outer colour; Red.
Base; Brass.
Closure; Six fold crimp.
Cap; Nickel.
Loading; Hull Cartridge Co.
Case by; Fiocchi.

© DN.3-1541. Revised; 21/12/08.

R. CLIMIE & SON:
Greenock, Renfrewshire (South-Clyde), Scotland.

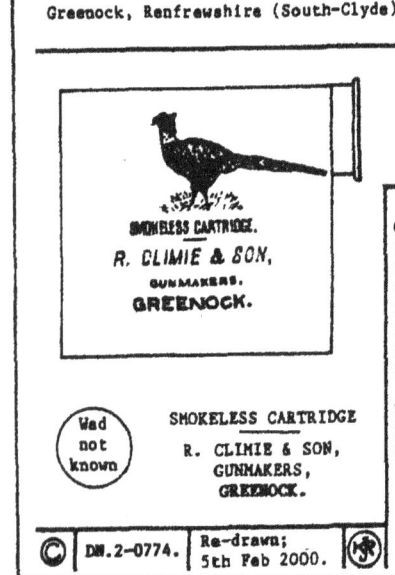

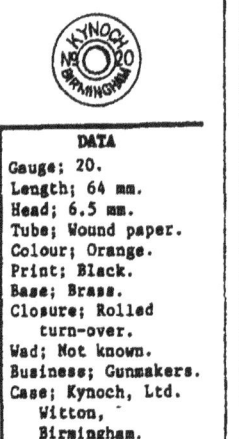

SMOKELESS CARTRIDGE
R. CLIMIE & SON,
GUNMAKERS,
GREENOCK.

DATA
Gauge; 20.
Length; 64 mm.
Head; 6.5 mm.
Tube; Wound paper.
Colour; Orange.
Print; Black.
Base; Brass.
Closure; Rolled turn-over.
Wad; Not known.
Business; Gunmakers.
Case; Kynoch, Ltd. Witton, Birmingham.

© DN.2-0774. Re-drawn; 5th Feb 2000.

CLINTON CARTRIDGE COMPANY (C.C.Co.):
Illinois, U.S.A.

This drawing was made from an unused case.

DATA
Gauge; 12.
Length; 66 mm.
Head; 7 mm.
Tube; Wound off-white paper.
Colour; Off-white with brown tinge.
Print; Dark blue.
Base; Brass.
Closure; Rolled turn-over.
Wad; Not known.
Business; Cartridge manufacturers.

© DN.2-1138. Re-drawn; 19th Jan 2000.

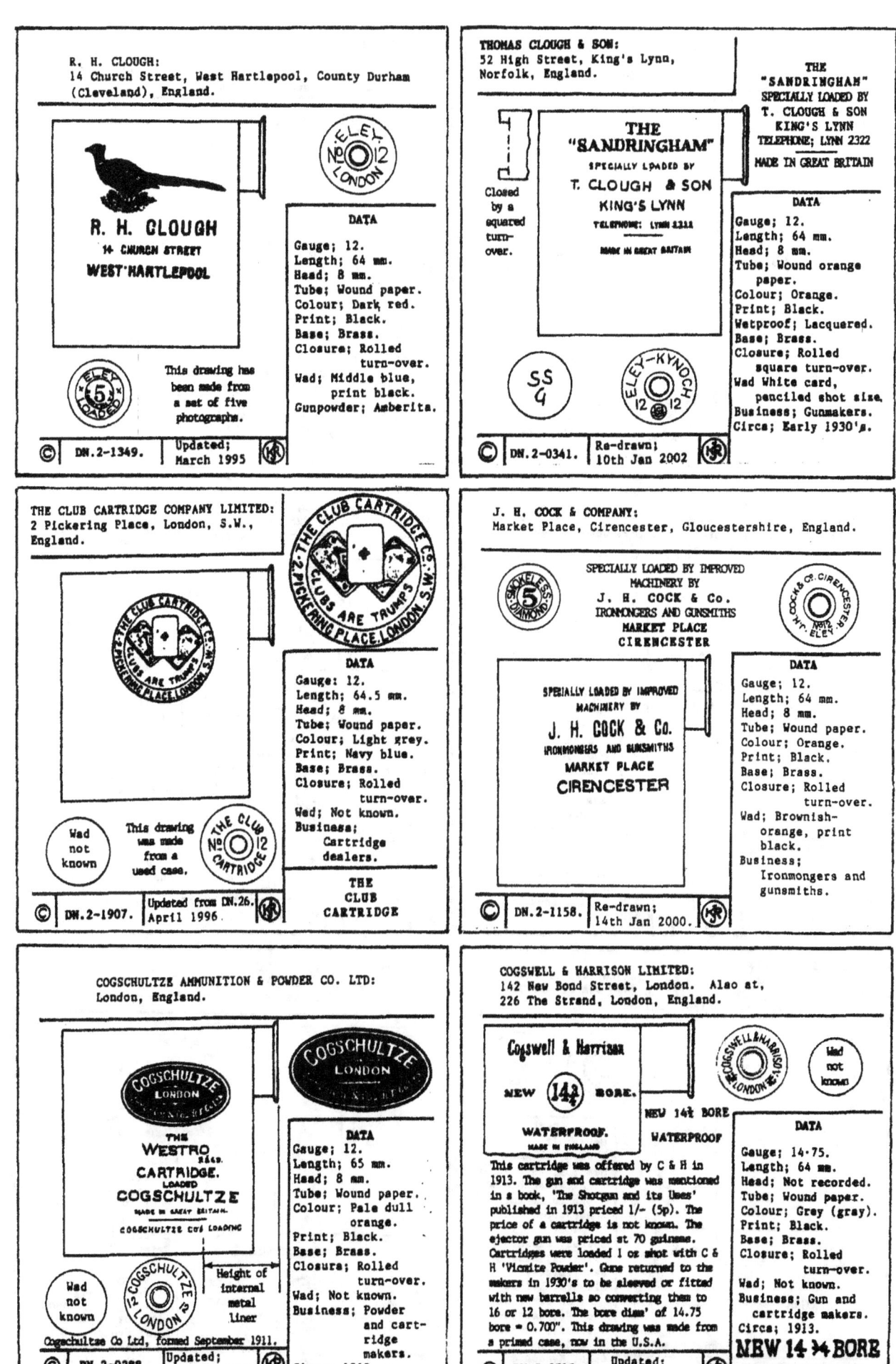

PLATE 57 [CLO - COG]

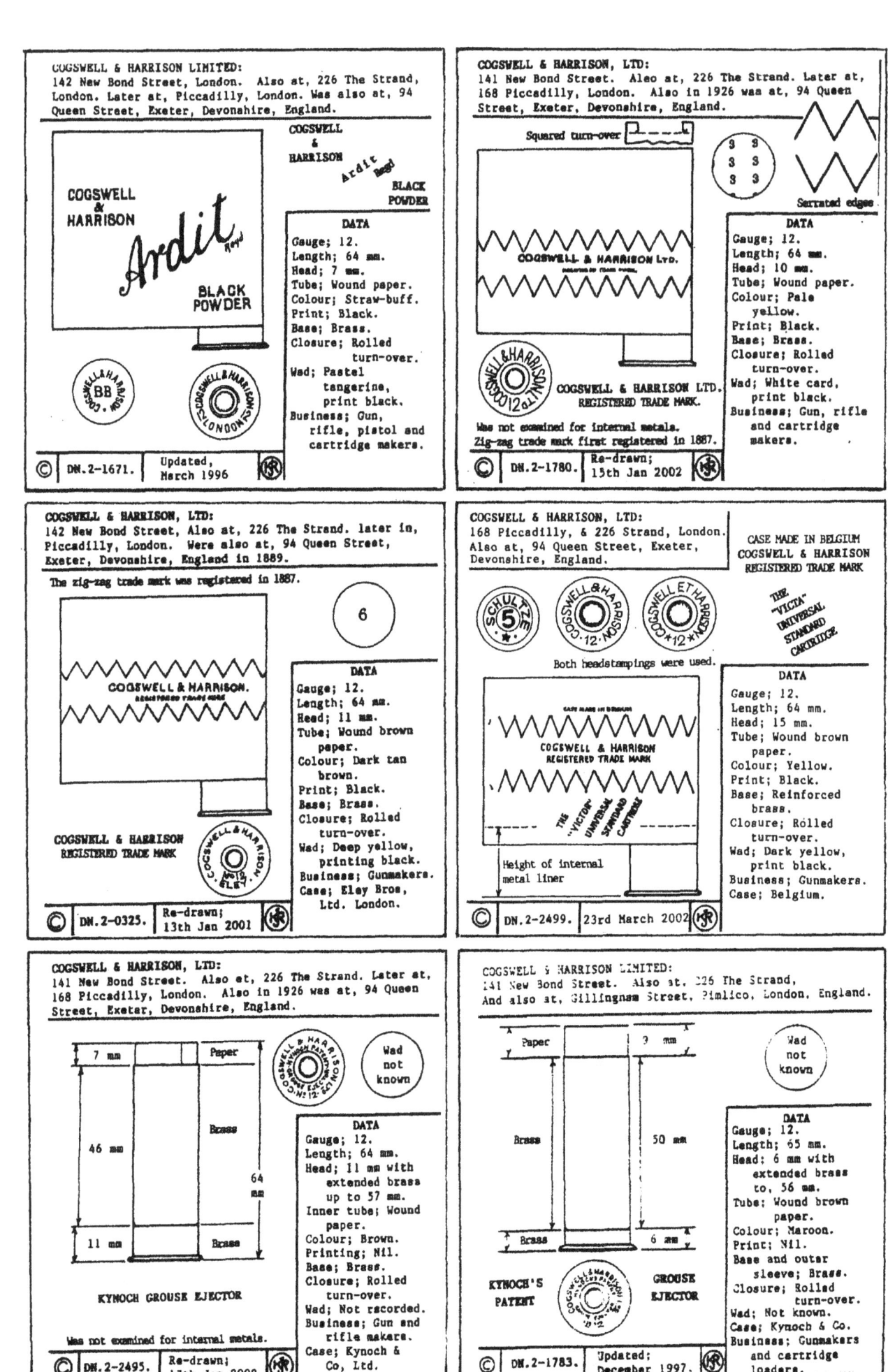
PLATE 58 [COG - COG]

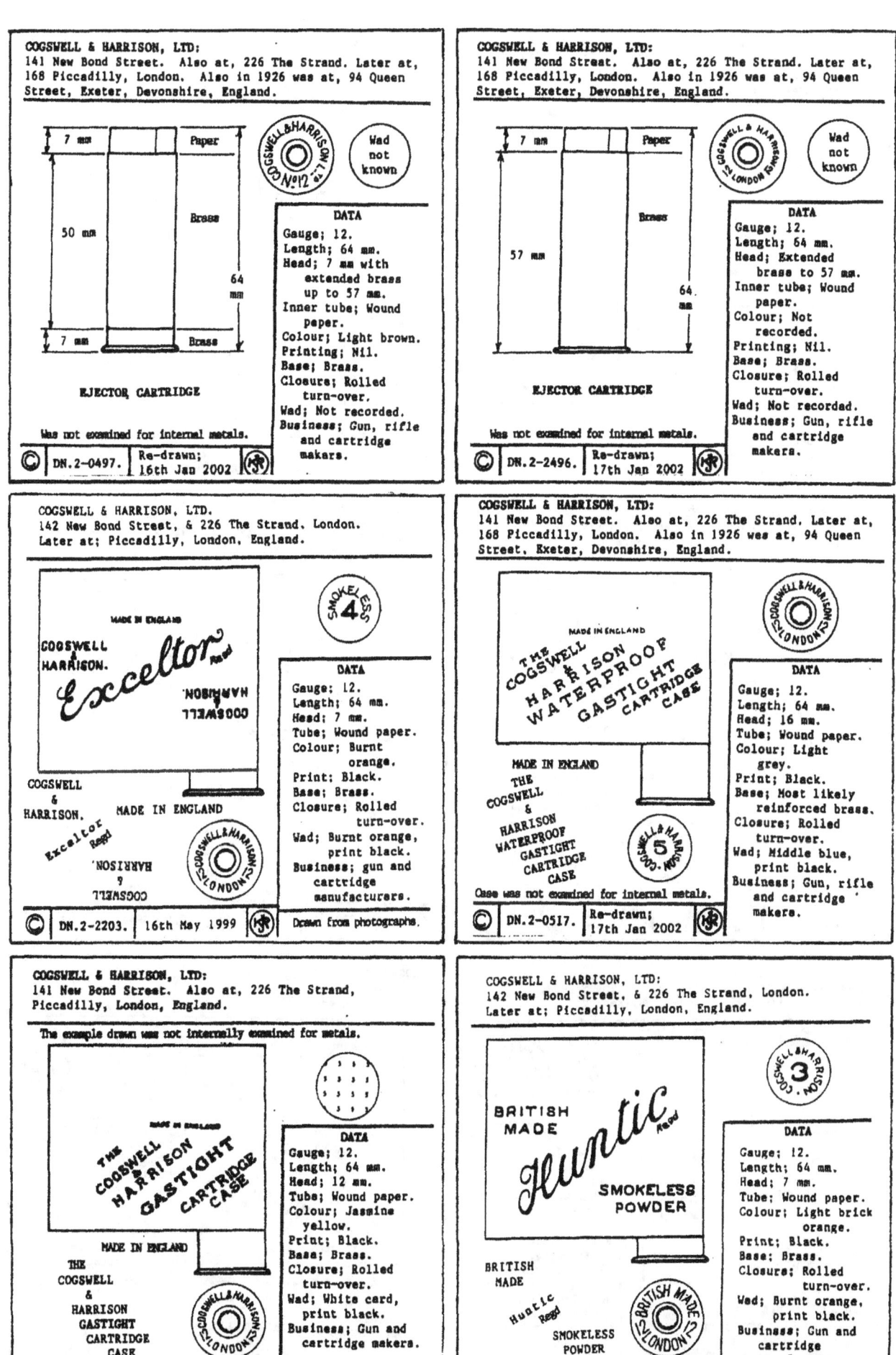

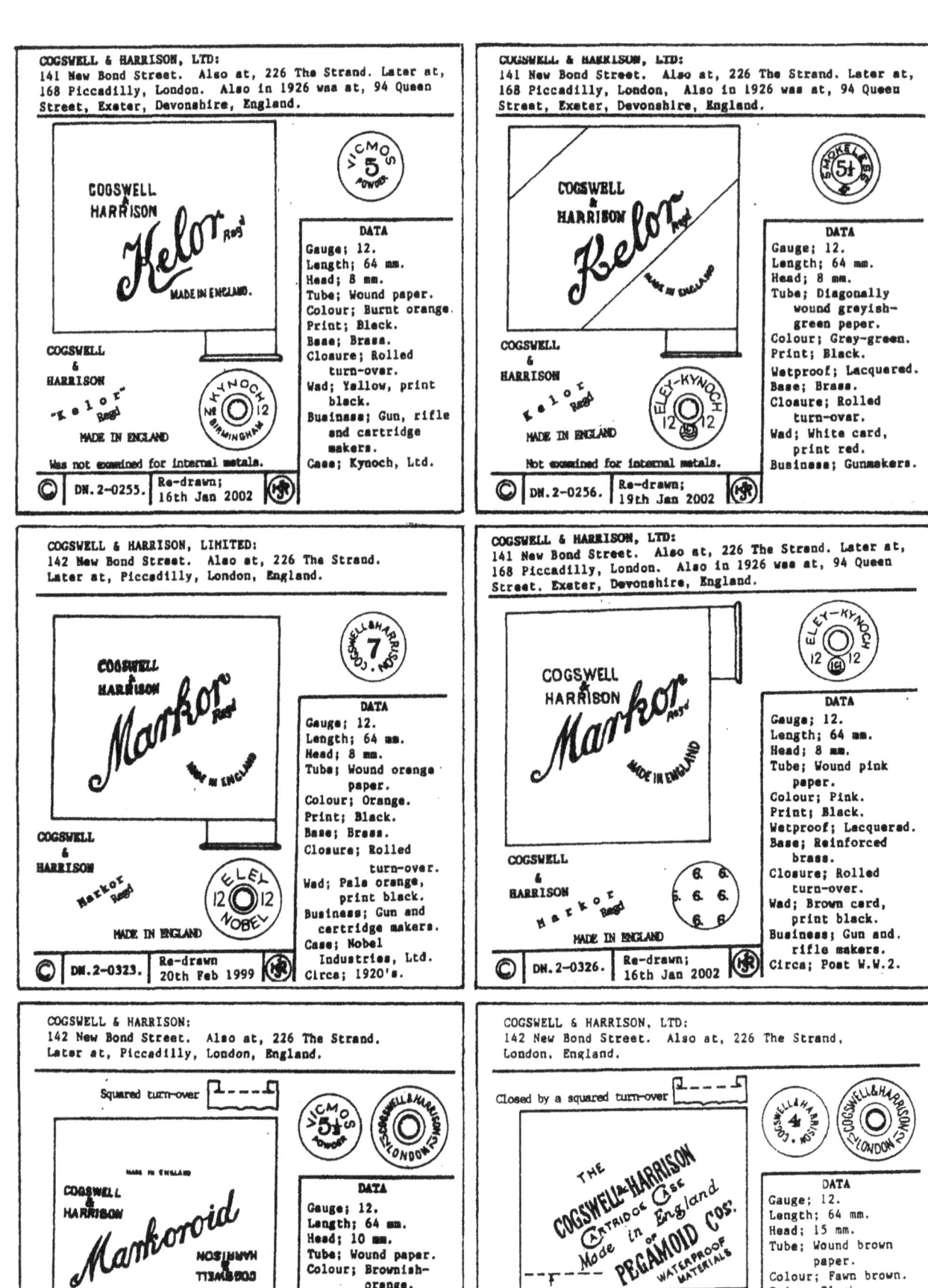

PLATE 60 [COG – COG]

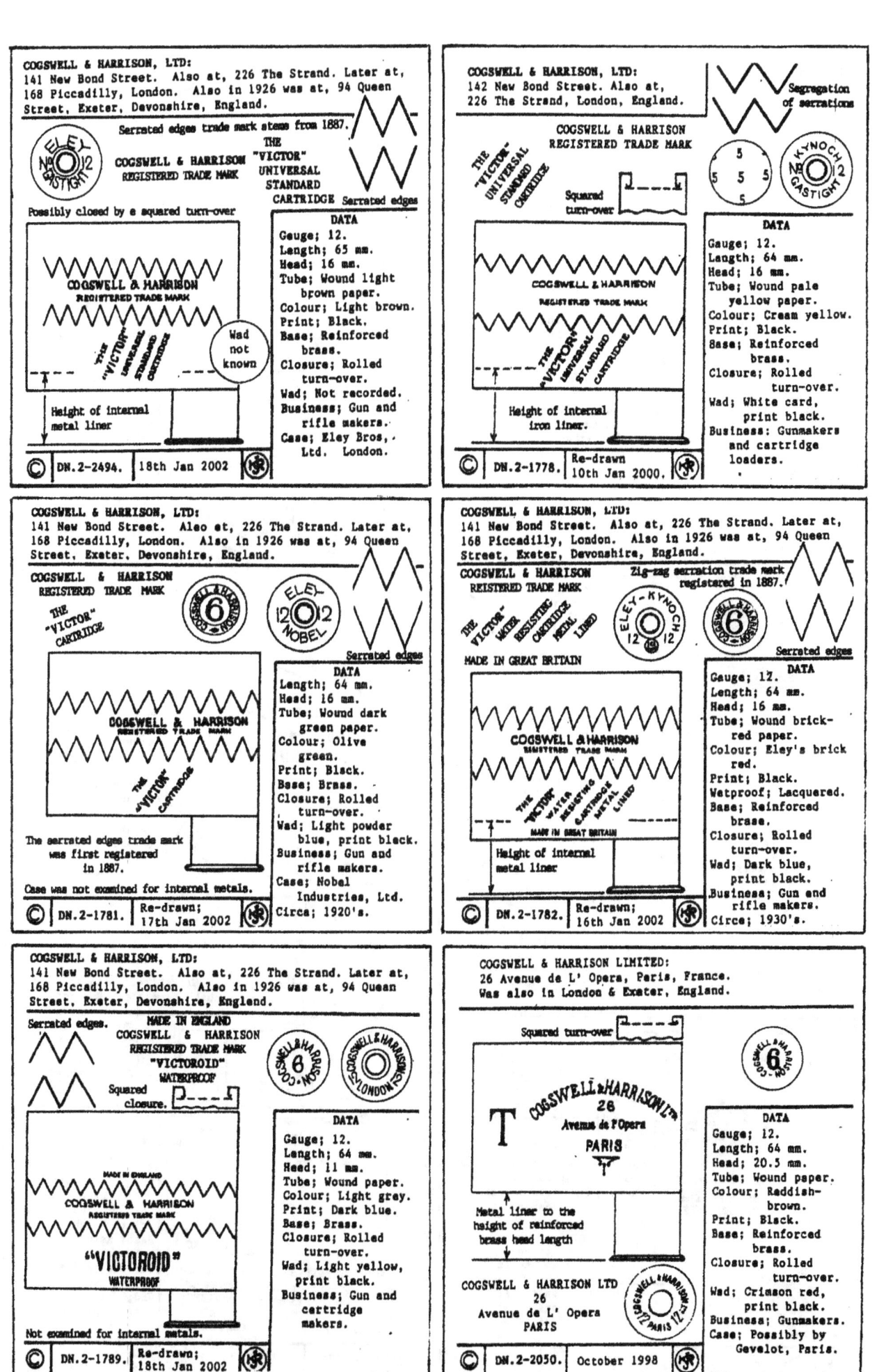

PLATE 61 [COG – COG]

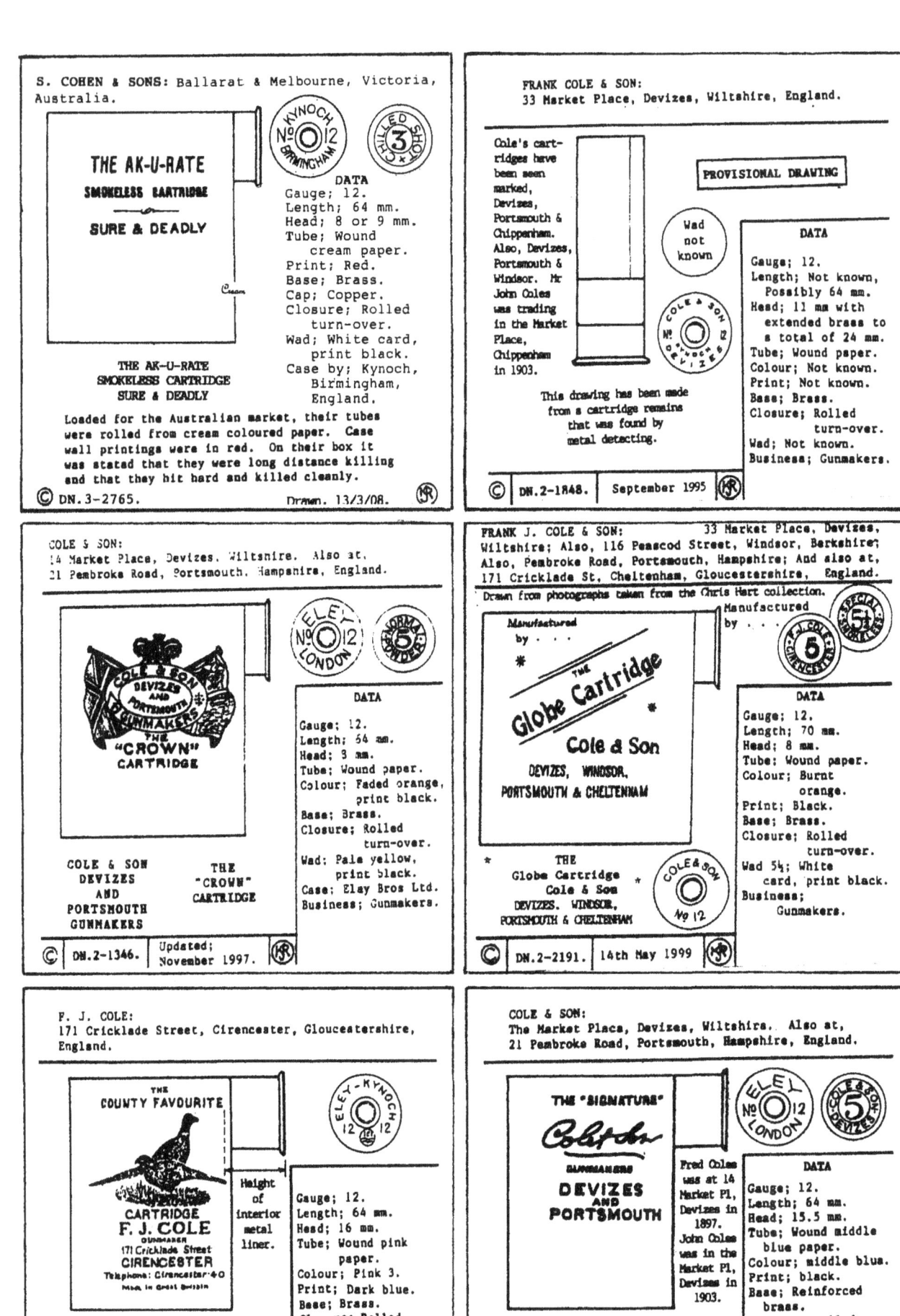

PLATE 62 [COH - COL]

WILHELM COLLATH:
Gewehr-u-Patronen (Gun, rifle & Cartridge Factory), Frankfurt A/O, East Germany.

DATA

Central Pinfire.
Gauge; (3).
Equivalent gauge; 14.
Length; 73.5 mm.
Head; 14 mm.
Tube; Wound paper.
Colour; Brownish cimson.
Print; Black.
Base; Brass.
Closure; Not known.
Business; Gun and cartridge maker.

TESCHNER-COLLATH
Spezialpatrone
Rauchlos
(Special cartridge, Smokeless)
Experimental central pinfire.

© DN.2-2018. November 1997.

WILHELM COLLATH & SOHNE:
Gewehr-u-Patronen (Gun, Rifle & Cartridge Factory), Frankfurt A/O, East Germany.

This cartridge had a bottle shaped head witha thin tapered rim. A large copper cap was fitted.

Collath gauge equivalents.

No, 0 = 10 gauge
No, 1 = 12 gauge
No, 2 Not used
No, 3 = 14 gauge
No, 4 = 16 gauge
No, 5 = 18 gauge
No, 6 = 20 gauge
No, 7 = 24 gauge
No, 8 = 28 gauge

DRAWING DIAMETERS

'A' = 0 666"
'B' = 0 705"
'C' = 0 731"
'D' = 0 803"

DATA

Gauge; (5).
Equivilent gauge; 18.
Length; 65 mm.
Head; 14 mm.
Tube; Wound paper.
Colour; Light redish brown.
Print; Nil.
Base; Brass.
Cap large copper.
Wetproof; Waxed.
Closure; Rolled turn-over.
Wad; Light sky blue, print black.
Business; Gun and cartridge maker.

© DN.2-1252. Updated; November 1997.

WILHELM COLLATH & SOHNE:
Gewehr-u-Patronen (Gun, Rifle & Cartridge Factory), Frankfurt A/O, East Germany.

Drawing made from a set of photographs.
"TESCO"
Experimental central pinfire.

DATA

Central Pinfire.
Gauge; (5).
Equivalent gauge; 18
Length; 74 mm.
Head; 12.5 mm.
Tube; Wound paper.
Colour; Greyish-green.
Print; Black.
Base; Brass.
Closure; Not known.
Business; Gun and cartridge maker.

© DN.2-2019. November 1997.

J. COLLIS, LTD:
Strood. Also in Rochester and Gravesend, Kent, England.

THE "ALL ROUND" SMOKELESS CARTRIDGE LOADED BY J.COLLIS LTD., STROOD, ROCHESTER AND GRAVESEND FOREIGN MADE CASE

DATA

Gauge; 16.
Length; 65 mm.
Head 7 mm.
Tube; Wound dark green paper.
Colour; Dark green.
Print; Black.
Base; Brass.
Closure; Rolled turn-over.
Wad; Not known.
Case; Imported.

The case was not internally examined.

© **DN.2-0089.** **Re-drawn; 10th Jan 2002**

COLONIAL AMMUNITION COMPANY, LIMITED:
Mount Eden, Auckland, New Zealand.

The COLONIAL AMMUNITION Coy.'s Gastight Cartridge Case.

DATA

Gauge; 12.
Length; 63 mm.
Head; 10 mm.
Tube; Wound paper.
Colour; Apple green.
Print; Black.
Base; Brass.
Closure; Rolled turn-over.
Wad; Not known.
Business; Ammunition manufacturers.

Drawn from photographs of a used case in the Jack Luttrell collection.

© **DN.2-2518.** 13th Sept 2002

COLONIAL AMMUNITION CO: Mount Eden, Auckland, New-Zealand.
(Business; Ammunition manufacturers).

GAME LOAD

The example from which this drawing was made had a soot black paper tube which was unprinted. The top wad was cut from white card with black printing. It was not examined for internal ferrous metals.

© DN.3-1170. Revised, 14/2/09.

PLATE 63 [COL – COL]

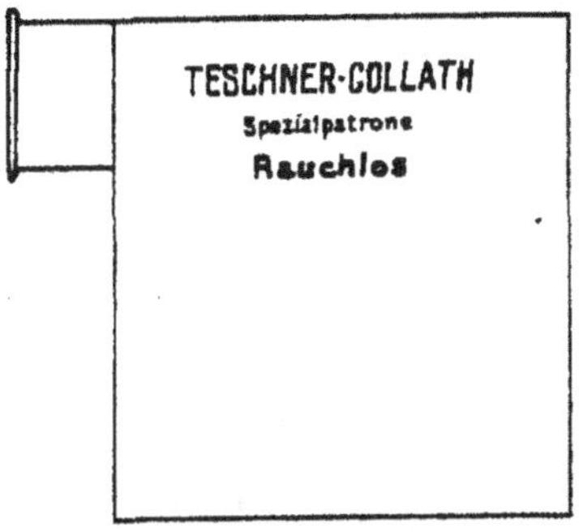

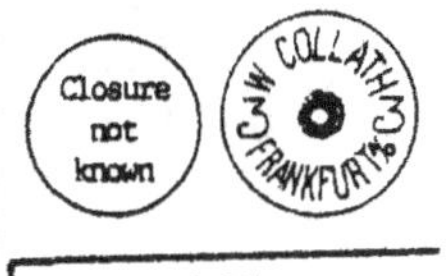

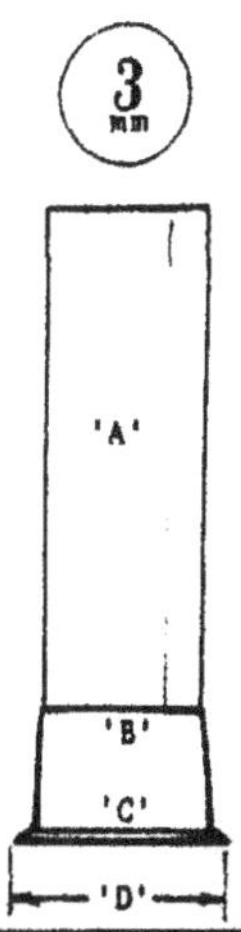

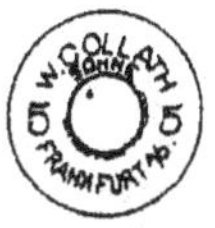

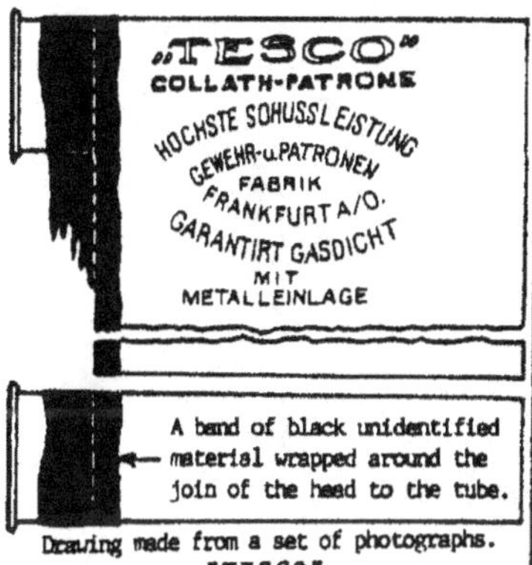

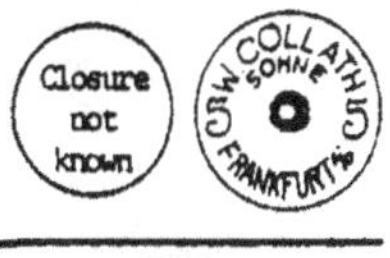

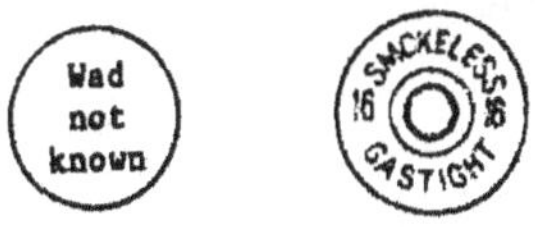

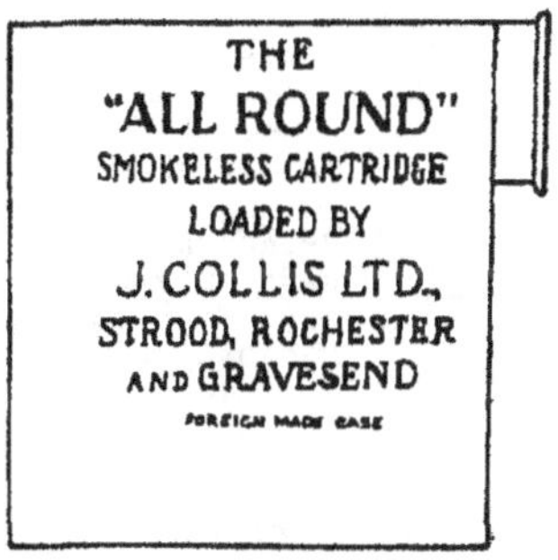

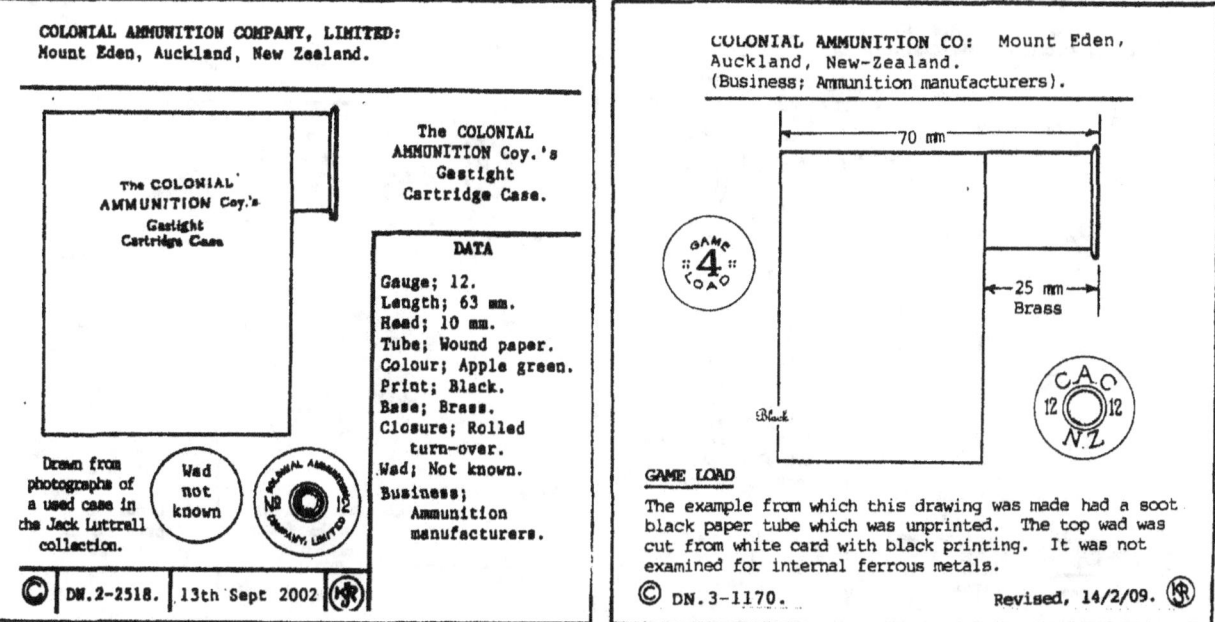

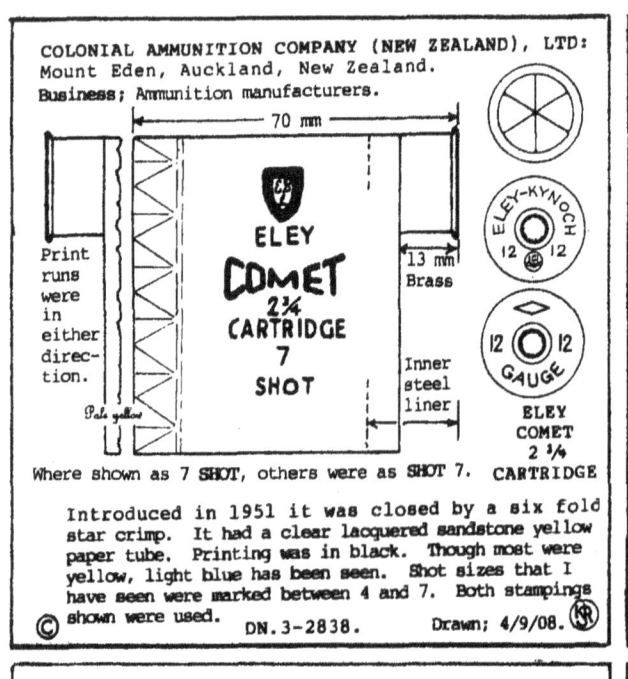
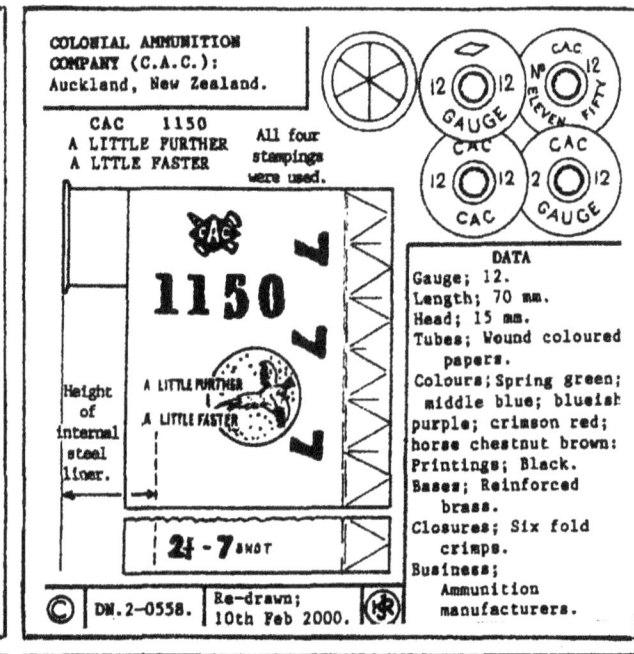
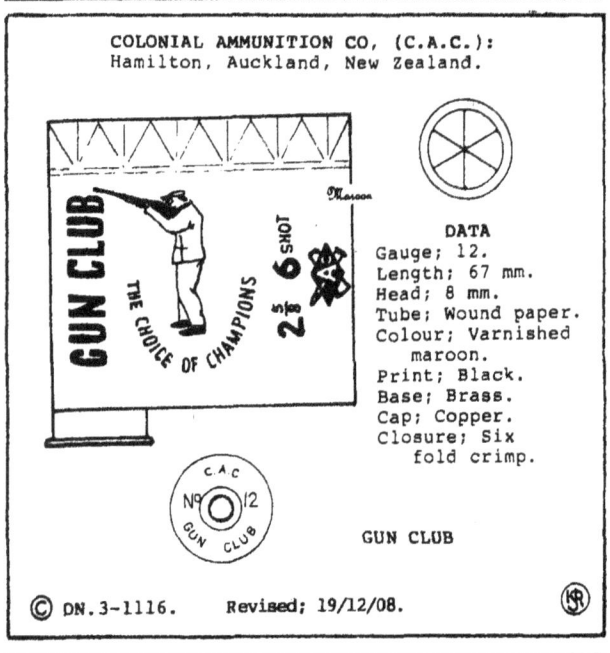
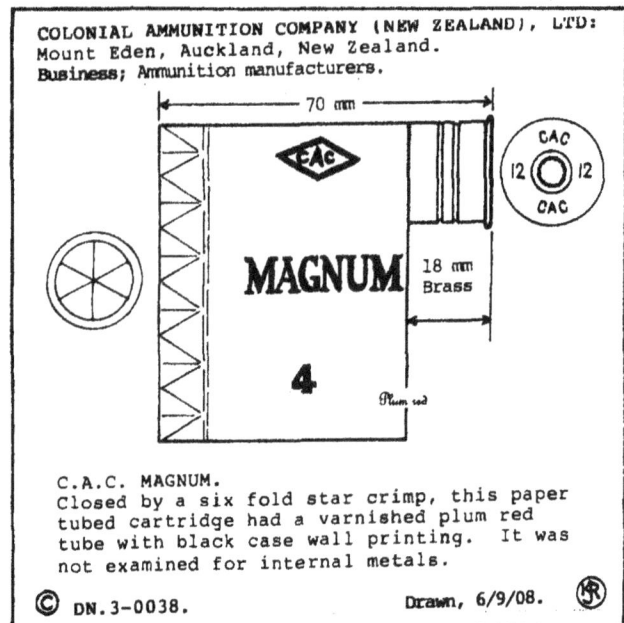
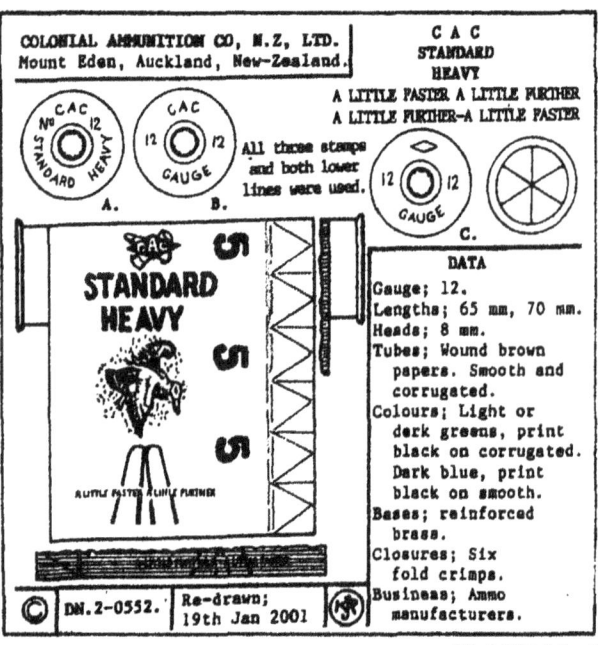
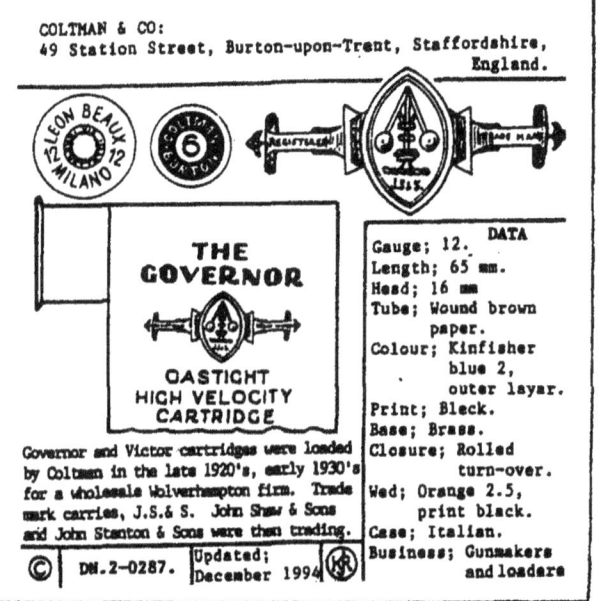

PLATE 64 [COL – COL]

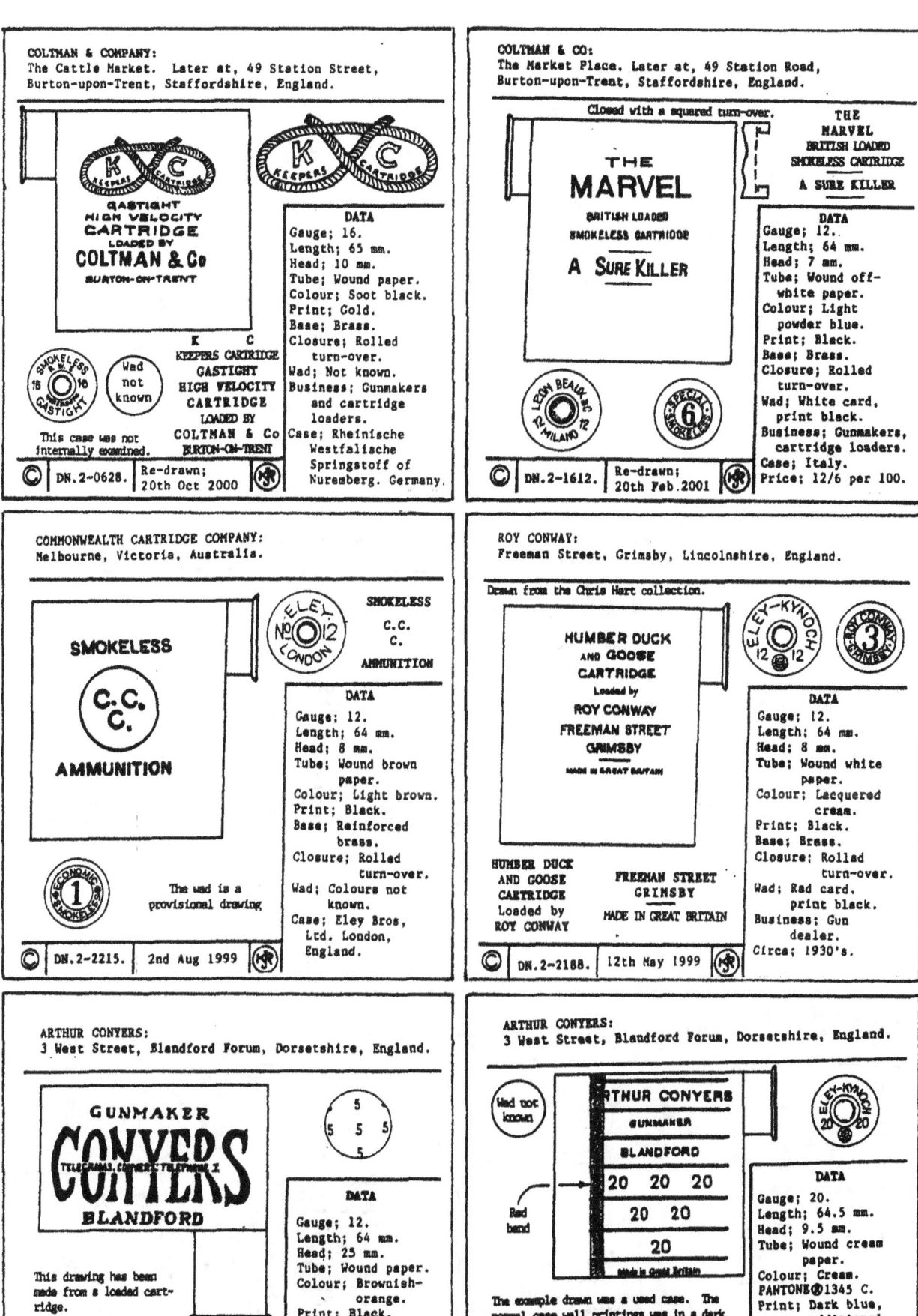

PLATE 65 [COL – CON]

ARTHUR CONYERS:
3 West Street, Blandford Forum, Dorsetshire, England.

ARTHUR CONYERS
GUN MAKER
BLANDFORD
TELEGRAMS:
CONYERS.BLANDFORD
TELEPHONE: N°7
CASE MADE IN BELGIUM

Wad not known

DATA
Gauge; 12.
Length; 64.5 mm.
Head; 8 mm.
Tube; Wound brown paper.
Colour; Crimson.
PANTONE® 194 C.
Print; Black.
Base; Brass.
Interior liner; Nil
Closure; Rolled turn-over.
Wad; Not known.
Business; Gunmaker.
Circa; 1930's.

This case would have been supplied by Jas R. Watson & Co, being of Cooppal manufacture. It is not known if Watsons' or Conyers loaded it. Note early telephone No.

© DN.2-1479. Updated, October 1995

ARTHUR CONYERS:
3 West Street, Blandford Forum, Dorsetshire, England.

THE "DORSET COUNTY"
CARTRIDGE
LOADED & GUARANTEED BY
ARTHUR CONYERS
BLANDFORD
TELEPHONE 7
TELEGRAMS: "CONYERS"
Made in Great Britain

DATA
Gauge; 12.
Length; 64 mm.
Head; 8 mm.
Tube; Wound eau-de-nil paper.
Colour; Eau-de-nil.
Print; Black.
Base; Brass.
Closure; Rolled turn-over.
Wad; Emerald green, print black.
Business; Gunmaker.
Circa; 1930.

© DN.2-1386. Re-drawn 16th Jan 1999

ARTHUR CONYERS: 3 West Street, Blandford Forum, Dorset, England.

DATA
Gauge; 12.
Head; 8 mm.
Tube; Wound paper.
Colour; Brownish straw-white.
Print; Black.
Base; Brass.
Cap; Copper.
Closure; Rolled turn-over.
Wad; White card, print navy-blue.
Business; Gunmaker.
Case by; Kynoch Nobel Industries.

"THE EXPRESS"
Loaded & Guaranteed by
ARTHUR CONYERS
BLANDFORD
Telegrams: "CONYERS BLANDFORD"
Telephone No 7.

Drawn from a set of photographs.

© DN.3-2610. Drawn, 8/11/07.

---

3 West Street, Blandford Forum, Dorsetshire, England.

"THE EXPRESS"
Loaded & Guaranteed by
ARTHUR CONYERS
BLANDFORD
Telegrams: "CONYERS, BLANDFORD"
Telephone: No.7
Made in Great Britain

Loaded & Guaranteed by
ARTHUR CONYERS
BLANDFORD
Telegrams: "Conyers, Blandford"
Telephone: No.7
Made in Great Britain

DATA
Gauges; 12, 16, 20.
Lengths; 64 mm.
Heads; 7 to 8 mm.
Tubes; Wound coloured papers.
Colours;
12, White or yellow, print black. Also, Eau-de-nil, print navy blue.
16, Dark blue, print navy blue or black.
20; Buff, print navy blue or black.
Bases; Brass.
Closures; Rolled turn-over.
Wad shown; Vermilion, print black.
Business; Gunmaker.

© DN.2-0478. Re-drawn; 22nd Feb 2000.

ARTHUR CONYERS & SONS:
3 West Street, Blandford Forum, Dorsetshire, England.

"THE EXPRESS"
ARTHUR CONYERS & SONS
CARTRIDGE MANUFACTURERS
BLANDFORD
DORSET
MADE IN GREAT BRITAIN

"THE EXPRESS"
ARTHUR CONYERS & SONS
CARTRIDGE MANUFACTURERS
BLANDFORD
DORSET
MADE IN GREAT BRITAIN

DATA
Gauge; 12.
Length; 64 mm.
Head; 8 mm.
Tube; Wound orange paper.
Colour; Orange.
Print; Black.
Base; Reinforced brass.
Closure; Rolled turn-over.
Watproof; Lacquered.
Wad; Brown card, print black.
Business; Gunmakers, cartridge loaders.
Circa; 1950.

© DN.2-0476. Re-drawn; 25th Feb 2001.

ARTHUR CONYERS:
3 West Street, Blandford Forum, Dorset, England.

"The EXPRESS"
DE LUXE
Loaded and Guaranteed by
ARTHUR CONYERS
BLANDFORD
Telegrams:
"Conyers. Blandford"
Telephone No.7
Made in Great Britain

Height of interior metal liner.

"THE EXPRESS" DE LUXE

The small wording read;
Loaded and Guaranteed by
Telegrams:
"Conyers. Blandford"
Telephone No. 7
Made in Great Britain

DATA
Gauge; 12.
Length; 64 mm.
Head; 16 mm.
Tube; Wound crimson paper.
Colour; Crimson red.
Print; Black.
Base; Brass.
Closure; Rolled turn-over.
Wad; Green card, print black.
Watproof; Lacquered.
Circa; Early 1930's.
Business; Gunmaker and cartridge loader.

© DN.2-1720. Updated; March 1995

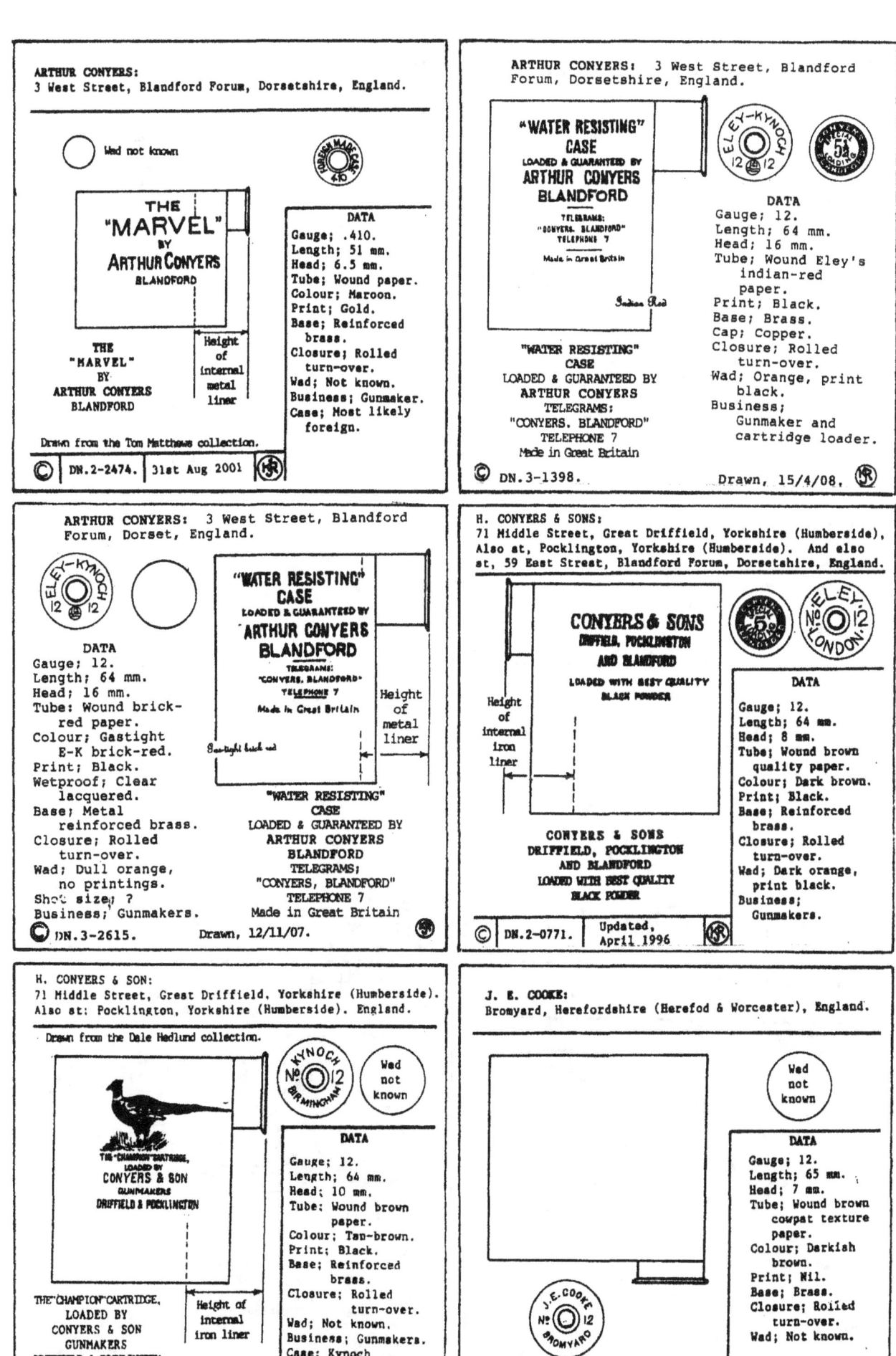

PLATE 67 [CON - COO]

GEORGE COONEY:
Cross Street / John Street Corner, Kells, County Meath, Republic of Ireland.

DATA
Gauge; 12.
Length; 64 mm.
Head; 26 mm.
Tube; Wound best quality brown paper.
Colour; Brown.
Print; Black.
Base; Brass.
Closure; Rolled turn-over.
Wad; Deep red, print black.
Business; Hardware merchant.
Case; Kynoch, Ltd. England.

Case was not examined for internal metals.

© | DN.2-1362. | Re-drawn; 14th Feb 2001

GEORGE COONEY:
Cross Street / John Street Corner, Kells, County Meath, Republic of Ireland.

Drawing made from a set of photographs taken of an unused case.
George closed his doors, circa 1932 - 1933.

DATA
Gauge; 12.
Length; 64.5 mm.
Head; 10 mm with extended brass to a total of 24 mm.
Tube; Wound paper.
Colour; Reddish-brown.
Print; Black.
Base; Double brass.
Internal liner; Not known.
Wad; Not known.
Case; Kynoch, Ltd. England.
Business; Hardware merchants

© | DN.2-1943. | December 1996

S. L. CORDEN:
37 High Street, Warminster, Wiltshire, England.

DATA
Gauge; 12.
Length; 65 mm.
Head; 9 mm.
Tube; Wound paper.
Colour; Dark crimson red.
Print; Black.
Base; Reinforced brass.
Closure; Rolled turn-over.
Wad; White card, print black.
Business; Ironmongers and general furnishing.
Case; Kynoch, Ltd.

Drawn from the Michael Snell Collection.

© | DN.2-2451. | 19th July 2001

S. L. CORDEN:
37 High Street, Warminster, Wiltshire, England.

DATA
Gauge; 12.
Length; 57 mm.
Head; 8-9 mm.
Tube; Wound paper.
Colour; Dark crimson.
Print; Black.
Base; Brass.
Closure; Rolled turn-over.
Wad; White card, print black.
Business; Ironmongers and general furnishing.
Case; Kynoch, Ltd.

Drawn from the Michael Snell Collection.

© | DN.2-2450. | 18th July 2001

SIDNEY LANCELOT CORDEN:
37 High Street, Warminster, Wiltshire, England.

DATA
Gauge; 12.
Length; 64 mm.
Head; 8 mm.
Tube; Wound paper.
Colour; Red.
Print; Black.
Base; Brass.
Closure; Rolled turn-over.
Wad; Not known.
Business; Ironmonger.
Case; Eley Bros, Ltd.

Drawing made from a used case.

© | DN.2-0234. | Re-drawn 6th Feb 1999

H. G. CORDES:
Bremerhaven, Nieder Sachsen, West Germany.
Factory at; Bischweiler, West Germany.

ENGLISH TRANSLATION
Extra Gastight Cartridge case by H. G. Cordes of Bremerhaven. Made from the very best materials of gastight quality with a metal liner.

DATA
Gauge; 12.
Length; 65 mm.
Head; 8 mm.
Tube; Wound brown paper.
Colour; Old brown.
Print, Black.
Base; reinforced brass.
Closure; Rolled turn-over.
Wad; White card, print red. 0 shot size in black.
Cap; Small copper.

© | DN.2-1969. | May 1997.

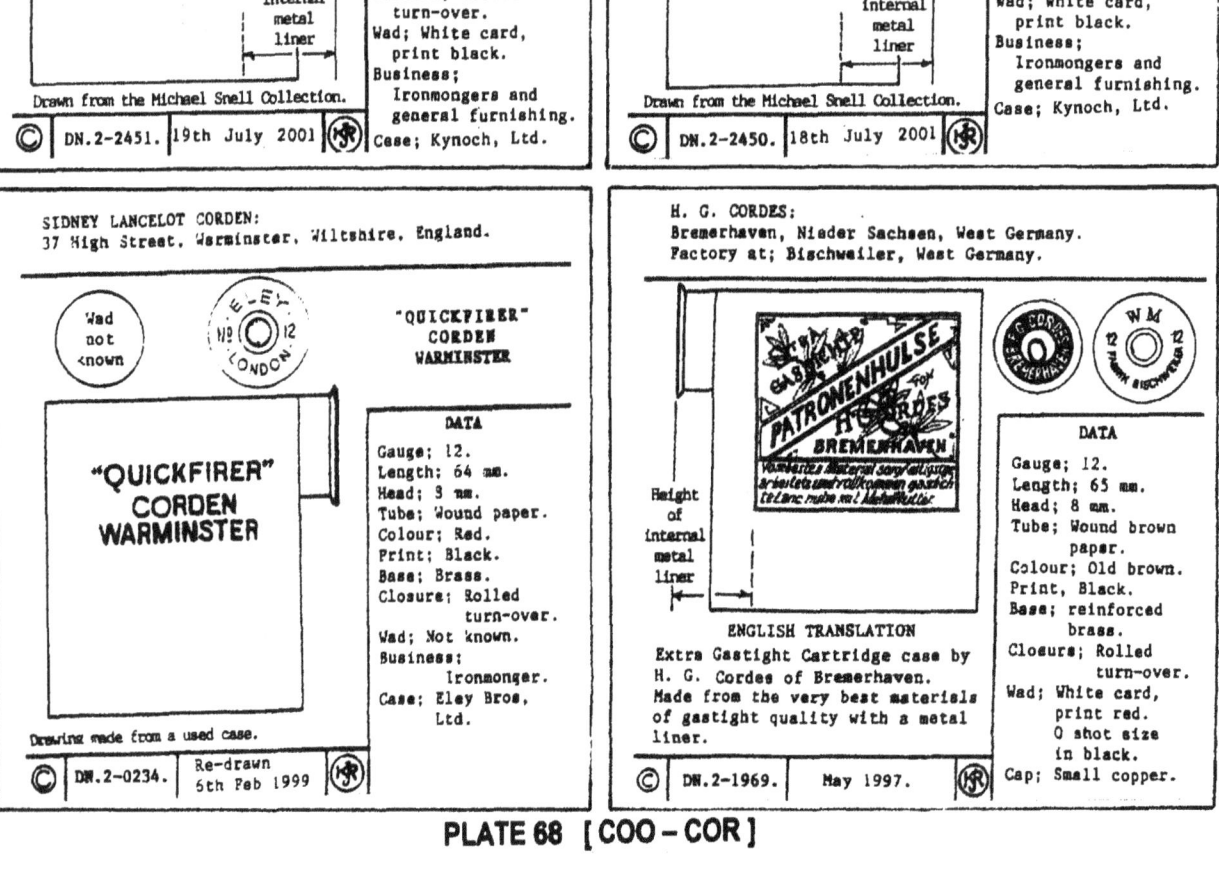

PLATE 68 [COO - COR]

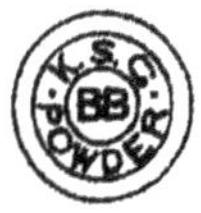

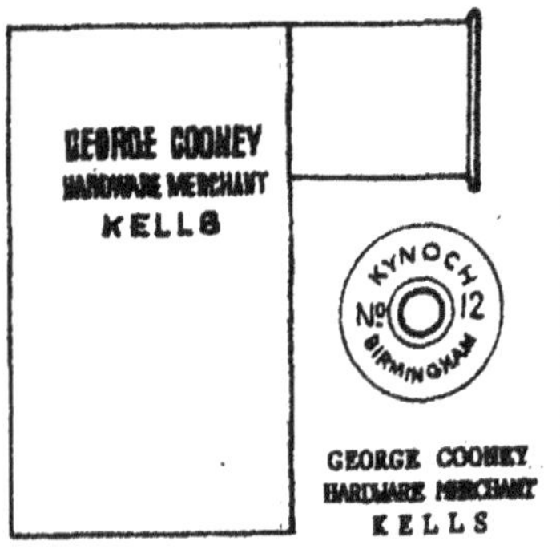

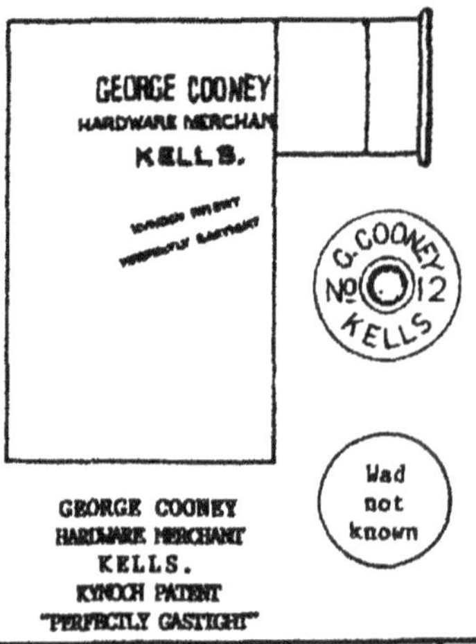

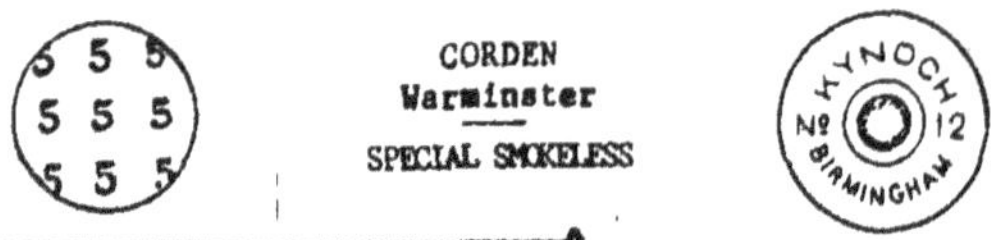

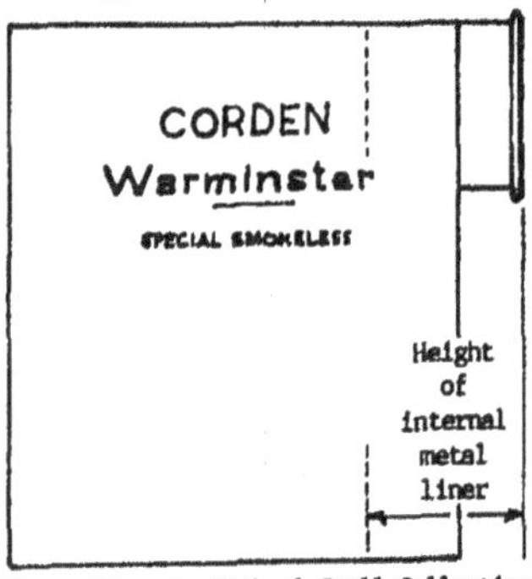

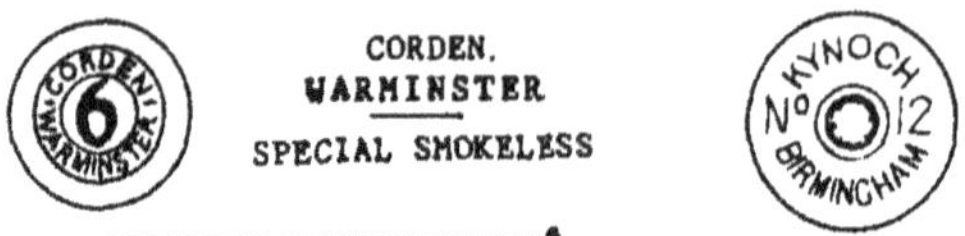

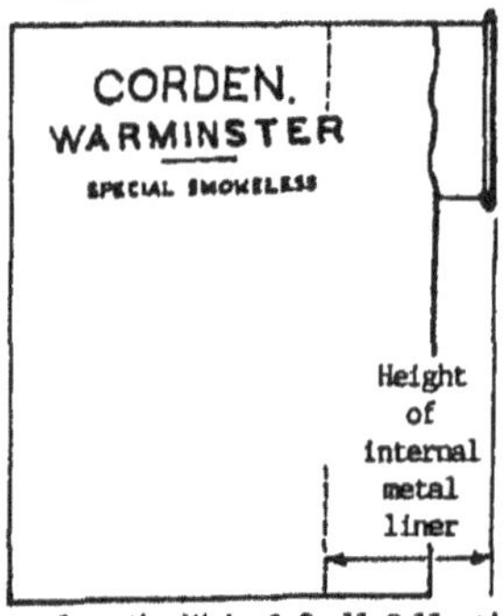

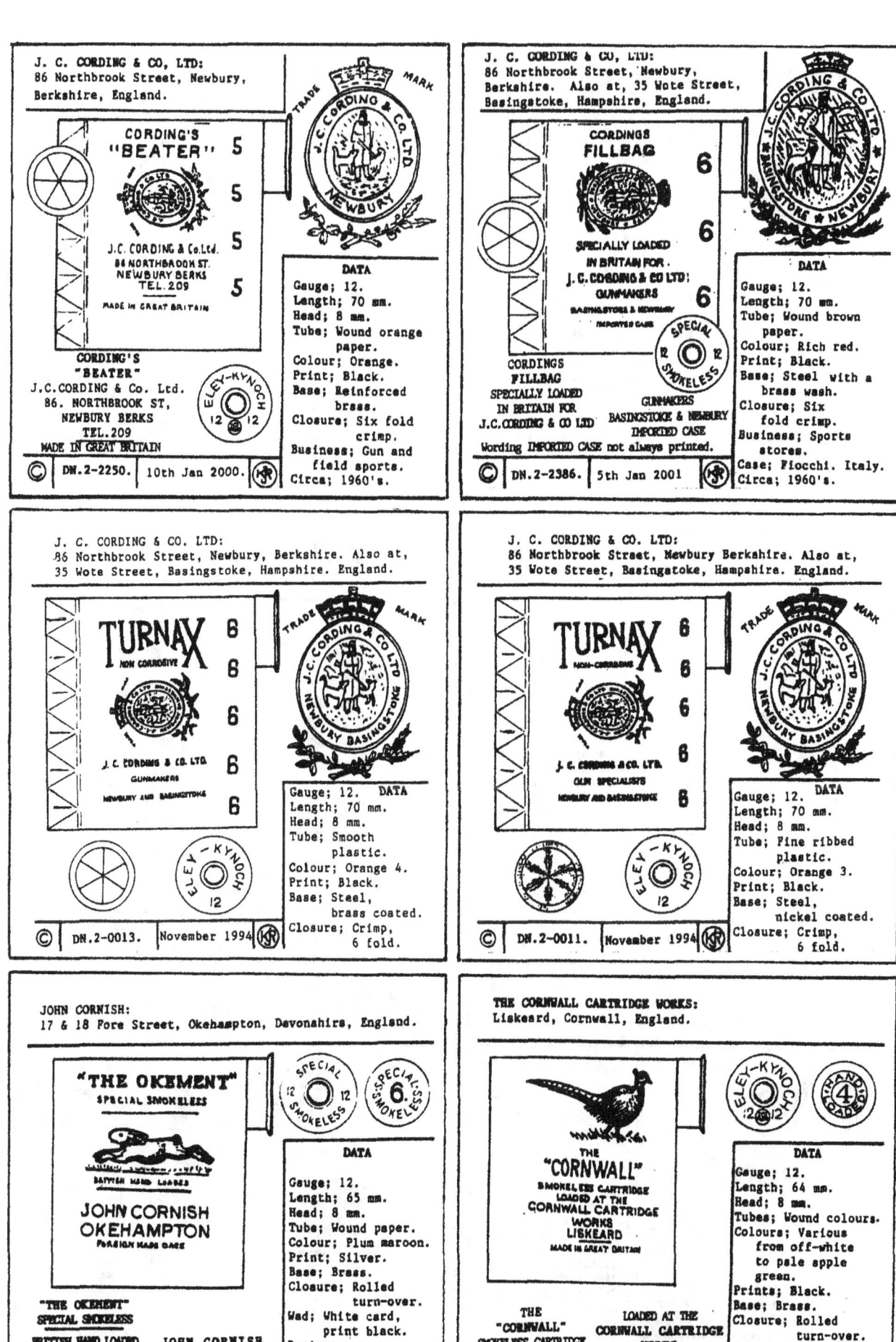

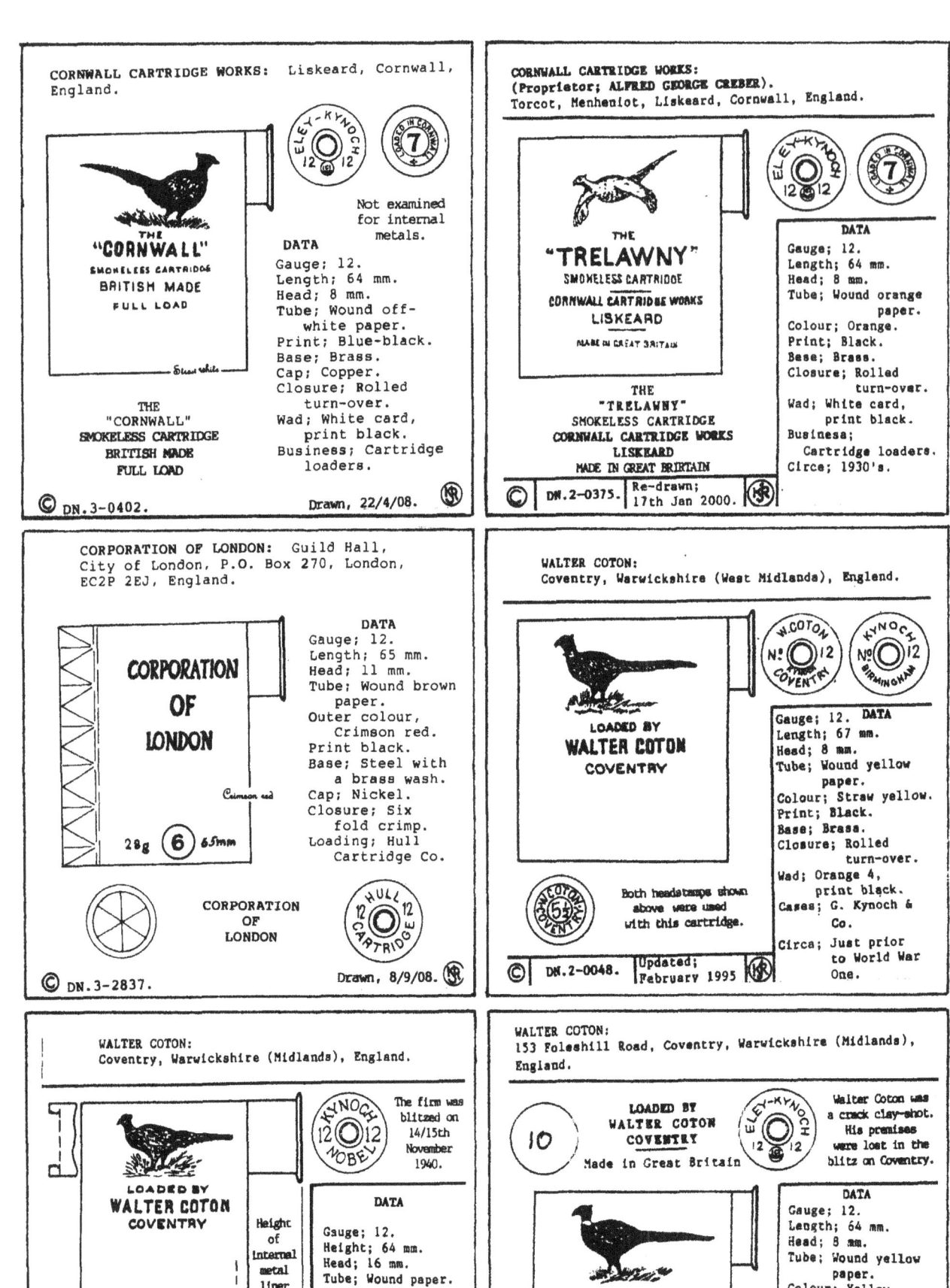

PLATE 70 [COR - COT]

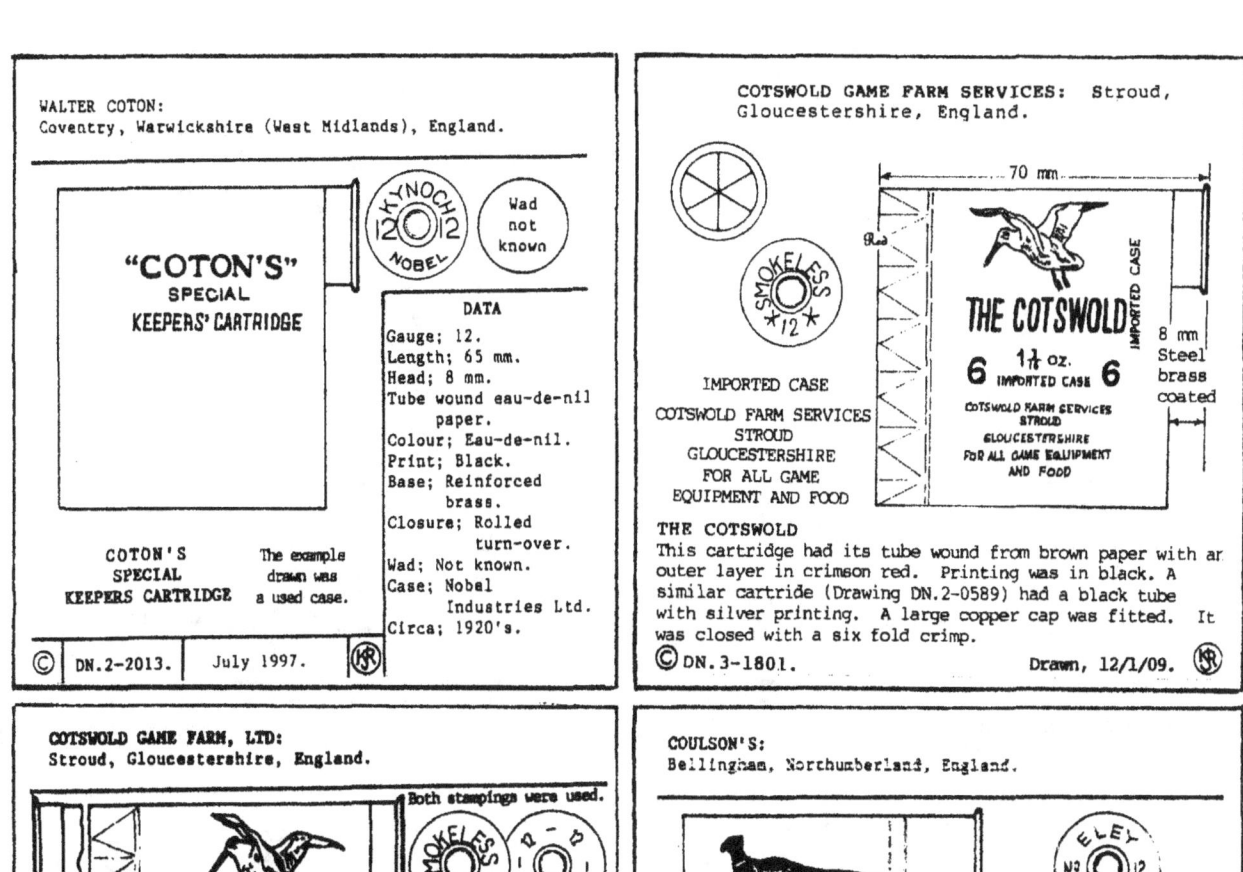
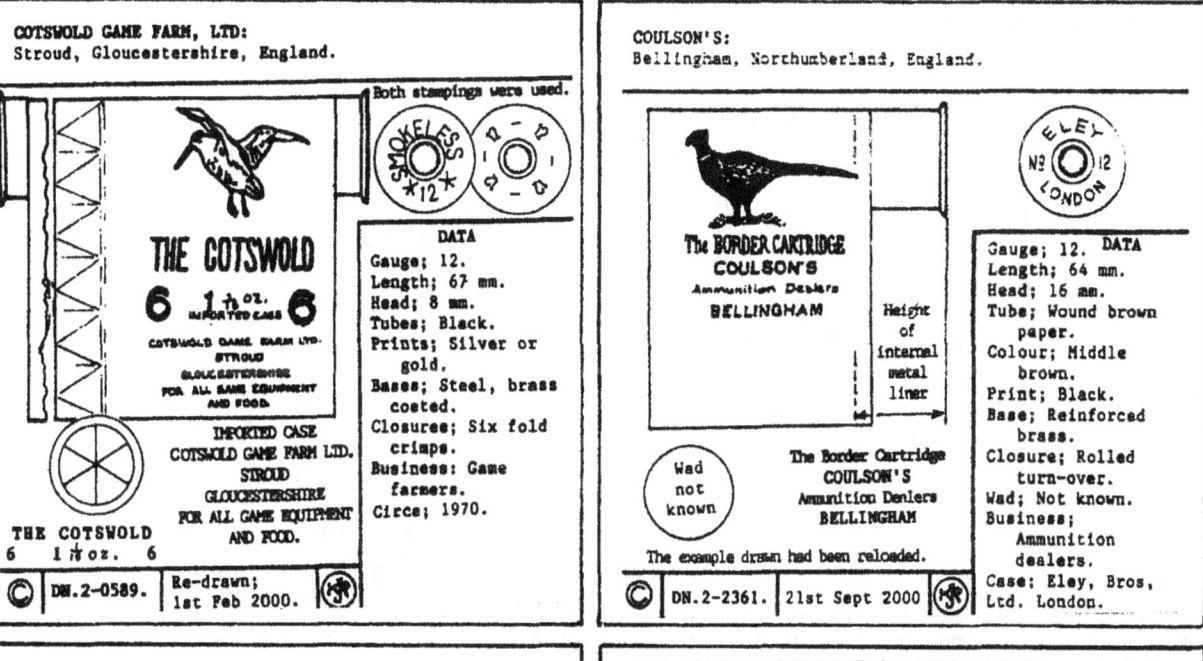
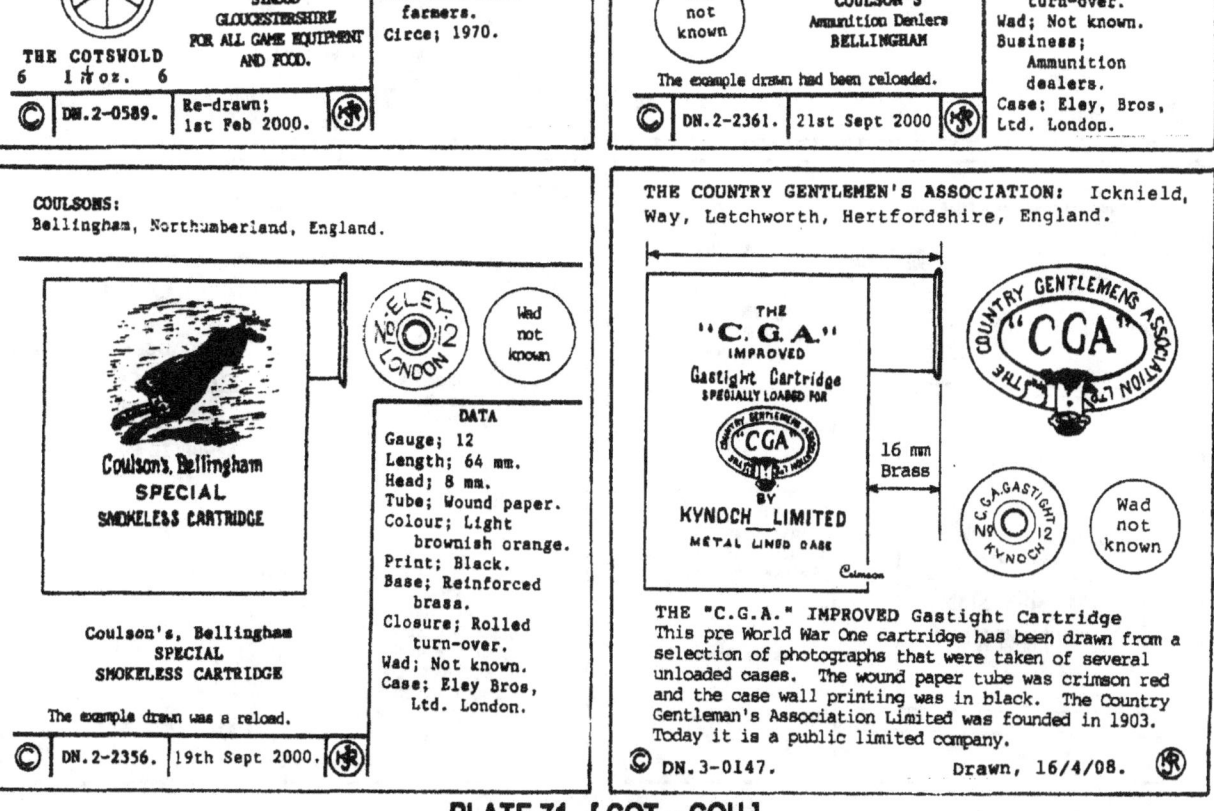

PLATE 71 [COT – COU]

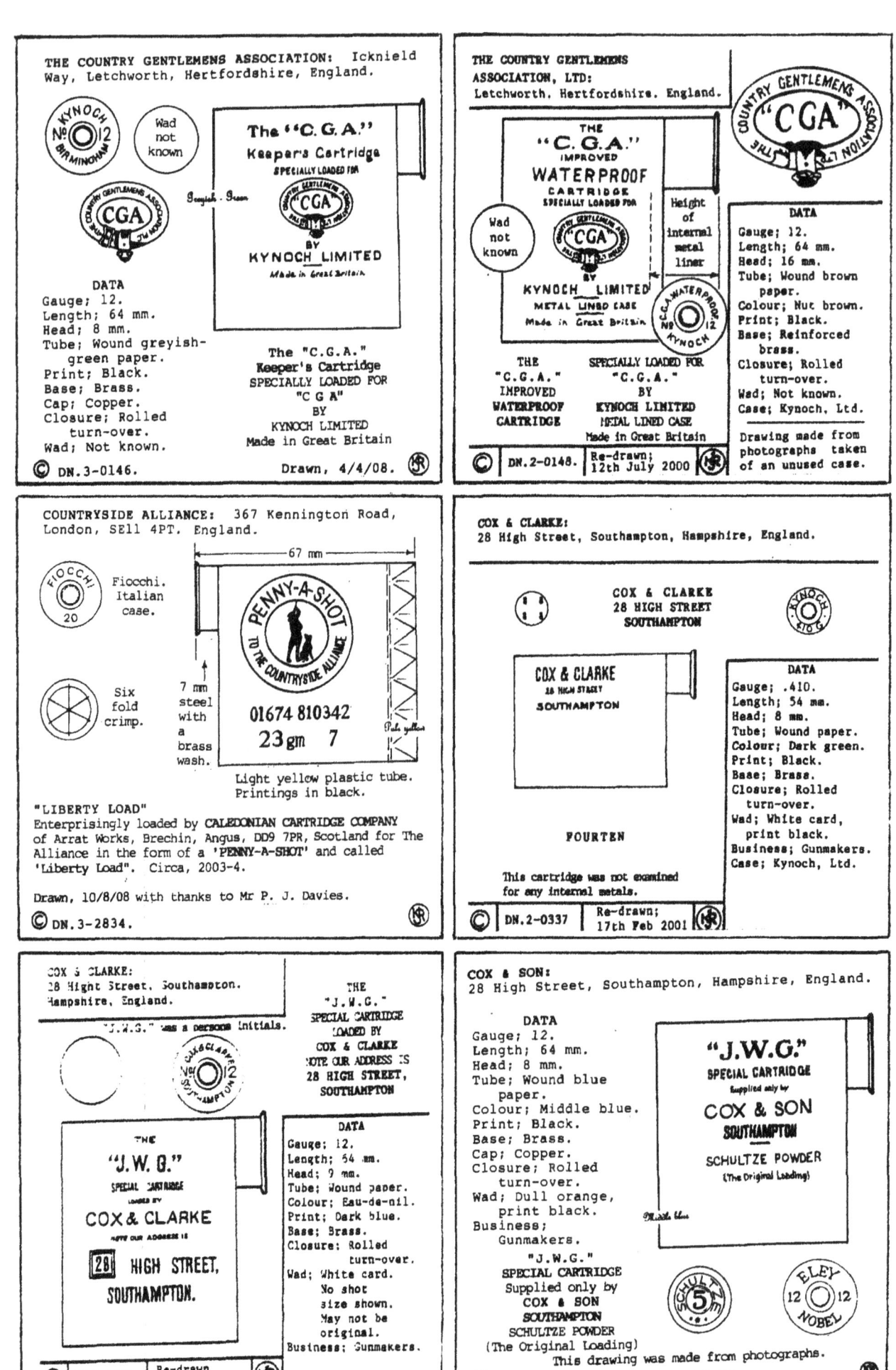

PLATE 72 [COU – COX]

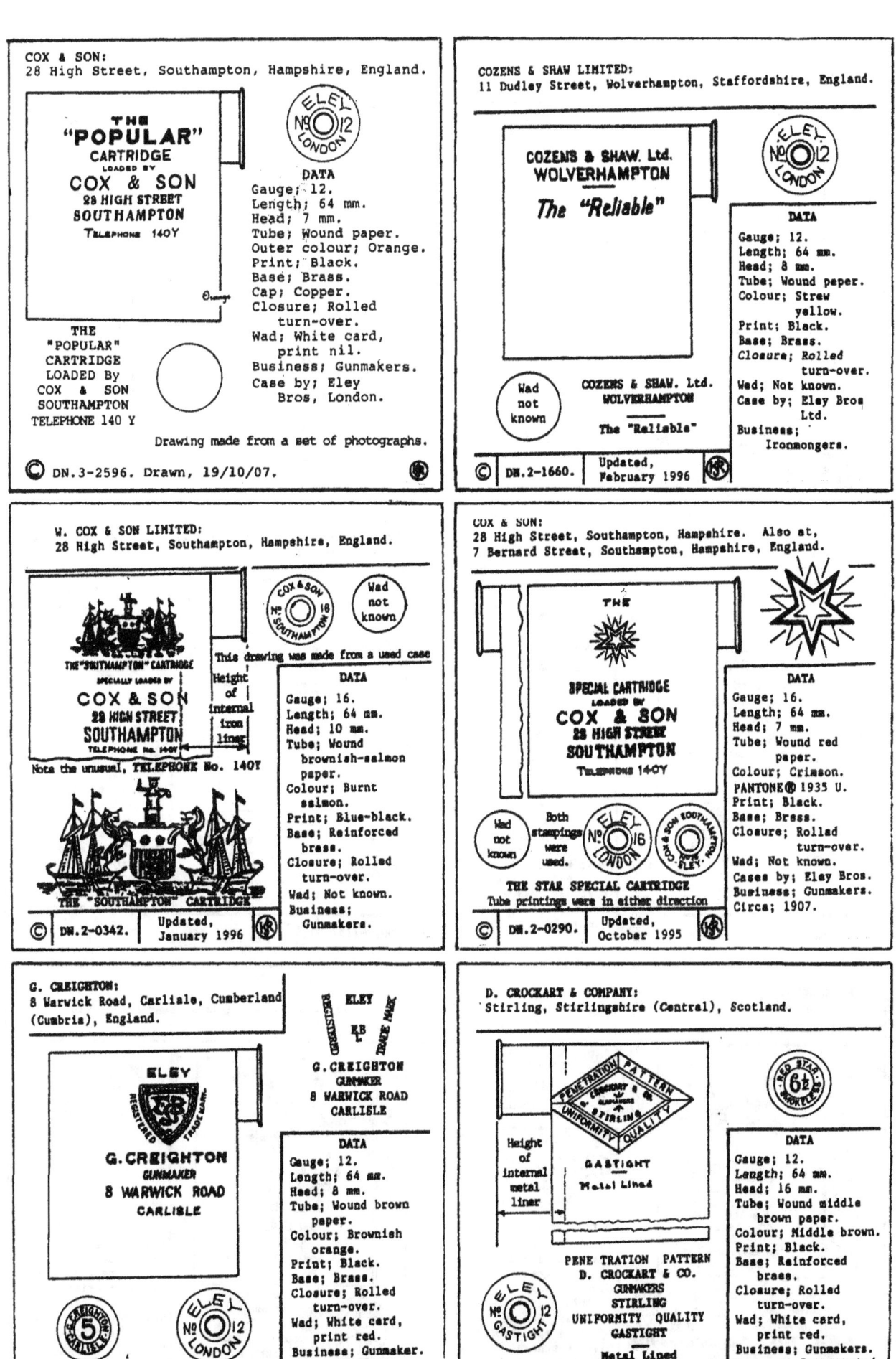

D. B. CROCKART:
33-35 County Place, Perth, Perthshire (Tayside), Scotland.

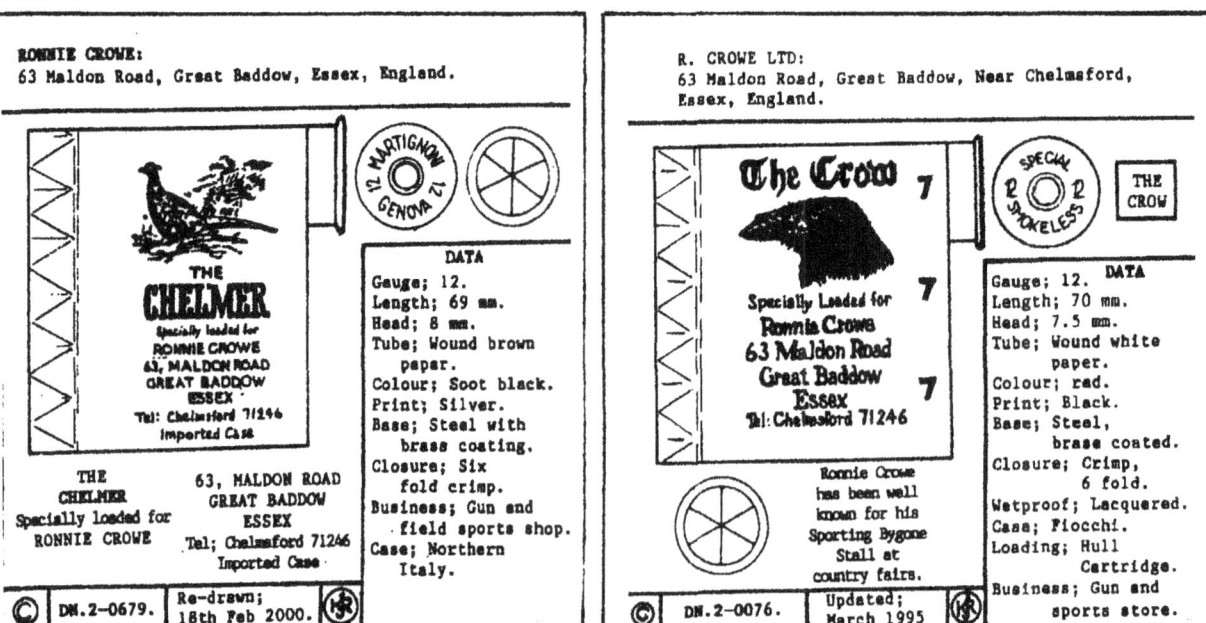

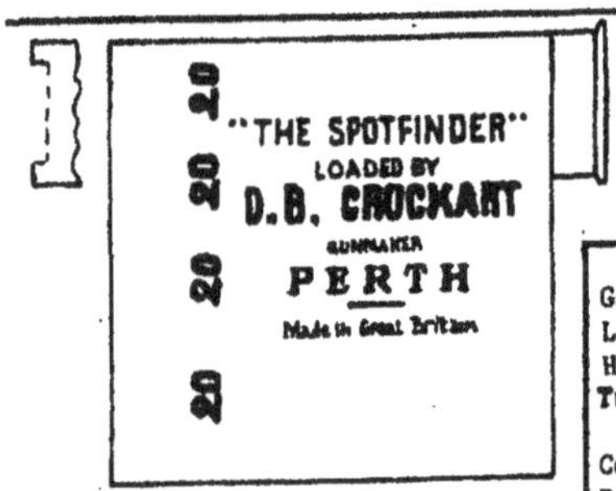

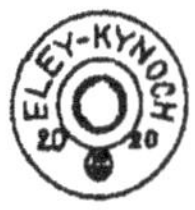

Closed by a squared turn-over.
The cartridge was not internally examined.

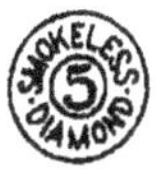

20 20 20 20
"THE SPOTFINDER"
LOADED BY
D.B. CROCKART
GUNMAKER
PERTH
Made in Great Britain

DATA
Gauge; 20.
Length; 64 mm.
Head; 7 mm.
Tube; Wound purple paper.
Colour; Rich purple.
Print; Silver.
Base; Brass.
Closure; Rolled turn-over.
Wad; White card, print black.
Wetproof; Lacquered.
Business; Gun and fishing tackle maker.

© DN.2-0477. Re-drawn; 16th March 2001

JAS CROCKART & SON: 26 Allan Street, Blairgowire, Perthshire (Tayside), Scotland.
Established, 1852.

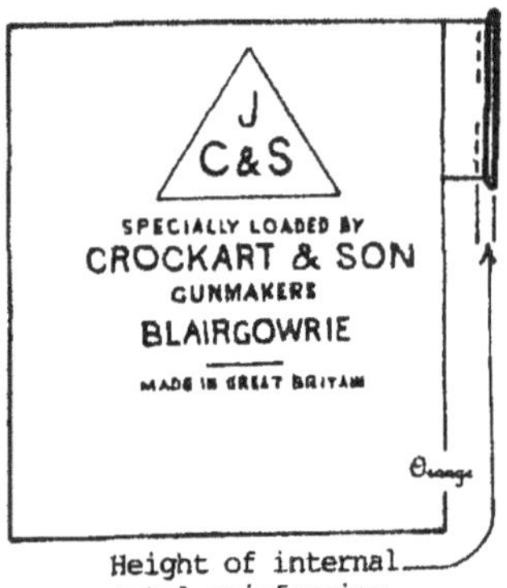

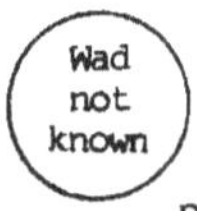

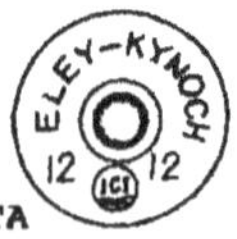

Height of internal metal reinforcing

J C & S
SPECIALLY LOADED BY
CROCKART & SON
GUNMAKERS
BLAIRGOWIRE
MADE IN GREAT BRITAIN

DATA
Gauge; 12.
Length; 64 mm.
Head; 8 mm.
Tube; Wound orange paper.
Colour; Orange.
Print; Black.
Base; Reinforced brass.
Cap; Copper.
Wetproof; Clear lacquered.
Closure; Rolled turn-over.
Wad; Not known.
Business: Gun rifle and fishing tackle makers.
Circa; 1930's.

© DN.3-2676. Drawn, 20/2/08.

CROSS BROTHERS, LTD:
Church Street. Also were at, 3 - 4 St. Mary's Street, Cardiff, Glamorgan, Wales.

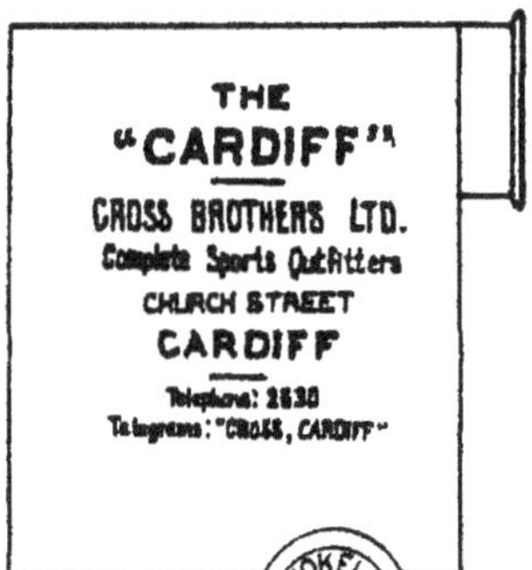

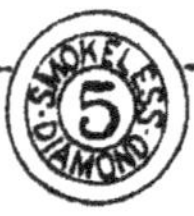

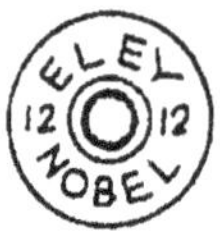

THE
"CARDIFF"
CROSS BROTHERS LTD.
Complete Sports Outfitters
CHURCH STREET
CARDIFF

Telephone: 2530
Telegrams: CROSS, CARDIFF"

DATA
Gauge; 12.
Length; 64 mm.
Head; 8 mm.
Tube; Wound orange paper.
Colour; Orange.
Print; Black.
Base; Reinforced brass.
Closure; Rolled turn-over.
Wad; White card, print black.
Business; Sports outfitters.
Circa; 1920's.

© DN.2-0458. 23rd Nov 1999

S. B. CROSS:
183 Price Street. Also at, 171 Chester Street, Birkenhead, Cheshire (Merseyside), England.

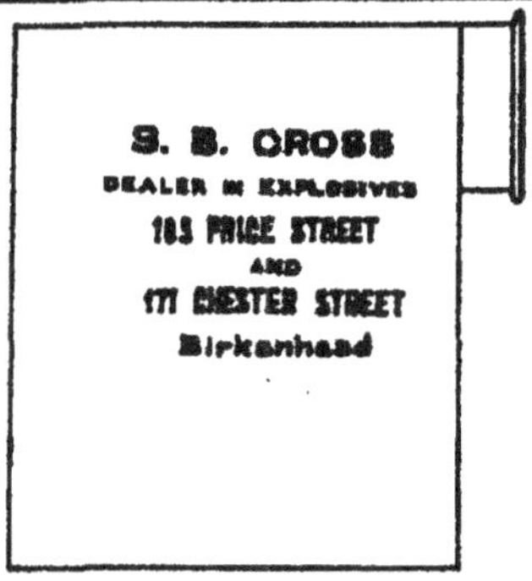

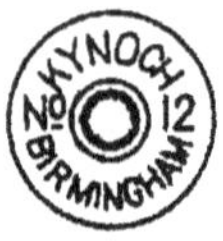

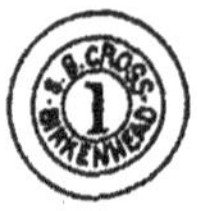

S. B. CROSS
DEALER IN EXPLOSIVES
163 PRICE STREET
AND
171 CHESTER STREET
Birkenhead

DATA
Gauge; 12.
Length; 64 mm.
Head; 8 mm.
Tube; wound paper.
Colour; Light apple green.
Print; Navy blue.
Base; Brass.
Closure; Rolled turn-over.
Wad; White card, print black.
Business; Dealers in explosives.
Case; Kynoch, Ltd.

© DN.2-1157. Redrawn; 17th Jan 2001

RONNIE CROWE:
63 Maldon Road, Great Baddow, Essex, England.

THE
CHELMER
Specially loaded for
RONNIE CROWE

63, MALDON ROAD
GREAT BADDOW
ESSEX
Tel; Chelmsford 71246
Imported Case

DATA
Gauge; 12.
Length; 69 mm.
Head; 8 mm.
Tube; Wound brown paper.
Colour; Soot black.
Print; Silver.
Base; Steel with brass coating.
Closure; Six fold crimp.
Business; Gun and field sports shop.
Case; Northern Italy.

© DN.2-0679. Re-drawn; 18th Feb 2000.

R. CROWE LTD:
63 Maldon Road, Great Baddow, Near Chelmsford, Essex, England.

Ronnie Crowe has been well known for his Sporting Bygone Stall at country fairs.

DATA
Gauge; 12.
Length; 70 mm.
Head; 7.5 mm.
Tube; Wound white paper.
Colour; red.
Print; Black.
Base; Steel, brass coated.
Closure; Crimp, 6 fold.
Wetproof; Lacquered.
Case; Fiocchi.
Loading; Hull Cartridge.
Business; Gun and sports store.

© DN.2-0076. Updated; March 1995

PLATE 74 [CRO - CRO]

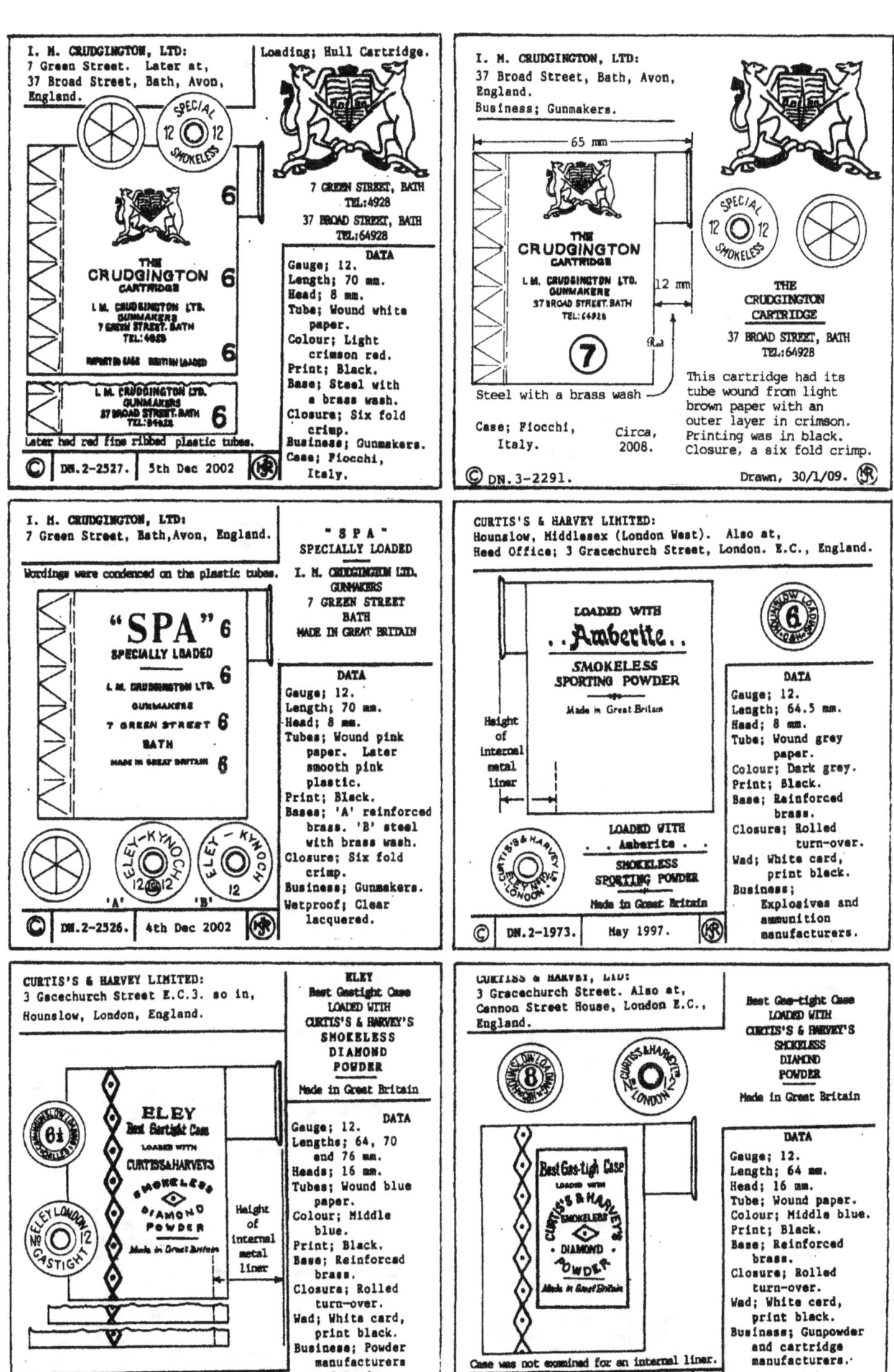

PLATE 75 [CRU – CUR]

Card 1 (top-left)

CURTIS'S & HARVEY LIMITED:
3 Gracechurch Street, London,
E.C.3., England.

"FEATHER WEIGHT"
(Registered)

CURTIS'S & HARVEY'S
"FEATHER WEIGHT"
SMOKELESS CARTRIDGE
LIGHT LOAD
FOR DRIVEN GAME

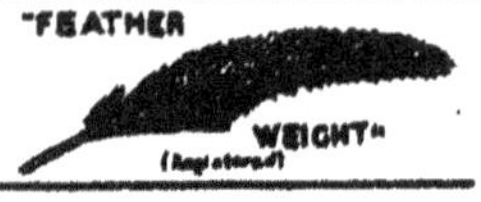

Most likely
Pegamoid
Brand
paper.

"FEATHER WEIGHT"

DATA
Gauge; 12.
Length; 64 mm.
Head; 10 mm.
Tube; Wound maroon paper.
Colour; Maroon.
Print; Black.
Base; Brass.
Closure; Rolled turn-over.
Wad; White card, print black.
Circa; 1907.
Business; Gunpowder and cartridge manufacturers.

© DN.2-1889. January 1996

Card 2 (top-right)

CURTIS'S & HARVEY, LTD:
3 Gracechurch Street. Also at,
Cannon Street House, London E.C., England.

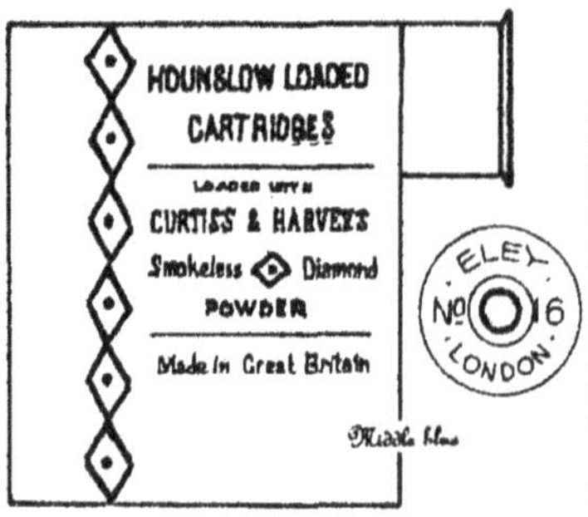

HOUNSLOW LOADED CARTRIDGES
LOADED WITH
CURTIS'S & HARVEY'S
Smokeless ◇ Diamond
POWDER
Made in Great Britain

Middle blue

HOUNSLOW LOADED CARTRIDGES

DATA
Gauge; 16.
Length; 64 mm.
Head; 14 mm.
Tube; Wound paper.
Outer colour; Middle blue.
Print; Black.
Base; Brass.
Cap; Copper.
Closure; Rolled turn-over.
Wad; White card, print black.
Main business; Explosives manufacturers.
Case by; Eley Bros Ltd, London.

Drawing made from a set of photographs.

© DN.3-2602.   Drawn, 5/11/07.

Card 3 (middle-left)

CURTIS'S & HARVEY LIMITED:
3 Gracechurch Street, London, England.

CURTIS'S & HARVEY'S
"MARVEL"
Smokeless Cartridge
Made in Great Britain

"MARVEL"

DATA
Gauge; 12.
Length; 64 mm.
Head; 8 mm.
Tube; Wound paper.
Colour; Greenish-grey 2.
Print; Black.
Base; Brass.
Closure; Rolled turn-over.
Wad; White card, print black.
Business; Explosives manufacturers.

© DN.2-1073. Updated; December 1994

Card 4 (middle-right)

CURTIS'S & HARVEY, LIMITED:
3 Gracechurch Street, London E.C.3., England.

No iron or steel was used in the case construction.

CURTIS'S & HARVEY'S
"MARVEL"
Smokeless Cartridge

CURTIS'S & HARVEY'S
"MARVEL"
Smokeless Cartridge

DATA
Gauge; 12.
Length; 65 mm.
Tube; Wound paper.
Colour; Crimson red.
Print; Black.
Base; Brass.
Closure; Rolled turn-over.
Wad shown; White card, print black.
Business; Explosives manufacturers.
Case; Remington. U.S.A.

© DN.2-2342. 18th Sept 2000

Card 5 (bottom-left)

CURTIS'S & HARVEY', LTD: 3 Gracechurch Street,
London E.C. Also at, Cannon Street House,
London E.C., England.

Business; Gunpowder and cartridge manufacturers.

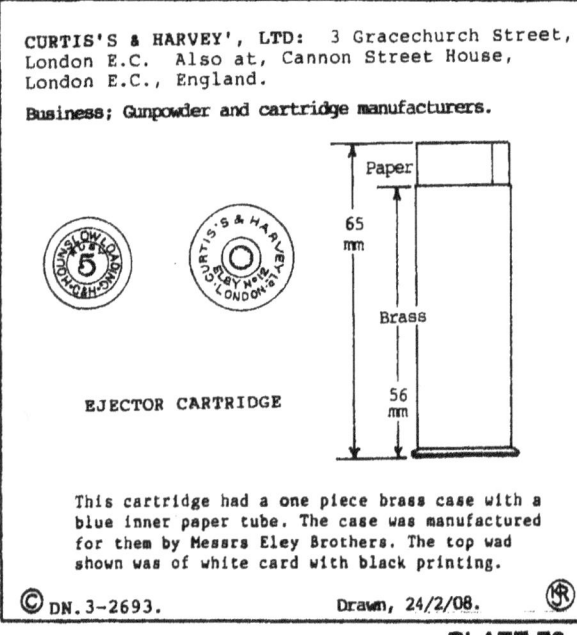

EJECTOR CARTRIDGE

Paper
65 mm
Brass
56 mm

This cartridge had a one piece brass case with a
blue inner paper tube. The case was manufactured
for them by Messrs Eley Brothers. The top wad
shown was of white card with black printing.

© DN.3-2693.   Drawn, 24/2/08.

Card 6 (bottom-right)

CURTIS'S & HARVEY LIMITED:
3 Gracechurch Street, London E.C.3., England.

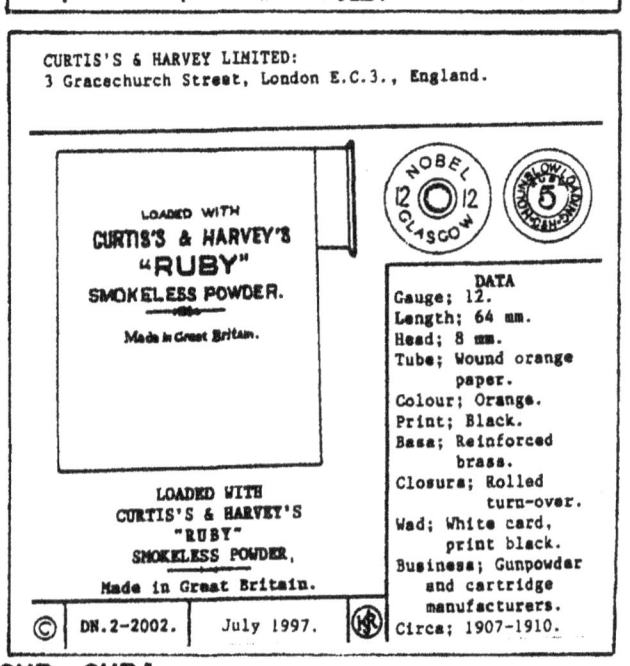

LOADED WITH
CURTIS'S & HARVEY'S
"RUBY"
SMOKELESS POWDER.
Made in Great Britain.

LOADED WITH
CURTIS'S & HARVEY'S
"RUBY"
SMOKELESS POWDER,
Made in Great Britain.

DATA
Gauge; 12.
Length; 64 mm.
Head; 8 mm.
Tube; Wound orange paper.
Colour; Orange.
Print; Black.
Base; Reinforced brass.
Closure; Rolled turn-over.
Wad; White card, print black.
Business; Gunpowder and cartridge manufacturers.
Circa; 1907-1910.

© DN.2-2002. July 1997.

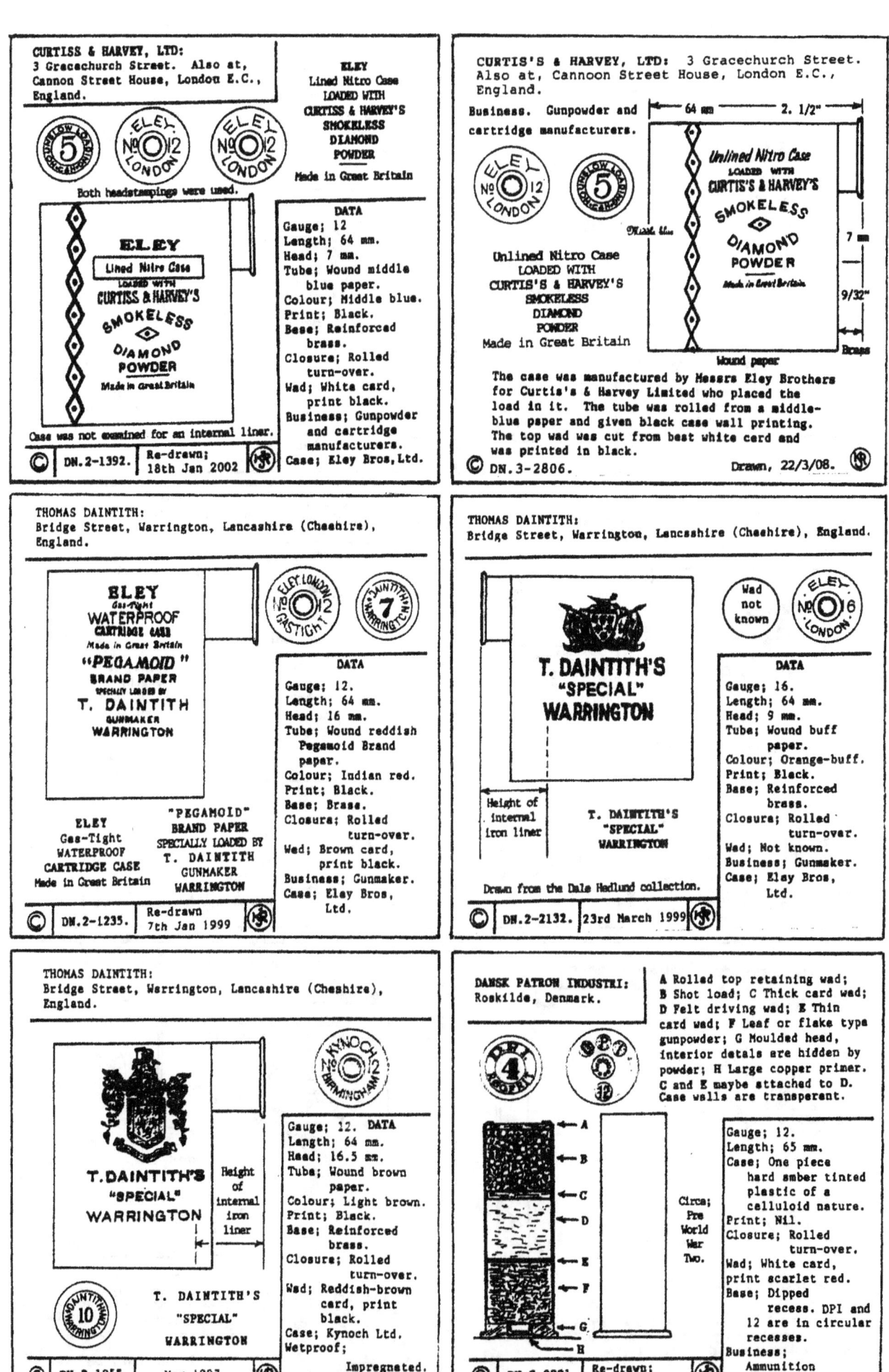

PLATE 77 [CUR – DAN]

WALTER DARLOW, LTD:
8 Orford Hill, Norwich, Norfolk, England.

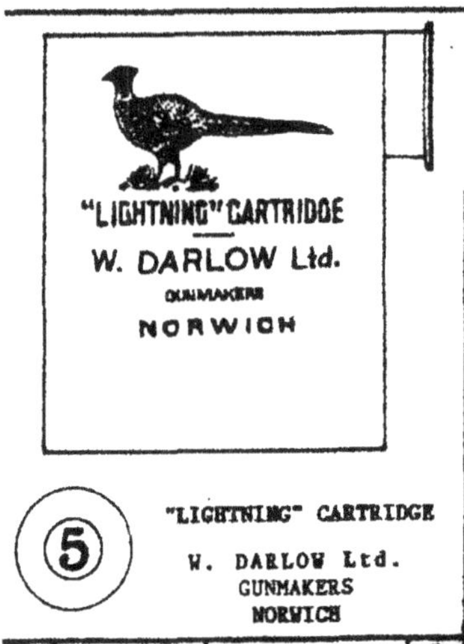

"LIGHTNING" CARTRIDGE
W. DARLOW Ltd.
GUNMAKERS
NORWICH

KYNOCH 12 BIRMINGHAM

(5)

"LIGHTNING" CARTRIDGE
W. DARLOW Ltd.
GUNMAKERS
NORWICH

DATA
Gauge; 12.
Length; 64 mm.
Head; 8 mm.
Tube; Wound paper.
Colour; Light applegreen.
Print; Black.
Base; Brass.
Closure; Rolled turn-over.
Wad; White card, print black.
Business; Gunmaker.
Note; 1916 trade directory listed the firm as Darlow & Co.

DN.2-1696. Re-drawn; 27th Jan 2000.

WALTER DARLOW, LTD:
8 Orford Hill, Norwich, Norfolk, England.

"LIGHTNING" CARTRIDGE
DARLOW LTD.
GUNMAKERS
NORWICH

SMOKELESS 5
KYNOCH 12 BIRMINGHAM

DATA
Gauge; 12.
Length; 64 mm.
Head; 8 mm.
Tube; Wound dark green paper.
Colour; Dark green.
Print; Black.
Base; Brass.
Closure; Rolled turn-over.
Wad; Off-white card, print black.
Wetproof; Wax impregnated.
Business; Gunmaker.

DN.2-0340. Re-drawn; 26th Feb 2000.

DARLOW & COMPANY:
8 Orford Hill, Norwich, Norfolk, England.

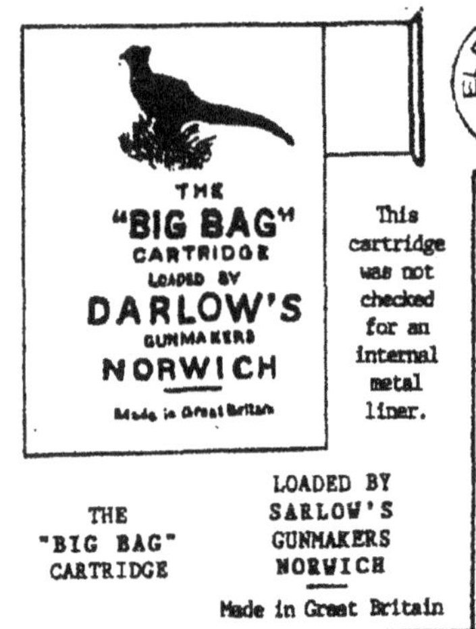

THE "BIG BAG" CARTRIDGE
LOADED BY DARLOW'S
GUNMAKERS
NORWICH
Made in Great Britain

ELEY-KYNOCH 12 12
DARLOW 5 NORWICH

This cartridge was not checked for an internal metal liner.

THE "BIG BAG" CARTRIDGE

LOADED BY DARLOW'S GUNMAKERS NORWICH

Made in Great Britain

DATA
Gauge; 12.
Length; 64 mm.
Head; 16 mm.
Tube; Wound middle blue paper.
Colour; Middle blue.
Print; Black or navy blue.
Base; Brass.
Closure; Rolled turn-over.
Wad; Buttercup yellow, print black.
Business; Gunmakers.
Circa; 1930's.

DN.2-0775. Re-drawn; 5th Feb 2000.

W. DARLOW & COMPANY:
8 Orford Hill, Norwich, Norfolk, England.

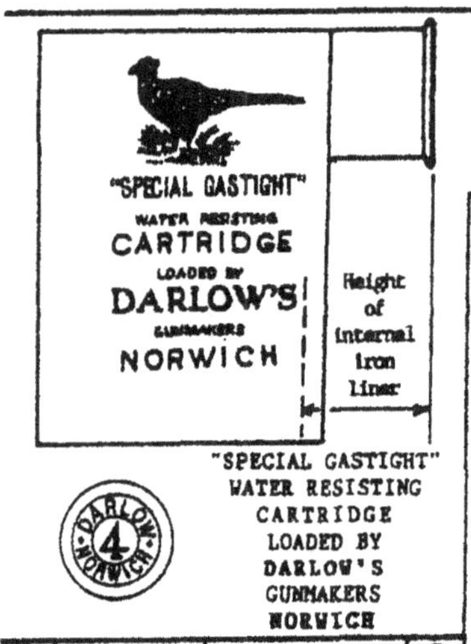

"SPECIAL GASTIGHT"
WATER RESISTING
CARTRIDGE
LOADED BY DARLOW'S
GUNMAKERS
NORWICH

KYNOCH 12 12 NOBEL
DARLOW 4 NORWICH

Height of internal iron liner.

"SPECIAL GASTIGHT" WATER RESISTING CARTRIDGE LOADED BY DARLOW'S GUNMAKERS NORWICH

DATA
Gauge; 12.
Length; 64 mm.
Head; 16 mm.
Tube; Wound brown paper.
Colour; Middle brown.
Print; Black.
Base; Reinforced brass.
Closure; Rolled turn-over.
Wad; Off-white card, print black.
Business; Gunmakers.
Case; Nobel Indidustries, Ltd.
Circa; 1920's.

DN.2-2107. November 1998.

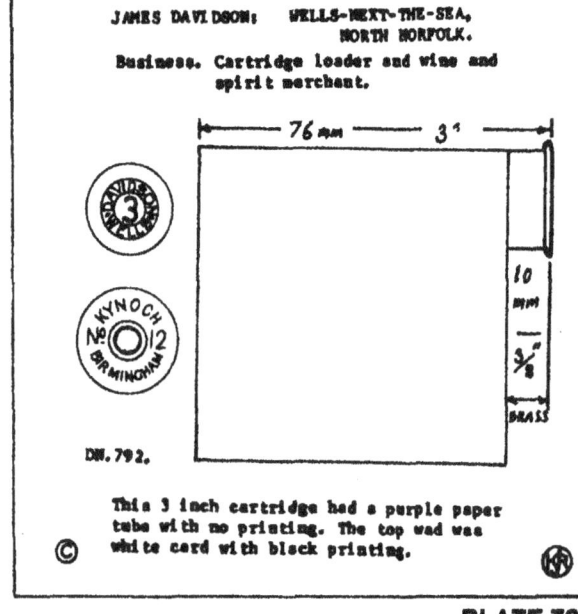

JAMES DAVIDSON: WELLS-NEXT-THE-SEA, NORTH NORFOLK.
Business. Cartridge loader and wine and spirit merchant.

DN.792.

This 3 inch cartridge had a purple paper tube with no printing. The top wad was white card with black printing.

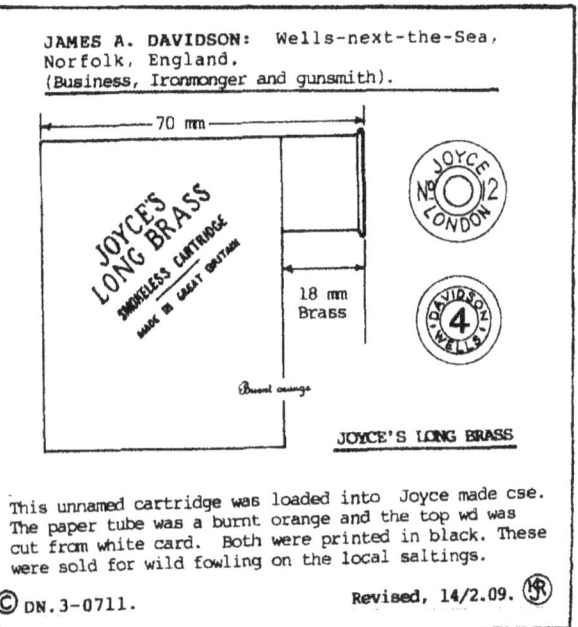

JAMES A. DAVIDSON: Wells-next-the-Sea, Norfolk, England.
(Business, Ironmonger and gunsmith).

JOYCE'S LONG BRASS
SMOKELESS CARTRIDGE
MADE IN GREAT BRITAIN

Burnt orange

JOYCE'S LONG BRASS

This unnamed cartridge was loaded into Joyce made cse. The paper tube was a burnt orange and the top wd was cut from white card. Both were printed in black. These were sold for wild fowling on the local saltings.

DN.3-0711. Revised, 14/2/09.

JAMES DAVIDSON:
Wells-next-the-Sea, North Norfolk, England.

From the Dale Hedlund collection

J. A. DAVIDSON
WELLS, (Norfolk)

The "NEW ERA"
CARTRIDGE

Made in Great Britain

Wad not known

DATA
Gauge; 12.
Length; 64 mm.
Head; 7 mm.
Tube; Wound paper.
Colour; Orange.
Print; Black.
Base; Brass.
Closure; Rolled turn-over.
Wad; Not known.
Business; Wine and spirit merchant. also cartridge loader.

© DN.2-2126. 20th March 1999 KR

FRANCIS DAVIE:
153 High Street, Elgin, Morayshire (Grampian), Scotland.

DATA
Gauge; 12.
Length; 64 mm.
Head; 8 mm.
Tube; Wound paper.
Colour; Light brown.
Print; Black.
Base; Brass.
Closure; Rolled turn-over.
Wad; Flesh pink, print black.
Case; Eley Bros Ltd.
Business; Gunmaker.

© DN.2-1632. Updated, January 1996 KR

HOWARD A. DAVIES:
6 Southgate Street, Winchester, Hampshire, England.

HOWARD A. DAVIES
WINCHESTER
MADE IN GREAT BRITAIN

DATA
Gauge; 12.
Length; 64 mm.
Head; 8 mm.
Tube; Wound dark green paper.
Colour; Dark green.
Print; Black.
Base; Brass.
Closure; Rolled turn-over.
Wad; Dark red card, print black.
Business; Gunmaker.
Circa; 1930's.

© DN.2-1036. Re-drawn; 19th Jan 2000. KR

HOWARD A. DAVIES:
6 Southgate Street,
Winchester, Hampshire, England.

"THE FLIGHT"
SMOKELESS CARTRIDGE
LOADED BY
HOWARD A. DAVIES
GUNMAKER

6 SOUTHGATE ST.
WINCHESTER
Phone WINCHESTER 935
Made in Great Britain

DATA
Gauge; 12.
Length; 64 mm.
Head; 8 mm.
Tube; Wound eau-de-nil paper.
Colour; Eley's eau-de-nil.
Print; Navy blue.
Base; Reinforced brass.
Closure; Rolled turn-over.
Wad; White card, print pink.
Business; Gunmaker.
Circa; 1930's.

© DN.2-1298. Updated, February 1996 KR

HOWARD A. DAVIES:
6 Southgate Street, Winchester, Hampshire, England.

THE "WINTON"

HOWARD A. DAVIES
GUNMAKER
6 SOUTHGATE STREET
WINCHESTER
Tel,: WINCHESTER 935
MADE IN GREAT BRITAIN

DATA
Gauge; 12.
Length; 64 mm.
Head; 8 mm.
Tube; Wound middle blue paper.
Colour; Middle blue.
Print; Black.
Wetproof; Lacquered.
Base; Reinforced brass.
Closure; Rolled turn-over.
Wad; Deep red, print black.
Business; Gunmaker.
Circa; 1930's.

© DN.2-1299. Updated, February 1996 KR

PETER J. DAVIES. 75th Birthday cartridge.
"Little Borings", Nettlesworth Lane,
Vine Cross, Heathfield, Sussex, England.

DATA
Gauge; 12.
Length; 67 mm.
Head; 7.5 mm.
Tube; Red fine ribbed plastic.
Print; Black.
Closure, Six fold crimp.
Base; Steel with a brass wash.
Business;
Private cartridge.
Circa; 2006.

LITTLE BORINGS Challenge

© DN.3-5501. Drawn, 25/5/2011. KR

PLATE 79 [DAV – DAV]

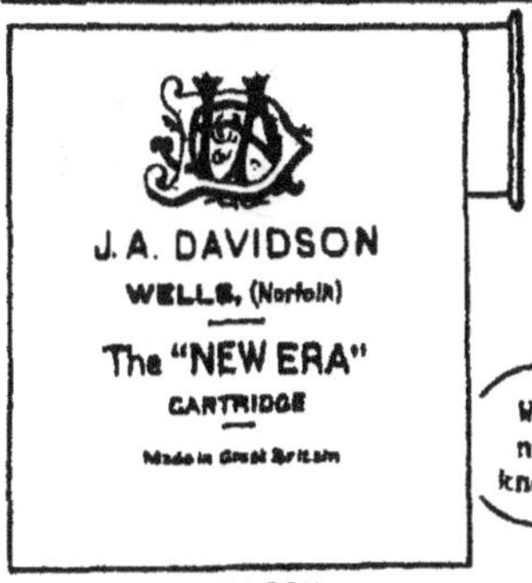

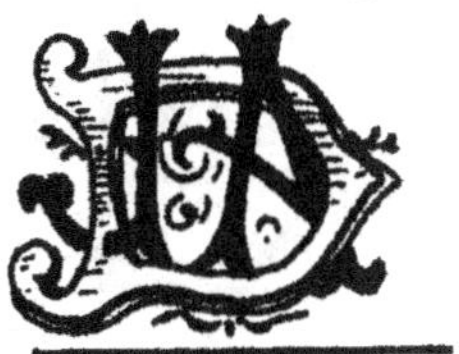

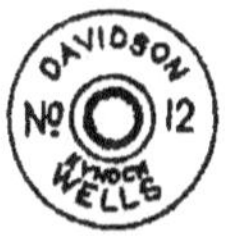

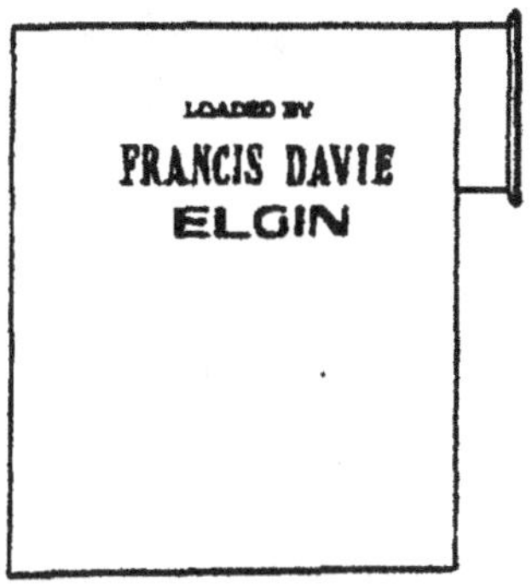

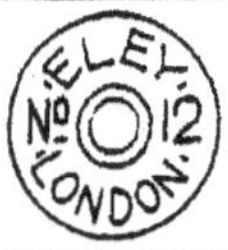

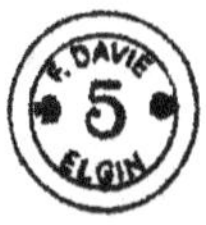

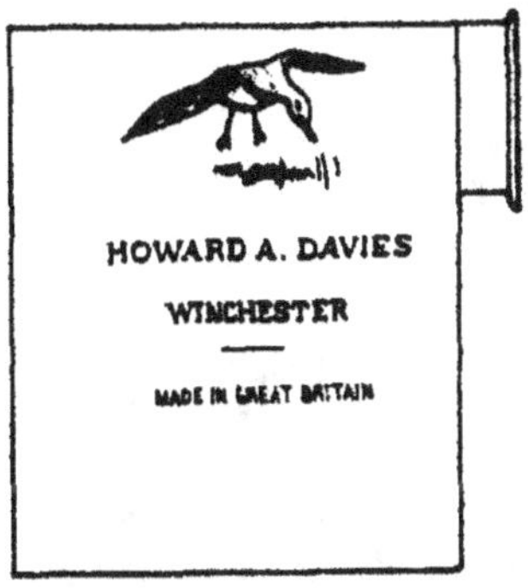

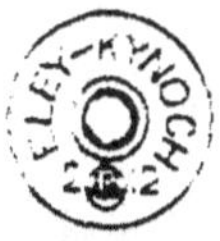

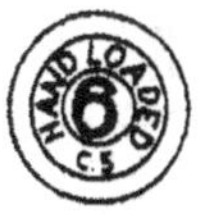

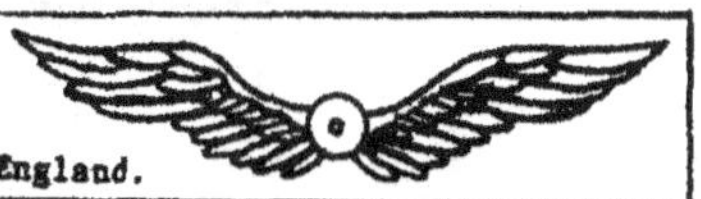

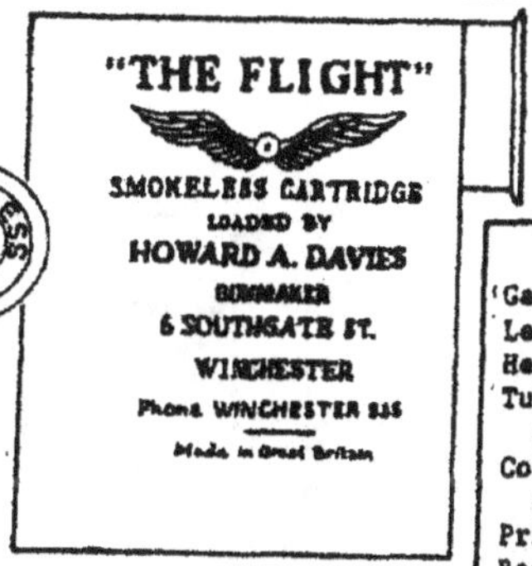

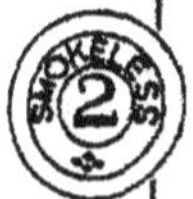

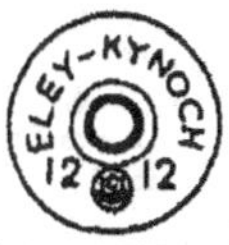

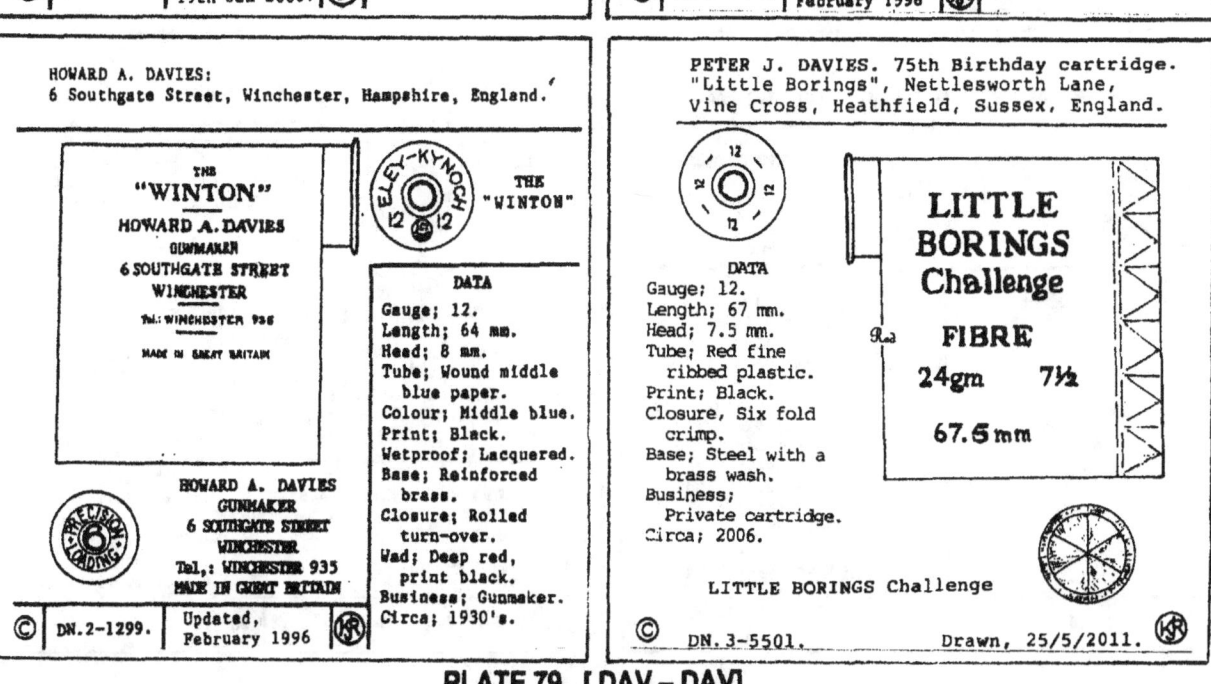

T. DAVIES:
Llandyssul, Cardiganshire (Dyfed), Wales.

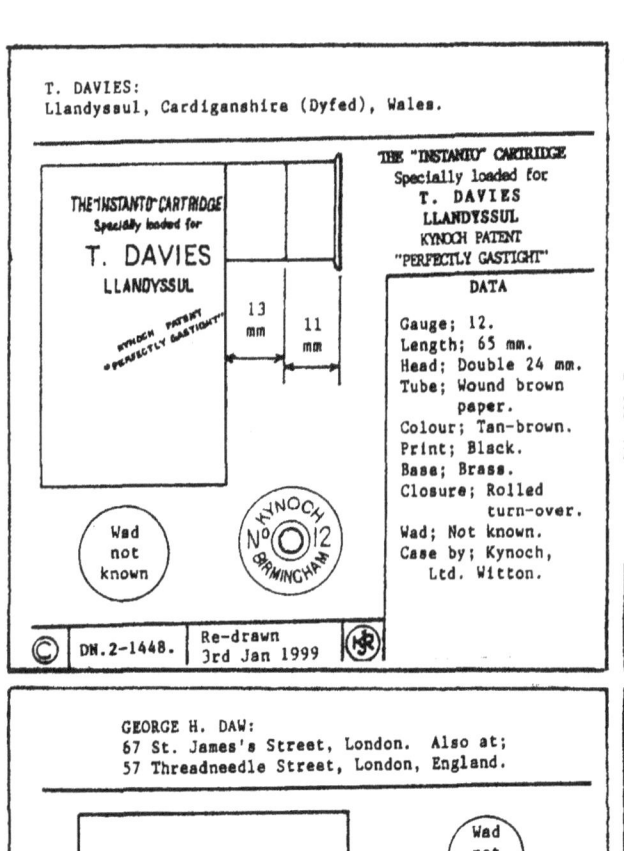

THE "INSTANTO" CARTRIDGE
Specially loaded for
T. DAVIES
LLANDYSSUL
KYNOCH PATENT
"PERFECTLY GASTIGHT"

DATA
Gauge; 12.
Length; 65 mm.
Head; Double 24 mm.
Tube; Wound brown paper.
Colour; Tan-brown.
Print; Black.
Base; Brass.
Closure; Rolled turn-over.
Wad; Not known.
Case by; Kynoch, Ltd. Witton.

DN.2-1448. Re-drawn 3rd Jan 1999

ALFRED DAVIS (FROM J. BLANCH & SON):
4 Bishopsgate Churchyard, Old Broad Street,
London E.C.2., England.

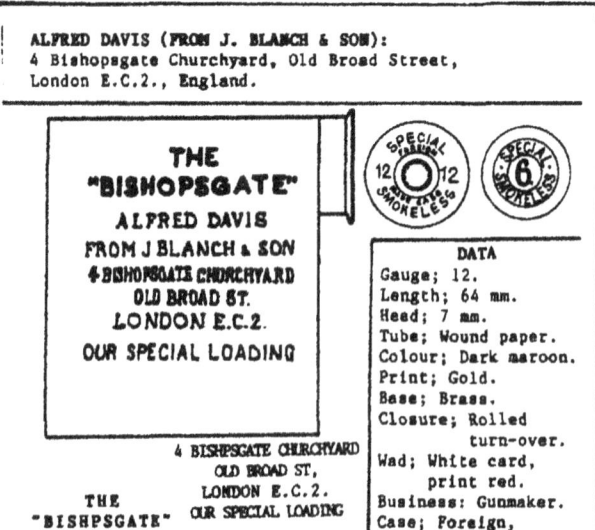

THE "BISHOPSGATE"
ALFRED DAVIS
FROM J BLANCH & SON
4 BISHOPSGATE CHURCHYARD
OLD BROAD ST.
LONDON E.C.2.
OUR SPECIAL LOADING

DATA
Gauge; 12.
Length; 64 mm.
Head; 7 mm.
Tube; Wound paper.
Colour; Dark maroon.
Print; Gold.
Base; Brass.
Closure; Rolled turn-over.
Wad; White card, print red.
Business: Gunmaker.
Case; Foreign, possibly German.

This cartridge was not examined for internal liner

DN.2-0793. Re-drawn; 10th Jan 2000.

GEORGE H. DAW:
67 St. James's Street, London. Also at;
57 Threadneedle Street, London, England.

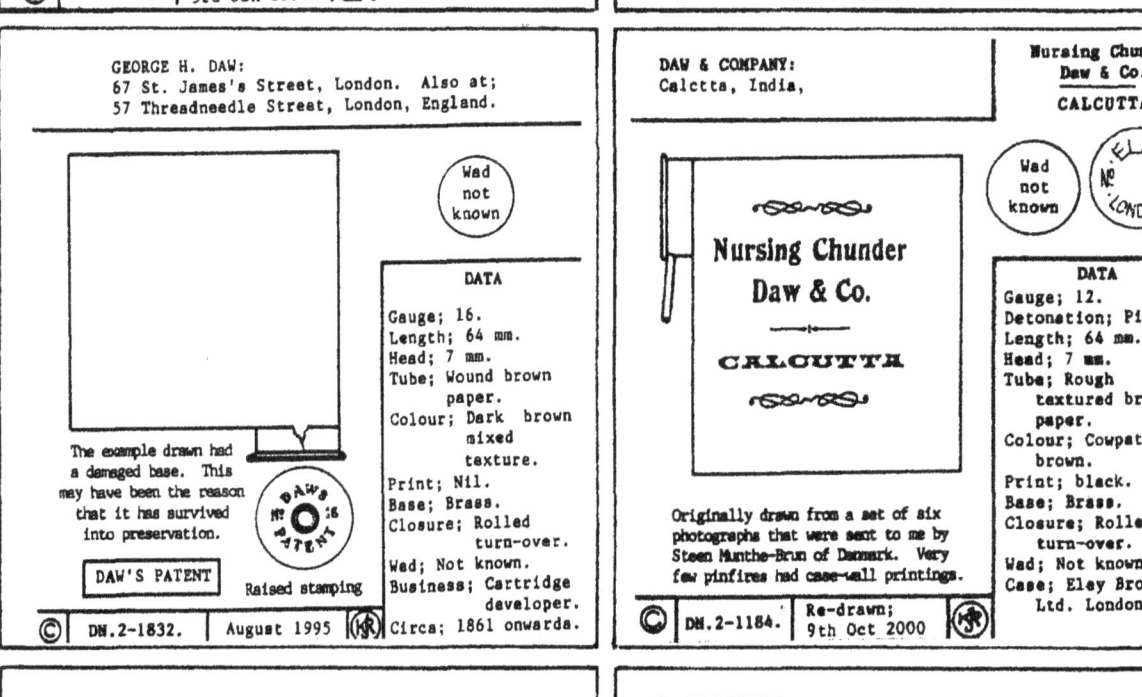

The example drawn had a damaged base. This may have been the reason that it has survived into preservation.

DAW'S PATENT   Raised stamping

DATA
Gauge; 16.
Length; 64 mm.
Head; 7 mm.
Tube; Wound brown paper.
Colour; Dark brown mixed texture.
Print; Nil.
Base; Brass.
Closure; Rolled turn-over.
Wad; Not known.
Business; Cartridge developer.
Circa; 1861 onwards.

DN.2-1832. August 1995

DAW & COMPANY:
Calcutta, India,

Nursing Chunder Daw & Co.
CALCUTTA

Nursing Chunder
Daw & Co.
CALCUTTA

Originally drawn from a set of six photographs that were sent to me by Steen Munthe-Brun of Denmark. Very few pinfires had case-wall printings.

DATA
Gauge; 12.
Detonation; Pinfire.
Length; 64 mm.
Head; 7 mm.
Tube; Rough textured brown paper.
Colour; Cowpat brown.
Print; black.
Base; Brass.
Closure; Rolled turn-over.
Wad; Not known.
Case; Eley Bros, Ltd. London.

DN.2-1184. Re-drawn; 9th Oct 2000.

F. DAWSON:
Altrincham, Cheshire (Great Manchester), England.

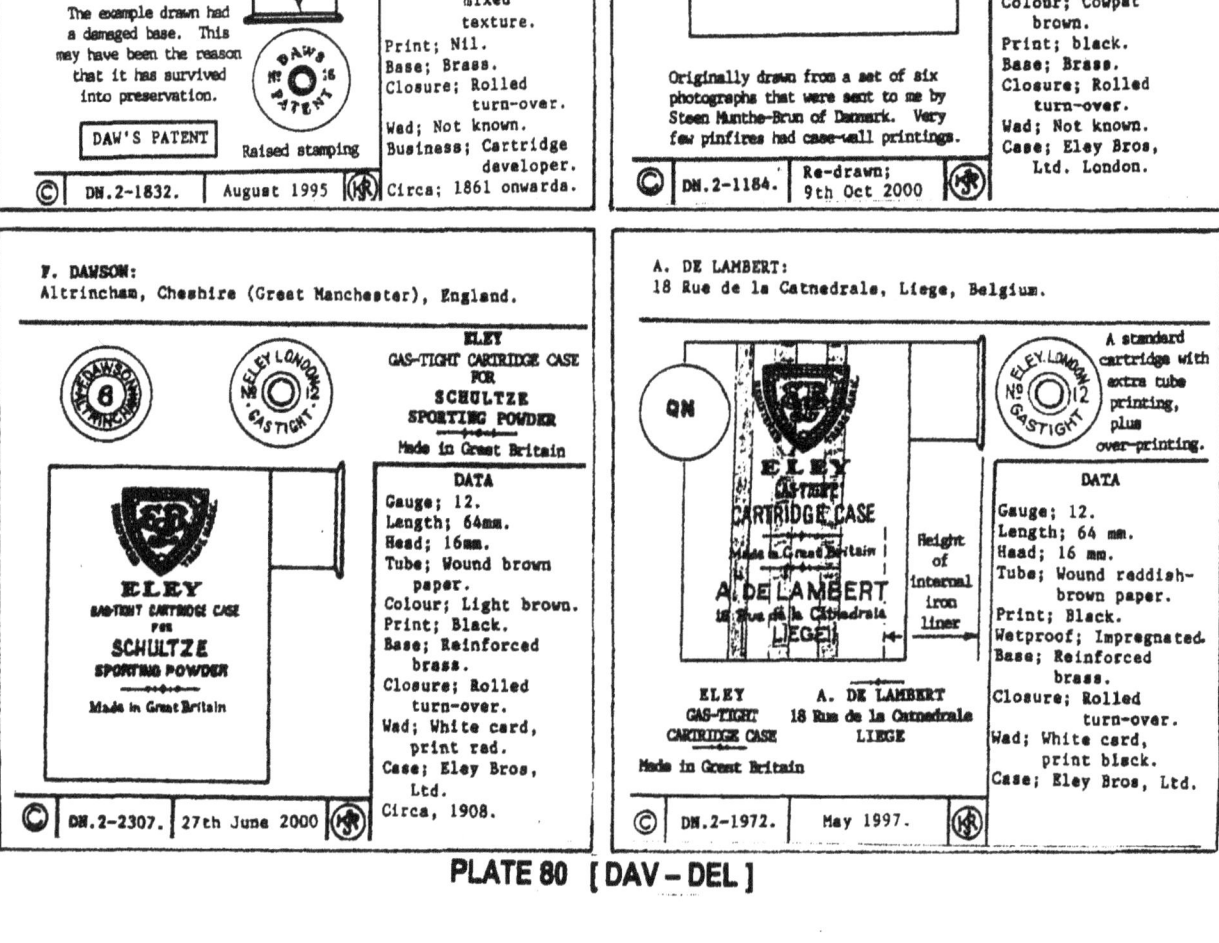

ELEY
GAS-TIGHT CARTRIDGE CASE
for
SCHULTZE
SPORTING POWDER
Made in Great Britain

DATA
Gauge; 12.
Length; 64mm.
Head; 16mm.
Tube; Wound brown paper.
Colour; Light brown.
Print; Black.
Base; Reinforced brass.
Closure; Rolled turn-over.
Wad; White card, print red.
Case; Eley Bros, Ltd.
Circa, 1908.

DN.2-2307. 27th June 2000

A. DE LAMBERT:
18 Rue de la Catnedrale, Liege, Belgium.

ELEY
GAS-TIGHT
CARTRIDGE CASE
Made in Great Britain

A. DE LAMBERT
18 Rue de la Catnedrale
LIEGE

A standard cartridge with extra tube printing, plus over-printing.

DATA
Gauge; 12.
Length; 64 mm.
Head; 16 mm.
Tube; Wound reddish-brown paper.
Print; Black.
Wetproof; Impregnated.
Base; Reinforced brass.
Closure; Rolled turn-over.
Wad; White card, print black.
Case; Eley Bros, Ltd.

DN.2-1972. May 1997.

PLATE 80 [DAV-DEL]

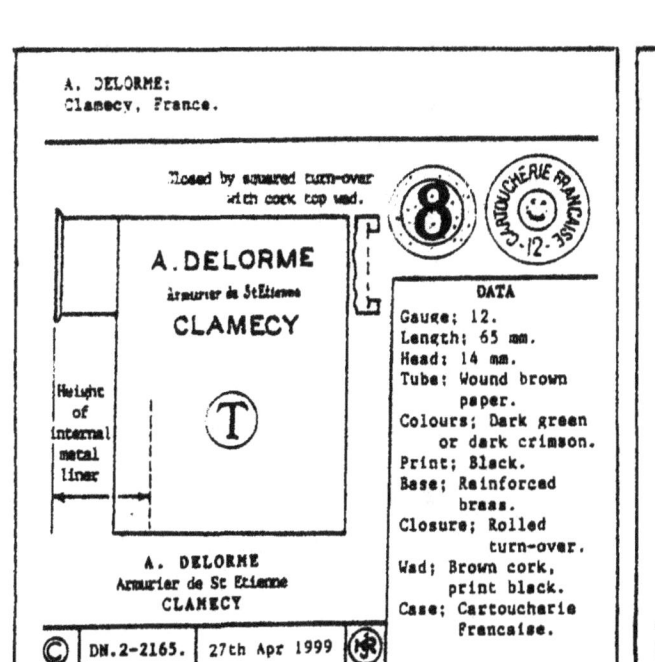
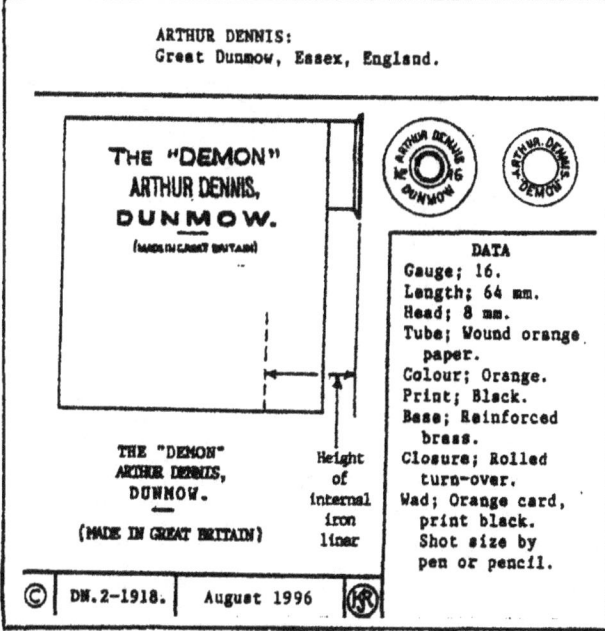
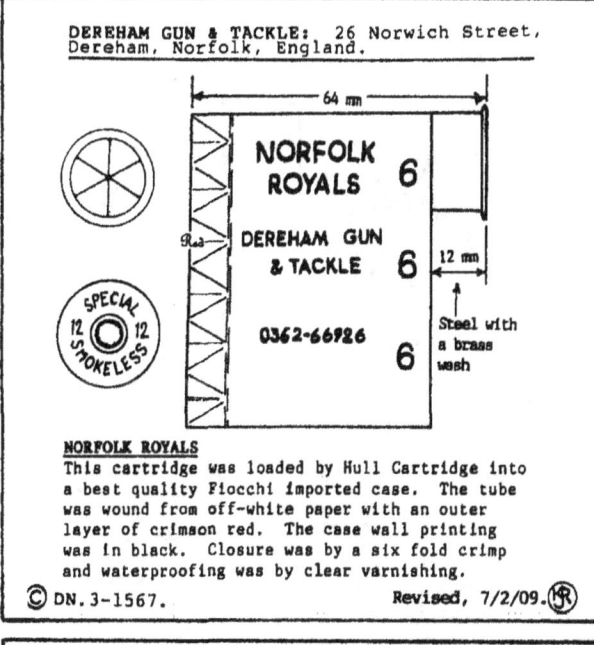
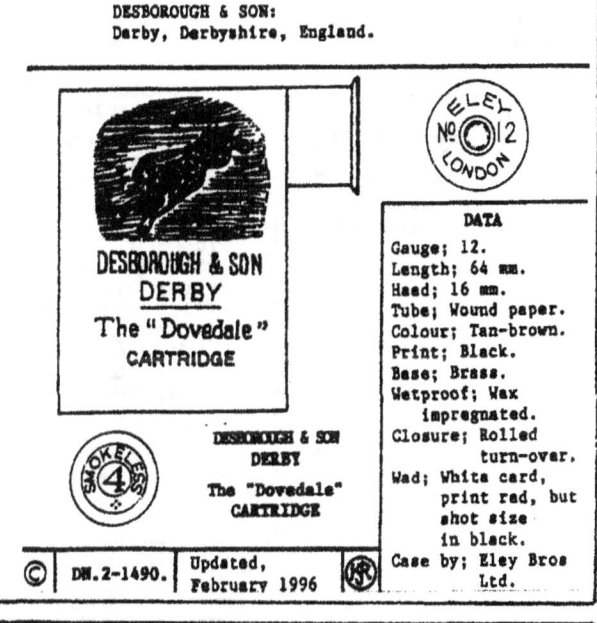
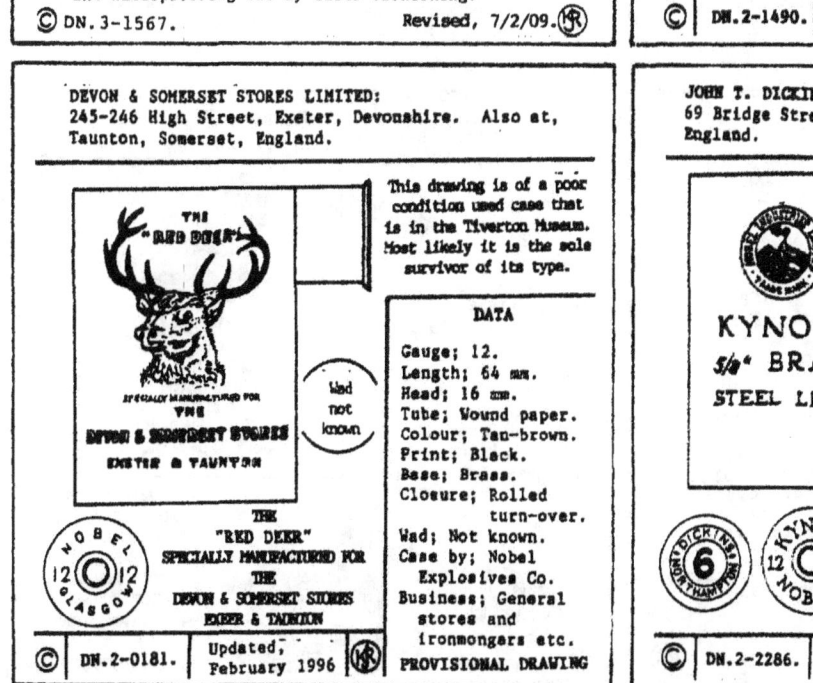

PLATE 81 [DEL – DIC]

JOHN T. DICKINS:
69 Bridge Street, Northampton, Northamptonshire, England.

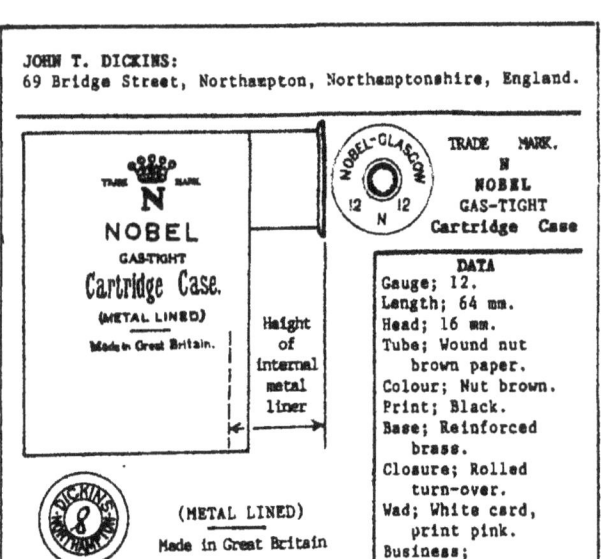

TRADE MARK.
N
NOBEL
GAS-TIGHT
Cartridge Case

DATA
Gauge; 12.
Length; 64 mm.
Head; 16 mm.
Tube; Wound nut brown paper.
Colour; Nut brown.
Print; Black.
Base; Reinforced brass.
Closure; Rolled turn-over.
Wad; White card, print pink.
Business; Ironmonger.
Case; Nobel Explosives Co, Ltd.

Shot size by pen and ink.

© DN.2-2298.   16th May 2000

JOHN DICKSON & SON:
63 Princes Street, Edinburgh, Midlothian, Scotland.

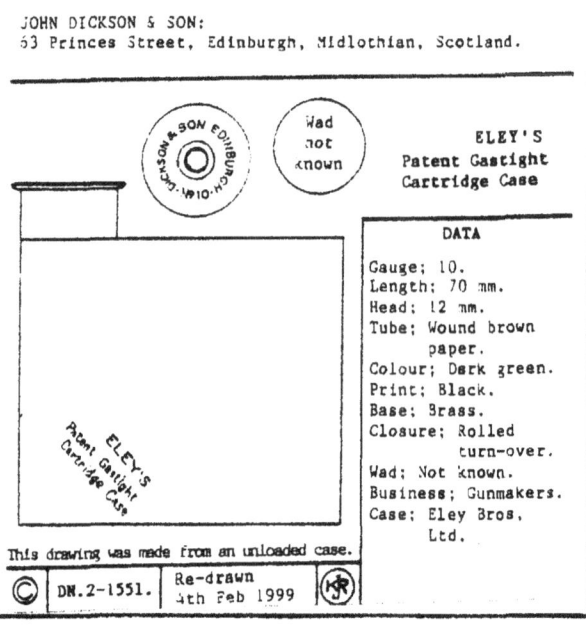

ELEY'S
Patent Gastight
Cartridge Case

DATA
Gauge; 10.
Length; 70 mm.
Head; 12 mm.
Tube; Wound brown paper.
Colour; Dark green.
Print; Black.
Base; Brass.
Closure; Rolled turn-over.
Wad; Not known.
Business; Gunmakers.
Case; Eley Bros, Ltd.

This drawing was made from an unloaded case.

© DN.2-1551.   Re-drawn 4th Feb 1999

JOHN DICKSON & SON:
20 Royal Exchange. Also at,
21 Frederick Street, Edinburgh, Midlothian, Scotland.

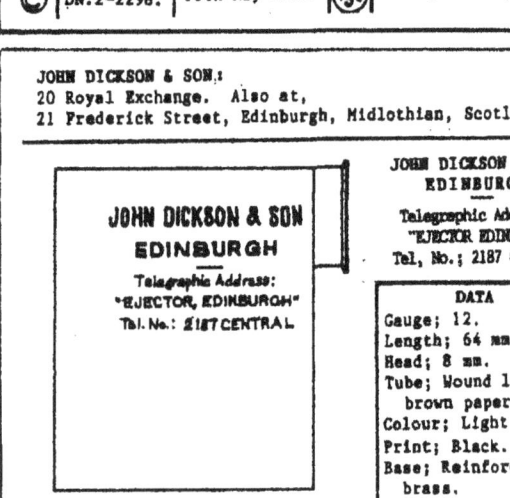

JOHN DICKSON & SON
EDINBURGH
Telegraphic Address;
"EJECTOR EDINBURGH"
Tel, No.; 2187 CENTRAL

DATA
Gauge; 12.
Length; 64 mm.
Head; 8 mm.
Tube; Wound light brown paper.
Colour; Light brown.
Print; Black.
Base; Reinforced brass.
Closure; Rolled turn-over.
Wad; White card, print shocking pink.
Business; Gunmakers.
Case; Kynoch, Ltd.

© DN.2-2405.   23rd Apr 2001

JOHN DICKSON & SON:
63 Princes Street, Edinburgh. Also in, Glasgow,
Kelso-on-Tweed, Roxburgh, Scotland.

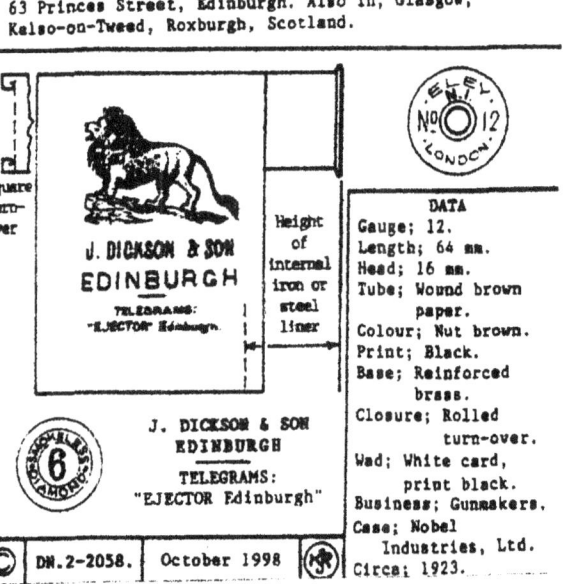

J. DICKSON & SON
EDINBURGH
TELEGRAMS:
"EJECTOR Edinburgh"

DATA
Gauge; 12.
Length; 64 mm.
Head; 16 mm.
Tube; Wound brown paper.
Colour; Nut brown.
Print; Black.
Base; Reinforced brass.
Closure; Rolled turn-over.
Wad; White card, print black.
Business; Gunmakers.
Case; Nobel Industries, Ltd.
Circa; 1923.

© DN.2-2058.   October 1998

JOHN DICKSON & SONS, LTD: 21 Frederick Street,
Edinburgh, Midlothian, Scotland.

J. DICKSON & SONS LTD.
INCORPORATING
MORTIMER & SON
EDINBURGH
TELEGRAMS
"EJECTOR, EDINBURGH"
MADE IN GREAT BRITAIN

DATA
Gauge; 20.
Length; 64 mm.
Head; 7 mm.
Tube; Wound buff paper.
Print; Black or dark blue.
Base; Brass.
Closure; Rolled turn-over.
Wad; Pink, print black.
Business; Gun and rifle makers.
Circa; 1930's.

J. DICKSON & SONS LTD.
INCORPORATING
MORTIMER & SON
EDINBURGH
TELEGRAMS
"EJECTOR, EDINBURGH"
MADE IN GREAT BRITAIN

© DN.3-0641.   Revised, 1/2.09.

JOHN DICKSON & SON, LTD: 20 Royal Exchange.
Also at, 21 Frederick Street, Edinburgh,
Midlothian, Scotland.

DATA
Gauge; 12.
Length; 64 mm.
Head; 8 mm.
Tube; Wound orange paper.
Print; Black.
Base; Reinforced brass.
Cap; Copper.
Closure; Rolled turn-over.
Wad; White card, print black.
Business; Gun and rifle makers.
Circa; 1930's.

J. DICKSON & SON Ltd.
INCORPORATING
MORTIMER & SON
EDINBURGH
TELEGRAMS:
"EJECTOR, EDINBURGH"
MADE IN GREAT BRITAIN

Inner steel

J. DICKSON & SON LTD.
INCORPORATING
MORTIMER & SON
EDINBURGH
TELEGRAMS:
"EJECTOR, EDINBURGH"
MADE IN GREAT BRITAIN

© DN.3-0283.   Drawn, 9/7/08.

PLATE 82 [DIC – DIC]

JOHN DICKSON & SON:
63 Princes Street, Edinburgh, Midlothian.
Also in, Glasgow, Kelso-on-Tweed, Roxburgh,
Scotland.

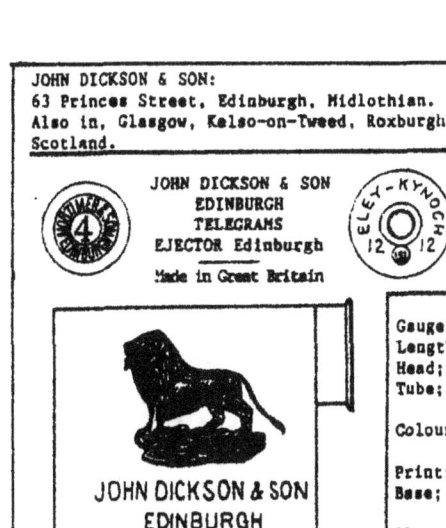

DATA
Gauge; 12.
Length; 64 mm.
Head; 8 mm.
Tube; Wound green paper.
Colour; Greyish-green.
Print; Black.
Base; Reinforced brass.
Closure; Rolled turn-over.
Wad; Emerald green, print black.
Business; Gun and rifle makers.
Circa; 1938-1939.

Note the Mortimer & Son Wad. This firm was incorporated into Dickson & Son in 1938.

DN.2-0284. Re-drawn 7th Jan 1999

JOHN DICKSON & SON, LTD: 21 Frederick Street.
Also at, Royal Exchange, Edinburgh, Midlothian, Scotland.

DATA
Gauge; 12.
Length; 64 mm.
Head; 16 mm.
Tube; Wound Eley's Gastight brick-red paper.
Print; Black.
Wetproof; Clear lacquered.
Base; Reinforced brass.
Closure; Rolled turn-over.
Wad; Light-brown card, print black.
Business; Gun and rifle makers.
Circa; 1955.

Brick Red

J.DICKSON & SON LTD.
INCORPORATING
MORTIMER & SON
EDINBURGH
TELEGRAMS
EJECTOR EDINBURGH
WATER RESISTING
MADE IN GREAT BRITAIN

Height of steel liner

DN.3-0286. Drawn, 4/4/08.

JOHN DICKSON & SON:
63 Princes Street, Edinburgh, Midlothian.
Also in, Glasgow, Kelso-on-Tweed, Roxburgh,
Scotland.

DICKSON'S
"FAVOURITE"
EDINBURGH
MADE IN GREAT BRITAIN

DATA
Gauge; 12.
Length; 64 mm.
Head; 16 mm.
Tube; Wound red paper.
Colour; Crimson.
Print; Black.
Waterproofed; Clear lacquer.
Base; Reinforced brass.
Closure; Rolled turn-over.
Wad; Crimson card, print black.
Business; Gun and rifle makers.

DN.2-0285. Re-drawn 7th Jan 1999

JOHN DICKSON & SON:
63 Princes Street, Edinburgh, Midlothian. Also in,
Glasgow, Kelso-on-Tweed, Roxburgh, Scotland.

DICKSON'S
"JUBILEE"
HIGH VELOCITY
MADE IN GREAT BRITAIN

DICKSON'S
"JUBILEE"
HIGH VELOCITY
MADE IN GREAT BRITAIN

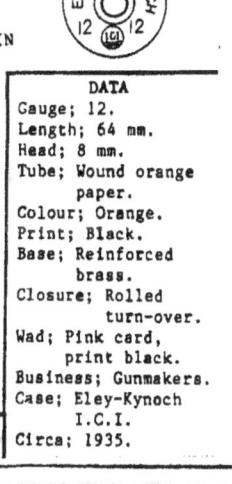

DATA
Gauge; 12.
Length; 64 mm.
Head; 8 mm.
Tube; Wound orange paper.
Colour; Orange.
Print; Black.
Base; Reinforced brass.
Closure; Rolled turn-over.
Wad; Pink card, print black.
Business; Gunmakers.
Case; Eley-Kynoch I.C.I.
Circa; 1935.

DN.2-0985. Re-drawn 9th Jan 1999

JOHN DICKSON & SON:
63 Princes Street, Edinburgh. Also in, Glasgow,
Kelso-on-Tweed, Roxburgh, Scotland.

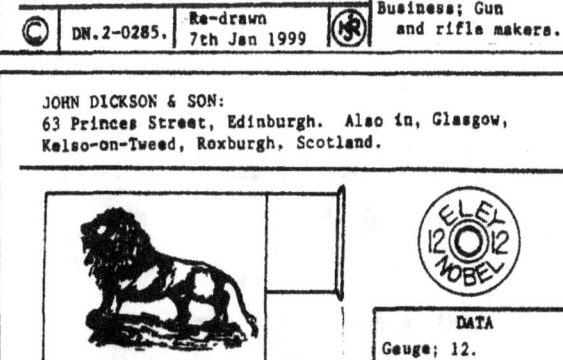

DICKSON'S
"SPECIAL BLUE SHELL"
HIGH VELOCITY
DAMP-PROOF

Height of internal iron or steel liner

DICKSON'S
"SPECIAL BLUE SHELL"
HIGH-VELOCITY
DAMP-PROOF

DATA
Gauge; 12.
Length; 64 mm.
Head; 16 mm.
Tube; Wound blue paper.
Colour; Middle blue.
Print; Black.
Base; Reinforced brass.
Closure; Rolled turn-over.
Wad; Oxford blue, print black.
Business; Gunmakers.
Case; Nobel Industries, Ltd.
Circa; Later 1920's.

DN.2-2059. October 1998

J. DICKSON & SON LTD. Inc, ALEX MARTIN LTD:
21 Frederick Street, Edinburgh, Scotland.
Also at, Glasgow, Aberdeen & Kelso.

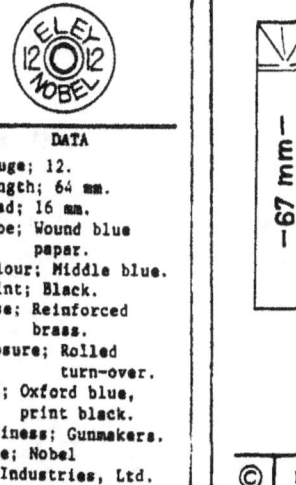

THE
CALEDONIAN
J. Dickson & Son
1 1/16 Oz.
6   6   6

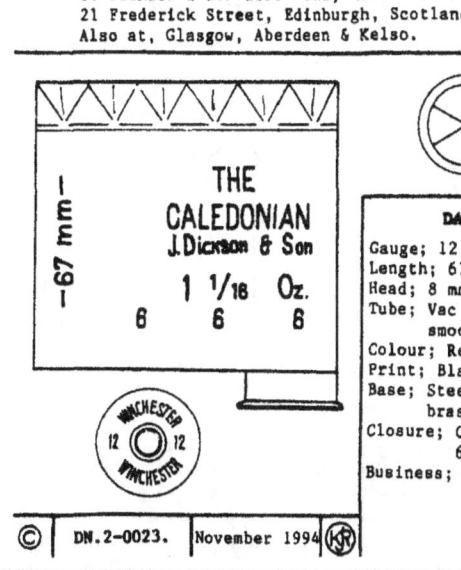

DATA
Gauge; 12.
Length; 67 mm.
Head; 8 mm.
Tube; Vac formed, smooth plastic.
Colour; Red 3.5.
Print; Black.
Base; Steel, brass coated.
Closure; Crimp, 6 fold.
Business; Gun and rifle makers.

DN.2-0023. November 1994

PLATE 83 [DIC - DIC]

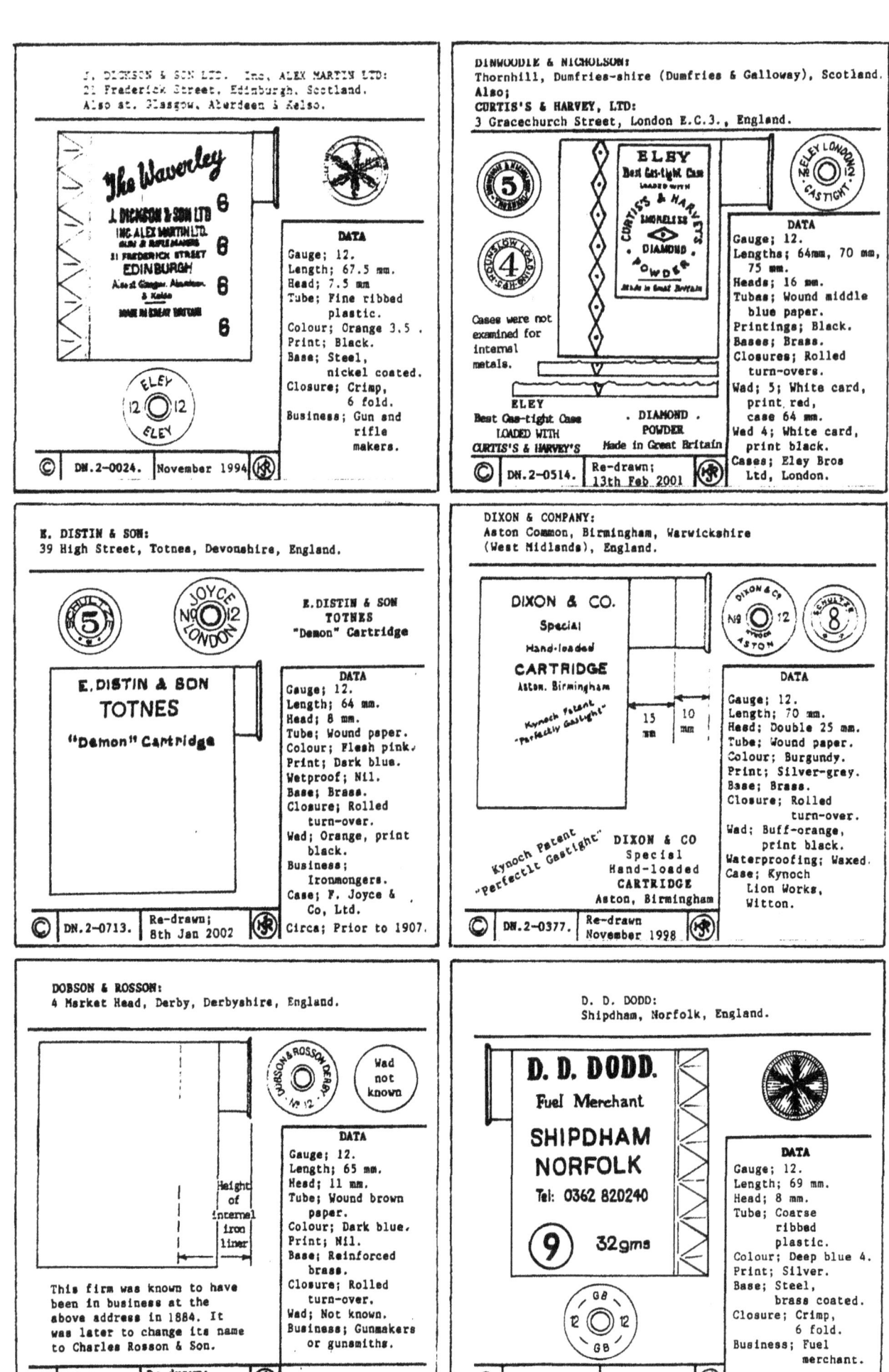

PLATE 84 [DIC - DOD]

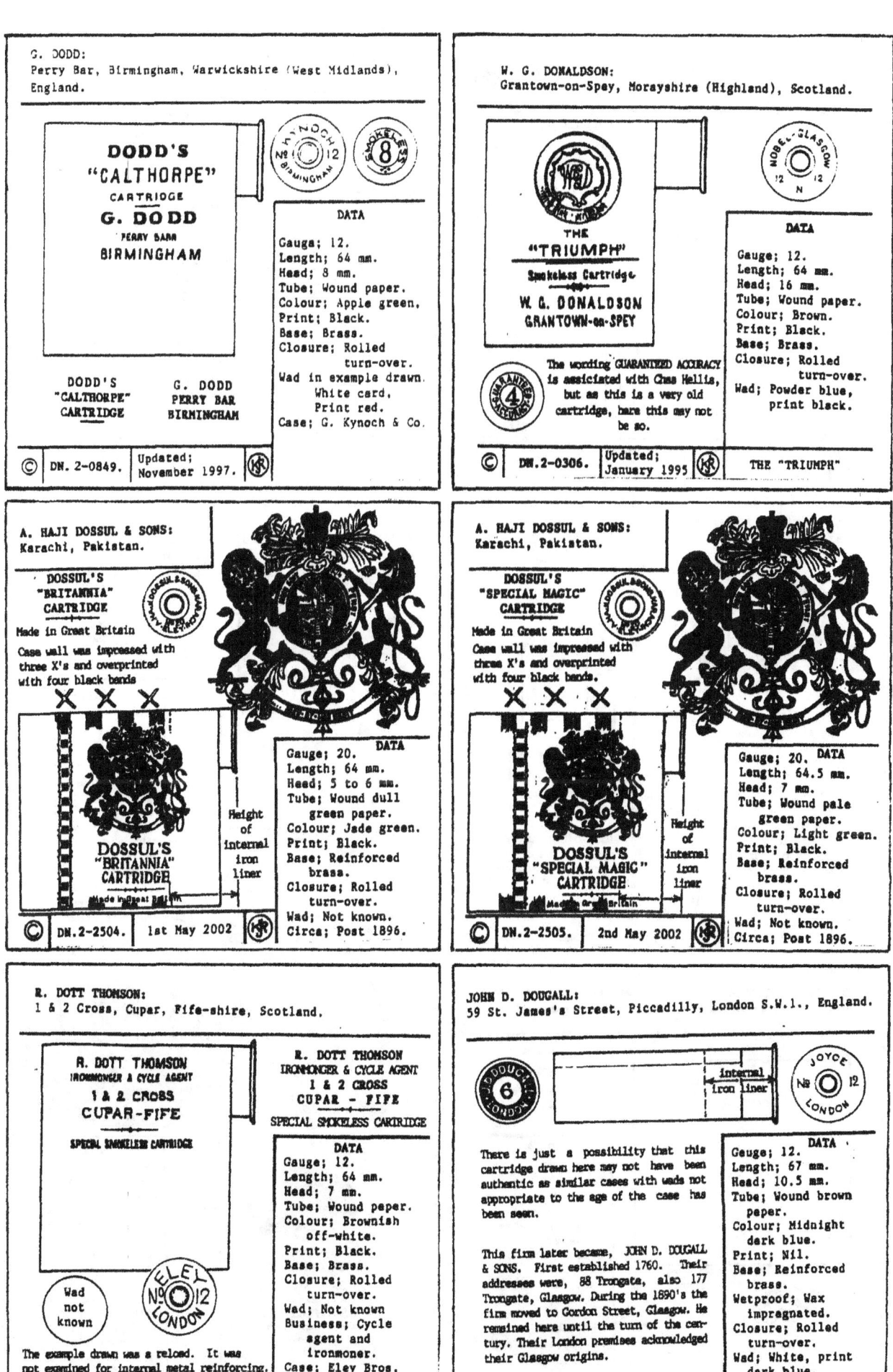

PLATE 85 [DOD - DOU]

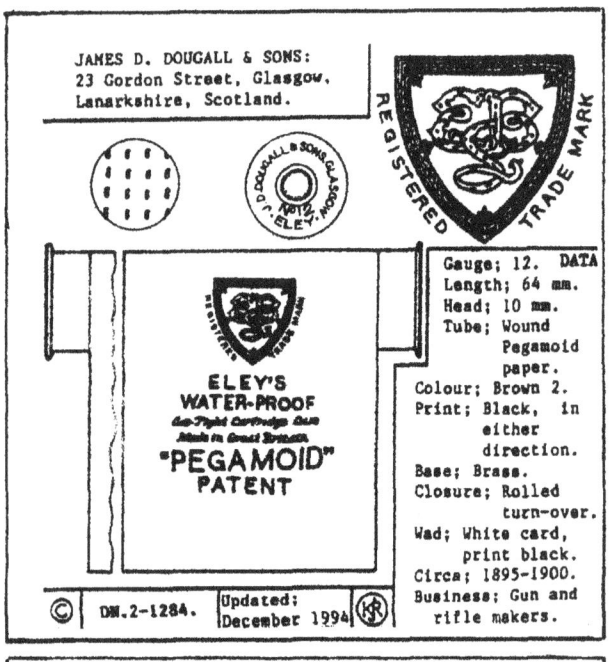
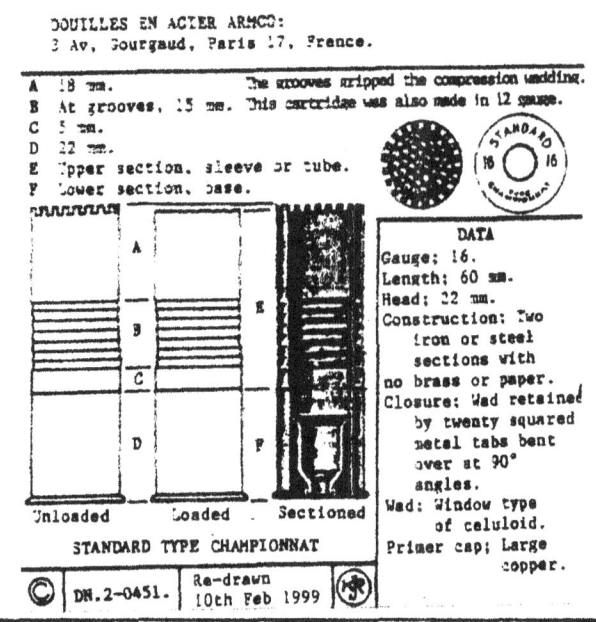
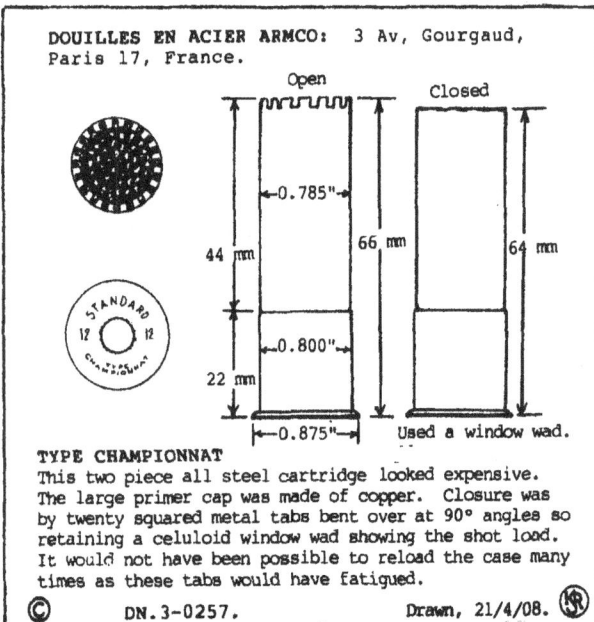
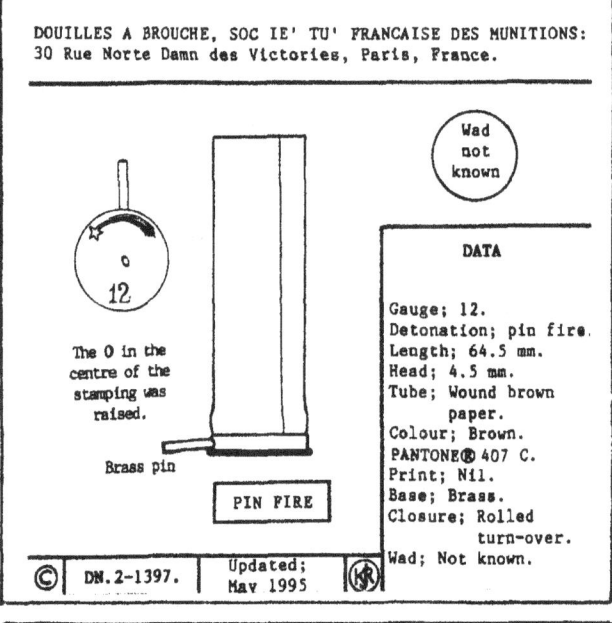
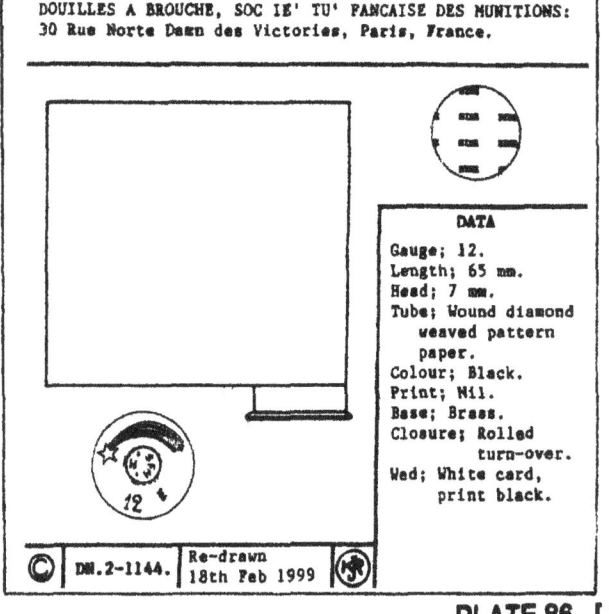

PLATE 86 [DOU - DOW]

DRETSE & COLLINSBUSCH:
Sommerda, Near Erfurt, East Germany.

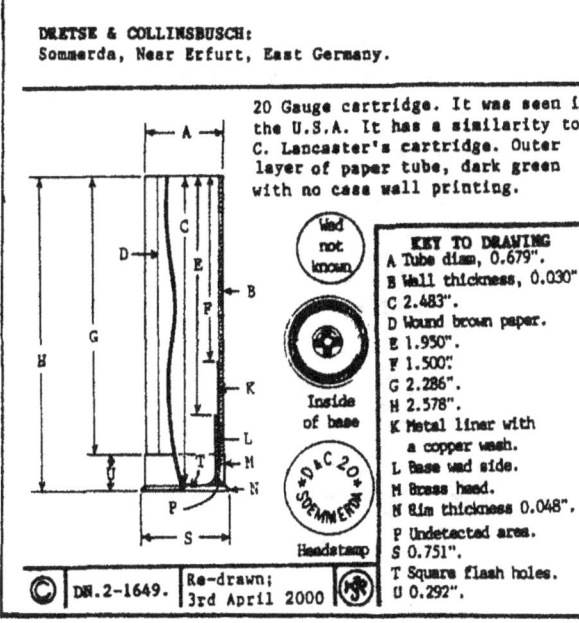

20 Gauge cartridge. It was seen in the U.S.A. It has a similarity to C. Lancaster's cartridge. Outer layer of paper tube, dark green with no case wall printing.

KEY TO DRAWING
A Tube diam. 0.679".
B Wall thickness, 0.030"
C 2.483".
D Wound brown paper.
E 1.950".
F 1.500".
G 2.286".
H 2.578".
K Metal liner with a copper wash.
L Base wad side.
M Brass head.
N Rim thickness 0.048".
P Undetected area.
S 0.751".
T Square flash holes.
U 0.292".

Headstamp

© DN.2-1649. Re-drawn; 3rd April 2000

FREDERICK VON DREYES:
Sommerda, Prussia (Erfurt, East Germany).

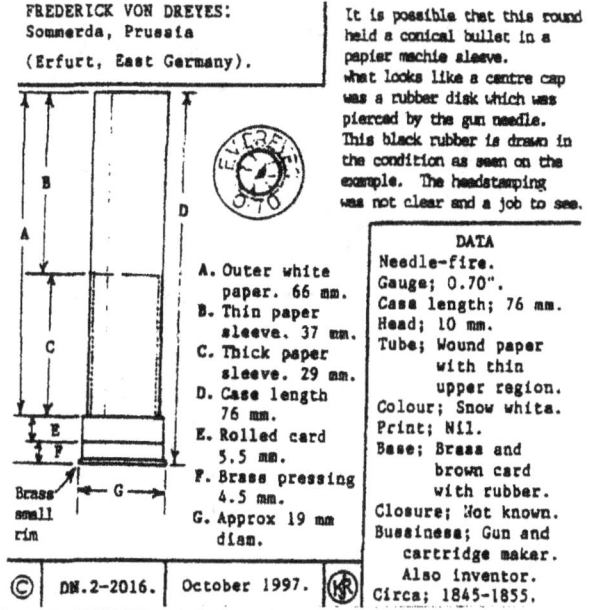

It is possible that this round held a conical bullet in a papier machie sleeve.
What looks like a centre cap was a rubber disk which was pierced by the gun needle. This black rubber is drawn in the condition as seen on the example. The headstamping was not clear and a job to see.

DATA
Needle-fire.
Gauge; 0.70".
Case length; 76 mm.
Head; 10 mm.
Tube; Wound paper with thin upper region.
Colour; Snow white.
Print; Nil.
Base; Brass and brown card with rubber.
Closure; Not known.
Business; Gun and cartridge maker. Also inventor.
Circa; 1845-1855.

A. Outer white paper. 66 mm.
B. Thin paper sleeve. 37 mm.
C. Thick paper sleeve. 29 mm.
D. Case length 76 mm.
E. Rolled card 5.5 mm.
F. Brass pressing 4.5 mm.
G. Approx 19 mm diam.

© DN.2-2016. October 1997.

DRUM SPORTS, LTD:
47 Courtnay Street, Newton Abbot, Devonshire, England.

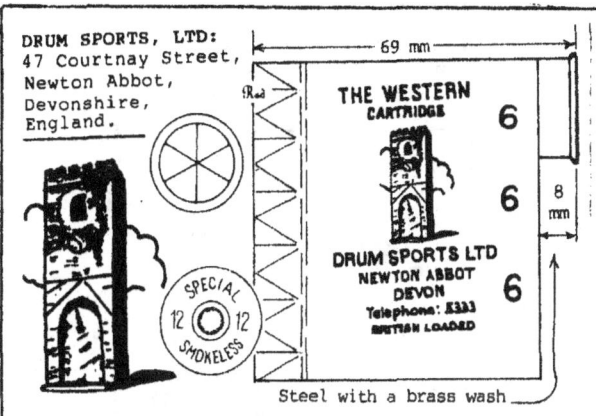

THE WESTERN CARTRIDGE
Loaded by the Hull Cartridge Co, into a paper tubed Fiocchi case with the outer layers in red, Case wall printing was black. Closed by a six fold crimp it had a nickel primer cap. It is believed that the tower is the one that was once attached to St Leonard's Church. If it is then its a poor illustration. The church was demolished in 1836.

© DN.3-1538. Revised; 27/12/08.

DUMOND:
21 Rue Ces d' Pyramides, Paris, France

This drawing has been made from a set of four photographs. These were sent to me from the U.S.A.

DATA
Gauge; 20.
Length; 63.5 mm.
Head; 24.5 mm.
Tube; Wound paper.
Colour; Crimson red.
Print; Black.
Base; Brass.
Closure; Rolled turn-over.
Wad; Not known.
Case; Eley Bros, Ltd. London.

The small case wall wording is,
DÉPOSÉE
21 RUE CES PYRAMIDES PARIS.
Importé d' Angleterre

© DN.2-1869. November 1995

A. H. DUNCALFE, LTD: 5 Merridale Road, Wolverhampton, Staffordshire (West Midlands), England.

YELLOW SEAL Mullerite SMOKELESS
Duncalfe's name had replaced the manufacturers address. This foreign cased cartridge that was loaded in Great Britain had a mustard-yellow waxed wetproof paper tube that was printed in black. The wad was a celandine yellow with scarlet red printing. This firm were sanitary ware manufacturers and ironmongers. They were listed in Kelly's Directory of Staffordshire 1932.

© DN.3-0871. Drawn, 26/3/08.

C. V. DUNCAN & CO: 136 Anlaby Road, Hull, Humberside, England.
Business; Gunmakers.

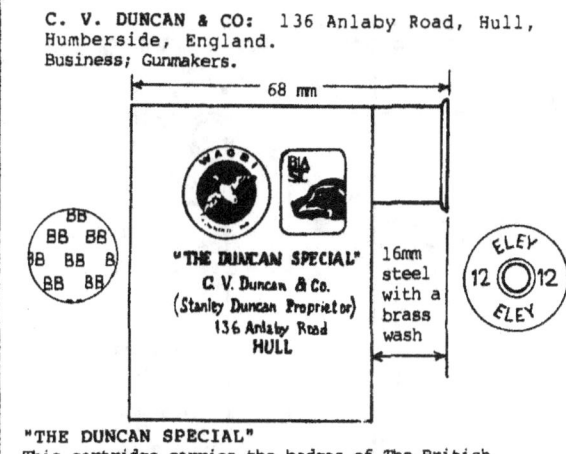

"THE DUNCAN SPECIAL"
This cartridge carries the badges of The British Association for Shooting and Conservation and The Wildfowlers Association of Great Britain & Ireland. This being founded by Stanley Duncan in 1908. The wound brown paper tube had an outer layer of crimson. The wad was of brown card. All printings were in black.

© DN.3-0618. Drawn, 2/7/08.

PLATE 87 [DRE - DUN]

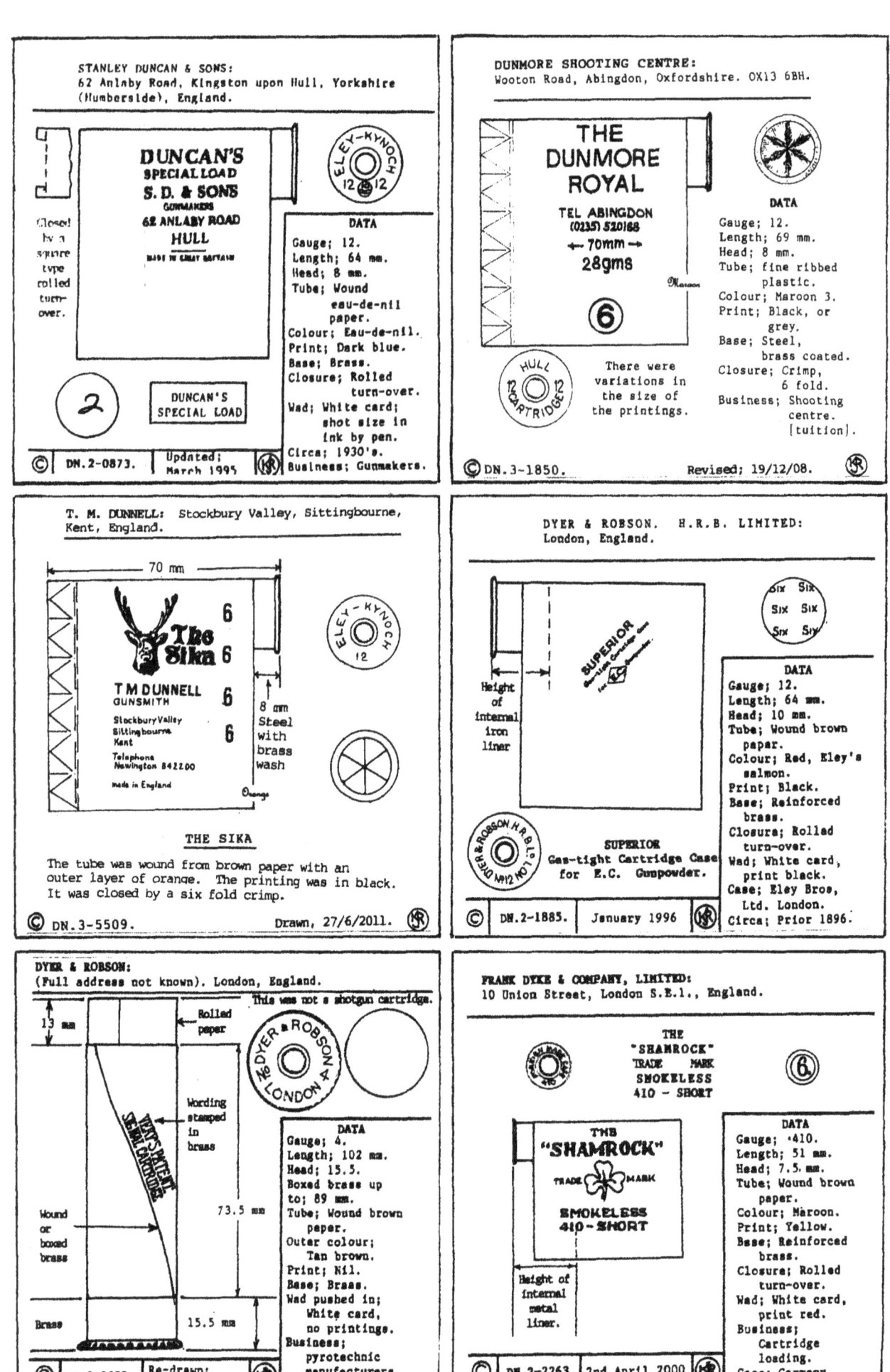

PLATE 88 [DUN – DYK]

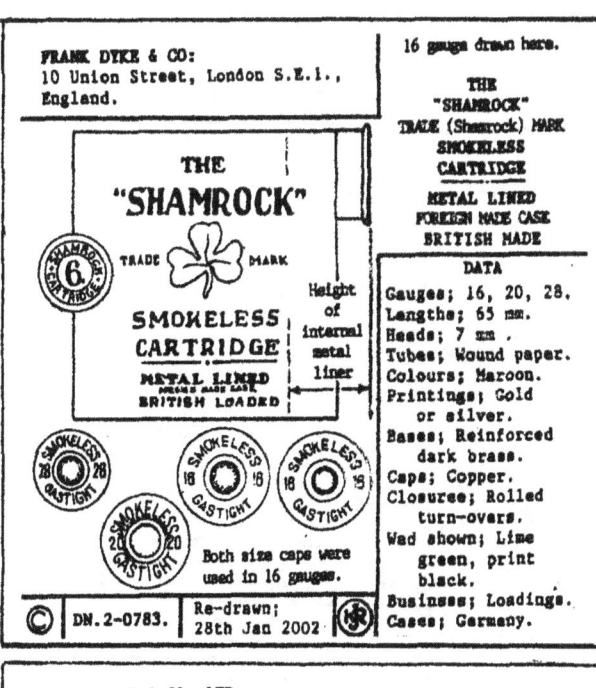
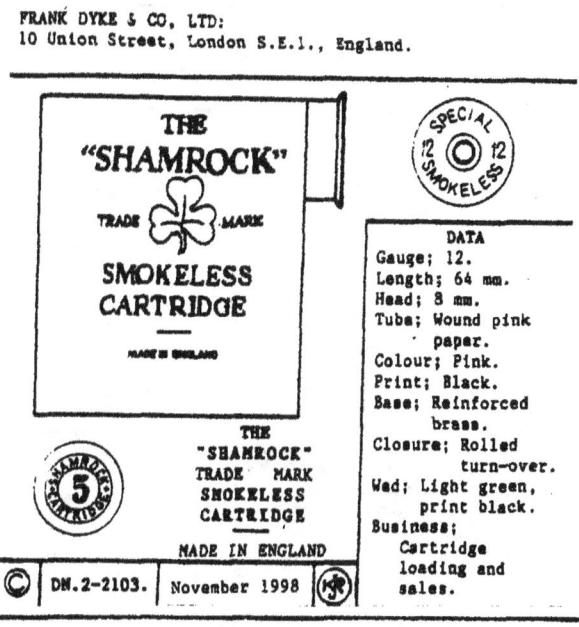
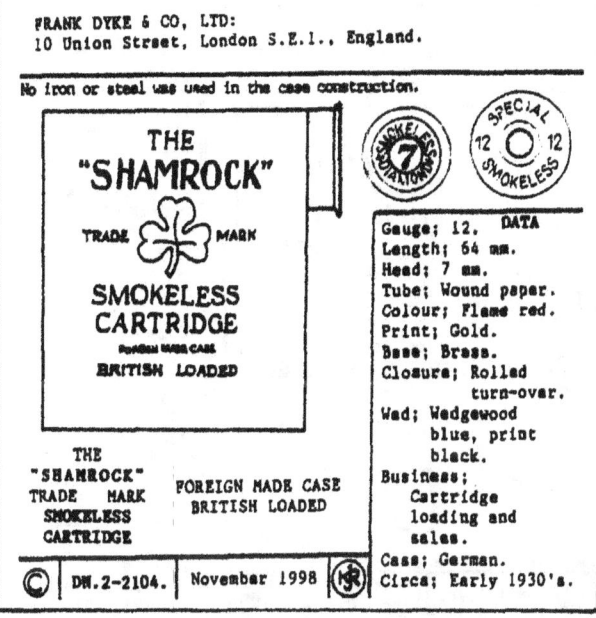
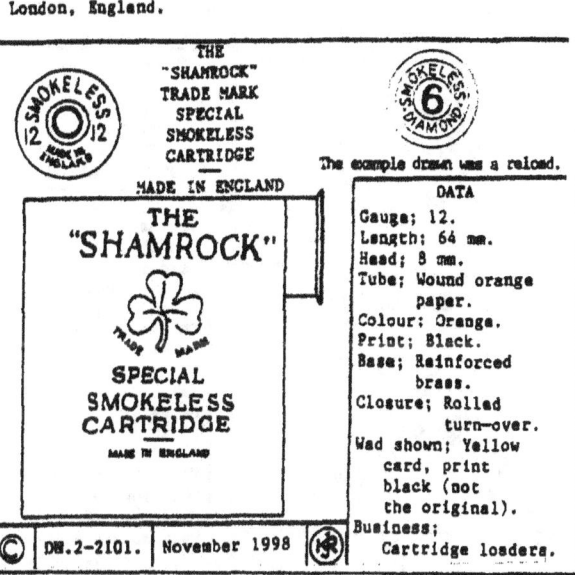
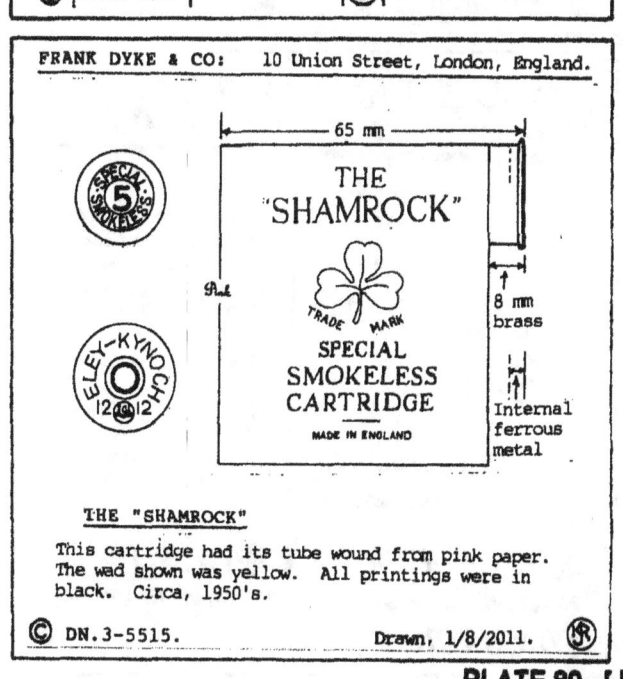
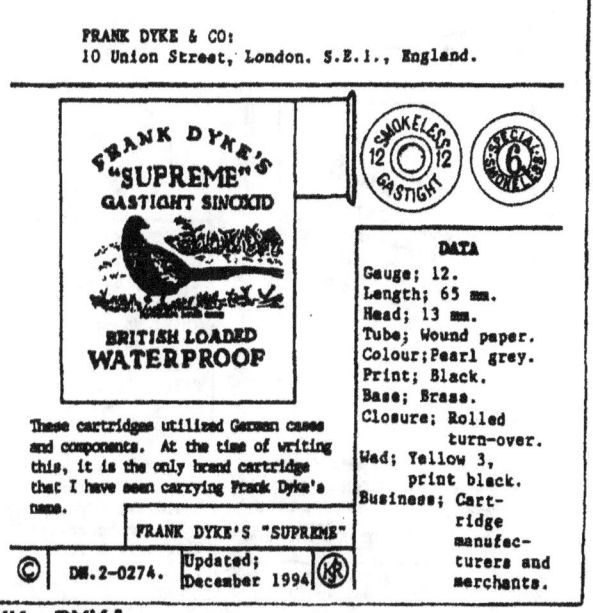

FRANK DYKE AND COMPANY LIMITED:
10 Union Street, Borough, London, S.E.1., England.

THE YELLOW WIZARD
SMOKELESS
SINOXID
RUSTLESS PRIMING
FOREIGN MADE CASE
LOADED IN ENGLAND

The very first Yellow Wizards were as the drawing, but minus case wall printings.

YELLOW WIZARD

DATA
Gauge; 12.
Length; 65 mm.
Head; 7 mm.
Tube; Wound paper.
Colour; Yellow 3.
Print; Black.
Base; coppery-brass.
Closure; Rolled turn-over.
Wad; Yellow card, print black.
Case; German.
Circa; Mid 1930's.
Business; Loaders and merchants.

DN.2-0073. Updated; February 1995

FRANK DYKE & COMPANY, LIMITED:
10 Union Street, London S.E.1., England.

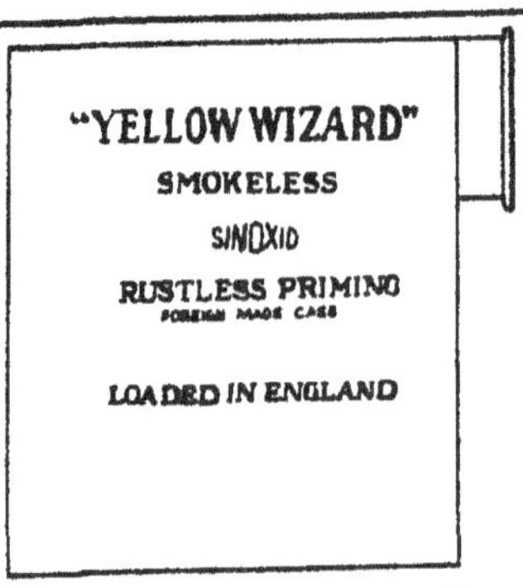

"YELLOW WIZARD"
SMOKELESS
SINOXID
RUSTLESS PRIMING
FOREIGN MADE CASE
LOADED IN ENGLAND

"YELLOW WIZARD"
SMOKELESS
SINOXID
RUSTLESS PRIMING
FOREIGN MADE CASE
LOADED IN ENGLAND

DATA
Gauge; 12.
Length; 65 mm.
Head; 7 mm.
Tube; Wound paper.
Colour; Buttercup yellow.
Print; Black.
Base; Brass.
Closure; Rolled turn-over.
Wad; Buttercup yellow, print black.
Business; Cartridge loading and sales.
Case; Germany.

DN.2-0124. Re-drawn 4th Jan 1999

FRANK DYKE & CO, LTD:
10 Union Street, S.E.1. Later at, 1 - 7 Ernest Avenue,
West Northwood, London N.W., England.

"Yellow Wizard Rustless"
COOPAL POWDER
BRITISH HAND LOADED
FOREIGN MADE CASE

16 Gauge drawn here

"Yellow Wizard Rustless"
COOPPAL POWDER
BRITISH HAND LOADED
FOREIGN MADE CASE

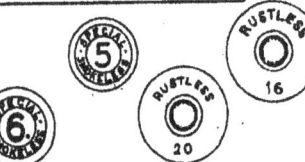

DATA
Gauges; 20, 16.
Lengths; 65 mm.
Heads; 7 mm.
Tubes; Wound light brown paper.
Colours; Dark yellow.
Printings; Black.
Bases; Brass.
Caps; Nickel.
Closures; Rolled turn-overs.
Wads; Canary yellow, prints black.
Business; Loadings.
Circa; 1965.

DN.2-0075. Re-drawn; 17th March 2001

FRANK DYKE & CO, LTD:
10 Union Street, S.E.1. Later at, 1 - 7 Ernest Avenue,
West Northwood, London N.W., England.

"Yellow Wizard Rustless"
COOPPAL POWDER
BRITISH HAND LOADED
FOREIGN MADE CASE

Crimped   Rolled turn-over

No iron or steel was used in the case.

"Yellow Wizard Rustless"
COOPALL POWDER
BRITISH HAND LOADED
FOREIGN MADE CASE

DATA
Gauges; 12.
Lengths; 65 mm with rolled turn-over.
70 mm with six fold crimp.
Heads; 8 mm.
Tubes; Wound light brown paper.
Colours; Dark yellow.
Printings; Black.
Bases; Brass.
Wad; Canary yellow, print black.
Cap; Nickel.
Business; Loadings.
Circa; 1960-1970.

DN.2-0074. Re-drawn; 17th March 2001

G. A. EARLE:
Bridgnorth, Shropshire, England.

EARLE'S
Special Cartridge
TELEPHONE NO. 2164
BRIDGNORTH
MADE IN GREAT BRITAIN

EARLE'S
Special Cartridge
TELEPHONE NO. 2164
BRIDGNORTH
MADE IN GREAT BRITAIN

DATA
Gauge; 12.
Length; 64 mm.
Head; 8 mm.
Tube; Wound orange paper.
Colour; Orange.
Print; Black.
Base; Brass.
Closure; Rolled turn-over.
Wad; Yellow card, print black.
Business; Ironmongers.
Circa: 1930's.

DN.2-0376. Re-drawn November 1998

REYNOLDS RICHARD EARLE.
High Street, Hungerford, Berkshire, England.

Rolled paper

This ironmonger was known to have been active somewhere in the High Street between 1877 and 1887. He was not listed in a directory for 1895.

Mr C. Silk has found three cartridge heads in the Lambourn area when metal detecting.

A PROVISIONAL DRAWING
This drawing is made to record the firm and its cartridge.
©DN.5-1010.

PLATE 90 [DYK-EAR]

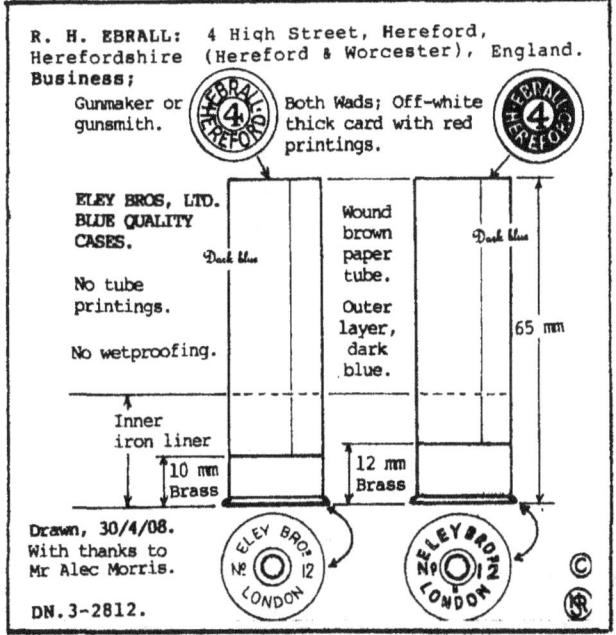
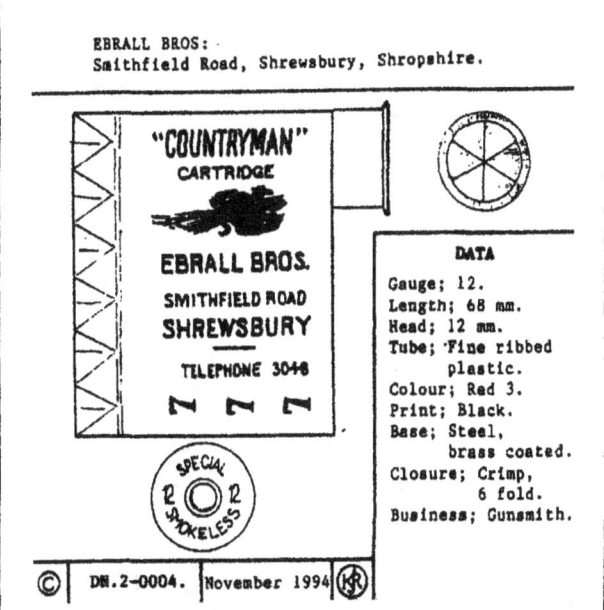
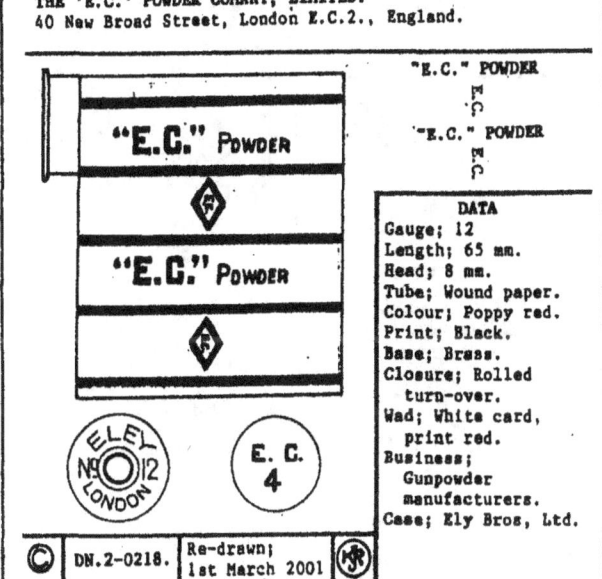
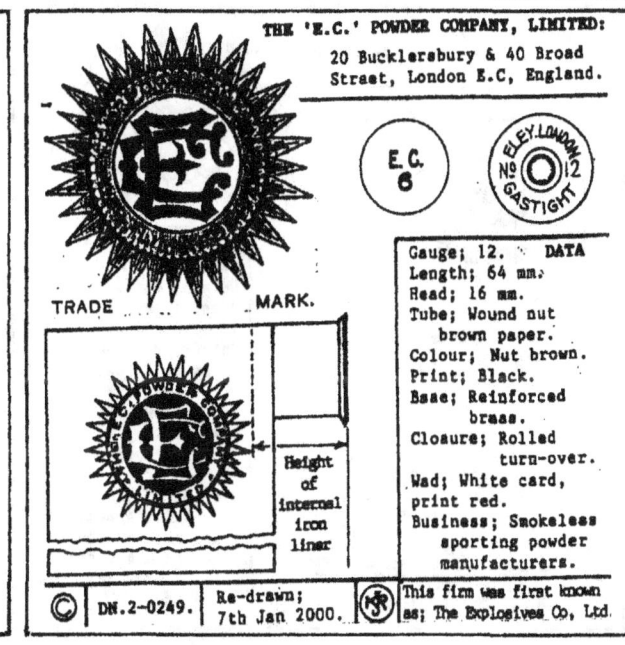
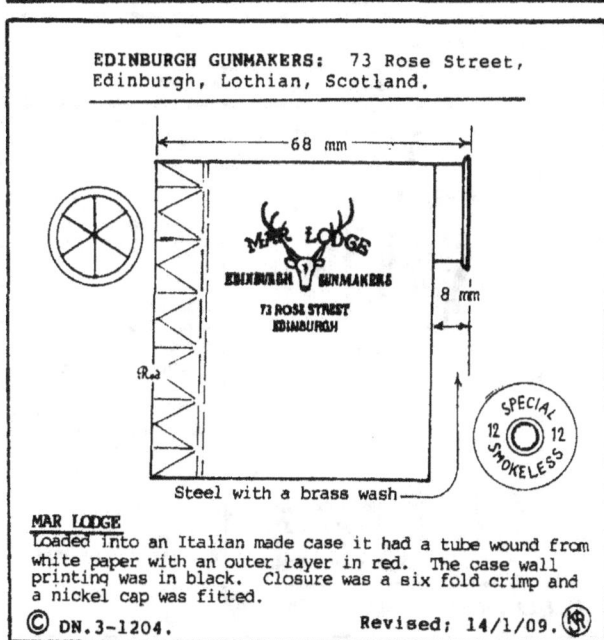
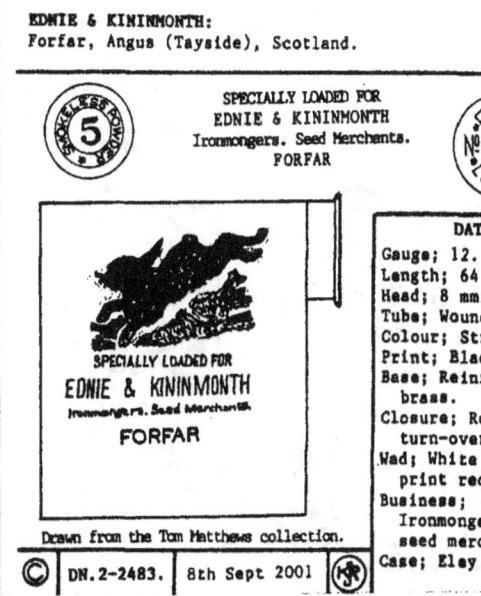

EDNIE & KININMONTH:
Forfar, Angus (Tayside), Scotland.

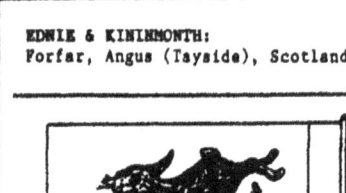

SPECIALLY LOADED FOR
EDNIE & KININMONTH
Ironmongers & Seed Merchants
FORFAR

DATA
Gauge; 12.
Length; 64 mm.
Head; 8 mm.
Tube; Wound paper.
Colour; Creamed yellow.
Print; Black.
Base; Reinforced brass.
Closure; Rolled turn-over.
Wad shown; White card, print red.
Business: Ironmongers and seed merchants.
Case; Eley Bros, Ltd.

SPECIALLY LOADED FOR
EDNIE & KININMONTH
Ironmongers & Seed Merchants
FORFAR

© DN.2-2326. 3rd Sept 2000

AUBREY EDWARDS & CO, LTD:
Swansea, West Glamorgan, Wales.

THE "ECLIPSE"
AUBREY EDWARDS & CO.
LIMITED
SWANSEA

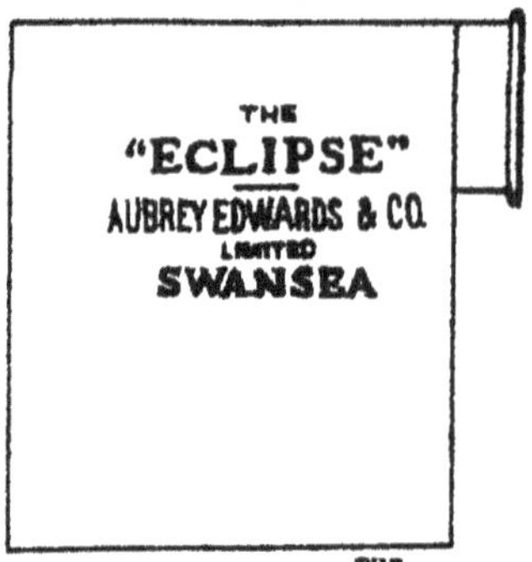

Wad not known

THE "ECLIPSE"
AUBREY EDWARDS & CO.
LIMITED
SWANSEA

Drawing made from a reloaded round.

DATA
Gauge; 12.
Length; 64 mm.
Head; 8 mm.
Tube; Wound paper.
Colour; Royal purple.
Print; Silver-white.
Base; Brass.
Closure; Rolled turn-over.
Wad; Not known.
Case; Kynoch.

© DN.2-2323. 2nd Sept 2000

EDWARDS, LIMITED:
Newport, Monmouthshire (Gwent), Wales.

THE "CHAMPION"
Loaded by
EDWARDS, Ltd.
Gun & Cartridge Makers
NEWPORT

DATA
Gauge; 12.
Length; 64 mm.
Head; 16 mm.
Tube; Wound paper.
Colour; Pinkish-mauve (possibly faded).
Print; Black.
Base; Brass.
Closure; Rolled turn-over.
Wad; Green card, print black.
Business; Gun and cartridge maker.
Case; Eley Bros, Ltd.

EDWARDS Ltd
Gun & Cartridge Makers
NEWPORT

Drawn from the Chris Hart collection.

© DN.2-2186. 12th May 1999

EDWARDS, LIMITED:
Newport, Monmouthshire (Gwent), Wales.

The "NEWPORT"
EDWARDS, Ltd.
Gun & Cartridge Makers
NEWPORT

DATA
Gauge; 12.
Length; 64 mm.
Head; 7 mm.
Tube wound paper.
Colour; Dark green.
Print; Black.
Base; Brass.
Closure; Rolled turn-over.
Wad; Green card, print black.
Business; Gun and cartridge makers.
Case; Eley Bros, Ltd.

The "NEWPORT"
EDWARDS, Ltd.
Gun & Cartridge Makers
NEWPORT

Drawn from the Chris Hart collection.

© DN.2-2187. 12th May 1999

AUBREY EDWARDS & COMPANY, LIMITED:
32 Oxford Street, Swansea, West Glamorgan, Wales.

The "GOWER"
LOADED BY
AUBREY EDWARDS & CO.
LIMITED
32 OXFORD STREET
SWANSEA

Wad not known

The "GOWER"
LOADED BY
AUBREY EDWARDS & CO.
LIMITED
32 OXFORD STREET
SWANSEA

DATA
Gauge; 12
Length; 64 mm.
Head; 8 mm.
Tube; Wound orange paper.
Colour; Redish orange.
Print; Black.
Base; Brass.
Closure; Rolled turn-over.
Wad; Not known.
Case; Kynoch, Ltd.

© DN.2-2338. 16th Sept 2000

C. G. EDWARDS & SON:
2 George Street. Also at, 1 Frankfort Lane, Plymouth, Devonshire, England.

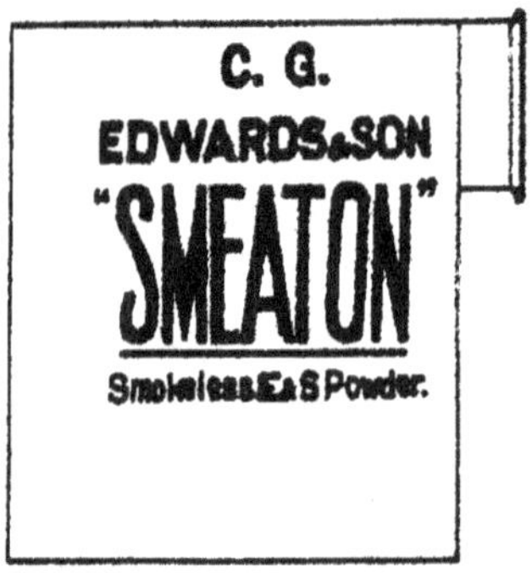

C. G.
EDWARDS&SON
"SMEATON"
Smokeless E&S Powder.

C. G.
EDWARDS&SON
"SMEATON"
Smokeless E&S Powder.

DATA
Gauge; 12.
Length; 64 mm.
Head; 8 mm.
Tube; Wound paper.
Colour; Greenish-grey.
Print; Black.
Base; Reinforced brass.
Closure; Rolled turn-over.
Wad; Yellow card, print black.
Business; Gunmakers.

© DN.2-2045. October 1998

PLATE 92 [EDN – EDW]

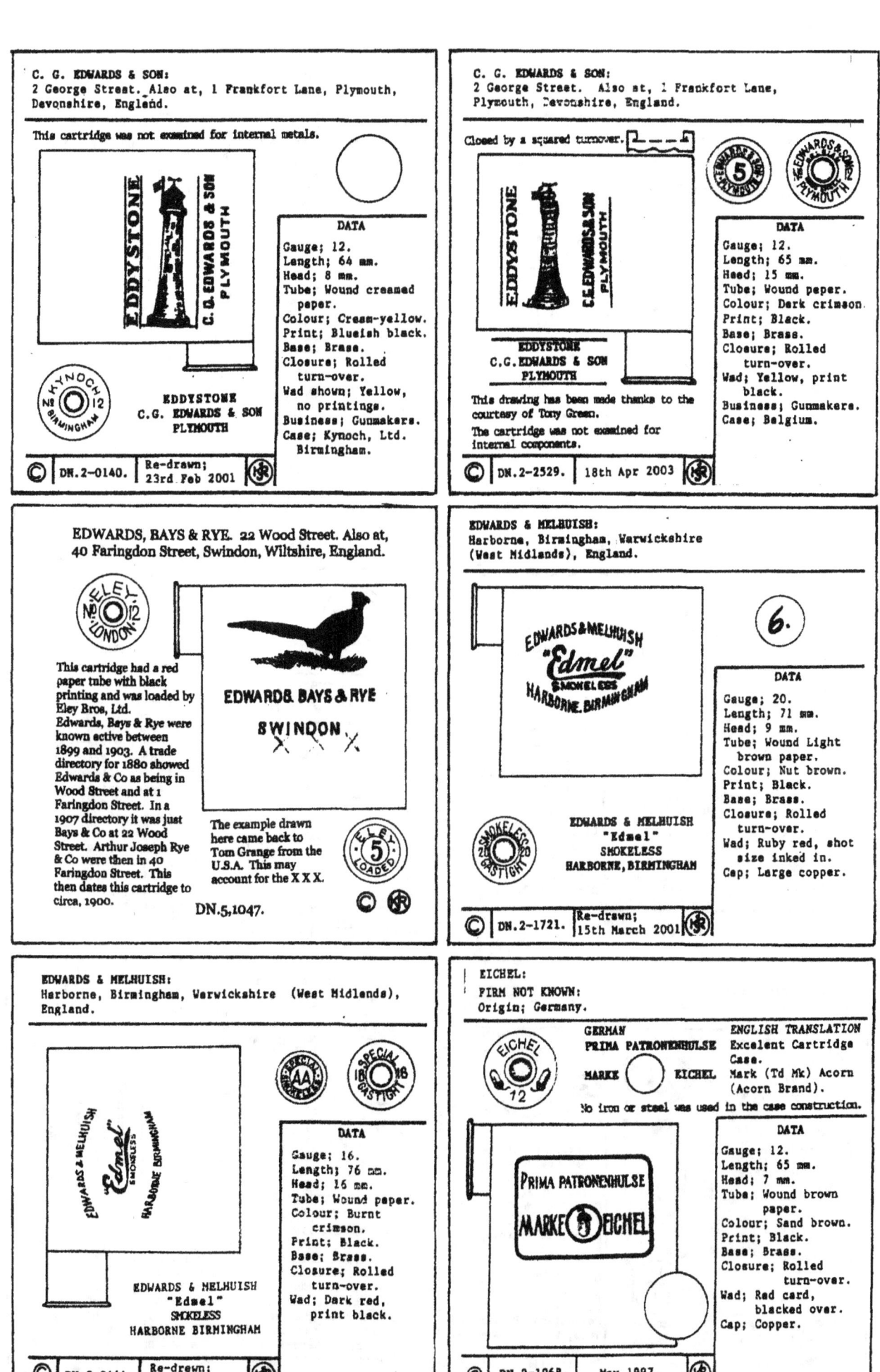

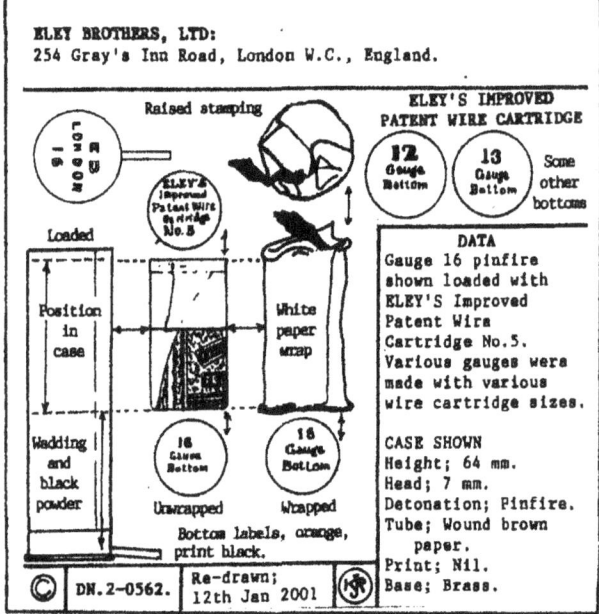

PLATE 94 [ELA – ELE]

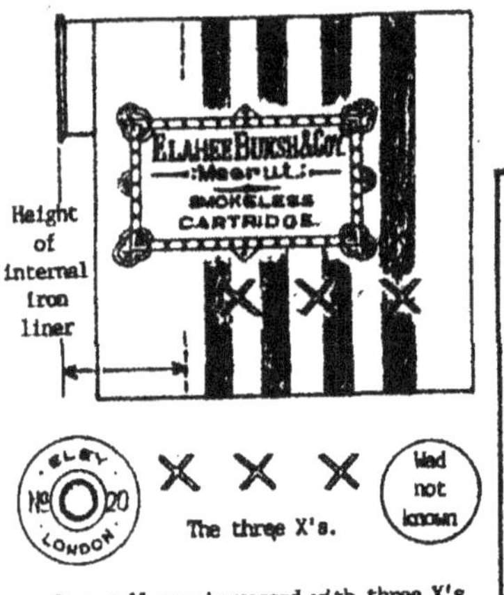

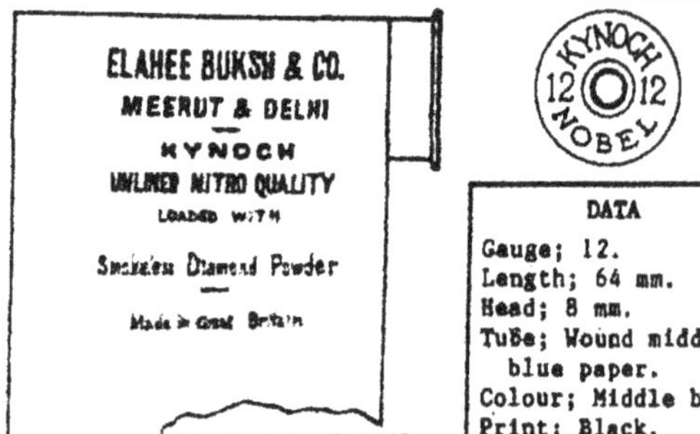

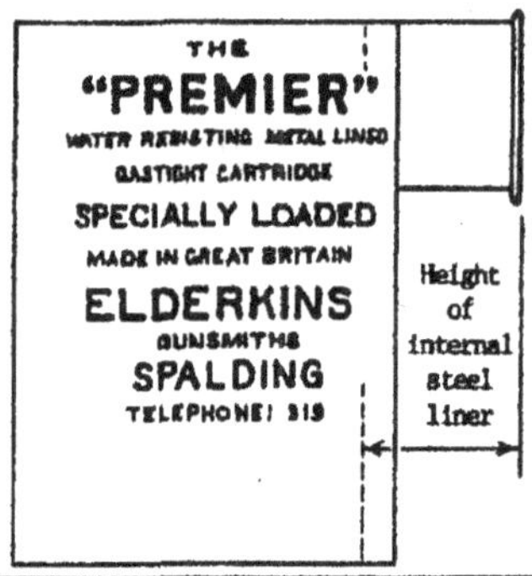

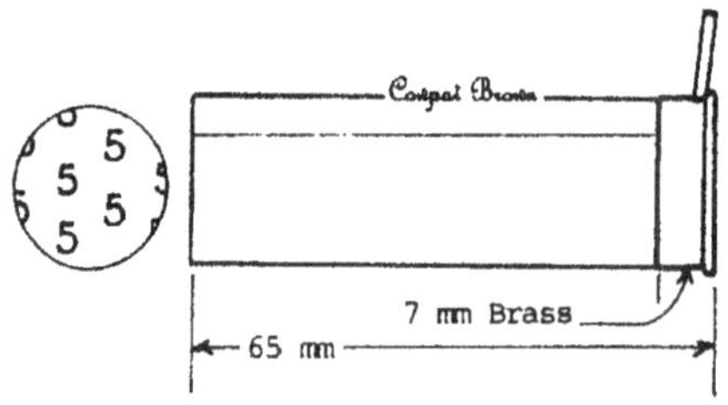

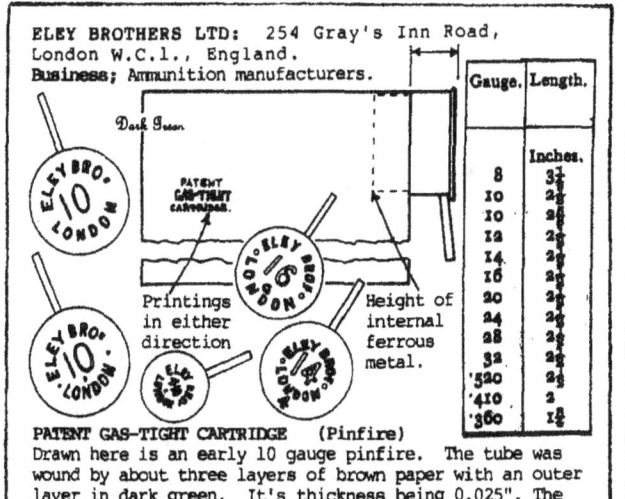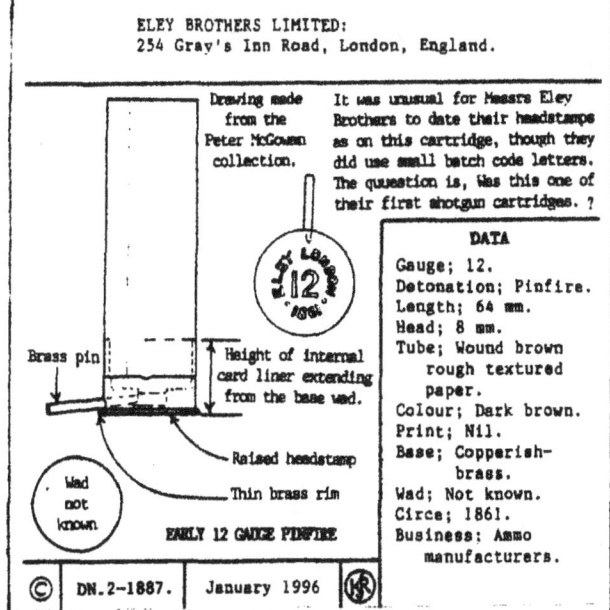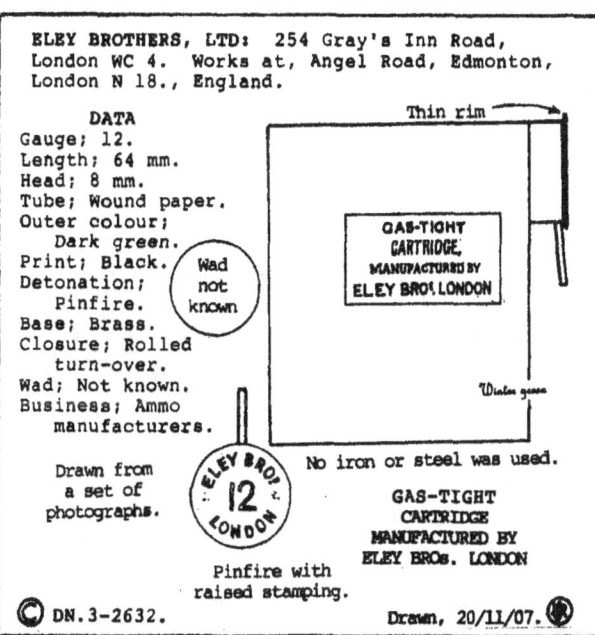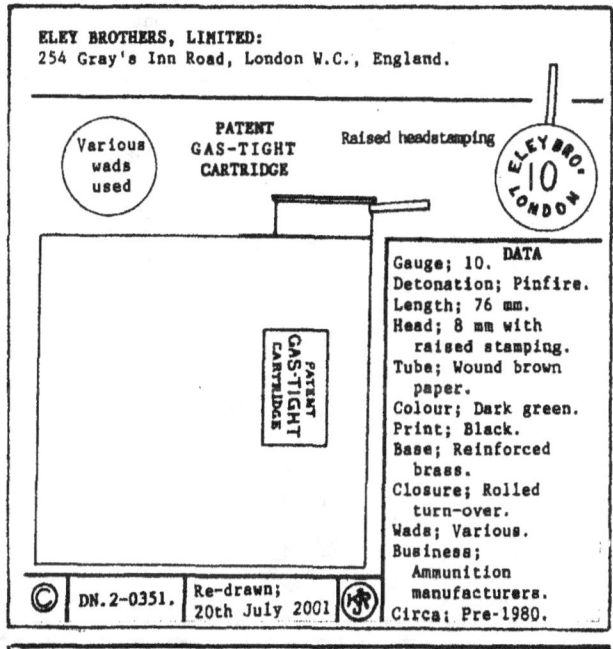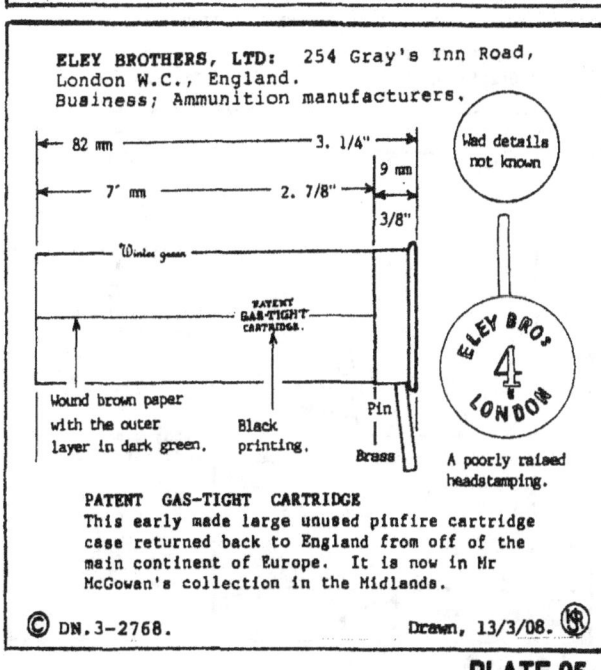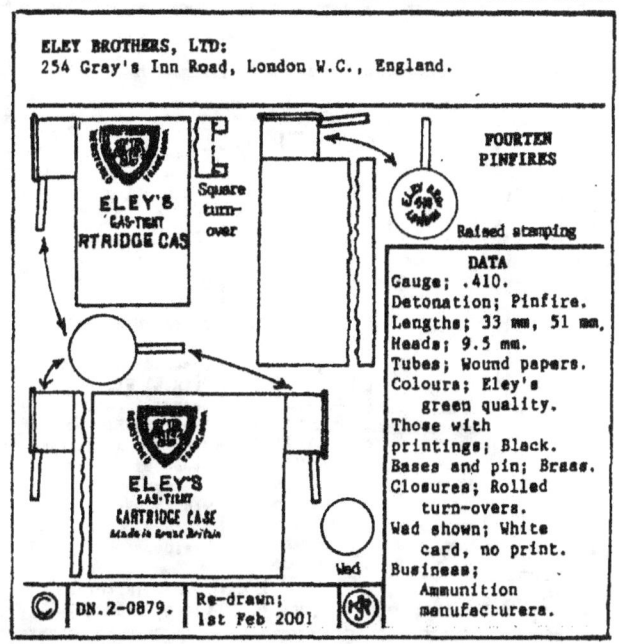

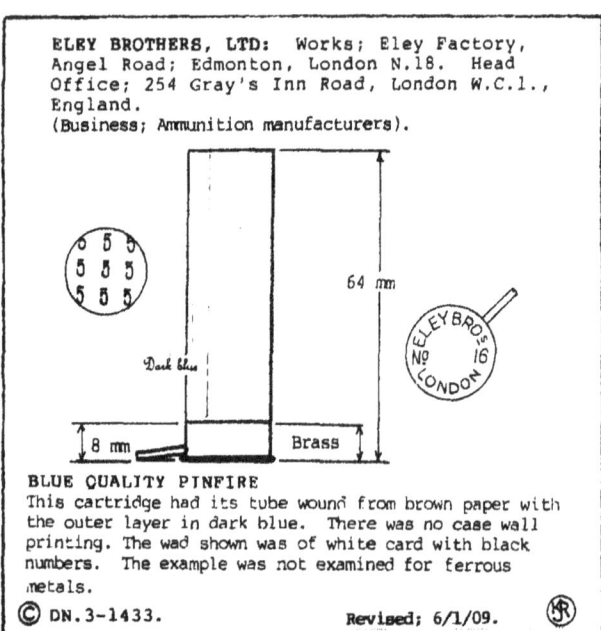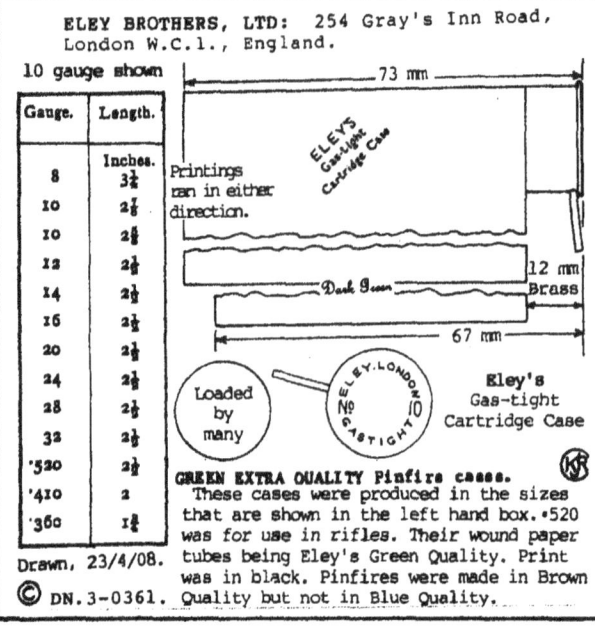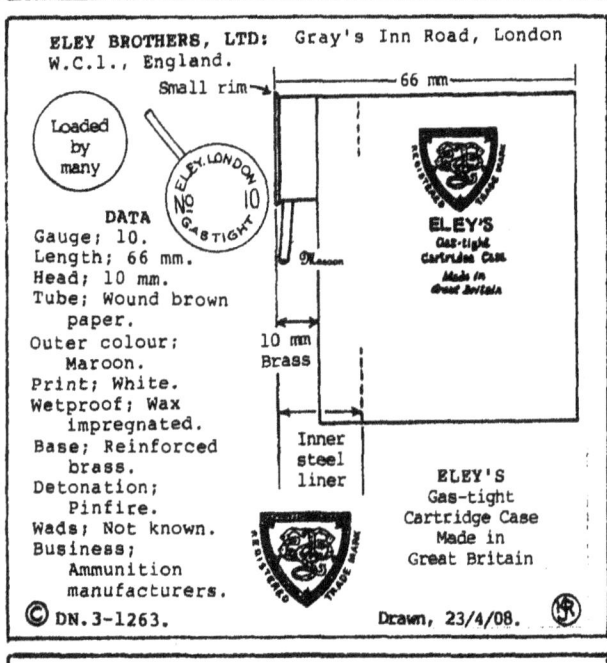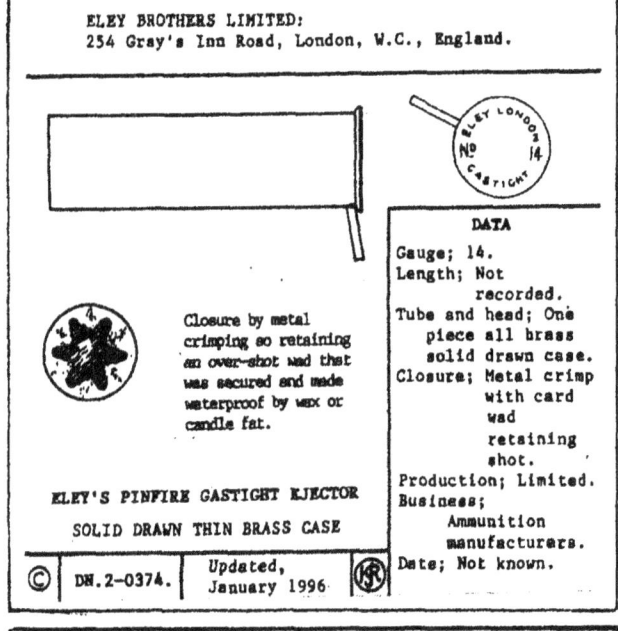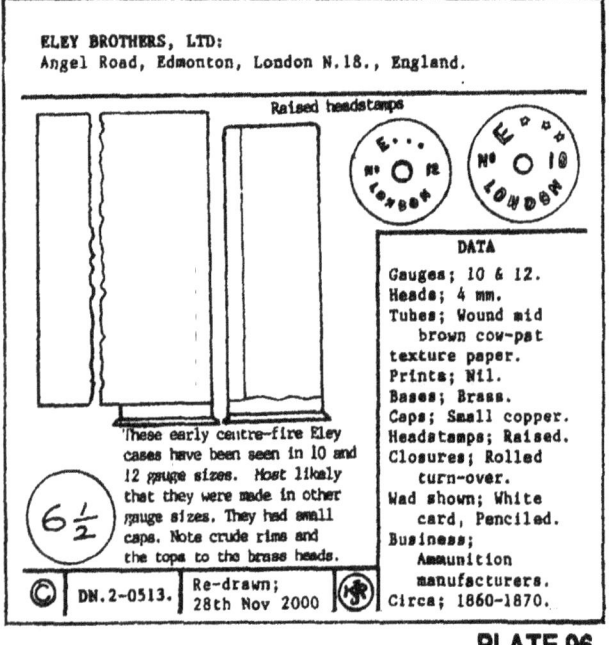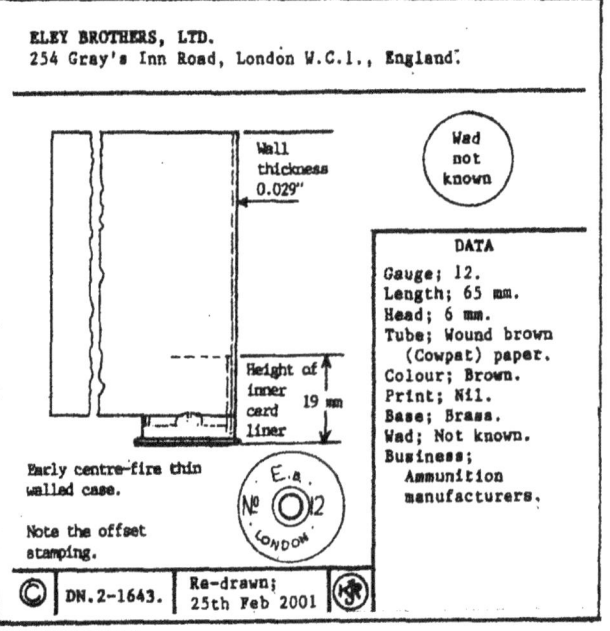

PLATE 96 [ELE-ELE]

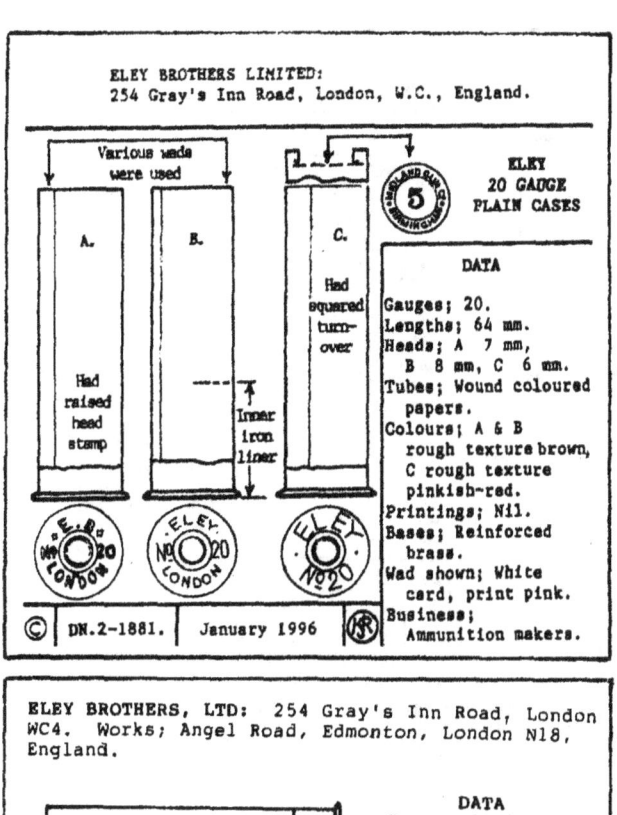

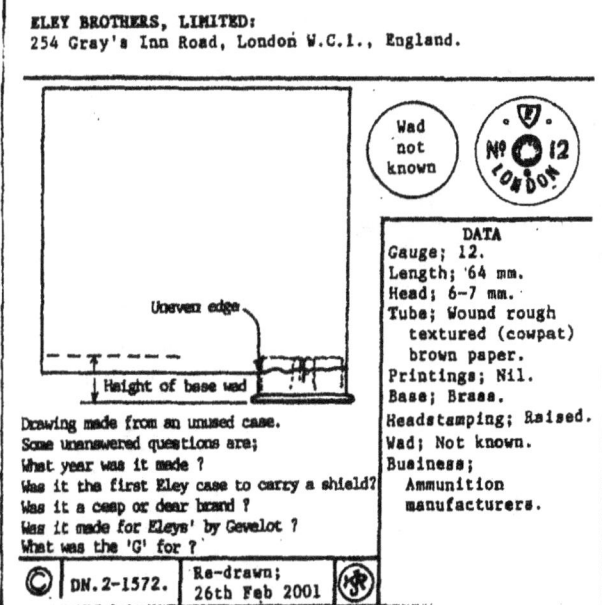

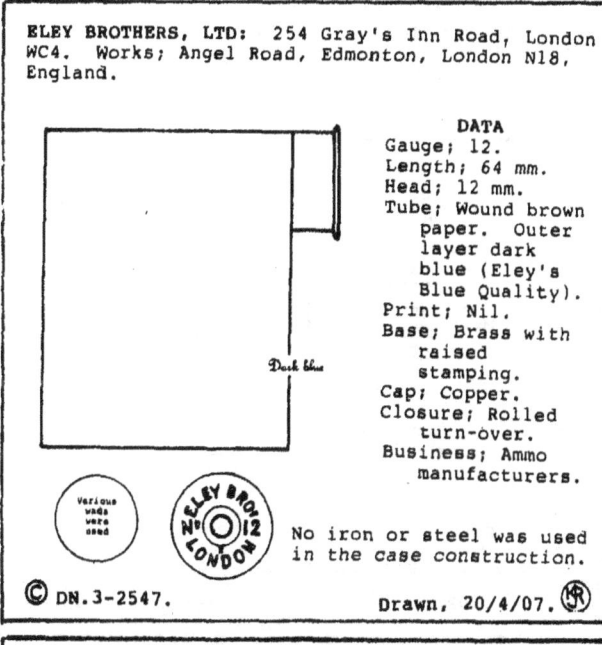

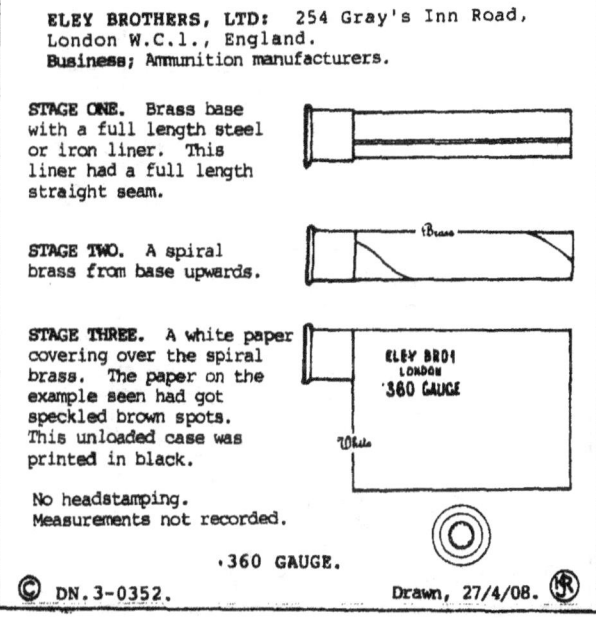

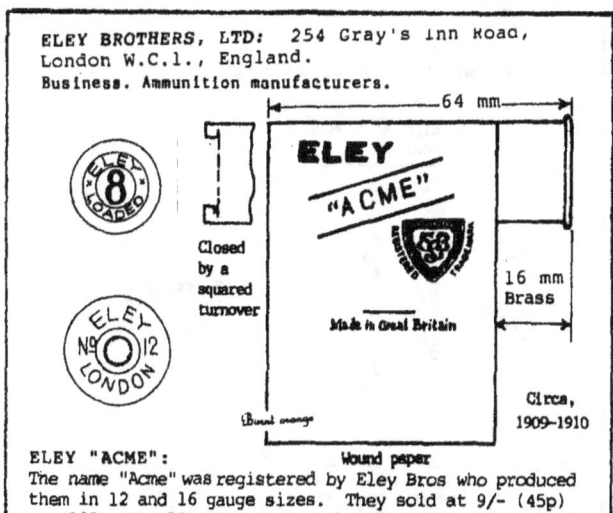

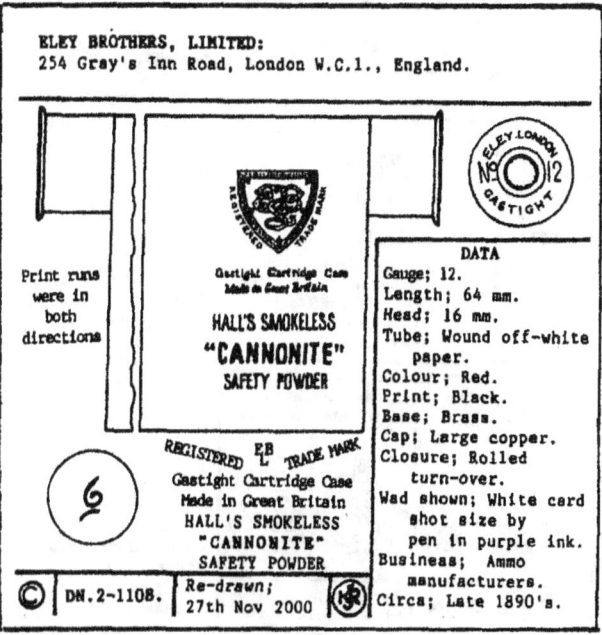

PLATE 97 [ELE – ELE]

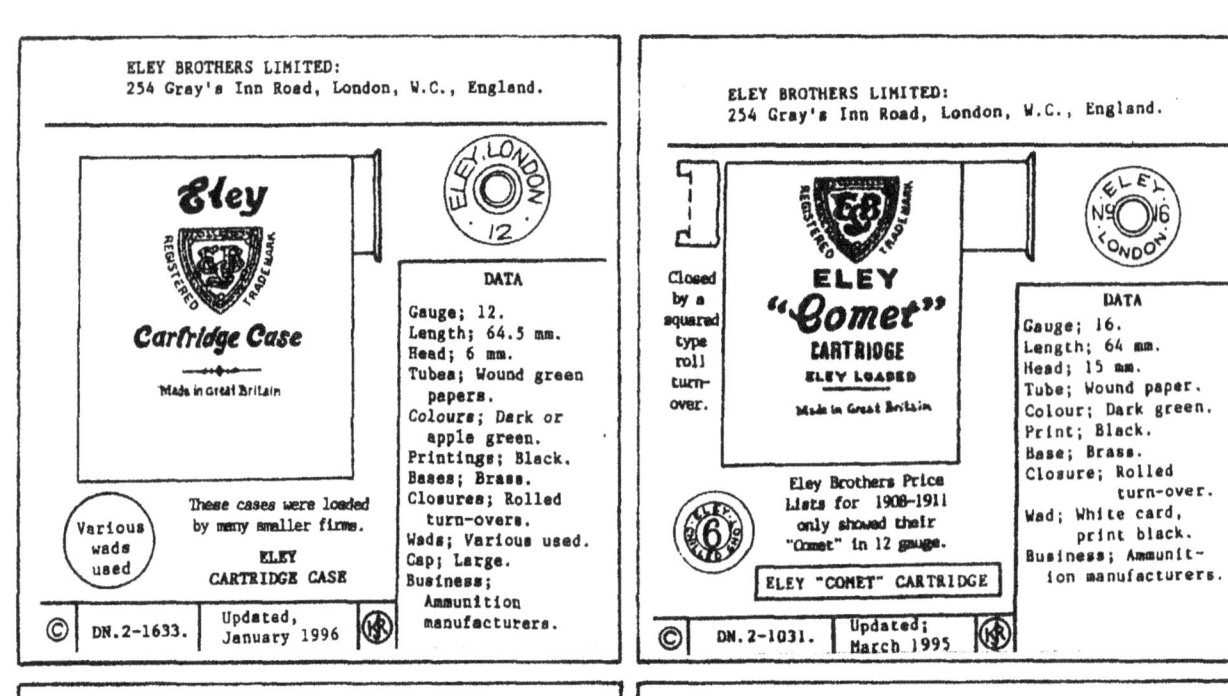

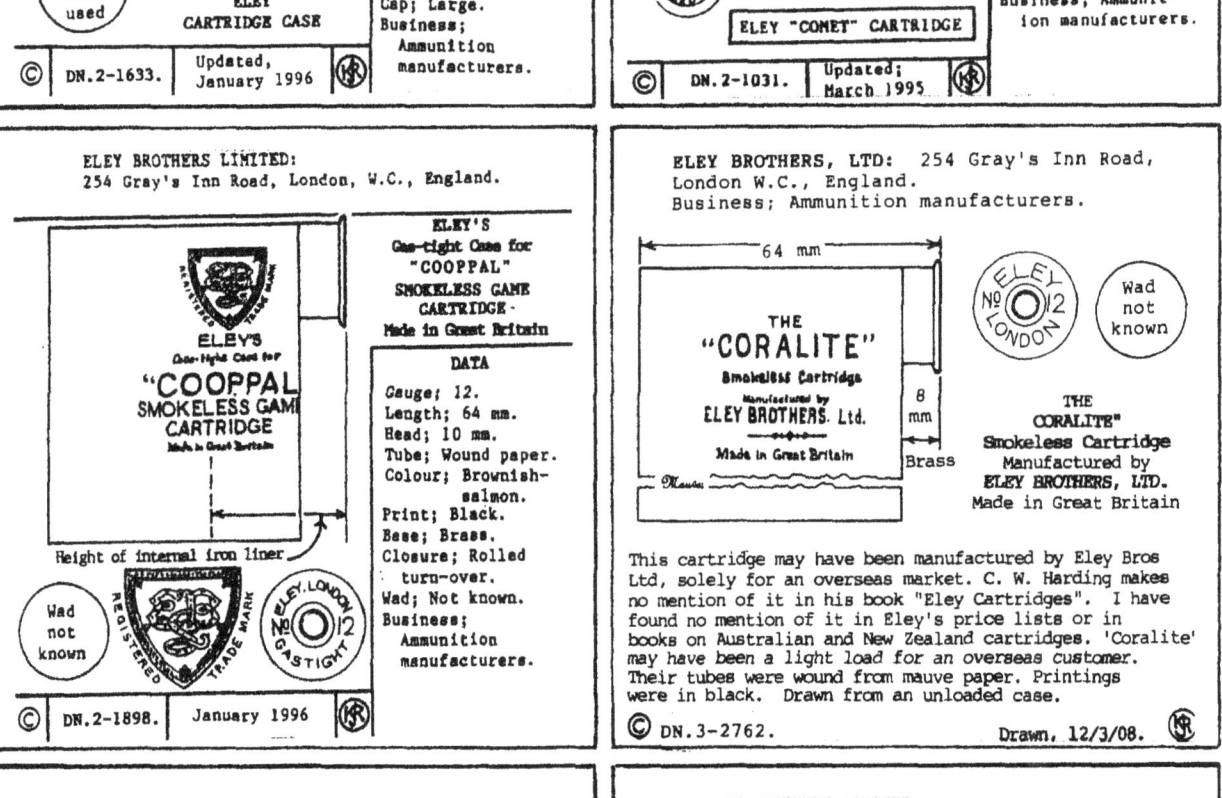

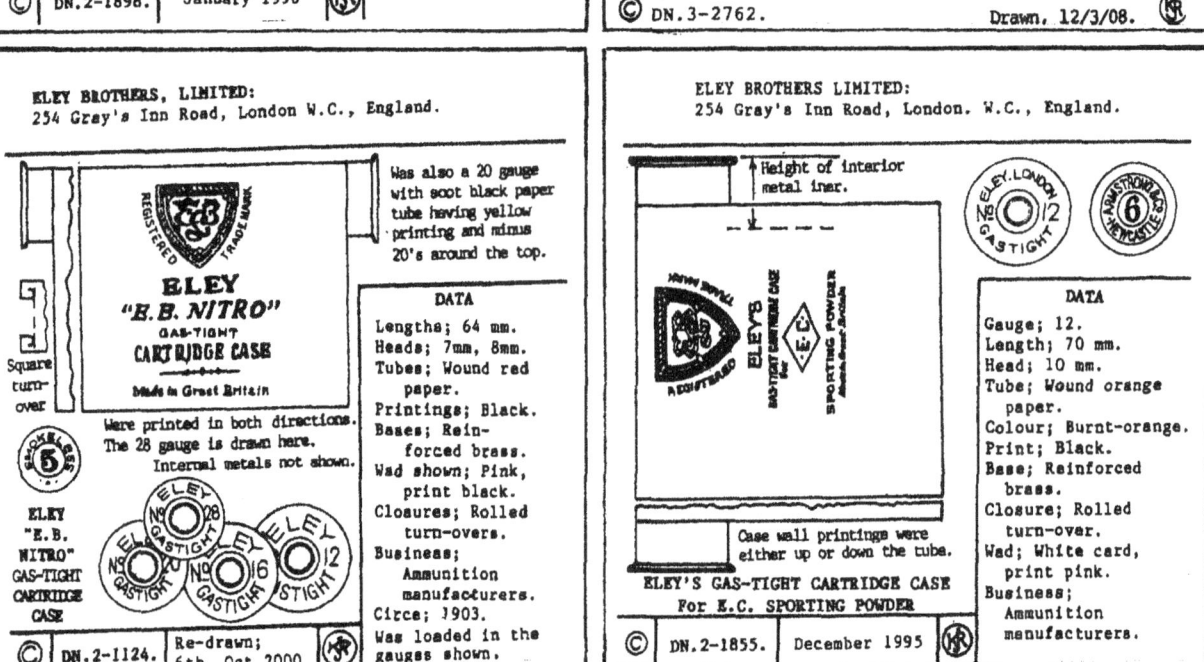

PLATE 98 [ELE - ELE]

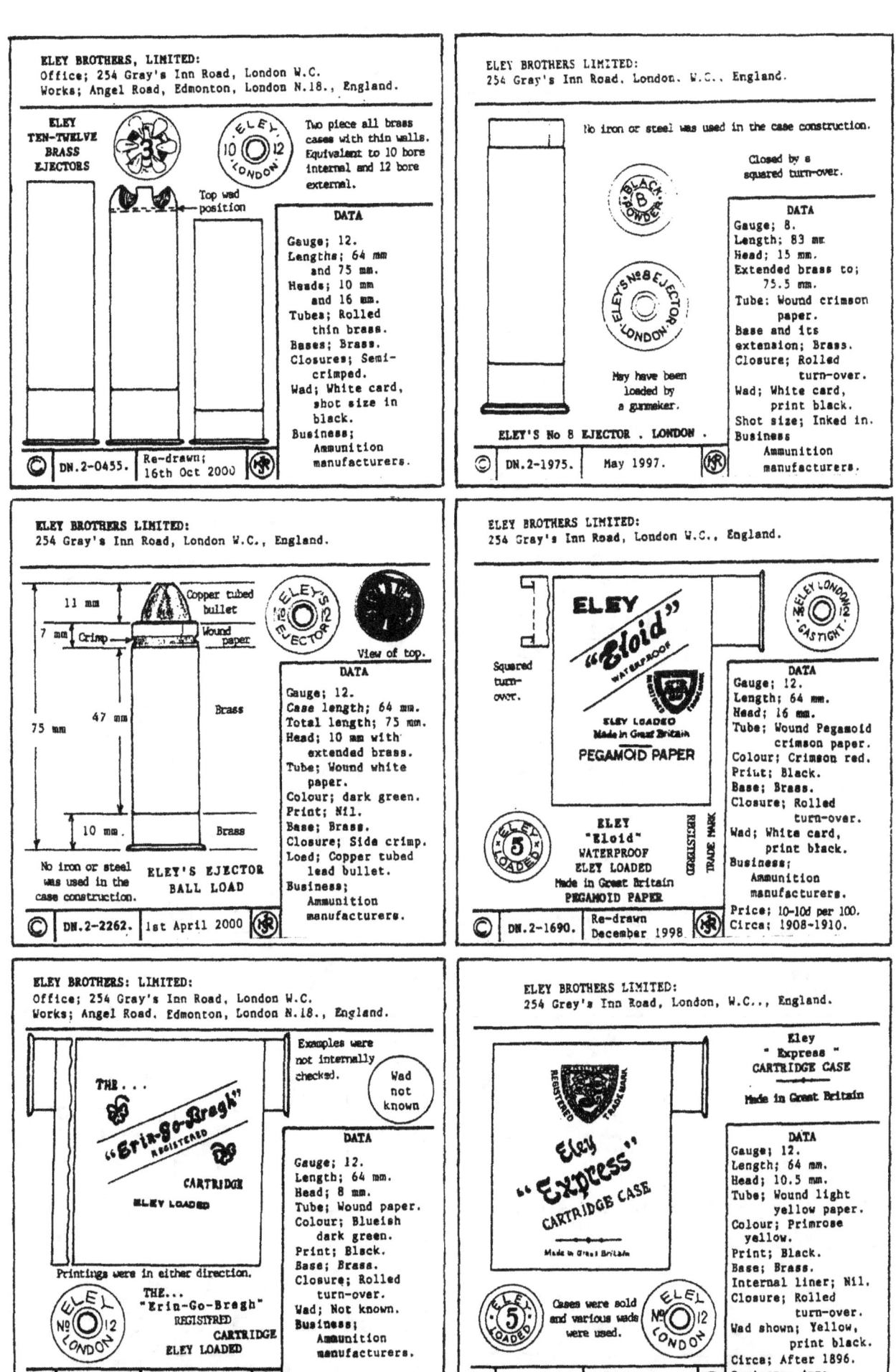

PLATE 99 [ELE – ELE]

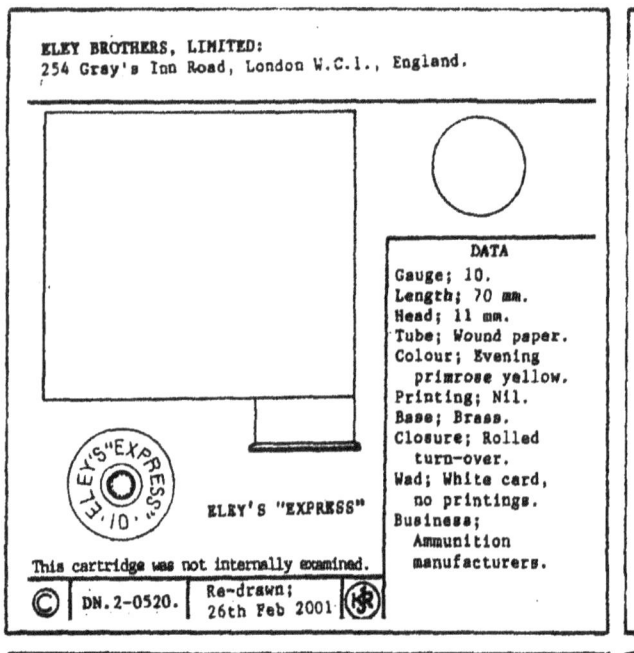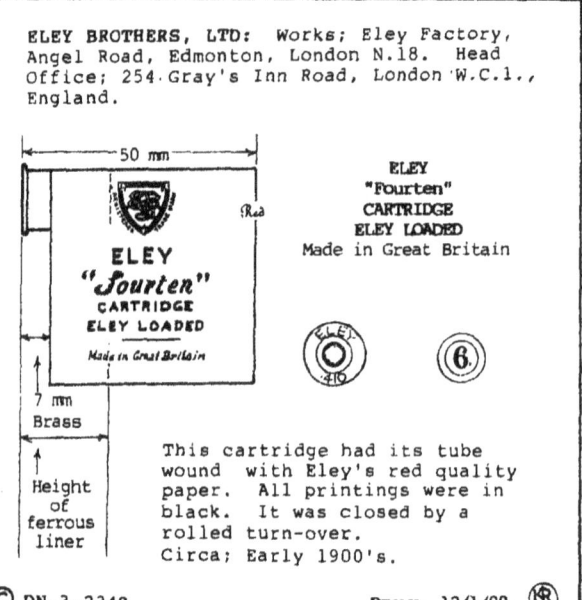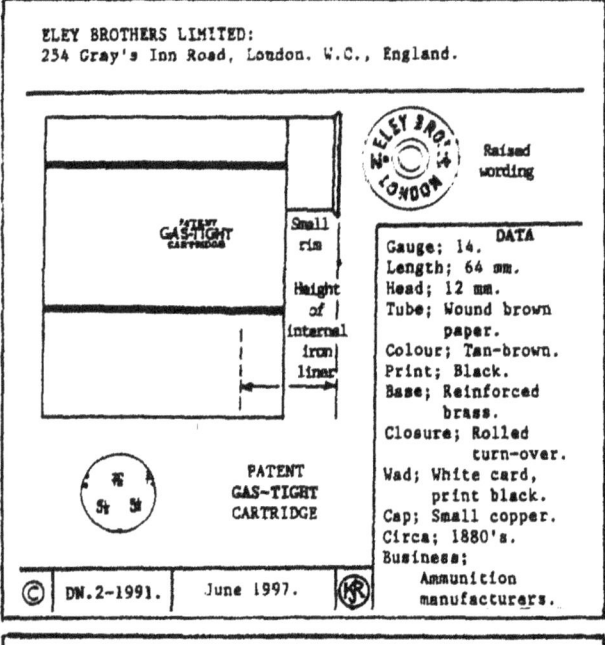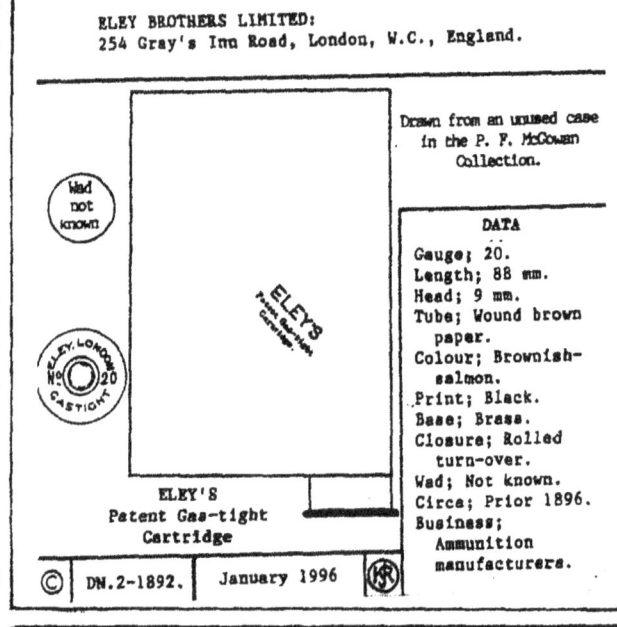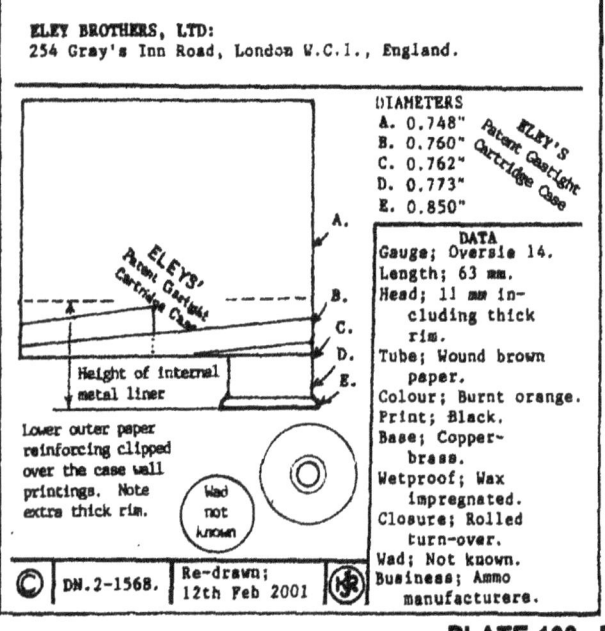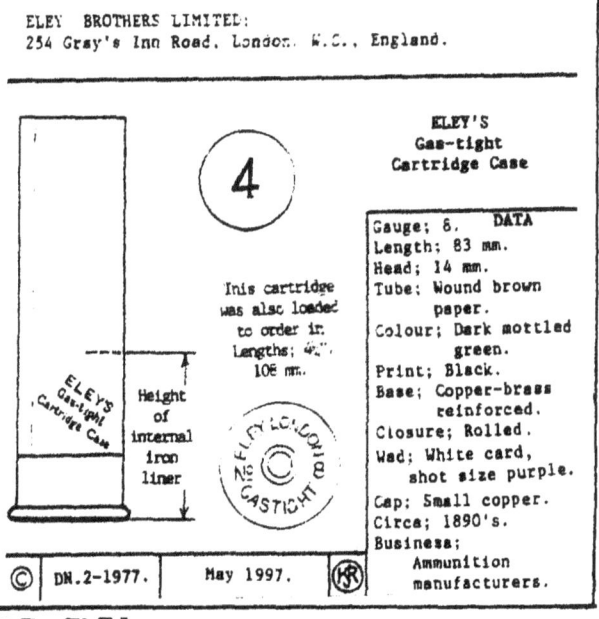

PLATE 100 [ELE - ELE]

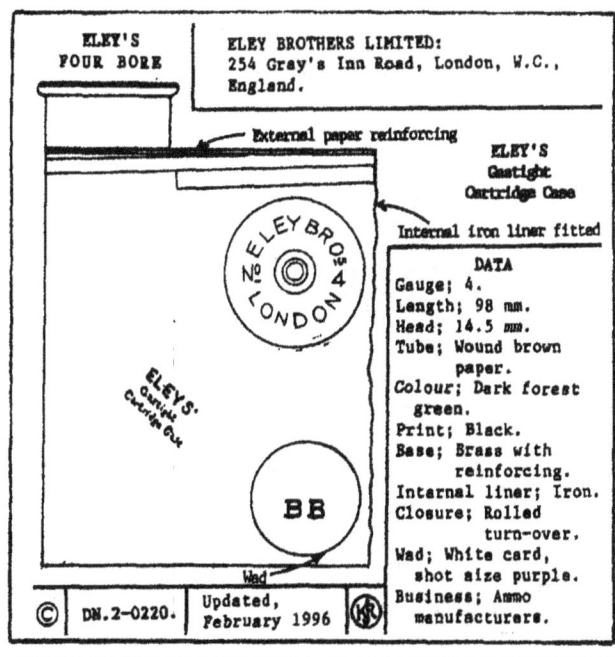
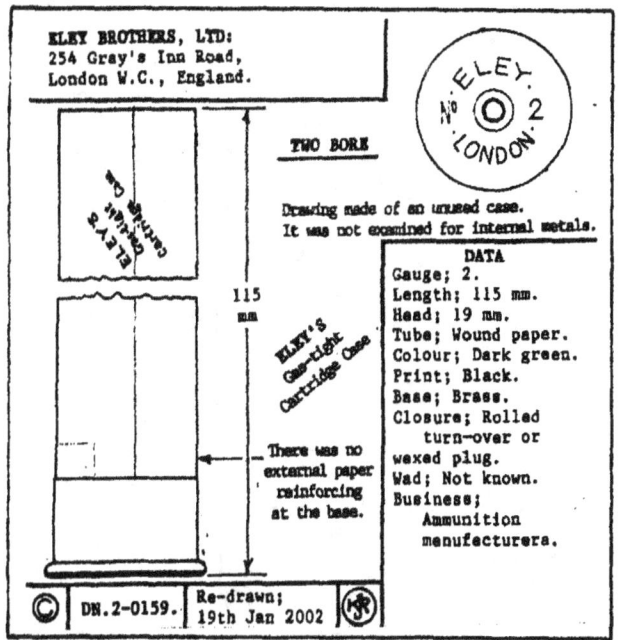
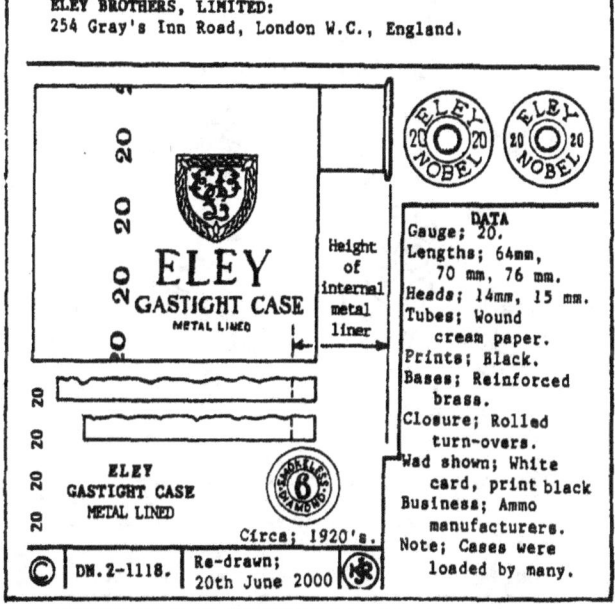
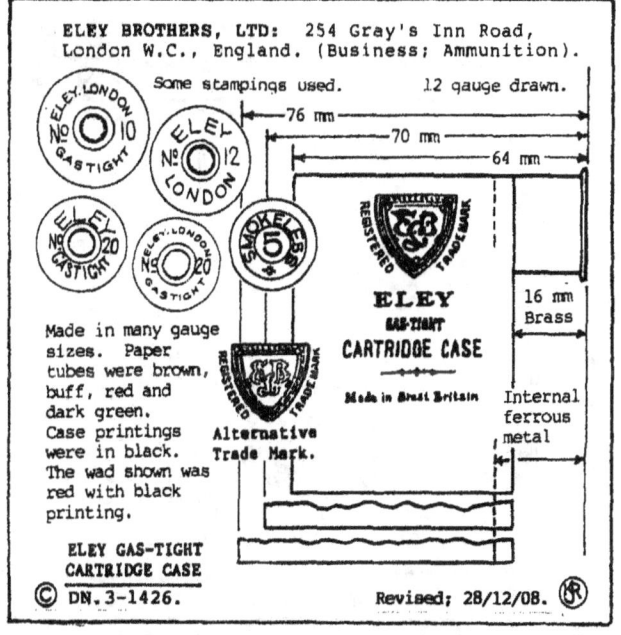
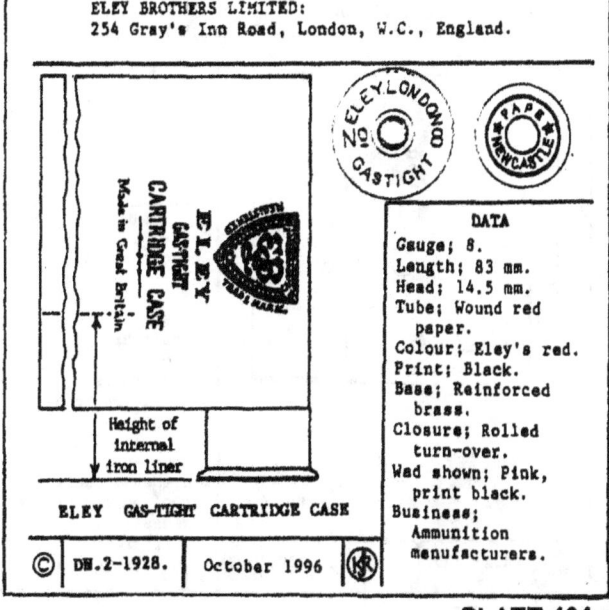
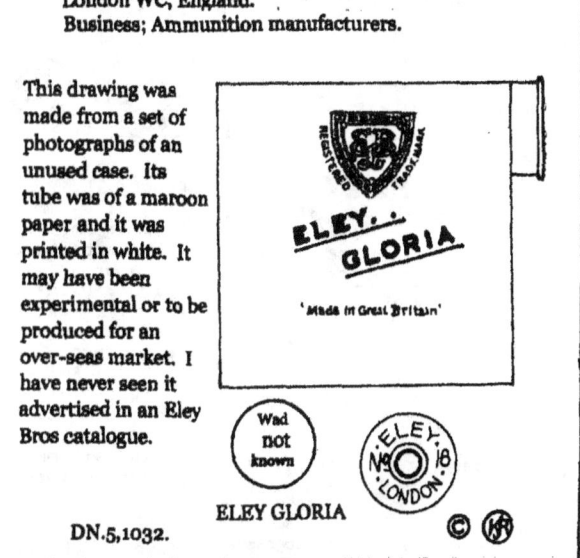

PLATE 101 [ELE – ELE]

ELEY BROTHERS LIMITED:
254 Gray's Inn Road, London. W.C., England.

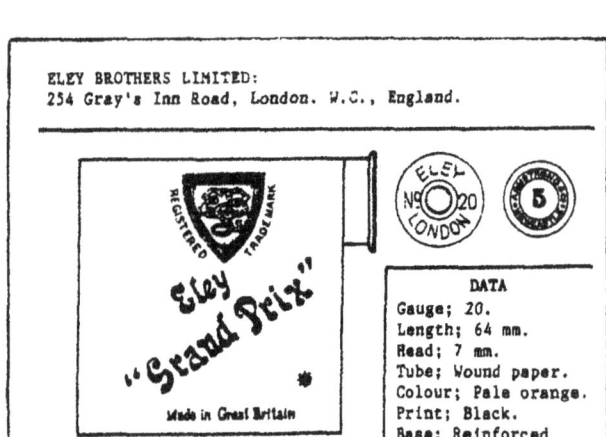

DATA
Gauge; 20.
Length; 64 mm.
Head; 7 mm.
Tube; Wound paper.
Colour; Pale orange.
Print; Black.
Base; Reinforced brass.
Closure; Rolled turn-over.
Wad shown; White card, print pink.
Business; Ammunition manufacturers.

I have headed this drawing Eley Bros Ltd. These case were purchased and loaded by many.

© DN.2-1990.   June 1997.

ELEY BROTHERS LIMITED:
254 Gray's Inn Road, London W.C., England.

DATA
Gauge; 20.
Length; 64 mm.
Head; 7.5 mm.
Tube; Wound black paper.
Colour; Soot black.
Print; Yellow.
Base; Reinforced brass.
Closure; Rolled turn-over.
Wad; White card, print red.
Business; Cartridge manufacturers.
Powder; Red Star.

© DN.2-2261.   31st March 2000

ELEY BROTHERS, LTD:
254 Gray's Inn Road, London. W.C., England.

Either round or squared rolls.

Also seen on an orange tan tube with the above trade mark. As on the drawing, it was made with a black tube and yellow print minus the ring of four 20's.

DATA
Gauge; 20.
Length; 64 mm.
Head; 7 mm.
Tube; Wound paper.
Colours; Cream, off-white, orange-tan, tan.
Print; Black.
Base; Brass.
Closure; Rolled turn-over.
Wad shown; White card red print.
Business; Manufacturers.

ELEY "GRAND PRIX"

© DN.2-1707.   Updated; February 1995

ELEY BROTHERS, LTD:
Head office; 254 Gray's Inn Road, London W.C.4. Works at; Angel Road, Edmonton, London N.18., England.

Most closed by a squared turnover — 64 mm — 8 mm Brass

Eley "Grand Prix"
Produced in 12 and 16 gauge with wound paper tubes of brownish-orange. 12's have also been seen in a few other colours, dark-tan, mid-blue and off-white. Case wall printings were in black. These other colours may have been products of World War One. The top card shown was of white card with red printing.

© DN.3-1709.   Drawn, 14/4/08.

ELEY BROTHERS, LTD: 254 Gray's Inn Road,
London WC.4. Works at, Angel Road, Edmonton, London N.18., England.

Plum red

ELEY
"Juno"
CARTRIDGE
ELEY LOADED
Made in Great Britain

DATA
Gauge; 16.
Length; 64 mm.
Head; 8 mm.
Tube; Wound red paper.
Colour; Plum-red.
Print; Black.
Base; Brass.
Cap; Copper.
Closure; Rolled turn-over.
Wad; White card, print black.
Business; Ammo manufacturers.

ELEY
"Juno"
CARTRIDGE
ELEY LOADED
Made in Great Britain

Drawn from a set of photographs.

© DN.3-2608.   Drawn, 9/11/07.

ELEY BROTHERS, LIMITED:
254 Gray's Inn Road, London W.C., England.

ELEY
LAB
CASE.
TRADE MARK
PROOF

Wad not known

Height of internal metal liner.

ELEY
LAB
CASE
TRADE
MARK
PROOF

DATA
Gauge; 12.
Length; 64 mm.
Head; 16 mm.
Tube; Wound buff paper.
Colour; Brownish buff.
Print; Black.
Base; Reinforced brass.
Closure; Rolled turn-over.
Wad; (Most likely a proof powder charge).
Business; Cartridge manufacturers.

© DN.2-2335.   15th Sept 2000

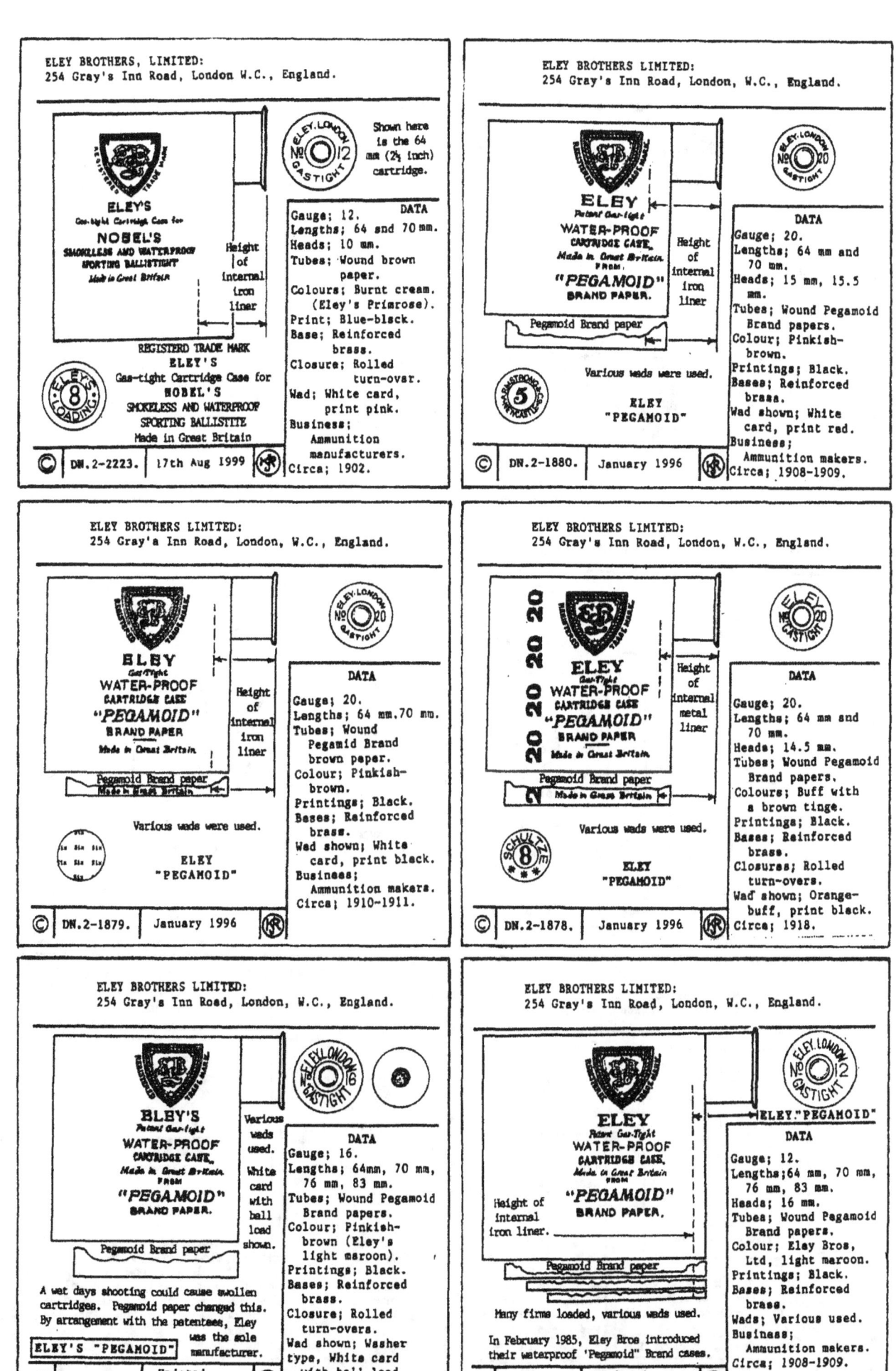

PLATE 103 [ELE - ELE]

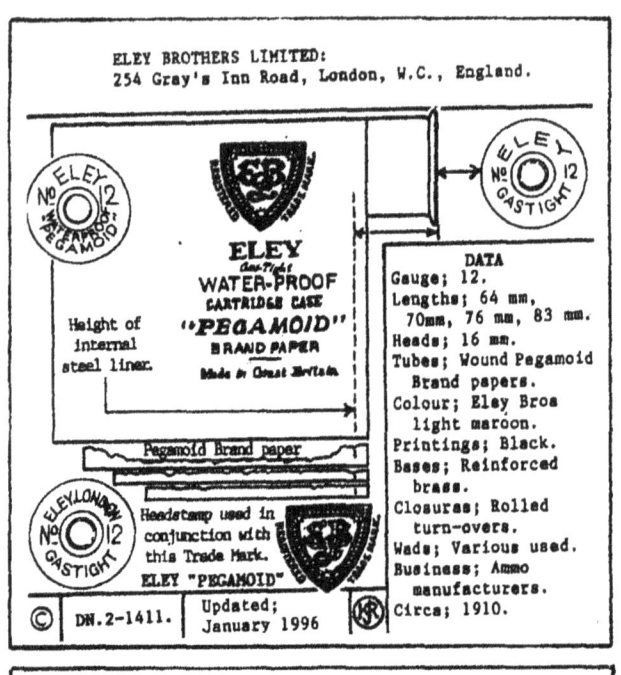
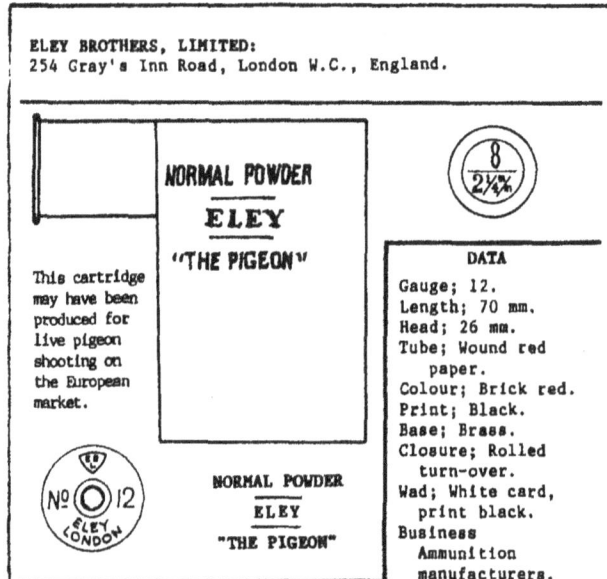

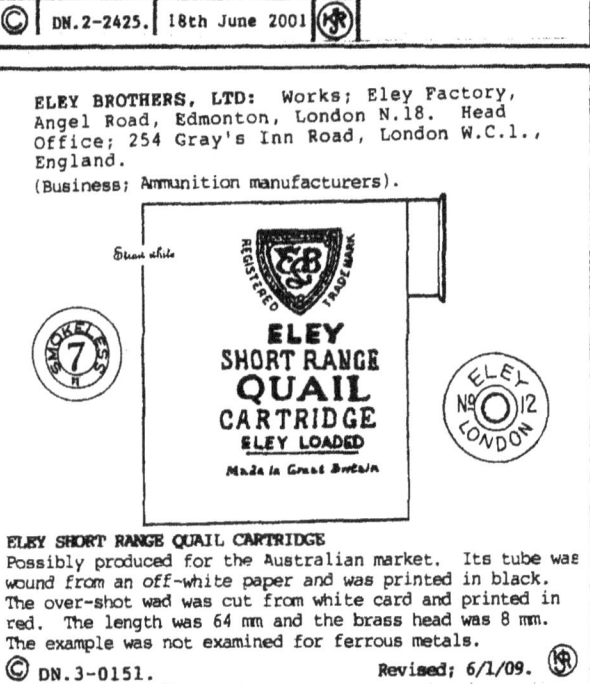

ELEY SHORT RANGE QUAIL CARTRIDGE
Possibly produced for the Australian market. Its tube was wound from an off-white paper and was printed in black. The over-shot wad was cut from white card and printed in red. The length was 64 mm and the brass head was 8 mm. The example was not examined for ferrous metals.

© DN.3-0151.   Revised; 6/1/09.

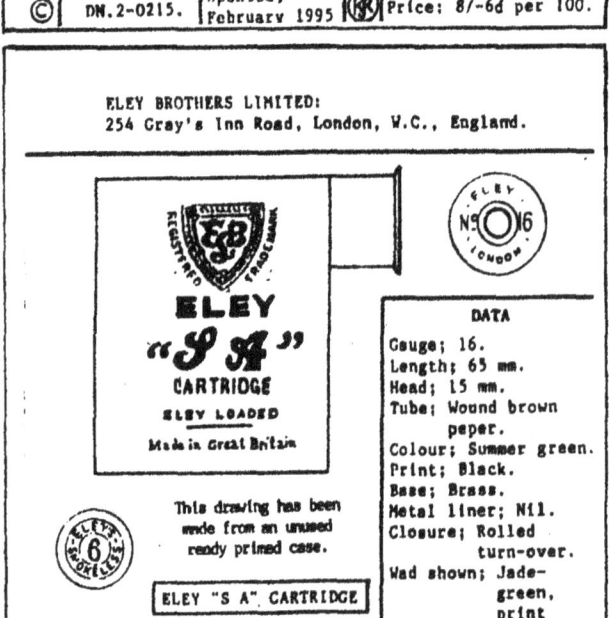
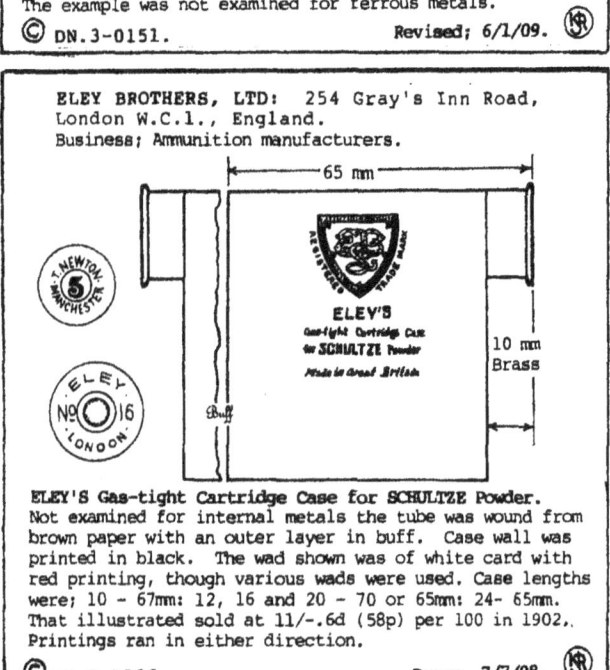

ELEY'S Gas-tight Cartridge Case for SCHULTZE Powder.
Not examined for internal metals the tube was wound from brown paper with an outer layer in buff. Case wall was printed in black. The wad shown was of white card with red printing, though various wads were used. Case lengths were; 10 - 67mm: 12, 16 and 20 - 70 or 65mm: 24- 65mm. That illustrated sold at 11/-.6d (58p) per 100 in 1902. Printings ran in either direction.

© DN.3-1126.   Drawn, 7/7/08.

PLATE 104 [ELE - ELE]

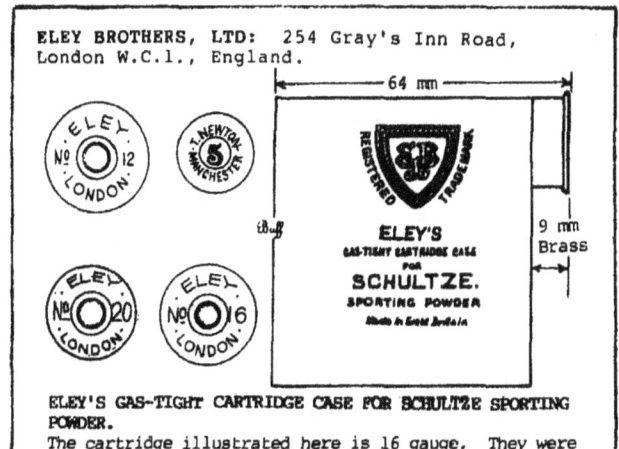

ELEY BROTHERS, LTD: 254 Gray's Inn Road, London W.C.1., England.

ELEY'S GAS-TIGHT CARTRIDGE CASE FOR SCHULTZE SPORTING POWDER.
The cartridge illustrated here is 16 gauge. They were also produced in other gauge sizes. Although not examined for internal metals, being Gas-tight I would expect the brass head to have been metal reinforced. The tube was wound from a pinkish-buff paper and printed in black. Case wall printings ran in either direction. These cases were loaded by many. The wad shown was white card with red printing.

© DN.3-1069.   Drawn, 3/5/08.

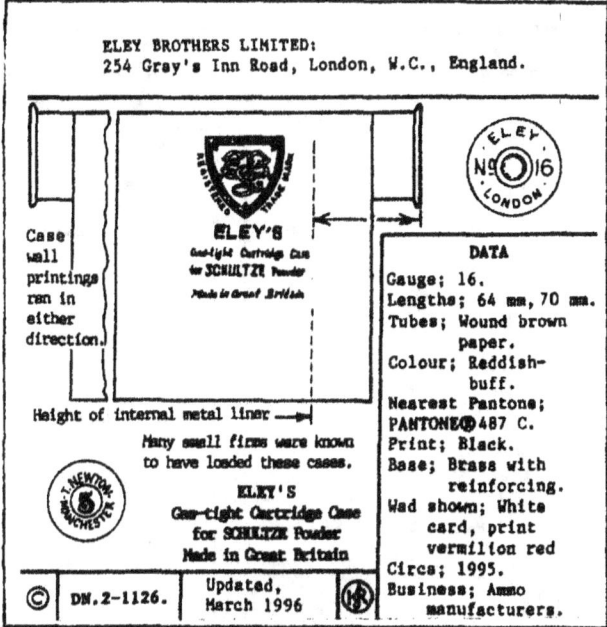

ELEY BROTHERS LIMITED: 254 Gray's Inn Road, London, W.C., England.

Case wall printings ran in either direction.

Height of internal metal liner

Many small firms were known to have loaded these cases.

ELEY'S Gas-tight Cartridge Case for SCHULTZE Powder Made in Great Britain

DATA
Gauge; 16.
Lengths; 64 mm, 70 mm.
Tubes; Wound brown paper.
Colour; Reddish-buff.
Nearest Pantone; PANTONE® 487 C.
Print; Black.
Base; Brass with reinforcing.
Wad shown; White card, print vermilion red
Circa; 1995.
Business; Ammo manufacturers.

© DN.2-1126.   Updated, March 1996

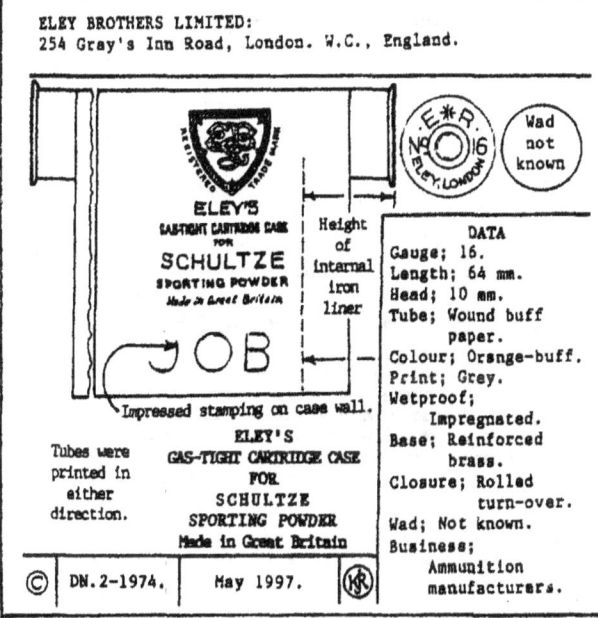

ELEY BROTHERS LIMITED: 254 Gray's Inn Road, London. W.C., England.

Impressed stamping on case wall.
Tubes were printed in either direction.

ELEY'S GAS-TIGHT CARTRIDGE CASE FOR SCHULTZE SPORTING POWDER Made in Great Britain

DATA
Gauge; 16.
Length; 64 mm.
Head; 10 mm.
Tube; Wound buff paper.
Colour; Orange-buff.
Print; Grey.
Wetproof; Impregnated.
Base; Reinforced brass.
Closure; Rolled turn-over.
Wad; Not known.
Business; Ammunition manufacturers.

© DN.2-1974.   May 1997.

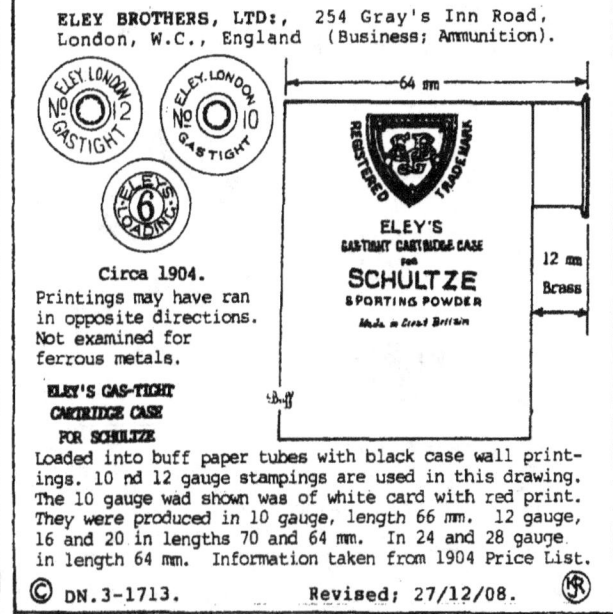

ELEY BROTHERS, LTD:, 254 Gray's Inn Road, London, W.C., England (Business; Ammunition).

Circa 1904.
Printings may have ran in opposite directions. Not examined for ferrous metals.

ELEY'S GAS-TIGHT CARTRIDGE CASE FOR SCHULTZE
Loaded into buff paper tubes with black case wall printings. 10 nd 12 gauge stampings are used in this drawing. The 10 gauge wad shown was of white card with red print. They were produced in 10 gauge, length 66 mm. 12 gauge, 16 and 20 in lengths 70 and 64 mm. In 24 and 28 gauge. in length 64 mm. Information taken from 1904 Price List.

© DN.3-1713.   Revised; 27/12/08.

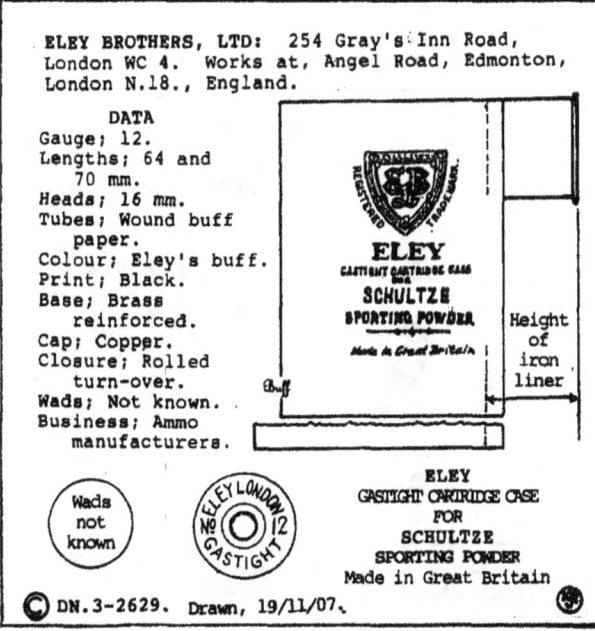

ELEY BROTHERS, LTD: 254 Gray's Inn Road, London WC 4. Works at, Angel Road, Edmonton, London N.18., England.

DATA
Gauge; 12.
Lengths; 64 and 70 mm.
Heads; 16 mm.
Tubes; Wound buff paper.
Colour; Eley's buff.
Print; Black.
Base; Brass reinforced.
Cap; Copper.
Closure; Rolled turn-over.
Wads; Not known.
Business; Ammo manufacturers.

ELEY GASTIGHT CARTRIDGE CASE FOR SCHULTZE SPORTING POWDER Made in Great Britain

© DN.3-2629. Drawn, 19/11/07.

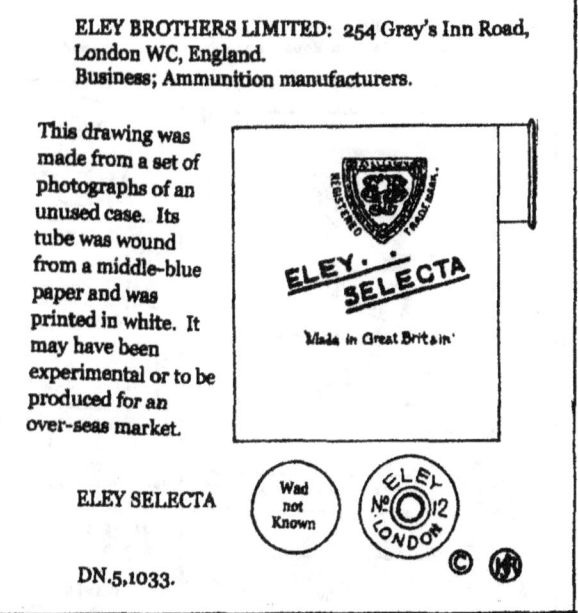

ELEY BROTHERS LIMITED: 254 Gray's Inn Road, London WC, England.
Business; Ammunition manufacturers.

This drawing was made from a set of photographs of an unused case. Its tube was wound from a middle-blue paper and was printed in white. It may have been experimental or to be produced for an over-seas market.

ELEY SELECTA

DN.5,1033.

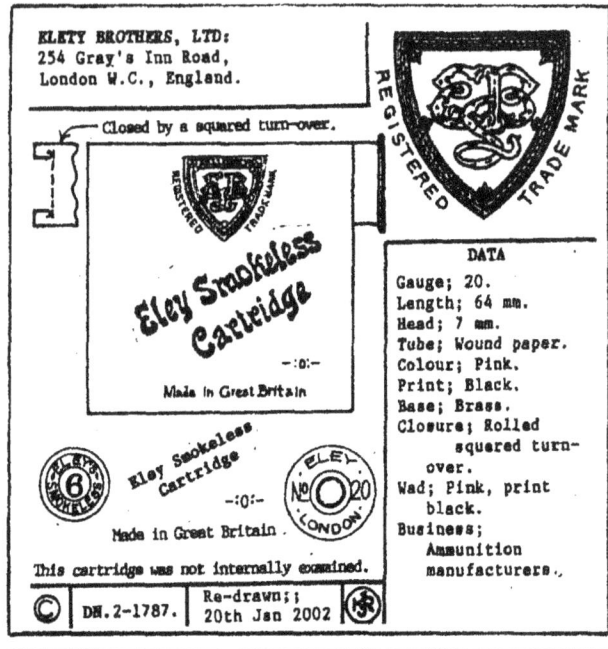

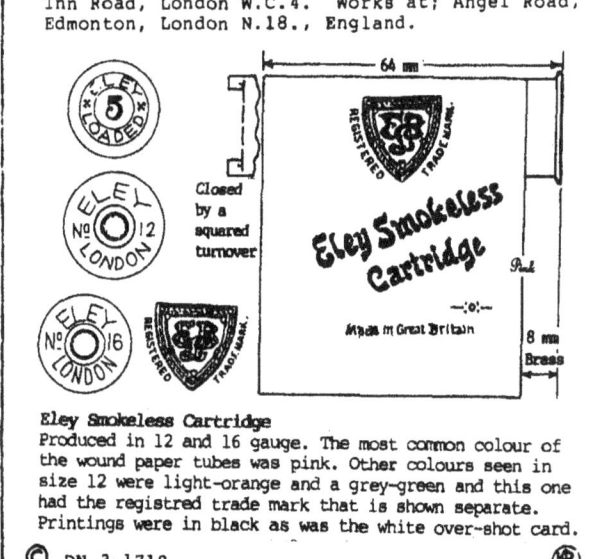
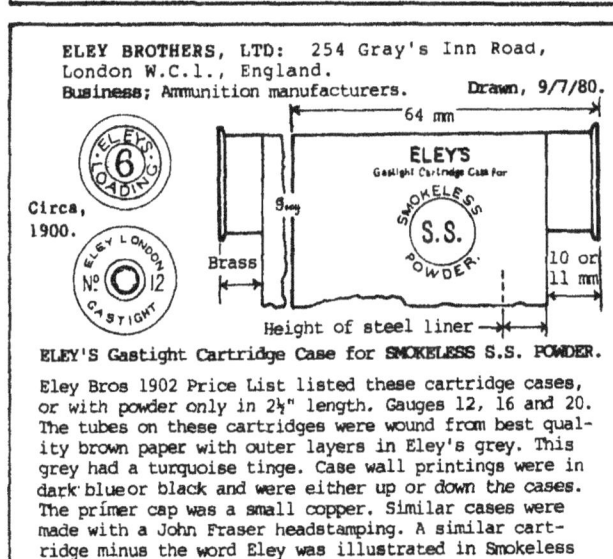
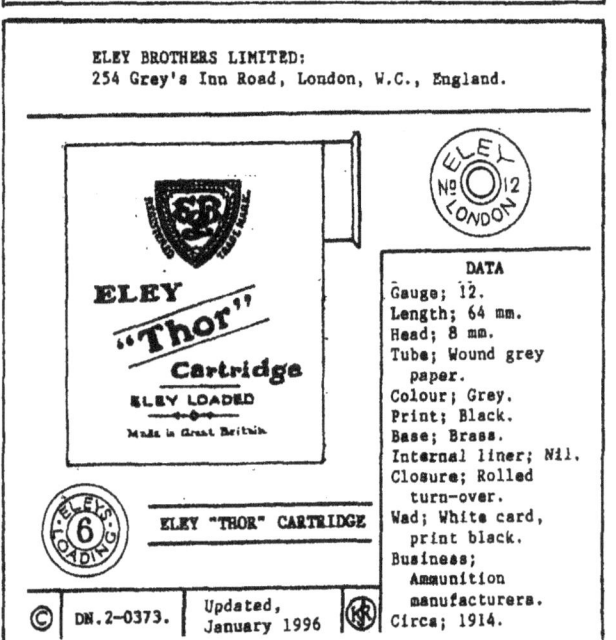
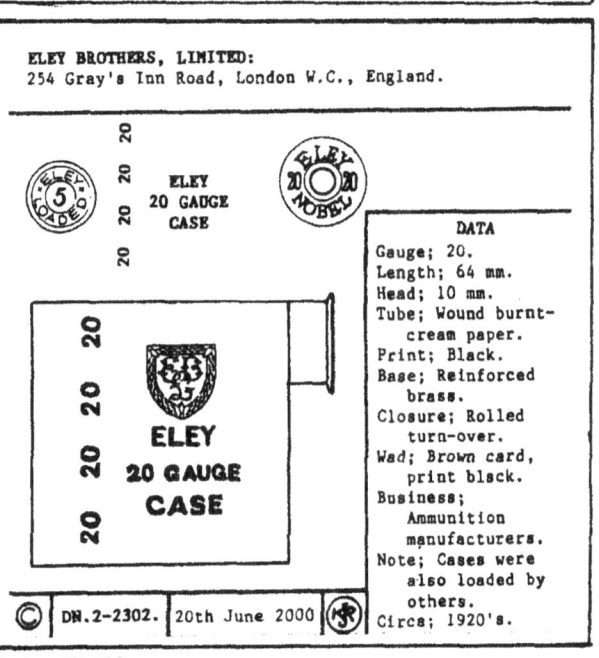

PLATE 106 [ELE – ELE]

ELEY BROTHERS LIMITED:
254 Gray's Inn Road, London, W.C., England.

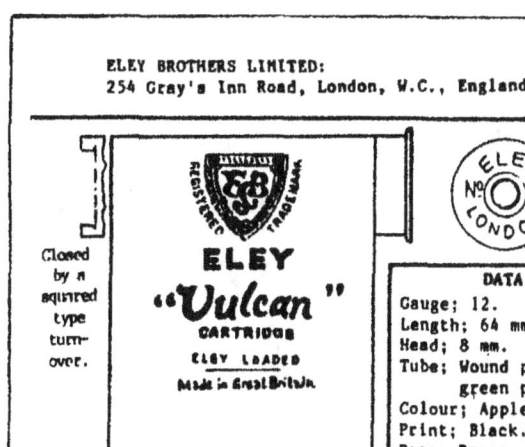

Closed by a squared type turn-over.

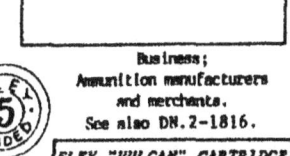

Business; Ammunition manufacturers and merchants. See also DN.2-1816.

ELEY "VULCAN" CARTRIDGE

DATA
Gauge; 12.
Length; 64 mm.
Head; 8 mm.
Tube; Wound pale green paper.
Colour; Apple green.
Print; Black.
Base; Brass.
Closure; Rolled turn-over.
Wad; Yellow, print black.
Powder; Eley 33 Gr Smokeless.
Shot charge; 15/16 oz.
Circa; 1910-1911.

© DN.2-0293.   Updated; February 1995

ELEY BROTHERS: 254 GRAY'S INN RD, LONDON. W.C.
Business. Ammunition manufacturers.

DN.5,1035.

ELEY "Vulcan"
These cartridges had an apple green paper tube with black case wall printing. Top wads with shot sizes 5 and 6 have been seen printed in black on yellow card. Closure was by a squared turn-over.

ELEY BROTHERS LIMITED:
254 Gray's Inn Road, London. W.C., England.

ELEY "UNIVERSAL" CARTRIDGE

DATA
Gauge; 20.
Length; 64.5 mm.
Head; 7 mm.
Tube; Wound paper.
Colour; Off-white.
Print; Black.
Base; Brass.
Closure; Rolled turn-over.
Wad; White card, print pinkish-red.
Business; Ammunition Manufacturers.

© DN.2-1074.   Updated; December 1994

ELEY BROTHERS, LTD: 254 Gray's Inn Road, London W.C., England.

ELEY "UNIVERSAL" CARTRIDGE
ELEY LOADED
Made in Great Britain

Pale brown
65 mm — 2. 1/2"
8 mm
5/16"
Brass
Wound paper

This cartridge had a tube which was wound from off-white, or so called, light brown paper. The case wall printing was in black. Eley Brothers limited produced their "Universal" cartridges in 12, 16 and 20 gauge sizes. The powder used was their Best T.S. Black. In 1909, these were sold at 7/- (35p) per 100.

© DN.3-2752.   Drawn, 10/3/08.

ELEY BROTHERS, LTD: 254 Gray's Inn Road, London WC 4. Works at, Angel Road, Edmonton, London N 18., England.

 Wad not known

Third quality. Indented three X's.

DATA
Gauge; 12.
Length; 64 mm.
Head; 19 mm.
Tube; Wound maroon paper.
Colour; Eley's light-maroon.
Print; Black.
Base; Brass.
Cap; Copper.
Closure; Rolled turn-over.
Wad; Not known.
Business; Ammo manufacturers.

ELEY'S
Gastight Cartridge Case for
WALSRODE
SMOKELESS & WATERPROOF
POWDER
Made in Great Britain

Drawn from a set of photographs.

© DN.3-2630.   Drawn, 19/11/07.

ELEY BROTHERS (CANADA) LTD: North Transcombe, Manitoba, Near Winnipeg, Canada.

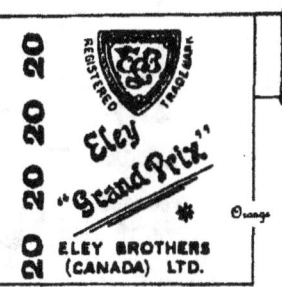

 Wad not known

Eley "Grand Prix"
ELEY BROTHERS (CANADA) LTD.

DATA
Gauge; 20.
Length; 64 mm.
Head; 8 mm.
Tube; Wound orange paper.
Print; Black.
Base; Brass.
Cap; Copper.
Business; Ammo manufacturers.
Circa, Prior to World War One.

The example taken for this drawing was a ready capped unused case. Its tube was rolled from orange paper and it had black case wall printing. The case was unvarnished.

© DN.3-2760.   Drawn, 12/3/08.

ELEY BROTHERS (CANADA) LTD: North Transcombe, Manitoba, Near Winnipeg, Canada.

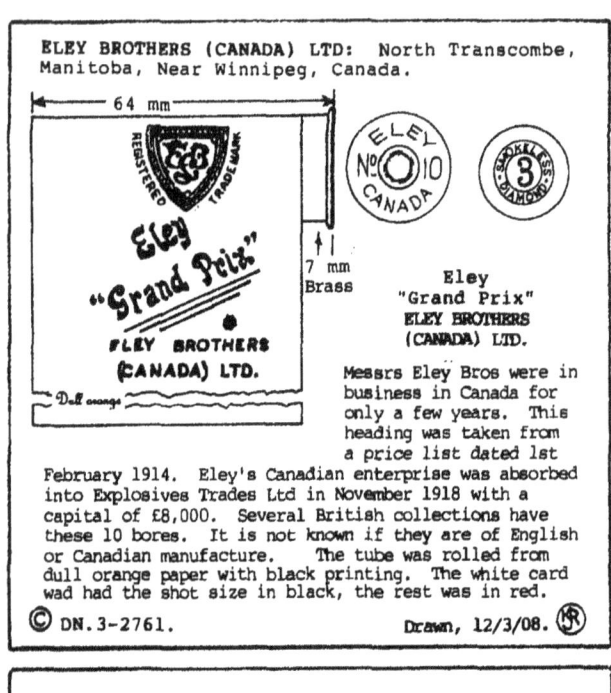

Eley "Grand Prix" ELEY BROTHERS (CANADA) LTD.

Messrs Eley Bros were in business in Canada for only a few years. This heading was taken from a price list dated 1st February 1914. Eley's Canadian enterprise was absorbed into Explosives Trades Ltd in November 1918 with a capital of £8,000. Several British collections have these 10 bores. It is not known if they are of English or Canadian manufacture. The tube was rolled from dull orange paper with black printing. The white card wad had the shot size in black, the rest was in red.

© DN.3-2761. Drawn, 12/3/08.

ELEY. P.O. Box 705, Witton, Birmingham, Midlands, England.

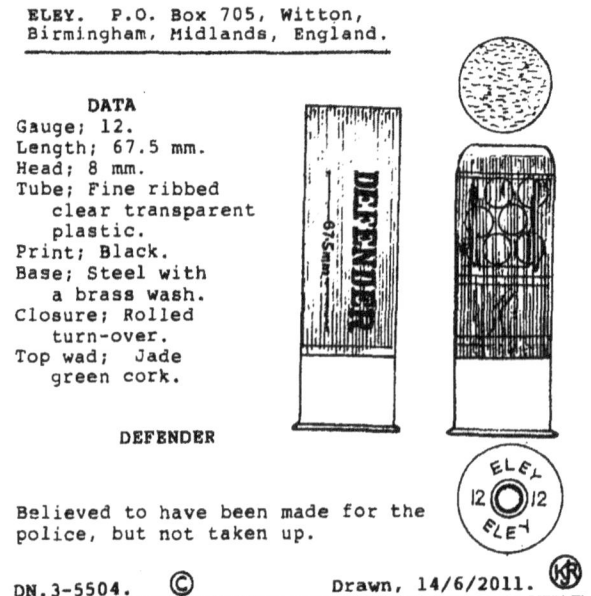

DATA
Gauge; 12.
Length; 67.5 mm.
Head; 8 mm.
Tube; Fine ribbed clear transparent plastic.
Print; Black.
Base; Steel with a brass wash.
Closure; Rolled turn-over.
Top wad; Jade green cork.

DEFENDER

Believed to have been made for the police, but not taken up.

DN.3-5504. © Drawn, 14/6/2011.

ELEY LIMITED:
P.O. Box 707, Witton, Birmingham, B6 7UX. England.

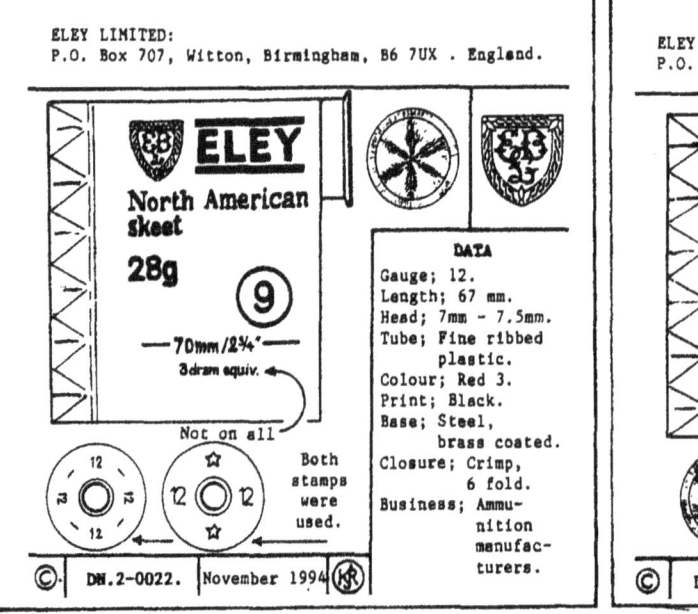

DATA
Gauge; 12.
Length; 67 mm.
Head; 7mm - 7.5mm.
Tube; Fine ribbed plastic.
Colour; Red 3.
Print; Black.
Base; Steel, brass coated.
Closure; Crimp, 6 fold.
Business; Ammunition manufacturers.

© DN.2-0022. November 1994

ELEY LIMITED:
P.O. Box 707, Witton, Birmingham, B6 7UX. England.

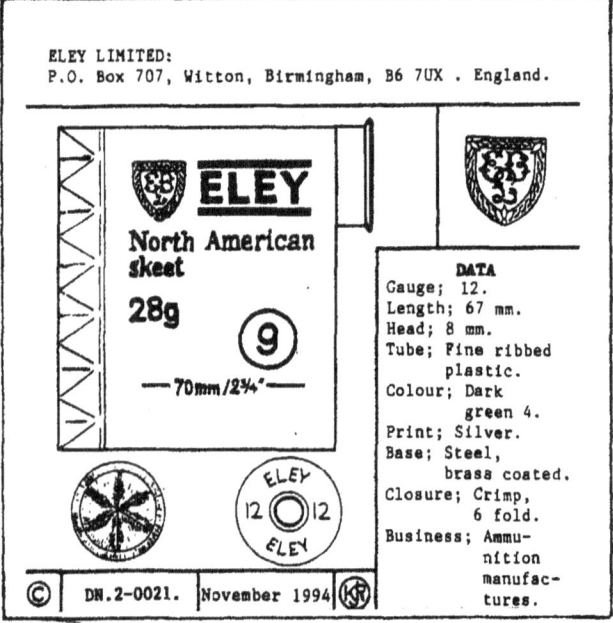

DATA
Gauge; 12.
Length; 67 mm.
Head; 8 mm.
Tube; Fine ribbed plastic.
Colour; Dark green 4.
Print; Silver.
Base; Steel, brass coated.
Closure; Crimp, 6 fold.
Business; Ammunition manufactures.

© DN.2-0021. November 1994

ELEY HAWK: PO Box 705, Witton, Birmingham, West Midlands B6 7UT, England

DATA
Gauge; 12.
Length; 67 mm.
Head; 16 mm.
Base; Steel with brass coating.
Closure; Six fold crimp.
For other details see below.

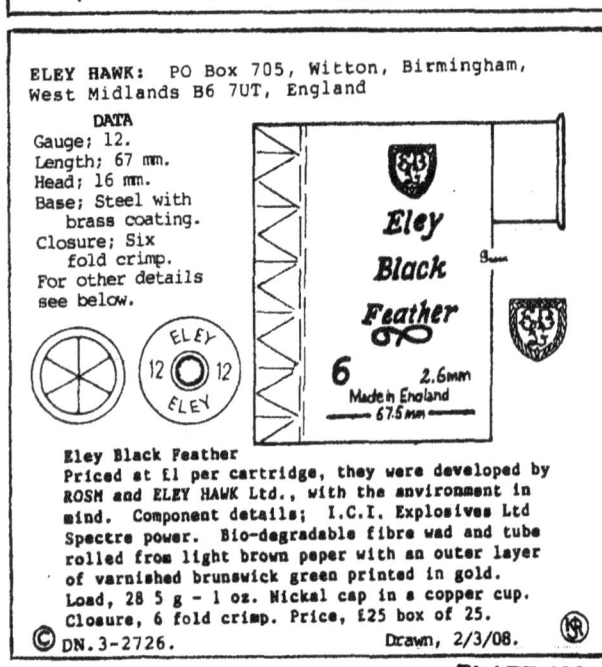

Eley Black Feather
Priced at £1 per cartridge, they were developed by ROSH and ELEY HAWK Ltd., with the environment in mind. Component details; I.C.I. Explosives Ltd Spectre power. Bio-degradable fibre wad and tube rolled from light brown paper with an outer layer of varnished brunswick green printed in gold. Load, 28.5 g - 1 oz. Nickel cap in a copper cup. Closure, 6 fold crimp. Price, £25 box of 25.
© DN.3-2726. Drawn, 2/3/08.

ELEY HAWK: PO Box 705, Witton, Birmingham, West Midlands B6 7UT, England.

DATA
Gauge; 12.
Length; 67 mm.
Head; 16 mm.
Base; Steel with brass coating.
Closure; Six fold crimp.
For other details see below.

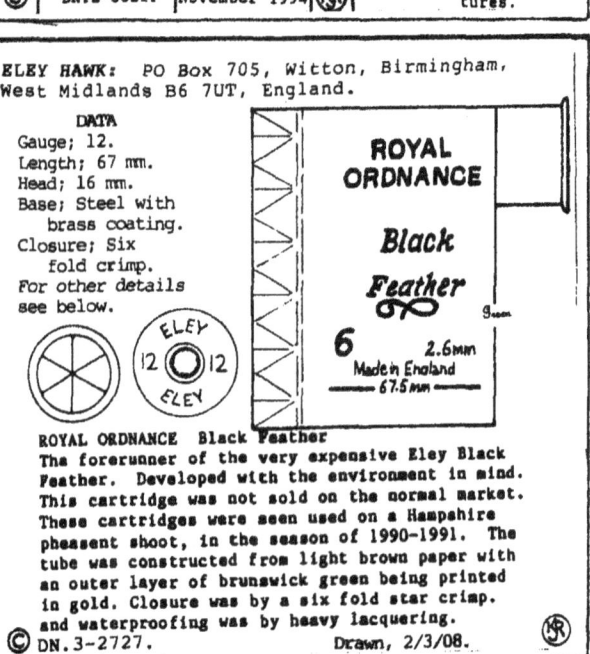

ROYAL ORDNANCE Black Feather
The forerunner of the very expensive Eley Black Feather. Developed with the environment in mind. This cartridge was not sold on the normal market. These cartridges were seen used on a Hampshire pheasant shoot, in the season of 1990-1991. The tube was constructed from light brown paper with an outer layer of brunswick green being printed in gold. Closure was by a six fold star crimp. and waterproofing was by heavy lacquering.
© DN.3-2727. Drawn, 2/3/08.

PLATE 108 [ELE - ELE]

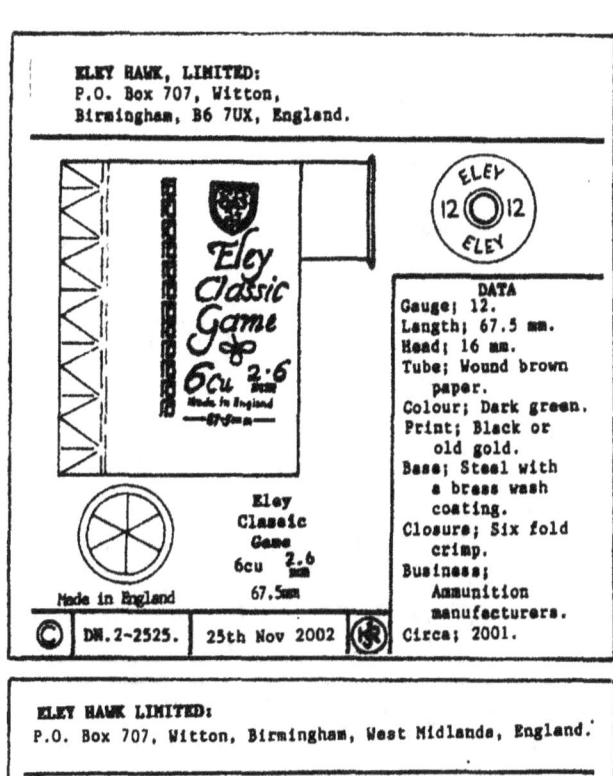
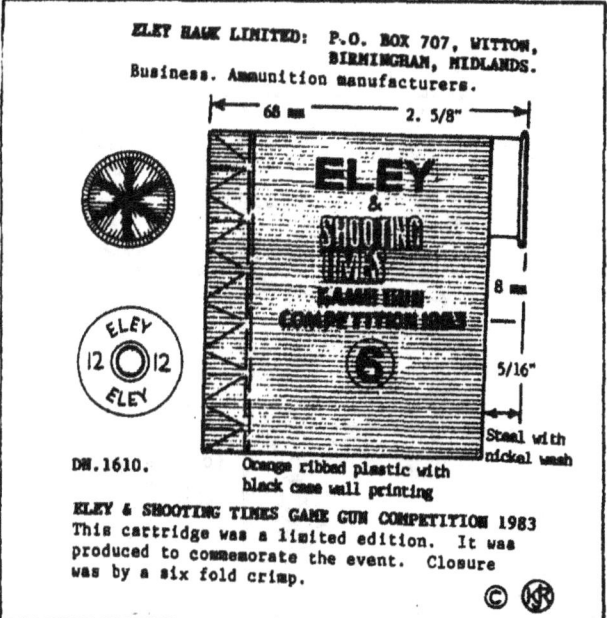
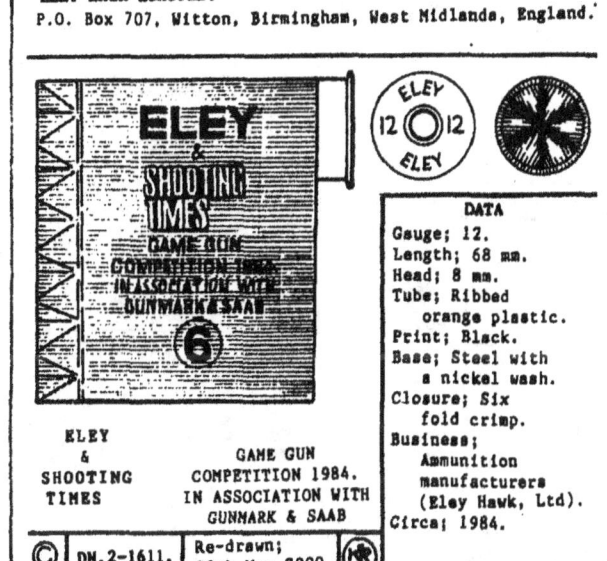
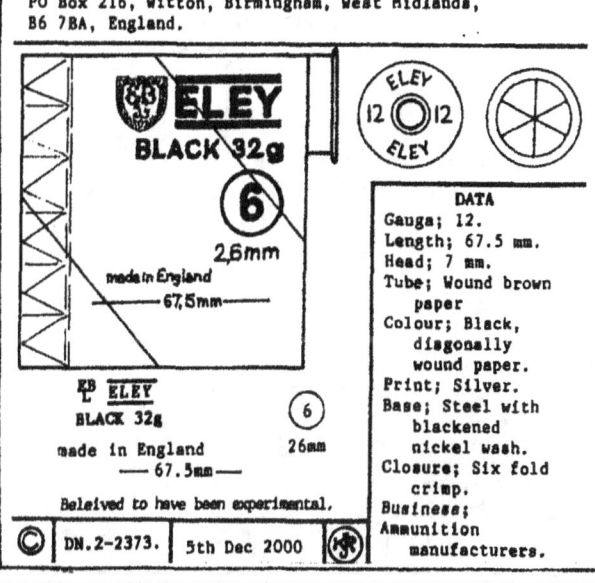
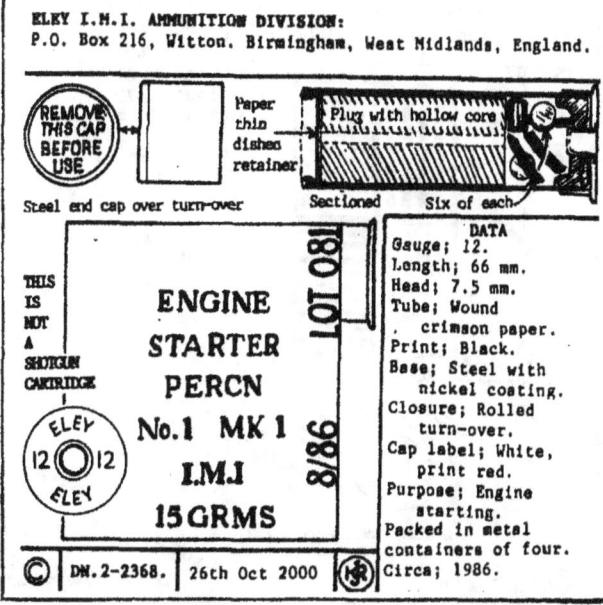
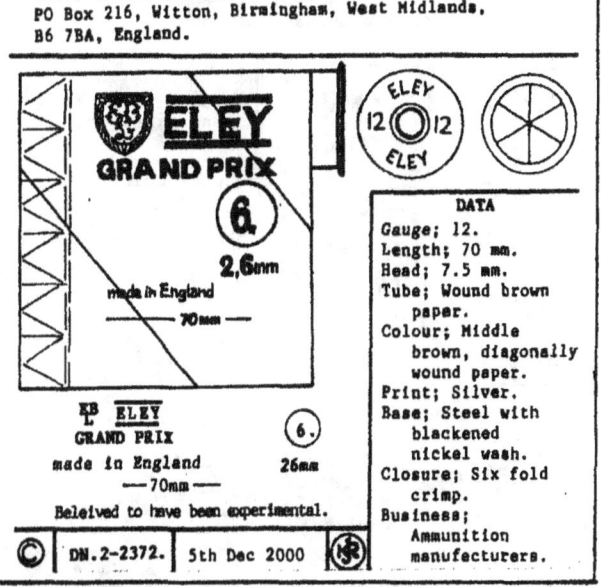

PLATE 109 [ELE – ELE]

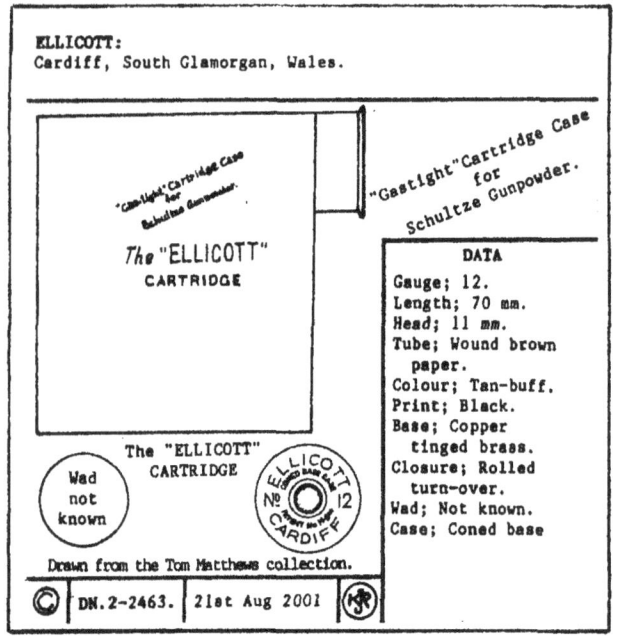
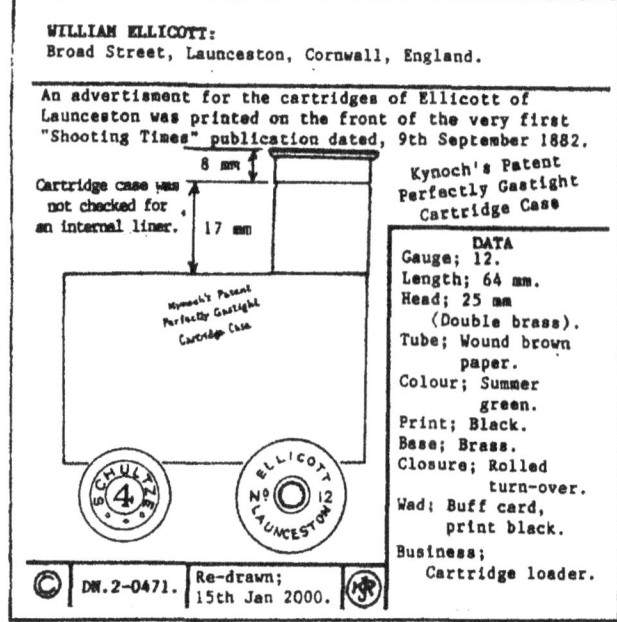
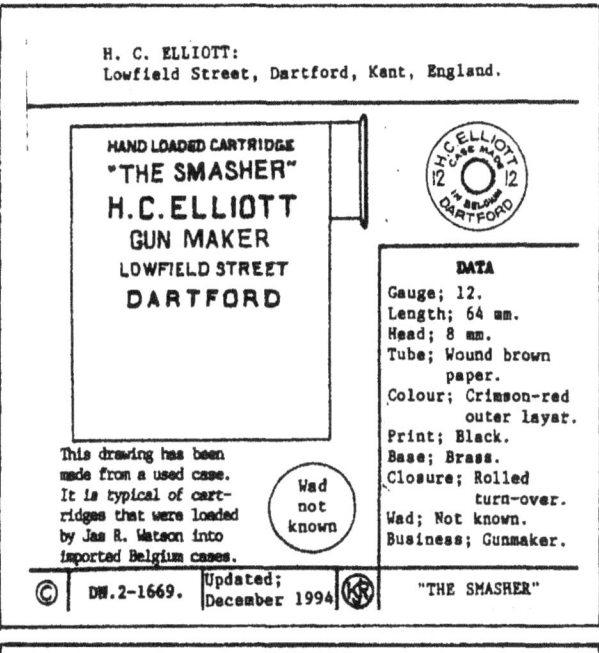
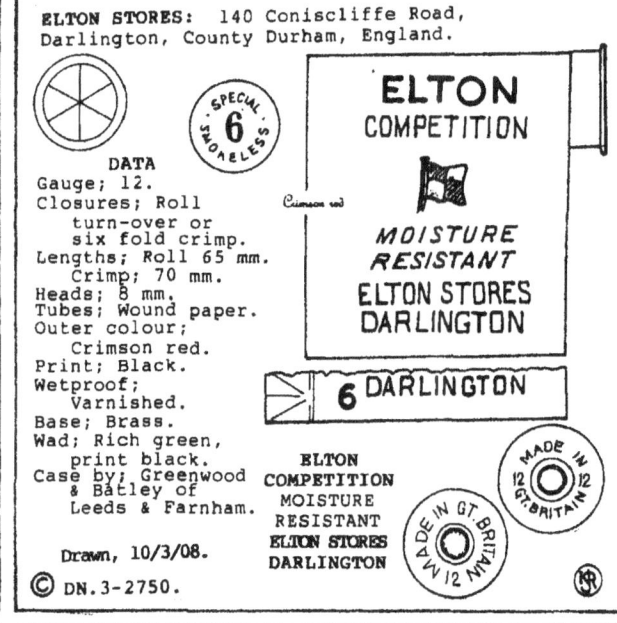
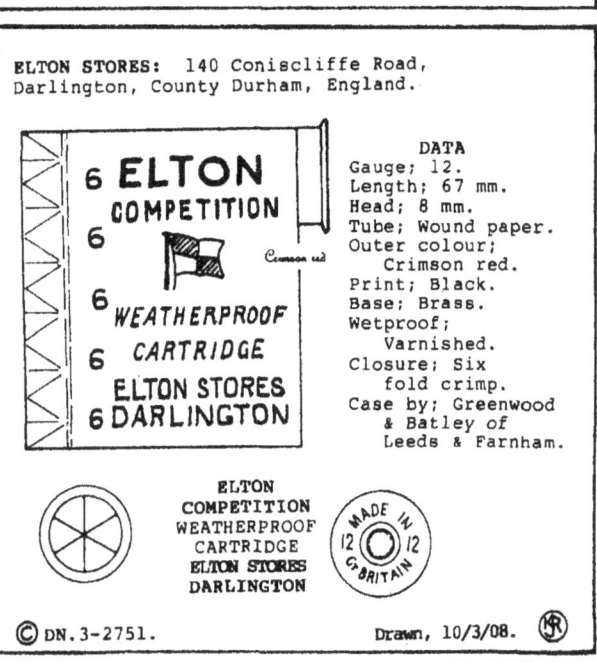
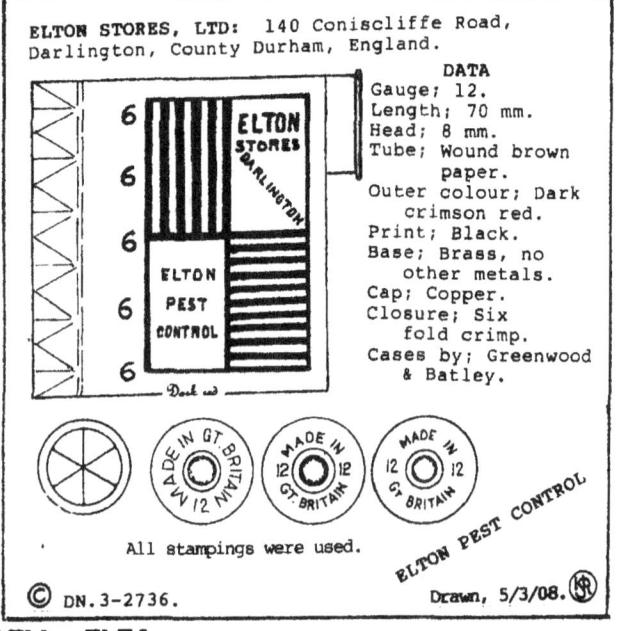

PLATE 110 [ELL – ELT]

ELTON STORES LIMITED:
140 Coniscliffe Road, Darlington, County Durham, England.

By Appointment To Her Majesty The Queen. Supliers of Cartridges.

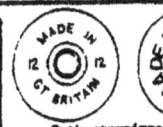

Both stampings were used.

The base as on the example drawn.

No iron or steel was used in the construction of this case.

DATA
Gauge; 12.
Length; 65 mm.
Head; 7.5 mm to 9.5 mm.
Tube; Wound orange paper.
PANTONE® 1595 C.
Print; Black.
Base; Brass.
Wetproof; Clear lacquered.
Closure; Rolled turn-over.
Wad; White card, print black.
Circa; 1960's.
Business; Stores.

© DN.2-0845. Updated, April 1996

ELVEDEN ESTATE:
Near Thetford, Suffolk bordering Norfolk, East Anglia, England.

This drawing has been taken from an unused primed case that was made by Eley Bros Ltd. It was probably sold through Cogswell & Harrison Ltd. Elveden was once owned by Maharajah Duleep Singh. It had 20,000 acres and a workforce of 70 men. (24 liveried men, 16 horsemen and 30 warreners). On the 8th September 1876, the Maharajah killed 780 partridges on Elveden using 1,000 cartridges.

Wad not known

ELVEDEN ESTATE

16 mm
8 mm

DATA
Gauge; 12.
Length; 64.5 mm.
Head; 24 mm.
Tube; Wound tan paper.
Colour; Brownish-tan.
Print; Black.
Base; Brass.
Closure; Rolled turn-over.
Wad; Not known.
Interior liner; Nil.
Business; Country estate.

© DN.2-0077. Updated; March 1995 ELVEDEN ESTATE

ELVEDEN ESTATE GUN CLUB:
Elveden Estate, Near Thetford, Norfolk/Suffolk. England.

ELVEDEN ESTATE GUN CLUB
← 67mm →
7½ - 32gms
7½ - 28gms

Blue, 28gms.
Red, 28gms.
Green, 32gms.

DATA
Gauge; 12.
Length; 67 mm.
Head; 7 mm.
Tube; Medium ribbed plastic.
Colours; Green 3, red 3, blue 4.
Print; Black.
Base; Steel, brass coated.
Closure; Crimp, 6 fold.
Business; Private gun club.

© DN.2-0015. November 1994

DAVID EMSLIE:
Elgin, Morayshire (Grampian), Scotland.

THE *Sniper* CARTRIDGE
Specially loaded for
DAVID EMSLIE
ELGIN
Tel. No. 555
Made in Great Britain

THE *Sniper* CARTRIDGE
Specially loaded for
DAVID EMSLIE
ELGIN
Tel. No. 555
Made in Great Britain

DATA
Gauge; 12.
Length; 64 mm.
Head; 8 mm.
Tube; Wound red or orange paper.
Colours; Vermilion or orange.
Printings; Black.
Base; Reinforced brass.
Closure; Rolled turn-over.
Wad; Yellow, print black.

© DN.2-0404. Re-drawn; 12th Oct 2000

S. ENTWISTLE:
151 Church Street, Blackpool, Lancashire, England.

LOADED BY
S. ENTWISTLE
GUNSMITH
151 CHURCH STREET
BLACKPOOL
Phone; 2192
MADE IN GREAT BRITAIN

LOADED BY
S. ENTWISTLE
GUNSMITH
151 CHURCH STREET
BLACKPOOL
Phone; 2192
MADE IN GREAT BRITAIN

This cartridge was not examined for internal metals.

 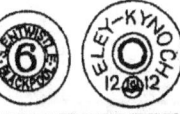

DATA
Gauge; 12.
Length; 64 mm.
Head; 8 mm.
Tube; Wound red paper.
Colour; Crimson.
Print; Black.
Base; Brass.
Closure; Rolled turn-over.
Wad; Red with black printing.
Business; Gunsmith.
Circa; 1930's.

© DN.2-1156. Re-drawn; 27th March 2001

ERRE:
Italy. Address not known.

I.G.I.
EXPORT
HIGH SPEED
smokeless powder
original loading
Erre

EXPORT
HIGH SPEED
smokeless powder
original loading
Erre

DATA
Gauge; 12.
Length; 66 mm.
Head; 3 mm.
Tube; Smooth black plastic.
Colour; Black.
Print; Gold.
Base; Steel with a brass coating.
Closure; Rolled turn-over.
Wad; Not known.

Drawing was made from a used case.

© DN.2-2275. 19th April 2000

PLATE 111 [ELT – ERR]

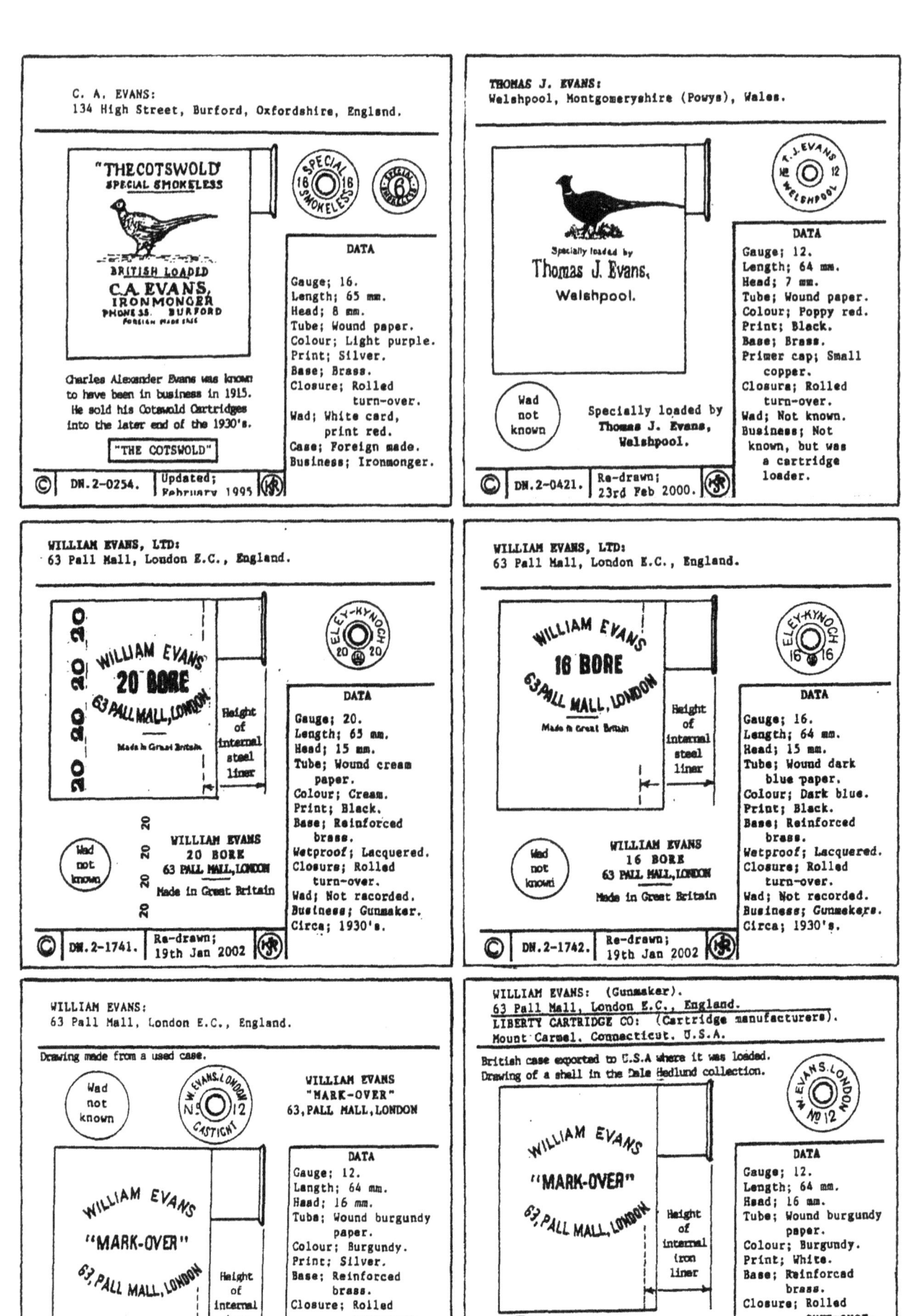

PLATE 112 [EVA - EVA]

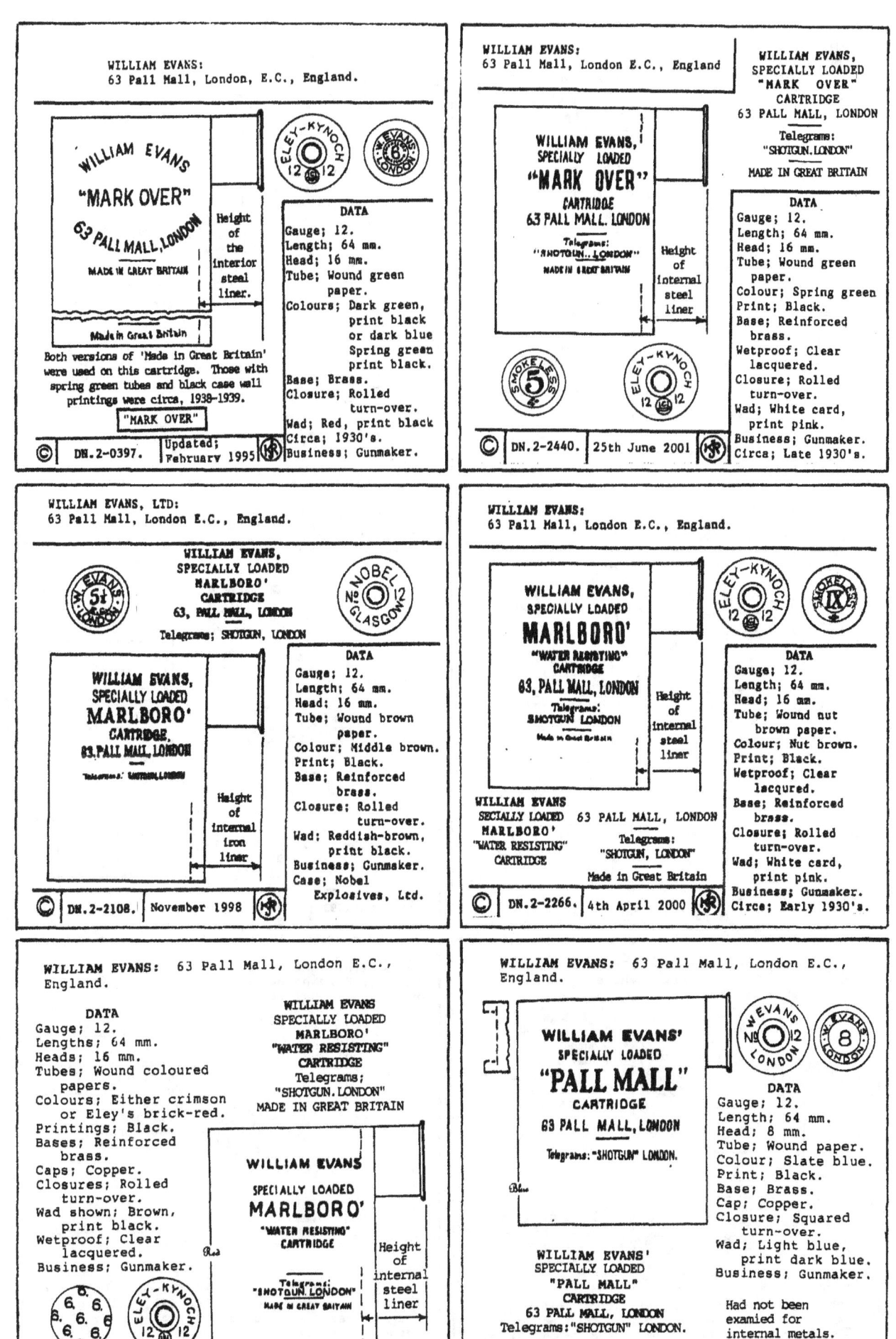

PLATE 113 [EVA - EVA]

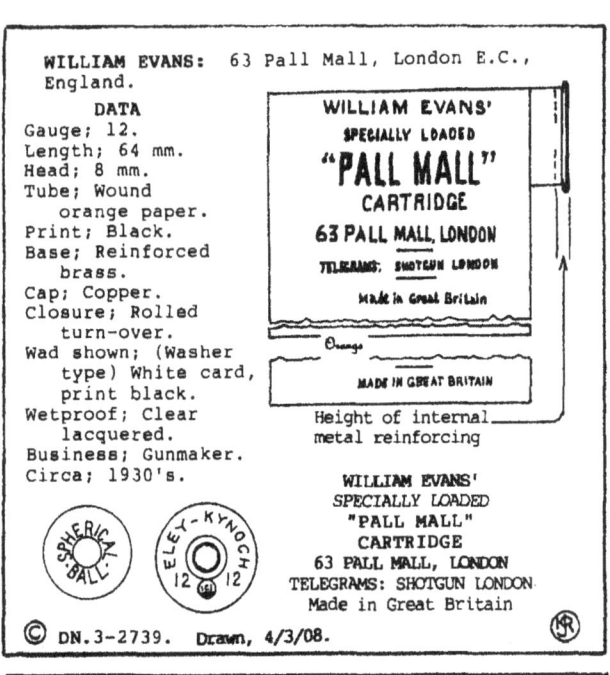
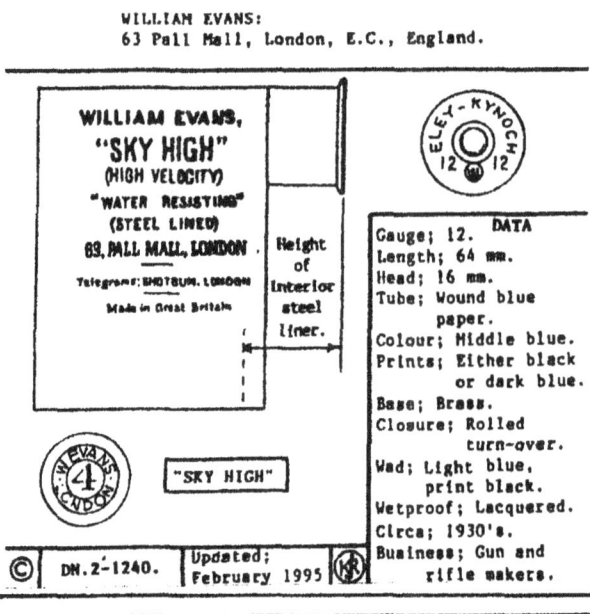
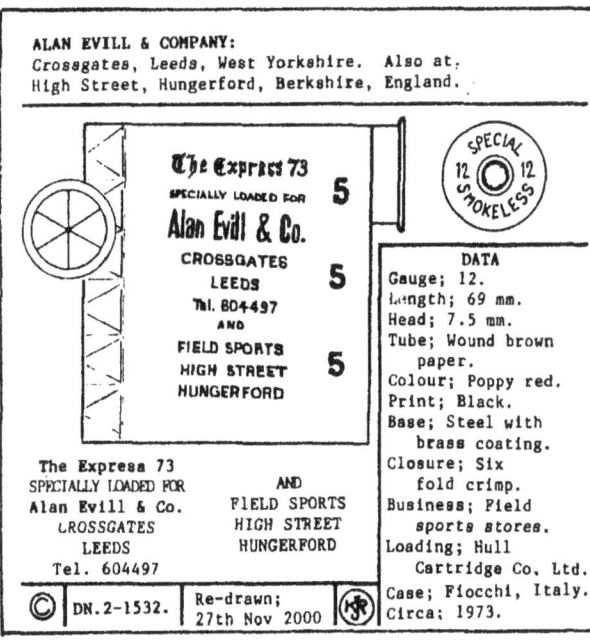
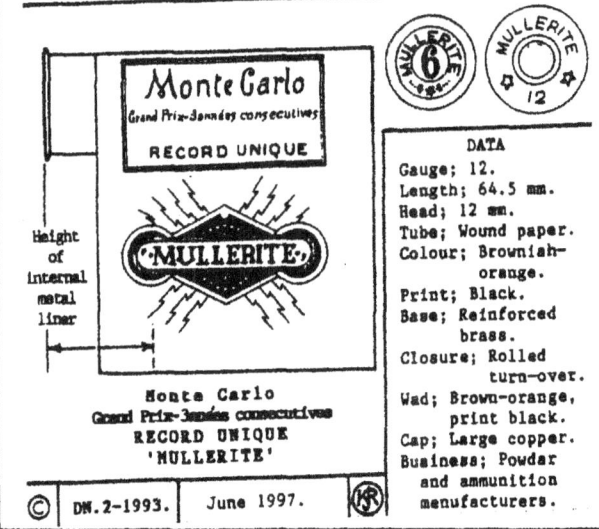
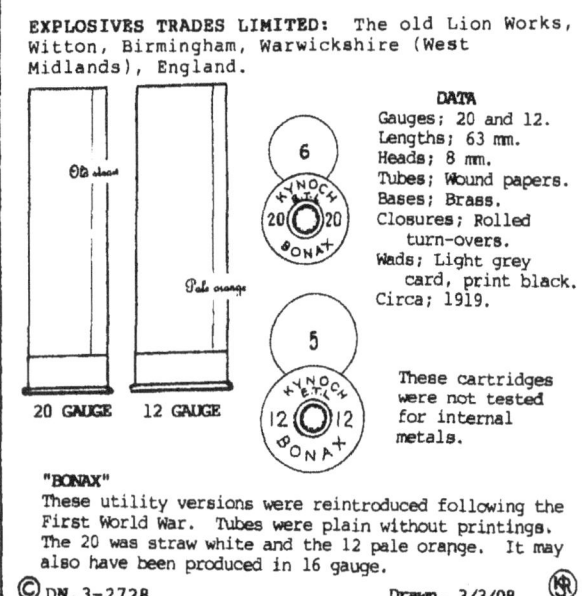
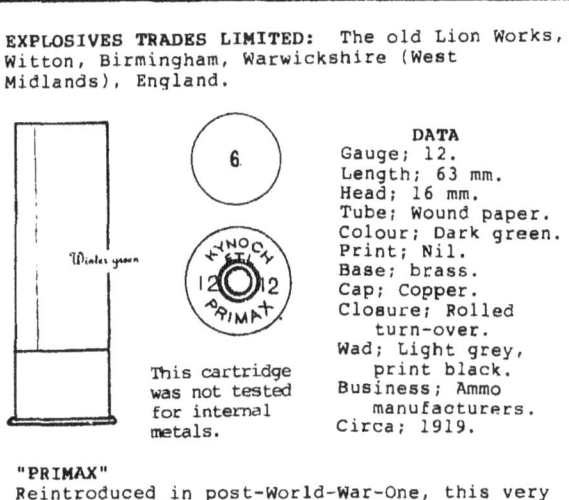

PLATE 114 [EVA – EXP]

EXPLOSIVES TRADES LTD: Witton, Birmingham, Warwickshire (West Midlands), England.

Ammunition manufacturers.

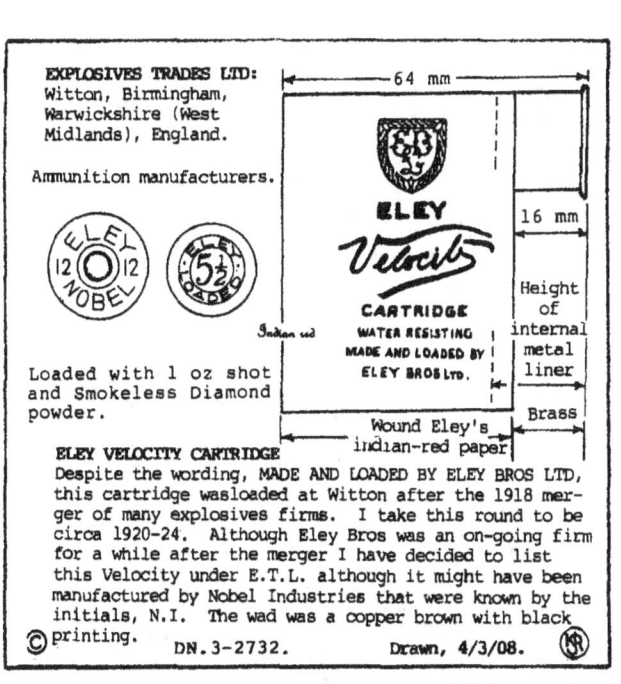

Loaded with 1 oz shot and Smokeless Diamond powder.

ELEY VELOCITY CARTRIDGE
Despite the wording, MADE AND LOADED BY ELEY BROS LTD, this cartridge was loaded at Witton after the 1918 merger of many explosives firms. I take this round to be circa 1920-24. Although Eley Bros was an on-going firm for a while after the merger I have decided to list this Velocity under E.T.L. although it might have been manufactured by Nobel Industries that were known by the initials, N.I. The wad was a copper brown with black printing.
© DN.3-2732. Drawn, 4/3/08.

FABRIQUE NATIONALE d'ARMES: de Guerre, Belgium.

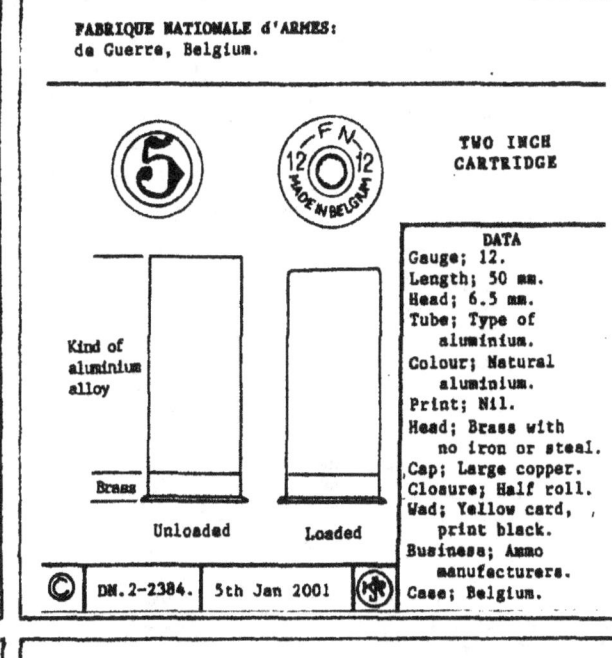

TWO INCH CARTRIDGE

DATA
Gauge; 12.
Length; 50 mm.
Head; 6.5 mm.
Tube; Type of aluminium.
Colour; Natural aluminium.
Print; Nil.
Head; Brass with no iron or steel.
Cap; Large copper.
Closure; Half roll.
Wad; Yellow card, print black.
Business; Ammo manufacturers.
Case; Belgium.

© DN.2-2384. 5th Jan 2001

FALKE (FALCON)
THIS GERMAN FIRM IS NOT KNOWN.

GERMAN
Beste Jagdpatronenhülse Marke "FALKE" für rauchschwaches Pulver

ENGLISH TRANSLATION
Best hunting cartridge shell, trade mark Falcon, for feeble smoking powder.

DATA
Gauge; 12
Length; 65 mm.
Head; 7 mm.
Tube; Wound brown paper.
Colour; Pale cream.
Print; Black.
Base; Brass.
Closure; Rolled turn-over.
Wad; Not known.
Cap; Large copper.
Origin; German.

© DN.3-2006. Revised, 1/2/09.

R. FARMER: 12 North Street, Leighton Buzzard, Bedfordshire, England

DATA
Gauge; 16.
Length; 64 mm.
Head; 24 mm.
Tube; Wound pale brown paper.
Colour; Grey/Gray.
PANTONE® 414 C.
Print; Dark blue.
PANTONE® 534 C.
Base; Double brass.
Closure; Rolled turn-over.
Wad; White card, print black.
Business; Gunmaker.

KYNOCH'S PATENT "PERFECTLY GASTIGHT"

© DN.2-0158. Updated; May 1995

RICHARD FARMER: 12 North Street, Leighton Buzzard, Bedfordshire, England.

DATA
Gauge; 16.
Length; 66 mm.
Head; 11 mm.
Tube; Wound brown paper.
Outer colour; Burgundy.
Print; Silver.
Base; Reinforced brass.
Internal liner; Was fitted with a metal but not measured for height.
Cap; Copper.
Closure; Rolled turn-over.
Wad; White card, print black.
Case by; Kynoch.
Business; Gunmaker.

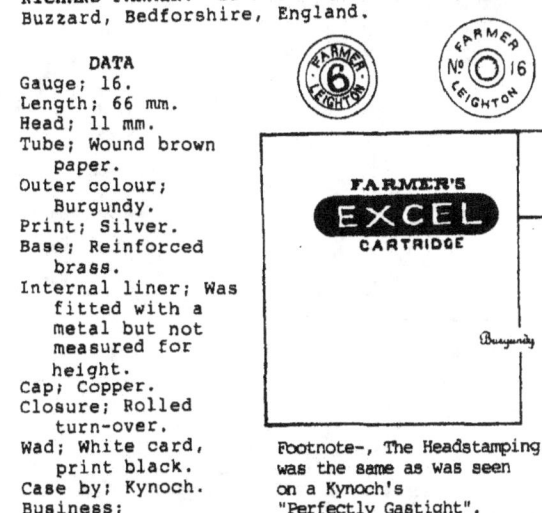

Footnote-, The Headstamping was the same as was seen on a Kynoch's "Perfectly Gastight".

FARMER'S "EXCEL" CARTRIDGE
© DN.3-2729. Drawn, 3/3/08.

FARM HEALTH, LTD: Cattle Market, Reading, Berkshire. Also at, Newman Lane, Alton, Hampshire, England.

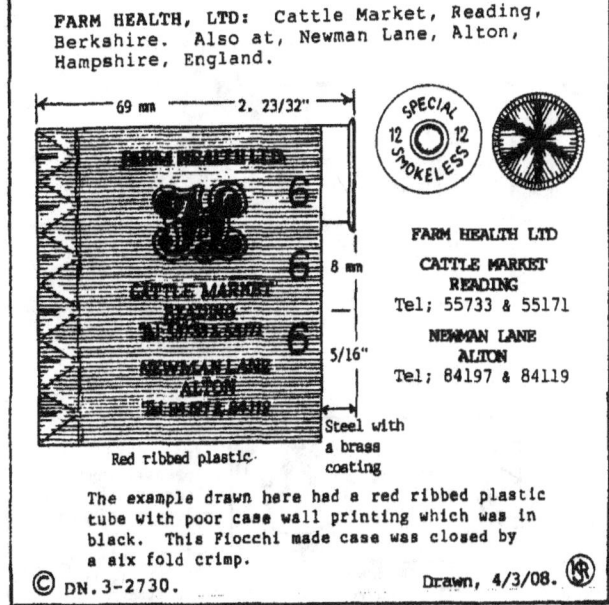

FARM HEALTH LTD
CATTLE MARKET
READING
Tel: 55733 & 55171

NEWMAN LANE
ALTON
Tel: 84197 & 84119

The example drawn here had a red ribbed plastic tube with poor case wall printing which was in black. This Fiocchi made case was closed by a six fold crimp.

© DN.3-2730. Drawn, 4/3/08.

G. F. FARRELL & SONS:
23 High Street, Chippenham, Wiltshire, England.

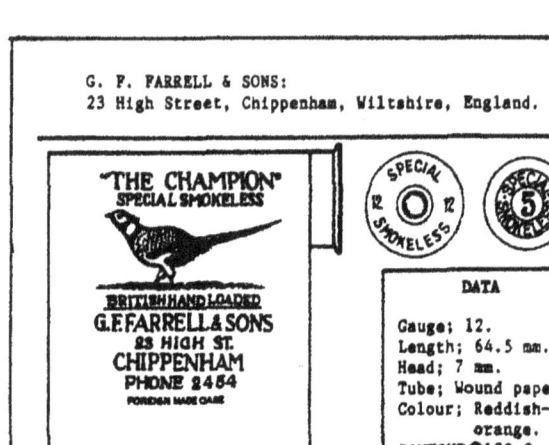

"THE CHAMPION"
SPECIAL SMOKELESS

This cartridge had no internal metal liner nor iron or steel in the construction of its head.

DATA
Gauge; 12.
Length; 64.5 mm.
Head; 7 mm.
Tube; Wound paper.
Colour; Reddish-orange.
PANTONE® 180 C.
Print; Black.
Base; Brass.
Closure; Rolled turn-over.
Wad; Yellow, print black.
PANTONE® Yellow 012 C.
Case; German.

© DN.2-1854.   November 1995

BRYAN FARRELLY & SONS:
Castle Street, Kells, County Meath, Republic of Ireland.

Drawn from a set of photographs

"KENLIS"
Specially loaded for
BRYAN FARRELLY & SONS
CASTLE STREET
KELLS
Tel; KELLS 18.
MANUFACTURED UNDER LICENCE BY
IRISH METAL INDUSTRIES LTD.

DATA
Gauge; 12.
Length; 64 mm.
Head; 8 mm.
Tube; Wound orange paper.
Colour; Reddish-orange.
Print; Black.
Base; Brass.
Closure; Rolled turn-over.
Wad; Brown card, print black.
Case, I.M.I. Ltd, Dublin & Galway, Republic of Ireland.

© DN.2-2032.   Amended: 1st May 1999

B. FINCH & SONS:
35 Bell Street, Reigate, Surrey, England.

"THE LONE FLYER"

DATA
Gauge; 12.
Length; 66 mm.
Head; 8.5 mm.
Tube; Wound red paper.
Colour; Crimson.
PANTONE® 193 U.
Print; Black.
Base; Brass.
Closure; Rolled turn-over.
Wad; White card, print red.
Powder; Walsrode.
Case; German.

© DN.2-1866.   November 1995

FIOCCHI USA/LMCS:
5030 Fremont Road, Ozark, Missouri MO 65721, U.S.A.

FIOCCHI
Louise Mandrell™
CELEBRITY SHOOT
1996

DATA
Gauge; 12.
Length; 68 mm.
Head; 9 mm.
Tube; Extra fine transparent ribbed plastic.
Colour; Pale mauve.
Print; Black.
Base; Steel with brass coating.
Closure; Eight fold star crimp.
Business; Ammunition manufacturers.
Circa; Fall, 1996.

© DN.2-2116.   16th Jan 1999

FIRLE SHOOT:
Firle, Near Lewes, Sussex, England.

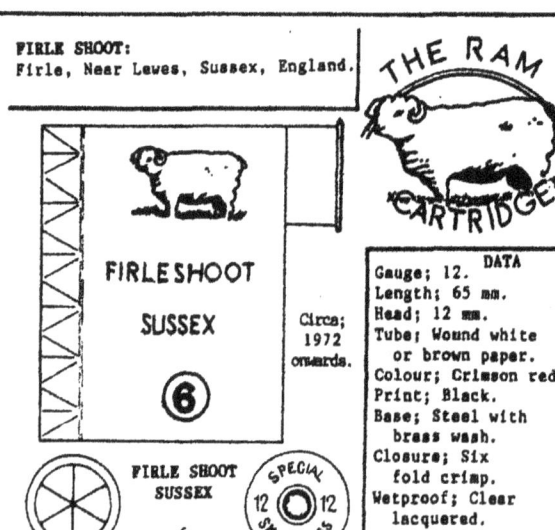

FIRLE SHOOT
SUSSEX
6

Shoot gamekeeper; Mr W. Young.

Circa; 1972 onwards.

DATA
Gauge; 12.
Length; 65 mm.
Head; 12 mm.
Tube; Wound white or brown paper.
Colour; Crimson red.
Print; Black.
Base; Steel with brass wash.
Closure; Six fold crimp.
Wetproof; Clear lacquered.
Business; Private shoot.
Loading; Hull Cartridge, Co, Ltd.
Case; Fiocchi.

© DN.2-1562.   Re-drawn; 14th Feb 2001

10TH F.I.T.A.S.C. CHAMPIONSHIPS: AUSTRALIA.

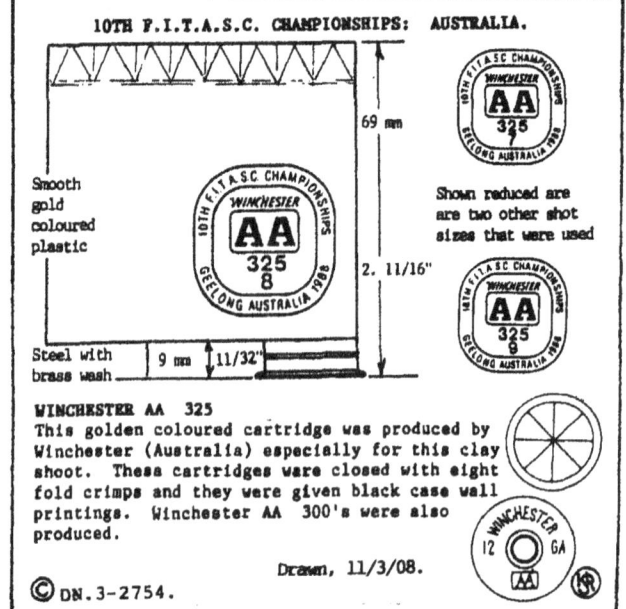

WINCHESTER AA 325
This golden coloured cartridge was produced by Winchester (Australia) especially for this clay shoot. These cartridges were closed with eight fold crimps and they were given black case wall printings. Winchester AA 300's were also produced.

Drawn, 11/3/08.

© DN.3-2754.

PLATE 116 [FAR – FIT]

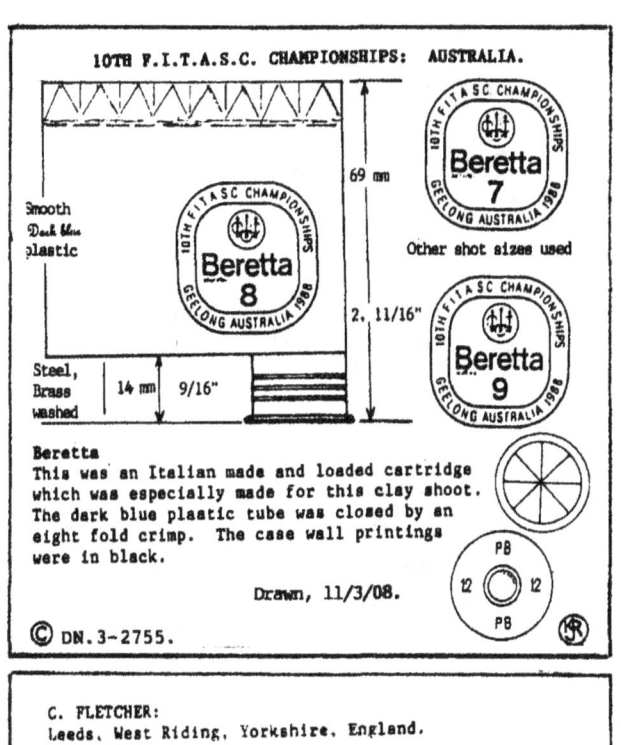
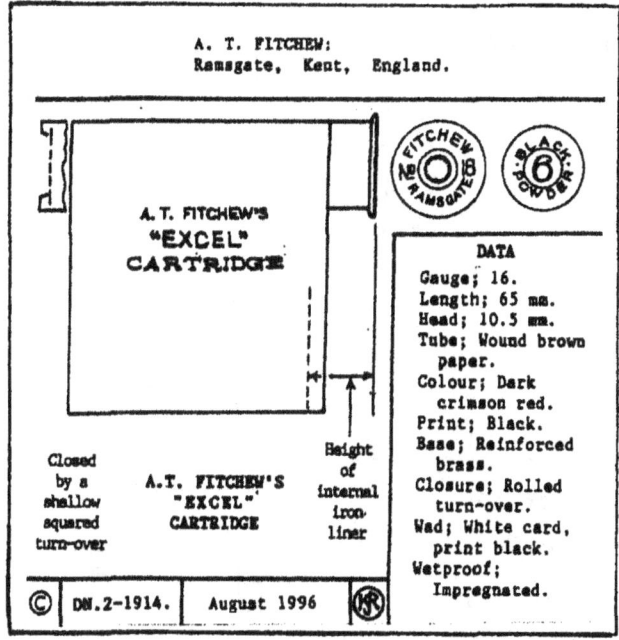
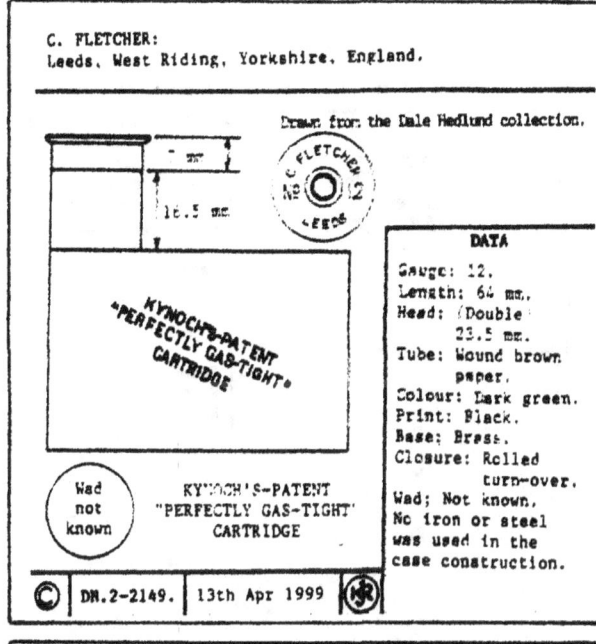
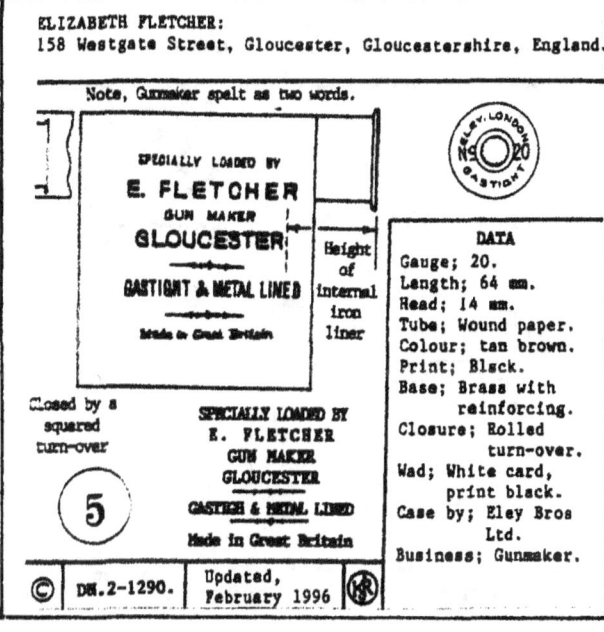
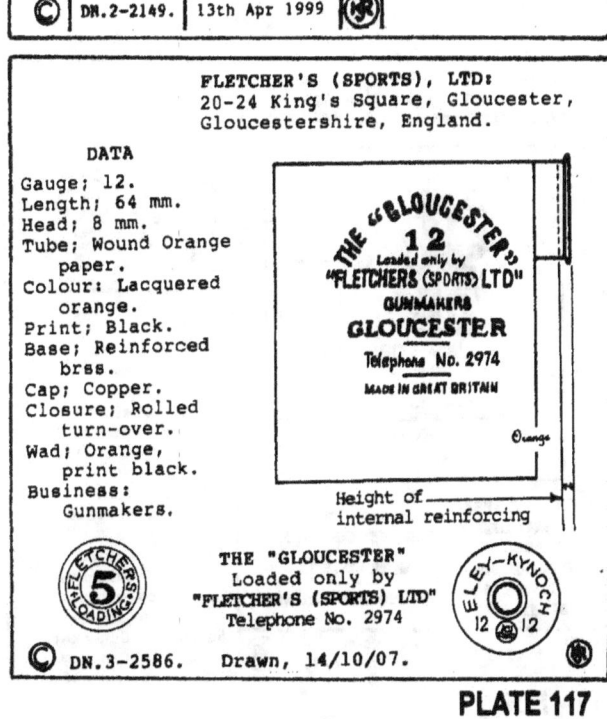
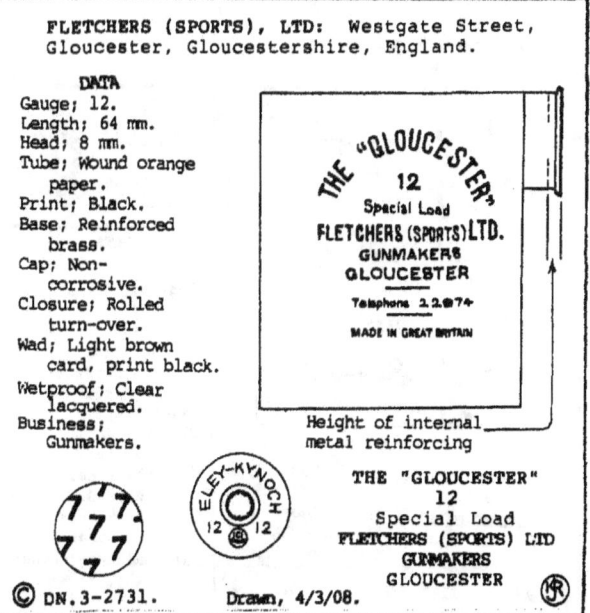

PLATE 117 [FIT – FLE]

H. & A. FLINT:
(Address not known. Most likely in the British Isles).

Most likely it was a New Explosives Co, Ltd, loading.

DATA

Gauge; 12.
Length; 64 mm.
Head; 7.5 mm.
Tube; Wound paper.
Colour; Primrose yellow.
Print; Black.
Base; Reinforced brass.
Closure; Rolled turn-over.
Wad shown; White card, print red.
Case; Eley Bros. Ltd. London.

H. & A. FLINT
"PRIMROSE"
Smokeless Cartridge

© | DN.2-2354. | 18th Sept 2000

FLOBERT:
3 Boulevard Saint Michel, Paris, France.

DATA

Gauge; 16.
Length; 64 mm.
Head; 14 mm.
Tube; Wound brown paper.
Colour; Burnt-orange.
Print; Black.
Base; Reinforced brass.
Closure; Rolled turn-over.
Wad; Brown cork, print black.
Business; Gun and ammunition manufacturer.

T

FLOBERT
ARMURIER
3,Boulevard Saint Michel
PARIS

© | DN.2-2174. | 6th May 1999

FLOBERT:
3 Boulevard Saint Michel, Paris, France.

DATA

Gauge; 16.
Length; 64 mm.
Head; 14 mm.
Tube; Wound brown paper.
Colour; Soot black.
Print; Silver.
Base; Reinforced brass.
Closure; Rolled turn-over.
Wad; Off-white card, print black.
Business; Gun and ammunition manufacturer.

T

FLOBERT
ARMURIER
3,Boulevard Saint Michel
PARIS

© | DN.2-2175. | 6th May 1999

FLOBERT:
3 Boulevard Saint Michel, Paris, France.

Wad not known

Also seen on an outer dark green paper with black printing but minus the letter T.

DATA

Gauge; 12.
Length; 65 mm.
Head; 15 mm.
Tube; Wound brown paper.
Colour; Black.
Print; Silver.
Base; Reinforced brass.
Closure; Rolled turn-over.
Wad; Not known.
Business; Gun and ammunition manufacturer.

ELOBERT
AMURIERBREVETE
3,BoulevardStMichel
PARIS

T

© | DN.2-2172. | 6th May 1999

G. FODEN:
Openshaw (District of Manchester, Lancashire (Greater Manchester), England.

DATA

Gauge; 12.
Length; 70 mm.
Head; 9 mm.
Tube; Wound paper.
Colour; Dark blueish green.
Print; Black.
Base; Brass.
Closure; Rolled turn-over.
Wad; White card, print red.
Case; Eley Bros, Ltd. London.
Internal metal liner; Height, 18 mm.

ELEY'S
GAS-TIGHT
CARTRIDGE CASE.

LOADED WITH
CURTIS'S & HARVEY'S
SMOKELESS
DIAMOND
GUNPOWDER
Made in Great Britain

© | DN.2-2283. | 18th April 2000

WILLIAM FORD:
15 St. Mary's Row, Birmingham, Warwickshire (West Midlands), England.

DATA

Gauge; 12.
Length; 64 mm.
Head; 16 mm.
Tube; Wound red paper.
Colour; E-K I.C.I. Gastight quality brick red.
Print; Black.
Base; Reinforced brass.
Closure; Rolled turn-over.
Wad; Middle blue, print black.
Business; Gunmaker.
Circa; 1930's.

THE "ECLIPSE"
CARTRIDGE
LOADED BY
WILLIAM FORD
GUNMAKER
BIRMINGHAM

TELEGRAMS: "ECLIPSE"
TELEPHONE: CENTRAL 5210
WATER RESISTING
Made in Great Britain

© | DN.2-1234. | Re-drawn 7th Jan 1999

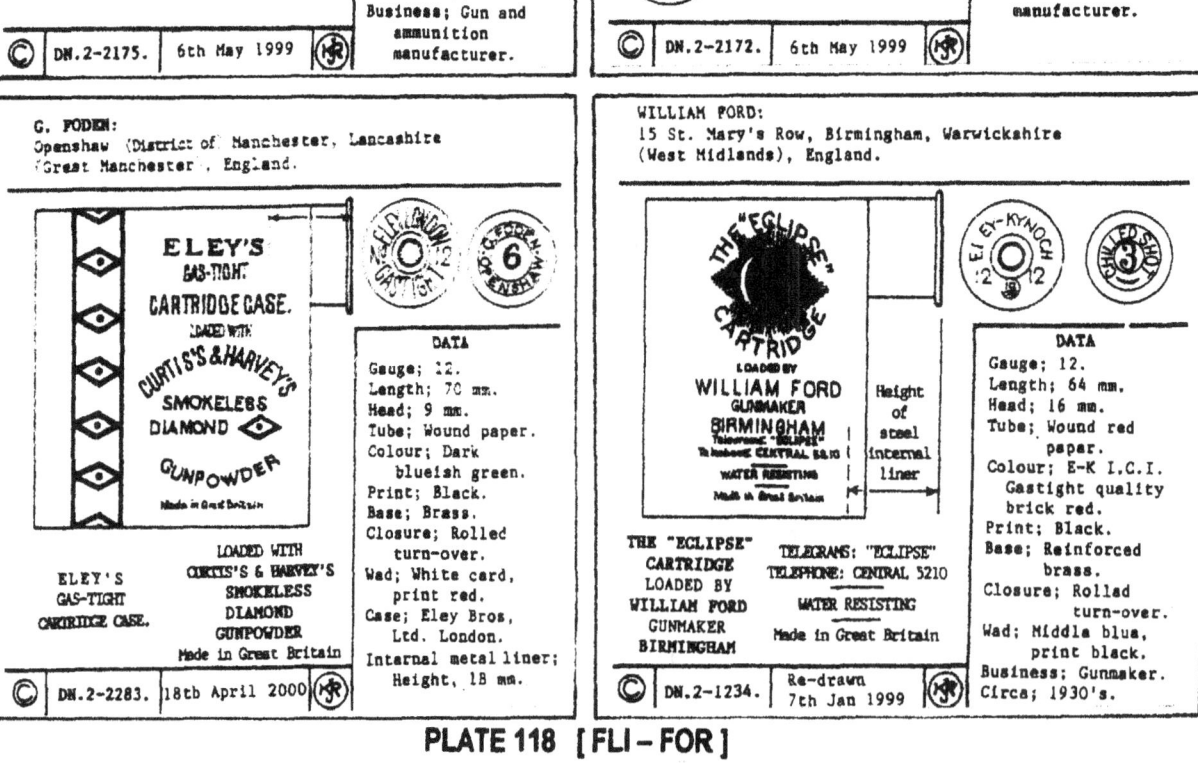

PLATE 118 [FLI – FOR]

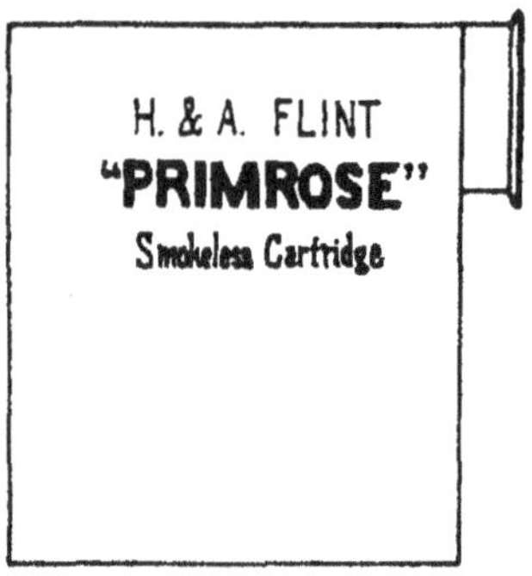

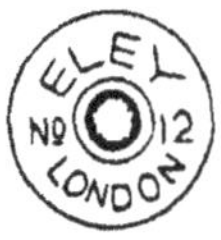

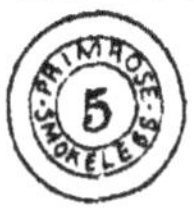

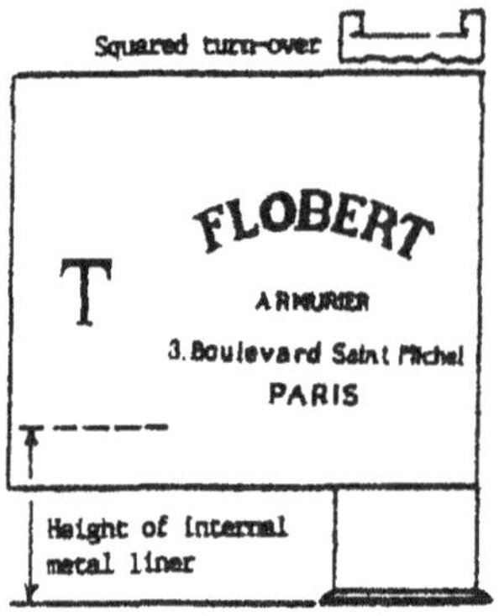

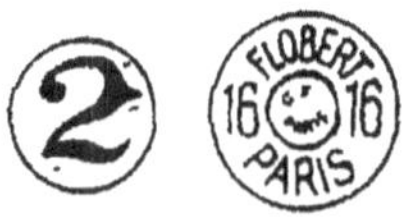

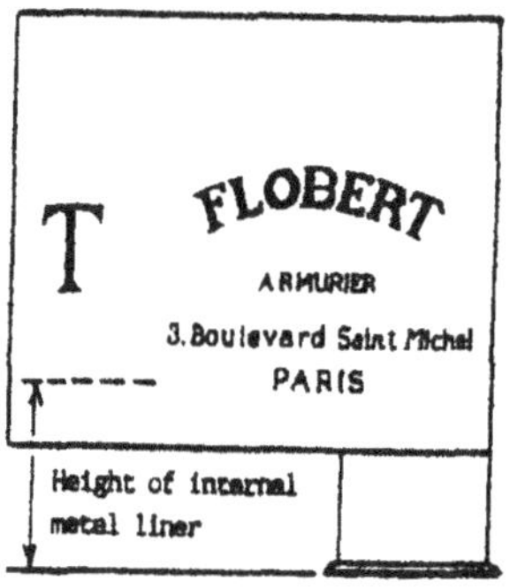

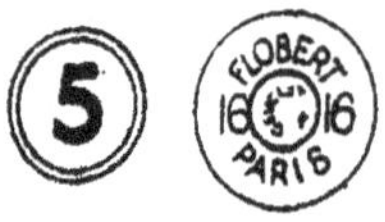

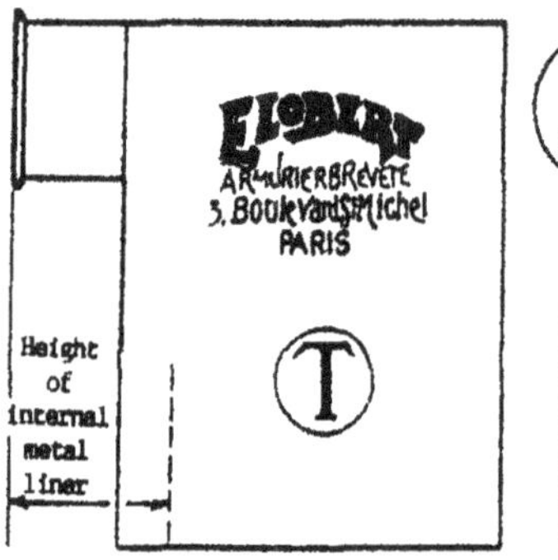

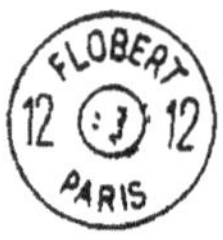

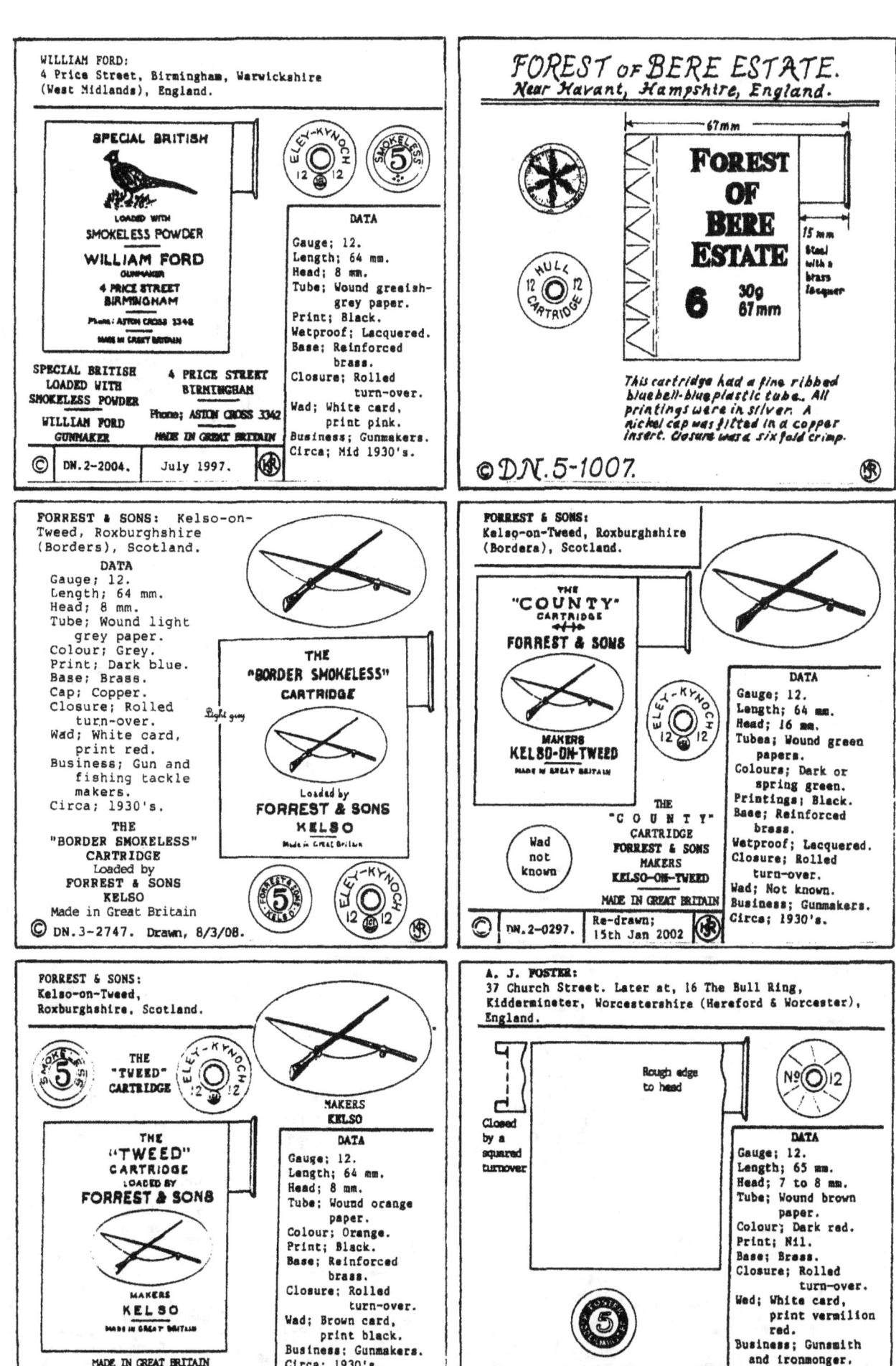

PLATE 119 [FOR - FOS]

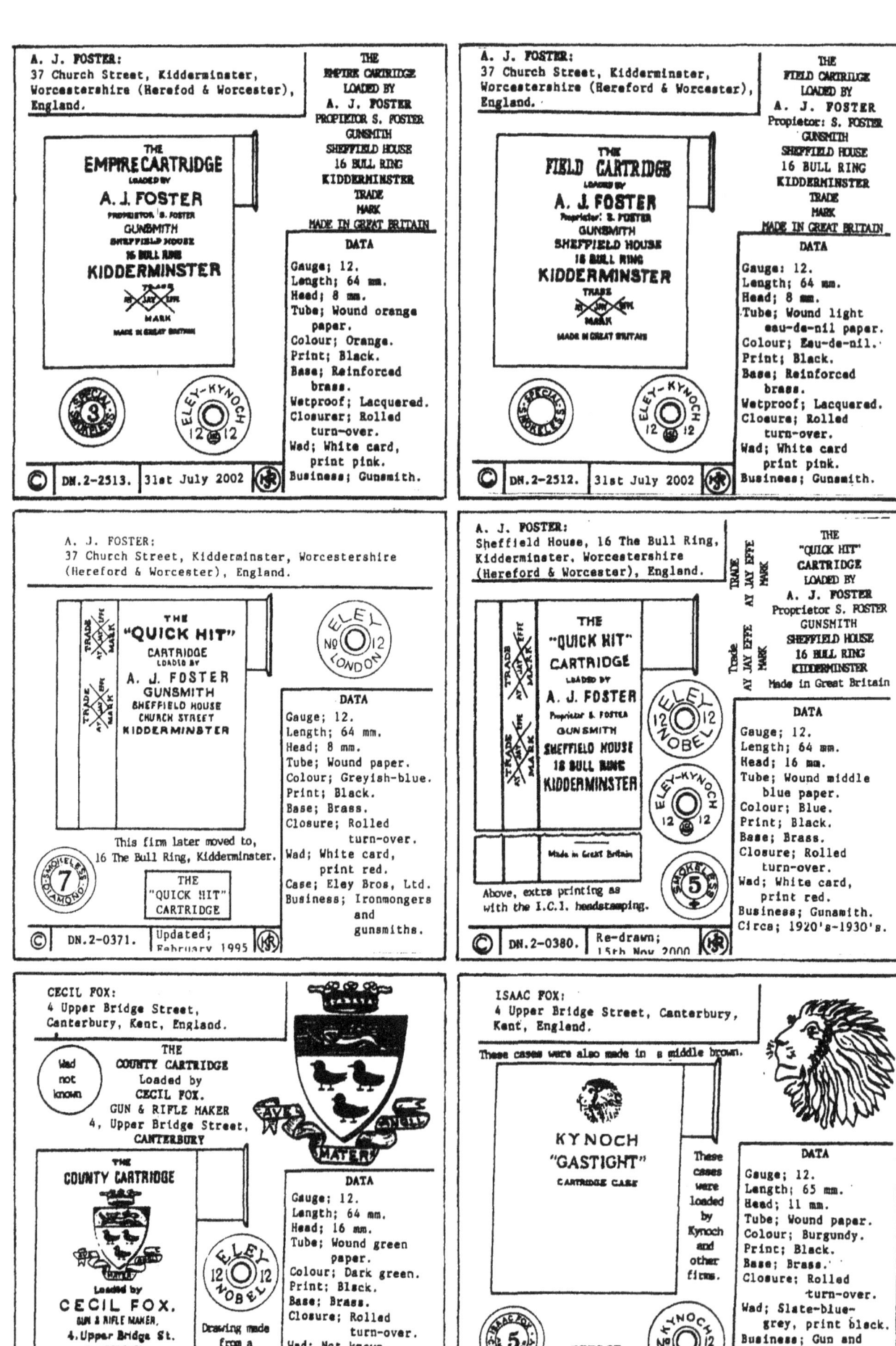

PLATE 120 [FOS-FOX]

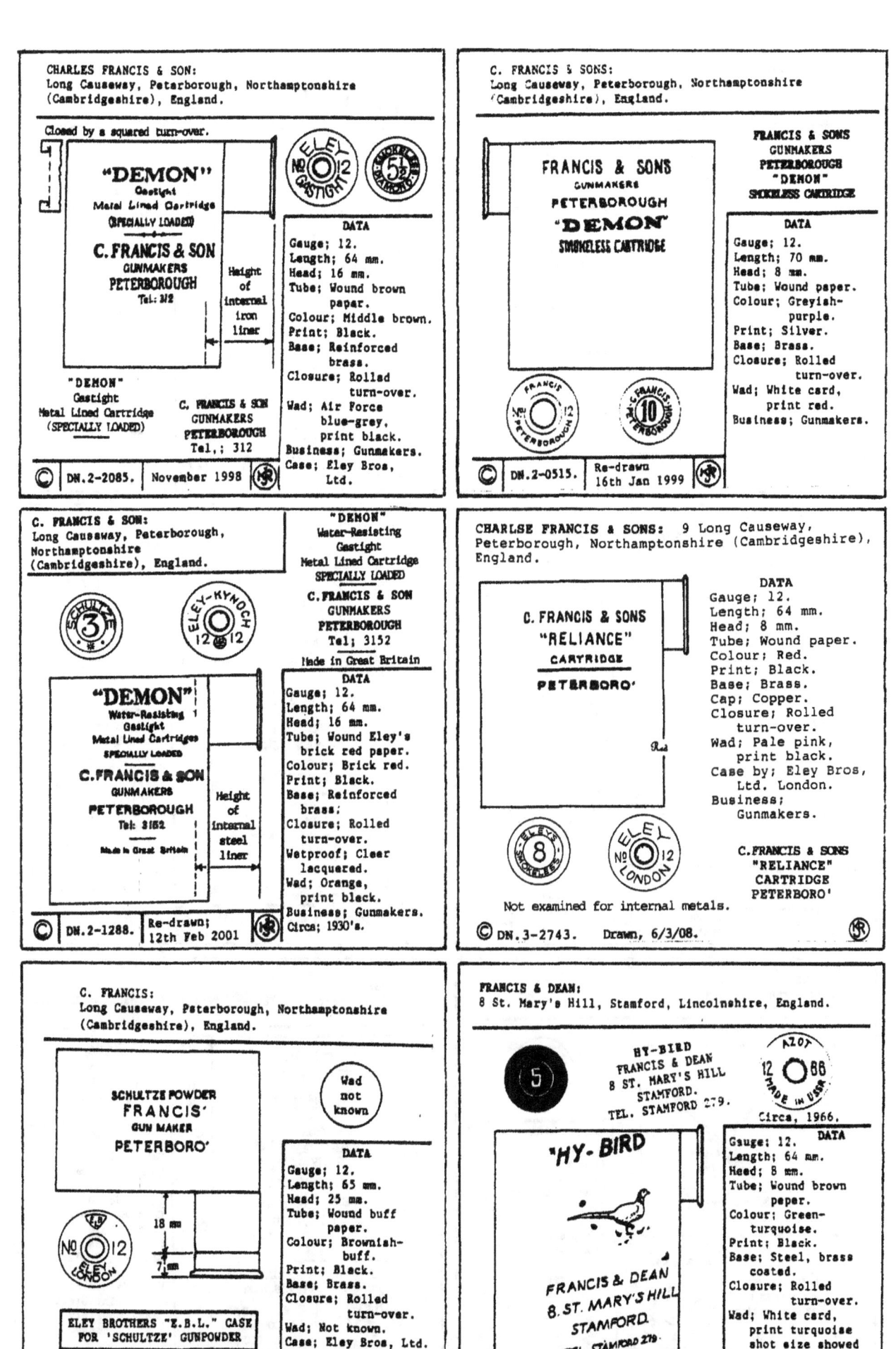

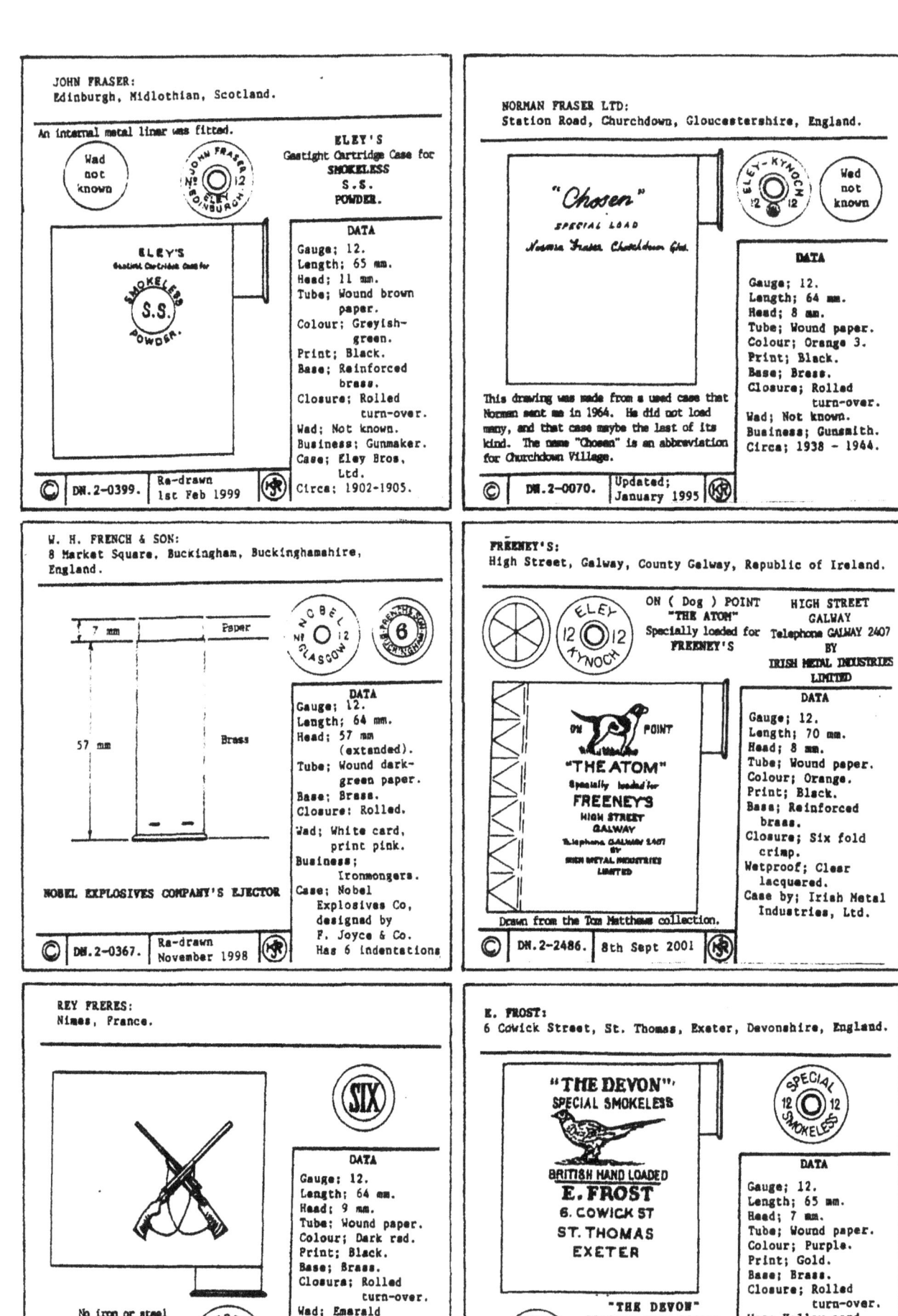

PLATE 122 [FRA - FRO]

EDWARD FROST:
Bridlington, East Riding, Yorkshire (Humberside), England.

EDWARD FROST

BRIDLINGTON

DATA

Gauge; 12.
Length; 65 mm.
Head; 8 mm.
Tube; Wound paper.
Colour; Poppy red.
Print; Black.
Base; Brass.
Closure; Rolled turn-over.
Wad; White card, no printing. (Blank load).
Case; Foreign.

© DN.2-0607. Re-drawn; 18th Feb 2000. KSR

JOHN FRY:
14 Sadler Gate, Derby, Derbyshire, England.

This drawing has been made from a set of five photographs of an unused case which was sent to me by Doug Culver of Eureka Springs, AR, U.S.A.

John Fry was in business at the above address between 1884 and 1910.

DATA

Gauge; 12.
Length; 66 mm.
Head; 16 mm.
Tube; Wound brown paper.
Colour; Flame red.
Print; Black.
Base; Brass.
Closure; Rolled turn-over.
Wad; Not known.
Business; Gunmaker.

© DN.2-1543. Updated, March 1996 KSR

FUSSELL'S, LTD: 118-119 Cheap Side, London E.C.2, England. Also in Wales at the following. See Welsh addresses below: Abergavenny, Monmouthshire (Gwnt); Port Talbot, West Glamorgan; Newport, Monmouthshire (Gwent).

25th Jan 2000.

DATA

Gauge; 12.
Length; 65 mm.
Head; 7 mm.
Tube; Wound paper.
Colour; Kingcup yellow.
Print; Black.
Base; Brass.
Closure; Rolled turn-over.
Wad; Primrose yellow, print black.
Business; Gunmakers.
Case; Possibly Germany.

"THE CLUB" NON-RUSTING SPECIAL SMOKELESS BRITISH HAND LOADED
FUSSELL'S GUN-MAKERS
118-119 CHEAPSIDE.LONDON. E.C.2.
55 CROSS ST. ABERGAVENNY
81 STATION ROAD, PORT TALBOT
2 DOCK ST STREET, NEWPORT, MON.
65 HIGH ST, NEWPORT, MON.
FOREIGN MADE CASE

© DN.2-2253. KSR

W. GALBRAITH:
22 St. Nicholas Street, Lancaster, Lancashire, England.

W Galbraith was known as at the above address between 1899-1901. The cartridge is circa to this.

DATA

Gauge; 12.
Length; 64 mm.
Head; 8 mm.
Tube; Wound paper.
Colour; Pink 2.5 .
Print; Black.
Base; Brass.
Wetproof; Impregnated.
Closure; Rolled turn-over.
Wad; Not known.
Business; General and furnishing, ironmonger and steel merchant.

© DN.2-0888. Updated; December 1994 KSR

EDWARD GALE & SON:
20 Joy Street, Barnstaple, Devonshire, England.

DATA

Gauge; 12.
Length; 64 mm.
Head; 16 mm.
Tube; Wound dark green paper.
Colour; Dark green.
Print; Black or navy blue.
Base; Reinforced brass.
Wetproof; Lacquered.
Closure; Rolled turn-over.
Wad; White card, print nil.
Business; Gunmakers.

"FIELD"

The example drawn was loaded with a plain white card top wad.

© DN.2-1835. August 1995 KSR

EDWARD GALE & SON: 20 Joy Street, Barnstaple. Also at, 2-3 Mill Street, Bideford, Devonshire, England.

DATA

Gauge; 12.
Length; 64 mm.
Head; 16 mm.
Tube; Wound spring-green paper.
Print; Black.
Base; Reinforced brass.
Cap; Copper.
Closure; Rolled turn-over.
Wad; Brown card, print black.
Business; Gunmakers.
Circa; 1938-39.

"FIELD"
E.GALE & SON
GUNMAKERS
BARNSTAPLE
AND
BIDEFORD
MADE IN GREAT BRITAIN

© DN.3-2725. Drawn, 1/3/08. KSR

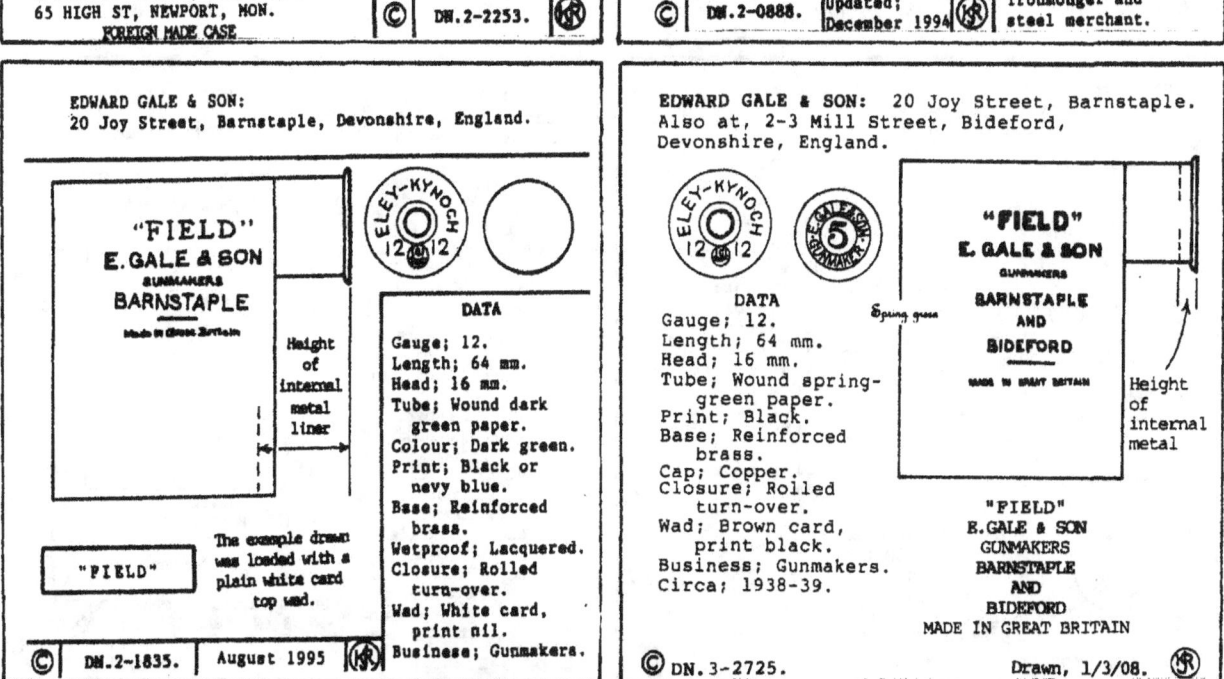

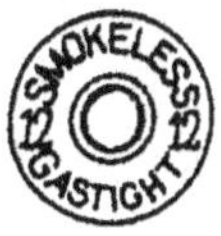

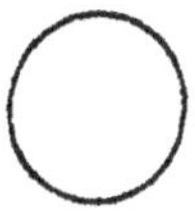

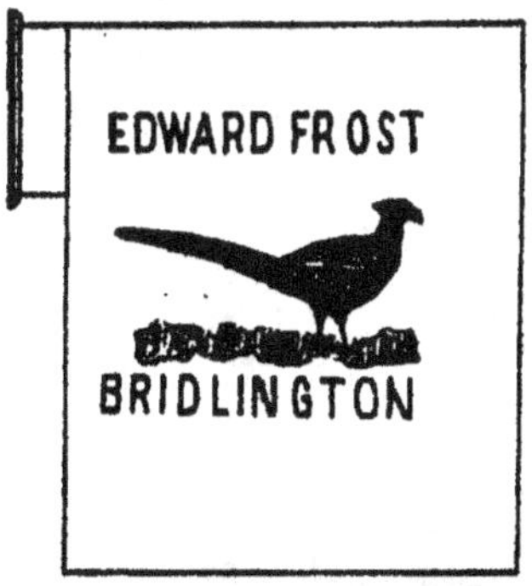

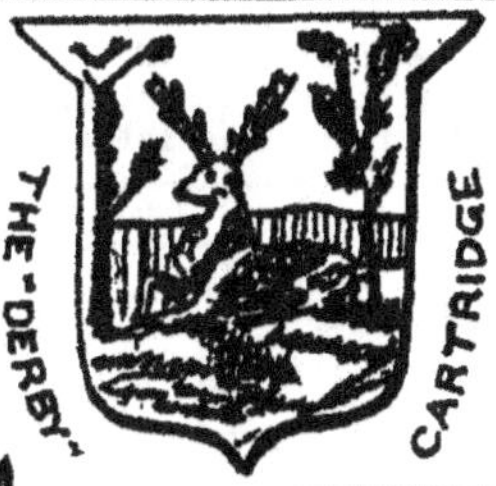

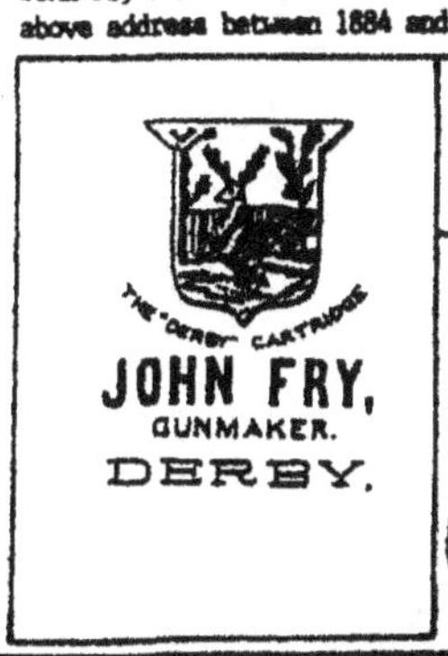

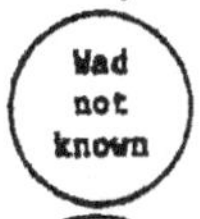

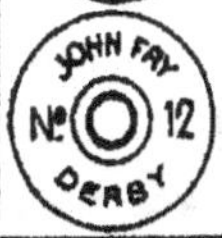

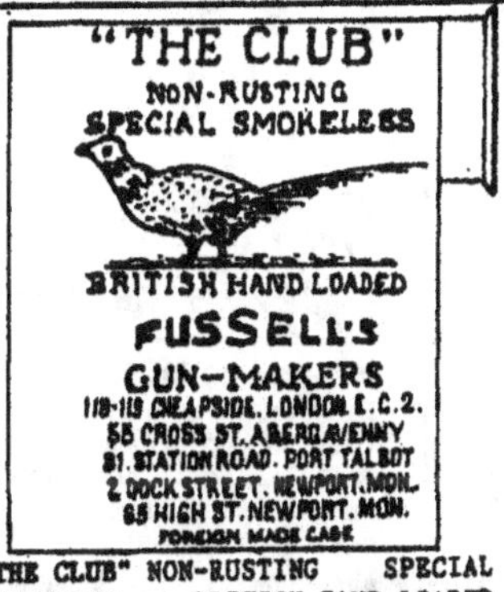

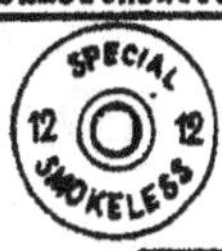

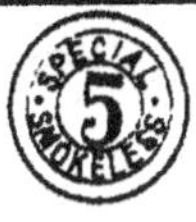

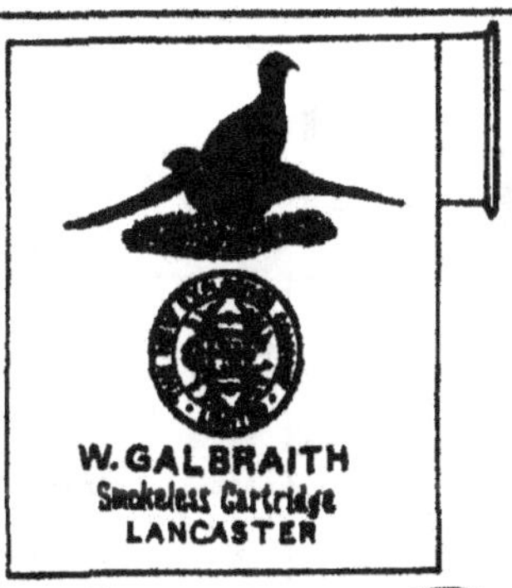

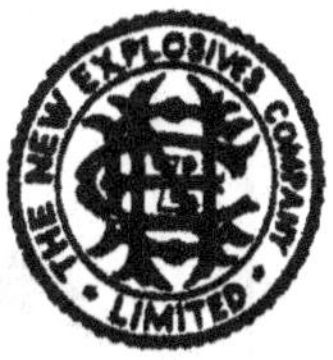

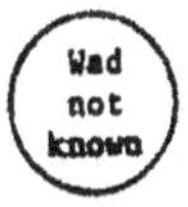

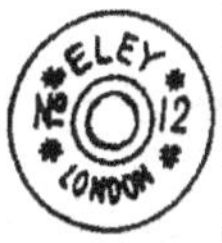

EDWARD GALE & SON:
Joy Street, Barnstaple. Also at, 2 and 3 Mill Street, Bideford, Devonshire, England.

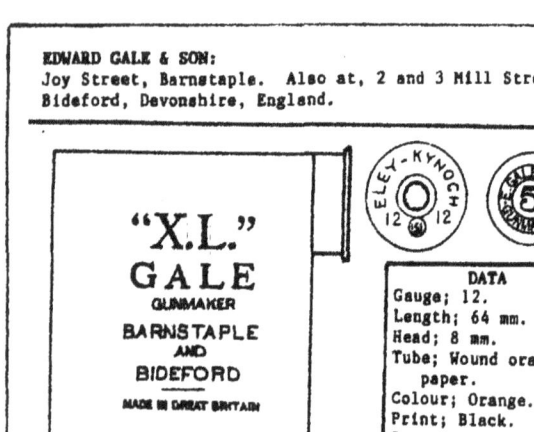

DATA
Gauge; 12.
Length; 64 mm.
Head; 8 mm.
Tube; Wound orange paper.
Colour; Orange.
Print; Black.
Base; Reinforced brass.
Wetproof; Clear lacquered.
Closure; Rolled turn-over.
Wad; Brown card, print black.
Business; Gunmakers.

DN.2-1440. Re-drawn; 3rd Dec 2000.

GALLYON & SONS, LTD:
66 Bridge Street, Cambridge, Cambridgeshire. Also at, 52 High Street, King's Lynn, Norfolk, England.

DATA
Gauge; 12.
Length; 64 mm.
Head; 8 mm.
Tube; Wound orange paper.
Colour; Orange.
Print; Black.
Base; Brass.
Closure; Rolled turn-over.
Wad; White card, inked with pen.
Business; Gunmakers.
Case; Eley-Kynoch Ammo Div.
Circa; 1930's.

DN.2-0295. Re-drawn; 11th Jan 2000.

GALLYONS & SONS, LTD:
66 Bridge Street, Cambridge, Cambridgeshire, England.

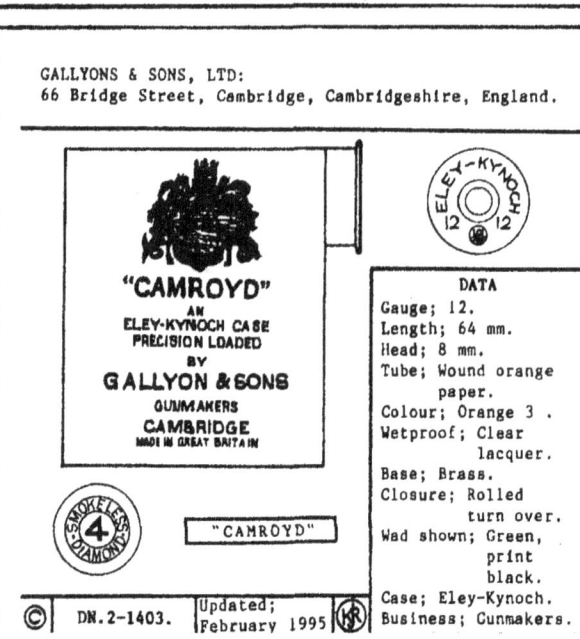

DATA
Gauge; 12.
Length; 64 mm.
Head; 8 mm.
Tube; Wound orange paper.
Colour; Orange 3.
Wetproof; Clear lacquer.
Base; Brass.
Closure; Rolled turn over.
Wad shown; Green, print black.
Case; Eley-Kynoch.
Business; Gunmakers.

DN.2-1403. Updated; February 1995.

GALLYON & SONS, LTD:
66 Bridge Street, Cambridge, Cambridgeshire. Also at, 52 High Street, King's Lynn, Norfolk, England.

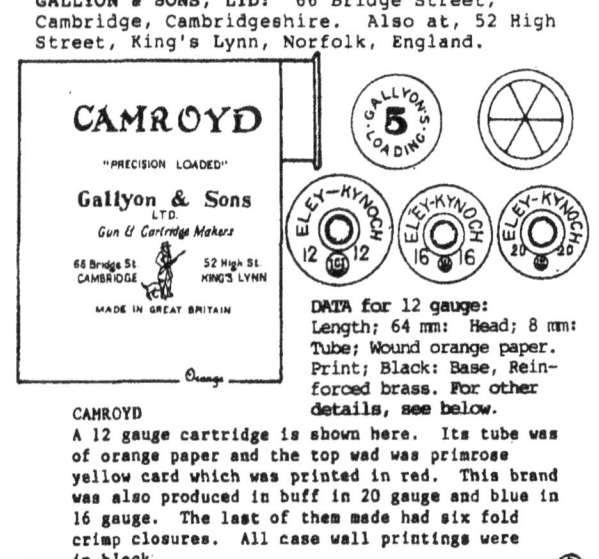

DATA for 12 gauge:
Length; 64 mm. Head; 8 mm:
Tube; Wound orange paper.
Print; Black: Base, Reinforced brass. For other details, see below.

CAMROYD
A 12 gauge cartridge is shown here. Its tube was of orange paper and the top wad was primrose yellow card which was printed in red. This brand was also produced in buff in 20 gauge and blue in 16 gauge. The last of them made had six fold crimp closures. All case wall printings were in black.

DN.3-2723. Drawn, 1/3/08.

GALLYON & SONS:
66 Bridge Street, Cambridge, Cambridgeshire, England.

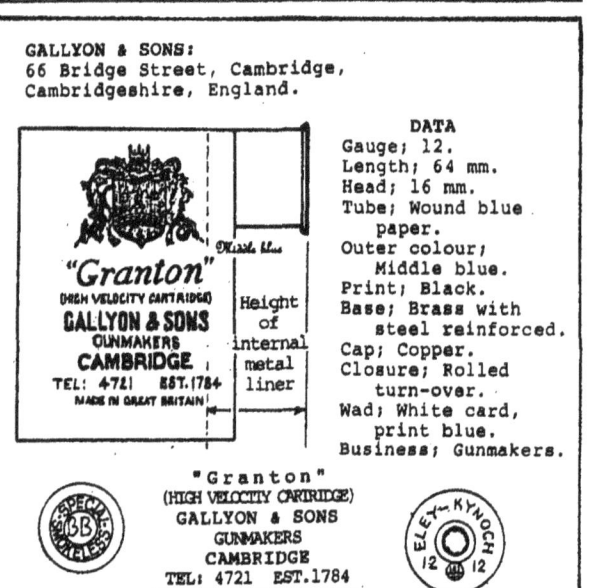

DATA
Gauge; 12.
Length; 64 mm.
Head; 16 mm.
Tube; Wound blue paper.
Outer colour; Middle blue.
Print; Black.
Base; Brass with steel reinforced.
Cap; Copper.
Closure; Rolled turn-over.
Wad; White card, print blue.
Business; Gunmakers.

DN.3-2597. Drawn, 19/10/07.

GALLYON & SONS, LTD:
66 Bridge Street, Cambridge, Cambridgeshire. Also at, 52 High Street, King's Lynn, Norfolk, England.

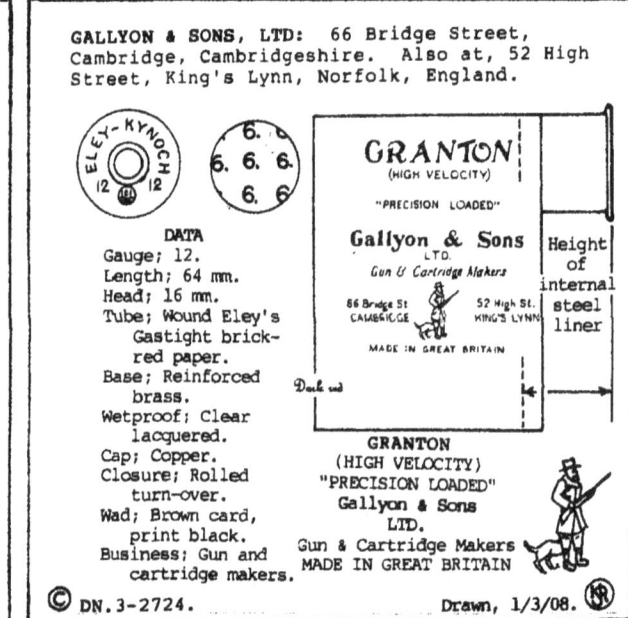

DATA
Gauge; 12.
Length; 64 mm.
Head; 16 mm.
Tube; Wound Eley's Gastight brick-red paper.
Base; Reinforced brass.
Wetproof; Clear lacquered.
Cap; Copper.
Closure; Rolled turn-over.
Wad; Brown card, print black.
Business; Gun and cartridge makers.

DN.3-2724. Drawn, 1/3/08.

GALLYON & SONS, LTD: 66 Bridge Street,
Cambridge, Cambridgeshire. Also at, 52 High
Street, King's Lynn, Norfolk, England.

KILHAM
"PRECISION LOADED"
Gallyon & Sons
LTD.
Gun & Cartridge Makers
66 Bridge St   52 High St
CAMBRIDGE   KING'S LYNN
MADE IN GREAT BRITAIN
Orange

Height of internal
metal reinforcing

KILHAM
"PRECISION LOADED"
Gallyon & Sons
LTD.
Gun & Cartridge Makers

DATA
Gauge; 12.
Length; 64 mm.
Head; 8 mm.
Tube; Wound orange
  paper.
Print; Black.
Wetproof; Clear
  lacquered.
Base; Reinforced
  brass.
Cap; Copper.
Closure; Rolled
  turn-over.
Wad; Brown card,
  print black.
Business; Gun and
  cartridge makers.

© DN.3-2722.   Drawn, 1/3/08.

GALLYON & SONS, LTD:
66 Bridge Street, Cambridge, Cambridgeshire. Also at,
52 High Street, King's Lynn, Norfolk, England.

SANDRINGHAM
"PRECISION LOADED"
Gallyon & Sons
LTD.
Gun & Cartridge Makers
66 Bridge St   52 High St
CAMBRIDGE   KING'S LYNN
MADE IN GREAT BRITAIN

SANDRINGHAM
"PRECISION LOADED"   66 Bridge St.
Gallyon & Sons   CAMBRIDGE
LTD.   52 High St.
Gun & Cartridge Makers KING'S LYNN
MADE IN GREAT BRITAIN

DATA
Gauge; 12.
Length; 64 mm.
Head; 8 mm.
Tube; Wound pink
  paper.
Colour; Pink.
Print; Black.
Wetproof; Clear
  lacquered.
Base; Reinforced
  brass.
Closure; Rolled
  turn-over.
Wad; Primrose yellow,
  print black.
Business; Gun and
  cartridge makers.

© DN.2-1401. Re-drawn; 11th July 2000

GALLYON & SONS, LTD:
66 Bridge Street, Cambridge, Cambridgeshire, England.

Loading possibly by H. Hodgson.

**The
VANGUARD
BY
GALLYON & SONS
GUNMAKERS
OF
CAMBRIDGE
Metal Lined Case**

The
VANGUARD   GUNMAKERS
BY   OF
GALLYON & SONS CAMBRIDGE
                Metal Lined Case

DATA
Gauge; 12.
Length; 64 mm.
Head; 8 mm.
Tube; Wound paper,
  rough textured.
Colour; Light brown.
Print; Black.
Base; Reinforced
  brass.
Closure; Rolled
  turn-over.
Wad; White card,
  print black.
Business; Gunmakers.
Circa; 1920's.
Case; France.

© DN.2-1209. Re-drawn; 22nd Nov 2000

GALLYON & SONS: 66 Bridge Street, Cambridge,
Cambridgeshire, England.

←— 65 mm —→

**The
VANGUARD
BY
GALLYON & SONS
GUNMAKERS
OF
CAMBRIDGE
Metal Lined Case**

17 mm
Brass

Grey

The VANGUARD
Drawn from a set of coloured photographs which was
sent to me by Mr B. Johnson, the paper tube has a
brownish grey appearance. The case wall printing
was in black. The top wad was of white card with
black printing.

© DN.3-1208.   Drawn, 9/7/08.

A. W. GAMAGE, LIMITED:
Holborn, London E.C.1., England.

**THE
A.W.G.
SPECIAL LONDON LOADED
SMOKELESS CARTRIDGE**

THE
A.W.G.
SPECIAL LONDON LOADED
SMOKELESS CARTRIDGE

DATA
Gauge; 16.
Length; 64 mm.
Head; 8 mm.
Tube; Wound brown
  paper.
Colour; Redish
  orange.
Print; Black.
Base; Brass.
Closure; Rolled
  turn-over.
Wad; White card,
  print deep pink.
Business; depart-
  mental stores.
Case; Germany.

© DN.2-0636. Re-drawn; 31st Oct 2000

A. W. GAMAGE, LTD:
Holborn, London E.C.1., England.

**THE
"A.W.G."
SPECIAL LONDON LOADED
SMOKELESS CARTRIDGE**

THE
"A.W.G."
SPECIAL LONDON LOADED
SMOKELESS CARTRIDGE

DATA
Gauge; 12.
Length; 65 mm.
Head; 8 mm.
Tube; Wound paper.
Colour; Pinkish-
  red.
Print; Black.
Base; Brass.
Closure; Rolled
  turn-over.
Wad; White card,
  print black.
Business;
  Department stores.
Case; Germany.

© DN.2-1746. Re-drawn; 10th Apr 2001

PLATE 125 [GAL – GAM]

JOHN G. GAMBLE: Magherafelt, Londonderry, Northern Ireland.

DATA
Gauge; 12.
Length; 64 mm.
Head; 8 mm.
Tube; Wound red paper.
Outer colour: Crimson red.
Print; Black.
Base; Brass.
Closure; Rolled turn-over.
Wad; White card, print red.
Business; Ammo merchant.
Circa, 1926.

"S W I F T"
Loaded by
JOHN G. GAMBLE
AMMUNITION MERCHANT
MAGHERAFELT

© DN.3-2556.   Drawn, 3/6/07.

JOHN G. GAMBLE: Magherafelt, Londonderry, Northern Ireland.

DATA
Gauge; 12.
Length; 64 mm.
Tube; Wound red paper.
Outer colour; Crimson red.
Print; Black.
Base; Brass.
Closure; Rolled turn-over.
Wad; White card, print black.
Business; Ammo merchant.
Circa; 1930's.

④

"S W I F T"
Loaded by
JOHN G. GAMBLE
AMMUNITION MERCHANT
MAGHERAFELT
MADE IN GREAT BRITAIN

© DN.3-2557.   Drawn, 3/6/07.

GAMEBORE CARTRIDGE COMPANY:
Great Union Street, Kingston upon Hull, Humberside, HU9 1AR., England.

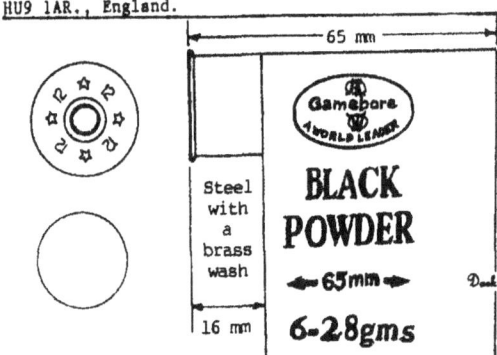

BLACK POWDER

One of the few black powder loaded cartridges in this day and age. It was aimed at those shooters who still enjoy shooting old damascus barreled guns. A market being found for these in America. The tube was wound brown paper with an outer layer of deep crimson. It was closed by a roll turn-over with a middle-green top wad. Printings were in black. Circa; 2004.

© DN.3-1790.   Drawn, 3/2/09.

GAMEBORE CARTRIDGE COMPANY; Great Union Street, Hull, Humberside, HU9 1AR, England.

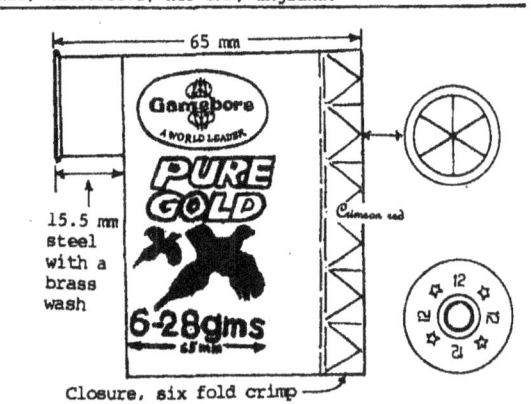

Closure, six fold crimp

This cartridge had its tube wound from brown paper with the outer layer in crimson red. The case wall printing was in black.

PURE GOLD

© DN.3-5518.   Drawn, 3/8/2011.

GAMEBORE CARTRIDGE COMPANY:
Great Union Street, Kingston upon Hull, Humberside, HU9 1AR., England.

DATA
Gauge; 16.
Length; 67 mm.
Head; 15 mm.
Tube; Fine ribbed red plastic.
Print; Black.
Base; Steel with a brass wash.
Closure; Six fold crimp.
Business; Shotgun cartridges.
Circa; Late 1990's.

Gamebore
A WORLD LEADER
Tin Shot
NON TOXIC
-67mm-
4-26gms

© DN.2-2383.   31st Dec 2000

GAMEBORE CARTRIDGE COMPANY; Great Union Street, Hull, Humberside, HU9 1AR, England.

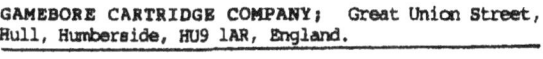

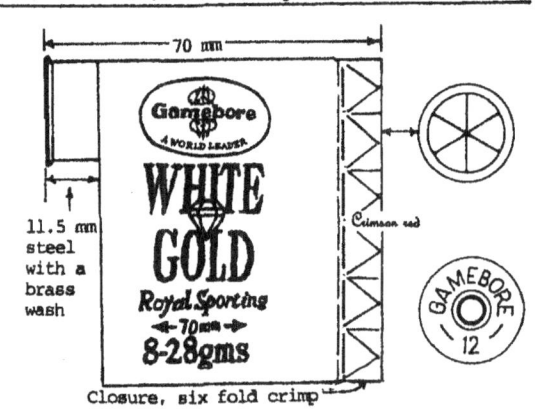

Closure, six fold crimp

This cartridge had its tube wound from brown paper with the outer layer in crimson red. The case wall printing was in black.

WHITE GOLD

© DN.3-5521.   Drawn, 5/8/2011.

PLATE 126 [GAM – GAM]

WILLIAM GARDEN:
122½ Union Street, Aberdeen, Aberdeenshire (Grampian), Scotland.

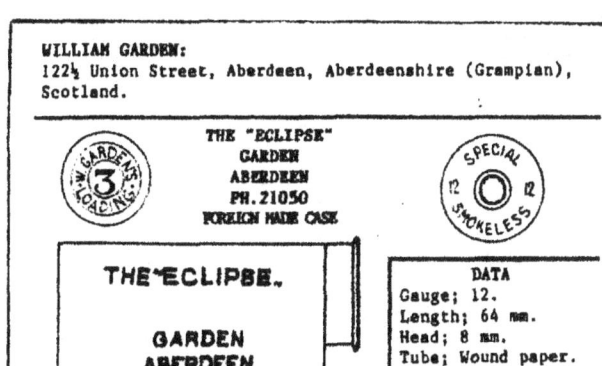

DATA
Gauge; 12.
Length; 64 mm.
Head; 8 mm.
Tube; Wound paper.
Colour; Red.
Print; Black.
Base; Brass.
Cap; nickel.
Wetproof; Clear lacquered.
Closure; Rolled turn-over.
Wad; Brown card, print black.
Business; Gunmaker.
Case; Fiocchi, Italy.

Cartridge was not internally examined.
DN.2-0411. Re-drawn; 16th Feb 2001.

T. M. GARDINER, LTD: Hoddesdon, Hertfordshire, England.
Business; Ammunition dealers.

This cartridge had a dull red paper tube that was printed in black. The over-shot wad was yellow and was printed in black.
Circa; 1930's.

DN.5,1036.

WILLIAM GARDNER:
6 High Street, Chippenham, Wiltshire, England.

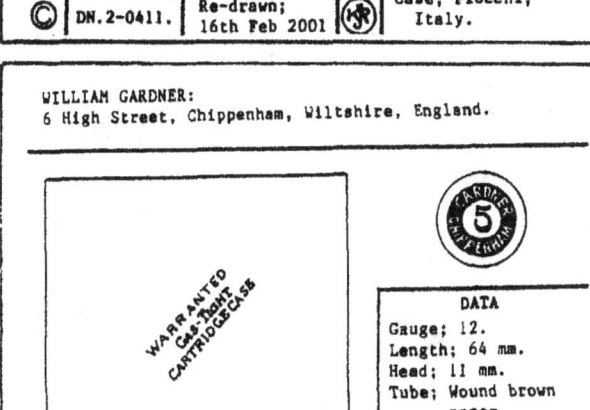

DATA
Gauge; 12.
Length; 64 mm.
Head; 11 mm.
Tube; Wound brown paper.
Colour; Dark green.
Print; Black.
Base; Brass.
Closure; Rolled turn-over.
Wad; White card, print red.
Business; Gunmaker.

DN.2-0394. Re-drawn 3rd Feb 1999.

M. GARNETT:
Crampton Court. Later at, 31 Parliament Street, Dublin, Republic of Ireland.

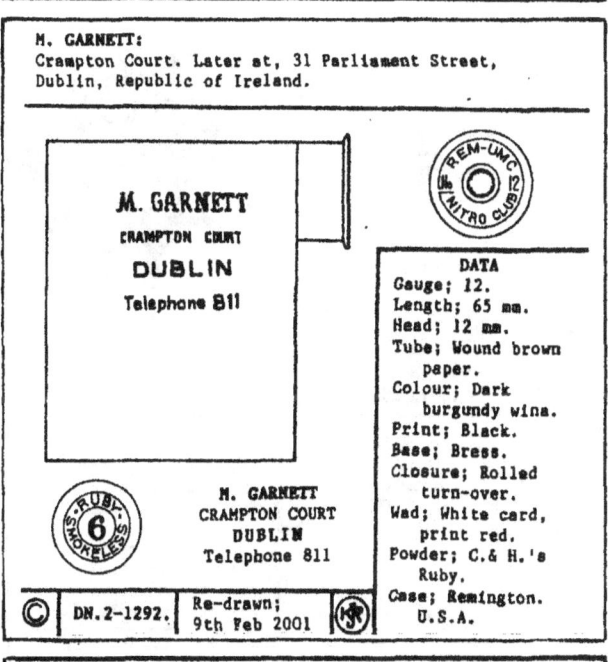

DATA
Gauge; 12.
Length; 65 mm.
Head; 12 mm.
Tube; Wound brown paper.
Colour; Dark burgundy wine.
Print; Black.
Base; Brass.
Closure; Rolled turn-over.
Wad; White card, print red.
Powder; C.& H.'s Ruby.
Case; Remington. U.S.A.

DN.2-1292. Re-drawn; 9th Feb 2001.

M. GARNETT & SON:
31 Parliament Street, Dublin, Republic of Ireland.

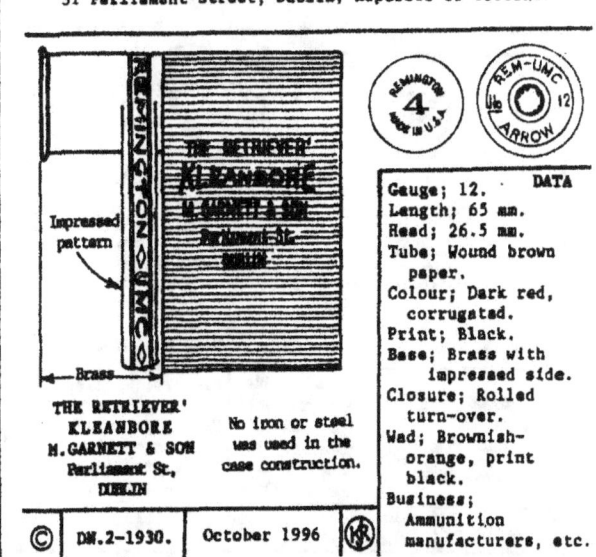

'THE RETRIEVER' KLEANBORE
M. GARNETT & SON
Parliament St,
DUBLIN

No iron or steel was used in the case construction.

Gauge; 12. DATA
Length; 65 mm.
Head; 26.5 mm.
Tube; Wound brown paper.
Colour; Dark red, corrugated.
Print; Black.
Base; Brass with impressed side.
Closure; Rolled turn-over.
Wad; Brownish-orange, print black.
Business; Ammunition manufacturers, etc.

DN.2-1930. October 1996.

FRANK GARRETT: 7¼ Bath Street, Birmingham, Warwickshire (West Midlands). Also at, Ilmington, Warwickshire. And also at, Evesham, Worcestershire (Hereford & Worcester, England.

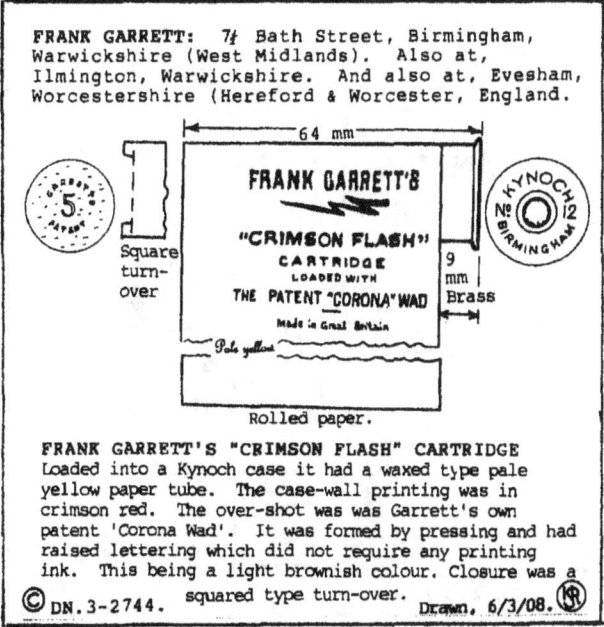

FRANK GARRETT'S "CRIMSON FLASH" CARTRIDGE
Loaded into a Kynoch case it had a waxed type pale yellow paper tube. The case-wall printing was in crimson red. The over-shot was was Garrett's own patent 'Corona Wad'. It was formed by pressing and had raised lettering which did not require any printing ink. This being a light brownish colour. Closure was a squared type turn-over.

DN.3-2744. Drawn; 6/3/08.

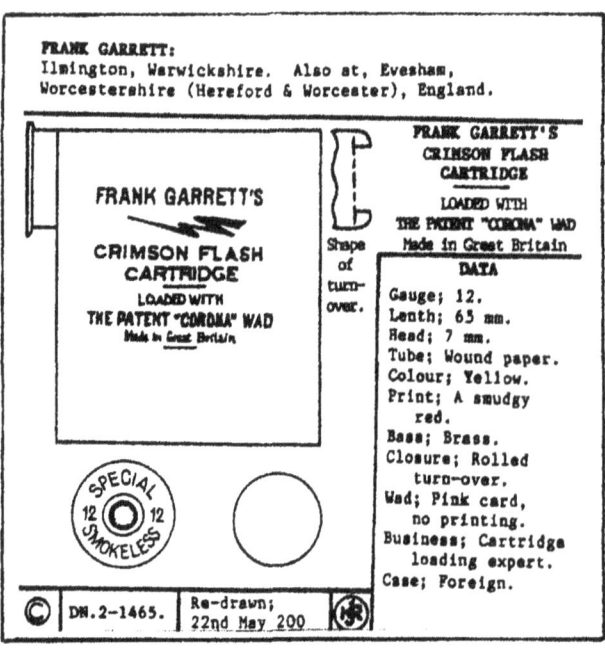

FRANK GARRETT:
Ilmington, Warwickshire. Also at, Evesham, Worcestershire (Hereford & Worcester), England.

FRANK GARRETT'S CRIMSON FLASH CARTRIDGE
LOADED WITH THE PATENT "CORONA" WAD
Made in Great Britain

DATA
Gauge; 12.
Length; 65 mm.
Head; 7 mm.
Tube; Wound paper.
Colour; Yellow.
Print; A smudgy red.
Base; Brass.
Closure; Rolled turn-over.
Wad; Pink card, no printing.
Business; Cartridge loading expert.
Case; Foreign.

DN.2-1465. Re-drawn; 22nd May 200

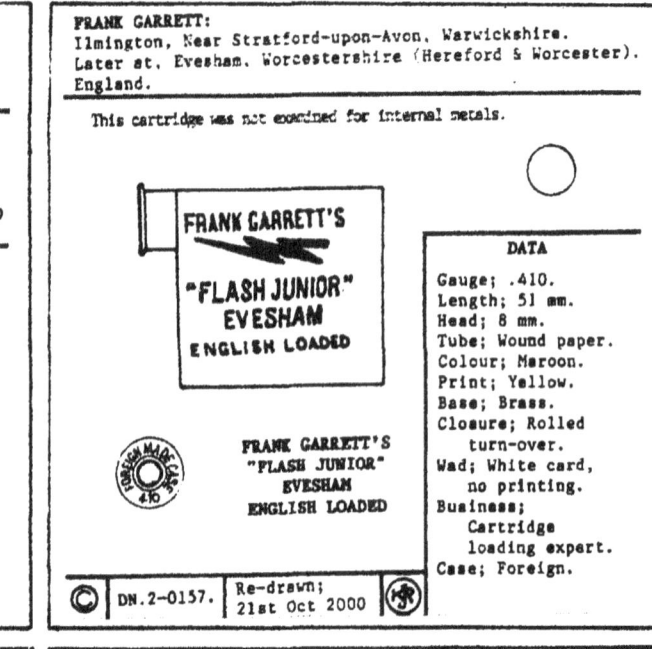

FRANK GARRETT:
Ilmington, Near Stratford-upon-Avon, Warwickshire. Later at, Evesham, Worcestershire (Hereford & Worcester). England.

This cartridge was not examined for internal metals.

FRANK GARRETT'S "FLASH JUNIOR" EVESHAM ENGLISH LOADED

DATA
Gauge; .410.
Length; 51 mm.
Head; 8 mm.
Tube; Wound paper.
Colour; Maroon.
Print; Yellow.
Base; Brass.
Closure; Rolled turn-over.
Wad; White card, no printing.
Business; Cartridge loading expert.
Case; Foreign.

DN.2-0157. Re-drawn; 21st Oct 2000

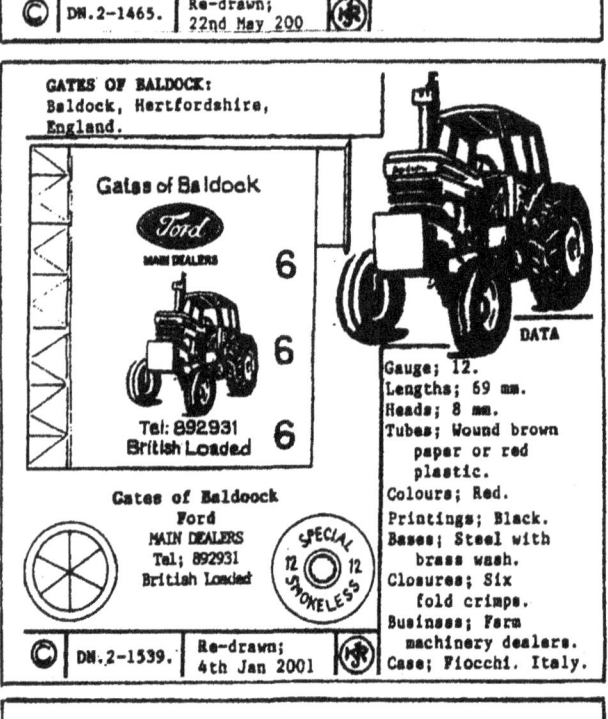

GATES OF BALDOCK:
Baldock, Hertfordshire, England.

Gates of Baldock
Ford MAIN DEALERS
Tel: 892931
British Loaded

DATA
Gauge; 12.
Lengths; 69 mm.
Heads; 8 mm.
Tubes; Wound brown paper or red plastic.
Colours; Red.
Printings; Black.
Bases; Steel with brass wash.
Closures; Six fold crimps.
Business; Farm machinery dealers.
Case; Fiocchi, Italy.

DN.2-1539. Re-drawn; 4th Jan 2001

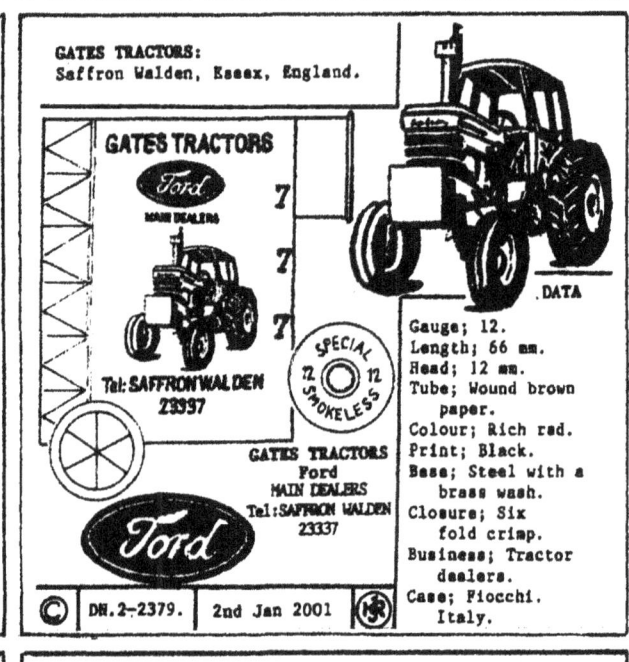

GATES TRACTORS:
Saffron Walden, Essex, England.

GATES TRACTORS
Ford MAIN DEALERS
Tel: SAFFRON WALDEN 23337

DATA
Gauge; 12.
Length; 66 mm.
Head; 12 mm.
Tube; Wound brown paper.
Colour; Rich red.
Print; Black.
Base; Steel with a brass wash.
Closure; Six fold crimp.
Business; Tractor dealers.
Case; Fiocchi. Italy.

DN.2-2379. 2nd Jan 2001

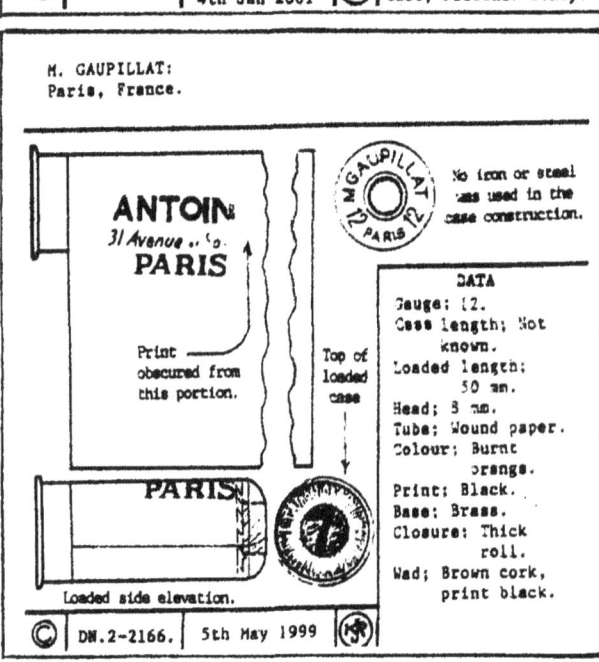

M. GAUPILLAT:
Paris, France.

ANTOIN
31 Avenue ..
PARIS

Print obscured from this portion.

Top of loaded case

PARIS

Loaded side elevation.

No iron or steel was used in the case construction.

DATA
Gauge; 12.
Case length; Not known.
Loaded length; 50 mm.
Head; 8 mm.
Tube; Wound paper.
Colour; Burnt orange.
Print; Black.
Base; Brass.
Closure; Thick roll.
Wad; Brown cork, print black.

DN.2-2166. 5th May 1999

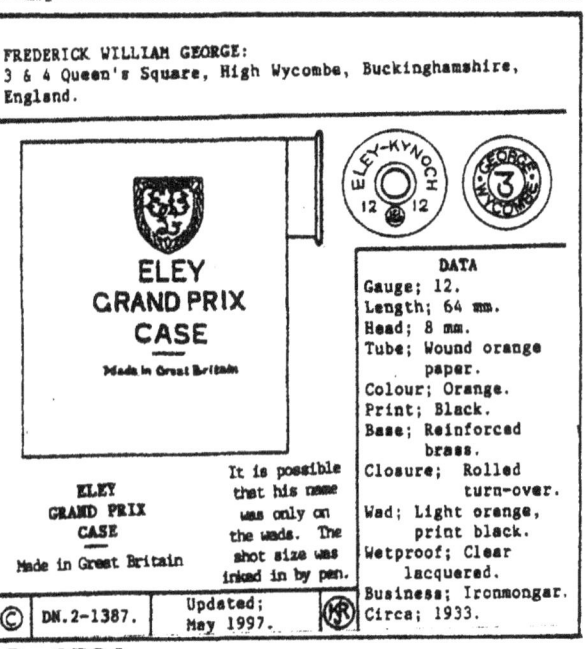

FREDERICK WILLIAM GEORGE:
3 & 4 Queen's Square, High Wycombe, Buckinghamshire, England.

ELEY GRAND PRIX CASE
Made in Great Britain

It is possible that his name was only on the wads. The shot size was inked in by pen.

DATA
Gauge; 12.
Length; 64 mm.
Head; 8 mm.
Tube; Wound orange paper.
Colour; Orange.
Print; Black.
Base; Reinforced brass.
Closure; Rolled turn-over.
Wad; Light orange, print black.
Wetproof; Clear lacquered.
Business; Ironmonger.
Circa; 1933.

DN.2-1387. Updated; May 1997.

PLATE 128 [GAR – GEO]

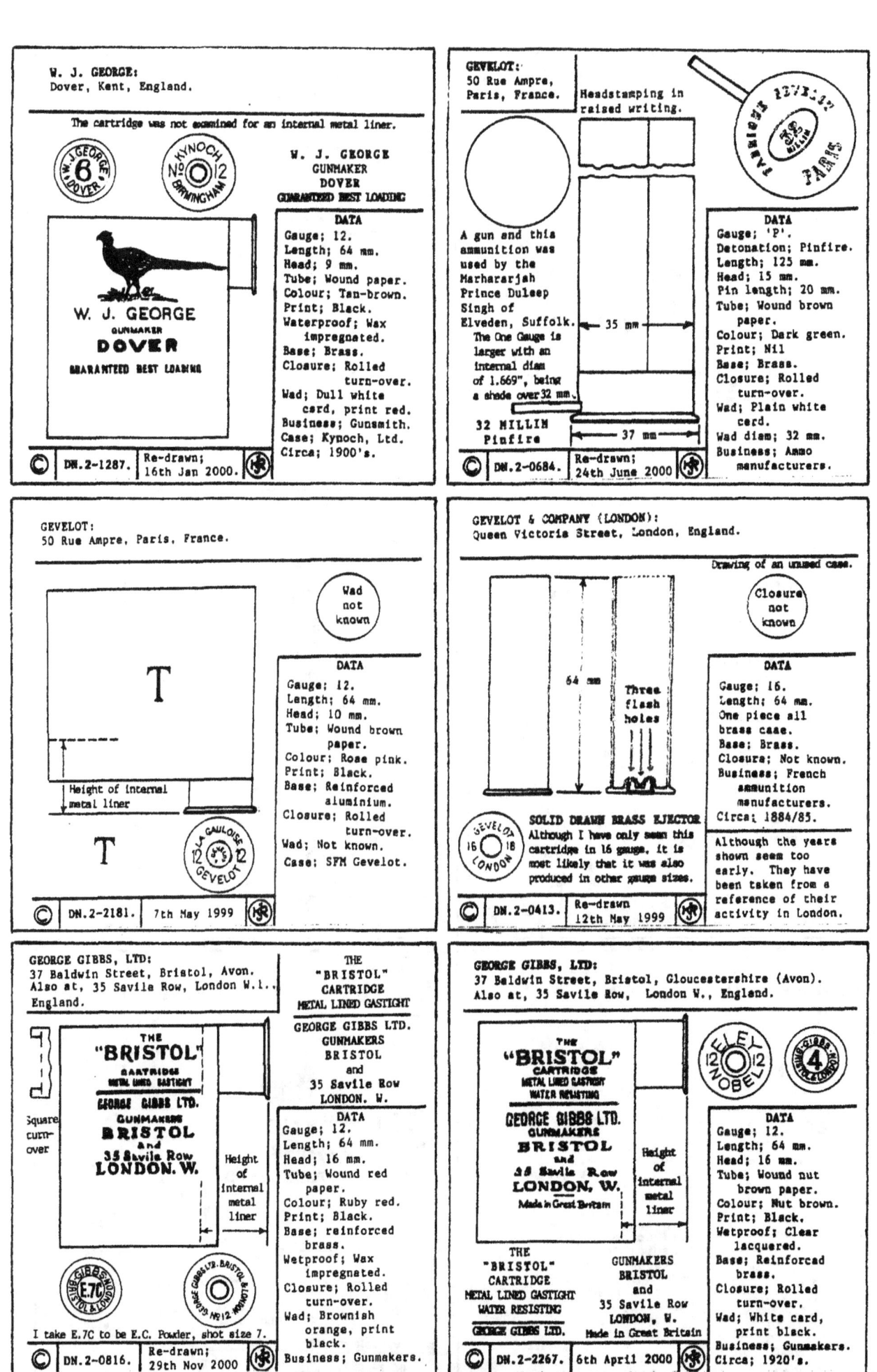

PLATE 129 [GEO - GIB]

GEORGE GIBBS, LTD: 37 Baldwin Street, Bristol, Gloucestershire (Avon), England.

The "BRISTOL"
METAL LINED CARTRIDGE
WATER RESISTING
GEORGE GIBBS Ltd.
37 Baldwin Street
BRISTOL
Made in Great Britan

DATA
Gauge; 16.
Length; 64 mm.
Head; 15 mm.
Tube; Wound blue paper.
Colour; Deep or mariner blue.
Print; Navy blue or black.
Base; Reinforced brass.
Cap; Copper.
Closure; Rolled turn-over.
Wad; White card, print black.
Business; Gunmakers.
Circa; 1930's.

© DN.3-0128. Drawn, 27/3/08.

GEORGE GIBBS, LTD: 37 Baldwin Street, Bristol, Gloucestershire (Avon), England.

"THE COUNTY"
GEORGE GIBBS LTD.
Gunmakers
37 Baldwin Street
BRISTOL
KEEP DRY
MADE IN GREAT BRITAIN

DATA
Gauge; 12.
Length; 64 mm.
Head; 8 mm.
Tube; Wound grey-green paper.
Print; Black.
Base; Reinforced brass.
Cap; Copper.
Closure; Rolled turn-over.
Wad; White card, print black.
Business; Gunmakers.
Circa; 1930's.

© DN.3-0118. Drawn, 20/4/08.

GEORGE GIBBS, LTD: 37 Baldwin Street, Bristol, Gloucestershire (Avon). Also at, 35 Savile Row, London W.1., England.

GEORGE GIBBS,
GUNMAKER,
BRISTOL,
AND
35 SAVILE ROW,
LONDON.
"FIELD CARTRIDGE"

DATA
Gauge; 12.
Length; 65 mm.
Head; 9 mm.
Tube; Wound paper.
Colour; Orange.
Print; Black.
Base; Brass. (Not internally examined).
Closure; Rolled turn-over.
Wad; White card, print black.
Business; Gunmaker.

© DN.3-1556. Drawn, 24/4/08.

GEORGE GIBBS, LTD: 37 Baldwin Street, Bristol, Gloucestershire (Avon), England.

The "FIELD"
GEORGE GIBBS LTD.
GUNMAKERS
37 Baldwin Street
BRISTOL
KEEP DRY
MADE IN GREAT BRITAIN

DATA
Gauge; 12.
Length; 64 mm.
Head; 8 mm.
Tube; Wound red paper.
Print; Black.
Base; Reinforced brass.
Cap; Copper.
Closure; Rolled turn-over.
Wad; Blue, print black.
Business; Gunmakers.
Circa; 1930's.

© DN.3-0120. Drawn, 14/4/08.

GEORGE GIBBS, LTD: 37 Baldwin Street, Bristol, Gloucestershire (Avon), England.

THE
"GIBBS"
GEORGE GIBBS LTD.
GUNMAKERS
37 Baldwin Street
BRISTOL
KEEP DRY
MADE IN GREAT BRITAIN

DATA
Gauge; 12.
Length; 64 mm.
Head; 16 mm.
Tube; Wound dark green paper.
Colour; Winter green.
Print; Navy blue or black.
Base; Reinforced brass.
Cap; Copper.
Closure; Rolled turn-over.
Wad; White card, print black.
Business; Gunmakers.
Circa; 1930's.
Not examined for internal metals.

© DN.3-2840. Drawn, 27/3/08.

GEORGE GIBBS, LIMITED: 39 Baldwin Street, Bristol 1, Gloucestershire (Avon). Also at, 35 Savile Row, London, England.

Closed by a squared turn-over.

KYNOCH
5/8" BRASS
STEEL LINED

KYNOCH
5/8" BRASS
STEEL LINED
Cases were sold and loaded by many.

DATA
Gauge; 12.
Lengths; 65 and 70 mm.
Head; 16 mm.
Tubes; Wound brown paper.
Colour; Middle brown.
Print; Black.
Base; Reinforced brass.
Closure; Rolled turn-over.
Wad; White card, print black.
Business; Gunmakers.

© DN.2-1082. Re-drawn December 1998

A. C. GILBERT & SON, LTD: Billinghay, Near Sleaford, Lincolnshire. England.

ACG

Loaded by the Hull Cartridge Company into an imported Fiocchi paper tubed case. It had black case wall printing on an outer layer of red paper and was waterproofed by clear varnishing. Closure was by a six fold crimp. A nickel cap was fitted.

© DN.3-1537. Revised; 12/1/09.

J. GILMAN & SON LTD:
Corners of, Stafford Street & Corporation Street, Birmingham, Midlands, England.

This drawing has been made from a set of photographs.

DATA

Gauge; 12.
Length; 64 mm.
Head; 8 mm.
Tube; Wound paper.
Colour; Red.
Print; Black.
Base; Brass.
Closure; Rolled turn-over.
Wad; White card, print black.

© DN.2-1285. Updated; December 1994 REGISTERED NO, 28596.

J. GILMAN & SON, LTD:
Corners of, Stafford Street & Corporation Street, Birmingham, (West Midlands), England.

Registered No> 28596.
J. GILMAN & SON LTD.
CORNER
STAFFORD STREET
AND
CORPORATION STREET
BIRMINGHAM
Made in Great Britain

DATA

Gauge; 12.
Length; 64 mm.
Head; 8 mm.
Tube Wound red paper.
Colour; Crimson.
Print; Black.
Base; Reinforced brass.
Closure; Rolled turn-over.
Wad; Yellow, print black.
Wetproof; Lacquered.

© DN. 2-2510. 18th July 2002

GIULIO FIOCCHI:
Lecco, Lombardi, Italy.

DATA

Gauge; 12.
Length; 64.5 mm.
Head; 25 mm.
Tube; Wound paper.
Colour; Pale mustard yellow.
Print; Black.
Base; Reinforced brass.
Closure; Rolled turn-over.
Wad; Light brown card, print grey.
Business; Ammunition manufacturers.

© DN.2-1959. May 1997.

GIULIO FIOCCHI:
Lecco, Lombardi, Italy.

Top view of cartridge

DATA

Gauge; 12.
Length; 64 mm.
Head; 10 mm.
Tube; Wound paper.
Colour; Dark red.
Print; Black.
Base; Brass reinforced.
Closure; Rolled turn-over.
Wad; Transparent celluloid.
Business; Ammunition manufacturers.

© DN.2-1984. June 1997.

J. GLIDDON & SONS (Agricultural engineers):
Williton. Also at Minehead, Somerset.
WILLIAM TARR & SONS (Hardware and agricultural):
Minehead, Somerset, England.

THE "EXMOOR" CARTRIDGE
Specially Loaded by
J. GLIDDON & SONS
WILLITON
W. TARR & SONS
MINEHEAD

DATA

Gauge; 12
Length; 64 mm.
Head; 8 mm.
Tube; Wound orange paper.
Print; Black.
Base; Reinforced brass.
Closure; Rolled.
Wad; White card, print rose-pink.
Business; In 1913, Gliddon purchased the business of W. Tarr & Sons.
Case; Nobel Industries, Ltd.
Circa; Mid 1920's.

© DN.2-2091. November 1998

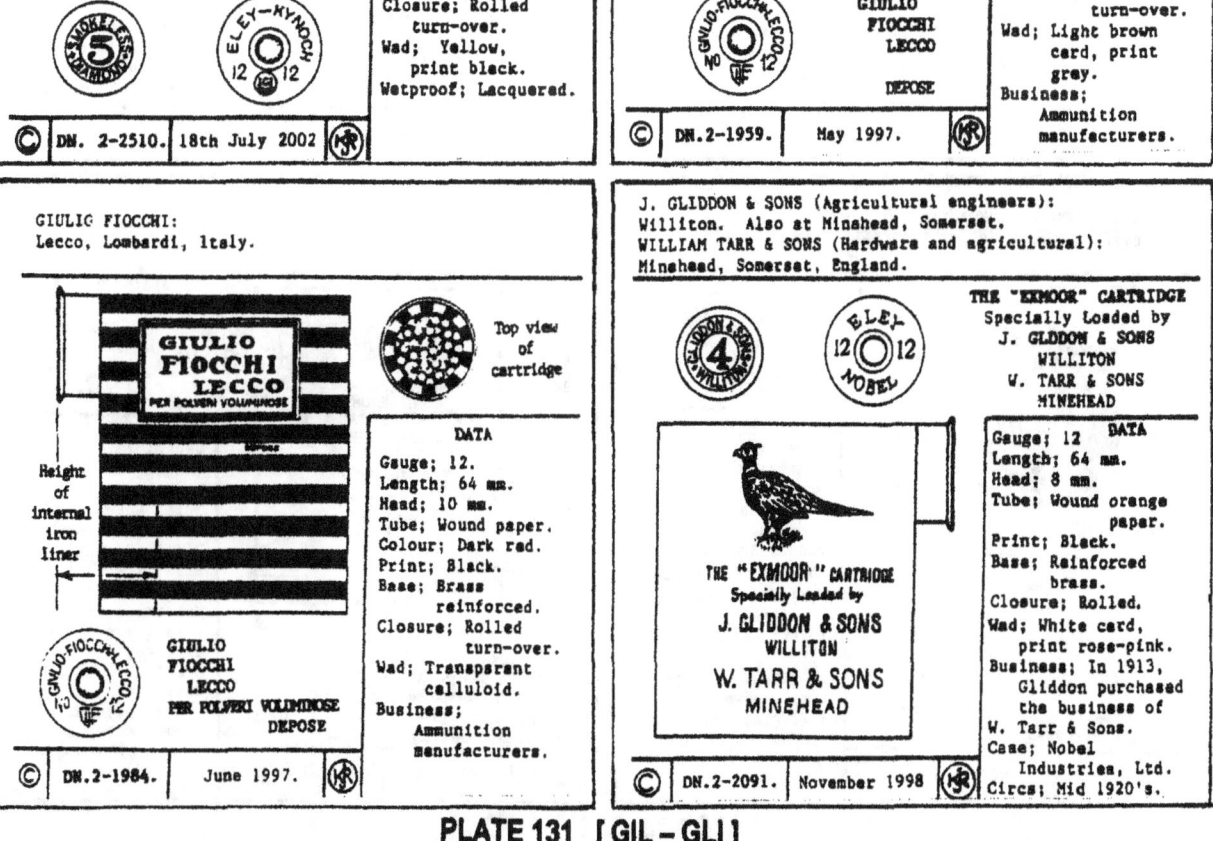

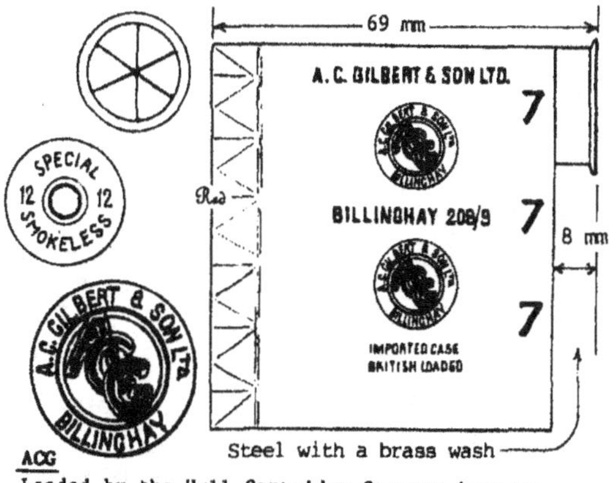

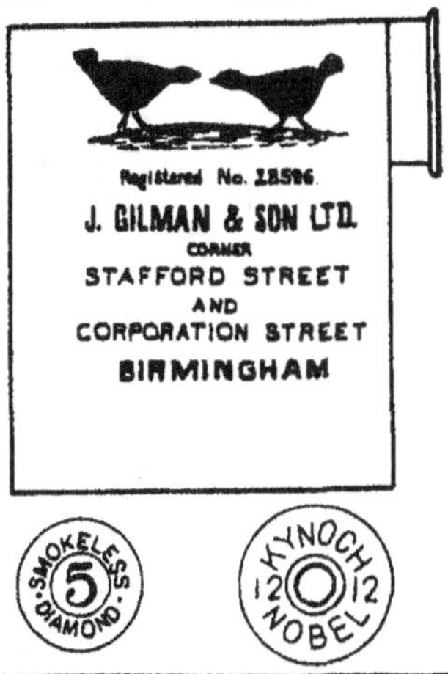

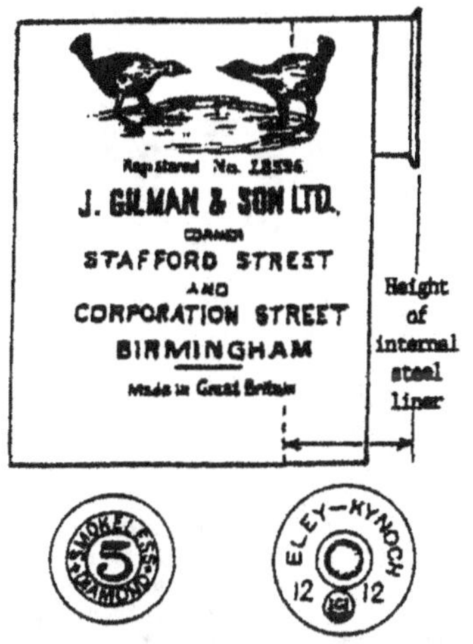

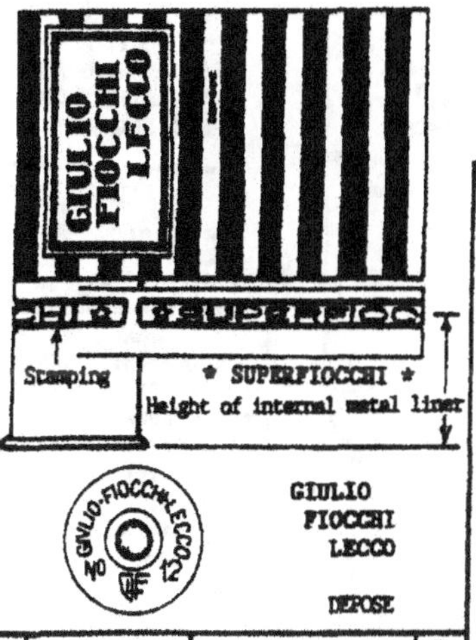

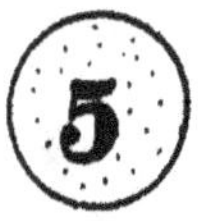

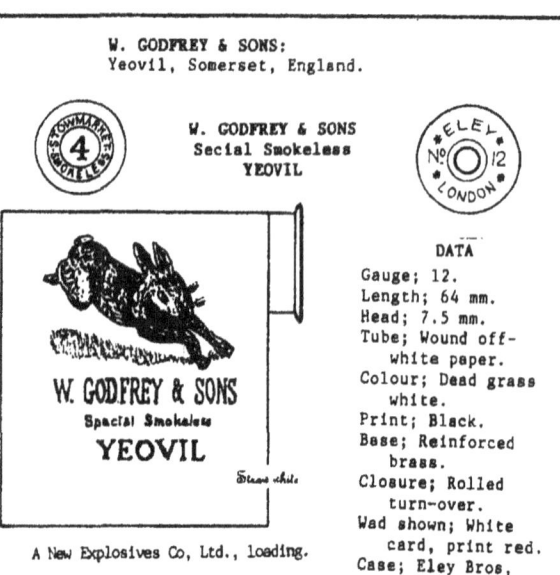
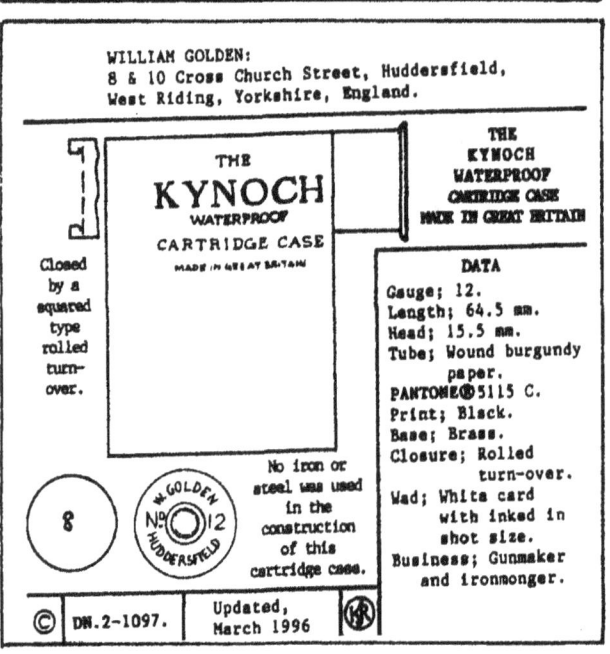
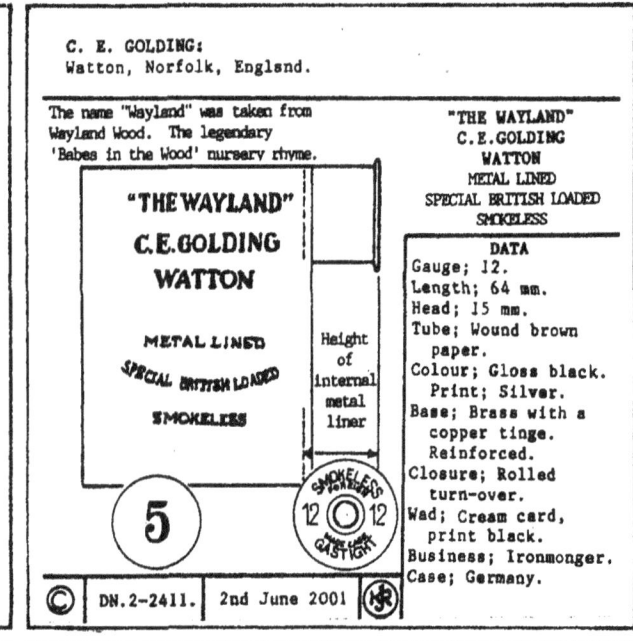
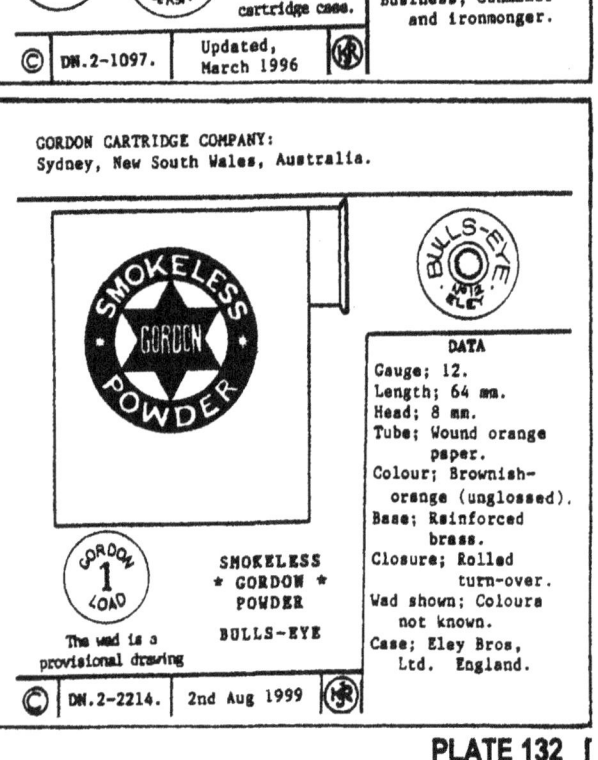
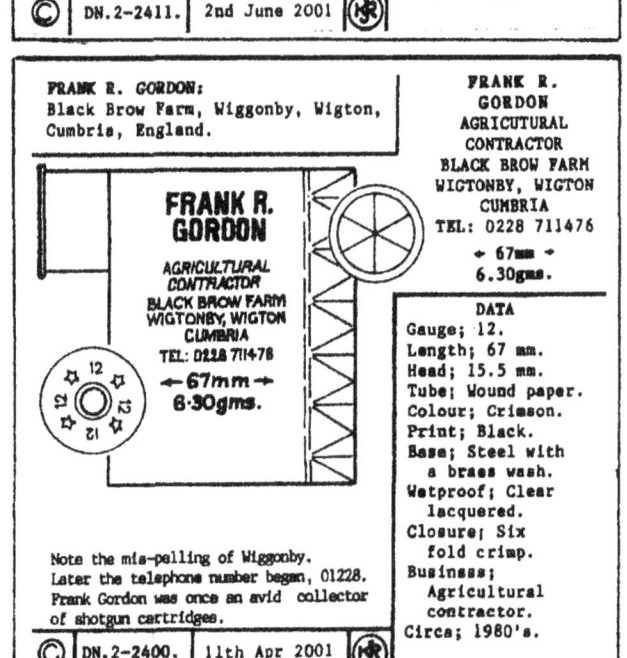

PLATE 132 [GLO - GOR]

JOHN R. GOW & SONS:
Dundee, Angus-shire (Tayside), Scotland.

DATA
Gauge; 12.
Length; 60 mm !.
Head; 8 mm.
Tube; Wound paper.
Colour; Orange.
Print; Black.
Base; Brass.
Closure; Rolled turn-over.
Wad; Not known.
Circa; 1907.
Business; Gunmakers.

This drawing has been made from a set of photographs that were taken of a possible cut down reload. The headstamping is very rare. Two similar heads with this stamping were once found in Oxfordshire.

© DN.2-1772. Updated; January 1995

JOHN R. GOW & SONS:
12 Union Street, Dundee, Angus-shire (Tayside), Scotland.

DATA
Gauge; 12.
Length; 64 mm.
Head; 8 mm.
Tube; Wound orange paper.
Colour; Orange.
Print; Black.
Base; Reinforced brass.
Closure; Rolled turn-over.
Wad; Bluaball blue card, print black.
Business; Gunmakers.
Circa; Late 1930's.

© DN.2-0686. Re-drawn; 20th May 2000

OLIVER J. GOWER, LTD:
31 High Street. Also at, 33 Marlowes, Hemel Hempstead, Hertfordshire, England.

DATA
Gauge; 12.
Length; 70 mm.
Head; 8 mm.
Tube; Wound white paper.
Outer colour; Red.
Print; Black.
Base; Brass.
Closure; Six fold crimp.
Loaded by; Hull Cartridge Co.
Case by; Fiocchi.

GOWERS

© DN.3-1191. Revised; 20/12/08.

G. P. GRAHAM:
Cockermouth, Cumberland (Cumbria), England.

Squared turn-over.

DATA
Gauge; 12.
Length; 64 mm.
Head; 8 mm.
Tube; Wound paper.
Colour; Pale apple green.
Print; Black.
Base; Brass.
Closure; Rolled turn-over.
Wad; White card, no print.
Business; Gunmaker.

© DN.2-0896. Re-drawn; 21st Jan 2000.

J. GRAHAM & CO, LTD:
27 Union Street, Inverness, Inverness-shire, Scotland.

"BON-TON"
Loaded by
J.GRAHAM & CO. LTD.
INVERNESS

DATA
Gauge; 12.
Length; 64 mm.
Head; 8 mm.
Tubes; Wound coloured papers.
Colours; Shades of middle or Jamaica blue with black or dark blue print. Also orange with black print.
Base; Brass.
Closure; Rolled.
Wad; Deep blue, print black.
Business; Gunmakers.

Tel. No.; 178 Inverness
Telegrams; "Graham Gunmakers. Inverness"
Made in Great Britain

© DN.0155. Re-drawn December 1998

JOHN GRAHAM & CO, LTD:
27 Union Street, Inverness, Inverness-shire (Highland), Scotland.

DATA
Gauge; 12.
Length; 64 mm.
Head; 16 mm.
Tube; Wound dark green paper.
Print; Black or navy blue.
Base; Brass.
Cap; Copper.
Closure; Rolled turn-over.
Wad; Deep blue, print black.
Business; Gun and fishing tackle makers.

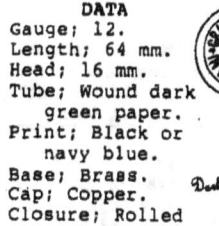  

"HIGHLAND"
LOADED BY
J.GRAHAM & CO. LTD.
GUNMAKERS
INVERNESS
Made in Great Britain

Not examined for internal metal

© DN.3-0154. Drawn, 4/4/08.

PLATE 133 [GOW - GRA]

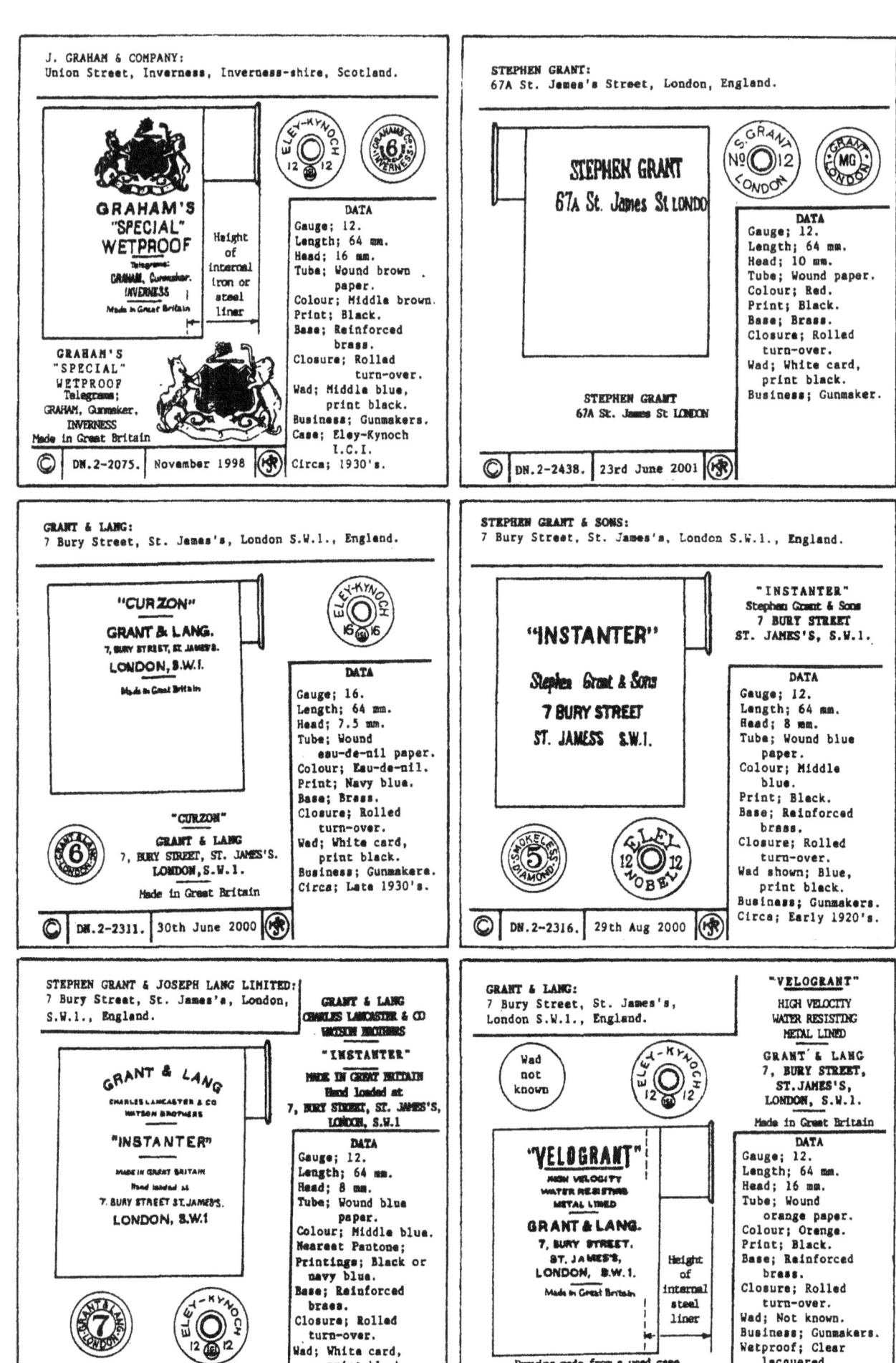

GRANT & LANG:
7 Bury Street, St. James's.
London S.W.1., England.

GRANT & LANG,
CHARLES LANCASTER & CO.
WATSON BROTHERS
"VELOGRANT"
HIGH VELOCITY
WATER RESISTING
METAL LINED

MADE IN GREAT BRITAIN
Hand loaded at
7, BURY STREET, ST.JAMES'S,
LONDON, S.W.1.

DATA
Gauge; 12.
Length; 64 mm.
Head; 16 mm.
Tube; Wound orange paper.
Print; Black.
Base; Reinforced brass.
Closure; Rolled.
Wad; White card, print black.
Business; Gunmakers.
Wetproof; Lacquered.
No shot size shown.

DN.2-2364. 3rd Oct 2000

D. GRAY & COMPANY:
30 Union Street, Inverness, Inverness-shire, Scotland.

ELEY EJECTOR

DATA
Gauge; 12.
Length; 64 mm.
Brass height; 57 mm.
Tube; Wound nut-brown paper.
Colour; Nut brown.
Print; Nil.
Base; Brass with reinforcing.
Closure; Rolled turn-over.
Wad; Pale orange, print black.
Case; Eley Bros Ltd.
Business; Gunmakers.

DN.2-1937. October 1996

D. GRAY & COMPANY:
30 Union Street, Inverness, Inverness-shire, Scotland.

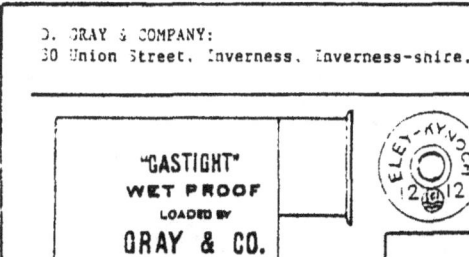

"GASTIGHT"
WET PROOF
LOADED BY
GRAY & CO.
GUNMAKERS
INVERNESS
Telegrams:
"SPORT, INVERNESS"
Telephone 225
MADE IN GREAT BRITAIN

DATA
Gauge; 12.
Length; 64 mm.
Head; 16 mm.
Tube; Wound brick red paper.
Print; Black.
Wetproof; Lacquered.
Base; Reinforced brass.
Closure; Rolled turn-over.
Wad; Brown card, print black.
Case; Eley-Kynoch I.C.I.
Business; Gunmakers.
Circa; 1930's.

DN.2-1739. Updated; December 1997.

DON GRAY GUNS: 7 Railway Street, Chatham, Kent, England.

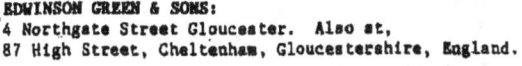

DON GRAY
SPORTS
6
Yellow

DATA
Gauge; 20.
Length; 64 mm.
Head; 7 mm.
Tube; Wound paper.
Outer colour; Buff-yellow.
Print; Black.
Base; Brass.
Cap; Nickle.
Closure; Six fold crimp.
Business; Gunshop.
Case; Fiocchi, Italy.
Possible loading; By Hull Cartridge.

DON GRAY SPORTS

No iron or steel was used in the case construction.

DN.3-2622. Drawn, 15/11/07.

REGINALD GRAY:
Doncaster, South Yorkshire, England.

Anti Corrosive foreign Cap&Case
LOADED IN GREAT BRITAIN

THE DON
REG. GRAY.
YOUR SPORTING
SPORTS DEALER
DONCASTER

DATA
Gauge; 12.
Length; 64.5 mm.
Head; 8 mm.
Tube; Wound brown paper.
Colour; Dark blue.
Print; Black.
Base; Brass.
Closure; Rolled turn-over.
Wad; Red card, print black.
Wetproof; Lacquered.
Case; Foreign.
Business; Sports dealer.

Note how the pheasant's neck includes the letter 'N' in Great Britain.

DN.2-0156. Updated; April 1995

EDWINSON GREEN & SONS:
4 Northgate Street Gloucester. Also at,
87 High Street, Cheltenham, Gloucestershire, England.

THE "Cotswold"
LOADED BY
EDWINSON GREEN & SONS
CHELTENHAM & GLOUCESTER.

DATA
Gauge; 12.
Length; 64 mm.
Head; 8 mm.
Tube; Wound paper.
Colour; Deep orange.
Print; Black.
Base; Brass.
Closure; Rolled turn-over.
Wad; White card, print red.
Business; Gunmakers.

THE "Cotswold"
LOADED BY
EDWINSON GREEN & SONS
CHELTENHAM & GLOUCESTER.

DN.2-1391. Re-drawn; 8th Jan 2002

PLATE 135 [GRA – GRE]

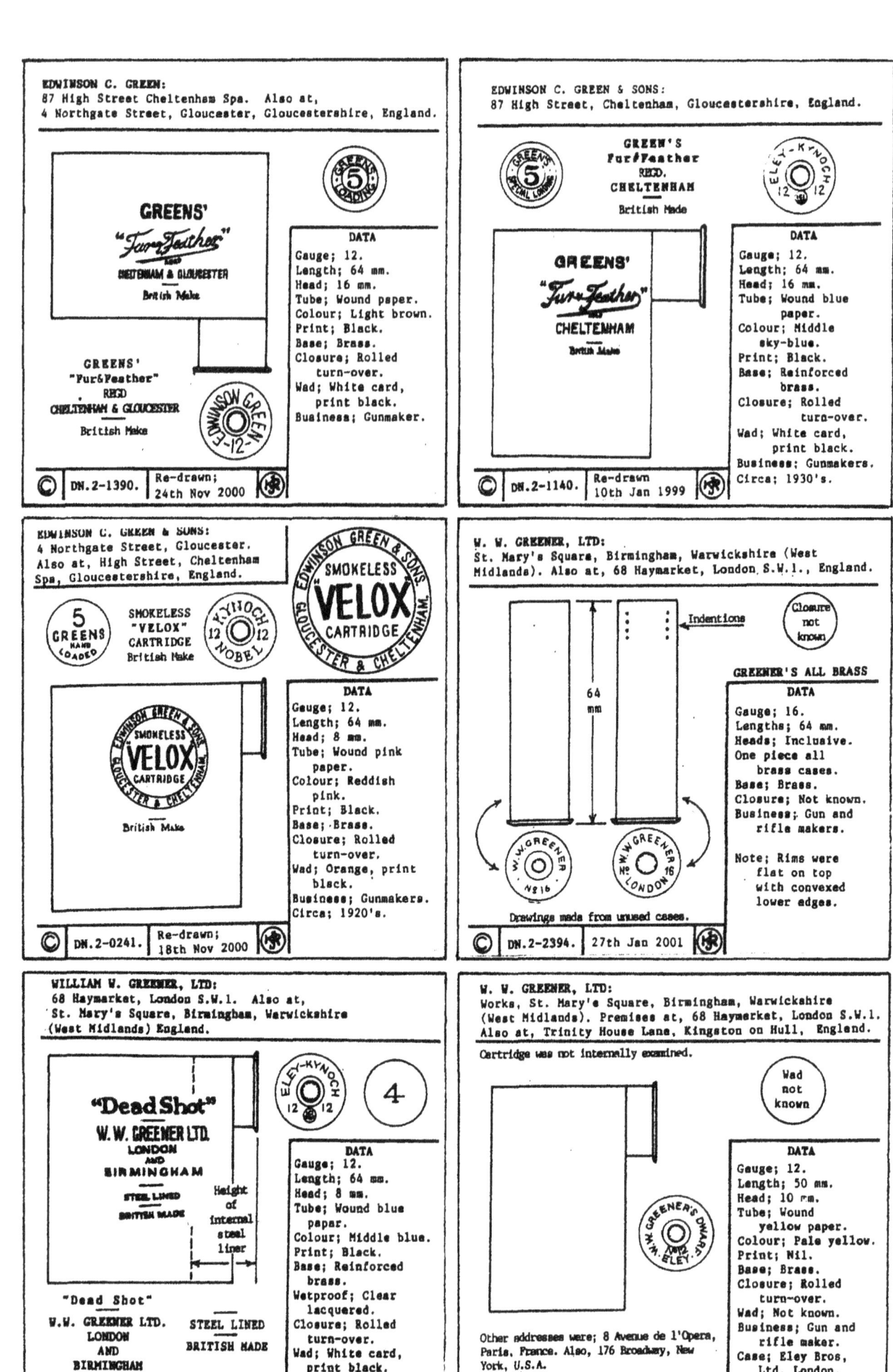

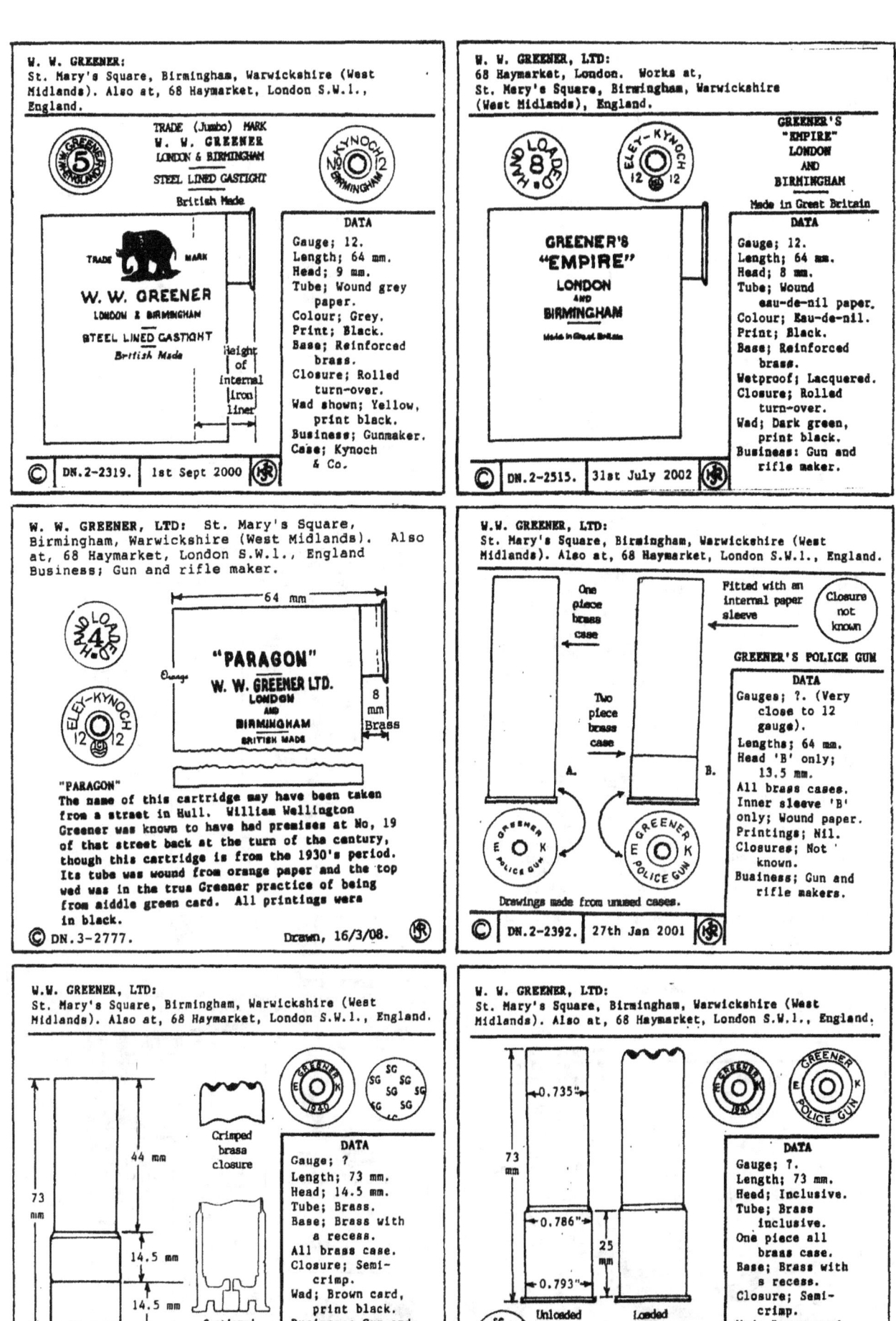

PLATE 137 [GRE - GRE]

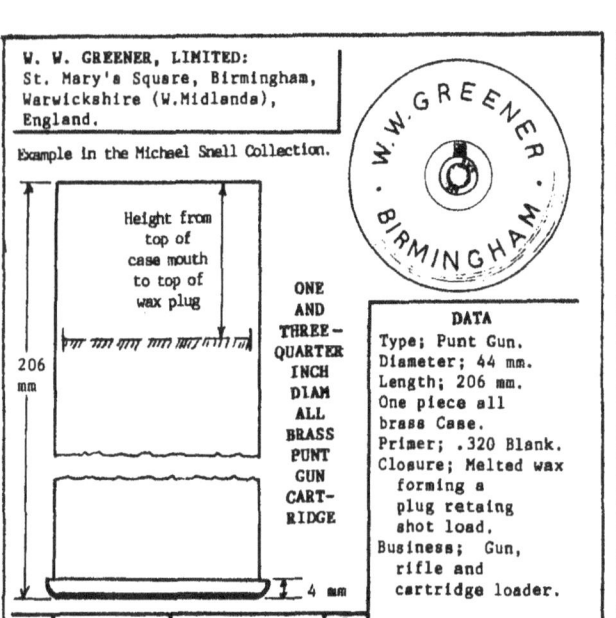

W. W. GREENER, LIMITED:
St. Mary's Square, Birmingham,
Warwickshire (W.Midlands),
England.

Example in the Michael Snell Collection.

ONE AND THREE-QUARTER INCH DIAM ALL BRASS PUNT GUN CARTRIDGE

Height from top of case mouth to top of wax plug
206 mm
4 mm

DATA
Type; Punt Gun.
Diameter; 44 mm.
Length; 206 mm.
One piece all brass Case.
Primer; .320 Blank.
Closure; Melted wax forming a plug retaing shot load.
Business; Gun, rifle and cartridge loader.

© DN.2-2443.   4th July 2001

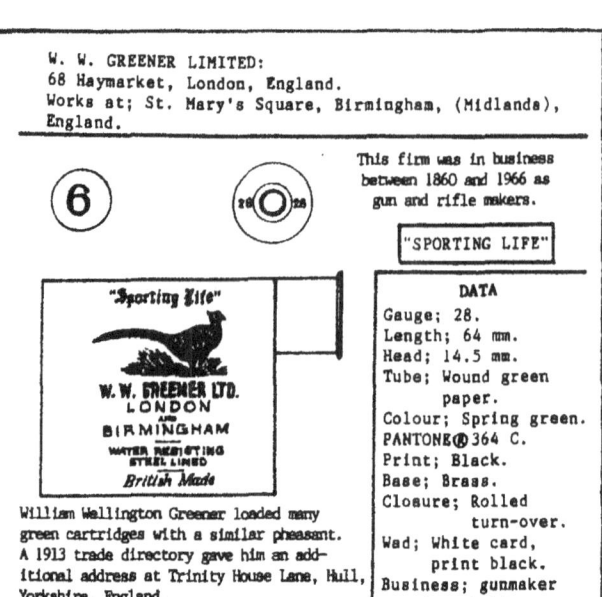

W. W. GREENER LIMITED:
68 Haymarket, London, England.
Works at; St. Mary's Square, Birmingham, (Midlands), England.

This firm was in business between 1860 and 1966 as gun and rifle makers.

"SPORTING LIFE"

DATA
Gauge; 28.
Length; 64 mm.
Head; 14.5 mm.
Tube; Wound green paper.
Colour; Spring green.
PANTONE® 364 C.
Print; Black.
Base; Brass.
Closure; Rolled turn-over.
Wad; White card, print black.
Business; gunmaker and cartridge loader.

William Wellington Greener loaded many green cartridges with a similar pheasant. A 1913 trade directory gave him an additional address at Trinity House Lane, Hull, Yorkshire, England.

© DN.2-1843.   September 1995

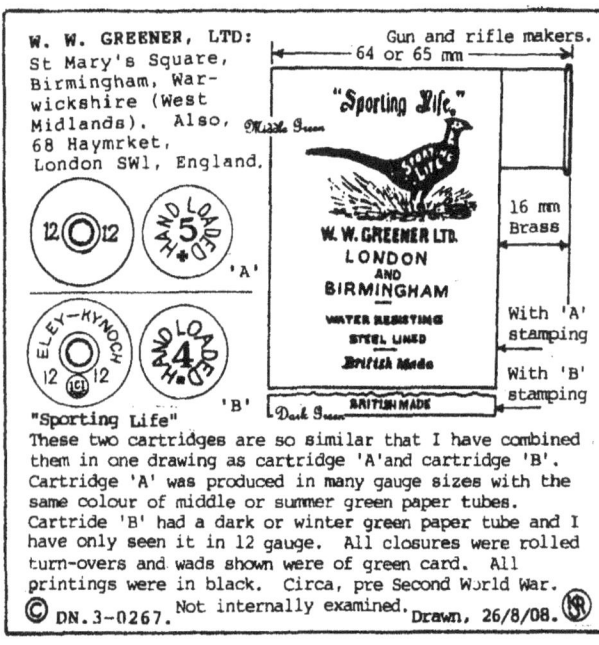

W. W. GREENER, LTD:
St Mary's Square, Birmingham, Warwickshire (West Midlands). Also, 68 Haymrket, London SW1, England.

Gun and rifle makers.
64 or 65 mm
16 mm Brass

With 'A' stamping
With 'B' stamping

"Sporting Life"

These two cartridges are so similar that I have combined them in one drawing as cartridge 'A' and cartridge 'B'. Cartridge 'A' was produced in many gauge sizes with the same colour of middle or summer green paper tubes. Cartrige 'B' had a dark or winter green paper tube and I have only seen it in 12 gauge. All closures were rolled turn-overs and wads shown were of green card. All printings were in black. Circa, pre Second World War.
© DN.3-0267.   Not internally examined.   Drawn, 26/8/08.

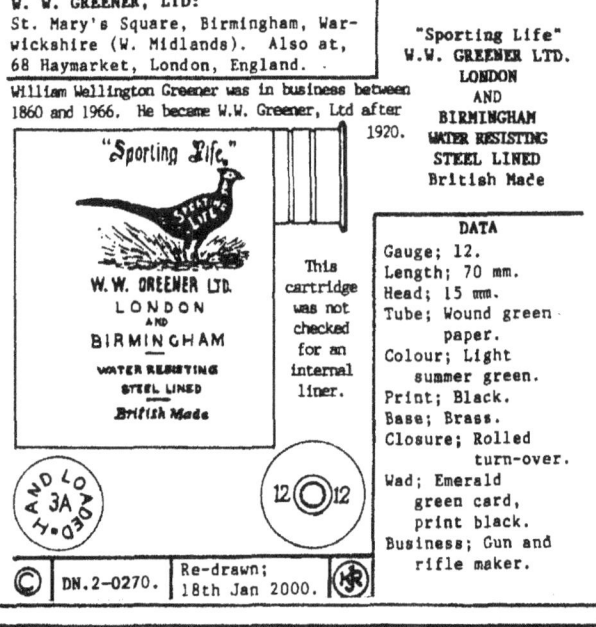

W. W. GREENER, LTD:
St. Mary's Square, Birmingham, Warwickshire (W. Midlands). Also at, 68 Haymarket, London, England.

William Wellington Greener was in business between 1860 and 1966. He became W.W. Greener, Ltd after 1920.

"Sporting Life"
W.W. GREENER LTD.
LONDON AND BIRMINGHAM
WATER RESISTING STEEL LINED
British Made

This cartridge was not checked for an internal liner.

DATA
Gauge; 12.
Length; 70 mm.
Head; 15 mm.
Tube; Wound green paper.
Colour; Light summer green.
Print; Black.
Base; Brass.
Closure; Rolled turn-over.
Wad; Emerald green card, print black.
Business; Gun and rifle maker.

© DN.2-0270.   Re-drawn; 18th Jan 2000.

W. W. GREENER: 68 Haymarket, London. Also at, St. Mary's Square, Birmingham, (W. Midlands), England.

"Sporting Life"
W. W. GREENER,
LONDON AND BIRMINGHAM
British Made

DATA
Gauge; 12.
Length; 65 mm.
Head; 11 mm.
Tube; Wound paper.
Colour; Summer-green.
Print; Black.
Base; Brass.
Closure; Rolled turn-over.
Wad; Lime-green, print black.
Business; Gun and rifle makers.

"Sporting Life"

© DN.3-2672.   Drawn, 16/2/08.

W. W. GREENER, LTD:
St. Mary's Square, Birmingham, Warwickshire (West Midlands). Also at, 68 Haymarket, London, England.

"Sporting Life"
W. W. GREENER LTD
LONDON AND BIRMINGHAM
STEEL LINED
British Made

This cartridge was not checked for an internal liner.

"Sporting Life"
W.W. GREENER LTD.
LONDON AND BIRMINGHAM
STEEL LINED
British Made

DATA
Gauge; 12.
Length; 64 mm.
Head; 16 mm.
Tube; Wound brown paper.
Colour; Nut brown.
Print; Black.
Base; Brass.
Closure; Rolled turn-over.
Load; Central rifled slug.
Business; Gun and rifle maker.
Circa; 1920's.

© DN.2-0269.   Re-drawn; 18th Jan 2000.

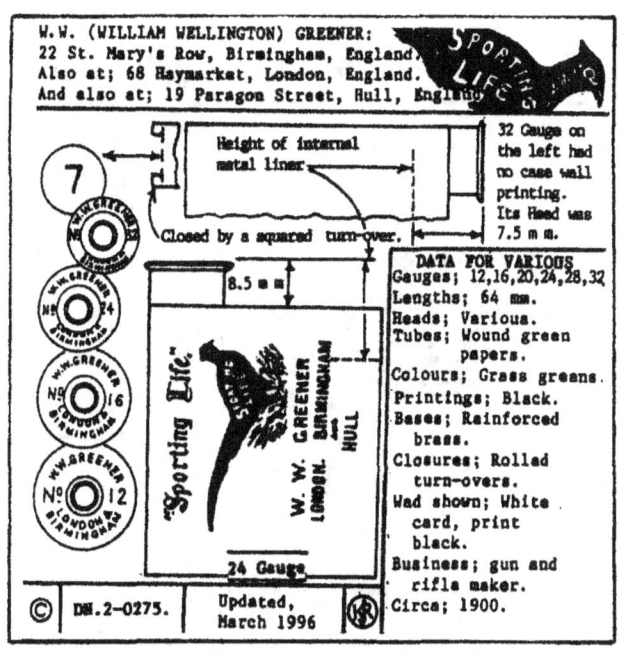
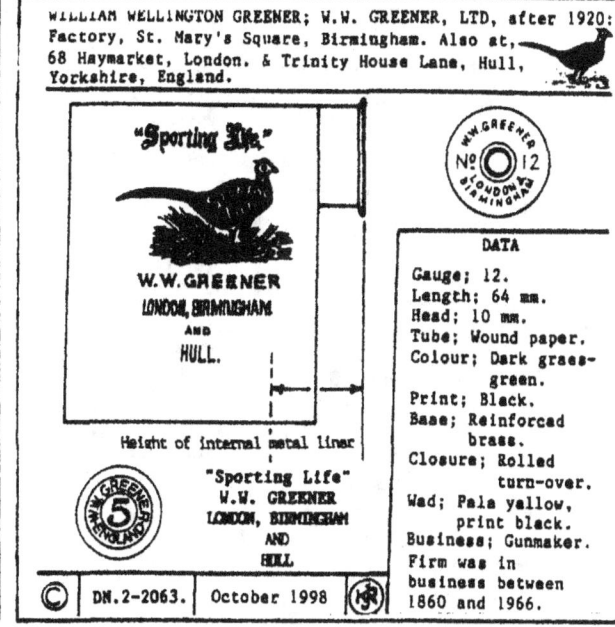
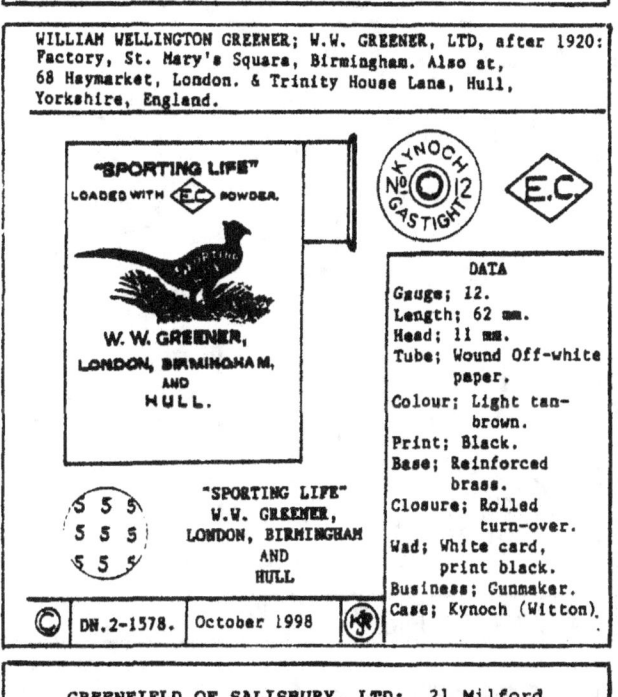
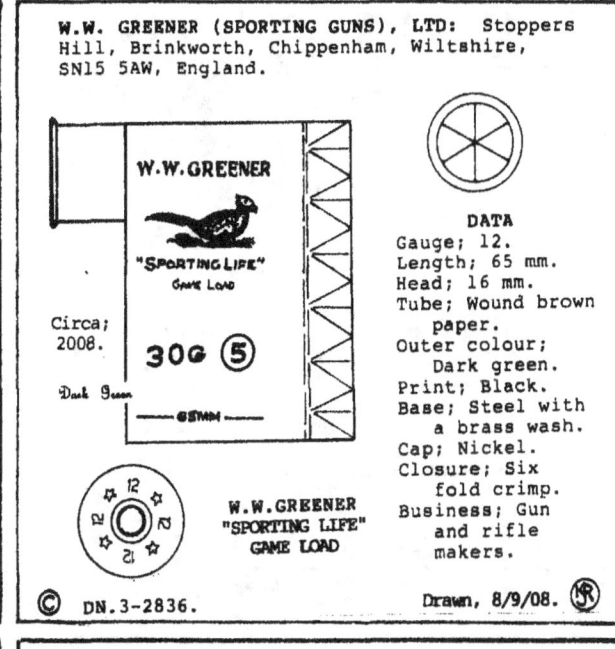
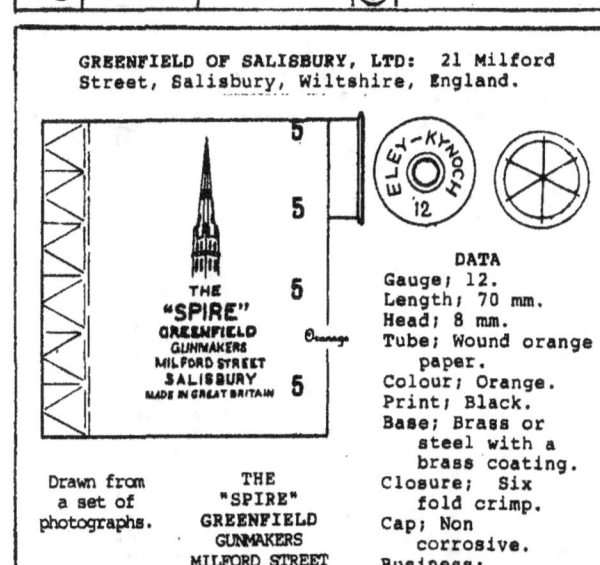
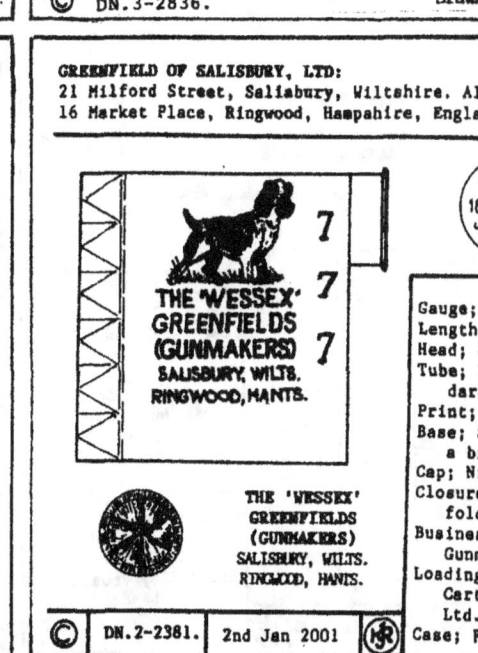

PLATE 139 [GRE – GRE]

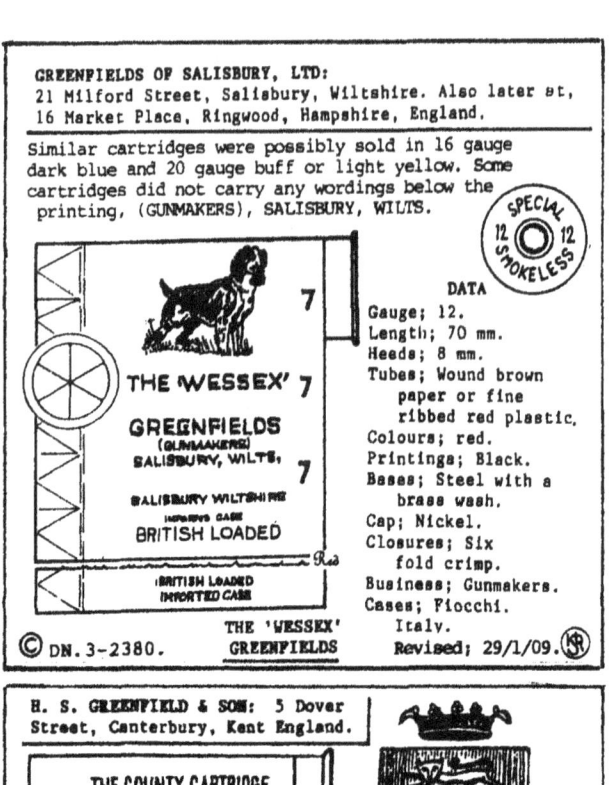
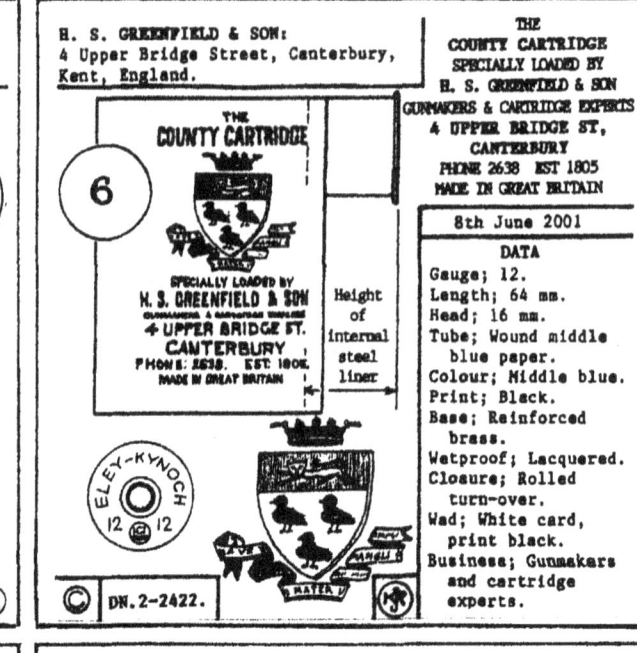
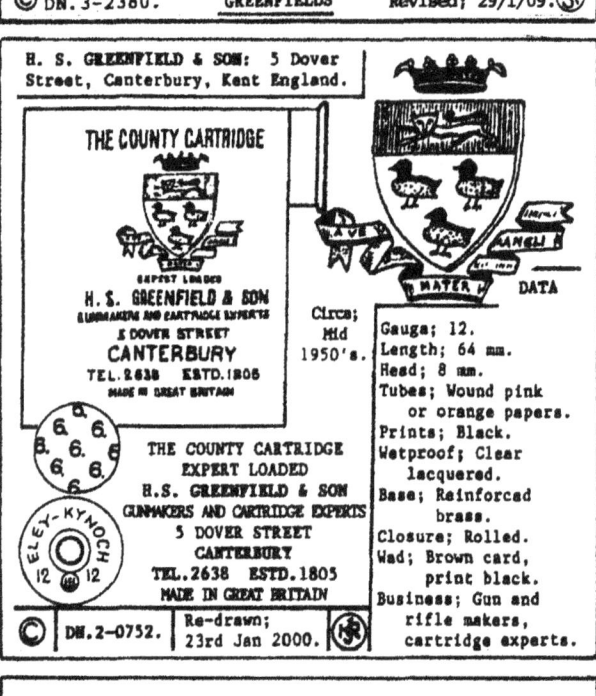
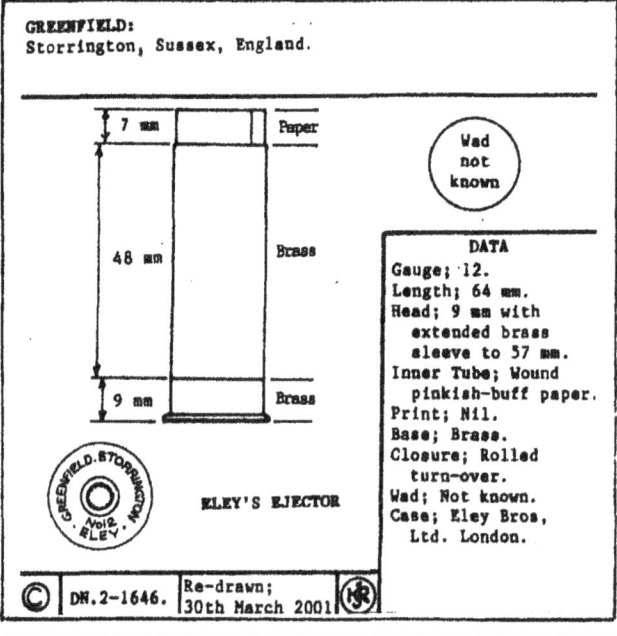
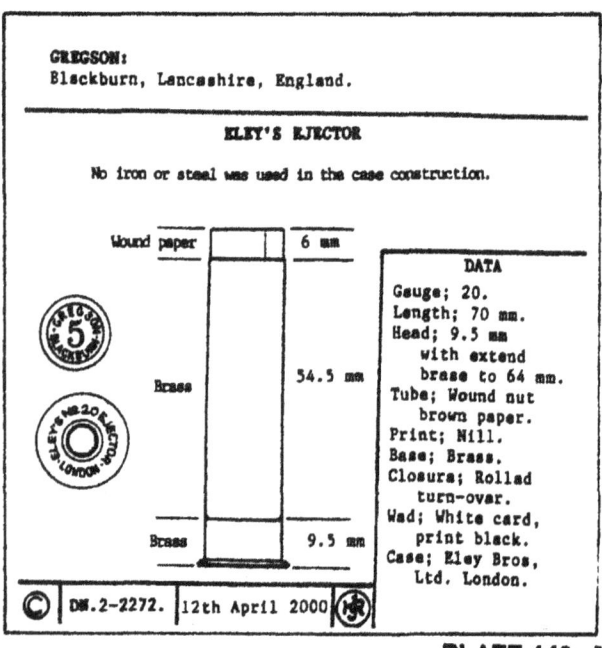
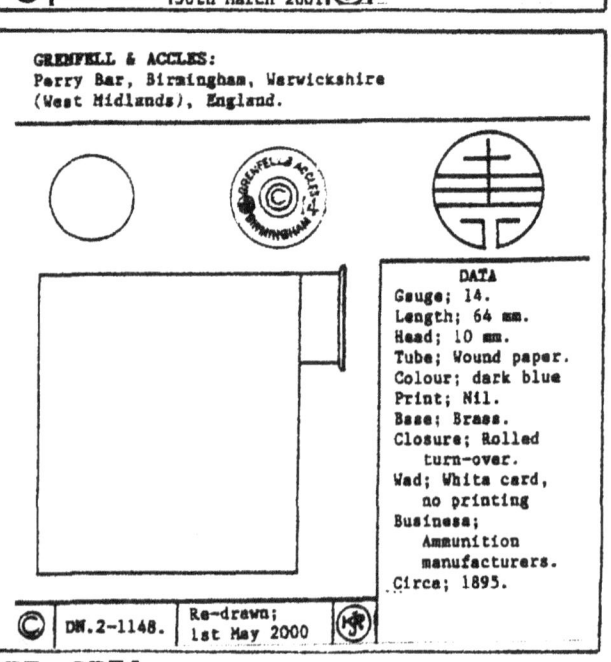

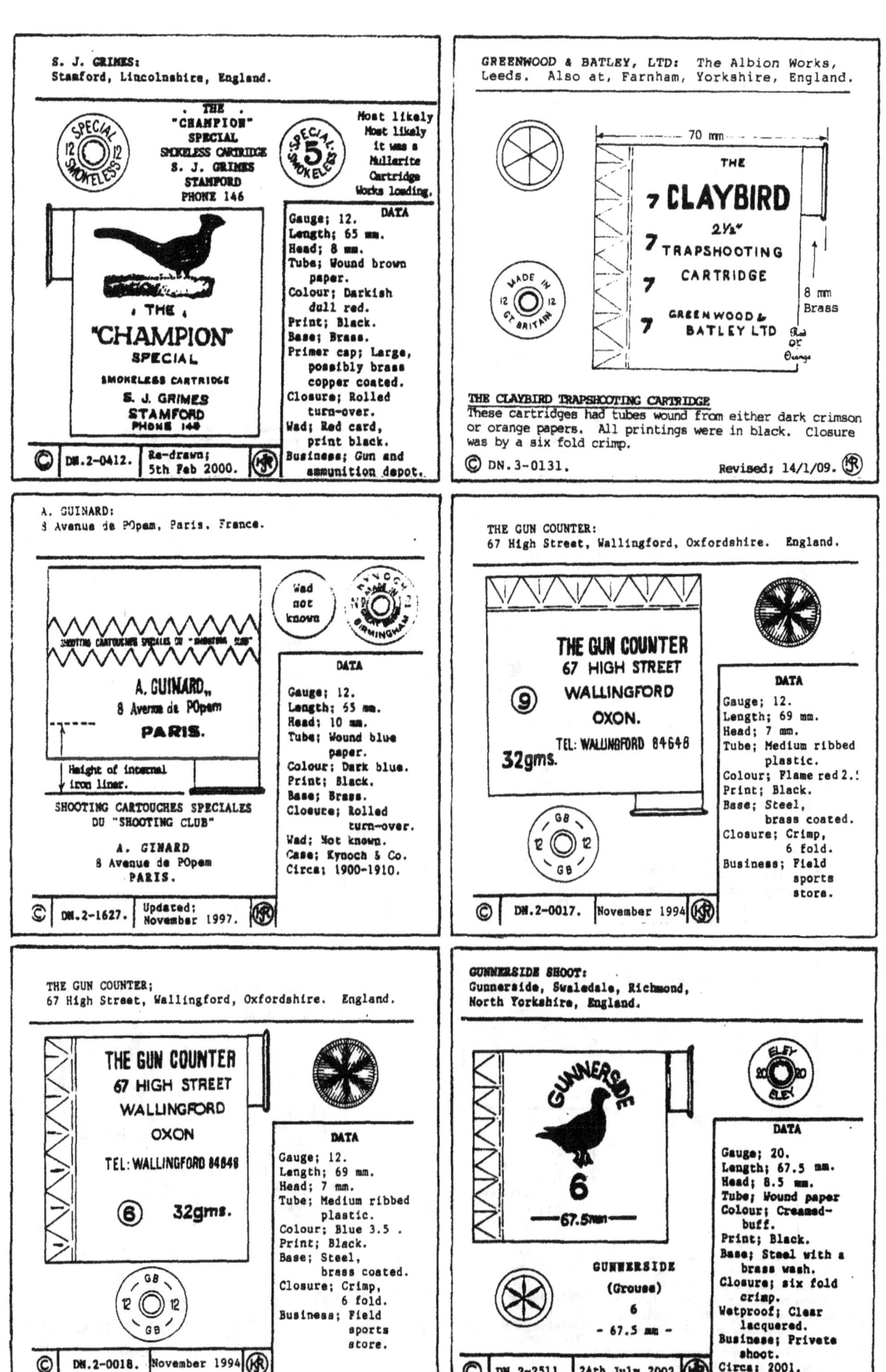

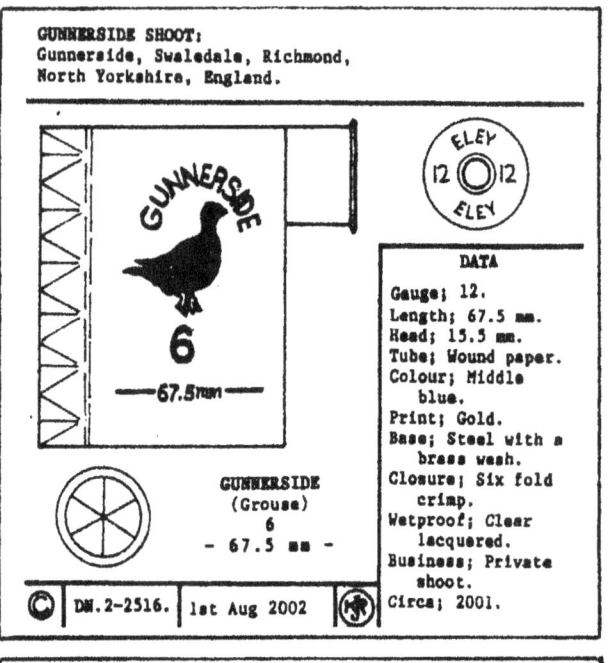
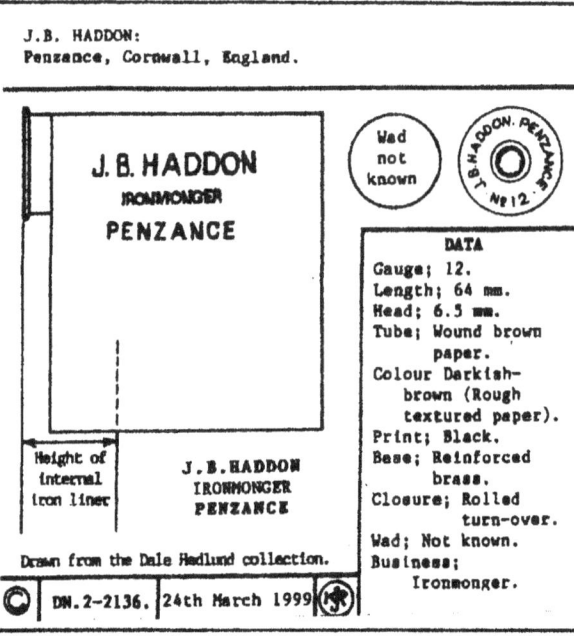

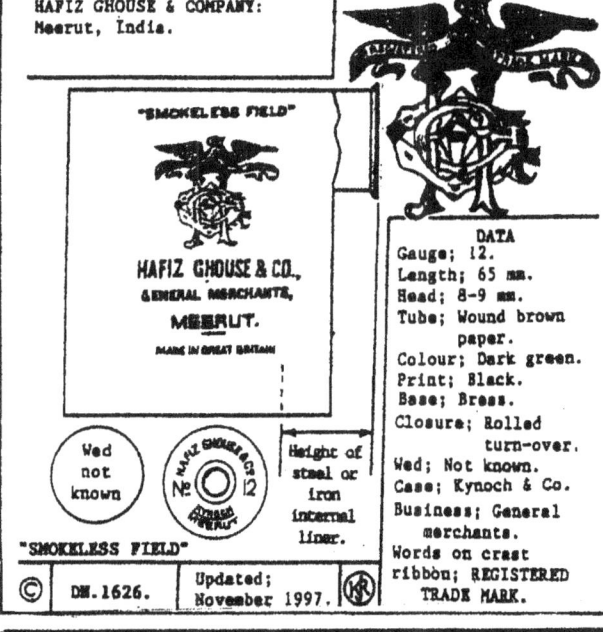
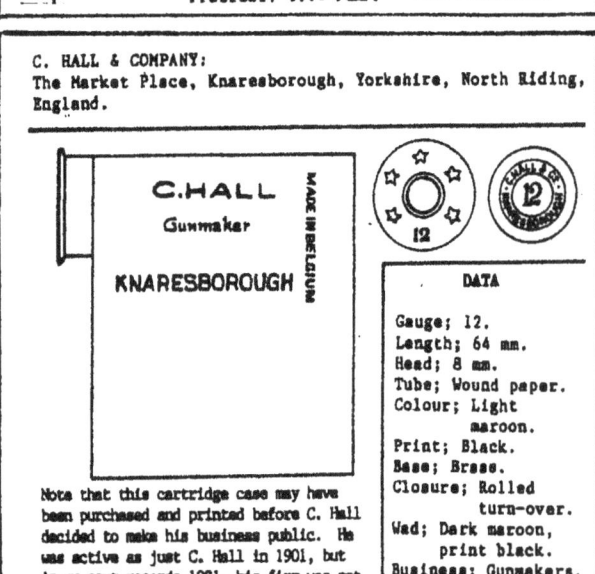
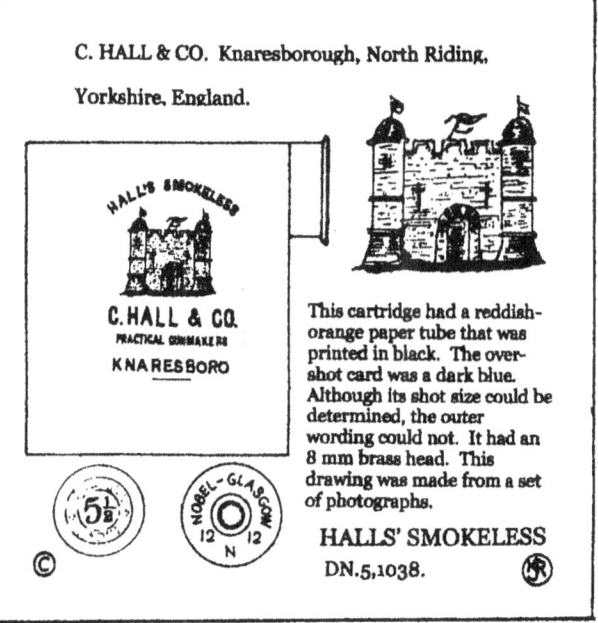

PLATE 142 [GUN - HAL]

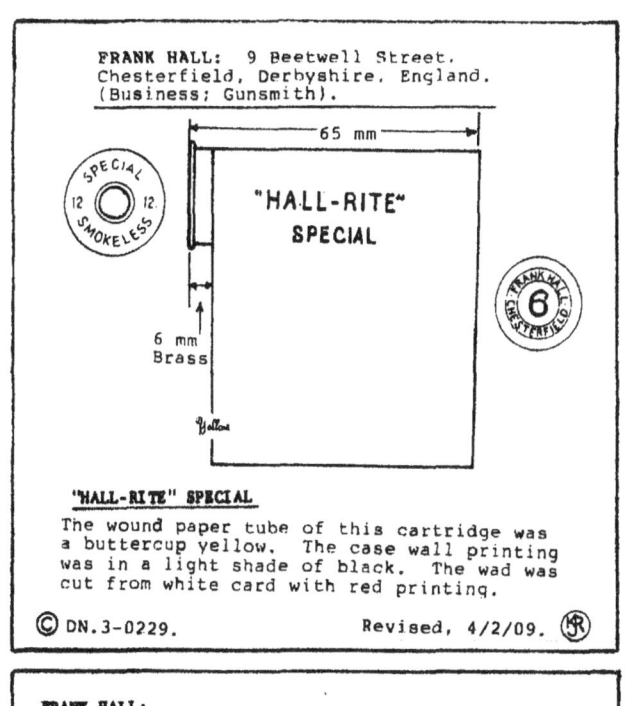
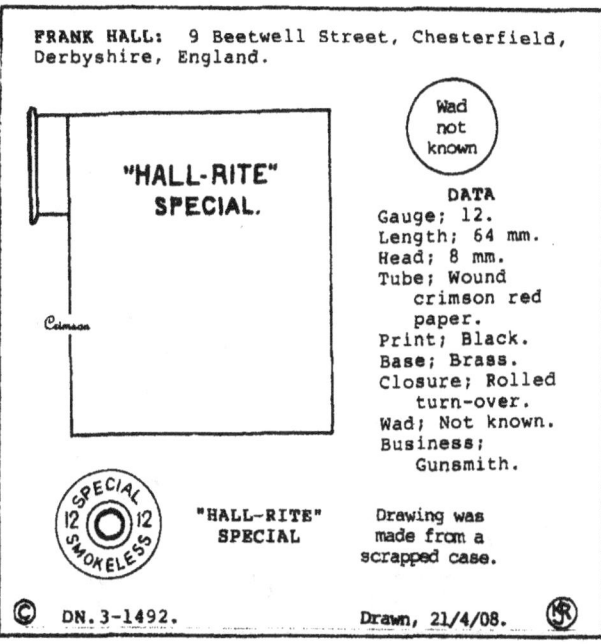
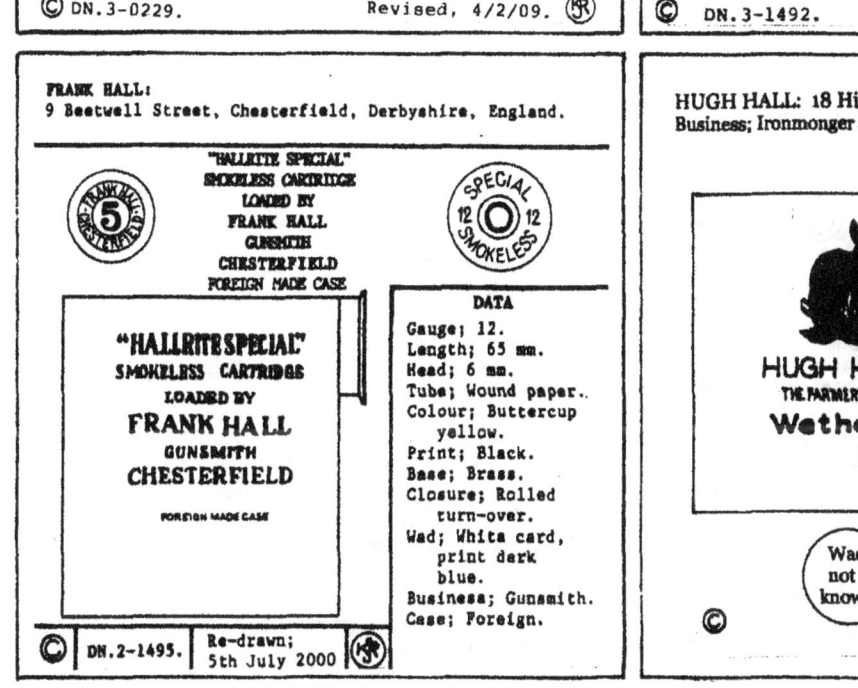

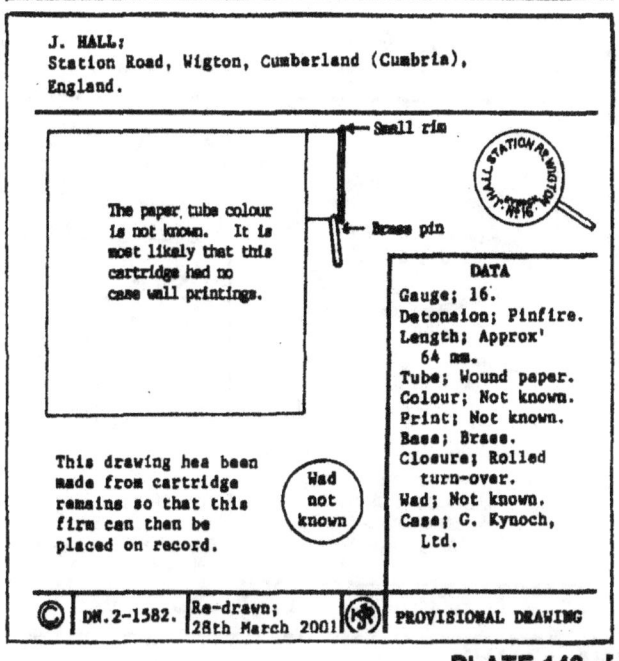
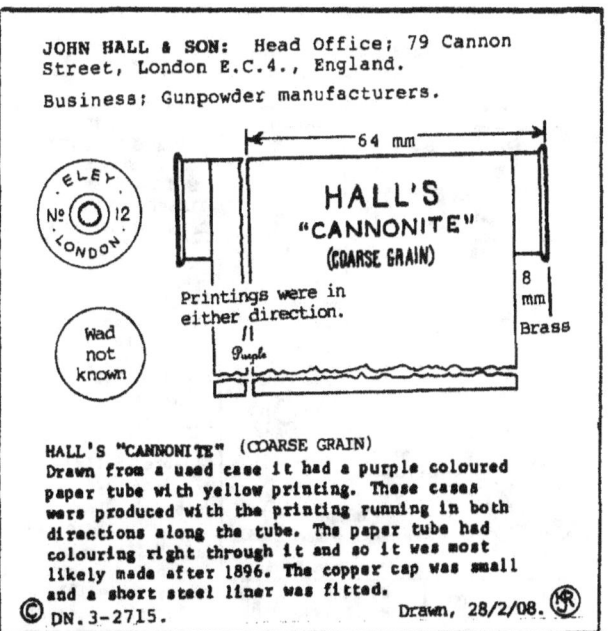

PLATE 143 [HAL – HAL]

```
JOHN HALL & SON:
Head office; 73 Cannon Street, London E.C.4., England.
Powder mills; Faversham, Kent, England. Also at,
Loch Fyne, Argyllshire (South Clyde), Scotland.
```

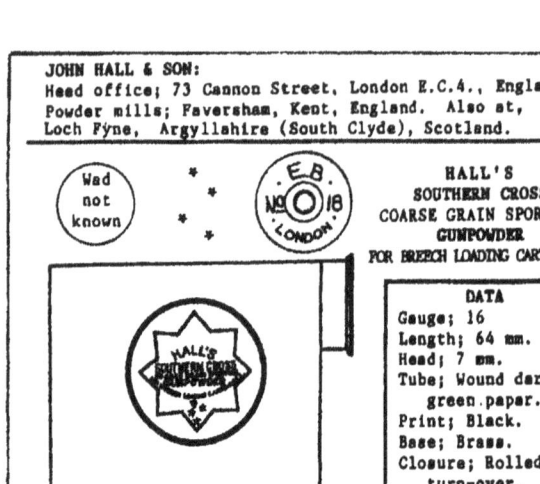

HALL'S
SOUTHERN CROSS
COARSE GRAIN SPORTING
GUNPOWDER
FOR BREECH LOADING CARTRIDGES

DATA
Gauge; 16
Length; 64 mm.
Head; 7 mm.
Tube; Wound dark green paper.
Print; Black.
Base; Brass.
Closure; Rolled turn-over.
Wad; Not known.
Business; Gunpowder manufacturers.
Case; Eley Bros, Ltd. London.
Circa; Between 1900 - 1914.

Drawing made from photographs of an unused case. No iron or steel was used in the case construction. Was made for exporting to Australasia in the then, British Empire.

© DN.2-2371. 1st Dec 2000

```
B. HALLIDAY & CO, LTD.
60 Queen Victoria Street. London, E.C.4. England.
```

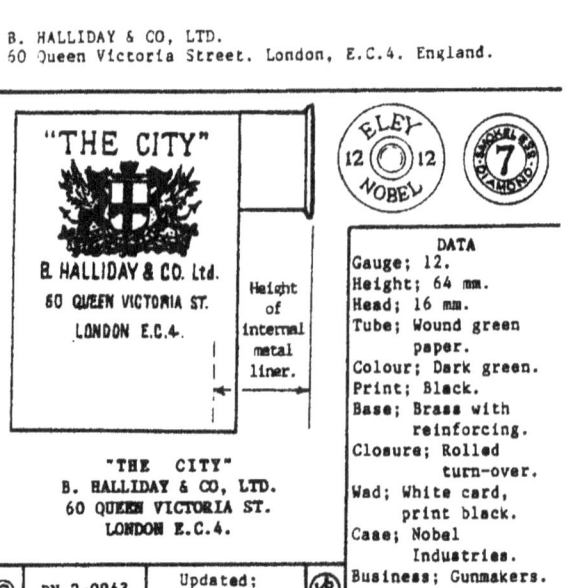

"THE CITY"
B. HALLIDAY & CO, LTD.
60 QUEEN VICTORIA ST.
LONDON E.C.4.

DATA
Gauge; 12.
Height; 64 mm.
Head; 16 mm.
Tube; Wound green paper.
Colour; Dark green.
Print; Black.
Base; Brass with reinforcing.
Closure; Rolled turn-over.
Wad; White card, print black.
Case; Nobel Industries.
Business; Gunmakers.
Circa; 1923.

© DN.2-0943. Updated; April 1997

```
B. HALLIDAY & COMPANY LIMITED:
63 Cannon Street, London, E.C.4., England.
```

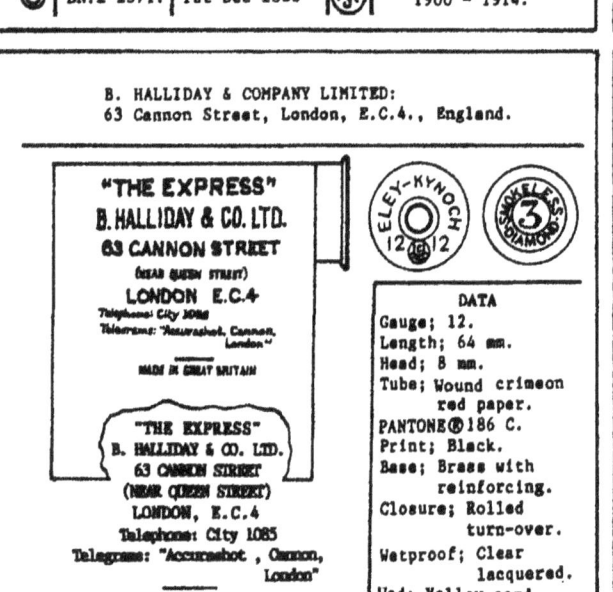

"THE EXPRESS"
B. HALLIDAY & CO. LTD.
63 CANNON STREET
(NEAR QUEEN STREET)
LONDON, E.C.4
Telephone: City 1085
Telegrams: "Accurashot, Cannon, London"
MADE IN GREAT BRITAIN

DATA
Gauge; 12.
Length; 64 mm.
Head; 8 mm.
Tube; Wound crimson red paper.
PANTONE® 186 C.
Print; Black.
Base; Brass with reinforcing.
Closure; Rolled turn-over.
Wetproof; Clear lacquered.
Wad; Yellow card, print black.
Circa; Late 1930's.
Business; Gunmakers.

© DN.2-0950. Updated, March 1996

```
B. HALLIDAY & CO, LTD:
63 Cannon Street, London E.C.4., England.
```

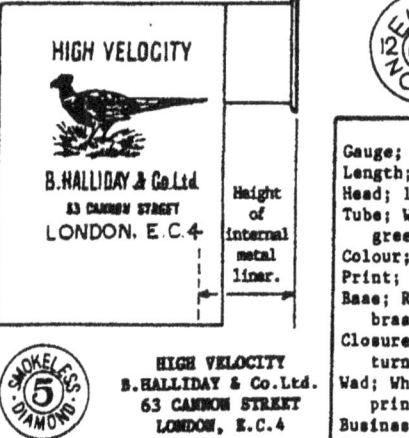

HIGH VELOCITY
B.HALLIDAY & Co.Ltd.
63 CANNON STREET
LONDON, E.C.4

DATA
Gauge; 12.
Length; 64 mm.
Head; 16 mm.
Tube; Wound dark green paper.
Colour; Dark green.
Print; Black.
Base; Reinforced brass.
Closure; Rolled turn-over.
Wad; White card, print black.
Business; Gunmakers.
Case; Nobel Industries, Ltd.
Circa; Late 1920's.

© DN.2-1196. Re-drawn; 24th Feb 2000.

```
B. HALLIDAY & COMPANY LIMITED:
63 Cannon Street, London, E.C.4., England.
```

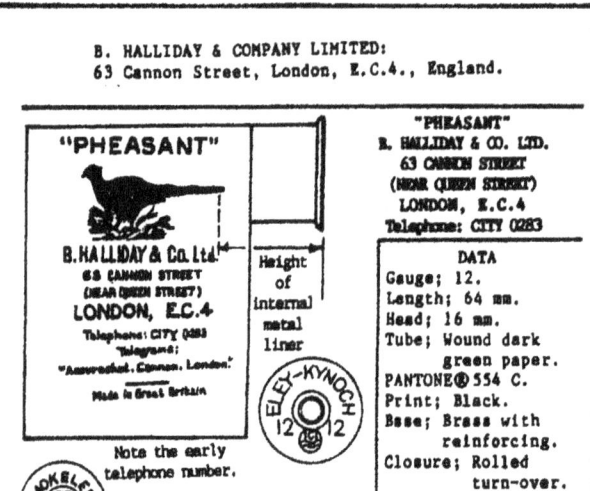

"PHEASANT"
B. HALLIDAY & CO. LTD.
63 CANNON STREET
(NEAR QUEEN STREET)
LONDON, E.C.4
Telephone: CITY 0283

DATA
Gauge; 12.
Length; 64 mm.
Head; 16 mm.
Tube; Wound dark green paper.
PANTONE® 554 C.
Print; Black.
Base; Brass with reinforcing.
Closure; Rolled turn-over.
Wetproof; Clear lacquered.
Wad; Yellow card, print black.
Circa; Early 1930's.
Business; Gunmakers.

Note the early telephone number.

Telegrams: "Accurashot, Cannon, London"
Made in Great Britain

© DN.2-0951. Updated, March 1996

```
B. HALLIDAY & CO, LTD:
60 Queen Victoria Street. London E.C.4., England.
```

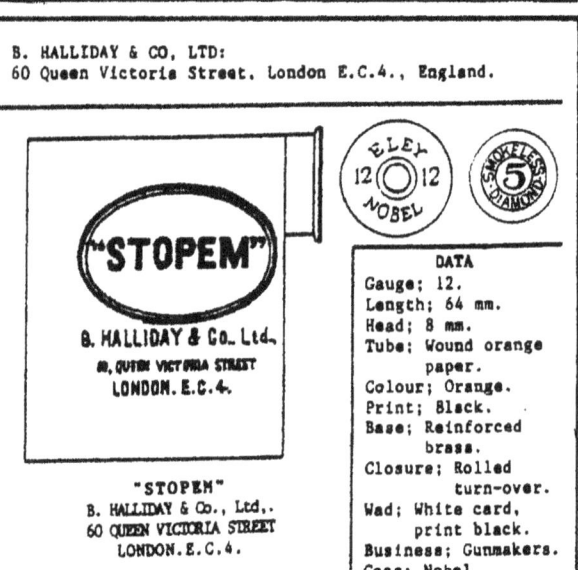

"STOPEM"
B. HALLIDAY & Co., Ltd,.
60 QUEEN VICTORIA STREET
LONDON. E.C.4.

DATA
Gauge; 12.
Length; 64 mm.
Head; 8 mm.
Tube; Wound orange paper.
Colour; Orange.
Print; Black.
Base; Reinforced brass.
Closure; Rolled turn-over.
Wad; White card, print black.
Business; Gunmakers.
Case; Nobel Industries, Ltd.
Circa; 1920's.

© DN.2-0955. November 1998

HAMMANT'S:
26 Bell Street, Henley-on-Thames, Oxfordshire, England.

HAMMANT'S
HENLEY-ON-THAMES
(GUN SPECIALISTS)
"BLUE ROCK"

DATA
Gauges; 12, 16.
Lengths; 65mm, 70 mm.
Heads; 8 mm, 7.5 mm.
Tubes; Wound papers.
Colours;
  12 gauge, Red.
  16 gauge, Blue.
12 gauge SMOKELESS
head had a crimson
tube.
Bases; Steel with
  brass coatings.
Closures; Six
  fold crimps.
Business; Dealers in
  guns, sports, TV's.
Loadings; Hull
  Cartridge Co, Ltd.

Shown here in gauges 12, 16. Not sure on 20.

DN.2-0939. Re-drawn; 16th Feb 2000.

HAMMOND BROTHERS; 40 Jewry Street, Winchester, Hampshire, England.

TRUSTY SERVANT
HAMMOND BROS.
GUNMAKERS
WINCHESTER
WATER RESISTING
Made in Great Britain

DATA
Gauge; 12.
Length; 64 mm.
Head; 16 mm.
Tube; Wound brown
  paper
Colour; Nut brown.
Print; Blck.
Base; Brass. Not
  examined for
  internal metal.
Cap; Copper.
Closure; Rolled
  turn-over.
Wad; Mustard
  yellow, print
  black.
Business;
  Gunmakers.
Established; 1828.

DN.3-0115. Drawn, 16/4/08.

HAMMOND BROTHERS: 40 Jewry Street, Winchester, Hampshire, England.

DATA
Gauge; 12.
Length; 64 mm.
Head; 16 mm.
Tube; Wound green
  papers.
Colours; First
  dark-green.
  Then in late
  1930's, in
  spring-green.
Wetproof; Clear
  lacquered.
Base; Reinforced
  brass.
Closure; Rolled
  turn-over.
Wad; White card,
  print red.
Business; Gunmakers.
Circa; 1930's.

TRUSTY SERVANT

DN.3-2675. Drawn; 19/2/08.

HAMMOND BROTHERS:
40 Jewry Street, Winchester, Hampshire, England.
(Established 1828)

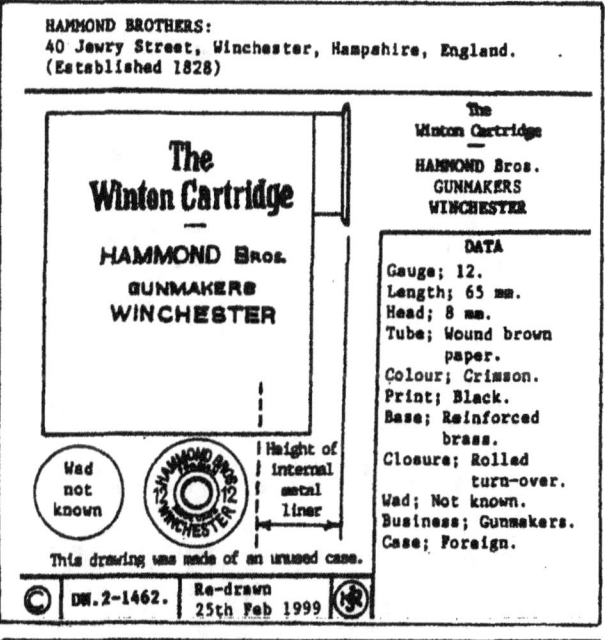

The Winton Cartridge
HAMMOND Bros.
GUNMAKERS
WINCHESTER

DATA
Gauge; 12.
Length; 65 mm.
Head; 8 mm.
Tube; Wound brown
  paper.
Colour; Crimson.
Print; Black.
Base; Reinforced
  brass.
Closure; Rolled
  turn-over.
Wad; Not known.
Business; Gunmakers.
Case; Foreign.

This drawing was made of an unused case.

DN.2-1462. Re-drawn 25th Feb 1999

HAMMOND BROTHERS:
40 Jewry Street, Winchester, Hampshire, England.

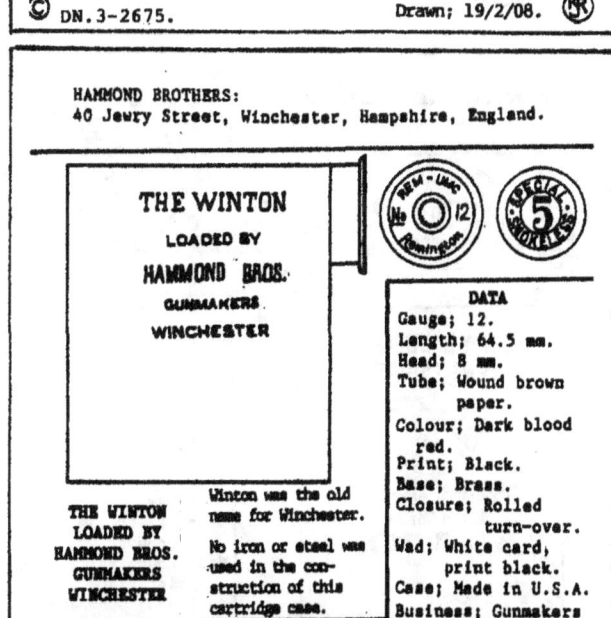

THE WINTON
LOADED BY
HAMMOND BROS.
GUNMAKERS
WINCHESTER

DATA
Gauge; 12.
Length; 64.5 mm.
Head; 8 mm.
Tube; Wound brown
  paper.
Colour; Dark blood
  red.
Print; Black.
Base; Brass.
Closure; Rolled
  turn-over.
Wad; White card,
  print black.
Case; Made in U.S.A.
Business; Gunmakers
  and cartridge
  loaders.

THE WINTON
LOADED BY
HAMMOND BROS.
GUNMAKERS
WINCHESTER

Winton was the old name for Winchester.
No iron or steel was used in the construction of this cartridge case.

DN.2-1043. Updated, March 1996

HAMPSHIRE ARMS COMPANY: Bughurst, Tadley, Hampshire, England.
(Business; Gun and carpet shop).

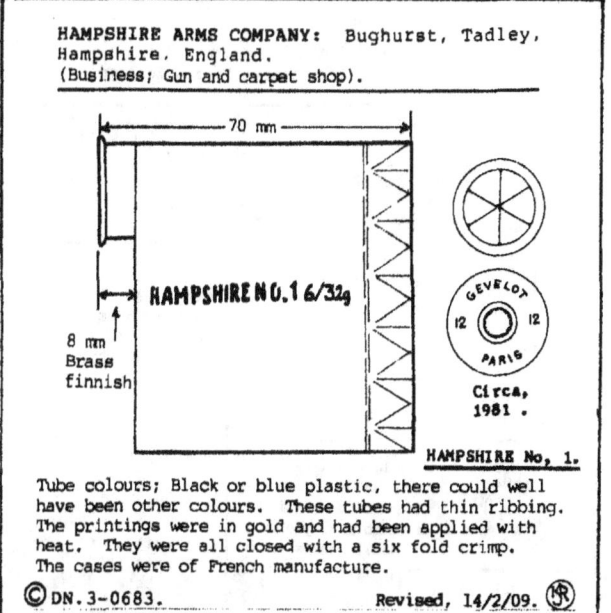

HAMPSHIRE NO.1 6/32g

8 mm Brass finnish

Circa, 1981.

HAMPSHIRE No. 1.

Tube colours; Black or blue plastic, there could well have been other colours. These tubes had thin ribbing. The printings were in gold and had been applied with heat. They were all closed with a six fold crimp. The cases were of French manufacture.

DN.3-0683. Revised, 14/2/09.

W. T. HANCOCK:
308 High Holborn, London, England.

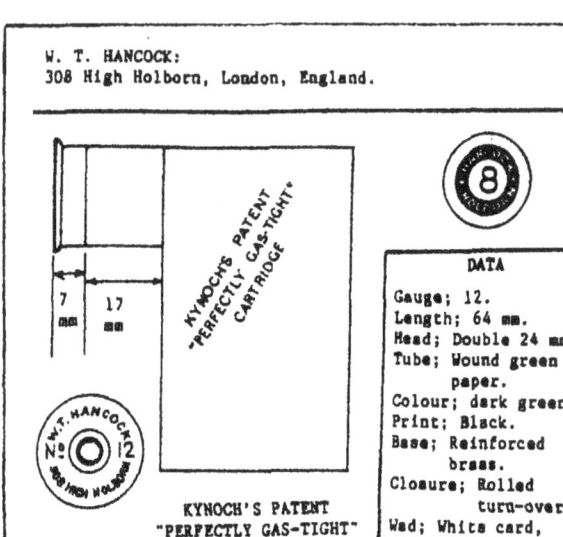

KYNOCH'S PATENT
"PERFECTLY GAS-TIGHT"
CARTRIDGE

DATA
Gauge; 12.
Length; 64 mm.
Head; Double 24 mm.
Tube; Wound green paper.
Colour; dark green.
Print; Black.
Base; Reinforced brass.
Closure; Rolled turn-over.
Wad; White card, print red.
Business; Gunmaker.
Case; Kynoch Works, Witton.

DN.2-0347. Re-drawn November 1998

HAND BROTHERS:
High Street, Odiham, Near Basingstoke, Hampshire, England.

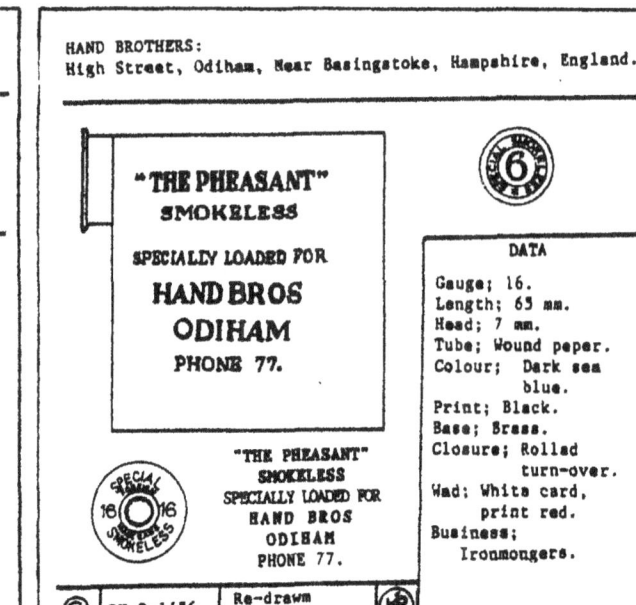

"THE PHEASANT"
SMOKELESS
SPECIALLY LOADED FOR
HAND BROS
ODIHAM
PHONE 77.

DATA
Gauge; 16.
Length; 65 mm.
Head; 7 mm.
Tube; Wound paper.
Colour; Dark sea blue.
Print; Black.
Base; Brass.
Closure; Rolled turn-over.
Wad; White card, print red.
Business; Ironmongers.

DN.2-1436. Re-drawn 4th Jan 1999

L. HANSON:
1 Cornhill, Lincoln, Lincolnshire, England.

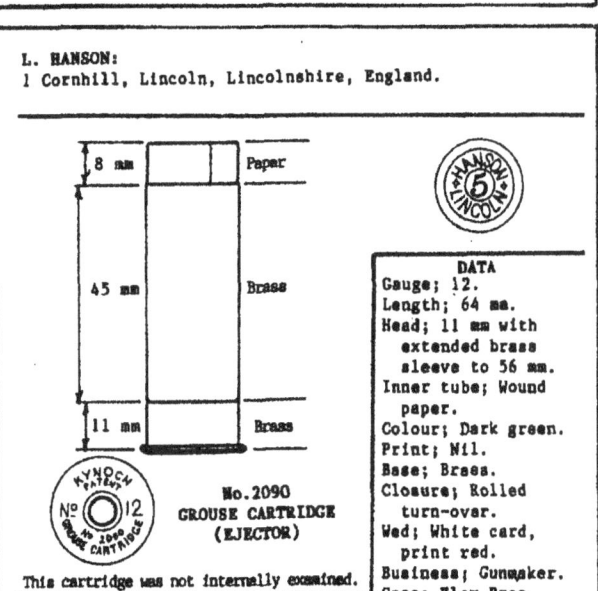

No.2090
GROUSE CARTRIDGE
(EJECTOR)

This cartridge was not internally examined.

DATA
Gauge; 12.
Length; 64 mm.
Head; 11 mm with extended brass sleeve to 56 mm.
Inner tube; Wound paper.
Colour; Dark green.
Print; Nil.
Base; Brass.
Closure; Rolled turn-over.
Wad; White card, print red.
Business; Gunmaker.
Case; Eley Bros, Ltd. London.

DN.2-1250. Re-drawn; 30th March 2001

G. J. HANDY & CO., LTD:
120 Victoria Road, Old Town, Swindon, Wiltshire, England.

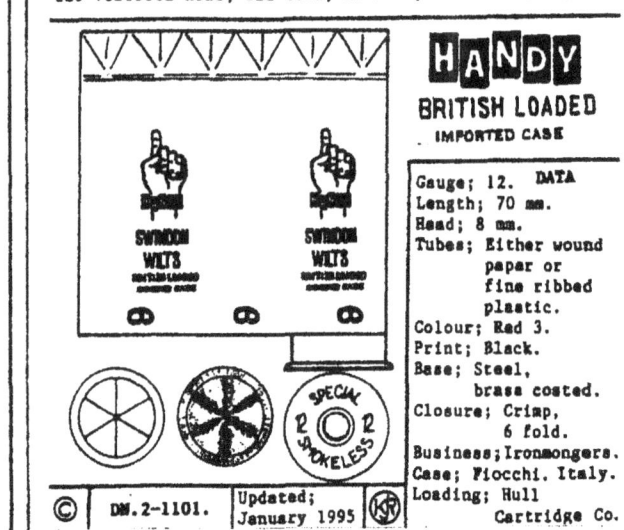

HANDY
BRITISH LOADED
IMPORTED CASE

DATA
Gauge; 12.
Length; 70 mm.
Head; 8 mm.
Tubes; Either wound paper or fine ribbed plastic.
Colour; Red 3.
Print; Black.
Base; Steel, brass coated.
Closure; Crimp, 6 fold.
Business; Ironmongers.
Case; Fiocchi. Italy.
Loading; Hull Cartridge Co.

DN.2-1101. Updated; January 1995

J. HARDING:
Benfleet, Thames Estuary, Essex, England.

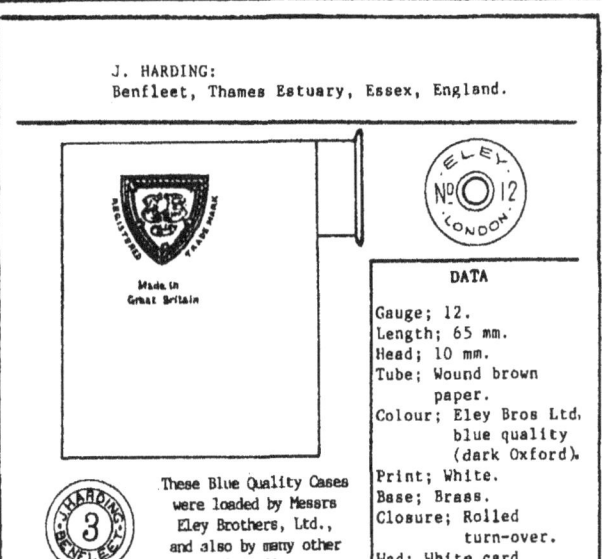

These Blue Quality Cases were loaded by Messrs Eley Brothers, Ltd., and also by many other smaller firms.

DATA
Gauge; 12.
Length; 65 mm.
Head; 10 mm.
Tube; Wound brown paper.
Colour; Eley Bros Ltd, blue quality (dark Oxford).
Print; White.
Base; Brass.
Closure; Rolled turn-over.
Wad; White card, print red.
Circa; Late 1800's.

DN.2-1758. Updated; February 1995

HARDY BROTHERS (ALNWICK), LTD:
Alnwick, Northumberland, England.

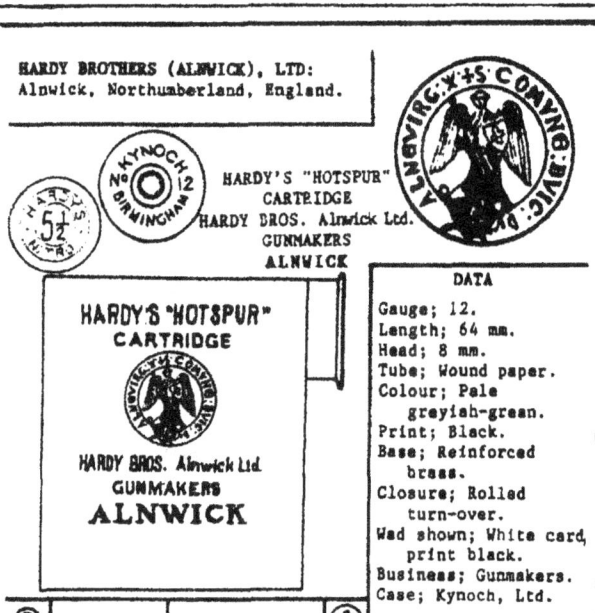

HARDY'S "HOTSPUR"
CARTRIDGE
HARDY BROS. Alnwick Ltd.
GUNMAKERS
ALNWICK

DATA
Gauge; 12.
Length; 64 mm.
Head; 8 mm.
Tube; Wound paper.
Colour; Pale greyish-green.
Print; Black.
Base; Reinforced brass.
Closure; Rolled turn-over.
Wad shown; White card, print black.
Business; Gunmakers.
Case; Kynoch, Ltd.

DN.2-2331. 13th Sept 2000

PLATE 146 [HAN - HAR]

HARDY BROTHERS, LTD: 101 Princes Street, Edinburgh, Scotland. Also, North British Works, Alnwick, Northumberland. And also, 12 & 14 Moult Street, Manchester, Lancashire (Great Manchester). and also, 61 Pall Mall, London S.W.1., England.

By Appointment to H.M. the King
HARDY'S "NORTHERN"
Smokeless Cartridge
HARDY BROTHERS LTD.
ALNWICK
RETAIL DEPOTS:
Edinburgh: 101 Princes St.
Manchester: 12 & 14 Moult St.
London: 61 Pall Mall, S.W.
Made in Great Britain

DATA
Gauge, 12; Length, 64 mm; Head, 8 mm; Tube, Wound off-white paper; Print, Black; Wad; White with black printing; Business, Gunmakers.

© DN.3-0232. Drawn, 16/4/08.

HARDY BROTHERS, LTD. Addresses at, Alnwick, Northumberland; Manchester, Lancashire; & London, England; Also at, Edinburgh, Midlothian, Scotland.

By Appointment Manufacturers to H. M. the King
HARDY'S "NORTHERN" Smokeless Cartridges
HARDY BROTHERS Ltd. ALNWICK RETAIL DEPOTS:
Edinburgh: 101 Princes St. Manchester:
12 & 14 Moult St. London: 61 Pall Mall. S.W.

DATA
Gauge; 12.
Length; 64 mm.
Head; 8 mm.
Tube; Wound off-
   white paper.
Colour; Brownish
   off-white.
Print; Black.
Base; Brass.
Closure; Rolled
   turn-over.
Wad; White card,
   print black.
Business; Gunmakers.
Case; Nobel
   Industries, Ltd.
Circa; 1920's.

© DN.2-1194. Re-drawn; 4th Feb 2000.

HARDY BROTHERS LIMITED: Alnwick, Northumberland. Also, London and Manchester, Lancashire (Gt Manchester), England. Also at, Edinburgh, Midlothian and Glasgow, Lanarkshire (S. Clyde), Scotland.

By Appointment to H.M. the King
HARDY'S "NORTHERN"
SMOKELESS CARTRIDGE
HARDY BROTHERS LTD.
ALNWICK (Tel;93)
London: 61 Pall Mall. S.W.
Tele; Whitehall 7577
and 12 Royal Exchange. E.C.3.
Tele; Mansion House 0853
Edinburgh 69 George St.
Tele; 23494
Manchester 12 Moult St.
Tele; Blackfriars 3796
Glasgow. 117 West George St.
Tele; Central 9427
MADE IN GREAT BRITAIN

DATA: Length, 64 mm; Head, 8 mm; Tubes; Wound yellow paper with black print or bone paper with blue print; Wad, yellow with black print; Base, Brass.

© DN.2-0090. Updated, January 1996

HARDY BROTHERS (ALNWICK) LIMITED: Branches at; 58 St. David Street, Edinburgh, Scotland. Also at, Alnwick, Northumberland; 12 & 14 Moult Street, Manchester; 61 Pall Mall, London S.W., England.

HARDY'S "RELIANCE"
SMOKELESS CARTRIDGE
HARDY BROS. (Alnwick)
LIMITED
GUNMAKERS
ALNWICK
BRANCHES—
Edinburgh: 58 St David Street
Manchester: 12 & 14 Moult Street
London: 61 Pall Mall. S.W.
MANUFACTORY, ALNWICK

HARDY'S "RELIANCE"
BRANCHES—
Edinburgh: 58 St David Street
Manchester: 12 & 14 Moult Street
London: 61 Pall Mall, S.W.
MANUFACTORY, ALNWICK

Closed by a squared turn-over.

DATA
Gauge; 12.
Length; 64 mm.
Head; 16 mm.
Tube; Wound paper.
Colour; Reddish-brown.
Print; Black.
Base; Reinforced brass.
Wad; Crimson red, print black.
Business; Gunmakers.
Case; Kynoch & Co.

© DN.2-2038. October 1998

HARDY BROTHERS, LTD: North British Gunworks, Alnwick, Northumberland, England. (Other addresses, see RETAIL DEPOTS).

By Appointment Manufacturers to H.M. the King
HARDY'S "RELIANCE"
Smokeless Cartridge
HARDY BROTHERS Ltd.
ALNWICK
RETAIL DEPOTS:
Edinburgh 101 Princes St.
Manchester; 12 & 14 Moult St.
London. 61 Pall Mall. S.W.

By Appointment Manufacturers
to H.M. the King
HARDY'S "RELIANCE"
Smokeless Cartridge
HARDY BROTHERS Ltd.
ALNWICK

RETAIL DEPOTS:
Edinburgh 101 Princes St,
Manchester; 12 & 14 Moult St,
London, 61 Pall Mall, S.W.

Circa; 1920's.

DATA
Gauge; 12.
Length; 64 mm.
Head; 16 mm.
Tube; Wound dark green paper.
Colour; Dark green.
Print; Black.
Base; Reinforced brass.
Closure; Squared turn-over.
Wetproof; Clear lacquered.
Wad; White card, print black.
Business; Gunmakers.

© DN.2-1088. Re-drawn; 1st Feb 2001

HARDY BROTHERS, LTD: Edinburgh, Scotland. Manchester & London, England.

By Appointment to H.M. the King
Smokeless Cartridges
HARDY BROTHERS Ltd.
ALNWICK
RETAIL DEPOTS;
Edinburgh; 101 Princes St.
Manchester; 12 & 14 Moult St.
London; 61 Pall Mall. S.W.
Made in Great Britain

By Appointment to H.M. the King
HARDY'S "RELIANCE"
Smokeless Cartridge
HARDY BROTHERS Ltd.
ALNWICK
RETAIL DEPOTS:
Edinburgh; 101 Princes St.
Manchester; 12 & 14 Moult St.
London; 61 Pall Mall. S.W.
Made in Great Britain

DATA
Gauge; 12.
Length; 64 mm.
Head; 16 mm.
Tube; Wound dark green paper.
Colour; Dark green.
Print; Black.
Base; Reinforced brass.
Wetproof; Lacquered.
Closure; Rolled turn-over.
Wad; White card, print black.
Business; Gunmakers.
Case; Nobel Industries, Ltd.
Circa; 1920's.

© DN.2-2417. 7th June 2001

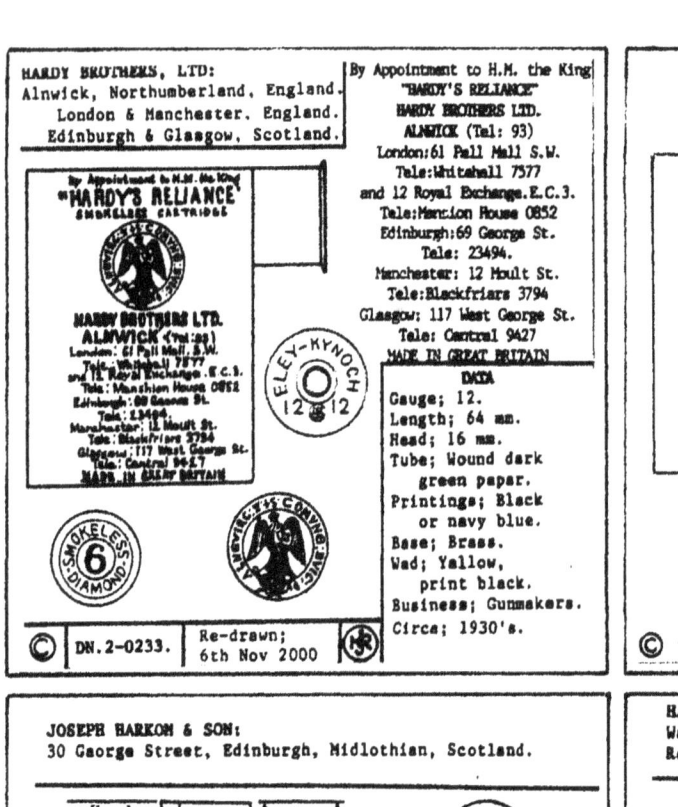
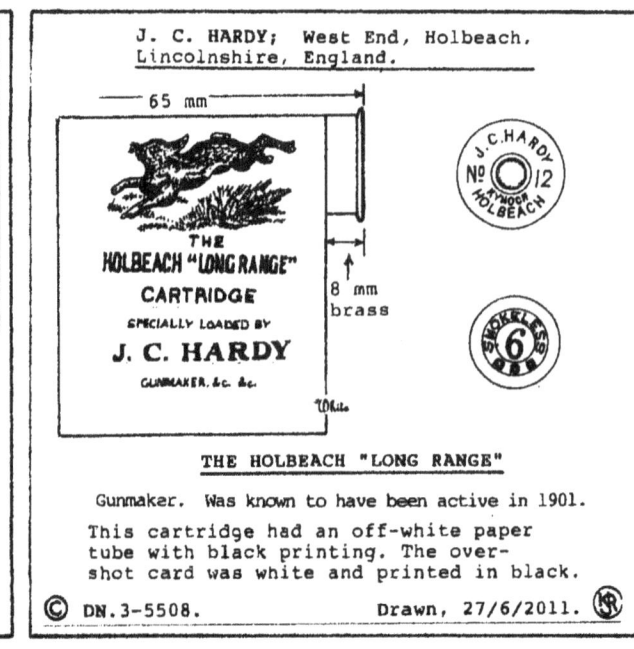
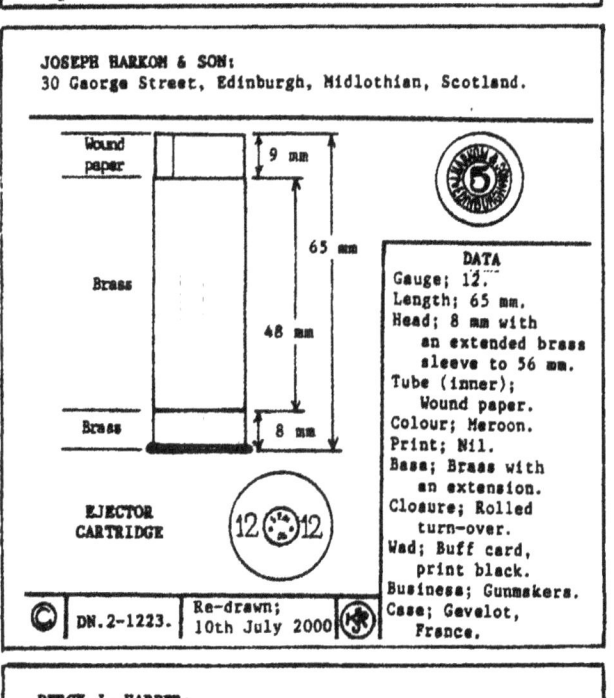
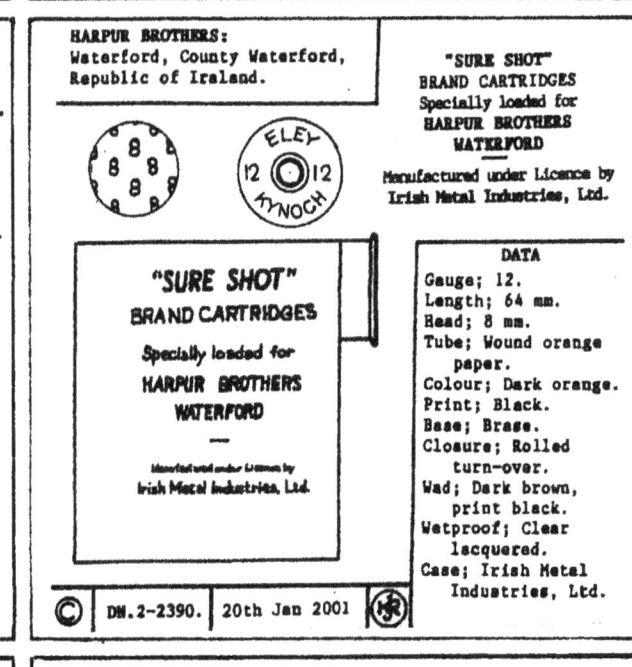
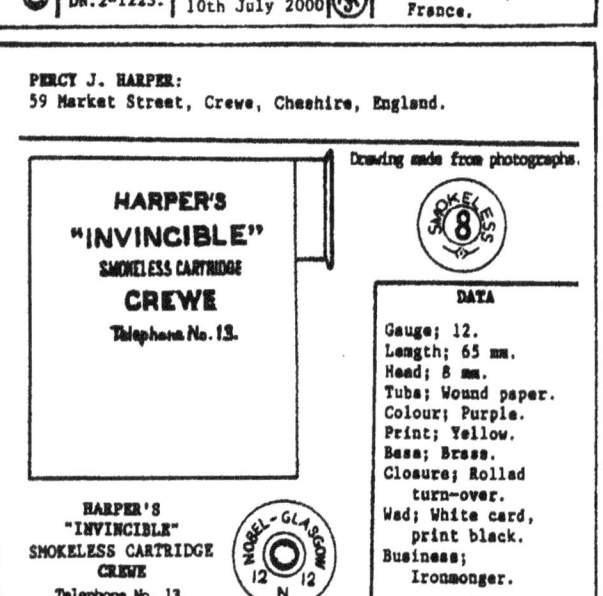
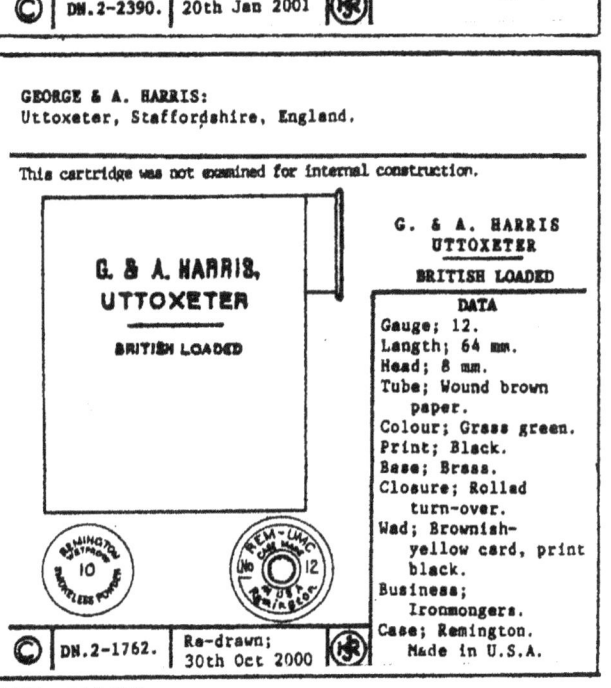

PLATE 148 [HAR – HAR]

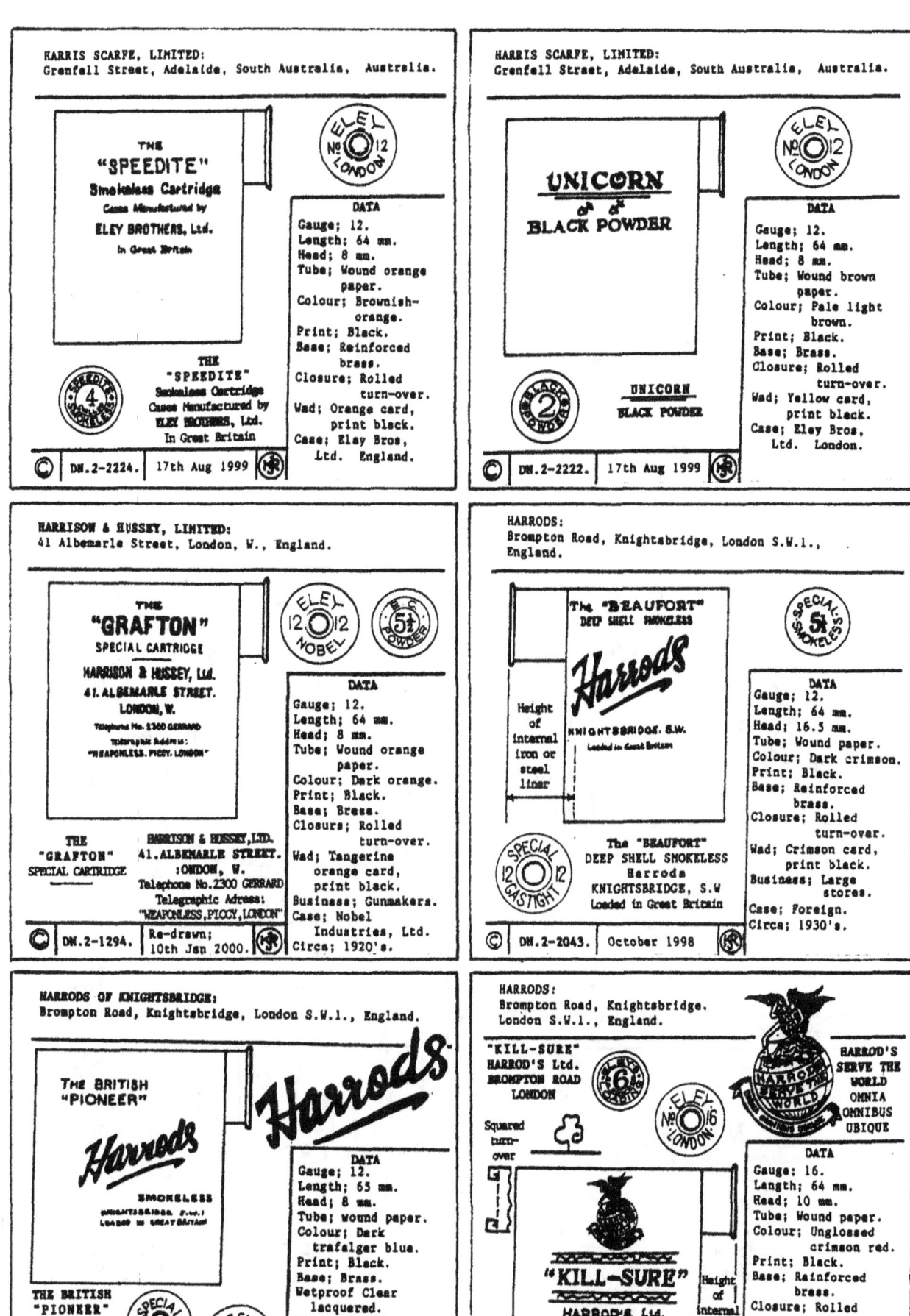

PLATE 149 [HAR – HAR]

HARRODS, LTD:
Brompton Road, Knightsbridge, London S.W.1., England.

Cartridge was not checked for an internal metal liner.

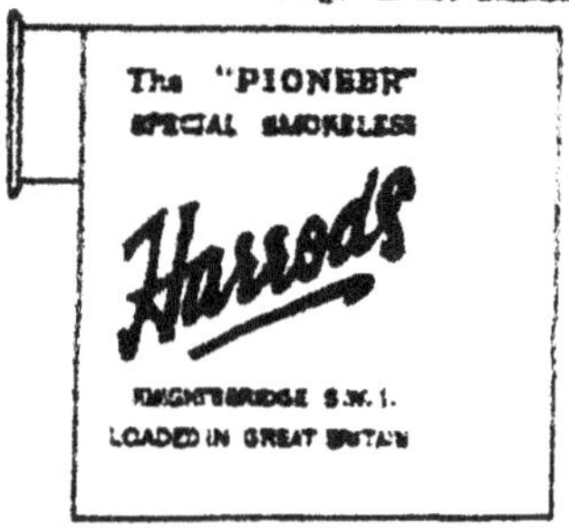

The "PIONEER" SPECIAL SMOKELESS
Harrods
KNIGHTSBRIDGE S.W.1.
LOADED IN GREAT BRITAIN

Headstamp: SPECIAL SMOKELESS 6
Base: SMOKELESS 20 20 GASTIGHT

The "PIONEER" SPECIAL SMOKELESS
Harrods
KNIGHTSBRIDGE S.W.1.
LOADED IN GREAT BRITAIN

DATA
Gauge; 20.
Length; 65 mm.
Head; 9 mm.
Tube; Wound paper.
Colour; Mustard yellow.
Print; Black.
Wetproof; Clear lacquered.
Base; Brass.
Closure; Rolled turn-over.
Wad; Deep crimson, print black.
Business; Department stores.

DN.2-1195. Re-drawn; 4th Feb 2000.

E. F. HART:
Clare, Suffolk, England.

E. F. HART
CLARE

Headstamp: E F HART CLARE 1912 ELEY
Base: E F HART CLARE 5

E. F. HART
CLARE

DATA
Gauge; 12.
Length; 64 mm.
Head; 8 mm.
Tube; Wound paper.
Colour; Dull orange.
Print; Black.
Base; Brass.
Closure; Rolled turn-over.
Wad; White card, print red.
Business; Ironmonger.
Case; Eley Bros, Ltd.

DN.2-0212. Re-drawn; 24th Jan 2000.

Fred W. HART:
39 Queen Street, Scarborough, Yorkshire, England.

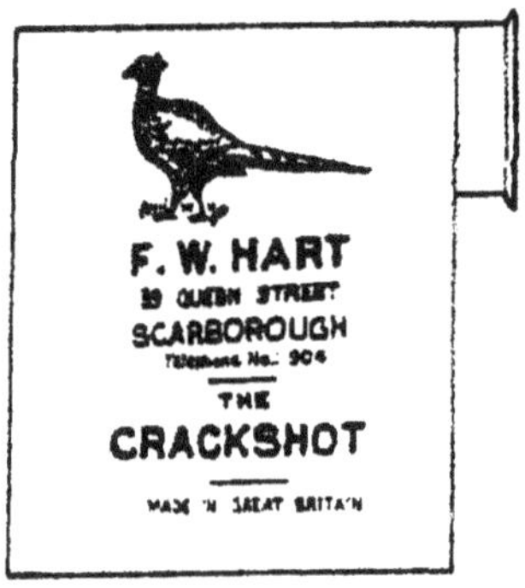

F. W. HART
39 QUEEN STREET
SCARBOROUGH
Telephone No. 904
THE
CRACKSHOT
MADE IN GREAT BRITAIN

Headstamp: ELEY-KYNOCH 12 12
Base: SMOKELESS 5

F. W. HART
39 QUEEN STREET
SCARBOROUGH

Telephone No; 904
THE CRACKSHOT
MADE IN GREAT BRITAIN

DATA
Gauge; 12.
Length; 64 mm.
Head; 8 mm.
Tube; Wound orange paper.
Colour; Orange.
Print; Black.
Base; Brass.
Closure; Rolled turn-over.
Wad; Brown card, print black.
Case; Eley-Kynoch I.C.I.
Circa; 1930's

DN.2-1297. Re-drawn November 1998

F. W. HART:
King Street, Scarborough, North Riding, Yorkshire, England.

Drawn from a set of photographs.

"THE EXPRESS"
Specially Loaded by
F. W. HART
39 QUEEN STREET
SCARBORO.
Telephone No. 904
Made in Great Britain

Headstamp: ELEY-KYNOCH 12 12
Base: F W HART SCARBORO 7

"THE EXPRESS" Specially Loaded by F. W. HART
39 QUEEN STREET SCARBORO
Telephone No, 904
Made in Great Britain

DATA
Gauge; 12.
Length; 62 mm.
Head; 16 mm.
Tube; Wound crimson paper.
Colour; Dark crimson.
Print; Black.
Base; Reinforced brass.
Closure; Rolled turn-over.
Wad; Yellow card, print black.
Business; Gunmaker.
Circa; 1930's.

DN.2-2312. 1st July 2000.

F. W. HART:
King Street, Scarborough, North Riding, Yorkshire, England.

ROCKET
LOADED BY
F. W. HART
GUNMAKER
KING STREET
SCARBOROUGH
Made in Great Britain

Headstamp: ELEY-KYNOCH 12 ICI 12
Base: F W HART SCARBOROUGH 6

ROCKET

DATA
Gauge; 12.
Length; 64 mm.
Head; 8 mm.
Tube; Wound paper.
Colour; Brownish-white.
Print; Black.
Base; Brass.
Closure; Rolled turn-over.
Wad; White card, print red.
Circa; 1930's.
Business; Gunmaker.

DN.2-0052. Updated; March 1995

HARTHAM PARK ESTATE: Corsham, Wiltshire, SN13 0RP, England.

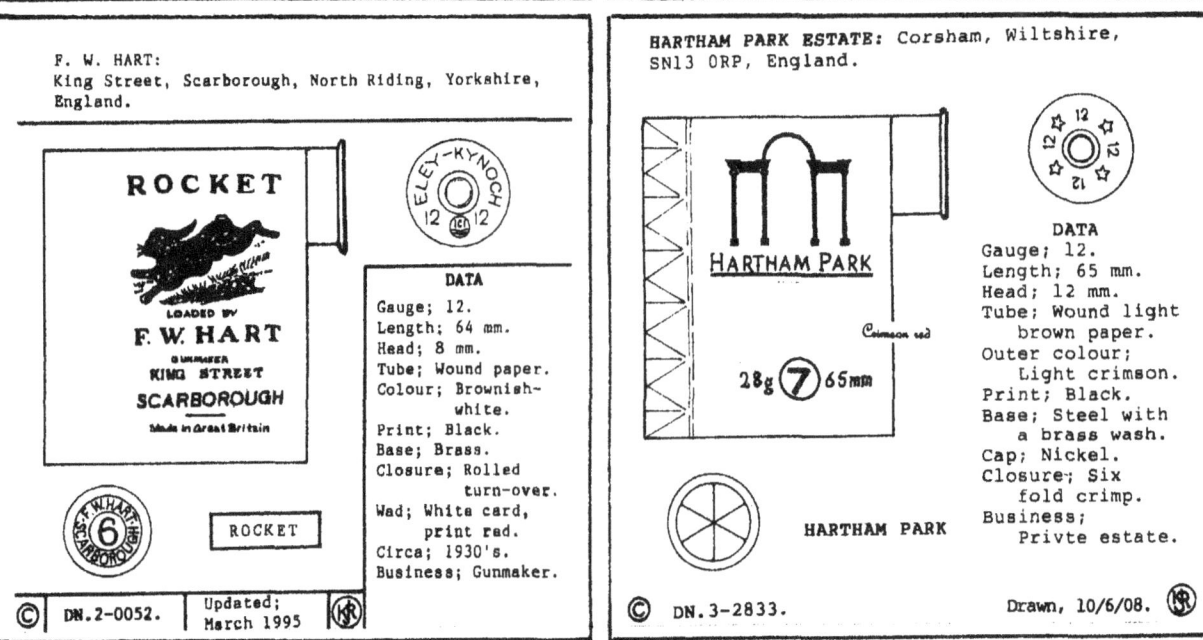

HARTHAM PARK
Crimson red
28g 7 65mm

Headstamp: 12 12 12 12
Base: HARTHAM PARK

DATA
Gauge; 12.
Length; 65 mm.
Head; 12 mm.
Tube; Wound light brown paper.
Outer colour; Light crimson.
Print; Black.
Base; Steel with a brass wash.
Cap; Nickel.
Closure; Six fold crimp.
Business; Privte estate.

DN.3-2833. Drawn, 10/6/08.

PLATE 150 [HAR – HAR]

HARTLEY'S SPORT STORE:
Flinders Street, Melbourne, Victoria, Australia.

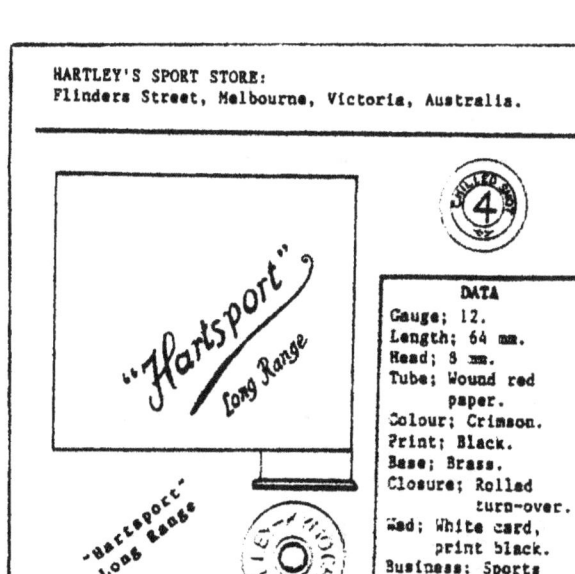

DATA
Gauge; 12.
Length; 64 mm.
Head; 8 mm.
Tube; Wound red paper.
Colour; Crimson.
Print; Black.
Base; Brass.
Closure; Rolled turn-over.
Wad; White card, print black.
Business; Sports stores.
Case; Eley-Kynoch I.C.I.

© DN.2-0545.   Re-drawn 1st Feb 1999

A. B. HARVEY & SON, LTD:
1 & 2 Market Strand, Falmouth, Cornwall, England.

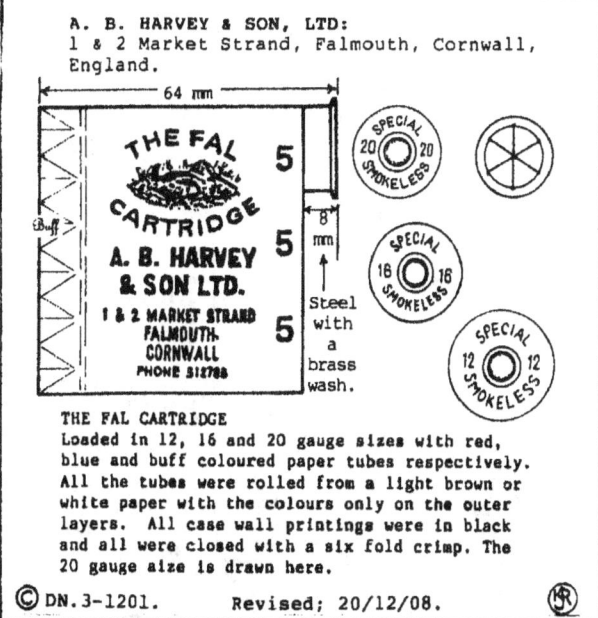

THE FAL CARTRIDGE
Loaded in 12, 16 and 20 gauge sizes with red, blue and buff coloured paper tubes respectively. All the tubes were rolled from a light brown or white paper with the colours only on the outer layers. All case wall printings were in black and all were closed with a six fold crimp. The 20 gauge size is drawn here.

© DN.3-1201.   Revised; 20/12/08.

A.B. HARVEY & SON, LTD: 1-2 Market Strand, Falmouth, Cornwall, TR11 3DA, England.

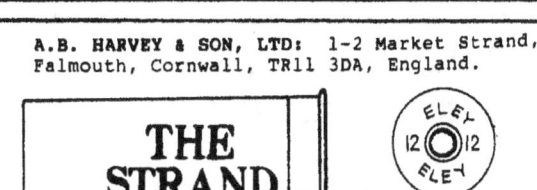

DATA
Gauge; 12.
Length; 65 mm.
Tube; Wound light brown paper.
Outer colour; Orange.
Print; Black.
Base; Steel with a brass wash.
Cap; Non corrosive.
Closure; Rolled turn-over.
Wad; Light grey card, print black.
Business; Gunsmiths.

THE STRAND
A.B. HARVEY & SON LTD
1-2 Market Strand
Falmouth, Cornwall
Made in Great Britain

© DN.3-1094.   Drawn, 9/7/08.

HARVEY SHAW SUCCESSORS:
560-6 Lonsdale Street, Melbourne, Victoria, Australia.

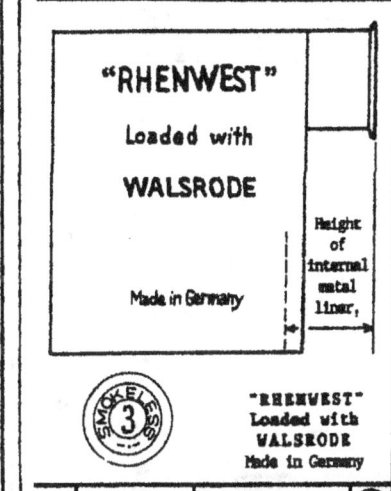

DATA
Gauge; 12.
Length; 69 mm.
Head; 15 mm.
Tube; Wound brown paper.
Colour; Yellow.
Print; Black.
Base; Reinforced brass.
Closure; Rolled turn-over.
Wad; Orange card, print black.
Business; Stores and cartridge loaders.
Case; Germany.
Circa; 1930's.

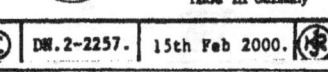

© DN.2-2257.   15th Feb 2000.

HARVEY SHAW SUCCESSORS:
560-6 Lonsdale Street, Melbourne, Victoria, Australia.

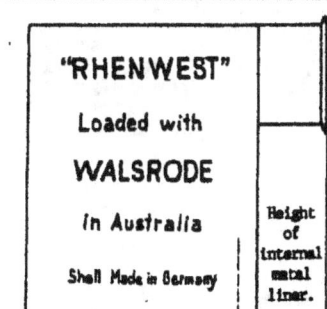

DATA
Gauge; 12.
Length; 64 mm.
Head; 15 mm.
Tube; Wound brown paper.
Colour; Yellow.
Print; Black.
Base; Reinforced brass.
Closure; Rolled turn-over.
Wad; Orange card, print black.
Business; Stores and cartridge loaders.
Case; Germany.
Circa; 1930's.

© DN.2-0980.   Re-drawn; 15th Feb 2000.

HARVEY SHAW SUCCESSORS: 560-6 Lonsdale Street, Melbourne. Victoria, Australia.
(Business; Cartridge loaders and merchants).

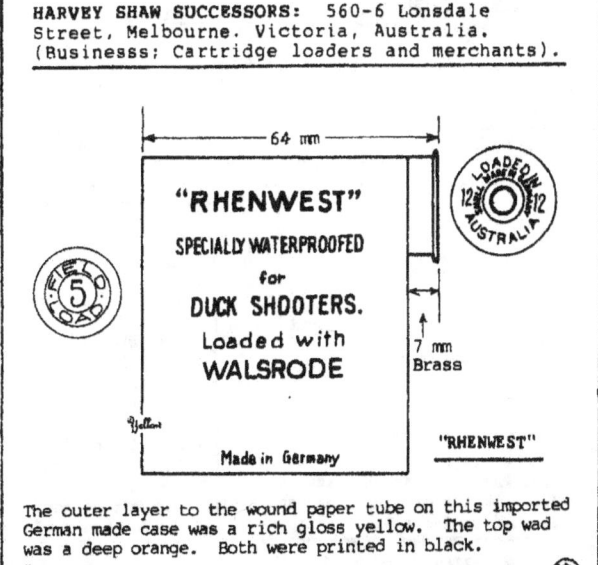

The outer layer to the wound paper tube on this imported German made case was a rich gloss yellow. The top wad was a deep orange. Both were printed in black.

© DN.3-0982.   Revised, 2/2/09.

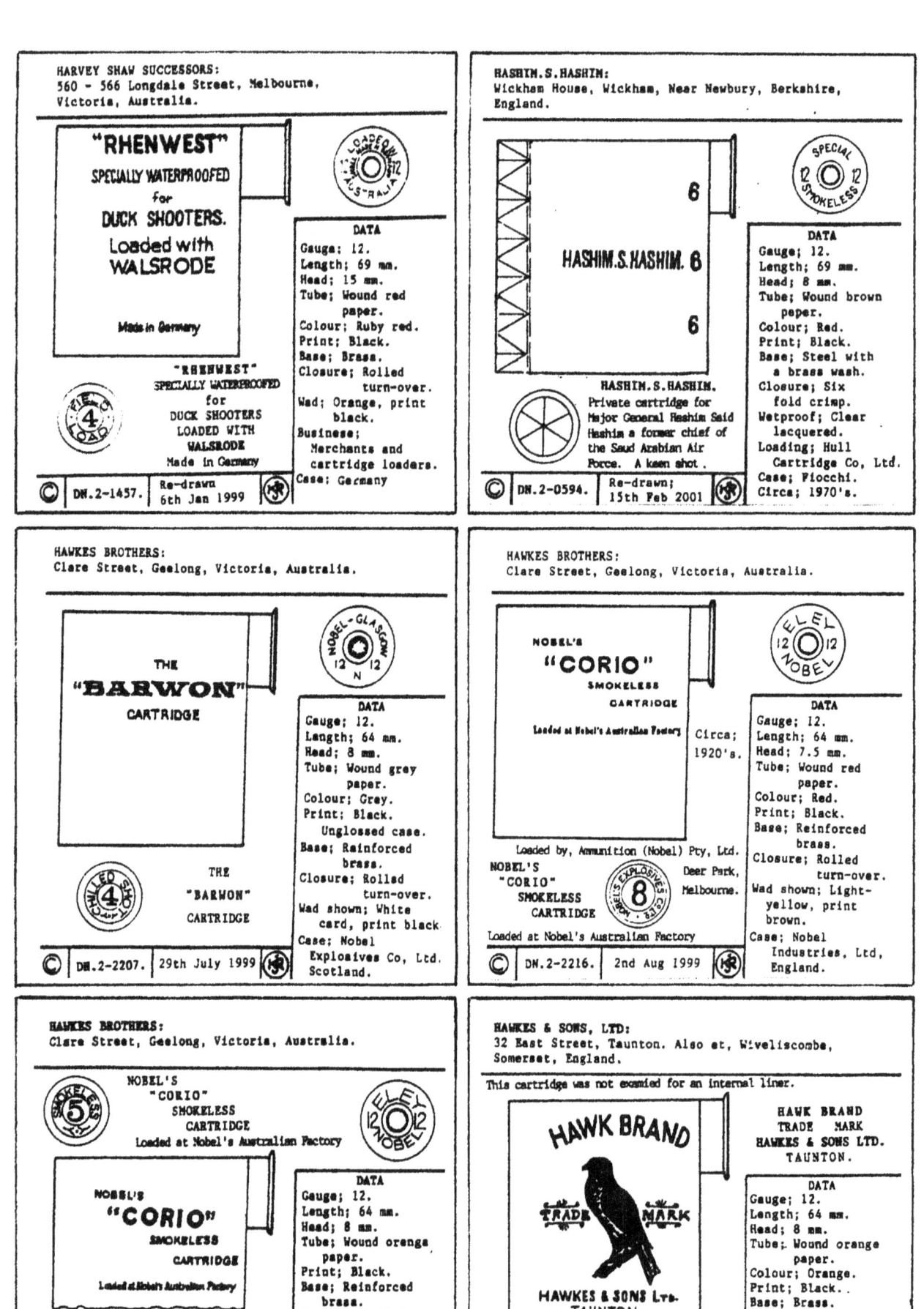

PLATE 152 [HAR – HAW]

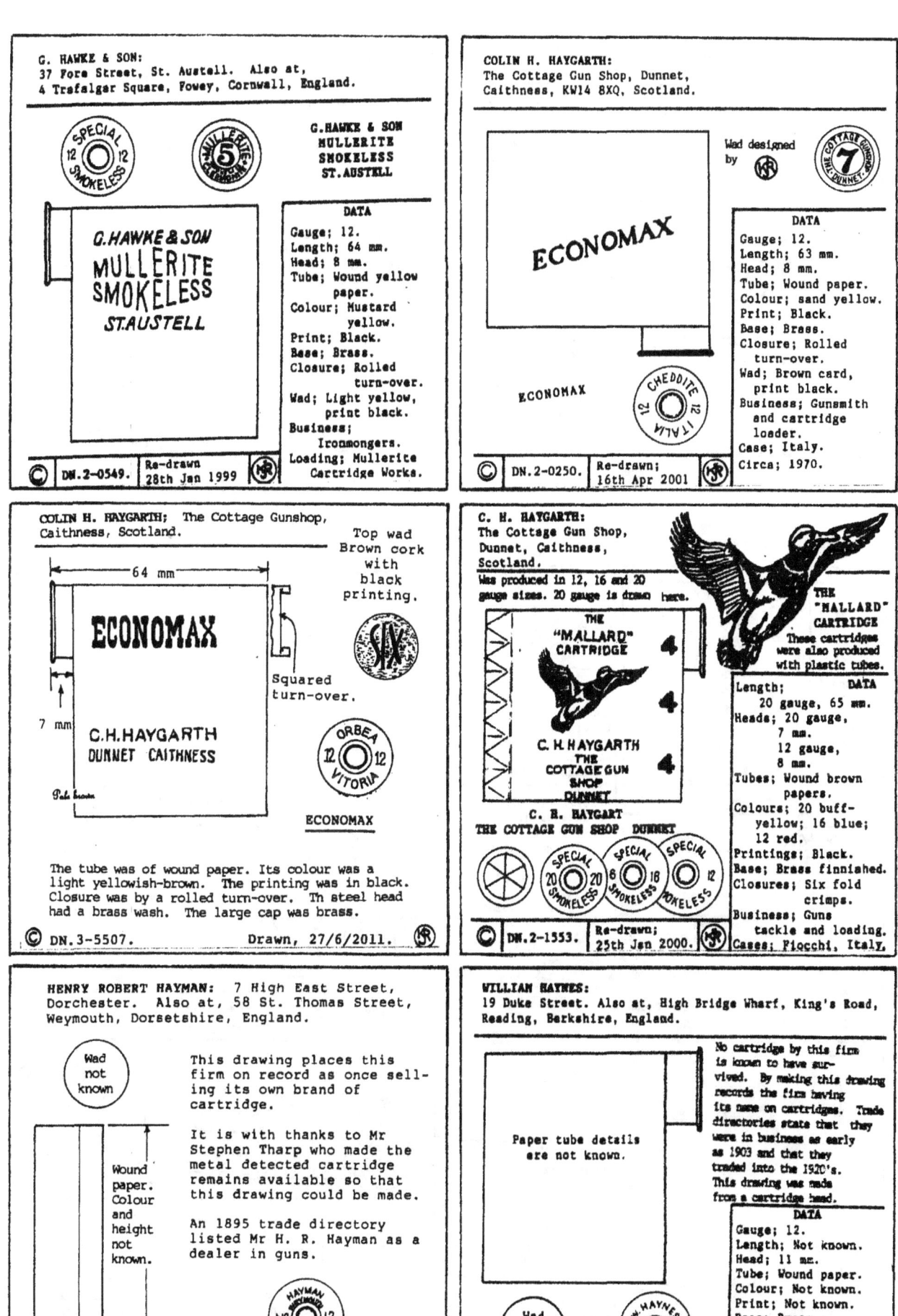

PLATE 153 [HAW – HAY]

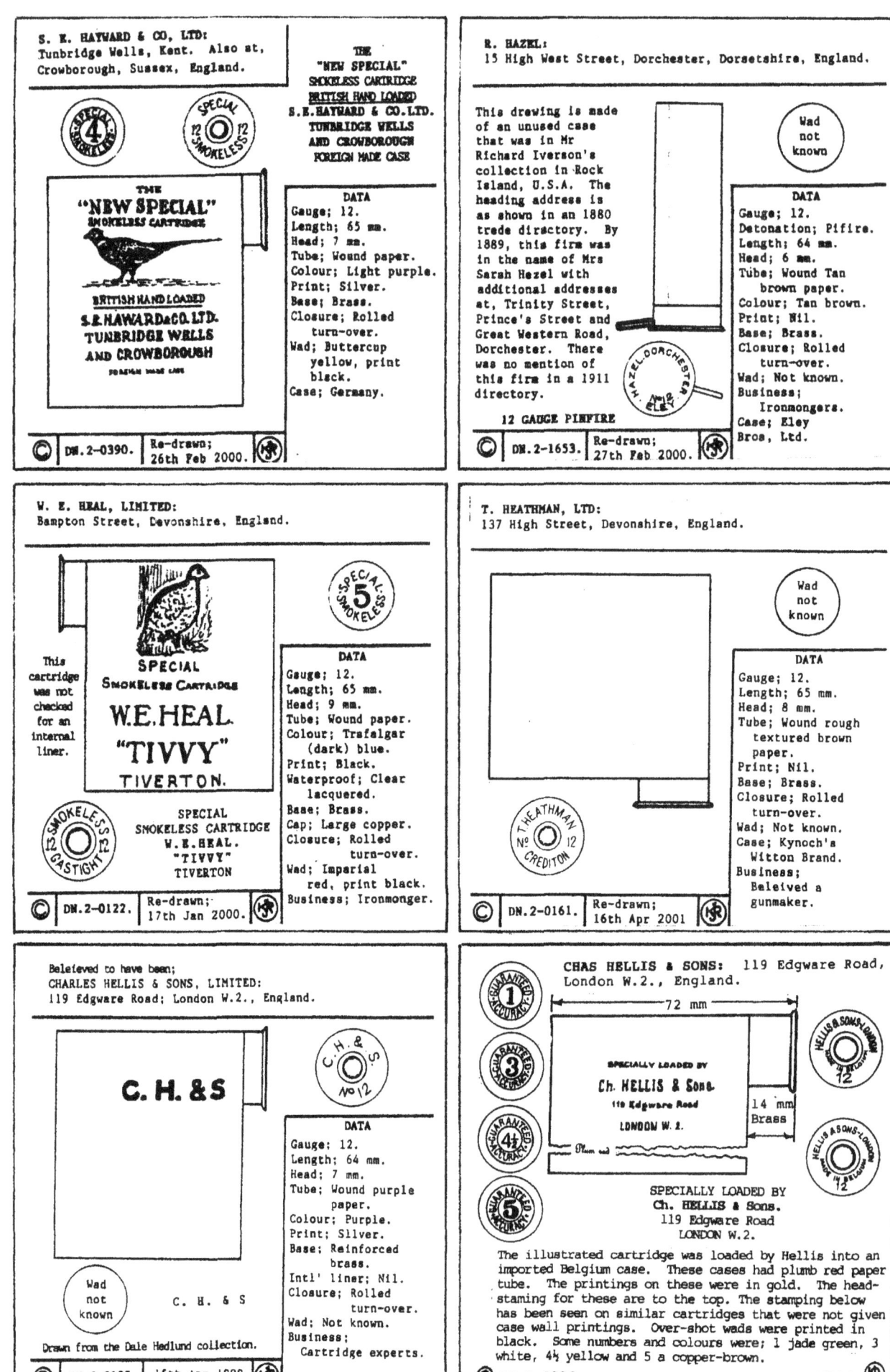

PLATE 154 [HAY - HEL]

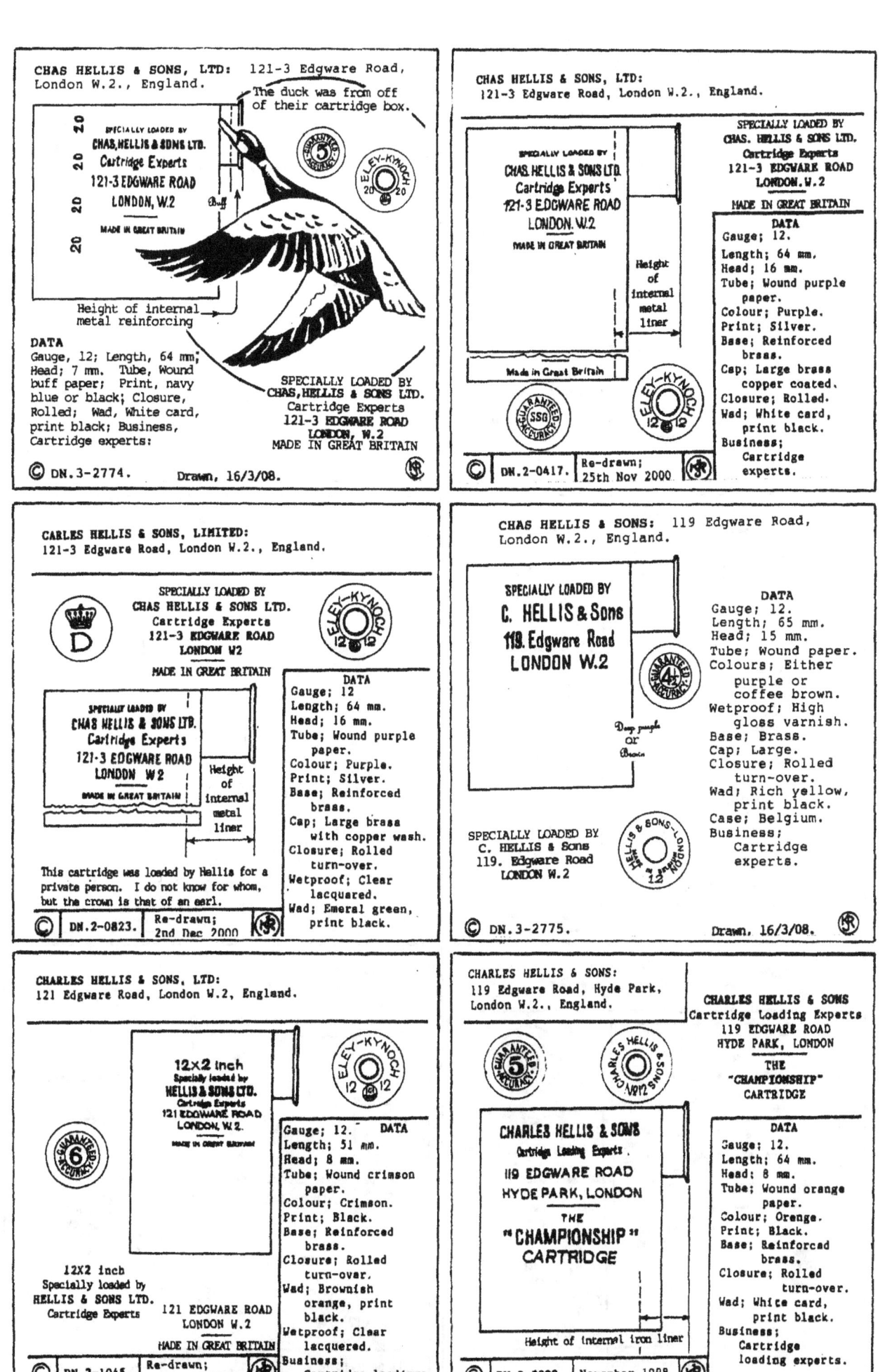

PLATE 155 [HEL - HEL]

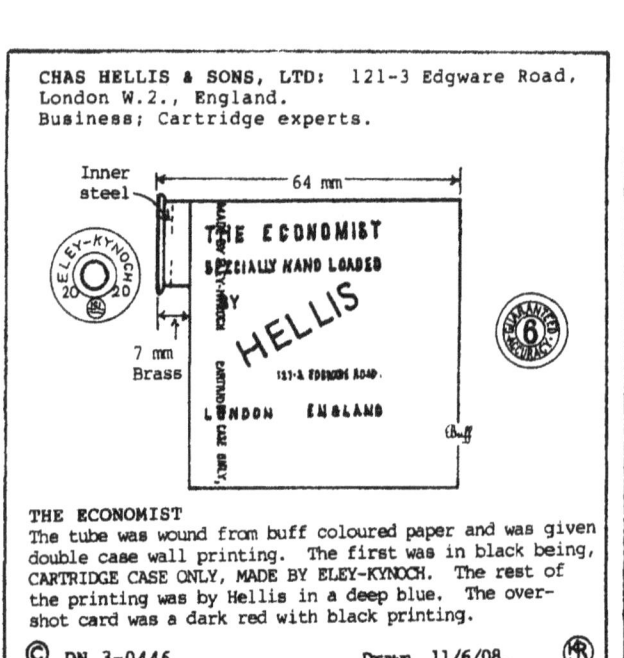
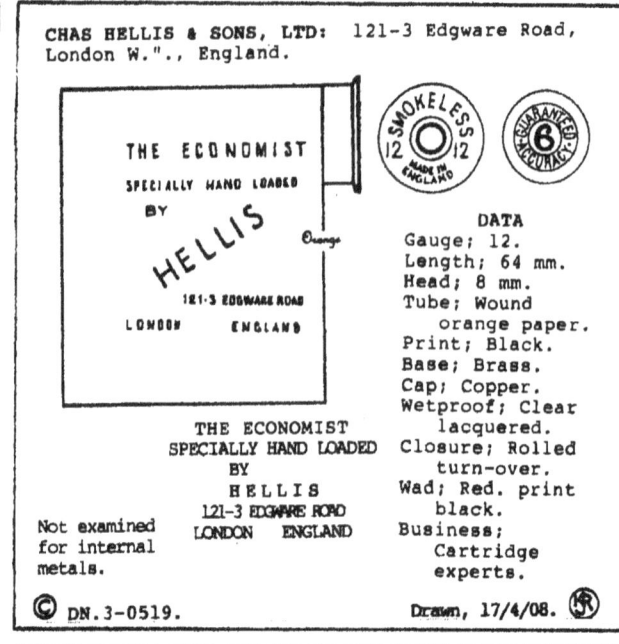
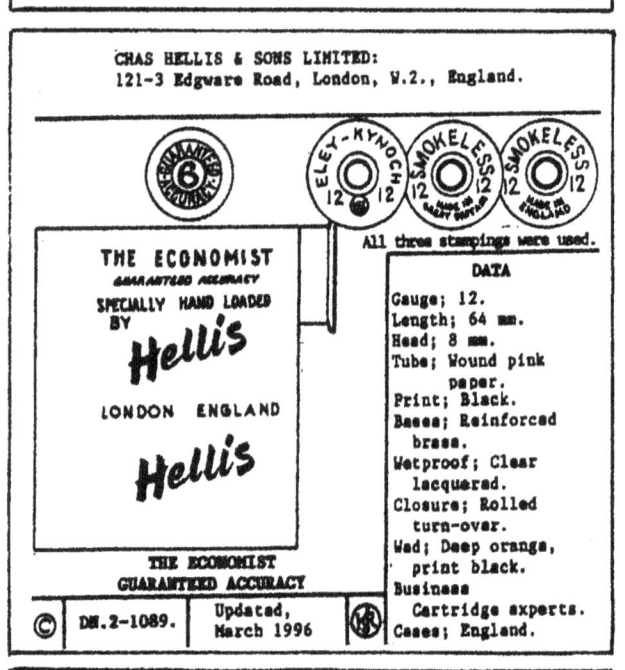
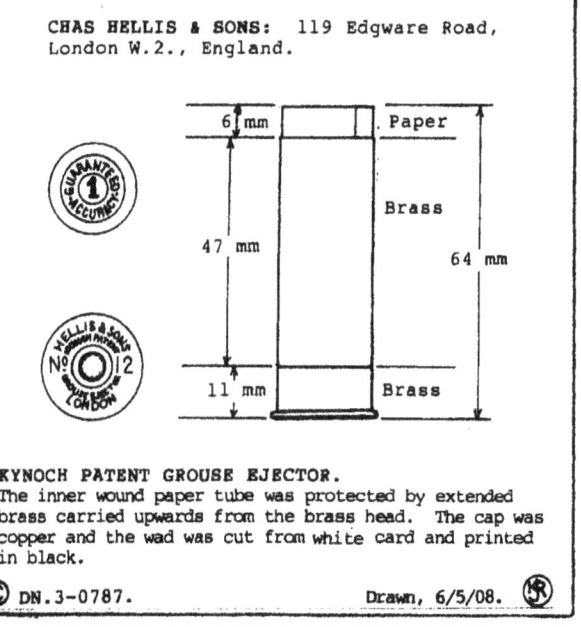
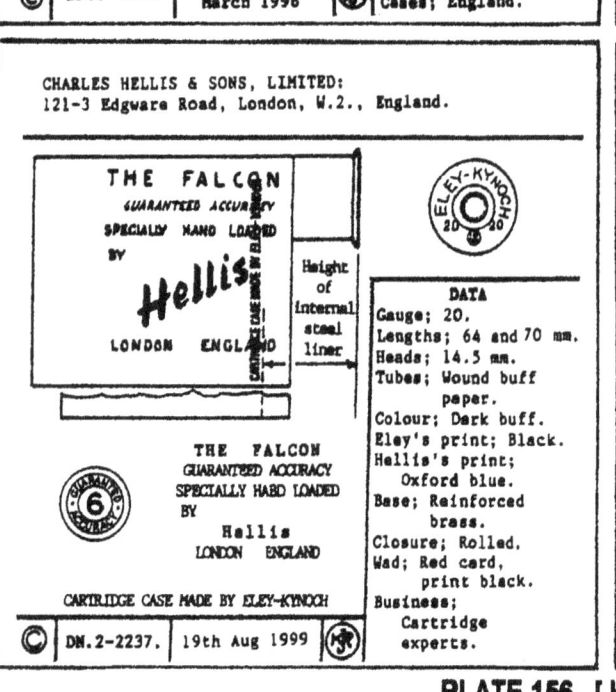
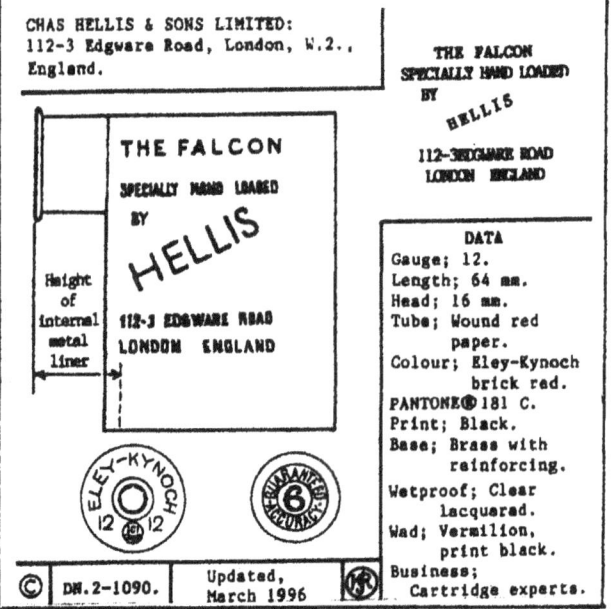

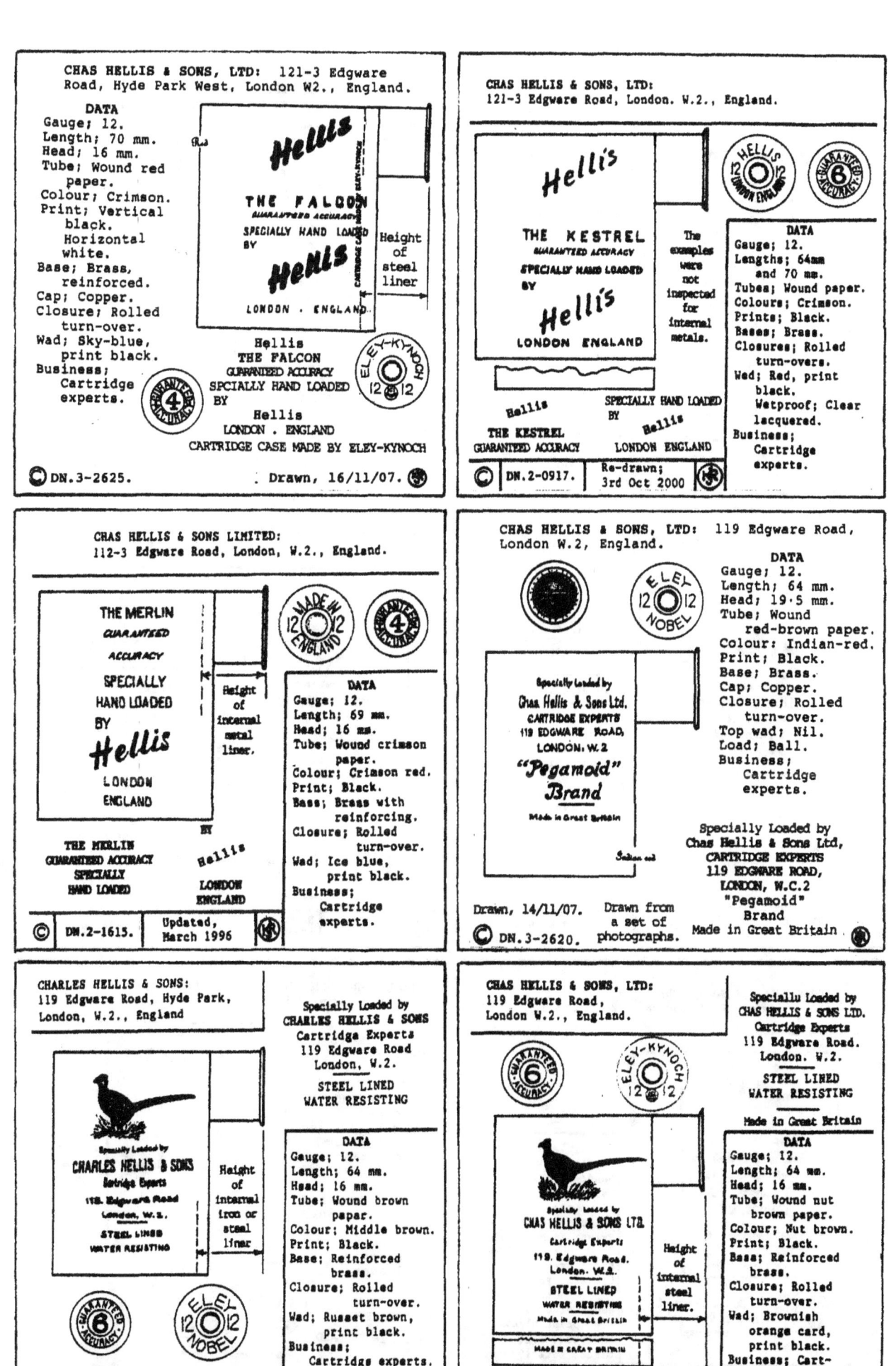

PLATE 157 [HEL – HEL]

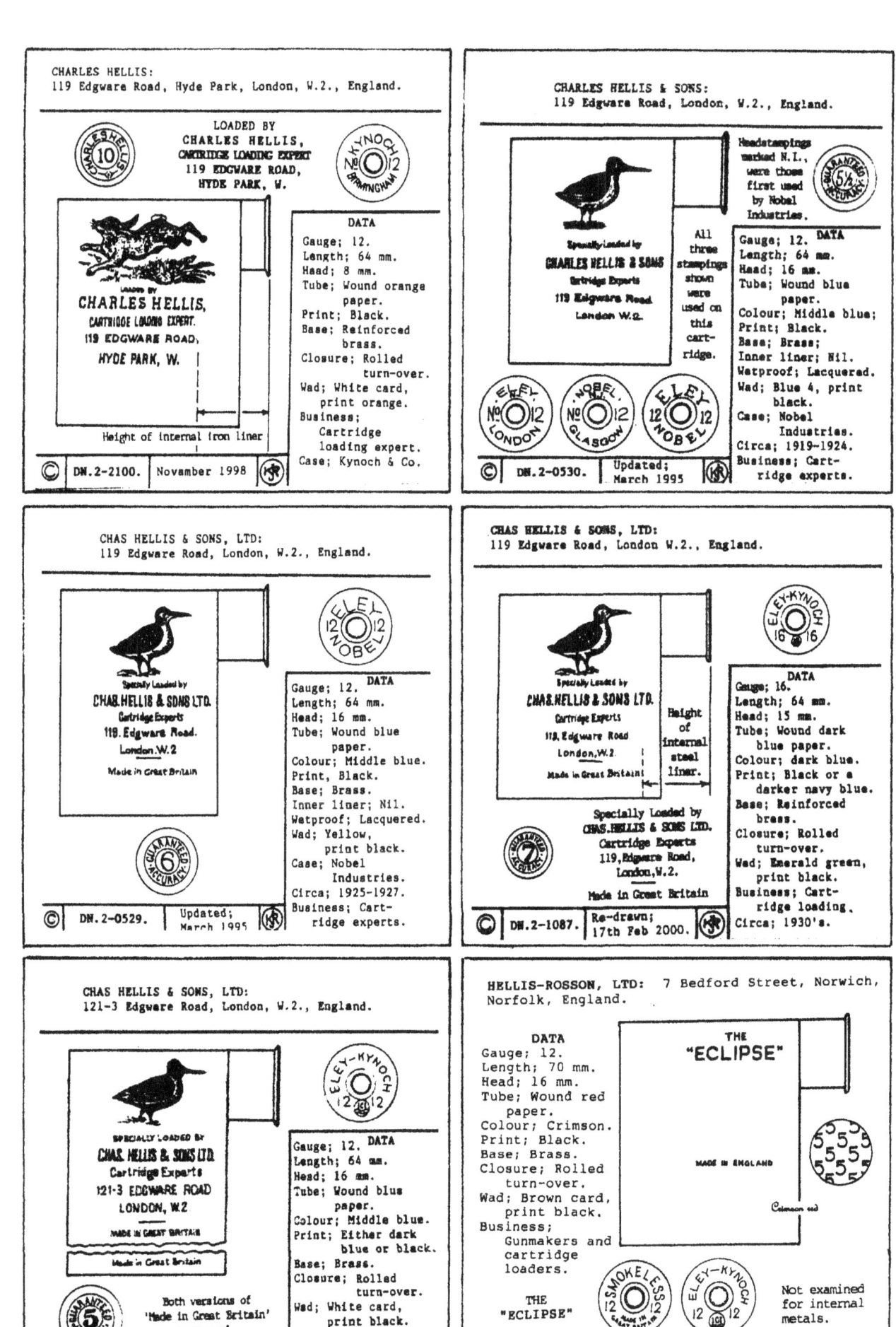

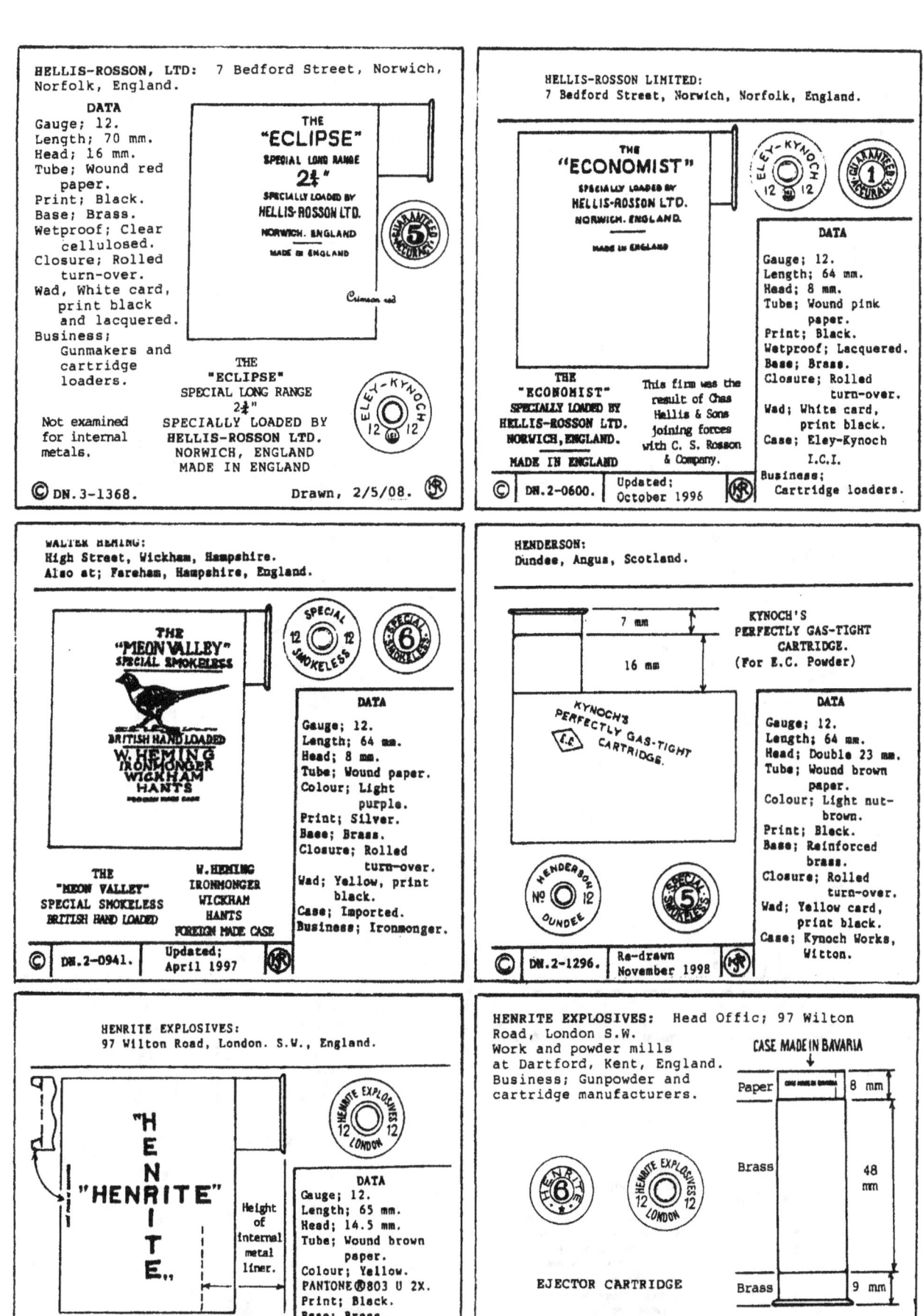

PLATE 159 [HEL - HEN]

T. HEPPLESTONE:
23 Shudehill, Manchester, Lancashire (Great Manchester), England.

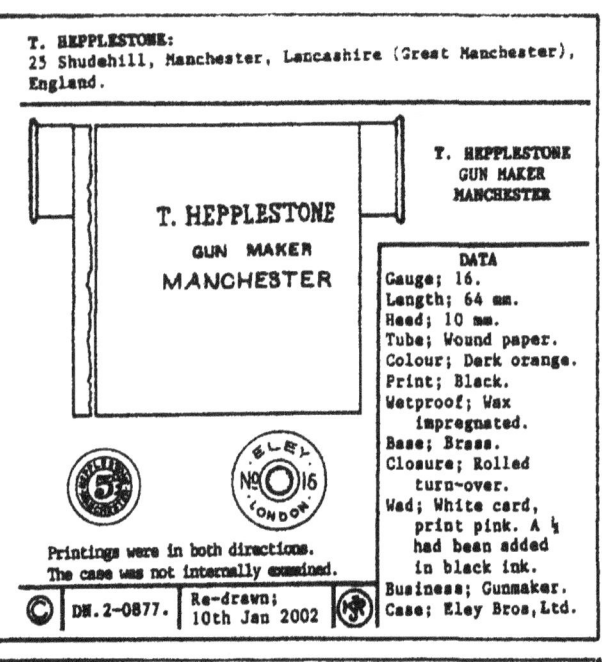

DATA
Gauge; 16.
Length; 64 mm.
Head; 10 mm.
Tube; Wound paper.
Colour; Dark orange.
Print; Black.
Wetproof; Wax impregnated.
Base; Brass.
Closure; Rolled turn-over.
Wad; White card, print pink. A ½ had been added in black ink.
Business; Gunmaker.
Case; Eley Bros, Ltd.

Printings were in both directions. The case was not internally examined.

DN.2-0877. Re-drawn; 10th Jan 2002

HERCULES ARMAMENT CO, LTD:
8 St. Martin's Street, Leicester Square, London W.C.2., England.

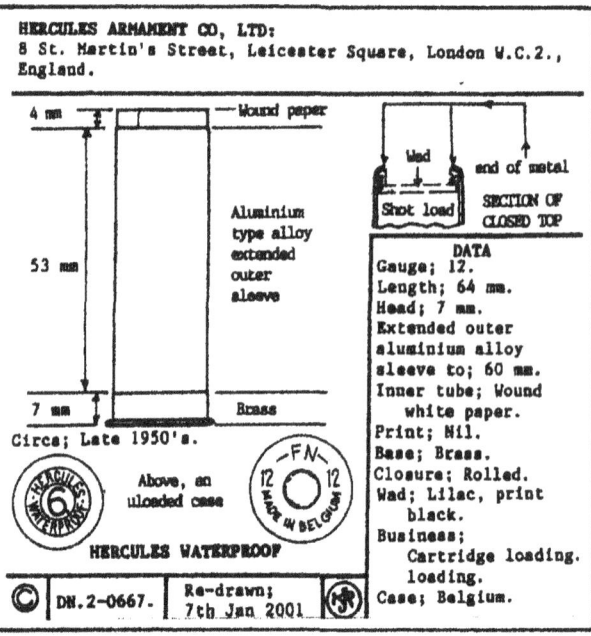

Circa; Late 1950's.

Above, an unloaded case

DATA
Gauge; 12.
Length; 64 mm.
Head; 7 mm.
Extended outer aluminium alloy sleeve to; 60 mm.
Inner tube; Wound white paper.
Print; Nil.
Base; Brass.
Closure; Rolled.
Wad; Lilac, print black.
Business; Cartridge loading.
Case; Belgium.

DN.2-0667. Re-drawn; 7th Jan 2001

HERCULES ARMAMENT CO, LTD:
8 St. Martins Street, Leicester Square, London W.C.2., England.

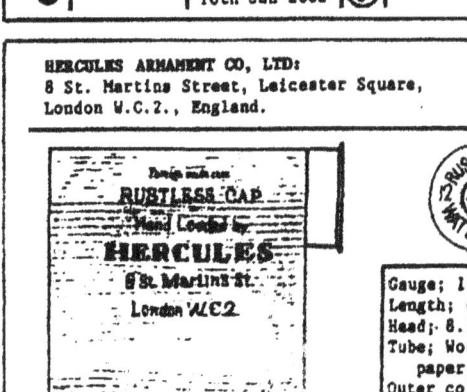

Foreign made case
RUSTLESS CAP
Hand Loaded by
HERCULES
8 St. Martins St.
London W.C.2.

DATA
Gauge; 12.
Length; 64 mm.
Head; 8.5 mm.
Tube; Wound brown paper.
Outer colours in corrugated papers; Royal purple, Buttercup yellow, For-get-me-not blue and signal red.
Printings; Black.
Base; Steel with brass wash.
Closure; Rolled.
Wad shown; Lilac, print black.

DN.2-0427. Re-drawn; 12th dec 2000

W. HERRING:
Street, Somerset, England.

Drawn from photographs of a reloaded round. It is believed that it was originally loaded for W. Herring by the New Explosives Co, Ltd.

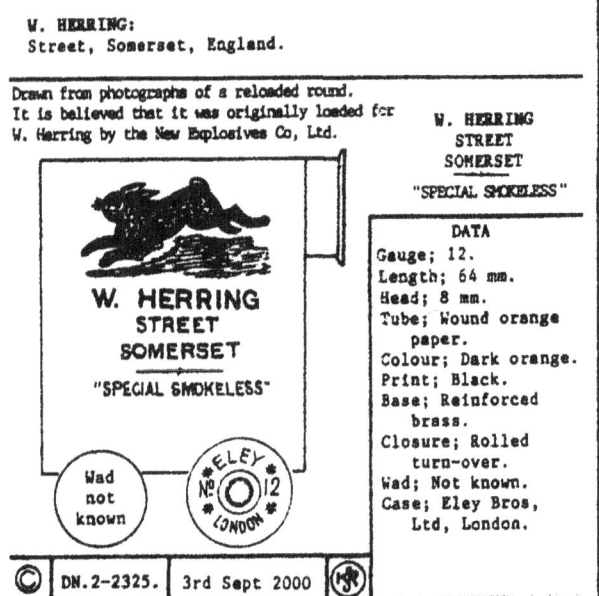

W. HERRING
STREET
SOMERSET

"SPECIAL SMOKELESS"

Wad not known

DATA
Gauge; 12.
Length; 64 mm.
Head; 8 mm.
Tube; Wound orange paper.
Colour; Dark orange.
Print; Black.
Base; Reinforced brass.
Closure; Rolled turn-over.
Wad; Not known.
Case; Eley Bros, Ltd, London.

DN.2-2325. 3rd Sept 2000

C. M. HESFORD & CO, LTD. Ormskirk, Lancashire, England.

"THE HESFORD" SPECIAL
C. M. HESFORD & CO. LTD.
ORMSKIRK
Made in Great Britain

The paper tube was wound from a middle blue paper and its printings were in a dark blue. The over-shot card was yellow with black printing. The brass head was 8 mm in height. This was a cartridge circa, the 1930's. This drawing was made from a set of photographs.

 "THE HESFORD" SPECIAL

DN.5,1039.

HESKETH ESTATE: Easton Neston Hall, Towcester, Northamptonshire, England.

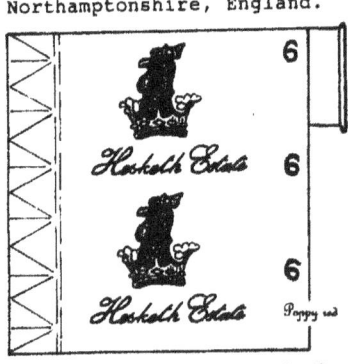

Hesketh Estate
This estate was sold, circa 2005.

DATA
Gauge; 12.
Length; 70 mm.
Head; 8 mm.
Tube; Light brown paper.
Outer colour; Poppy red.
Print; Black.
Base; Steel with a brass wash.
Cap; Nickel.
Closure; Six fold crimp.
Case by; Fiocchi.
Business; Private estate.
Circa; 1990's.

DN.3-2825. Drawn, 16/6/08.

CHARLES A. HEYER & COMPANY:
Nairobi, Kenya.

Made in Great Britain
Loaded expressly for
CHAS. A. HEYER & CO.,
NAIROBI

ELEY
GAS-TIGHT CARTRIDGE CASE
FOR
SCHULTZE
SPORTING POWDER

DATA
Gauge; 12.
Length; 64 mm.
Head; 16 mm.
Tube; Wound brown paper.
Colour; Middle brown.
Print; Black.
Base; Reinforced brass.
Closure; Rolled turn-over.
Wad White card. Washer type.
Load; Lethal ball.
Case; Eley Bros, Ltd.

© DN.2-0062. Re-drawn November 1998

CHARLES A. HEYER & COMPANY:
Nairobi, Kenya.

Simba
Specially loaded
for
Chas A.Heyer & Co,
Nairobi

DATA
Gauge; 12.
Length; 64 mm.
Head; 15 mm.
Tube; Wound paper.
Colour; Burnt orange.
Print; Black.
Base; Reinforced brass.
Closure; Rolled turn-over.
Wad; White card, print black.

© DN.2-2152. Updated; 19th Sept 2000

Drawn from the Bob Cameron collection.

HEYWOOD & HODGE:
Torrington, Devonshire, England.

The Reliable
Loaded with Schultze Powder
HEYWOOD & HODGE
TORRINGTON

Squared turn-over.

DATA
Gauge; 12.
Length; 64 mm.
Head; 8 mm.
Tube; Rolled paper.
Colour; Straw-yellow.
Print; Black.
Base; Brass.
Closure; Rolled turn-over.
Wad; Dark-yellow, print black.
Loading; Probably by Cogschultze & Ammunition Powder Company. Founded August 1911 and in business up in to 1914 war.

© DN.2-1281. Re-drawn November 1998

W. G. HIBBARD, F. P. SPENCER & A. L. BARTLETT:
Chicago, Illinois, United States of America.

Brass with six corrugated links

STAR
BRAND
MADE IN
U.S.A.

DATA
Gauge; 12.
Length; 66 mm.
Head; 14.5 mm.
Tube; Wound brown paper.
Colour; Red plum.
Print; Nil
Iternal liner; Nil.
Base; Brass.
Closure; Rolled turn-over.
Wad; Not known.
Produced by; Peters Cartridge Company of Cincinnati, Ohio.

© DN.2-1143. Updated, February 1996

HARRY HIGGINS:
46-48 Theme Street, Tenbury Wells, Worcestershire
(Hereford & Worcester), England.

This drawing has been made from
two used cases and a live cartridge.

HARRY HIGGINS "SPECIAL"

DATA
Gauge; 12.
Length; 64 mm.
Head; 8 mm.
Tube; Wound paper.
Colour; Pink 2.5.
Prints; Either black or dark blue.
Base; Brass.
Closure; Rolled turn-over.
Wad; Yellow, print black.
Wetproof; Clear lacquer.
Circa; Mid 1930's.

© DN.2-0125. Updated; December 1994

E. & G. HIGHAM: 4 Chapel Street, Liverpool,
Lancashire (Merseyside), England.
Business; Gunmkers.

PATENT GASTIGHT CARTRIDGE
This very old cartridge had raised writing on the headstamp. It had a summer green paper tube with black case wall printing. The top wad was just plain yellow card and may not have been the original.

© DN.3-0807. Drawn, 9/7/08.

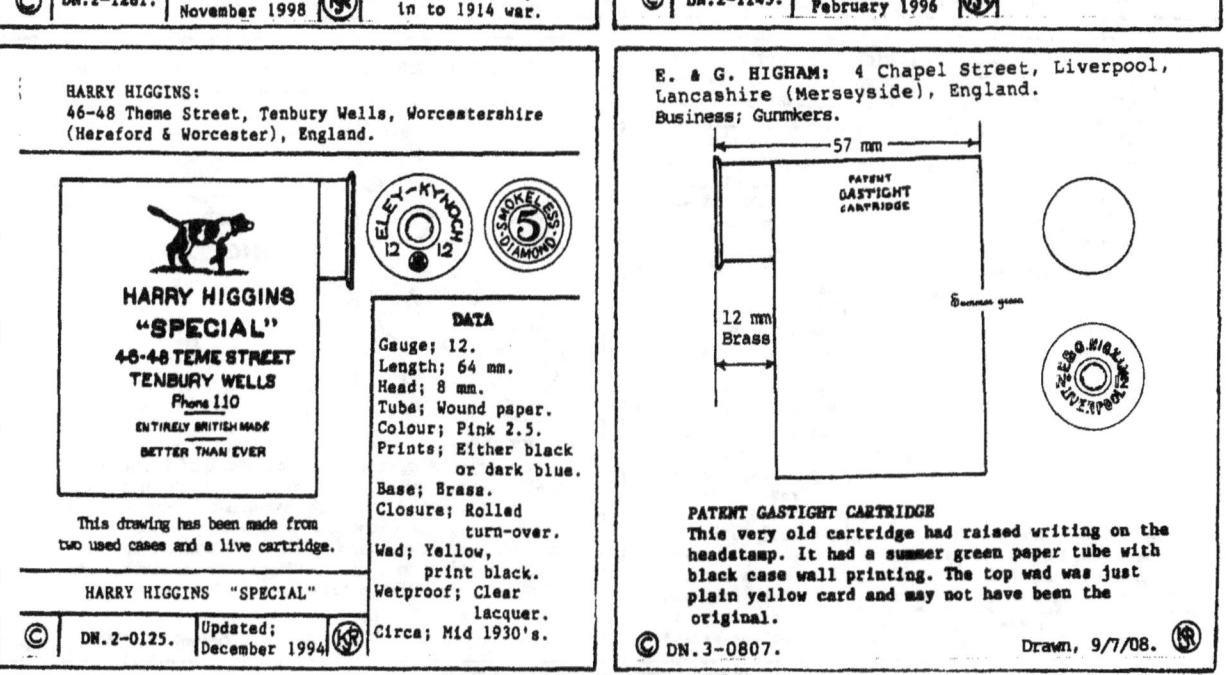

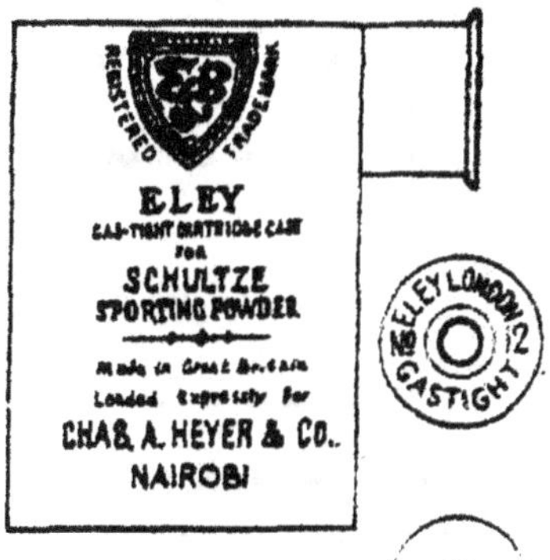

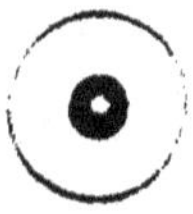

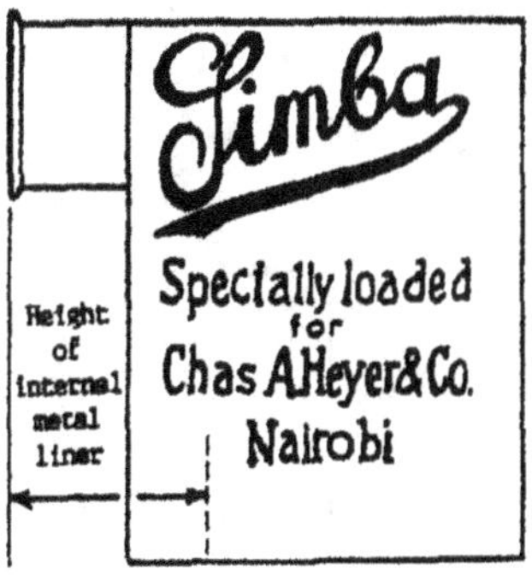

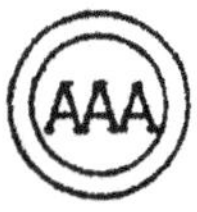

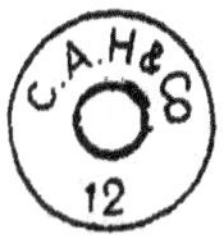

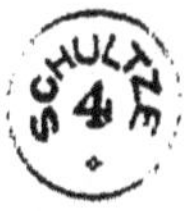

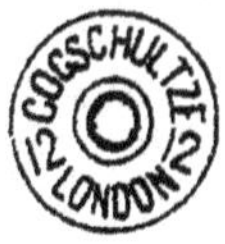

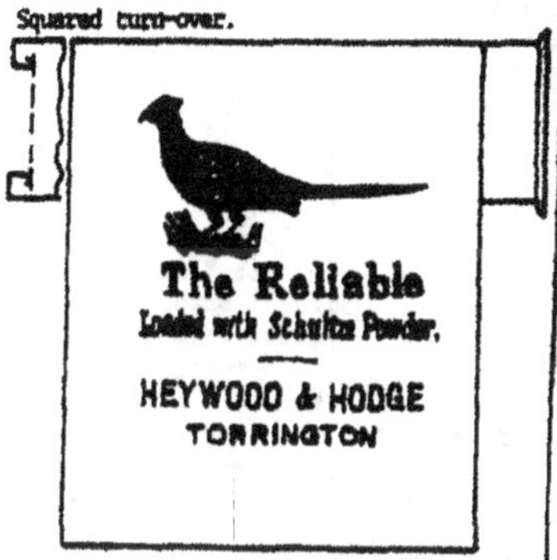

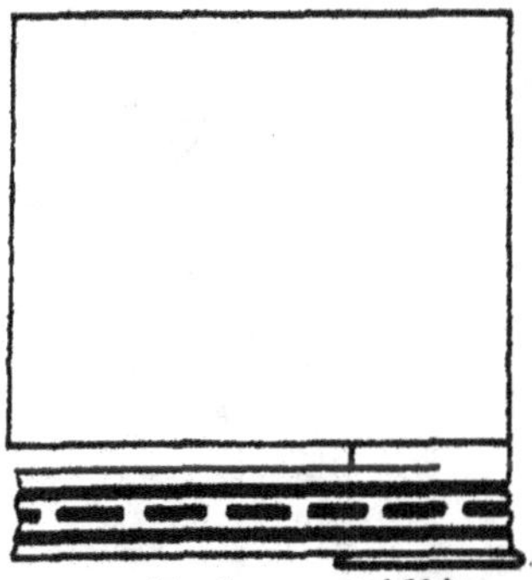

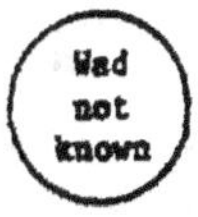

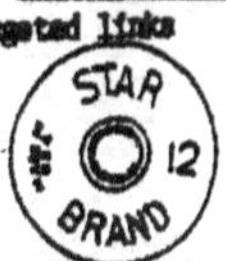

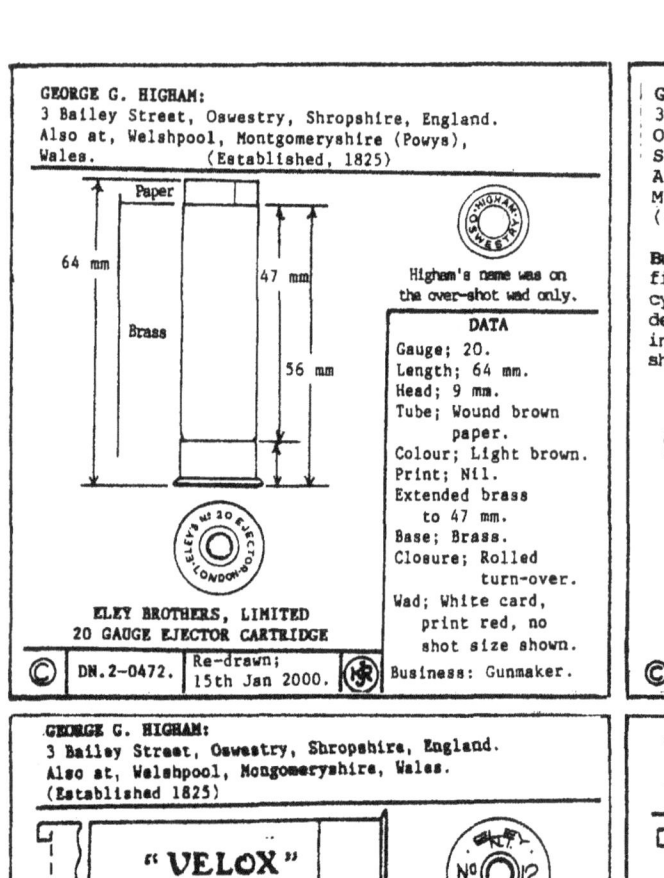
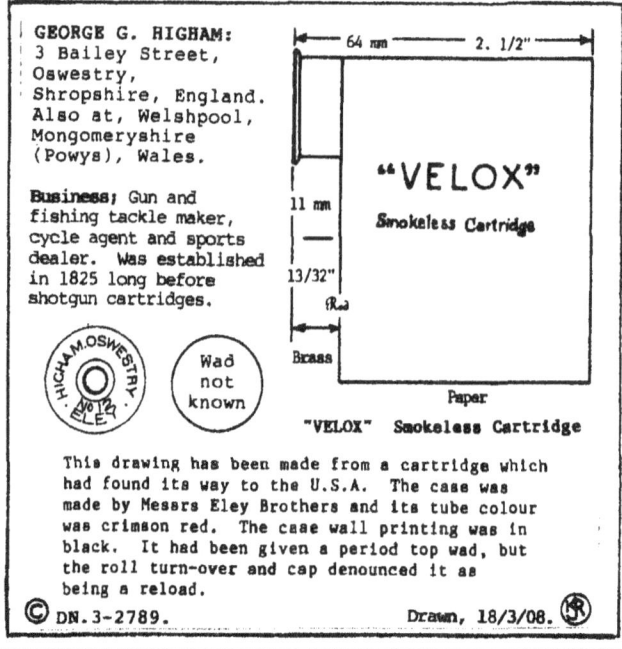
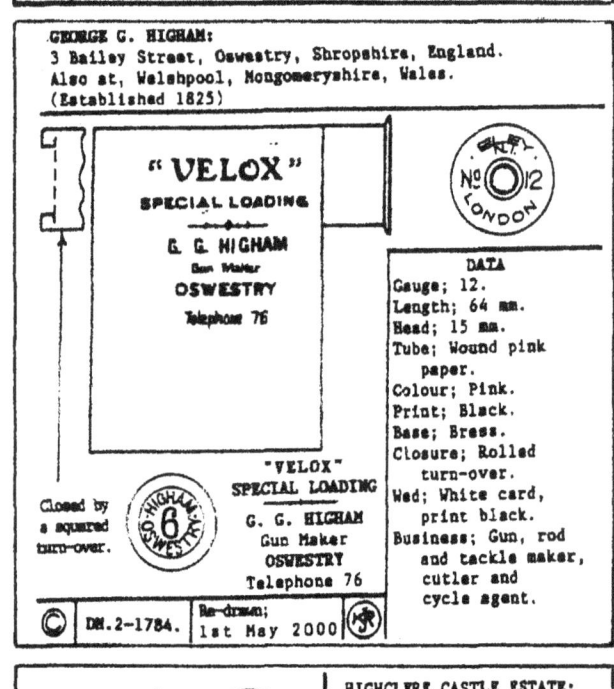
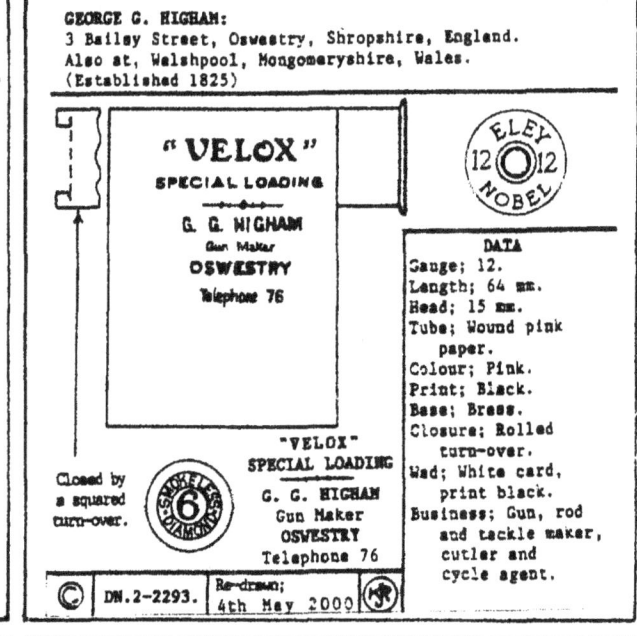
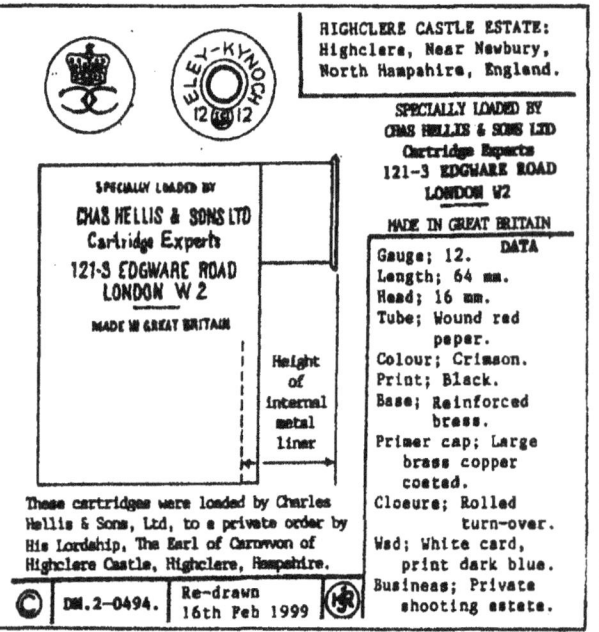
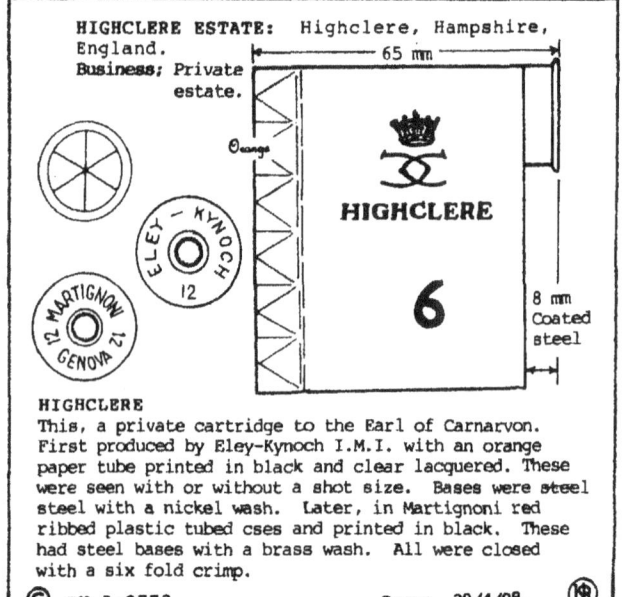

PLATE 162 [HIG – HIG]

HIGHCLERE ESTATE:
Highclere Park, Highclere, North Hampshire, England.

Head gamekeeper, Mr E. Hughes.

DATA
Gauge; 12.
Length; 67 mm.
Head; 8.5 mm.
Tube; flame red ribbed plastic.
Printing; As shown was in gold. Also black used but printed in other direction.
Head; Steel with a brass wash.
Closure; Six fold crimp.
Business; Private.
Case; Caledonian Cartridge Co.
Circa; 1992-1993.

Private cartridge to His Lordship, Earl of Carnarvon. One small batch printed in gold, the first to portray Highclere Castle.

© DN.2-1617. Re-drawn; 1st March 2001

HIGHCLERE ESTATE:
Hioghclere Park, Highclere, North Hampshire, England.

DATA
Gauge; 12.
Length; 67 mm.
Head; 12 mm.
Tube; Black ribbed plastic.
Printing; Gold.
Base; Steel with a brass wash.
Closure; Six fold crimp.
Business; Private estate.
Circa; 1993-1994.

Private cartridge to His Lordship, Earl of Carnarvon. Highclere Castle.
Head gamekeeper, Mr E. Hughes.

© DN.2-1573. Re-drawn; 1st March 2001

ARTHUR HILL & SON: 9 Market Place, Horncastle, Lincolnshire, England.

DATA
Gauge; 12.
Length; 64 mm.
Head; 16 mm.
Tube; Wound green paper.
Colour; Dark green.
Print; Black.
Base; Brass (not examined for internal mtals).
Closure; Rolled turn-over.
Wad; White card, by pen 6 or 9 ?
Business; Gunmakers.
Circa; 1920's.

THE "CHAMPION"
CARTRIDGE
SPECIALLY LOADED BY
H I L L & S O N
GUNMAKERS
HORNCASTLE

© DN.3-0473. Drawn, 26/4/08.

ARTHUR HILL & SON:
9 The Market Place, Horncastle, Lincolnshire, England.

THE RELIABLE
CARTRIDGE
SPECIALLY LOADED BY
HILL & SON
GUNMAKERS
HORNCASTLE
Telephone; 3366
MADE IN GREAT BRITAIN

DATA
Gauge; 12.
Length; 64 mm.
Head; 8 mm.
Tube; Wound pink paper.
Colour; Pink.
Print; Black.
Base; Brass.
Closure; Rolled turn-over.
Wad; Brown card, print black.
Business; Gunmakers.
Case; Eley-Kynoch I.C.I.
Circa; Mid 1930's.

© DN.2-1224. Re-drawn; 12th Oct 2000

RUSSELL HILLSDON:
Chichester, West Sussex.
Also at; Worthing, West Sussex, England.

Height of internal metal liner.

DATA
Gauge; ·410.
Length; 51 mm.
Head; 7 mm.
Tube; Wound light brown paper.
Colour; Spring green.
Print; Black.
Base; Reinforced brass.
Closure; Rolled turn-over.
Wad; Spring green, print black.
Case; Foreign.

GUARANTEED
accurately loaded in
ENGLAND
RUSSELL HILLSDIN
Chichester and Worthing:
FOREIGN MADE CASE

© DN.2-1964. May 1997.

RUSSELL HILLSDON: Chichester, Horsham & Worthing, Sussex. Also, Farnham, Surrey. & Birmingham, Warwickshire (W. Midlands), England.

Not examined for internal metal

DATA
Gauge; 12.
Length; 64 mm.
Head; 8 mm.
Tube; Wound blue paper.
Colour; Middle blue.
Print; Black or navy blue.
Base; Brass.
Cap; Copper.
Closure; Rolled turn-over.
Wad; Powder blue, print darker blue.
Business; Gun and sports.
Circa; Mid 1930's.

THE
"GOODWOOD"
Hand loaded by
RUSSELL HILLSDON
CHICHESTER
HORSHAM
AND
WORTHING
Made in Great Britain

DN.3-0370.

© Drawn, 4/4/08.

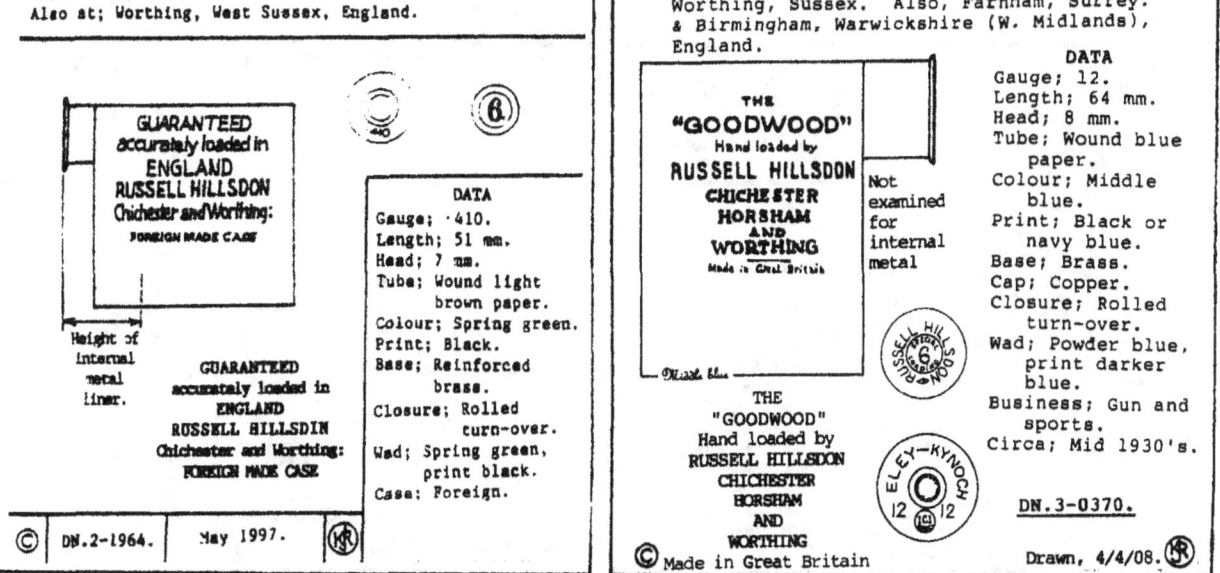

PLATE 163 [HIG – HIL]

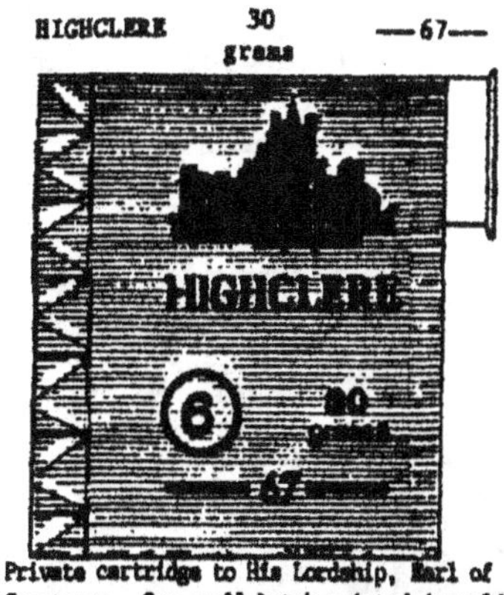

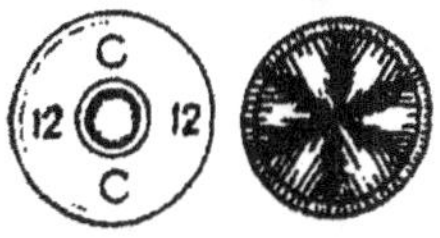

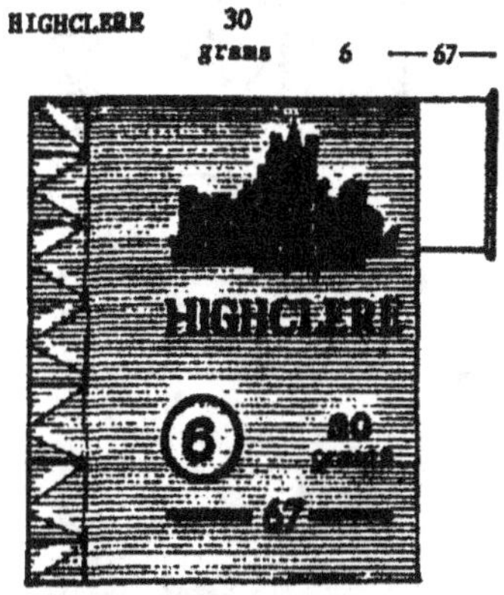

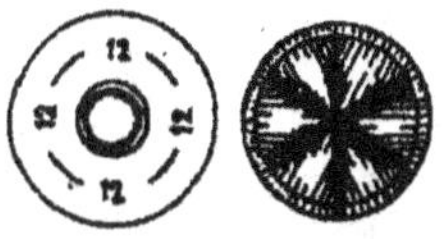

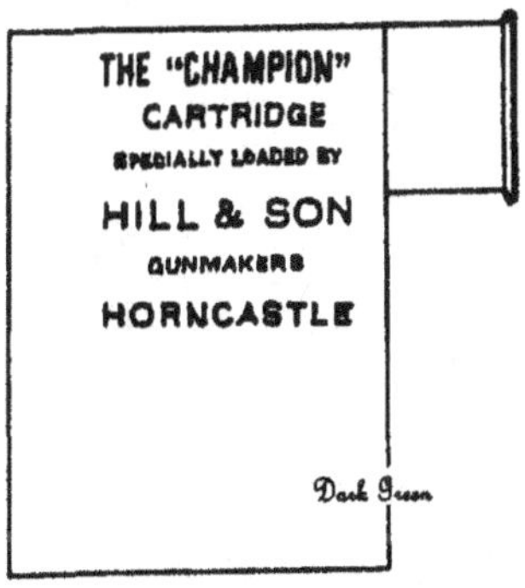

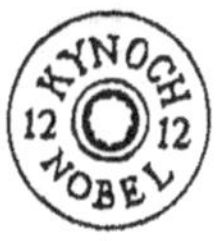

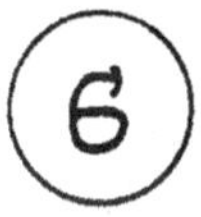

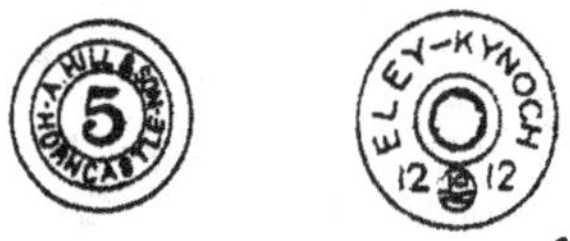

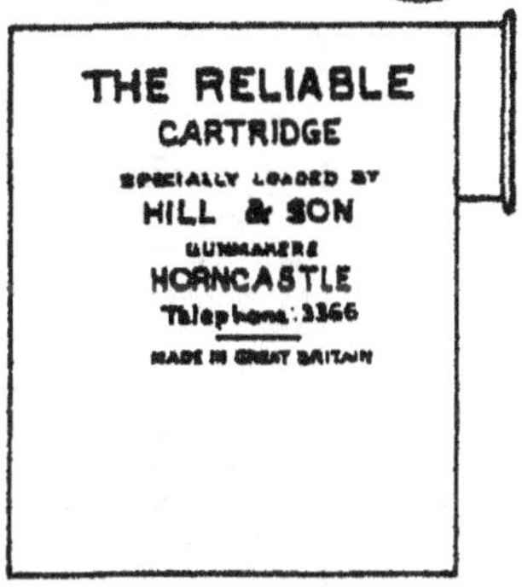

THE HINGSTON-SMITH ARMS COMPANY LIMITED:
Winnipeg, Manitoba, Canada.

NORMAL
SPORTING POWDER
SMOKELESS
AND
WATERPROOF

WINNIPEG
CANADIAN AGENTS
The Hingston Smith Arms Co.

I have never seen the actual cartridge. Its details were sent to me along with a sketch. The nationality must be Canadian although it was loaded at Hendon, London, England. The case was French and the powder came out of Switzerland. I do not know where the shot and wadding came from. H.R.H. The Prince of Wales used their shells in 1902.

DATA
Gauge; 12.
Length; Approx 64 mm.
Head; Not known.
Tube; Wound paper.
Colour; Vermilion.
Print; Black.
Base; Brass.
Closure; Rolled turn-over.
Wad; Yellow card, print black.
Business; Canadian agents, arms and sports dealers.

DN.2-0360. Updated, April 1996. PROVISIONAL DRAWING

GEORGE HINTON & SONS, LTD:
5 Fore Street, Taunton, Somerset, England.

HINTON'S
ECLIPSE GAMEKEEPERS
6/6 PER 100 CARTRIDGE

Drawn from a set of photographs

Using black powder and loaded into Kynoch's cheapest 'Witton' brand cases with the small primer caps they were aimed at country estates for issuing to their gamekeepers. Note the price of 6/- 6d on the case wall.

DATA
Gauge; 12.
Length; 64 mm.
Head; 7 to 8 mm.
Tube; Wound brown rough textured paper.
Colour; Dark brown.
Print; Black.
Base; Brass.
Closure; Rolled turn-over.
Wad; White card, print black.
Business; Gunmakers.
Case; G. Kynoch.

DN.2-2030. October 1998. ECLIPSE GAMEKEEPERS 6/6 PER 100 CARTRIDGE

GEORGE HINTON & SONS, LTD:
5 Fore Street, Taunton, Somerset, England.

SPECIALLY HAND LOADED BY
GEO. HINTON & SONS LTD.
GUNMAKERS
TAUNTON
MADE IN GREAT BRITAIN

 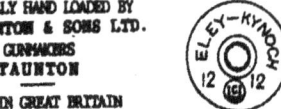 

SPECIALLY HAND LOADED BY
GEO. HINTON & SONS LTD.
GUNMAKERS
TAUNTON
MADE IN GREAT BRITAIN

DATA
Gauge; 12.
Length; 64 mm.
Head; 8 mm.
Tube; Wound; pink paper.
Colour; Pink.
Print; Black.
Base; Reinforced brass.
Closure; Rolled turn-over.
Wad shown; White card, print black except the shot size that was purple.
Business; Gunmakers.

DN.2-1093. Re-drawn; 4th March 2001.

GEO HINTON & SONS, LTD:
5 Fore Street, Taunton, Somerset, England.

THE
"TAUNTON"
CARTRIDGE
LOADED BY
GEO. HINTON & SONS Ltd.
GUNMAKERS
TAUNTON
MADE IN GREAT BRITAIN

LOADED BY
GEO. HINTON & SONS Ltd.
GUNMAKERS
TAUNTON
MADE IN GREAT BRITAIN

THE "TAUNTON" CARTRIDGE

DATA
Gauge; 12
Length; 64 mm.
Head; 8 mm.
Tube; Wound gray paper.
Colour; Grey.
Print; Black.
Base; Brass.
Closure; Rolled turn-over.
Wad; Yellow card, print black.
Business; Gunmakers.

DN.2-0905. Re-drawn; 2nd May 2000.

GEO HINTON & SONS, LTD:
5 Fore Street, Taunton, Somerset, England.
(Established 1815).

THE "STANDARD"
CARTRIDGE
LOADED BY
GEO. HINTON & SONS LTD.
GUNMAKERS
TAUNTON
MADE IN GREAT BRITAIN

This cartridge was not checked for an internal liner.

LOADED BY
GEO. HINTON & SONS LTD.
GUNMAKERS
TAUNTON
MADE IN GREAT BRITAIN

THE "STANDARD" CARTRIDGE

DATA
Gauge; 12.
Length; 64 mm.
Head; 16 mm.
Tube; Wound rich blue paper.
Colour; Rich middle blue.
Print; Black.
Base; Brass.
Closure; Rolled turn-over.
Wad; Buttercup yellow card, print black.
Business; Gunmakers.
Circa; 1930's.

DN.2-1236. Re-drawn; 20th Feb 2000.

HIRTENBERG:
? Austria.

Schnepf
ANTIKORRID
Hirtenberg
Geveloтzündung
Made in Austria

This cartridge case was not checked for an internal metal liner.

Wad not known

HIRTENBERG *12*

DATA
Gauge; 12.
Length; 68 mm.
Head; 16 mm.
Tube; Wound brown paper.
Colour; Soot black.
Print; Gold.
Base; Brass.
Closure; Rolled turn-over.
Wad; Not known.
Business; Ammunition manufacturers.
Case; Austria.

DN.2-0970. Re-drawn; 16th Feb 2000.

H. M. GOVERNMENT OF GREAT BRITAIN:
The Royal Armed Forces.

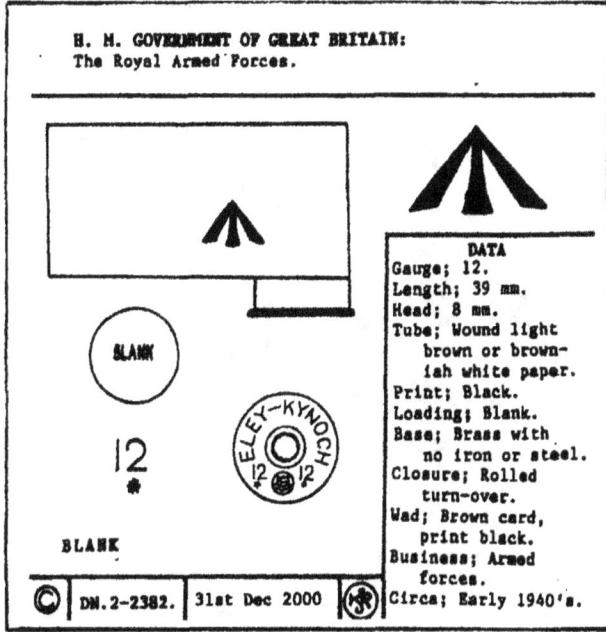

DATA
Gauge; 12.
Length; 39 mm.
Head; 8 mm.
Tube; Wound light brown or brownish white paper.
Print; Black.
Loading; Blank.
Base; Brass with no iron or steel.
Closure; Rolled turn-over.
Wad; Brown card, print black.
Business; Armed forces.
Circa; Early 1940's.

BLANK

DN.2-2382.   31st Dec 2000

H. M. GOVERNMENT OF GREAT BRITAIN: The Houses of Parliament, Westminster, London S.W.1., England.

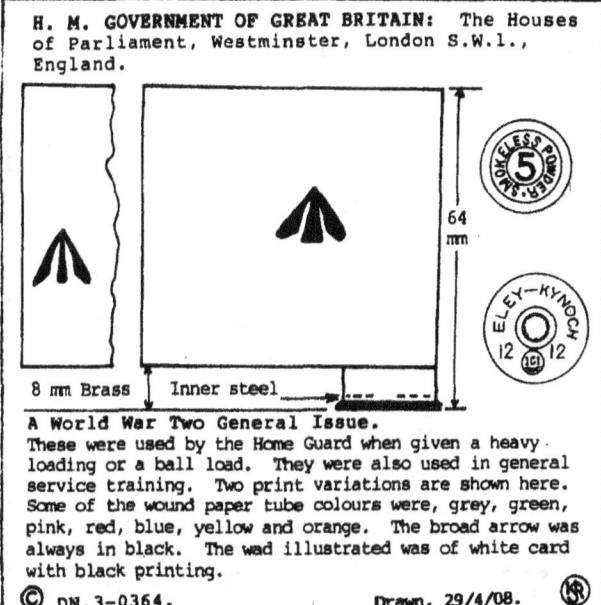

A World War Two General Issue.
These were used by the Home Guard when given a heavy loading or a ball load. They were also used in general service training. Two print variations are shown here. Some of the wound paper tube colours were, grey, green, pink, red, blue, yellow and orange. The broad arrow was always in black. The wad illustrated was of white card with black printing.

DN.3-0364.   Drawn, 29/4/08.

H. M. GOVERNMENT OF GREAT BRITAIN: The Houses of Parliament, Westminster, London S.W.1., England.

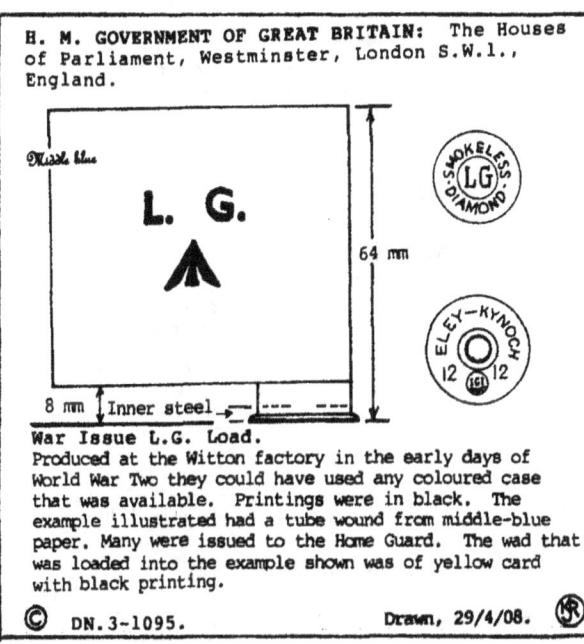

War Issue L.G. Load.
Produced at the Witton factory in the early days of World War Two they could have used any coloured case that was available. Printings were in black. The example illustrated had a tube wound from middle-blue paper. Many were issued to the Home Guard. The wad that was loaded into the example shown was of yellow card with black printing.

DN.3-1095.   Drawn, 29/4/08.

H. M. GOVERNMENT OF GREAT BRITAIN: The Houses of Parliament, Westminster, London S,W,1., England.

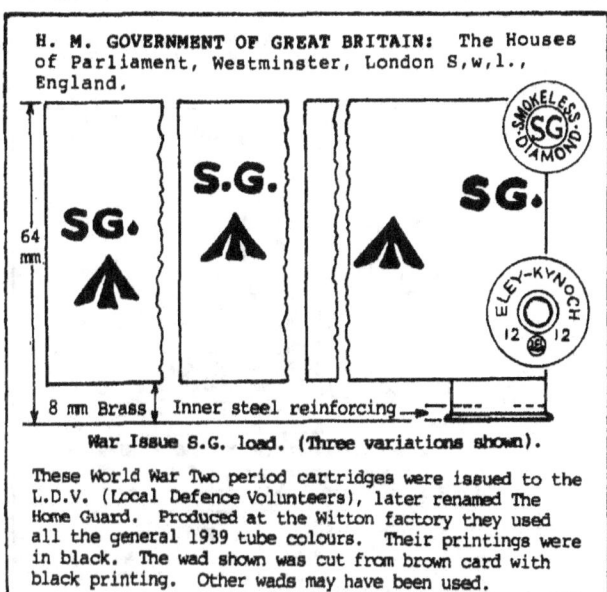

War Issue S.G. load. (Three variations shown).

These World War Two period cartridges were issued to the L.D.V. (Local Defence Volunteers), later renamed The Home Guard. Produced at the Witton factory they used all the general 1939 tube colours. Their printings were in black. The wad shown was cut from brown card with black printing. Other wads may have been used.

DN.3-0363.   Drawn, 29/4/08.

H. M. GOVERNMENT OF GREAT BRITAIN:: The Houses of Parliament, Westminster, Londn, England.

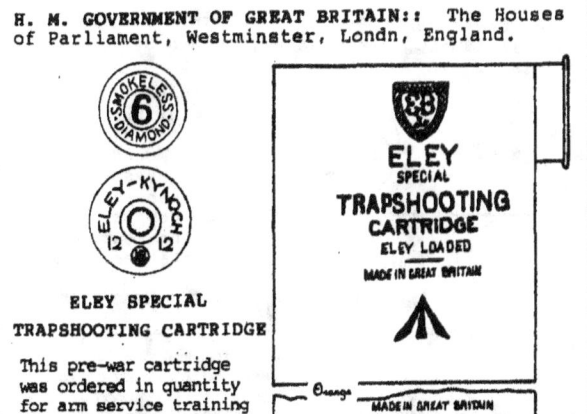

ELEY SPECIAL TRAPSHOOTING CARTRIDGE

This pre-war cartridge was ordered in quantity for arm service training during the Second World war. Tubes were wound from light or dark orange papers. Some also from off-white (old straw, known by Eleys' as being light brown paper). All case wall printings were in black. Wetproof was by clear Varnish. Wads were of yellow or brown card and printed in black.
DATA: Length 64 mm; Head 8 mm; Base Reinforced brass.

DN.3-0998.   Drawn, 27/3/08.

H. M. GOVERNMENT OF GREAT BRITAIN: The Houses of Parliament, Westminster, London S.W.1., England.

T R E N T

Trent Guns & Cartridges. Ltd.

DATA
Gauge; 12.
Length; 65 mm.
Head; 8 mm.
Tube; Wound paper.
Colour; Ruby red.
Print; Black.
Base; Brass.
Cap; Large.
Closure; Rolled turn-over.
Wad; Brown card, no printing.
Loading; Trent Guns & Cartridges, Ltd.

DN.3-0197.   Drawn, 29/4/08.

PLATE 165 [HMG – HMG]

H. M. GOVERNMENT OF GREAT BRITAIN: The Houses of Parliament, Westminster, London S.W.1., England.

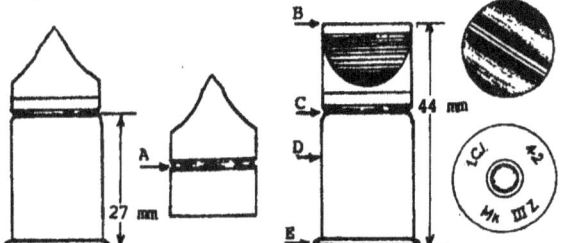

CARTRIDGE CABLE CUTTER Mk III Z.
A one piece thin brass case of 12 gauge size loaded with a high speed chisel edged cutting projectile. Used by the R.A.F. during World War Two in aircraft mainplanes for cutting the cables of barrage balloons. The internal components consisted of, Ballistite gunpowder in the base followed by a one sixteenth inch card wad, a one eighth inch felt compression wad and then the hardened steel projectile. 42 on the stamping is for 1942, the year of manufacture. Letters to the drawing; A, recess. B, ground cutting rdge. C, top of brass case cleaved into recess groove. D, thin brass case. E, Rim. Not to be used in a shotgun. DN.3-0927.

H. M. GOVERNMENT OF GREAT BRITAIN: The Houses of Parliament, Westminster, London S.W.1., England.

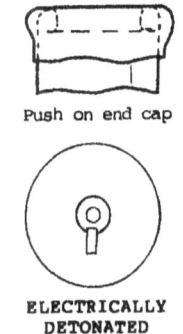

Push on end cap

ELECTRICALLY DETONATED ENGINE STARTER CARTRIDGE

For starting R.A.F. and R.N. aircraft engines. The tubes were wound from purple paper and were printed in black. The Lot Batch numbers were printed in black on the brass heads. An aluminium alloy protection cap had to be removed before use.

DN.3-0965.   **NOT TO BE USED IN SHOTGUNS**

H. M. GOVERNMENT OF GREAT BRITAIN. DEPT, R.A.F.: Houses of Parliament, Westminster, London S.W.1, England.

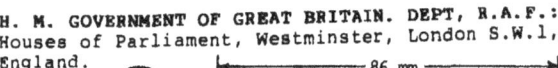
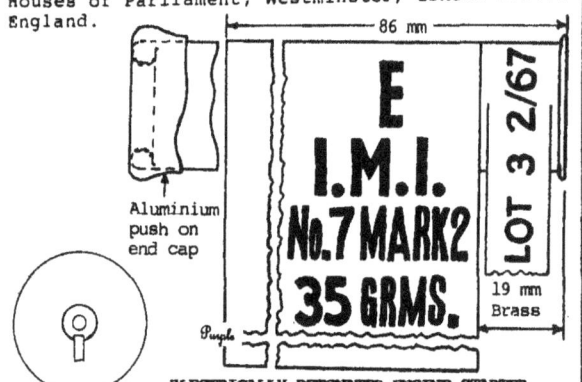

ELECTRICALLY DETONATED ENGINE STARTER
The example shown was used to start a R.R. Griffon engine in a Spitfire Mk P.R. XIX that was a part of the Battle of Britain Flight when based at R.A.F. Coltishall. The aircraft was either PM631 or PS853. Used in a Plessy Coffman starter coupled to a Mk VIII breach. The tube was wound purple paper and printed in black. **NOT TO BE USED IN SHOTGUNS.**
DN.3-0966.   Drawn, 2/5/08.

H. M. GOVERNMENT OF GREAT BRITAIN. Agricultural Executive Committee.

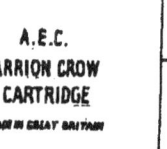

A.E.C. CARRION CROW CARTRIDGE
MADE IN GREAT BRITAIN

DATA
Gauge; 12.
Length; 64 mm.
Head; 8 mm.
Tube; Orange paper.
Print; Black.
Base; Reinforced brass.
Case; Lacquered.
Over shot card; Blue-grey with mottled orange.
Print size in black.
Circa, Late 1940's.

A.E.C. CARRION CROW

DN.3-5502.   Drawn, 27/5/2011.

H. M. GOVERNMENT OF GREAT BRITAIN: The Houses of Parliament, Westminster, London, England.

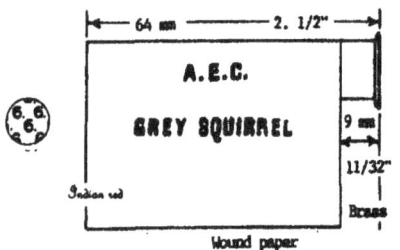

410 A.E.C. GREY SQUIRREL.
The 2½ inch pest control cartridge had the tube wound from Eley's indian red paper. The above shot wad was cut from brown card. Both the tube and the wad were printed in black. The letters A.E.C stood for 'Agricultural Executive Committee. Circa, Late 1940's and 1950's.
Drawn, 18/3/08.
DN.3-2788.

H. M. GOVERNMENT OF GREAT BRITAIN: The Houses of Parliament, Westminster, London S.W.1., England.

DATA
Length; 65 mm.
Head; 10 mm.
Tube; Wound paper.
Base; Brass with no inner metal.
Cap; Copper.
For the rest of details see below.

"A.E.C." PEST CONTROL
MADE BY GREENWOOD & BATLEY LTD LEEDS

"A.E.C." PEST CONTROL
This cartridge was produced for the A.E.C. by Greenwood & Batley of Leeds. These initials stood for, Agricultural Executive Committe and not for Associated Equipment Company. Tubes were orange and over-shot cards were of white card. All printings were in black. Waterproofing was a heavy coat of clear varnish.

Drawn, 27/2/08.
DN.3-2706.

PLATE 166 [HMG – HMG]

H. M. GOVERNMENT OF GREAT BRITAIN: The Houses of Parliament, Westminster, London S.W.1., England.

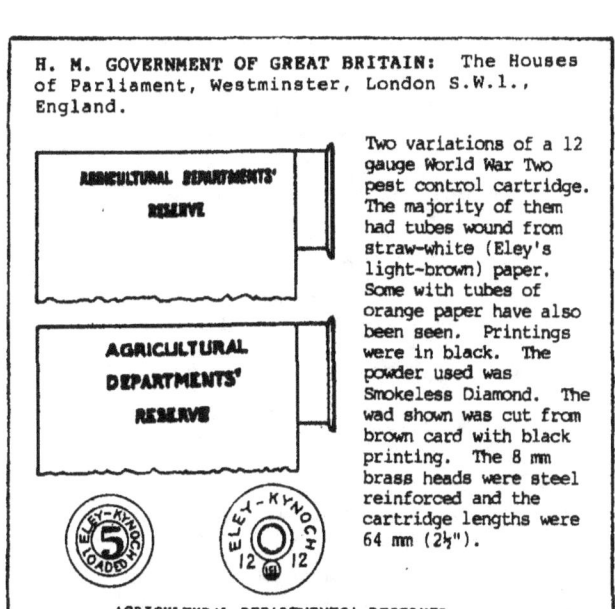

Two variations of a 12 gauge World War Two pest control cartridge. The majority of them had tubes wound from straw-white (Eley's light-brown) paper. Some with tubes of orange paper have also been seen. Printings were in black. The powder used was Smokeless Diamond. The wad shown was cut from brown card with black printing. The 8 mm brass heads were steel reinforced and the cartridge lengths were 64 mm (2½").

AGRICULTURAL DEPARTMENTS' RESERVED

© DN.3-1009. Drawn, 29/4/08.

H. M. GOVERNMENT OF GREAT BRITAIN. DEPT, FORESTRY COMMISSION: The Houses of Parliament, Westminster, London S.W.1., England.

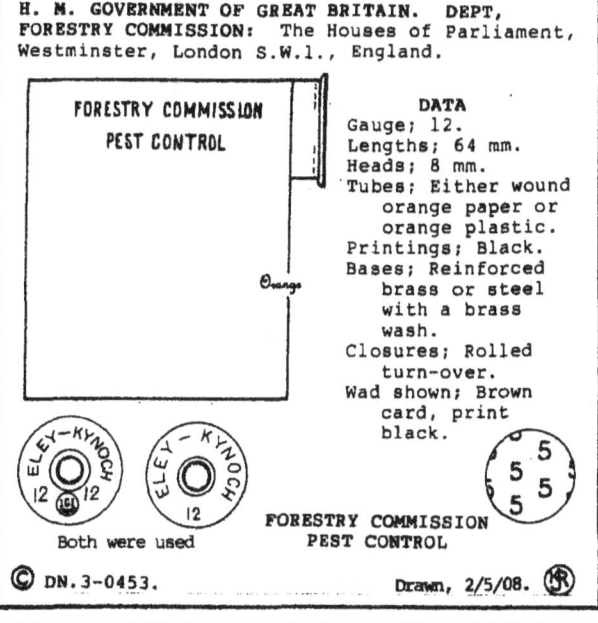

DATA
Gauge; 12.
Lengths; 64 mm.
Heads; 8 mm.
Tubes; Either wound orange paper or orange plastic.
Printings; Black.
Bases; Reinforced brass or steel with a brass wash.
Closures; Rolled turn-over.
Wad shown; Brown card, print black.

Both were used

FORESTRY COMMISSION PEST CONTROL

© DN.3-0453. Drawn, 2/5/08.

H. M. GOVERNMENT OF GREAT BRITAIN: The Houses of Parliament, Westminster, London S.W.1., England.

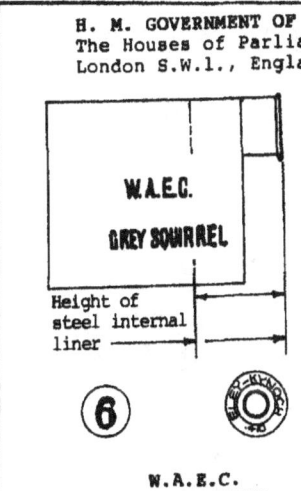

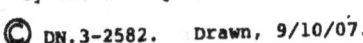

DATA
Gauge; .410.
Length; 51 mm.
Head; 8.5 mm.
Tube and colour; Wound Indian-red paper.
Print; Black.
Base; Brass with internal metal.
Cap; Copper.
Closure; Rolled turn-over.
Wad; Brown card, print black.
Case by; Eley-Kynoch I.C.I.

W.A.E.C. GREY SQUIRREL

A World War Two pest control cartridge issued by the War Agricultural Executive Committee.

© DN.3-2582. Drawn, 9/10/07.

J. HOBSON: 64 Regent Street, Leamington Spa, Warwickshire, England.

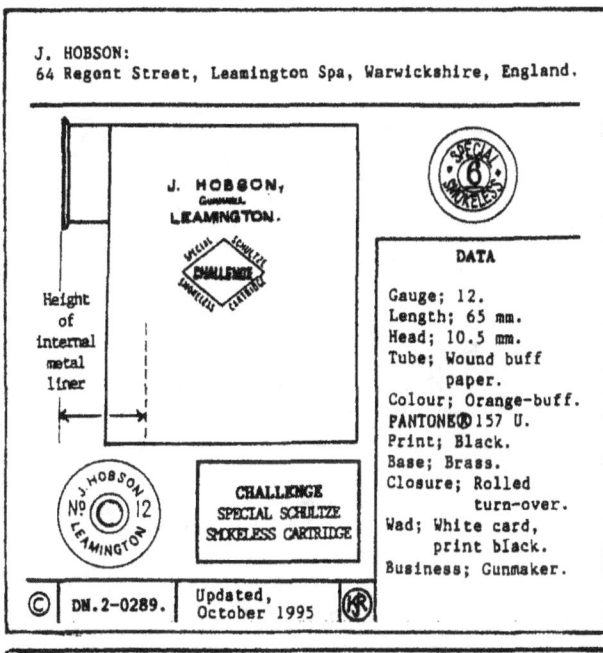

DATA
Gauge; 12.
Length; 65 mm.
Head; 10.5 mm.
Tube; Wound buff paper.
Colour; Orange-buff.
PANTONE® 157 U.
Print; Black.
Base; Brass.
Closure; Rolled turn-over.
Wad; White card, print black.
Business; Gunmaker.

© DN.2-0289. Updated, October 1995

J. HOBSON: Leamington Spa, Warwickshire, England.

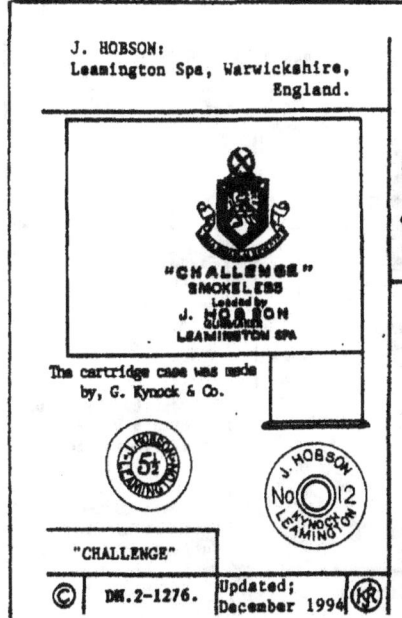

The cartridge case was made by, G. Kynoch & Co.

DATA
Gauge; 12.
Length; 64 mm.
Head; 16 mm.
Tube; Wound paper.
Colour; Brown 215.
Print; Dark blue.
Base; Brass.
Closure; Rolled turn-over.
Wad; White card, print black.
Business; Gunmaker.
Watproof; Lacquer.

"CHALLENGE"

© DN.2-1276. Updated; December 1994

A.S. HOCKNELL: Eccleshall, Staffordshire, England.

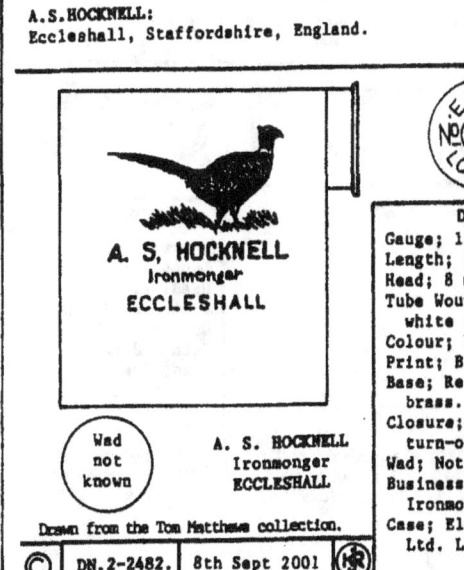

DATA
Gauge; 12.
Length; 64 mm.
Head; 8 mm.
Tube Wound pinkish-white paper.
Colour; Pale pink.
Print; Black.
Base; Reinforced brass.
Closure; Rolled turn-over.
Wad; Not known.
Business; Ironmonger.
Case; Eley Bros, Ltd. London.

Wad not known

A. S. HOCKNELL Ironmonger ECCLESHALL

Drawn from the Tom Matthews collection.

© DN.2-2482. 8th Sept 2001

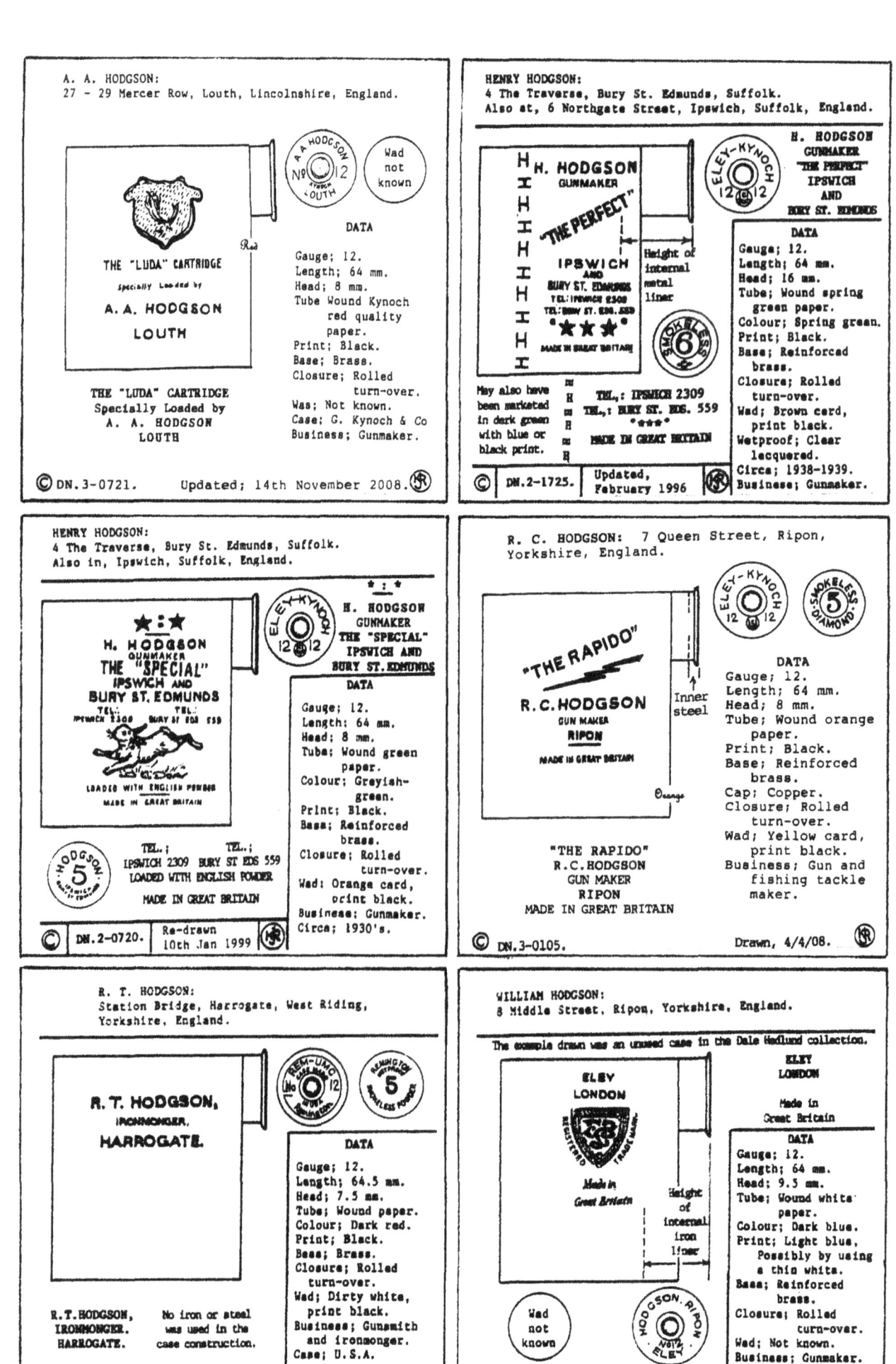

PLATE 168 [HOD – HOD]

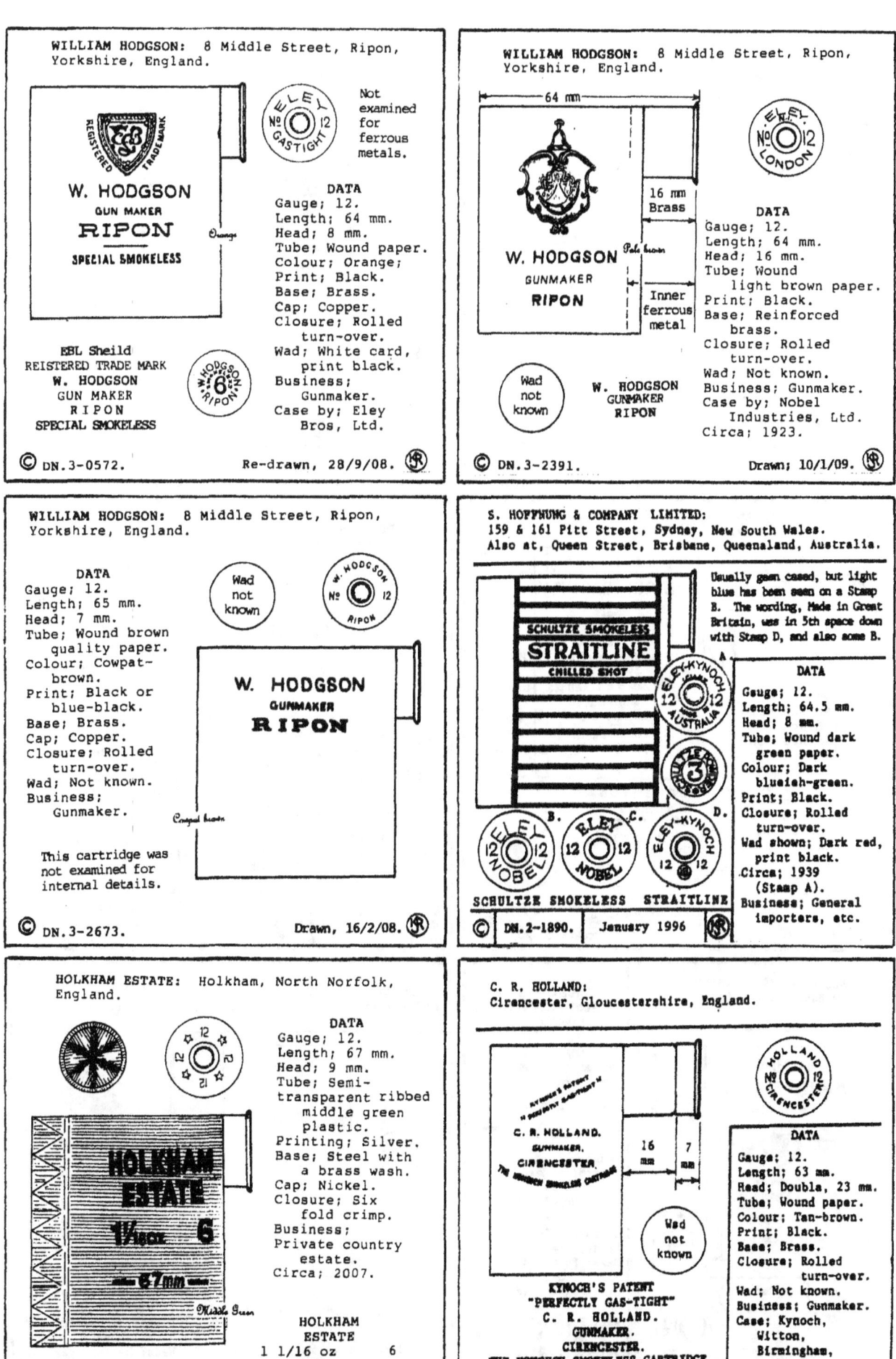

PLATE 169 [HOD – HOL]

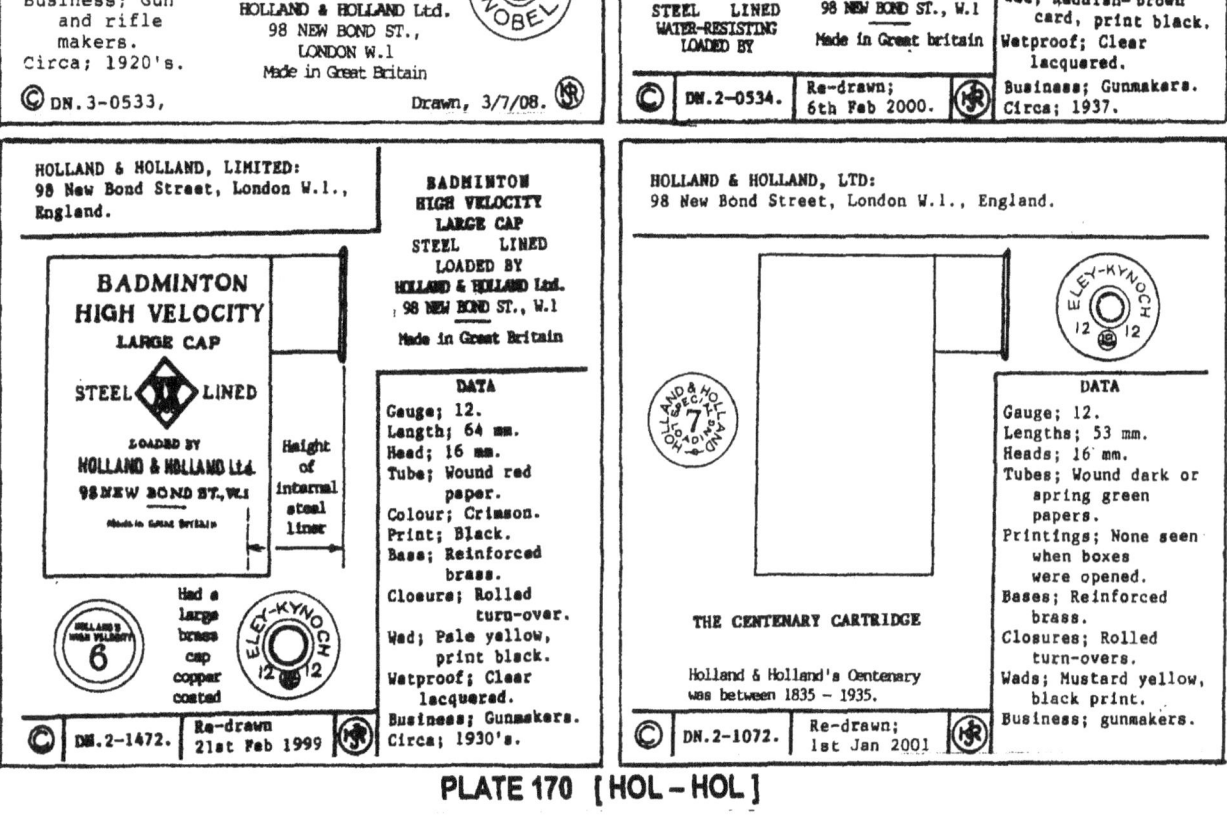

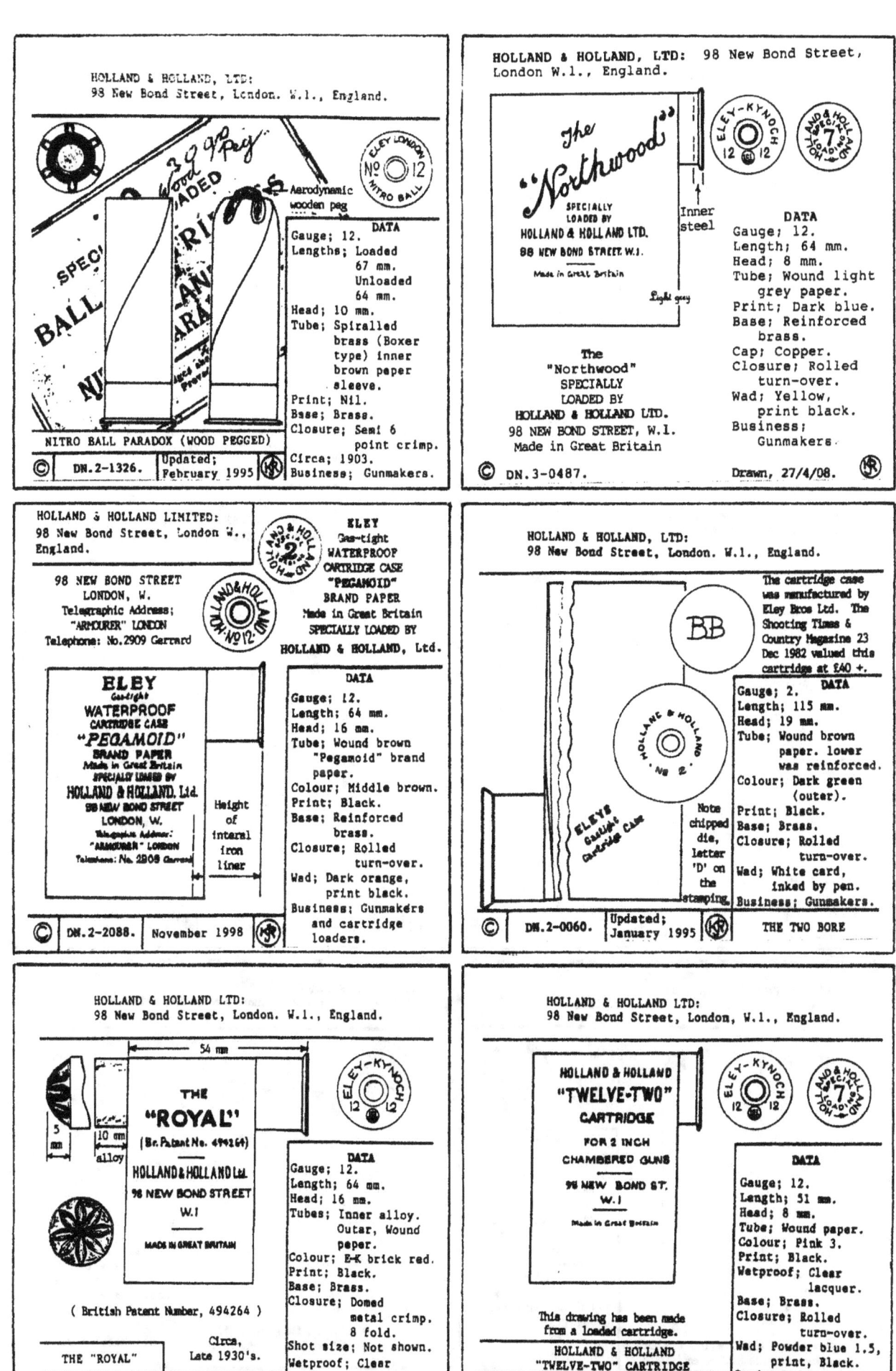

PLATE 171 [HOL - HOL]

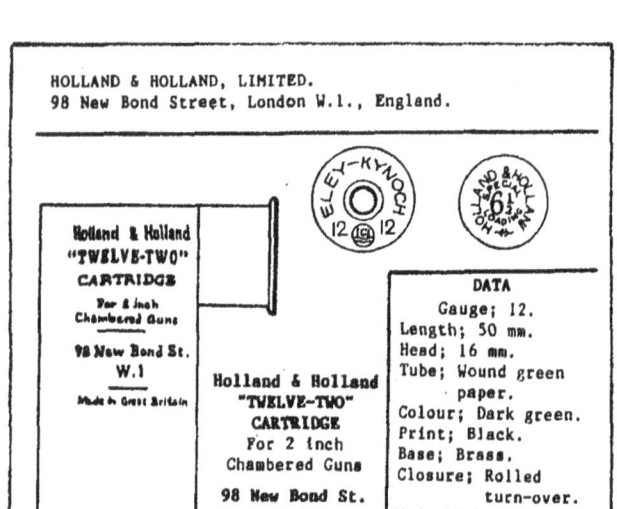
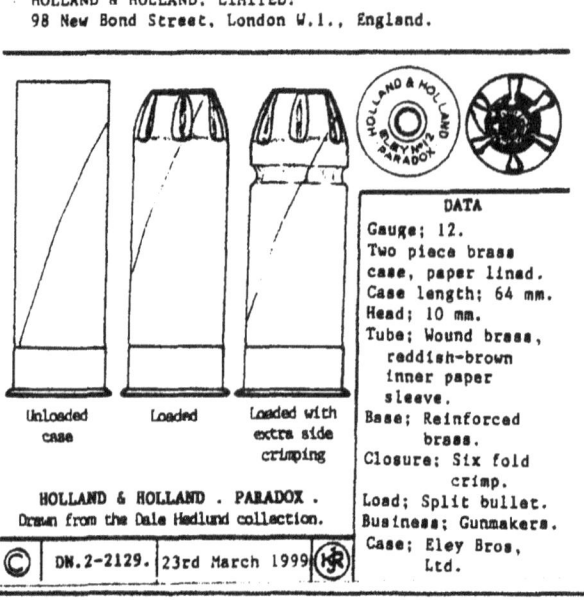

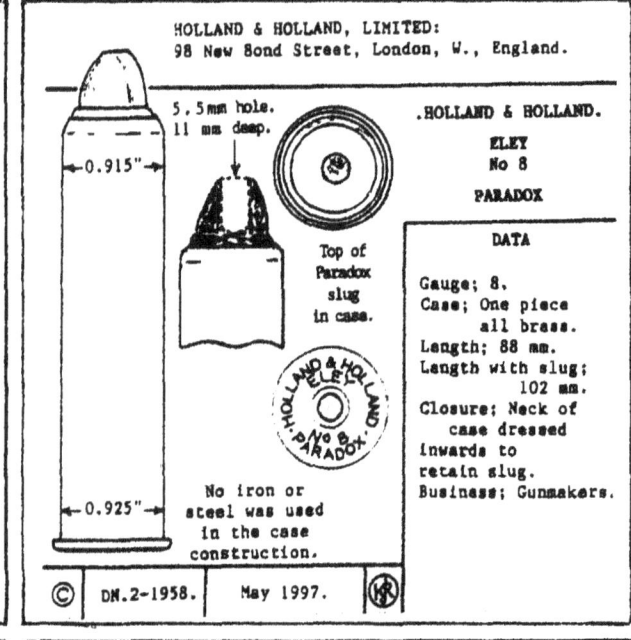
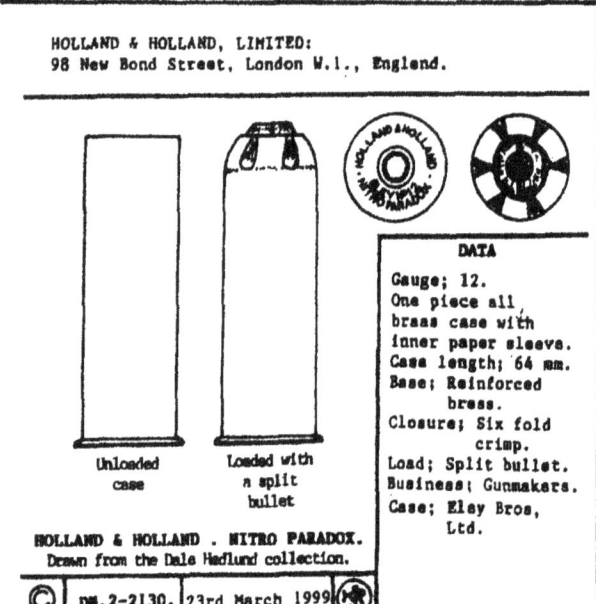
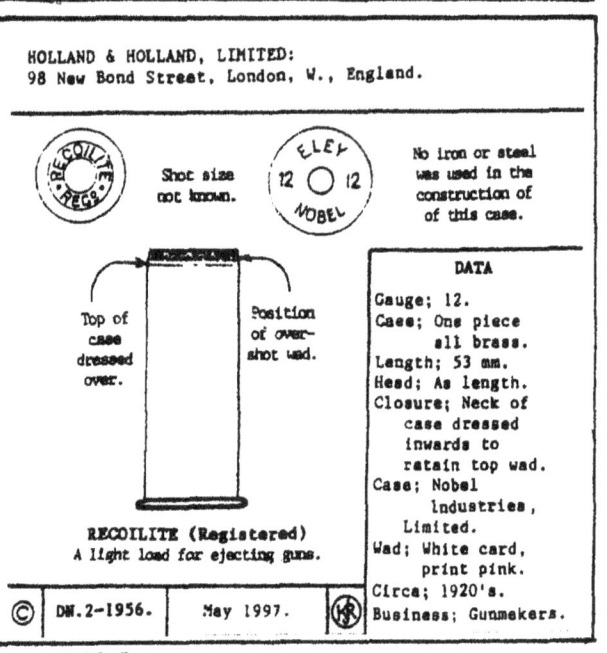

ISAAC HOLLIS:
Weaman Row, Lench Street, Birmingham,
Warwickshire (West Midlands), England.

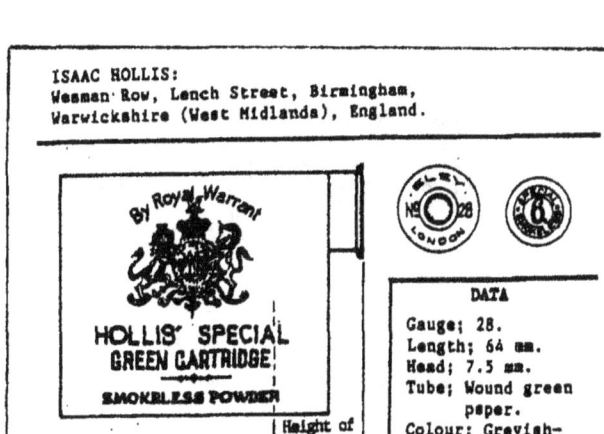

HOLLIS' SPECIAL
GREEN CARTRIDGE
SMOKELESS POWDER

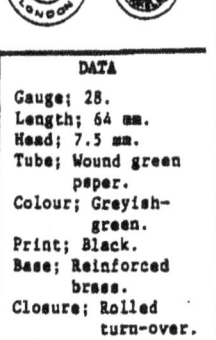

DATA
Gauge; 28.
Length; 64 mm.
Head; 7.5 mm.
Tube; Wound green paper.
Colour; Greyish-green.
Print; Black.
Base; Reinforced brass.
Closure; Rolled turn-over.
Wad; White card, print black.

DN.2-2217.   2nd Aug 1999

HOLTON:
243 London Road (South), Lowestoft, Suffolk, England.

The example was not detected for internal metal.

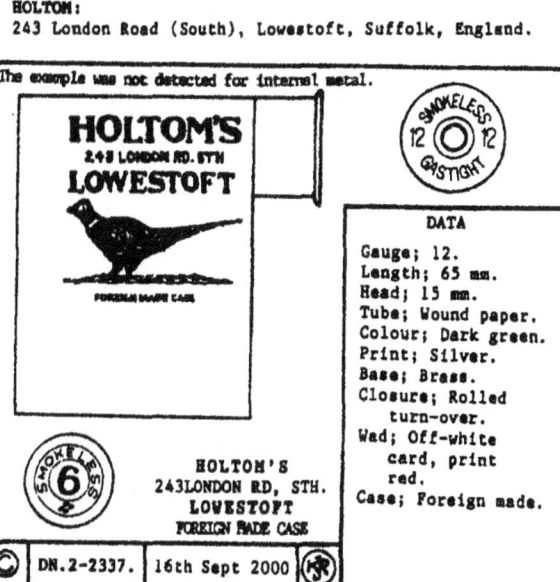

DATA
Gauge; 12.
Length; 65 mm.
Head; 15 mm.
Tube; Wound paper.
Colour; Dark green.
Print; Silver.
Base; Brass.
Closure; Rolled turn-over.
Wad; Off-white card, print red.
Case; Foreign made.

HOLTOM'S
243 LONDON RD, STH.
LOWESTOFT
FOREIGN MADE CASE

DN.2-2337.   16th Sept 2000

HOLTOM'S: 243 London Road (South), Lowestof, Suffolk, England.

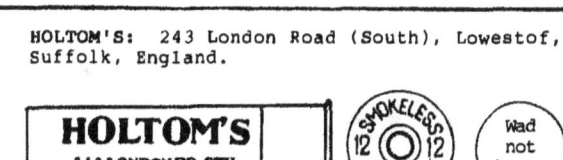

 Wad not known

DATA
Gauge; 12.
Length; 65 mm.
Head; 15 mm.
Tube; Wound paper.
Colour; Middle green.
Print; Silver.
Base; Brass.
Cap; Copper.
Closure; Rolled turn-over.
Wad; Not known.
Case; Imported.

HOLTOM'S
243 LONDON RD. STH.
LOWESTOF
FOREIGN MADE CASE
OUR SPECIAL LOADING

Not examined for internal metals.

DN.3-2823.   Drawn, 15/6/08.

HOME :
43 Friar Street, Reading, Berkshire, England.

At the time of making this drawing, I have not been able to obtain any history about this firm.

HOME'S
SPECIAL LOADING

DATA
Gauge; 12.
Length; 64 mm.
Head; 9.5 mm.
Tube; Wound paper.
Colour; Eley's buff.
Print; Black.
Base; Brass.
Closure; Rolled turn-over.
Wad; Pale pink, print black.
Case; Eley Bros, Ltd.

DN.3-1815.   Updated; 14th November 2008.

T. J. HOOKE & SON:
The Pavement, Coppergate, York, Yorkshire, England.

The example was not tested for internal metal reinforcing.

"EBOR CARTRIDGE
410 SHORT
T.J.HOOKE & SON
GUNMAKERS
COPPERGATE
YORK

DATA
Gauge; .410.
Length; 51 mm.
Head; 7.5 mm.
Tube; Wound paper.
Colour; Buttercup yellow.
Print; Black.
Base; Brass.
Closure; Rolled turn-over.
Wad; Light yellow, print black.
Business; Gunmakers.

(5)   "EBOR CARTRIDGE
410 SHORT
T.J.HOOKE & SON
GUNMAKERS
COPPERGATE
YORK

DN.2-2350.   22nd Sept 2000

HOOTON & JONES:
60 Dale Street, Liverpool, Lancashire (Merseyside), England.

HOOTON & JONES'S
"SPECIAL"
60, DALE ST., LIVERPOOL.

HOOTON & JONES'S
"SPECIAL"
60, DALE ST., LIVERPOOL

DATA
Gauge; 12.
Length; 64 mm.
Head; 10 mm.
Tube; Wound paper.
Colour; Ruby red.
Print; Black.
Base; Brass.
Closure; Rolled turn-over.
Wad; Brownish orange, print black.
Business; Gunmakers.
Case; Eley Bros, Ltd. London.

DN.2-0761.   Re-drawn; 30th Nov 2000

PLATE 173 [HOL – HOO]

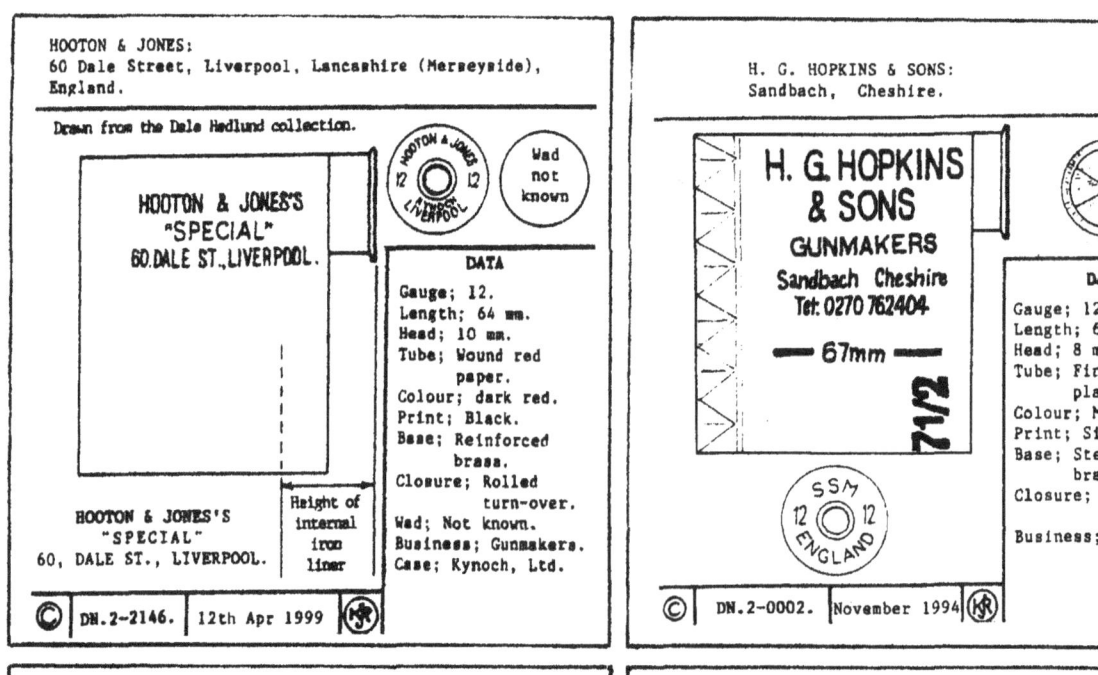

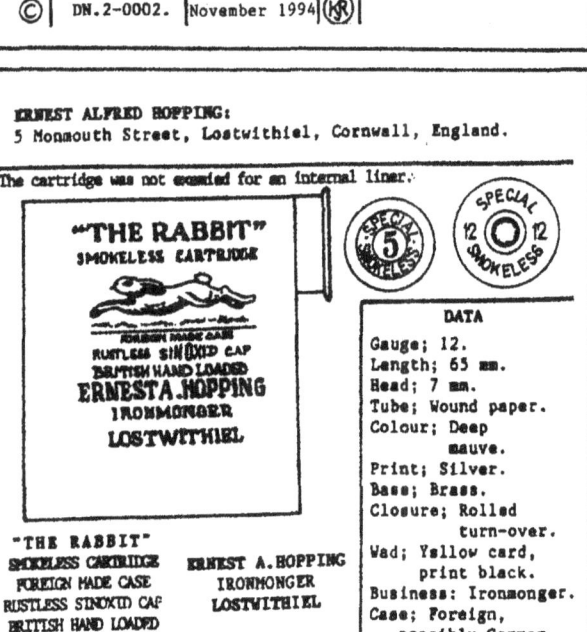
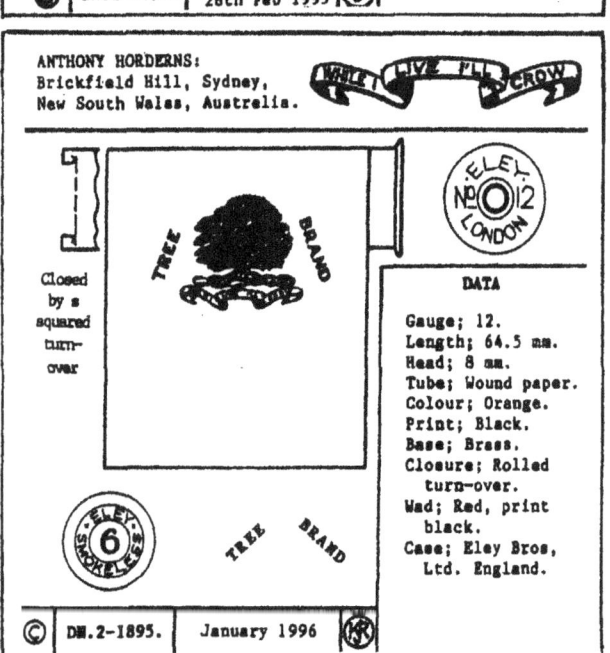
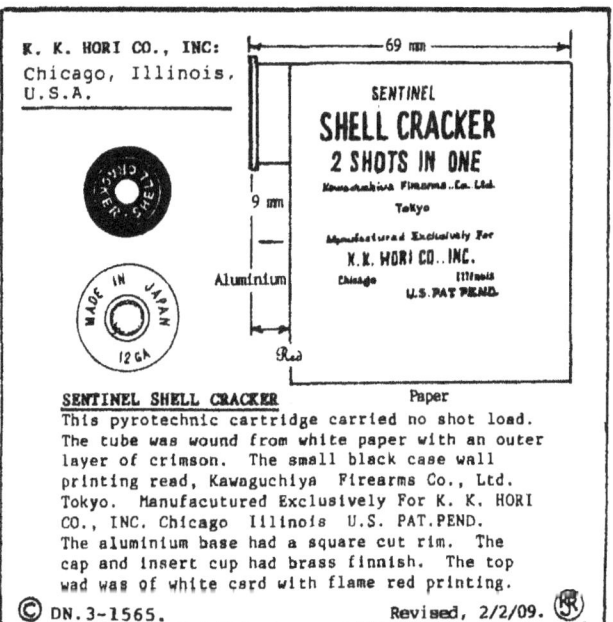

PLATE 174 [HOO - HOR]

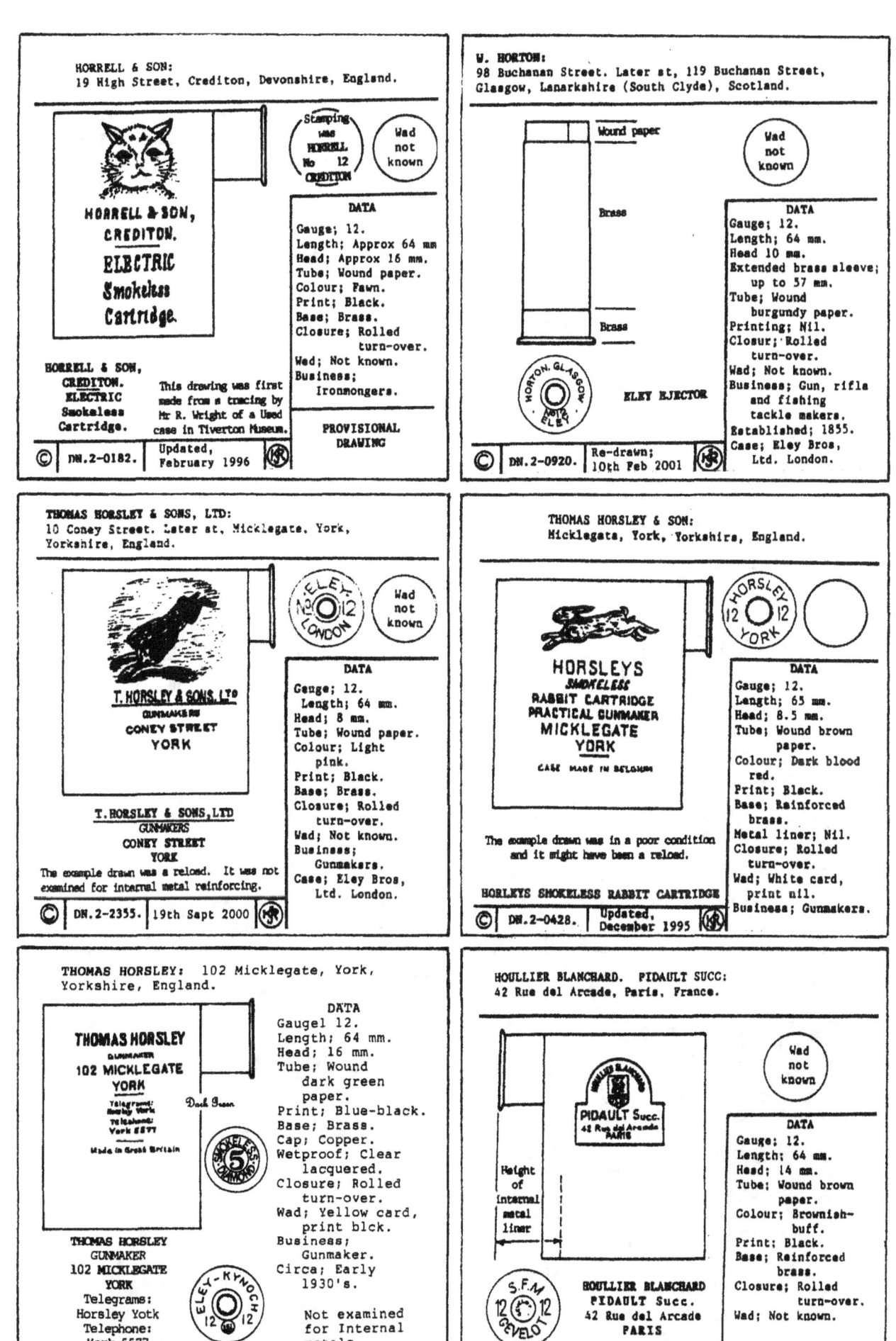

PLATE 175 [HOR - HOU]

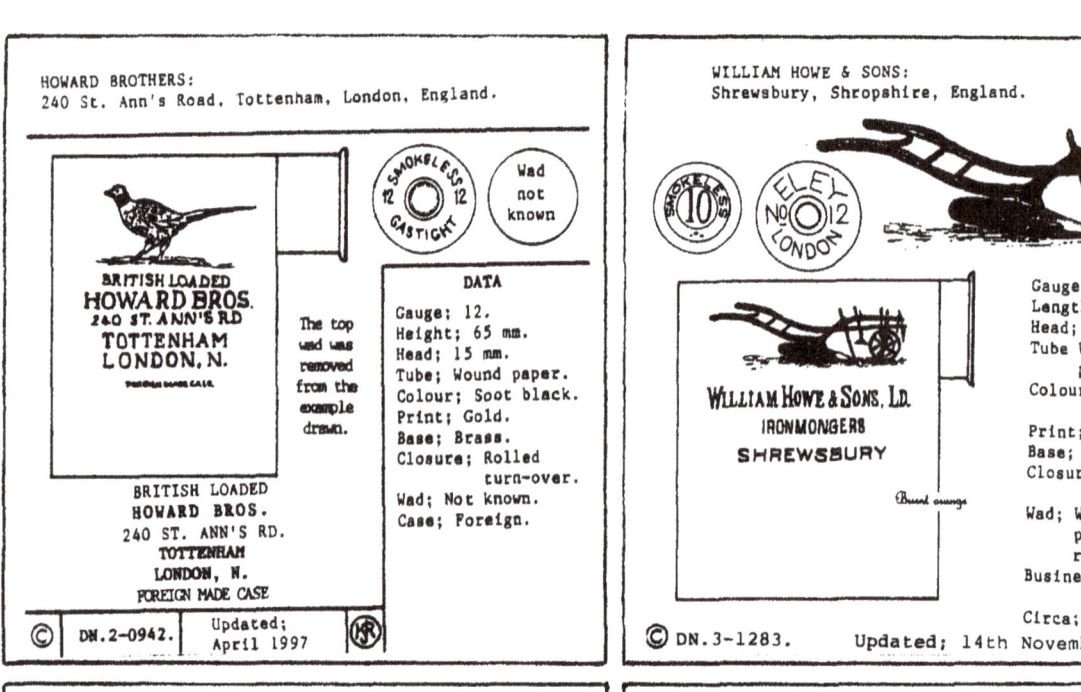
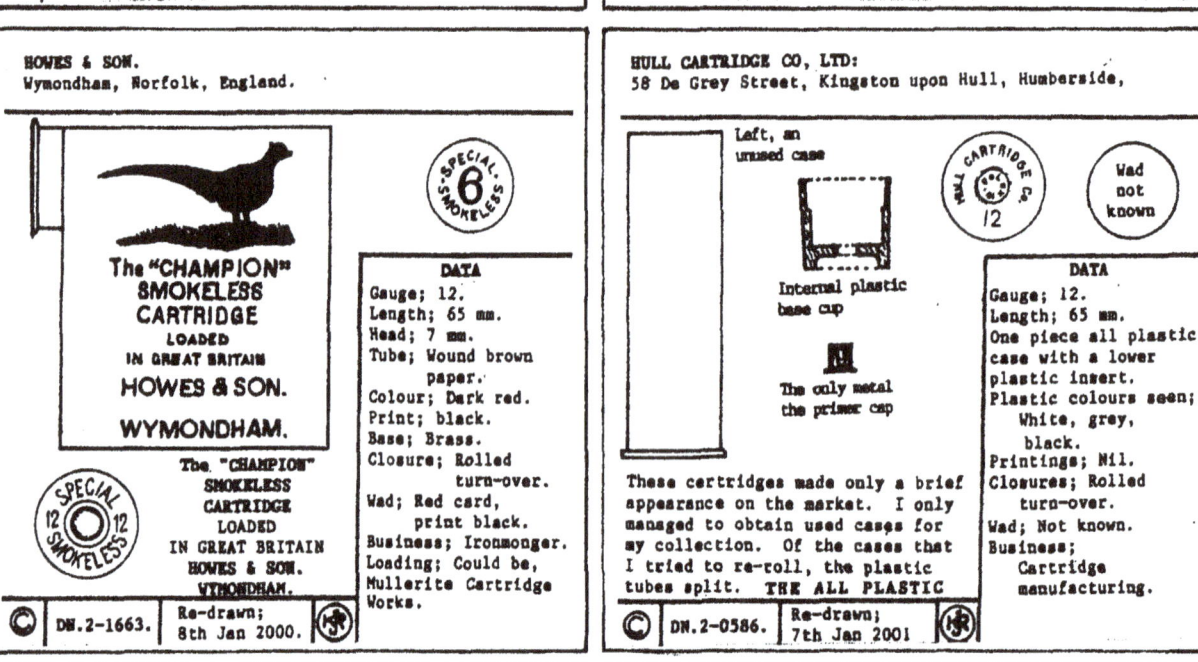
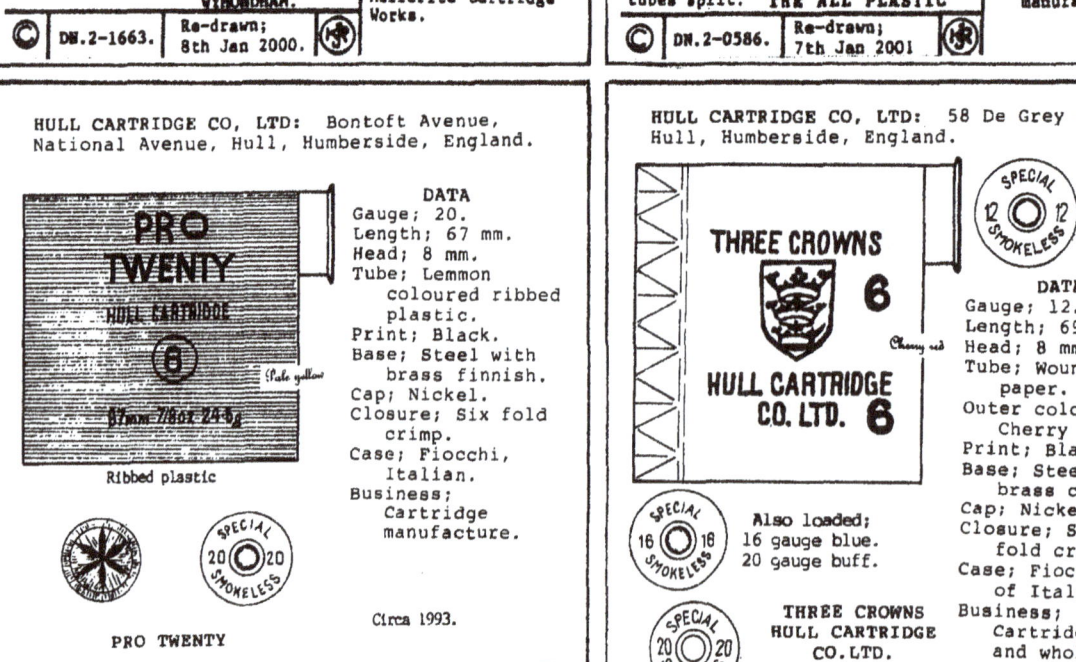

PLATE 176 [HOW – HUL]

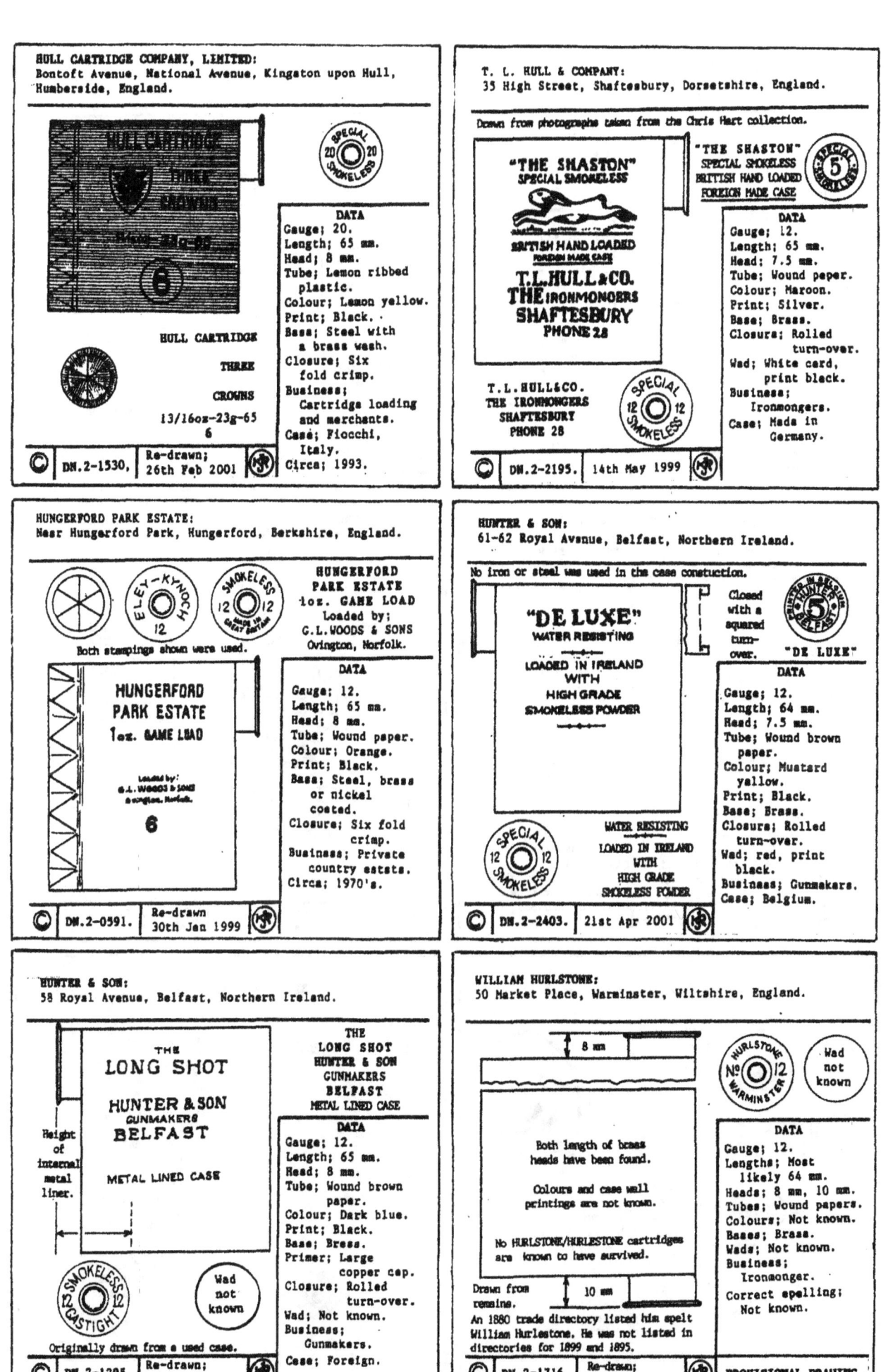

H. J. HUSSEY (Late of, LANG & HUSSEY, LTD):
81 New Bond Street, St. James's.
Also at, 88 Jermyn Street, London, England.

This cartridge is unusual as the case was made by Messrs Eley Brothers, Ltd and the over-shot wad is by The Midland Gun Company and loaded for a London gunmaker.

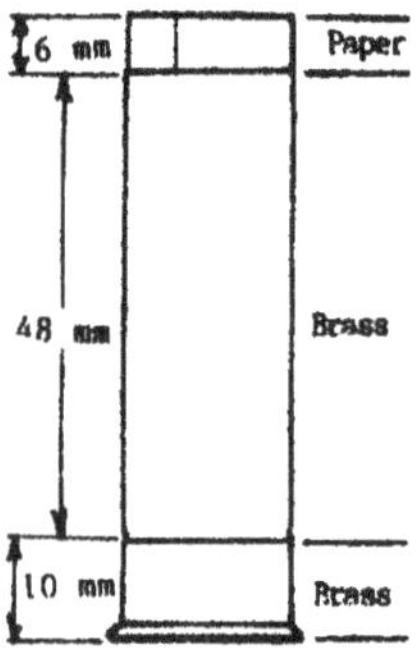

HIGH BRASS EJECTOR CARTRIDGE

DATA
Gauge; 16.
Length; 64 mm.
Head; 10 mm.
Tube; Wound light brown paper.
Outer brass sleeve; Up to 58 mm.
Base; Brass.
Closure; Rolled turn-over.
Wad; Yellow card, print red.
Business; Gunmaker.
Case; Eley Bros, Ltd.

DN.2-0493. Re-drawn 16th Feb 1999

H. J. HUSSEY:
81 New Bond Street, London W.1., England.

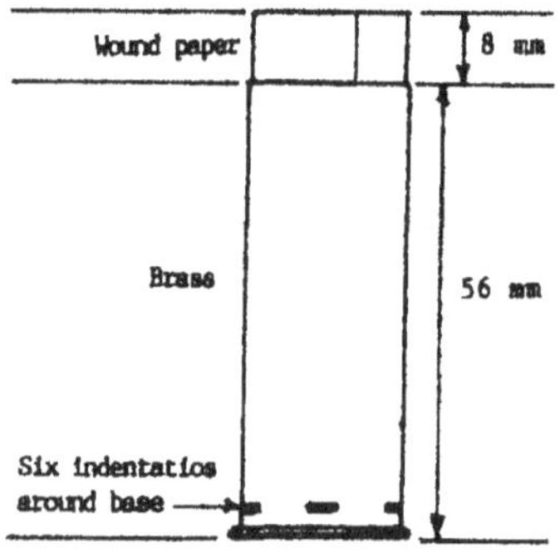

F. JOYCE & CO's EJECTOR

DATA
Gauge; 12.
Height; 64 mm.
Head being extended one piece brass; 56 mm.
Inner tube; Brown paper.
Printing; Nil.
Base; Brass.
Closure; Rolled turn-over.
Wad; Not known.
Business; Gunmaker.
Case; F. Joyce & Co, Ltd. London.
Circa; 1904. Prior to 1907.

DN.2-0794. Re-drawn; 14th Jan 2001

H. J. HUSSEY, LTD (Late of LANG & HUSSEY, LTD):
88 Jermyn Street. Was also at,
81 New Bond Street, St. James's, London, England.

The example was not checked for internal metals.

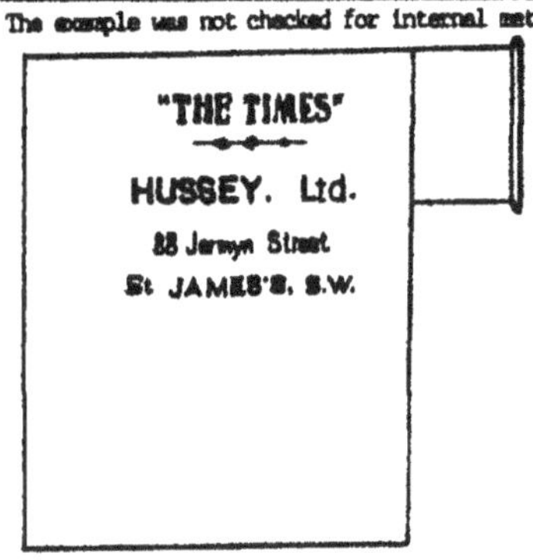

"THE TIMES"
HUSSEY. Ltd.
88 Jermyn Street
St JAMES'S. S.W.

E.C. 5¼

"THE TIMES"
HUSSEY, Ltd
88 Jermyn Street
St JAMES'S S.W.

DATA
Gauge; 12.
Length; 65 mm.
Head; 16 mm.
Tube; Wound red paper.
Colour; Crimson red.
Print; Black.
Base; Brass.
Closure; Rolled turn-over.
Wad; White card, print red.
Powder; E.C.
Business; Gunmaker.
Case; Eley Bros, Ltd. London.

DN.2-2437. 23rd June 2001

HUTCHINSON:
Kendal, Westmorland (Cumbria), England.

NOBEL'S "SPORTING BALLISTITE"
Special Cartridge
GUN MAKER
KENDAL

NOBEL'S "SPORTING BALLISTITE"
Special Cartridge
HUTCHINSON
GUN MAKER
KENDAL

DATA
Gauge; 12.
Length; 64 mm.
Head; 10 mm.
Tube; Wound paper.
Colour; Primrose yellow.
Print; Light brown.
Base; Brass.
Closure; Rolled turn-over.
Wad; White card, print vermilion red.
Business; Gunmaker.
Case; Eley Bros, Ltd.

DN.2-1748. Re-drawn December 1998

ILCHESTER ESTATES: Estate Office, Melbury Sampford, Dorset, DT2 0LF, England.

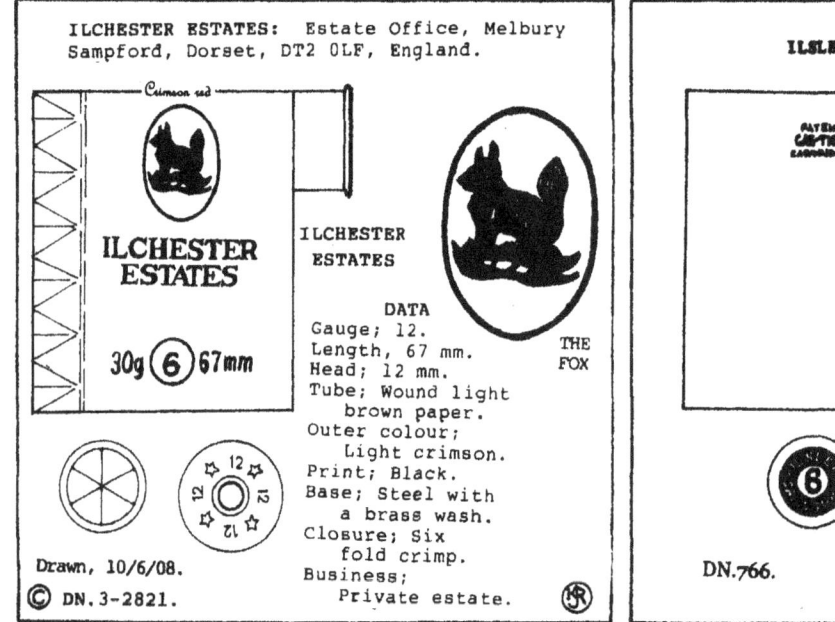

ILCHESTER ESTATES

30g 6 67mm

ILCHESTER ESTATES

THE FOX

DATA
Gauge; 12.
Length, 67 mm.
Head; 12 mm.
Tube; Wound light brown paper.
Outer colour; Light crimson.
Print; Black.
Base; Steel with a brass wash.
Closure; Six fold crimp.
Business; Private estate.

Drawn, 10/6/08.
DN.3-2821.

ILSLEY: SALISBURY, WILTSHIRE.

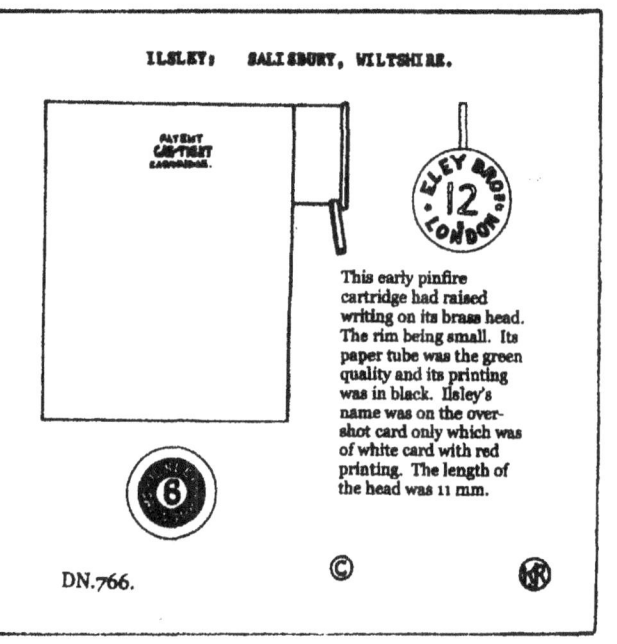

This early pinfire cartridge had raised writing on its brass head. The rim being small. Its paper tube was the green quality and its printing was in black. Ilsley's name was on the over-shot card only which was of white card with red printing. The length of the head was 11 mm.

DN.766.

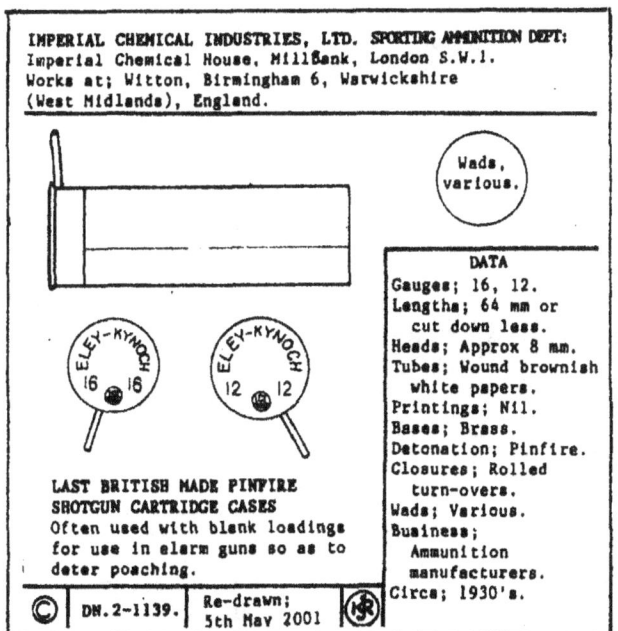
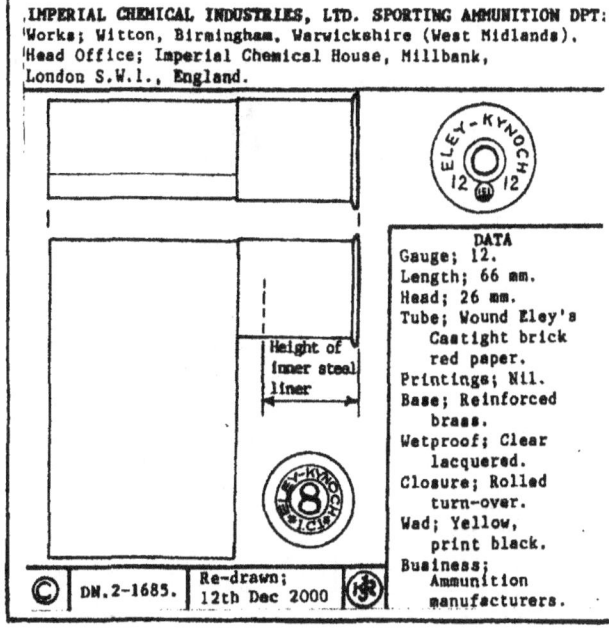
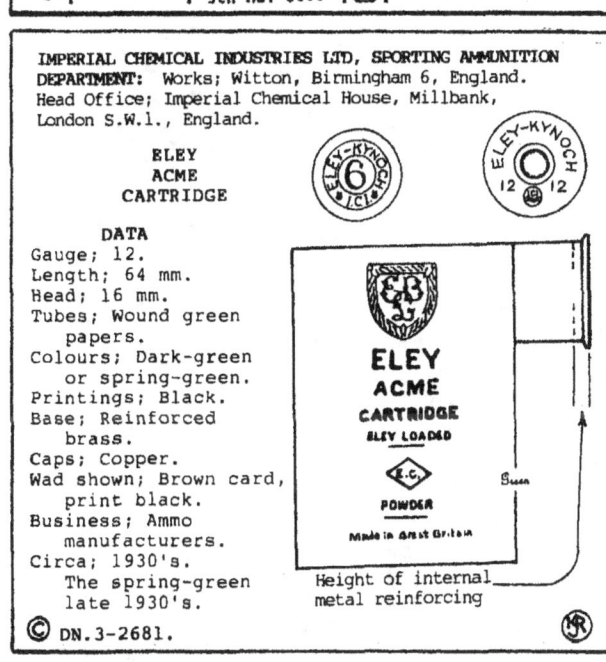
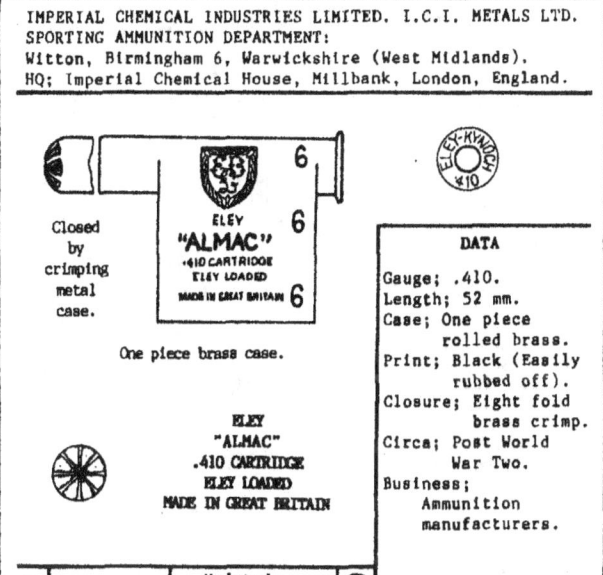
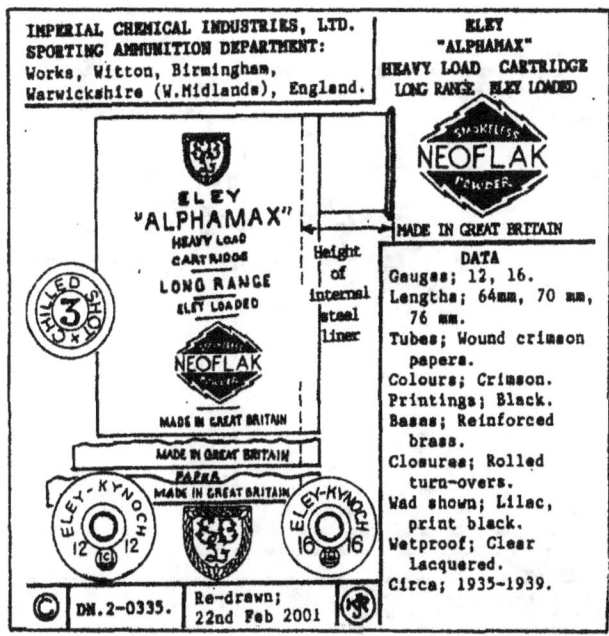
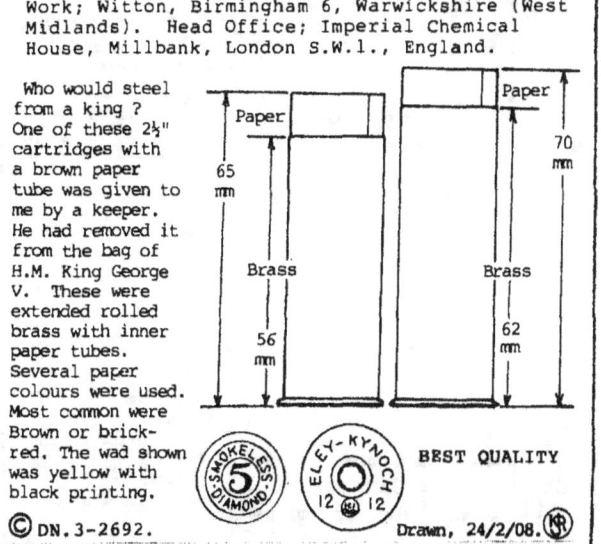

PLATE 179 [ICI – ICI]

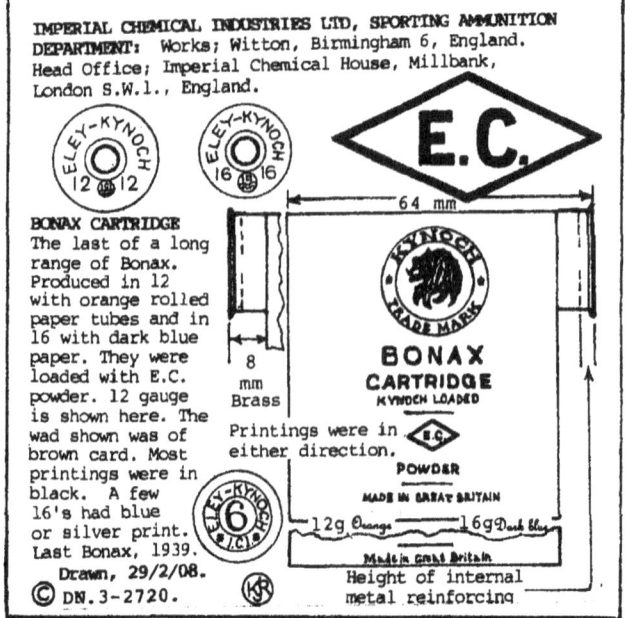
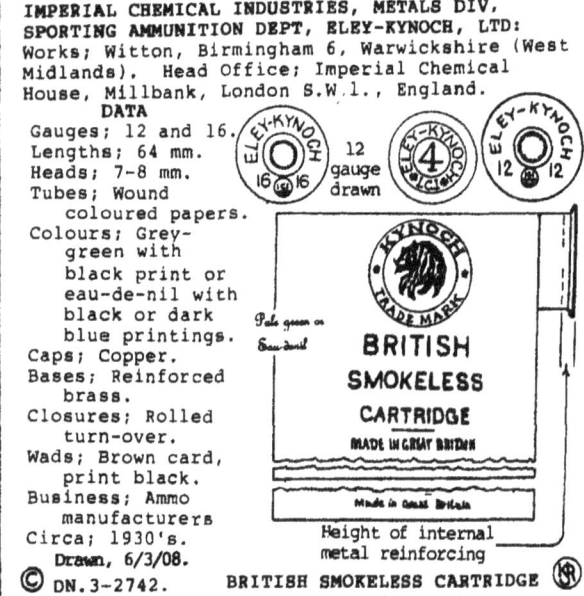

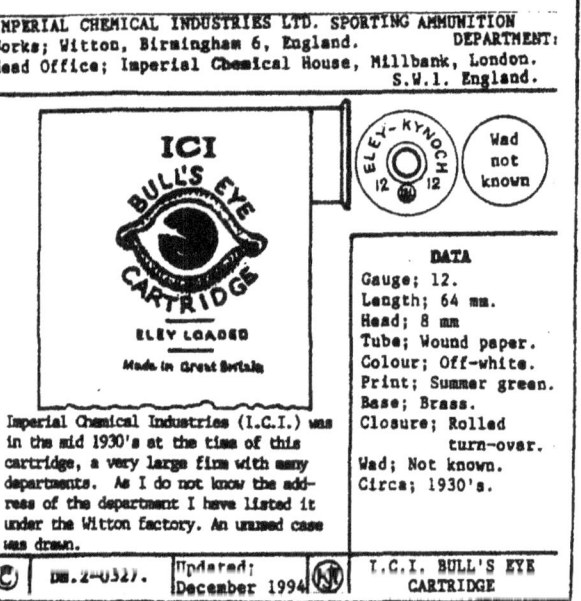

PLATE 180 [ICI – ICI]

IMPERIAL CHEMICAL INDUSTRIES (ICI) METALS
Witton, Birmingham, England.
Business; Ammunition manufacturers.

This was a one inch two piece brass case loaded with a high speed chisel cutting projectile. The Mk II was similar except that the upper brass portion extended above the rolled groove which retained the chisel and formed a waterproof seal. Cable cutters were fitted to the leading edges of some aircraft wings for cutting the cables of barrage balloons.
THIS IS NOT A SHOTGUN CARTRIDGE

CABLE CUTTER Mk I CARTRIDGE

DN.133.

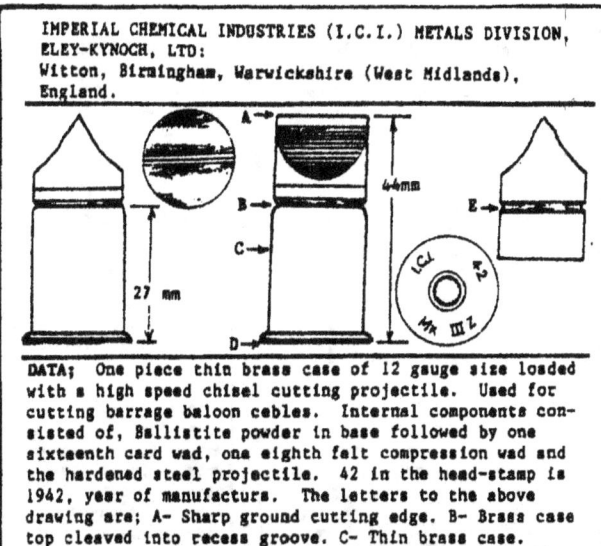

IMPERIAL CHEMICAL INDUSTRIES (I.C.I.) METALS DIVISION, ELEY-KYNOCH, LTD:
Witton, Birmingham, Warwickshire (West Midlands), England.

DATA; One piece thin brass case of 12 gauge size loaded with a high speed chisel cutting projectile. Used for cutting barrage baloon cables. Internal components consisted of, Ballistite powder in base followed by one sixteenth card wad, one eighth felt compression wad and the hardened steel projectile. 42 in the head-stamp is 1942, year of manufacture. The letters to the above drawing are; A- Sharp ground cutting edge. B- Brass case top cleaved into recess groove. C- Thin brass case. D- Rim. E- Recess. This was not a shotgun cartridge. Often used in devise fitted in leading-edges of aircraft.

© DN.2-0927. Re-drawn November 1998. CARTRIDGE FOR CABLE CUTTER. Mk III Z.

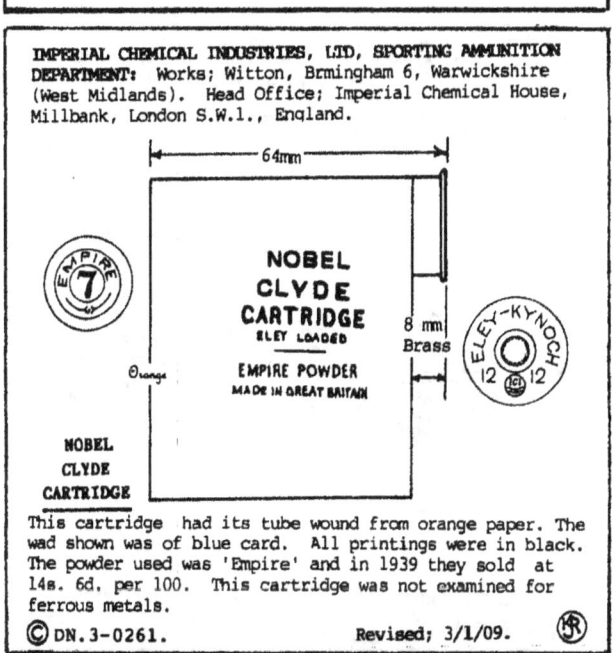

IMPERIAL CHEMICAL INDUSTRIES, LTD, SPORTING AMMUNITION DEPARTMENT: Works; Witton, Brmingham 6, Warwickshire (West Midlands). Head Office; Imperial Chemical House, Millbank, London S.W.1., England.

NOBEL CLYDE CARTRIDGE

This cartridge had its tube wound from orange paper. The wad shown was of blue card. All printings were in black. The powder used was 'Empire' and in 1939 they sold at 14s. 6d. per 100. This cartridge was not examined for ferrous metals.

© DN.3-0261. Revised; 3/1/09.

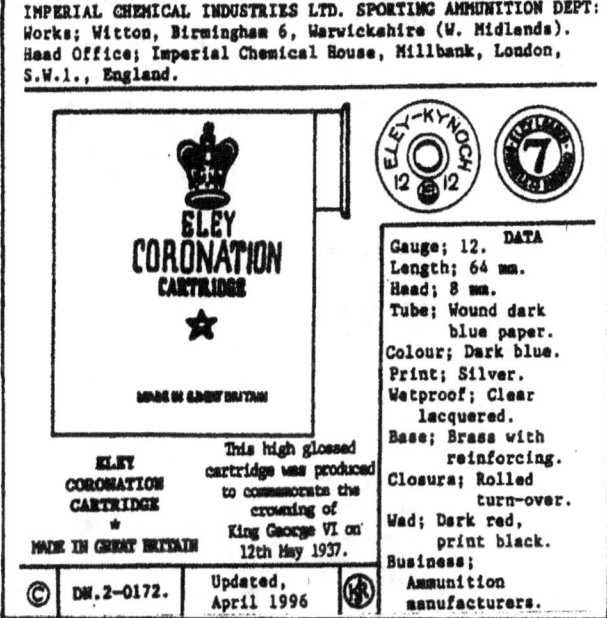

IMPERIAL CHEMICAL INDUSTRIES LTD. SPORTING AMMUNITION DEPT: Works; Witton, Birmingham 6, Warwickshire (W. Midlands). Head Office; Imperial Chemical House, Millbank, London, S.W.1., England.

DATA
Gauge; 12.
Length; 64 mm.
Head; 8 mm.
Tube; Wound dark blue paper.
Colour; Dark blue.
Print; Silver.
Wetproof; Clear lacquered.
Base; Brass with reinforcing.
Closure; Rolled turn-over.
Wad; Dark red, print black.
Business; Ammunition manufacturers.

This high glossed cartridge was produced to commemorate the crowning of King George VI on 12th May 1937.

© DN.2-0172. Updated, April 1996.

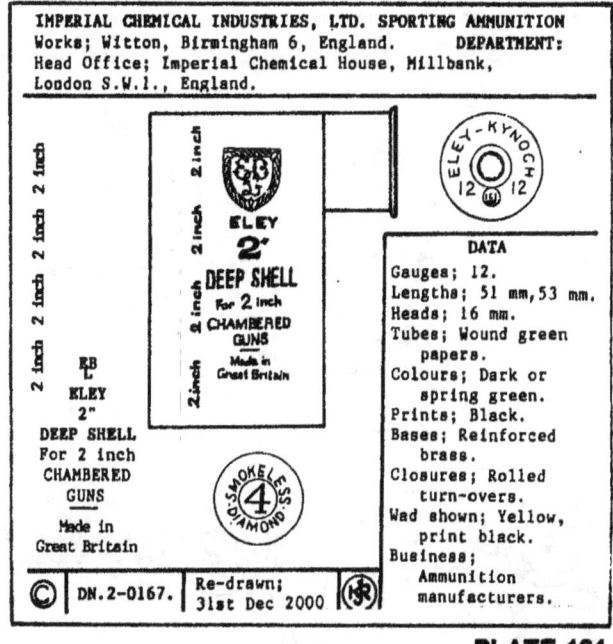

IMPERIAL CHEMICAL INDUSTRIES, LTD, SPORTING AMMUNITION DEPARTMENT: Works; Witton, Birmingham 6, England. Head Office; Imperial Chemical House, Millbank, London S.W.1., England.

ELEY 2" DEEP SHELL For 2 inch CHAMBERED GUNS
Made in Great Britain

DATA
Gauges; 12.
Lengths; 51 mm, 53 mm.
Heads; 16 mm.
Tubes; Wound green papers.
Colours; Dark or spring green.
Prints; Black.
Bases; Reinforced brass.
Closures; Rolled turn-overs.
Wad shown; Yellow, print black.
Business; Ammunition manufacturers.

© DN.2-0167. Re-drawn; 31st Dec 2000.

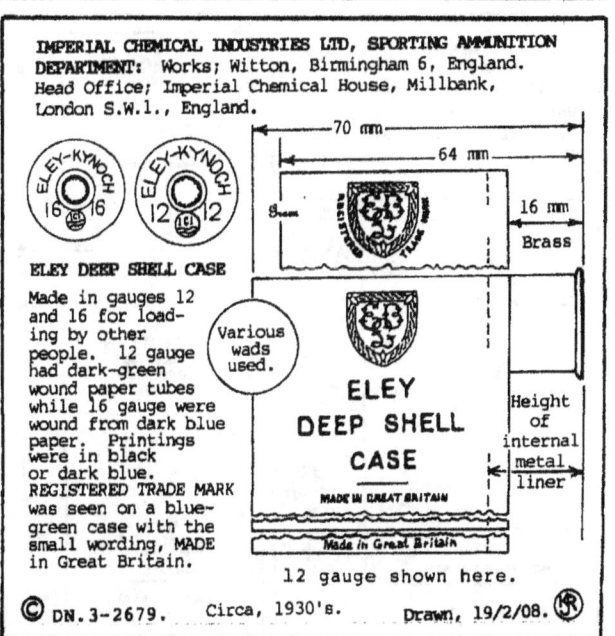

IMPERIAL CHEMICAL INDUSTRIES LTD, SPORTING AMMUNITION DEPARTMENT: Works; Witton, Birmingham 6, England. Head Office; Imperial Chemical House, Millbank, London S.W.1., England.

ELEY DEEP SHELL CASE
Made in gauges 12 and 16 for loading by other people. 12 gauge had dark-green wound paper tubes while 16 gauge were wound from dark blue paper. Printings were in black or dark blue. REGISTERED TRADE MARK was seen on a blue-green case with the small wording, MADE in Great Britain.

12 gauge shown here.

© DN.3-2679. Circa, 1930's. Drawn, 19/2/08.

PLATE 181 [ICI – ICI]

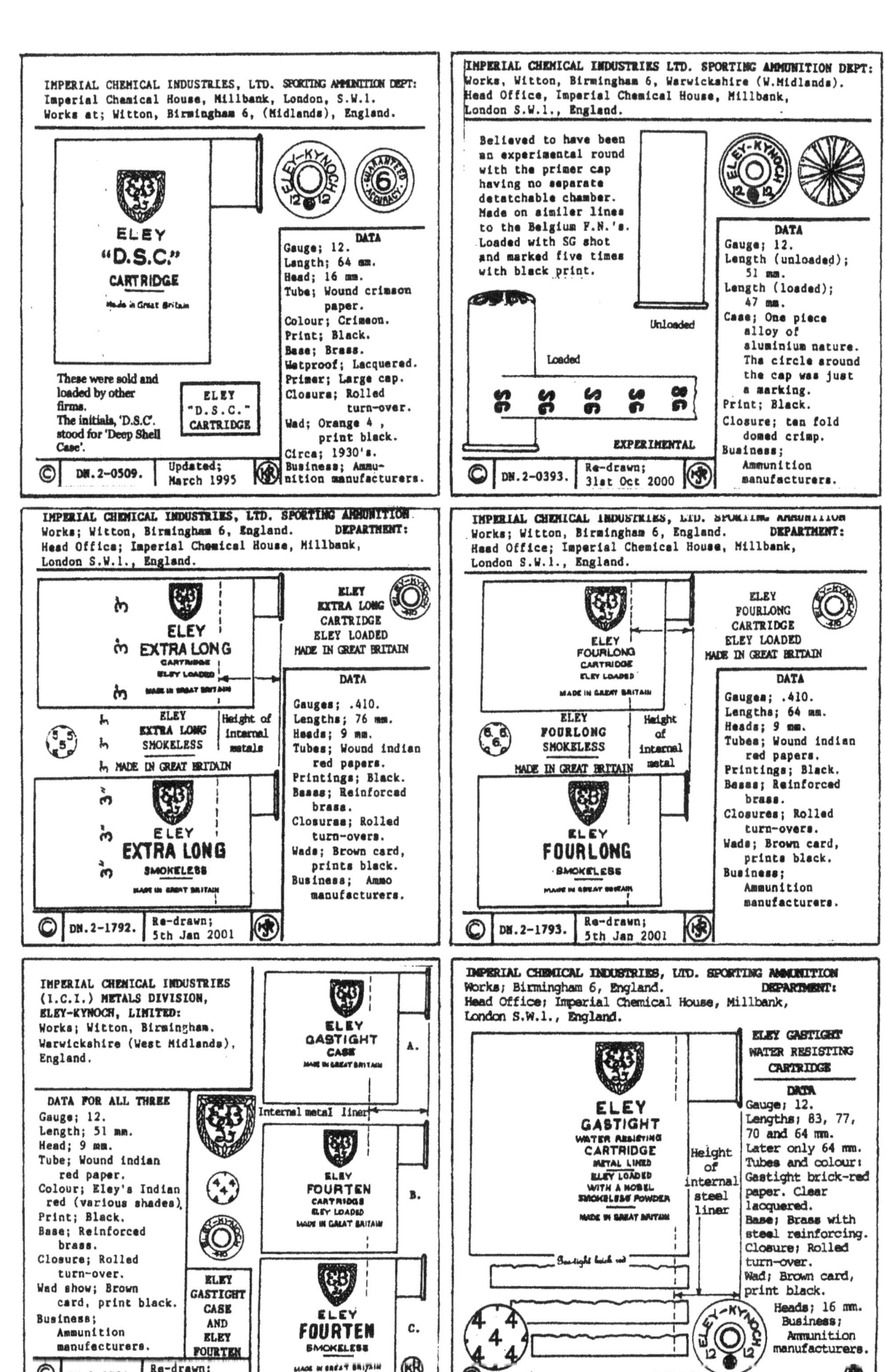

PLATE 182 [ICI – ICI]

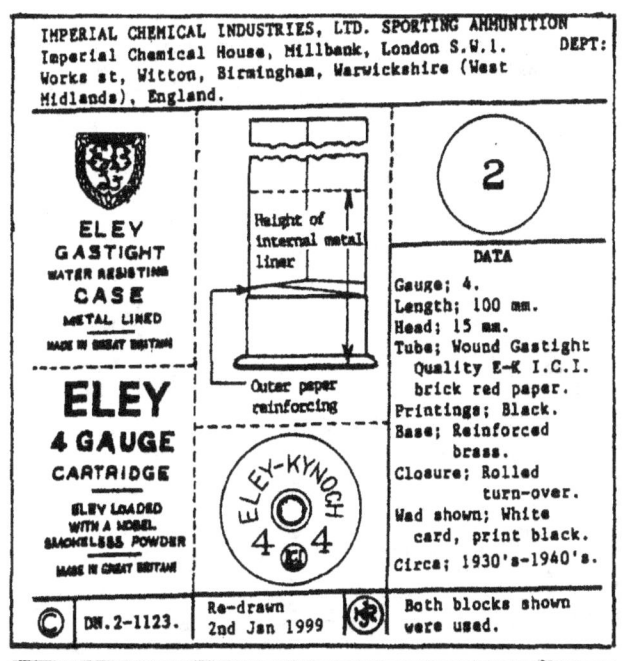
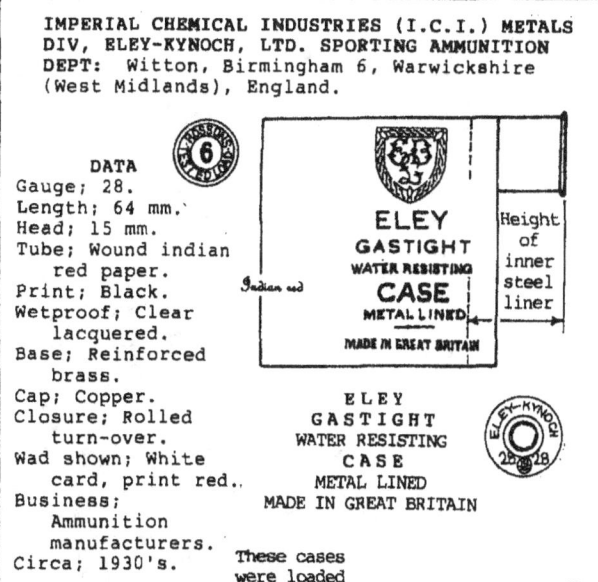
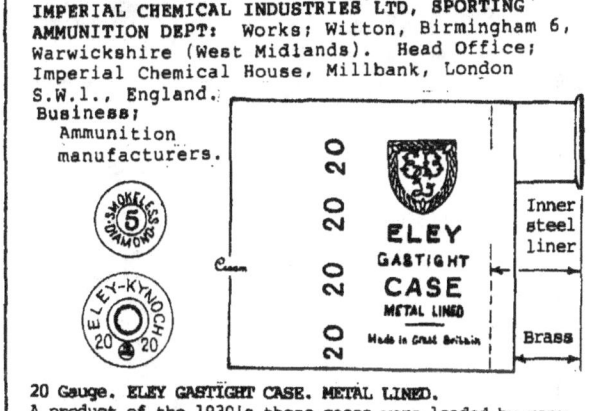
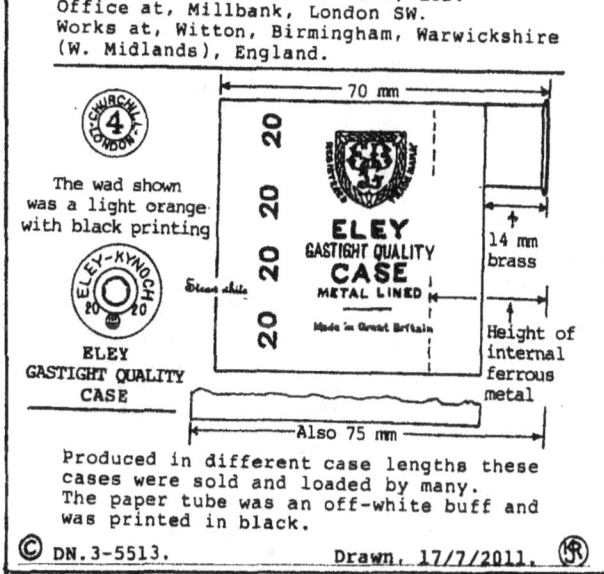
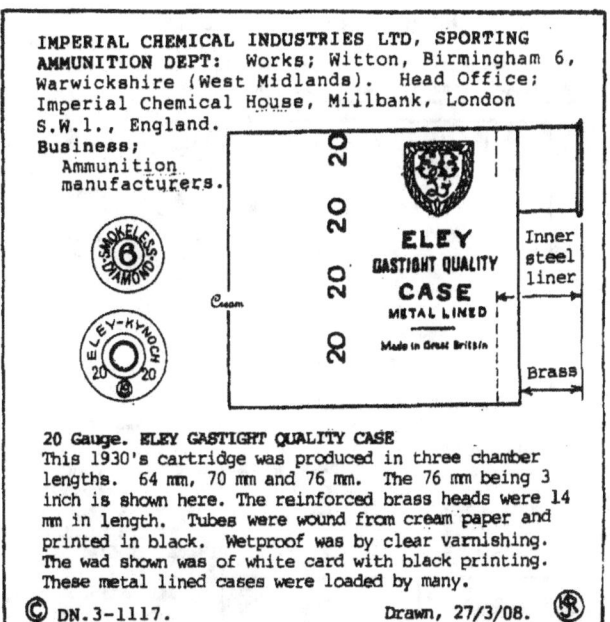
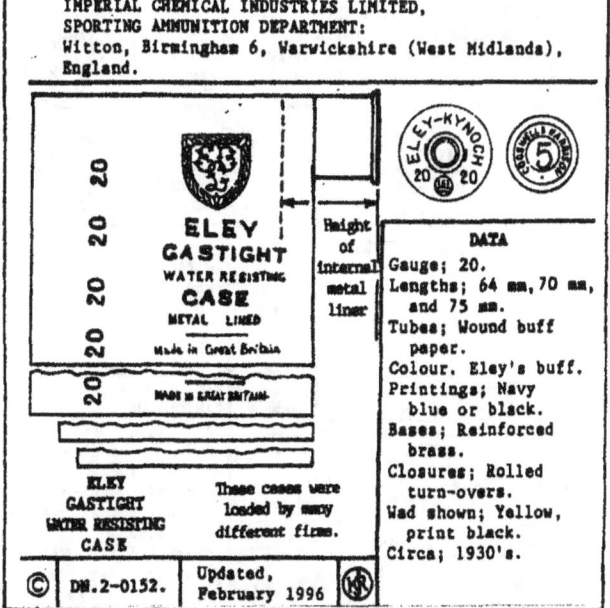

PLATE 183 [ICI – ICI]

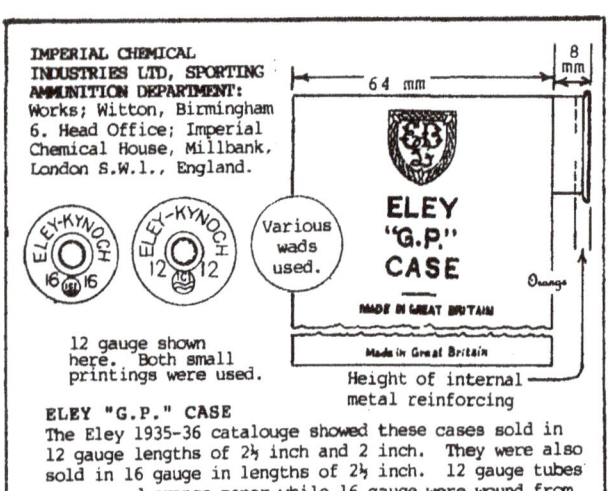
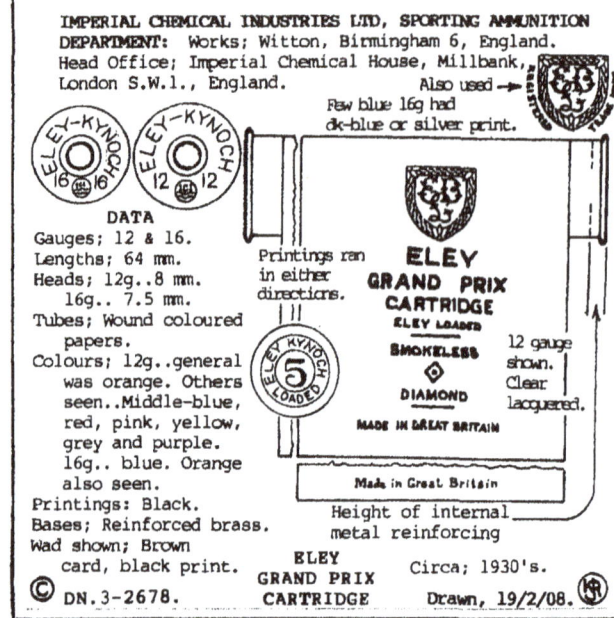
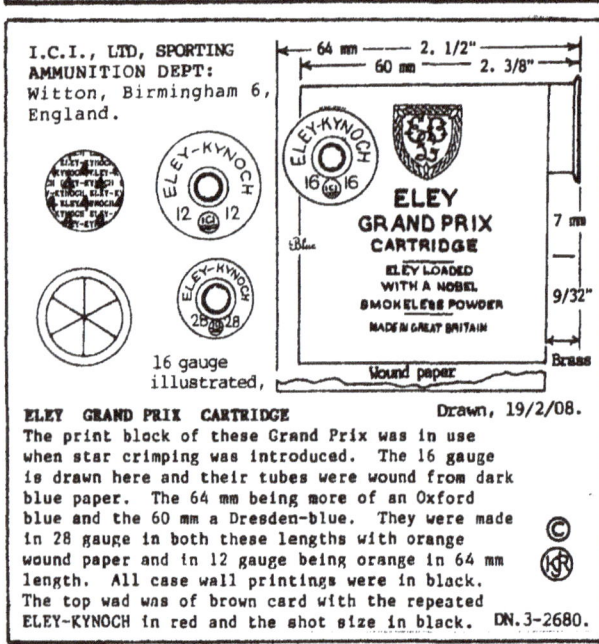
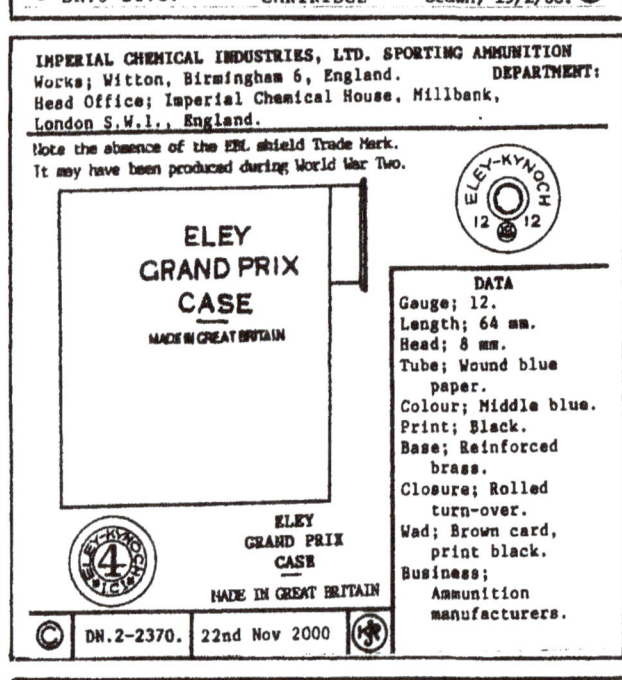
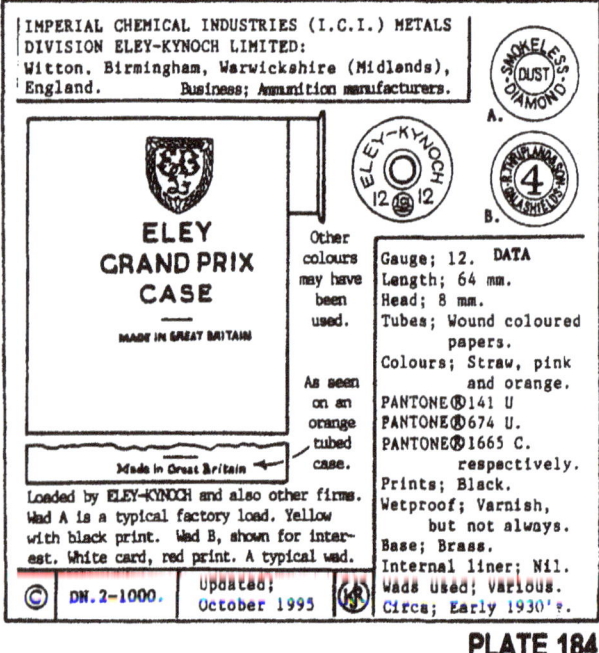
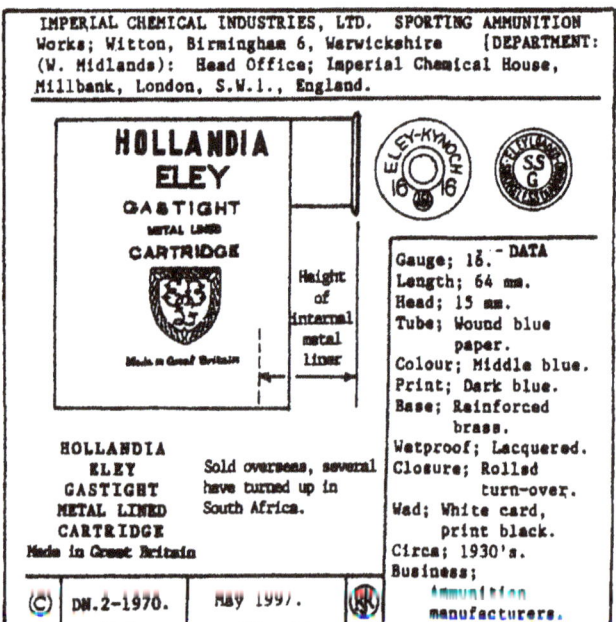

PLATE 184 [ICI – ICI]

IMPERIAL CHEMICAL INDUSTRIES, LTD. SPORTING AMMUNITION
Works; Witton, Birmingham 6, Warwickshire [DEPARTMENT:
(W. Midlands): Head Office; Imperial Chemical House,
Millbank, London, S.W.1., England.

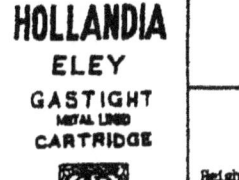
HOLLANDIA
ELEY
GASTIGHT
METAL LINED
CARTRIDGE

Made in Great Britain

Height of internal metal liner

HOLLANDIA
ELEY
GASTIGHT
METAL LINED
CARTRIDGE

Made in Great Britain
Sold overseas, several have turned up in South Africa.

DATA
Gauge; 12.
Lengths; 70 mm and 64 mm.
Tubes; Wound brown paper.
Colour; Brown.
Print; Black.
Wetproof; Lacquered
Base; Reinforced brass.
Closure; Rolled turn-over.
Wads; Blue-grey or light blue, prints black.
Business; Ammunition manufacturers.

© DN.2-1971. May 1997.

IMPERIAL CHEMICAL INDUSTRIES, LTD. SPORTING AMMUNITION DEPT:
Imperial Chemical House, Millbank, London S.W.1.
Works at; Witton, Birmingham 6, (Midlands), England.

KYNOCH
TRADE MARK
"JUNO"
SMOKELESS CARTRIDGE
Made in Great Britain

"JUNO"
SMOKELESS CARTRIDGE
Made in Great Britain

Using an ex Eley Brothers brand name and honouring the name of Kynoch, it was produced for export, possibly to the U.S.A. Drawn from the Dale Hedlund collection.

DATA
Gauge; 12.
Length; 64 mm.
Head; 8 mm.
Tube; Wound eau-de-nil paper.
Colour; Eau-de-nil.
Print; Dark blue.
Base; Reinforced brass.
Closure; Rolled turn-over.
Wad; Brown card, print black.
Business; Ammunition manufacturers.

© DN.2-2133. 24th March 1999. Circa; 1930's.

IMPERIAL CHEMICAL INDUSTRIES (I.C.I.) METALS DIVISION, ELEY-KYNOCH, LTD:
Witton, Birmingham, Warwickshire (West Midlands), England.

ELEY
HEAVY LOAD
"MAXIMUM"
LONG RANGE
NEOFLAK
ELEY LOADED
MADE IN GREAT BRITAIN

"MAXIMUM" NEOFLAK SMOKELESS POWDER
One batch of 12 gauge had deep pink paper tubes with black printings. A sample box of 12 gauge seen had paper tubes with the colours, dark blue, vermilion red, burgundy and deep blueish-green. All had white print.

DATA
Gauges; 12, 16.
Lengths; 64 mm.
Heads; 8 mm, 7 mm.
Tubes; Wound crimson paper.
Printings; black.
Bases; Reinforced brass.
Closures; Rolled turn-over.
Wad shown; Brown card, print black.
Wetproof; Lacquered.
Powder Neoflak.
Business; Ammo manufacturers.

© DN.2-0334. Re-drawn; 26th Feb 2001. Circa; 1935-1939.

IMPERIAL CHEMICAL INDUSTRIES (ELEY-KYNOCH) LTD, SPORTING AMMUNITION DEPT: Imperial Chemical House, Millbank, London, S.W.1. Works at; Witton, Birmingham, Midlands, England.

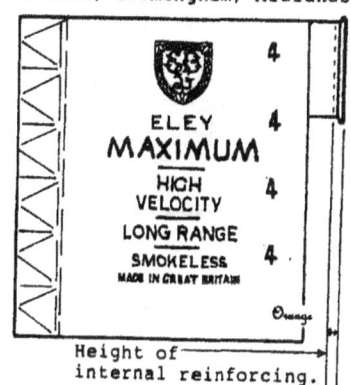

ELEY
MAXIMUM
HIGH VELOCITY
LONG RANGE
SMOKELESS
MADE IN GREAT BRITAIN

Height of internal reinforcing.

DATA
Gauge; 12.
Length; 70 mm.
Head; 8 mm.
Tube; Wound orange paper then clear lacquered.
Print; Black.
Base; Reinforced brass.
Closure; Six fold crimp.
Business; Ammo manufacturers.

ELEY
MAXIMUM
HIGH VELOCITY
LONG RANGE
SMOKELESS
MADE IN GREAT BRITAIN

© DN.3-2569. Drawn, 14/6/07.

IMPERIAL CHEMICAL INDUSTRIES, LTD, SPORTING AMMUNITION DEPARTMENT: Works; Witton, Birmingham 6, Warwickshire (West Midlands). Head Office; Imperial Chemical House, Millbank, London S.W.1., England.
(Business; Ammunition manufacturers).

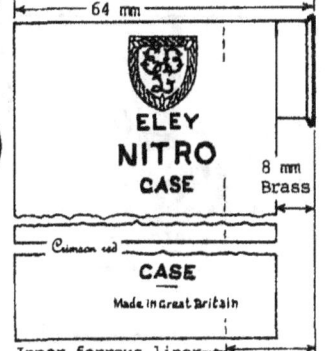

64 mm

ELEY
NITRO
CASE

8 mm Brass

Crimson red

CASE
Made in Great Britain

Inner ferrous liner

ELEY
NITRO
CASE

Produced in 64 mm lengths in 12 and 16 gauge and sold as primed empty cases. In 1939 their last year of manufacture they sold at £2. 12s. 6d. per 100. 12 tubes were of wound crimson paper while 16 gauge were from dark blue. Printings were generally in black. Drawn here is 12 gauge. The wad shown was white card with pink printing. DN.3-0768. Revised; 5/1/09.

IMPERIAL CHEMICAL INDUSTRIES, LTD. SPORTING AMMUNITION DPT: Works; Witton, Birmingham, Warwickshire (West Midlands). Head Office; Imperial Chemical House, Millbank, London S.W.1., England.

ELEY
NONEKA
CARTRIDGE
Specially loaded for
LIGHT GUNS
MADE IN GREAT BRITAIN

EB
ELEY
NONEKA
CARTRIDGE

Specially loaded for
LIGHT GUNS
MADE IN GREAT BRITAIN

DATA
Gauge; 12.
Lengths; 64 mm.
Heads; 16 mm.
Tubes; Wound green papers.
Colours; Dark green with black or navy blue printing. Spring green with black printing.
Base; reinforced brass.
Closure; Rolled.
Wad shown; Yellow, print black.
Loadings; 1 oz. 'E.C.' or Smokeless Diamond.

© DN.2-0983. Re-drawn; 12th Dec 2000.

PLATE 185 [ICI – ICI]

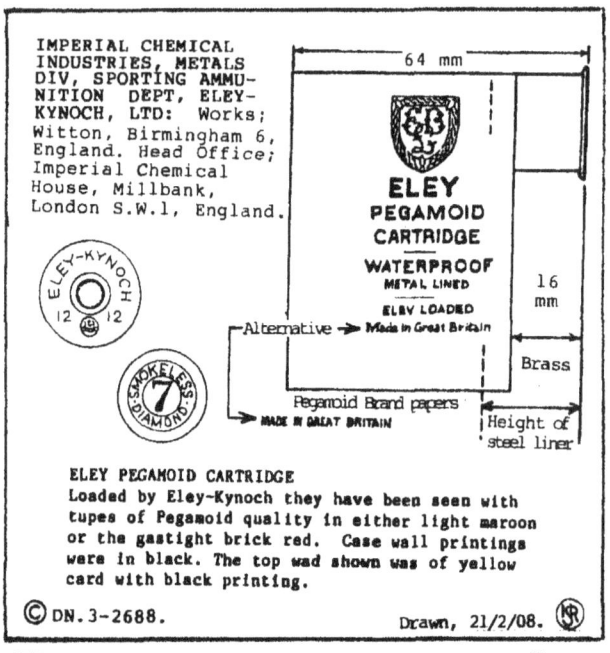

ELEY PEGAMOID CARTRIDGE
Loaded by Eley-Kynoch they have been seen with tupes of Pegamoid quality in either light maroon or the gastight brick red. Case wall printings were in black. The top wad shown was of yellow card with black printing.

© DN.3-2688. Drawn, 21/2/08.

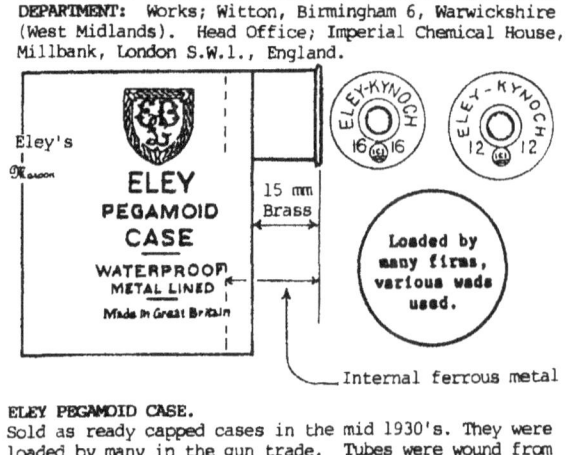

ELEY PEGAMOID CASE.
Sold as ready capped cases in the mid 1930's. They were loaded by many in the gun trade. Tubes were wound from 'Pegamoid' brand paper in Eley's Light Maroon. This was a cross between Eley's Indian red and pink. All printings were in black. Case lengths were; 12 gauge 64 and 70 mm. 16 Gauge 64 mm only. Illustration is 16 gauge.

© DN.3-1420. Revised; 21/12/08.

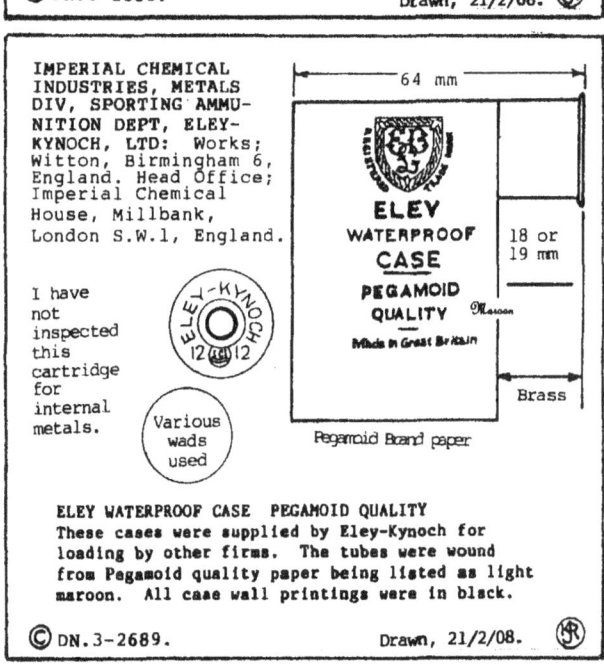

ELEY WATERPROOF CASE PEGAMOID QUALITY
These cases were supplied by Eley-Kynoch for loading by other firms. The tubes were wound from Pegamoid quality paper being listed as light maroon. All case wall printings were in black.

© DN.3-2689. Drawn, 21/2/08.

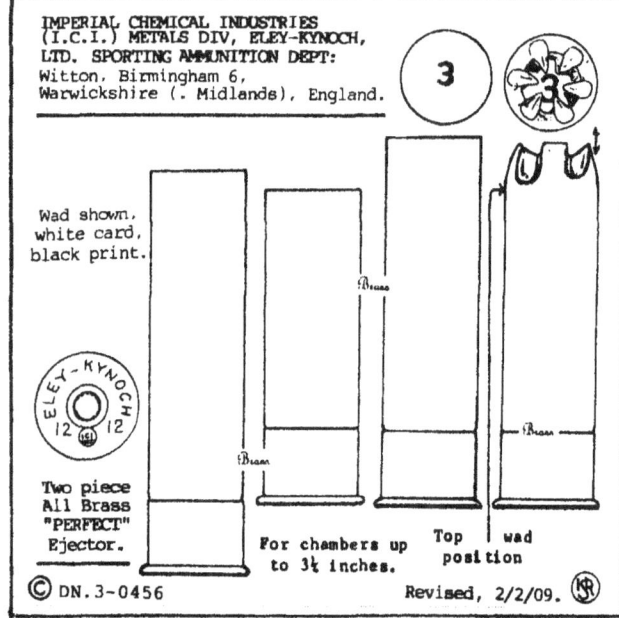

Two piece All Brass "PERFECT" Ejector. For chambers up to 3¼ inches. Top wad position. Wad shown, white card, black print.

© DN.3-0456. Revised, 2/2/09.

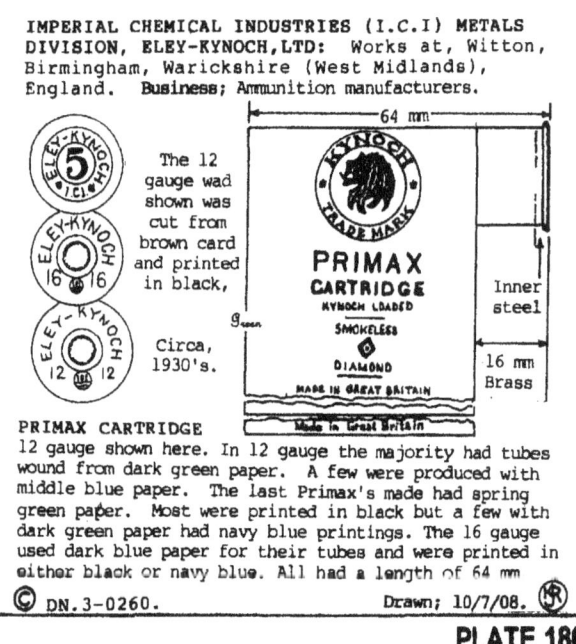

PRIMAX CARTRIDGE
12 gauge shown here. In 12 gauge the majority had tubes wound from dark green paper. A few were produced with middle blue paper. The last Primax's made had spring green paper. Most were printed in black but a few with dark green paper had navy blue printings. The 16 gauge used dark blue paper for their tubes and were printed in either black or navy blue. All had a length of 64 mm

© DN.3-0260. Drawn; 10/7/08.

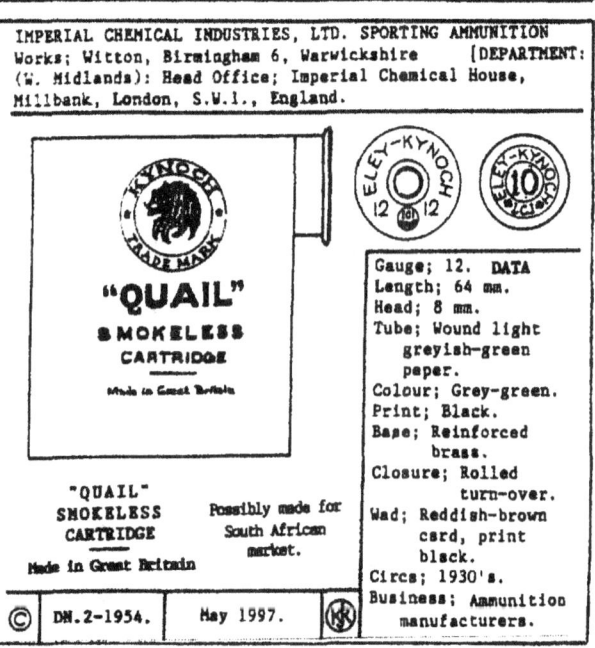

"QUAIL" SMOKELESS CARTRIDGE
Made in Great Britain
Possibly made for South African market.

DATA
Gauge; 12.
Length; 64 mm.
Head; 8 mm.
Tube; Wound light greyish-green paper.
Colour; Grey-green.
Print; Black.
Base; Reinforced brass.
Closure; Rolled turn-over.
Wad; Reddish-brown card, print black.
Circa; 1930's.
Business; Ammunition manufacturers.

© DN.2-1954. May 1997.

PLATE 186 [ICI – ICI]

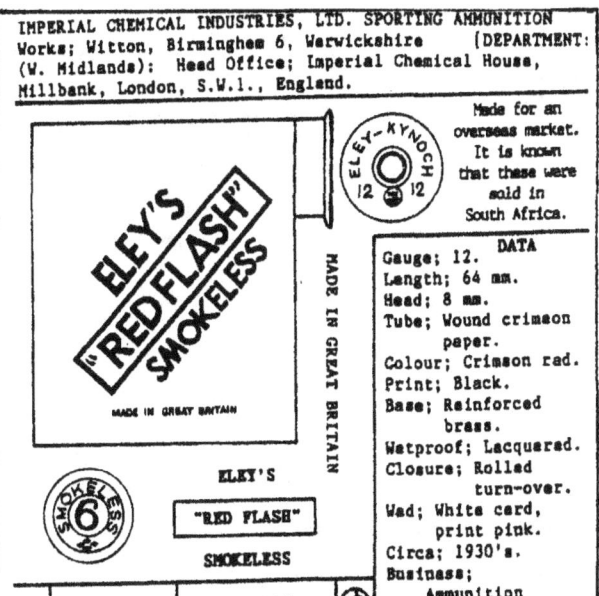

IMPERIAL CHEMICAL INDUSTRIES, LTD. SPORTING AMMUNITION
Works; Witton, Birmingham 6, Warwickshire [DEPARTMENT:
(W. Midlands): Head Office; Imperial Chemical House,
Millbank, London, S.W.1., England.

Made for an overseas market. It is known that these were sold in South Africa.

DATA
Gauge; 12.
Length; 64 mm.
Head; 8 mm.
Tube; Wound crimson paper.
Colour; Crimson red.
Print; Black.
Base; Reinforced brass.
Watproof; Lacquered.
Closure; Rolled turn-over.
Wad; White card, print pink.
Circa; 1930's.
Business; Ammunition manufacturers.

© DN.2-1966.   May 1997.

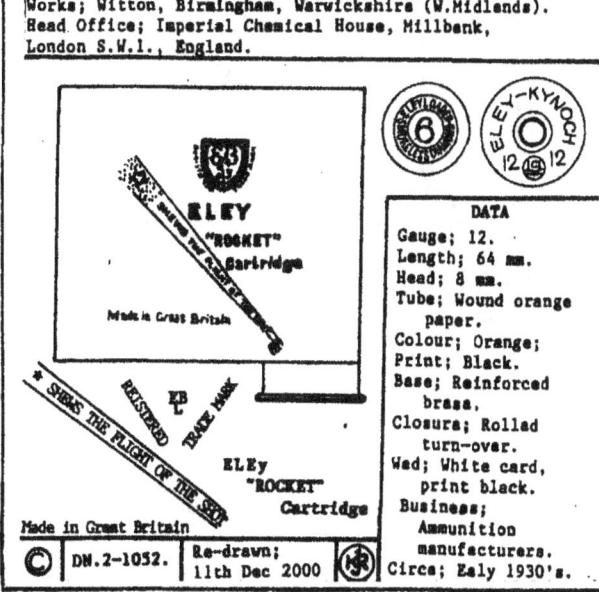

IMPERIAL CHEMICAL INDUSTRIES, LTD. SPORTING AMMUNITION DPT;
Works; Witton, Birmingham, Warwickshire (W. Midlands).
Head Office; Imperial Chemical House, Millbank,
London S.W.1., England.

DATA
Gauge; 12.
Length; 64 mm.
Head; 8 mm.
Tube; Wound orange paper.
Colour; Orange;
Print; Black.
Base; Reinforced brass.
Closure; Rolled turn-over.
Wad; White card, print black.
Business; Ammunition manufacturers.
Circa; Ealy 1930's.

© DN.2-1052.   Re-drawn; 11th Dec 2000

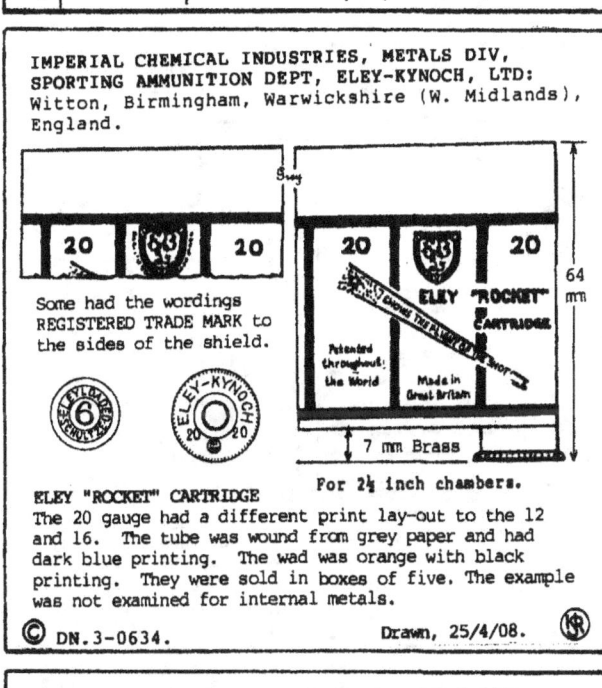

IMPERIAL CHEMICAL INDUSTRIES, METALS DIV,
SPORTING AMMUNITION DEPT, ELEY-KYNOCH, LTD:
Witton, Birmingham, Warwickshire (W. Midlands),
England.

Some had the wordings REGISTERED TRADE MARK to the sides of the shield.

For 2½ inch chambers.

ELEY "ROCKET" CARTRIDGE
The 20 gauge had a different print lay-out to the 12 and 16. The tube was wound from grey paper and had dark blue printing. The wad was orange with black printing. They were sold in boxes of five. The example was not examined for internal metals.

© DN.3-0634.   Drawn, 25/4/08.

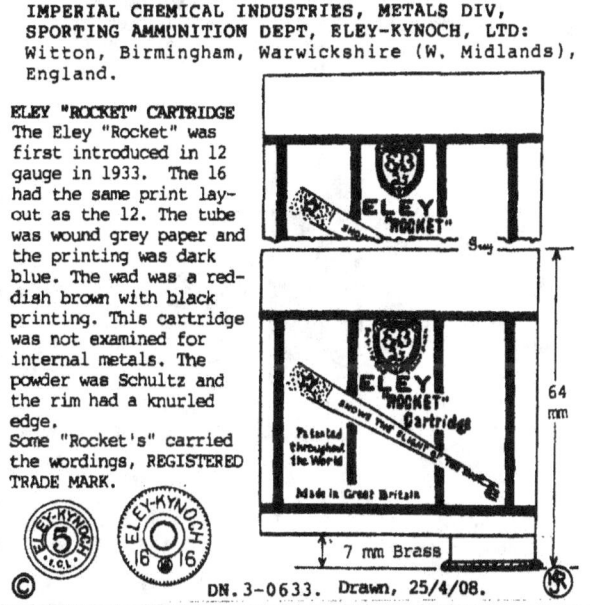

IMPERIAL CHEMICAL INDUSTRIES, METALS DIV,
SPORTING AMMUNITION DEPT, ELEY-KYNOCH, LTD:
Witton, Birmingham, Warwickshire (W. Midlands),
England.

ELEY "ROCKET" CARTRIDGE
The Eley "Rocket" was first introduced in 12 gauge in 1933. The 16 had the same print lay-out as the 12. The tube was wound grey paper and the printing was dark blue. The wad was a reddish brown with black printing. This cartridge was not examined for internal metals. The powder was Schultz and the rim had a knurled edge.
Some "Rocket's" carried the wordings, REGISTERED TRADE MARK.

© DN.3-0633.   Drawn, 25/4/08.

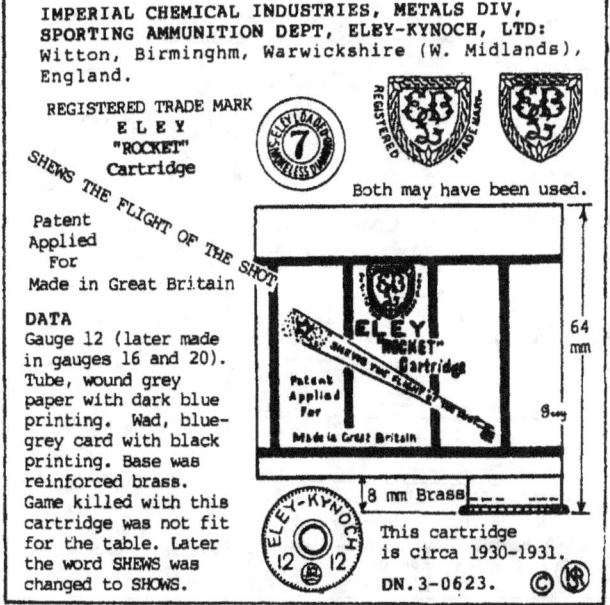

IMPERIAL CHEMICAL INDUSTRIES, METALS DIV,
SPORTING AMMUNITION DEPT, ELEY-KYNOCH, LTD:
Witton, Birminghm, Warwickshire (W. Midlands),
England.

REGISTERED TRADE MARK
ELEY "ROCKET" Cartridge

Both may have been used.

Patent Applied For
Made in Great Britain

DATA
Gauge 12 (later made in gauges 16 and 20).
Tube, wound grey paper with dark blue printing. Wad, blue-grey card with black printing. Base was reinforced brass.
Game killed with this cartridge was not fit for the table. Later the word SHEWS was changed to SHOWS.

This cartridge is circa 1930-1931.
DN.3-0623.

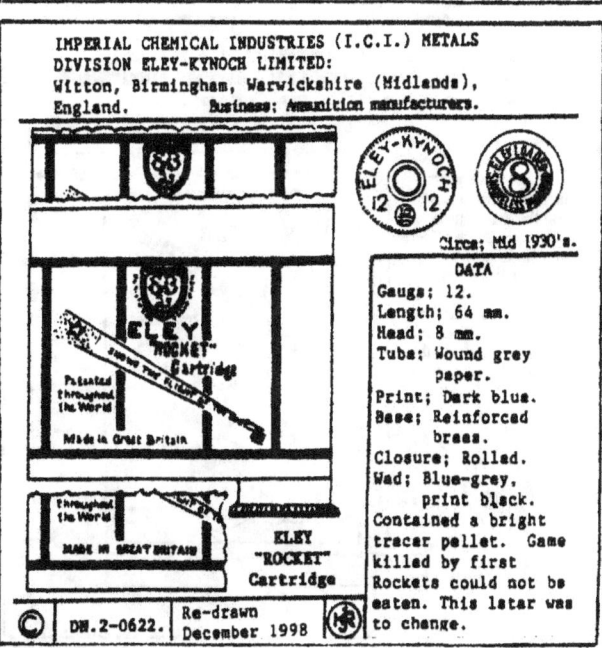

IMPERIAL CHEMICAL INDUSTRIES (I.C.I.) METALS
DIVISION ELEY-KYNOCH LIMITED:
Witton, Birmingham, Warwickshire (Midlands),
England.   Business; Ammunition manufacturers.

Circa; Mid 1930's.

DATA
Gauge; 12.
Length; 64 mm.
Head; 8 mm.
Tube; Wound grey paper.
Print; Dark blue.
Base; Reinforced brass.
Closure; Rolled.
Wad; Blue-grey, print black.
Contained a bright tracer pellet. Game killed by first Rockets could not be eaten. This later was to change.

© DN.2-0622.   Re-drawn December 1998

PLATE 187 [ICI – ICI]

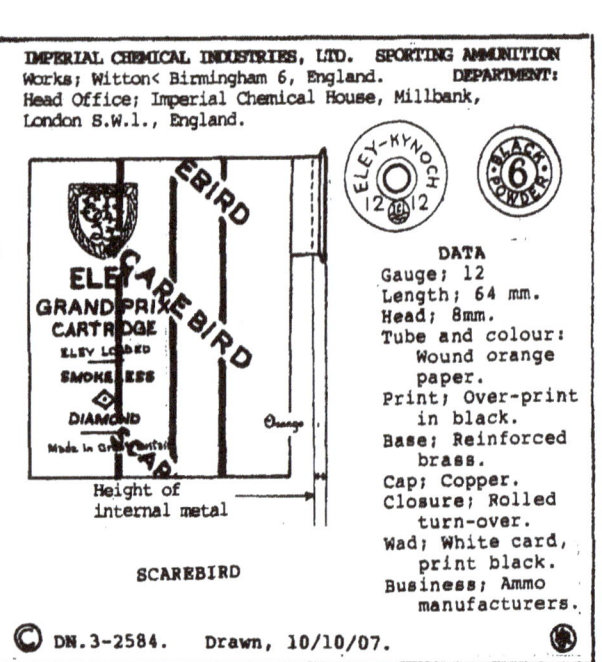
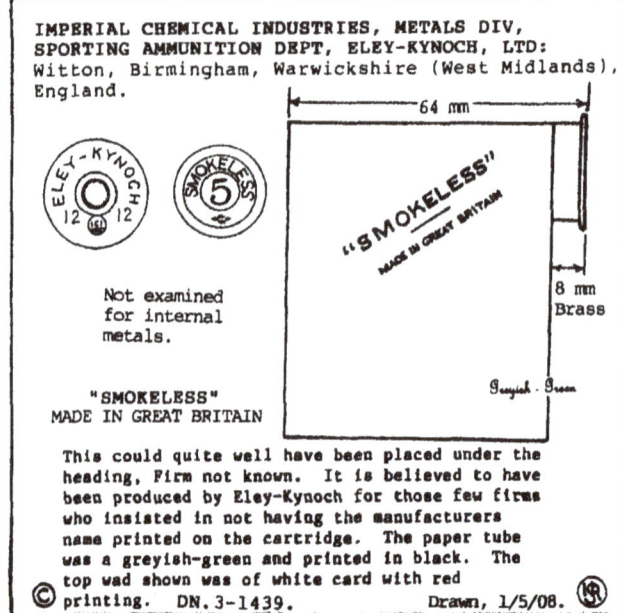
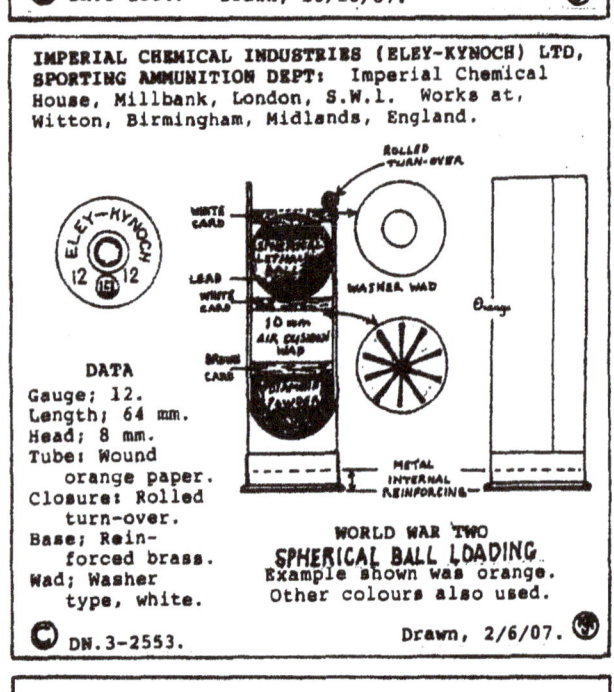
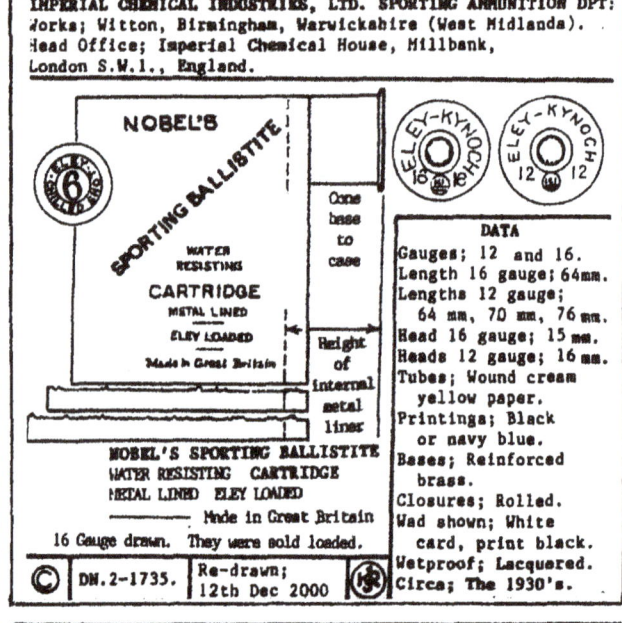
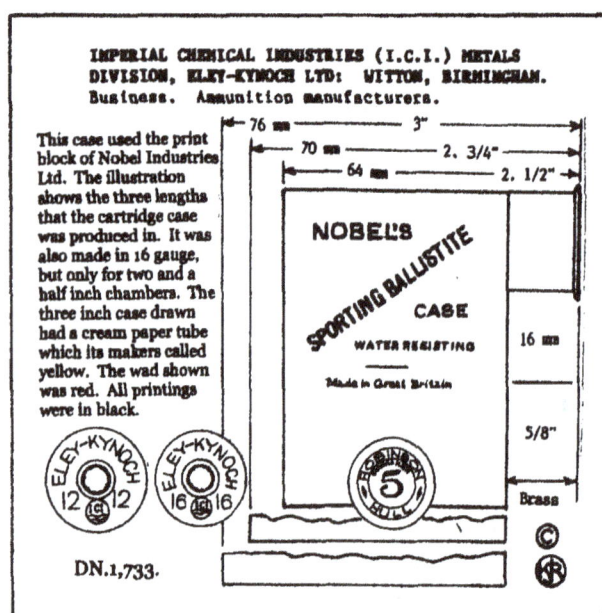
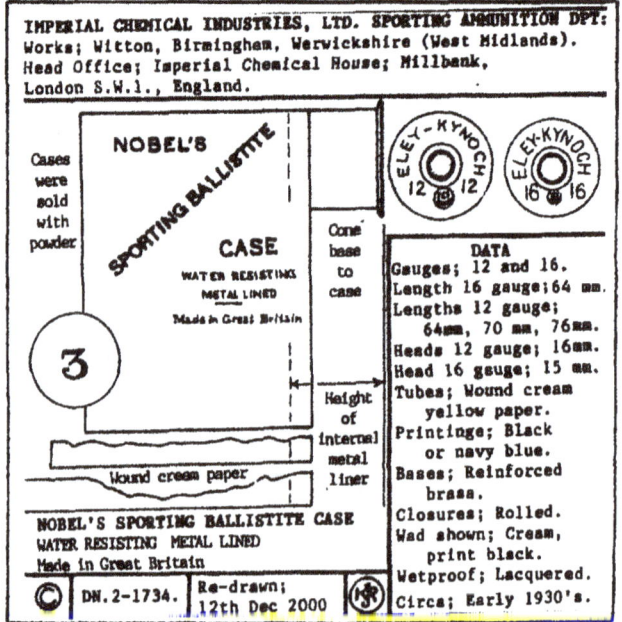

PLATE 188 [ICI – ICI]

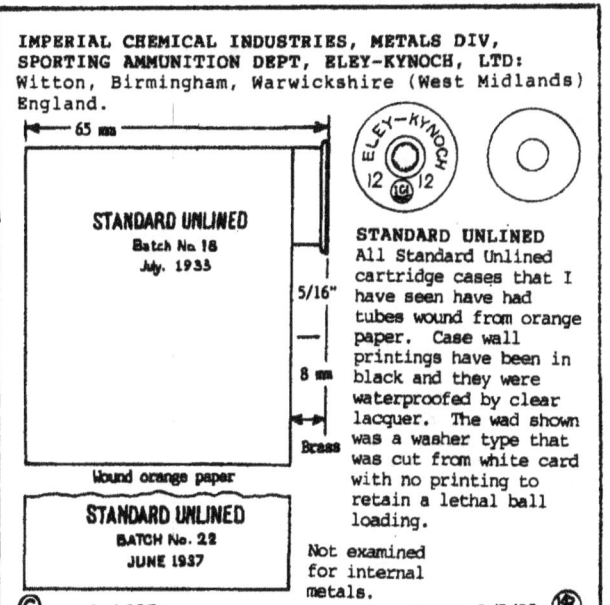
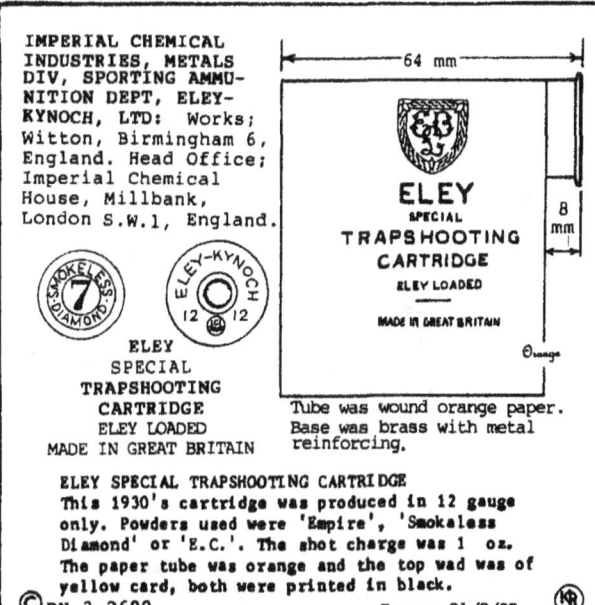
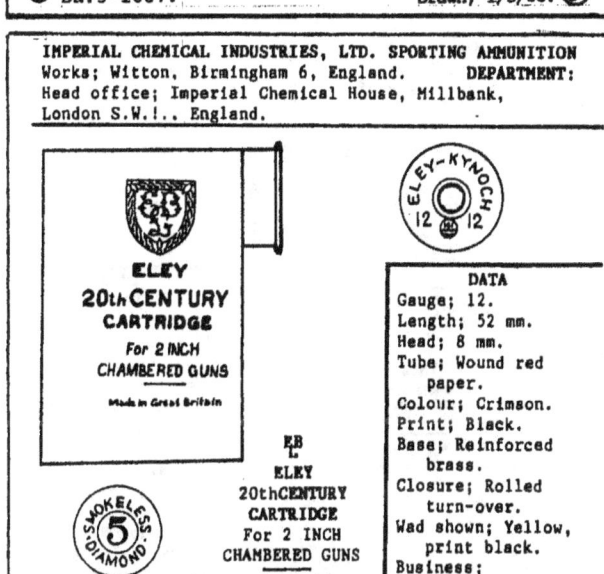
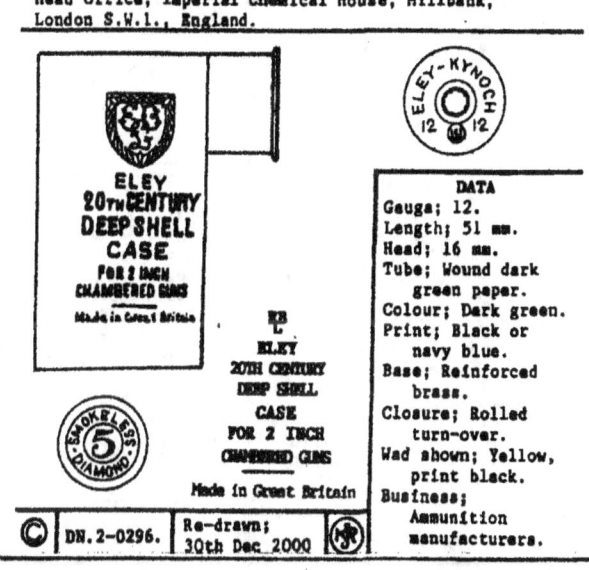
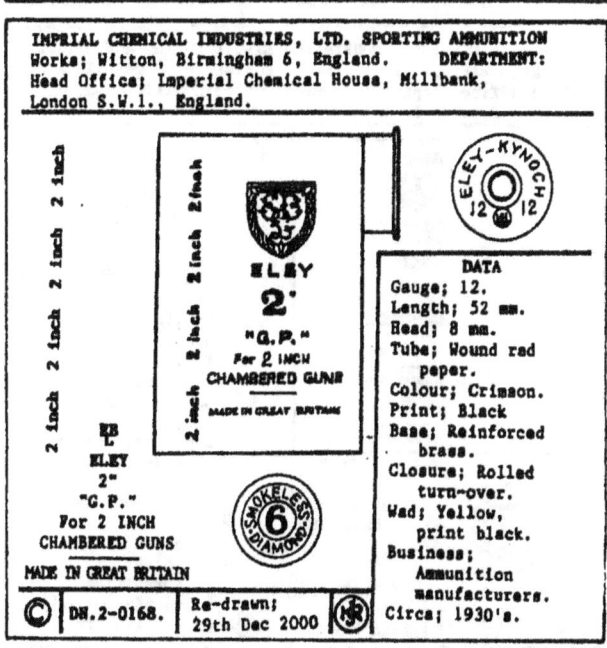
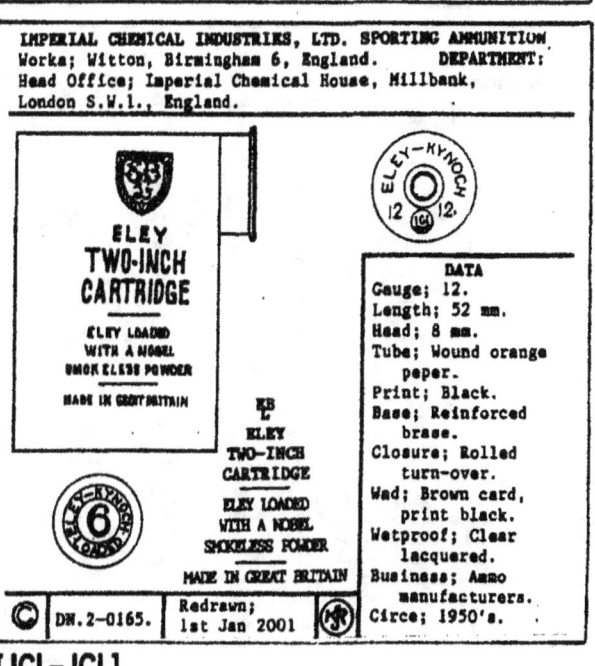

PLATE 189 [ICI – ICI]

IMPERIAL CHEMICAL INDUSTRIES LTD. SPORTING AMMUNITION DEPT.
Works; Witton, Birmingham 6, Warwickshire (W. Midlands).
Head Office; Imperial Chemical House, Millbank, London
S.W.1., England

ELEY UNIVERSAL (KYBLACK) CARTRIDGE
ELEY LOADED
BLACK POWDER
MADE IN GREAT BRITAIN

DATA
Gauges; 12 & 16.
(12 illustrated).
Length; 64 mm.
Head; 8 mm.
Tube; Wound off-white paper.
Colour; E-K I.C.I. light brown.
Printings; Black.
Base; Brass.
Closure; Rolled turn-over.
Wad; White card, print black.
Business; Ammunition manufacturers.

© DN.2-0396. Re-drawn 7th Jan 1999

IMPERIAL CHEMICAL INDUSTRIES, METALS DIV, SPORTING AMMUNITION DEPT, ELEY-KYNOCH, LTD: Works; Witton, Birmingham 6, England. Head Office; Imperial Chemical House, Millbank, London S.W.1, England.

ELEY UNIVERSAL CARTRIDGE
ELEY LOADED
BLACK POWDER
Made in Great Britain

65 mm / 2.1/2"
8 mm
5/16"
Wound paper
Brass

ELEY UNIVERSAL CARTRIDGE
Eley's Universal was a cartridge for those people who still used guns which were only proofed for black powders. Its tube was wound from what Eleys' called light brown paper. This was more of a dead grass colour. The case wall printing was in black. The top wad shown was cut from white card and was printed in black. Note the black powder marks below the 12's on the headstamping.

© DN.3-2691. Drawn, 21/2/08.

IMPERIAL CHEMICAL INDUSTRIES, LTD. SPORTING AMMUNITION DEPARTMENT:
Works; Witton, Birmingham 6, England.
Head Office; Imperial Chemical House, Millbank, London S.W.1., England.

The case was not examined for internal metals. May have been produced for an overseas market.

ELEY UNLINED NITRO LOADED WITH CURTISS & HARVEY'S SMOKELESS DIAMOND POWDER
MADE IN GREAT BRITAIN

DATA
Gauge; 12
Length; 64 mm.
Head; 8 mm.
Tube; Wound middle blue paper.
Colour; Middle blue.
Print; Black.
Wetproof; Lacquered.
Base; Brass.
Closure; Rolled turn-over.
Wad; Brown card, print black.
Business; Ammunition manufacturers.

© DN.2-1393. Re-drawn; 19th Jan 2002

IMPERIAL CHEMICAL INDUSTRIES LTD. SPORTING AMMUNITION DEPT.
Works, Witton, Birmingham 6, Warwickshire (West Midlands), England.

ELEY Velocity CARTRIDGE
WATER RESISTING
METAL LINED
ELEY LOADED
Made in Great Britain

Height of internal steel liner

DATA
Gauge; 12.
Length; 64 mm.
Head; 16 mm.
Tubes Wound coloured papers.
Colours; Brown or Eley's brick red.
Base; Reinforced brass.
Closure; Rolled turn-over.
Wad shown; Blue-grey, print black.
Wetproof; Lacquered.
Business; Ammo manufacturers.
Circa; 1930's.

© DN.2-0725. Re-drawn; 16th March 2001

IMPERIAL CHEMICAL INDUSTRIES, LTD. SPORTING AMMUNITION DEPARTMENT: Works; Witton, Birmingham 6, Warwickshire (West Midlands). Head Office; Imperial Chemical House, Millbank, London S.W.1., England.

64 mm

ELEY WESTMINSTER CARTRIDGE
ELEY LOADED
SCHULTZE POWDER
MADE IN GREAT BRITAIN

Height of internal ferrous metal.
16 mm

ELEY WESTMINSTER CARTRIDGE.
12 Gauge illustrated.

Produced in gauges 12 and 16. The 12 gauge were first marketed with wound dark green paper tubes with black or navy blue printings. Later, circa 1939 used spring green paper with black printing. The 16 gauge used dark blue paper with black or navy blue printings. The wad shown was of brown card printed in black.

© DN.3-0639. Revised: 20/12/08.

IMPERIAL CHEMICAL INDUSTRIES, LTD. SPORTING AMMUNITION
Works, Witton, Birmingham 6, England. DEPARTMENT:
Head Office, Imperial Chemical House, Millbank, London S.W.1., England.

ELEY SPECIAL WILDFOWLING CARTRIDGE
ELEY MADE AND LOADED
MADE IN GREAT BRITAIN

DATA
Gauge; 12.
Length; 64 mm.
Head; 8 mm.
Tube; Wound red paper.
Colour; Crimson red.
Print; Black.
Base; Reinforced brass.
Closure; Rolled turn-over.
Wad; Dark orange, print black.
Business; Ammunition manufacturers.
Circa; 1935-1939.

© DN.2-0999. Re-drawn; 13th Nov 2000

PLATE 190 [ICI - ICI]

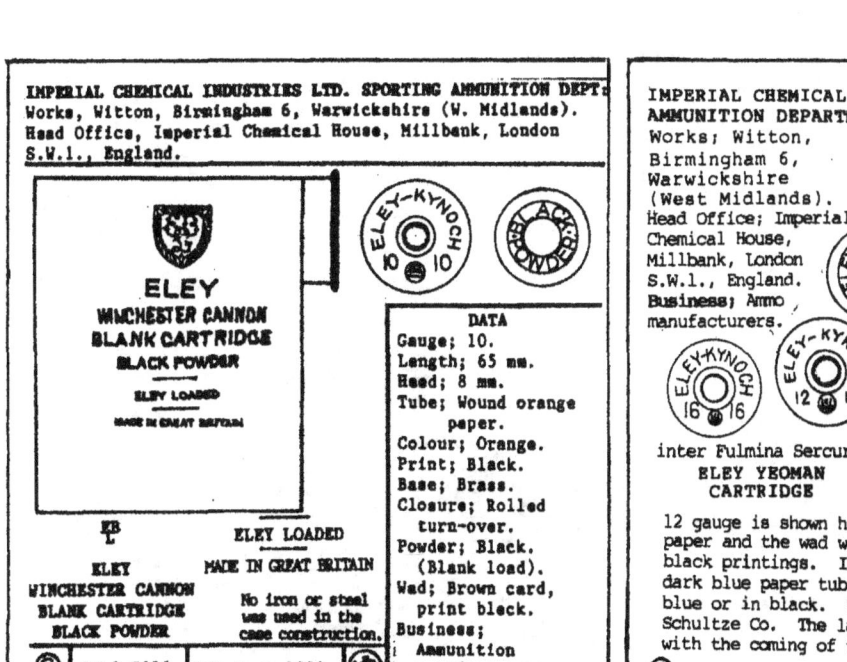
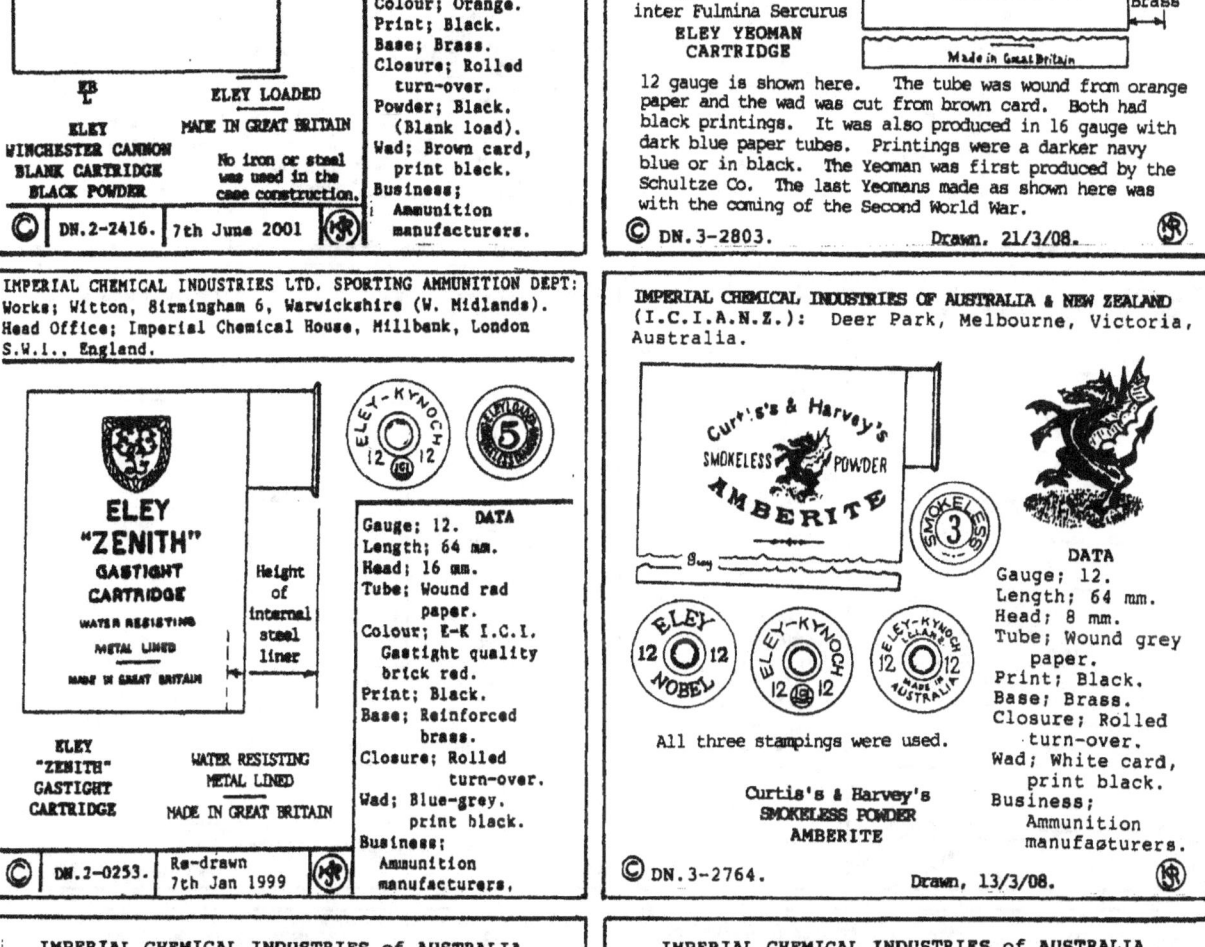
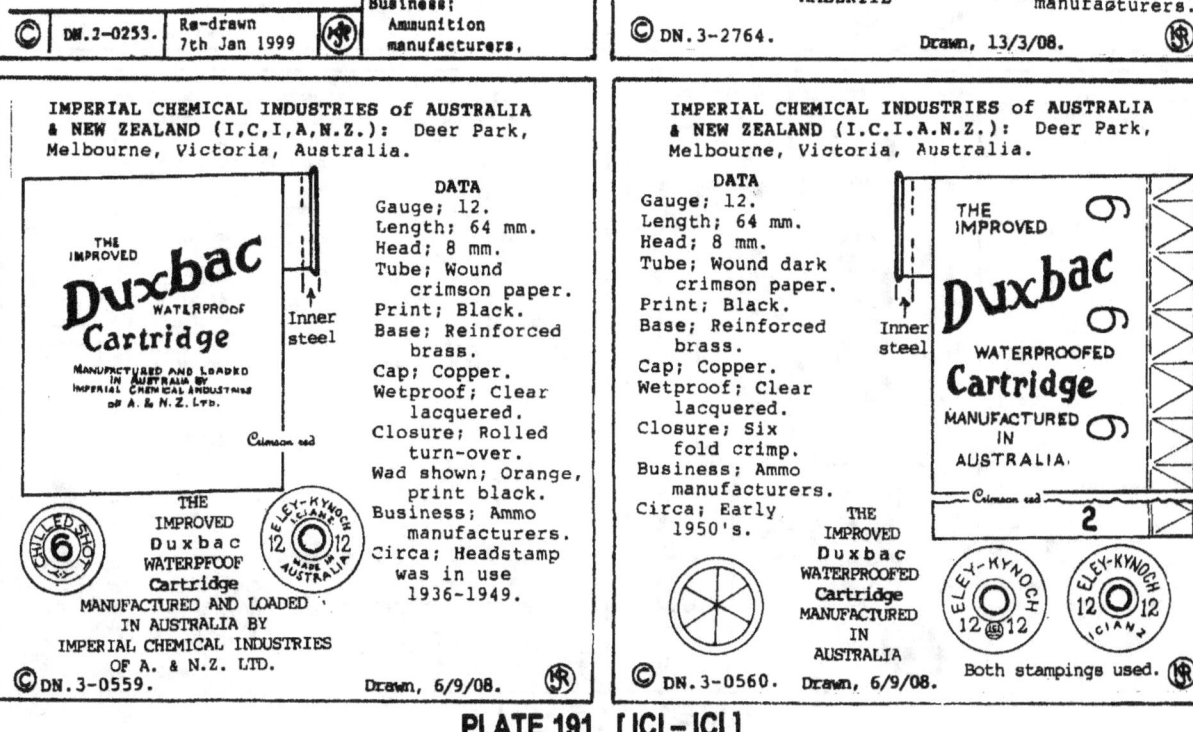

PLATE 191 [ICI – ICI]

IMPERIAL CHEMICAL INDUSTRIES of AUSTRALIA & NEW ZEALAND (I.C.I.A.N.Z.): Deer Park, Melbourne, Victoria, Australia.

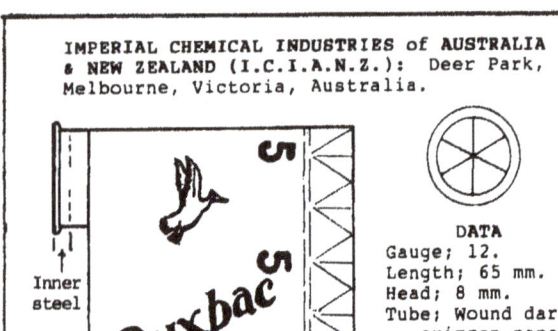

DATA
Gauge; 12.
Length; 65 mm.
Head; 8 mm.
Tube; Wound dark crimson paper.
Print; Black.
Base; Reinforced brass.
Cap; Copper.
Closure; Six fold crimp.
Wetproofed; Clear lacquered.
Business; Ammunition manufacturers.

Duxbac WATERPROOFED Cartridge

© DN.3-2824.   Drawn, 4/9/08.

IMPERIAL CHEMICAL INDUSTRIES OF AUSTRALIA & NEW ZEALAND (I.C.I.A.N.Z.): Deer Park, Melbourne, Victoria, Australia.

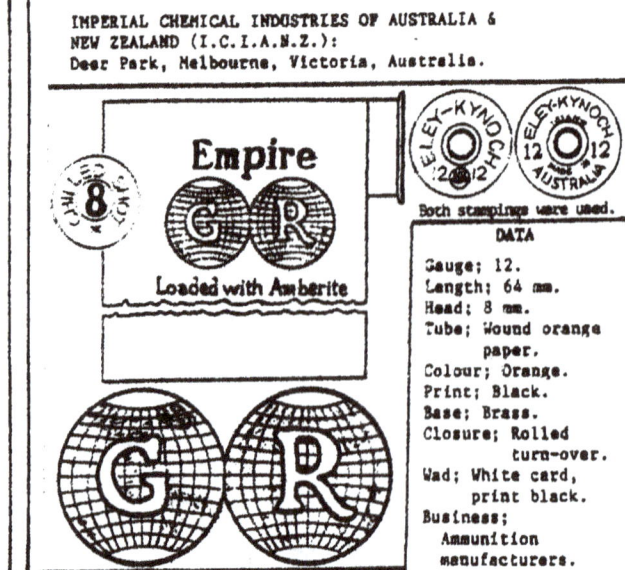

Both stampings were used.

DATA
Gauge; 12.
Length; 64 mm.
Head; 8 mm.
Tube; Wound orange paper.
Colour; Orange.
Print; Black.
Base; Brass.
Closure; Rolled turn-over.
Wad; White card, print black.
Business; Ammunition manufacturers.

© DN.2-1458. Re-drawn 6th Jan 1999

IMPERIAL CHEMICAL INDUSTRIES OF AUSTRALIA & NEW-ZEALAND (I.C.I.A.N.Z): Deer Park, Melbourne, Victoria, Australia.

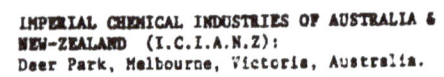

EMPRESS
Made & Loaded in Great Britain

I saw this cartridge when I visited Australia during 1985. As it states that it was made and loaded in Great Britain, I take it to have been loaded for the Australian market and to have been marketed by I.C.I.A.N.Z. It was not listed in Eley-Kynoch ammunition catalogues for Great Britain.

DATA
Gauge; 12.
Length; 64 mm.
Head; 8 mm.
Tube; Wound grey paper.
Colour; Grey.
Print; Black.
Base; Brass.
Closure; Rolled turn-over.
Wad; Not known.
Business; Ammunition manufacturers.

© DN.2-1466. Re-drawn; 6th Oct 2000

IMPERIAL CHEMICAL INDUSTRIES OF AUSTRALIA & NEW-ZEALAND (I.C.I.A.N.Z.): Deer Park, Melbourne, Victoria, Australia.
Business. Ammunition manufacturers.

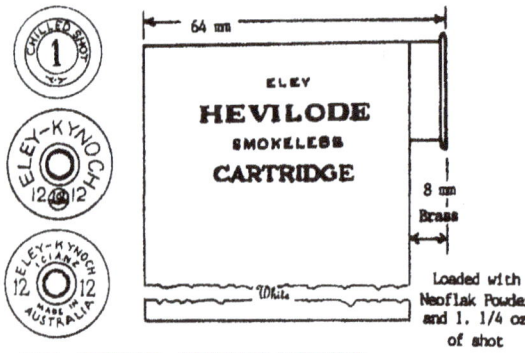

Loaded with Neoflak Powder and 1. 1/4 oz of shot

ELEY HEVILODE SMOKELESS CARTRIDGE
This cartridge had an unlined case with its tube wound from an off-white creamed coloured paper. The case wall printing was black. The top wad was cut from white card and printed in black. Both headstamps shown here have been used.

© DN.3-1743.   Revised; 3/1/09.

IMPERIAL CHEMICAL INDUSTRIES OF AUSTRALIA & NEW-ZEALAND. (I.C.I.A.N.Z.):

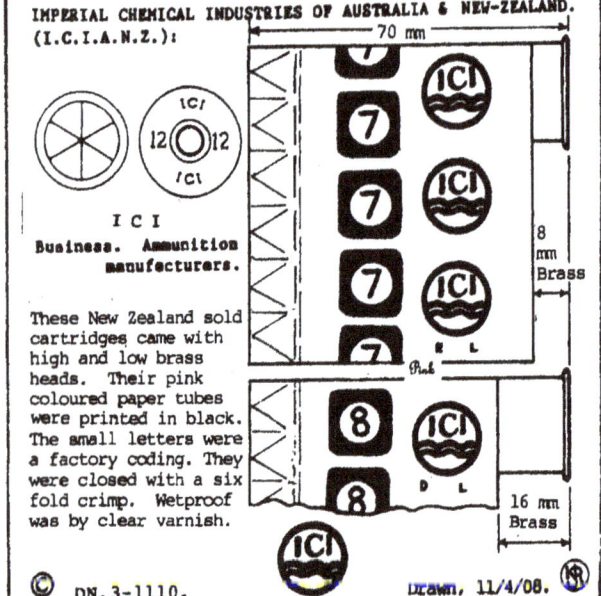

I C I
Business. Ammunition manufacturers.

These New Zealand sold cartridges came with high and low brass heads. Their pink coloured paper tubes were printed in black. The small letters were a factory coding. They were closed with a six fold crimp. Wetproof was by clear varnish.

© DN.3-1110.   Drawn, 11/4/08.

IMPERIAL CHEMICAL INDUSTRIES of AUSTRALIA & NEW ZEALAND (I.C.I.A.N.Z.): Deer Park, Melbourne, Victoria, Australia.
Business, Ammunition manufacturers.

DATA
Gauge; 12.
Length; 70 mm.
Head; 16 mm.
Tube; Wound crimson red paper.
Print; Black.
Wad shown; Orange, print black.
Cap; Copper.
Circa; Late 1930's.

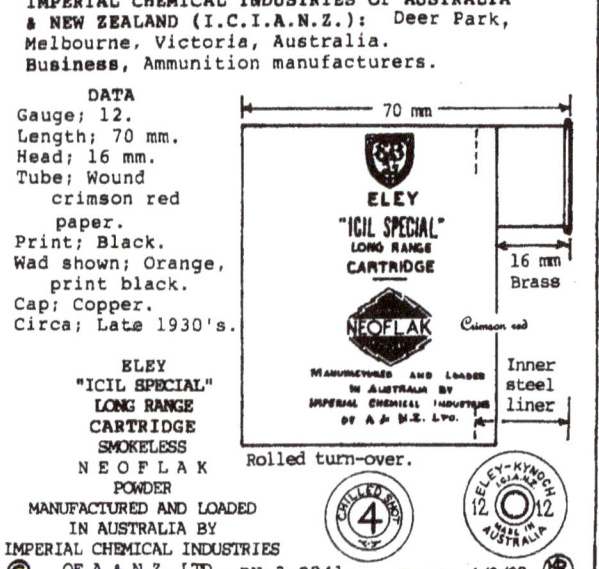

ELEY "ICIL SPECIAL" LONG RANGE CARTRIDGE SMOKELESS NEOFLAK POWDER MANUFACTURED AND LOADED IN AUSTRALIA BY IMPERIAL CHEMICAL INDUSTRIES OF A & N.Z. LTD.

© DN.3-2841.   Drawn, 4/9/08.

PLATE 192 [ICI – ICI]

IMPERIAL CHEMICAL INDUSTRIES OF AUSTRALIA &
NEW ZEALAND (I.C.I.A.N.Z.): Deer Park,
Melbourne, Victoria, Australia.
Business; Ammunition manufacturers.

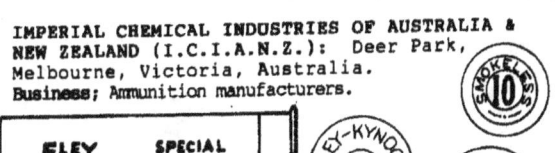

DATA
Gauge; 12.
Length; 64 mm.
Head; 8 mm.
Tube; Wound orange paper.
Print; Black.
Base; Brass.
Cap; Copper.
Closure; Rolled turn-over.
Wad; Orange, print black.
Business; Ammunition manufacturers.

ELEY SPECIAL QUAIL. Loaded in shot sizes 8, 10 and 12 only. Not all of them carried the wording, MANUFACTURED AND LOADED IN AUSTRALIA BY IMPERIAL CHEMICAL INDUSTRIES OF A. & N.Z. LTD.
Not examined for internal metals.
© DN.3-0555. Drawn, 25/3/08.

IMPERIAL CHEMICAL INDUSTRIES OF AUSTRALIA
& NEW-ZEALAND (I.C.I.A.N.Z.), LTD:
Deer Park, Melbourne, Victoria, Australia.

DATA
Gauge; 12.
Lengths; 64 mm.
Heads; 8 mm.
Tubes; Wound coloured papers.
Colours; Grey, orange or red.
Printings; Black.
Bases; Reinforced brass.
Closures; Rolled turn-overs.
Wad shown; White card, print black.
Business; Ammo manufacturers.
Circa; 1939.

ELEY REX CARTRIDGE MANUFACTURED AND LOADED IN AUSTRALIA BY IMPERIAL CHEMICAL INDUSTRIES OF A. & N.Z. LTD.

© DN.2-0548. Re-drawn; 23rd Feb 2001

IMPERIAL CHEMICAL INDUSTRIES OF
AUSTRALIA & NEW ZEALAND LIMITED:
Deer Park, Melbourne, Victoria, Australia.

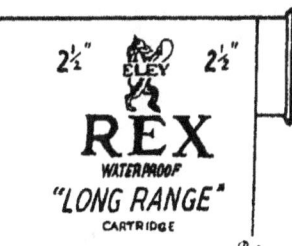

DATA
Gauge; 12.
Length; 64 mm.
Head; 8 mm.
Tube; Wound crimson red paper.
Colour; Crimson red.
Print; Black.
Wetproof; Lacquered.
Base; Brass.
Closure; Rolled turn-over.
Wad; White card, print black.
Circa; Between 1936 - 1949.
Business; Ammo manufacturers.

ELEY REX WATERPROOF "LONG RANGE" CARTRIDGE

© DN.3-1893. Revised; 17/12/08.

IMPERIAL CHEMICAL INDUSTRIES OF AUSTRALIA &
NEW-ZEALAND (I.C.I.A.N.Z.):
Deer Park, Melbourne, Victoria, Australia.

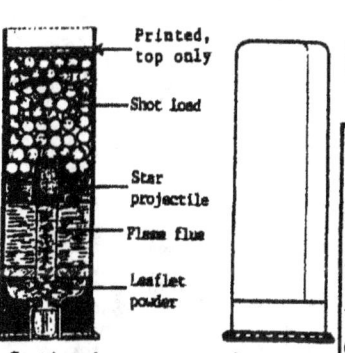

DATA
Gauge; 12.
Length; 63 mm.
Head; 8 mm.
Tube; Wound blue paper.
Colour; Greyish blue.
Print; Nil.
Base; Reinforced brass.
Closure; Rolled turn-over.
Wads; White or grey cards, print black.
Business; Ammunition manufacturers.
Circa; Late 1930's.

ELEY ROCKET CARTRIDGE
SHOWS THE FLIGHT OF THE SHOT

© DN.2-0632. Re-drawn; 28th Aug 2000.

IMPERIAL CHEMICAL INDUSTRIES OF AUSTRALIA &
NEW ZEALAND (I.C.I.A.N.Z.): Deer Park,
Melbourne, Victoria, Australia.   Drawn, 25/3/08.
Business; Ammunition manufacturers.

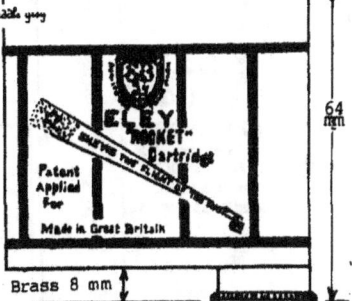

ELEY "ROCKET" Cartridge (* SHEWS THE FLIGHT OF THE SHOT). The cartridge case was made in England. It is not known if it was loaded in England or in Australia. It is known that it was sold on the New Zealand market. The base was brass and the tube was wound from grey paper and was printed with dark blue ink. The wad was a light grey and printed in black. A tracer pellet accompanied the shot string. A possibility, May have been imported
© DN.3-1104. by the Colonial Cartridge Co.

IMPERIAL CHEMICAL INDUSTRIES OF AUSTRALIA &
NEW-ZEALAND, LTD. (I.C.I.A.N.Z.):
Deer Park, Melbourne, Victoria, Australia.

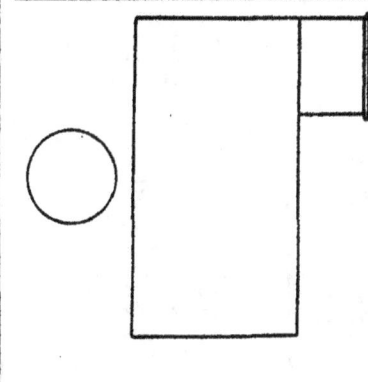

DATA
Gauge; 12.
Length; 52 mm.
Head; 16 mm.
Tube; Wound Eley's brick red paper.
Printing; nil.
Base; reinforced brass.
Closure; rolled turn-over.
Wad; White card, no printing.
Business; Ammunition manufacturers.
Circa; 1949 - 1956.

NOBEL SCAREBIRD CARTRIDGES

© DN.2-1129. Re-drawn; 1st Jan 2001

PLATE 193 [ICI – ICI]

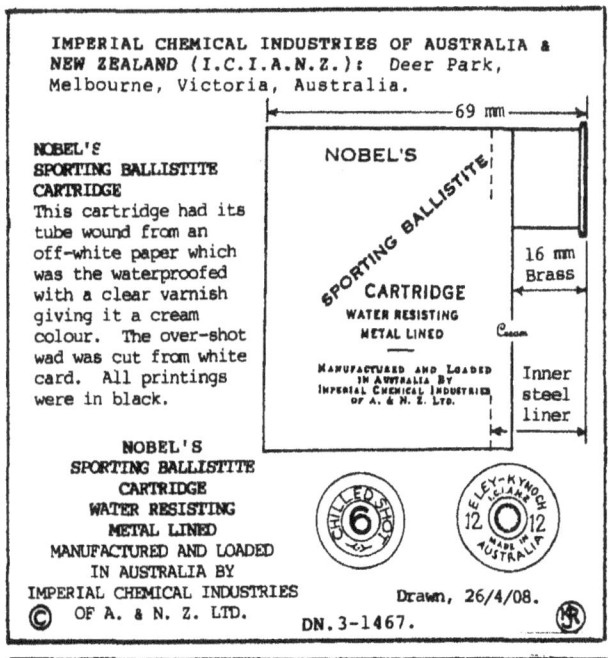
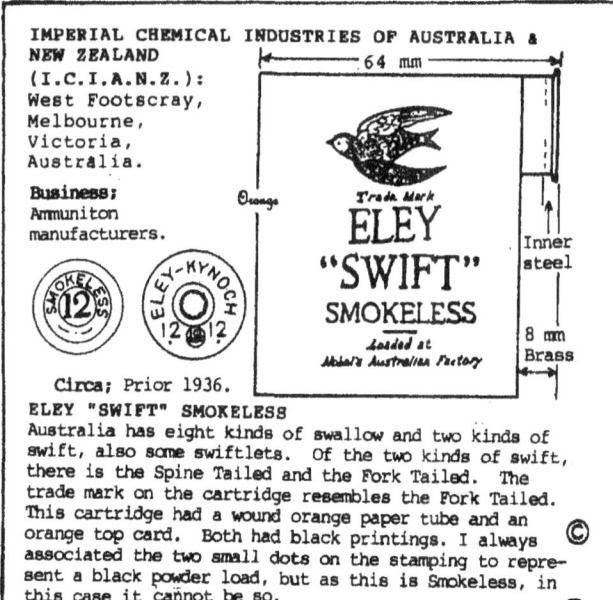
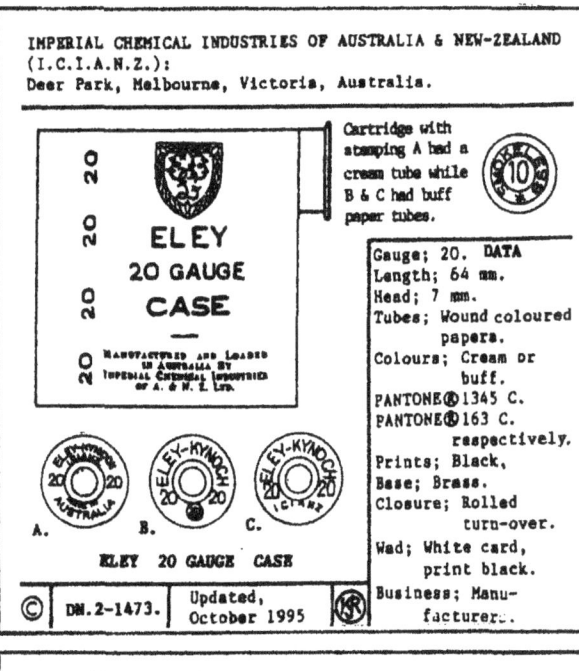
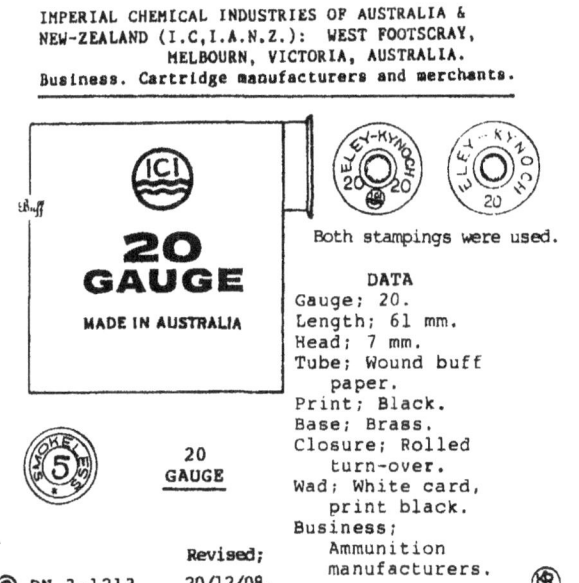
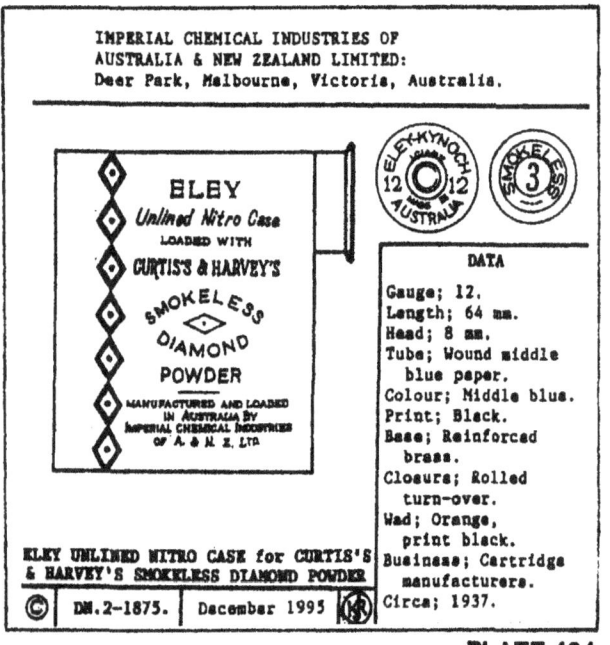
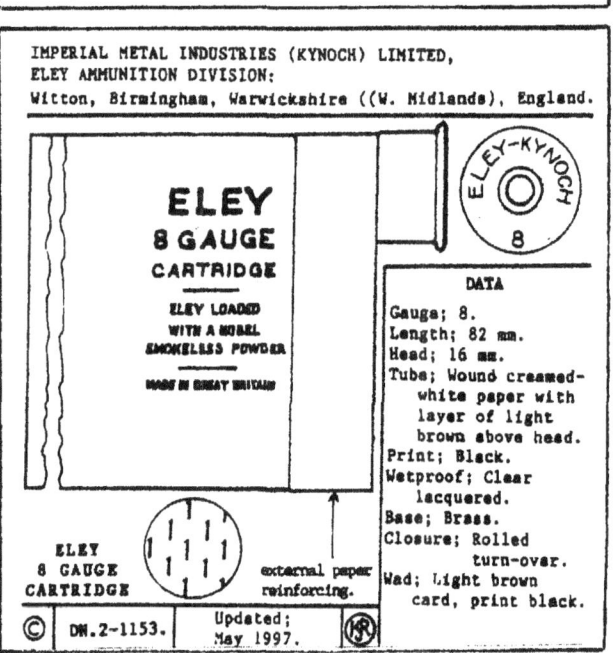

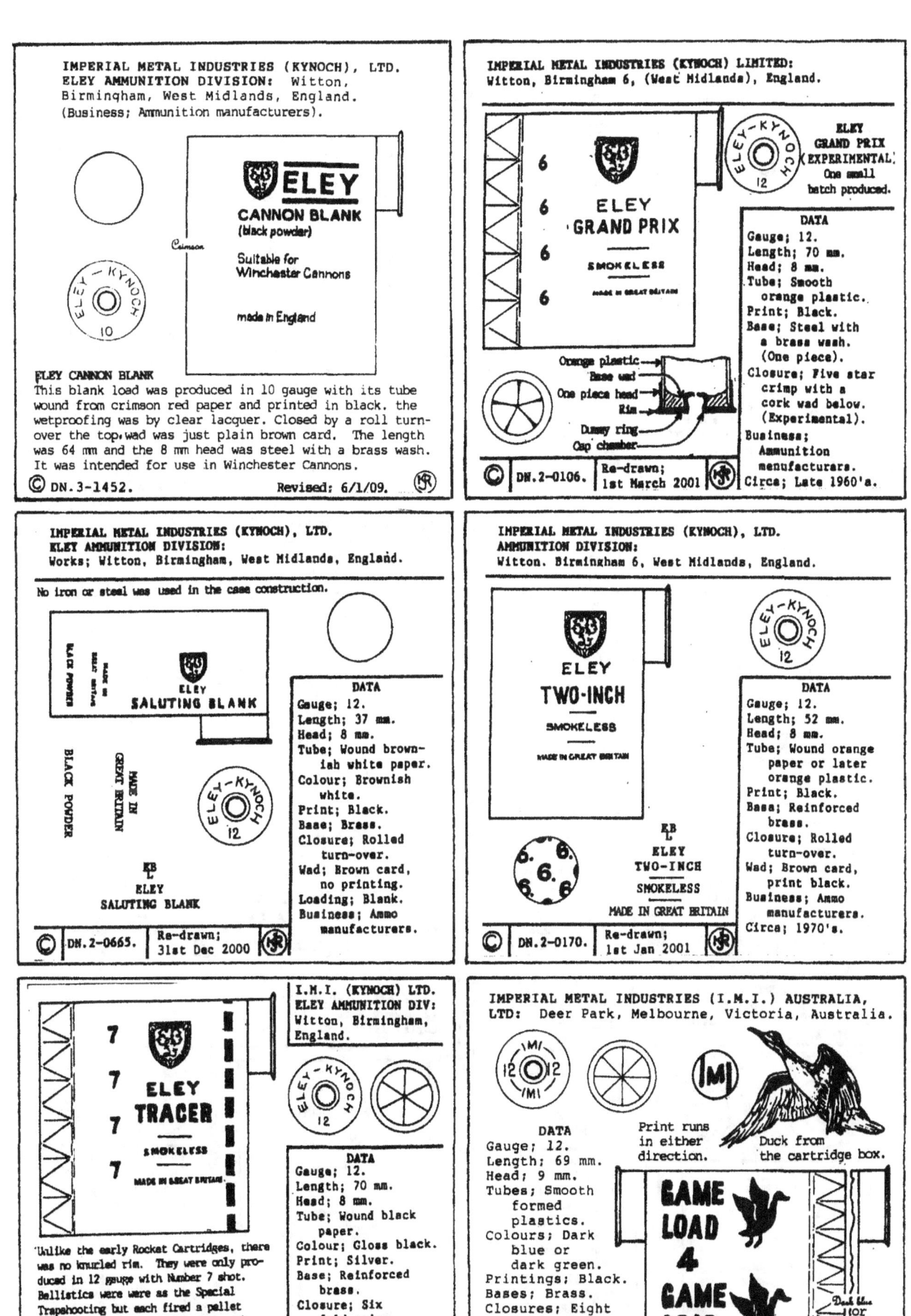

PLATE 195 [IMI – IMI]

IRISH METAL INDUSTRIES LIMITED:
12 Dawson Street, Dublin, Republic of Ireland. Also at, Earles Island, Galway, Republic of Ireland.

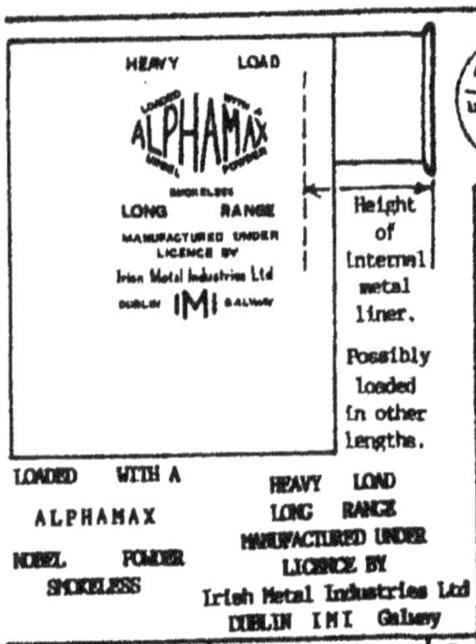

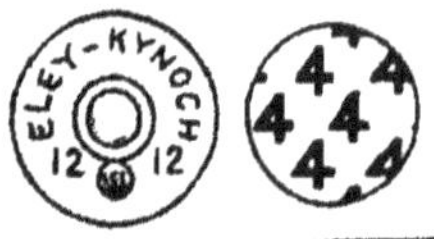

DATA
Gauge; 12.
Length; 69.5 mm.
Head; 16 mm.
Tube; Wound crimson red paper.
PANTONE® 187 C.
Print; Black.
Base; Brass with reinforcing.
Wetproof; Lacquered.
Closure; Rolled turn-over.
Wad; Brown card, print black.
Circa; 1950's.
Business; Ammo manufacturers.

© | DN.2-1906. | March 1996

IRISH METAL INDUSTRIES LIMITED:
19 Dawson Street, Dublin, Republic of Ireland.

Believed to have been made for an overseas market, possibly Ireland. Automatically its name associates one with black powder, but smokeless was used. Most likely, Smokeless Diamond.

BLACKTHORN CARTRIDGE

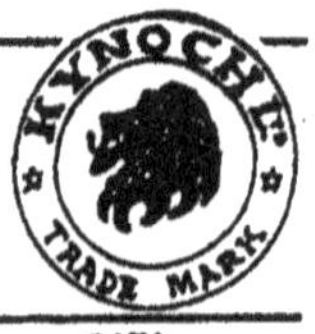

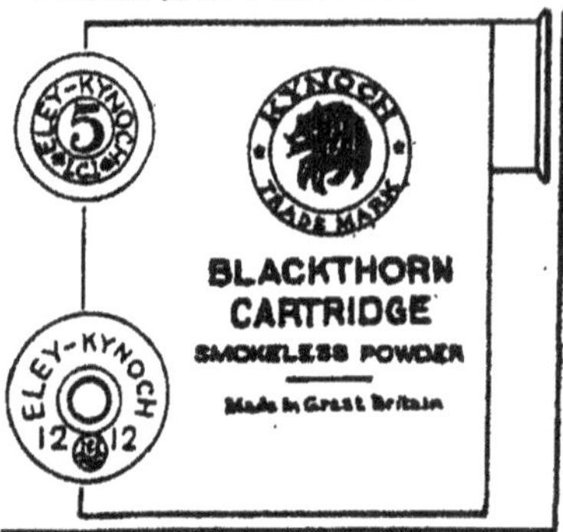

DATA
Gauge; 12.
Length; 64 mm.
Head; 8 mm.
Tube; Wound paper eau-de-nil.
Colour; Eley's eau-de-nil.
Print; Navy blue.
Base; Reinforced brass.
Closure; Rolled turn-over.
Wad; Brown card, print black.
Circa; 1930's.
Business; Ammunition makers. manufacturers.

© | DN.2-1657. | Updated, February 1996

IRISH METAL INDUSTRIES LIMITED:
12 Dawson Street, Dublin, Republic of Ireland. Also at, Earles Island, Galway, Republic of Ireland.

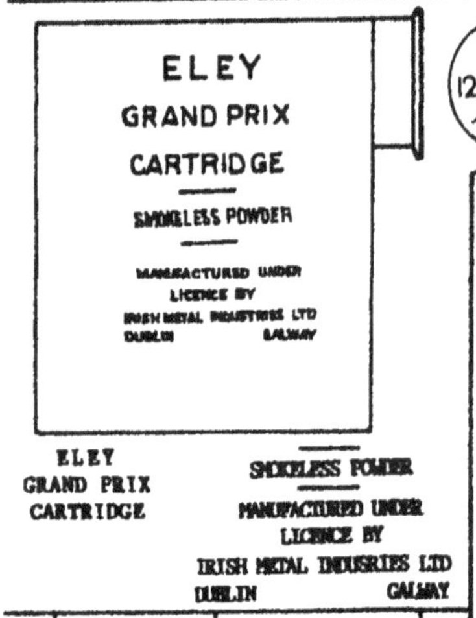

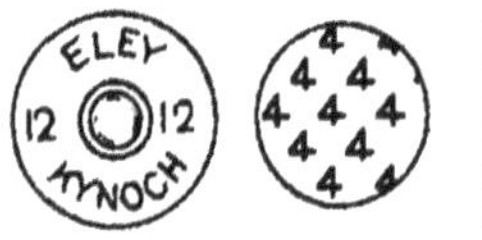

DATA
Gauge; 12.
Length; 64 mm.
Head; 8 mm.
Tube; Wound dark orange paper.
PANTONE® 180 C.
Print; Black.
Base; Brass with reinforcing.
Wetproof; Clear lacquered.
Closure; Rolled turn-over.
Wad; Brown card, print black.
Business; Ammo manufacturers.

© | DN.2-1905. | March 1996

IRISH METAL INDUSTRIES, LTD:
12 Dawson Street, Dublin.
Also at, Earles Island, Galway, Republic of Ireland.

The example was not examined for internal metals.

ELEY
(Name in Gaelic)
CARTRIDGE
Eley Made and Loaded
Specially suitable for
WILDFOWLING
MADE IN GREAT BRITAIN

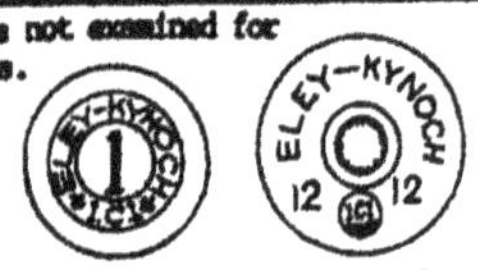

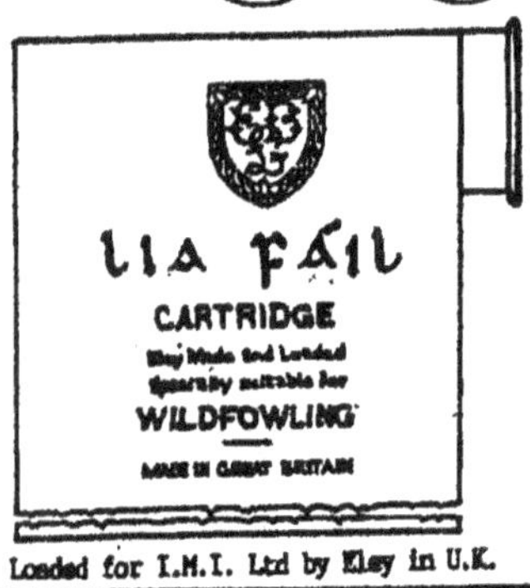

Loaded for I.M.I. Ltd by Eley in U.K.

DATA
Gauge; 12.
Length; 64 mm.
Head; 8 mm.
Tube; Wound orange paper.
Colour; Orange.
Print; Black.
Base; Brass.
Closure; Rolled turn-over.
Wad; Brown card, print black.
Wetproof; Lacquered.
Business; Ammunition manufacturers.

© | DN.2-2442. | 29th June 2001

IRISH METAL INDUSTRIES, LTD:
12 Dawson Street, Dublin.
Also at, Earles Island, Galway, Republic of Ireland.

The example was not examined for internal metals.

ELEY
(Name in Gaelic)
CARTRIDGE
Specially loaded for
WILDFOWLING
MANUFACTURED UNDER LICENCE
BY
IRISH METAL INDUSTRIES

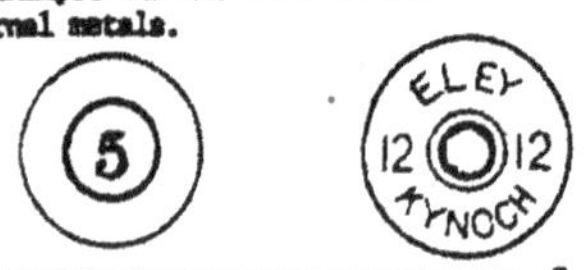

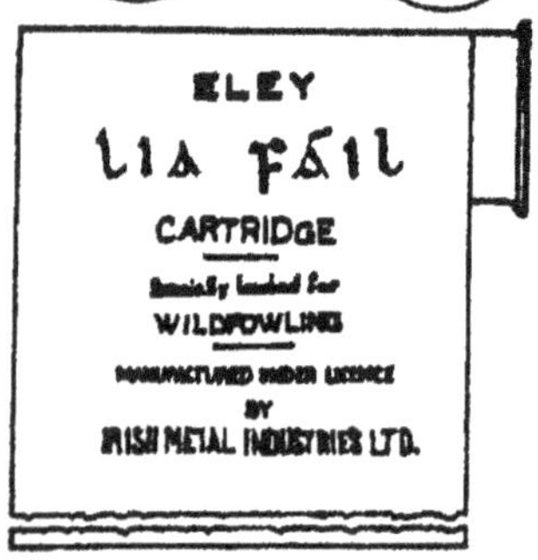

DATA
Gauge; 12.
Length; 64 mm.
Head; 8 mm.
Tube; Wound grey-green paper.
Colour; Greyish-green.
Print; Black.
Base; Brass.
Closure; Rolled turn-over.
Wad; Crimson, print black.
Business; Ammunition manufacturers.

© | DN.2-2441. | 29th June 2001

IRISH METAL INDUSTRIES LIMITED:
12 Dawson Street, Dublin, Republic of Ireland. Also at, Earles Island, Galway, Republic of Ireland.

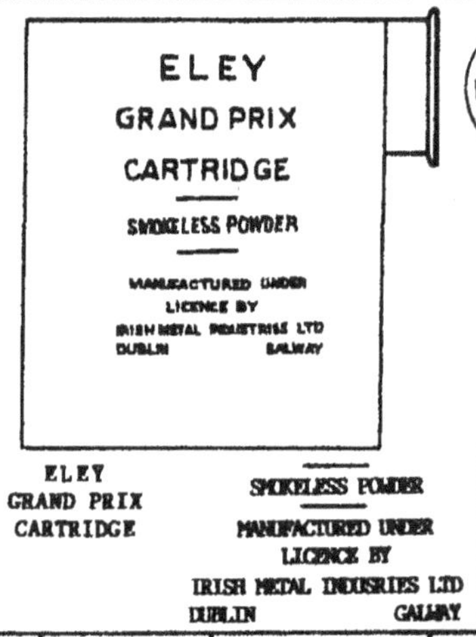

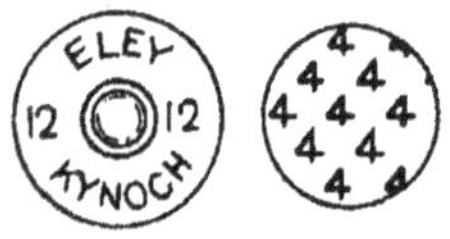

DATA
Gauge; 12.
Length; 64 mm.
Head; 8 mm.
Tube; Wound dark orange paper.
PANTONE® 180 C.
Print; Black.
Base; Brass with reinforcing.
Wetproof; Clear lacquered.
Closure; Rolled turn-over.
Wad; Brown card, print black.
Business; Ammo manufacturers.

© | DN.2-1905. | March 1996

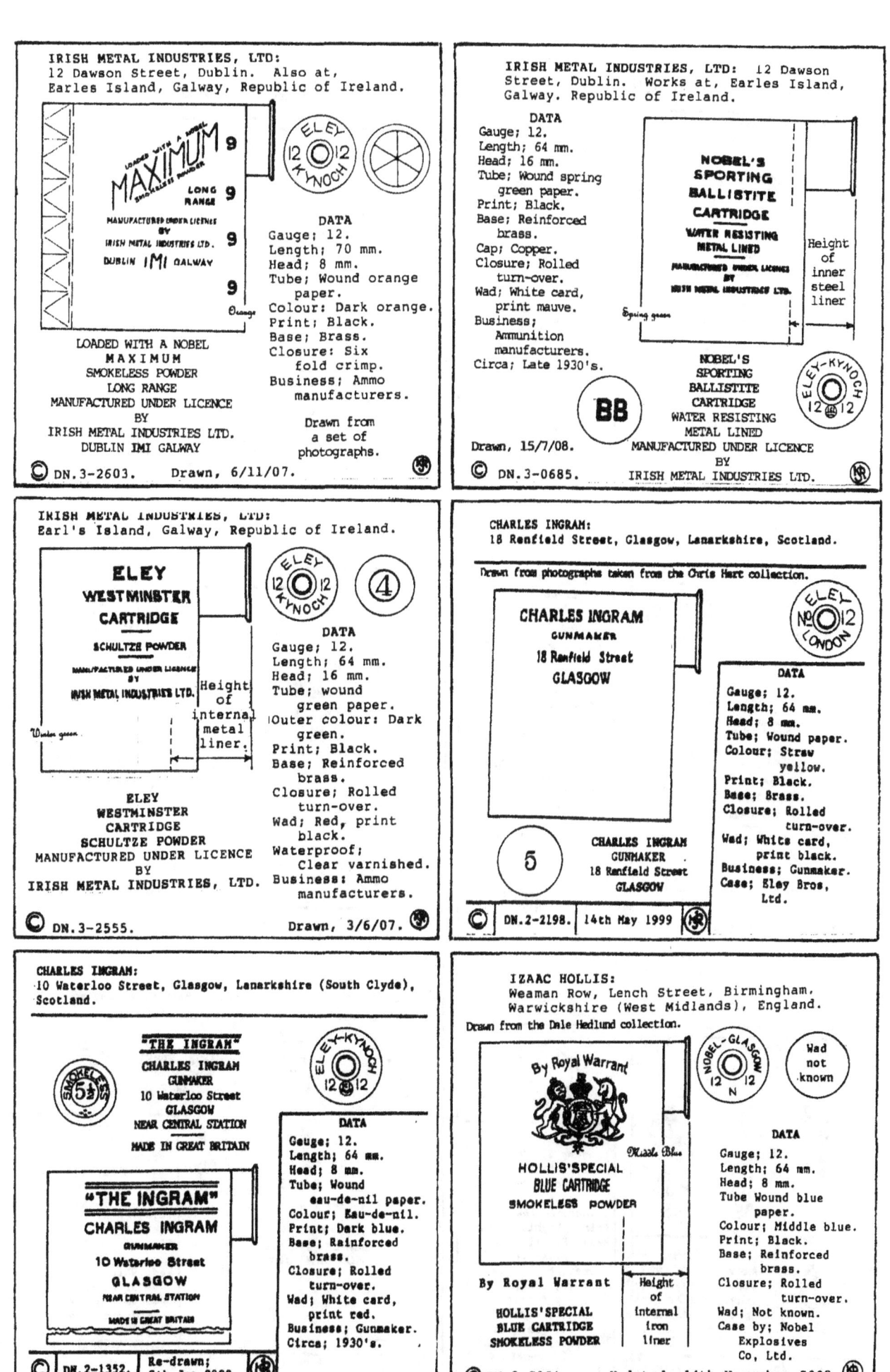

PLATE 197 [IMI - IZA]

JACKSON & SON:
Gainsborough, Lincolnshire, England.

THE PHEASANT LOADING
JACKSON & SON
GUNMAKERS   GAINSBOROUGH
                         LINCS.
Telephone No 101
Made in Great Britain

DATA
Gauge; 12.
Length; 64 mm.
Head; 8 mm.
Tube; Wound crimson paper.
Colour; Crimson.
Print; Black.
Base; Reinforced brass.
Closure; Rolled turn-over.
Wad; Yellow card, print black.
Business; Gunmakers.
Circa; 1930's.

DW.2-2281. 15th April 2000

JACKSON & SON:
Gainsborough, Lincolnshire, England.

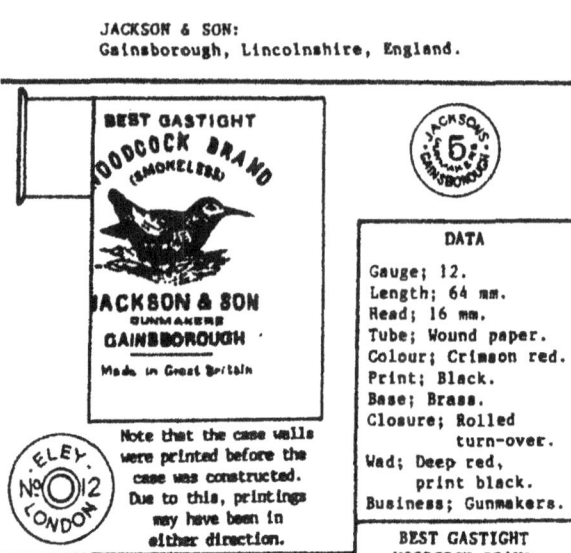

DATA
Gauge; 12.
Length; 64 mm.
Head; 16 mm.
Tube; Wound paper.
Colour; Crimson red.
Print; Black.
Base; Brass.
Closure; Rolled turn-over.
Wad; Deep red, print black.
Business; Gunmakers.

Note that the case walls were printed before the case was constructed. Due to this, printings may have been in either direction.

DW.2-1745. Updated; February 1995

BEST GASTIGHT
WOODCOCK BRAND
(SMOKELESS)

ALFRED JACKSON:
Abergavenny, Monmouthshire (Gwent), Wales.

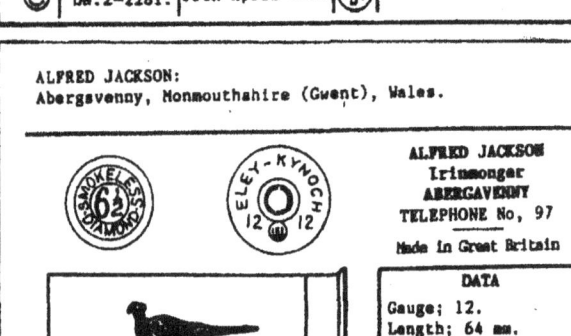

ALFRED JACKSON
Ironmonger
ABERGAVENNY
TELEPHONE No, 97
Made in Great Britain

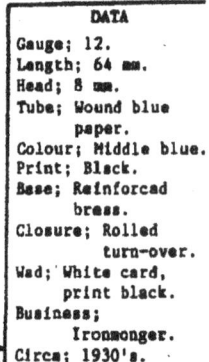

ALFRED JACKSON
Ironmonger
ABERGAVENNY
TELEPHONE No. 97
Made in Great Britain

DATA
Gauge; 12.
Length; 64 mm.
Head; 8 mm.
Tube; Wound blue paper.
Colour; Middle blue.
Print; Black.
Base; Reinforced brass.
Closure; Rolled turn-over.
Wad; White card, print black.
Business; Ironmonger.
Circa; 1930's.

DW.2-0894. Re-drawn 15th Feb 1999

WILLIAM JACKSON:
41 Silver Street, Gainsborough, Lincolnshire, England.

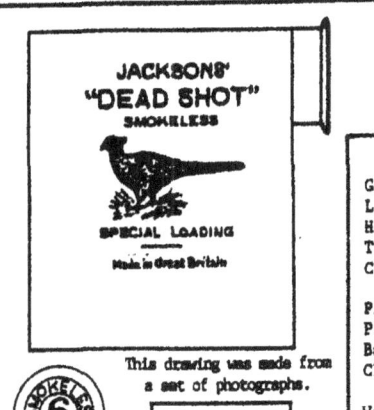
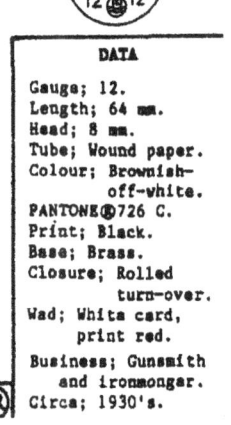

JACKSONS'
"DEAD SHOT"
SMOKELESS

SPECIAL LOADING
Made in Great Britain

This drawing was made from a set of photographs.

JACKSONS'
"DEAD SHOT"
SMOKELESS

DATA
Gauge; 12.
Length; 64 mm.
Head; 8 mm.
Tube; Wound paper.
Colour; Brownish-off-white.
PANTONE®726 C.
Print; Black.
Base; Brass.
Closure; Rolled turn-over.
Wad; White card, print red.
Business; Gunsmith and ironmonger.
Circa; 1930's.

DW.2-1842. September 1995

JAKTKLUBB:
Sweden.

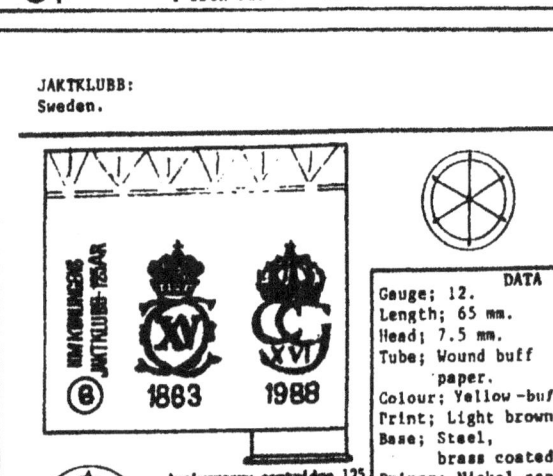

Anniversary cartridge 125 years of the field sports club. King Carl Gustav of Sweden club president.
HM KONUNGENS

DATA
Gauge; 12.
Length; 65 mm.
Head; 7.5 mm.
Tube; Wound buff paper.
Colour; Yellow-buff.
Print; Light brown.
Base; Steel, brass coated.
Primer; Nickel cap.
Closure; Crimp, 6 fold.
Wetproof; Clear lacquered.
Business; National sports club
Circa; 1988.

DW.2-1814. February 1995

JAMES & COMPANY:
Great Western Mills, Hungerford, Berkshire, England.

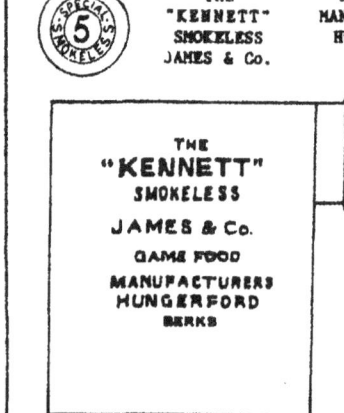
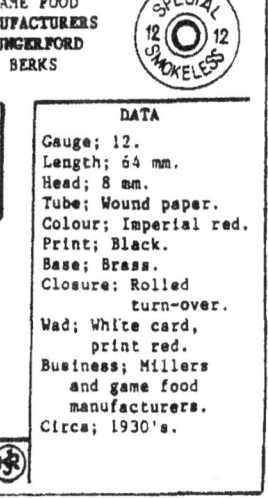

THE
"KENNETT"
SMOKELESS
JAMES & Co.
GAME FOOD
MANUFACTURERS
HUNGERFORD
BERKS

THE
"KENNETT"
SMOKELESS
JAMES & Co.
GAME FOOD
MANUFACTURERS
HUNGERFORD
BERKS

DATA
Gauge; 12.
Length; 64 mm.
Head; 8 mm.
Tube; Wound paper.
Colour; Imperial red.
Print; Black.
Base; Brass.
Closure; Rolled turn-over.
Wad; White card, print red.
Business; Millers and game food manufacturers.
Circa; 1930's.

DW.2-2243. Re-drawn 23rd Nov 1999

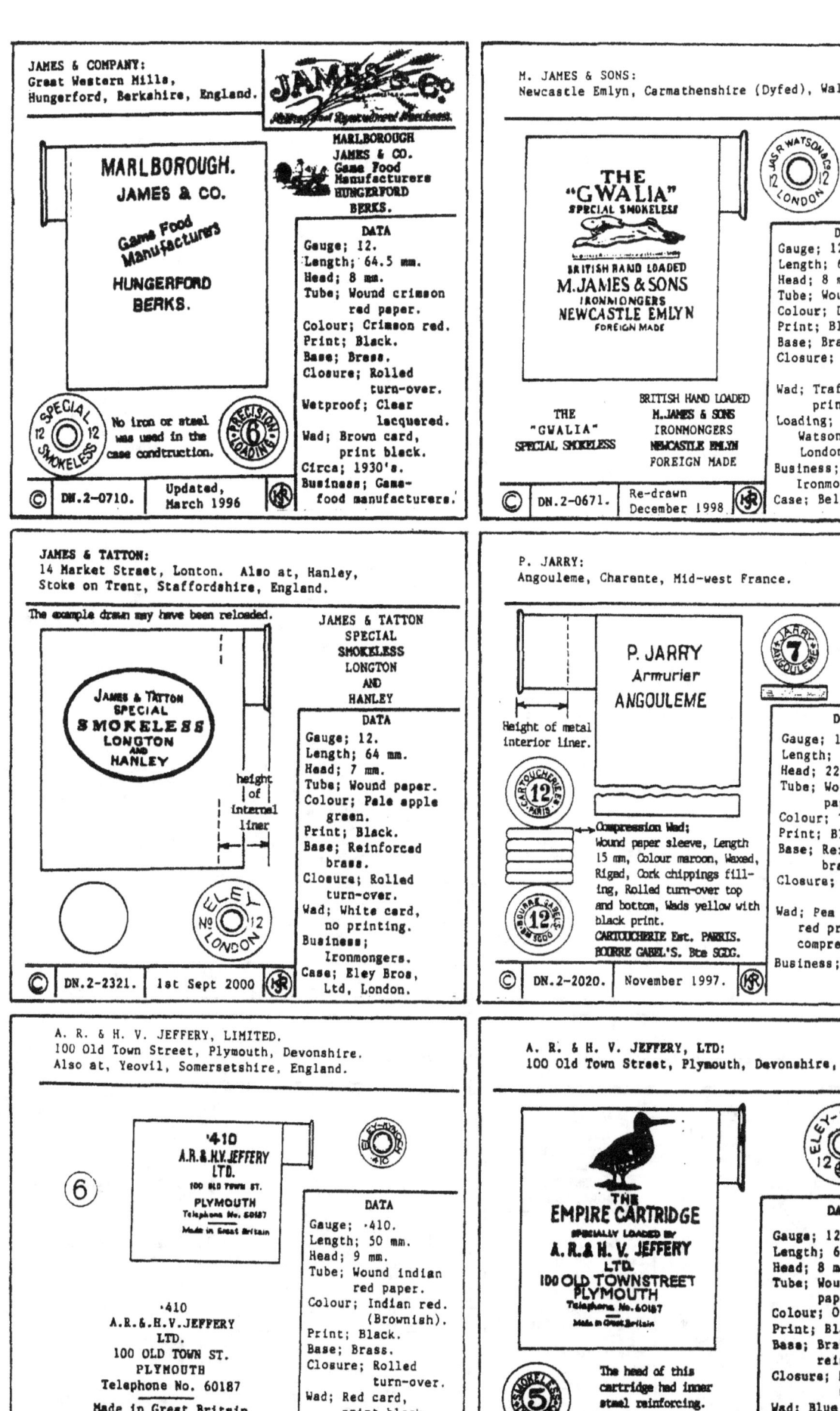

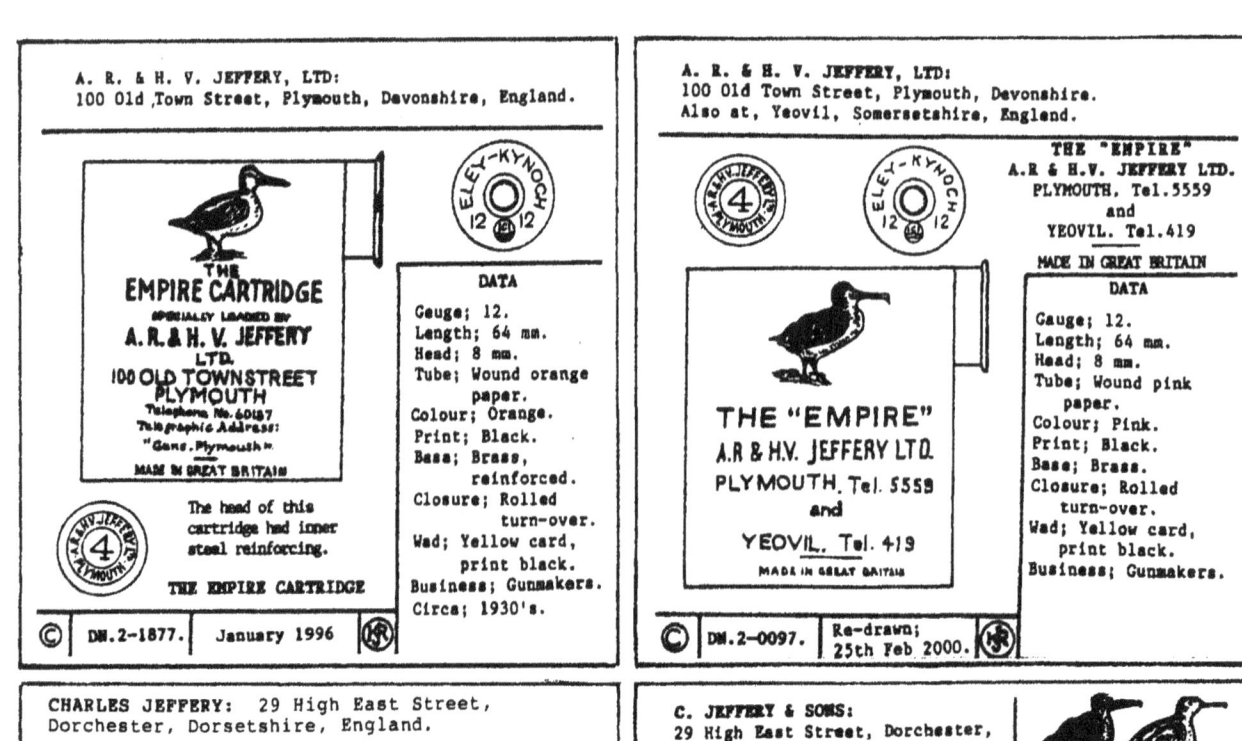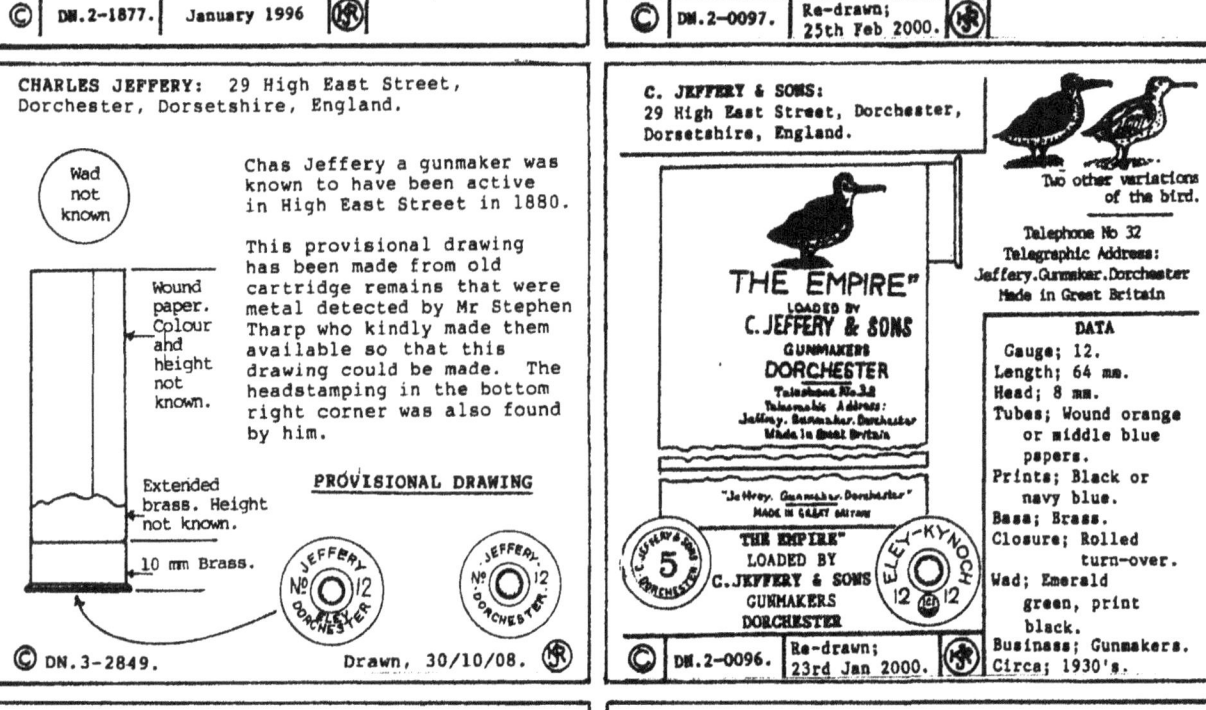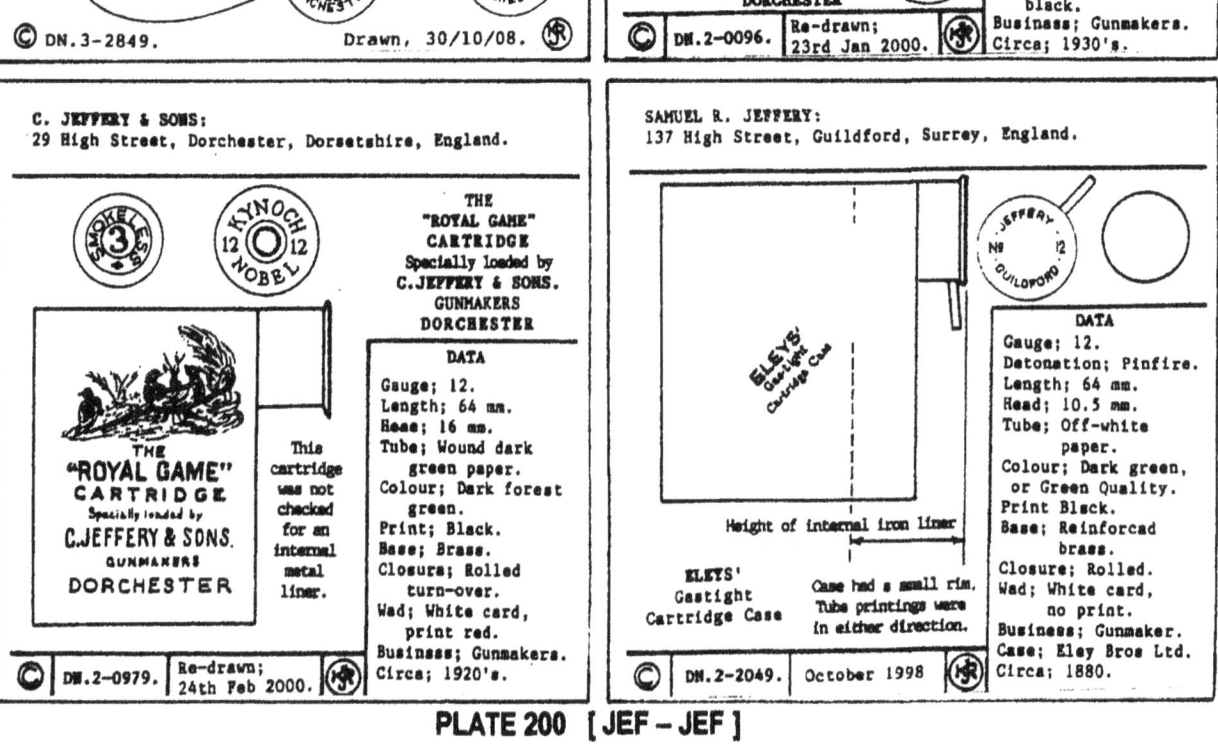

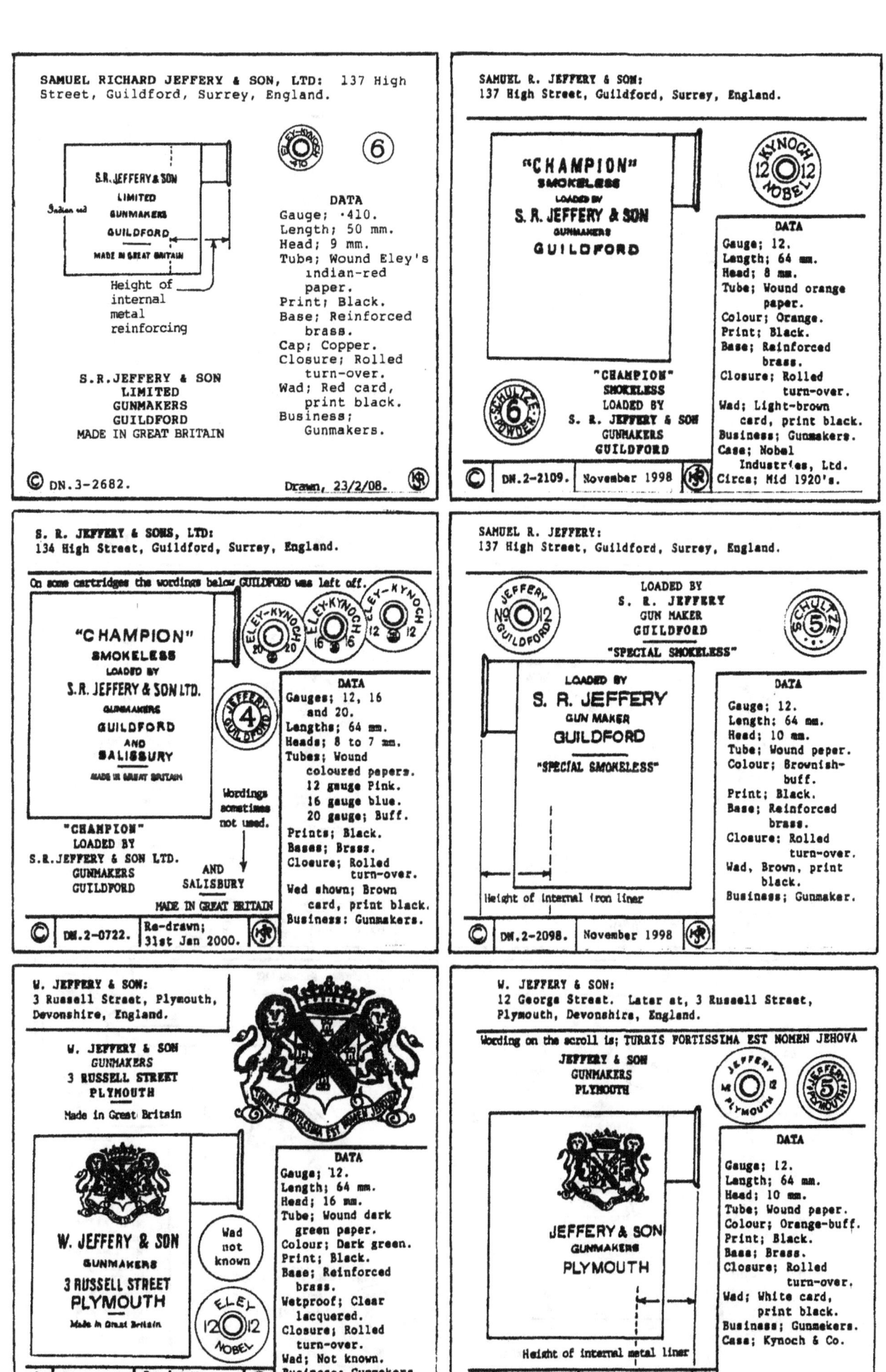

PLATE 201 [JEF - JEF]

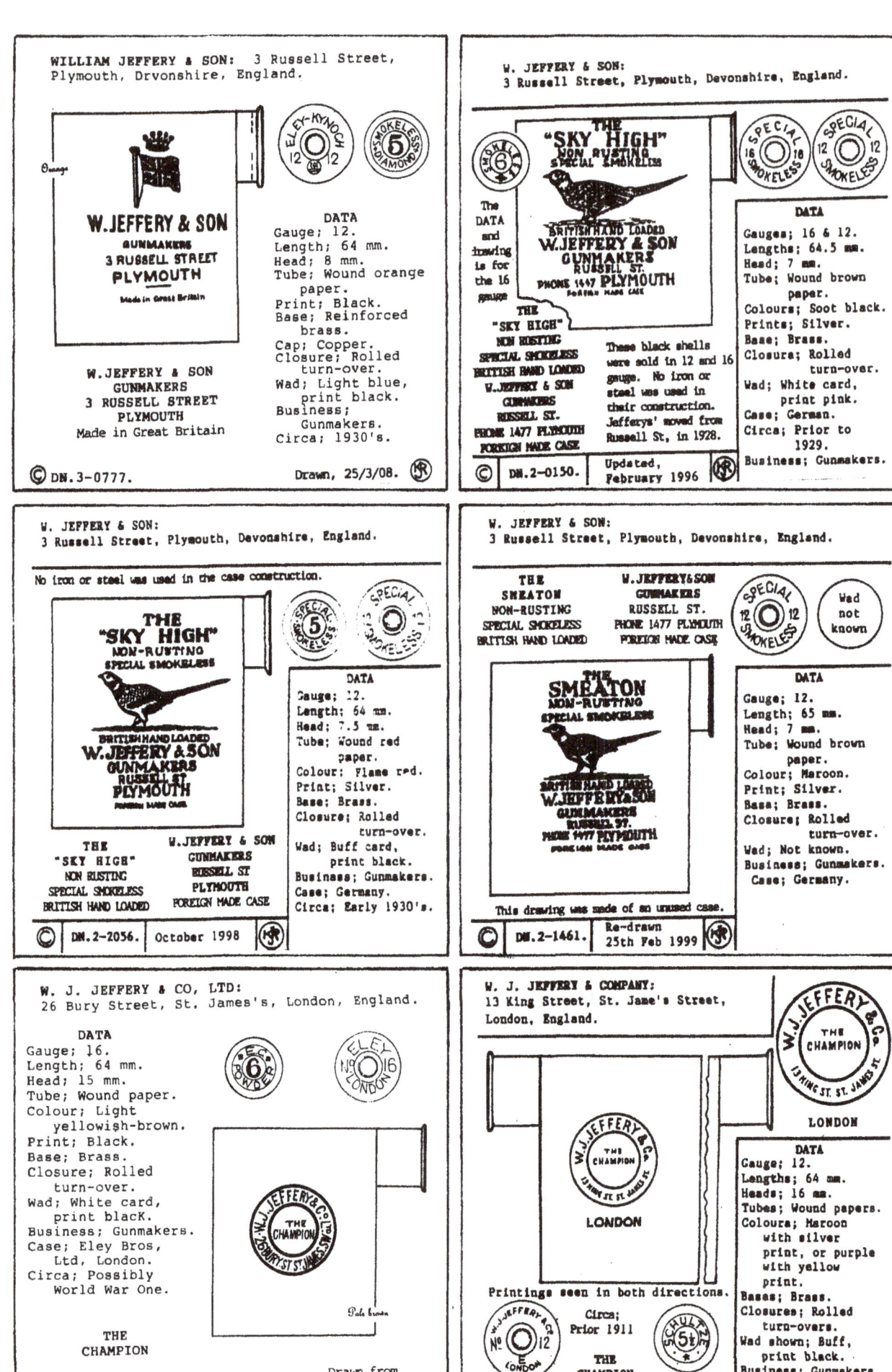

PLATE 202 [JEF–JEF]

W. J. JEFFERY & CO, LTD:
13 King Street, St. James's Street, London, England.

W.J.JEFFERY & CO.LTD.
THE
CHAMPION
13 KING ST. ST.JAMES ST.

DATA
Gauge; 12.
Length; 65 mm.
Head; 16 mm.
Tube; Wound purple paper.
Colour; Purple.
Print; Yellow.
Base; Brass.
Wetproof; Wax impregnated.
Closure; Rolled turn-over.
Wad; Scarlet red, print black.
Business; Gunmakers.
Case; Kynoch, Ltd.

DN.2-0227. Re-drawn; 18th Jan 2001

W. J. JEFFERY & CO, LTD: 9 Golden Square, Regent Street, London W.1., England.

DATA
Gauge; 12.
Length; 64 mm.
Head; 16 mm.
Tube; Wound Eley's brick red paper.
Print; Black.
Wetproof; Clear lacquered.
Base; Reinforced brass.
Cap; Copper.
Closure; Rolled turn-over.
Wad; Yellow, print black.
Business; Gunmakers.
Circa; 1930's.

WATER RESISTING
THE
CHAMPION
LONDON, W.1
MADE IN GREAT BRITAIN

DN.3-0228. Drawn, 6/7/08.

W. J. JEFFERY & CO, LTD:
26 Bury Street, St. James's,
London S.W., England.

W.J.JEFFERY & Co,LTD
THE
CLUB
26 BURY ST.ST.JAMES'S.S.W.
LONDON
Made in Great Britain

DATA
Gauge; 12.
Length; 64 mm.
Head; 8 mm.
Tube; Wound paper.
Colour; Straw yellow.
Print; Black.
Base; Brass.
Closure; Rolled turn-over.
Wad; Orange, print black.
Business; Gunmakers.
Case; Kynoch, of Witton.

Other London addresses of this firm were; 60 Queen Victoria Street, E.C. (Were known there in 1905); 13 King Street, St. James's. (known to have been in 1905-1911); 9 Golden Square, Regent Street, E.C.; Known to have been at 26 Bury Street in 1921.

DN.2-1199. Re-drawn 27th Jan 1999

W. J. JEFFERY & COMPANY:
26 Bury Street, St. James'. London S.W., England.

JEFFERY'S
"CLUB" SMOKELESS
26 Bury St. St James
London S.W.
Trade J Mark

DATA
Gauge; 12.
Length; 64 mm.
Head; 8 mm.
Tube; Wound paper.
Colour; Yellow.
Print; Black.
Base; Brass.
Closure; Rolled turn-over.
Wad; Scarlet red, print black.
Business; Gunmakers.
Case; Bavarian.

JEFFERY'S
"CLUB" SMOKELESS
26 Bury St. St James
London S.W.
Trade J Mark

This example was not examined internally.

DN.2-1202. Re-drawn; 6th Nov 2000

W. J. JEFFERY & CO, LTD:
9 Golden Square, Regent Street, London W.1., England.
(They were also in at least three other London addresses)

HIGH VELOCITY
"THE JEFFERY"
CARTRIDGE
9 Golden-Square
Regent Street
London W.1.

DATA
Gauge; 16.
Length; 64 mm.
Head; 15 mm.
Tube; Wound paper.
Colour; Crimson.
Print; Black.
Base; Reinforced brass.
Closure; Rolled turn-over.
Wad; White card, print rose-pink.
Business; Gunmakers.
Case; Foreign made.

HIGH VELOCITY
"THE JEFFERY"
CARTRIDGE
9 Golden - Square
Regent Street
London W.1.

DN.3-2092. Revised; 17/12/08.

W. J. JEFFERY & CO: 26 Bury Street, St.James's, London, England.

JEFFERY'S
"SHARPSHOOTER"
26 BURY STREET
St. JAMES', LONDON, S.W.

Height of internal metal reinforcing

DATA
Gauge; 12.
Length; 64 mm.
Head; 8 mm.
Tube wound red paper.
Colour; Crimson.
Print; Black.
Base; Reinforced brass.
Cap; copper.
Closure; Rolled turn-over.
Wad; Not known.
Business; Gunmakers.
Circa; 1920's.

FOR ONE AND ALL

JEFFERY'S
"SHARPSHOOTER"
26 BURY STREET
St.JAMES' LONDON.S.W.

DN.3-2684. Drawn, 23/2/08.

PLATE 203 [JEF – JEF]

W. J. JEFFERY & CO: 9 Golden Square, London W.1., England.

DATA
Gauge; 12.
Length; 64 mm.
Head; 8 mm.
Tube; Wound red paper.
Print; Black.
Base; Brass (not examined for internal metals).
Cap; Copper.
Closure; Rolled turn-over.
Wad; Green, print black.
Business; Gunmakers.
Circa; 1920's.

JEFFERY'S "SHARPSHOOTER"
9, GOLDEN SQUARE,
REGENT STREET, LONDON, W.1.

Drawn, 26/4/08.
DN. 3-0236.

W. J. JEFFERY & CO, LTD: 9 Golden Square, Regent Street, London W.1., England.

JEFFERY'S "SHARPSHOOTER"
9, GOLDEN SQUARE
REGENT STREET, LONDON, W.1.
MADE IN GREAT BRITAIN

DATA
Gauge; 12.
Lengths; 64 mm.
Heads; 8 mm.
Tubes; Wound red or orange papers.
Colours; Red, later orange.
Printings; Black.
Bases; reinforced brass.
Closures; Rolled turn-overs.
Wad shown; White card, print black (Washer type).
Business; Gunmakers.
Circa; 1930's.

DN.2-0237. Re-drawn; 31st Jan 2001

W. J. JEFFERY & COMPANY: 13 King Street, St. James' Street, London S.W.1., England.

JEFFERY'S "SHARPSHOOTERS"
13, KING-ST., ST. JAMES' ST.,
LONDON S.W.

DATA
Gauge; 20.
Length; 64 mm.
Head; 7 mm.
Tube; Wound paper.
Colour; Unglossed crimson red.
Print; Black.
Base; Brass.
Closure; Rolled turn-over.
Wad; Buff, print black.
Business; Gunmakers.
Circa; 1901-1910.

No iron or steel was used in the case construction.

DN.2-2042. October 1998

W. J. JEFFERY & CO: 13 King Street, St. James, London., S.W. Also at, 60 Queen Victoria Street, London, E.C. England.

Squared rolled turn-over.

JEFFERY'S "Sharpshooters"
13. KING STREET, ST. JAMES STREET,
LONDON S.W.
(AND 60, QUEEN VICTORIA STREET, E.C.)
MADE IN GREAT BRITAIN

DATA
Gauge; 12.
Length; 64 mm.
Head; 7 mm.
Tube; Wound paper.
Colour; Dark red 4.
Print; Black.
Base; Brass.
Closure; Rolled turn-over.
Wad; Powder blue 1.5, print dark blue.
Powder; Nobel's Empire.
Circa; 1907.
Business; Gun and rifle makers.

DN.2-0239. Updated; February 1995

W. J. JEFFERY & CO: 13 King Street, St. James, London, S.W. Also at, 60 Queen Victoria Street, London, E.C. England.

JEFFERY'S "SHARPSHOOTERS"
13 KING ST., ST. JAMES ST., S.W.
AND
60 QUEEN VICTORIA ST., E.C.
LONDON

DATA
Gauge; 12.
Length; 64 mm.
Head; 8.5 mm.
Tube; Wound paper.
Colour; Dark red 4.
Print; Black.
Base; Brass.
Closure; Rolled turn-over.
Wad; White card, print vermilion.
Circa; 1908.
Business; Gun and rifle makers.

DN.2-0240. Updated; February 1995

W. J. JEFFERY & COMPANY: 9 Golden Square, Regent Street, London W.1., England.

JEFFERY'S
XXX
CARTRIDGE
9 GOLDEN SQUARE
REGENT ST., LONDON. W.1.
Made in Great Britain

DATA
Gauge; 12.
Length; 64 mm.
Head; 16 mm.
Tube; Wound pink paper.
Printings; Either black or navy blue.
Base; Brass.
Wetproof; Clear lacquered.
Closure; rolled turn-over.
Wad; Buttercup yellow, print black.
Business; Gunmakers.
Circa; 1930's.

DN.2-0490. Re-drawn; 7th Feb 2001

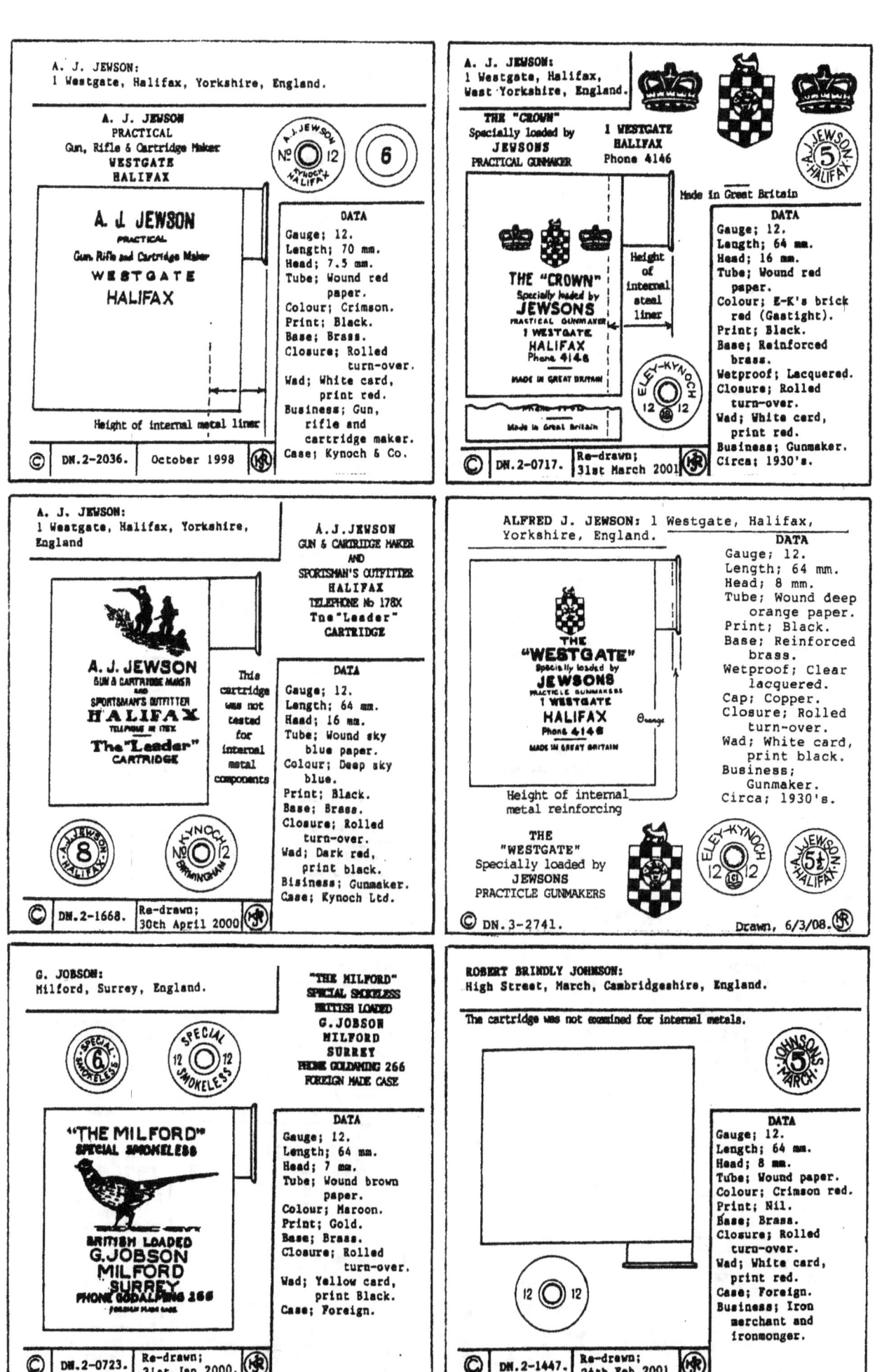

PLATE 205 [JEW – JOH]

THOMAS JOHNSON & SON: Market Place, Swaffham, Norfolk, England.

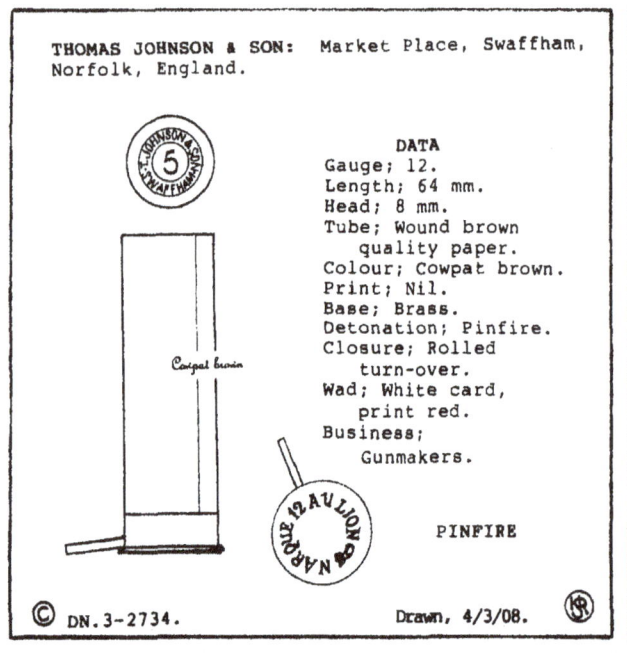

DATA
Gauge; 12.
Length; 64 mm.
Head; 8 mm.
Tube; Wound brown quality paper.
Colour; Cowpat brown.
Print; Nil.
Base; Brass.
Detonation; Pinfire.
Closure; Rolled turn-over.
Wad; White card, print red.
Business; Gunmakers.

PINFIRE

© DN.3-2734.   Drawn, 4/3/08.

THOMAS JOHNSON & SON: Market Place, Swaffham, Norfolk, England.

Drawn from photographs taken from the Chris Hart collection.

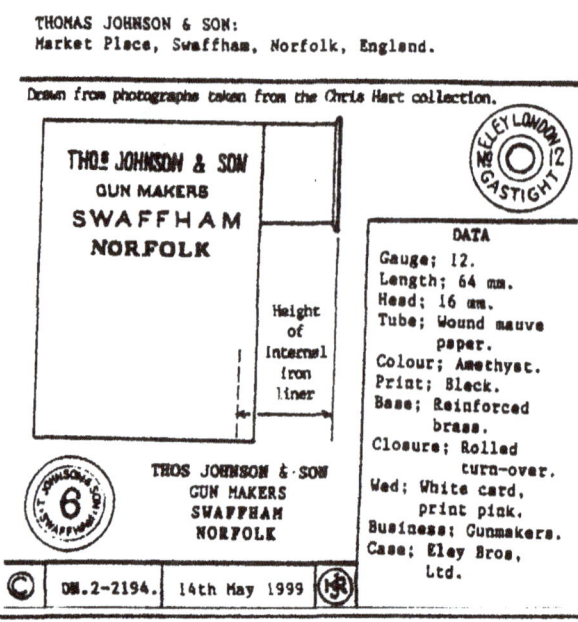

DATA
Gauge; 12.
Length; 64 mm.
Head; 16 mm.
Tube; Wound mauve paper.
Colour; Amethyst.
Print; Black.
Base; Reinforced brass.
Closure; Rolled turn-over.
Wad; White card, print pink.
Business; Gunmakers.
Case; Eley Bros, Ltd.

© DN.2-2194.   14th May 1999

JOHNSON & REID: Darlington, Yorkshire (County Durham), England.

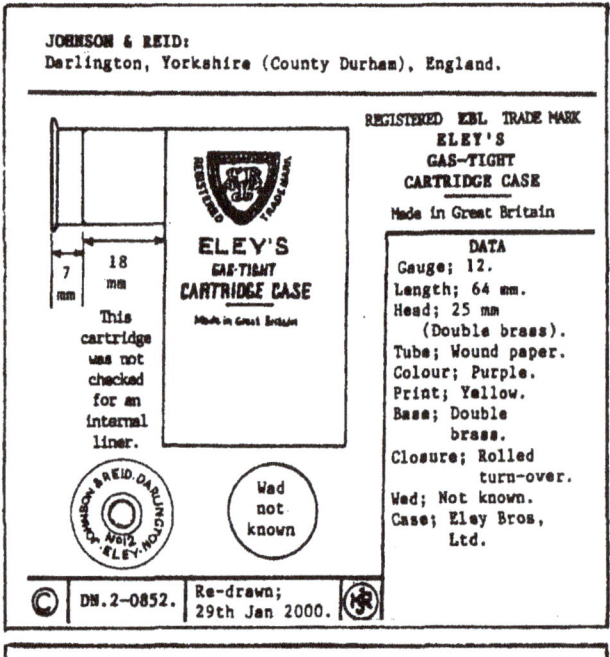

REGISTERED EBL TRADE MARK
ELEY'S
GAS-TIGHT
CARTRIDGE CASE
Made in Great Britain

DATA
Gauge; 12.
Length; 64 mm.
Head; 25 mm (Double brass).
Tube; Wound paper.
Colour; Purple.
Print; Yellow.
Base; Double brass.
Closure; Rolled turn-over.
Wad; Not known.
Case; Eley Bros, Ltd.

© DN.2-0852. Re-drawn; 29th Jan 2000.

JOHNSON & WRIGHT: 23A Gold Street, Northampton. Also at; Woolmonger Street, Northampton, Northamptonshire, England.

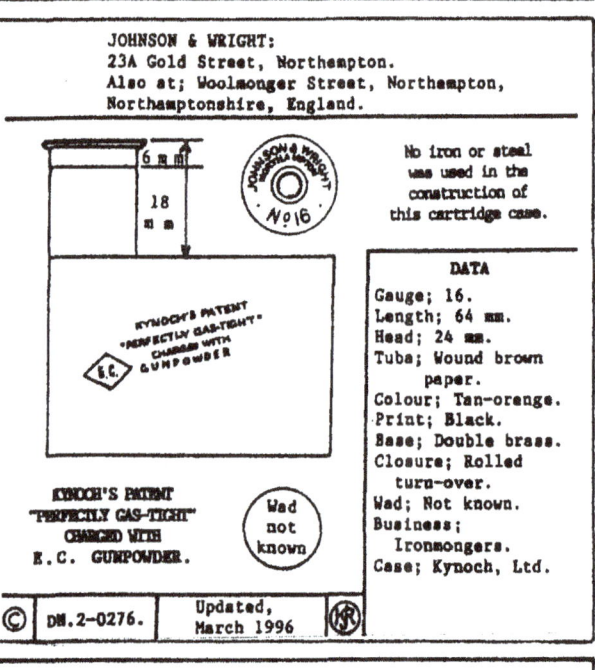

No iron or steel was used in the construction of this cartridge case.

DATA
Gauge; 16.
Length; 64 mm.
Head; 24 mm.
Tube; Wound brown paper.
Colour; Tan-orange.
Print; Black.
Base; Double brass.
Closure; Rolled turn-over.
Wad; Not known.
Business; Ironmongers.
Case; Kynoch, Ltd.

© DN.2-0276.   Updated, March 1996

JOHNSON & WRIGHT, LTD: 23A Gold Street. Also at, Woolmonger Street, Northampton, Northamptonshire, England.

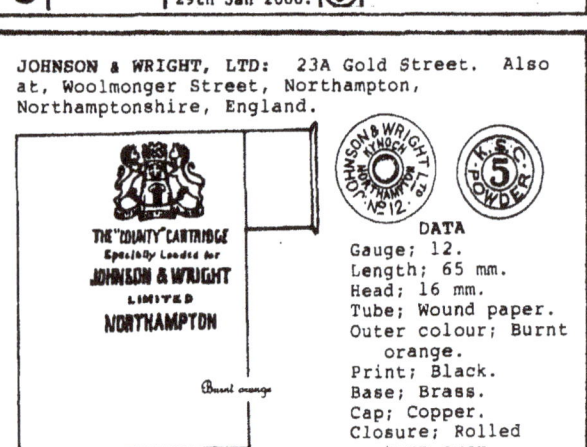

DATA
Gauge; 12.
Length; 65 mm.
Head; 16 mm.
Tube; Wound paper.
Outer colour; Burnt orange.
Print; Black.
Base; Brass.
Cap; Copper.
Closure; Rolled turn-over.
Wad; Red, print black.
Case by; Kynoch.
Business; Ironmongers etc.

THE "COUNTY" CARTRIDGE
Specially Loaded for
JOHNSON & WRIGHT
LIMITED
NORTHAMPTON

Footnote-, They were known as being active between 1894-1924.

It was not tested for internal metals.

© DN.3-2737.   Drawn, 5/3/08.

JONES & SON: Oxford Street and Gloucester Street, Malmesbury, Wiltshire, England.

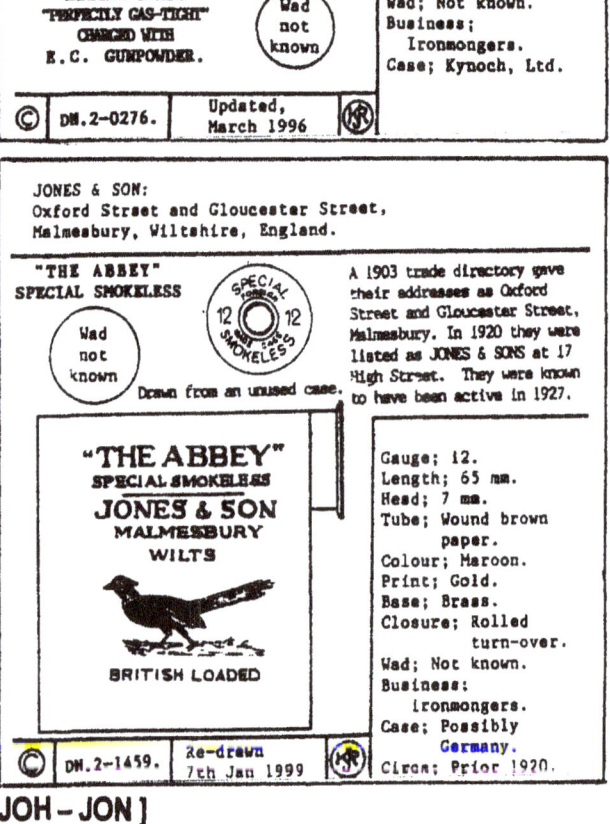

A 1903 trade directory gave their addresses as Oxford Street and Gloucester Street, Malmesbury. In 1920 they were listed as JONES & SONS at 17 High Street. They were known to have been active in 1927.

Gauge; 12.
Length; 65 mm.
Head; 7 mm.
Tube; Wound brown paper.
Colour; Maroon.
Print; Gold.
Base; Brass.
Closure; Rolled turn-over.
Wad; Not known.
Business; Ironmongers.
Case; Possibly Germany.

© DN.2-1459. Re-drawn 7th Jan 1999   Circa; Prior 1920.

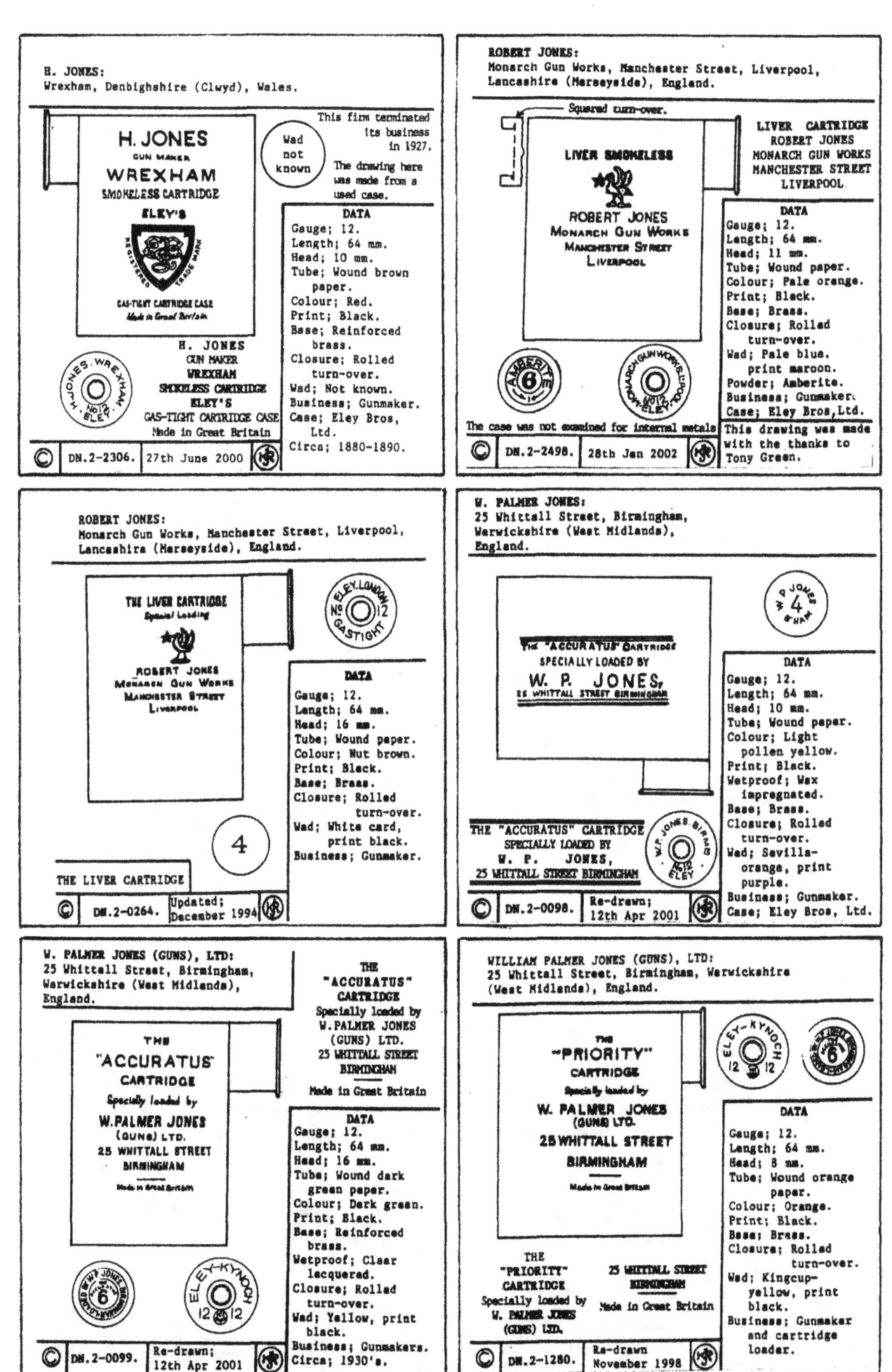

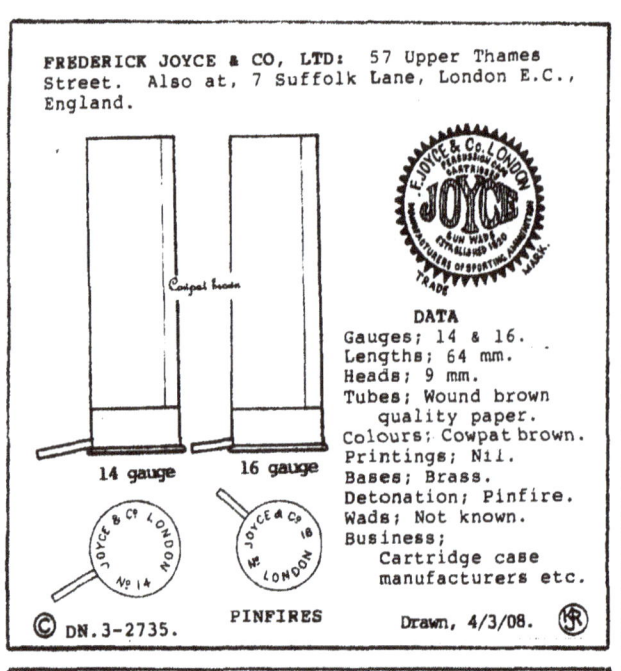
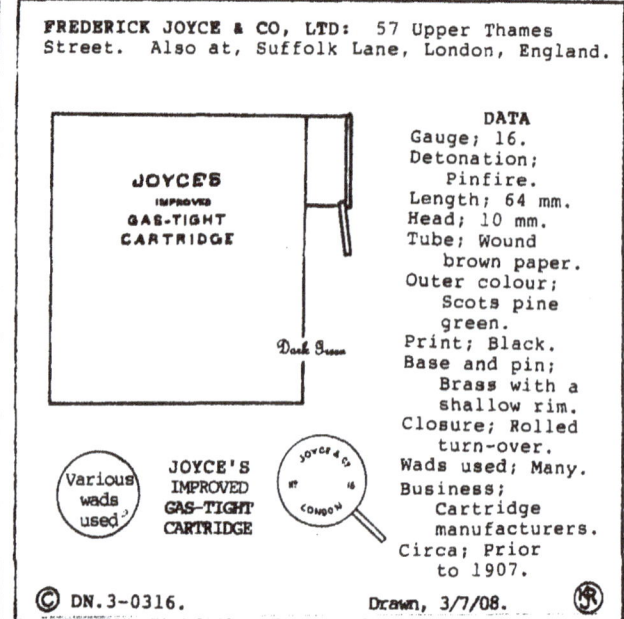
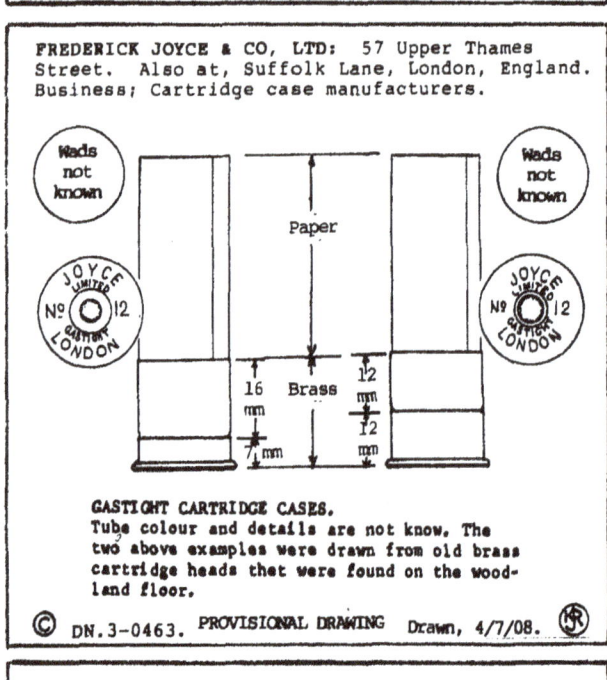
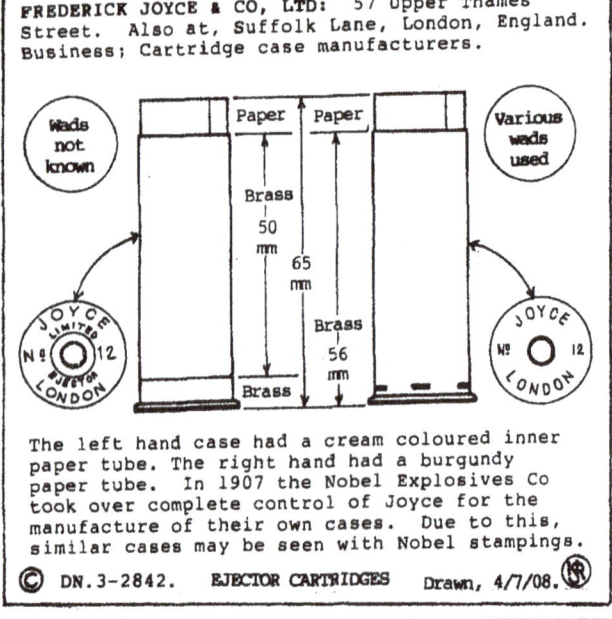
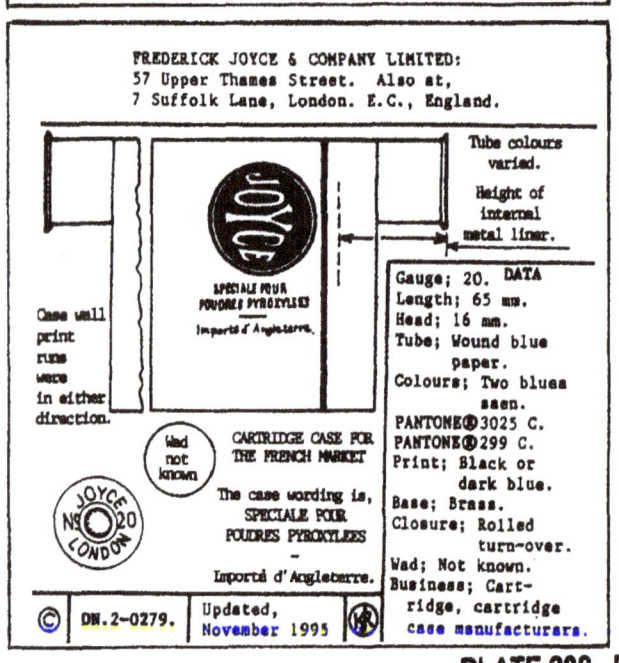

PLATE 208 [JOY – JOY]

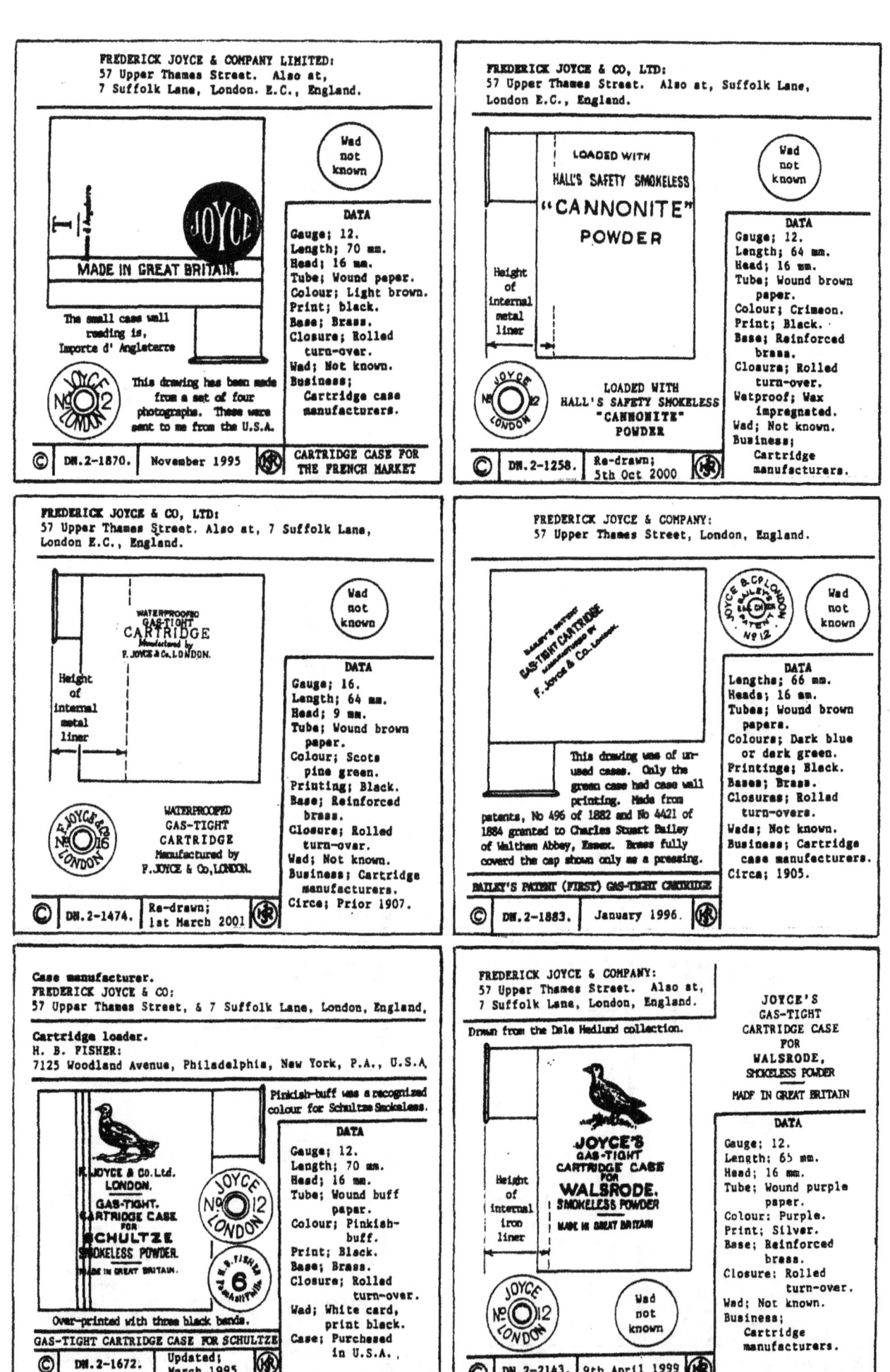

PLATE 209 [JOY – JOY]

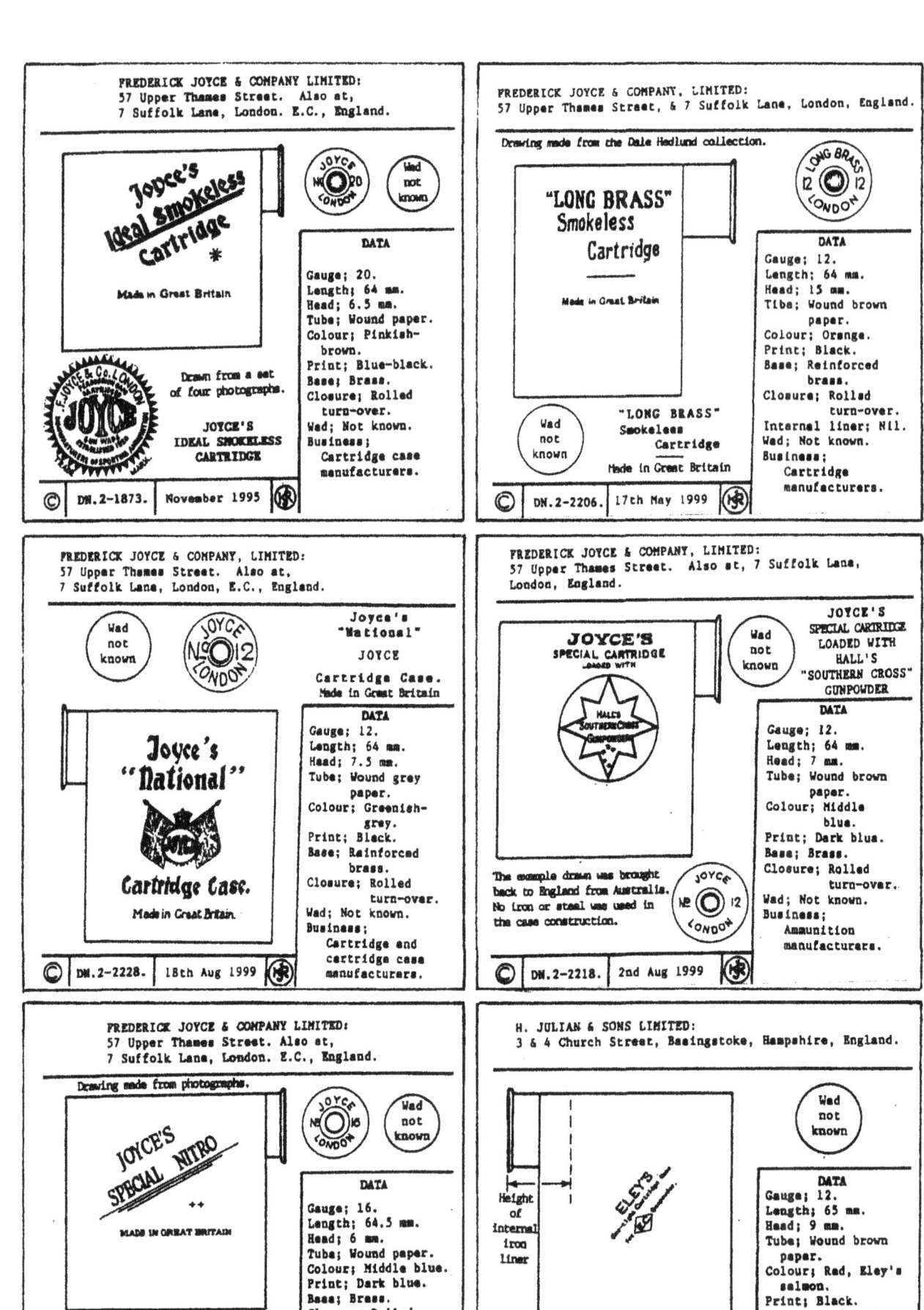

WILLIAM KAVANAGH & SON:
12 Dame Street, Dublin, Republic of Ireland.

Curtis's & Harvey's
SMOKELESS POWDER
AMBERITE
Made in Great Britain

Wad shown may not be correct for this cartridge

Height of internal iron liner

DATA
Gauge; 12.
Length; 64 mm.
Head; 16 mm.
Tube; Wound gray paper.
Colour; Grey.
Print; Black.
Base; Reinforced brass.
Closure; Rolled turn-over.
Wad shown; White card, print black.
Business; Gunmakers.

Drawn from the Dale Hedlund collection.

© DN.2-2138.   25th March 1999

W. KAVANAGH & SON: 12 Dame Street, Dublin, Republic of Ireland.

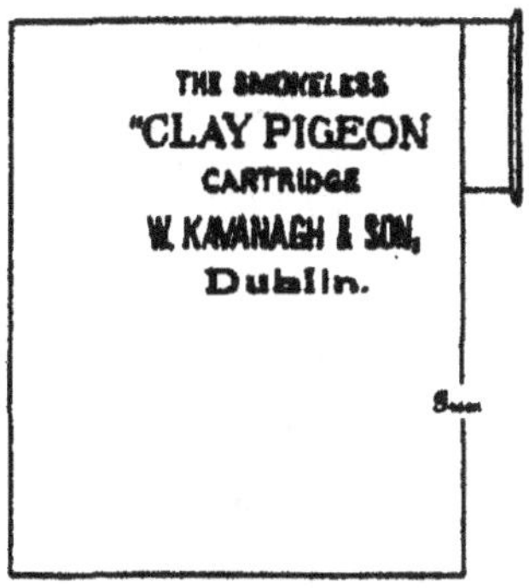

THE SMOKELESS
"CLAY PIGEON"
CARTRIDGE
W. KAVANAGH & SON,
Dublin.

DATA
Gauge; 12.
Length; 64 mm.
Head; 8 mm.
Tube; Wound paper.
Outer colour; Middle green.
Print; Black.
Base; Brass.
Closure; Rolled turn-over.
Wad; White card, print red.
Business; Gun and rifle makers.

 THE SMOKELESS CLAY PIGEON CARTRIDGE

© DN.3-2567.   Drawn, 8/6/07.

WILLIAM KAVANAGH & SON:
12 Dame Street, Dublin, Republic of Ireland.

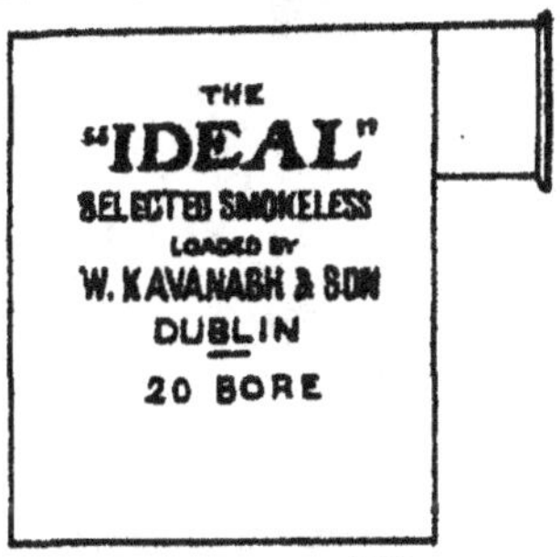

THE
"IDEAL"
SELECTED SMOKELESS
LOADED BY
W. KAVANAGH & SON
DUBLIN
20 BORE

DATA
Gauge; 20.
Length; 64 mm.
Head; 14 mm.
Tube; Wound paper.
Colour; Black.
Print; Silver.
Base; Brass with reinforcing.
Closure; Rolled turn-over.
Wad; Kingfisher blue, print black.
Business; Gunmakers and cartridge loaders.
Case; Kynoch, Ltd.

THE "IDEAL" SELECTED SMOKELESS LOADED BY W. KAVANAGH & SON DUBLIN 20 BORE

© DN.2-1934.   October 1996

WILLIAM KAVANAGH & SON:
12 Dame Street, Dublin, County Dublin, Republic of Ireland.

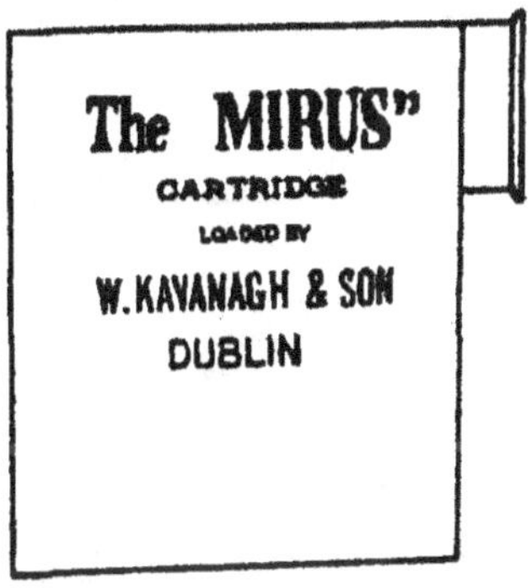

The "MIRUS"
CARTRIDGE
LOADED BY
W. KAVANAGH & SON
DUBLIN

DATA
Gauge; 12.
Lengths; 64 mm.
Heads; 8 mm.
Tubes; Wound papers.
Colours; Grey or light burnt orange.
Printings; Black.
Bases; brass.
Closures; rolled turn-overs.
Wad shown; Middle blue, print black.
Business; Gunmakers.

The "MIRUS" CARTRIDGE LOADED BY W. KAVANAGH & SON DUBLIN

© DN.2-1259.   Re-drawn; 27th Nov 2000

WILLIAM KAVANAGH & SON:
12 Dame Street, Dublin, County Dublin, Republic of Ireland.

THE
"Mirus"
Smokeless Cartridge
W. KAVANAGH & SON
DUBLIN

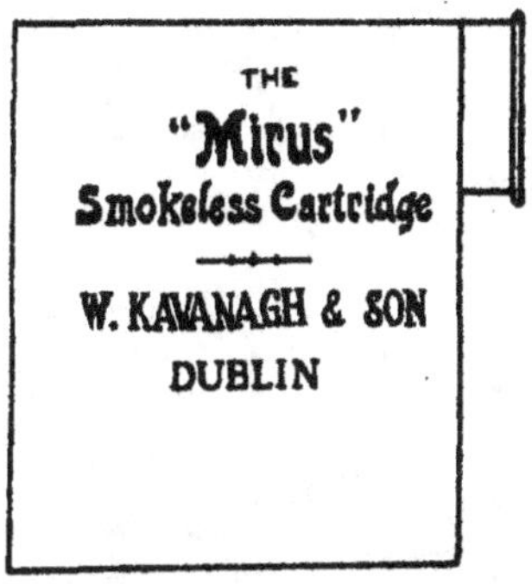

DATA
Colour; Gauge; 12.
Length; 64 mm.
Head; 8 mm.
Tube; Wound brown paper.
Colour; Brown, (Rough texture).
Print; Black.
Base; Brass.
Closure; Rolled turn-over.
Wad; Brownish yellow, print black.
Business; Gunmakers.
Case; Elay Bros, Ltd. London.

THE "Mirus" Smokeless Cartridge W. KAVANAGH & SON DUBLIN

© DN.2-2389.   20th Jan 2001

L. KEEGAN:
3 Inns Quay, Dublin, Republic of Ireland.

Drawn from the Dale Hedlund collection.

"The Emerald Isle"
SMOKELESS CARTRIDGE
LOADED BY
L. KEEGAN,
GUNMAKER
3. INNS QUAY,
DUBLIN.

Some scroll wording was obscured

Wad not known

DATA
Gauge; 12.
Length; 64 mm.
Head; 8 mm.
Tube; Wound green paper.
Colour; Middle green.
Print; Black.
Base; Reinforced brass.
Closure; Rolled turn-over.
Wad; Not known.
Business; Gunmaker.

"The Emerald Isle" SMOKELESS CARTRIDGE LOADED BY L. KEEGAN, GUNMAKER 3, INNS QUAY, DUBLIN.

© DN.2-2128.   22nd March 1999

PLATE 211 [KAV – KEE]

H. KEMPTON:
Bloomfield Road, Woolwich, London. S.E.18., England.

Basically drawn in the negative due to its soot black case wall, this German made cartridge was produced for the London firm. The small printing below EXPRESS was HARD HITTING. Around each oval was, ROTTWEIL POWDER FACTORIES UNITED COLOGNE. TRADE MARK.

DATA
Gauge; 12.
Length; 70 mm.
Head; 8 mm.
Tube; Wound paper.
Colour; Soot-black.
Print; Silver.
Base; Brass.
Closure; Rolled turn-over.
Wad; White card, print red.
Note; A similar 3 inch has been seen.

© DN.2-1726. Updated; December 1994 EXPRESS HARD HITTING

ALFRED KENT & SON:
Market Place, Wantage, Berkshire (Oxfordshire), England.

DATA
Gauge; 12.
Detonation; Pinfire.
Head; 12 mm.
Length; 65 mm.
Tube; Wound brown paper.
Colour; Dark green.
Print; Black.
Base; Reinforced brass.
Rim; Small.
Closure; Rolled turn-over.
Wad; White card, print red.
Business; Ironmongers.

© DN.2-0904. Re-drawn; 19th Jan 2001

ALFRED KENT & SON:
Market Place, Wantage, Berkshire (Oxfordshire), England.

KENT & SON
CHEAP
CARTRIDGE

DATA
Gauge; 12.
Length; 64 mm.
Head; 7 mm.
Tube; Wound brown paper.
Colour; Cow-pat brown.
Print; Nil.
Base; Brass.
Closure; Rolled turn-over.
Wad; White card, print black.
Business; Ironmongers and cartridge loaders.

© DN.2-0903. Re-drawn; 14th Nov 2000

ALFRED KENT & SON: Market Place, Wantage, Berkshire (Oxfordshire, England.

This cartridge had the tube wound from brown paper with the outer layer being in Eley's Green Quality. This was a dark green. Due to this type of construction it was made prior to 1896. Many firms of that period loaded these cases having their own names on the brass stampings. The small cap was copper and it ws fitted with an internal metal liner that is not shown on this drawing. The wad was cut from white card with red printing. Black powder was used. Kent's business then was furnishings, ironmongery and cartridge loadings, etc.

© DN.3-2773. Drawn, 16/3/08.

ALFRED KENT & SON, LTD: Maeket Place, Wantage, Berkshire (Oxfordshire), England.

Have been seen with printings in both directions.

KYNOCH'S PATENT "PERFECTLY GAS-TIGHT"
KYNOCH'S PATENT "PERFECTLY GAS-TIGHT" CHARGED WITH E.C. GUNPOWDER SPECIALLY LOADED BY KENT & SON WANTAGE

DATA
Gauge; 12.

Gauge; 12.
Length; 65 mm.
Head; Double, 24 mm.
Tube; Wound brown paper.
Colour; Brownish-orange.
Print; Black.
Base; Brass.
Closure; Rolled turn-over.
Wad; White card, print red.
Business; Ironmongers.
Case; Kynoch Works.

© DN.3-0111. Revised; 18/12/08.

ALFRED KENT & SON:
Market Place, Wantage, Berkshire (Oxfordshire), England.

Drawing made from photographs of an unused case.

THE
"Wantage" Cartridge
SPECIALLY MANUFACTURED
FOR
KENT & SON.
KYNOCH PATENT
"PERFECTLY GASTIGHT"

Wad not known

DATA
Gauge; 12.
Length; 64.5 mm.
Head; 10 mm with extended brass to a total of 24 mm.
Tube; Wound paper.
Colour; Redish-brown. PANTONE® 472 U.
Print; Black.
Base; Double brass.
Int' liner; Not known
Wad; Not known.
Case; G. Kynoch & Co.
Business; General furnishing, coach hire and ironmongers.

© DN.2-1941. December 1996

PLATE 212 [KEM – KEN]

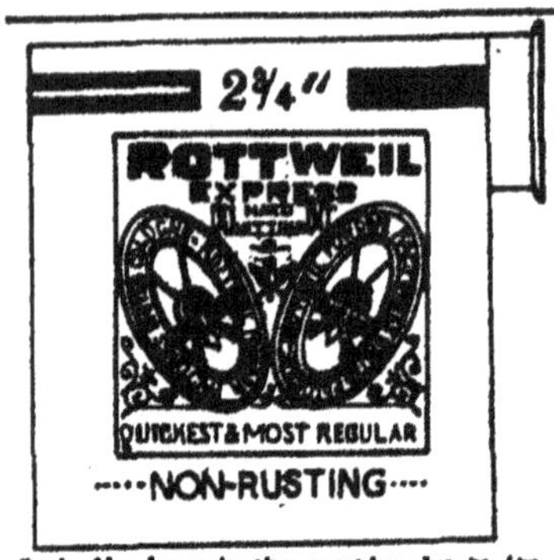

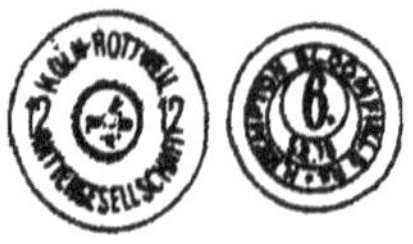

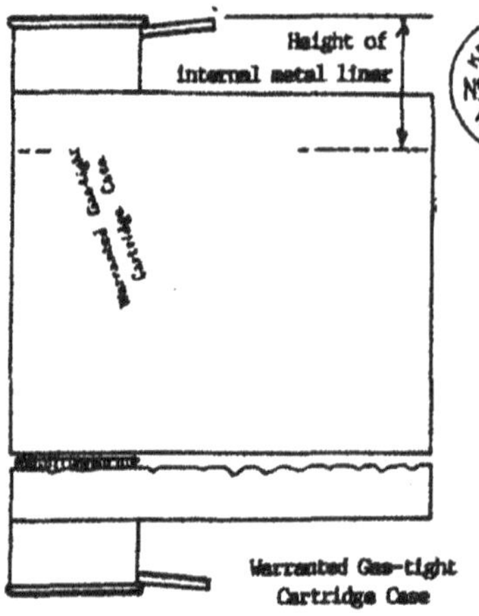

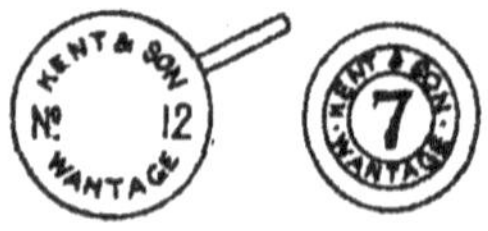

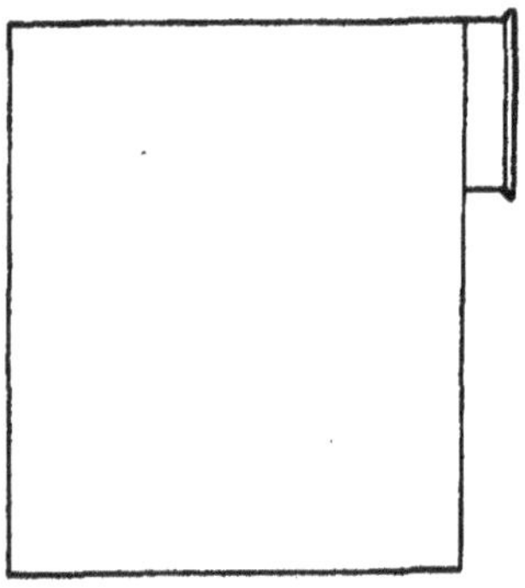

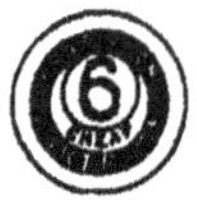

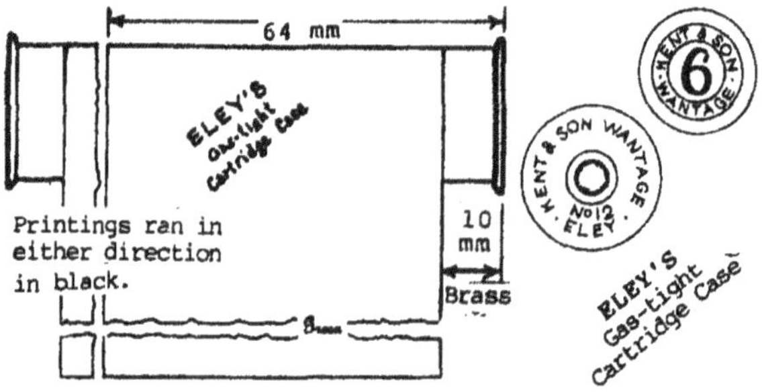

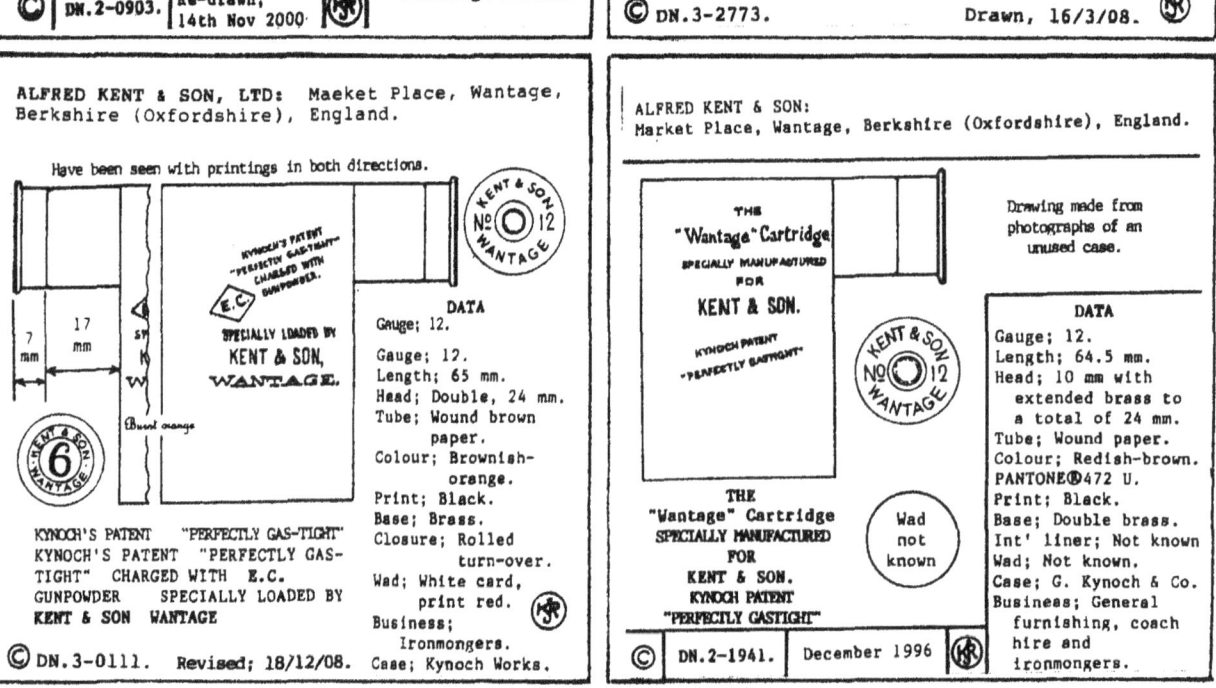

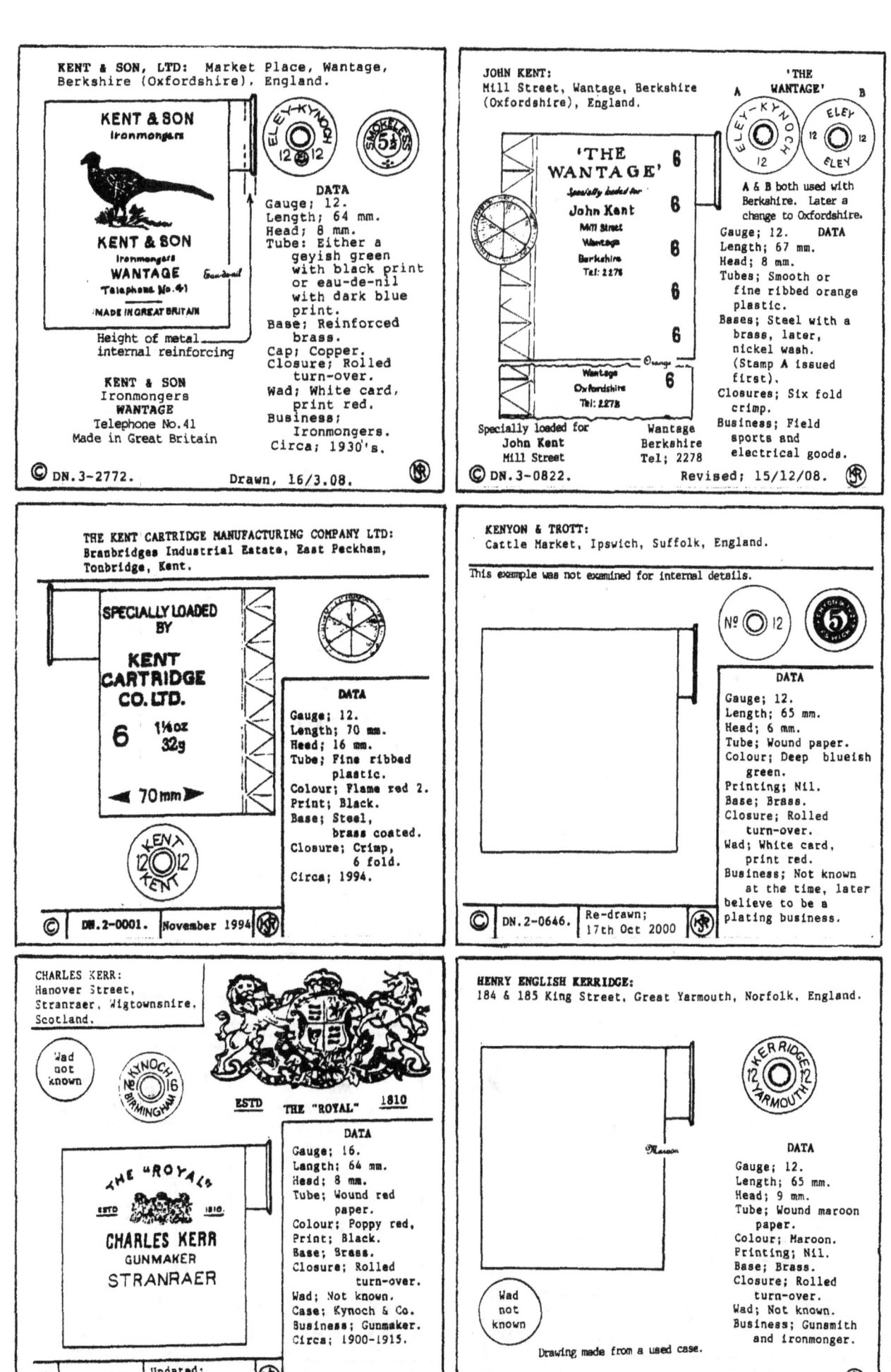

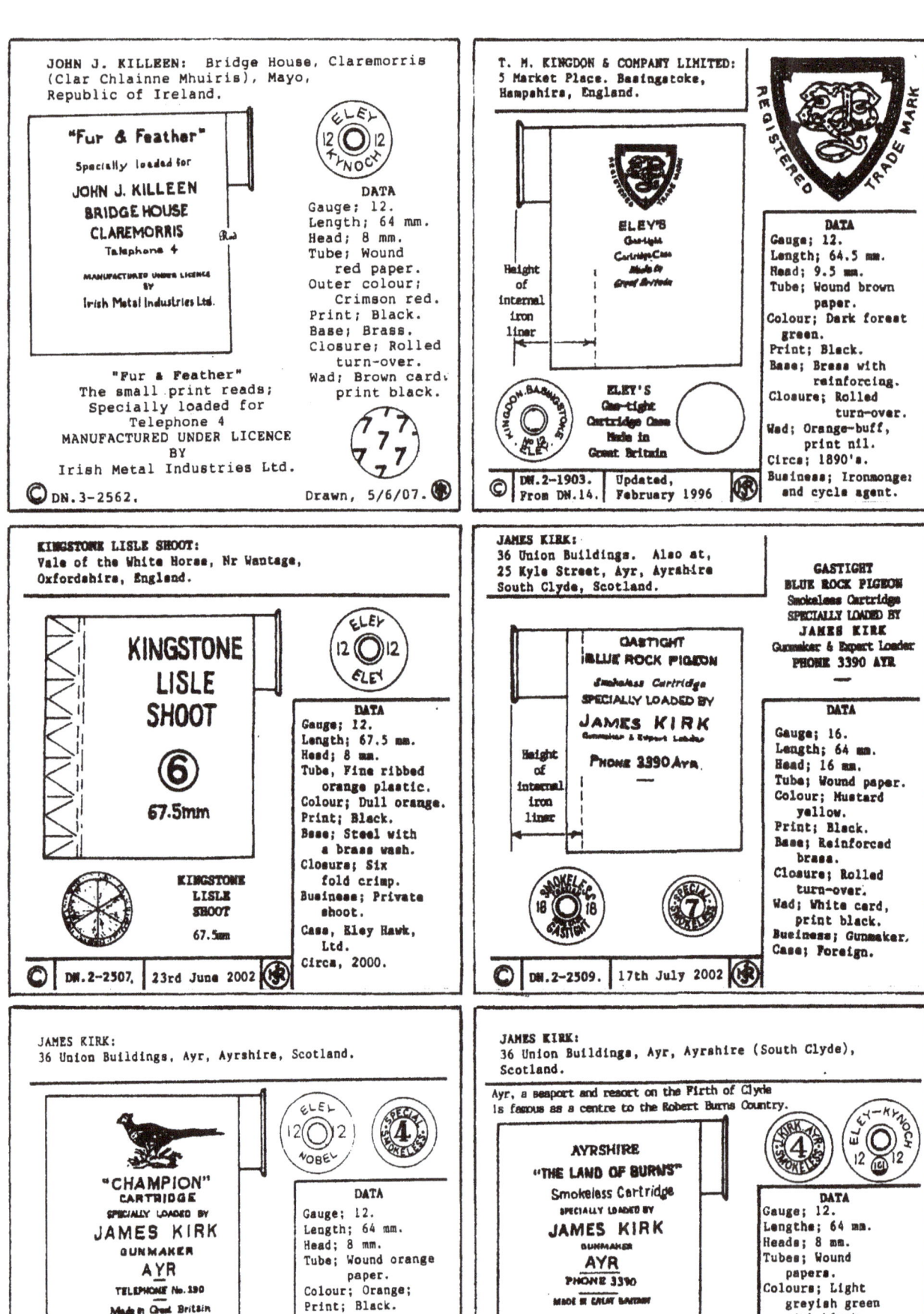

PLATE 214 [KIL - KIR]

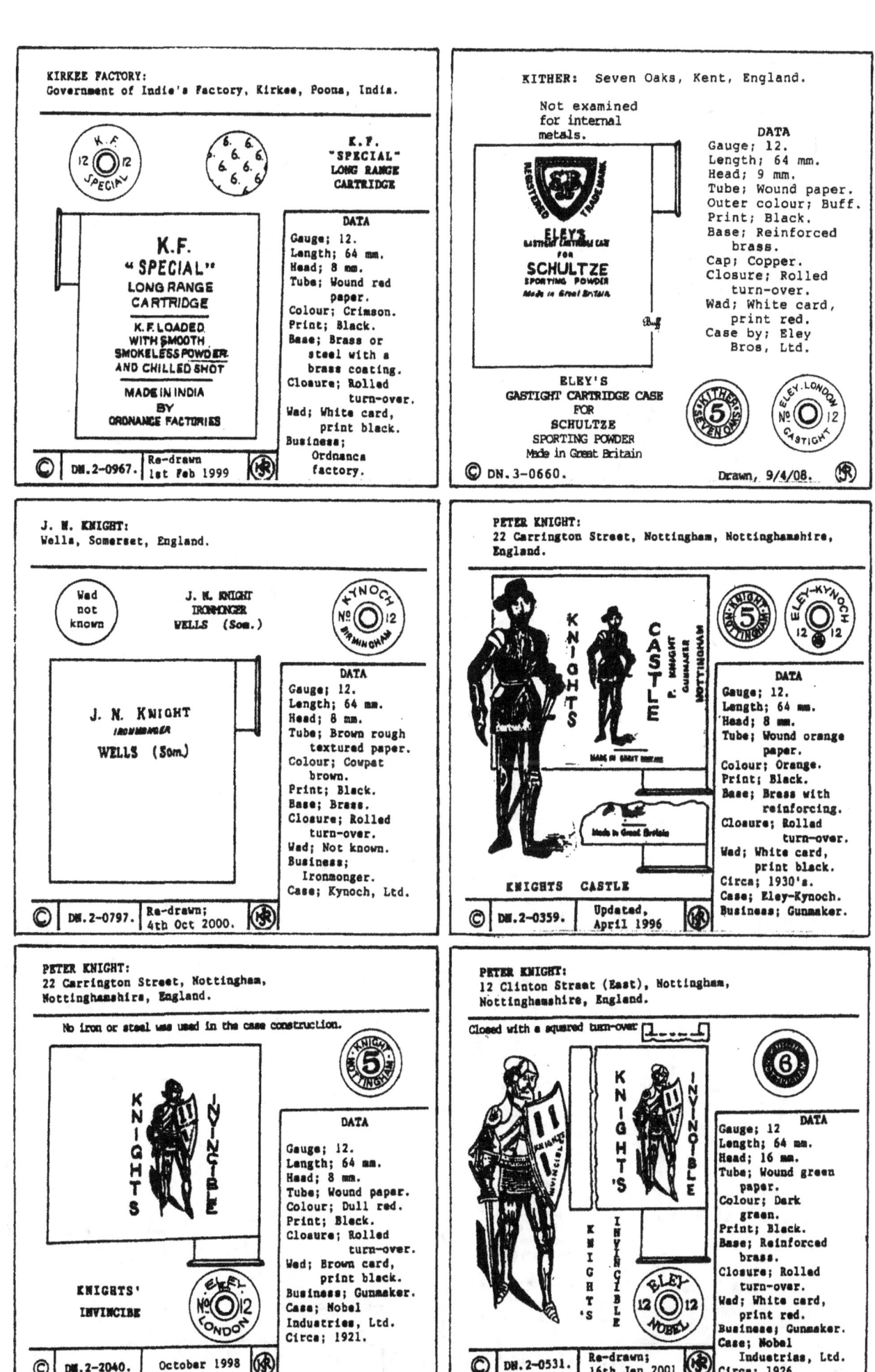

PLATE 215 [KIR – KNI]

PETER KNIGHT:
12 Clinton Street (East), Nottingham, Nottinghamshire, England.

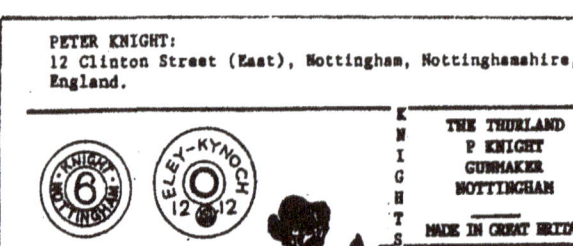

KNIGHTS

THE THURLAND
P KNIGHT
GUNMAKER
NOTTINGHAM

MADE IN GREAT BRITAIN

DATA
Gauge; 12.
Length; 64 mm.
Head; 8 mm.
Tube; Wound greyish-green paper.
Colour; Greyish-green.
Print; Black.
Base; Reinforced brass.
Closure; Rolled turn-over.
Wad; White card, print black.
Wetproof; Lacquered.
Business; Gunmaker.
Circa; 1930's.

© DN.2-1501. Updated, February 1996.

KOLN-ROTTWEILER AG:
Troisdorf, Western Germany.

HEADSTAMPING; VEREINIGTE KOLN-ROTTWEILER PULVERFABRIKEN

GERMAN	ENGLISH TRANSLATION
Rottweiler	Rottweiler
Jagdpatrone	Hunting cartridge
Kriegsjahr 1915	War year 1915
Rauchloses	Smokeless
Jagdpulver	Hunting powder

DATA
Gauge; 12.
Length; 64 mm.
Head; 7 mm.
Tube; Wound brown paper.
Colour; Dirty grey.
Print; Black.
Base; Iron or steel.
Closure; Squared turn-over.
Wad; White card, print black.
Cap; Large brass.
Business; Powder and ammunition manufacturers.
Circa; 1915-1918.

© DN.2-1998. July 1997.

JOHN KRIDER:
Philadelphia, Pennsylvania, United States of America.

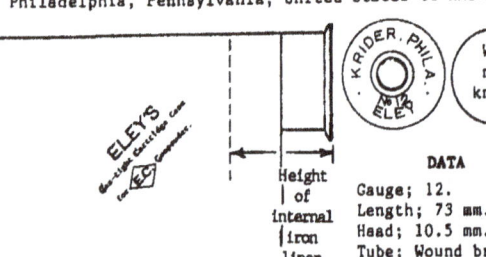  

John Krider imported cartridge cases (shells) from Eley Brothers Ltd, of London, England. Note, extra large cap.

ELEY'S
Gas-tight Cartridge Case
for E.C. Gunpowder.

DATA
Gauge; 12.
Length; 73 mm.
Head; 10.5 mm.
Tube; Wound brown paper.
Colour; Red, Eleys' Salmon.
Print; Black.
Base; Reinforced brass.
Closure; Rolled turn-over.
Wad; Not known.
Business; Gunmaker.
Circa; Prior to 1896.

© DN.3-1888. Revised; 17/12/08.

KRUKCL (KEN RUTTERFORD'S UNITED KINGDOM COLLECTORS LIST):
White Gates, Wickham, Newbury, Berkshire, England.

A very limited run was loaded into a Federal Gold Medal Target Load Shell. Mr D.J. Hedlund had these specially loaded in the U.S.A. for a KRUKCL exchange meeting held in Boxford Village Hall, Berkshire, Newbury, England.

DATA
Gauge; 12.
Length; 68 mm.
Head; 12 mm.
Tube; Burgundy ribbed plastic.
Print; Golden yellow.
Base; Reinforced brass.
Closure; Eight fold pie crimp.
Business; Private cartridge collectors club.
Case; Federal Cartridge Corp, Minnesota, U.S.A.

© DN.2-0123. Re-drawn 4th Jan 1999.

GEORGE KYNOCH, LTD. Or, G. KYNOCH & CO, LTD:
The Lion Works, or Kynoch Works, Witton, Birmingham, (West Midlands), England.

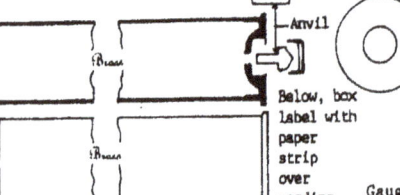

PRECISION MADE ALL BRASS CASE FOR RELOADERS.

Plain head

Below, box label with paper strip over wording

KYNOCH'S
CENTRAL FIRE No. 20
FOR SPORTING GUNS
Warranted to Re-load 100 Times and not to miss fire or split at the rim.

DATA
Gauge shown; 20.
Length; 64 mm.
One piece all brass case for reloaders.
Warranted to re-load 100 times without any failures.
Closure; Most likely a wax plug.

© DN.3-0063. Revised; 17/12/08.

GEORGE KYNOCH, LTD: or, G. KYNOCH & CO, LTD:
The Lion Works; or, Kynoch Works, Witton, Birmingham, Warwickshir (West Midlands), England.

Drawing of an unused case in the Dale Hedlund collection.

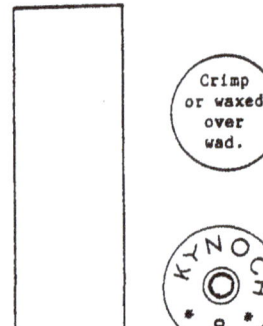

Crimp or waxed over wad.

This shell was also manufactured in other gauges.

DATA
Gauge; 8.
One piece all brass case.
Length; 77 mm.
Head; Continuous with case body.
Closures; Various.
Rim; Chamfered on lower edge.
Business; Manufacturers of gas engines, cycles, candles and other goods including explosives and ammunition.

© DN.2-2232. 23rd May 1999.

G. KYNOCH & COMPANY, LIMITED:
"Kynoch Lion Works", Witton, Birmingham, Warwickshire
(West Midlands), England.

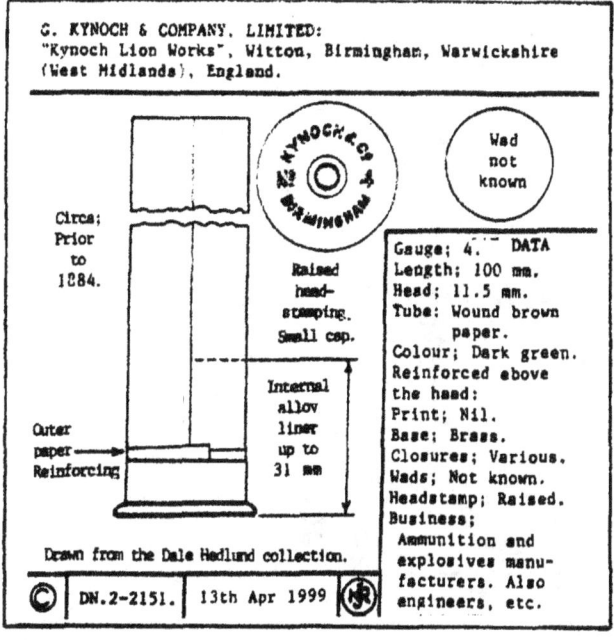

Circa; Prior to 1884.

Raised head-stamping. Small cap.

Wad not known

Outer paper Reinforcing

Internal alloy liner up to 31 mm

Drawn from the Dale Hedlund collection.

DATA
Gauge; 4.
Length; 100 mm.
Head; 11.5 mm.
Tube: Wound brown paper.
Colour; Dark green.
Reinforced above the head;
Print; Nil.
Base; Brass.
Closures; Various.
Wads; Not known.
Headstamp; Raised.
Business;
Ammunition and explosives manufacturers. Also engineers, etc.

© DN.2-2151.   13th Apr 1999

G. KYNOCH & CO, LTD. Lion Works, Witton, Birmingham, England.

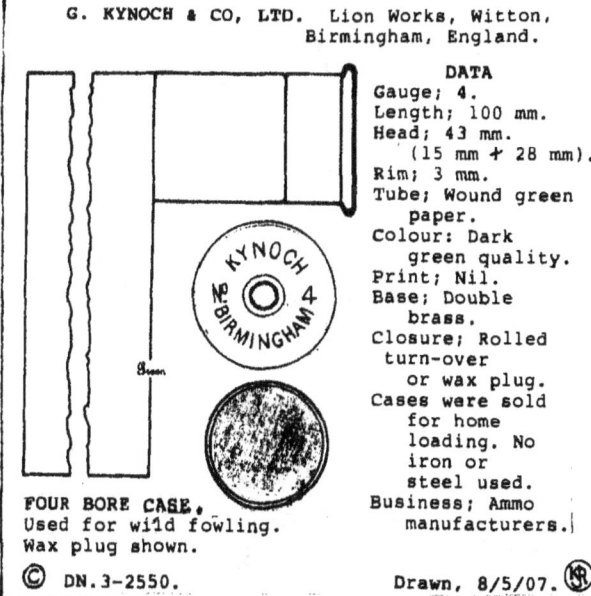

FOUR BORE CASE.
Used for wild fowling.
Wax plug shown.

DATA
Gauge; 4.
Length; 100 mm.
Head; 43 mm.
   (15 mm + 28 mm).
Rim; 3 mm.
Tube; Wound green paper.
Colour: Dark green quality.
Print; Nil.
Base; Double brass.
Closure; Rolled turn-over or wax plug.
Cases were sold for home loading. No iron or steel used.
Business; Ammo manufacturers.

© DN.3-2550.   Drawn, 8/5/07.

G.KYNOCH, LTD:
Lion Works, Witton, Birmingham, Warwickshire (West Midlands), England.

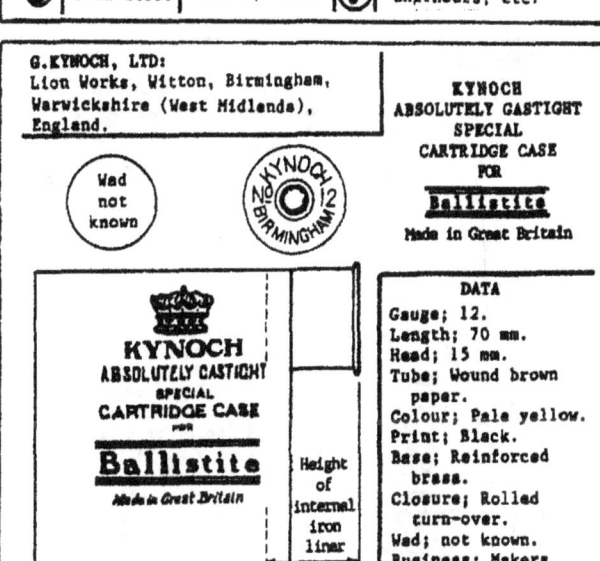

KYNOCH ABSOLUTELY GASTIGHT SPECIAL CARTRIDGE CASE FOR Ballistite Made in Great Britain

Height of internal iron liner

Drawn from the Tom Matthews collection.

DATA
Gauge; 12.
Length; 70 mm.
Head; 15 mm.
Tube; Wound brown paper.
Colour; Pale yellow.
Print; Black.
Base; Reinforced brass.
Closure; Rolled turn-over.
Wad; not known.
Business; Makers of ammunition, candles, cycles, gas engines, etc.

© DN.2-2461.   21st Aug 2001

GEORGE KYNOCH, LTD. Or, G. KYNOCH & CO, LTD:
The Lion Works, or Kynoch Works, Witton, Birmingham, Warwickshire (West Midlands), England.

Drawn from the George Crouch collection.

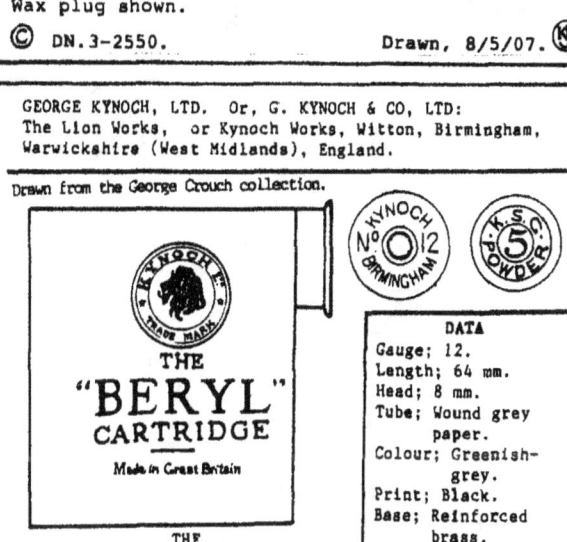

THE "BERYL" CARTRIDGE Made in Great Britain

THE "BERYL" CARTRIDGE Made in Great Britain
Possibly produced for the Australian market.

DATA
Gauge; 12.
Length; 64 mm.
Head; 8 mm.
Tube; Wound grey paper.
Colour; Greenish-grey.
Print; Black.
Base; Reinforced brass.
Closure; Rolled turn-over.
Wad; Dark red, print black.
Business; Explosives and general manufacturers.

© DN.2-2208.   29th July 1999

GEORGE KYNOCH & CO: The Lion Works, Witton, Birmingham, Warwickshire (West Midlands), England.

Business; Manufacturers of gas-engines, ammunition of all types, candles and cycles, etc.

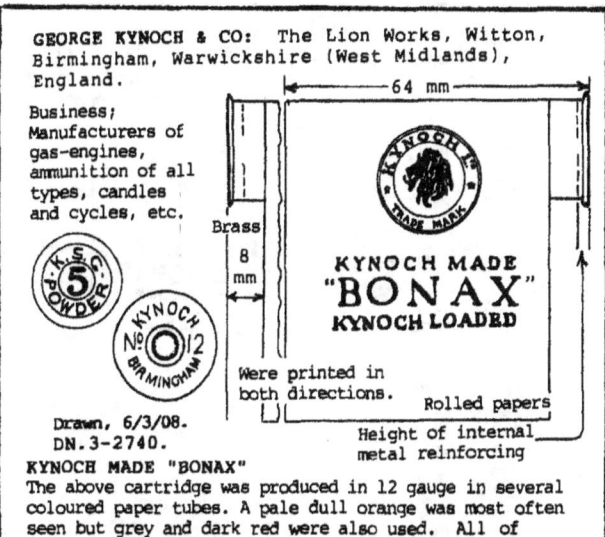

← 64 mm →

KYNOCH MADE "BONAX" KYNOCH LOADED

Brass 8 mm

Were printed in both directions.
Rolled papers
Height of internal metal reinforcing

Drawn, 6/3/08.
DN.3-2740.

KYNOCH MADE "BONAX"
The above cartridge was produced in 12 gauge in several coloured paper tubes. A pale dull orange was most often seen but grey and dark red were also used. All of these had their case-wall printings in black. The wad shown was made from white or red card and also had black printing. First introduced in 1905 they were made in the gauges 10, 12, 16 and 20. Shown here is 12.

G. KYNOCH & CO: THE LION WORKS, WITTON, BIRMINGHAM (MIDLANDS).
Business. Manufacturers and merchants.

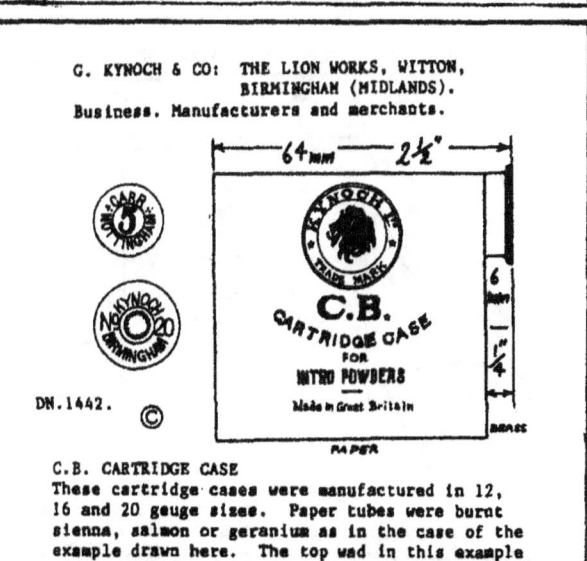

← 64 mm → ← 2½" →

C.B. CARTRIDGE CASE FOR NITRO POWDERS Made in Great Britain

DN.1442. ©

PAPER

C.B. CARTRIDGE CASE
These cartridge cases were manufactured in 12, 16 and 20 gauge sizes. Paper tubes were burnt sienna, salmon or geranium as in the case of the example drawn here. The top wad in this example was of white card with red printing having been loaded by Carr of Nottingham. All case wall printings were in black.

PLATE 217 [KYN – KYN]

KYNOCH & COMPANY LIMITED: Lion Works, Witton, Birmingham, Warwickshire (West Midlands), England.

A. B.

Some were closed with a squared turn-over.

First produced by Kynoch & Co with stamping A.
After the merger by Nobel Industries with stamping B.
Was loaded by many, various wads were used.

DATA

Gauge; 16.
Length; 64 mm.
Head; 8 mm.
Tube; Wound mauve paper.
Colour; Amethyst.
Print; Black.
Base; Brass.
Cosure; Rolled turn-over.
Wad shown; White card, print red.
Business; Explosives and ammunition manufacturers.
Circa; 1917-1920.

© DN.2-1575. Updated; November 1997.

KYNOCH LIMITED: Lion Works, Witton, Birmingham, Warwickshire (West Midlands), England.

C.B.
CARTRIDGE CASE
LOADED WITH
CURTIS'S & HARVEY'S
SMOKELESS
DIAMOND
POWDER

DATA

Gauge; 12.
Length; 64 mm.
Head; 8 mm.
Tube; Wound paper.
Colour; Dirty middle blue.
Print; Black.
Base; Reinforced brass.
Closure; Rolled turn-over.
Wad; Light blue, print black.
Business; Ammunition, cycle and gas engine manufacturers.

© DN.2-1997. July 1997.

KYNOCH LIMITED: The Lion Works, Witton, Birmingham, Warwickshire (West Midlands), England.

TWO INCH

THE KYNOCH .410 & "PERFECTLY GASTIGHT"

A.

No iron or steel was used in the construction of these cases.

B.

KYNOCH'S PATENT "PERFECTLY GASTIGHT"

DATA

Gauges; .410.
Lengths; 51 mm.
Heads; A 10 mm. B 14 + 7 mm, = 21 mm.
Tubes; Wound brown papers.
Colours; A Old straw. B Burgundy.
Printings; Black.
Bases; Brass.
Closures; Rolled turn-overs.
Wads; White card, printings black.
Business; Ammo makers and engineers, etc.

© DN.2-1882. January 1996

KYNOCH LIMITED: The Lion Works, Witton, Birmingham, Warwickshire (West Midlands), England.

TWO INCH

THE KYNOCH .410

A.

Height of internal iron liners

B.

DATA

Gauges; .410.
Lengths; 51 mm.
Heads; A 7.5 mm, B 13 mm.
Tubes; Wound coloured papers.
Colours; A Purple with yellow print. B Brown with black print.
Bases; Brass.
Closures; Rolled turn-overs.
Wads; White cards, printings black.
Business; Ammo makers engineers, etc.

© DN.2-0355. Updated, January 1996

KYNOCH LIMITED: The Lion Works, Witton, Birmingham, Warwickshire (West Midlands), England. Business; Ammunition manufacturers, etc.

©

Not examined for internal metals.

KYNOCH "GASTIGHT" CARTRIDGE CASE. Circa around 1910, these cases have been seen with both brown and burgundy paper tubes. Kynochs' may have had other names for these colours. Printings seen were in black. They could well have ben produced in other colours and gauge sizes. A 12 gauge is shown here. The wad shown was of white card with black printing.

DN.3-0656. Drawn, 31/3/08.

G. KYNOCH & CO: The Lion Works, Witton, Birmingham, Warwickshire (West Midlands), England.

DATA

Gauge; 12.
Length; 64 mm.
Head; 14 mm.
Tube; Wound paper.
Colour; Brick red.
Print; Black.
Base; Reinforced brass.
Cap; Copper.
Closure; Rolled turn-over.
Wad; White card, print black.
Business; Ammunition, explosives, gas engines, cycles and candle manufacturers, etc.

KYNOCH
"GASTIGHT"
CARTRIDGE CASE
Made in Great Britain

© DN.3-1785. Drawn, 23/4/08.

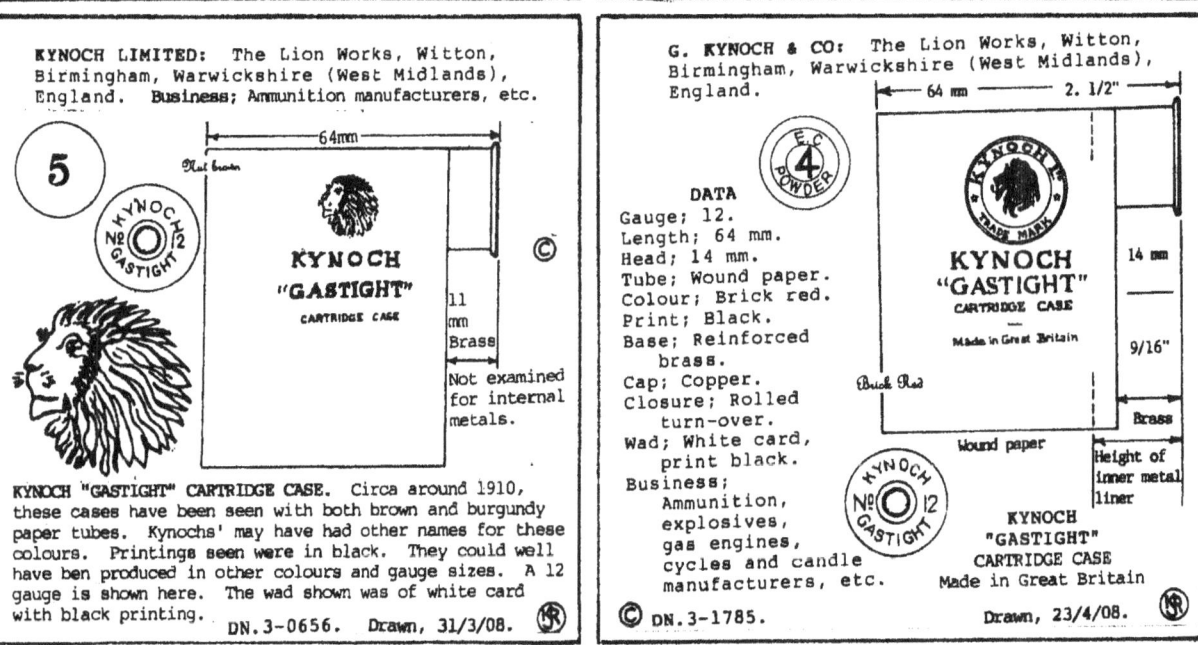

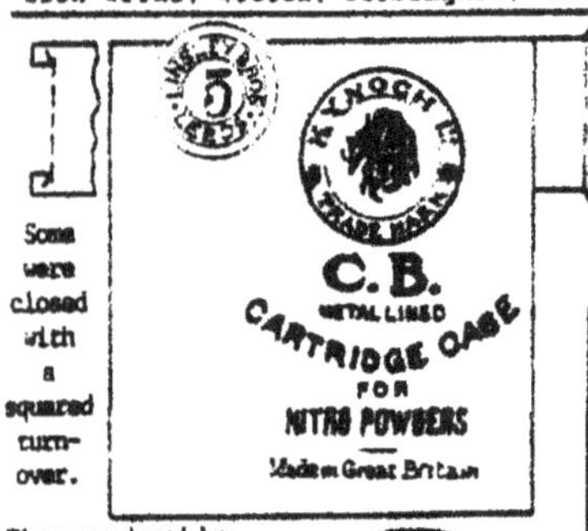

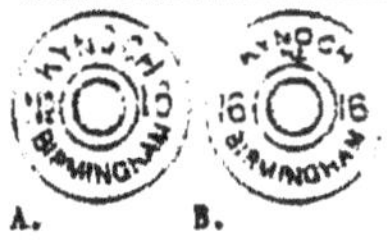

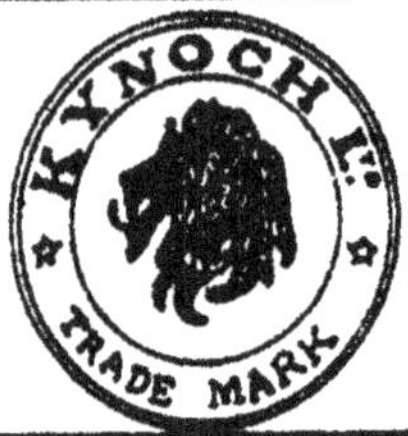

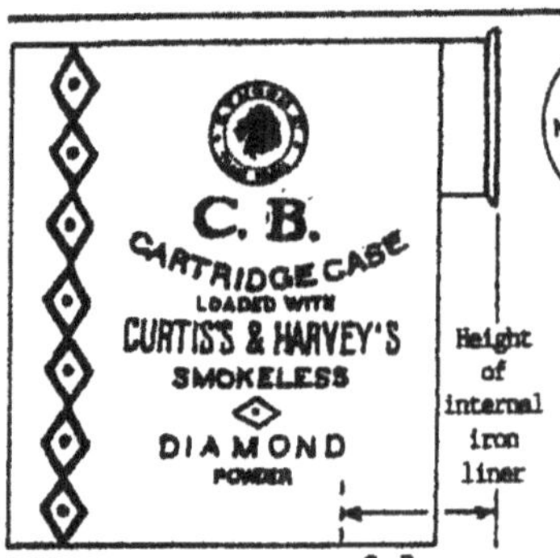

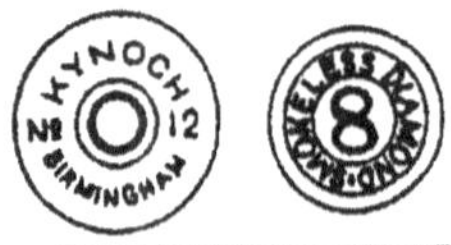

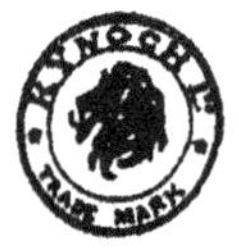

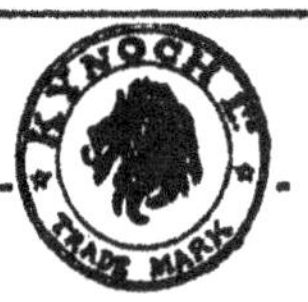

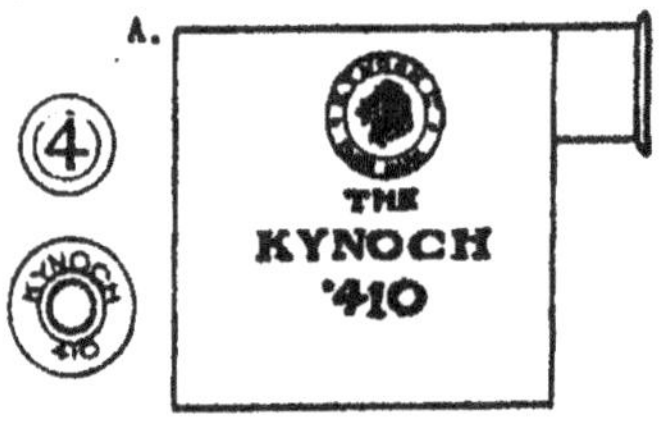

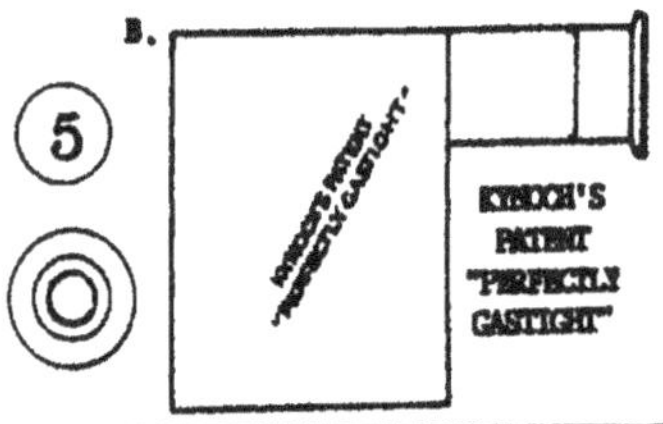

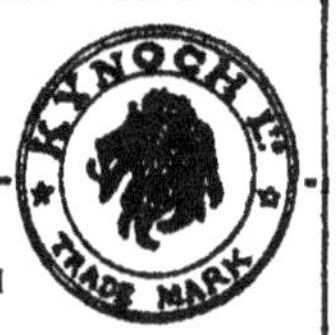

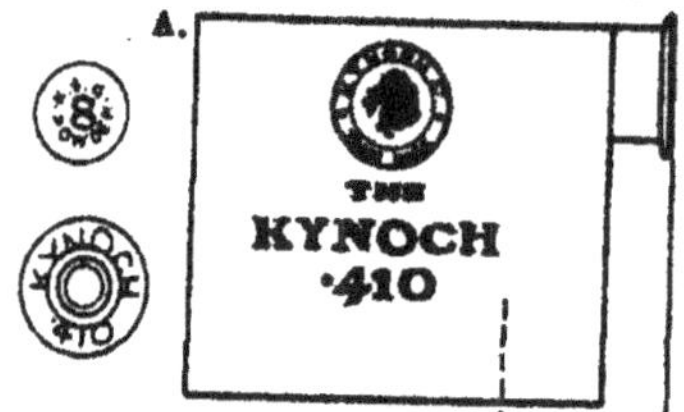

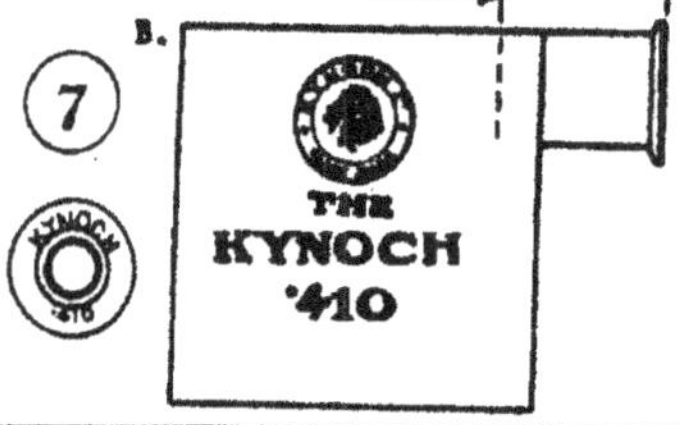

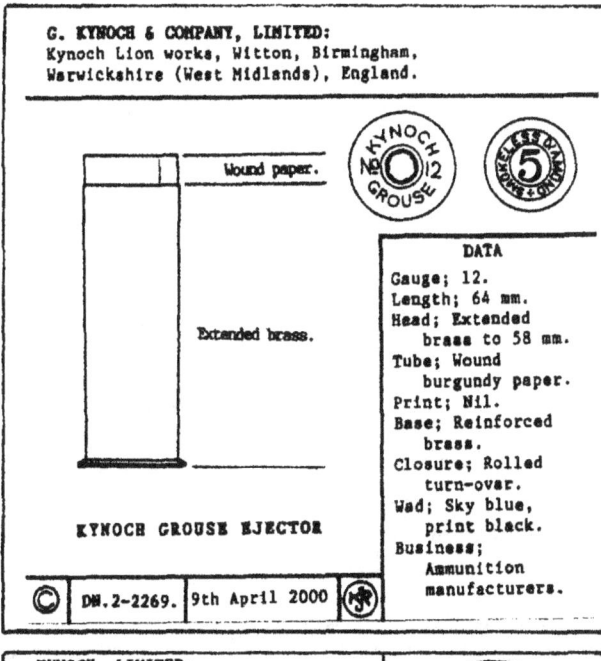
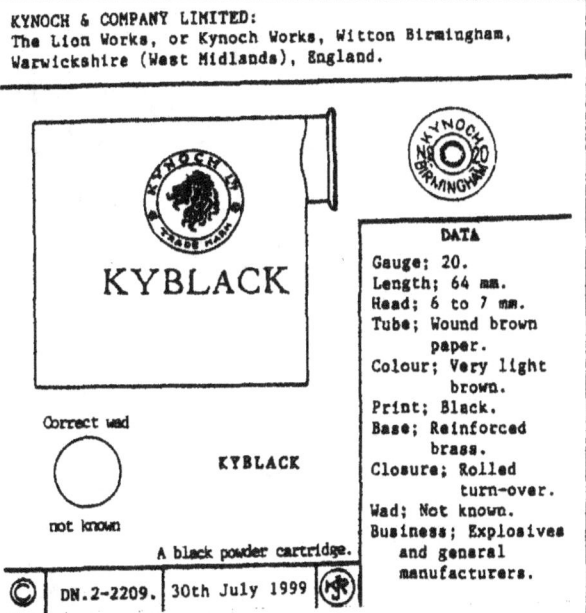

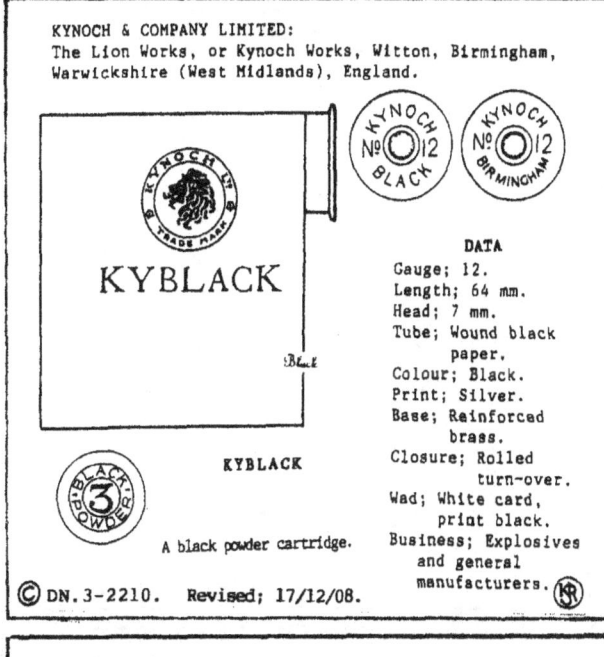
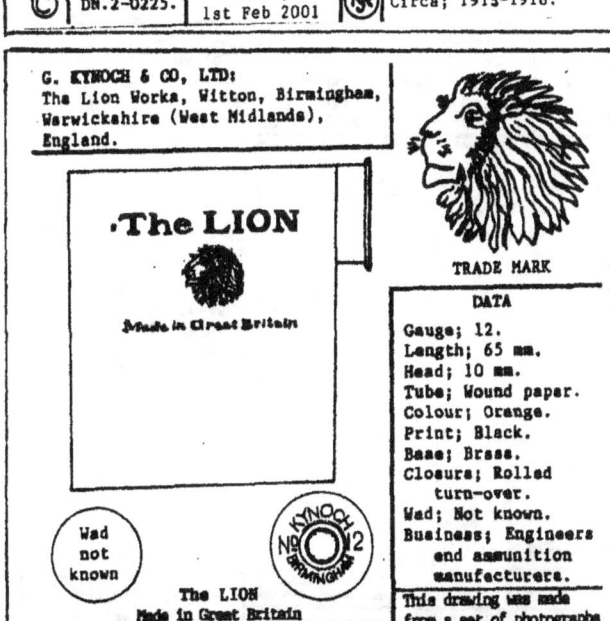
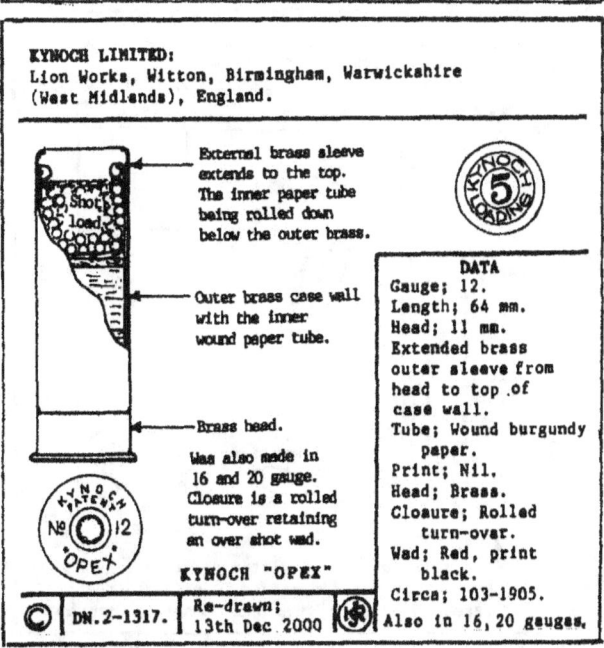

PLATE 219 [KYN – KYN]

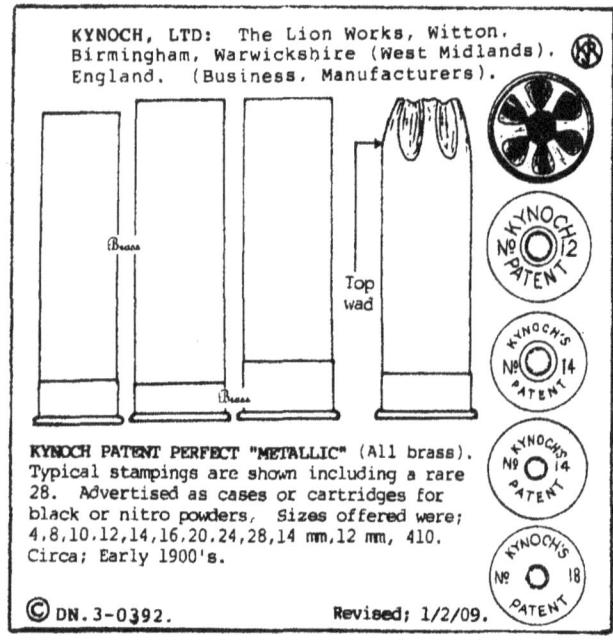

KYNOCH, LTD: The Lion Works, Witton, Birmingham, Warwickshire (West Midlands). England. (Business, Manufacturers).

KYNOCH PATENT PERFECT "METALLIC" (All brass). Typical stampings are shown including a rare 28. Advertised as cases or cartridges for black or nitro powders. Sizes offered were; 4,8,10,12,14,16,20,24,28,14 mm,12 mm, 410. Circa; Early 1900's.

© DN.3-0392.   Revised; 1/2/09.

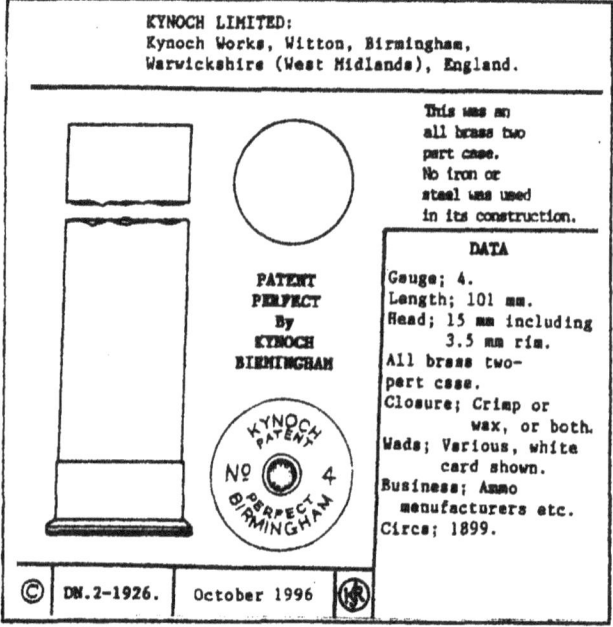

KYNOCH LIMITED: Kynoch Works, Witton, Birmingham, Warwickshire (West Midlands), England.

This was an all brass two part case. No iron or steel was used in its construction.

DATA
Gauge; 4.
Length; 101 mm.
Head; 15 mm including 3.5 mm rim.
All brass two-part case.
Closure; Crimp or wax, or both.
Wads; Various, white card shown.
Business; Ammo manufacturers etc.
Circa; 1899.

© DN.2-1926.   October 1996

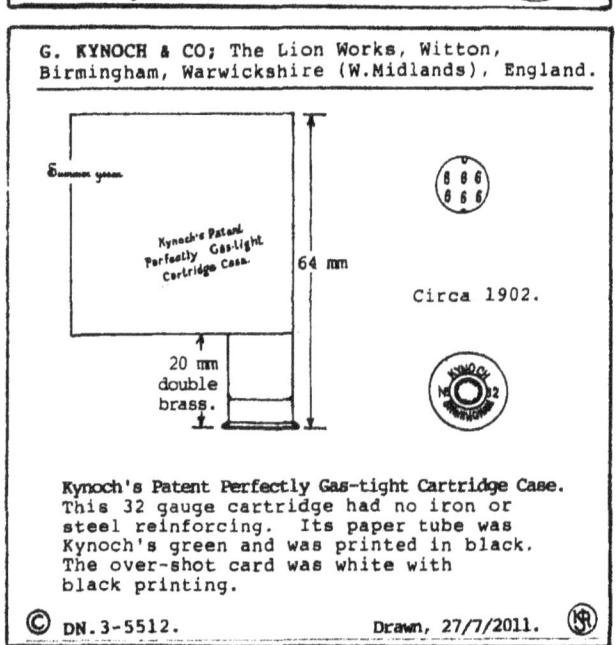

G. KYNOCH & CO; The Lion Works, Witton, Birmingham, Warwickshire (W.Midlands), England.

Circa 1902.

Kynoch's Patent Perfectly Gas-tight Cartridge Case. This 32 gauge cartridge had no iron or steel reinforcing. Its paper tube was Kynoch's green and was printed in black. The over-shot card was white with black printing.

© DN.3-5512.   Drawn, 27/7/2011.

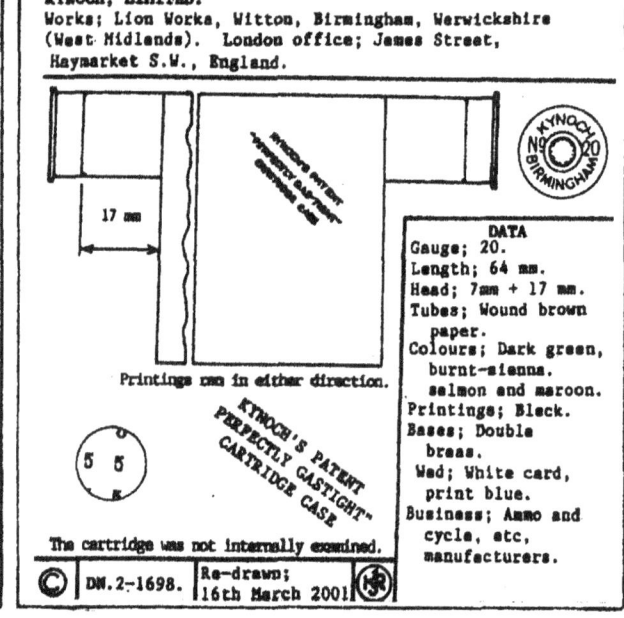

KYNOCH, LIMITED: Works; Lion Works, Witton, Birmingham, Warwickshire (West Midlands). London office; James Street, Haymarket S.W., England.

Printings run in either direction.

The cartridge was not internally examined.

DATA
Gauge; 20.
Length; 64 mm.
Head; 7mm + 17 mm.
Tubes; Wound brown paper.
Colours; Dark green, burnt-sienna, salmon and maroon.
Printings; Black.
Bases; Double brass.
Wad; White card, print blue.
Business; Ammo and cycle, etc, manufacturers.

© DN.2-1698.   Re-drawn; 16th March 2001

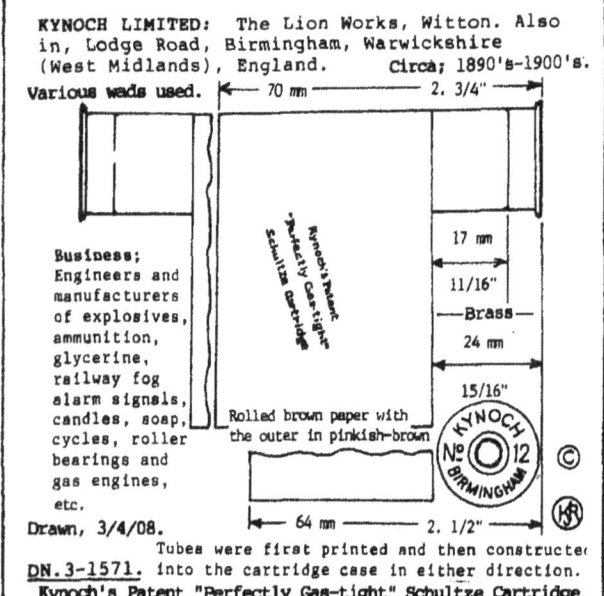

KYNOCH LIMITED: The Lion Works, Witton. Also in, Lodge Road, Birmingham, Warwickshire (West Midlands), England.   Circa; 1890's-1900's.

Various wads used.

Business; Engineers and manufacturers of explosives, ammunition, glycerine, railway fog alarm signals, candles, soap, cycles, roller bearings and gas engines, etc.

Drawn, 3/4/08.
DN.3-1571.   Tubes were first printed and then constructed into the cartridge case in either direction.
Kynoch's Patent "Perfectly Gas-tight" Schultze Cartridge

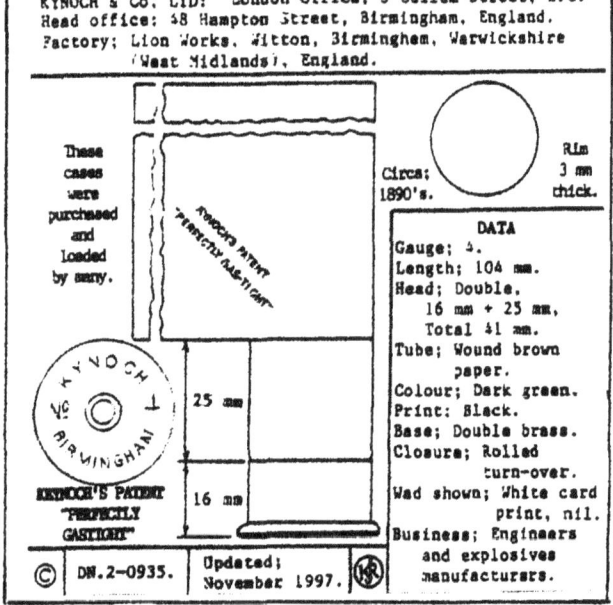

KYNOCH & Co, LTD: London office; 3 Cullum Street, E.C. Head office; 48 Hampton Street, Birmingham, England. Factory; Lion Works, Witton, Birmingham, Warwickshire (West Midlands), England.

These cases were purchased and loaded by many.

Circa; 1890's.

Rim 3 mm thick.

DATA
Gauge; 4.
Length; 104 mm.
Head; Double. 16 mm + 25 mm. Total 41 mm.
Tube; Wound brown paper.
Colour; Dark green.
Print; Black.
Base; Double brass.
Closure; Rolled turn-over.
Wad shown; White card print, nil.
Business; Engineers and explosives manufacturers.

© DN.2-0935.   Updated; November 1997.

PLATE 220 [KYN - KYN]

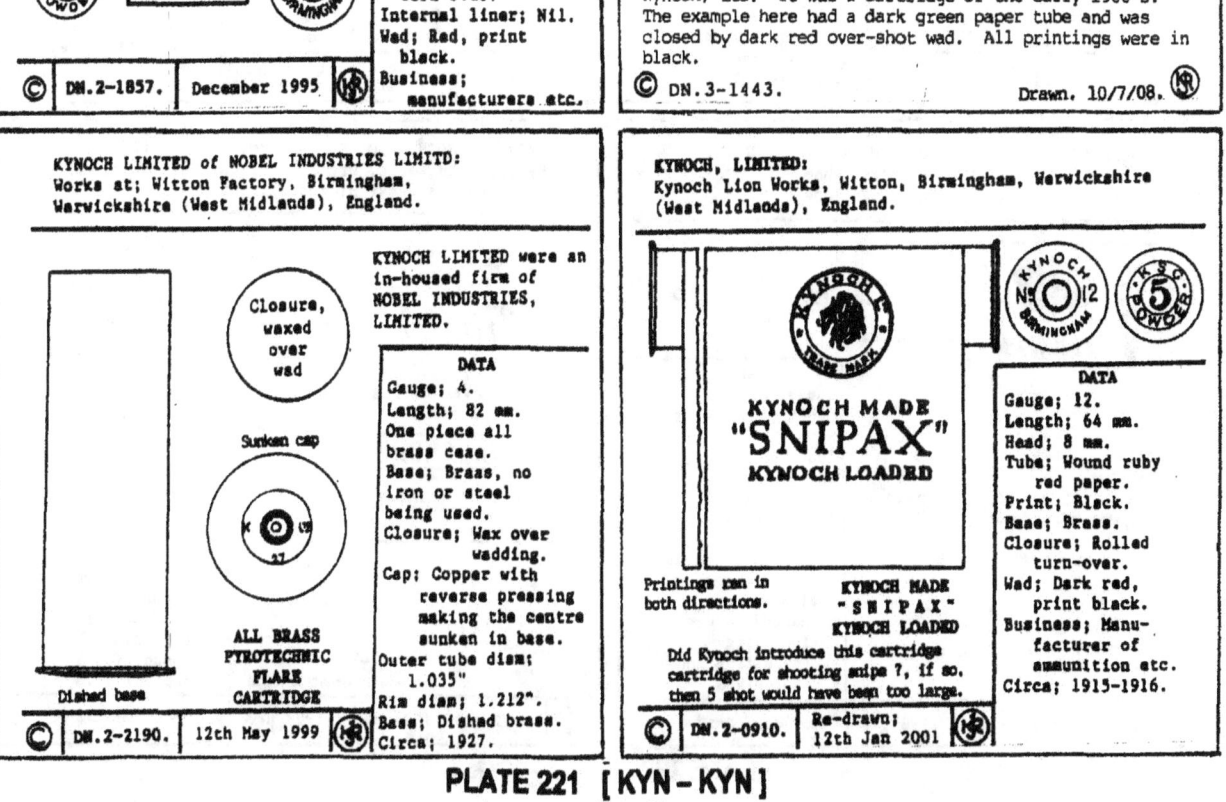

PLATE 221 [KYN - KYN]

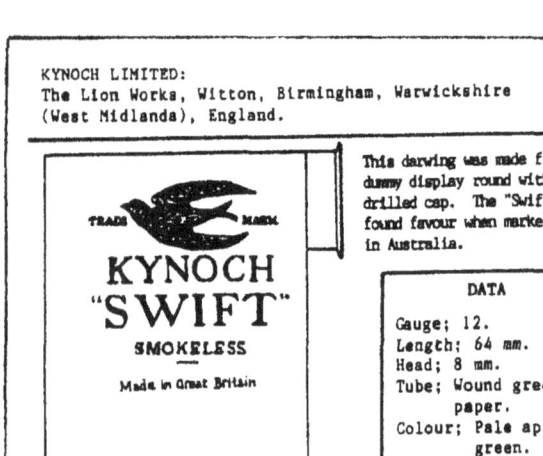
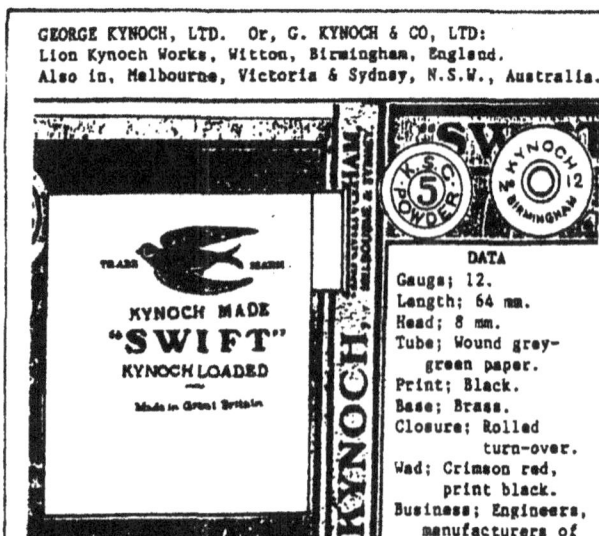
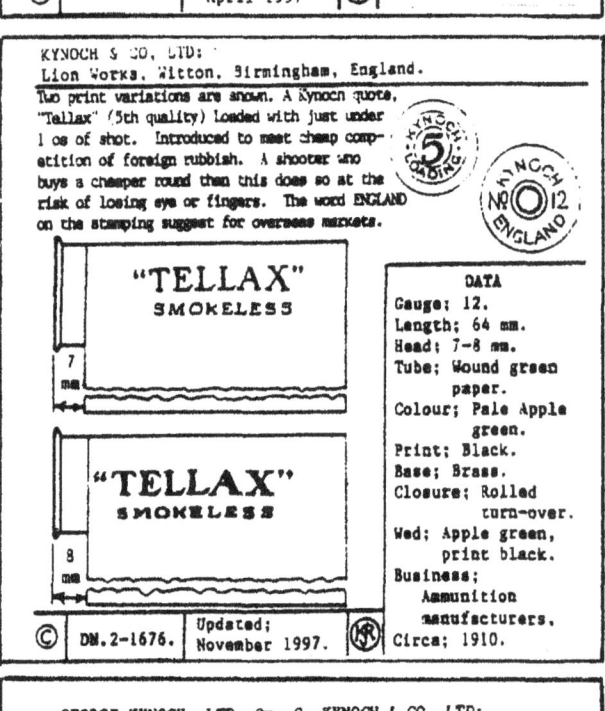

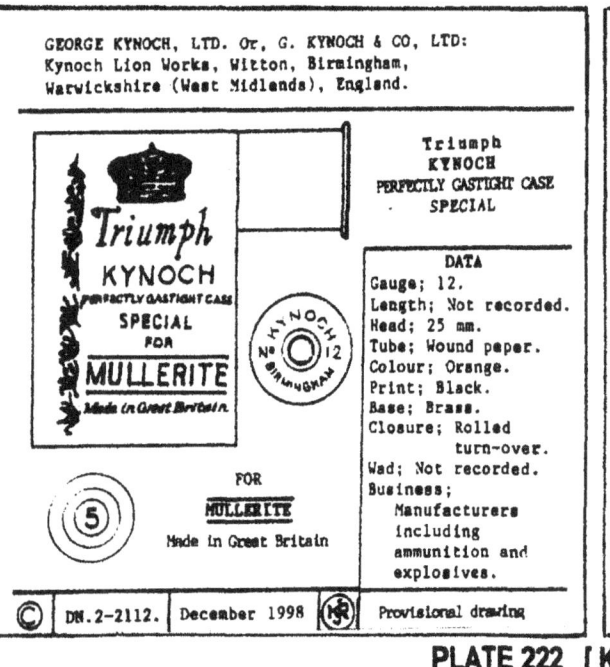
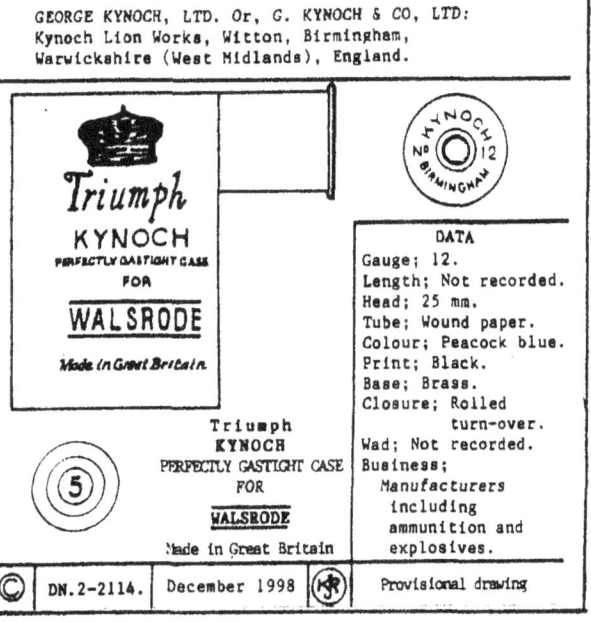

PLATE 222 [KYN – KYN]

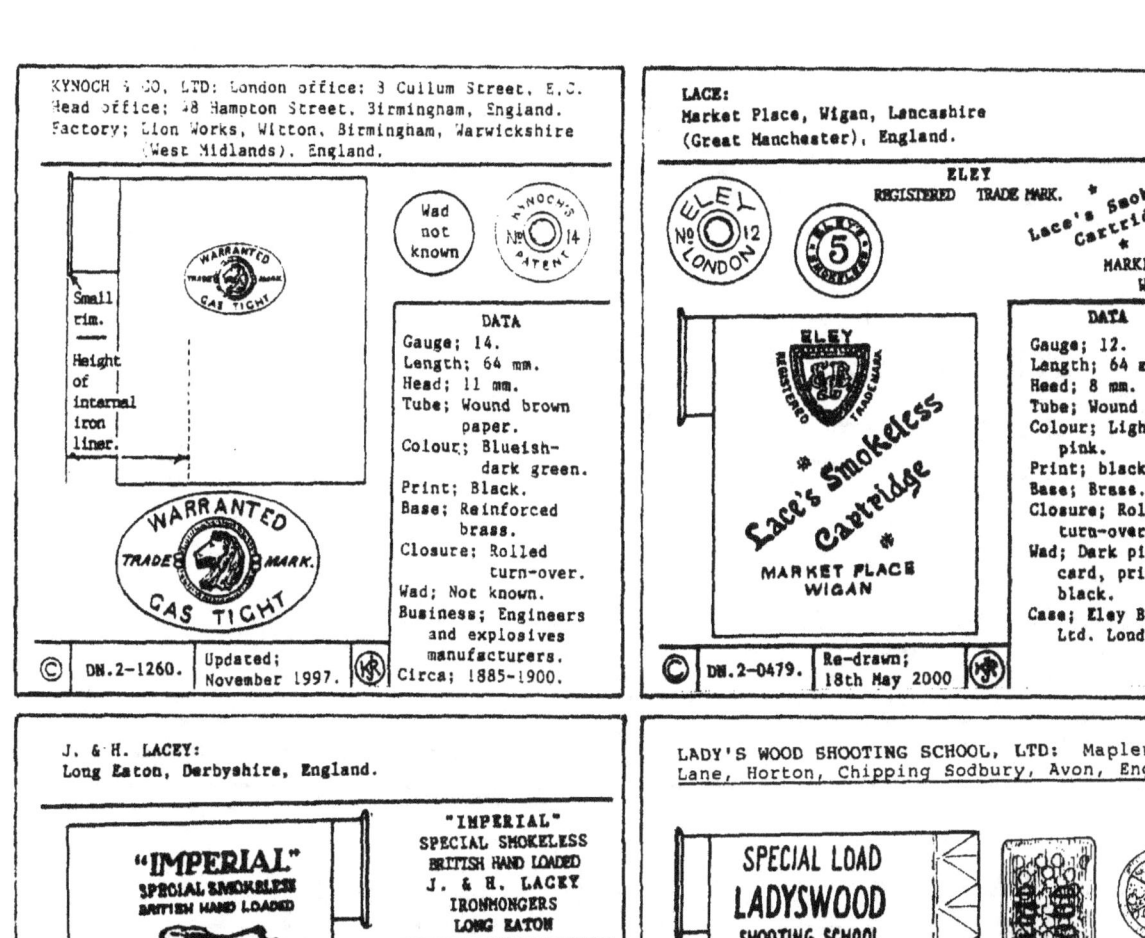
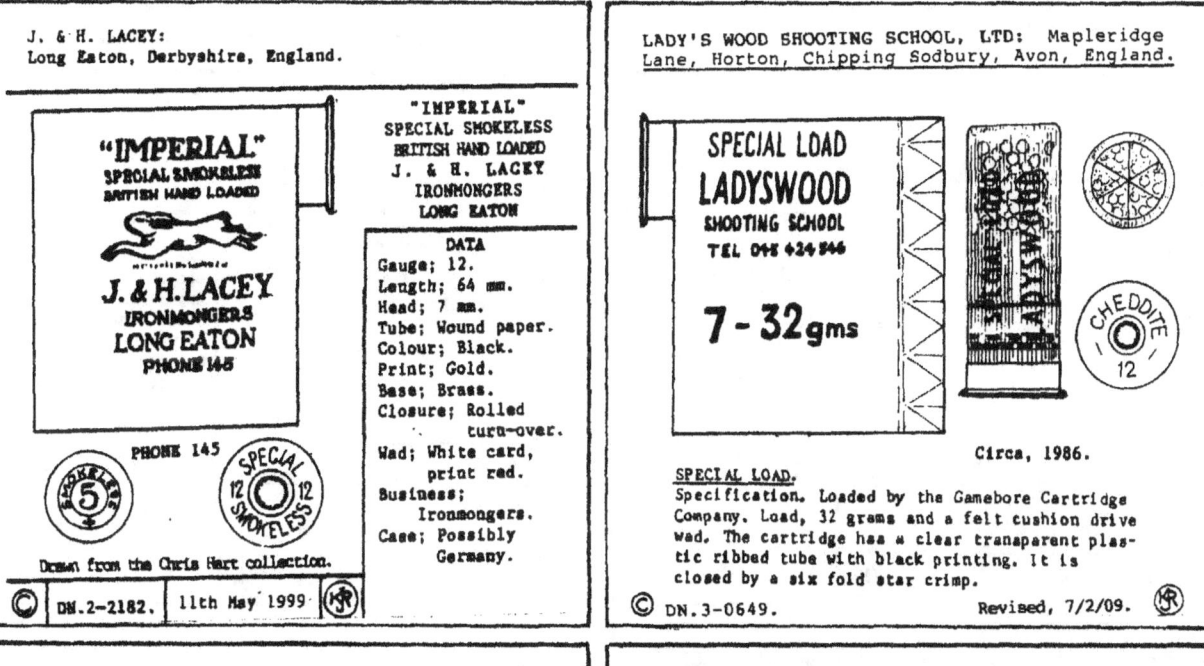
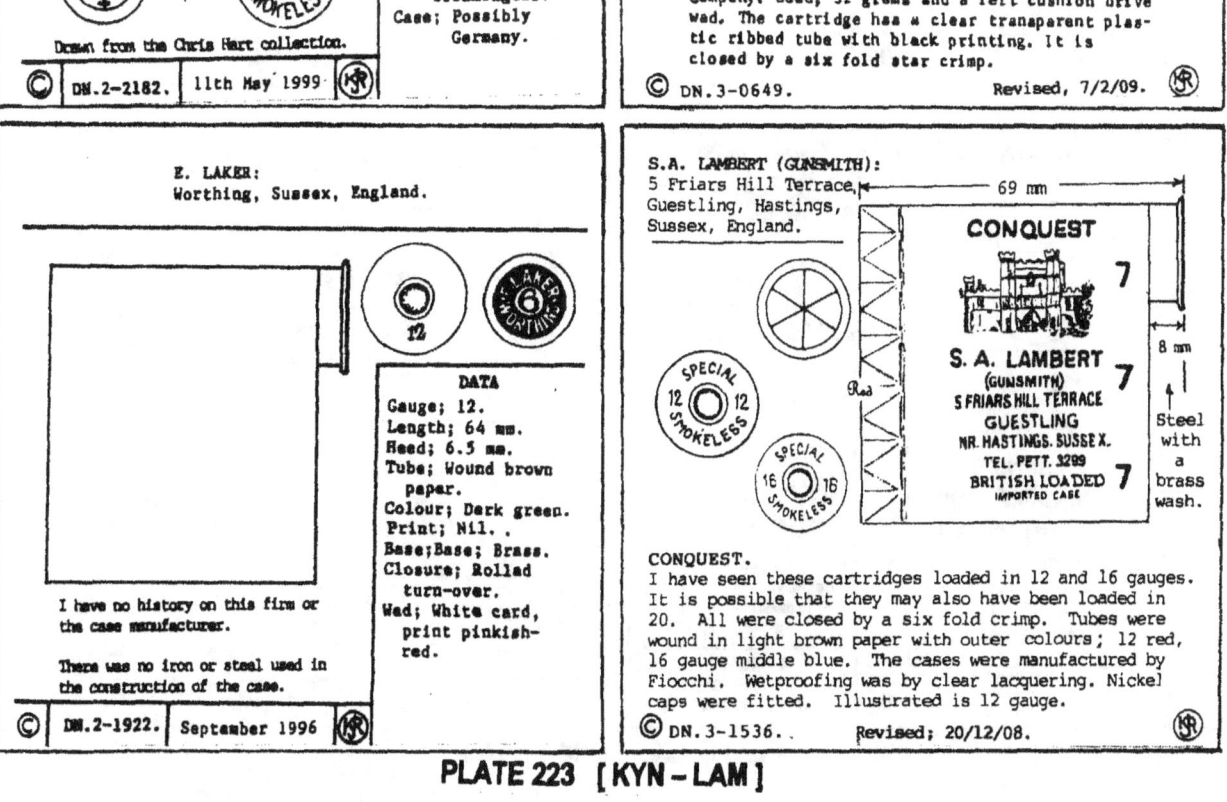

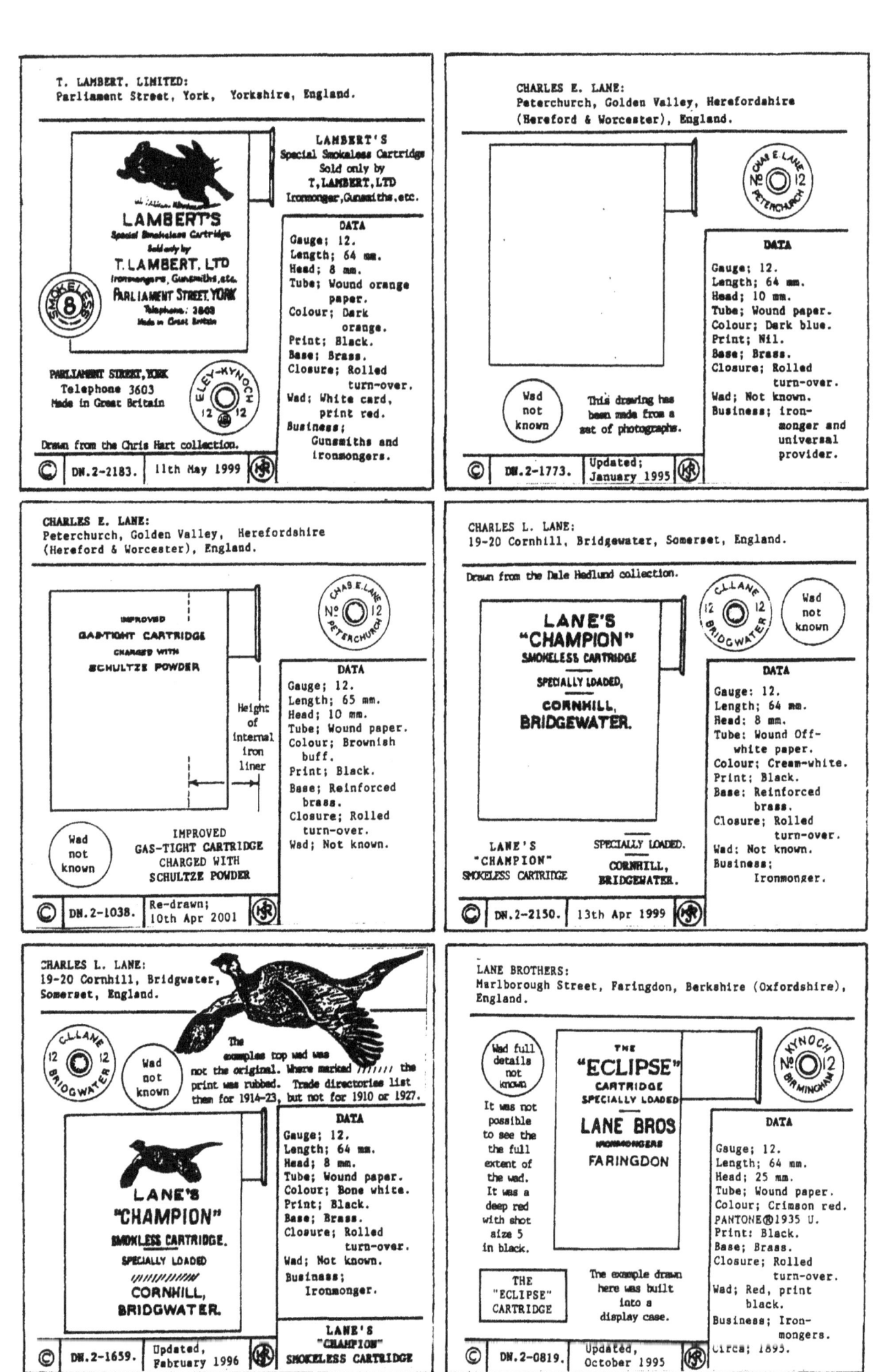

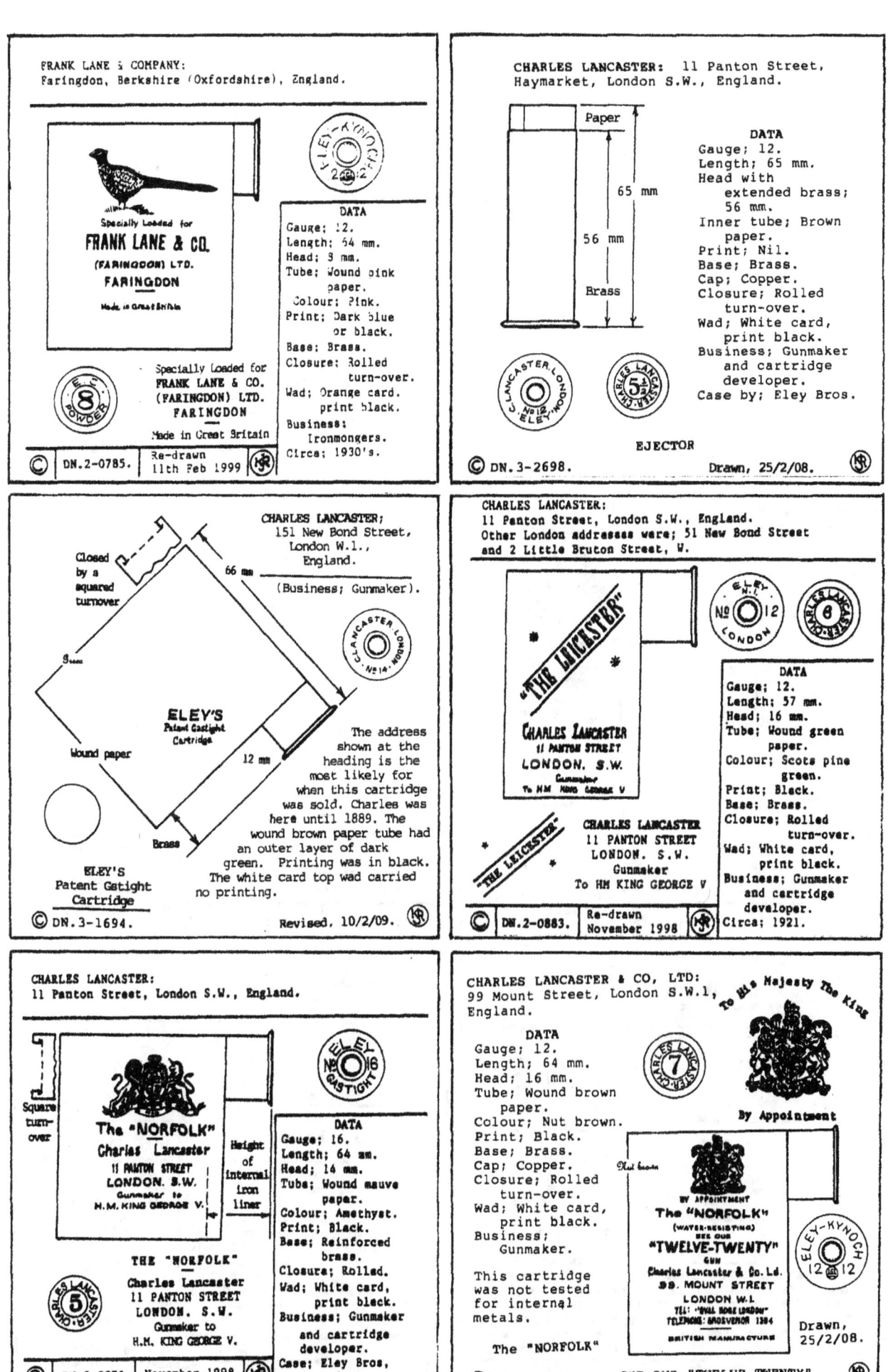

PLATE 225 [LAN-LAN]

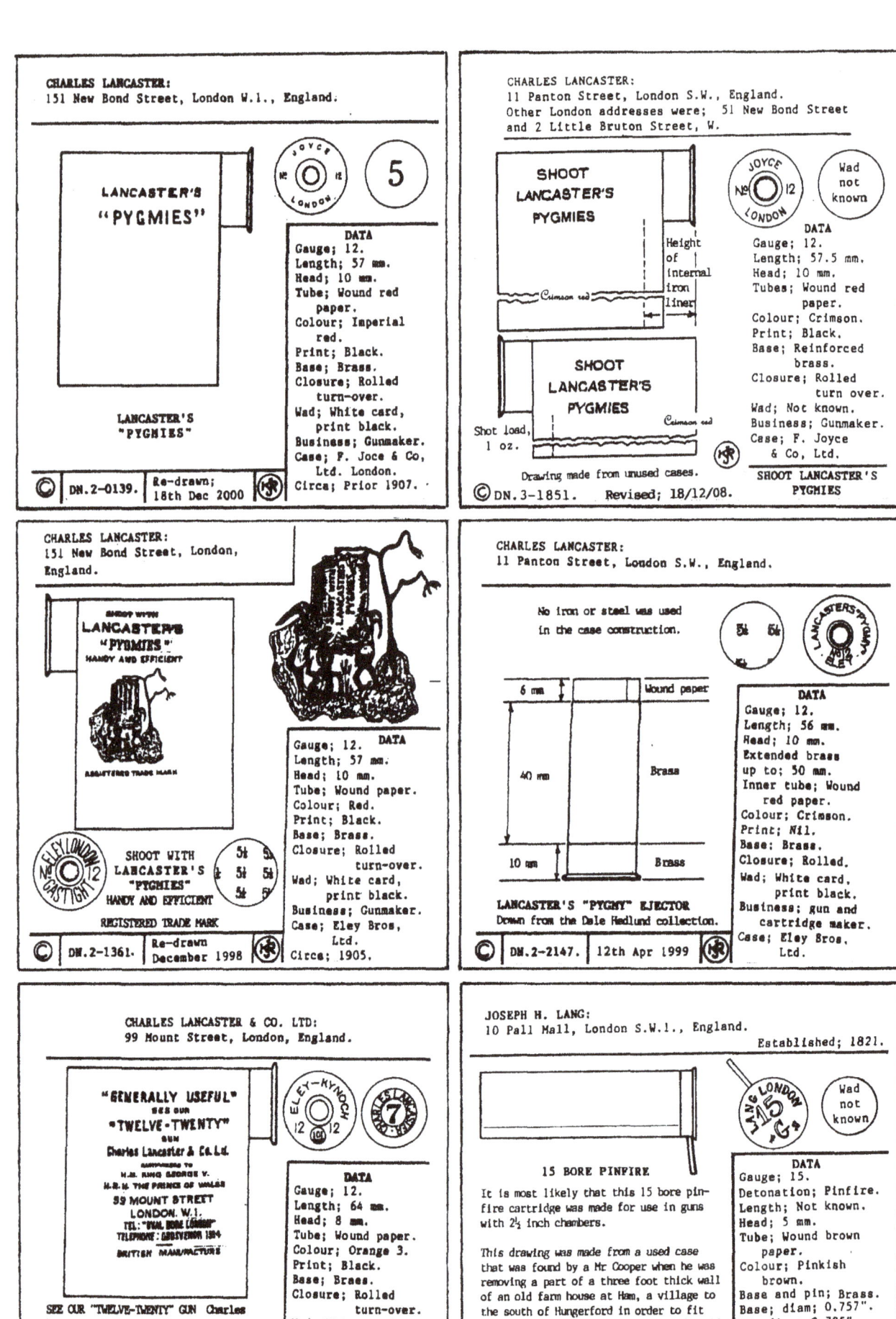

PLATE 226 [LAN-LAN]

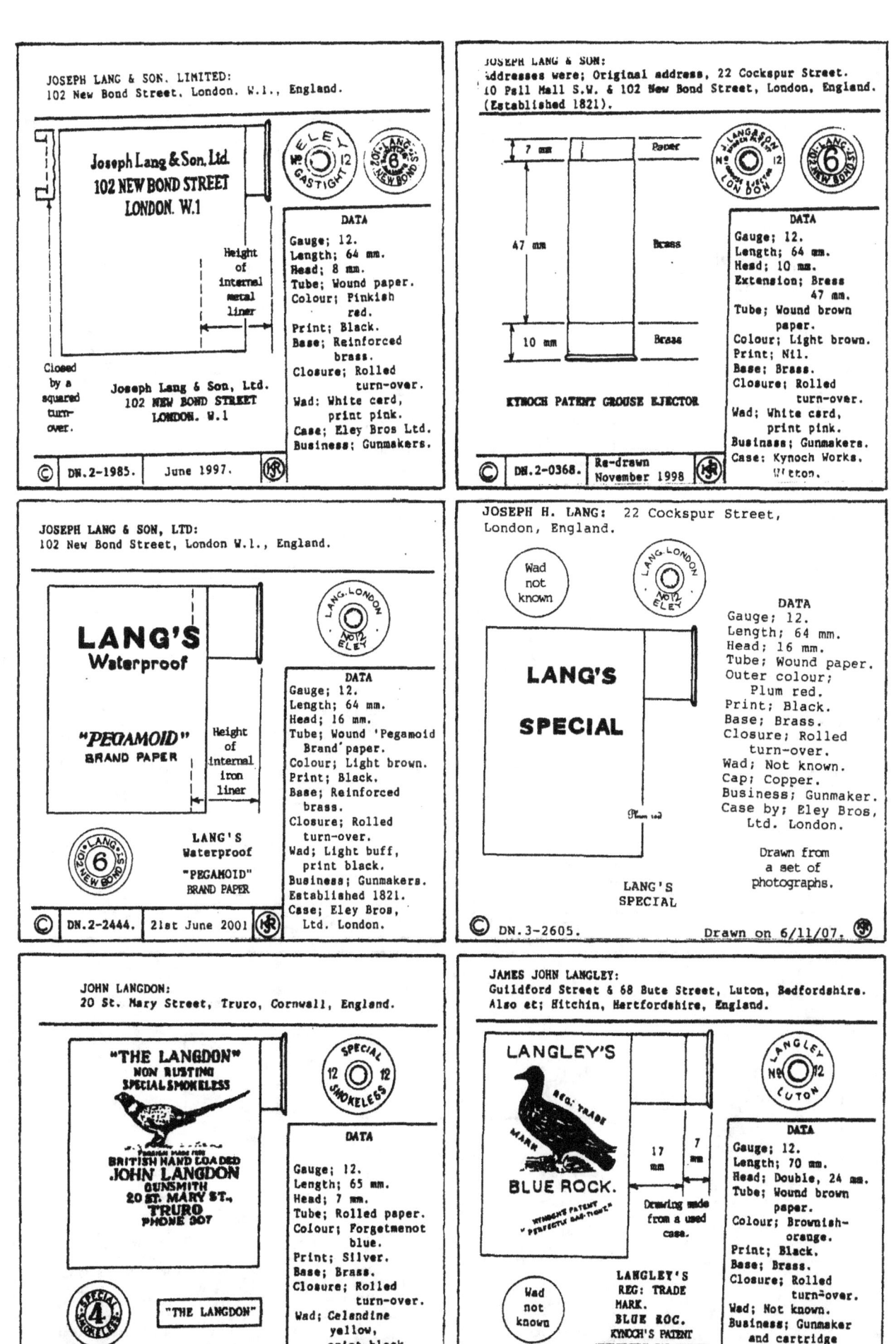

JAMES JOHN LANGLEY:
Guildford Street, and at, 68 Bute Street, Luton, Bedfordshire. Also at, Hitchin, Hertfordshire, England.

The example is believed to have been reloaded.

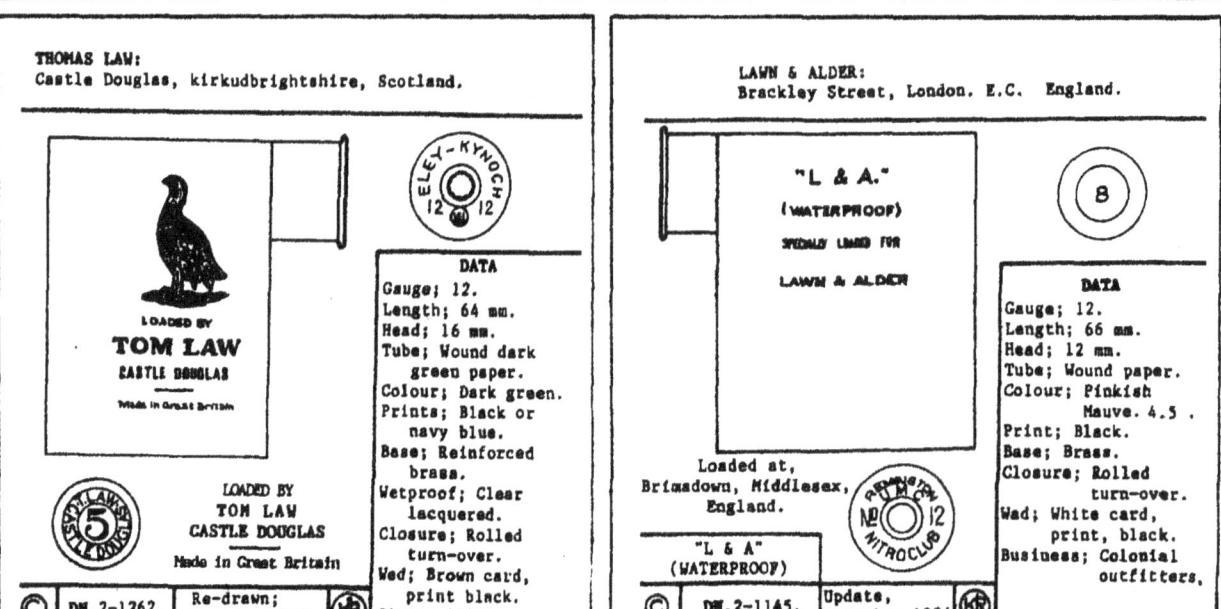

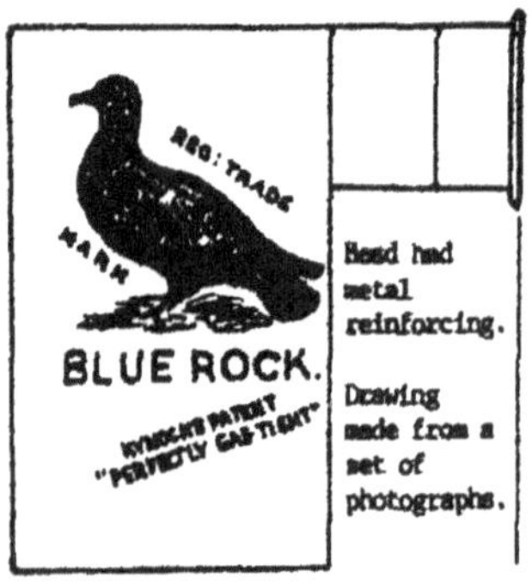

Head had metal reinforcing.

Drawing made from a set of photographs.

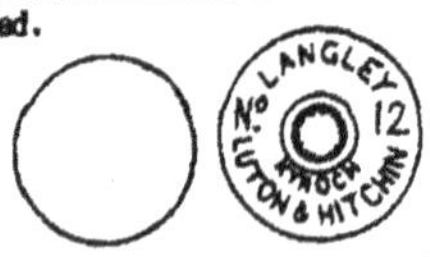

REG: TRADE
MARK
BLUE ROC

KYNOCH'S PATENT
"PERFECTLY GAS-TIGHT"

DATA
Gauge; 12.
Length; 64 mm.
Head; Double brass, 11 mm + 13 mm.
Tube; Wound paper.
Colour; Light tan brown.
Print; Blue-black.
Base; Reinforced brass.
Closure; Rolled turn-over.
Wad; White card, no printing.
Business; Gun and cartridge maker.
Case; Kynoch, Ltd.

© | DN.2-2343. | 19th Sept 2000 | KR

LANGLEY & LEWIS:
Park Square, Luton, Bedfordshire.
Also at; Maldon, Essex, England.

Height of interior metal liner.

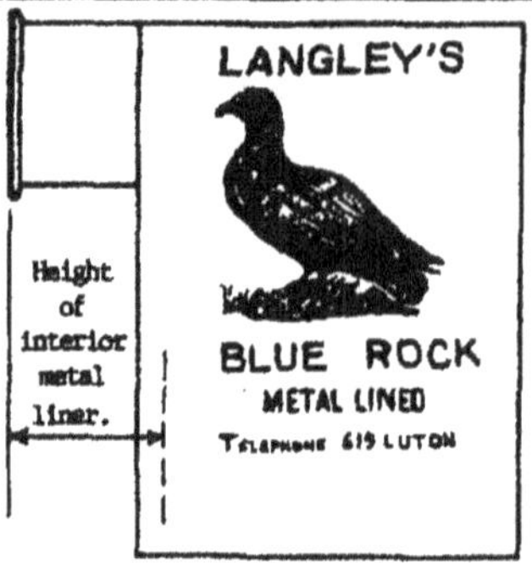

This drawing has been made from a used case. It is from the period when Langley and Lewis were partners.

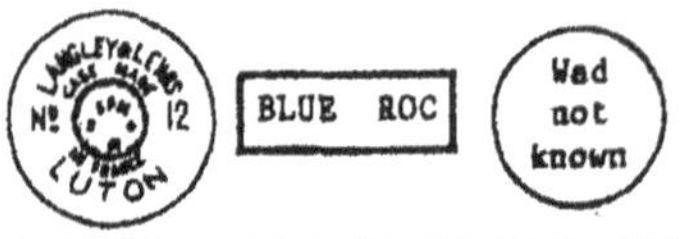

DATA
Gauge; 12.
Length; 64 mm.
Head; 16 mm.
Tube; Wound brown paper.
Colour; Schultze's buff.
Print; Black.
Base; Brass.
Closure; Rolled turn-over.
Wad; Not known.
Case; French, possibly Gevelot.
Business; Gunmakers, cartridge loaders.

© | DN.2-0336. | Updated March 1995 | KR

LANGLEY & LEWIS: Park Square, Luton, Bedfordshire. Also at, Maldon, Essex, England.

DATA
Gauge; 12.
Base; Brass.
Cap; Copper.
Tube; Wound off-white paper.
Business; Gunmakers.
All other details below.

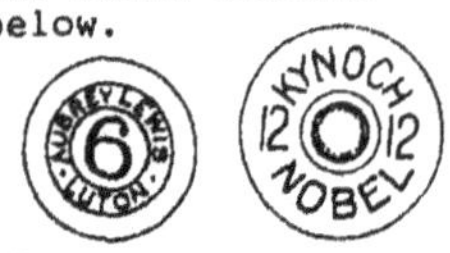

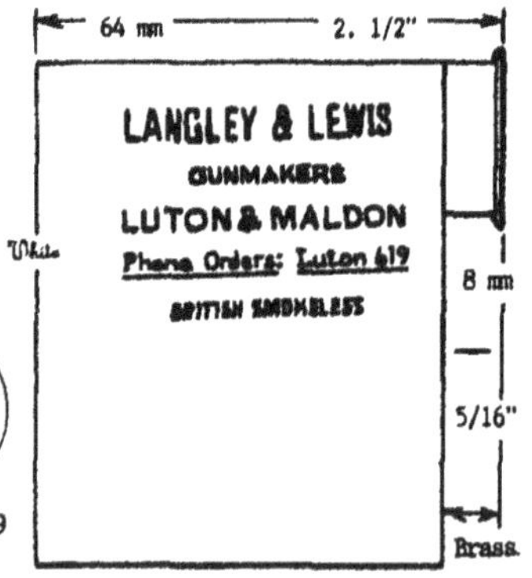

Phone Orders: Luton 619
BRITISH SMOKELESS

This plain looking cartridge from the early 1920's had its tube wound from off-white paper. The case wall printing was in black. James John Langley had his premises burnt down in 1914. For a few years he went into partnership with Aubrey Lewis. The orange top wad was one of Aubrey's and so the cartridge may have been loaded after their partnership was dissolved. All the printings were in black. DN.3-2710. Drawn; 28/2/08.

© KR

THOMAS LAW (JUNIOR):
Castle Douglas, Kirkudbrightshire (Dumfries & Galloway), Scotland.

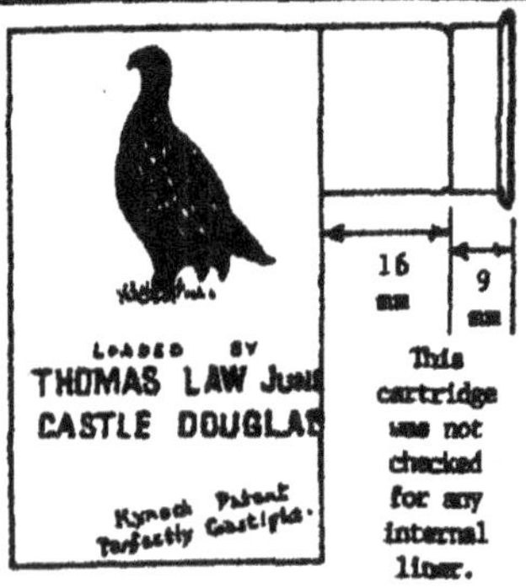

LOADED BY
THOMAS LAW JUNR
CASTLE DOUGLAS

Kynoch Patent
Perfectly Gastight

This cartridge was not checked for any internal liner.

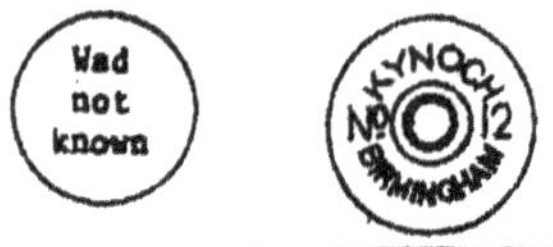

DATA
Gauge; 12.
Length; 64 mm.
Head; 25 mm (Double brass).
Tube; Wound paper.
Colour; Light blue.
Print; Dark blue.
Base; Brass.
Closure; Rolled turn-over.
Wad; Not known.
Business; Gunmaker or gunsmith.
Case; Kynoch, Witton, Birmingham.

© | DN.2-0214. | Re-drawn; 24th Jan 2000. | KR

THOMAS LAW:
Castle Douglas, kirkudbrightshire, Scotland.

LOADED BY
TOM LAW
CASTLE DOUGLAS
Made in Great Britain

DATA
Gauge; 12.
Length; 64 mm.
Head; 16 mm.
Tube; Wound dark green paper.
Colour; Dark green.
Prints; Black or navy blue.
Base; Reinforced brass.
Wetproof; Clear lacquered.
Closure; Rolled turn-over.
Wad; Brown card, print black.
Circa; 1930's.

© | DN.2-1262. | Re-drawn; 2nd Dec 2000 | KR

LAWN & ALDER:
Brackley Street, London. E.C. England.

Loaded at, Brimsdown, Middlesex, England.

"L & A"
(WATERPROOF)

DATA
Gauge; 12.
Length; 66 mm.
Head; 12 mm.
Tube; Wound paper.
Colour; Pinkish Mauve. 4.5 .
Print; Black.
Base; Brass.
Closure; Rolled turn-over.
Wad; White card, print, black.
Business; Colonial outfitters.

© | DN.2-1145. | Update, November 1994 | KR

PLATE 228 [LAN – LAW]

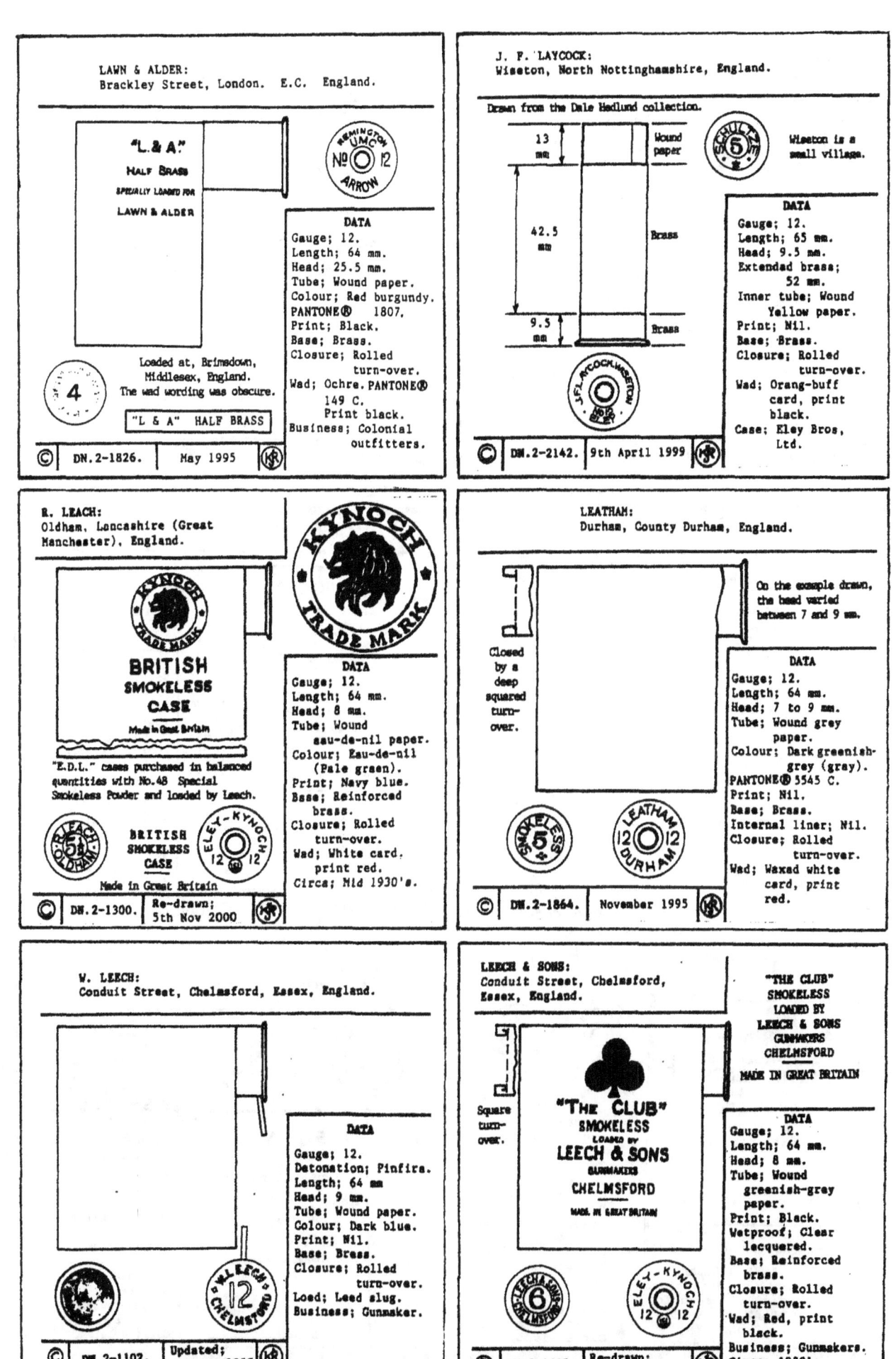

PLATE 229 [LAW-LEE]

W. LEECH & SONS:
Conduit Street, Chelmsford, Essex, England.

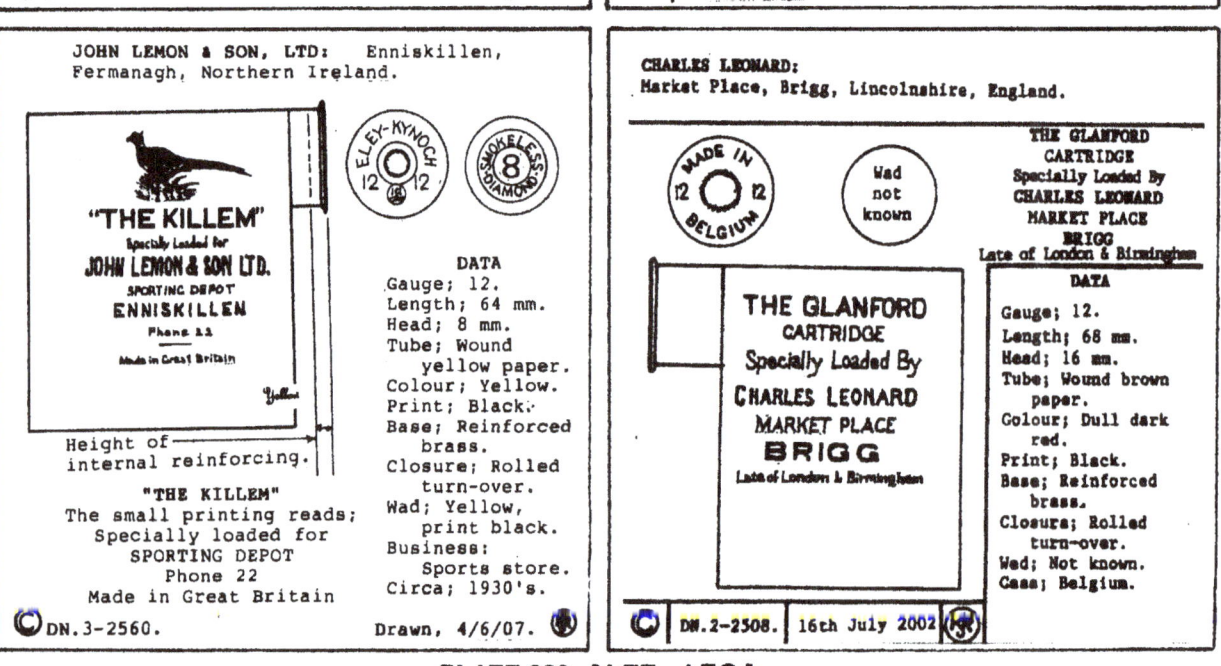

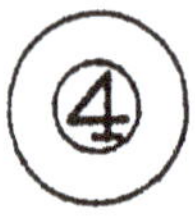

LEECH & SONS
GUNMAKERS
CHELMSFORD
PIGEON CARTRIDGE

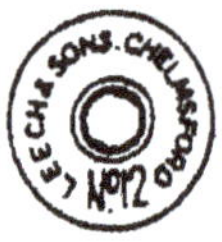

Drawn from a set of coloured photographs.

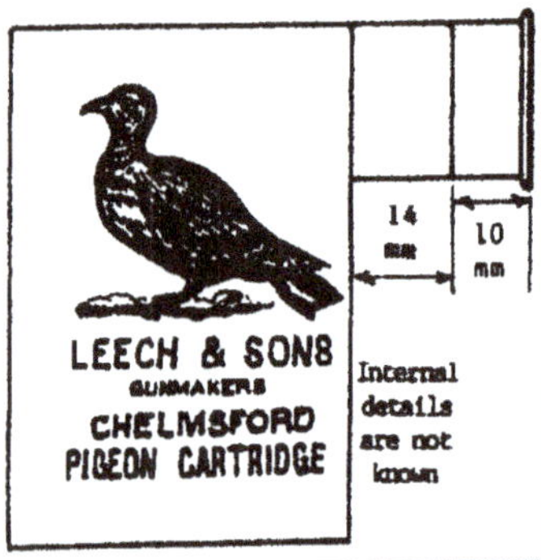

DATA

Gauge; 12.
Length; Approx 70 mm.
Head; Double 24 mm.
Tube; Wound paper.
Colour; Dark crimson.
Print; Black.
Base; Double brass.
Closure; Rolled turn-over.
Wad; White card, print black.
Business; Gunmakers.
Case; Most likely, Kynoch.

W. LEECH & SONS:
Conduit Street, Chelmsford, Essex, England.

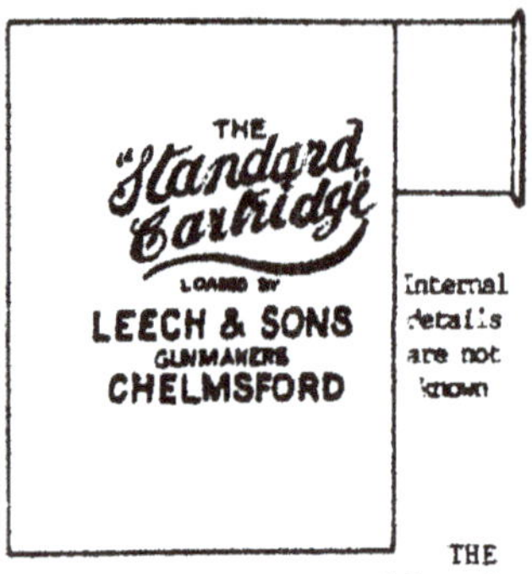

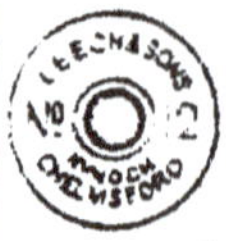

Drawn from a set of coloured photographs.

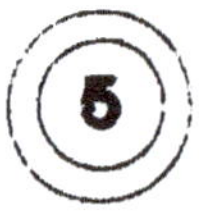

THE
"Standard
Cartridge"
LOADED BY
LEECH & SONS
GUNMAKERS
CHELMSFORD

DATA

Gauge; 12.
Length; Approx 65 mm.
Head; 16 mm.
Tube; Wound paper.
Colour; Dark crimson.
Print; Black.
Base; Brass.
Closure; Rolled turn-over.
Wad; White card, print black.
Business; Gunmakers.
Case; Kynoch.

WILLIAM LEECH & SONS: Conduit Street, Chelmsford, Essex, England.

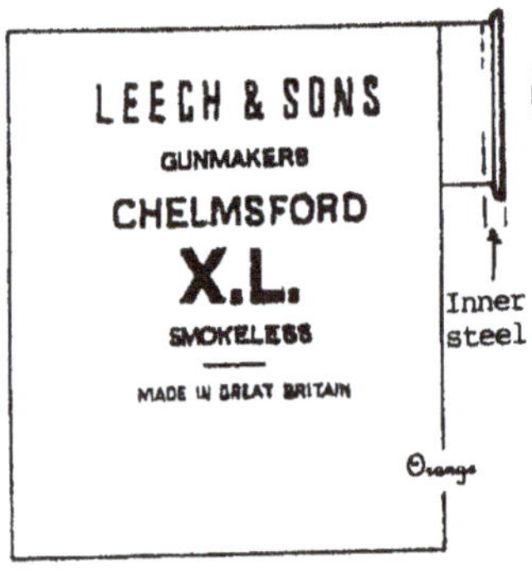

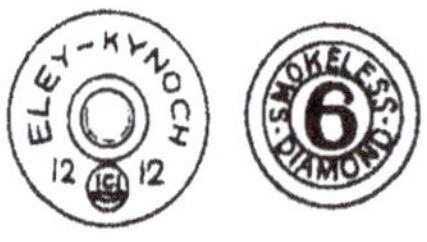

LEECH & SONS
GUNMAKERS
CHEMSFORD
X.L.
SMOKELESS
MADE IN GREAT BRITAIN

DATA

Gauge; 12.
Length; 64 mm.
Head; 8 mm.
Tube; Wound orange paper.
Print; Black.
Base; Reinforced brass.
Cap; Copper.
Closure; Rolled turn-over.
Wad; Yellow, print black.
Business; Gunmakers.

 Drawn, 27/4/08.

HERBERT E. LEGGETT:
Broad Street, Eye, Suffolk, England.

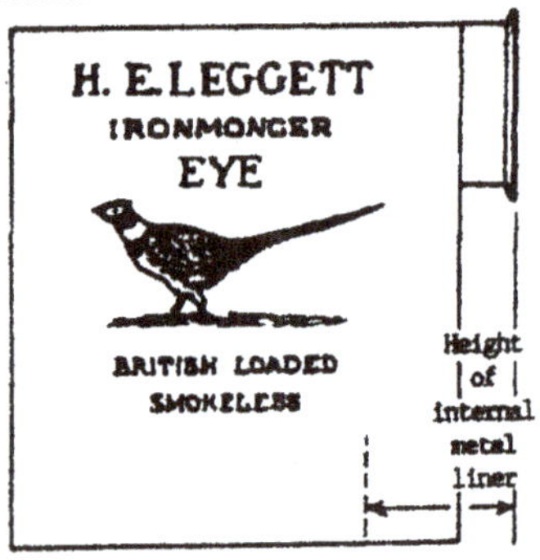

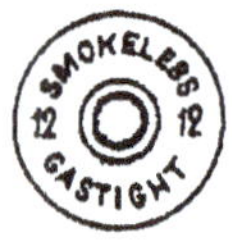

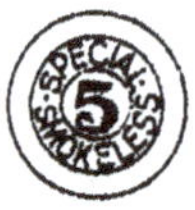

H. E. LEGGETT
IRONMONGER
EYE
BRITISH LOADED
SMOKELESS

DATA

Gauge; 12.
Length; 65 mm.
Head; 7.5 mm.
Tube; Wound brown paper.
Colour; Pinkish Salmon.
Print; Black.
Base; Reinforced brass.
Closure; Rolled turn-over.
Wad; Yellow, print black.
Business; Ironmonger.
Case; Germany.

JOHN LEMON & SON, LTD: Enniskillen, Fermanagh, Northern Ireland.

Height of internal reinforcing.

"THE KILLEM"
The small printing reads;
Specially loaded for
SPORTING DEPOT
Phone 22
Made in Great Britain

DATA

Gauge; 12.
Length; 64 mm.
Head; 8 mm.
Tube; Wound yellow paper.
Colour; Yellow.
Print; Black.
Base; Reinforced brass.
Closure; Rolled turn-over.
Wad; Yellow, print black.
Business: Sports store.
Circa; 1930's.

 Drawn, 4/6/07.

CHARLES LEONARD:
Market Place, Brigg, Lincolnshire, England.

Wad not known

THE GLANFORD
CARTRIDGE
Specially Loaded By
CHARLES LEONARD
MARKET PLACE
BRIGG
Late of London & Birmingham

DATA

Gauge; 12.
Length; 68 mm.
Head; 16 mm.
Tube; Wound brown paper.
Colour; Dull dark red.
Print; Black.
Base; Reinforced brass.
Closure; Rolled turn-over.
Wad; Not known.
Case; Belgium.

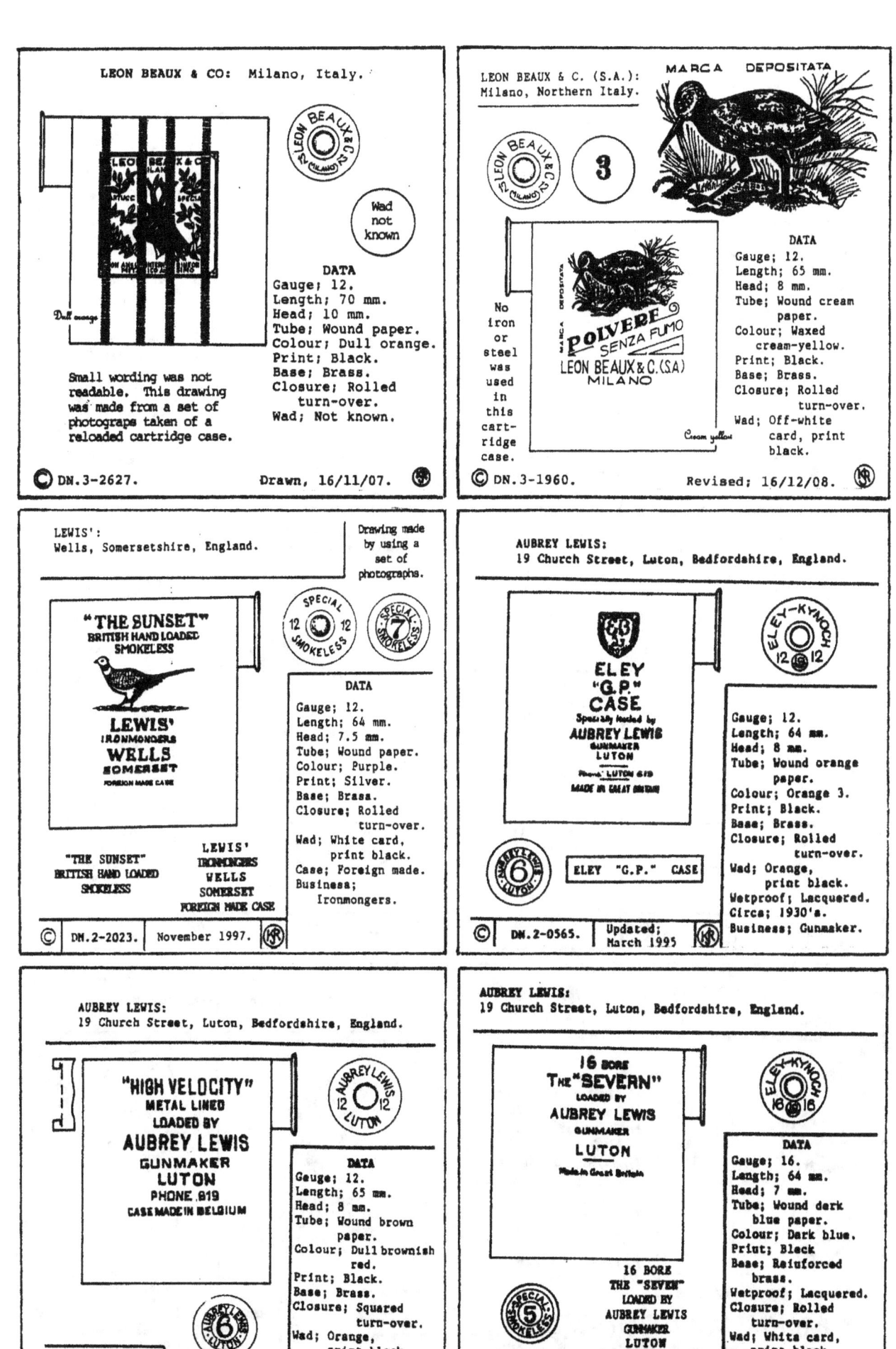

PLATE 231 [LEO - LEW]

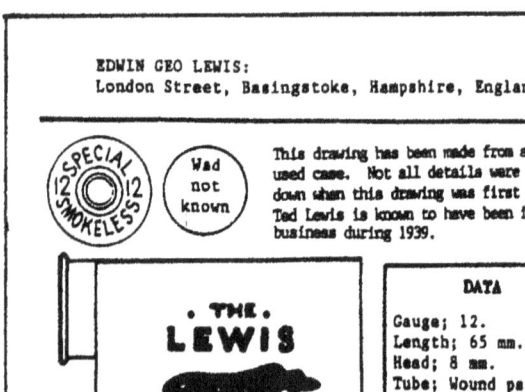
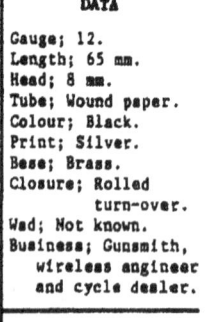
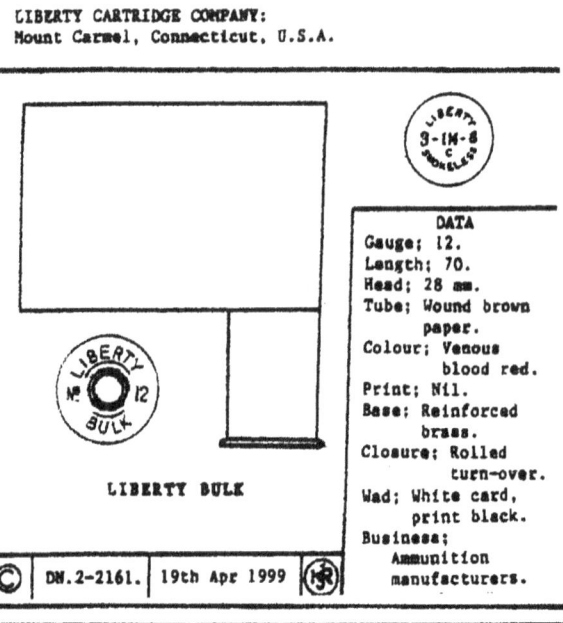
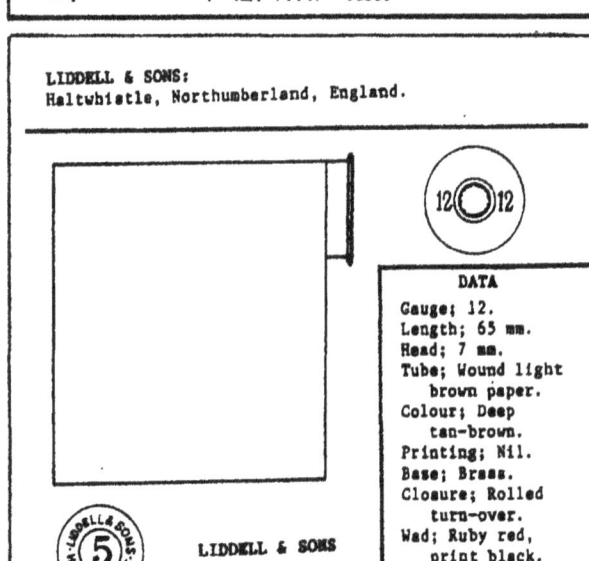
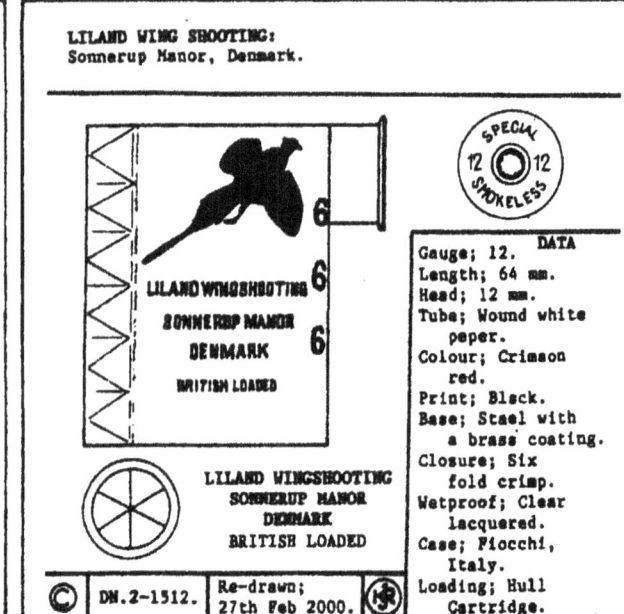
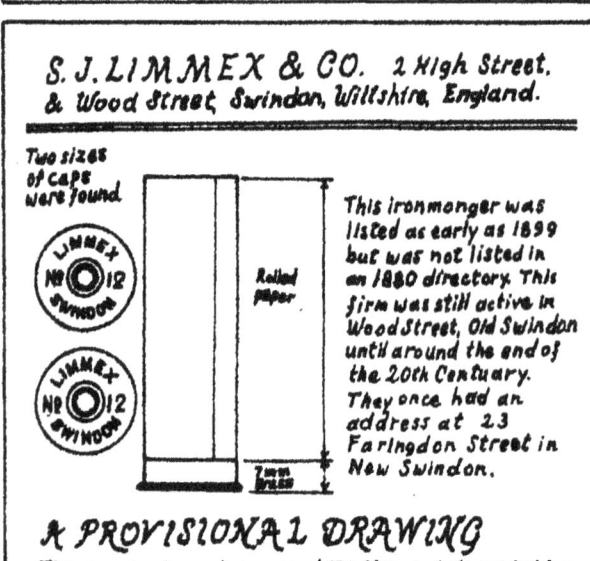
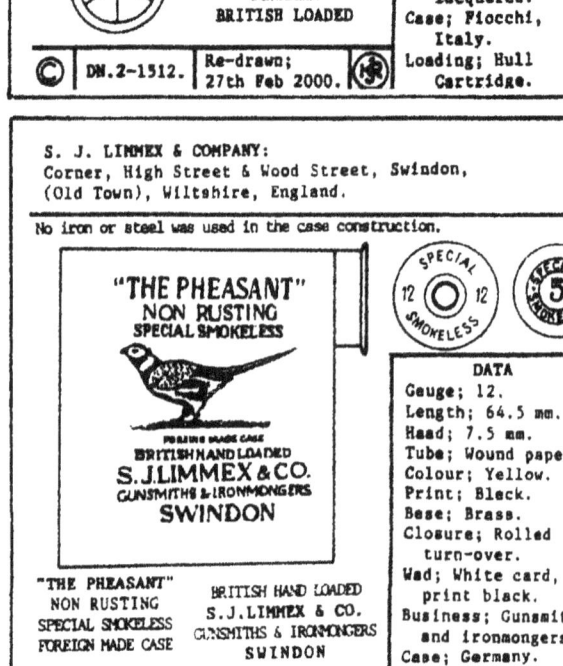

PLATE 232 [LEW – LIM]

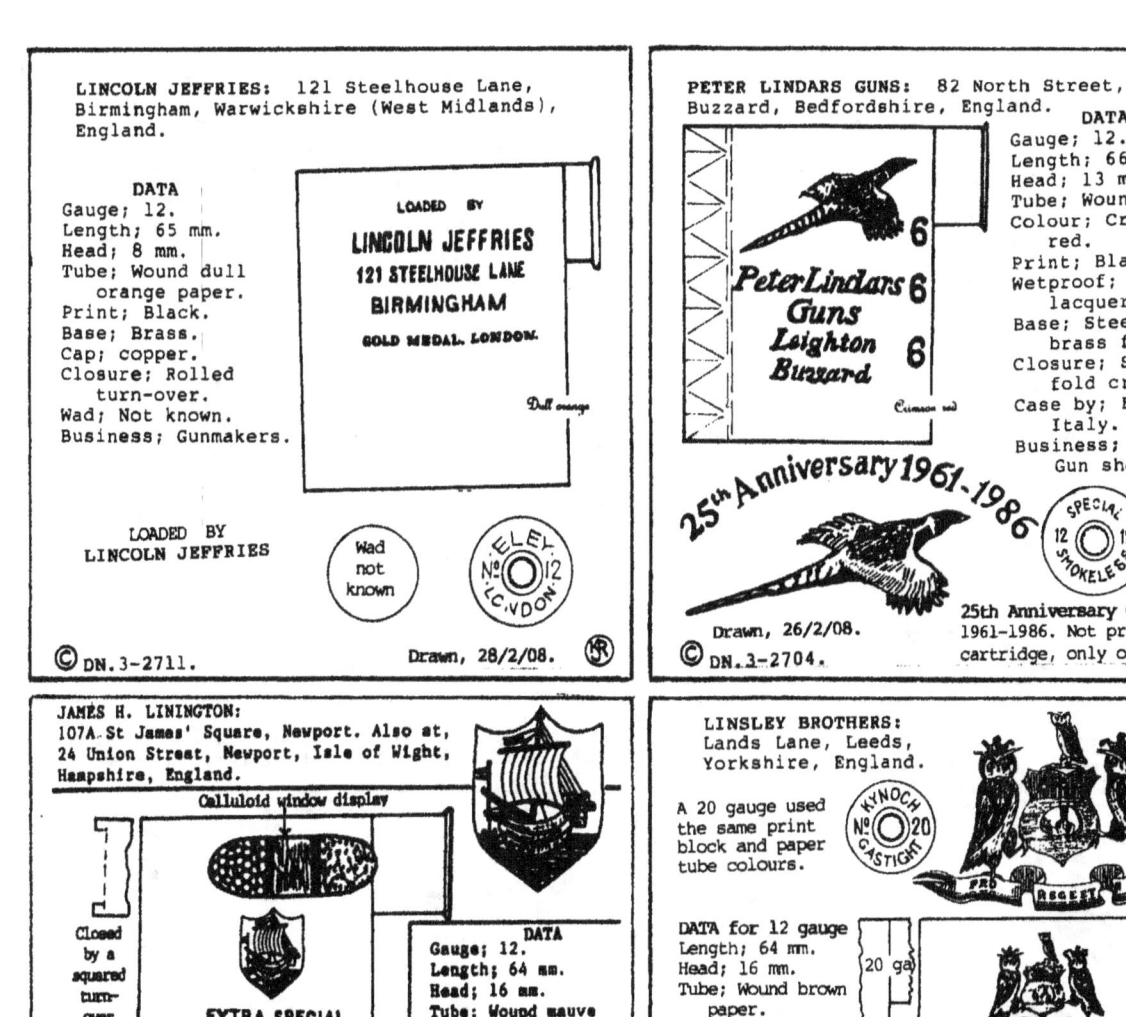
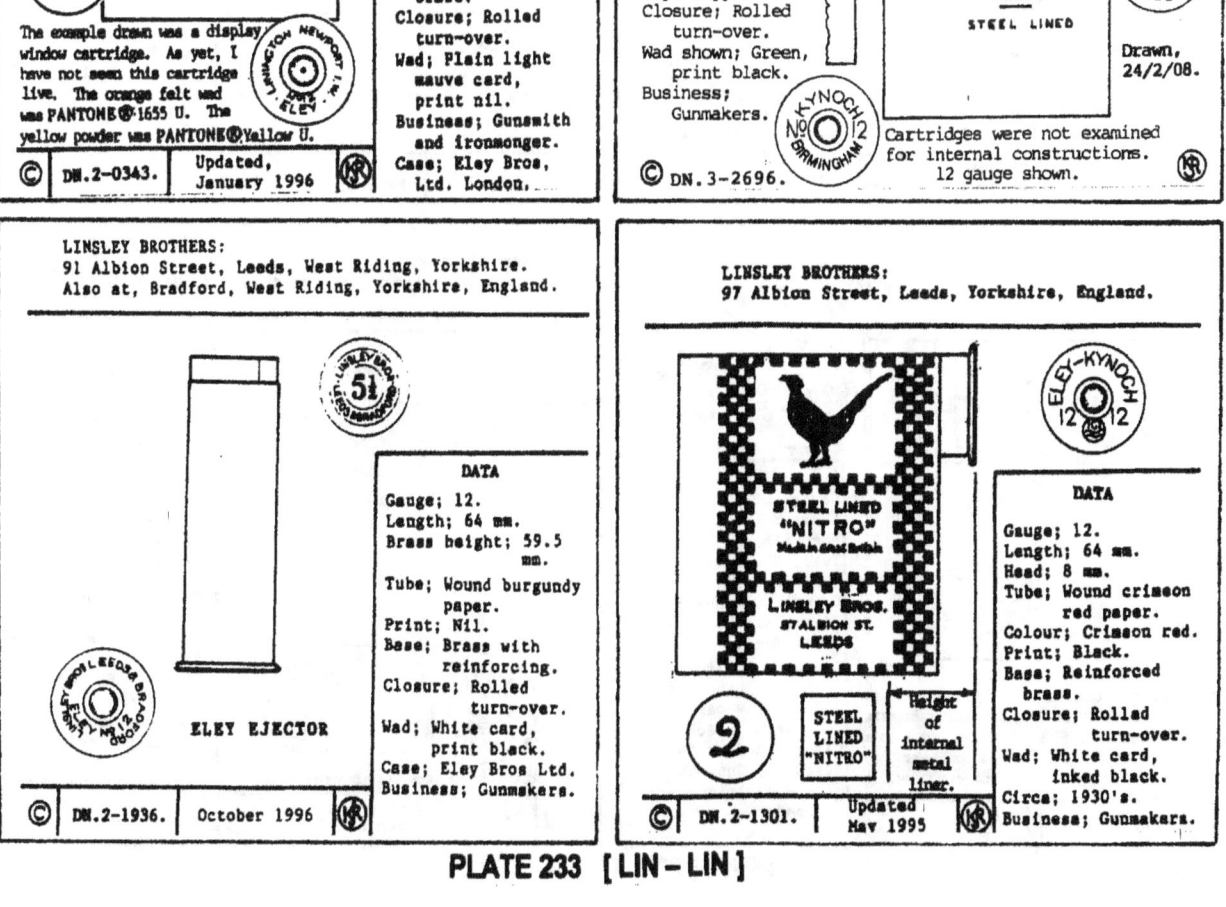

PLATE 233 [LIN – LIN]

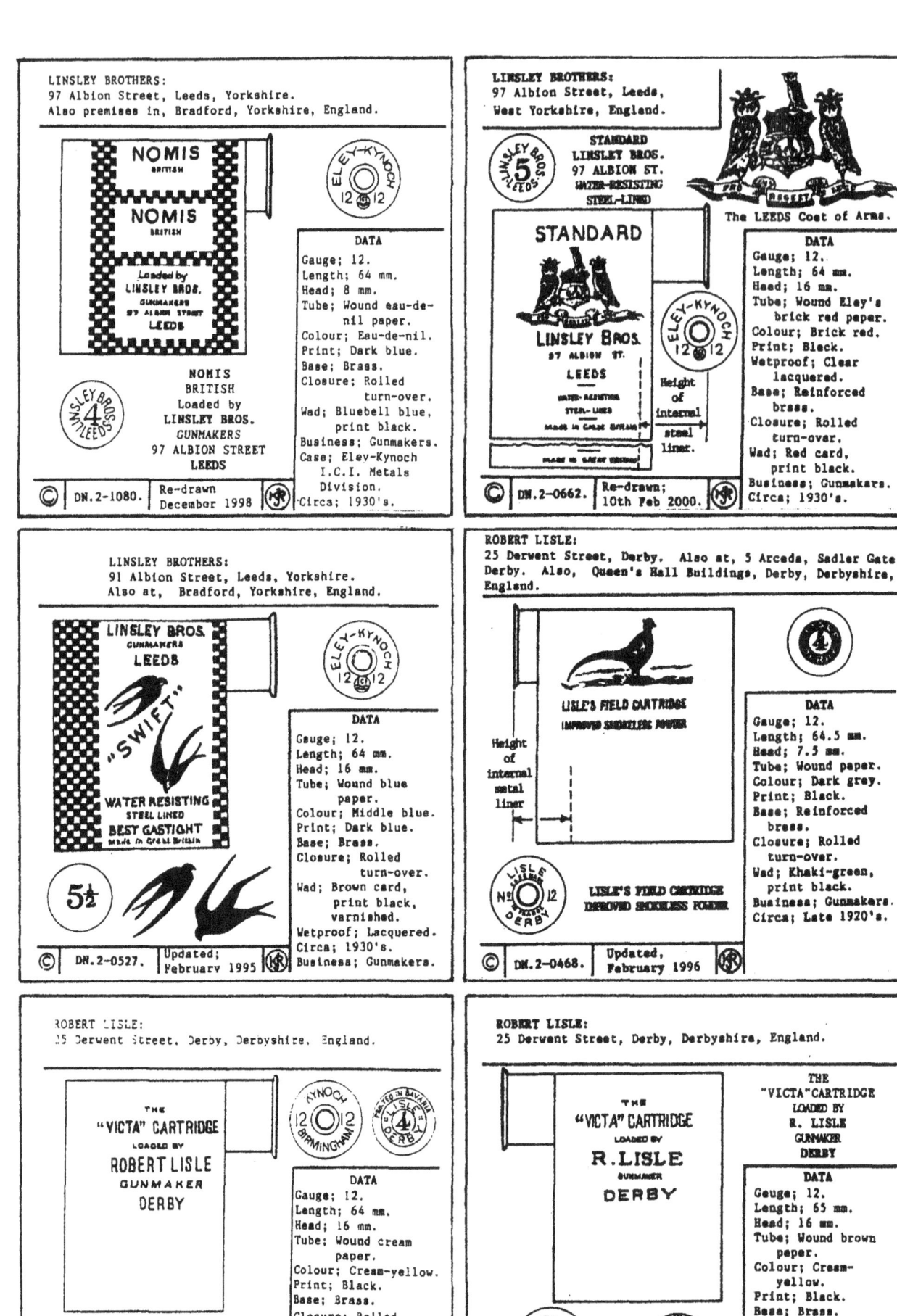

PLATE 234 [LIN – LIS]

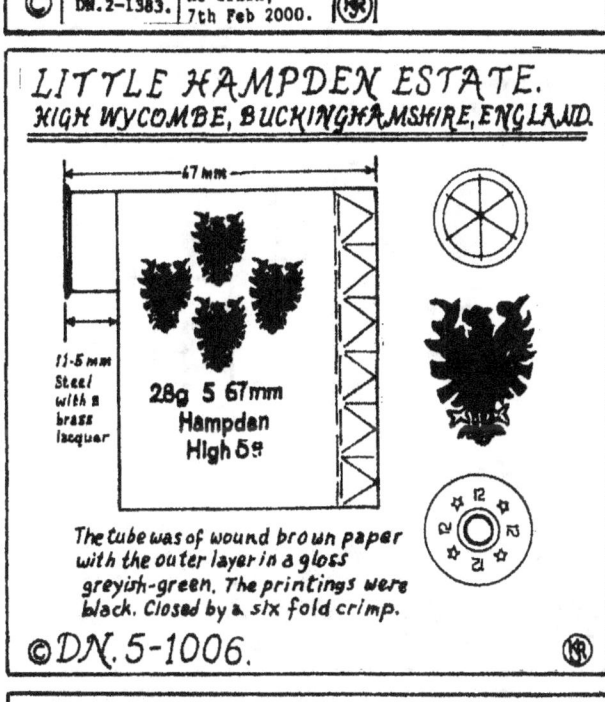
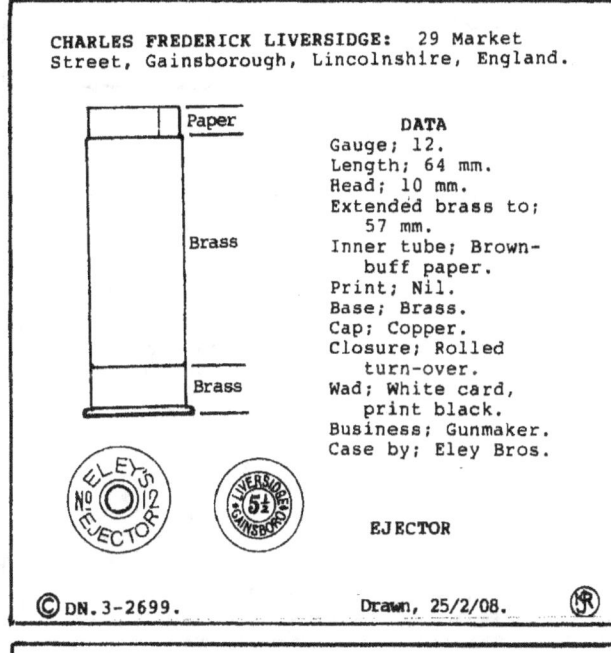
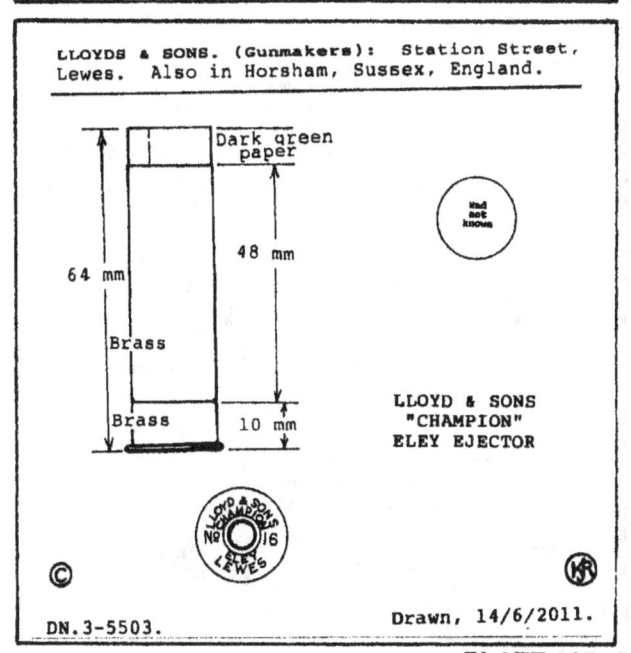
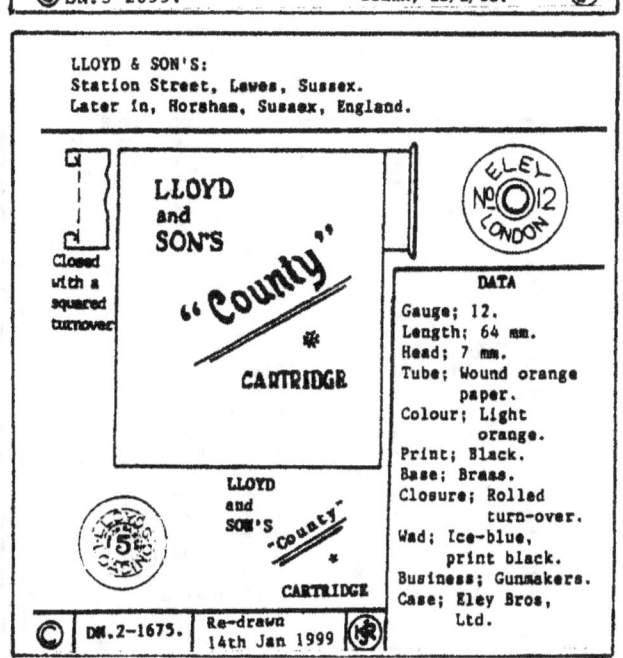

PLATE 235 [LIT – LLO]

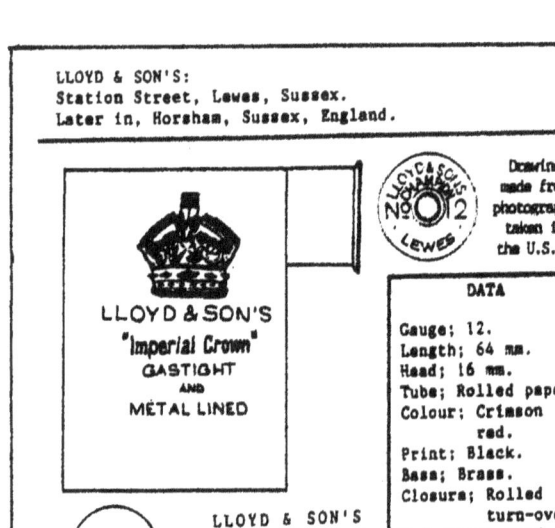
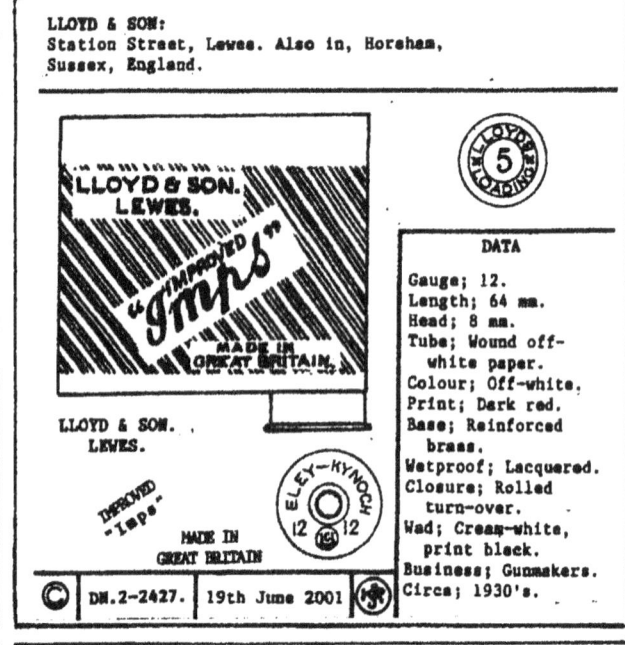
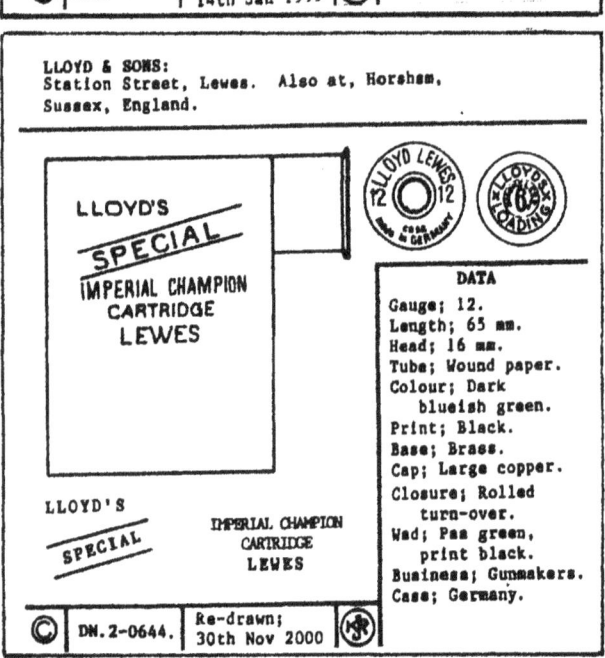
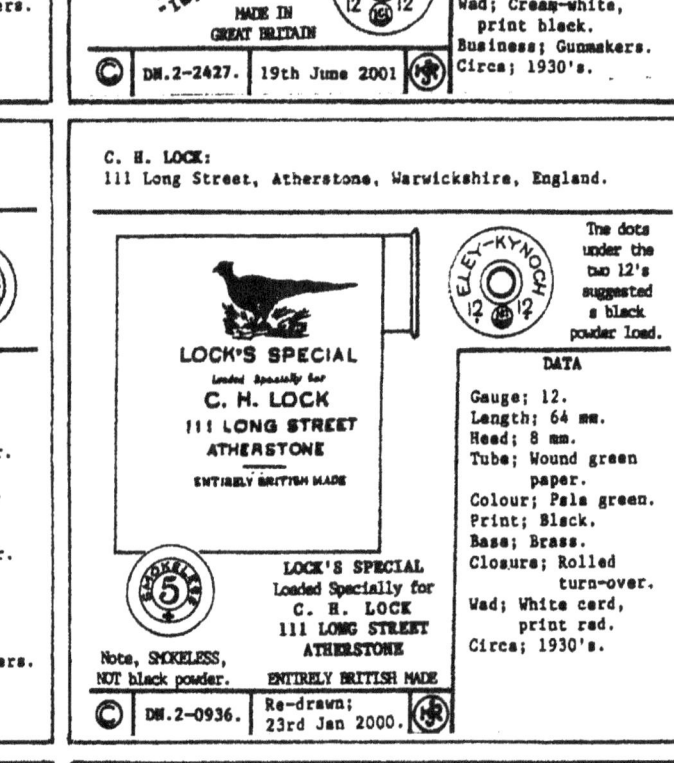
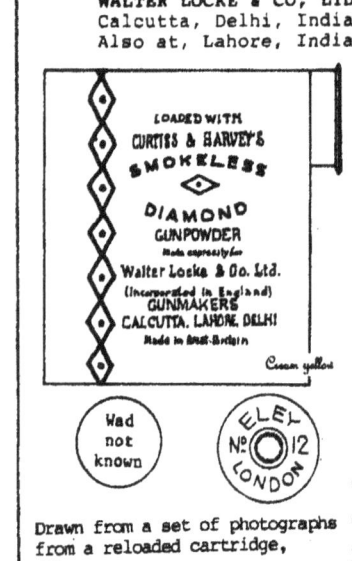
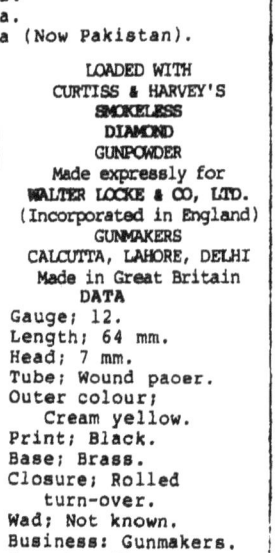
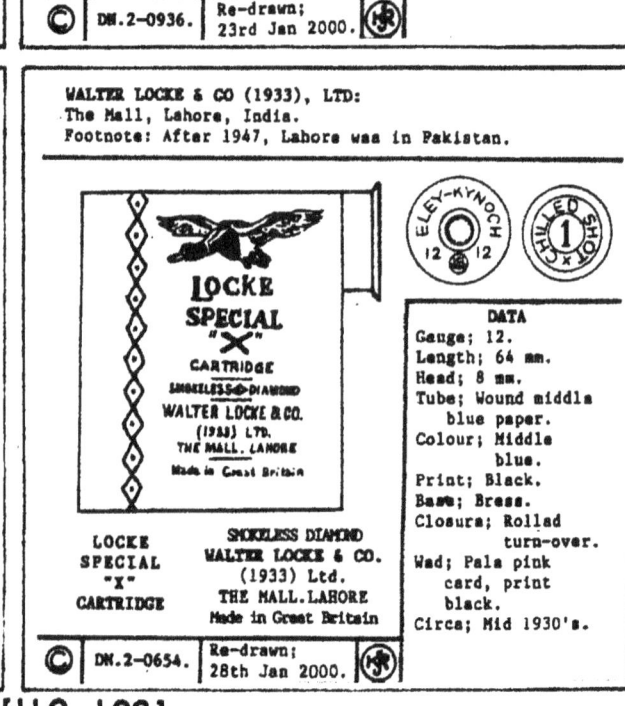

PLATE 236 [LLO – LOC]

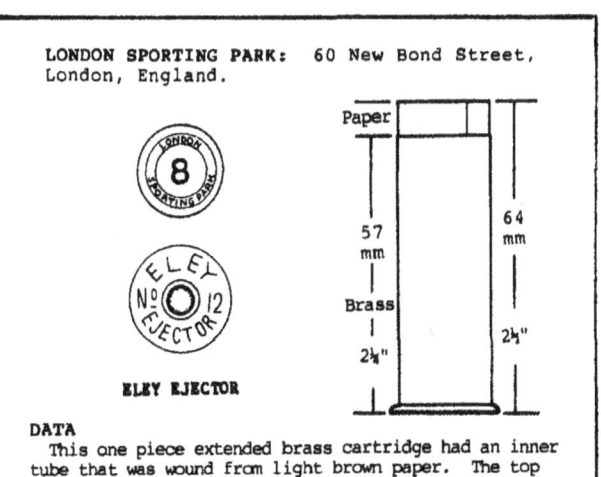
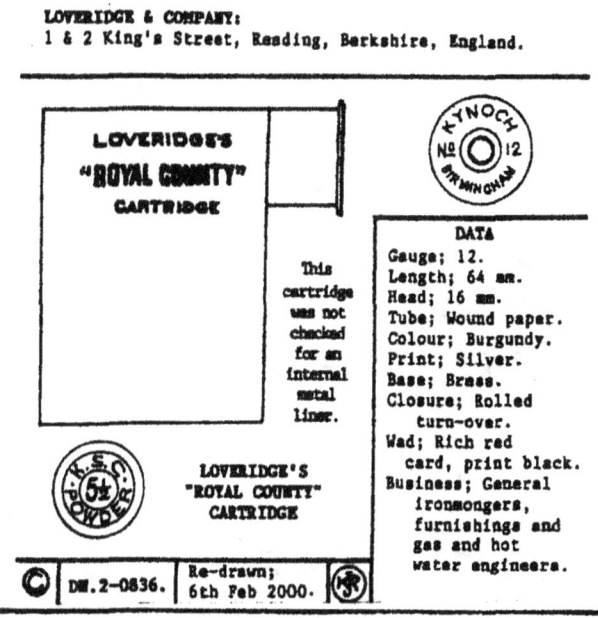
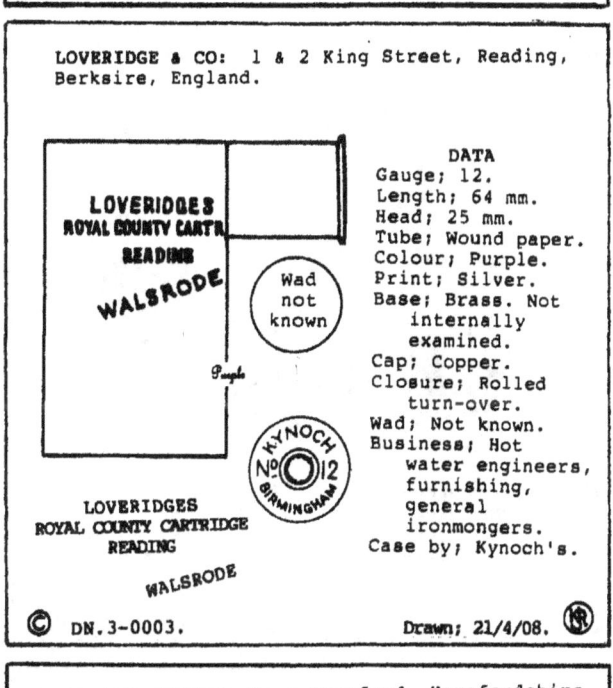
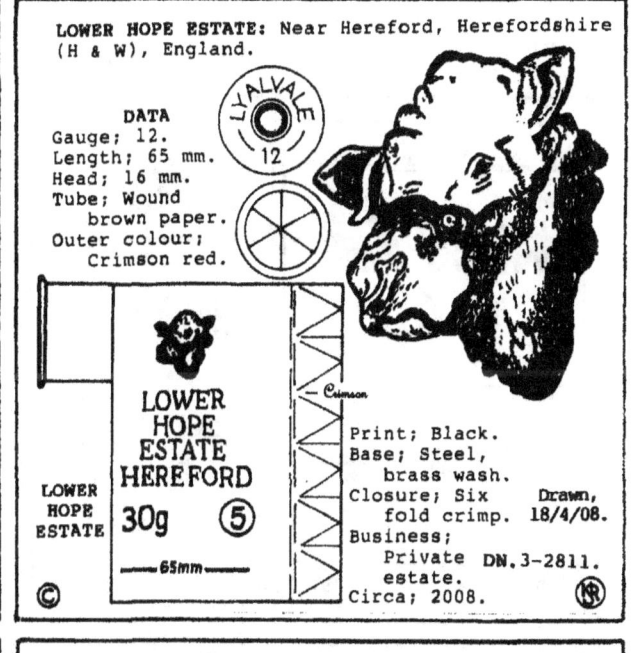
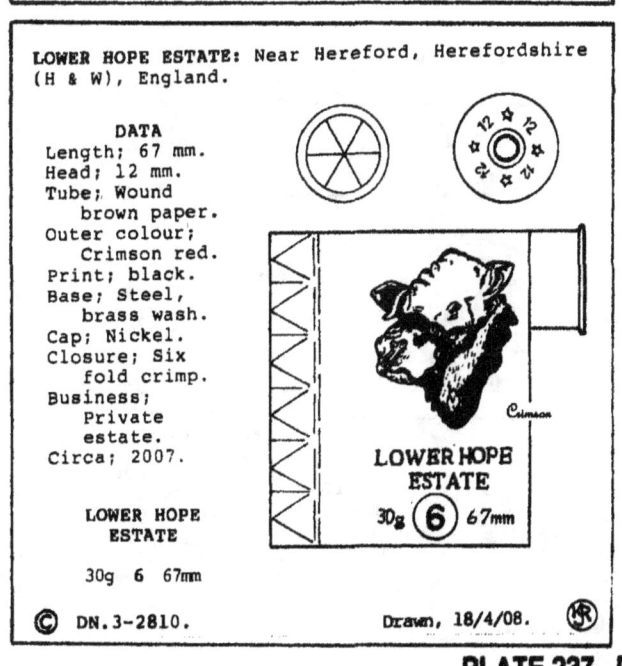

PLATE 237 [LON – LUC]

LYALVALE LIMITED:
1650 Pershore Road, Birmingham, B30 3BL. England.

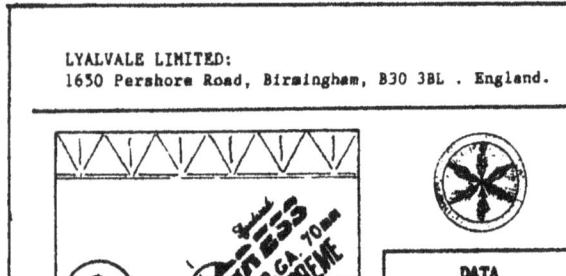

DATA
Gauge; 12.
Length; 68.5 mm.
Head; 26 mm.
Tube; Fine ribbed plastic.
Colour; Maroon 3.
Print; Gold.
Base; Steel, brass coated.
Closure; Crimp, 6 fold.
Circa; 1994.

© DN.2-0005. November 1994

LYALVALE LIMITED:
1650 Pershore Road, Birmingham, B30 3BL. England.

DATA
Gauge; 12.
Length; 69 mm.
Head; 16 mm.
Tube; Fine ribbed plastic.
Colour; Kingfisher blue 2.
Print; Old gold 4.
Base; Steel, brass coated.
Closure; Crimp, 6 fold.
Circa; 1994.

© DN.2-0020. November 1994

LYALVALE LIMITED:
1650 Pershore Road, Birmingham, B30 3BL. England.

DATA
Gauge; 12.
Length; 69 mm.
Head; 16 mm.
Tube; Fine ribbed plastic.
Colour; Kingfisher blue 2.
Print; Old gold 4.
Base; Steel, brass coated.
Closure; Crimp, 6 fold.
Circa; 1994.

© DN.2-0019. November 1994

LYON & LYON, LTD: Chowringhee, Calcutta, India.

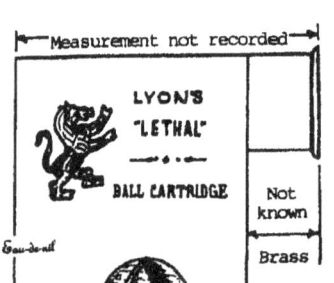

LYON'S "LETHAL" BALL CARTRIDGE

The example drawn here was loaded into a German manufactured case that was fractured. It had a pale blueish-green paper tube with blue-black case wall printing. Lyon & Lyon Ltd were gunmakers.

© DN.3-2758. PROVISIONAL DRAWING Drawn, 12/3/08.

LYON & LYON, LTD: Chowringhee, Calcutta, India.

LYON & LYON CALCUTTA "THE TIMES" SMOKELESS

DATA
Gauge; 12.
Length; 64 mm.
Head; 16 mm.
Tube; Wound paper.
Outer colour; Dark brown.
Print; Black.
Base; Brass.
Closure; Rolled turn-over.
Wad; (Washer type) white card.
Load; Ball.
Business; Gunmakers.
This cartridge was not internally examined.

© DN.3-2757. Drawn, 11/3/08.

LYON & LYON, LTD: Chowringhee, Calcutta, India.

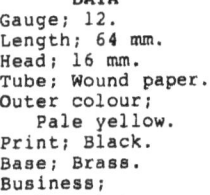

LYON & LYON CALCUTTA "THE TIMES" SMOKELESS

DATA
Gauge; 12.
Length; 64 mm.
Head; 16 mm.
Tube; Wound paper.
Outer colour; Pale yellow.
Print; Black.
Base; Brass.
Business; Gunmakers.
Load shown; Lyon & Lyon's 'Lethal Bullet' (For short range smooth barreled guns at big game).
This cartridge was not internally examined.

© DN.3-2756. Drawn, 11/3/08.

PLATE 238 [LYA – LYO]

Mc and MAC are both treated as "MAC" in this entry. The next letter determines entry.

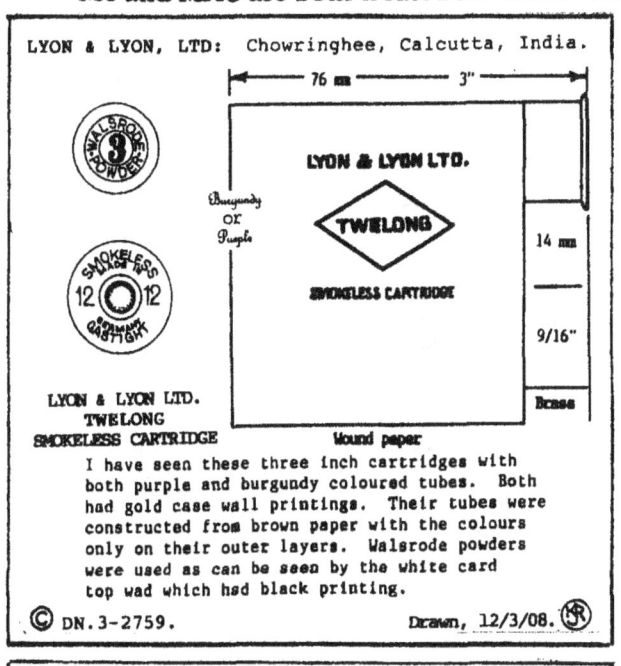

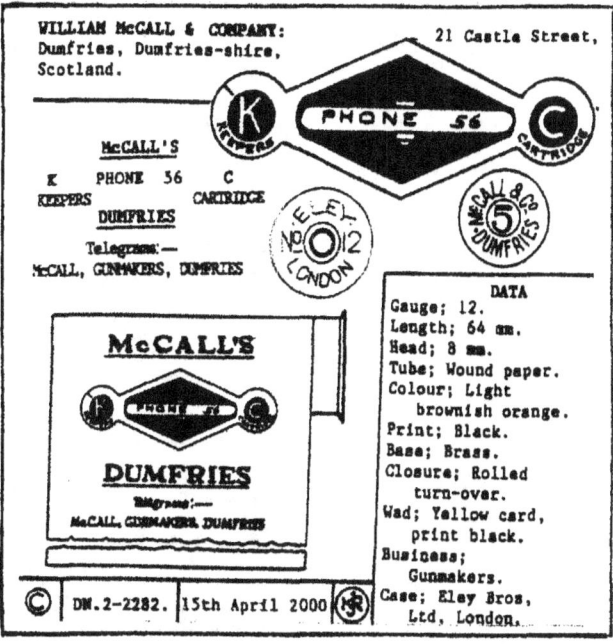

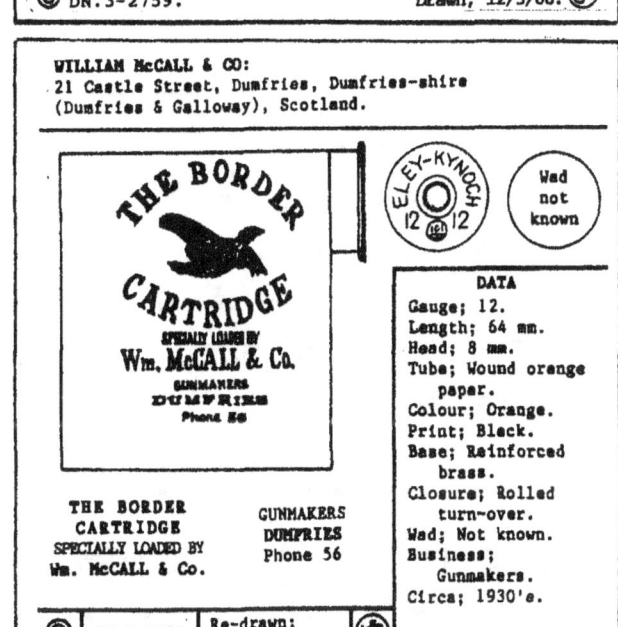

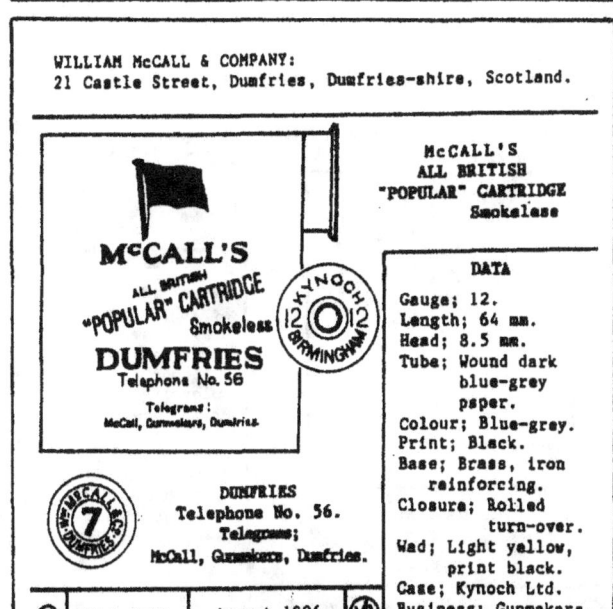

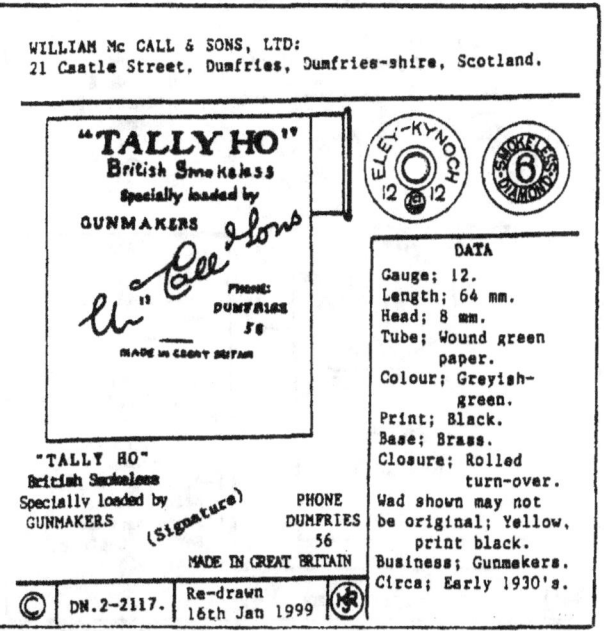

PLATE 239 [LYO – MAC]

Mc and MAC are both treated as "MAC" in this entry. The next letter determines entry.

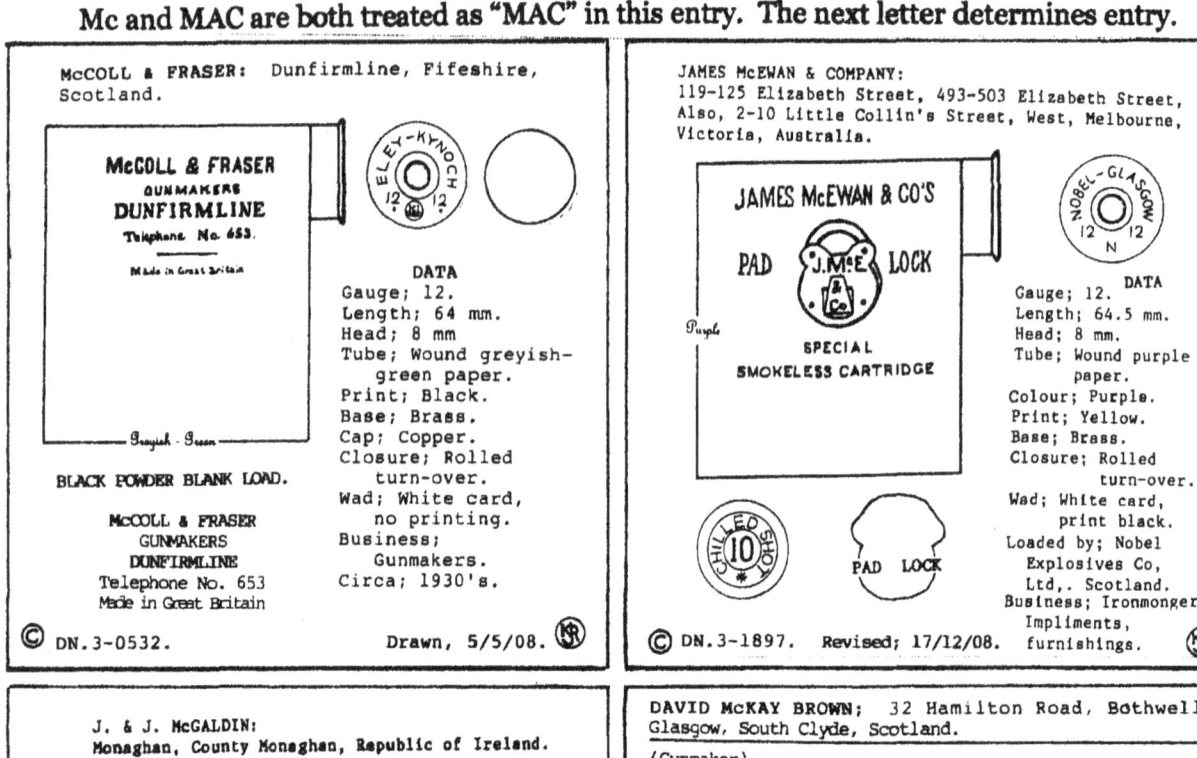

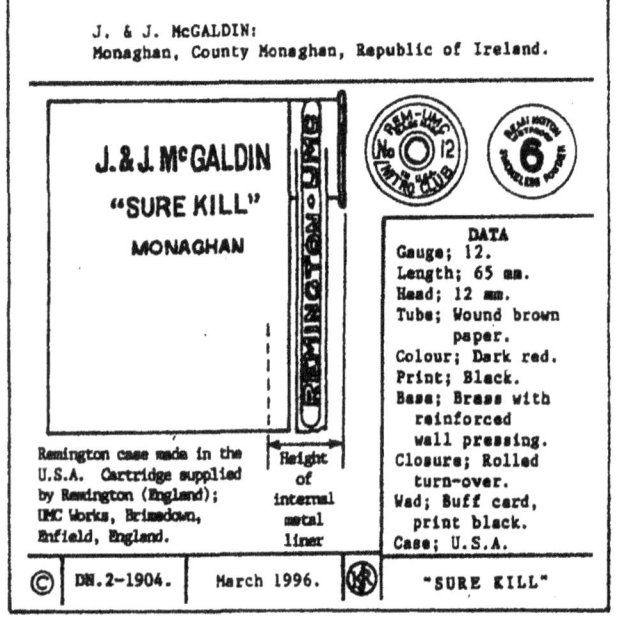

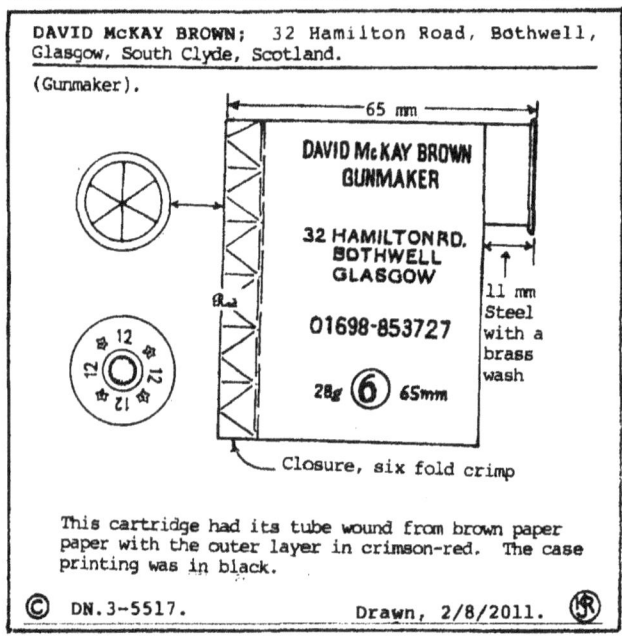

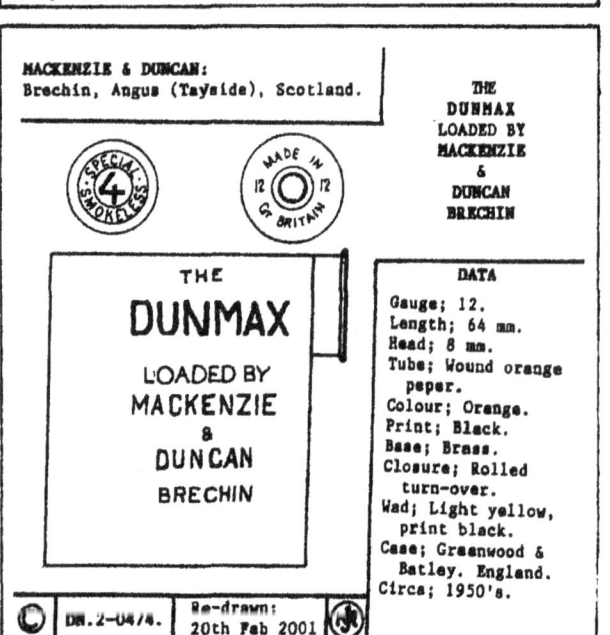

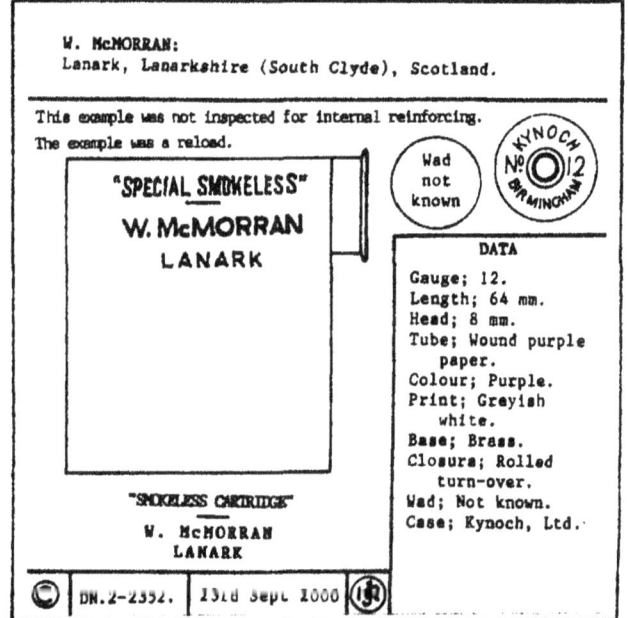

PLATE 240 [MAC – MAC]

Mc and MAC are both treated as "MAC" in this entry. The next letter determines entry.

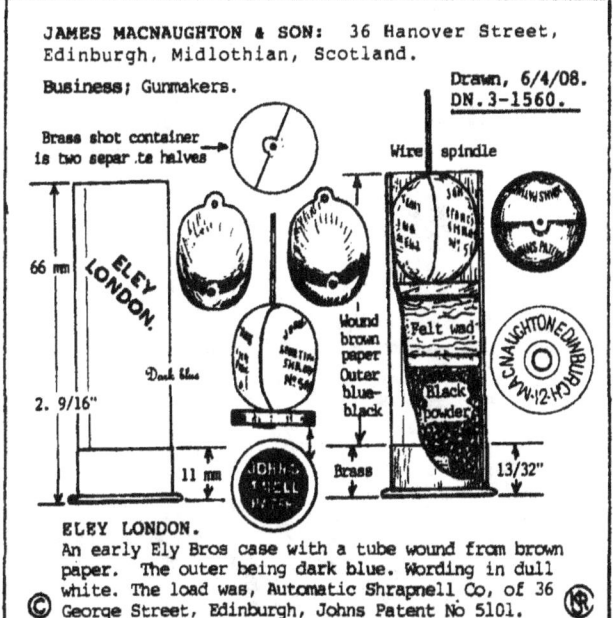

JAMES MACNAUGHTON & SON: 36 Hanover Street, Edinburgh, Midlothian, Scotland.

Business; Gunmakers.

Drawn, 6/4/08.
DN. 3-1560.

ELEY LONDON.
An early Ely Bros case with a tube wound from brown paper. The outer being dark blue. Wording in dull white. The load was, Automatic Shrapnell Co, of 36 George Street, Edinburgh, Johns Patent No 5101.

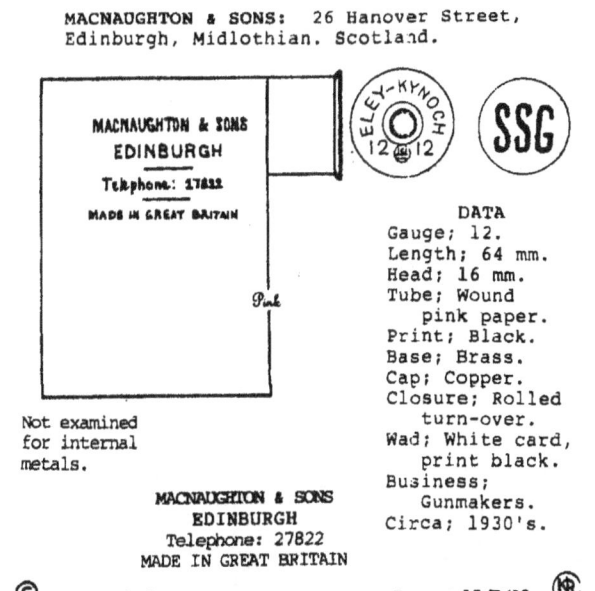

MACNAUGHTON & SONS: 26 Hanover Street, Edinburgh, Midlothian, Scotland.

DATA
Gauge; 12.
Length; 64 mm.
Head; 16 mm.
Tube; Wound pink paper.
Print; Black.
Base; Brass.
Cap; Copper.
Closure; Rolled turn-over.
Wad; White card, print black.
Business; Gunmakers.
Circa; 1930's.

MACNAUGHTON & SONS
EDINBURGH
Telephone: 27822
MADE IN GREAT BRITAIN

DN.3-0045.   Drawn, 15/7/08.

JOHN MACPHERSON: Inverness, Inverness-shire, Scotland.

DATA
Gauge; 12.
Height; 64 mm.
Head; 16 mm.
Tube; Wound gastight quality paper.
Colour; Eley-Kynoch brick red.
Base; Brass.
Closure; Rolled turn-over.
Wetproof; Lacquered.
Wad; Light pink, print black.
Circa; 1930's.
Business; Gunmaker.

DN.2-1380.   Updated; March 1995

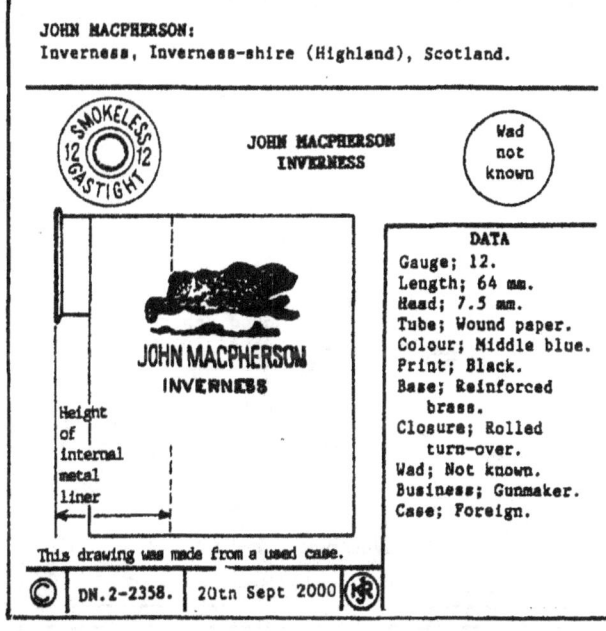

JOHN MACPHERSON: Inverness, Inverness-shire (Highland), Scotland.

DATA
Gauge; 12.
Length; 64 mm.
Head; 7.5 mm.
Tube; Wound paper.
Colour; Middle blue.
Print; Black.
Base; Reinforced brass.
Closure; Rolled turn-over.
Wad; Not known.
Business; Gunmaker.
Case; Foreign.

This drawing was made from a used case.

DN.2-2358.   20th Sept 2000

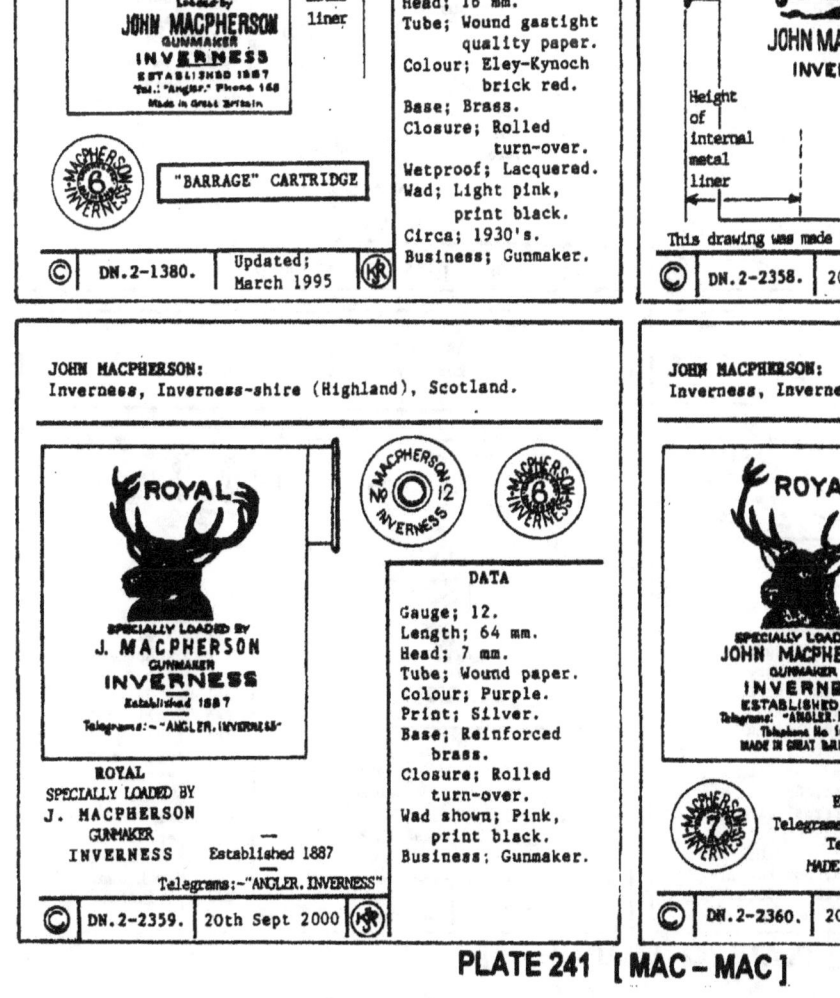

JOHN MACPHERSON: Inverness, Inverness-shire (Highland), Scotland.

DATA
Gauge; 12.
Length; 64 mm.
Head; 7 mm.
Tube; Wound paper.
Colour; Purple.
Print; Silver.
Base; Reinforced brass.
Closure; Rolled turn-over.
Wad shown; Pink, print black.
Business; Gunmaker.

ROYAL
SPECIALLY LOADED BY
J. MACPHERSON
GUNMAKER
INVERNESS   Established 1887
Telegrams:-"ANGLER.INVERNESS"

DN.2-2359.   20th Sept 2000

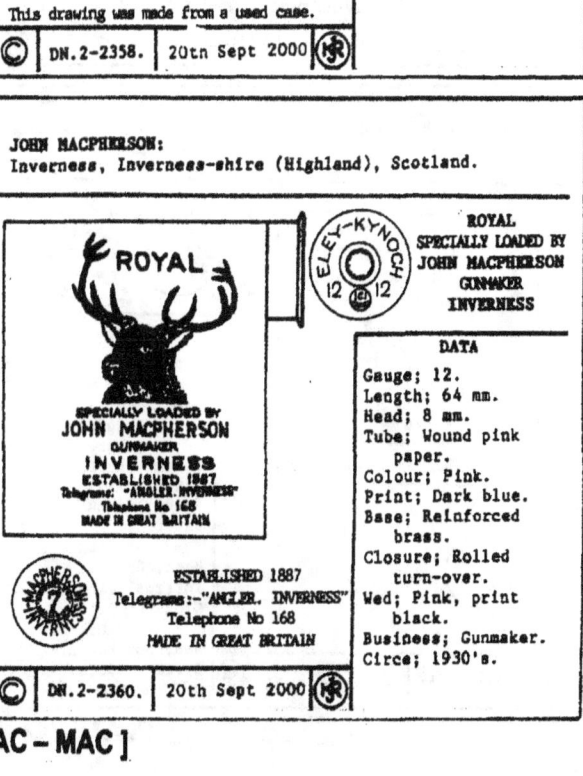

JOHN MACPHERSON: Inverness, Inverness-shire (Highland), Scotland.

ROYAL
SPECIALLY LOADED BY
JOHN MACPHERSON
GUNMAKER
INVERNESS

DATA
Gauge; 12.
Length; 64 mm.
Head; 8 mm.
Tube; Wound pink paper.
Colour; Pink.
Print; Dark blue.
Base; Reinforced brass.
Closure; Rolled turn-over.
Wad; Pink, print black.
Business; Gunmaker.
Circa; 1930's.

DN.2-2360.   20th Sept 2000

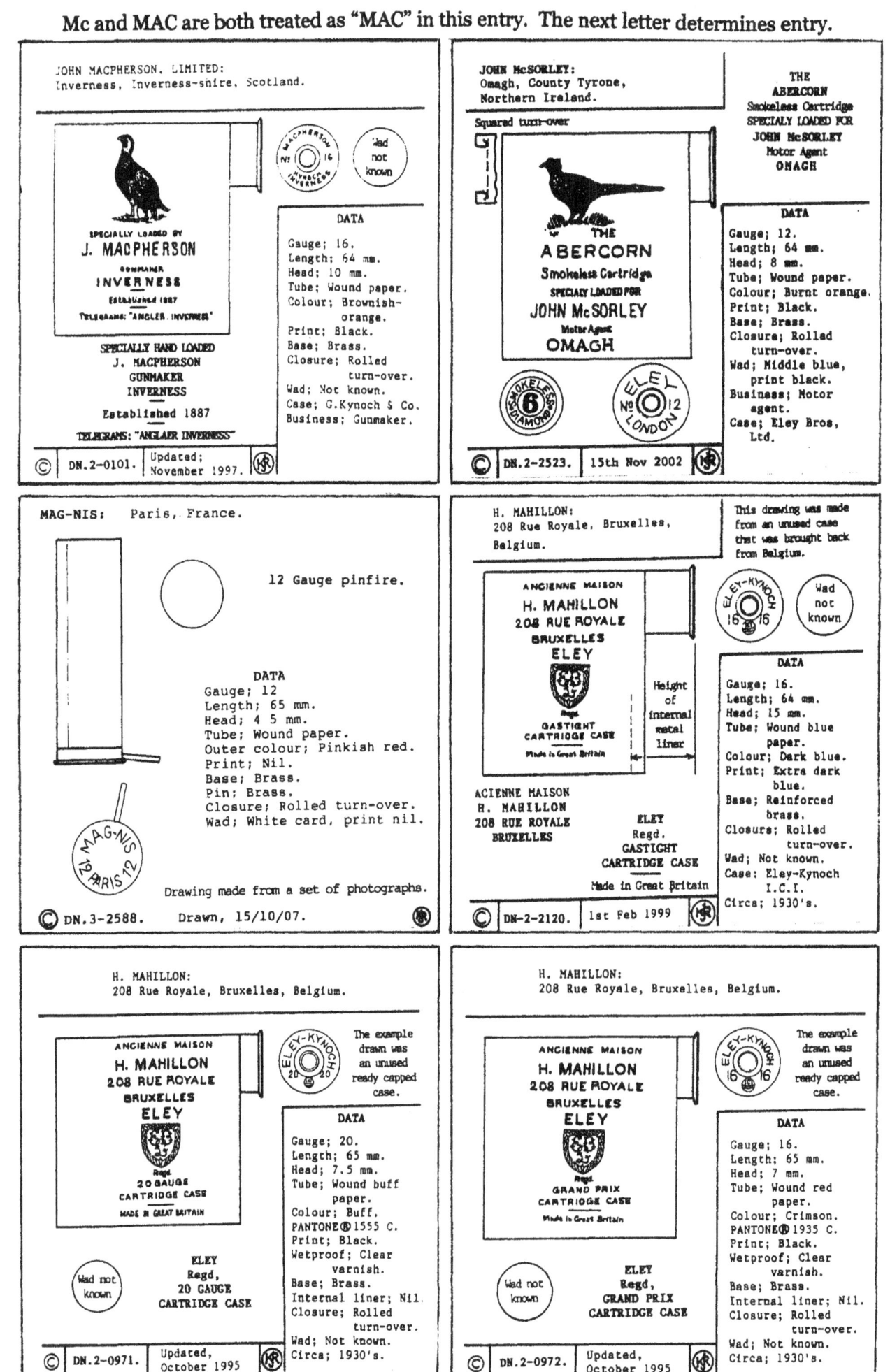

PLATE 242 [MAC – MAH]

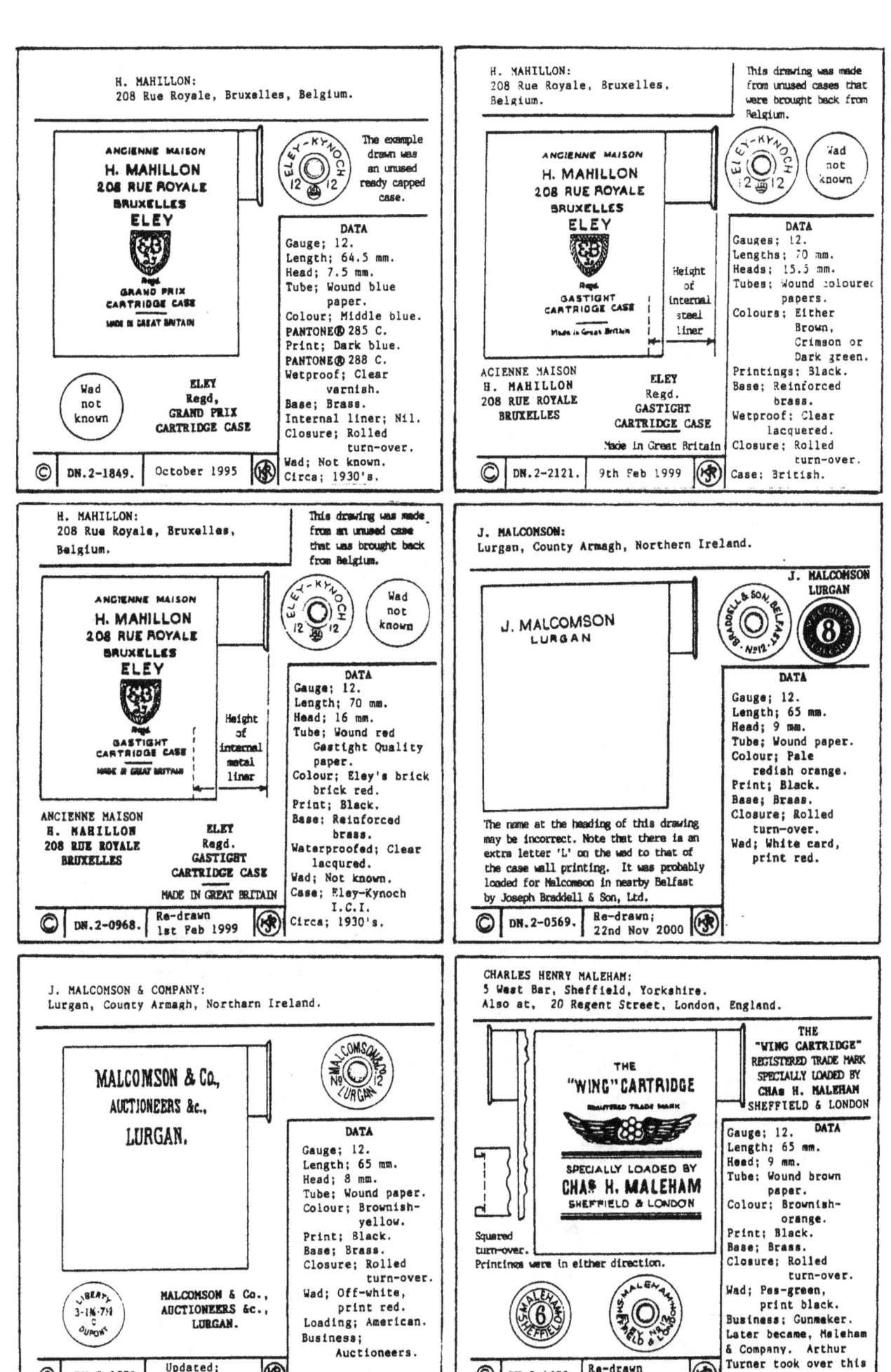

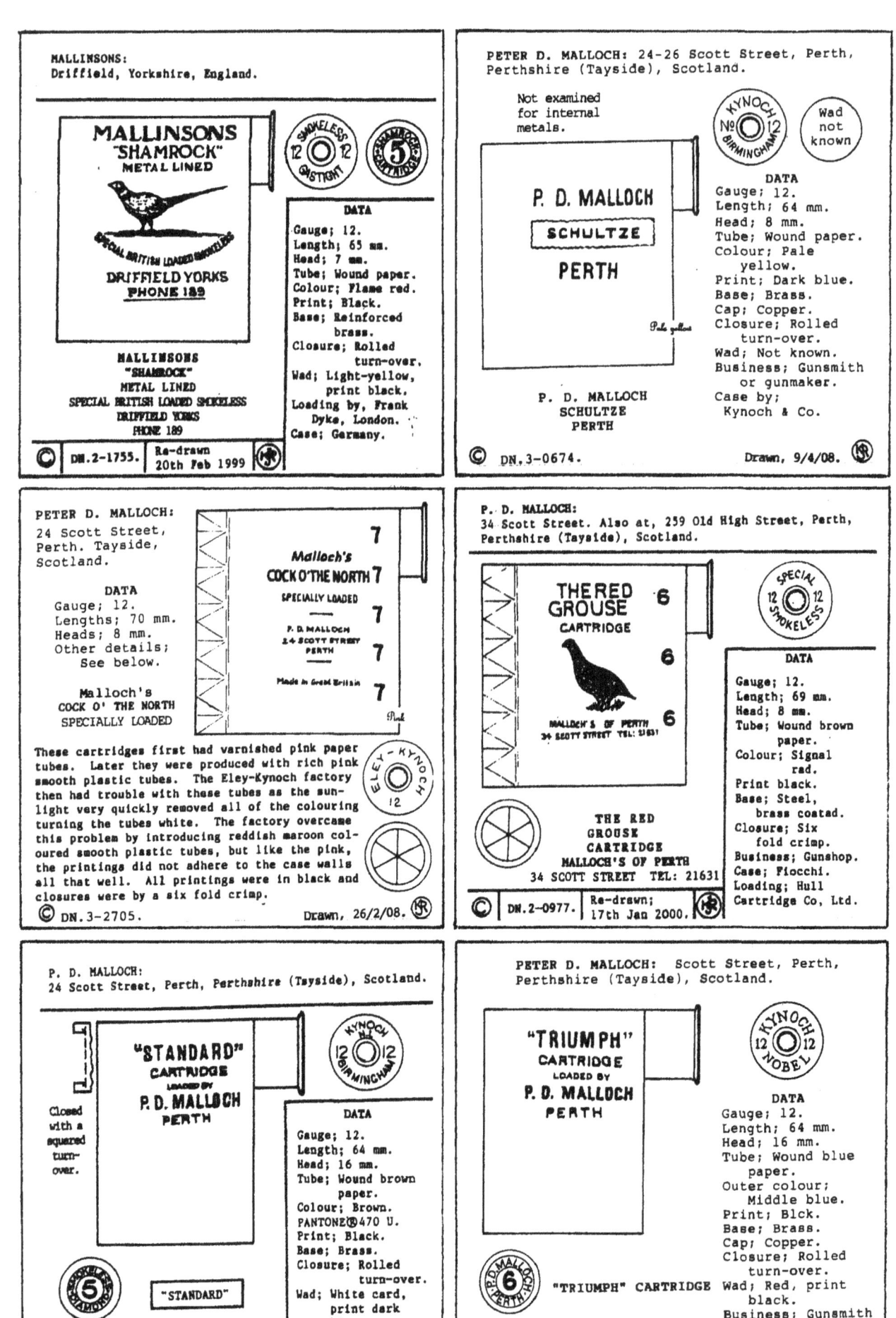

PLATE 244 [MAL – MAL]

F. MANBY & BROTHER:
62 The High Street, Skipton, North Riding, Yorkshire, England.

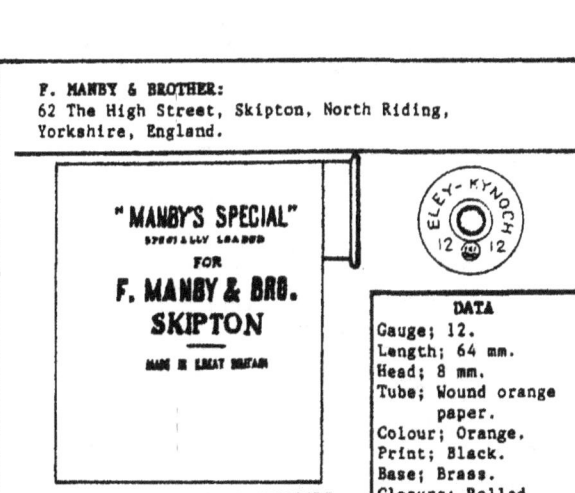

DATA
Gauge; 12.
Length; 64 mm.
Head; 8 mm.
Tube; Wound orange paper.
Colour; Orange.
Print; Black.
Base; Brass.
Closure; Rolled turn-over.
Wad; Buttercup yellow, print black.
Business; Ironmongers
Circa; Early 1930's.

DN.2-0727. Re-drawn; 9th Jan 2000.

ALLAN MANBY:
62 High Street, Southwold, Sussex, England.
(Was known to have been active in 1925).

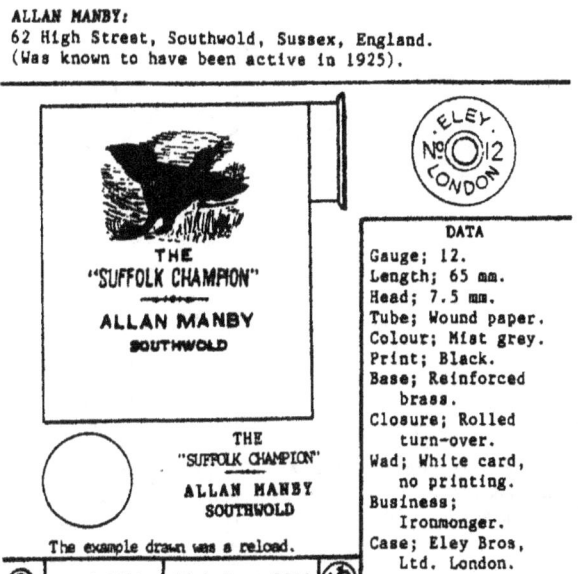

DATA
Gauge; 12.
Length; 65 mm.
Head; 7.5 mm.
Tube; Wound paper.
Colour; Mist grey.
Print; Black.
Base; Reinforced brass.
Closure; Rolled turn-over.
Wad; White card, no printing.
Business; Ironmonger.
Case; Eley Bros, Ltd. London.

DN.2-2330. 12th Sept 2000

MANOR OF CADLAND ESTATE; Fawley, Southampton, Hampshire, England.

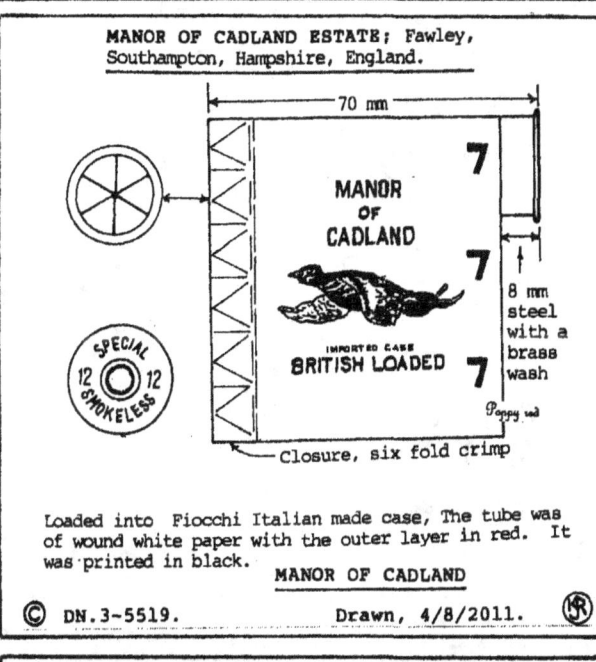

Loaded into Fiocchi Italian made case, The tube was of wound white paper with the outer layer in red. It was printed in black.

MANOR OF CADLAND

DN.3-5519. Drawn, 4/8/2011.

MANTON & COMPANY LIMITED:
Calcutta & New Delhi, India. Also in, London, England.

Shown on this Contractile are three exit holes for barrel lubrication.

That with the ELEY NOBEL headstamping was minus the wording, 'Made in Great Britain'.

DATA
Gauge; 12.
Length; 65 mm.
Head; 16 mm.
Tube; Wound orange paper.
Colour; Brownish-orange.
Print; Black.
Base; Brass.
Closure; Rolled turn-over.
Load; Contractile.
Wad; Nil.
Circa; 1920's-1930's.
Business; Gun and rifle makers.

DN.2-0065. Updated; February 1995

MANTON & COMPANY:
Calcutta, India.

MANTON'S SPECIAL EXPRESS CARTRIDGE
Smokeless Diamond Powder

Note the Curtis's & Harvey's Ltd, Diamond Powder chain decoration.

DATA
Gauge; 12.
Length; 64 mm.
Head; 8 mm.
Tube; Wound blue Paper.
Colour; Middle blue.
Print; Black.
Base; Brass.
Closure; Rolled turn-over.
Wad; Green card, print black.
Business; Gun and rifle makers.
Circa; 1930's

DN.2-1776. Re-drawn; 18th Jan 2000.

MANTON & COMPANY LIMITED:
Calcutta & New Delhi, India. Also in, London, England.

Closed by a squared type rolled turn-over.

MANTON'S "FORINDIA" SMOKELESS CARTRIDGE

Powders were, Smokeless Diamond or 'E.C.'

DATA
Gauge; 12.
Length; 64 mm.
Head; 8 mm.
Tube; Wound red paper.
Colour Crimson red.
Print; Black.
Base; Brass.
Closure; Rolled turn-over.
Wad; Orange 4, print black.
Wetproof; Lacquered.
Circa; 1930's.
Business; Gun and rifle makers.

DN.2-0669. Updated; February 1995

MANTON & COMPANY LIMITED: Calcutta & New Delhi, India. Also in, London, England.

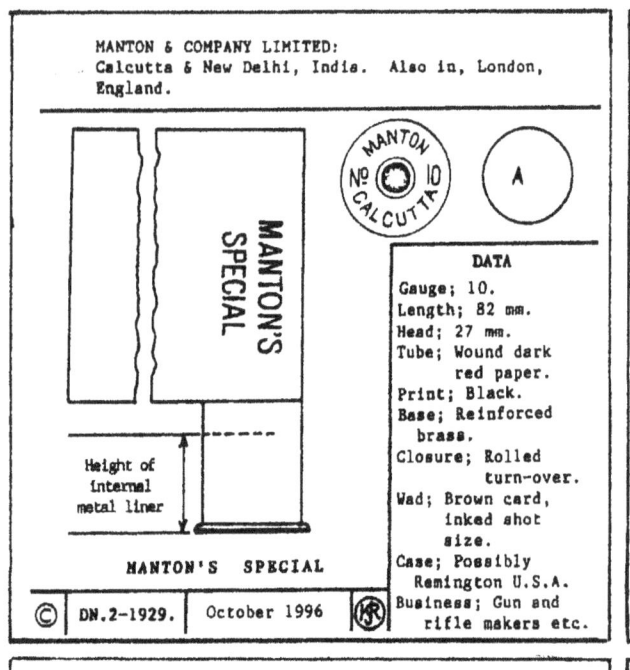

DATA
Gauge; 10.
Length; 82 mm.
Head; 27 mm.
Tube; Wound dark red paper.
Print; Black.
Base; Reinforced brass.
Closure; Rolled turn-over.
Wad; Brown card, inked shot size.
Case; Possibly Remington U.S.A.
Business; Gun and rifle makers etc.

MANTON'S SPECIAL

© DN.2-1929.   October 1996

MANTON & CO: 13 Old Court House Street, Dalhousie Square, Calcutta, India. Once was at, 116 Jermyn Street, London S.W.1., England.

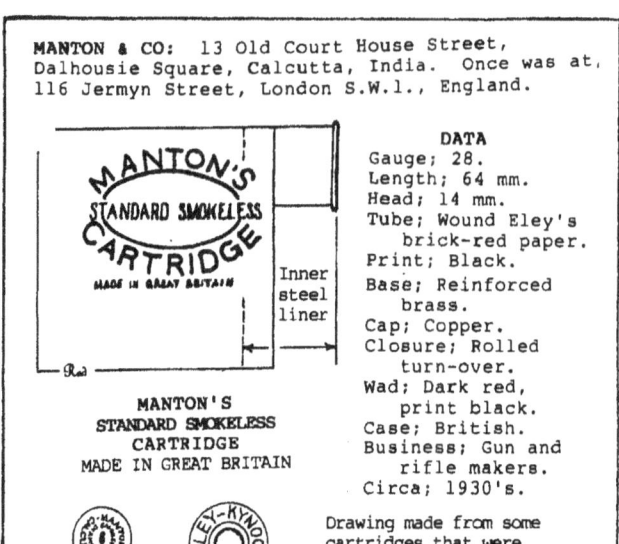

DATA
Gauge; 28.
Length; 64 mm.
Head; 14 mm.
Tube; Wound Eley's brick-red paper.
Print; Black.
Base; Reinforced brass.
Cap; Copper.
Closure; Rolled turn-over.
Wad; Dark red, print black.
Case; British.
Business; Gun and rifle makers.
Circa; 1930's.

MANTON'S STANDARD SMOKELESS CARTRIDGE MADE IN GREAT BRITAIN

Drawing made from some cartridges that were brought back from India. Shot sizes were 4 and 6.

© DN.3-0909.   Drawn, 25/3/08.

MANTON & CO: 13 Old Court House Street, Dalhousie Square, Calcutta, India. Once was at, 116 Jermyn Street, London S.W.1., England.

DATA
Gauge; 20.
Length; 64 mm.
Head; 14 mm
Tube; Wound Dull orange paper.
Print; Black.
Base; Reinforced brass.
Cap; Copper.
Closure; Rolled turn-over.
Wad; Not known.
Case; Brittish.
Business; Gun and rifle makers.
Circa; Late 1920's.

MANTON'S STANDARD SMOKELESS CARTRIDGE

© DN.3-0066.   Drawn, 25/3/08.

MANTON & CO: 13 Old Court House Street, Dalhousie Square, Calcutta, India. Once was at, 116 Jermyn Street, London S.W.1., England.

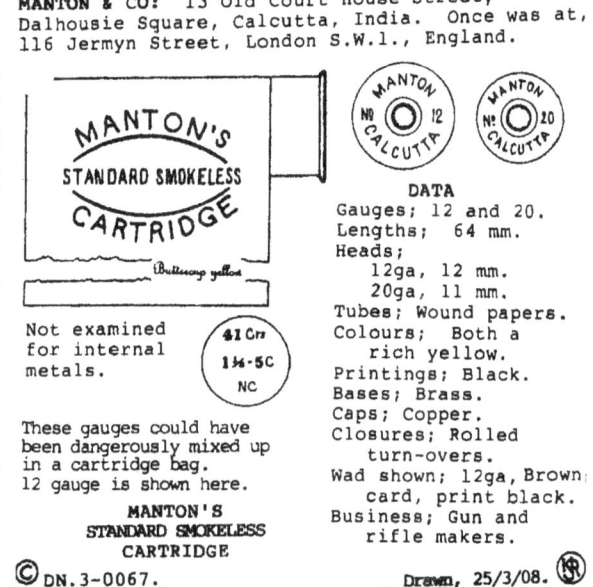

Not examined for internal metals.

These gauges could have been dangerously mixed up in a cartridge bag. 12 gauge is shown here.

MANTON'S STANDARD SMOKELESS CARTRIDGE

DATA
Gauges; 12 and 20.
Lengths; 64 mm.
Heads;
  12ga, 12 mm.
  20ga, 11 mm.
Tubes; Wound papers.
Colours; Both a rich yellow.
Printings; Black.
Bases; Brass.
Caps; Copper.
Closures; Rolled turn-overs.
Wad shown; 12ga, Brown card, print black.
Business; Gun and rifle makers.

© DN.3-0067.   Drawn, 25/3/08.

MANTON & COMPANY LIMITED: Calcutta & New Delhi, India. Also in, London, England.

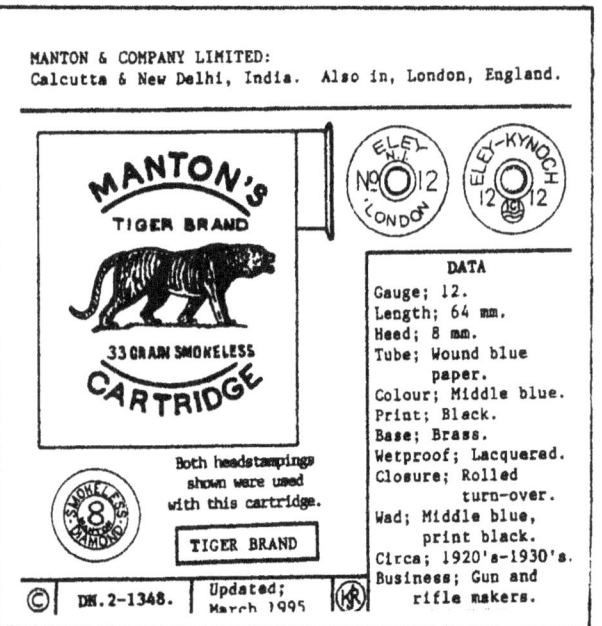

TIGER BRAND

DATA
Gauge; 12.
Length; 64 mm.
Head; 8 mm.
Tube; Wound blue paper.
Colour; Middle blue.
Print; Black.
Base; Brass.
Wetproof; Lacquered.
Closure; Rolled turn-over.
Wad; Middle blue, print black.
Circa; 1920's-1930's.
Business; Gun and rifle makers.

Both headstampings shown were used with this cartridge.

© DN.2-1348.   Updated; March 1995

MANUFACTURE FRANCAISE D'ARMES: (Loire) De Saint-Etienne, France. Depot at, Rue Du Louvre / Rue Coquillere, Paris, France.

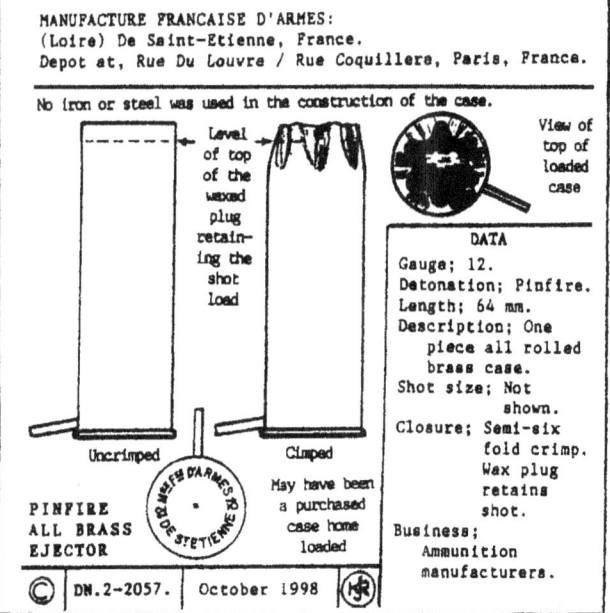

PINFIRE ALL BRASS EJECTOR

DATA
Gauge; 12.
Detonation; Pinfire.
Length; 64 mm.
Description; One piece all rolled brass case.
Shot size; Not shown.
Closure; Semi-six fold crimp. Wax plug retains shot.
Business; Ammunition manufacturers.

May have been a purchased case home loaded

© DN.2-2057.   October 1998

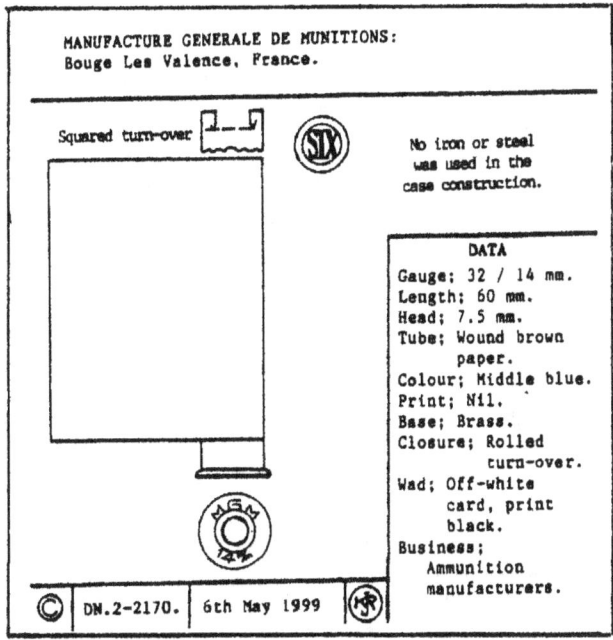
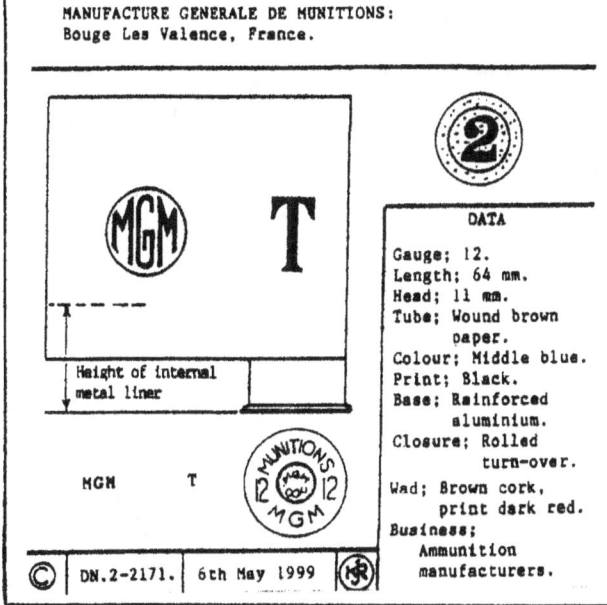
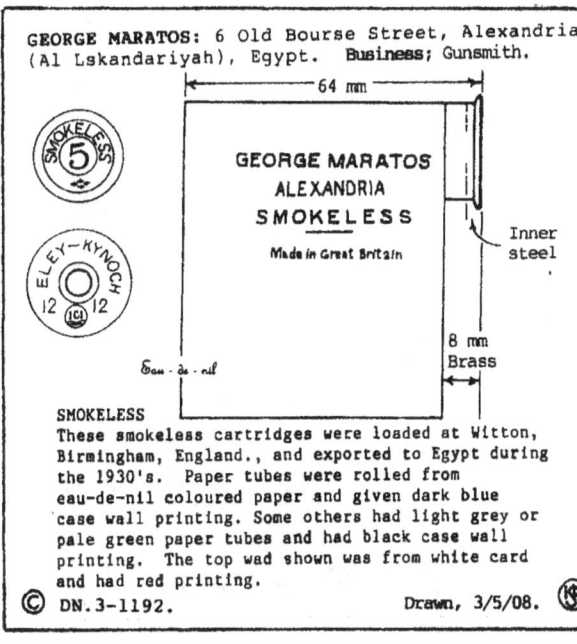
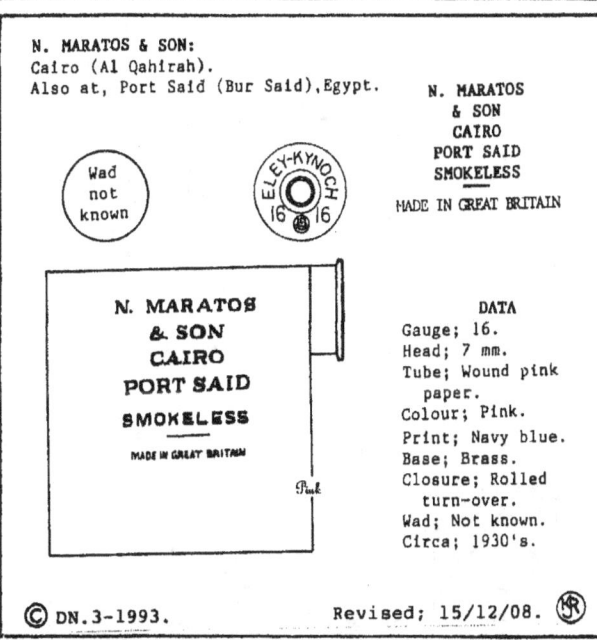
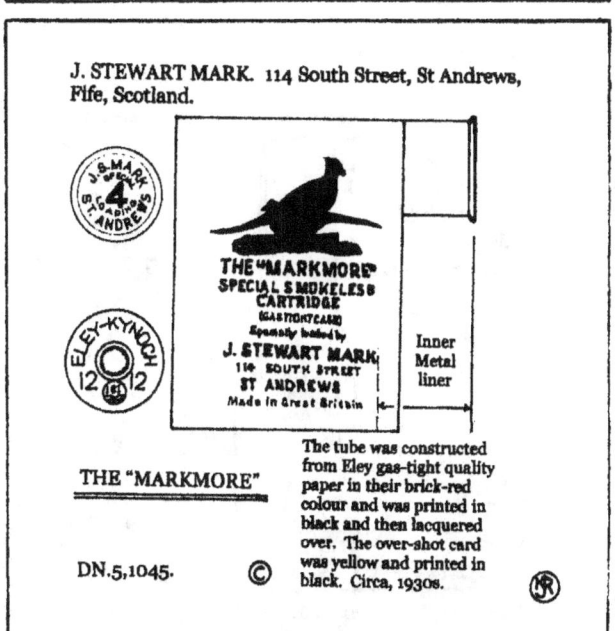
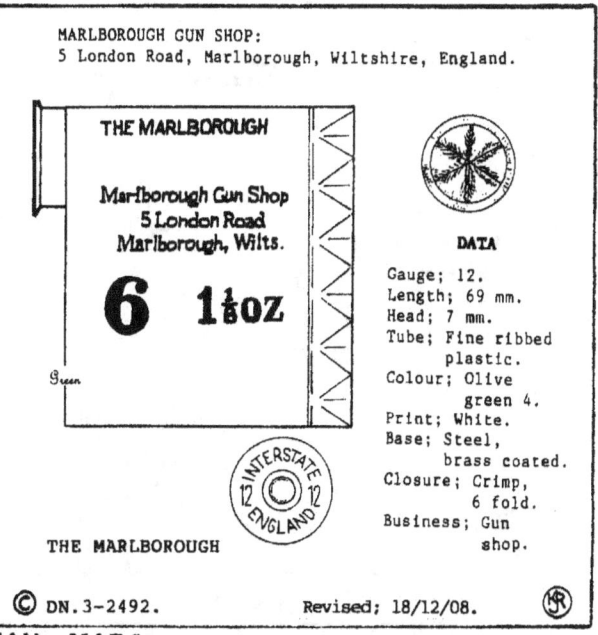

PLATE 247 [MAN – MAR]

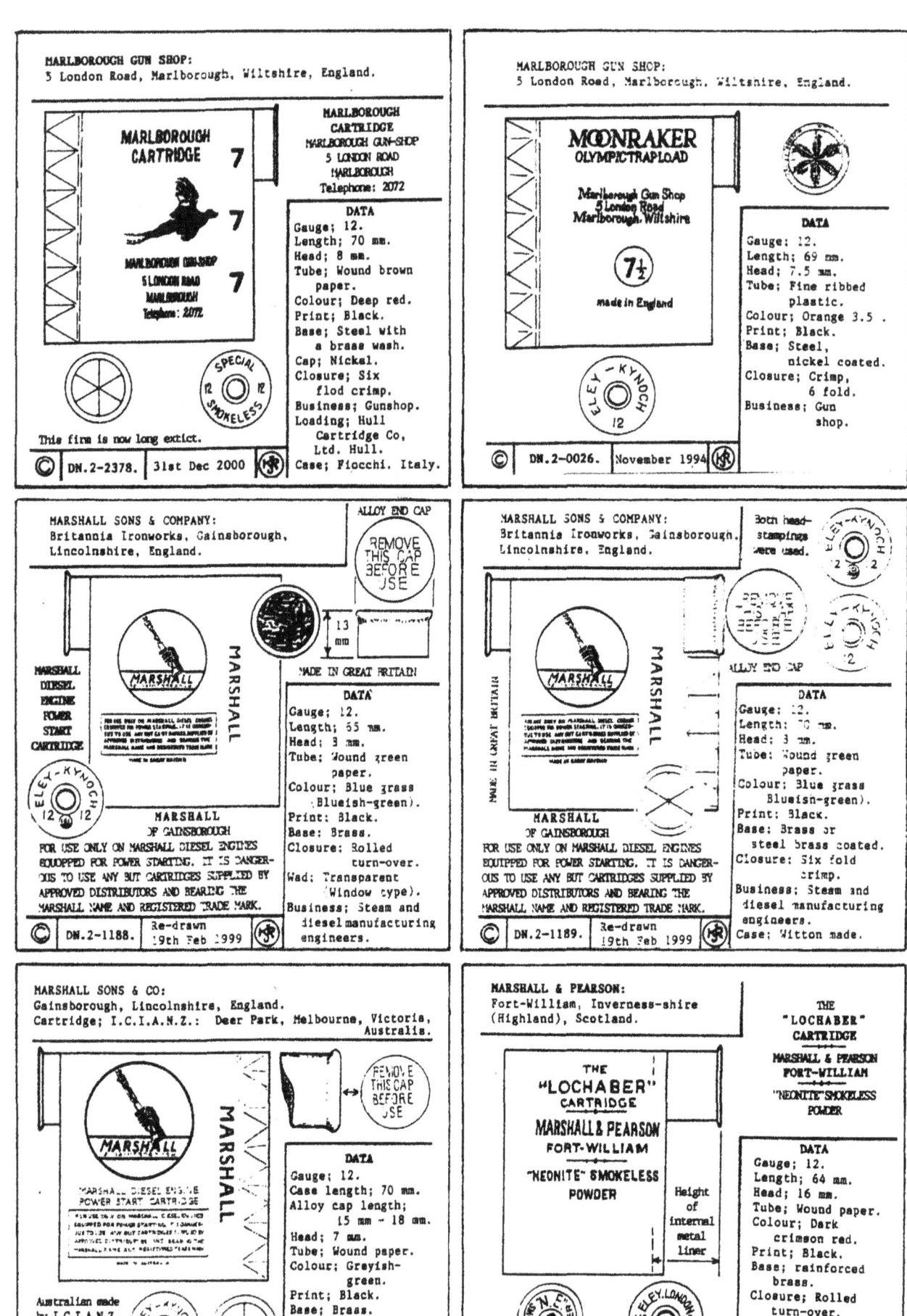

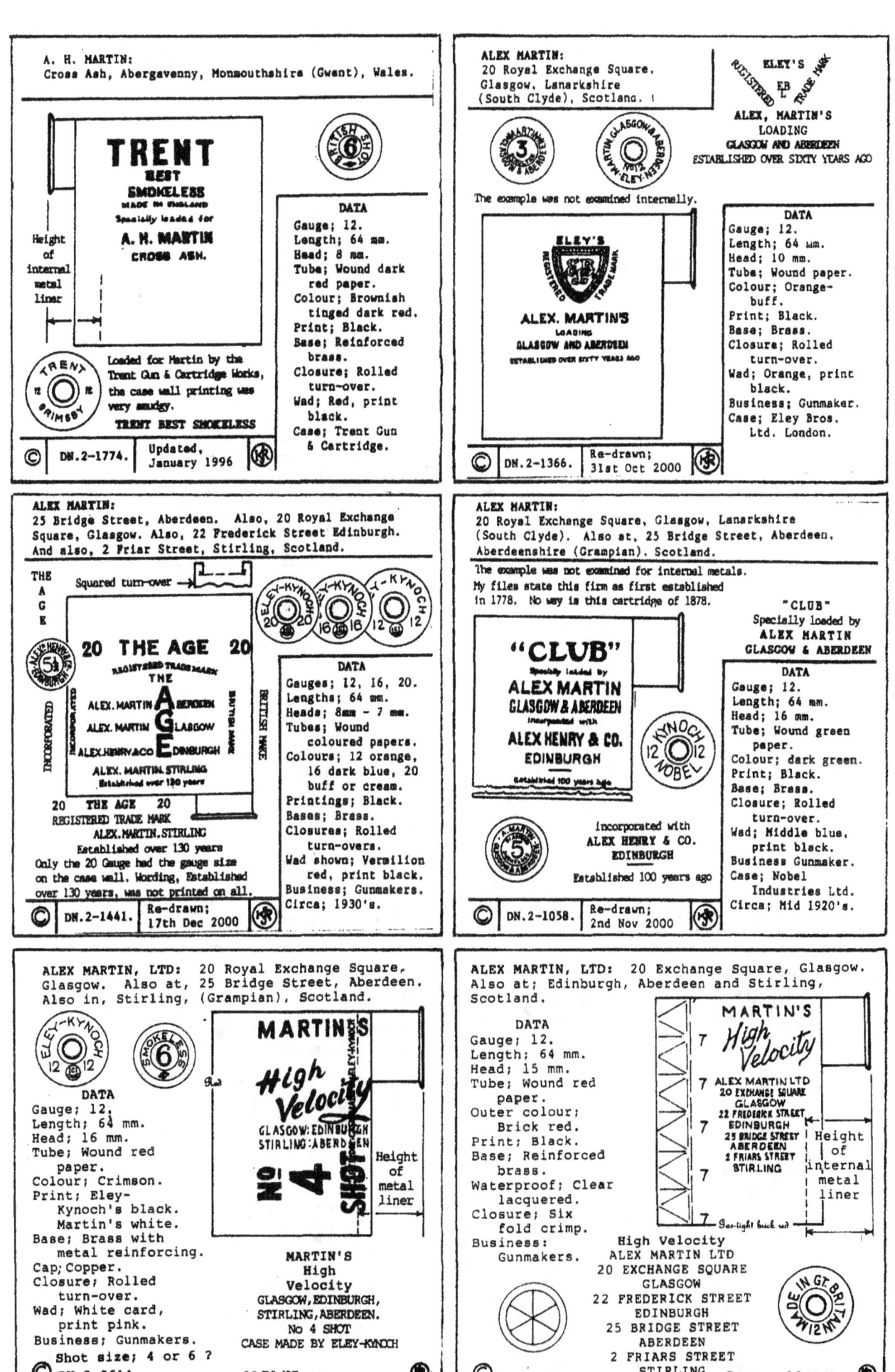

PLATE 249 [MAR - MAR]

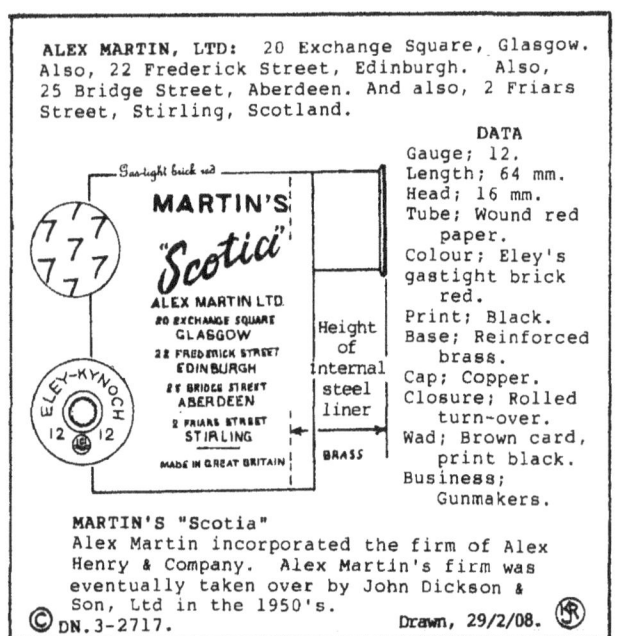
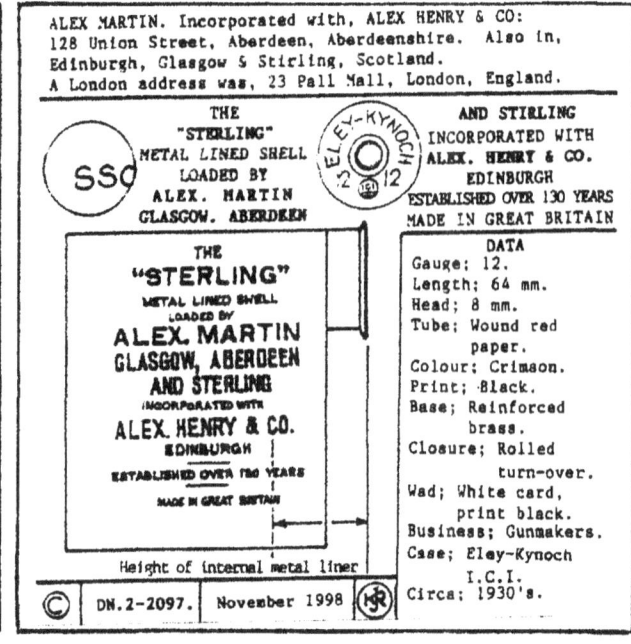
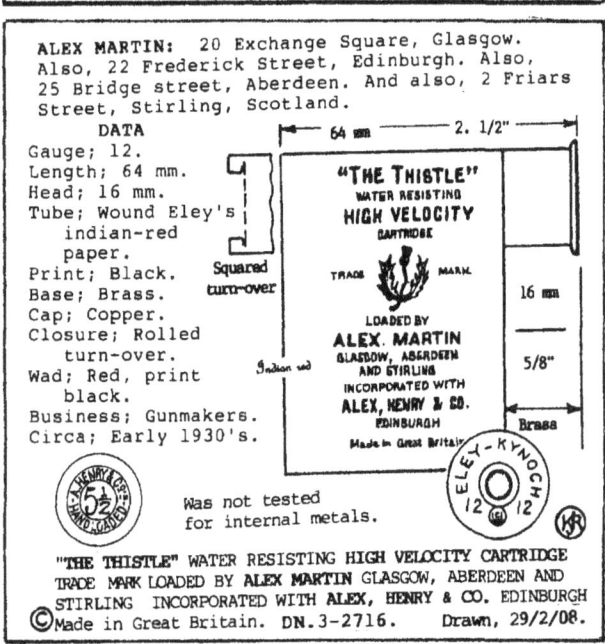
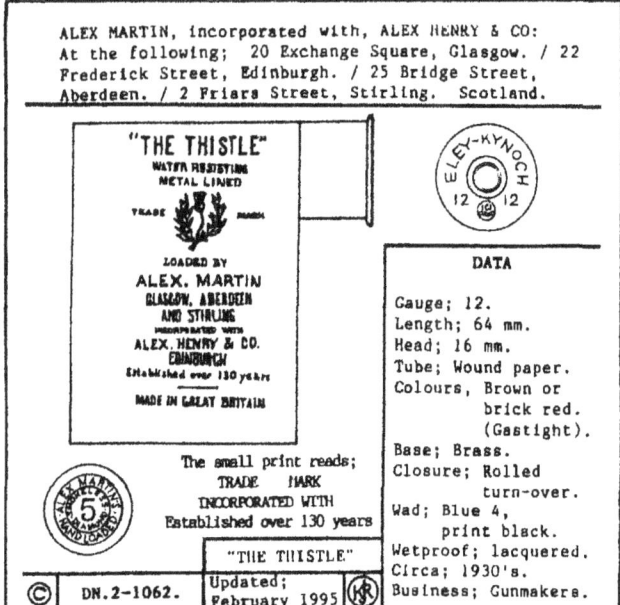
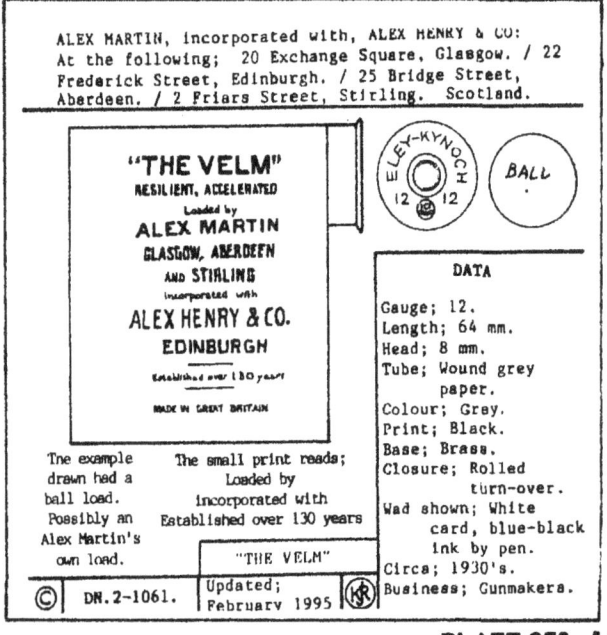
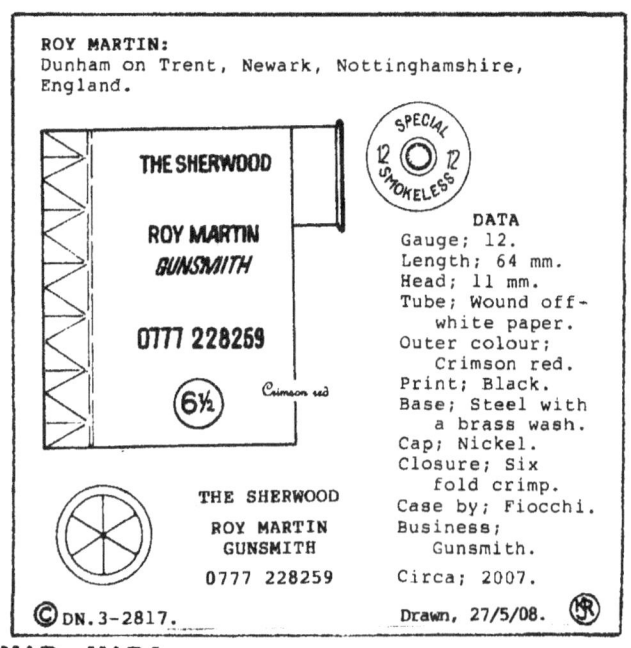

MARTIN DYMOND:
Callington, Cornwall, England.

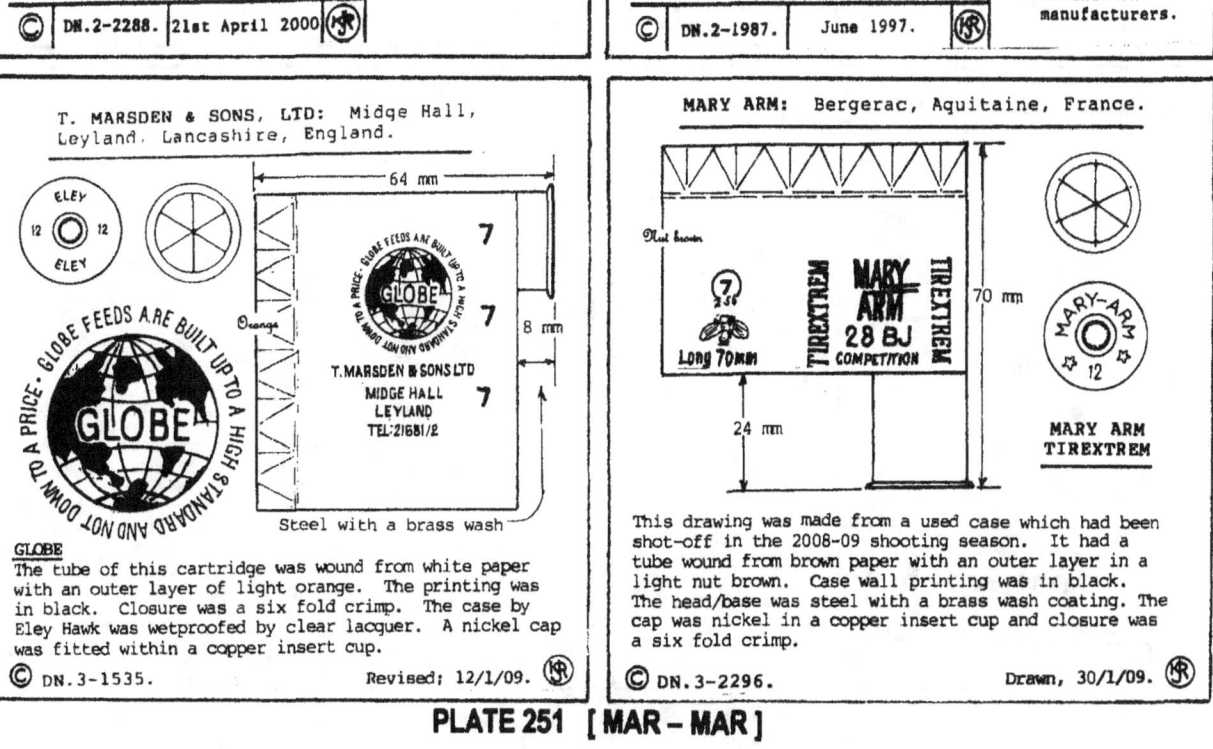

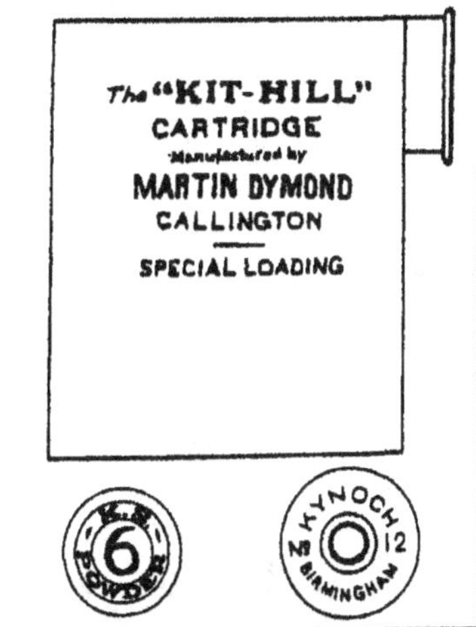

The "KIT-HILL" CARTRIDGE Manufactured by MARTIN DYMOND CALLINGTON SPECIAL LOADING

DATA

Gauge; 12.
Length; 64 mm.
Head; 8 mm.
Tube; Wound paper.
Colour; Burgundy.
Print; Black.
Base; Brass.
Closure; Rolled turn-over.
Wad; Dull orange, print black.
Case; G. Kynoch & & Co.

© DN.2-1947. April 1997

MARTIGNONI. Genova, North Italy.

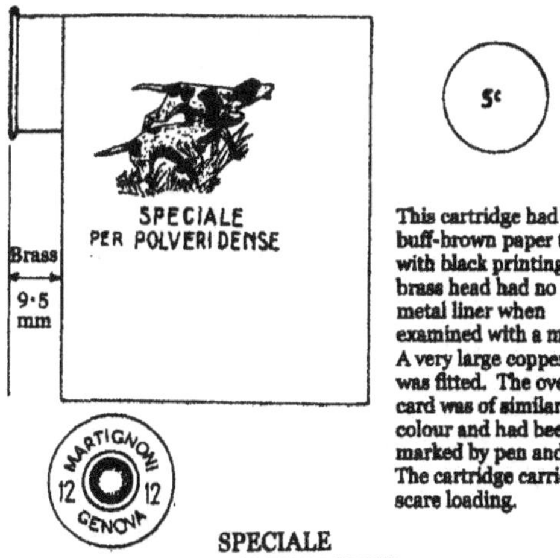

This cartridge had a light buff-brown paper tube with black printing. The brass head had no inner metal liner when examined with a magnet. A very large copper cap was fitted. The over-shot card was of similar colour and had been marked by pen and ink. The cartridge carried a scare loading.

SPECIALE
PER PLOVERI DENSE

DN.5,1048. ©

MARTIGNONI:
Genova, North Italy.

No iron or steel was used in the case construction.

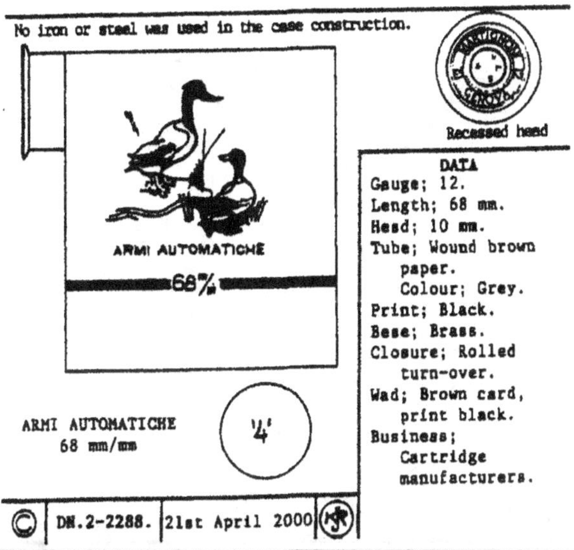

ARMI AUTOMATICHE
68 mm/mm

DATA

Gauge; 12.
Length; 68 mm.
Head; 10 mm.
Tube; Wound brown paper. Colour; Grey.
Print; Black.
Base; Brass.
Closure; Rolled turn-over.
Wad; Brown card, print black.
Business; Cartridge manufacturers.

© DN.2-2288. 21st April 2000

MARTIGNONI:
Genova, Northern Italy.

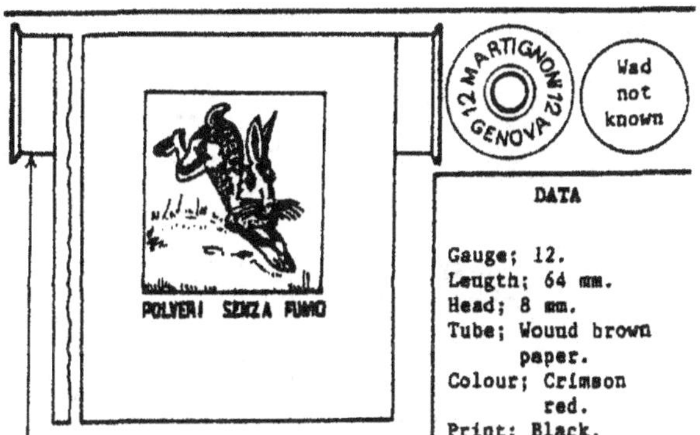

Printings may run in either direction.

No iron or steel was used in the case construction.

Drawing made from home loaded examples.

DATA

Gauge; 12.
Length; 64 mm.
Head; 8 mm.
Tube; Wound brown paper.
Colour; Crimson red.
Print; Black.
Base; Brass.
Closure; Rolled turn-over.
Wad; Not known.
Business; Ammunition manufacturers.

© DN.2-1987. June 1997.

T. MARSDEN & SONS, LTD: Midge Hall,
Leyland, Lancashire, England.

GLOBE

The tube of this cartridge was wound from white paper with an outer layer of light orange. The printing was in black. Closure was a six fold crimp. The case by Eley Hawk was wetproofed by clear lacquer. A nickel cap was fitted within a copper insert cup.

© DN.3-1535. Revised; 12/1/09.

MARY ARM: Bergerac, Aquitaine, France.

MARY ARM
TIREXTREM

This drawing was made from a used case which had been shot-off in the 2008-09 shooting season. It had a tube wound from brown paper with an outer layer in a light nut brown. Case wall printing was in black. The head/base was steel with a brass wash coating. The cap was nickel in a copper insert cup and closure was a six fold crimp.

© DN.3-2296. Drawn, 30/1/09.

J. F. MASON Esquire:
Eynsham Hall, Eynsham, Oxfordshire, England.

Gauge; 12.
Type; Ejector.
Length; 64 mm.
Head; 9 mm.
Extended brass; brass; 48 mm.
Tube; Wound paper.
Colour; Brown 3.
Print; Nil.
Base; Brass.
Closure; Rolled turn-over.
Wad; Unglossed white card, print, red.
Business; Private estate.

DATA

Manufactured by Messrs Eley Brothers Ltd, for J. F. Mason Esq. It was not a common practice for a country hall to have its name on the wad and head stamping. This drawing has been made from a live cartridge.

ELEY EJECTOR

© DN.2-0273. Updated; December 1994

J. MATHER & COMPANY: Nottinghamshire, ENGLAND.
Castle Gate, Kirkgate & Bargate,
Works at Lombard St, Newark; Also at
King St, Southwell & Market Pl, Bingham.

DATA

Gauge; 12.
Length; 64.5 mm.
Head; 8 mm.
Tube; Wound brown paper.
Colour; Dark crimson.
Print; Black.
Base; Brass.
Closure; Rolled turn-over.
Wad; Crimson, black print.
Case; Belgium made.
Business; iron-mongers, Automobile and agricultural engineers.

© DN.2-1487. Updated, January 1996

W. MAWBY & SON:
Birkenhead, Cheshire (Merseyside), England.

Manufactured by Nobel Explosives Co, Ltd, with its main factory at Ardeer, Ayrshire (South Clyde), Scotland. It was closed by a squared turn-over.

DATA

Gauge; 12.
Length; 64 mm.
Head; 7 mm.
Tube; Wound paper.
Colour; Light orange.
Print; Black.
Base; Brass.
Closure; Rolled turn-over.
Wad; Dark orange, print black.

© DN.2-1476. Updated, October 1995

NOBEL'S "CLYDE" SMOKELESS CARTRIDGE

MAWER & SAUNDERS:
The Square, Market Harborough, Leicestershire, England.

Drawing taken from an unused case.

DATA

Gauge; 12.
Length; 64 mm.
Head; 8 mm.
Tube; Wound paper.
Colour; Purple.
Print; Silver.
Base; Brass.
Closure; Rolled turn-over.
Wad; Not known.
Case; F.Joyce & Co, Ltd.
Business; Ironmongers.

© DN.2-0719. Updated; May 1997.

THE MEMBURY ESTATE:
Membury, Near Axminster, Devonshire, England.

DATA

Gauge; 12.
Length; 65 mm.
Head; 12 mm.
Tube; Wound brown paper.
Colour; Pine green.
Print; Black.
Base; Steel, brass coated.
Closure; Six fold crimp.
Wetproof; Clear lacquered.
Business; Private estate.
Clear; 1999.

© DN.2-2119. 26th Jan 1999

B. MEGGINSON:
Atherstone, Warwickshire, England.

PROVISIONAL DRAWING

DATA

This drawing has been made so that this firm can be recorded in history. At the time of writing this, I have no informtion of the firms long gone activitys. This provisional drawing has been compiled from old cartridge remains found on the Marlborough Downs in Wiltshire by metal detecting. These remains are now in the collection of Mr A. Richardson.

© DN.3-2591. Drawn, 16/10/07.

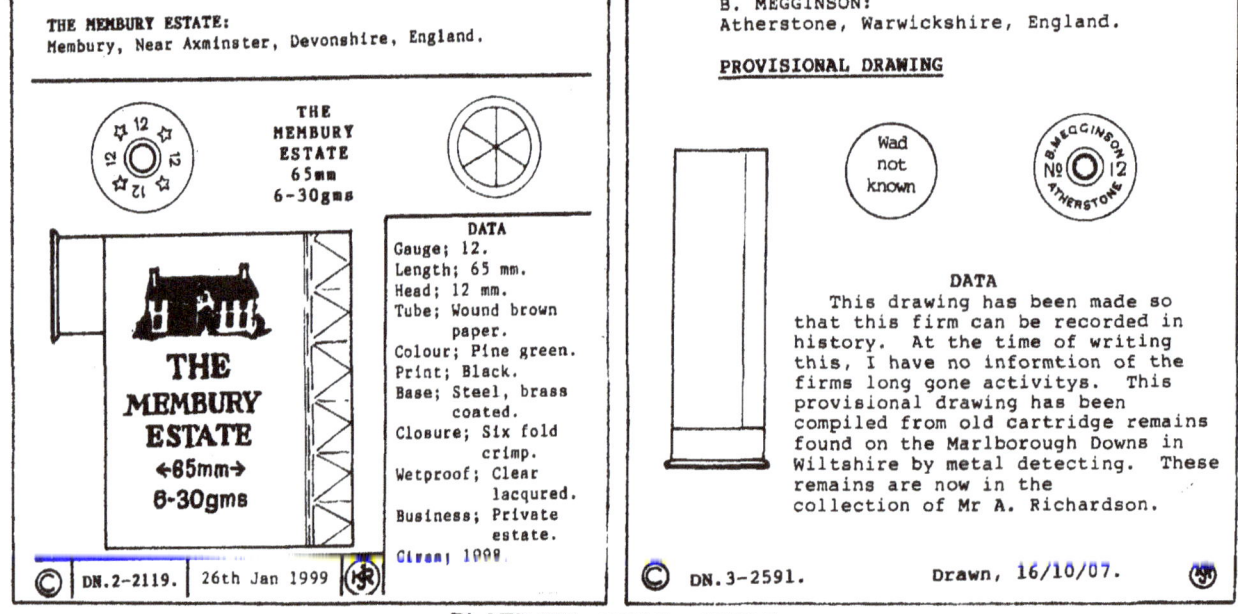

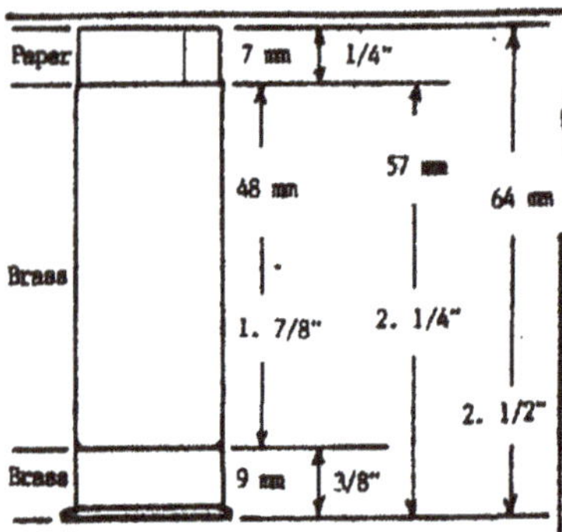

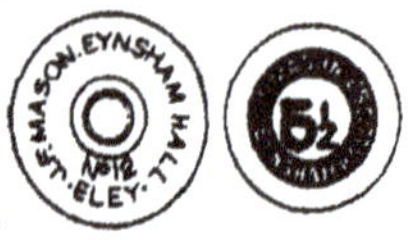

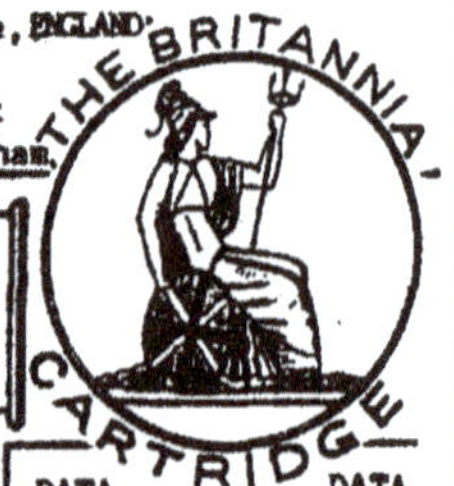

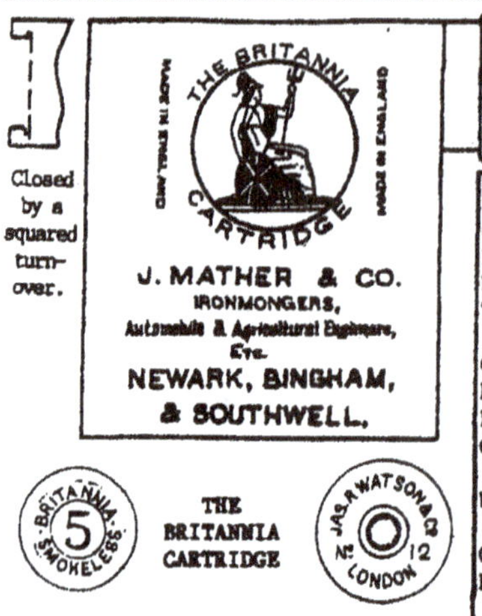

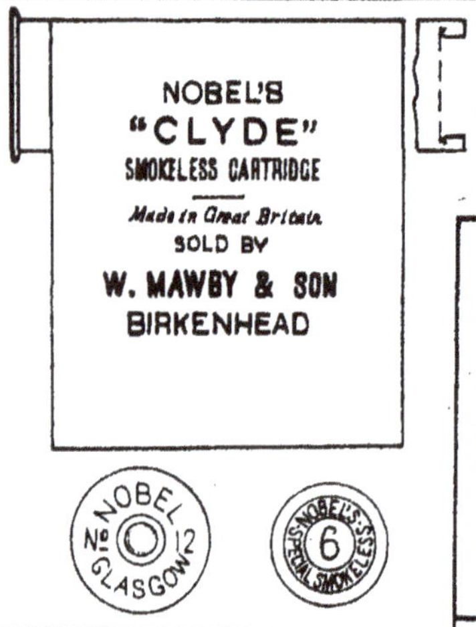

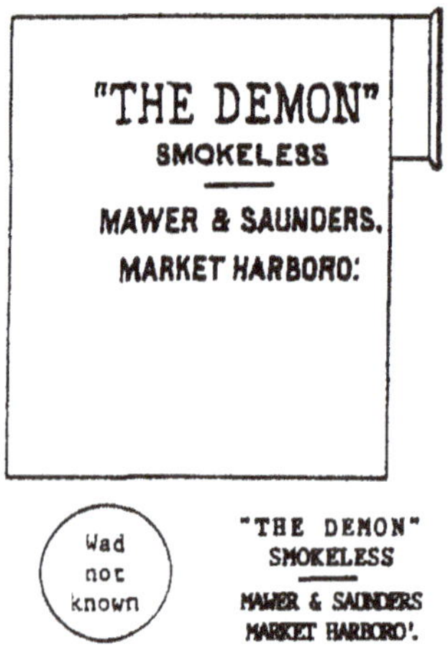

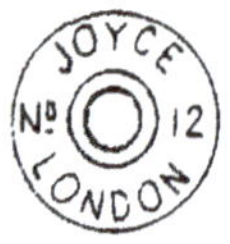

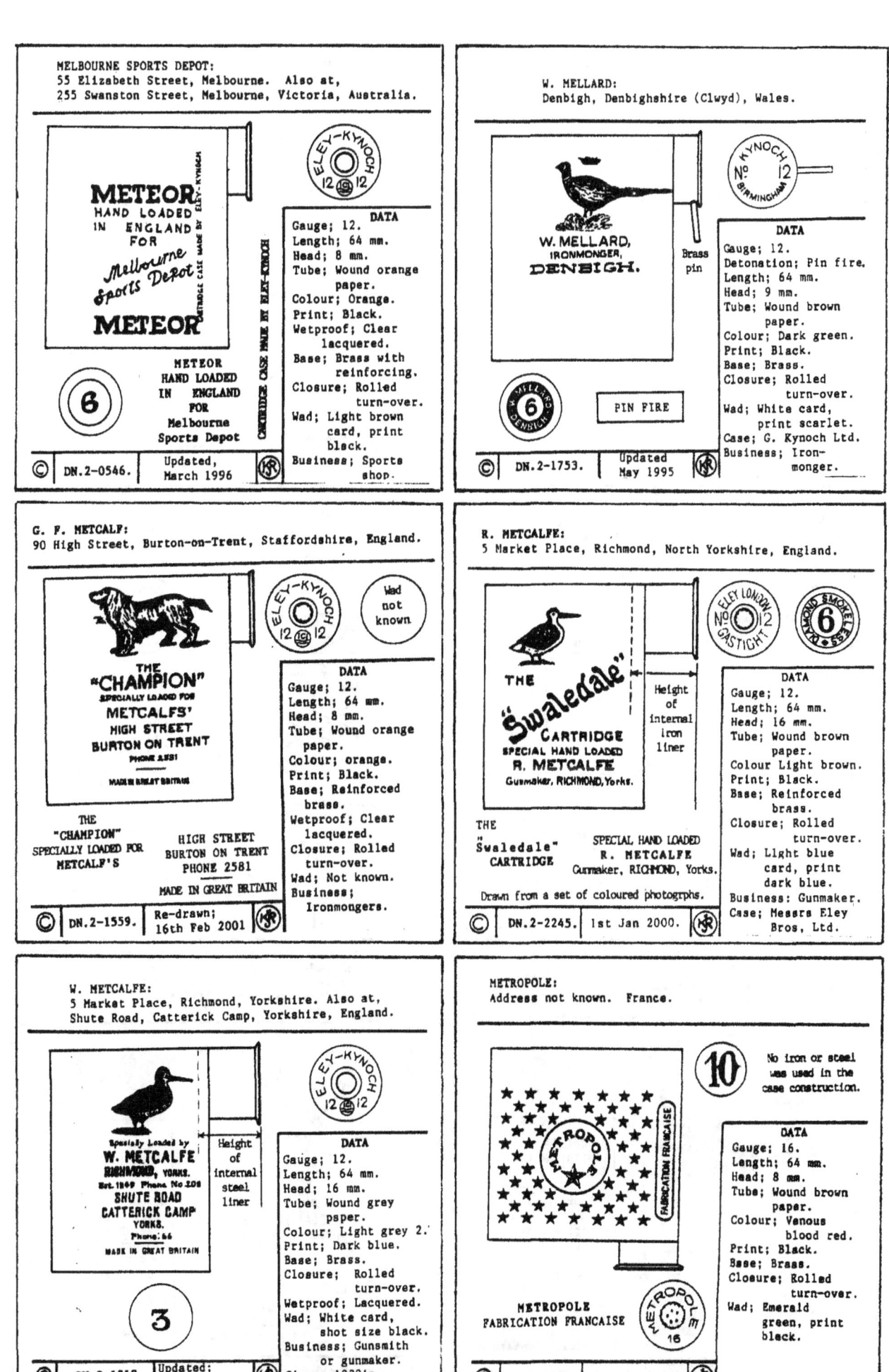

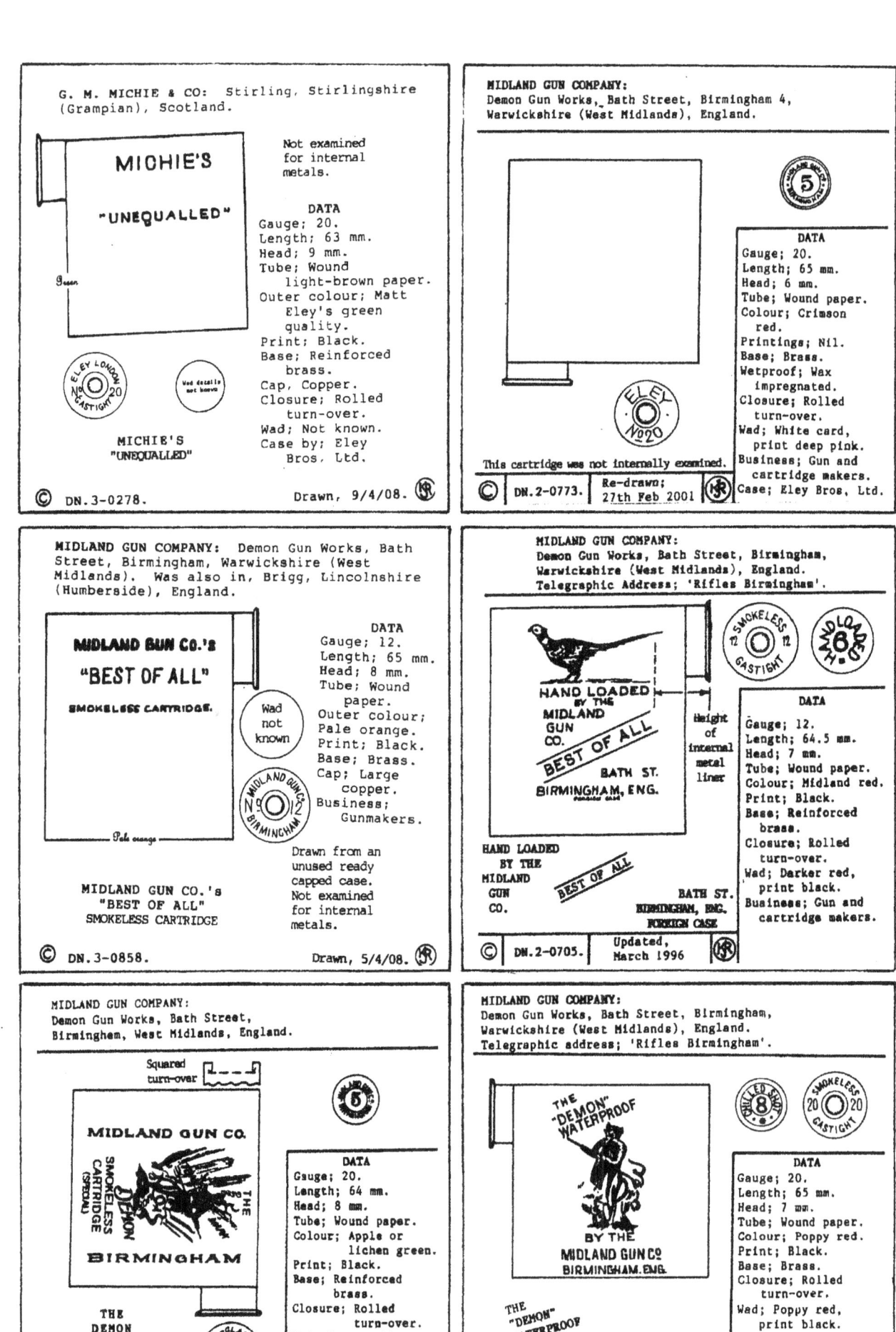

PLATE 254 [MIC – MID]

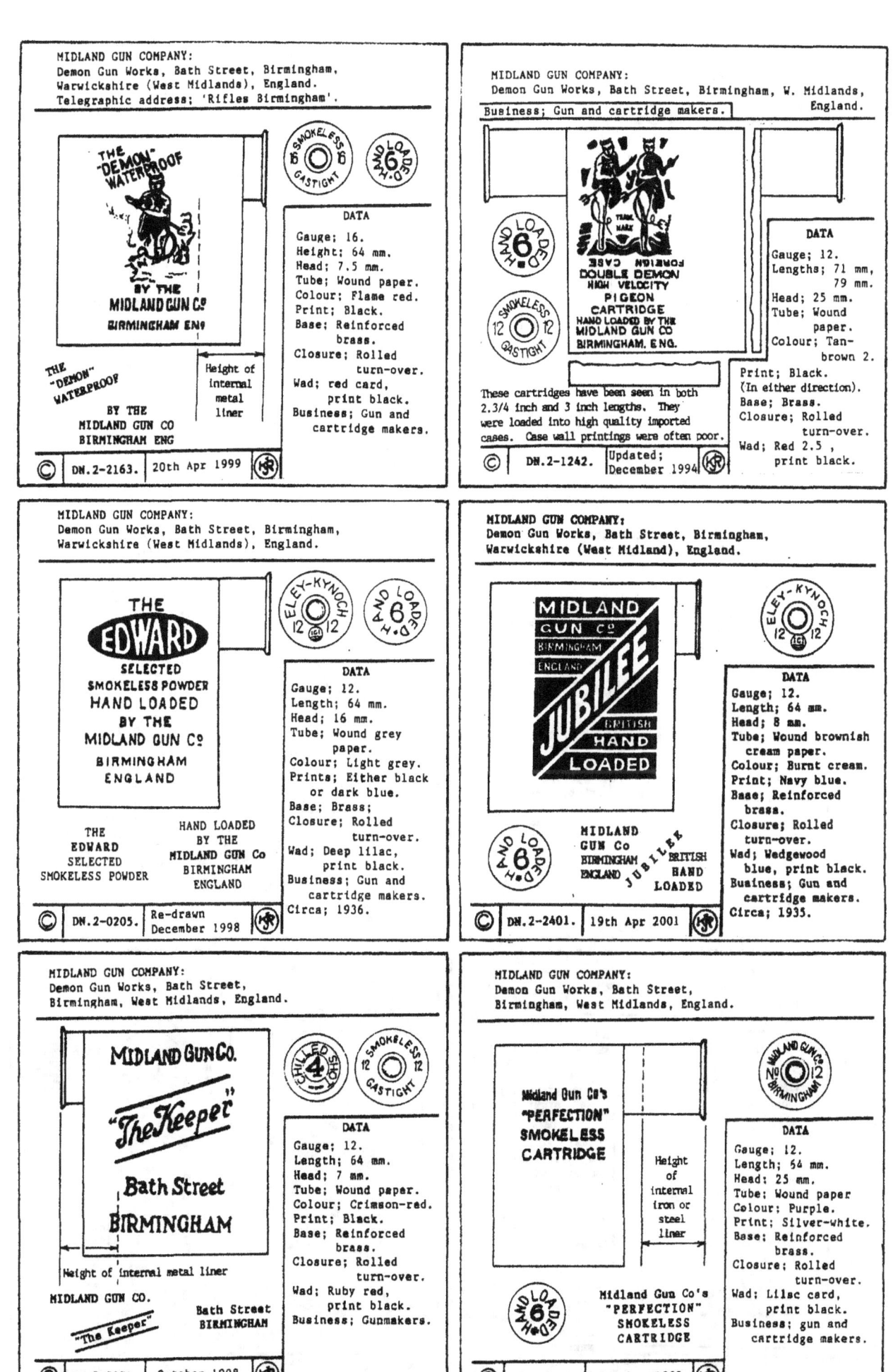

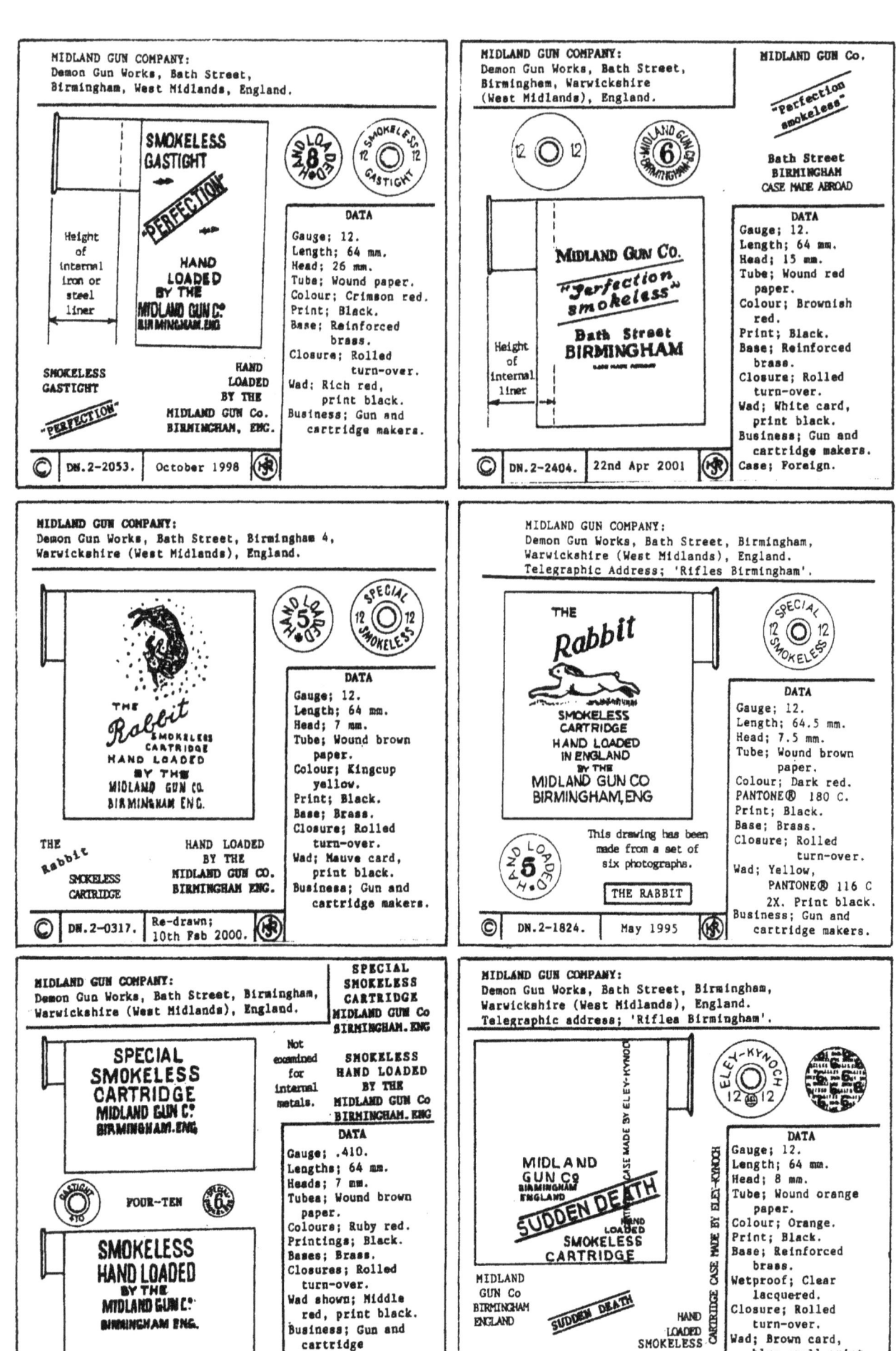

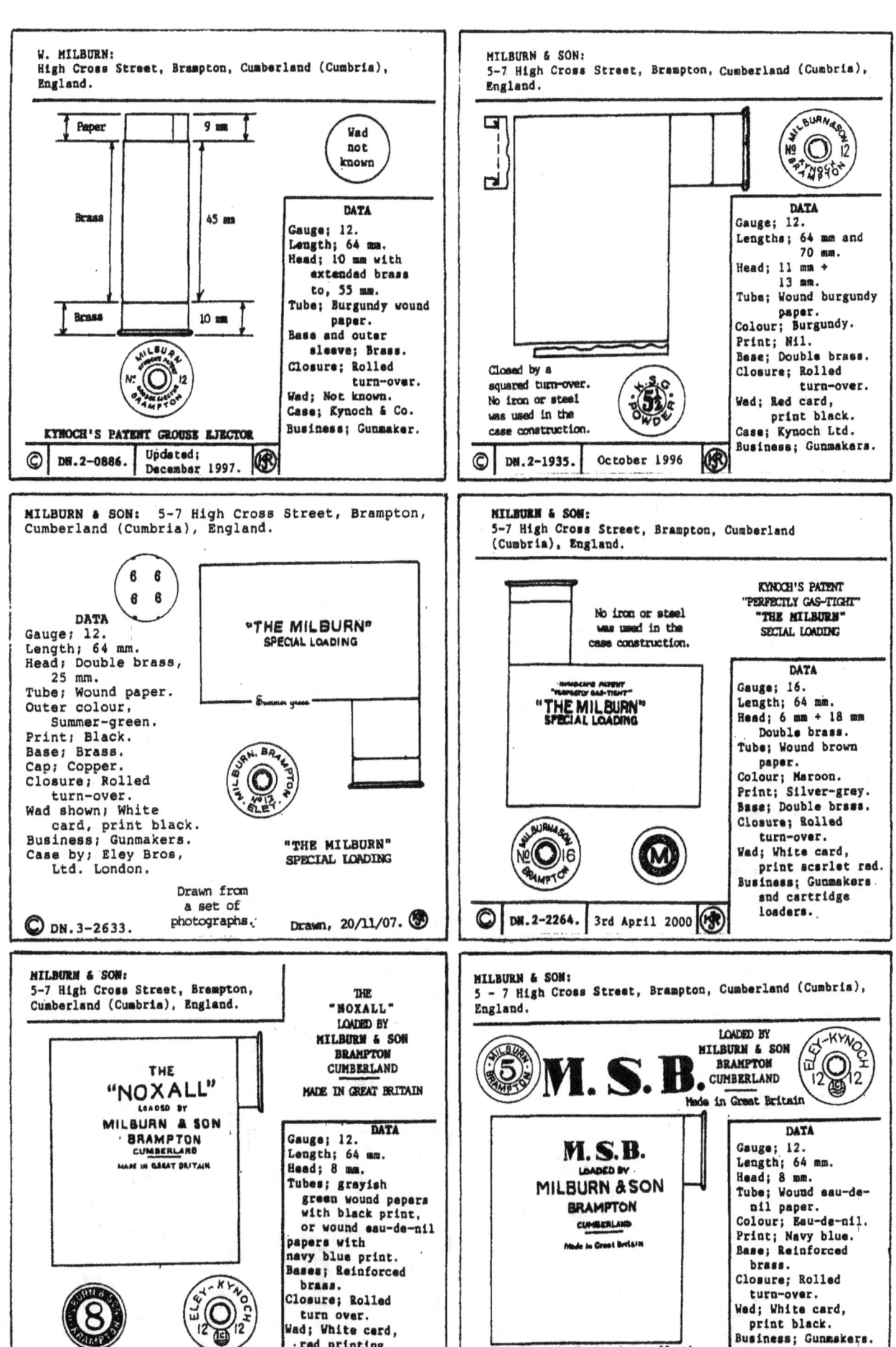

MILLS BROTHERS:
137 High Street, Crediton,
Devonshire, England.

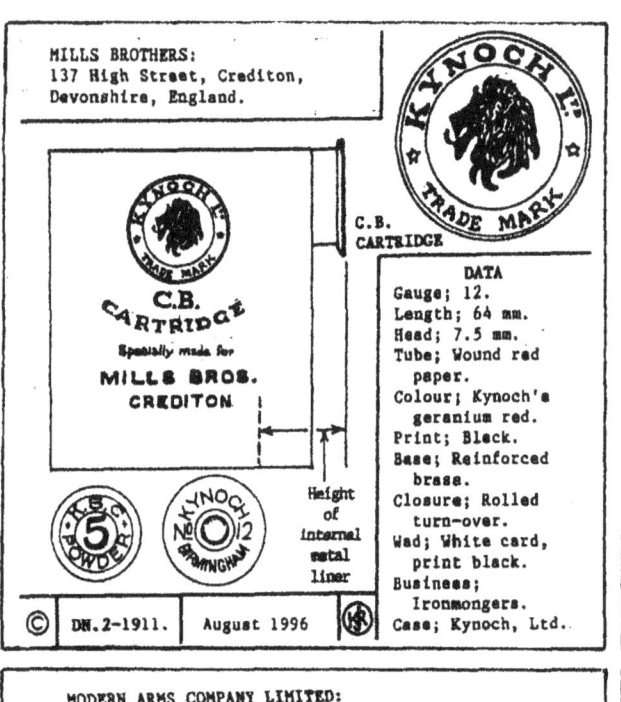

DATA
Gauge; 12.
Length; 64 mm.
Head; 7.5 mm.
Tube; Wound red paper.
Colour; Kynoch's geranium red.
Print; Black.
Base; Reinforced brass.
Closure; Rolled turn-over.
Wad; White card, print black.
Business; Ironmongers.
Case; Kynoch, Ltd.

© DW.2-1911.   August 1996

MODERN ARMS CO, LTD:
58 Southwark Ridge Road, London S.E.1.,
England.

DATA
Gauge; .410.
Length; 51 mm.
Head; 7 mm.
Tube; Wound paper.
Outer colour; Dark blood-red.
Print; Black.
Base; Brass.
Cap; Copper.
Closure; Rolled turn-over.
Wad; red, print black.
Case; German import.

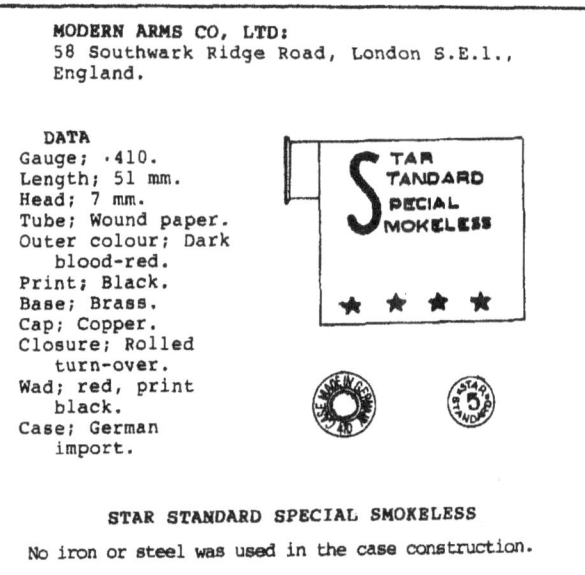

STAR STANDARD SPECIAL SMOKELESS

No iron or steel was used in the case construction.

© DW.3-2583.   Drawn, 9/10/07.

MODERN ARMS COMPANY LIMITED:
58 Southwark Bridge Road, London, S.E.1. England.
Works at; Bromley, Kent, England.

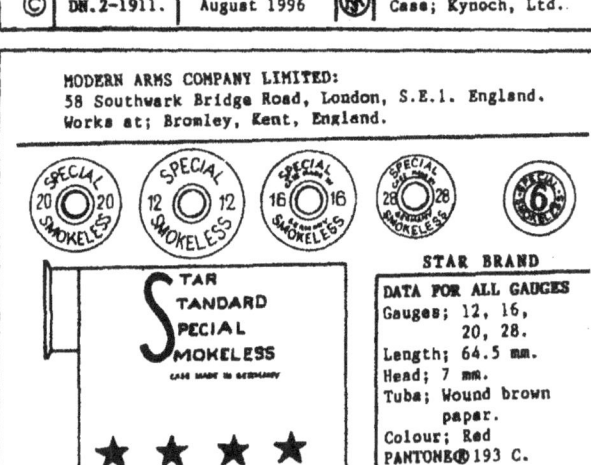

STAR BRAND

DATA FOR ALL GAUGES
Gauges; 12, 16, 20, 28.
Length; 64.5 mm.
Head; 7 mm.
Tube; Wound brown paper.
Colour; Red PANTONE® 193 C.
Print; Black.
Base; Brass.
Closure; Rolled turn-over.
Wad; White card, print black.
Circa; Mid 1930's.
Business; Arms, ammo and fishing.

No iron or steel was used in the case constructions. Where, CASE MADE IN GERMANY was shown on the stampings, it was not printed on the case walls. Caps were Synoxide and the powder was Walsrode. A 20 gauge is illustrated here.

© DW.2-0907.   Updated, March 1996

B. D. MOGG & SON:
Wells, Somerset, England.

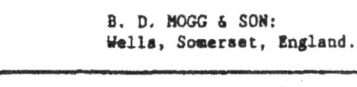
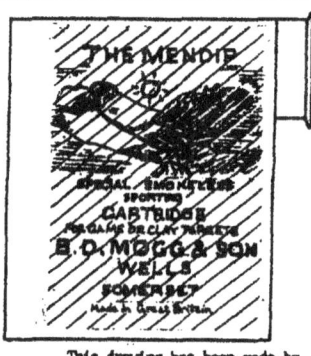

DATA
Gauge; 12.
Length; 64 mm.
Head; 8 mm.
Tube; Wound eau-de-nil paper.
Colour; Eau-de-nil.
Print; Navy blue.
Base; Reinforced brass.
Closure; Rolled turn-over.
Wad; White card, print red.
Wetproof; Lacquered.
Circa; 1930's.

This drawing has been made by the use of a set of six photographs. The small wording reads as follows,
THE   SPECIAL SMOKELESS SPORTING
MENDIP   FOR GAME OR CLAY TARGETS
          Made in Great Britain

© DW.2-1828.   May 1995.

MONARCH GUNWORKS:
Liverpool, Lancashire (Merseyside), England.

EJECTOR CARTRIDGE

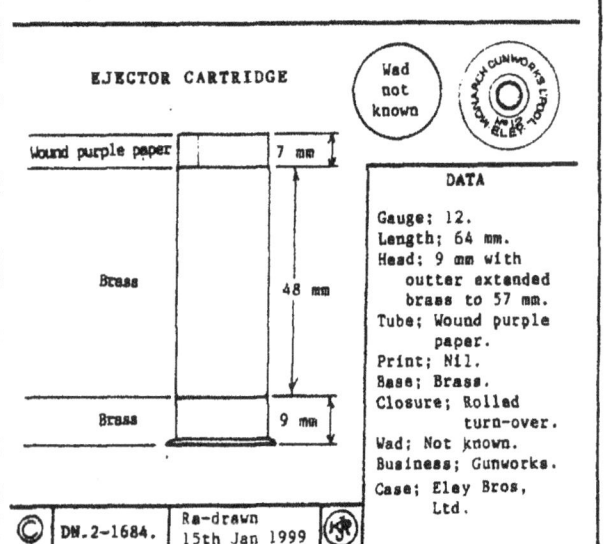

DATA
Gauge; 12.
Length; 64 mm.
Head; 9 mm with outter extended brass to 57 mm.
Tube; Wound purple paper.
Print; Nil.
Base; Brass.
Closure; Rolled turn-over.
Wad; Not known.
Business; Gunworks.
Case; Eley Bros, Ltd.

© DW.2-1684.   Re-drawn 15th Jan 1999

W. HENRY MONK:
77 Foregate Street, Chester, Cheshire, England.

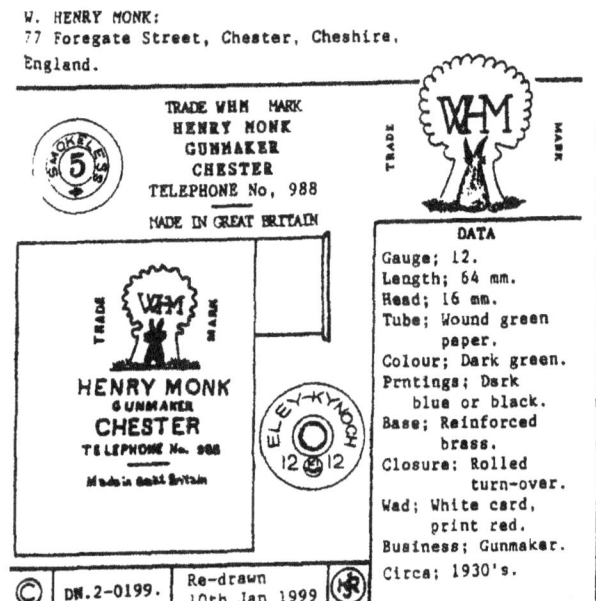

DATA
Gauge; 12.
Length; 64 mm.
Head; 16 mm.
Tube; Wound green paper.
Colour; Dark green.
Printings; Dark blue or black.
Base; Reinforced brass.
Closure; Rolled turn-over.
Wad; White card, print red.
Business; Gunmaker.
Circa; 1930's.

© DW.2-0199.   Re-drawn 10th Jan 1999

PLATE 258   [MIL – MON]

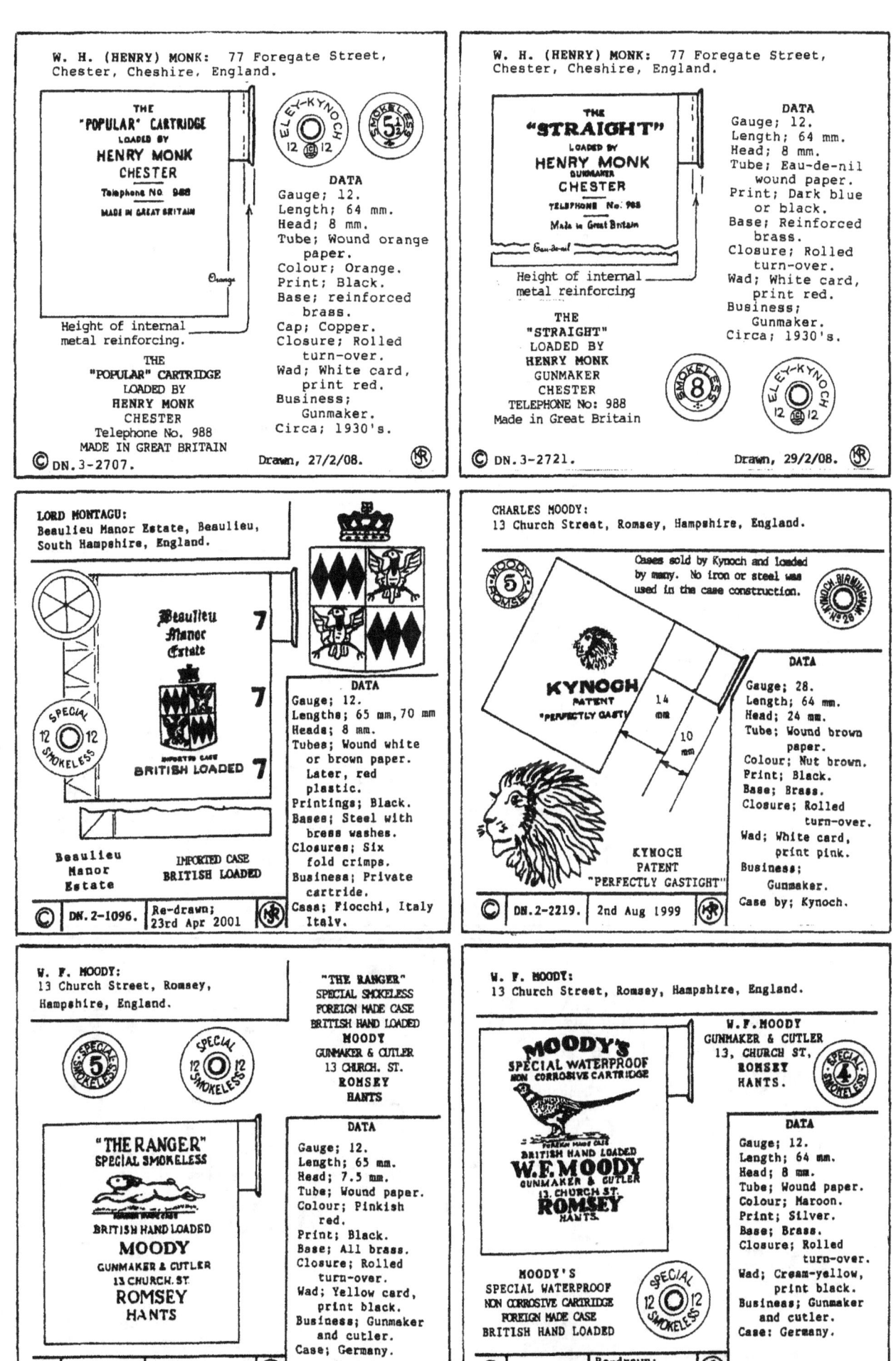

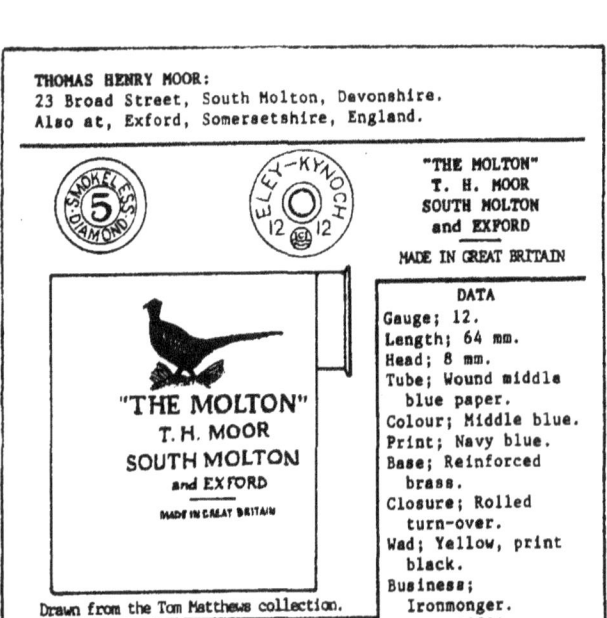
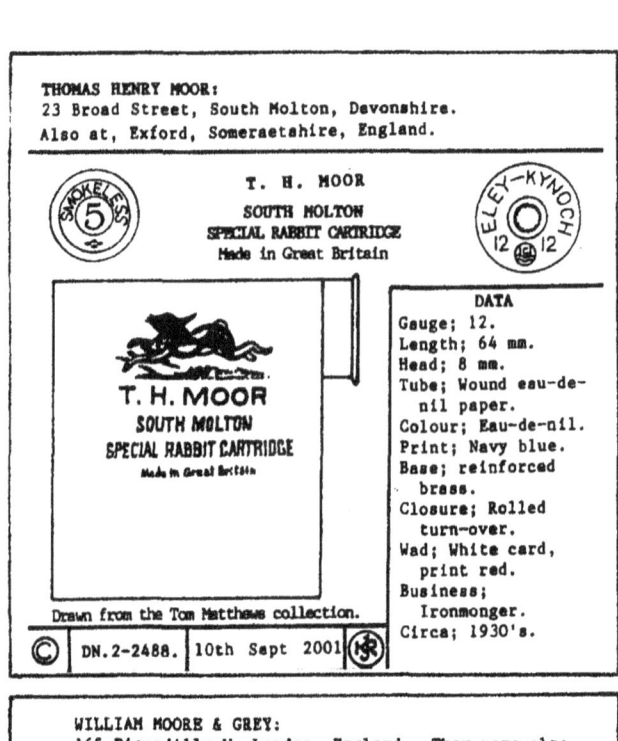
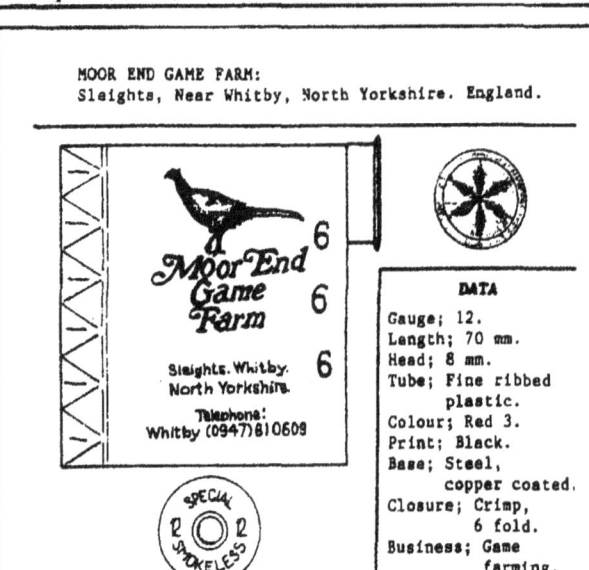
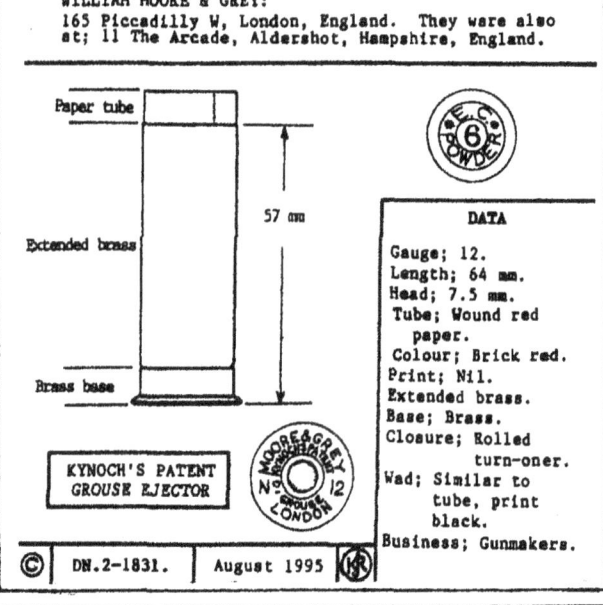
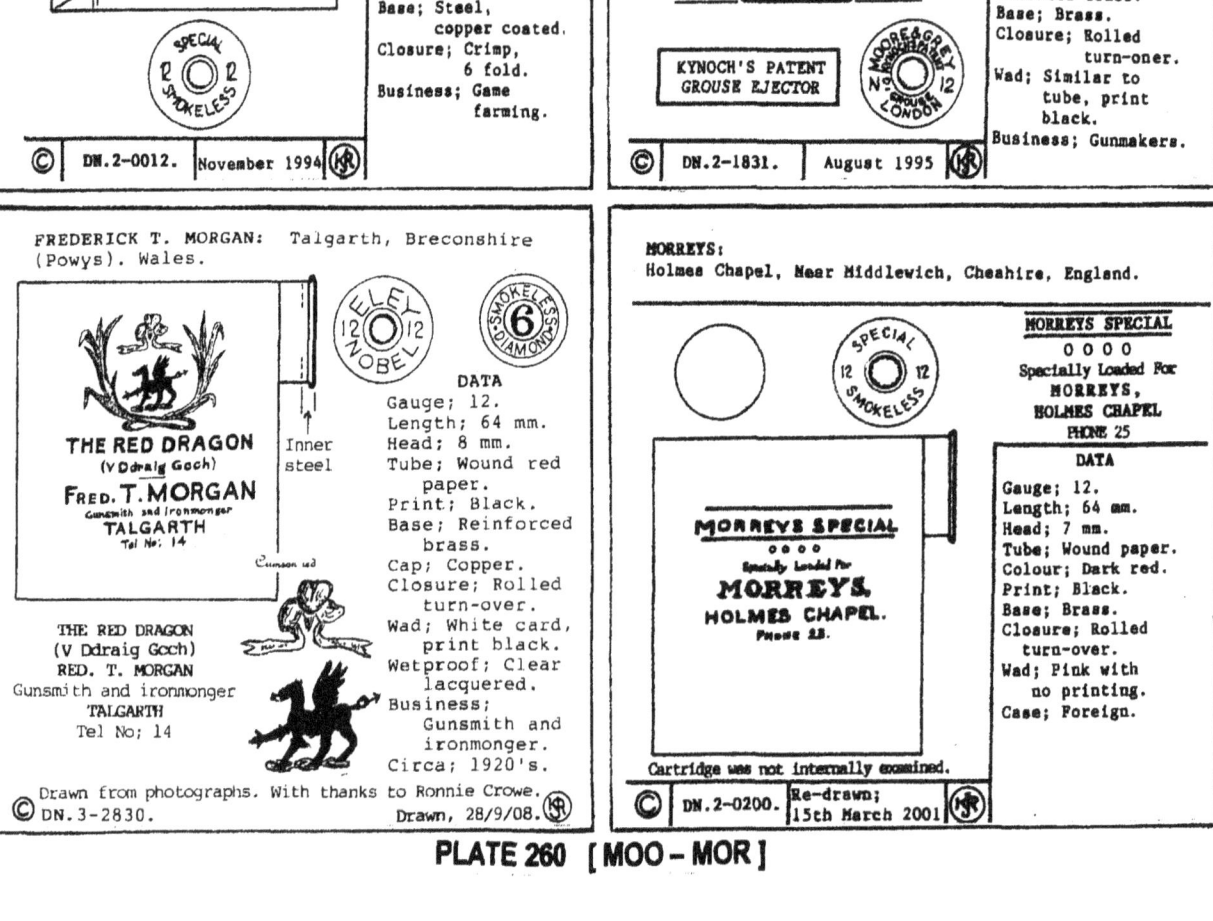

PLATE 260 [MOO – MOR]

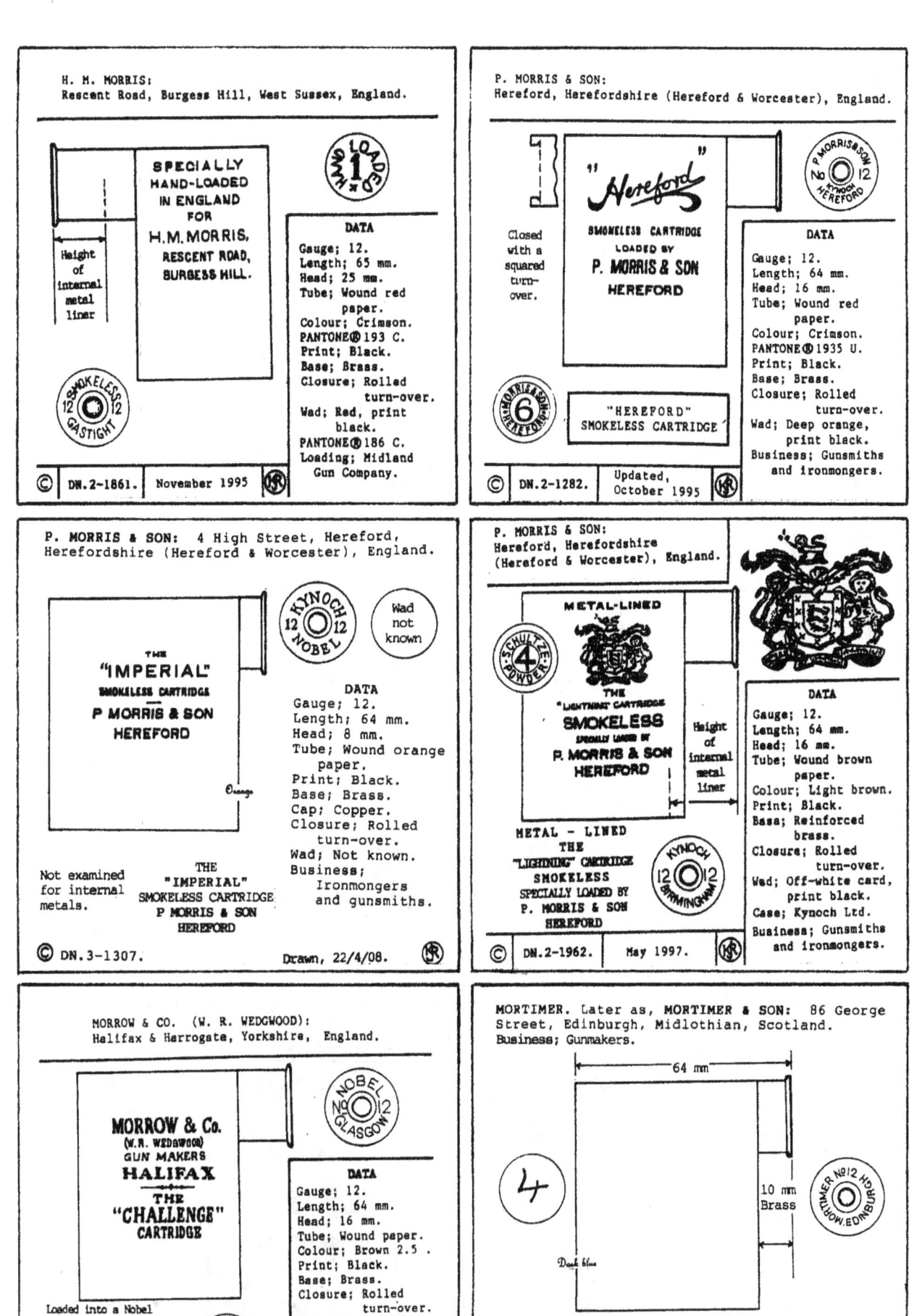

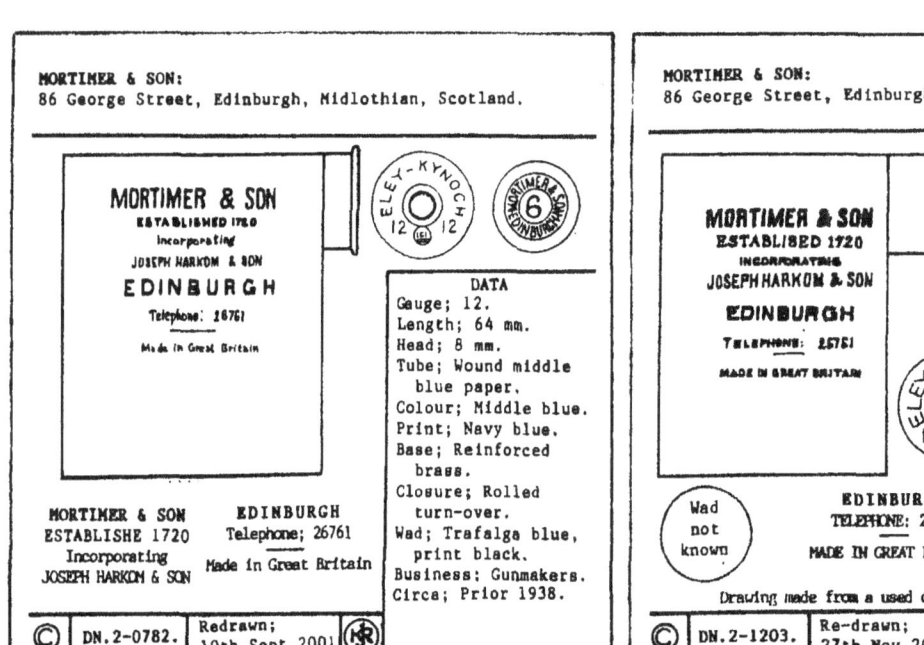
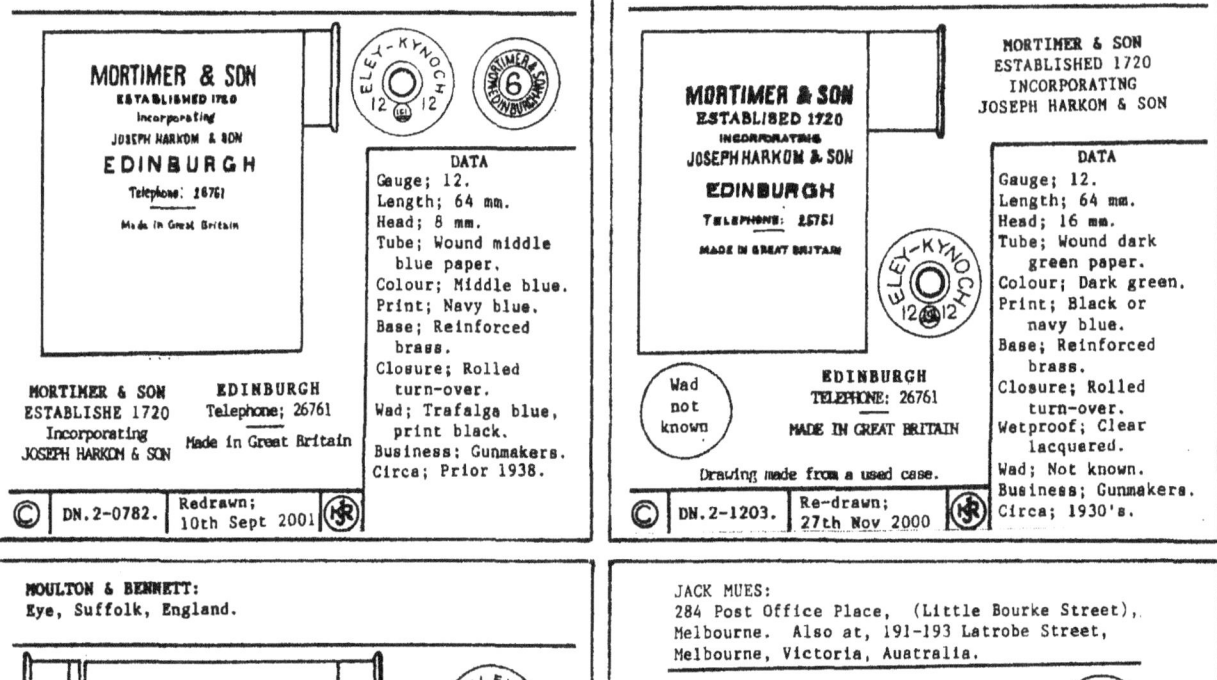
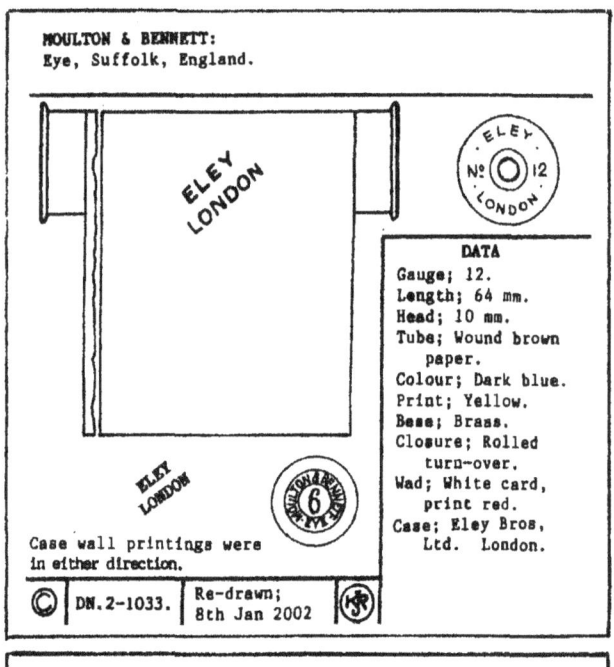
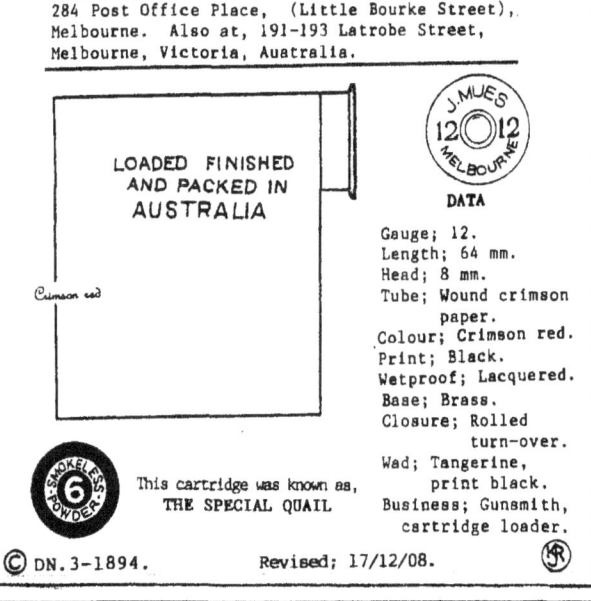
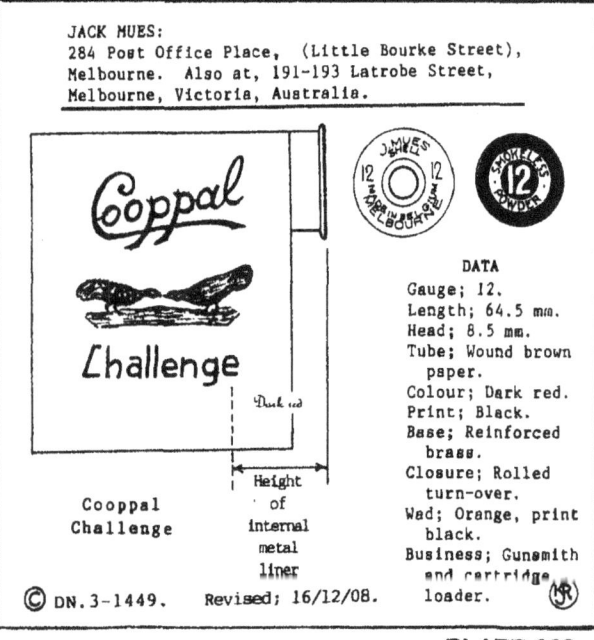
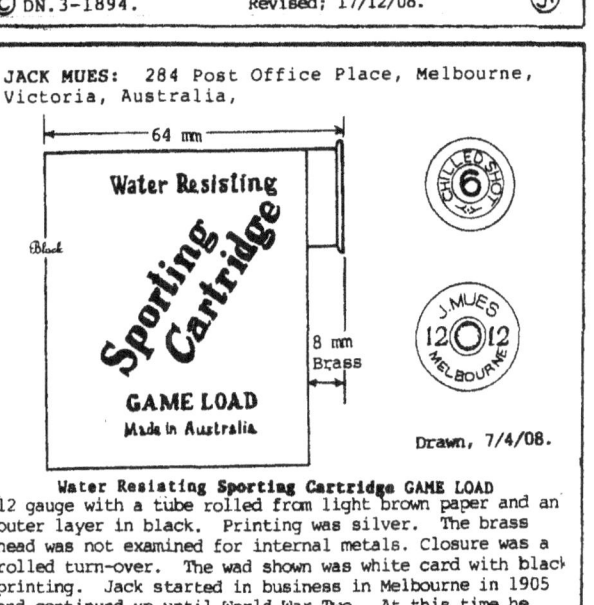

PLATE 262 [MOR – MUE]

MUNITIONSWERKE:
Schoenebeck A/E, Germany.

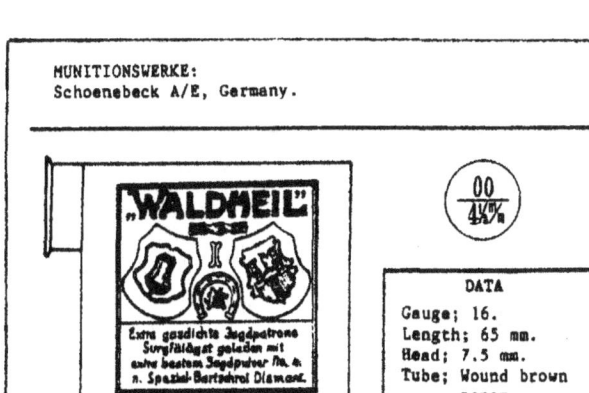

"WALDHEIL"

DATA
Gauge; 16.
Length; 65 mm.
Head; 7.5 mm.
Tube; Wound brown
 paper.
Colour; Dark brown.
Print; Black.
Base; Reinforced
 brass.
Closure; Rolled
 turn-over.
Wad; Shocking-
 pink card,
 print black.
Origin; Germany.

© DN.2-2073. November 1998

MULLERITE CARTRIDGE WORKS:
59 Bath Street, Birmingham. Also at,
St. Mary's Row, Birmingham, (W.Midlands), England.

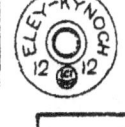

THE ACE

DATA
Gauge; 12.
Length; 64 mm.
Head; 8 mm.
Tube; Wound paper.
Colour; Orange.
Print; Black.
Base; Brass.
Closure; Rolled
 turn-over.
Wads; Both shown
 brown card,
 Shot 5 in
 black, shot 2
 in mauve.
Cases; Eley-Kynoch.
Business; Manu-
 facturers.

© DN.2-1767. Updated; January 1995

MULLERITE CARTRIDGE WORKS:
59 Bath Street, Birmingham. Also at,
St. Mary's Row, Birmingham, (W.Midlands), England.

THE ACE

DATA
Gauge; 12.
Lengths; 64 mm, 69
 mm, 75 mm.
Head; 16 mm.
Tubes; Wound brown
 paper.
Ext' colours; Orange
 or light
 brown.
Base; Brass.
Closure; Rolled
 turn-over.
Wad; Red 3,
 print black.
Business; Manu-
 facturers.

© DN.2-1768. Updated; January 1995

BRITISH MULLERITE: Proprietors; MARTIN PULVERMAN &
COMPANY LIMITED:
Mullerite Cartridge Works, St. Mary's Row, Birmingham 4,
Also at, 59 Bath Street, Birmingham, (Midlands), England.

THE BLACK PRINCE

BLACK POWDER
CARTRIDGE.

Wad not known

This drawing has been made
of an unused case which was
portrayed on a set of six
photographs. Its head had
signs of double stamping.

DATA
Gauge; 12.
Length; 66 mm.
Head; 7 mm.
Tube; Wound brown
 paper.
Colour; Old bone.
PANTONE® 727 C.
Print; Black.
Base; Brass.
Closure; Rolled.
Circa; 1934-1935.
Business;
 Ammunition
 manufacturers.

© DN.2-1825. Updated, March 1996   THE BLACK PRINCE

MULLERITE CARTRIDGE WORKS:
59 Bath Street. Also at, St. Mary's Row, Birmingham 4,
Warwickshire (West Midlands), England.

The "CHAMPION"
SMOKELESS
CARTRIDGE

Anti-Corrosive Foreign Cap and Case
LOADED IN
GREAT BRITAIN

The "CHAMPION"
SMOKELESS
CARTRIDGE
Anti-Corrosive Foreign Cap and Case
LOADED IN
GREAT BRITAIN

DATA
Gauge; 12.
Length; 65 mm.
Head; 8 mm.
Tube; Wound paper.
Colour; Dark blue.
Print; Black.
Base; Brass.
Primer cap; Large.
Wetproof; Clear
 lacquered.
Closure; Rolled
 turn-over.
Wad; Red card,
 print black.
Business;
 Cartridge
 manufacturers.

© DN.2-0738. Re-drawn; 5th Feb 2000.

MULLERITE CARTRIDGE WORKS:
59 Bath Street. Also at, St. Mary's Row, Birmingham 4,
Warwickshire,(West Midlands), England.

The "CHAMPION"
SMOKELESS
CARTRIDGE
LOADED
IN GREAT BRITAIN

The "CHAMPION"
SMOKELESS
CARTRIDGE
LOADED
IN GREAT BRITAIN

DATA
Gauge; 12.
Length; 65 mm.
Head; 8 mm.
Tube; Wound brown
 paper.
Colour; Dull
 brownish red.
Print; Black.
Base; Brass.
Closure; Rolled
 turn-over.
Wad; red card,
 print black.
Business;
 Cartridge
 manufacturers.
Case; Foreign.

© DN.2-0736. Re-drawn; 5th Feb 2000.

MULLERITE CARTRIDGE WORKS:
59 Bath Street, Birmingham. Also at, St. Mary's Row,
Birmingham, Warwickshire (West Midlands), England.

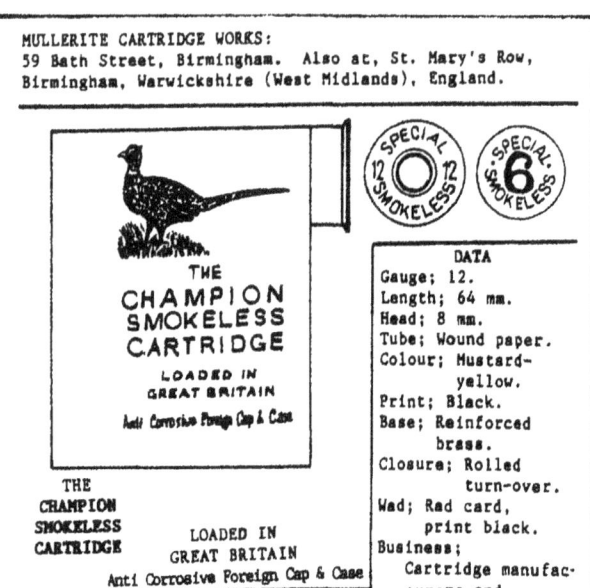

THE
CHAMPION
SMOKELESS
CARTRIDGE
Mullerite
LOADED IN
GREAT BRITAIN
Anti Corrosive Foreign Cap & Case

DATA
Gauge; 12.
Length; 64 mm.
Head; 8 mm.
Tube; Wound paper.
Colour; Mustard-yellow.
Print; Black.
Base; Reinforced brass.
Closure; Rolled turn-over.
Wad; Red card, print black.
Business; Cartridge manufacturers and merchants.

© DN.2-2084. November 1998

THE MULLERITE CARTRIDGE WORKS:
59 Bath Street, Birmingham. Also at,
St. Mary's Row, Birmingham, West Midlands, England.

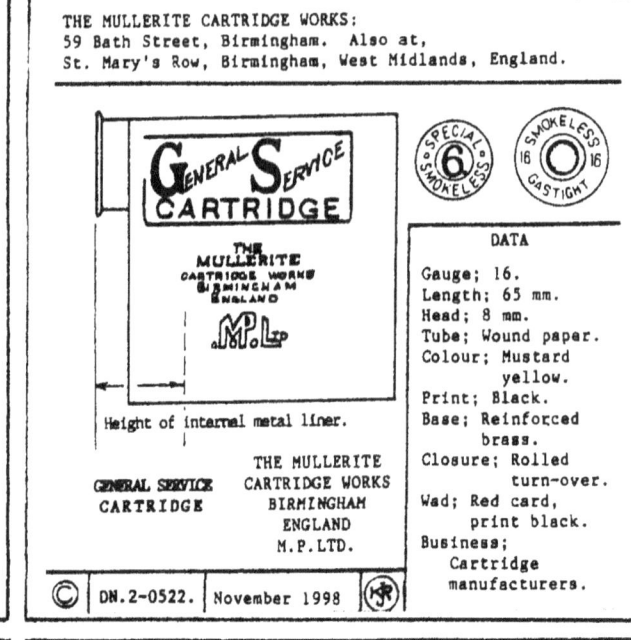

GENERAL SERVICE CARTRIDGE
THE MULLERITE CARTRIDGE WORKS BIRMINGHAM ENGLAND M.P.LTD.

DATA
Gauge; 16.
Length; 65 mm.
Head; 8 mm.
Tube; Wound paper.
Colour; Mustard yellow.
Print; Black.
Base; Reinforced brass.
Closure; Rolled turn-over.
Wad; Red card, print black.
Business; Cartridge manufacturers.

© DN.2-0522. November 1998

THE MULLERITE CARTRIDGE WORKS, MARTIN PULVERMANN LTD:
59 Bath Street, Birmingham. Also at, St. Mary's Row,
Birmingham, Warwickshire (West Midlands), England.

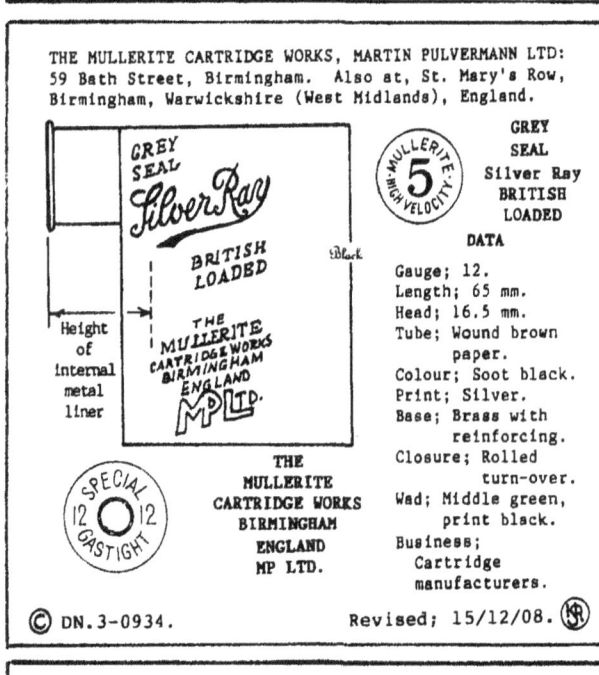

GREY SEAL
Silver Ray
BRITISH LOADED

DATA
Gauge; 12.
Length; 65 mm.
Head; 16.5 mm.
Tube; Wound brown paper.
Colour; Soot black.
Print; Silver.
Base; Brass with reinforcing.
Closure; Rolled turn-over.
Wad; Middle green, print black.
Business; Cartridge manufacturers.

THE MULLERITE CARTRIDGE WORKS BIRMINGHAM ENGLAND MP LTD.

© DN.3-0934. Revised; 15/12/08.

THE MULLERITE CARTRIDGE WORKS, MARTIN PULVERMANN LTD:
59 Bath Street, Birmingham. Also at, St. Mary's Row,
Birmingham, Warwickshire (West Midlands), England.

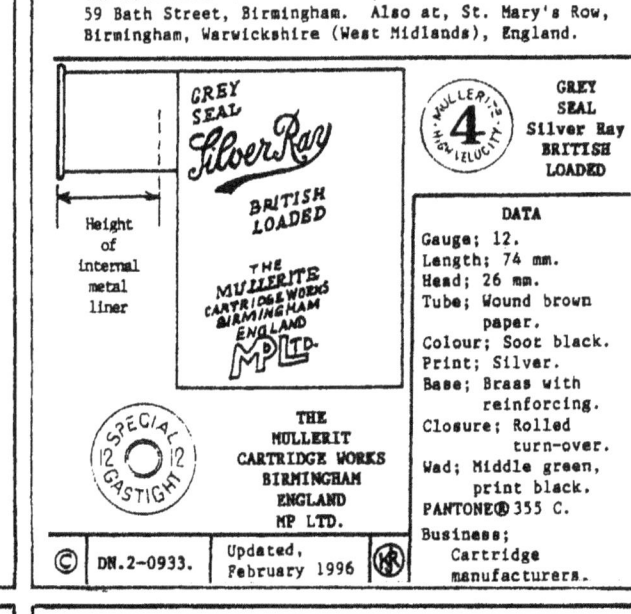

GREY SEAL
Silver Ray
BRITISH LOADED

DATA
Gauge; 12.
Length; 74 mm.
Head; 26 mm.
Tube; Wound brown paper.
Colour; Soot black.
Print; Silver.
Base; Brass with reinforcing.
Closure; Rolled turn-over.
Wad; Middle green, print black.
PANTONE® 355 C.
Business; Cartridge manufacturers.

THE MULLERIT CARTRIDGE WORKS BIRMINGHAM ENGLAND MP LTD.

© DN.2-0933. Updated, February 1996

MULLERITE CARTRIDGE WORKS: 59 Bath Street, &
St. Mary's Row, Birmingham, Warwickshire
(West Midlands), England.
MPL =Proprietors; MARTIN PULVERMANN & CO, LTD:

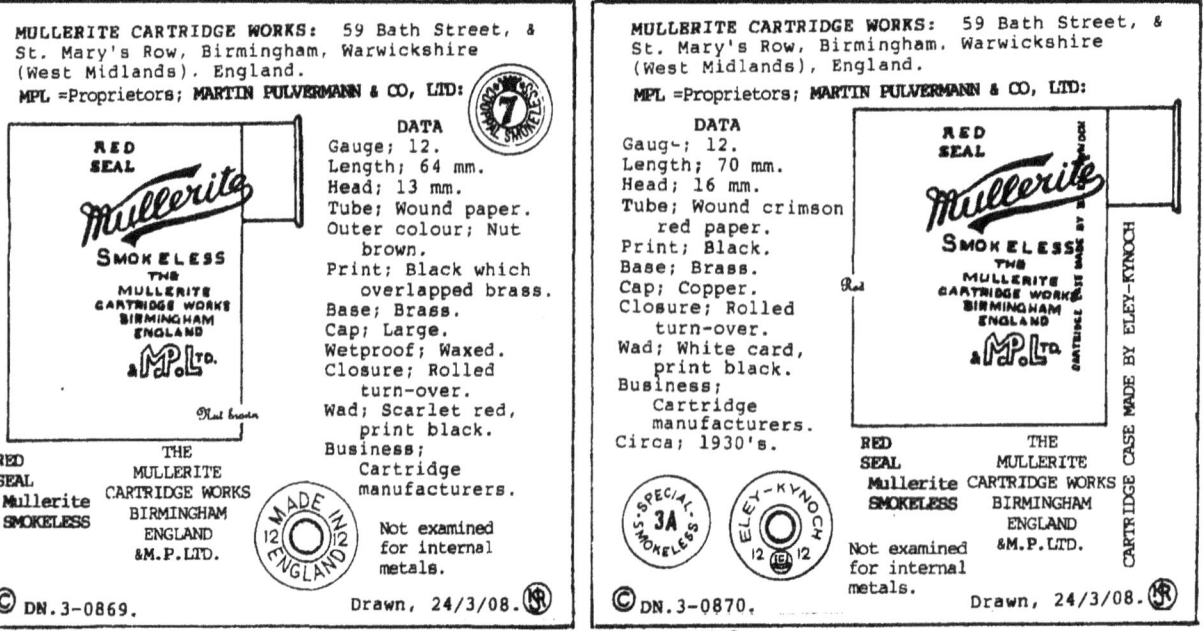

RED SEAL
Mullerite
SMOKELESS
THE MULLERITE CARTRIDGE WORKS BIRMINGHAM ENGLAND &M.P.LTD.

DATA
Gauge; 12.
Length; 64 mm.
Head; 13 mm.
Tube; Wound paper.
Outer colour; Nut brown.
Print; Black which overlapped brass.
Base; Brass.
Cap; Large.
Wetproof; Waxed.
Closure; Rolled turn-over.
Wad; Scarlet red, print black.
Business; Cartridge manufacturers.
Not examined for internal metals.

© DN.3-0869. Drawn, 24/3/08.

MULLERITE CARTRIDGE WORKS: 59 Bath Street, &
St. Mary's Row, Birmingham, Warwickshire
(West Midlands), England.
MPL =Proprietors; MARTIN PULVERMANN & CO, LTD:

DATA
Gauge; 12.
Length; 70 mm.
Head; 16 mm.
Tube; Wound crimson red paper.
Print; Black.
Base; Brass.
Cap; Copper.
Closure; Rolled turn-over.
Wad; White card, print black.
Business; Cartridge manufacturers.
Circa; 1930's.

RED SEAL
Mullerite
SMOKELESS
THE MULLERITE CARTRIDGE WORKS BIRMINGHAM ENGLAND &M.P.LTD.
CARTRIDGE CASE MADE BY ELEY-KYNOCH

Not examined for internal metals.

© DN.3-0870. Drawn, 24/3/08.

MULLERITE CARTRIDGE WORKS: 59 Bath Street, & St. Mary's Row, Birmingham, Warwickshire (West Midlands). And also, MARTIN PULVERMANN & CO, LTD: 31 Minories, London E.C.3., England.

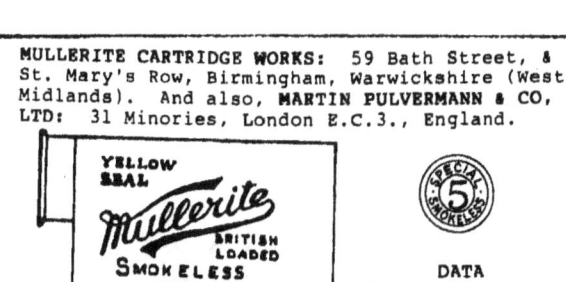

DATA
Gauge; 16.
Length; 64 mm.
Head; 8 mm.
Tube; Wound red paper.
Print; Black.
Base; Brass.
Wetproof; Waxed.
Closure; Rolled turn-over.
Wad; Red, print black.
Business; Manufacturers and merchants.

YELLOW SEAL
MULLERITE
BRITISH LOADED
SMOKELESS
THE
MULLRITE
CARTRIDGE WORKS
BIRMINGHAM
ENGLAND
& MP CO LTD.

© DN.3-0867.   Drawn, 30/4/08.

MULLERITE CARTRIDGE WORKS: 59 Bath Street, & St. Mary's Row, Birmingham, Warwickshire (West Midlands), England.
MPL =Proprietors; MARTIN PULVERMANN & CO, LTD.

Not examined for internal metals.

DATA
Gauge; 12.
Length; 64 mm.
Head; 9 mm.
Tube; Wound paper.
Outer colour; Mustard yellow.
Print; Black.
Wetproof; Waxed.
Base; Brass.
Cap; Large copper.
Closure; Rolled turn-over.
Wads shown; Celandine yellow, prinings black.
Case; Foreign.
Business; Cartridge manufacturers.

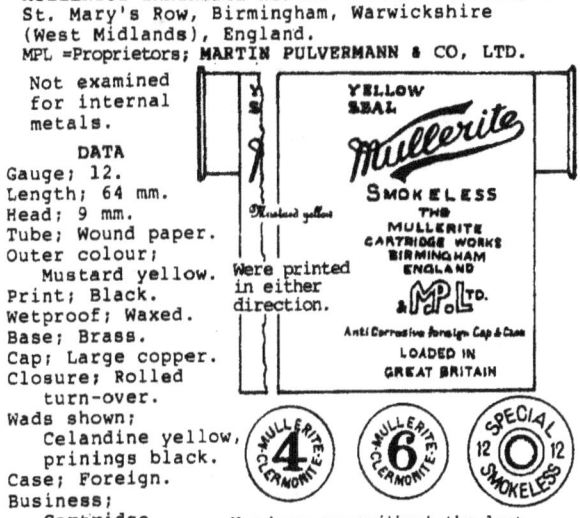

Were printed in either direction.

Has been seen without the last three printed lines.

© DN.3-0866. YELLOW SEAL Mullerite   Drawn, 25/3/08.

MULLERITE CARTRIDGE WORKS: 59 Bath Street, & St. Mary's Row, Birmingham, Warwickshire (West Midlands), England.
MPL =Proprietors; MARTIN PULVERMANN & CO, LTD:

DATA
Gauge; 12.
Length; 70 mm.
Head; 7 mm.
Tube; Wound paper.
Colour; Mustard yellow.
Print; Black.
Wetproof; Waxed.
Base; Brass.
Cap; Large.
Closure; Rolled turn-over.
Wad; Celandine yellow, print black.
Business; Cartridge manufacturers.
Case; Foreign.

Not examined for internal metals.

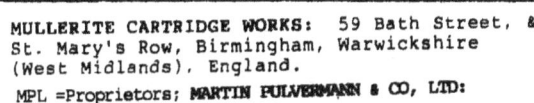

MULLERITE
SMOKELESS

© DN.3-0169.   Drawn, 24/3/08.

MULLERITE CARTRIDGE WORKS:
59 Bath Street, Birmingham. Also at, St. Mary's Row, Birmingham, Warwickshire (West Midlands), England.

WAD; MULLERITE. SMOKELESS CLERMONITE. 5½.

20 GAUGE 20
SMOKELESS
GASTIGHT
CARTRIDGE
LOADED
IN GREAT BRITAIN

Height of internal metal liner

20 GAUGE 20
SMOKELESS
GASTIGHT
CARTRIDGE
LOADED
IN GREAT BRITAIN

DATA
Gauge; 20.
Length; 64 mm.
Head; 16.5 mm.
Tube; Wound paper.
Colour; Nut brown.
Print; Black.
Base; Reinforced brass.
Closure; Rolled turn-over.
Wad; Celandine yellow, print black.
Cap; Large copper.
Business; Ammunition manufacturers.

© DN.2-2005.   July 1997.

MULLERITE CARTRIDGE WORKS: 59 Bath Street, Also at, St. Mary's Row, Birmingham, Warwickshire (W. Midlands), England.

MULLERITE
SPECIAL
CLAYKING
LOW RECOIL

DATA
Gauge; 20.
Length; 64 mm.
Head; 8.5 mm.
Tube; Wound paper.
Outer colour; Mustard yellow.
Print; Black.
Base; Brass.
Cap; Large copper.
Closure; Rolled turn-over.
Wad; Light yellow, print black.
Business; Cartridge manufacturers.

MULLERITE
SPECIAL
CLAY KING
LOW RECOIL

Drawn from a set of photographs.

© DN.3-2606.   Drawn on 7/11/07.

MULLERITE CARTRIDGE WORKS: 59 Bath Street, & St. Mary's Row, Birmingham, Warwickshire (West Midlands), England.

MULLERITE
SPECIAL
CLAYKING

Dark blue

DATA
Gauge; 12.
Length; 65 mm.
Head; 8 mm.
Tube; Wound paper.
Colour; Very dark blue.
Print; Black.
Base; Brass.
Cap; Large copper.
Closure; Rolled turn-over.
Wad; Light powder blue, print black.
Business; Ammo manufacturers.

MULLERITE
SPECIAL
CLAYKING

Not examined for internal metals.

© DN.3-0526.   Drawn, 30/4/08.

PLATE 265 [MUL - MUL]

MULLERITE CARTRIDGE WORKS: 59 Bath Street, & St. Mary's Row, Birmingham, Warwickshire (West Midlands). And also, **MARTIN PULVERMANN & CO, LTD:** 31 Minories, London E.C.3., England.

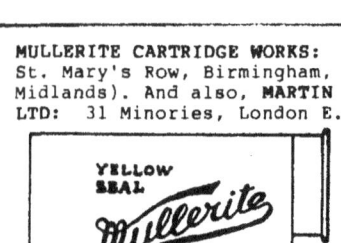

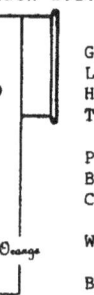

DATA
Gauge, 12.
Length; 64 mm.
Head; 8 mm.
Tube; Wound orange paper.
Print; Black.
Base; Brass.
Closure; Rolled turn-over.
Wad; Light brown, print black.
Business;; Manufacturers and merchants.

YELLOW SEAL
MULLERITE
SMOKELESS
THE
MULLERITE
CARTRIDGE WORKS
BIRMINGHAM
ENGLAND
& MP CO LTD.

Both were used.

© DN.3-0868.   Drawn, 30/4/08.

MULTI-SPORTS; 225 Old Christchurch Road, Bournemouth, Hampshire, England.

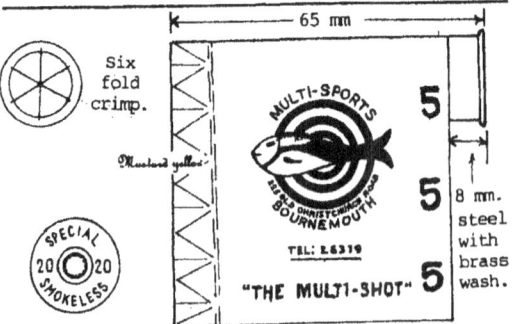

"THE MULTI-SHOT"

This cartridge was loaded by Hull Cartridge into a best quality Fiocchi imported case. The tube was wound from off-white paper with an outer layer of buff-yellow. The case wall printing was in black. Closure was by a six fold crimp and waterproofing was by clear varnishing.

© DN.3-5500.   Drawn, 26/6/2011.

MULTI-SPORTS; 225 Old Christchurch Road, Bournemouth, Hampshire, England.

"THE MULTI-SHOT"

This cartridge was loaded by Hull Cartridge into a best quality Fiocchi imported case. The tube was wound from off-white paper with an outer layer of crimson red. The case wall printing was in black. Closure was by a six fold crimp and waterproofing was by clear varnishing.

© DN.3-5505.   Drawn, 26/6/2011.

S. MUNTHE-BRUN: Gartnervej, Naestved, Denmark.

(A private cartridge).

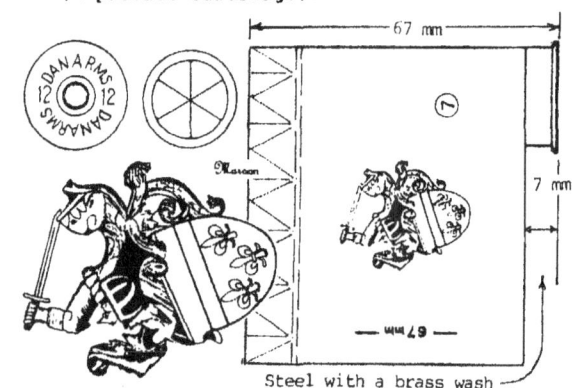

Steel with a brass wash

Manufactured by DAN-ARMS at Frederickavaerk, its tube was wound from brown paper with an outer layer of maroon. The case wall printing was in black. Closure was by a six fold star crimp.

© DN.3-1313.   Revised; 12/1/09.

T. W. MURRAY & CO, LTD: The Munster Armoury, 87 Patrick Street, Cork, Republic of Ireland.

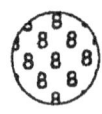 

(Dog)
TRADE MARK
"MURRAY'S RELIABLE
TWM
SMOKELESS CARTRIDGE
GUARANTEED BEST LOADING
MANUFACTURED UNDER LICENCE
BY
IRISH METAL INDUSTRIES LTD.

DATA
Gauge; 12.
Length; 64 mm.
Head; 8 mm.
Tube; Wound orange paper.
Colour; Orange.
Print; Black.
Base; Reinforced brass.
Wetproof; Lacquered.
Closure; Rolled turn-over.
Wad; Brown card, print black.
Business; Gunmakers.
Case; Republic of Ireland.

© DN.2-2415.   5th June 2001

T. NAUGHTON & SONS: Shop Street, Galway, County Galway, Republic of Ireland.

"THE BLAZER"
Special Loading

DATA
Gauge; 12.
Length; 64 mm.
Head; 8 mm.
Tube; Wound grey paper.
Colour; Light grey.
Print; Black.
Base; Brass.
Closure; Rolled turn-over.
Wad; Yellow, print black.
Business: Sports dealers, ironmongers, furnishings.
Circa; 1930's.

© DN.3-2561.   Drawn, 5/6/07.

PLATE 266 [MUL – NAU]

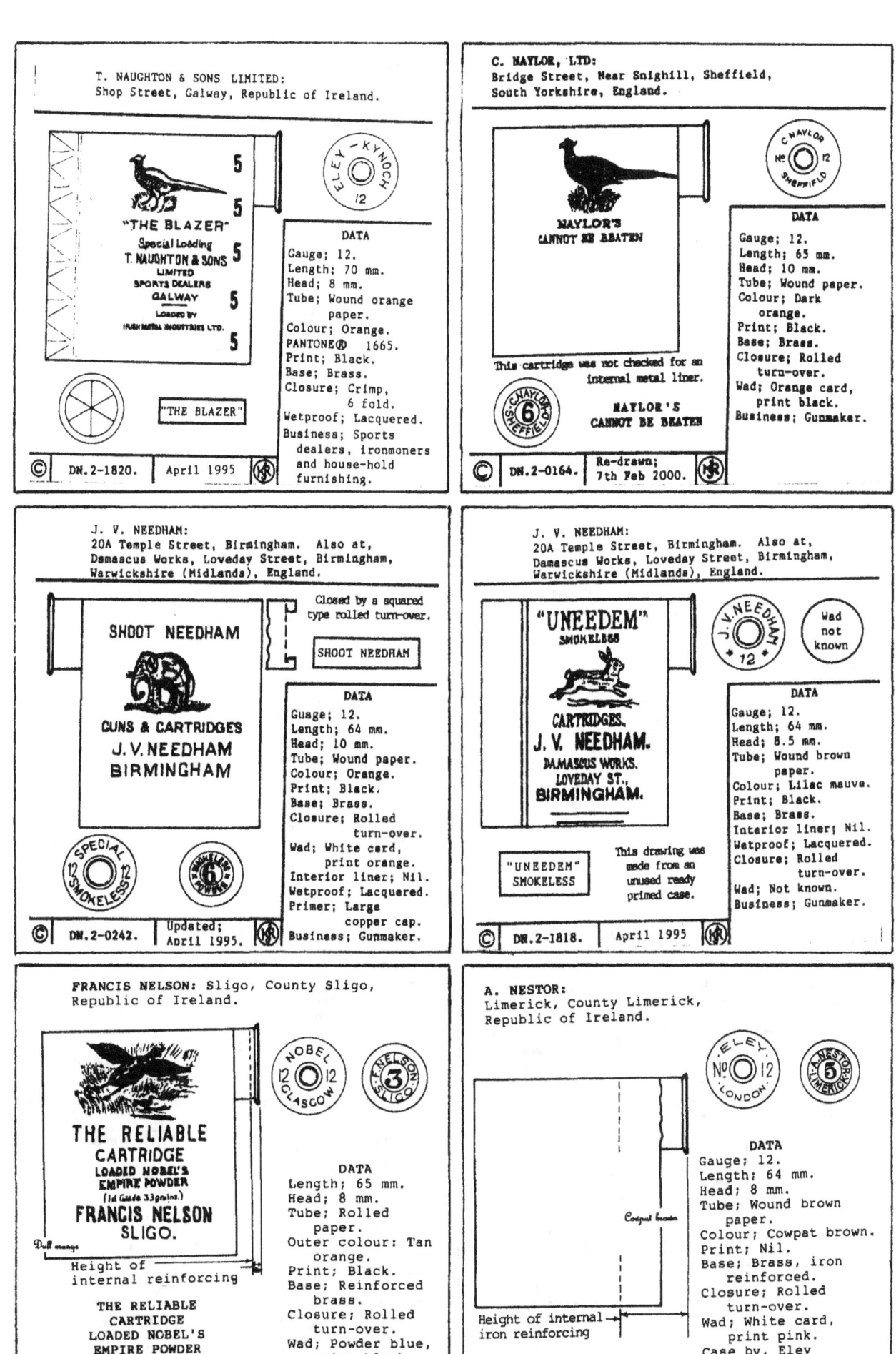

PLATE 267 [NAU – NES]

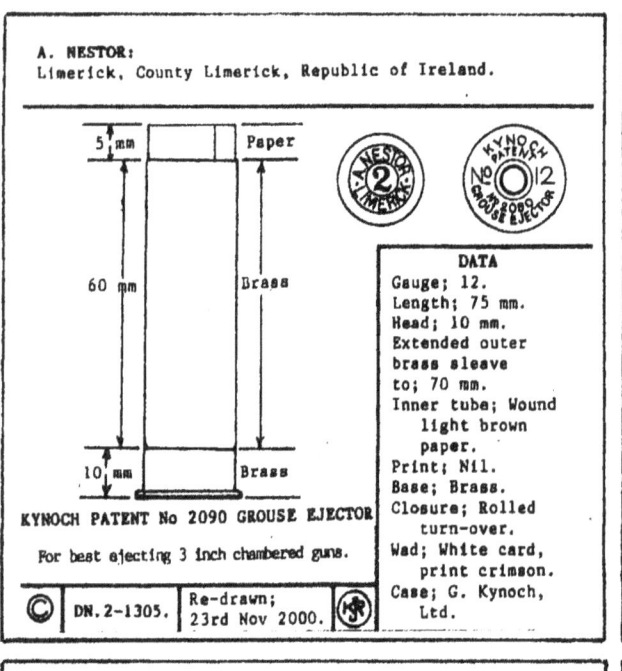
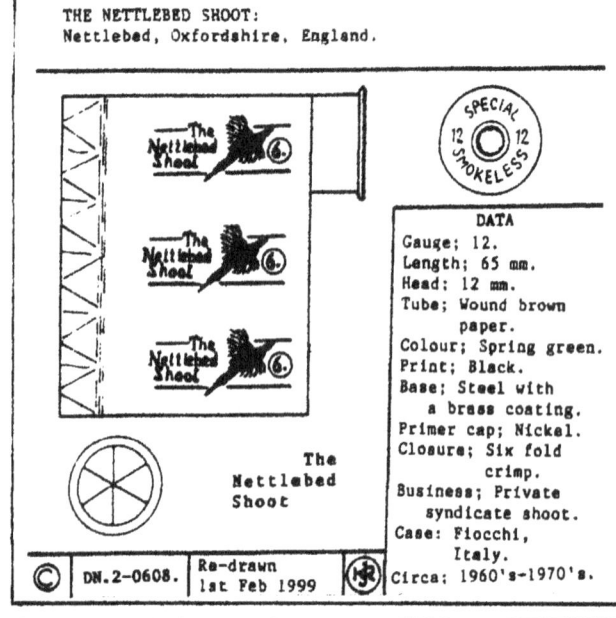
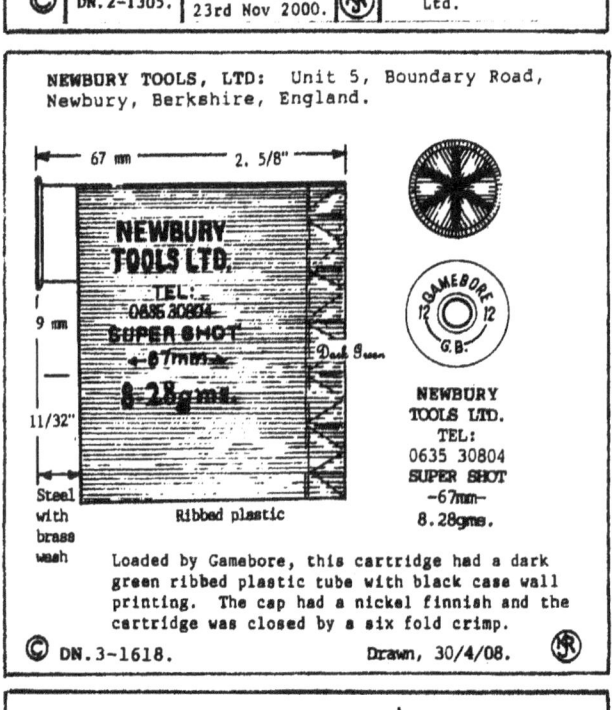
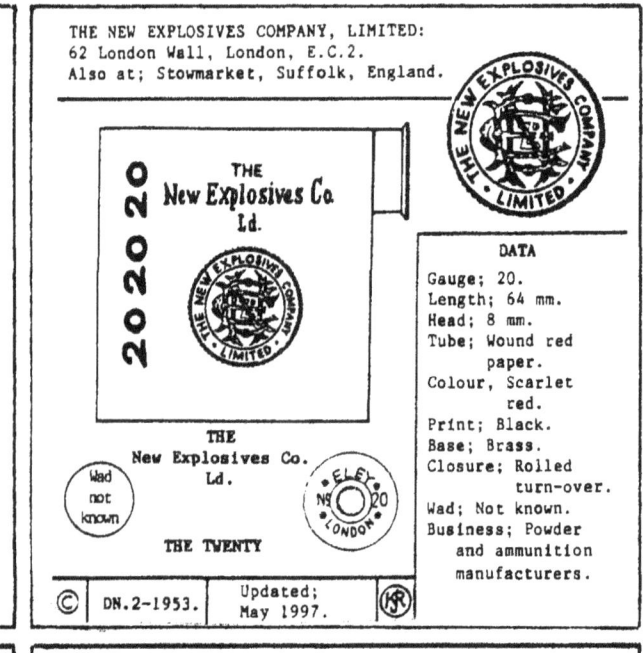

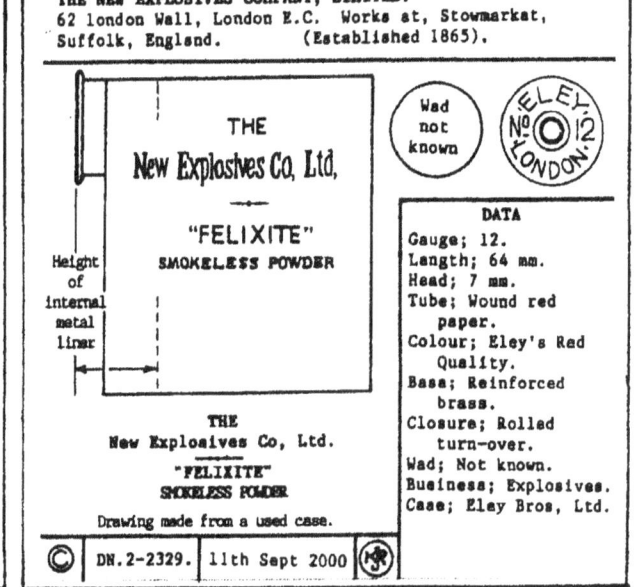

PLATE 268 [NES – NEW]

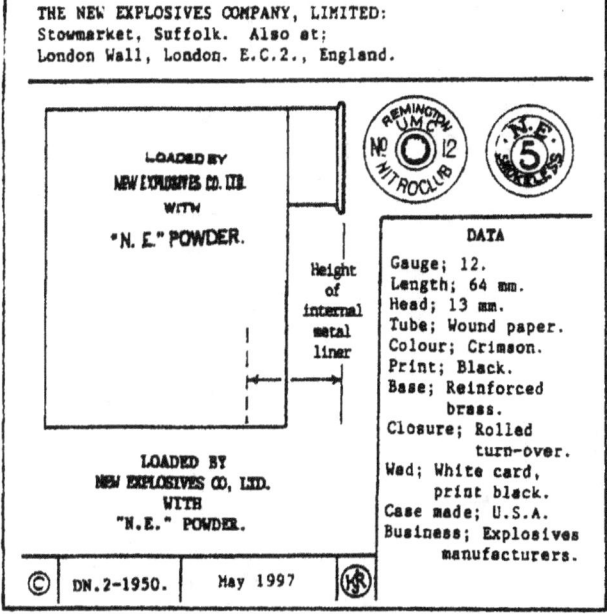
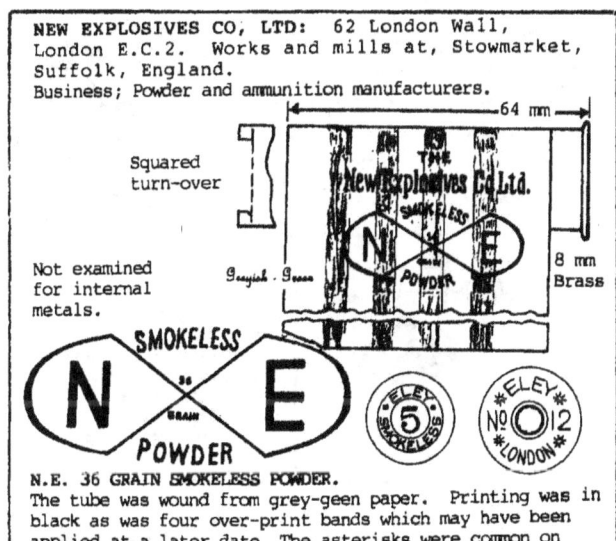
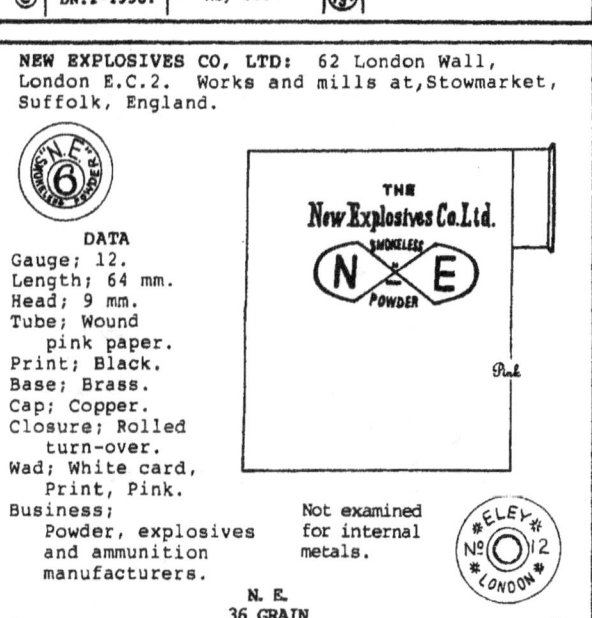

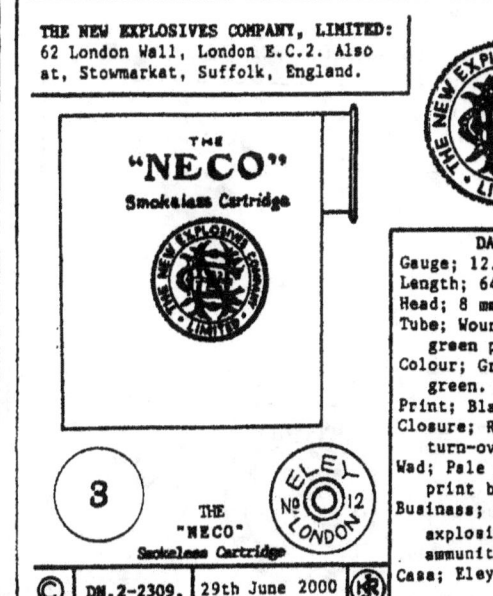

PLATE 269 [NEW – NEW]

Panel 1 (top left)

NEW EXPLOSIVES COMPANY LIMITED:
Stowmarket, Suffolk. Also at,
62 London Wall, London E.C., England.

THE New Explosives Co.,Ld. WATERPROOF CARTRIDGE CASE "Pegamoid" Brand Paper LOADED WOTH "NEONITE" SMOKELESS POWDER

Made in Great Britain

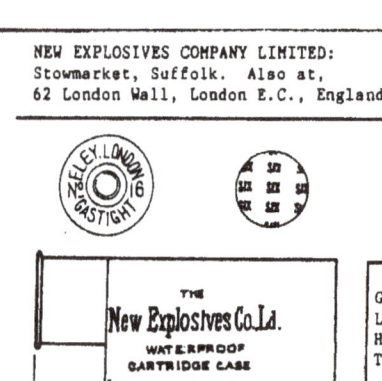

DATA
Gauge; 16.
Length; 64 mm.
Head; 15 mm.
Tube; Wound brown paper.
Colour; Middle brown.
Print; Black.
Base; Reinforced brass.
Closure; Rolled turn-over.
Wad; White card, print black.
Business; Gunpowder and ammunition manufacturers.
Case; Eley Bros, Ltd.

© DN.2-2067. October 1998

Panel 2 (top right)

THE NEW EXPLOSIVES COMPANY, LIMITED.
62 London Wall, London E.C., England.
Works at: Stowmarket, Suffolk, England.
(Established 1865).

THE "PREMIER" Smokeless Cartridge LOADED WITH "NEONITE"

THE "PREMIER" Smokeless Cartridge LOADED WITH "NEONITE"

Drawn from the Dale Hedlund collection.

DATA
Gauge; 12.
Length; 64 mm.
Head; 16 mm.
Tube; Wound brownish-buff paper.
Print; Black.
Intl' liner; Nil.
Base; Reinforced brass.
Closure; Rolled.
Wad shown; White card, print red.
Business; Explosives and cartridge manufacturers.
Circa; Post 1906.

© DN.2-2144. 10th Apr 1999

Panel 3 (middle left)

THE NEW EXPLOSIVES COMPANY, LIMITED:
62 London Wall, London E.C. Works at, Stowmarket, Suffolk, England. (Established 1865).

Drawing made from photographs of what may have been a reloaded round.

THE "PREMIER" Smokeless Cartridge LOADED WITH "NEONITE"

Pale brown

DATA
Gauge; 12.
Length; 64 mm.
Head; 16 mm.
Tube; Wound brownish buff paper.
Print; Black.
Base; Reinforced brass.
Closure; Rolled turn-over.
Wad; White card, no printing.
Business; Explosives and cartridge manufacturers.
Case; Eley Bros, Ltd.

© DN.3-2327. Revised; 14/12/08.

Panel 4 (middle right)

THE NEW EXPLOSIVES CO., LTD:
Stowmarket, Suffolk. Also at,
62 London Wall, London E.C., England.

THE New Explosives Co.,Ld.

DATA
Gauge; 12.
Length; 64 mm.
Head; 9 mm.
Tube; Wound paper.
Colour; Pink.
Print; Black.
Base; Brass.
Closure; Rolled turn-over.
Wad; White card, print pink.
Business; Powder and ammunition manufacturers.
Case; Eley Bros, Ltd. London.

© DN.2-2497. 19th Jan 2002

Panel 5 (bottom left)

NEW EXPLOSIVES CO, LTD:
62 London Wall, London EC.2. Works and mills at Stowmarket, Suffolk, England.

THE New Explosives Co.,Ld.

PRIMROSE POWDER

Drawn from a set of photographs.
Drawn on 6/11/07.

DATA
Gauge; 12.
Length; 64 mm.
Head; 8 mm.
Tube; Wound pink paper.
Colour; Pale pink.
Print; Black.
Base; Brass.
Cap; Copper.
Closure; Rolled turn-over.
Wad; White card, print red.
Business; Ammo and gunpowder manufacturers.
Case; Eley Bros, Ltd. London.

© DN.3-2604.

Panel 6 (bottom right)

NEW EXPLOSIVES COMPANY LIMITED:
Stowmarket, Suffolk. Also at,
62 London Wall, London E.C., England.

THE "Red Rival" SMOKELESS CARTRIDGE

THE "Red Rival" SMOKELESS CARTRIDGE

DATA
Gauge; 12.
Length; 64 mm.
Head 16 mm.
Tube; Wound brown paper.
Colour; Nut brown.
Print; Black.
Base; Reinforced brass.
Closure; Rolled turn-over.
Wad; White card, print black.
Business; Gunpowder and ammunition manufacturers.
Case; Eley Bros, Ltd.

© DN.2-1034. October 1998

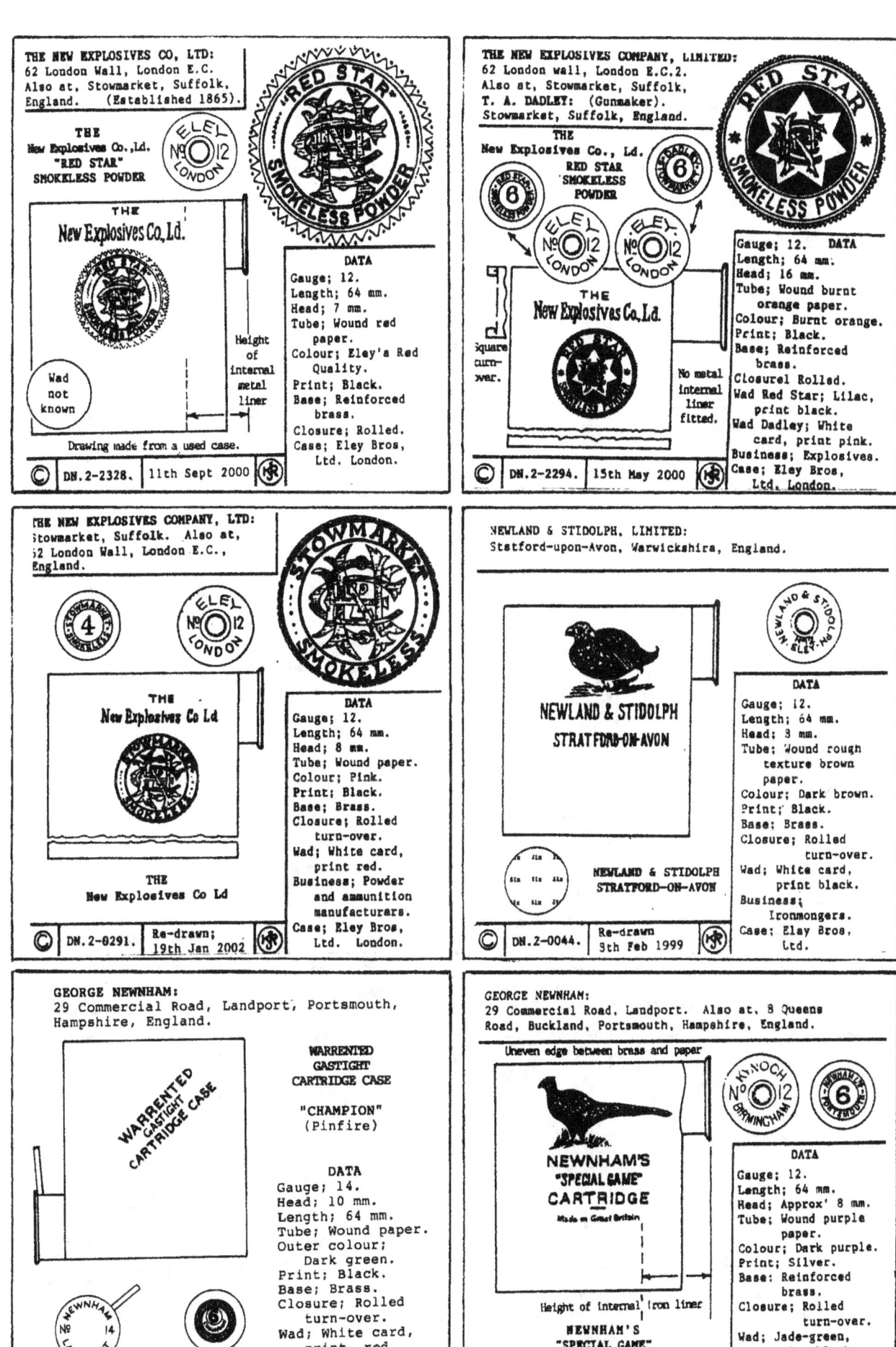

PLATE 271 [NEW – NEW]

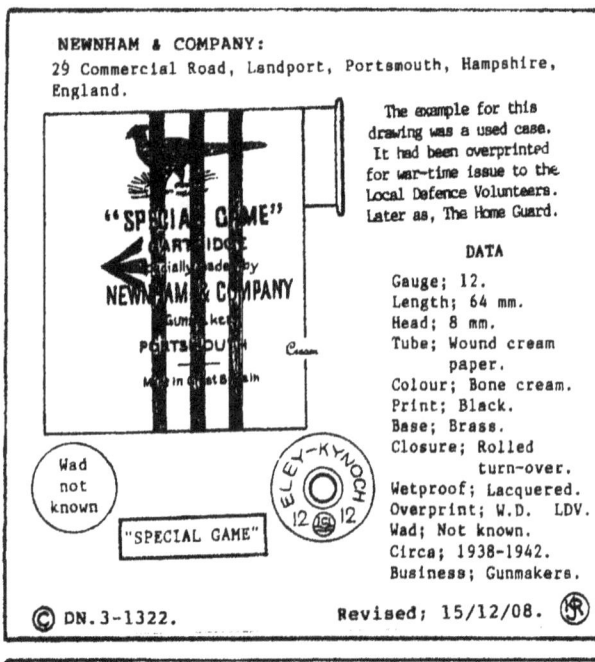
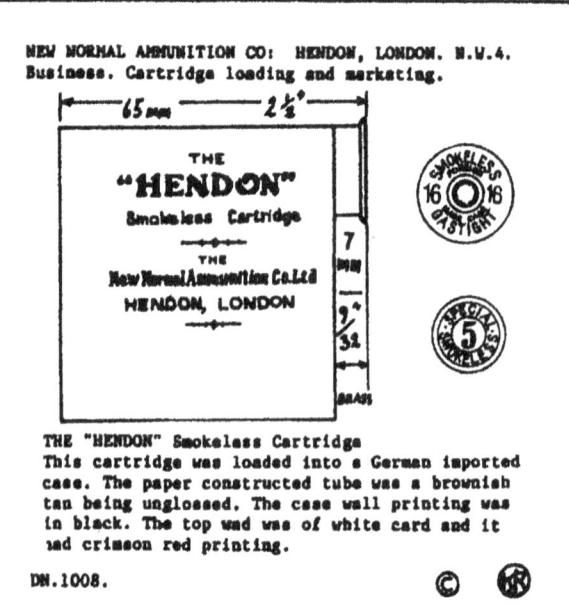
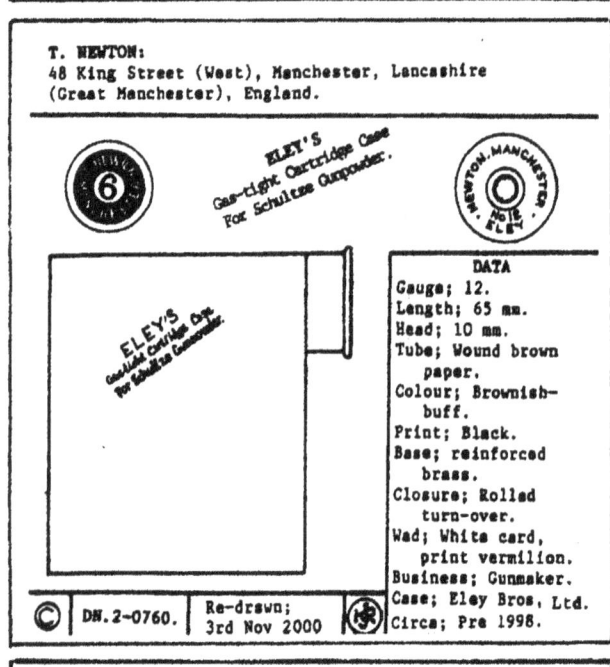
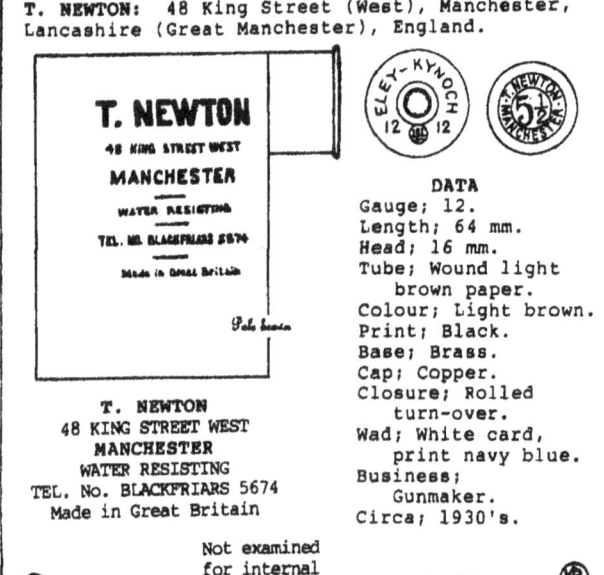
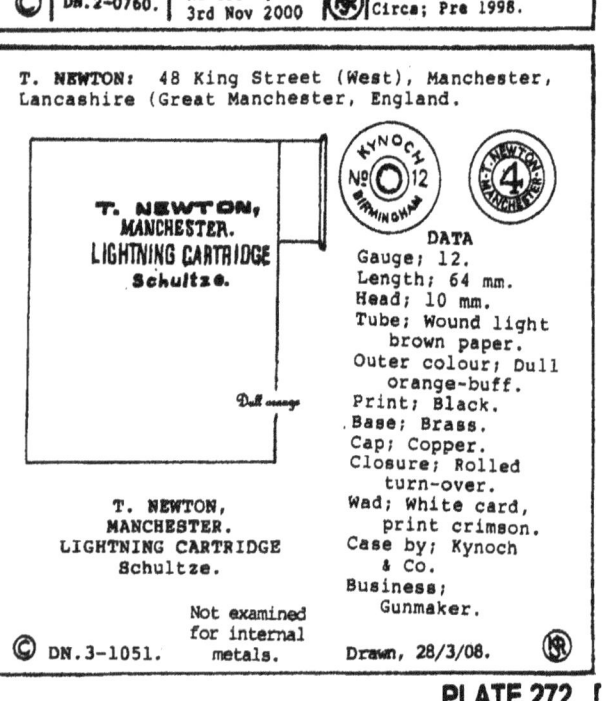
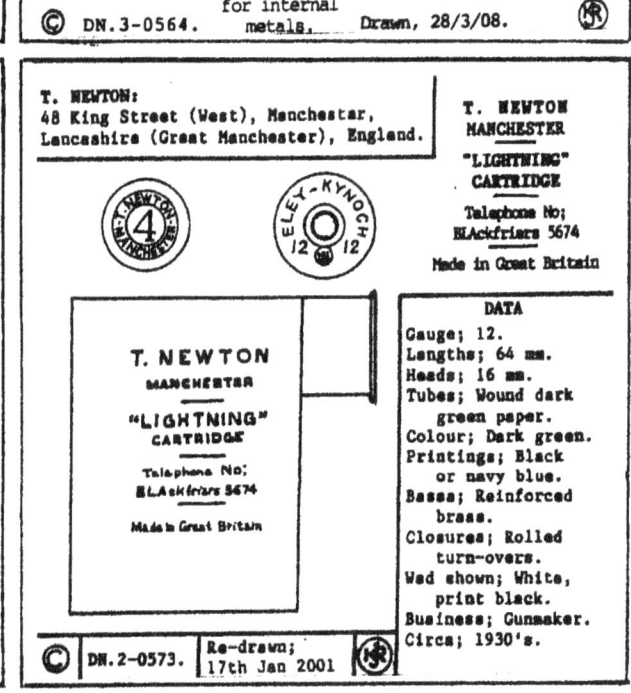

NEW ZEALAND CARTRIDGE COLLECTORS CLUB:
Upper Hutt, North Island (South), New Zealand.

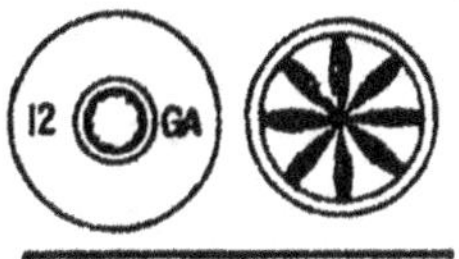

NEW ZEALAND C.C.C. • 25 • YEARS 1961 - 1986 ACE - 32 - 7

These shotshell cases were imported into N-Z from Winchester Division, Olin, Australia Ltd. where they were produced at East Geelong, Victoria. They were then loaded for the New Zealand Cartridge Collectors Club by Don Leslie.

DATA
Gauge; 12.
Length; 70 mm.
Head; 8.5 mm.
Tube; vacuum formed gold plastic.
Print; Black.
Base; Steel with brass wash.
Closure; 8 fold crimp.
Business; Collectors Club.
Circa; 1986.

© DN.2-1580. Re-drawn; 1st Dec 2000. COMMEMORATED 25 YEARS OF SERVICE TO MEMBERS

A. P. NIGHTINGALE & SON, LTD:
47 Canal, Salisbury, Wiltshire, England.

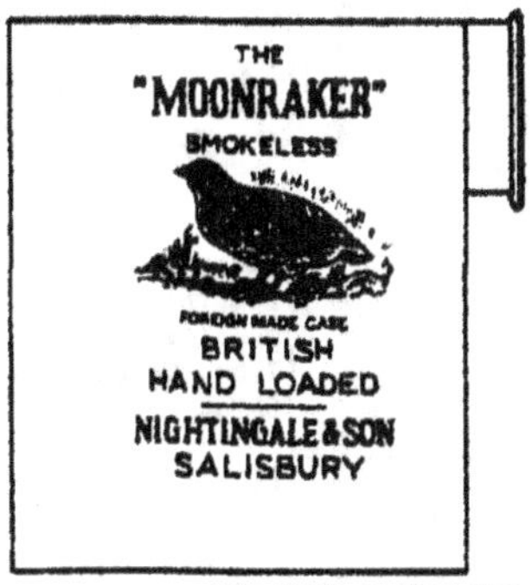

THE "MOONRAKER" SMOKELESS — FOREIGN MADE CASE — BRITISH HAND LOADED — NIGHTINGALE & SON SALISBURY

The fable is that some yokels near Devizes were caught trying to rake the reflection of the full moon from a pond. They thought it a cheese.

DATA
Gauge; 12.
Length; 64 mm.
Heads; 7.5 - 9 mm.
Tube; Wound brown paper.
Colour; Dark orange.
PANTONE® 159 C.
Print; Black.
Bases; Brass.
Closure; Rolled turn-over.
Wad; Orange.
PANTONE® 180 C.
Print black.
Business; Iron-mongers.

© DN.2-0135. Updated; April 1995.

DAVID NICKERSON (TATHWELL), LTD: The Old Vicarage, Tathwell, Louth, Lincolnshire, LN11 9ST, England.

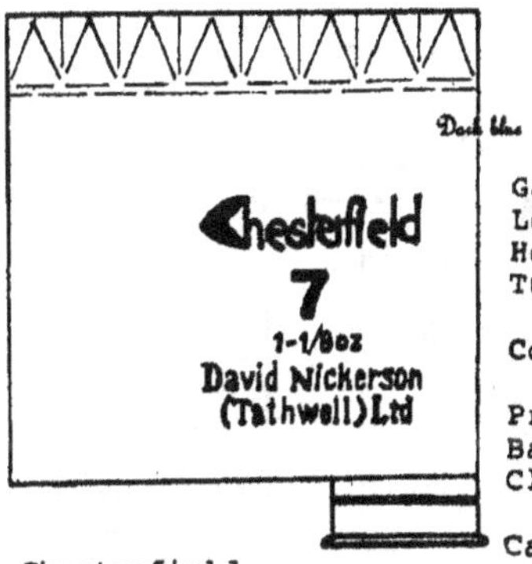

Dark blue

Chesterfield 7 1-1/8oz David Nickerson (Tathwell) Ltd

DATA
Gauge; 12.
Length; 70 mm.
Head; 9 mm.
Tube; Vac-formed plastic.
Colour; Bluebell blue.
Print; Black.
Base; Brass.
Closure; Eight fold crimp.
Case by; Winchester Australia.
Business; Gun shop.

Chesterfield 7 1-1/8oz David Nickerson (Tathwell) Ltd

© DN.3-1197. Drawn, 19/4/08.

NITRO NOBEL (Division Sport):
S-71030, Gyttorp, Sweden.

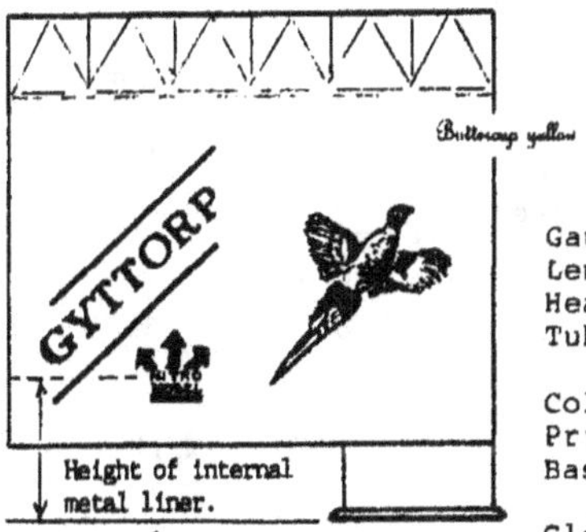

Buttercup yellow

GYTTORP — Height of internal metal liner. — GYTTORP NITRO NOBEL

DATA
Gauge; 12.
Length; 65 mm.
Head; 10 mm.
Tube; Wound brown paper.
Colour; Yellow.
Print; Black.
Base; Steel with brass coating.
Closure; Six fold ctimp.
Business; Ammunition manufacturers.
Circa; 1970's.

© DN.3-0962. Revised; 15/12/08.

NITROKOL POWDER COMPANY:
London, England.

Drawing was made from an unused case. It was not examined for internal metals.

Wad not known

THE NITROKOL POWDER CO's "REDSKIN" SMOKELESS CARTRIDGE Best British Loading — Made in France

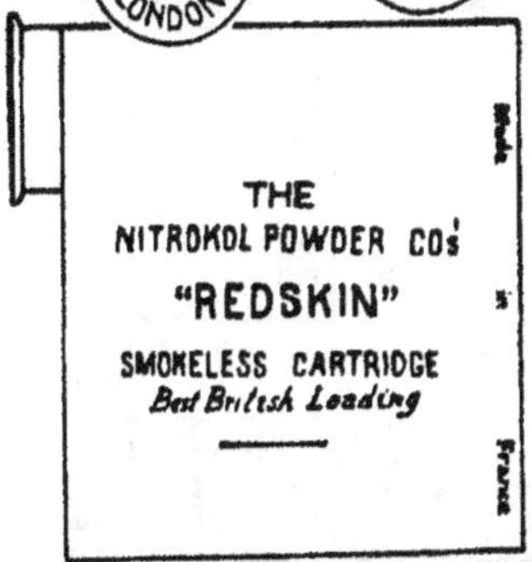

DATA
Gauge; 12.
Length; 65 mm.
Head; 6 mm.
Tube; Wound brown paper.
Colour; Salmon red.
Print; Black.
Base; Brass.
Closure; Rolled turn-over.
Wad; Not known.
Case; French.

© DN.2-0637. Re-drawn; 3rd Nov 2000.

NITROKOL POWDER COMPANY: London, England.
(The full address is not known).

Wad not known

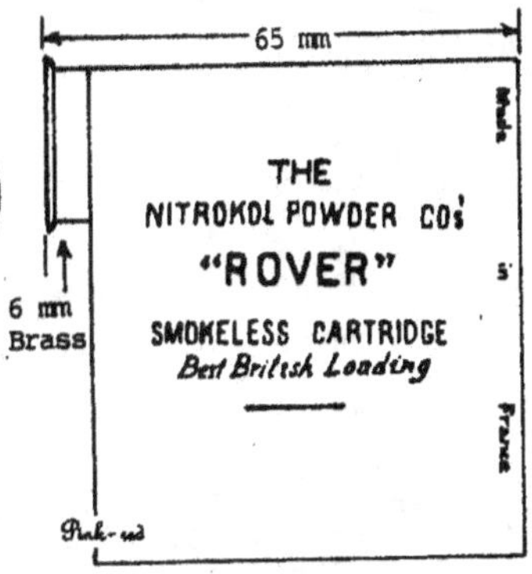

65 mm

6 mm Brass

THE NITROKOL POWDER CO's "ROVER" SMOKELESS CARTRIDGE Best British Loading

Pink-ud

THE NITROKOL POWDER CO's "ROVER" SMOKELESS CARTRIDGE Best British Loading Made in France

This case was identical to that of the "Redskin" differing only by the name change to "Rover". I have only seen un-used cases. Tubes were wound from brown paper with the outer layer in a pinkish-red. Printings were in black. A copper cap was fitted into copper insert cup. Cases were not examined for inner ferrous metals.

© DN.3-0638. Drawn, 15/7/08.

SYDNEY A. NOBBS:
2 Norman Street, Lincoln, Lincolnshire, England.

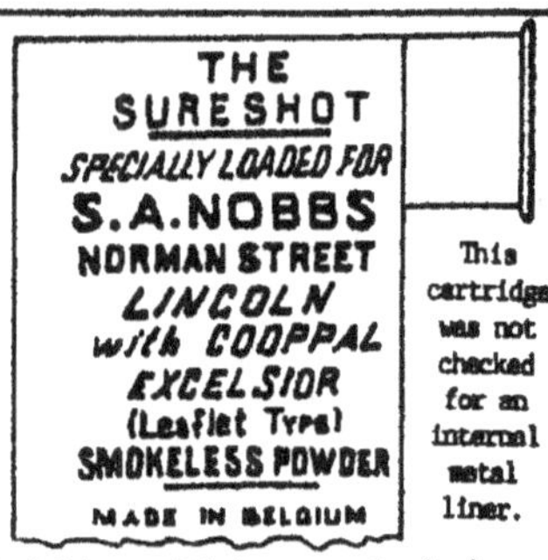

THE SURESHOT
SPECIALLY LOADED FOR
S.A. NOBBS
NORMAN STREET
LINCOLN
with *COOPPAL*
EXCELSIOR
(Leaflet Type)
SMOKELESS POWDER
MADE IN BELGIUM

This cartridge was not checked for an internal metal liner.

Loaded into a Belgium case, its loaders were probably Jas R. Watson & Company of Queen Victoria Street, London. Sydney Nobbs was first recorded in Kelly's 1913 directory as a naturalist. His business in fishing tackle came after The Great War. After World War Two, this shop then sold sports goods and toys.

DATA
Gauge; 12.
Length; 64 mm.
Head; 16 mm.
Tube; Wound paper.
Colour; Brownish red.
Print; Black.
Base; Brass.
Closure; Rolled turn-over.
Wad; Dark red, print black.
Business; Fishing tackle dealer and taxidermist.

© DN.2-1028. Re-drawn; 11th Feb 2000. THE SURESHOT

NOBEL EXPLOSIVES CO, LTD:
195 West George Street, Glasgow, Lanarkshire (Strathclyde), Scotland. Also at, College Hall Chambers, Cannon Street, London E.C.4., England.

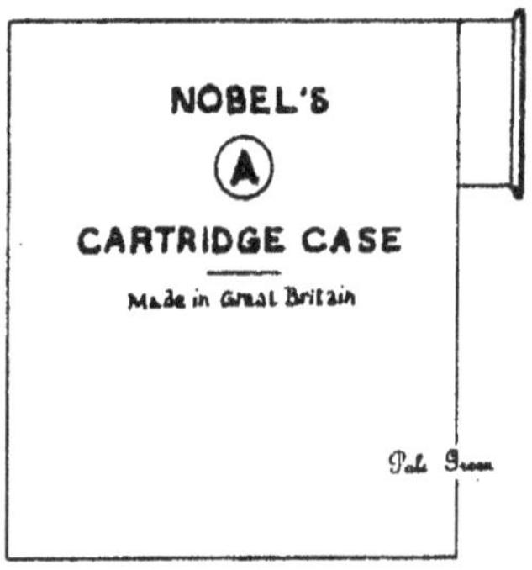

NOBEL'S
Ⓐ
CARTRIDGE CASE
Made in Great Britain

Pale Green

NOBEL'S A CARTRIDGE CASE
Made in Great Britain

DATA
Gauge; 12.
Length; 64 mm.
Head; 8 mm.
Tube; Wound paper.
Colour; Pale green.
Print; Black.
Base; Brass.
Cap; Copper.
Closure; Rolled turn-over.
Wad; White card, print black.
Business; Explosives and ammunition manufacturers.

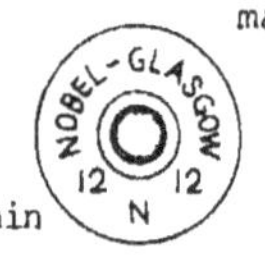

Not examined for internal metals.

© DN.3-0696. Drawn, 14/7/08.

NOBEL EXPLOSIVES CO, LTD:
195 West George Street, Glasgow, Scotland. Also at, College Hill Chambers, Cannon Street, London E.C.4., England.

DATA
Gauge; 12.
Length; 64 mm.
Head; 8 mm
Tube; Wound paper.
Colour, Light green.
Print; Black.
Base; Brass.
Cap; Copper.
Closure; Rolled turn-over.
Wad; White card, print black.
Business; Explosives and ammunition manufacturers.

NOBEL'S
"AJAX"
SMOKELESS CARTRIDGE.
Made in Great Britain

Light Green

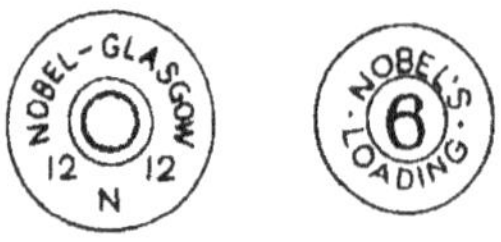

NOBEL'S "AJAX"

© DN.3-0688. Revised, 1/2/09.

NOBEL EXPLOSIVES COMPANY, LIMITED:
195 West George Street, Glasgow, Scotland. Also at, College Hall Chambers, Cannon Street, London. E.C., England.

The example drawn was brought back from Australia.

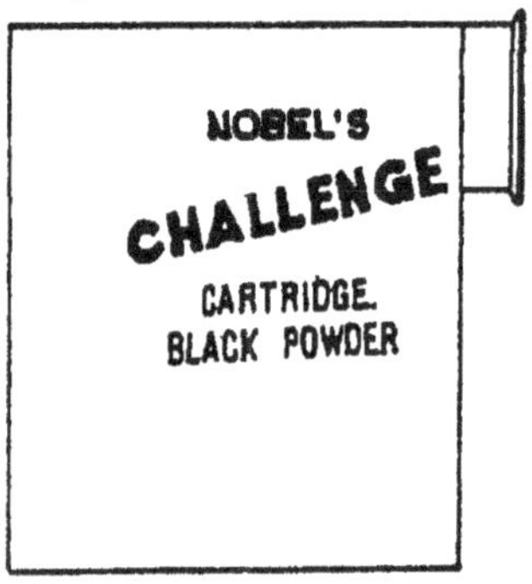

NOBEL'S
CHALLENGE
CARTRIDGE.
BLACK POWDER

Wad not known

NOBEL'S CHALLENGE CARTRIDGE. BLACK POWDER

DATA
Gauge; 12.
Length; 65 mm.
Head; 8 mm.
Tube; Wound maroon paper.
Colour; Maroon.
Print; Yellow.
Base; Reinforced brass.
Closure; Rolled turn-over.
Wad; Not known.
Business; Explosives and cartridge manufacturers.

© DN.2-2230. 18th Aug 1999

NOBEL EXPLOSIVES CO, LTD:
149 & 195 West George Street, Glasgow, Lanarkshire (Strathclyde), Scotland. Also at, College Hall Chambers, Cannon Street. And also at, 1 Arundal Street, The Strand, London W.C.1., England.

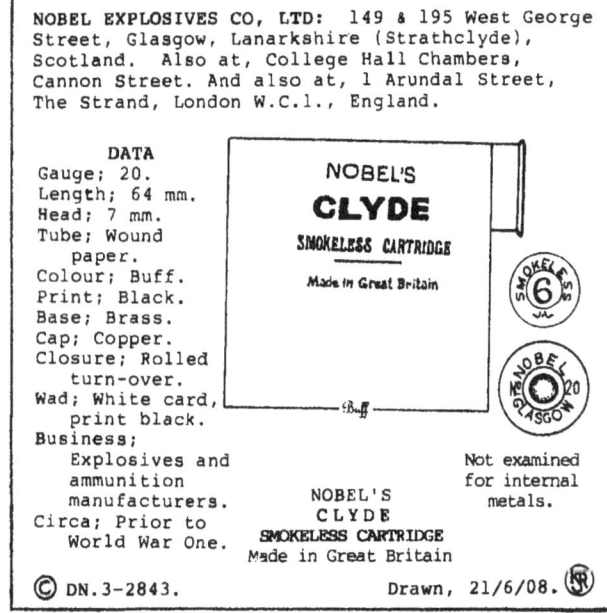

DATA
Gauge; 20.
Length; 64 mm.
Head; 7 mm.
Tube; Wound paper.
Colour; Buff.
Print; Black.
Base; Brass.
Cap; Copper.
Closure; Rolled turn-over.
Wad; White card, print black.
Business; Explosives and ammunition manufacturers.
Circa; Prior to World War One.

NOBEL'S CLYDE SMOKELESS CARTRIDGE Made in Great Britain

Not examined for internal metals.

© DN.3-2843. Drawn, 21/6/08.

NOBEL EXPLOSIVES COMPANY:
Offices; 195 West George Street, Glasgow, Lanarkshire (South Clyde), Scotland. Also at, College Hill Chambers, Cannon Street, London. E.C., England.

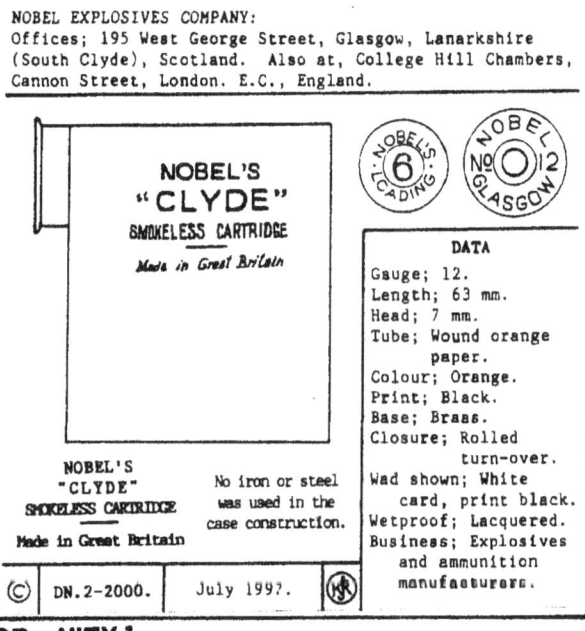

NOBEL'S "CLYDE" SMOKELESS CARTRIDGE Made in Great Britain

No iron or steel was used in the case construction.

DATA
Gauge; 12.
Length; 63 mm.
Head; 7 mm.
Tube; Wound orange paper.
Colour; Orange.
Print; Black.
Base; Brass.
Closure; Rolled turn-over.
Wad shown; White card, print black.
Wetproof; Lacquered.
Business; Explosives and ammunition manufacturers.

© DN.2-2000. July 199?.

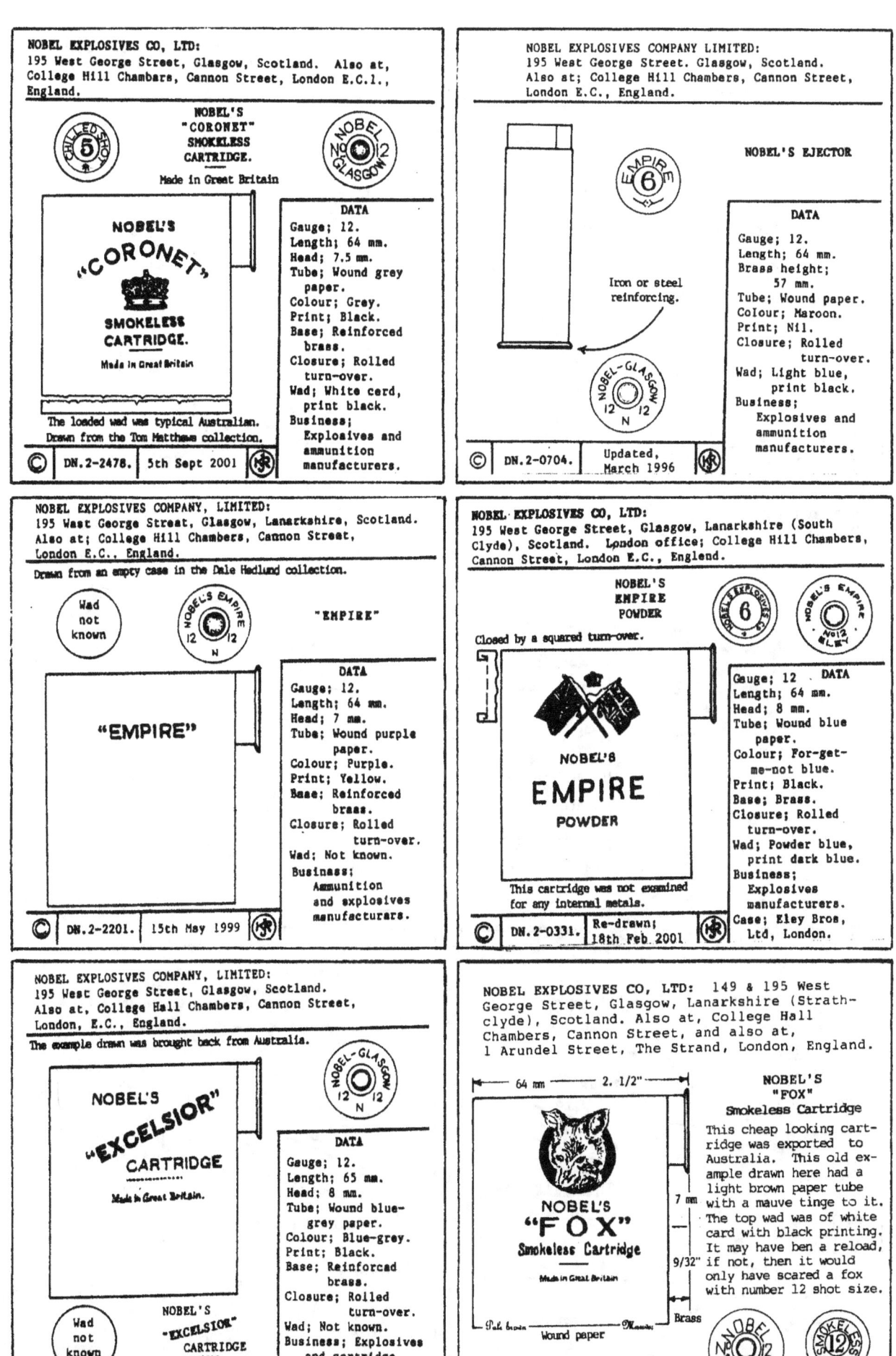

PLATE 275 [N'EX – N'EX]

NOBEL EXPLOSIVES COMPANY, LIMITED:
195 West George Street, Glasgow, Lanarkshire, Scotland.
Also at, College Hill Chambers, Cannon Street,
London E.C. 4., England.

TRADE MARK
N
NOBEL'S
CARTRIDGE
CASE

Made in Great Britain

DATA
Gauge; 12.
Length; 64 mm.
Head; 25 mm.
Tube; Wound paper.
Colour; Maroon.
Print; Silver.
Base; Reinforced brass.
Closure; Rolled turn-over.
Wad; Light blue, print dark blue.
Business; Explosives manufacturers.

This cartridge was not internally examined.

© DN.2-0690. Re-drawn; 16th Dec 2000

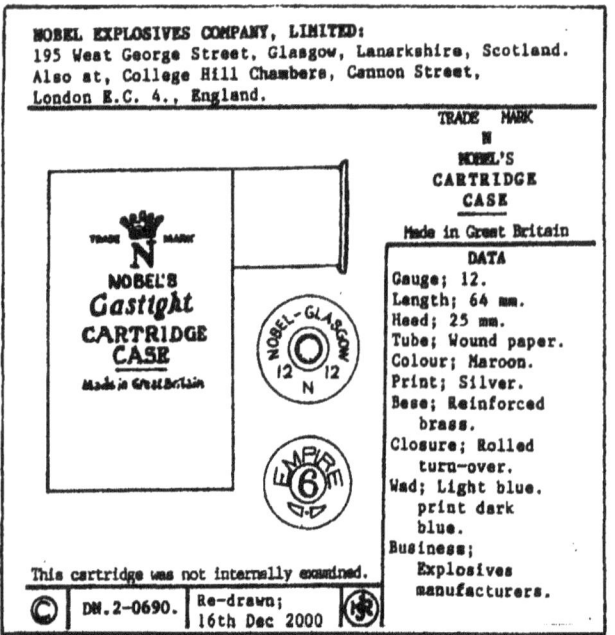

NOBEL EXPLOSIVES CO, LTD: 195 West George
Street, Glasgow, Lanarkshire (Strathclyde),
Scotland. Also at, College Hall Chambers,
Cannon Street, London E.C.4., England.

DATA
Gauge; 12.
Length; 64 mm.
Head; 8 mm.
Tube; Wound paper.
Colour; Poppy red.
Print; Black.
Base; Brass.
Cap; Copper.
Closure; Rolled turn-over.
Wad; White card, print black.
Business; Explosives and ammunition manufacturers.

Not examined for internal metals.

© DN.3-0689. Drawn, 14/7/08.

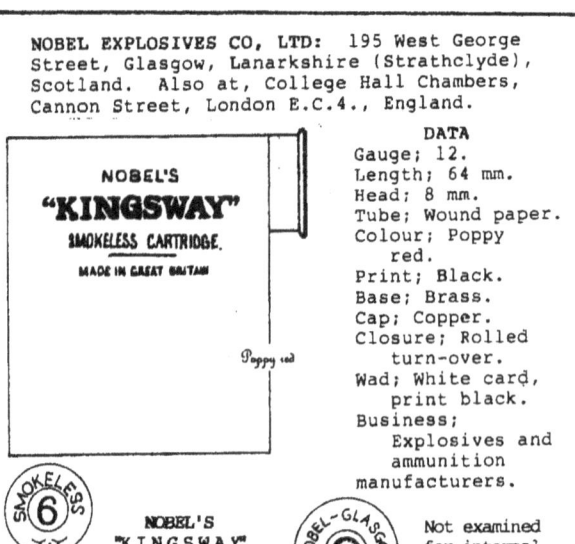

NOBEL EXPLOSIVES CO, LTD:
195 West George Street, Glasgow, Scotland.
Also at; College Hill Chambers, Cannon Street, London E.C.
England.

THE NATIONAL

DATA
Gauge; 16.
Length; 64 mm.
Head; 9 mm.
Tube; Wound paper.
Colour; Pale blue.
PANTONE® 317 U.
Print; Black.
Base; Brass.
Closure; Rolled turn-over.
Wad; Purple, print silver.
PANTONE® 2735 C.
Business; Cartridge manufacturers.

This cartridge case was manufactured by Frederick Joyce & Company of 57 Upper Thames Street, London, and 7 Suffolk Lane, London E.C. England. Nobels bought out Joyce in 1907 and would then have used up this case prior to making their own.

© DN.2-1837. August 1995

NOBEL EXPLOSIVES COMPANY, LIMITED:
195 West George Street, Glasgow, Scotland.
Also at, College Hall Chambers, Cannon Street,
London, E.C., England.

The example drawn was brought back to England from Australia.

NOBEL'S
"New Era"
BLACK POWDER.
Made in Great Britain.

DATA
Gauge; 16.
Length; 64 mm.
Head; 8 mm.
Tube; Wound brown paper.
Colour; Rough texture brown.
Print; Maroon.
Base; Reinforced brass.
Closure; Rolled turn-over.
Wad; White card, print black.
Business; Explosives and cartridge manufacturers.

NOBEL'S
"New Era"
BLACK POWDER
Made in Great Britain

© DN.2-2233. 19th Aug 1999

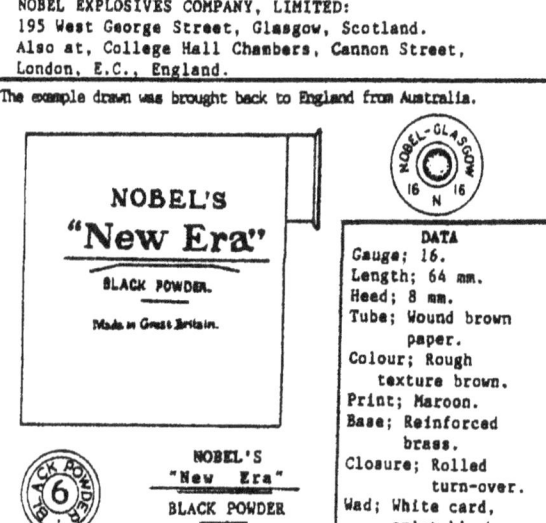

NOBEL EXPLOSIVES CO, LTD: 195 West George
Street, Glasgow, Lanarkshire (Strathclyde),
Scotland. Also at, College Hall Chambers,
Cannon Street, London E.C.4., England.

DATA
Gauge; 12.
Length; 64 mm.
Head; 8 mm.
Tube; Wound paper.
Colour; Maroon, print yellow.
Base; Brass.
Cap; Copper.
Closure; Rolled turn-over.
Wad; Yellow, print black.
Business; Explosives and ammunition manufacturers.

NOBEL'S
"Nile"
Cartridge
Loaded with
SPORTING BALLISTITE
Made in Great Britain

Not examined for internal metals.

© DN.3-0694. Drawn, 14/7/08.

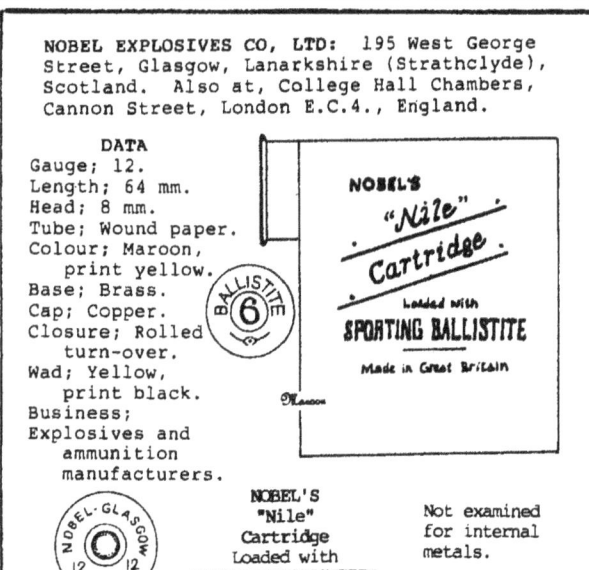

NOBEL EXPLOSIVES COMPANY, LIMITED:
195 West George Street, Glasgow, Scotland.
Also at; College Hill Chambers, Cannon Street,
London E.C., England.

"Nile"
Cartridge
Loaded with
SPORTING BALLISTITE
Made in Great Britain

DATA
Gauge; 12.
Length; 64 mm.
Head; 7.5 mm.
Tube; Wound maroon paper.
Colour; Maroon.
Print; Yellow.
Base; Reinforced brass.
Closure; Rolled turn-over.
Wad; Not known.
Business; Explosives and cartridge manufacturers.

Wad not known

Drawn from the Bob Cameron collection.

© DN.2-2140. 8th April 1999

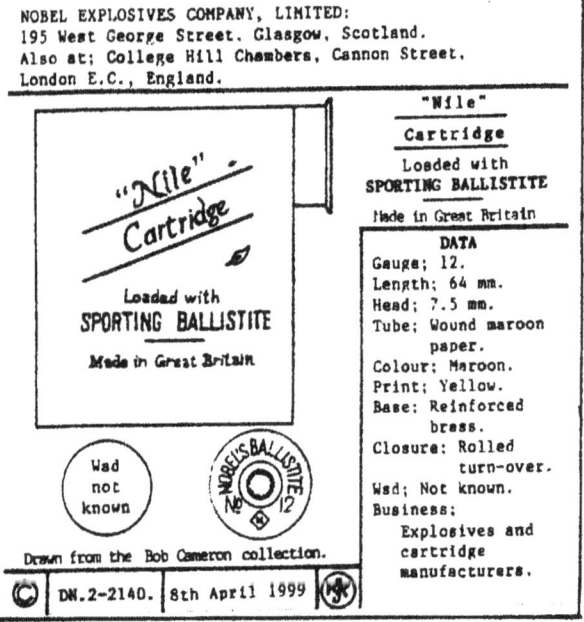

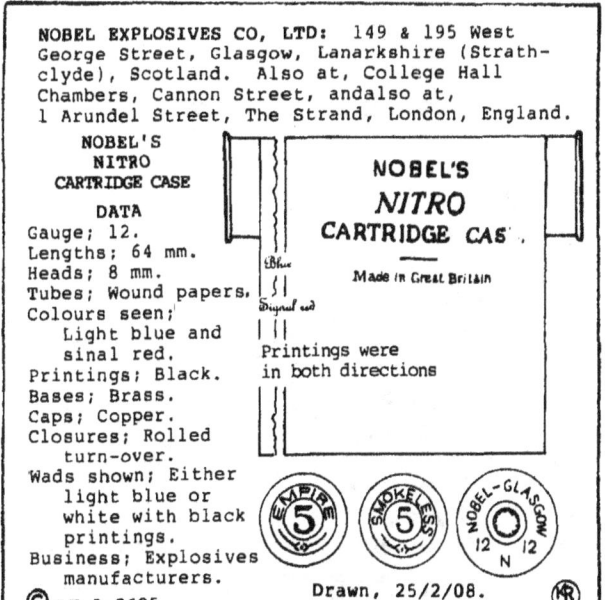
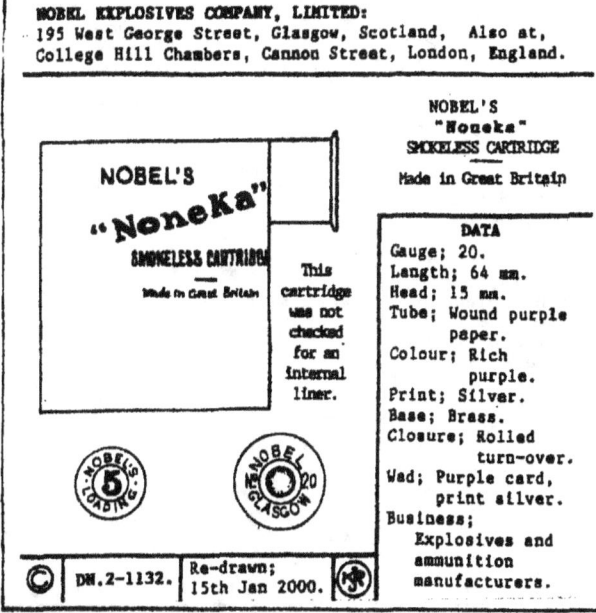
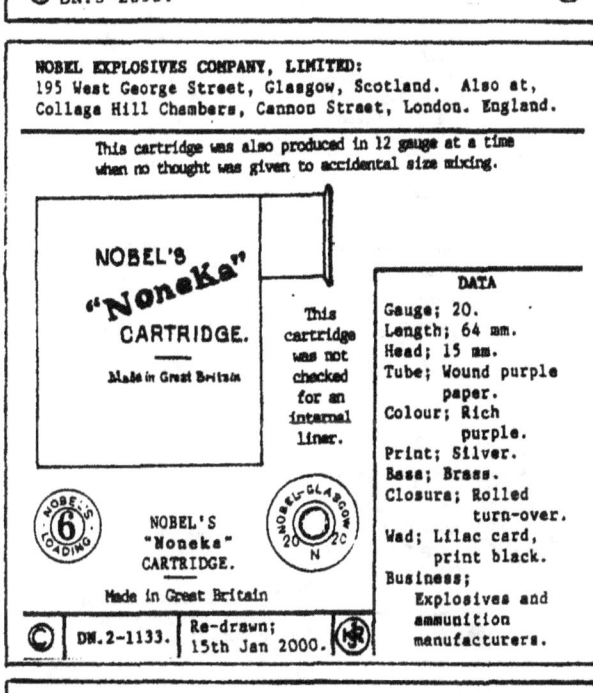
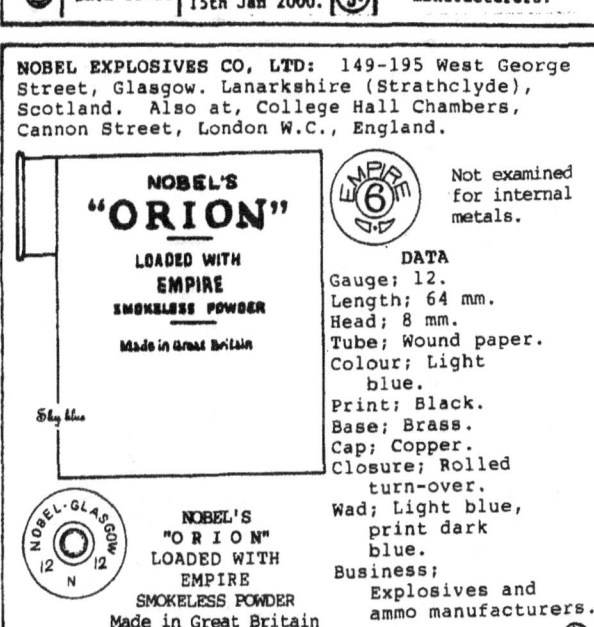
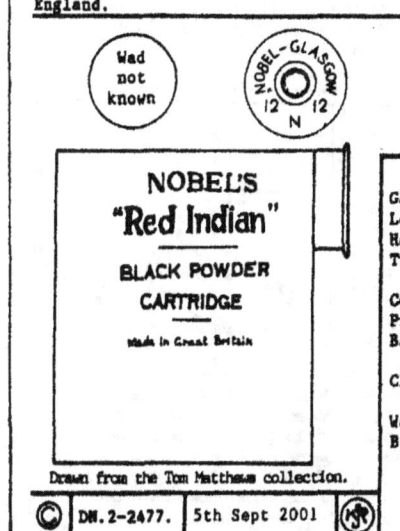

PLATE 277 [N'EX – N'EX]

NOBEL EXPLOSIVES CO, LTD: 149-195 West George Street, Glasgow, Lanarkshire (Strathclyde), Scotland. Also at, College Hall Chambers, Cannon Street, London W.C.1., England.

DATA
Gauge; 12.
Length; 65 mm.
Head; 8 mm.
Tube; Wound paper.
Colour; Burnt orange.
Print; Black.
Base; Brass.
Cap; Copper.
Closure; Rolled turn-over.
Wad; Red, print black.
Business; Explosives and ammunition manufacturers.

TRADE N MARK
NOBEL'S "REGENT" SMOKELESS CARTRIDGE
Made in Great Britain

Not examined for internal metals.

© DN.3-0697.   Drawn, 22/6/08.

NOBEL EXPLOSIVES COMPANY, LTD: 195 West George Street, Glasgow, Scotland. Offices at; College Hill Chambers, Cannon Street, London E.C., England.

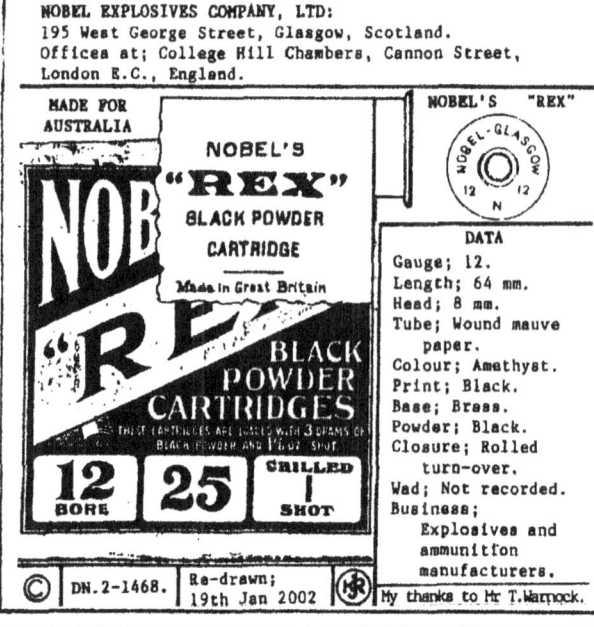

DATA
Gauge; 12.
Length; 64 mm.
Head; 8 mm.
Tube; Wound mauve paper.
Colour; Amethyst.
Print; Black.
Base; Brass.
Powder; Black.
Closure; Rolled turn-over.
Wad; Not recorded.
Business; Explosives and ammunition manufacturers.

© DN.2-1468. Re-drawn; 19th Jan 2002
My thanks to Mr T.Warnock.

NOBEL EXPLOSIVES COMPANY, LIMITED: 195 West George Street, Glasgow, Scotland. Also at; College Hill Chambers, Cannon Street, London. E.C., England.

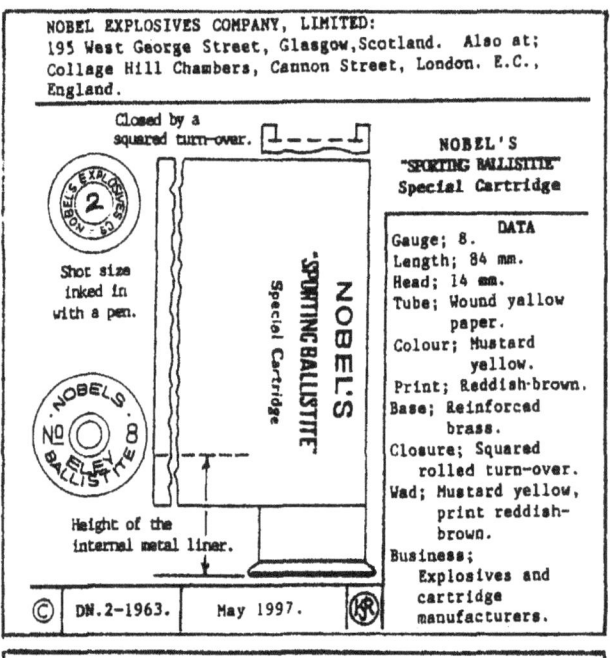

DATA
Gauge; 8.
Length; 84 mm.
Head; 14 mm.
Tube; Wound yellow paper.
Colour; Mustard yellow.
Print; Reddish-brown.
Base; Reinforced brass.
Closure; Squared rolled turn-over.
Wad; Mustard yellow, print reddish-brown.
Business; Explosives and cartridge manufacturers.

© DN.2-1963.   May 1997.

NOBEL EXPLOSIVES CO, LTD: 195 West George Street, Glasgow, Scotland. Also at; College Hill Chambers, Cannon Street, London, E.C., England.

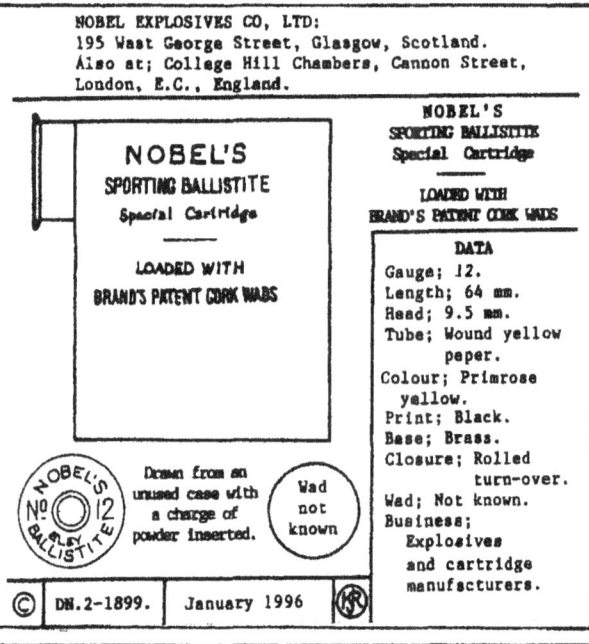

DATA
Gauge; 12.
Length; 64 mm.
Head; 9.5 mm.
Tube; Wound yellow paper.
Colour; Primrose yellow.
Print; Black.
Base; Brass.
Closure; Rolled turn-over.
Wad; Not known.
Business; Explosives and cartridge manufacturers.

© DN.2-1899.   January 1996

NOBEL EXPLOSIVES CO, LTD: 195 West George Street, Glasgow, Scotland. Also at, College Hill Chambers, Cannon Street, London E.C.4., England.

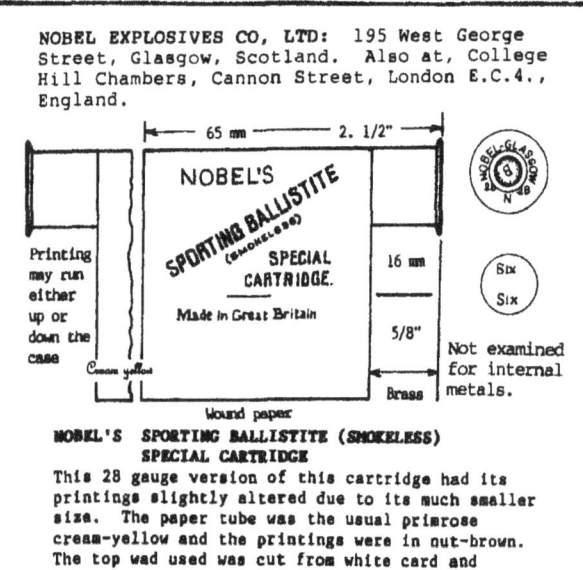

NOBEL'S SPORTING BALLISTITE (SMOKELESS) SPECIAL CARTRIDGE

This 28 gauge version of this cartridge had its printings slightly altered due to its much smaller size. The paper tube was the usual primrose cream-yellow and the printings were in nut-brown. The top wad used was cut from white card and had the shot size printed in black.

© DN.3-1731.   Drawn, 17/4/08.

NOBEL EXPLOSIVES CO, LTD: 149 & 195 West George Street, Glasgow, Lanarkshire (Strathclyde), Scotland. Also at, College Hall Chambers, Cannon Street. Also at, 1 Arundel Street, The Strand, London W.C., England.
Business; Explosives and ammunition manufacturers.

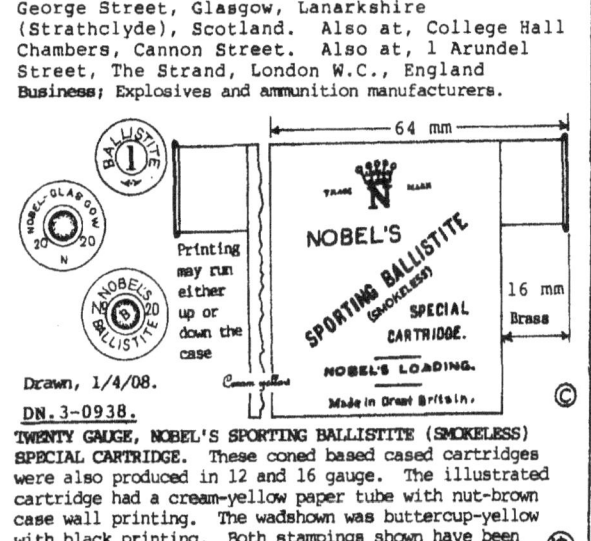

Drawn, 1/4/08.
DN.3-0938.

TWENTY GAUGE, NOBEL'S SPORTING BALLISTITE (SMOKELESS) SPECIAL CARTRIDGE. These coned based cased cartridges were also produced in 12 and 16 gauge. The illustrated cartridge had a cream-yellow paper tube with nut-brown case wall printing. The wad shown was buttercup-yellow with black printing. Both stampings shown have been seen. It was not examined for internal metals.

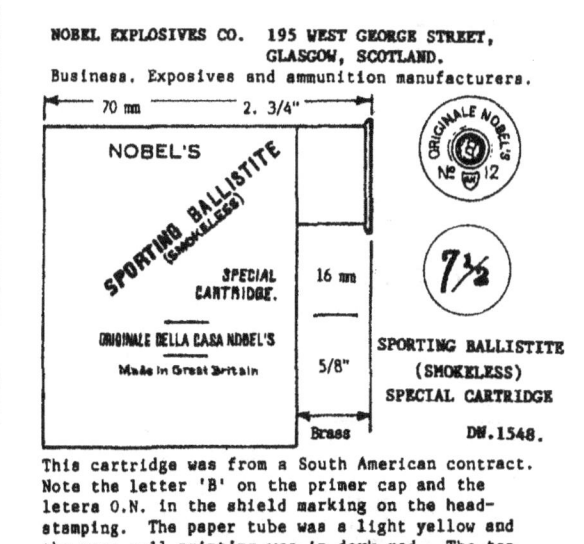
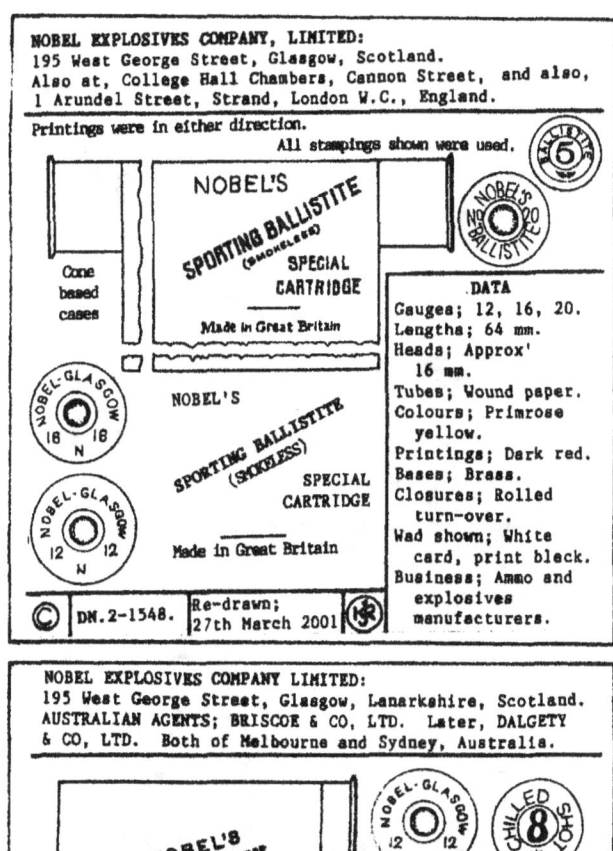
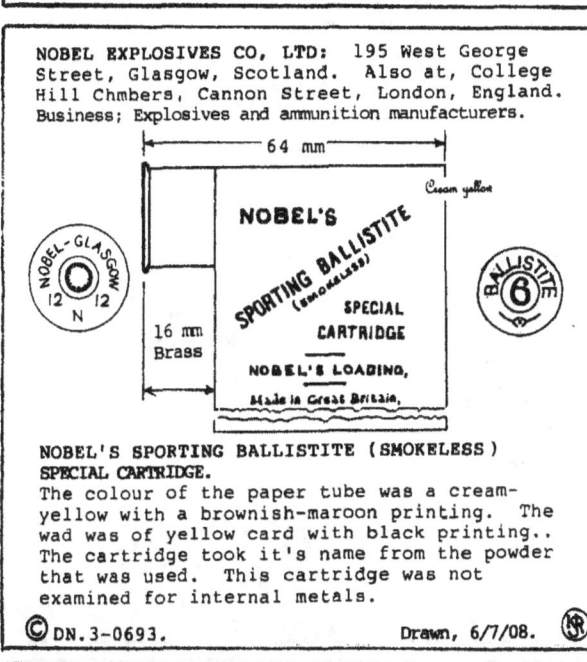
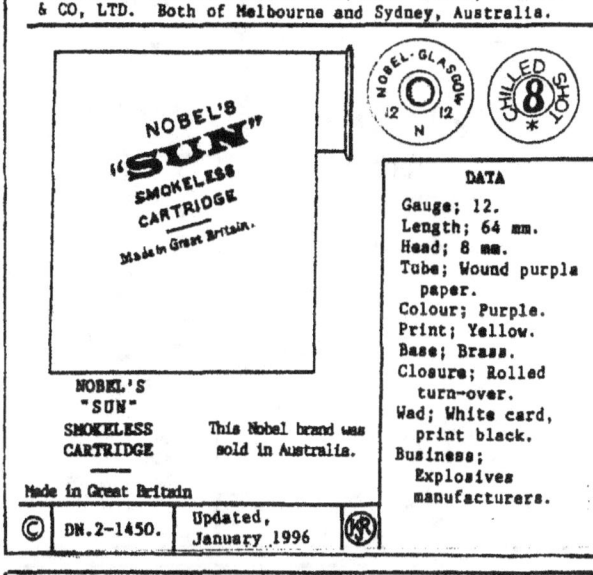

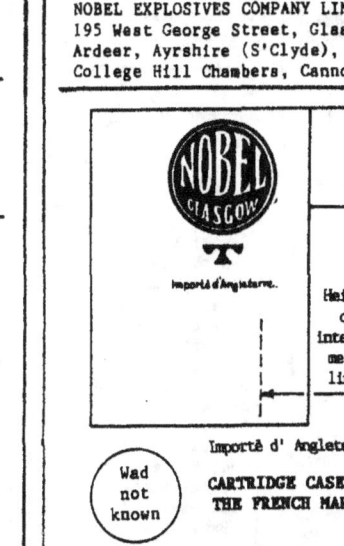
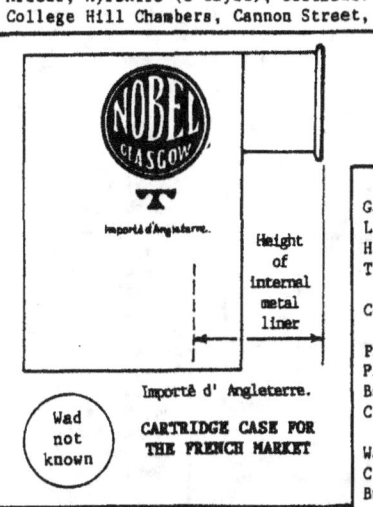
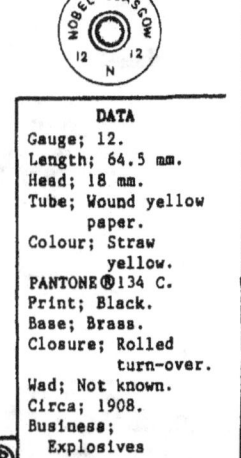
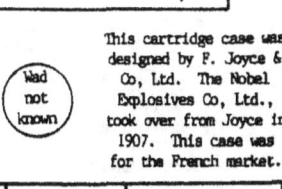
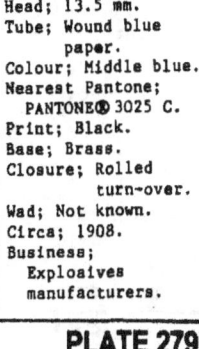

PLATE 279 [N'EX – N'EX]

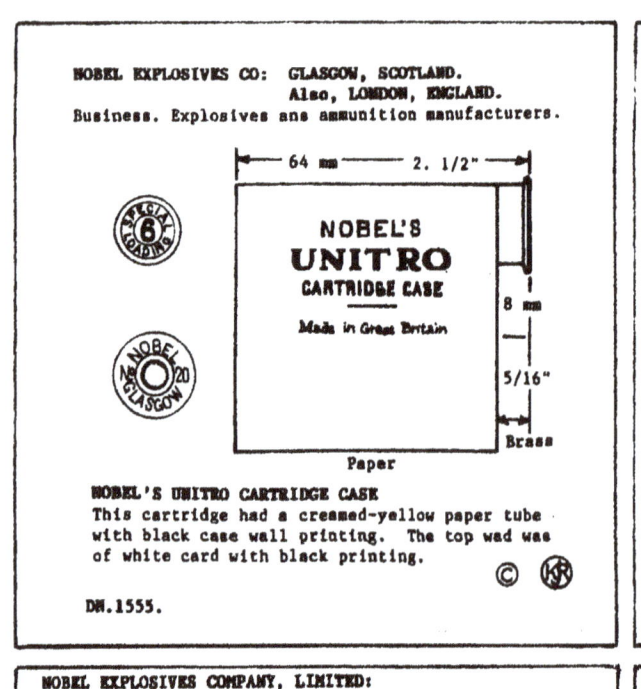
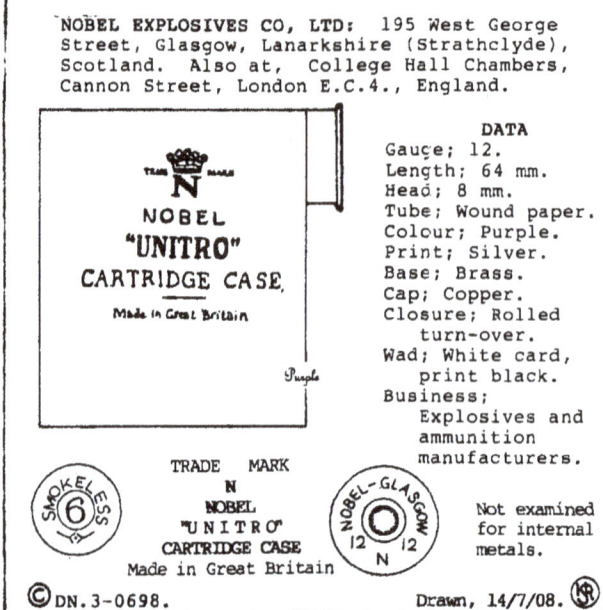
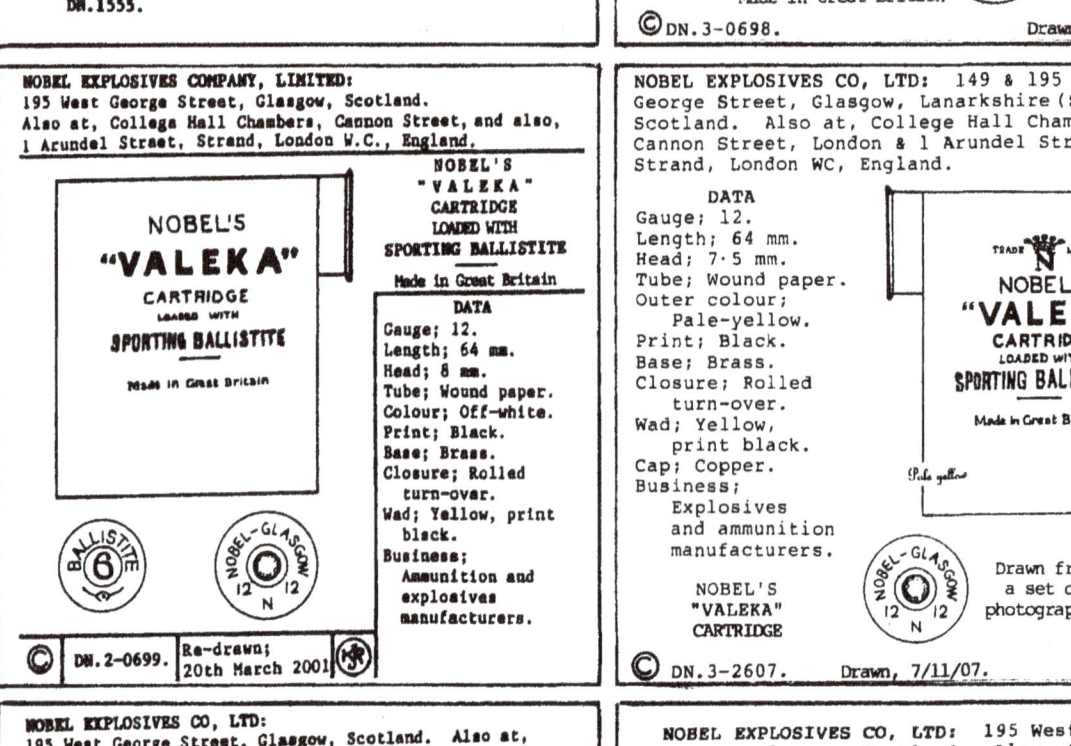
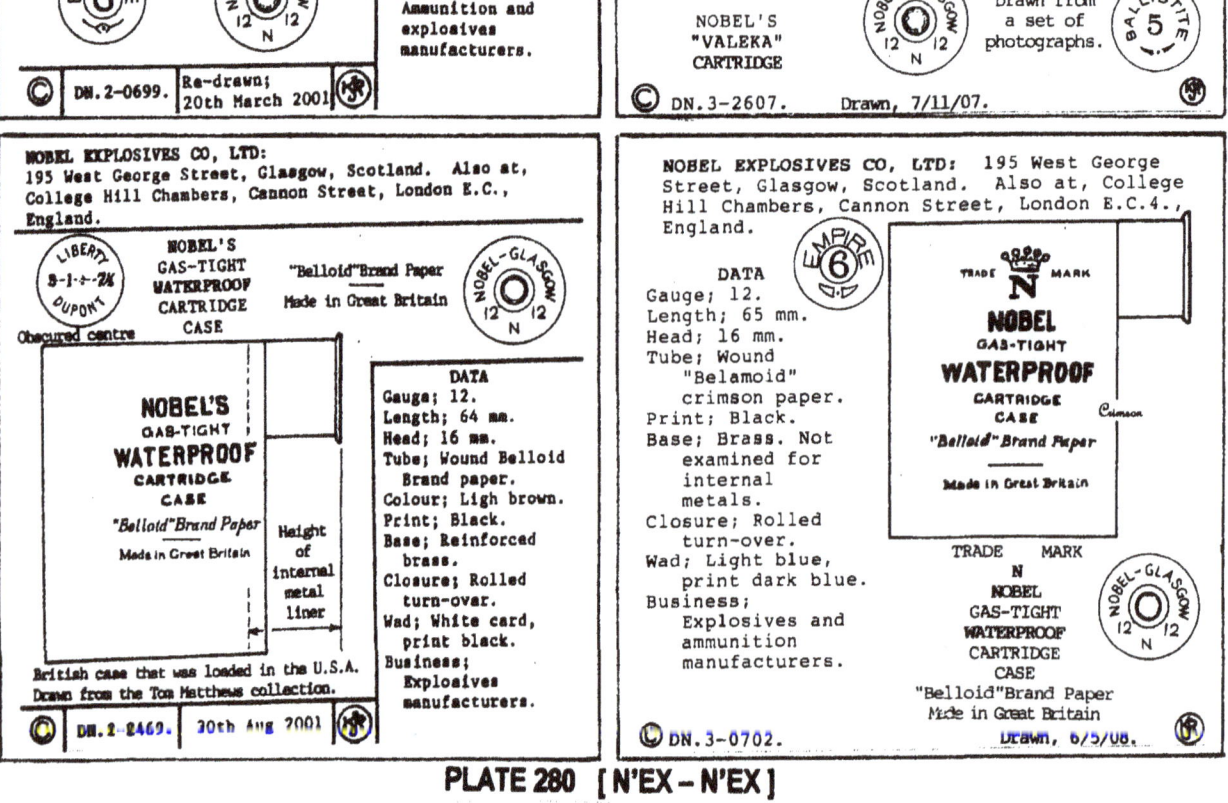

NOBEL INDUSTRIES, LIMITED:
Works at, Witton, Birmingham, Warwickshire (West Midlands). Offices at, Nobel House, London, England.

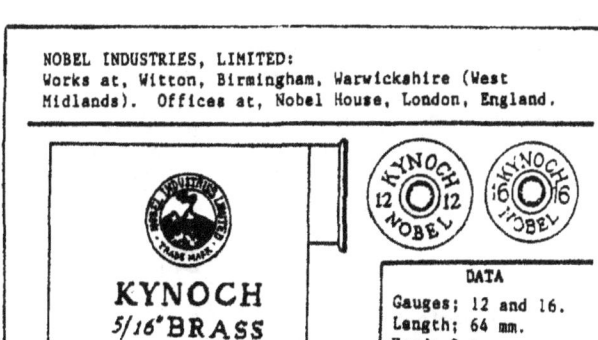

KYNOCH 5/16" BRASS

12 gauge drawn here.

KYNOCH 5/16" BRASS

DATA
Gauges; 12 and 16.
Length; 64 mm.
Head; 9 mm.
Tubes; Wound orange paper.
Printings; Black.
Base; Brass.
Wad 12g; Brown card, print black.
Wad 16g; White card, print black.
Business; Ammunition manufacturers.
Were loaded by many.

© DN.2-1079. Re-drawn December 1998

NOBEL INDUSTRIES LIMITED: Works at; Witton, Birmingham, Warwickshire (West Midlands). Head Office; Nobel House, Buckingham Gate, London S.W.1., England.

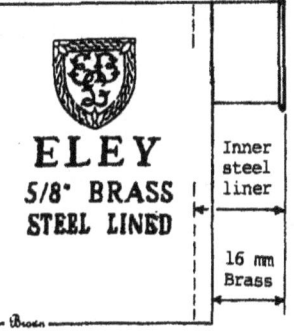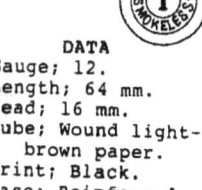

ELEY 5/8" BRASS STEEL LINED

Inner steel liner

16 mm Brass

ELEY 5/8" BRASS STEEL LINED

DATA
Gauge; 12.
Length; 64 mm.
Head; 16 mm.
Tube; Wound light-brown paper.
Print; Black.
Base; Reinforced brass.
Cap; Copper.
Closure; Rolled turn-over.
Wad shown; White card, print black.
Business; Ammunition manufacturers.
Circa; 1920's.

© DN.3-0217.   Drawn, 5/4/08.

NOBEL INDUSTRIES, LIMITED:
Witton, Birmingham, Warwickshire (West Midlands), England.

KYNOCH 5/8" BRASS

KYNOCH 5/8" BRASS

Cases were sold and loaded by many.

DATA
Gauge; 16.
Length; 64 mm.
Head; 15 mm.
Tube; Wound green paper.
Colour; Dark green.
Print; Black.
Base; Brass.
Closure; Rolled turn-over.
Wad shown; White card with lead penciled in shot size.
Business; Ammunition manufacturers.

© DN.2-1081. Re-drawn December 1998

NOBEL INDUSTRIES LIMITED: Works at, Witton, Birmingham, Warwickshire (W. Midlands), England.

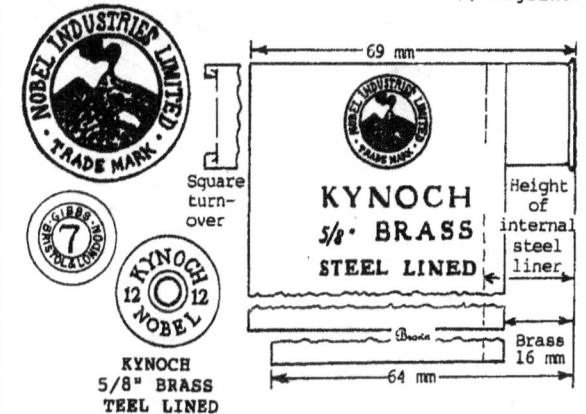

KYNOCH 5/8" BRASS STEEL LINED

This cartridge had a tube rolled from brown paper with black case wall printing. Loaded by many, the example drawn was by George Gibbs who closed it with a squared turn-over. The white card wad was printed in black.

© DN.3-2749.   Drawn, 10/3/08.

NOBEL INDUSTRIES LIMITED: Works; Witton, Birmingham, Warwickshire (West Midlands). Head Office; Nobel House, Buckingham Gate, London S.W.1., England.

ELEY CARTRIDGE CASE

DATA
Gauge; .360.
Length; 47 mm.
Head; 8 mm.
Tube; Eley's wound indian-red paper.
Print; Black.
Base; Brass.
Closure; Rolled turn-over.
Wad; White card, print black.
Business; Ammo manufacturers.

© DN.3-2712.   Drawn, 28/2/08.

NOBEL INDUSTRIES LIMITED: Works; Witton, Birmingham. Head Office; Nobel House, Buckingham Gate, London S.W.1, England.

DATA
Gauge; 12
Case; Unlined.
Base; Brass.
Cap; Copper.
Business; Ammo manufacturers.
Circa; 1923-24.
For other details, see below.

Eley Acme
E.C. POWDER
Made in Great Britain

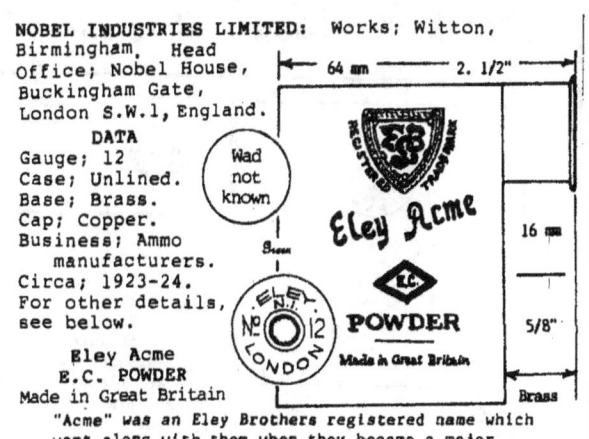

"Acme" was an Eley Brothers registered name which went along with them when they became a major part of Nobel Industries Limited. The example from which this drawing was made was a used, or so called fired case. The tube was wound from dark green paper and the case wall printing was in black. "Acme" were produced in both 12 and 16 gauge sizes. They were loaded into dark green cases and used E.C. Powder.

© DN.3-2713.   Drawn, 28/2/08.

PLATE 281 [N'IN – N'IN]

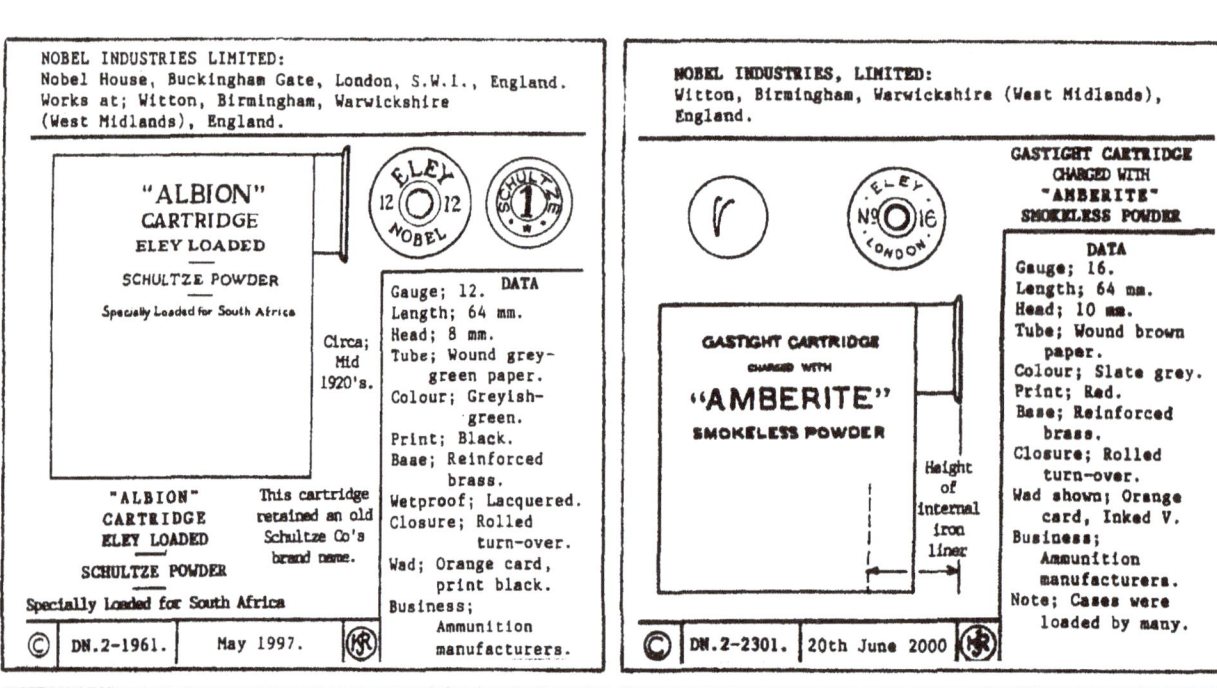
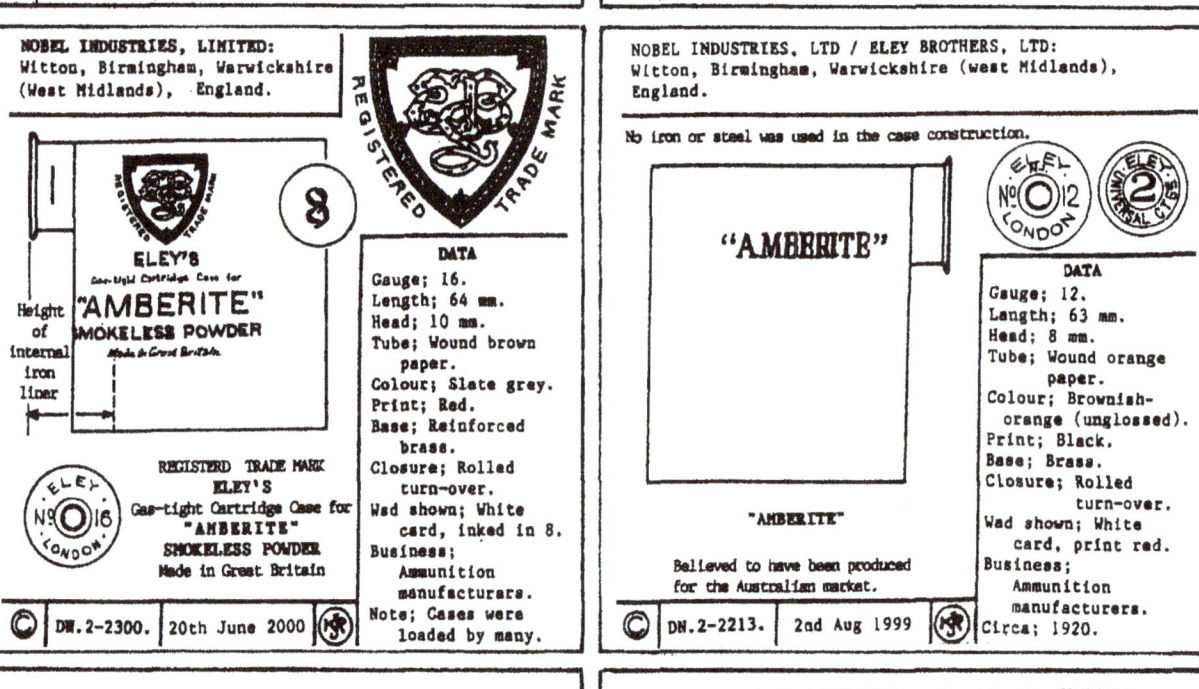
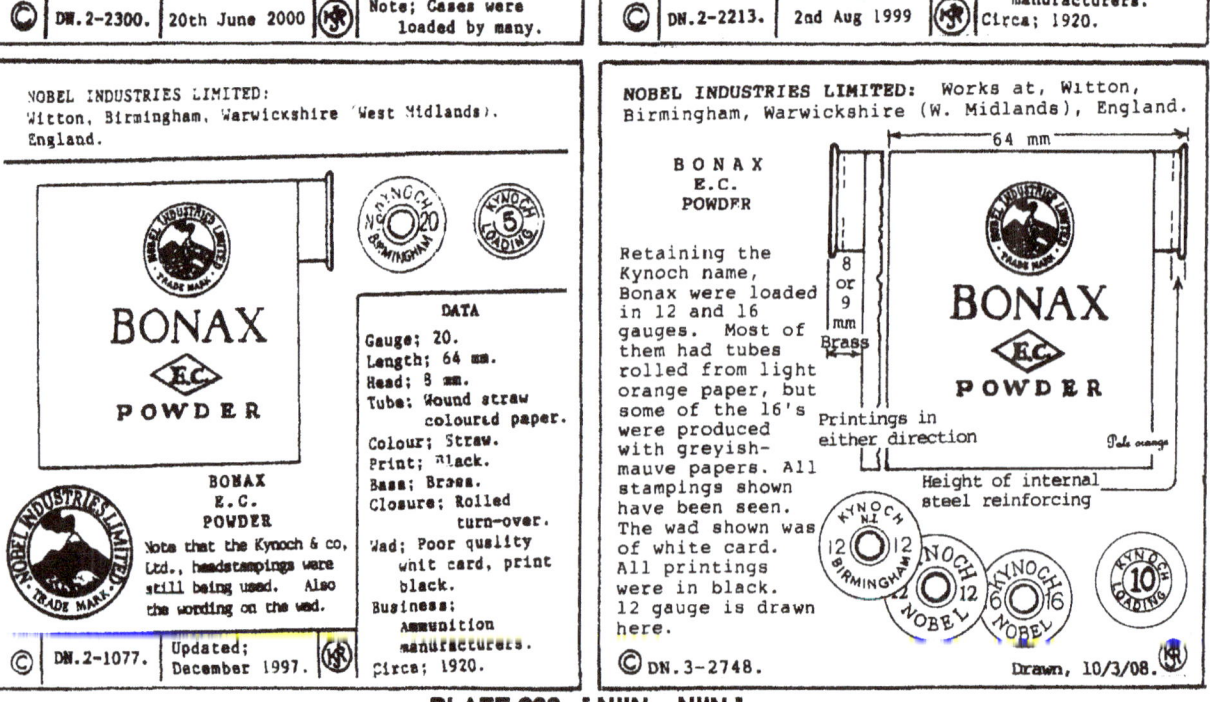

PLATE 282 [N'IN – N'IN]

NOBEL INDUSTRIES, LTD: Works; Witton, Factory, Birmingham, Warwickshire (West Midlands). Head Office; Nobel House, Buckingham Gate, London S.W.1., England. (Business; Ammunition manufacturers).

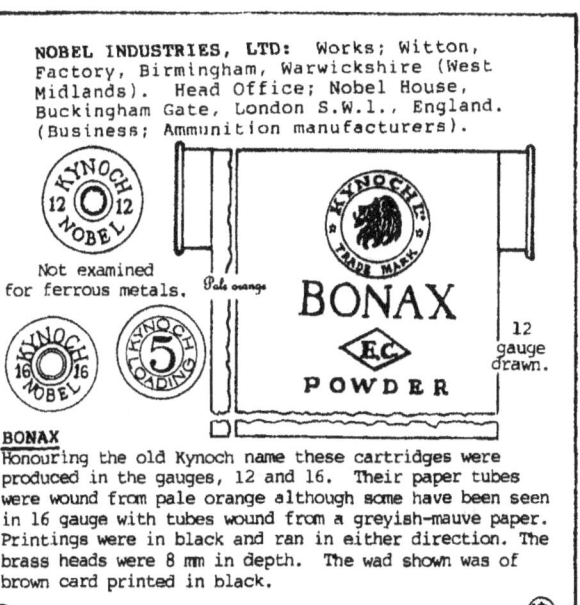

Not examined for ferrous metals. Pale orange. 12 gauge drawn.

BONAX

Honouring the old Kynoch name these cartridges were produced in the gauges, 12 and 16. Their paper tubes were wound from pale orange although some have been seen in 16 gauge with tubes wound from a greyish-mauve paper. Printings were in black and ran in either direction. The brass heads were 8 mm in depth. The wad shown was of brown card printed in black.

© DN.3-0333.   Circa; 1920's.   Revised; 30/12/08.

NOBEL INDUSTRIES, LIMITED:
Works; Witton, Birmingham, Warwickshire (West Midlands). Head Office; Nobel House, Buckingham Gate, London S.W.1., England.

DATA
Gauge; 12.
Length; 64 mm.
Head; 8 mm.
Tube; Wound orange paper.
Colour; Orange.
Print; Black.
Base; Reinforced brass.
Closure; Rolled turn-over.
Wad; Red with shot size in black.
Wetproof; Clear lacquered.
Business; Ammo manufacturers.

© DN.2-1681.   Re-drawn; 24th Feb 2001

NOBEL INDUSTRIES LIMITED; Subsidiary, KYNOCH LIMITED:
Witton, Birmingham, Warwickshire (Midlands), England.

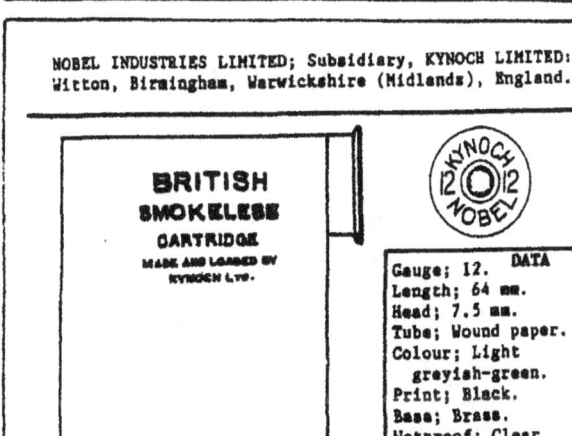

DATA
Gauge; 12.
Length; 64 mm.
Head; 7.5 mm.
Tube; Wound paper.
Colour; Light greyish-green.
Print; Black.
Base; Brass.
Wetproof; Clear lacquered.
Closure; Rolled turn-over.
Wad; Pink, print blck.
Business; Ammunition manufacturers.

© DN.2-1834.   August 1995   Circa; Mid 1920's.

NOBEL INDUSTRIES LIMITED: Works at; Witton, Birmingham, Warwickshire (West Midlands). Head Office; Nobel House, Buckingham Gate, London S.W.1., England. Business; Ammunition manufacturers.

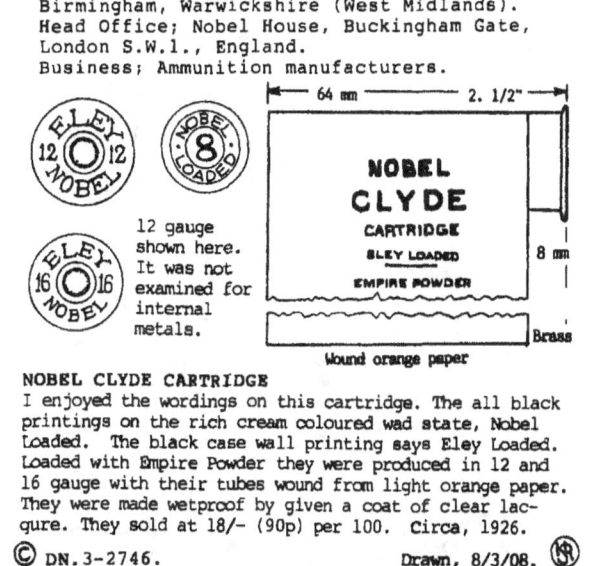

12 gauge shown here. It was not examined for internal metals.

NOBEL CLYDE CARTRIDGE

I enjoyed the wordings on this cartridge. The all black printings on the rich cream coloured wad state, Nobel Loaded. The black case wall printing says Eley Loaded. Loaded with Empire Powder they were produced in 12 and 16 gauge with their tubes wound from light orange paper. They were made wetproof by given a coat of clear lacqure. They sold at 18/- (90p) per 100. Circa, 1926.

© DN.3-2746.   Drawn, 8/3/08.

NOBEL INDUSTRIES LIMITED: Works; Witton, Birmingham, Warwickshire (West Midlands). Head Office; Nobel House, Buckingham Gate, London S.W.1., England.

DATA
Gauge; 12.
Length; 64 mm.
Head; 8 mm.
Tube; Wound deep orange paper.
Print; Black.
Base; Brass (not examined for internal metals.
Closure; Rolled turn-over.
Wad; Cream card, print black.
Business; Ammunition manufacturers.

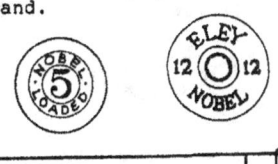

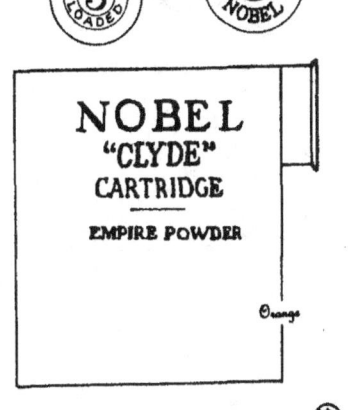

NOBEL
"CLYDE"
CARTRIDGE
EMPIRE POWDER

DN.3-0216.   Drawn, 27/4/08.

NOBEL INDUSTRIES LIMITED: Works; Witton, Birmingham, Warwickshire (West Midlands). Head Office; Nobel House, Buckingham Gate, London S.W.1., England.

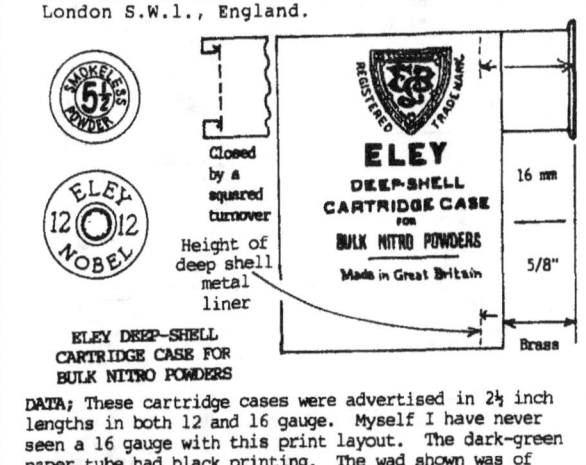

Closed by a squared turnover.
Height of deep shell metal liner.

ELEY DEEP-SHELL CARTRIDGE CASE FOR BULK NITRO POWDERS

DATA; These cartridge cases were advertised in 2½ inch lengths in both 12 and 16 gauge. Myself I have never seen a 16 gauge with this print layout. The dark-green paper tube had black printing. The wad shown was of white card with red printing. The cap was copper.

© DN.3-2709.   Drawn, 27/2/08.

PLATE 283 [N'IN – N'IN]

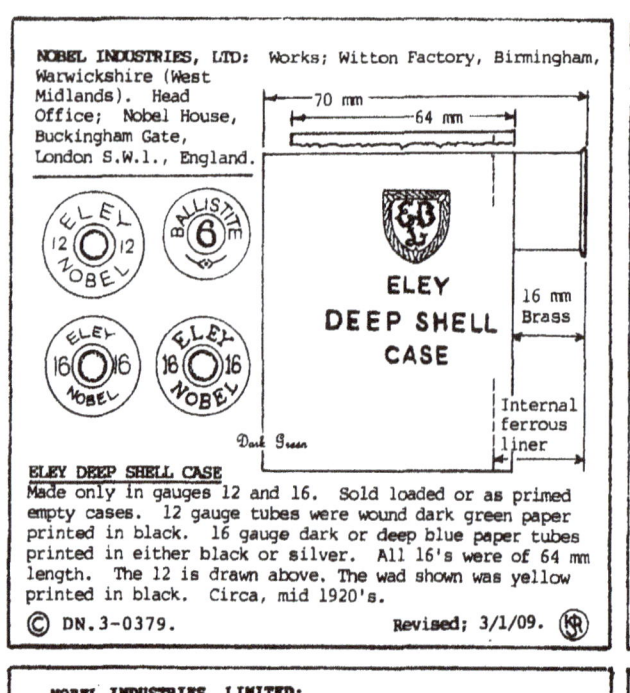

NOBEL INDUSTRIES, LTD: Works; Witton Factory, Birmingham, Warwickshire (West Midlands). Head Office; Nobel House, Buckingham Gate, London S.W.1., England.

ELEY DEEP SHELL CASE
Made only in gauges 12 and 16. Sold loaded or as primed empty cases. 12 gauge tubes were wound dark green paper printed in black. 16 gauge dark or deep blue paper tubes printed in either black or silver. All 16's were of 64 mm length. The 12 is drawn above. The wad shown was yellow printed in black. Circa, mid 1920's.

© DN.3-0379. Revised; 3/1/09.

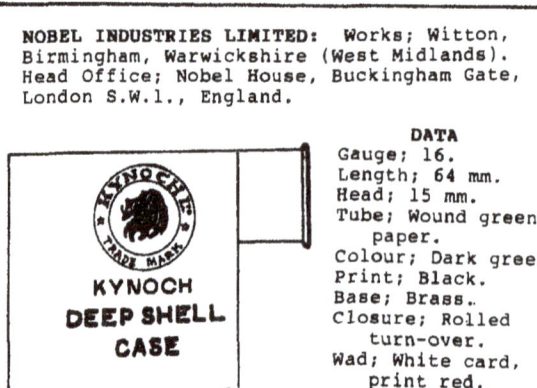

NOBEL INDUSTRIES LIMITED: Works; Witton, Birmingham, Warwickshire (West Midlands). Head Office; Nobel House, Buckingham Gate, London S.W.1., England.

DATA
Gauge; 16.
Length; 64 mm.
Head; 15 mm.
Tube; Wound green paper.
Colour; Dark green.
Print; Black.
Base; Brass.
Closure; Rolled turn-over.
Wad; White card, print red.
Business; Ammo manufacturers.
Circa; 1925.
This cartridge was not examined for any internal metals. These cases were loaded by many.

© DN.3-2770. Drawn, 14/3/08.

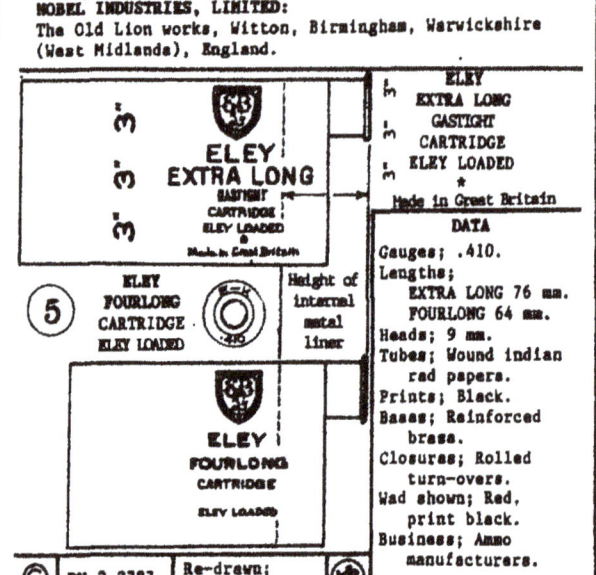

NOBEL INDUSTRIES, LIMITED: The Old Lion works, Witton, Birmingham, Warwickshire (West Midlands), England.

DATA
Gauges; .410.
Lengths;
 EXTRA LONG 76 mm.
 FOURLONG 64 mm.
Heads; 9 mm.
Tubes; Wound indian red papers.
Prints; Black.
Bases; Reinforced brass.
Closures; Rolled turn-overs.
Wad shown; Red, print black.
Business; Ammo manufacturers.

© DN.2-2387. Re-drawn; 5th Jan 2001

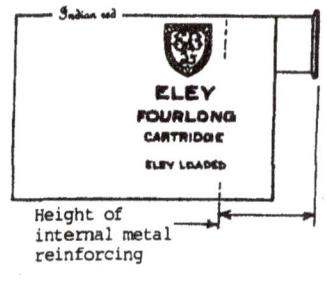

NOBEL INDUSTRIES LIMITED: Works at; Witton, Birmingham, Warwickshire (West Midlands). Head Office; Nobel House, Buckingham Gate, London S.W.1., England.

ELEY FOURLONG CARTRIDGE ELEY LOADED

DATA
Gauge; .410.
Length; 64 mm.
Head; 9 mm.
Tube; Wound Eley Indian-red paper.
Print; Black.
Base; Reinforced brass.
Cap; Copper.
Closure; Rolled turn-over.
Wad shown; Red print black.
Business; Ammo manufacturers.
Circa; 1920's.

© DN.3-2687. Drawn, 19/2/08.

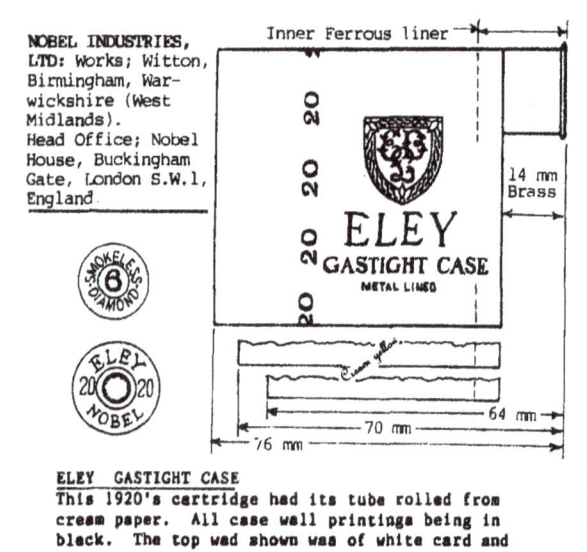

NOBEL INDUSTRIES, LTD: Works; Witton, Birmingham, Warwickshire (West Midlands). Head Office; Nobel House, Buckingham Gate, London S.W.1, England.

ELEY GASTIGHT CASE
This 1920's cartridge had its tube rolled from cream paper. All case wall printings being in black. The top wad shown was of white card and it too was printed in black.

© DN.3-1118. Revised; 6/1/09.

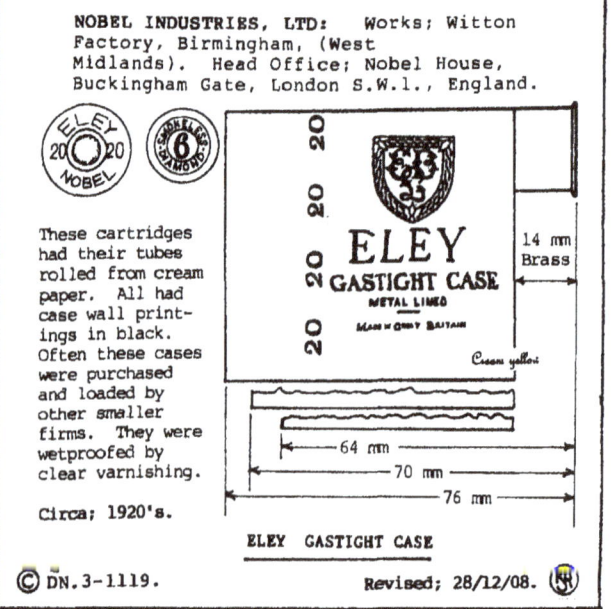

NOBEL INDUSTRIES, LTD: Works; Witton Factory, Birmingham, (West Midlands). Head Office; Nobel House, Buckingham Gate, London S.W.1., England.

These cartridges had their tubes rolled from cream paper. All had case wall printings in black. Often these cases were purchased and loaded by other smaller firms. They were wetproofed by clear varnishing.

Circa; 1920's.

ELEY GASTIGHT CASE

© DN.3-1119. Revised; 28/12/08.

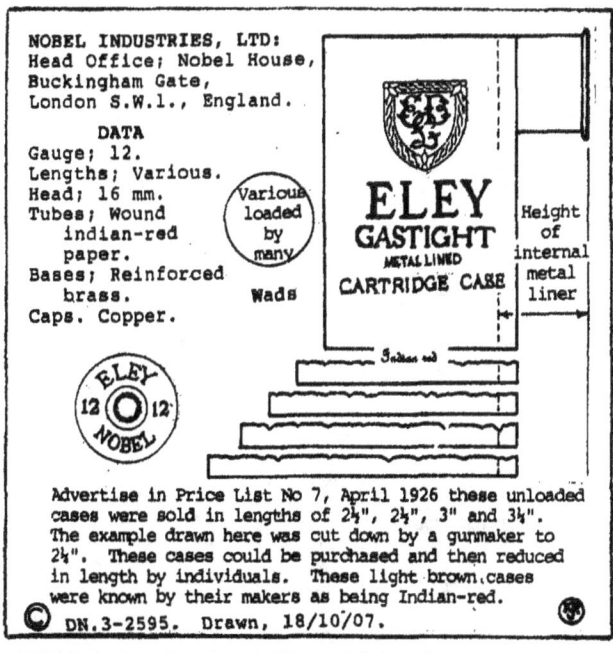
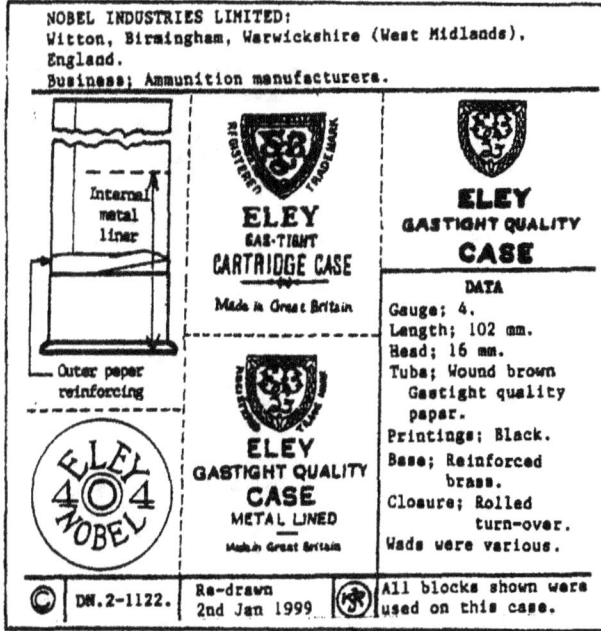
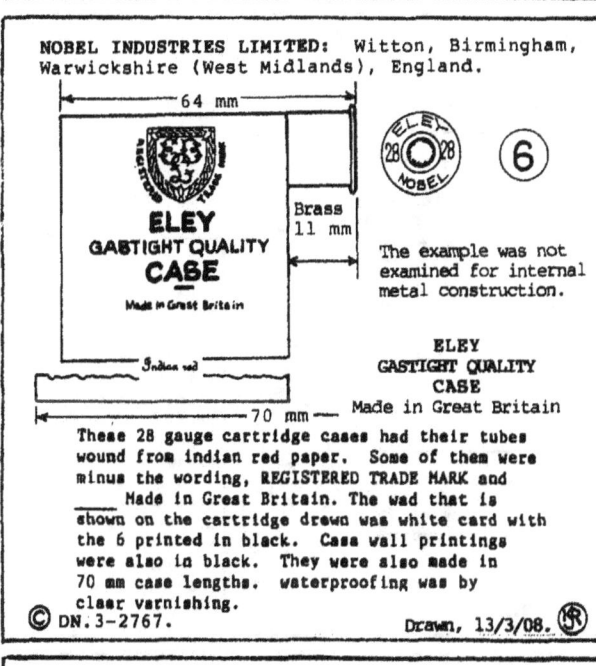
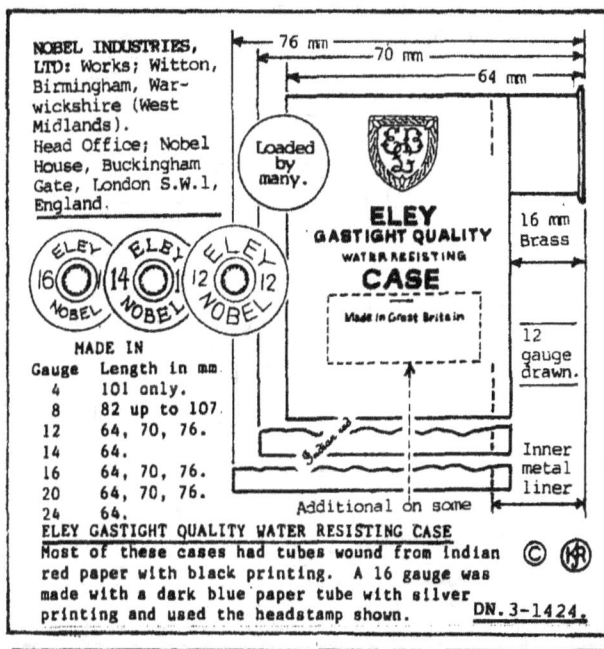
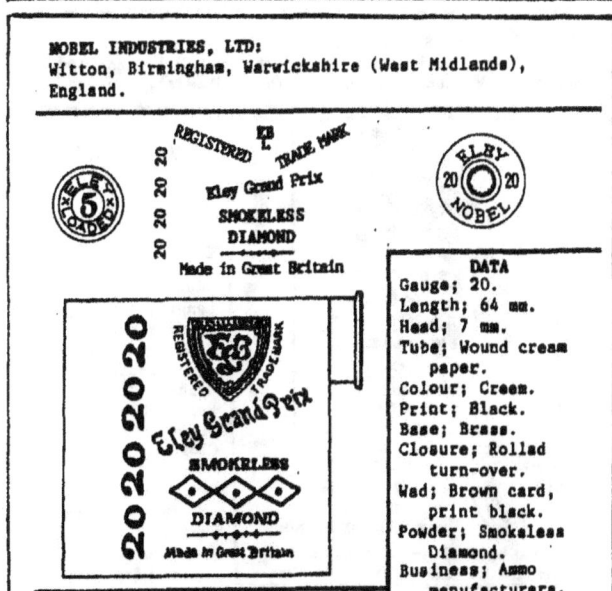
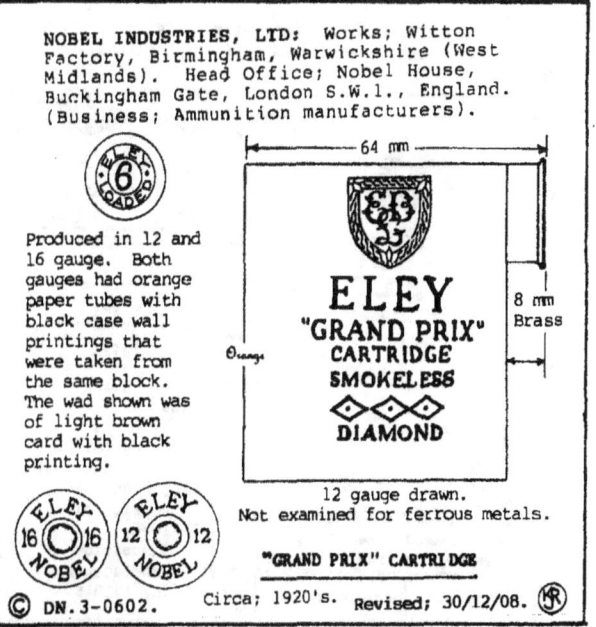

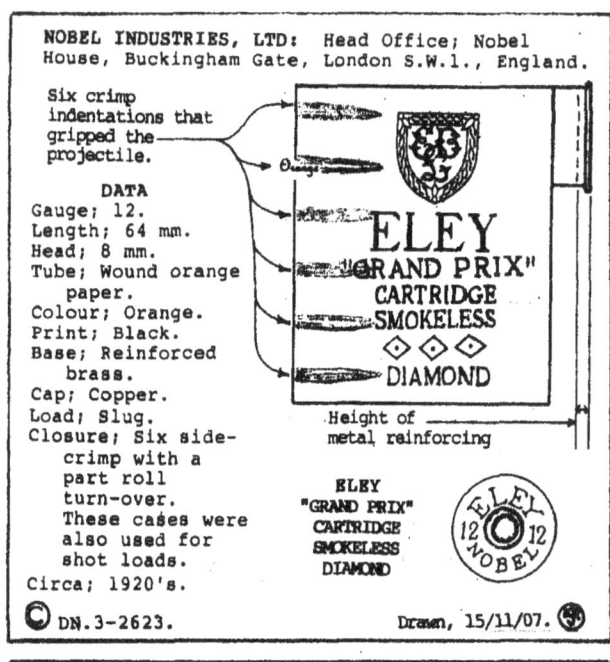
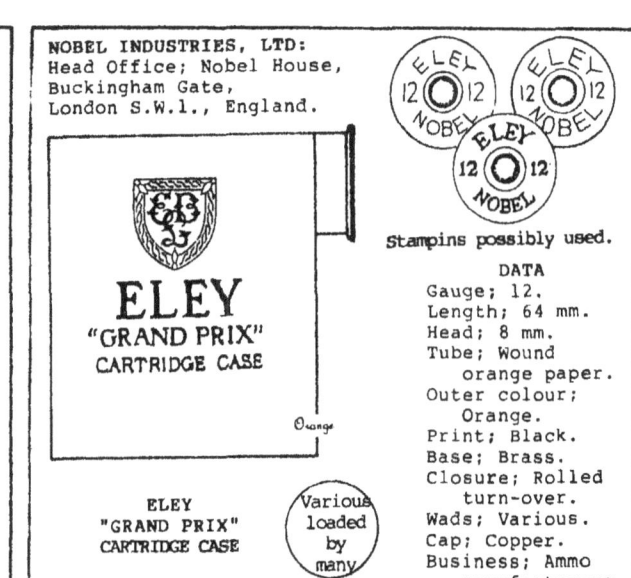
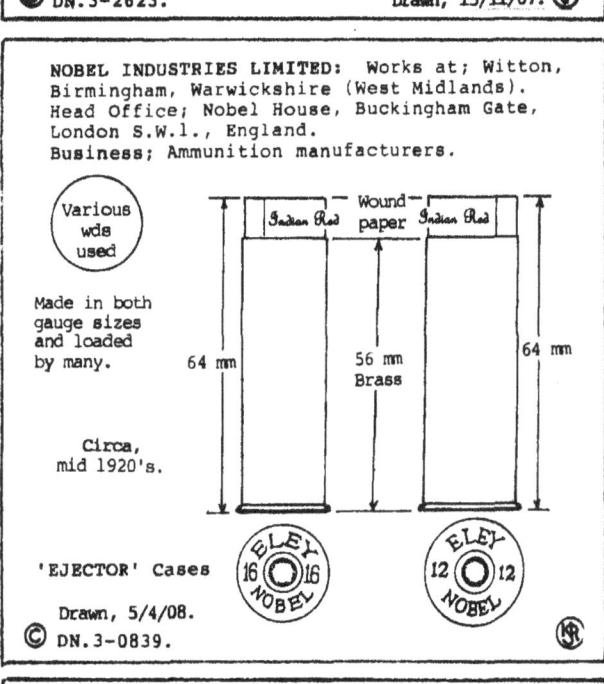
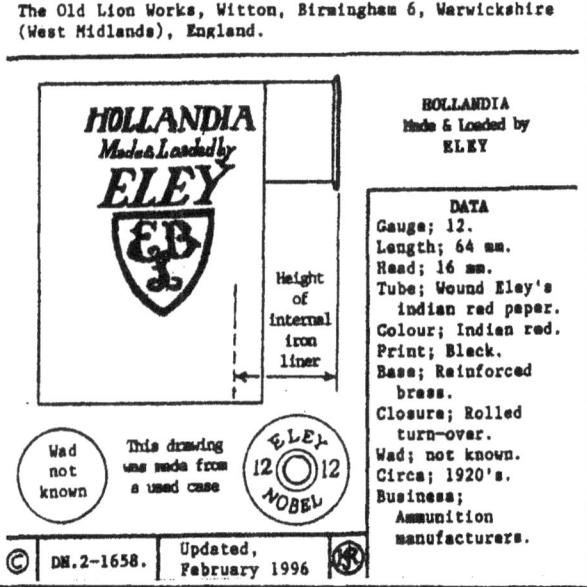

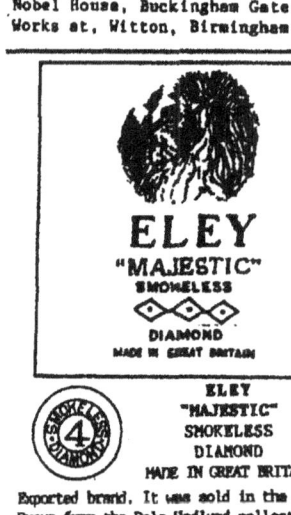

PLATE 286 [N'IN – N'IN]

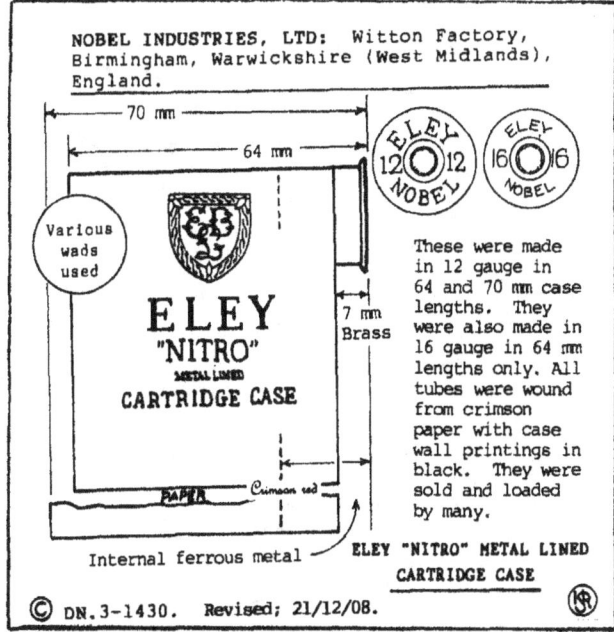
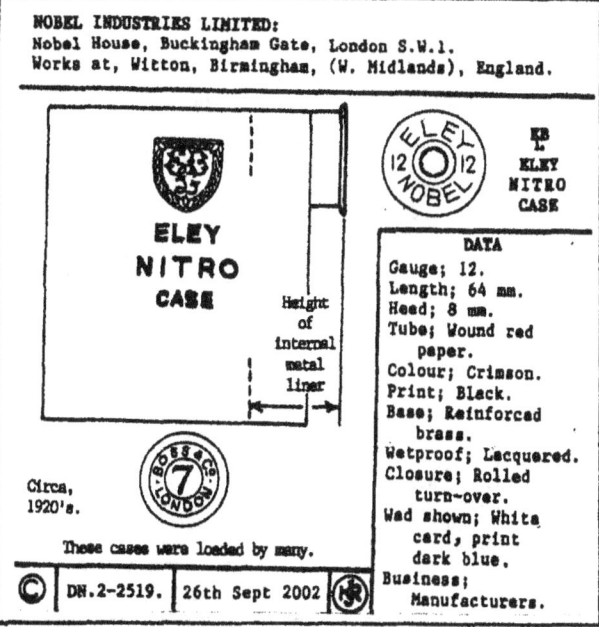

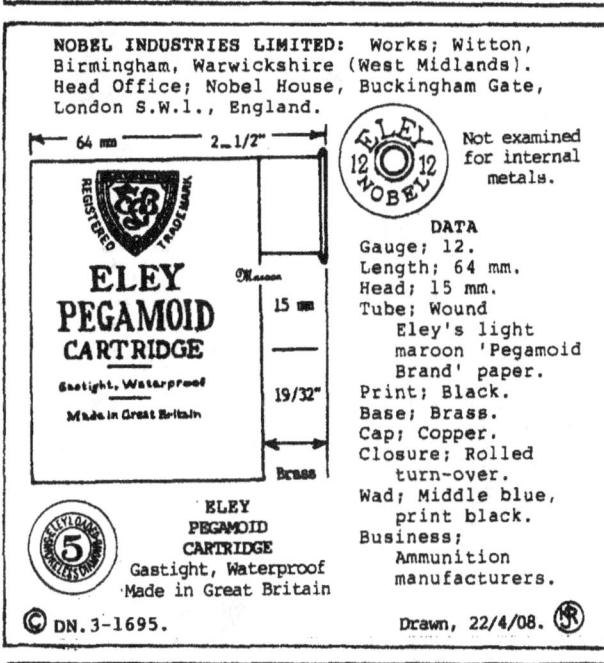
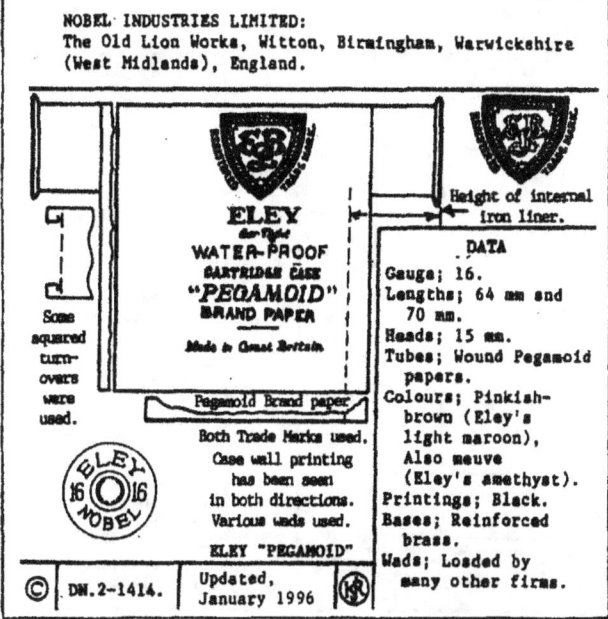
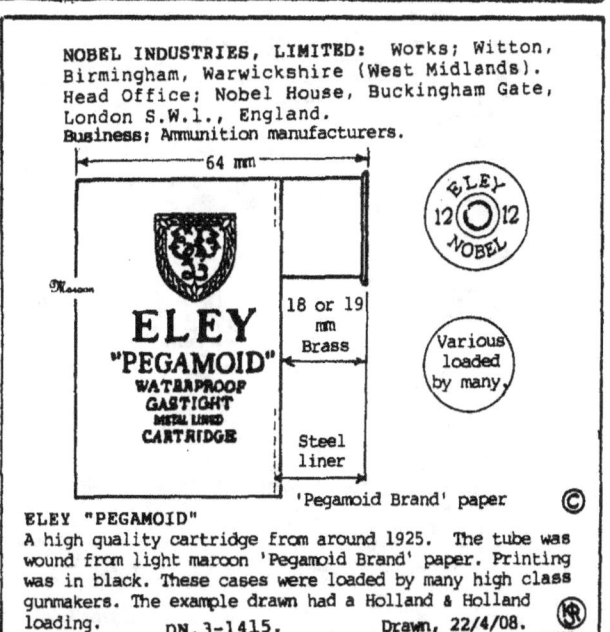

PLATE 287 [N'IN – N'IN]

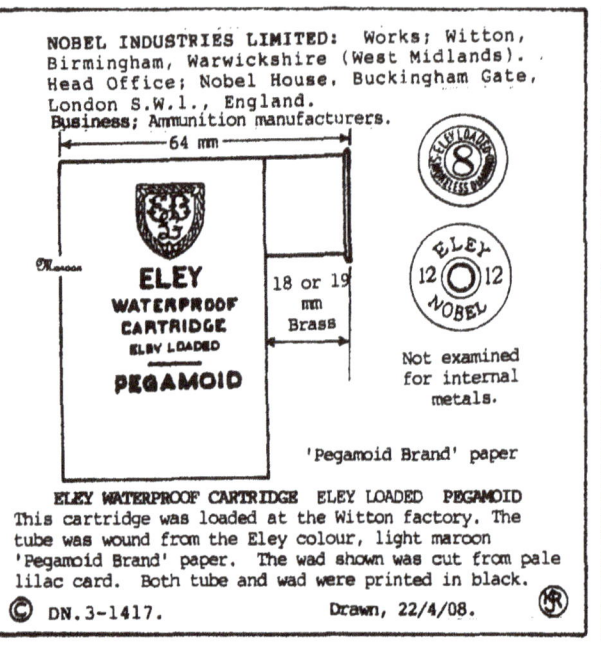

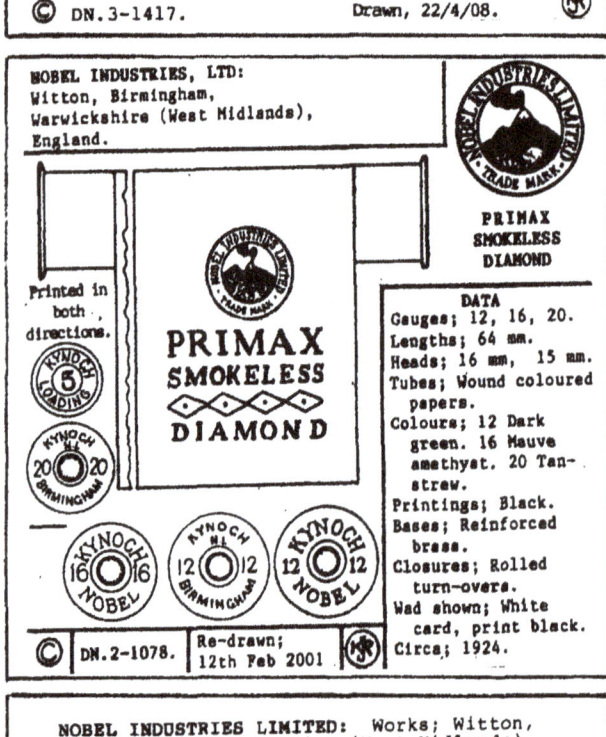
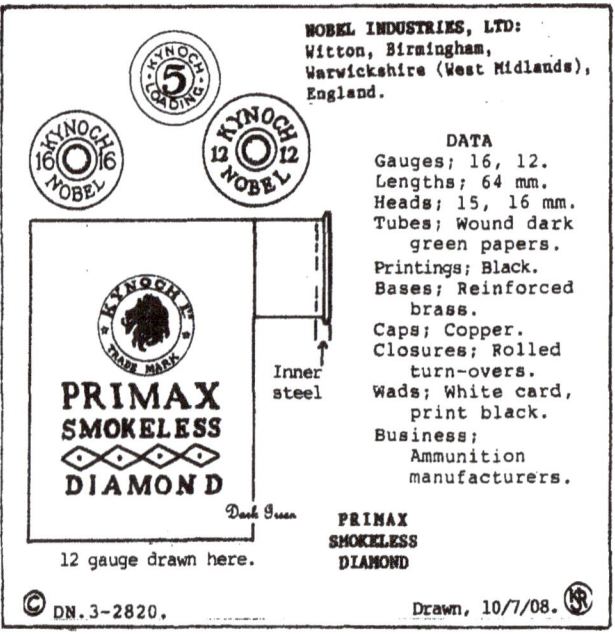
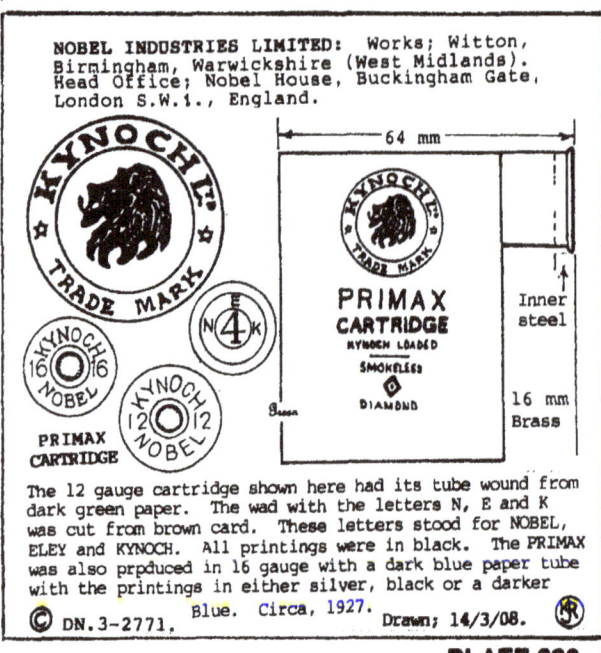
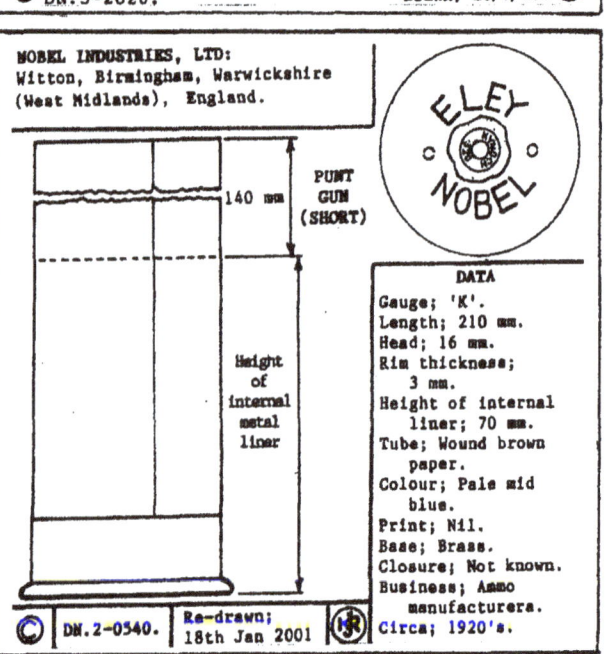

PLATE 288 [N'IN – N'IN]

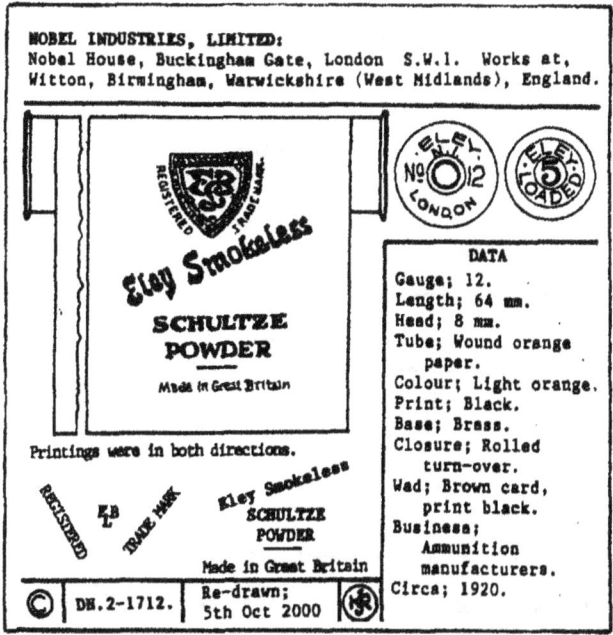
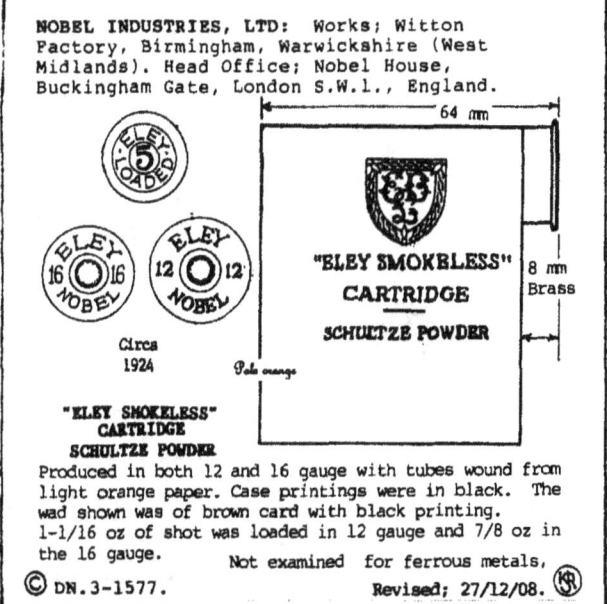

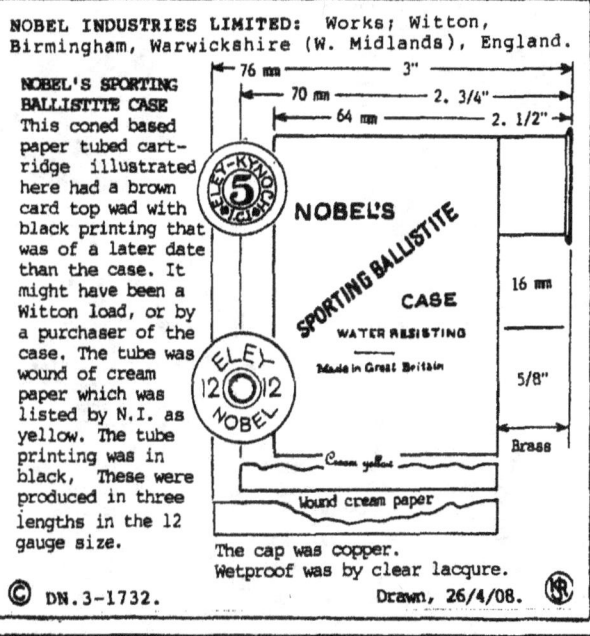

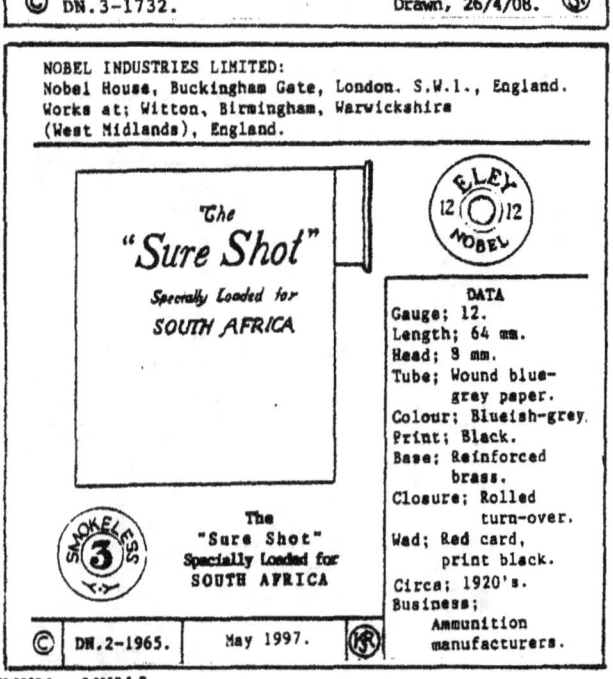

NOBEL INDUSTRIES LIMITED:
Office, Nobel House, Buckingham Gate, London S.W.1.
Works, Witton, Birmingham, Warwickshire (West Midlands),
England.

Loaded in 12 gauge only
in what Eley's called
light orange cases.
Powders were Empire,
Smokeless Diamond or 'E.C'.

ELEY SPECIAL TRAPSHOOTING CARTRIDGE

DATA
Gauge; 12.
Length; 65 mm.
Head; 8 mm.
Tube; Wound orange paper.
Colour; Orange.
Print; Black.
Base; Reinforced brass.
Closure; Rolled turn-over.
Wad shown; Blue, print black.
Business; Ammunition manufacturers.

ELEY SPECIAL TRAPSHOOTING CARTRIDGE

© DN.2-1703. Re-drawn; 28th Oct 2000

NOBEL INDUSTRIES, LTD / ELEY BROTHERS, LTD.
Witton, Birmingham, Warwickshire
(West Midlands), England.

ELEY 20 GAUGE CASE

DATA
Gauge; 20.
Length; 64 mm.
Head; 10 mm.
Tube; Wound burnt-cream paper.
Print; Black.
Base; Reinforced brass.
Closure; Rolled turn-over.
Wad; Brown card, print black.
Business; Ammunition manufacturers.
Note; Cases were also loaded by others.
Circa; 1920's.

© DN.3-2302. Revised, 14/12/08.

NOBEL INDUSTRIES LIMITED:
Witton, Birmingham, England.
London address; Nobel House,
S.W.1., England.

"WESTMINSTER" DEEP SHELL CARTRIDGE — SCHULTZE POWDER

DATA
Gauge; 12.
Length; 64 mm.
Head; 16 mm.
Tube; Wound green paper.
Colour; Dark pine green.
Print; Black.
Base; Brass.
Closure; Rolled turn-over.
Wad; Buff card, print black.
Business; Ammunition manufacturers.
Circa; 1920's.

REGISTERED TRADE MARK.
"WESTMINSTER" DEEP SHELL CARTRIDGE — SCHULTZE POWDER

© DN.2-1114. Re-drawn November 1998

NOBEL INDUSTRIES, LTD:
Witton, Birmingham,
Warwickshire
(W. Midlands), England.

YEOMAN SCHULTZE POWDER
Made in Great Britain

Wad not known

YEOMAN SCHULTZE POWDER Made in Great Britain

DATA
Gauge; 12.
Length; 64 mm.
Head; 8 mm.
Tube; Wound off-white paper.
Colour; Eley's light brown.
Print; Black.
Base; Brass.
Closure; Rolled turn-over.
Powder; Schultze.
Wad; Not known.
Business; Ammunition manufacturers.
Circa; 1921.

© DN.2-1702. Re-drawn; 12th Jan 2002

NOBEL INDUSTRIES LIMITED: Works; Witton,
Birmingham, Warwickshire (West Midlands).
Head Office; Nobel House, Buckingham Gate,
London S.W.1., England.

DATA
Gauge; 12.
Length; 64 mm.
Head; 16 mm.
Tube; Wound indian red paper.
Print; Black.
Base; Reinforced brass.
Cap; Copper.
Closure; Rolled turn-over.
Wad; Pale lilac, print black.
Business; Ammunition manufacturers.

ELEY "ZENITH" GASTIGHT CARTRIDGE WATER RESISTING METAL LINER

Indian red
Steel liner

ELEY "ZENITH" GASTIGHT CARTRIDGE
WATER RESISTING METAL LINED

© DN.3-1429. Drawn; 27/4/08.

NOBEL INDUSTRIES, LIMITED:
The Old Lion Works, Witton, Birmingham,
Warwickshire (West Midlands), England.

Drawn from the Dale Hedlund collection.

Lead ball-bullet
64 mm
Recess
43 mm
Rim's lower radius

THIS CASE HAD NO IRON OR STEEL IN ITS CONSTRUCTION

DATA
Gauge; 4.
One piece all brass case.
Case length; 107 mm.
Loaded round length; 125 mm.
Cap; Flat copper.
Business; Engineers and ammunition manufacturers.

Case tapered in at the mouth by approximately 1 mm.

KYNOCH 4 4 NOBEL

© DN.2-2135. 24th March 1999

NOBEL INDUSTRIES LIMITED:
Works at, Witton, Birmingham, Warwickshire (West Midlands). Offices at, Nobel House, London, England.

CARTRIDGE SHAPED CIGARETTE LIGHTER
Circa 1920's, it fooled many.

MEASUREMENTS
A, 61 mm; B, 44 mm; C, 15 mm; D, 46 mm; E, 27 mm.

© DN.2-1438. Re-drawn December 1998

NOBEL INDUSTRIES (AUSTRALIA), LTD:
Nobel Factory, West Footscray, Melbourne, Victoria, Australia.

ELEY
DUXBAC
WATERPROOF
LOADED WITH
SMOKELESS
DIAMOND

DATA
Gauge; 12.
Length; 64 mm.
Head; 8 mm.
Tube; Wound crimson paper.
Colour; Crimson red.
Print; Black.
Base; Reinforced brass.
Closure; Rolled turn-over.
Wad; White card, print dark pink.
Business; Sale of ammunition, etc.
Circa; Early 1920's.

Most likely loaded in Great Britain.
Drawn from the Tom Matthews collection.

© DN.2-2471. 30th Aug 2001

NORMAL POWDER COMPANY:
Hendon, London W., England.

DATA
Gauge; 16.
Length; 64 mm.
Head; 14 mm.
Tube; Wound paper.
Colour; Reddish-brown.
Print; Black.
Base; Reinforced brass.
Closure; Rolled turn-over.
Wad; Pink card, print black.
Business; Gunpowder and cartridge manufacturers.
Case; Kynoch & Co.

NORMAL
SPORTING POWDER,
SMOKELESS
AND
WATERPROOF.

© DN.2-2095. November 1998

NORMAL POWDER COMPANY:
Hendon, London N.W.4., England.

DATA
Gauge; 12.
Length; 64 mm.
Head; 6 mm.
Tube; Wound paper.
Colour; Orange.
Print; Black.
Base; Reinforced brass.
Closure; Rolled turn-over.
Wad; Pink card, print black.
Business; Powder manufacturing and cartridge loading.
Case; Belgium made.

NORMAL
SMOKELESS POWDER
NO BLOW - BACKS
NO GUN - HEADACHE

© DN.2-2083. November 1998

NORMAL POWDER COMPANY. Later known as, NORMAL POWDER & AMMUNITION CO, LTD: 2 Bank Buildings, Cricklewood. Also at, Hendon, London N.W.4., England.

DATA
Gauge; 12.
Length; 64 mm.
Head; 8 mm.
Tube; Wound paper.
Colour; Ruby red.
Print; Black.
Base; Brass.
Cap; Copper.
Wetproof; Waxed process.
Closure; Squared turn-over.
Wad; Light yellow, print black.
Business; Gunpowder manufacturers and cartridge loaders.

NORMAL
SPORTING POWDER
SMOKELESS
AND
WATERPROOF.

© DN.3-2745. Drawn, 6/3/08.

NORMAL POWDER COMPANY:
Hendon, London N.W.4., England.

LOADED WITH
HENDON
NORMAL POWDER

KYNOCH PATENT
"PERFECTLY GASTIGHT"

DATA
Gauge; 12.
Length; 65 mm.
Head; 24 mm.
Tube; Wound paper.
Colour; Crimson.
Print; Black.
Base; Brass.
Wetproof; Wax impregnated.
Closure; Rolled turn-over.
Wad; Light blue, print dark blue.
Business; Powder manufacturers and cartridge loaders.
Case; Kynoch.

© DN.2-1029. Re-drawn; 1st Feb 2001

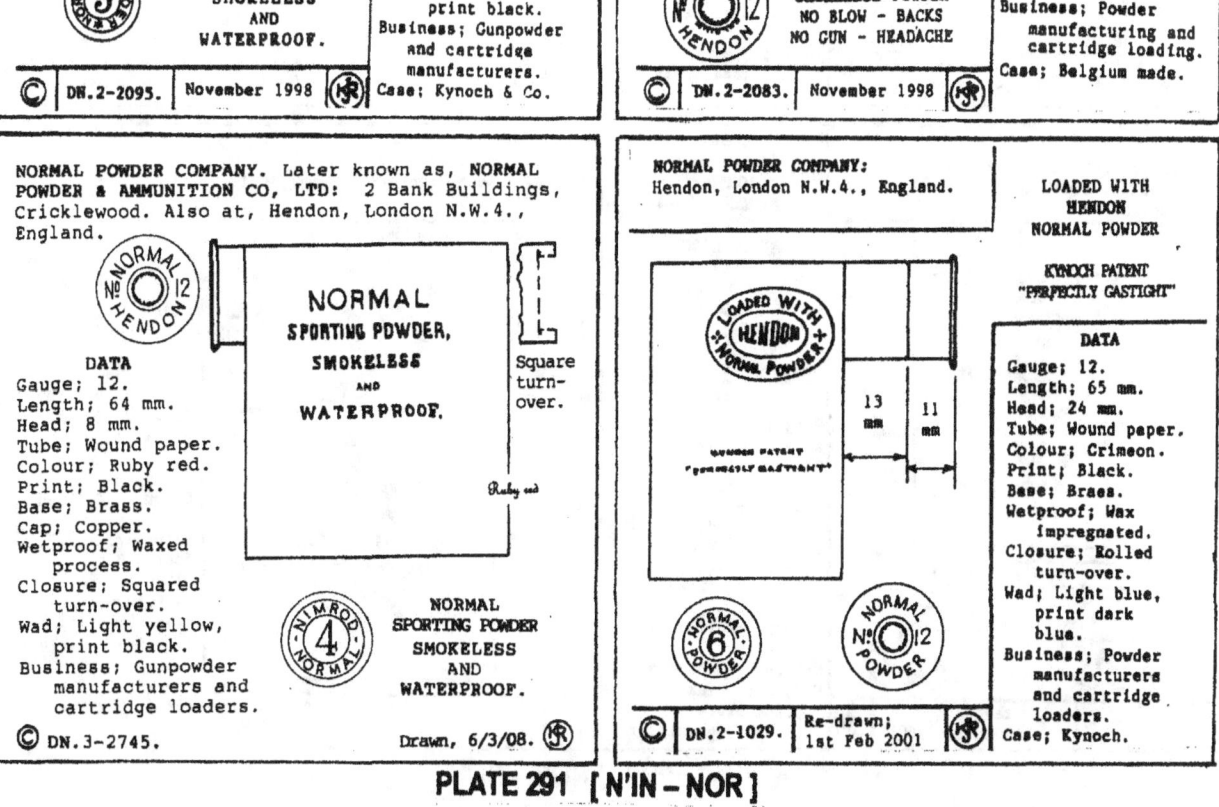

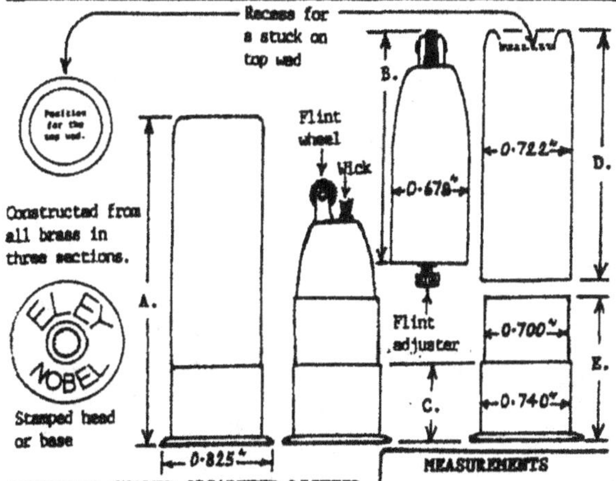

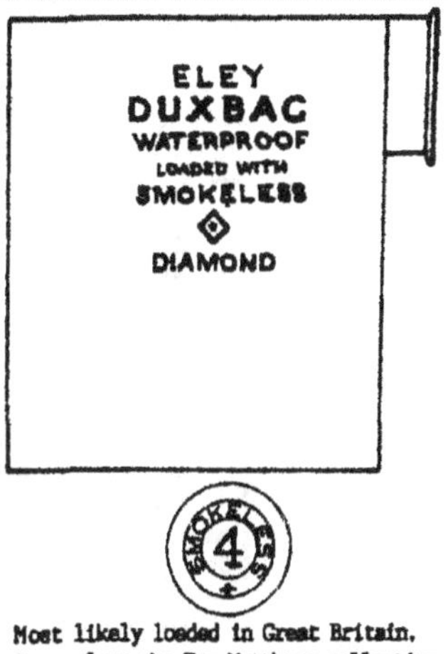

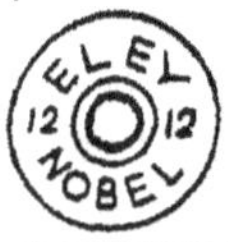

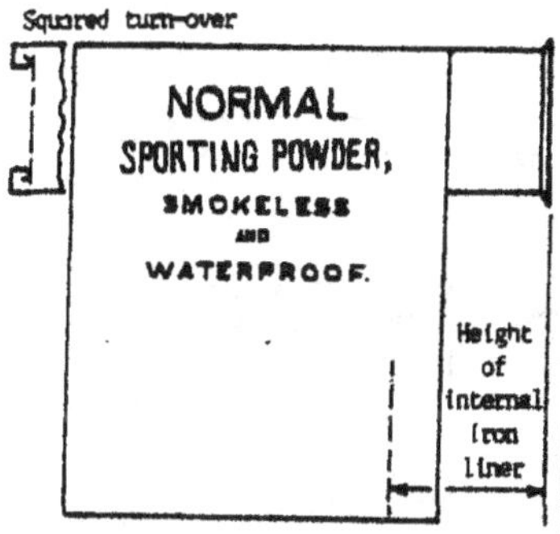

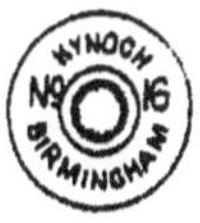

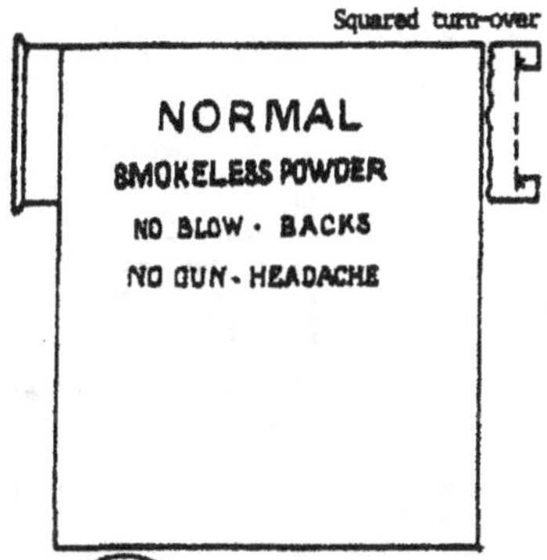

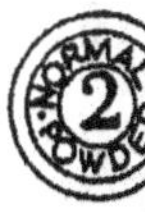

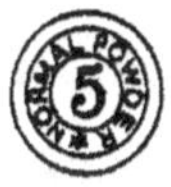

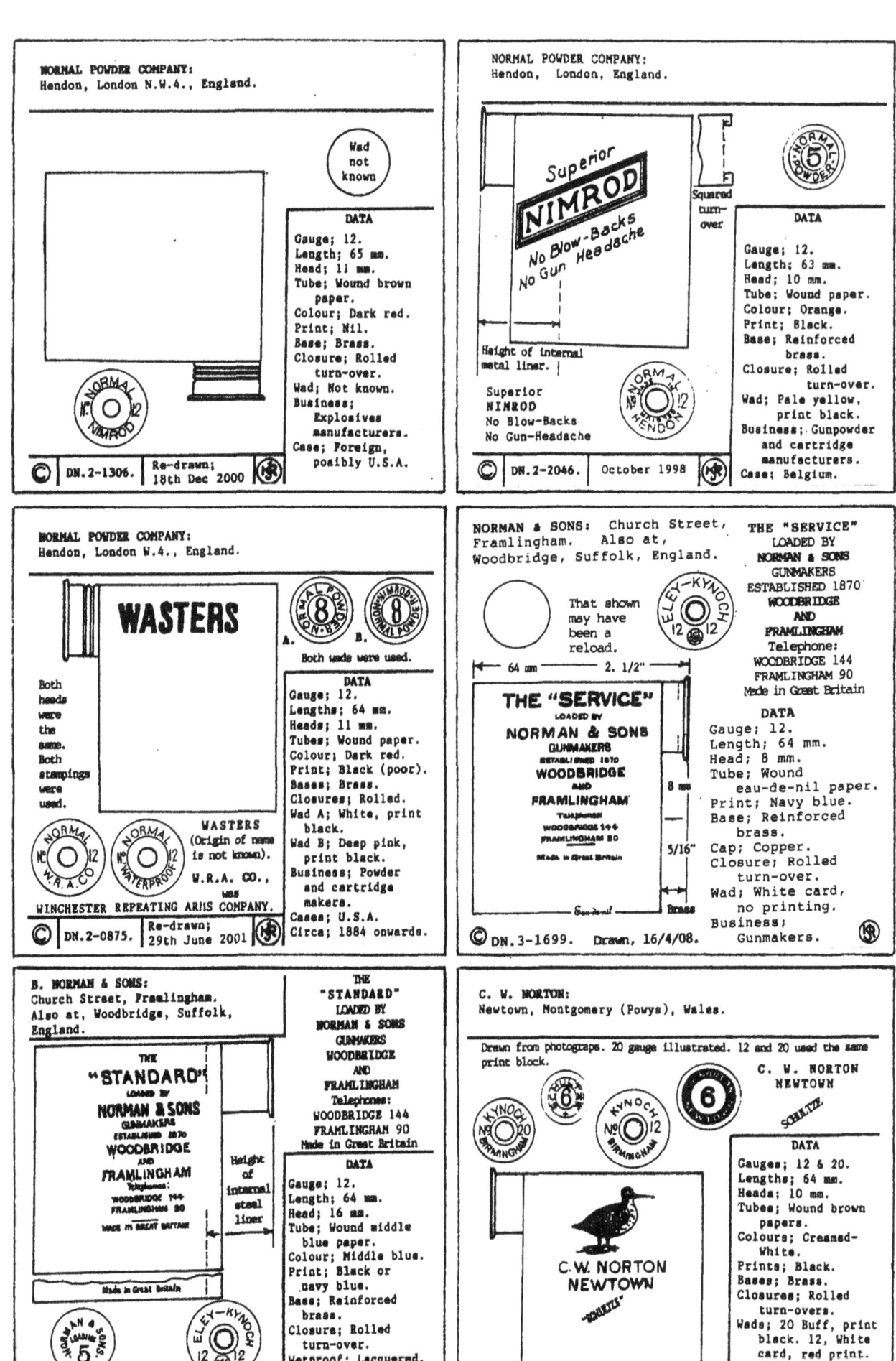

PLATE 292 [NOR – NOR]

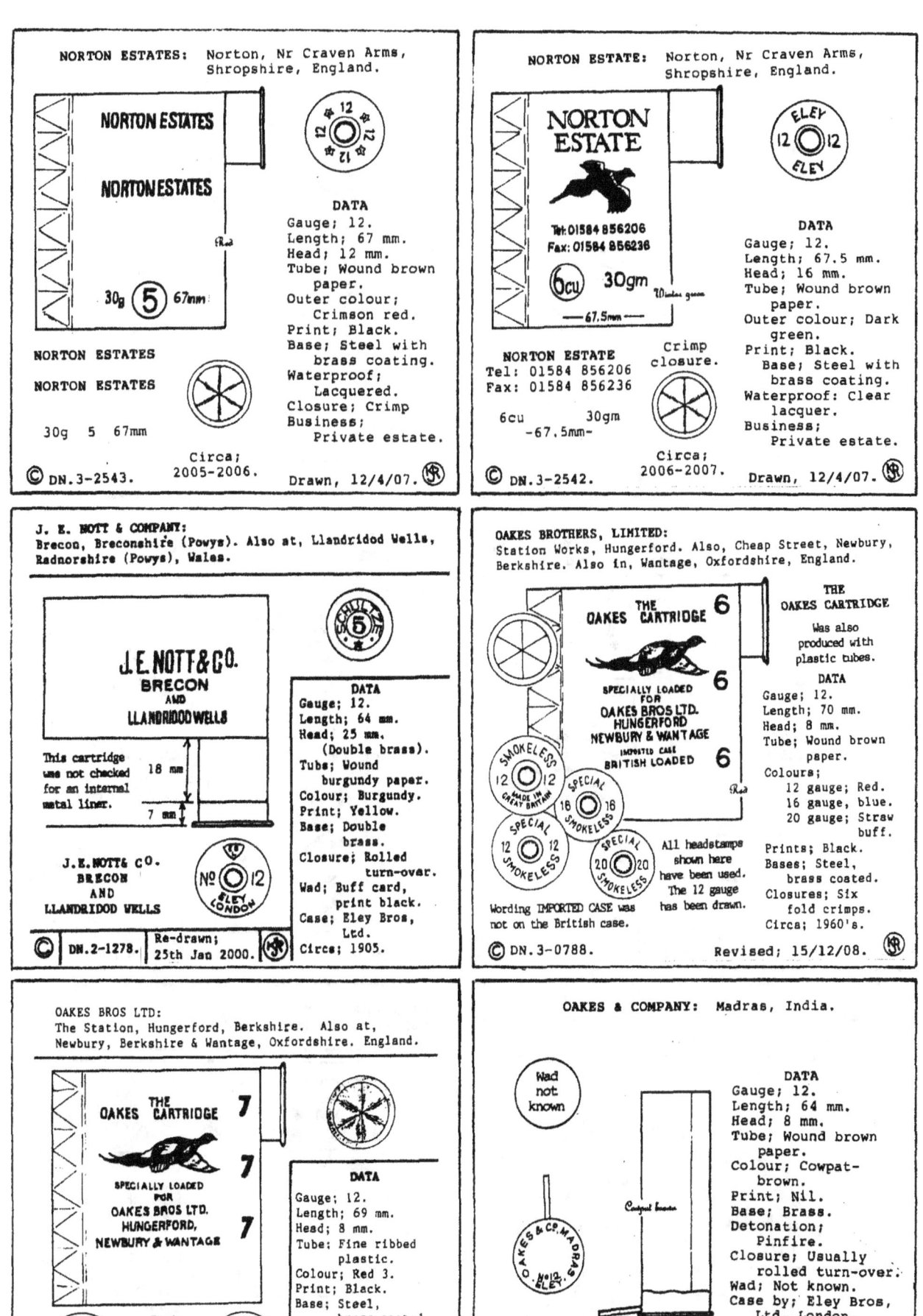

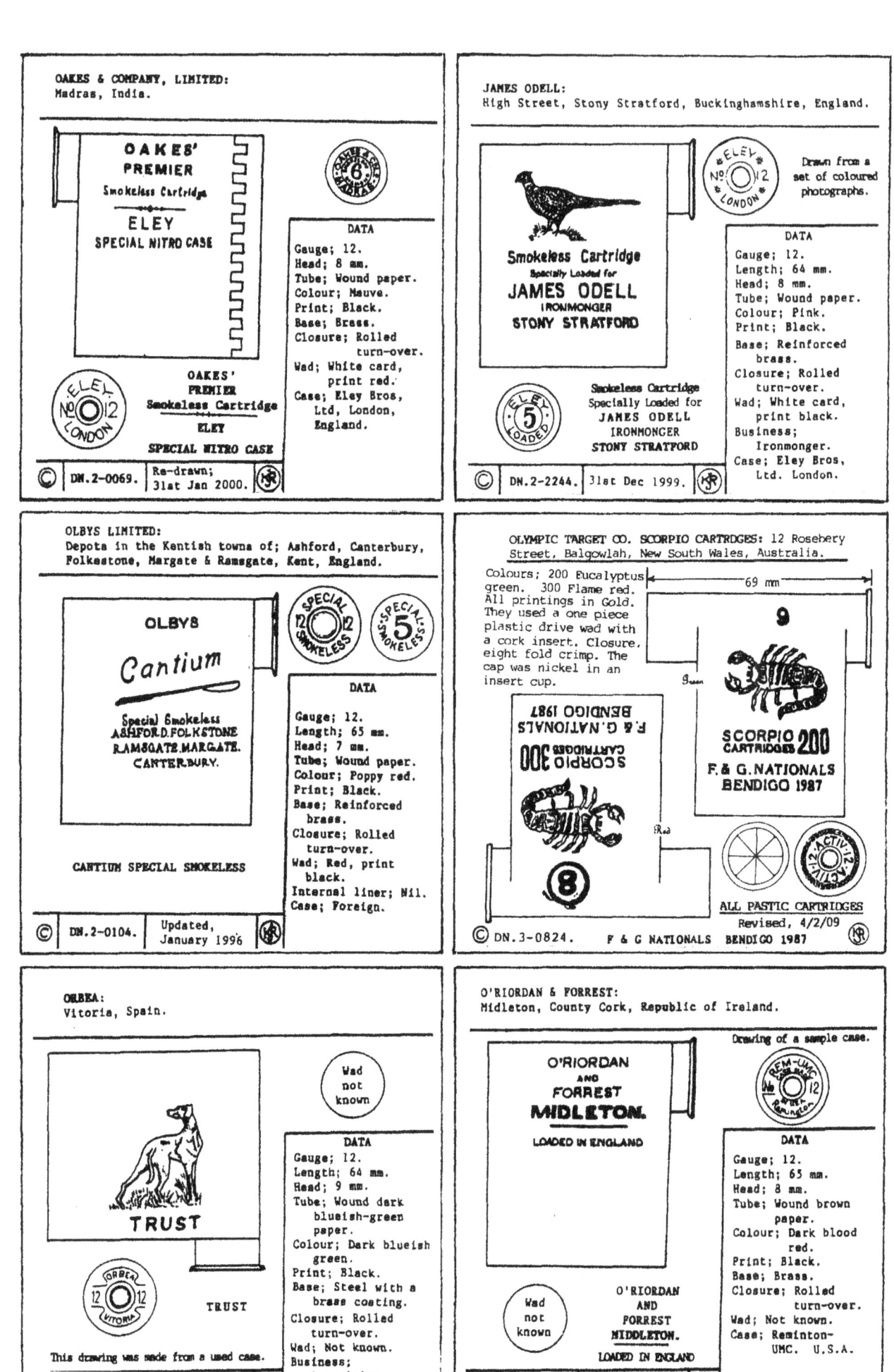

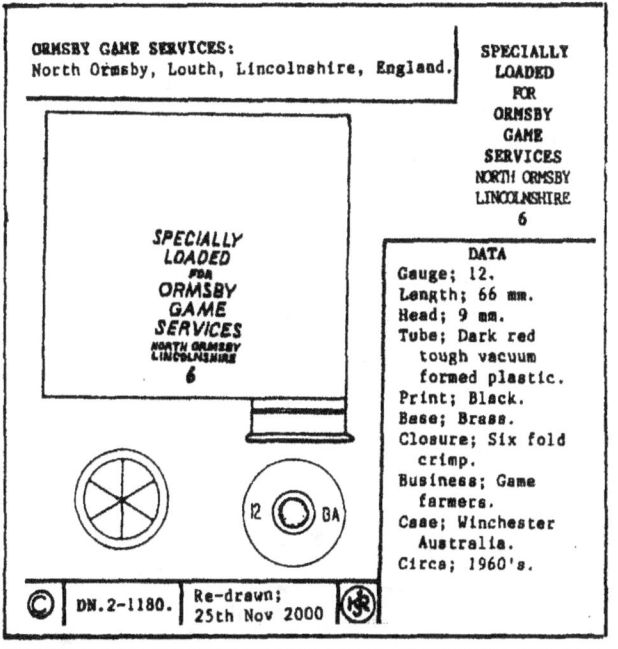
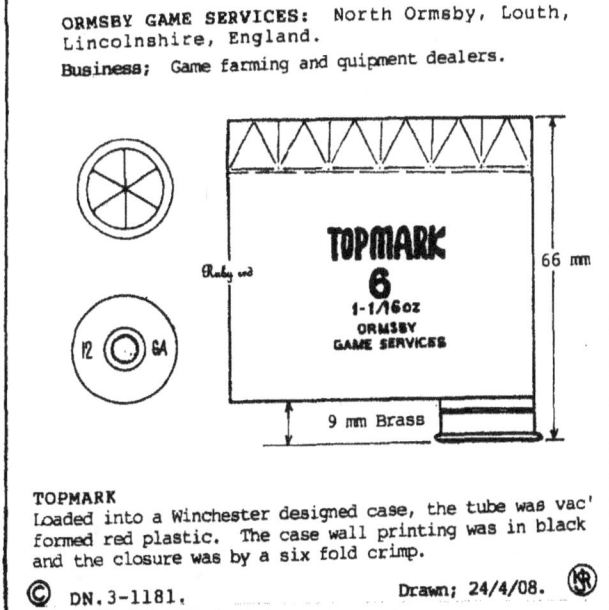
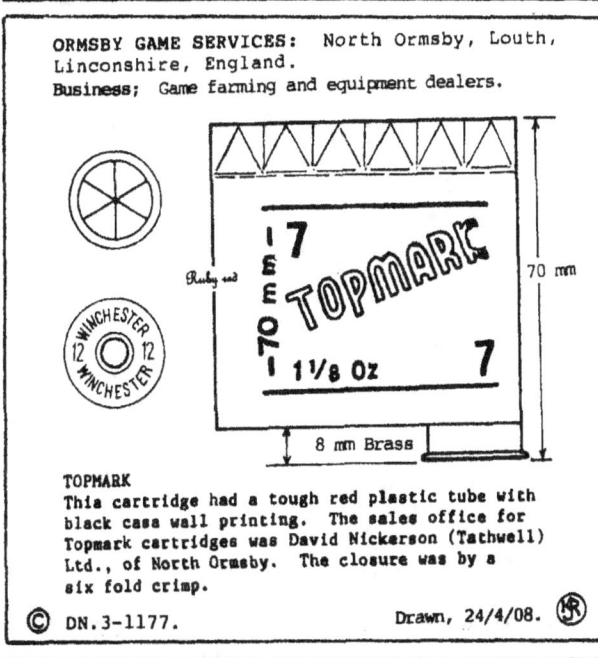
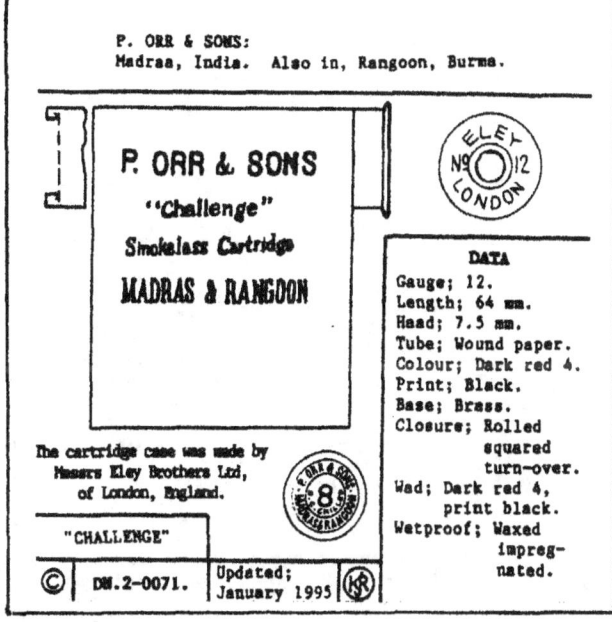
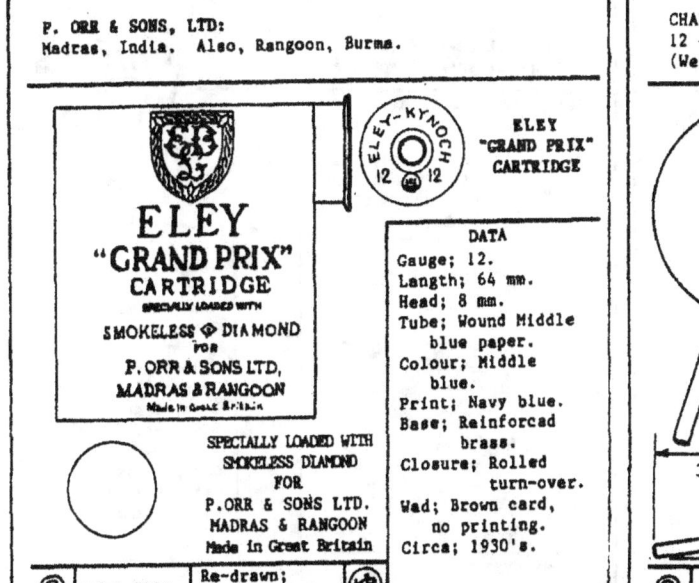
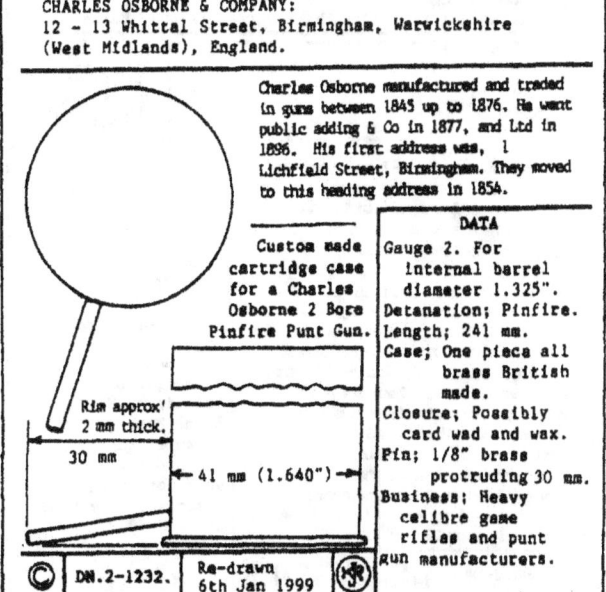

PLATE 295 [ORM – OSB]

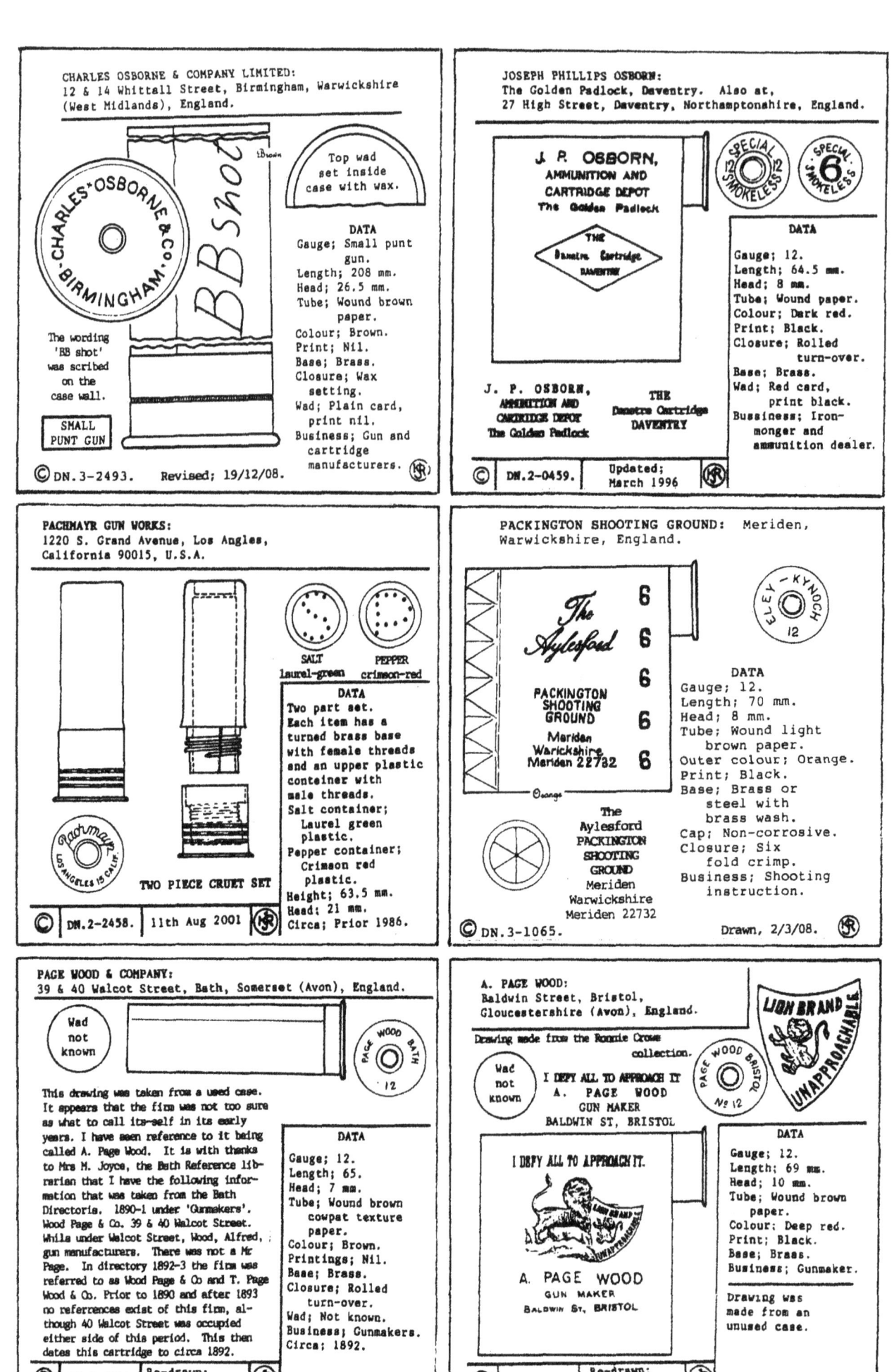

T. PAGE-WOOD:
17 Nicholas Street, Bristol. Gloucestershire (Avon), England.

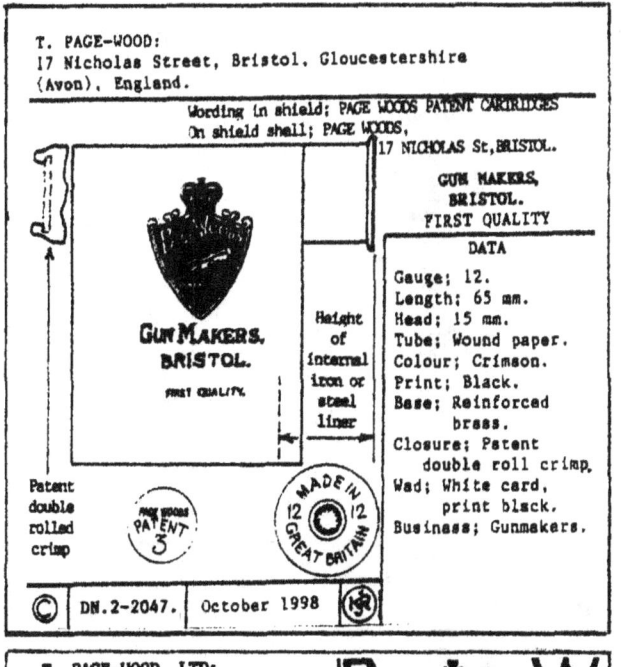

DATA

Gauge; 12.
Length; 65 mm.
Head; 15 mm.
Tube; Wound paper.
Colour; Crimson.
Print; Black.
Base; Reinforced brass.
Closure; Patent double roll crimp.
Wad; White card, print black.
Business; Gunmakers.

DN.2-2047. October 1998

THOMAS PAGE WOOD, LTD:
9 Old Paqrk Hill, Park Row, Bristol. Also at,
8 Pipe Lane, Tramway Centre, Bristol, Gloucestershire (Avon), England.

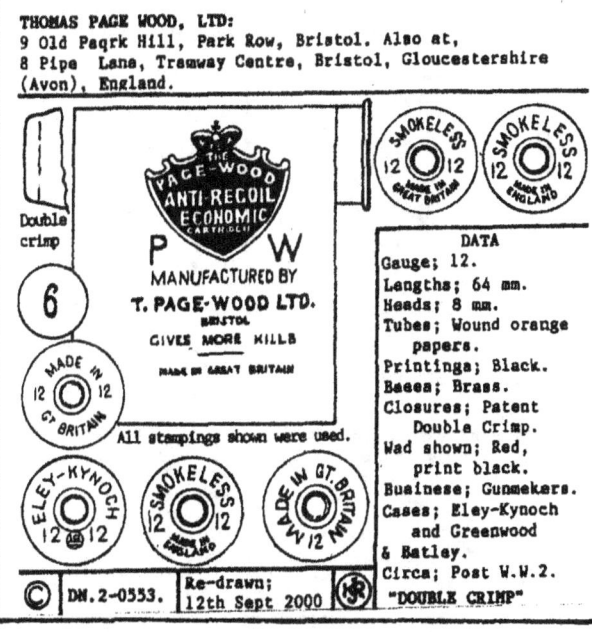

DATA

Gauge; 12.
Lengths; 64 mm.
Heads; 8 mm.
Tubes; Wound orange papers.
Printings; Black.
Bases; Brass.
Closures; Patent Double Crimp.
Wad shown; Red, print black.
Business; Gunmakers.
Cases; Eley-Kynoch and Greenwood & Batley.
Circa; Post W.W.2.

DN.2-0553. Re-drawn; 12th Sept 2000 "DOUBLE CRIMP"

T. PAGE-WOOD, LTD:
17 Nicholas Street, Bristol, Gloucestershire (Avon), England.

DATA

Gauge; 12.
Lengths; 64 mm.
Heads; 7 to 9 mm.
Tubes; Wound orange papers.
Printings; Black.
Bases; Brass with no iron or steel.
Closures; Rolled turn-overs.
Wad shown; Yellow, print black.
Business; Gunmakers.
Cases; Greenwood & Batley
Circa; Post W.W.2.

DN.2-0537. Re-drawn; 9th Sept 2000

T. PAGE-WOOD, LTD:
17 Nicholas Street. Later at 18 Pipe Lane, Bristol, Gloucestershire (Avon), England.

The example drawn was not checked for internal metal reinforcing.

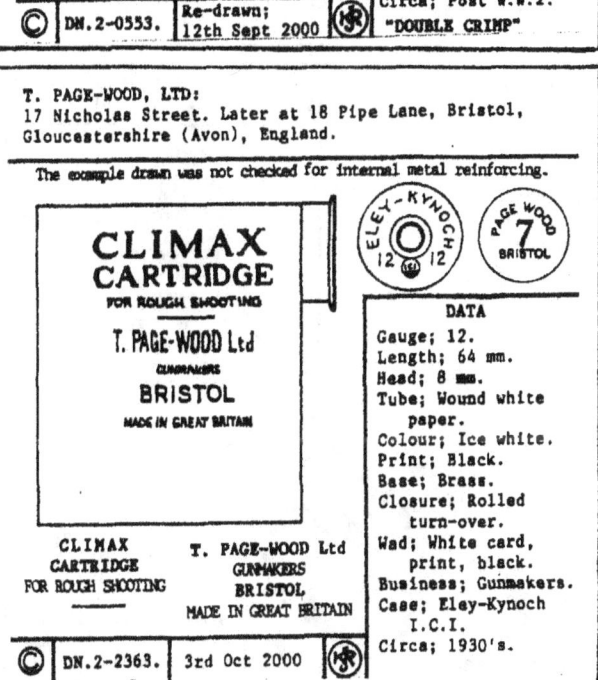

DATA

Gauge; 12.
Length; 64 mm.
Head; 8 mm.
Tube; Wound white paper.
Colour; Ice white.
Print; Black.
Base; Brass.
Closure; Rolled turn-over.
Wad; White card, print, black.
Business; Gunmakers.
Case; Eley-Kynoch I.C.I.
Circa; 1930's.

DN.2-2363. 3rd Oct 2000

T. PAGE-WOOD, LTD:
17 Nicholas Street, Bristol, Gloucestershire (Avon), England.

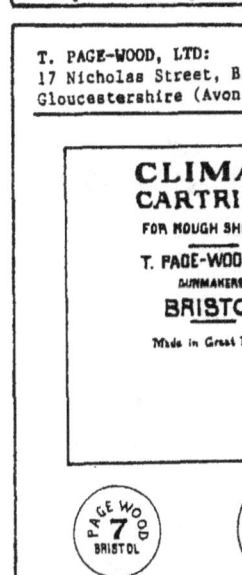

CLIMAX
CARTRIDGE
FOR ROUGH SHOOTING
T. PAGE-WOOD Ltd.
GUNMAKERS
BRISTOL
Made in Great Britain

DATA

Gauge; 12.
Lengths; 64 mm.
Heads; 8 mm.
Tubes; Wound coloured papers.
Colours; Grey-green with black print, or eau-de-nil with navy blue print.
Bases; Reinforced brass.
Closures; Rolled turn-overs.
Wad; White card, print black.
Business; Gunmakers.

DN.3-1037. Revised; 16/12/08.

T. PAGE-WOOD, LTD.
17 Nicholas Street, Bristol, Gloucestershire (Avon), England.

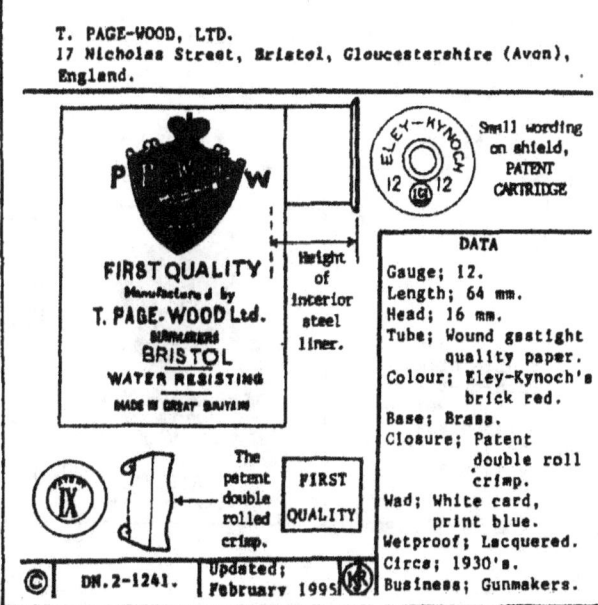

DATA

Gauge; 12.
Length; 64 mm.
Head; 16 mm.
Tube; Wound gastight quality paper.
Colour; Eley-Kynoch's brick red.
Base; Brass.
Closure; Patent double roll crimp.
Wad; White card, print blue.
Wetproof; Lacquered.
Circa; 1930's.
Business; Gunmakers.

DN.2-1241. Updated; February 1995

PLATE 297 [PAG – PAG]

T. PAGE-WOOD:
17 Nicholas Street, Bristol, Gloucestershire (Avon), England.

Closed by a patent double-crimp rolled turn-over.

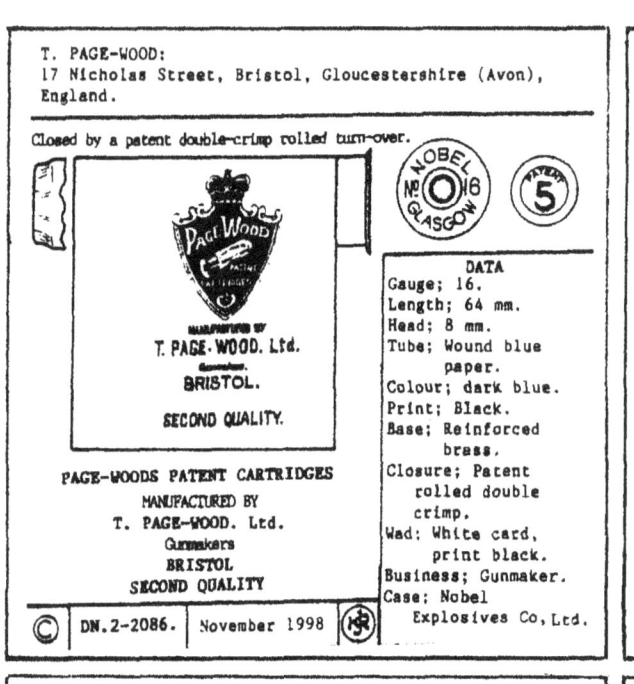

DATA
Gauge; 16.
Length; 64 mm.
Head; 8 mm.
Tube; Wound blue paper.
Colour; dark blue.
Print; Black.
Base; Reinforced brass.
Closure; Patent rolled double crimp.
Wad; White card, print black.
Business; Gunmaker.
Case; Nobel Explosives Co, Ltd.

PAGE-WOODS PATENT CARTRIDGES
MANUFACTURED BY
T. PAGE-WOOD. Ltd.
Gunmakers
BRISTOL
SECOND QUALITY

© DN.2-2086.   November 1998

T. PAGE-WOOD, LTD: 17 Nicholas Street. Later at, Pipe Lane, Bristol, Gloucestershire (Avon), England.

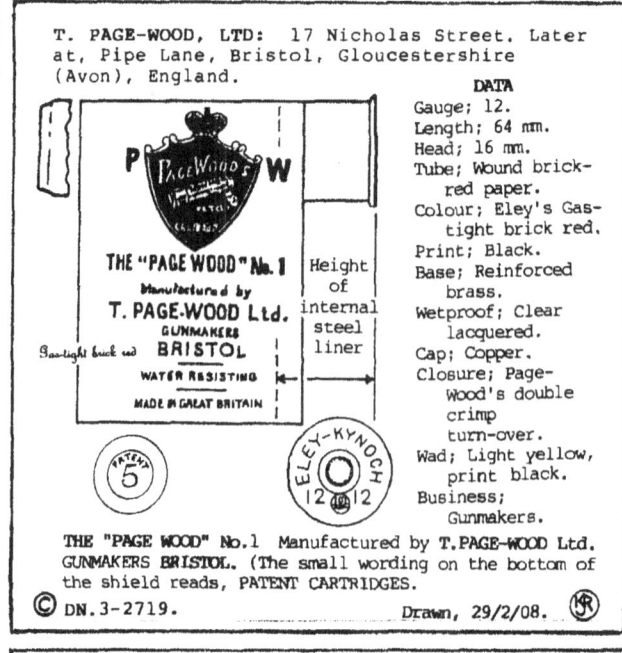

DATA
Gauge; 12.
Length; 64 mm.
Head; 16 mm.
Tube; Wound brick-red paper.
Colour; Eley's Gas-tight brick red.
Print; Black.
Base; Reinforced brass.
Wetproof; Clear lacquered.
Cap; Copper.
Closure; Page-Wood's double crimp turn-over.
Wad; Light yellow, print black.
Business; Gunmakers.

THE "PAGE WOOD" No.1 Manufactured by T.PAGE-WOOD Ltd. GUNMAKERS BRISTOL. (The small wording on the bottom of the shield reads, PATENT CARTRIDGES.

© DN.3-2719.   Drawn, 29/2/08.

T. PAGE-WOOD, LTD: 17 Nicholas Street, Bristol, Gloucestershire (Avon), England.

DATA
Gauge; 12.
Length; 64 mm.
Head; 16 mm.
Tube; Wound crimson paper.
Print; Black.
Base; Brass.
Cap; Copper.
Closure; Double rolled top.
Wad; Canary-yellow, print black.
Business; Gunmakers.

Not examined internally.

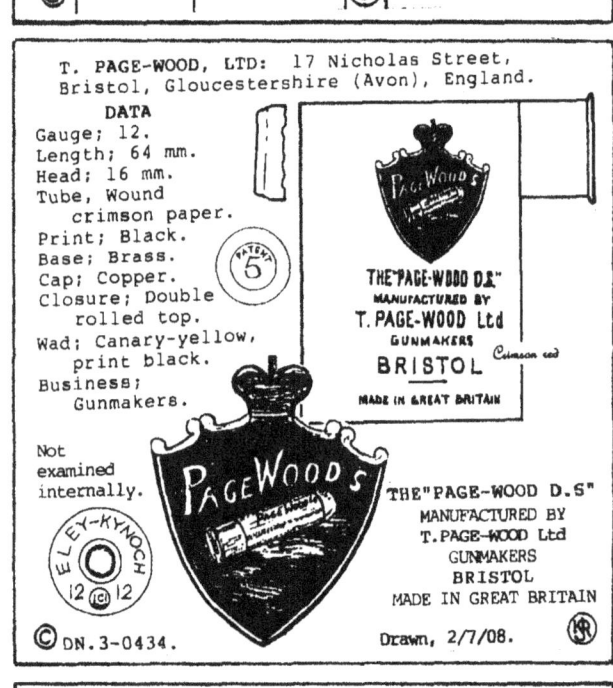

THE "PAGE-WOOD D.S"
MANUFACTURED BY
T. PAGE-WOOD Ltd
GUNMAKERS
BRISTOL
MADE IN GREAT BRITAIN

© DN.3-0434.   Drawn, 2/7/08.

T. PAGE-WOOD, LTD: 17 Nicholas Street. Bristol, Gloucestershire (Avon), England.

DATA
Gauge; 12.
Length; 64 mm.
Head; 8 mm.
Tube; Wound eau-de-nil paper.
Print; Black or dark blue.

Inner steel

Base; Reinforced brass.
Closure; Patent rolled double crimp.
Wad; Red, print black.
Business; Gunmakers and cartridge loaders.

© DN.3-0437.   Drawn, 6/5/08.

T. PAGE-WOOD, LTD: 17 Nicholas Street. Later at, 18 Pipe Lane, Bristol, Gloucestershire (Avon), England.

DATA
Gauge; 12.
Length; 64 mm.
Head; 8 mm.
Tube; Wound papers.
Colours; Grey-green or eau-de-nil.
Printings; Black or dark blue.
Base; Reinforced brass.
Closure; Page-Wood's double crimp turn-over.
Wad; Light yellow, print black.
Business; Gunmakers.

THE "PAGE WOOD SHIELD"

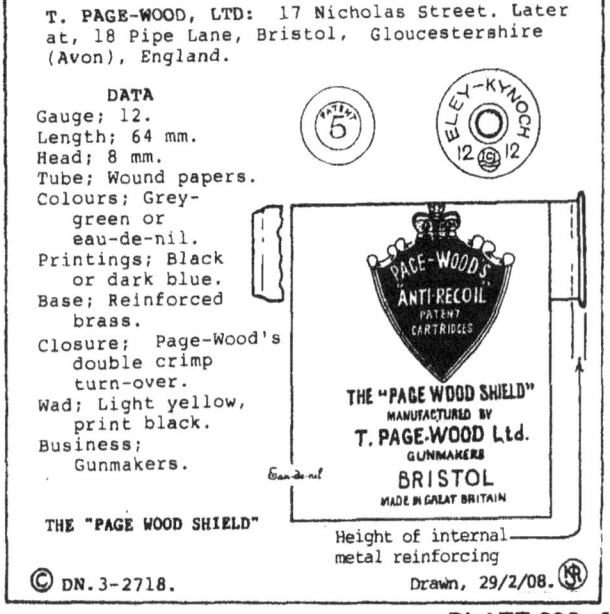

Height of internal metal reinforcing

© DN.3-2718.   Drawn, 29/2/08.

T. PAGE-WOOD, LTD:
17 Nicholas Street, Bristol, Gloucestershire (Avon), England.

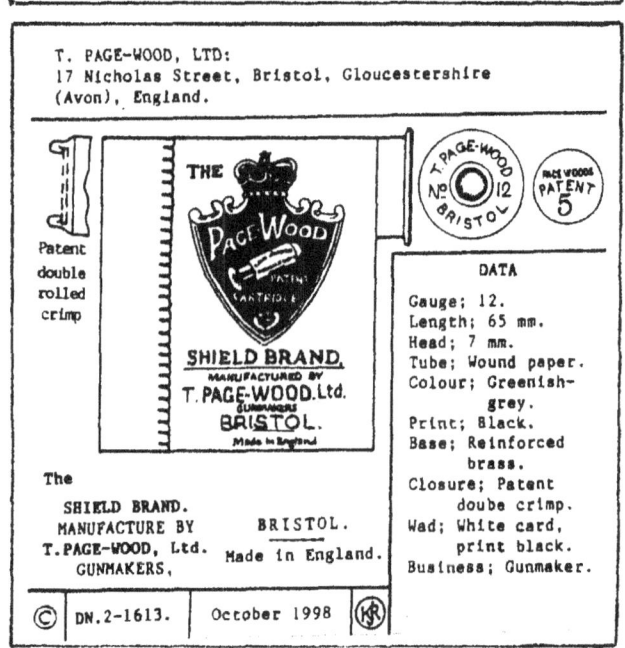

Patent double rolled crimp

DATA
Gauge; 12.
Length; 65 mm.
Head; 7 mm.
Tube; Wound paper.
Colour; Greenish-grey.
Print; Black.
Base; Reinforced brass.
Closure; Patent doube crimp.
Wad; White card, print black.
Business; Gunmaker.

The
SHIELD BRAND.
MANUFACTURE BY
T. PAGE-WOOD, Ltd.
GUNMAKERS,
BRISTOL.
Made in England.

© DN.2-1613.   October 1998

PLATE 298 [PAG - PAG]

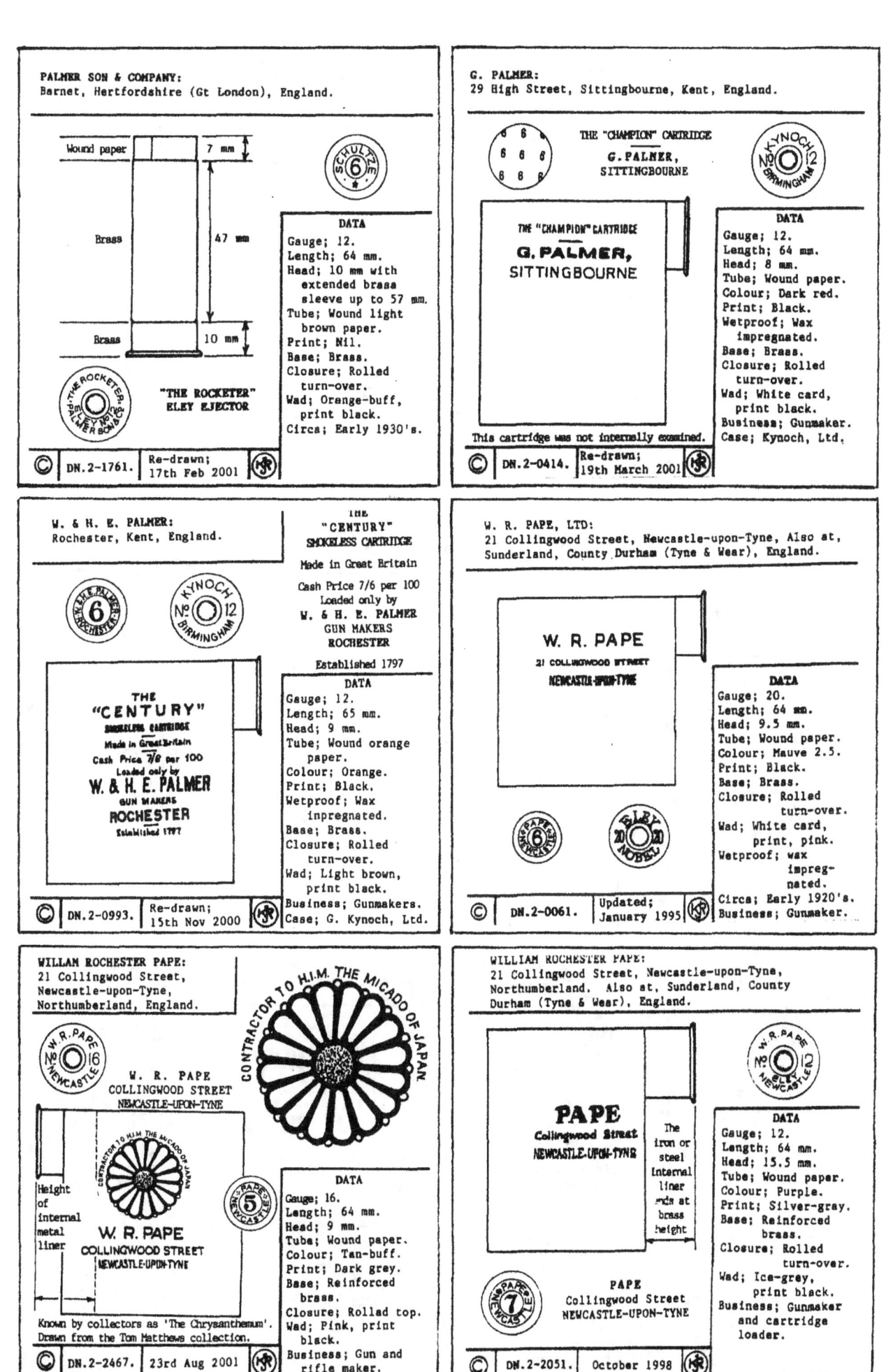

PLATE 299 [PAL - PAP]

WILLIAM ROCHESTER PAPE:
21 Collingwood Street, Newcastle-upon-Tyne, Northumberland. Also at, Sunderland, County Durham (Tyne & Wear), England

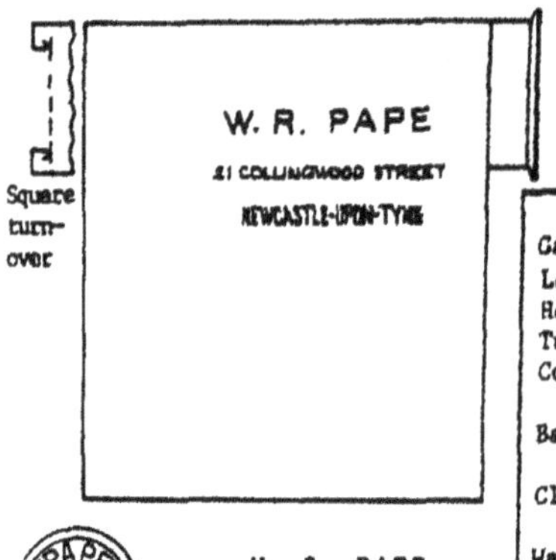

W. R. PAPE
21 COLLINGWOOD STREET
NEWCASTLE-UPON-TYNE

W. R. PAPE
21 COLLINGWOOD STREET
NEWCASTLE-UPON-TYNE

Square turn-over

Headstamp: KYNOCH NOBEL 12 12
Headstamp: PAPE NEWCASTLE No 6

DATA
Gauge; 12.
Length; 64 mm.
Head; 7.5 mm.
Tube; Wound paper.
Colour; Pinkish-red.
Base; Reinforced brass.
Closure; Rolled turn-over.
Wad; White card, print pink.
Business; Gunmaker.
Case; Nobel Industries, Ltd.
Circa; 1920's.

© DN.2-2044.   November 1998

WILLIAM ROCHESTER PAPE:
21 Collingwood Street, Newcastle-upon-Tyne, Northumberland. Also at, Sunderland, County Durham (Tyne & Wear), England.

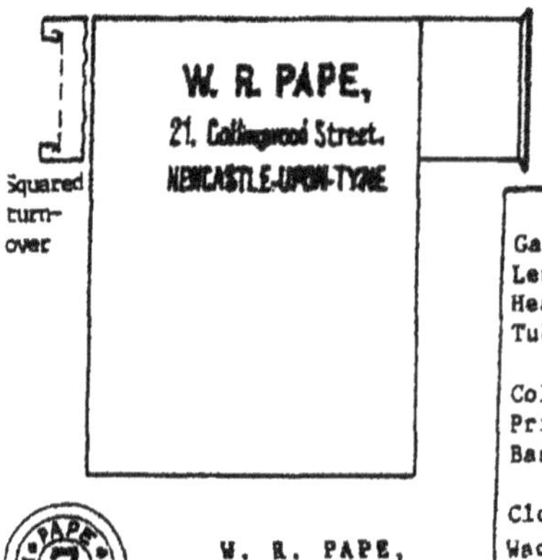

W. R. PAPE,
21. Collingwood Street.
NEWCASTLE-UPON-TYNE

W. R. PAPE,
21, Collingwood Street,
NEWCASTLE-UPON-TYNE

Squared turn-over

Headstamp: ELEY NOBEL 12 12
Headstamp: PAPE NEWCASTLE No 7

DATA
Gauge; 12.
Length; 64 mm.
Head; 16 mm.
Tube; Wound green paper.
Colour; Dark green.
Print; Black.
Base; Reinforced brass.
Closure; Rolled.
Wad; White card, print red.
Business; Gunmaker and cartridge loader.
Case; Nobel Industries, Ltd.

© DN.2-2068.   October 1998

W. R. PAPE:
21 Collingwood Street. Newcastle-upon-Tyne, Northumberland (Tyne & Wear). Also in, Sunderland, County Durham (Tyne & Wear), England.

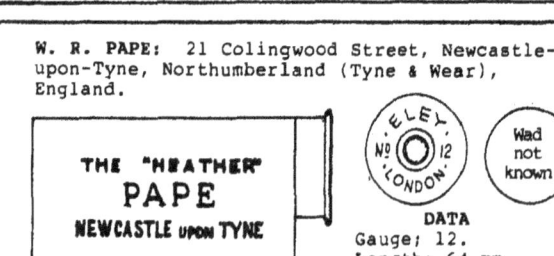

Headstamp: PAPE NEWCASTLE No 4
Headstamp: W R PAPE ELEY NEWCASTLE No 12

DATA
Gauge; 12.
Length; 64 mm.
Head; 10 mm.
Tube; Wound paper.
Colour; Dull orange.
Print; Black.
Base; Brass.
Closure; Rolled turn-over.
Wad; Pink 3, print black.
Business; Gun and rifle maker.

The case wall printing on this cartridge is a picture of Pape's gun and rifle works. On the actual cartridge, guns can be seen displayed in the shop window.

© DN.2-0064.   Updated; February 1995

W. R. PAPE: 21 Colingwood Street, Newcastle-upon-Tyne, Northumberland (Tyne & Wear), England.

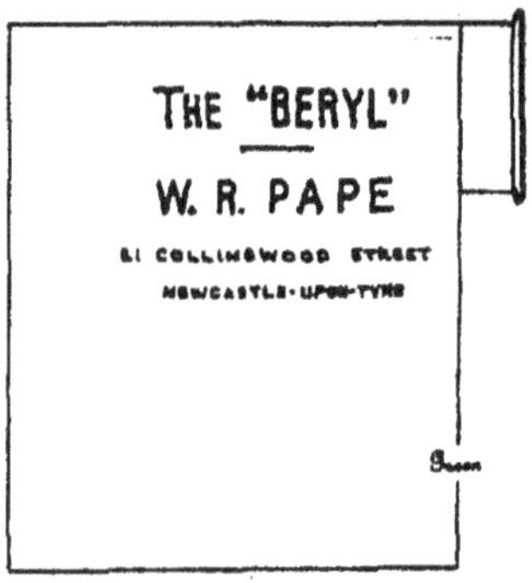

THE "BERYL"
W. R. PAPE
21 COLLINGWOOD STREET
NEWCASTLE-UPON-TYNE

THE "BERYL"
W. R. PAPE
21 COLINGWOOD STREET
NEWCASTLE-UPON-TYNE

Headstamp: KYNOCH BIRMINGHAM No 12
Wad not known

DATA
Gauge; 12
Length; 64 mm.
Head; 8 mm.
Tube; wound paper.
Colour; Greyish-green.
Print; Black.
Base; Brass.
Cap; Copper.
Closure; Rolled turn-over.
Wad; Not known.
Business; Gunmaker.
Case by; Kynoch & Co.

This cartridge was named after William Pape's wife.

Drawn, 18/3/08.
© DN.3-2783.

W. R. PAPE: 21 Colingwood Street, Newcastle-upon-Tyne, Northumberland (Tyne & Wear), England.

THE "HEATHER"
PAPE
NEWCASTLE upon TYNE

THE "HEATHER"
PAPE
NEWCASTLE UPON TYNE

Headstamp: ELEY LONDON No 12
Wad not known

DATA
Gauge; 12.
Length; 64 mm.
Head; 8 mm.
Tube; Wound paper.
Colour; Mauve.
Print; Black.
Base; Brass.
Cap; Copper.
Closure; Rolled turn-over.
Wad; Not known.
Business; Gunmaker.
Case by; Eley Bros, Ltd.

This cartridge may have been named after William Pape's daughter.

Drawn, 18/3/08.
© DN.3-2782.

THE PARAGON GUN SPECIALISTS: 43 Ann Street, Belfast, Northern Ireland.

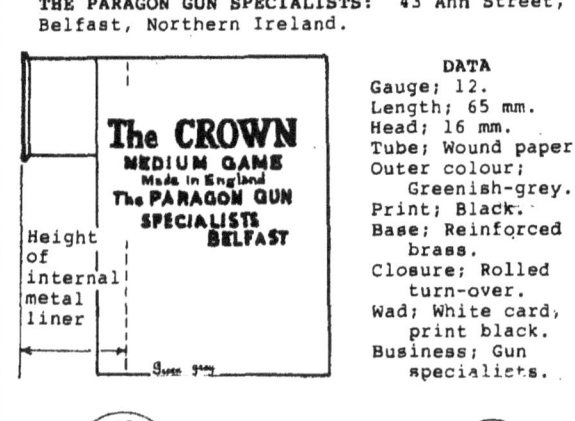

The CROWN
MEDIUM GAME
Made in England
The PARAGON GUN SPECIALISTS
BELFAST

The CROWN
MEDIUM GAME

Height of internal metal liner

Headstamp: SPECIAL SMOKELESS 12 12

DATA
Gauge; 12.
Length; 65 mm.
Head; 16 mm.
Tube; Wound paper.
Outer colour; Greenish-grey.
Print; Black.
Base; Reinforced brass.
Closure; Rolled turn-over.
Wad; White card, print black.
Business; Gun specialists.

© DN.3-2564.   Drawn, 6/6/07.

PLATE 300 [PAP – PAR]

HUGH PARKER:
Port Elizabeth, Cape of Good Hope (Cape Province), Republic of South Africa.

DATA
- Gauge; 12.
- Length; 64 mm.
- Head; 16 mm.
- Tube; Wound red paper.
- Colour; Eley's brick red.
- Print; Black.
- Base; Reinforced brass.
- Closure; Rolled turn-over.
- Wad; Brown card, print black.
- Wetproof; Clear lacquered.
- Circa; 1930's.

"HUGH PARKER'S SPECIAL"
PORT ELIZABETH
MADE IN GREAT BRITAIN

DN.2-2357. 20th Sept 2000

TOM PARKINSON:
Ulverston, Lancashire (Cumbria), England.

This drawing was made from a part loaded case.

TOM PARKINSON ULVERSTON.

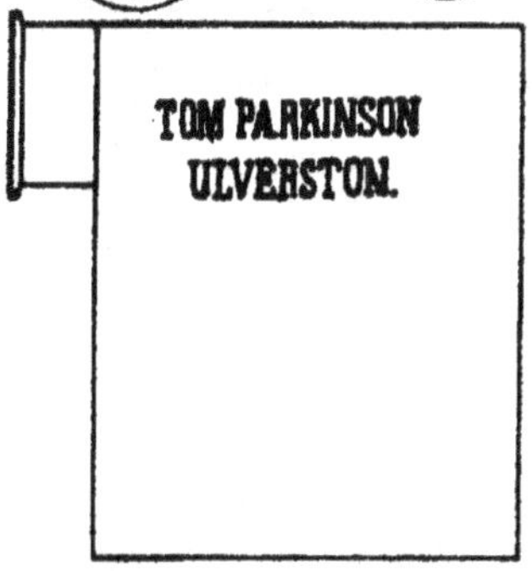

DATA
- Gauge; 12.
- Length; 65 mm.
- Head; 11 mm.
- Tube; wound brown paper.
- Colour; Maroon.
- Print; Silvery-gold.
- Base; Brass.
- Closure; Rolled turn-over.
- Wad; Not known

DN.2-0892. Re-drawn 18th Feb 1999

C. PARSONS:
Nuneaton. Also, Coventry Warwickshire (Midlands). Also at, Hinkley, Leicestershire, England.

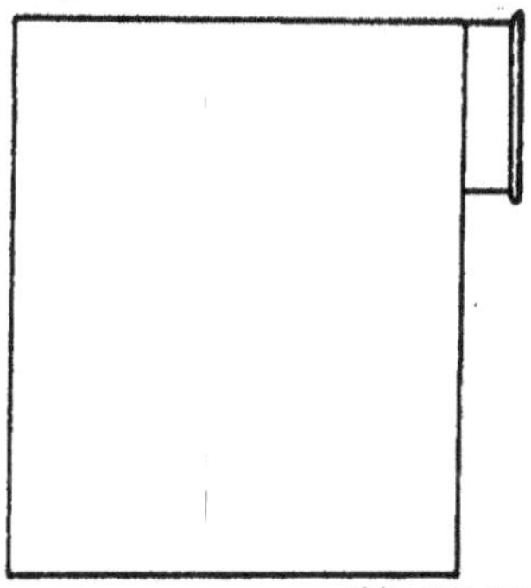

This firm later became, Parsons Sherwin & Company.

DATA
- Gauge; 12
- Length; 64 mm.
- Head; 8 mm.
- Tube; Wound brown (Rough quality) paper.
- Printings; Nil.
- Base; Brass.
- Closure; Rolled turn-over.
- Wad; White card, print black.
- Business; Agricultural and hardware merchants. Also cartridge loaders.

This case may have been made by Kynoch as one of their 'Witton Brand' cases.

DN.2-0424. Updated; 8th June 2001

C. PARSON:
Nuneaton, Warwickshire. Also at, Hinckley, Leicestershire, England.

DATA
- Gauge; 12.
- Length; 64 mm.
- Head; 8 mm.
- Tube; Wound brown paper.
- Colour; Cowpat-brown.
- Print; Black.
- Wad; Not known.
- Base; Brass.
- Cap; Copper.
- Business; Agricultural and hardware merchants.

PARSON'S
SPECIAL LOADING,
NUNEATON, HINCKLEY
AND
COVENTRY

Drawn from photographs of an unused case.

DN.3-2611. Drawn, 8/11/07.

C. PARSONS:
Nuneaton, Warwickshire. Also at, Hinckley, Leicestershire, England.

PARSON'S
SPECIAL LOADING,
NUNEATON, HINCKLEY,
AND
COVENTRY.

DATA
- Gauge; 12.
- Length; 65 mm.
- Head; 7 mm.
- Tube; Wound paper.
- Colour; Turquoise.
- Print; Dark blue.
- Base; Brass.
- Closure; Rolled turn-over.
- Wad; White card, print black.
- Business; Agricultural and hardware merchants.
- Circa; 1920's.

DN.2-0742. Re-drawn; 7th Feb 2000.

PARSONS, SHERWIN & CO, LTD:
Station Road, Hinckley, Leicestershire. Also at, Nuneaton, Warwickshire, England.

The drawn example was not tested for internal metal reinforcing.

Parsons, Sherwin & Co, Ld
NUNEATON & HINCKLEY
SPECIAL LOADING

DATA
- Gauge; 12.
- Length; 64 mm.
- Head; 8 mm.
- Tube; Wound paper.
- Colour; Pale greenish-grey.
- Print; Black.
- Base; Brass.
- Closure; Rolled turn-over.
- Wad shown; dark orange, print black.
- Business; Agricultural and hardware.

DN.2-2362. 21st Sept 2000

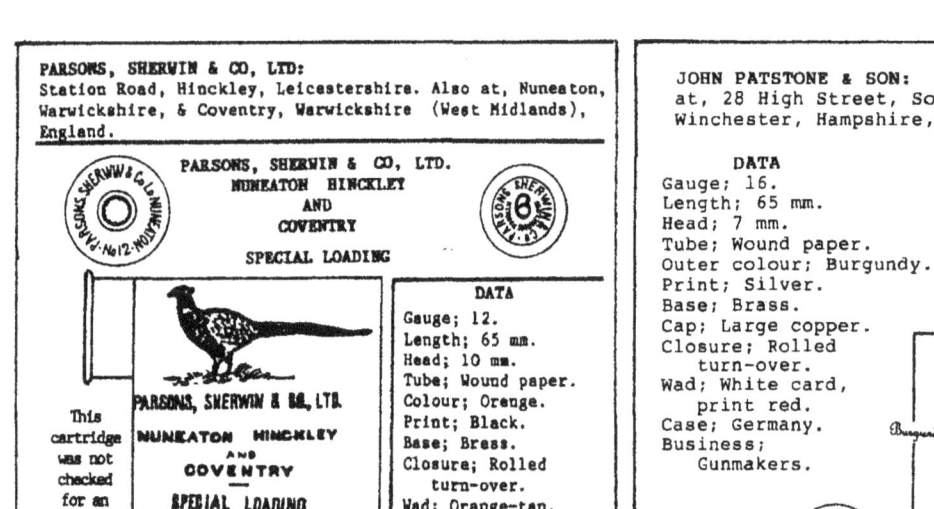
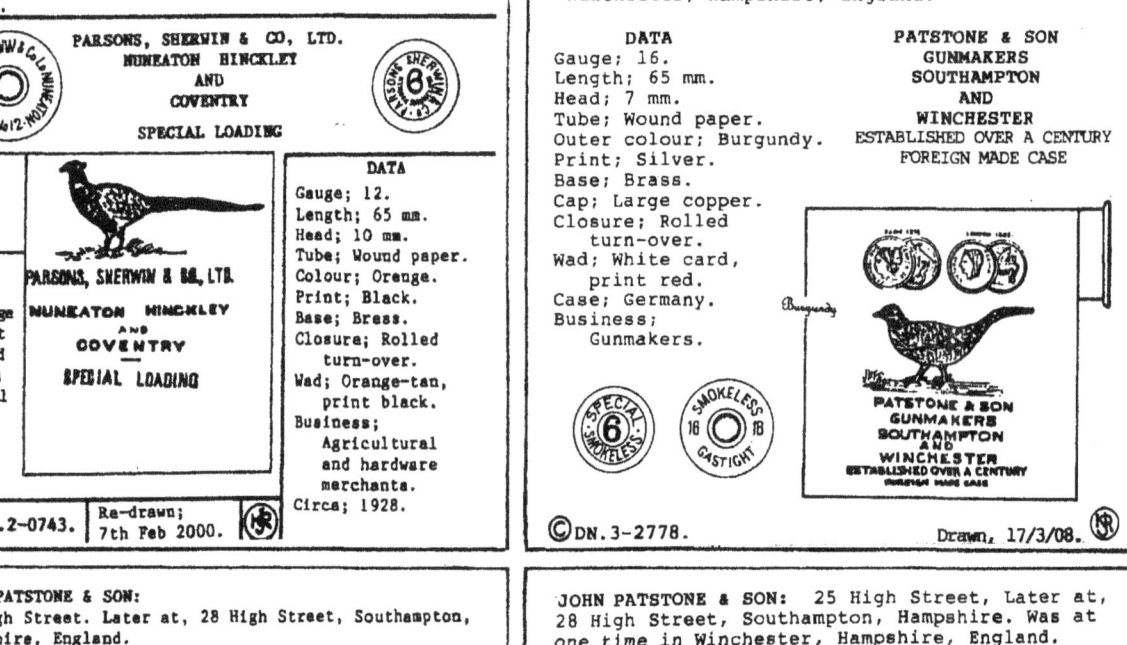
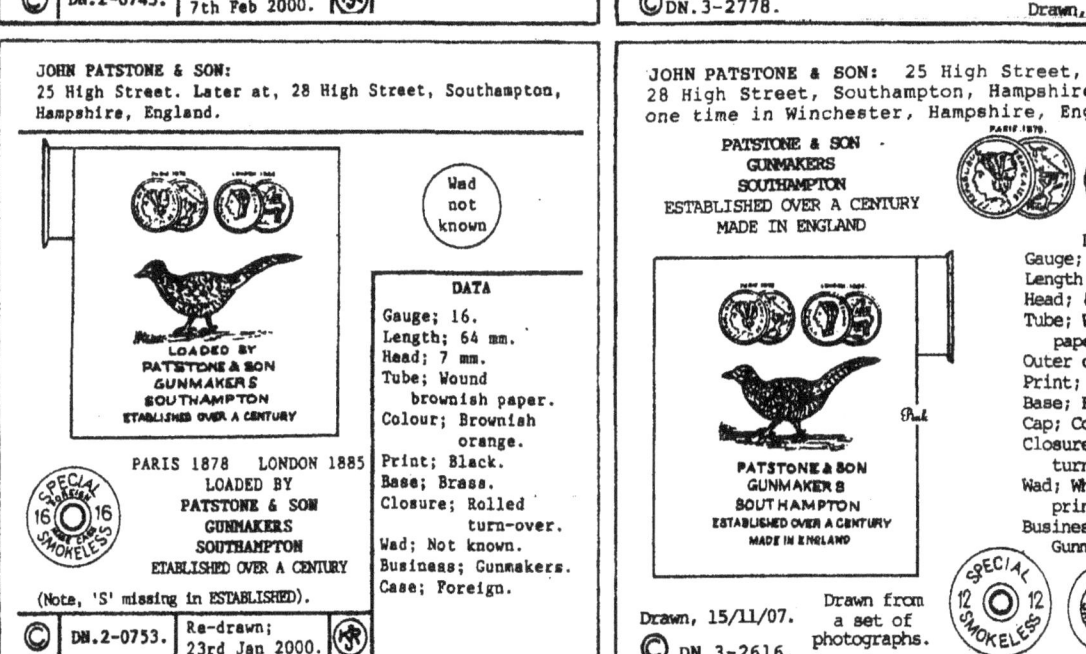
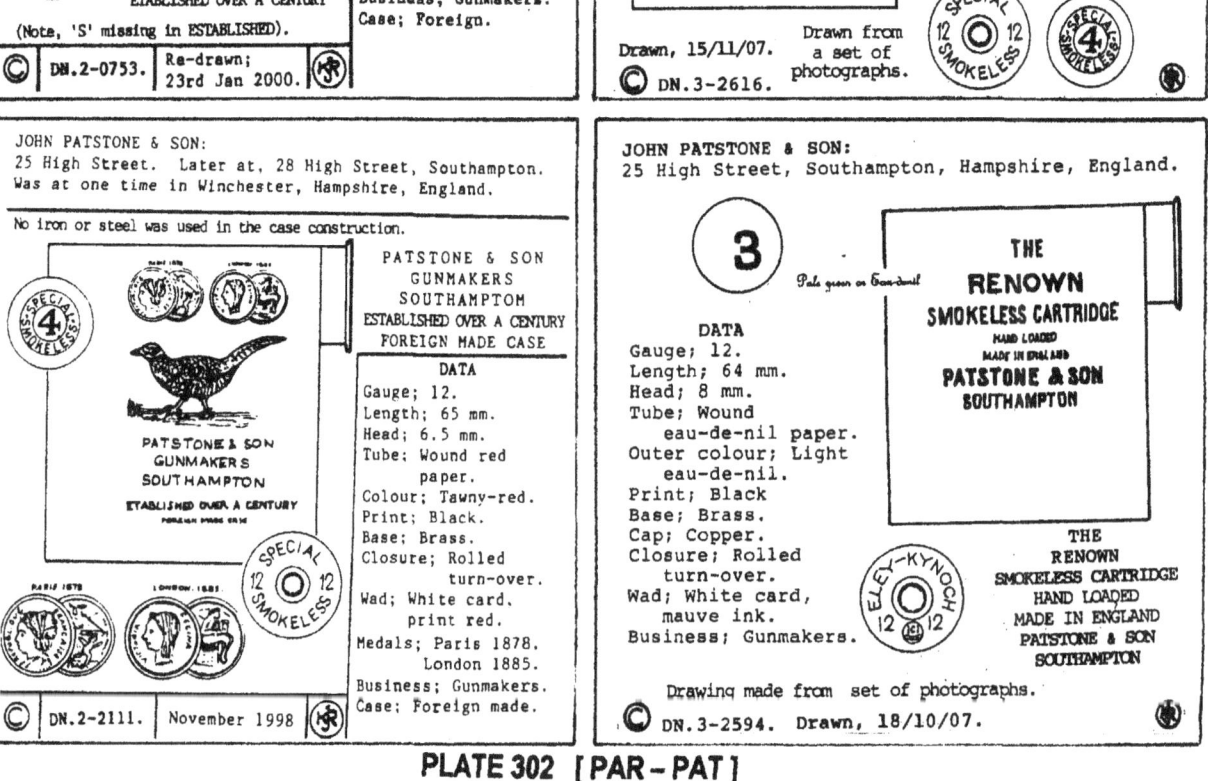

PLATE 302 [PAR - PAT]

PATSTONE & COX:
28 High Street, Also at, 7 Bernard Street, Southampton, Hampshire; England.

DATA
Gauge; 12.
Length; 64 mm.
Head; 8 mm.
Tube; Wound orange paper.
Colour; Orange.
Print; Black.
Base; Reinforced brass.
Closure; Rolled turn-over.
Wad; Brown card, print black.
Wetproof; Clear lacquered.
Business; Gunmakers.
Circa; 1938.

DN.2-1337. Re-drawn; 17th dec 2000

PATSTONE & COX: 25 HIGH STREET, SOUTHAMPTON, HAMPSHIRE.
Business. Gunmakers.

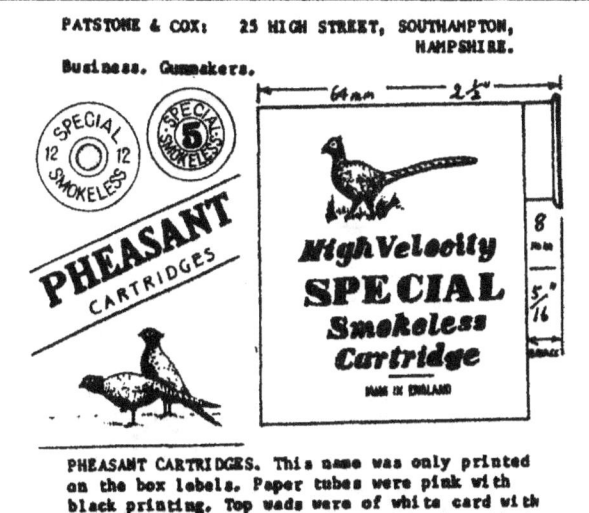

PHEASANT CARTRIDGES. This name was only printed on the box labels. Paper tubes were pink with black printing. Top wads were of white card with red printing. Some of these cartridge boxes had printed on the side, W. A. WELCH, Saddler and Pathletic outfitter. 90-92 Southampton Road and also at, 2e High Street, Eastleigh.
DN.818.

S. PAXTON & COMPANY:
High Street, Stokesley, North Riding, Yorkshire, England.

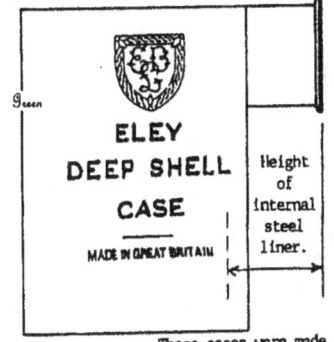

Height of internal steel liner.

ELEY DEEP SHELL CASE

These cases were made in lengths of 51 mm, 64mm and 70 mm. They were purchased and loaded by many of the smaller firms.

(Firm now extinct).

DATA
Gauge; 12.
Length; 64 mm.
Head; 16 mm.
Tube: Wound dark green paper.
Colour; Dark green.
Print; Black.
Wetproof; Clear lacquered.
Base; Brass with reinforcing.
Closure; Rolled.
Wad; White card, print black.
Circa; 1937.
Business; Ironmongers.

DN.3-2522. Revised;19/12/08.

JOSEPH PEACE, LIMITED:
Darlington, County Durham, England.

ELEY "G.P." CASE
Made in Great Britain

Formerly known as Grand Prix Quality Case, they were loaded by many. This example drawn was loaded by J. Peace.

ELEY "G.P." CASE

DATA
Gauge; 12.
Length; 64 mm.
Head; 8 mm.
Tube; Wound orange paper.
Colour; Orange 3.
Print; Black.
Base; Brass.
Closure; Rolled turn-over.
Wad; Dark blue, print black.
Wetproof; Lacquered.
Circa; Early 1930's.
Business; Gunmaker and sports outfitter.

DN.2-1311. Updated; February 1995

PEARSON & COMPANY:
Grimsby, Lincolnshire (Humberside), England.

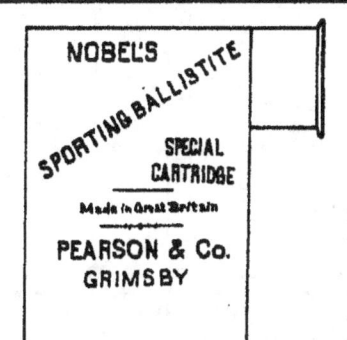

This drawing was made from a set of photographs.

NOBEL'S SPORTING BALLISTITE SPECIAL CARTRIDGE

DATA
Gauge; 12.
Length; 64 mm.
Head; 16 mm.
Tube; Wound paper.
Colour; Old straw white.
Print; Black.
Base; Brass.
Closure; Rolled turn-over.
Wad; Red, print black.

DN.2-1839. September 1995

CAPTAIN E. PELLIER-JOHNSON:
Address not know. Believed in Great Britain.

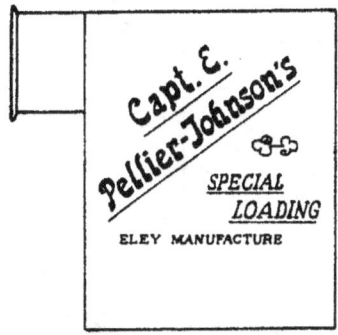

Wad not known

Drawing made by using a set of photographs.

Capt. E. Pellier-Johnson's SPECIAL LOADING ELEY MANUFACTURE

DATA
Gauge; 12.
Length; 70 mm.
Head; 16 mm.
Tube; Wound paper.
Colour; Crimson red.
Print; Black.
Base; Brass.
Closure; Rolled turn-over.
Wad; Not known.
Case; Eley Bros Ltd.
Business; Private cartridge.

DN.2-2021. November 1997.

PLATE 303 [PAT - PEL]

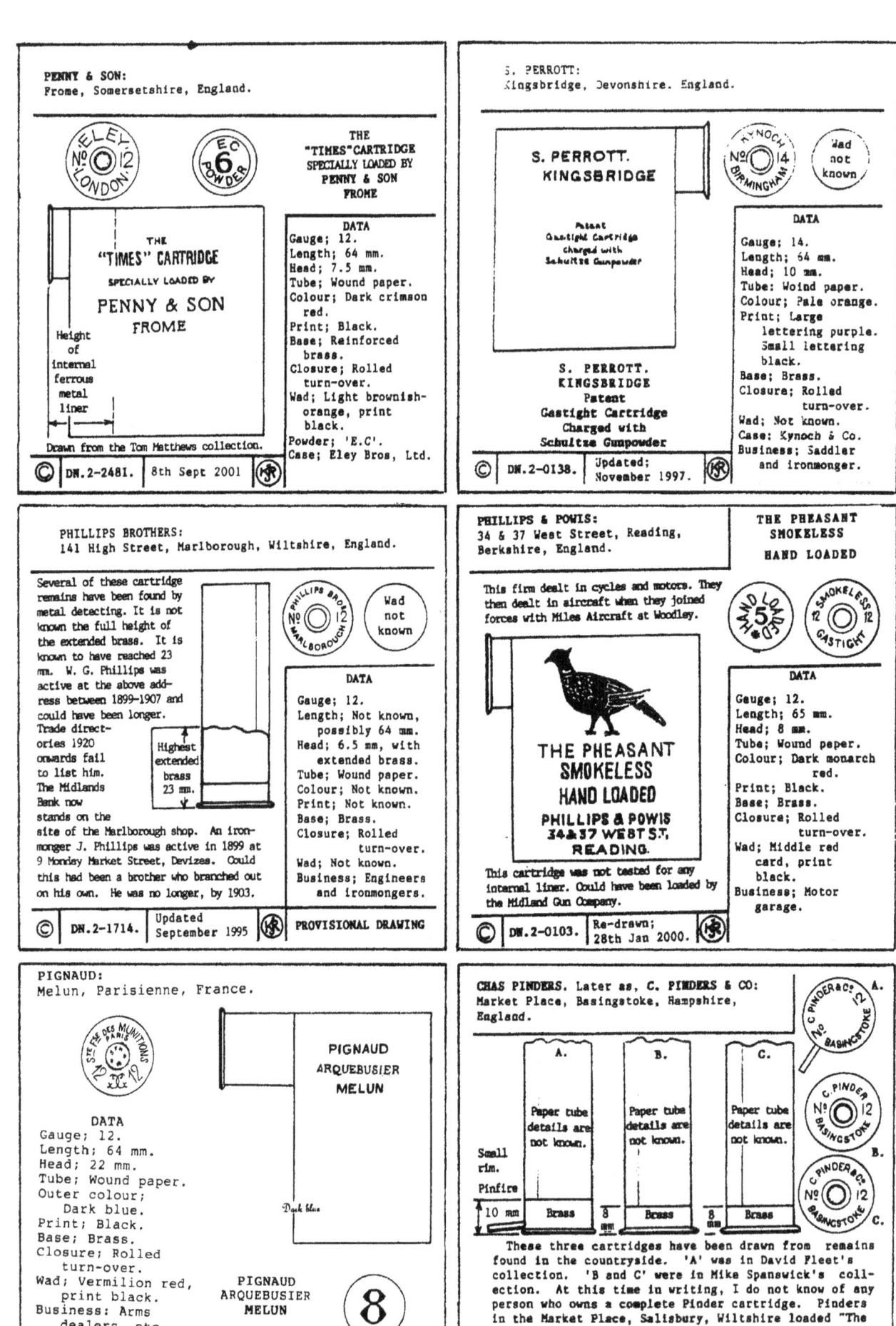

J. E. PINDER:
1 Winchester Street, (Market Place), Salisbury, Wiltshire, England.

Drawing made from the Michael Snell Collection.

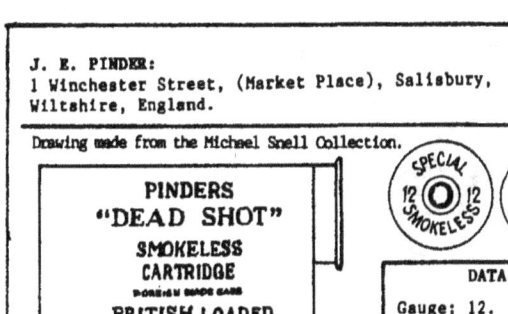

PINDERS
"DEAD SHOT"
SMOKELESS
CARTRIDGE
FOREIGN MADE CASE
BRITISH LOADED
PINDERS
IRONMONGERS
MARKET PLACE
SALISBURY

DATA
Gauge; 12.
Length; 65 mm.
Head; 6 mm.
Tube; Wound brown paper.
Colour; Yellow.
Print; Black.
Base; Brass.
Closure; Rolled turn-over.
Wad; Yellow, print black.
Business; Ironmonger.
Case; Germany.

© DN.2-2445. 10th July 2001

HERBERT B. PITT:
7 Silver Street, Trowbridge, Wiltshire, England.

H. B. PITT'S "PREMIER" CARTRIDGE
LOADED WITH
SCHULTZE POWDER
No. 7 Silver Street
TROWBRIDGE

This cartridge was not checked for any internal metal components

DATA
Gauge; 12.
Length; 64 mm.
Head; 16 mm.
Tube; Wound brown paper.
Colour; Pale brown.
Print; Black.
Base; Brass.
Closure; Rolled turn-over.
Wad; Pinkish orange card, print black.
Business; Ironmonger.
Case; Kynoch, Ltd.
Circa; 1920.

© DN.2-1039. Re-drawn; 2nd May 2000

S. PLUMBERS, LIMITED:
Great Yarmouth, Norfolk, England.

"NORFOLK"
HIGH Velocity LOAD
PLUMBERS LTD
GT YARMOUTH.
GUNS & AMMUNITION

Wad not known

Drawing taken from an unused case.

DATA
Gauge; 12.
Length; 65 mm.
Head; 10 mm.
Tube; Wound brown paper.
Colour; Dull orange.
Print; Black.
Wetproof; Nil.
Internal liner; Nil.
Base; Brass.
Closure; Rolled turn-over.
Wad; Not known.
Business; Dealer in guns and ammunition.

"NORFOLK"
HIGH Velocity LOAD
SP LTD
PLUMBERS LTD
GT YARMOUTH
GUNS & AMMUNITION

© DN.2-0902. Updated; May 1997.

PLUMBERS, LTD:
Great Yarmouth, Norfolk, England.

"THE ORIGINAL NORFOLK"
PLUMBERS LD
GT YARMOUTH

The example drawn was not internally examined for any internal metal structures.

DATA
Gauge; 12.
Length; 65 mm.
Head; 8 mm.
Tube; Wound paper.
Colour; Greyish blue.
Print; Black.
Base; Brass.
Closure; Rolled turn-over.
Wad; Dark red, print black.
Business; Dealers in guns and ammunition.

"THE ORIGINAL NORFOLK"
PLUMBERS LD
GT YARMOUTH

© DN.2-1445. Re-drawn; 1st Nov 2000

PNEUMATIC CARTRIDGE CO, LTD: Bristol, Gloucestershire (Avon), England.

"PNEUMATIC"
CARTRIDGE
SOLE MANUFACTURERS
"PNEUMATIC" CARTRIDGE
CO. LTD.
BRISTOL
MADE IN GREAT BRITAIN

Pink

DATA
Gauge; 12.
Length with roll; 64 mm.
Head; 8 mm.
Tubes; Wound pink papers.
Print; Black.
Bases; Steel reinforced brass. Later, Steel with brass coating.
Closures; Roll turn-over and later six fold crimp.
Wad; Brown card, print black.
Business; Loading shotgun ammo.
Circa; Post World War Two.

All above stampings were used.

"PNEUMATIC"
CARTRIDGE
SOLE MANUFACTURERS
"PNEUMATIC" CARTRIDGE
CO. LTD.
BRISTOL
MADE IN GREAT BRITAIN

© DN.3-2804. Drawn, 21/3/08.

PNEUMATIC CARTRIDGE CO, LTD: 96-98 Holyrood Road, Edinburgh, Midlothian, Scotland.

Trade { "PNEUMA" / "PNEUMATIC" } Marks
"PNEUMATIC" No.1
(METAL LINED)
Sole Manufacturers:
"Pneumatic" Cartridge Co. Ltd.
EDINBURGH
Made in Great Britain

Red

Height of internal steel liner

DATA
Gauge; 12.
Length; 70 mm.
Head; 16 mm.
Tube; Wound red paper.
Colour; Crimson.
Print; Black.
Base; Reinforced brass.
Closure; Rolled turn-over.
Wad; Brown card, print black.
Business; cartridge experts.

"PNEUMATIC" No.1
(METAL LINED)
Sole Manufacturers:
"Pneumatic" Cartridge Co. Ltd.
EDINBURGH
Made in Great Britain

© DN.3-2780. Drawn, 17/3/08.

PLATE 306 [PNE – PNE]

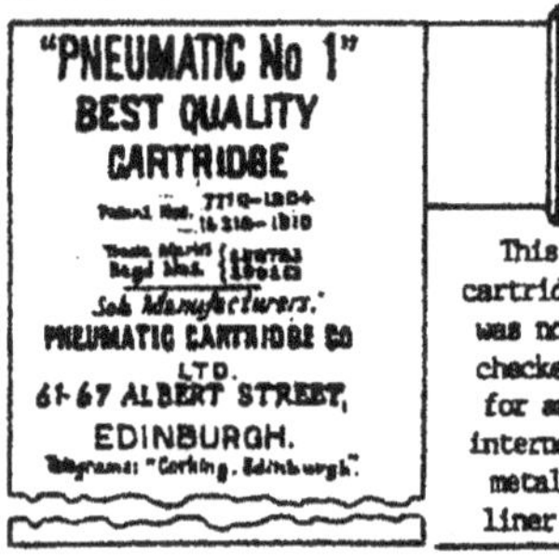

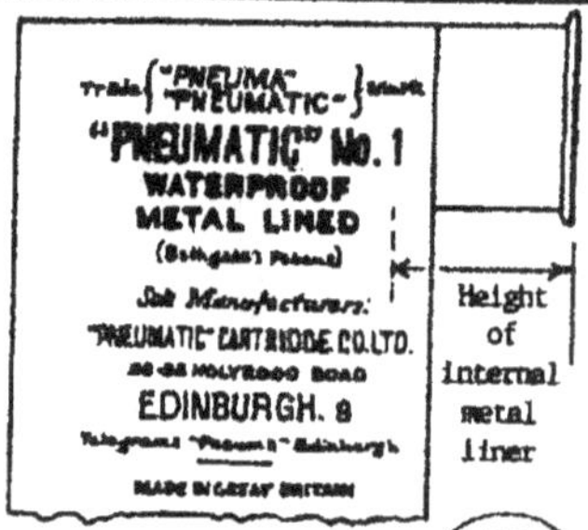

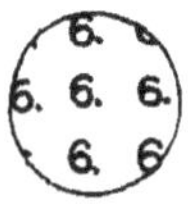

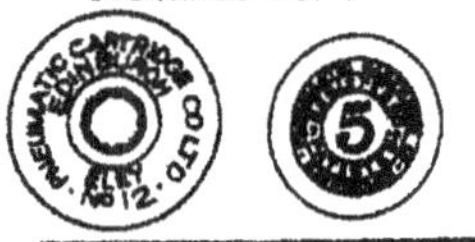

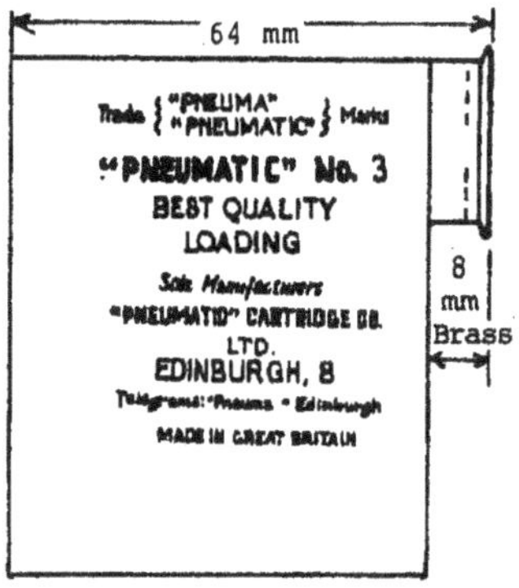

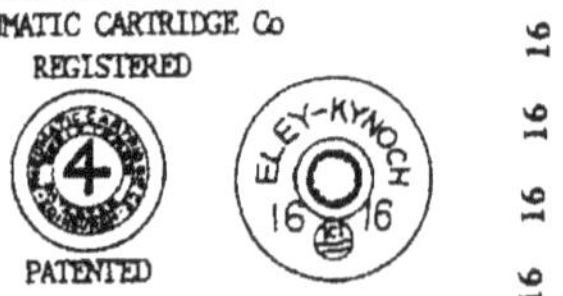

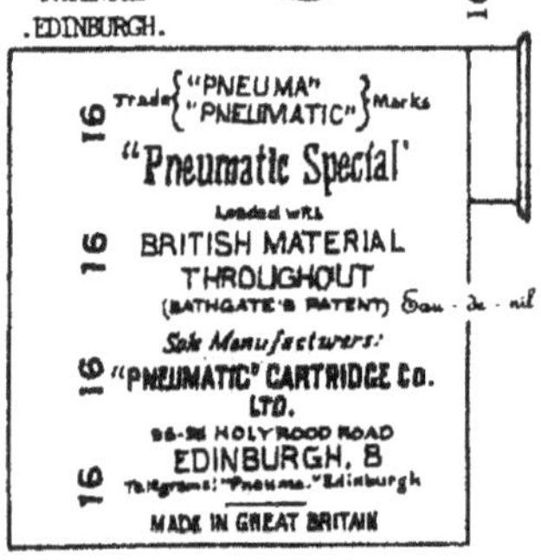

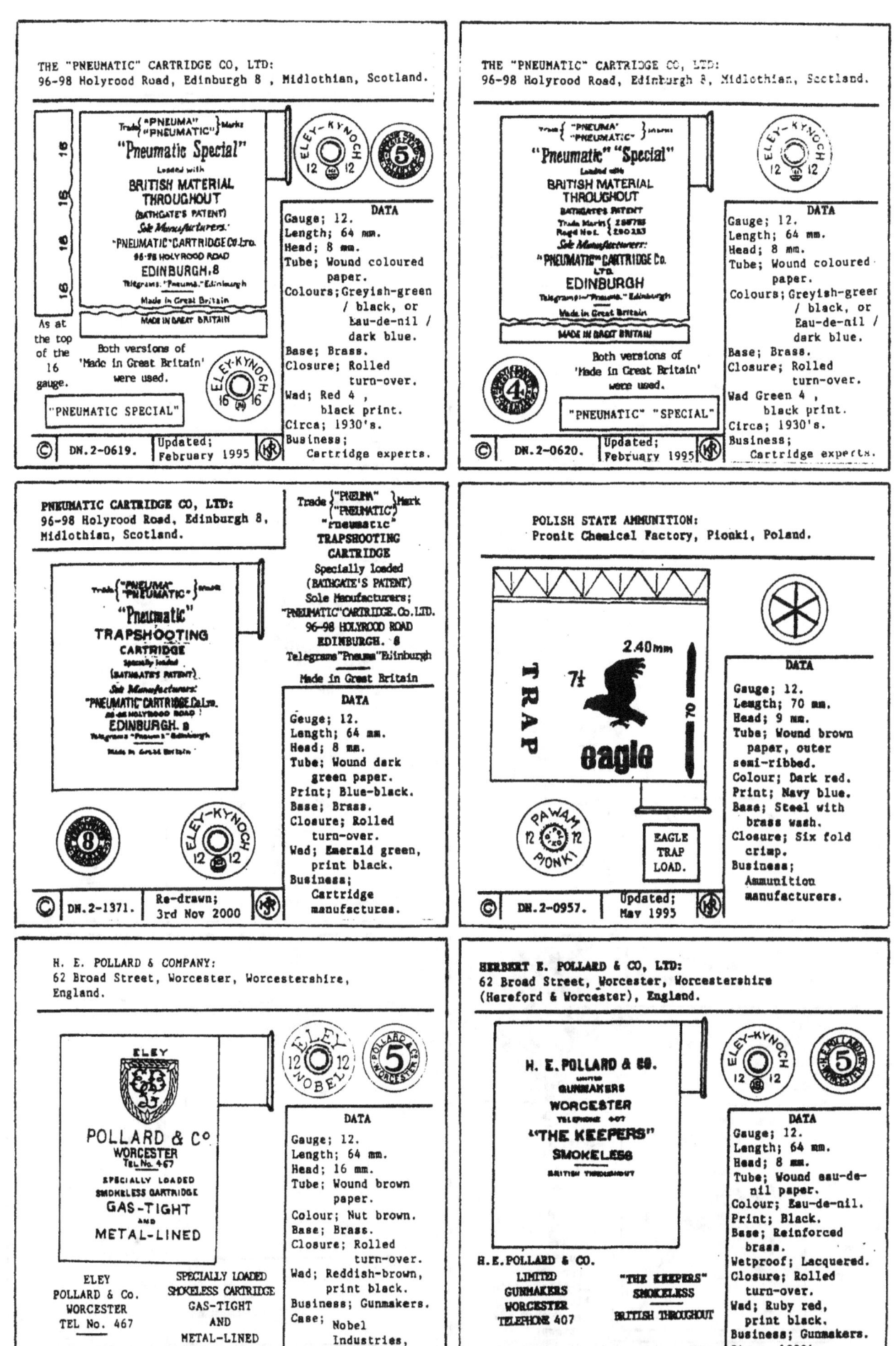

PLATE 307 [PNE - POL]

HERBERT E. POLLARD & COMPANY:
62 Broad Street, Worcester, Worcestershire
(Hereford & Worcester), England.

DATA

Gauge; 16.
Length; 64 mm.
Head; 8 mm.
Tube; Wound paper.
Colour; Crimson.
Print; Black.
Base; Brass.
Closure; Rolled turn-over.
Wad; Buff card, print black.
Business; Gunmakers.
Case; Nobel Explosives, Ltd.

© DN.2-1216. Re-drawn; 27th Nov 2000

HERBERT E. POLLARD & COMPANY:
62 Broad Street, Worcester, Worcestershire
(Hereford & Worcester), England.

DATA

Gauge; 12.
Length; 64 mm.
Head; 16 mm.
Tube; Wound blue paper.
Colour; Middle blue. PANTONE® 312C.
Print; Black.
Base; Brass.
Closure; Rolled turn-over.
Wad; White card, print red.
Circa; 1924.
Business; Gunmakers.

© DN.2-1829. May 1995

POND & SON:
Market Place, Blandford Forum, Dorsetshire, England.

This drawing was made from an unused case. Its rim was hardly worth calling a rim. The firms telephone number was Blandford 1.

DATA

Detonation; Pinfire.
Gauge; 12.
Length; 65 mm.
Head; 12 mm.
Tube; Wound brown paper.
Colour; Dark blue 4.5 outer layer.
Print; Nil.
Base; Brass.
Closure; Rolled turn-over.
Business; Ironmonger

© DN.2-0581. Updated; December 1994

S. E. PORTER & CO:
Whitchurch (Mediolanum), Shropshire, England.

DATA

Gauge; 12.
Length; 64 mm.
Head; 7.5 mm.
Tube; Wound pink paper.
Colour; Mauveish light pink.
Print; Black.
Base; Brass.
Closure; Rolled turn-over.
Wad; White card, print black.
Case; Nobel Industries, Ltd.

© DM.2-2277. 14th April 2000

S. E. PORTER & COMPANY:
Whitchurch, Shropshire, England.

DATA

Gauge; 12.
Length; 64 mm.
Head; 8 mm.
Tube; Wound paper.
Colour; Dark pink.
Print; Black.
Base; Reinforced brass.
Closure; Rolled turn-over.
Wad; Lilac, print black.
Case; Sweden. By Gyttorp.

© DM.2-1921. September 1996

J. M. POSTANS:
Walton-on-Naze, Essex, England.

DATA

Gauge; 12.
Length; 64 mm.
Head; Not recorded.
Tube; Wound paper.
Colour; Reddish-brown.
Print; Nil.
Base; Brass.
Closure; Rolled turn-over.
Wad; White card, print pink.

© DN.2-0657. Re-drawn November 1998

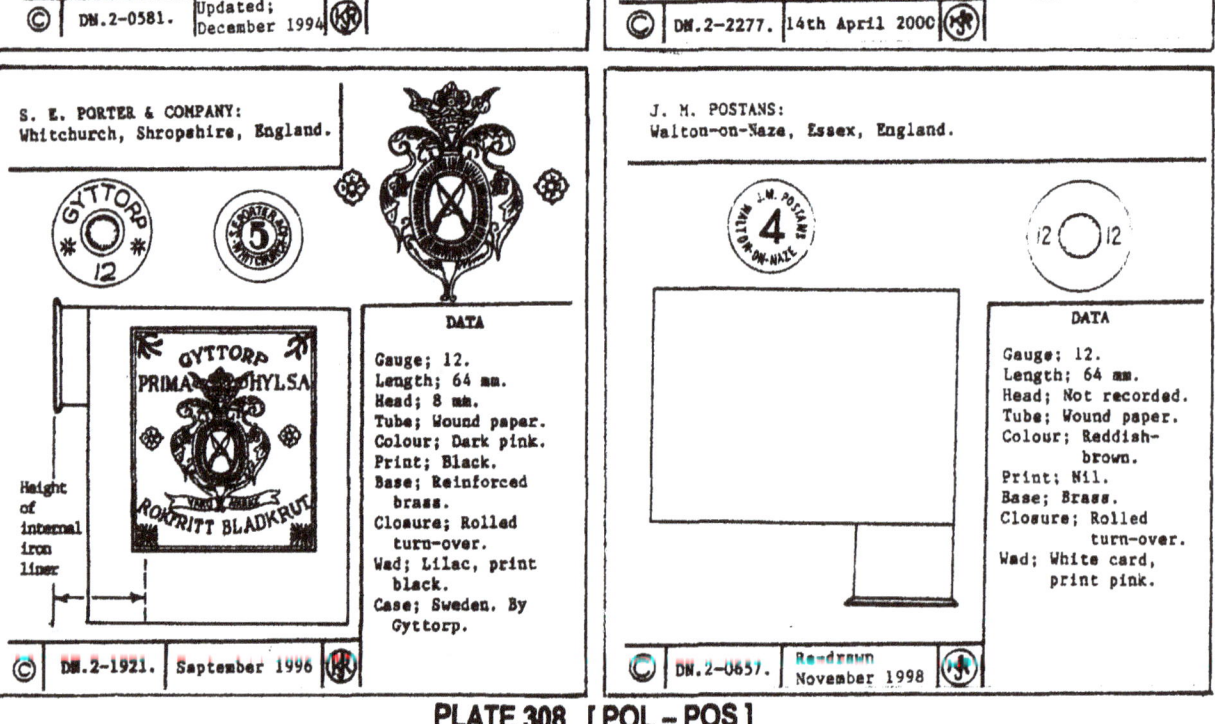

PLATE 308 [POL – POS]

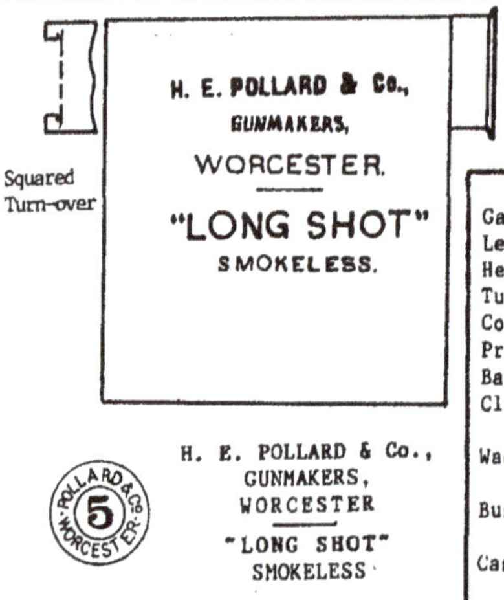

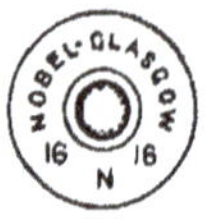

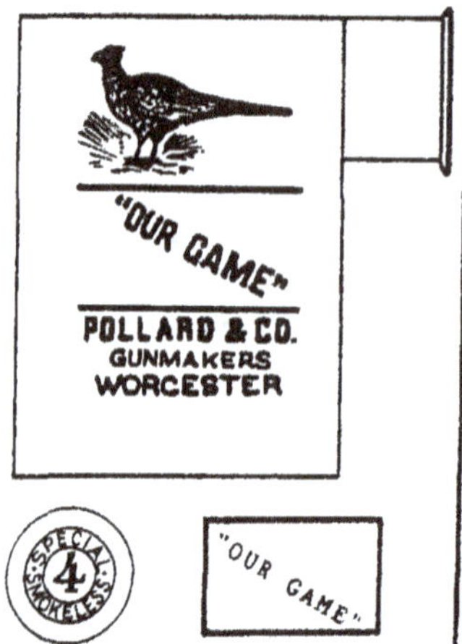

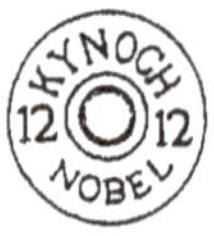

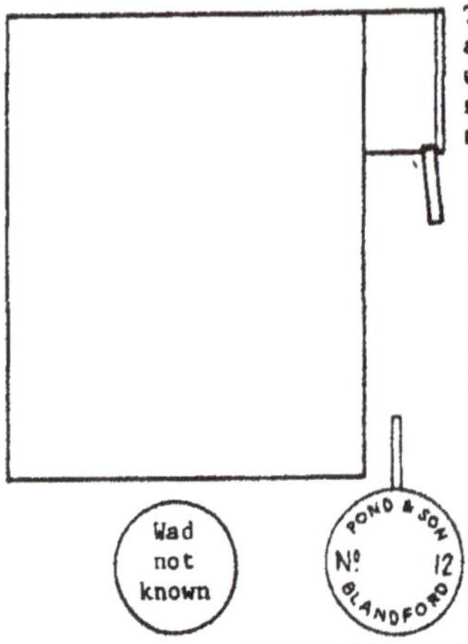

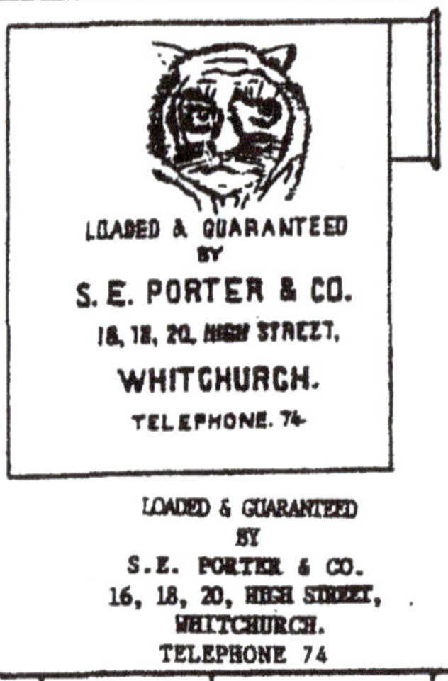

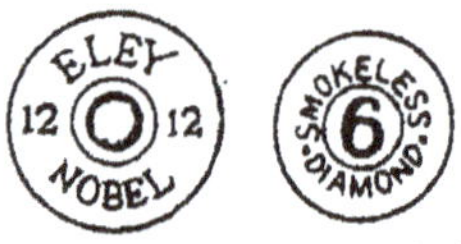

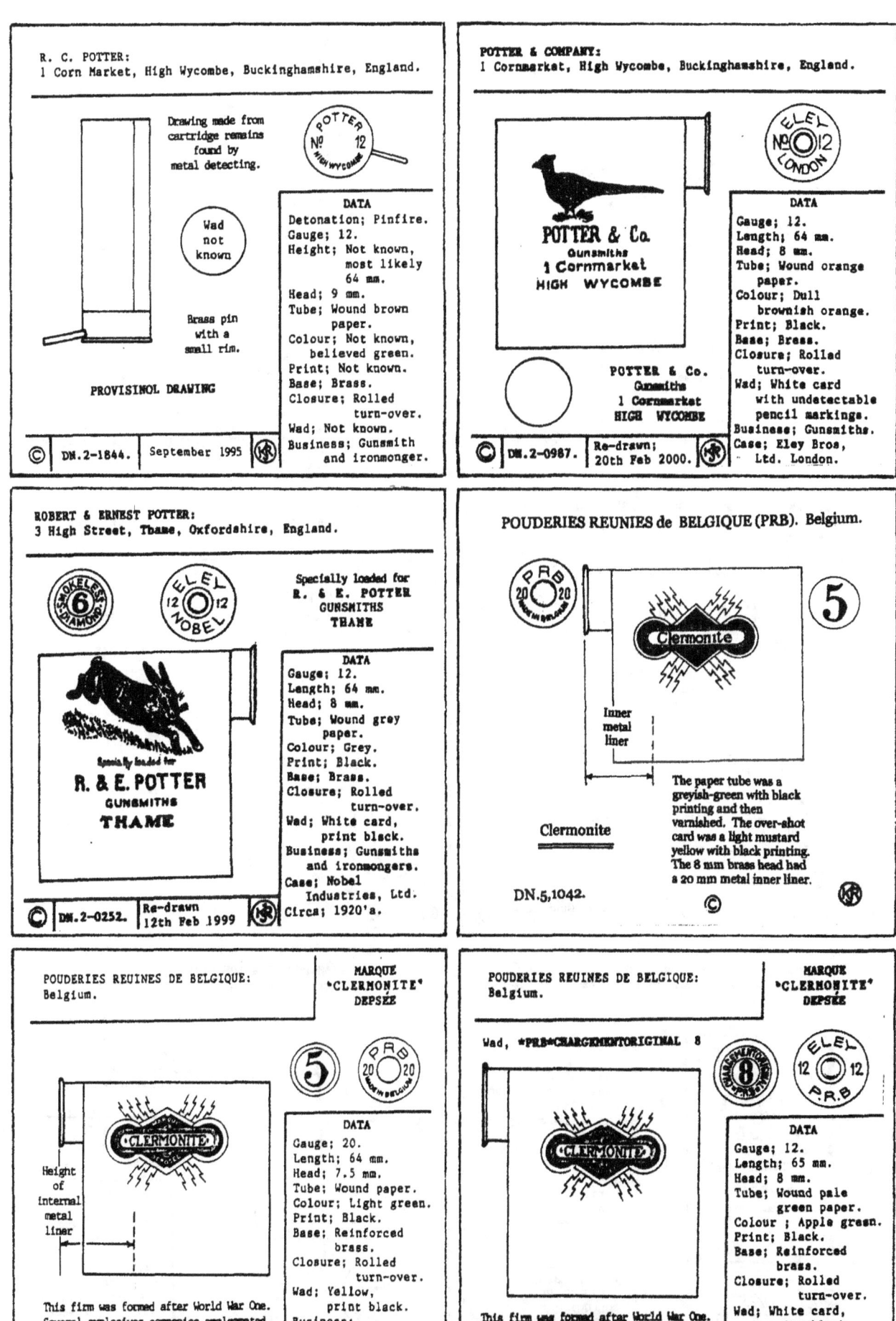

PLATE 309 [POT – POU]

POUDERIES REUNIES de BELGIQUE (PRB). Belgium.

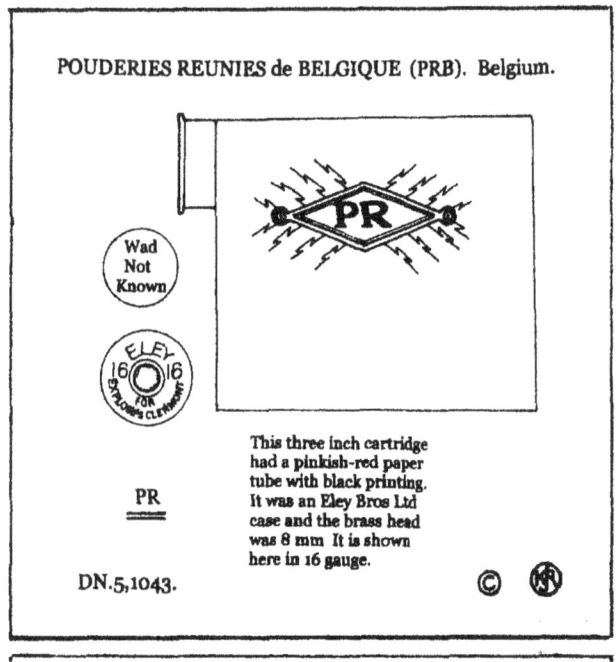

This three inch cartridge had a pinkish-red paper tube with black printing. It was an Eley Bros Ltd case and the brass head was 8 mm. It is shown here in 16 gauge.

PR

DN.5,1043.

T. POWELL & COMPANY, LIMITED:
Bemberton, Salisbury, Wiltshire, England.

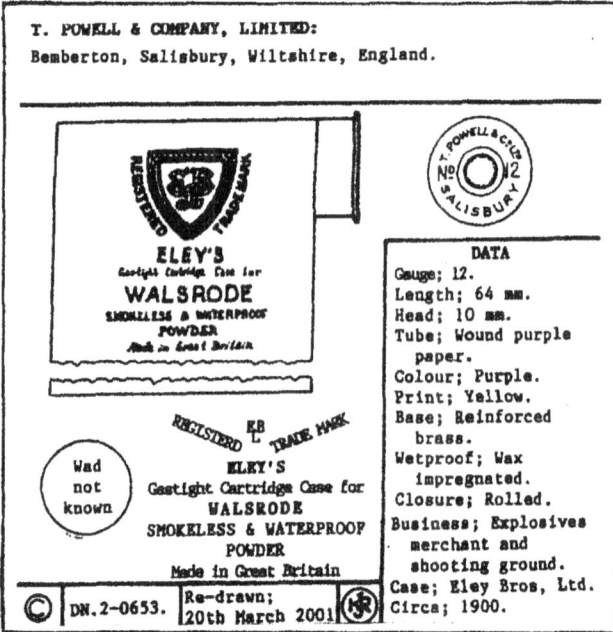

DATA
Gauge; 12.
Length; 64 mm.
Head; 10 mm.
Tube; Wound purple paper.
Colour; Purple.
Print; Yellow.
Base; Reinforced brass.
Wetproof; Wax impregnated.
Closure; Rolled.
Business; Explosives merchant and shooting ground.
Case; Eley Bros, Ltd.
Circa; 1900.

DN.2-0653. Re-drawn; 20th March 2001

WILLIAM POWELL & SON (GUNMAKERS), LTD:
35 Carrs Lane, Birmingham 4, Warwickshire
(West Midlands), England.

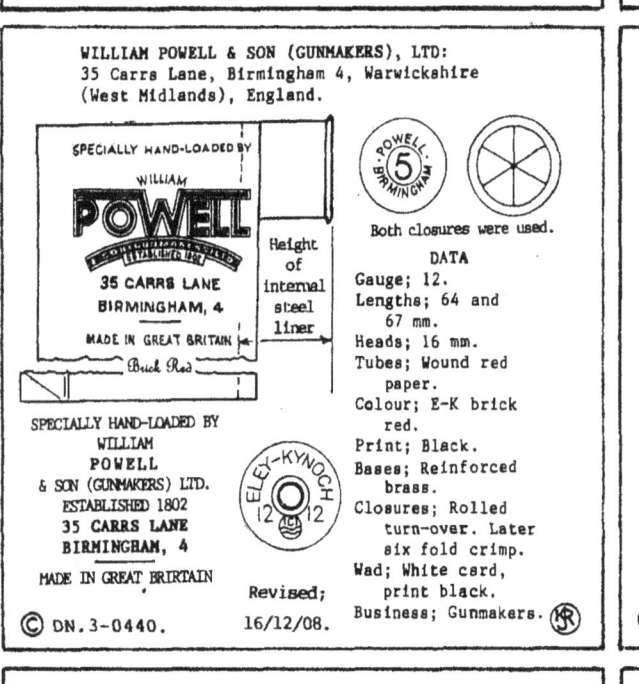

Both closures were used.

DATA
Gauge; 12.
Lengths; 64 and 67 mm.
Heads; 16 mm.
Tubes; Wound red paper.
Colour; E-K brick red.
Print; Black.
Bases; Reinforced brass.
Closures; Rolled turn-over. Later six fold crimp.
Wad; White card, print black.
Business; Gunmakers.

DN.3-0440. Revised; 16/12/08.

WILLIAM POWELL & SON, LTD.
35 Carrs Lane, Birmingham 4, Warwickshire (West Midlands), England.

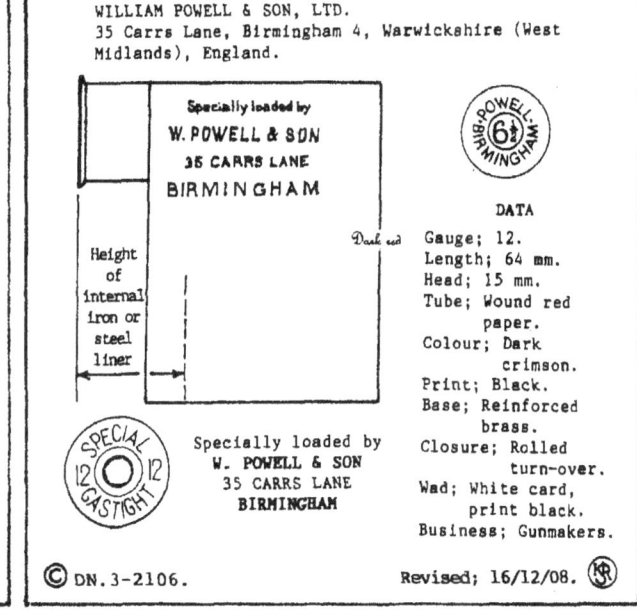

DATA
Gauge; 12.
Length; 64 mm.
Head; 15 mm.
Tube; Wound red paper.
Colour; Dark crimson.
Print; Black.
Base; Reinforced brass.
Closure; Rolled turn-over.
Wad; White card, print black.
Business; Gunmakers.

DN.3-2106. Revised; 16/12/08.

WILLIAM POWELL & SON (GUNMAKERS), LTD: 35 Carrs Lane, Birmingham 4, Warwickshire (West Midlands), England.

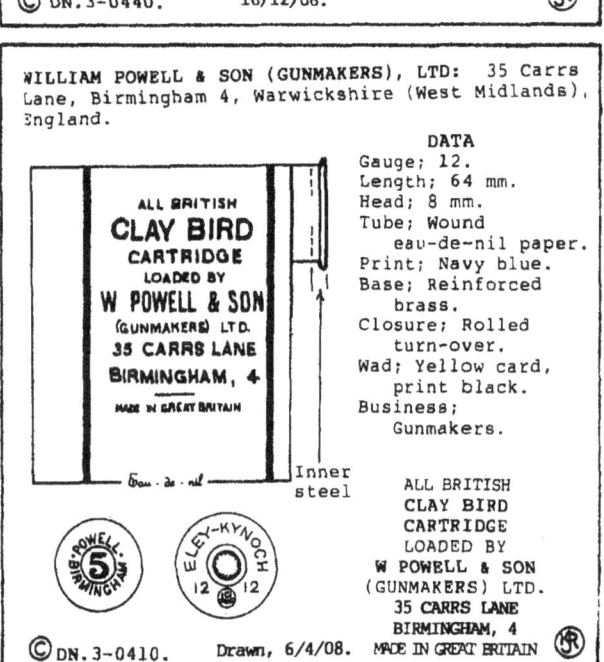

DATA
Gauge; 12.
Length; 64 mm.
Head; 8 mm.
Tube; Wound eau-de-nil paper.
Print; Navy blue.
Base; Reinforced brass.
Closure; Rolled turn-over.
Wad; Yellow card, print black.
Business; Gunmakers.

ALL BRITISH CLAY BIRD CARTRIDGE LOADED BY W POWELL & SON (GUNMAKERS) LTD. 35 CARRS LANE BIRMINGHAM, 4 MADE IN GREAT BRITAIN

DN.3-0410. Drawn, 6/4/08.

WILLIAM POWELL & SON LIMITED:
35 Carrs Lane, Birmingham 4, Warwickshire (West Midlands), England.

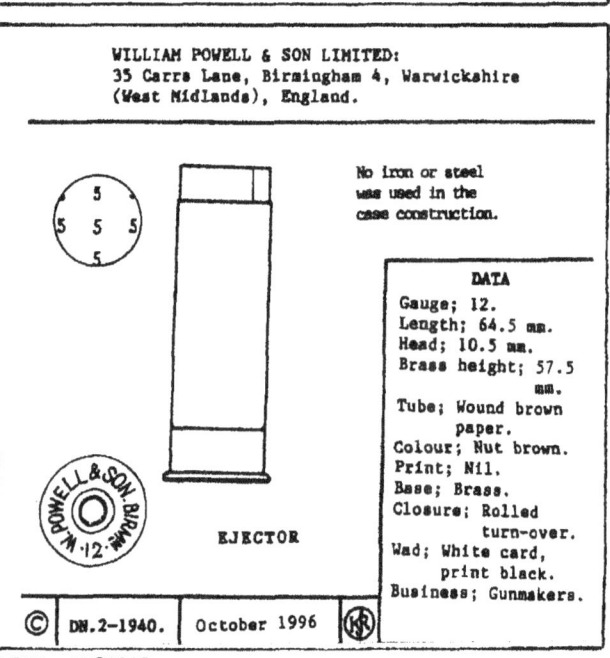

No iron or steel was used in the case construction.

DATA
Gauge; 12.
Length; 64.5 mm.
Head; 10.5 mm.
Brass height; 57.5 mm.
Tube; Wound brown paper.
Colour; Nut brown.
Print; Nil.
Base; Brass.
Closure; Rolled turn-over.
Wad; White card, print black.
Business; Gunmakers.

DN.2-1940. October 1996

WILLIAM POWELL & SON (GUNMAKERS) LIMITED:
35 Carrs Lane, Birmingham 4, Warwickshire
(West Midlands), England.

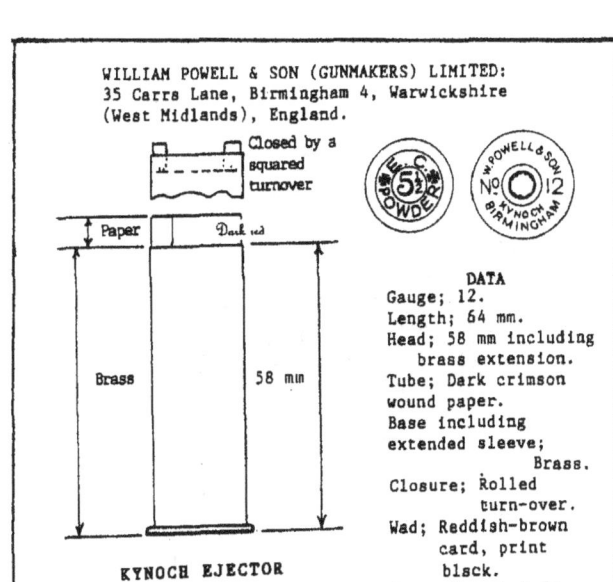

DATA
Gauge; 12.
Length; 64 mm.
Head; 58 mm including brass extension.
Tube; Dark crimson wound paper.
Base including extended sleeve; Brass.
Closure; Rolled turn-over.
Wad; Reddish-brown card, print black.
Case; Kynoch & Co.
Business; Gunmakers.

© DN.3-1740. Revised; 16/12/08.

WILLIAM POWELL & SON (GUNMAKERS) LTD:
35 Carrs Lane, Birmingham 4, Warwickshire
(West Midlands), England.

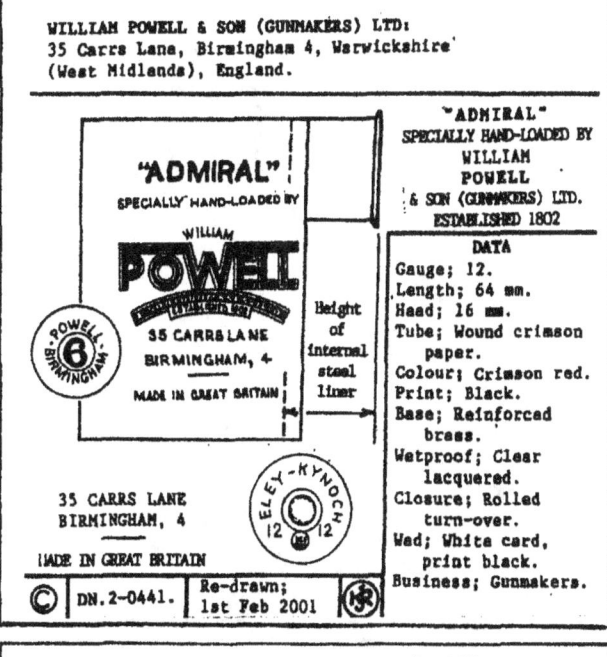

"ADMIRAL"
SPECIALLY HAND-LOADED BY
WILLIAM POWELL
& SON (GUNMAKERS) LTD.
ESTABLISHED 1802

DATA
Gauge; 12.
Length; 64 mm.
Head; 16 mm.
Tube; Wound crimson paper.
Colour; Crimson red.
Print; Black.
Base; Reinforced brass.
Wetproof; Clear lacquered.
Closure; Rolled turn-over.
Wad; White card, print black.
Business; Gunmakers.

© DN.2-0441. Re-drawn; 1st Feb 2001

WILLIAM POWELL & SON (GUNMAKERS), LTD: 35 Carrs Lane, Birmingham 4, Warwickshire (West Midlands), England.

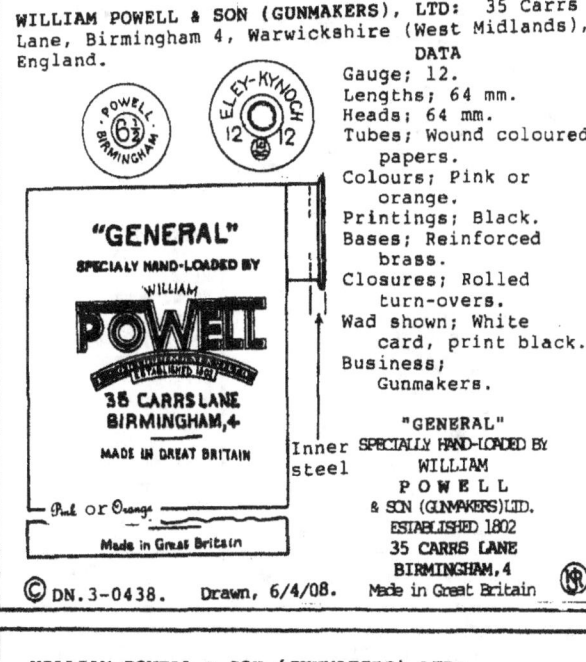

DATA
Gauge; 12.
Lengths; 64 mm.
Heads; 64 mm.
Tubes; Wound coloured papers.
Colours; Pink or orange.
Printings; Black.
Bases; Reinforced brass.
Closures; Rolled turn-overs.
Wad shown; White card, print black.
Business; Gunmakers.

"GENERAL"
SPECIALLY HAND-LOADED BY
WILLIAM POWELL
& SON (GUNMAKERS) LTD.
ESTABLISHED 1802
35 CARRS LANE
BIRMINGHAM, 4
Made in Great Britain

© DN.3-0438. Drawn, 6/4/08.

WILLIAM POWELL & SON (GUNMAKERS), LTD:
35-37 Carrs Lane, Birmingham, West Midlands,
B4 7SX, England. (Established 1802).

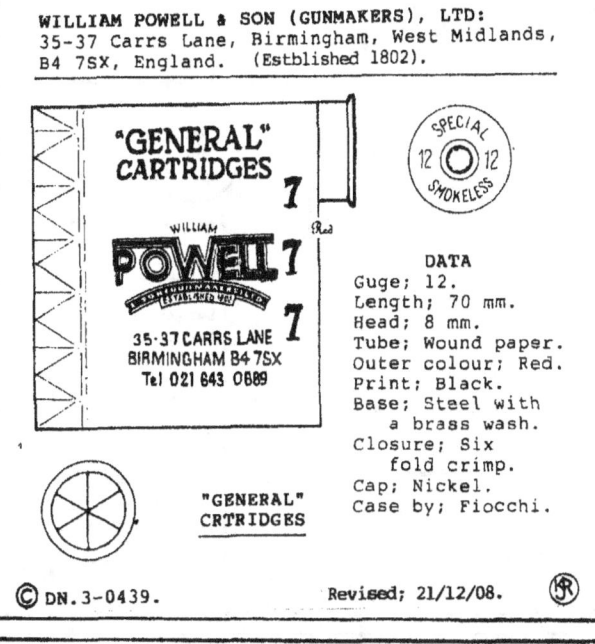

DATA
Guge; 12.
Length; 70 mm.
Head; 8 mm.
Tube; Wound paper.
Outer colour; Red.
Print; Black.
Base; Steel with a brass wash.
Closure; Six fold crimp.
Cap; Nickel.
Case by; Fiocchi.

© DN.3-0439. Revised; 21/12/08.

WILLIAM POWELL & SON (GUNMAKERS) LTD:
35 Carrs Lane, Birmingham 4, Warwickshire (West Midlands), England.

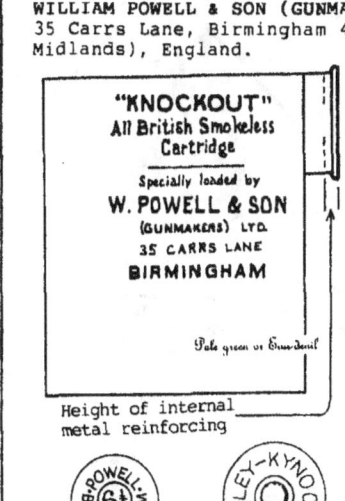
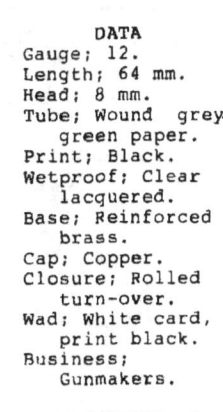
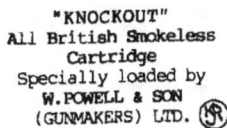

DATA
Gauge; 12.
Length; 64 mm.
Head; 8 mm.
Tube; Wound grey-green paper.
Print; Black.
Wetproof; Clear lacquered.
Base; Reinforced brass.
Cap; Copper.
Closure; Rolled turn-over.
Wad; White card, print black.
Business; Gunmakers.

"KNOCKOUT"
All British Smokeless Cartridge
Specially loaded by
W. POWELL & SON
(GUNMAKERS) LTD.

© DN.3-2701. Drawn, 25/2/08.

WILLIAM POWELL & SON (GUNMAKERS), LTD:
35 Carrs Lane, Birmingham, Warwickshire
(West Midlands), England.

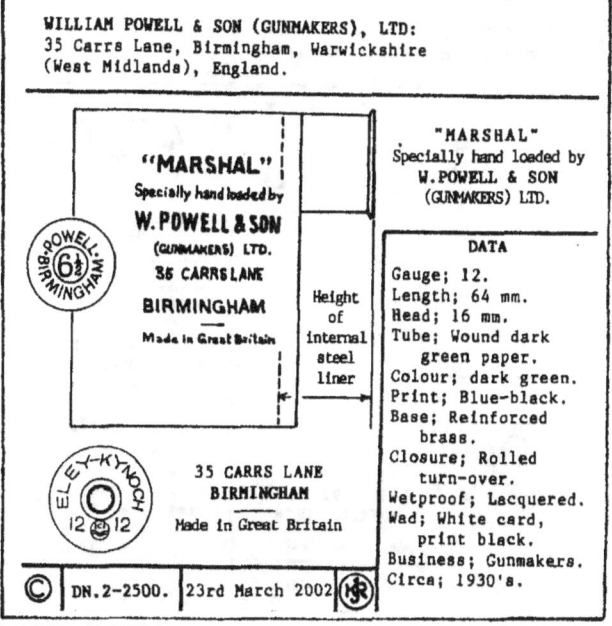

"MARSHAL"
Specially hand loaded by
W. POWELL & SON
(GUNMAKERS) LTD.

DATA
Gauge; 12.
Length; 64 mm.
Head; 16 mm.
Tube; Wound dark green paper.
Colour; dark green.
Print; Blue-black.
Base; Reinforced brass.
Closure; Rolled turn-over.
Wetproof; Lacquered.
Wad; White card, print black.
Business; Gunmakers.
Circa; 1930's.

© DN.2-2500. 23rd March 2002

PLATE 311 [POW – POW]

W. J. POWELL:
Leiston, Suffolk, East Anglia, England.

THE
"LIGHTNING"
SMOKELESS

W.J.POWELL,
Practical Gunmaker.
LEISTON

The black band was a cancellation mark.
Drawn from the Bob Cameron collection.

DATA

Gauge; 12.
Length: 64 mm.
Head; 8 mm.
Tube; Wound green paper.
Colour; Greyish-green.
Print; Black.
Base; Reinforced brass.
Closure; Rolled turn-over.
Wad; Not known.
Business; Gunmaker.

© | DN.2-2141. | 8th April 1999 | KSR

ALBERT PRATT:
Knaresborough, North Yorkshire, England.

THE "FYSCHE"
Specially loaded by
ALBERT PRATT
Ironmonger and
Ammunition Dealer
KNARESBOROUGH
PHONE 200
Made in Great Britain

DATA

Gauge; 12.
Length; 64 mm.
Head; 8 mm.
Tube; Wound pale yellow paper.
Colour; Pale yellow.
Print; Black.
Base; Brass.
Closure; Rolled turn-over.
Wad; Darker yellow, print; Black.
Business; Ironmonger and ammunition dealer.
Circa; 1930's.

© | DN.2-0571. | Re-drawn; 16th Feb 2001 | KSR

THOMAS PRENTICE & COMPANY:
Stowmarket, Suffolk, England.

PATENT
GUN COTTON CARTRIDGES,
MANUFACTURED BY
THOS PRENTICE & CO.
STOWMARKET.

Drawn from the Michael Snell Collection.

DATA

Gauge; 12.
Detonation; Pinfire.
Length; 64 mm.
Head; 6 mm.
Tube; Wound brown paper.
Colour; Dark green.
Print; Black.
Base; Brass with raised head stamp.
Closure; Rolled turn-over.
Wad; Not known.
Case; Eley Bros, Ltd. London.

© | DN.2-2447. | 28th July 2001 | KSR

PRESTON & DISTRICT FARMERS TRADING SOCIETY, LIMITED:
Preston, Lancashire, England.

FARMERS
GENERAL PURPOSE
OBTAINABLE ONLY AT
ALL BRANCHES OF

THE
PRESTON & DISTRICT
FARMERS
TRADING SOC. LTD
PRESTON

DATA

Gauge; 12.
Length; 64 mm.
Head; 8 mm.
Tube; Wound orange paper.
Colour; Orange.
Print; Black.
Wetproof; Clear lacquered.
Base; Reinforced brass.
Closure; Rolled turn-over.
Wad; Brown card, print black.
Business; Agricultural traders.

© | DN.2-2259. | 29th March 2000 | KSR

PRESTWICH & SONS:
Longridge, Lancashire, England.

REGISTERED
TRADE MARK
ELEY'S
E.B. "NITRO"
CARTRIDGE CASE
Made in Great Britain

DATA

Gauge; 20.
Length; 64 mm.
Head; 7.5 mm.
Tube; Wound crimson paper.
Print; Black.
Base; Reinforced brass.
Closure; Rolled turn-over.
Wad; White card, print red.
Case; Eley Bros, Ltd. London.

© | DN.2-2258. | 28th March 2000 | KSR

THE PROGRESSIVE CARTRIDGE CO:
Chandlersford, Hampshire, England.

DATA

Gauge; 12.
Length; 65 mm.
Head; 7 mm.
Tube; Wound paper.
Colour; Jade Green.
Print; Black.
Base; Brass.
Closure; Rolled turn-over.
Wad; White card, no printing, no shot load.

© | DN.2-1460. | Re-drawn 7th Jan 1999 | KSR

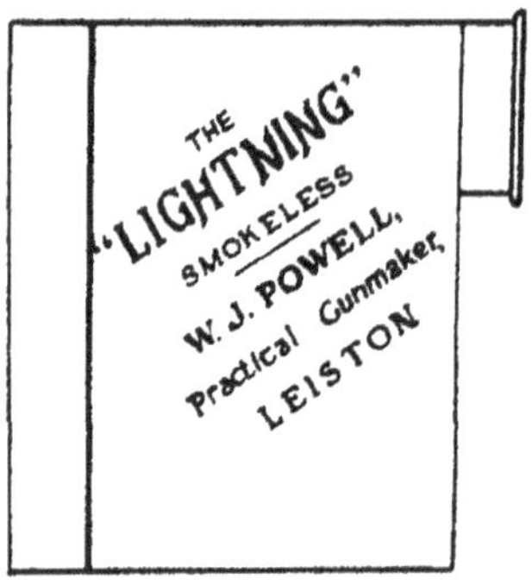

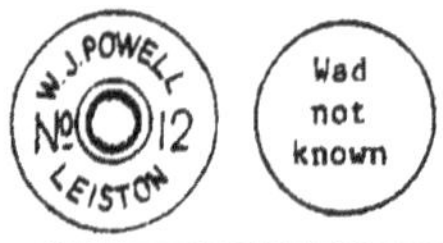

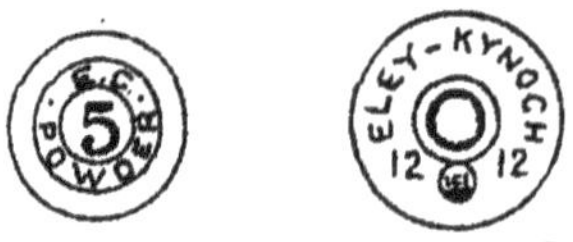

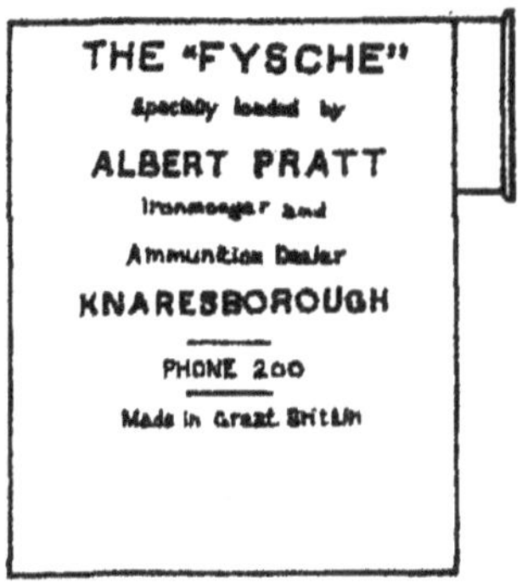

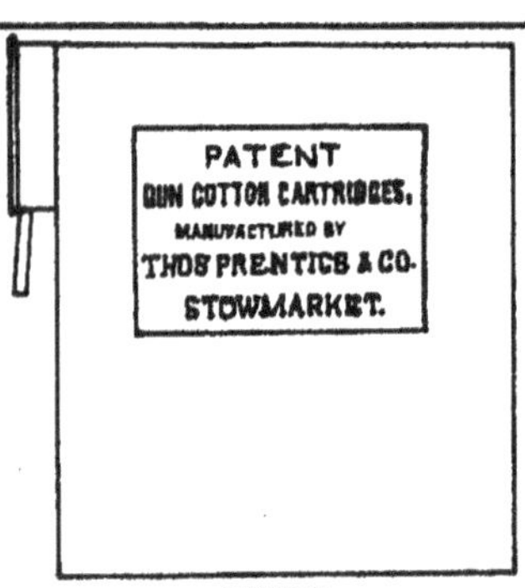

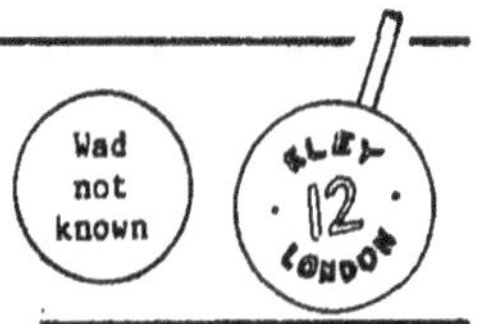

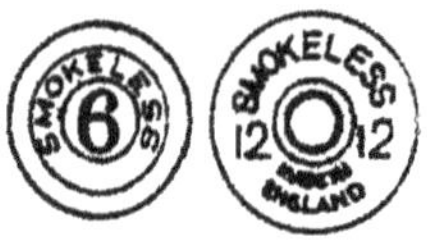

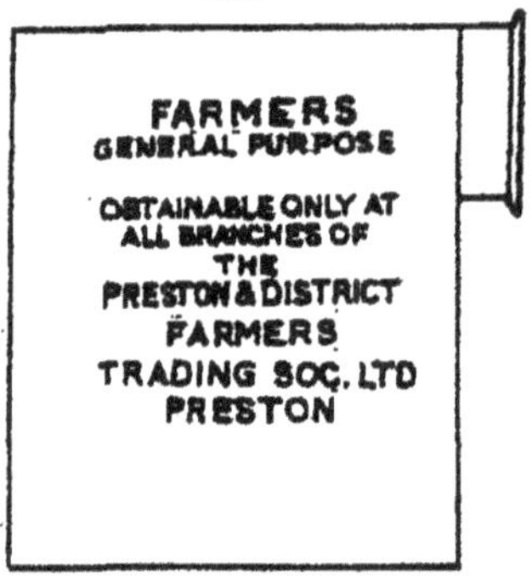

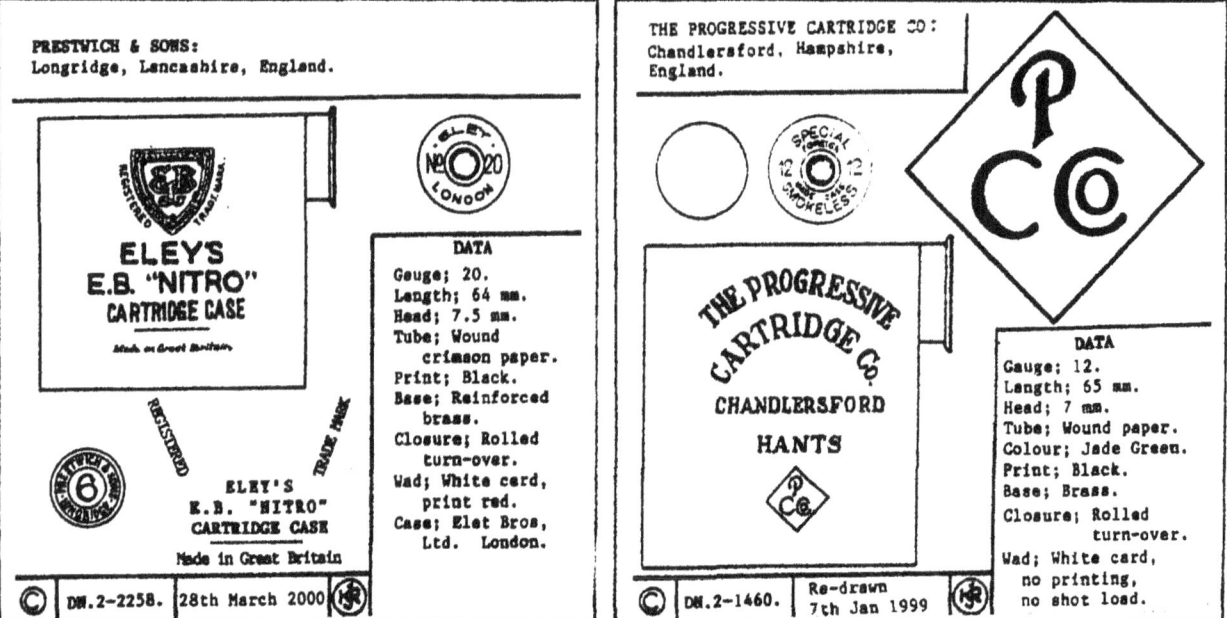

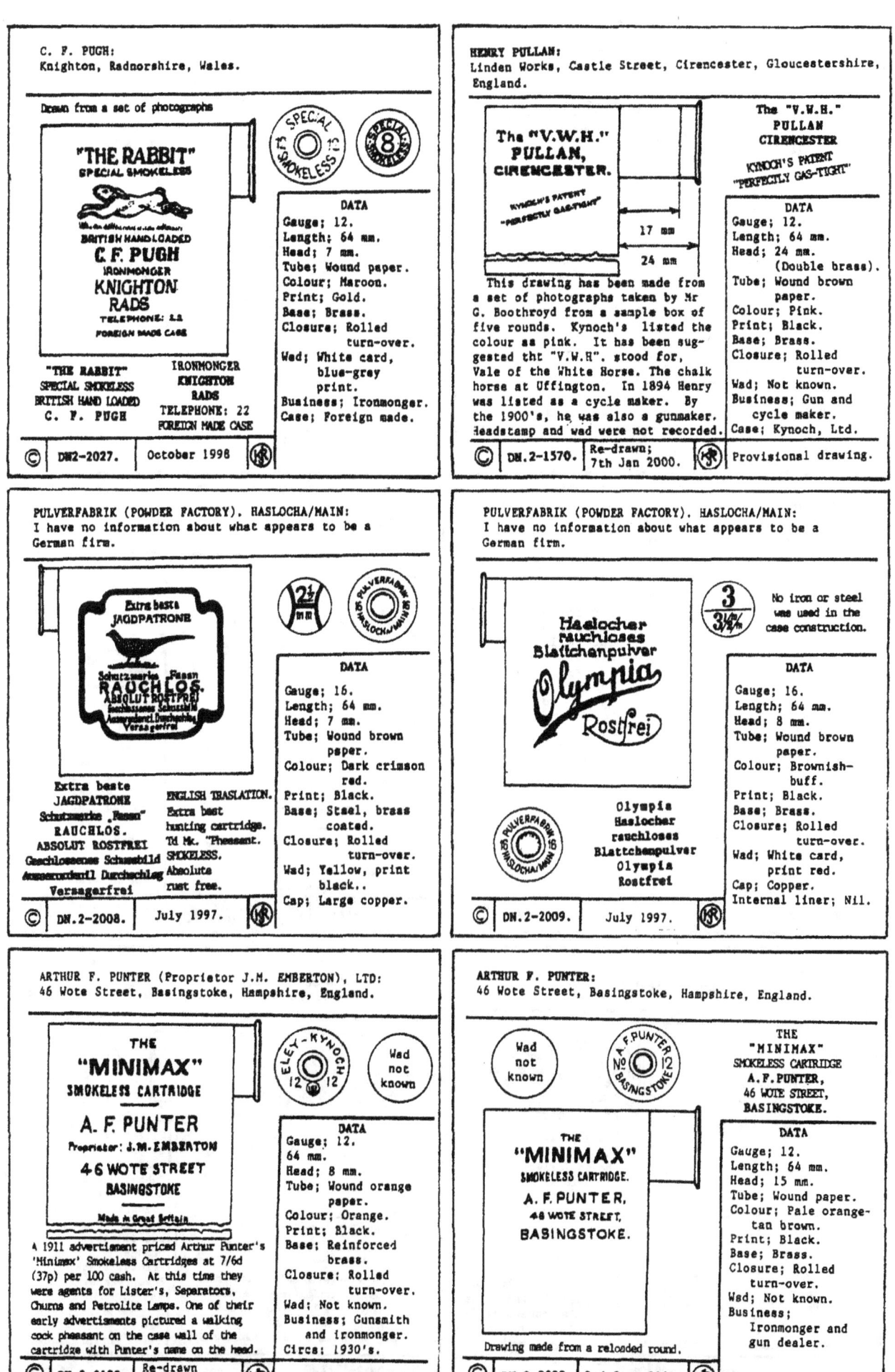

ARTHUR F. PUNTER (Proprietor; J. M. EMBERTON):
46 Wote Street, Basingstoke, Hampshire, England.

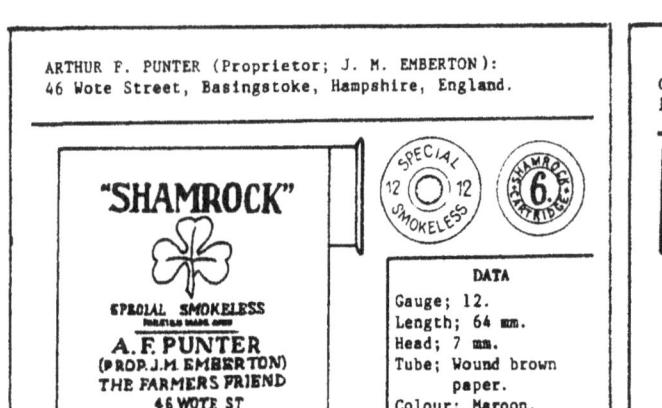

"SHAMROCK"
"SHAMROCK"
SPECIAL SMOKELESS
FOREIGN MADE CASE

A.F. PUNTER
(PROP. J.M. EMBERTON)
THE FARMERS FRIEND
46 WOTE ST
BASINGSTOKE

DATA
Gauge; 12.
Length; 64 mm.
Head; 7 mm.
Tube; Wound brown paper.
Colour; Maroon.
Print; Gold.
Base; Brass with reinforcing.
Closure; Rolled turn-over.
Wad shown; Lime green, print black.
Case; German.
Business; Ironmonger.

DN.2-0940. Updated; April 1997

C. PURCELL:
10 Worcester Street, Gloucester, Gloucestershire, England.

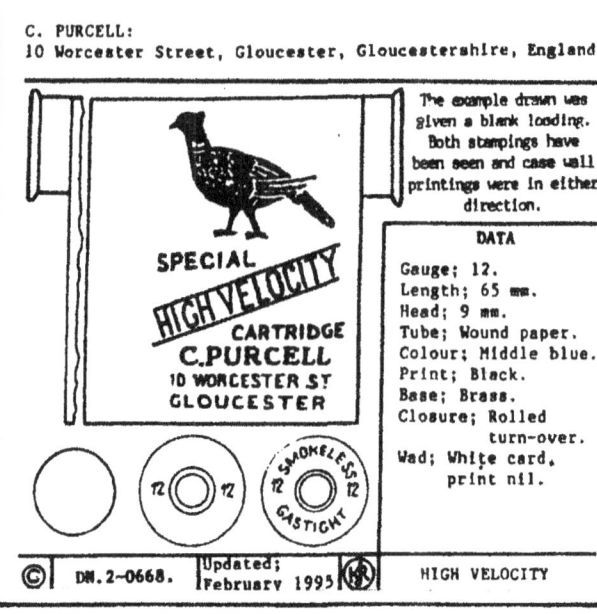

The example drawn was given a blank loading. Both stampings have been seen and case wall printings were in either direction.

DATA
Gauge; 12.
Length; 65 mm.
Head; 9 mm.
Tube; Wound paper.
Colour; Middle blue.
Print; Black.
Base; Brass.
Closure; Rolled turn-over.
Wad; White card, print nil.

DN.2-0668. Updated; February 1995   HIGH VELOCITY

JAMES PURDEY: 314½ Oxford Street, Near Hanover Square, London W.1., England.

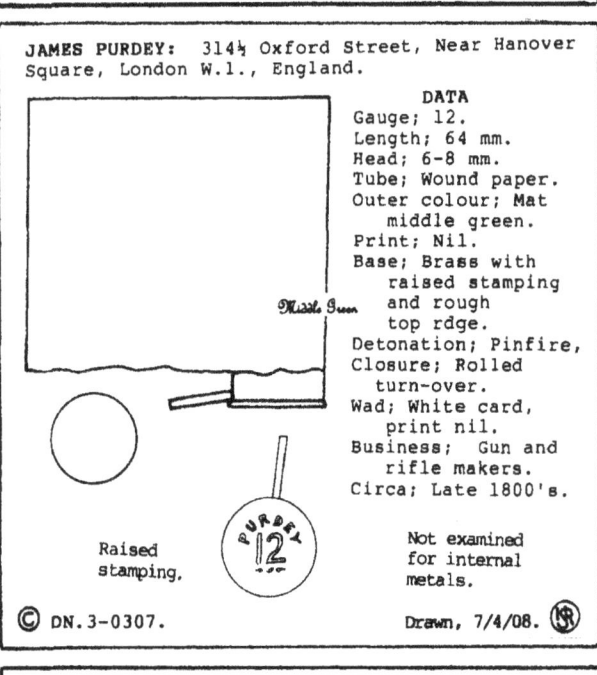

Raised stamping.

DATA
Gauge; 12.
Length; 64 mm.
Head; 6-8 mm.
Tube; Wound paper.
Outer colour; Mat middle green.
Print; Nil.
Base; Brass with raised stamping and rough top ridge.
Detonation; Pinfire.
Closure; Rolled turn-over.
Wad; White card, print nil.
Business; Gun and rifle makers.
Circa; Late 1800's.

Not examined for internal metals.

DN.3-0307.   Drawn, 7/4/08.

JAMES PURDEY:
South Audley Street, London W.1., England.

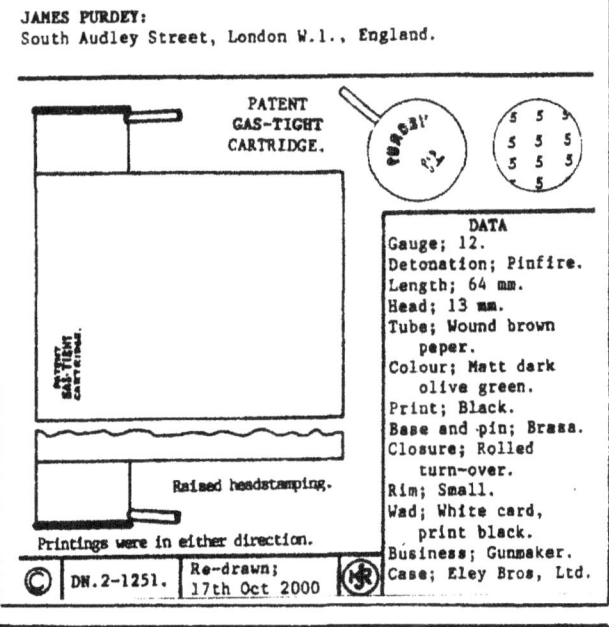

PATENT GAS-TIGHT CARTRIDGE.

Raised headstamping.
Printings were in either direction.

DATA
Gauge; 12.
Detonation; Pinfire.
Length; 64 mm.
Head; 13 mm.
Tube; Wound brown paper.
Colour; Matt dark olive green.
Print; Black.
Base and pin; Brass.
Closure; Rolled turn-over.
Rim; Small.
Wad; White card, print black.
Business; Gunmaker.
Case; Eley Bros, Ltd.

DN.2-1251. Re-drawn; 17th Oct 2000

JAMES PURDEY:
314½ Oxford Street, London, England.

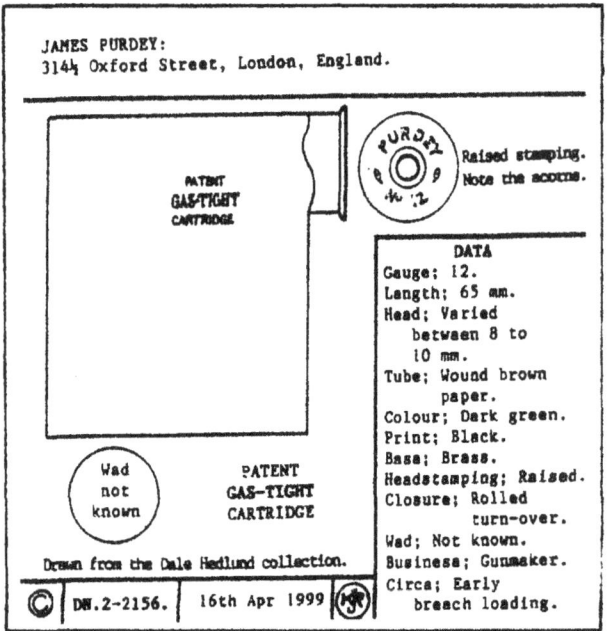

PATENT GAS-TIGHT CARTRIDGE

Raised stamping.
Note the scorns.

Wad not known

Drawn from the Dale Hedlund collection.

DATA
Gauge; 12.
Length; 65 mm.
Head; Varied between 8 to 10 mm.
Tube; Wound brown paper.
Colour; Dark green.
Print; Black.
Base; Brass.
Headstamping; Raised.
Closure; Rolled turn-over.
Wad; Not known.
Business; Gunmaker.
Circa; Early breach loading.

DN.2-2156. 16th Apr 1999

JAMES PURDEY & SONS, LTD:
Audley House, South Audley Street, London, W.1., England.

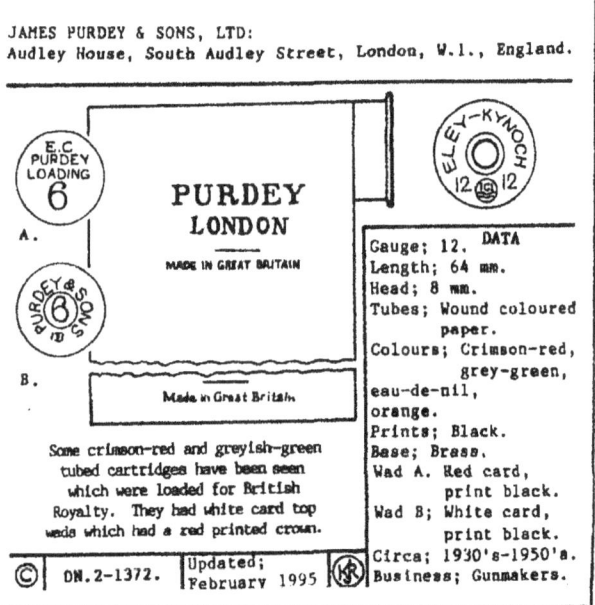

A.
PURDEY
LONDON
MADE IN GREAT BRITAIN

B.
Made in Great Britain

Some crimson-red and greyish-green tubed cartridges have been seen which were loaded for British Royalty. They had white card top wads which had a red printed crown.

DATA
Gauge; 12.
Length; 64 mm.
Head; 8 mm.
Tubes; Wound coloured paper.
Colours; Crimson-red, grey-green, eau-de-nil, orange.
Prints; Black.
Base; Brass.
Wad A. Red card, print black.
Wad B; White card, print black.
Circa; 1930's-1950's.
Business; Gunmakers.

DN.2-1372. Updated; February 1995

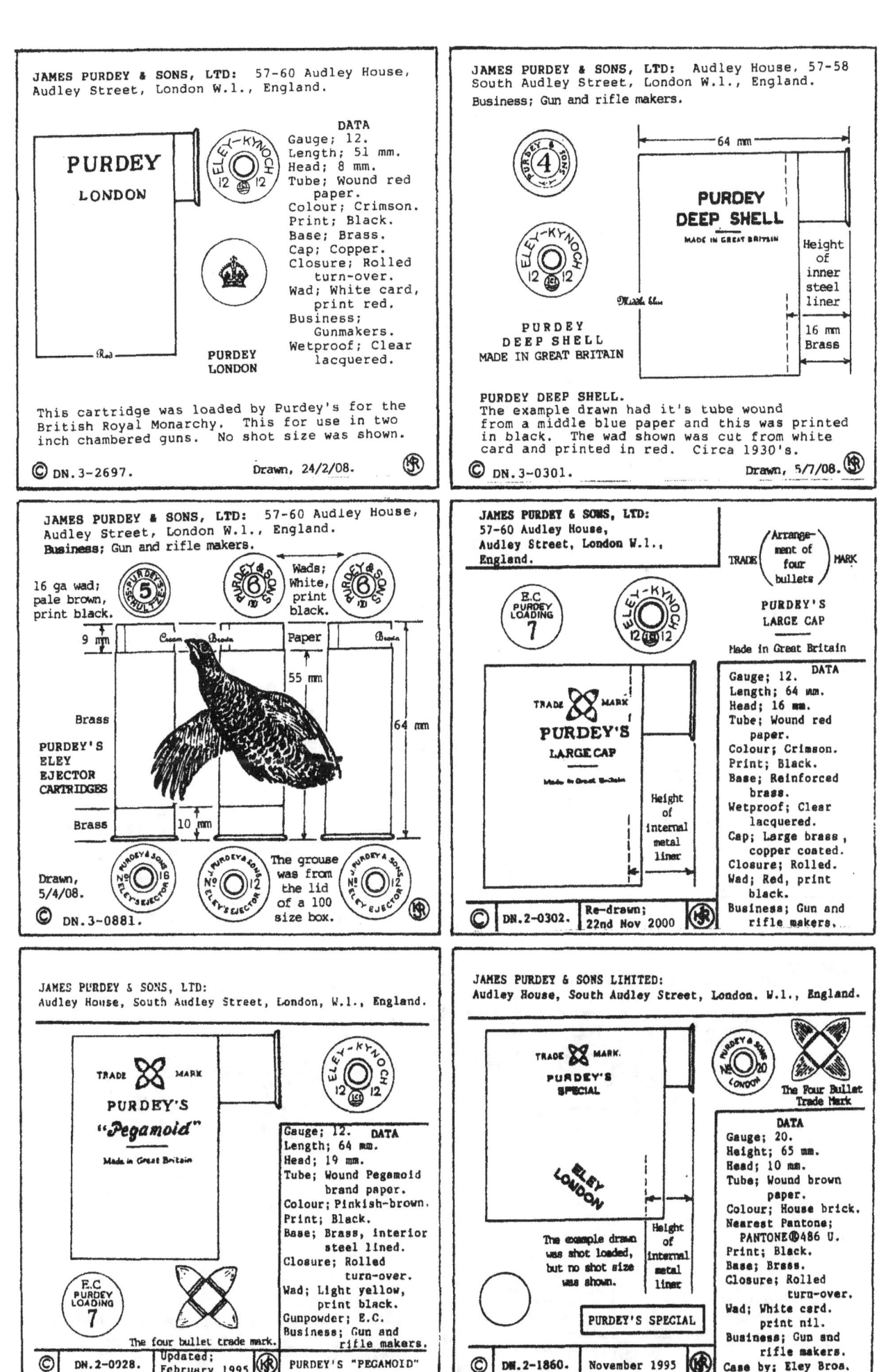

PLATE 315 [PUR – PUR]

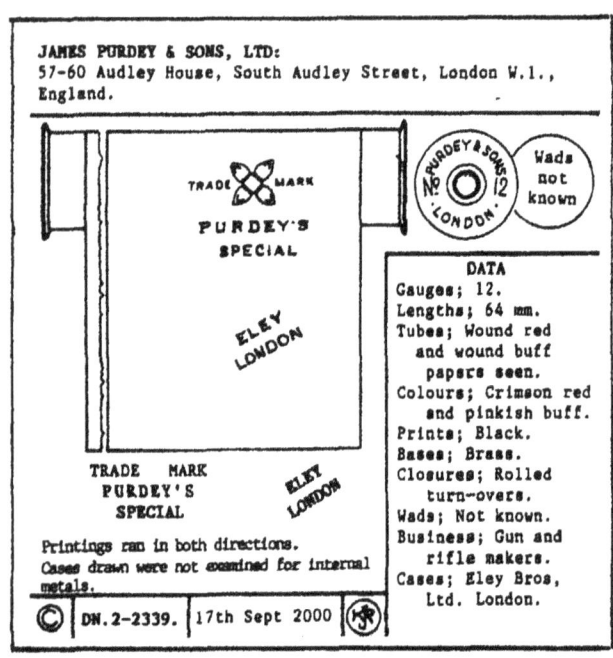
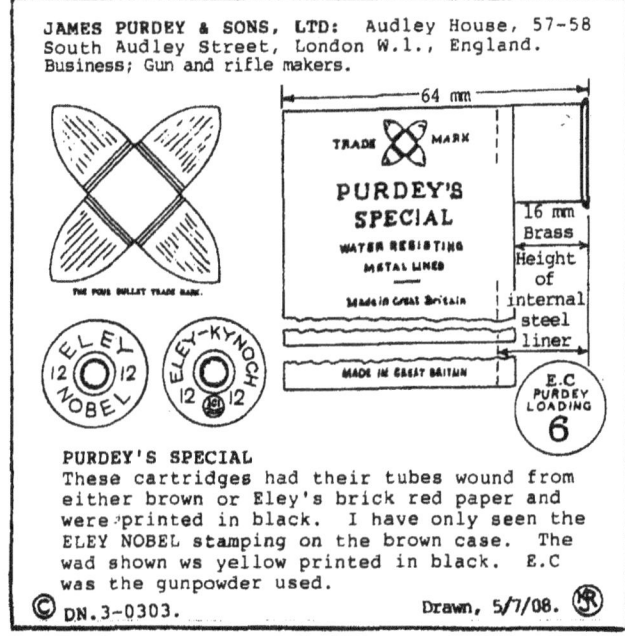
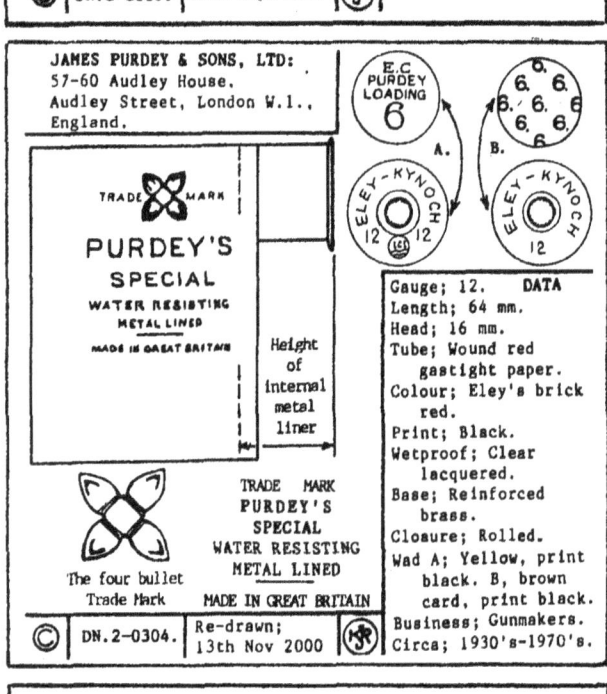
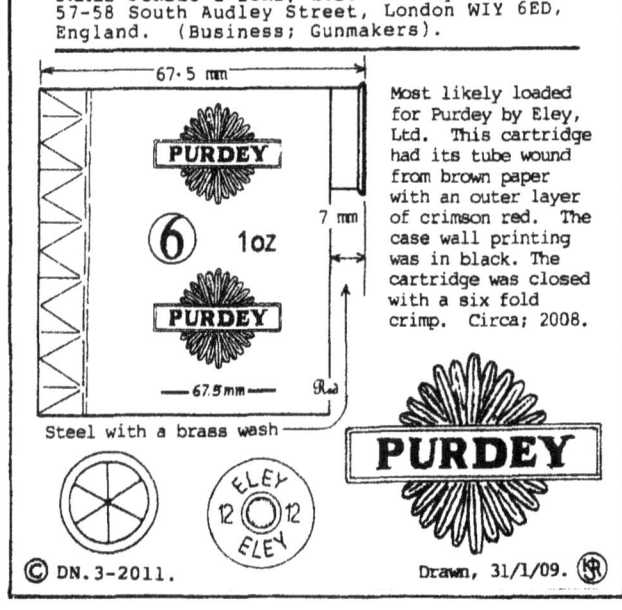
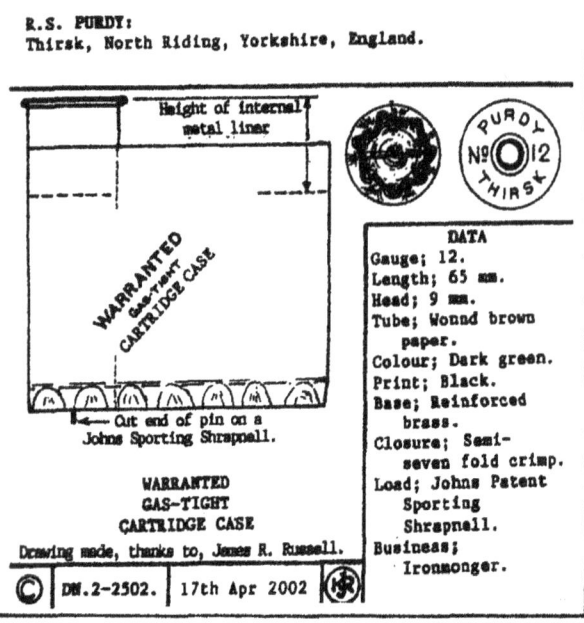
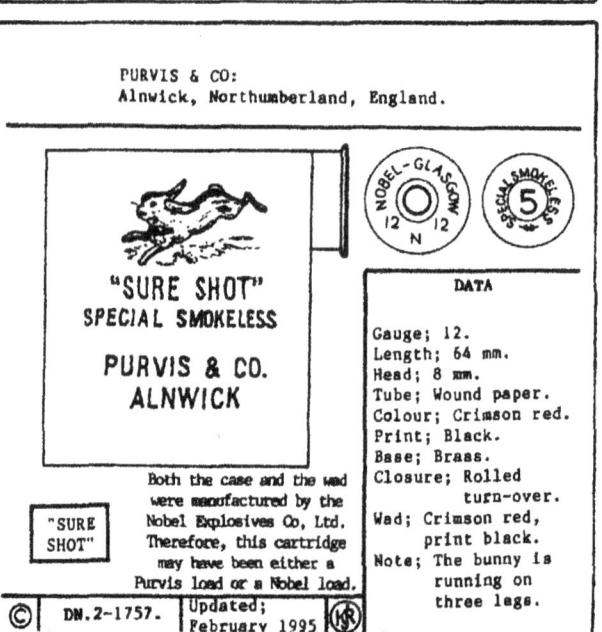

PLATE 316 [PUR – PUR]

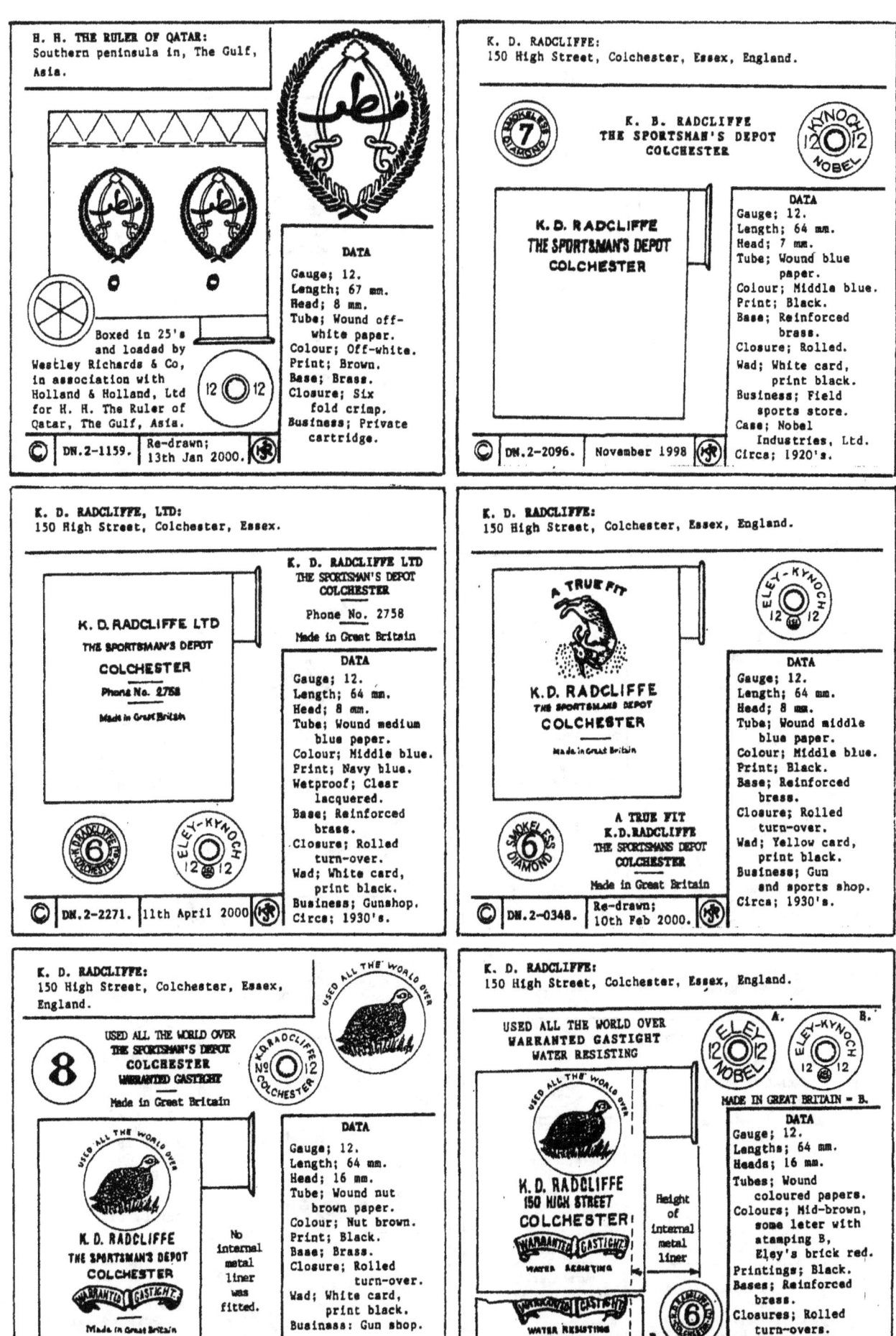

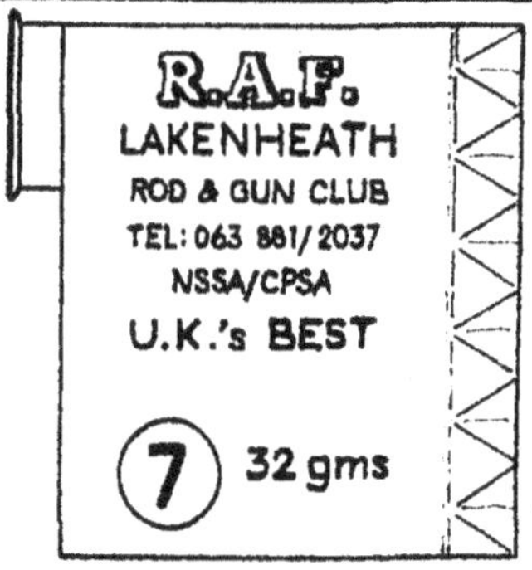

R.A.F. LAKENHEATH ROD & GUN CLUB:
R.A.F. Lakenheath Air Force Base, Suffolk.

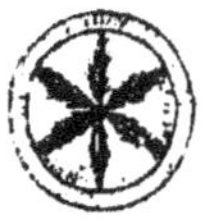

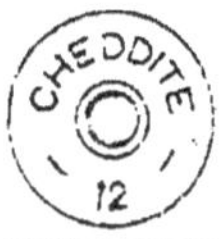

DATA
Gauge; 12.
Length; 67 mm.
Head; 7 mm.
Tube; Medium ribbed plastic.
Colour; Summer Green 3.
Print; Black.
Base; Steel, brass coated.
Closure; Crimp, 6 fold.
Business; Armed Service field sports.

© DN.2-0006. November 1994

RAINE BROTHERS:
Carlisle, Cumberland (Cumbria), England.

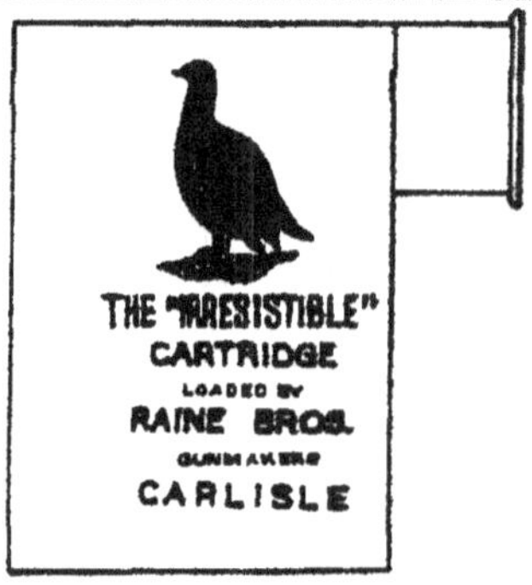

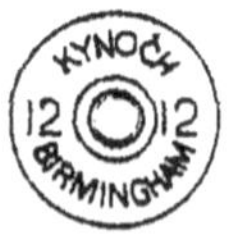

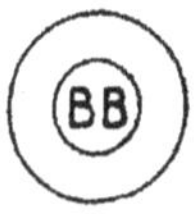

THE "IRRESISTIBLE"

DATA
Gauge; 12.
Length; 64 mm.
Head; 16 mm.
Tube; Wound brown paper.
Colour; Dark green.
Print; Black.
Base; Brass.
Inner liner; Nil.
Closure; Rolled turn-over.
Wad; White card, print black.
Business; Gunmakers.

© DN.2-1381. Updated; March 1995

RAKER:
2 Josselin Court, Burnt Mills Industrial Estate, Basildon, Essex, England.

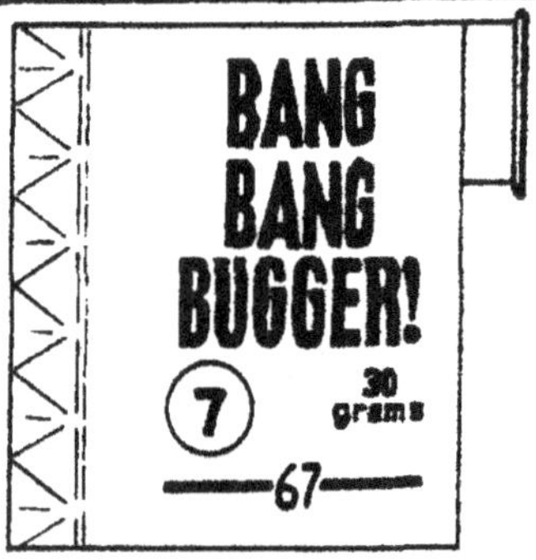

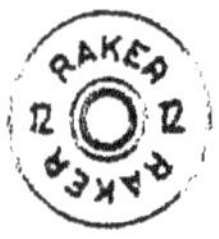

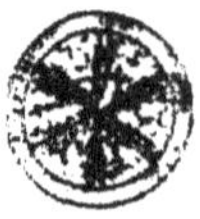

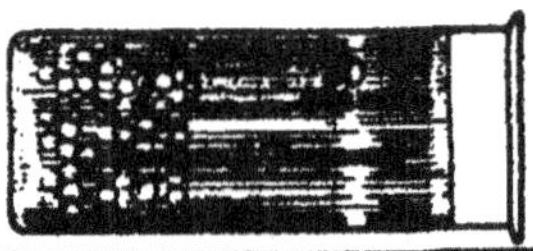

DATA
Gauge; 12.
Length; 67 mm.
Head; 8 mm.
Tube; Fine ribbed transparent plastic.
Colour; Water clear.
Print; Black.
Base; steel, brass coated.
Closure; Crimp, 6 fold.
Business; Loading and sales.

© DN.2-1817. Updated; March 1995 | BANG BANG BUGGER!

R. RAMSBOTTOM:
Manchester, Lancashire (Great Manchester), England.

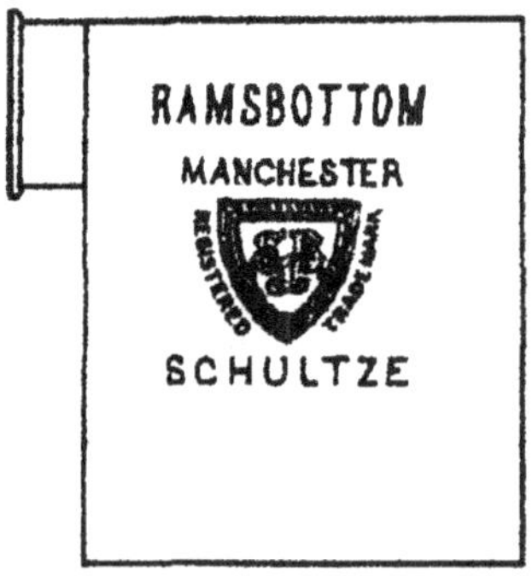

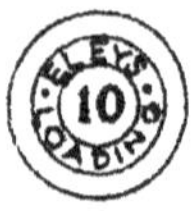

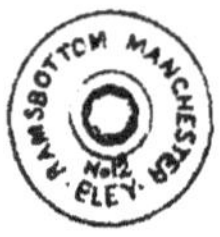

RAMSBOTTOM
MANCHESTER
REGISTERED TRADE MARK
SCHULTZE

DATA
Gauge; 12.
Length; 64 mm.
Head; 10 mm.
Tube; Wound paper.
Colour; Dull peach.
Print; Blue-black.
Base; Brass.
Closure; Rolled turn-over.
Wad; White card, print red.
Business; Sports depot.
Case; Eley Bros, Ltd.

© DN.2-0208. Re-drawn; July 2000

F. RANDELL LIMITED:
Market Place, North Walsham. Also at, Cromer, Norfolk, England.

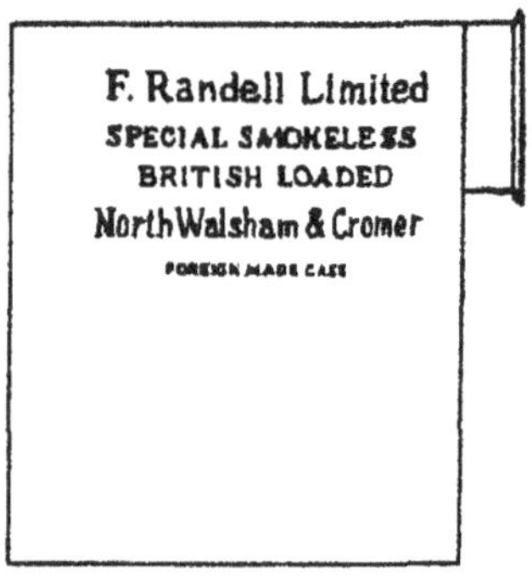

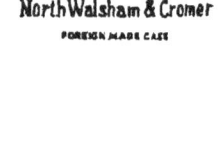

F. Randell Limited
SPECIAL SMOKELESS
BRITISH LOADED
North Walsham & Cromer
FOREIGN MADE CASE

DATA
Gauge; 12.
Length; 64 mm.
Head; 8 mm.
Tube; Wound paper.
Colour; Light turquoise.
Print; Black.
Base; Brass.
Closure; Rolled turn-over.
Wad; Yellow, print black.
Business; Ironmongers.
Case; Imported.
Circa; 1920's.

© DN.2-1509. Re-drawn; 29th Nov 2000

RANSTON ESTATE:
The Estate Office, Ranston, Iwerne Courtney, Blandford Forum, Dorset, DT11 8PU, England.

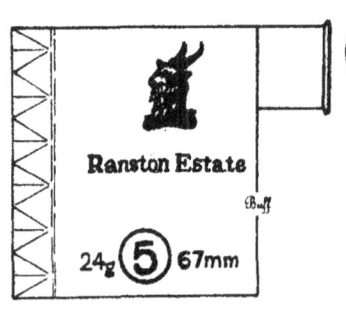

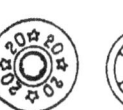

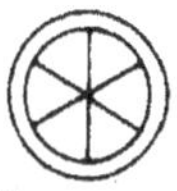

DATA
Gauge; 20.
Length; 67 mm.
Head; 15 mm.
Tube; Wound brown paper.
Outer colour; Dark buff.
Print; Black.
Base; Steel with a brass wash.
Cap; Nickel.
Closure; Six fold crimp.
Business; Private estate.

Ranston Estate
24g 67mm

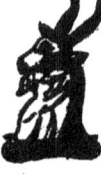

© DN.3-2815. Drawn, 21/5/08.

PLATE 318 [RAF – RAN]

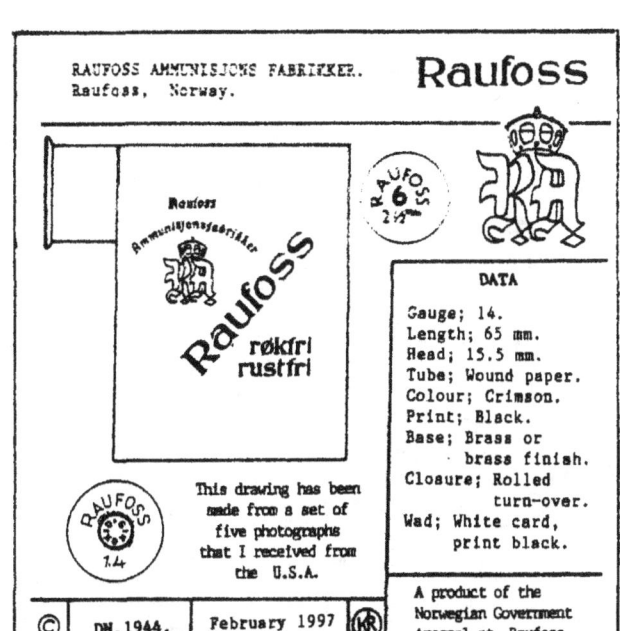
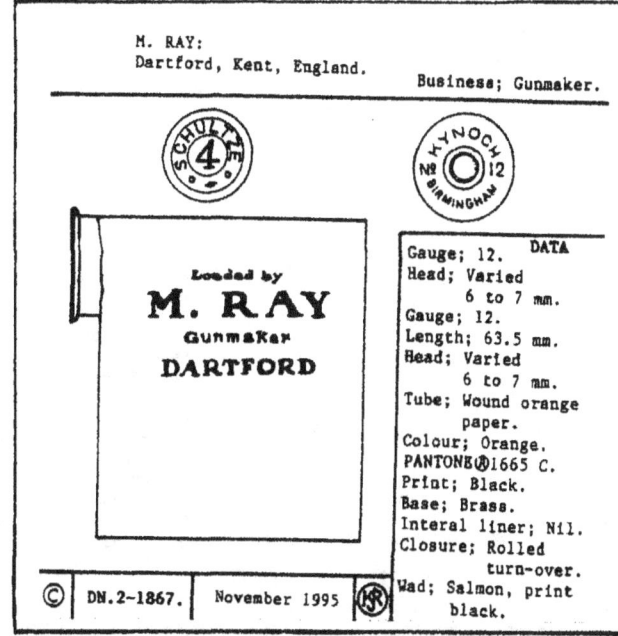
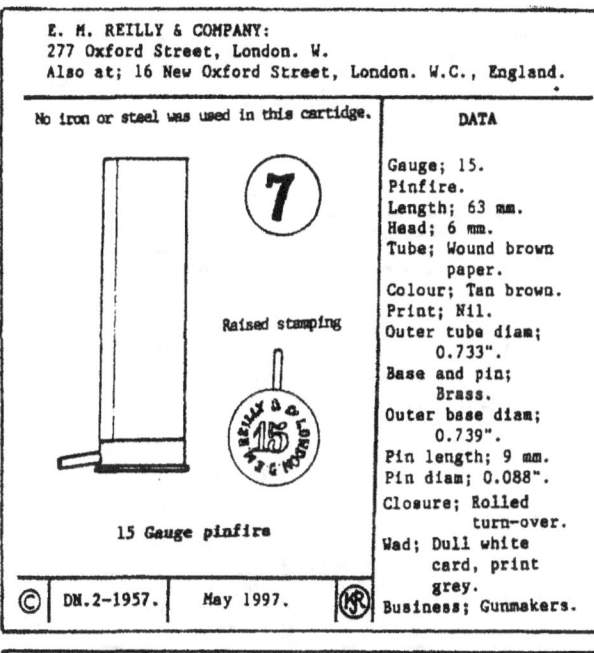
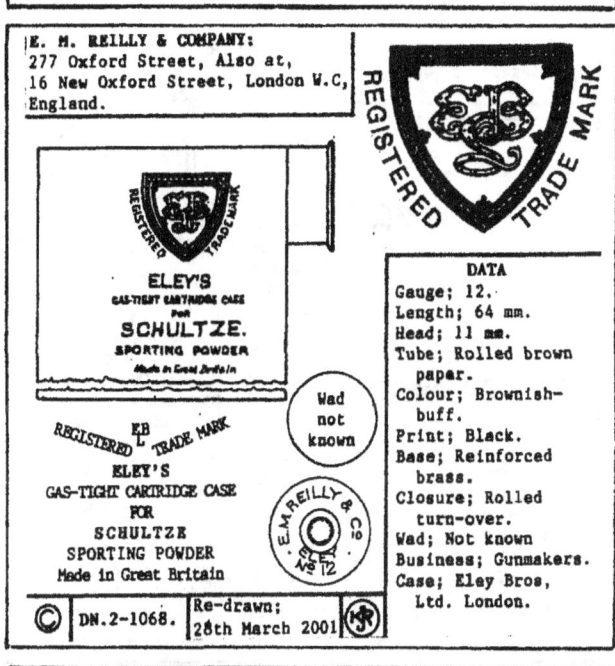
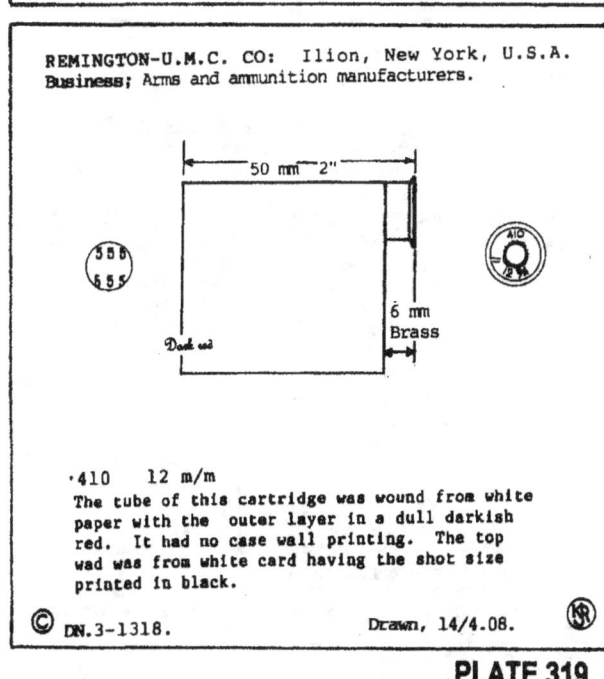
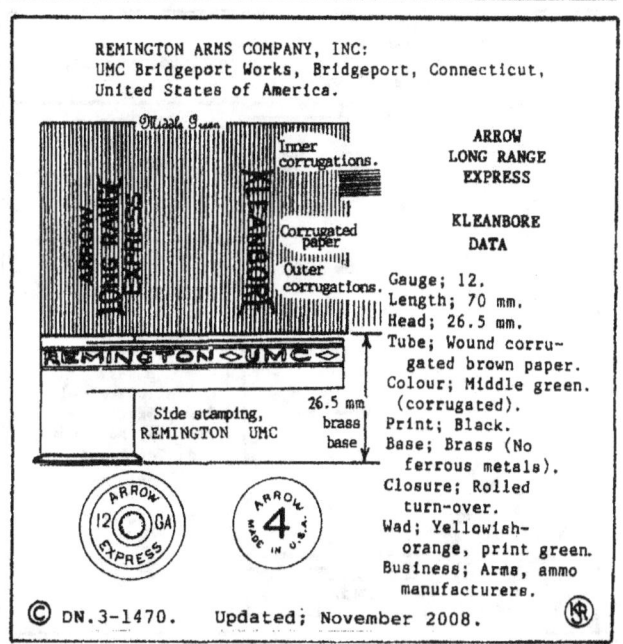

PLATE 319 [RAU – REM]

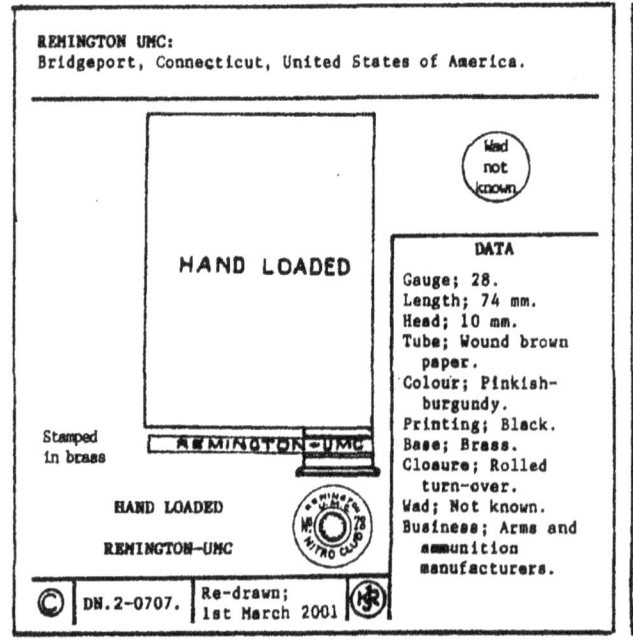
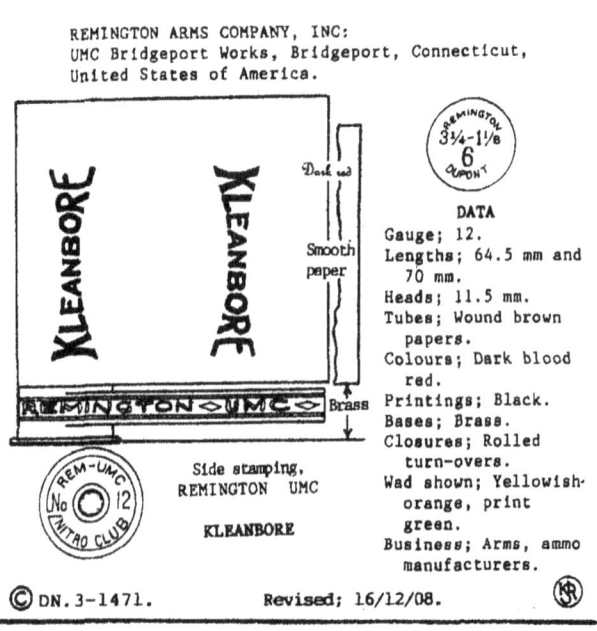
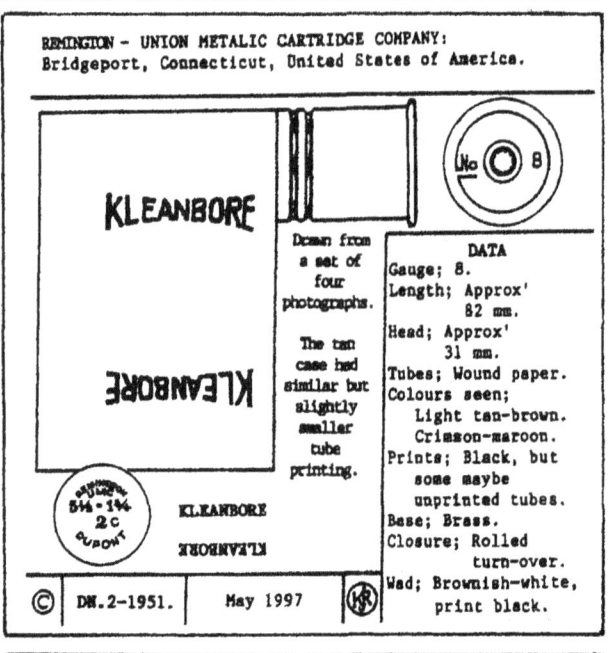
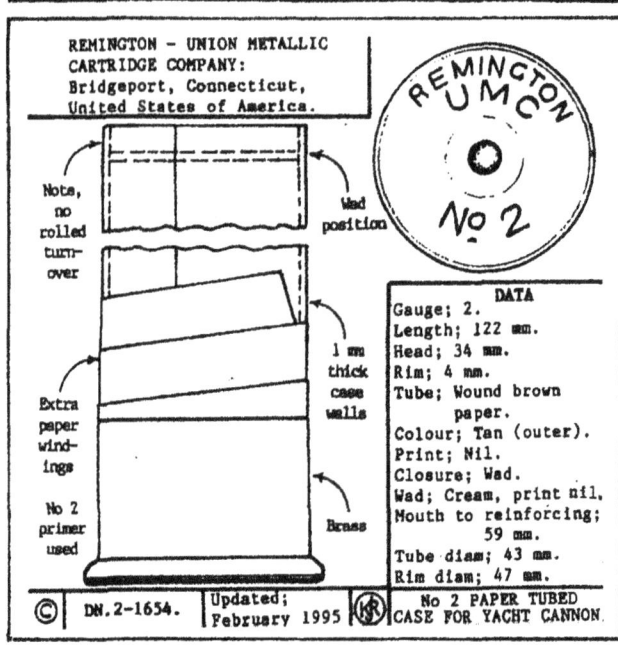
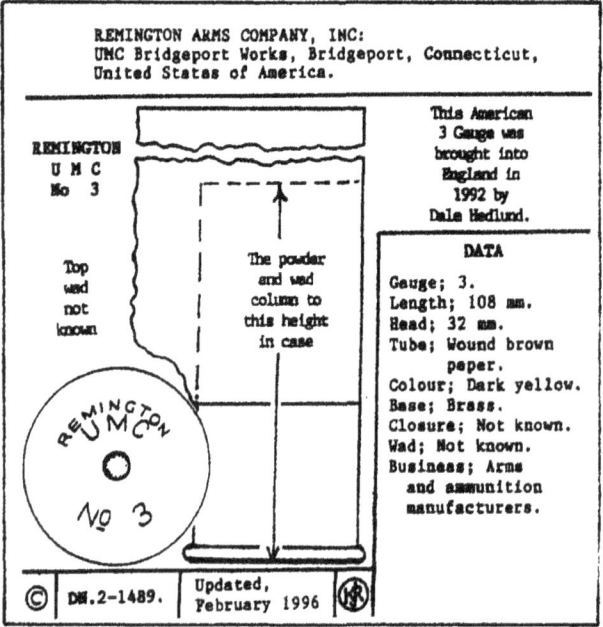
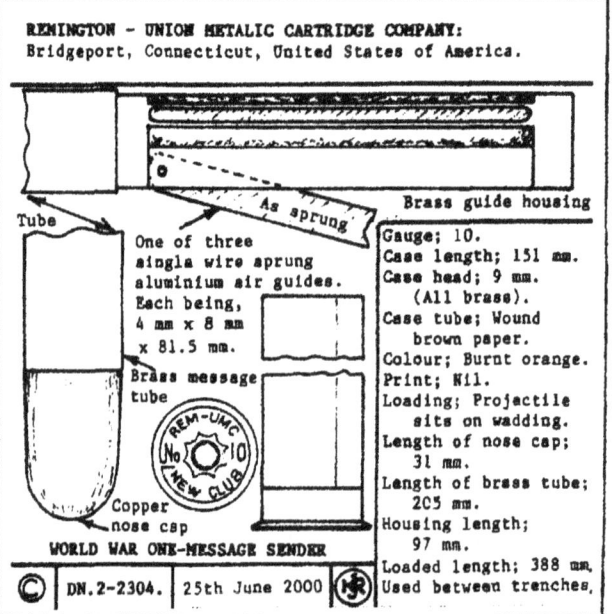

PLATE 320 [REM – REM]

REMINGTON (ENGLAND): Remington UMC Works, Brimsdown, Enfield, Middlesex (London), England.

REMINGTON NITRO CLUB

Drawing was made from a used case.
Wad not known.

Loaded at Remington UMC Works Brimsdown England
Pressing in brass: REMINGTON-UMC

DATA
Gauge; 20.
Length; 68 mm.
Head; 11 mm.
Tube; Wound brown paper.
Colour; Blotchy dark red.
Print; Black.
Base; Brass.
Wetproof; Wax impregnated.
Closure; Rolled turn-over.
Wad; Not known.
Business; Ammo manufacturers.
Case; U.S.A.

DN.2-0666. Re-drawn; 26th March 2001

REMINGTON (ENGLAND): UMC Works, Brimsdown, Enfield, Middlesex, England.

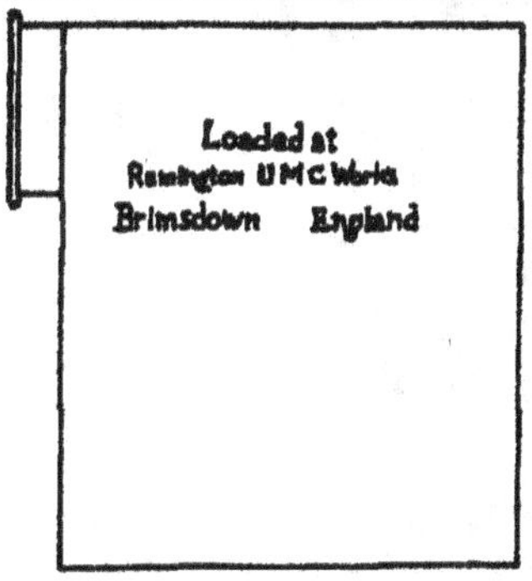

Loaded at Remington UMC Works Brimsdown England
Wad not known. This drawing has been made from a used case.

DATA
Gauge; 12.
Length; 65 mm.
Head; 7 mm.
Tube; Wound brown paper.
Colour; Dark blood red.
Print; Black.
Base; Brass.
Interior liner; Nil.
Closure; Rolled turn-over.
Wad; Not known.
Case; Made in U.S.A.
Business; American arms and ammunition manufacturers.

DN.2-1379. Updated; February 1995

REMINGTON (ENGLAND): UMC Works, Brimsdown, Enfield, Middlesex, England.

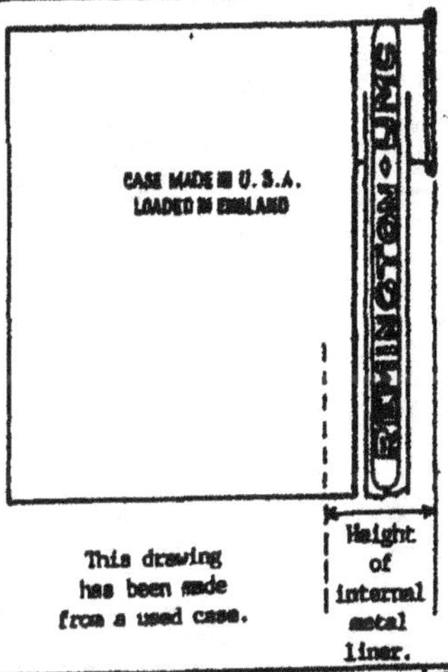

CASE MADE IN U.S.A. LOADED IN ENGLAND
REMINGTON-UMC
Wad not known.
This drawing has been made from a used case.
Height of internal metal liner.

DATA
Gauge; 12.
Length; 65 mm.
Head; 12 mm.
Tube; Wound brown paper.
Colour; Dark red.
Print; Black.
Base; Brass.
Closure; Rolled turn-over.
Wad; Not known.
Case; Made in U.S.A.
Business; American arms and ammunition manufacturers.

DN.2-1378. Updated; February 1995

REMINGTON (ENGLAND): UMC Works, Brimsdown, Enfield, Middlesex, England.

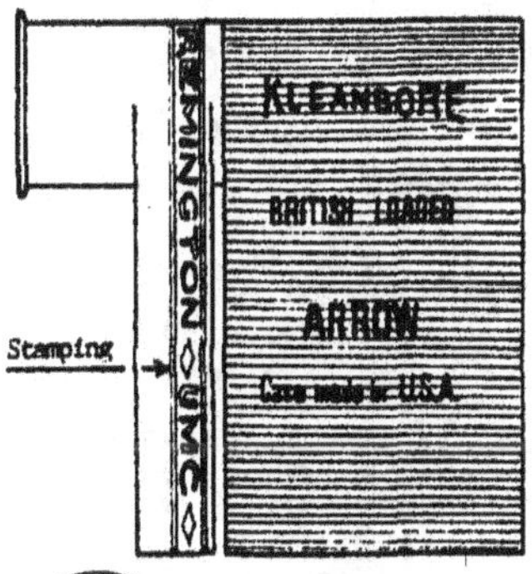

REMINGTON-UMC
Stamping →
KLEANBORE BRITISH LOADED ARROW
Case made in U.S.A.

KLEANBORE BRITISH LOADED ARROW
Case made in U.S.A.

DATA
Gauge; 12.
Length; 65 mm.
Head; 27 mm.
Tube; Wound brown corrugated paper.
Colour; Rich middle green.
Print; Black.
Base; Brass.
Closure; Rolled turn-over.
Wad; Brownish-yellow, print black.
Business; American arms and ammunition manufacturers.

DN.2-0969. Updated; April 1997

REMINGTON (ENGLAND): UMC Works, Brimsdown, Enfield, Middlesex, England.

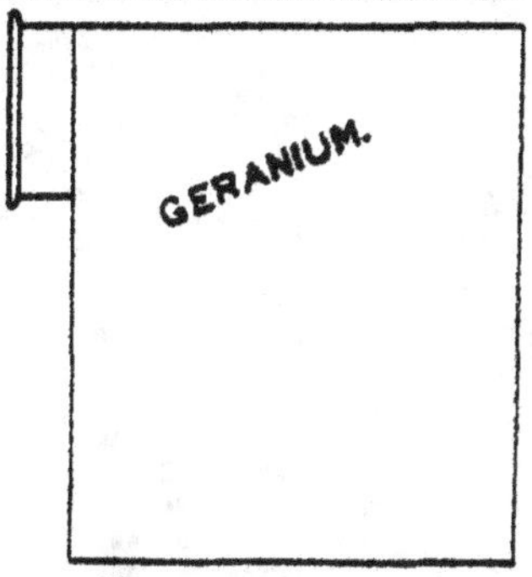

GERANIUM.
No iron or steel was used in the case construction.
GERANIUM. REMILION.

DATA
Gauge; 12.
Length; 65 mm.
Head; 8.5 mm.
Tube; Wound paper.
Colour; Geranium red.
Print; Black.
Base; Brass.
Closure; Rolled turn-over.
Wad; White card, print black.
Business; Cartridge loading etc.
Case; Remington U.M.C. Made in U.S.A.

Drawn from the Dale Hedlund collection.
DN.2-2154. 15th Apr 1999

REMINGTON (ENGLAND): U.M.C. Works, Brimsdown, Enfield, Middlesex (London), England.

KLEANBORE NITRO LOADED Remington
Case made in U.S.A.

KLEANBORE BRITISH LOADED Remington Case Made in U.S.A.

DATA
Gauges; 12, 16, 20.
Lengths; 64 mm.
Heads; 7-8 mm.
Tubes; Wound brown paper.
Colour; Dark green with corrugations.
Printings; Black, ran in either direction.
Bases; Brass with no internal steel.
Closures; Rolled turn-overs.
Wads; brownish-yellow, print black.
Business; American arms and ammo manufacturers.
Cases; Made in U.S.A.

DN.2-0207. Re-drawn; 27th Feb 2001

REMINGTON (ENGLAND):
UMC Works, Brimsdown, Enfield, Middlesex, England.

DATA
Gauge; 12.
Length; 64.5 mm.
Head; 12 mm.
Tube; Wound brown paper.
Colour; Mid-green. (Corrugated).
Ferrous metal; Nil.
Print; Black.
Base; Brass.
Closure; Rolled.
Wad; Yellowish-orange, print black.
Business; Arms manufacturers etc.

© DN.2-1923. September 1996

E. G. E. REYNOLDS:
Saxmundham, Suffolk, East Anglia, England.

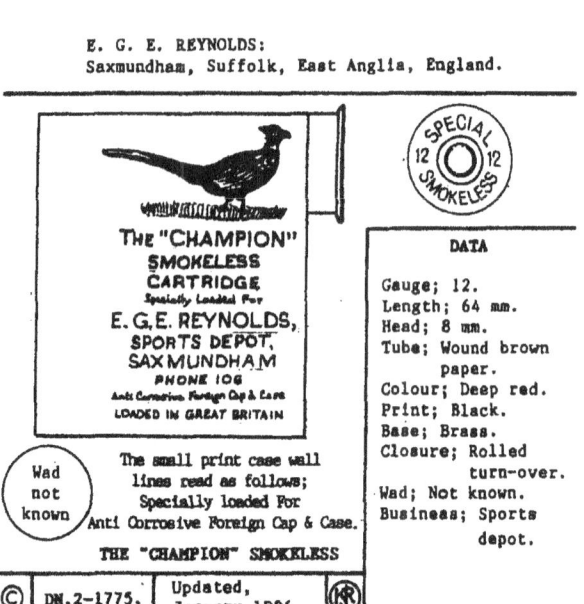

DATA
Gauge; 12.
Length; 64 mm.
Head; 8 mm.
Tube; Wound brown paper.
Colour; Deep red.
Print; Black.
Base; Brass.
Closure; Rolled turn-over.
Wad; Not known.
Business; Sports depot.

© DN.2-1775. Updated, January 1996

J. REYNOLDS:
Cullompton, Devonshire, England.

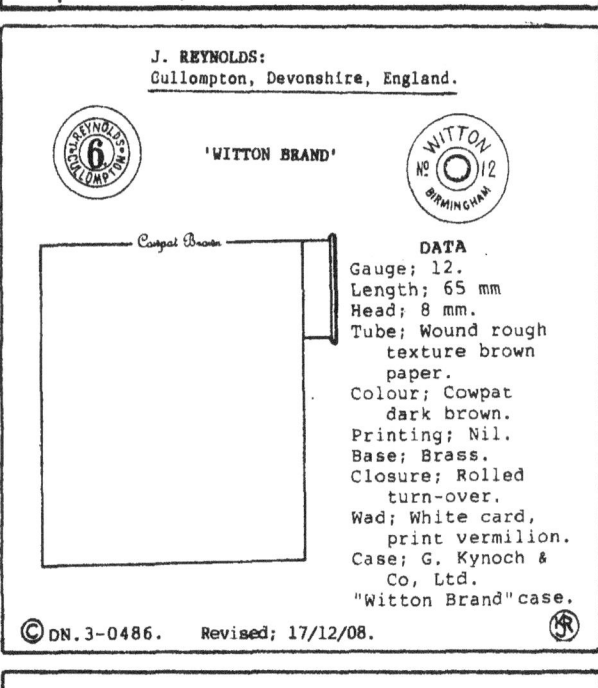

DATA
Gauge; 12.
Length; 65 mm.
Head; 8 mm.
Tube; Wound rough texture brown paper.
Colour; Cowpat dark brown.
Printing; Nil.
Base; Brass.
Closure; Rolled turn-over.
Wad; White card, print vermilion.
Case; G. Kynoch & Co, Ltd. "Witton Brand" case.

© DN.3-0486. Revised; 17/12/08.

RHEINISCHE WESTFALISCHE SPRINGSTOFF:
Nurnberg, Germany.

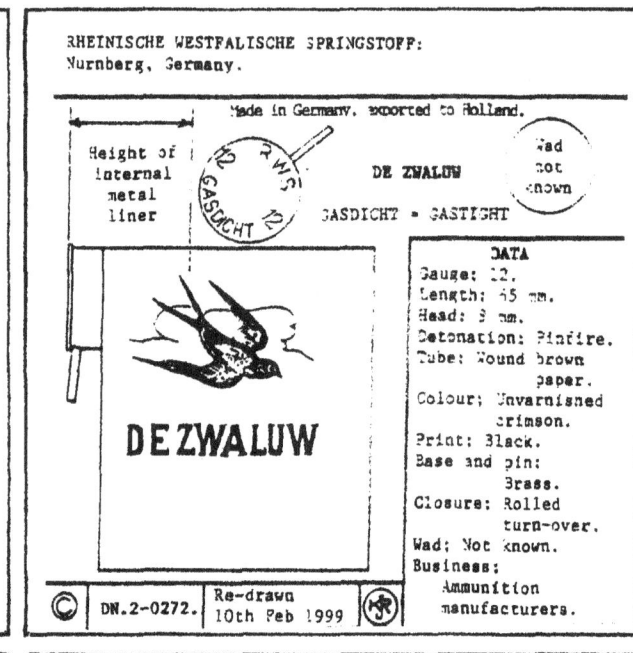

DATA
Gauge; 12.
Length; 65 mm.
Head; 8 mm.
Detonation; Pinfire.
Tube; Wound brown paper.
Colour; Unvarnished crimson.
Print; Black.
Base and pin; Brass.
Closure; Rolled turn-over.
Wad; Not known.
Business; Ammunition manufacturers.

© DN.2-0272. Re-drawn 10th Feb 1999

RHEINISCHE WESTFALISCHE SPRINGSTOFF:
Nurnberg, Germany.

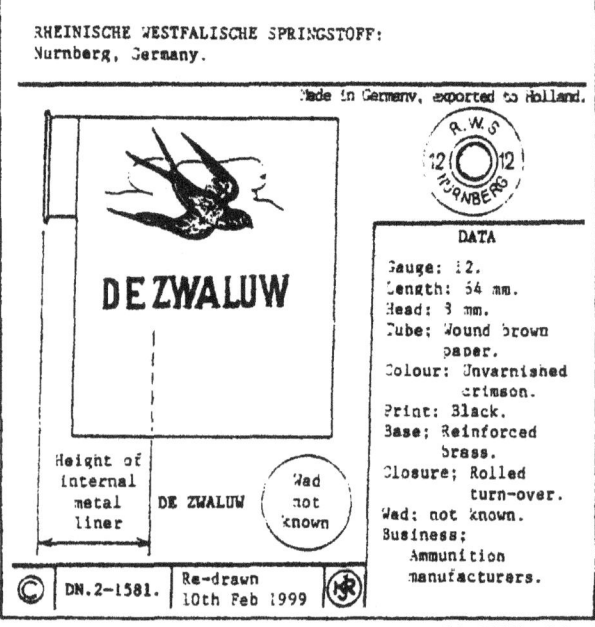

DATA
Gauge; 12.
Length; 64 mm.
Head; 8 mm.
Tube; Wound brown paper.
Colour; Unvarnished crimson.
Print; Black.
Base; Reinforced brass.
Closure; Rolled turn-over.
Wad; not known.
Business; Ammunition manufacturers.

© DN.2-1581. Re-drawn 10th Feb 1999

RHEINISCHE-WESTFALISCHE SPRENGSTOFF, A.G:
Nurnberg, West Germany.

DATA
Gauge; 16.
Length; 65 mm.
Head; 6.5 mm.
Tube; Wound brown paper.
Colour; Salmon red.
Print; Black.
Base; Reinforced brass.
Closure; Rolled turn-over.
Wad; White card, print black.
Case; H. Utendoerffer.
Cap; R.W.S. (brass).
Business; Ammunition manufacturers.

GERMAN	ENGLISH TRANSLATION
MARKE EINHORN	Mark (Td Mk) Unicorn
RAUCHLOS	Smokeless
Rostfrei	Rust free

© DN.2-1967. May 1997.

PLATE 322 [REM - RHE]

C. C. RICHARDS: Wiveliscombe, Somerset, England.

"THE WIVEY" SPECIAL SMOKELESS
BRITISH HAND LOADED
C.C. RICHARDS
IRONMONGER
WIVELISCOMBE
PHONE 29
FOREIGN MADE CASE

Drawn from a set of photographs

DATA
Gauge; 12.
Length; 64 mm.
Head; 7 mm.
Tube; Wound paper.
Colour; Light purple.
Print; Silver.
Base; Brass.
Closure; Rolled turn-over.
Wad; Yellow, print black.
Business; Ironmonger.
Case; Foreign made.

© DN.2-2028. October 1998

WILLIAM RICHARDS (LIVERPOOL), LTD: 27 Old Hall Street, Liverpool, Lancashire (Merseyside). Also at, 44 Fisher Gate, Preston, Lancashire, England.

SPECIALLY LOADED BY W. RICHARDS (Liverpool) LTD.
LIVERPOOL & PRESTON
"THE CASTLE"
SMOKELESS CARTRIDGE
SMOKELESS CARTRIDGE
Tel: "Shooting Liverpool".
" Richard Gunmakers Preston
Dark Green

DATA
Gauge; 12.
Length; 64 mm.
Head; 16 mm.
Tube; Wound dark green paper.
Print; Black.
Base; Reinforced brass.
Cap; Copper.
Closure; Rolled turn-over.
Wad; Deep orange, print black.
Business; Gunmakers.
Circa; 1920's.

DN.3-0320. © Redrawn, 8/7/08.

WILLIAM RICHARDS (LIVERPOOL), LTD: 27 Old Hall Street, Liverpool, Lancashire (Merseyside). Also at, 44 Fisher Gate, Preston, Lancashire, England.

DATA
Gauge; 12.
Length; 64 mm.
Head; 16 mm.
Tube; Wound dark green paper.
Print; Black or navy blue.
Base; Reinforced brass.
Wad; White card, print black.
Business; Gunmakers.

SPECIALLY LOADED BY W. RICHARDS (Liverpool) LTD.
LIVERPOOL & PRESTON
"THE CASTLE"
SMOKELESS CARTRIDGE
Tel: "Shooting Liverpool".
" Richard Gunmakers Preston
Made in Great Britain
Dark Green

DN.3-0315. © Redrawn, 8/7/08.

WILLIAM RICHARDS: 27 Old Hall Street, Liverpool, Lancashire (Merseyside), England.

W. RICHARDS LIVERPOOL — Telephone No. 6925 Central
THE "EXPRESS" CARTRIDGE (SMOKELESS)
Telegraphic Address } "Shooting" Liverpool

W. RICHARDS LIVERPOOL
THE "EXPRESS" CARTRIDGE (SMOKELESS)
Telephone No. 6925 Central
Telegraphic Address } "Shooting" Liverpool

DATA
Gauge; 12.
Length; 65 mm.
Head; 15 mm.
Tube; Wound yellow paper.
Colour; Pale yellow.
Print; Black.
Base; Reinforced brass.
Closure; Rolled turn-over.
Wad shown; White card, print black.
Business; Gunmaker.

© DN.2-2367. 26th Oct 2000

WILLIAM RICHARDS: 1 Tithebarn Street, Liverpool, Lancashire (Merseyside), England.

DATA
Gauge; 12.
Length; 64 mm.
Head; 8 mm.
Tube; Wound paper.
Colour; Burnt orange.
Print; Black.
Base; Brass.
Cap; Copper.
Closure; Rolled turn-over.
Wad; Buttercup-yellow, print black.
Business; Gunmaker.
Case by; Eley Bros, Ltd.

"Grand Prix"
W. RICHARDS
GUNMAKER
LIVERPOOL
TELEPHONE No. 6926
Burnt orange

"Grand Prix"
W. RICHARDS
GUNMAKER
LIVERPOOL
TELEPHONE No. 6926

Not examined for internal metals.

© DN.3-0483. Drawn, 6/4/08.

WILLIAM RICHARDS (LIVERPOOL), LTD: 27 Old Hall Street, Liverpool, Lancashire (Merseyside). Also at, 44 Fishergate, Preston, Lancashire, England.

SPECIALLY LOADED
W. RICHARDS (Liverpool) LTD.
LIVERPOOL & PRESTON
THE "MARK DOWN" SMOKELESS CARTRIDGE
Tel: "Shooting Liverpool"
" "Richards Gunmakers, Preston"
MADE IN GREAT BRITAIN

DATA
Gauge; 12.
Length; 64 mm.
Head; 8 mm.
Tube; Wound pink paper.
Colour; Pink.
Printings; Black or navy blue.
Base; Reinforced brass.
Closure; Rolled turn-over.
Wetproof; Clear lacquered.
Wad; Brown card, print black.
Business; Gunmakers.
Circa: 1930's.

© DN.2-0313. Re-drawn; 12th Feb 2001

PLATE 323 [RIC - RIC]

WILLIAM RICHARDS:
44 Fishergate, Preston. Also at, 27 Old Hall Street, Liverpool, Lancashire, England.

The example drawn was old, faded and reloaded.

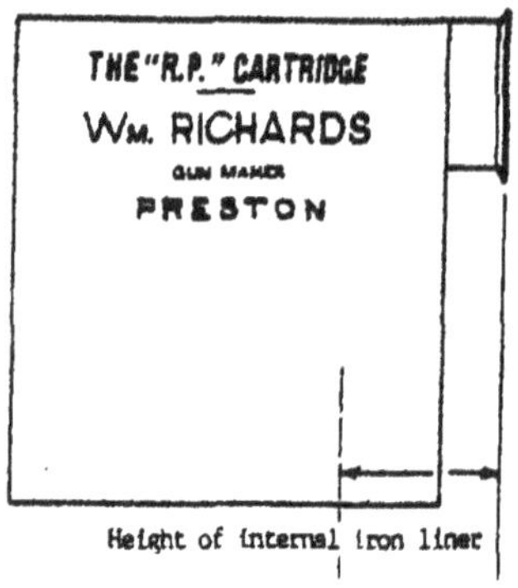

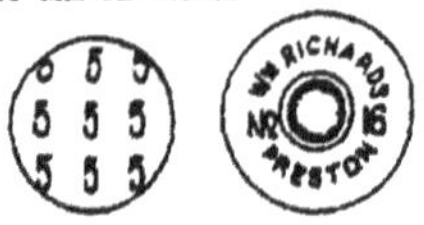

THE "R.P." CARTRIDGE
Wm. RICHARDS
GUN MAKER
PRESTON

DATA
Gauge; 16.
Length; 64 mm.
Head; 8 mm.
Tube; Wound red paper.
Colour; Dull red.
Print; Black.
Base; Reinforced brass.
Closure; Rolled turn-over.
Wad shown; White card, print black. (Not original).
Business; Gunmaker.

© DN.2-2094. November 1998

W. RICHARDS:
44 Fishergate, Preston, Lancashire, England.

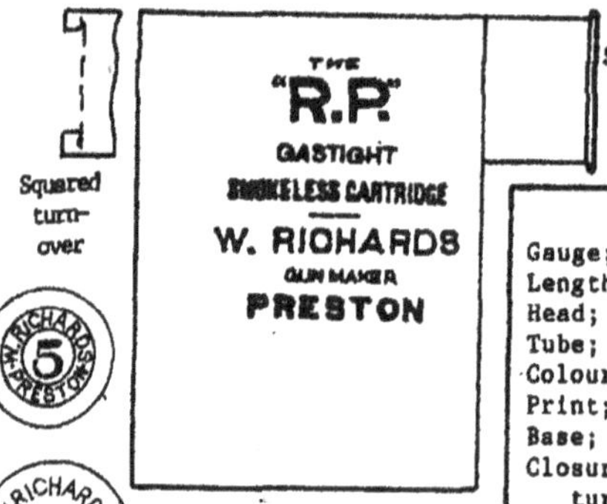

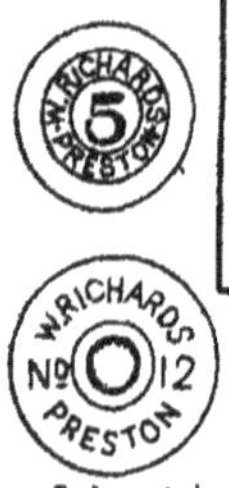

THE
"R.P."
GASTIGHT
SMOKELESS CARTRIDGE
W. RICHARDS
GUNMAKERS
PRESTON

DATA
Gauge; 12.
Length; 64 mm.
Head; 16 mm.
Tube; Wound paper.
Colour; Off-white.
Print; Black.
Base; Brass.
Closure; Rolled turn-over.
Wad; Pea green, print black.
Business; Gunmaker.

I do not know why the letters 'R.P.' Guessing, perhaps, Richards Preston.

© DN.2-1340. Re-drawn; 8th Feb 2001

A. RICHARDSON & SONS : 32 Quay Street, Halesworth, Suffolk, England.

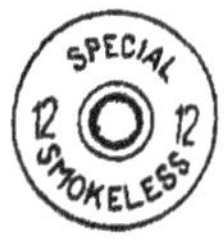

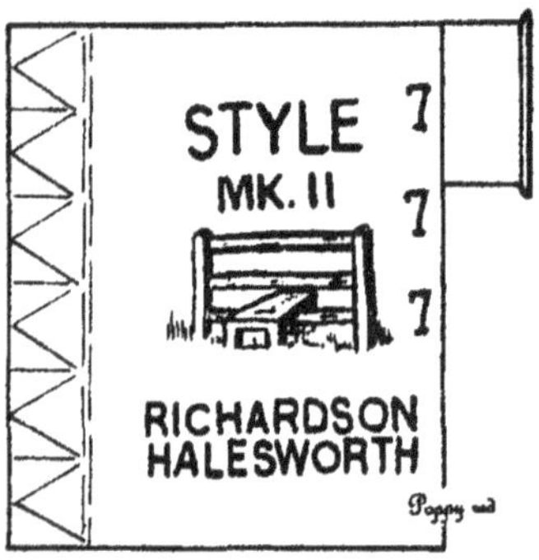

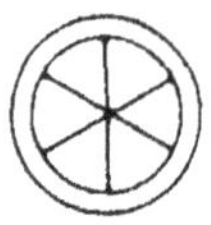

STYLE
MK. II
RICHARDSON
HALESWORTH

DATA
Gauge; 12.
Length; 69 mm.
Head; 12 mm.
Tube; Wound white paper.
Outer colour; Red.
Print; Black.
Base; Steel with a brass wash.
Cap; Nickel.
Closure; Six fold crimp.
Case by, Fiocchi.
Load by, Hull Cartridge.
Business; Gunsmiths.

© DN.3-0975. Drawn, 27/4/08.

G. M. RICHARDSON: Dumfries, Dumfries-shire, Scotland.

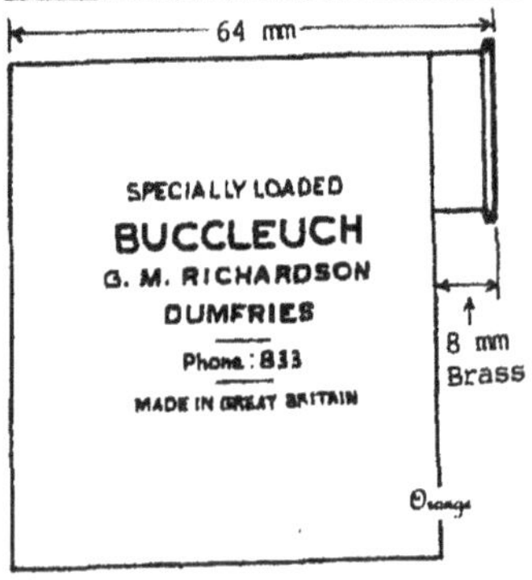

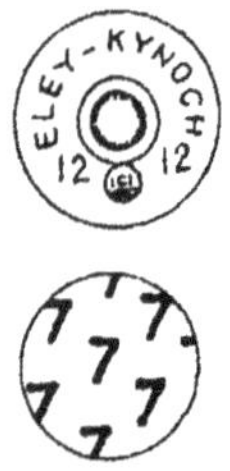

SPECIALLY LOADED
BUCCLEUCH
G.M.RICHARDSON
DUMFRIES
Phone:833
MADE IN GREAT BRITAIN

The tube on this cartridge was wound from orange paper. The top wad was from brown card. Both the case wall and the wad were printed in black.

© DN.3-1344. Revised, 9/2/09.

WILLIAM G. RICHARDSON: Barnard Castle, County Durham, England.

Was not internally examined.

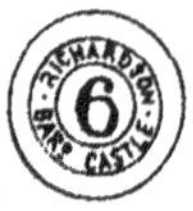

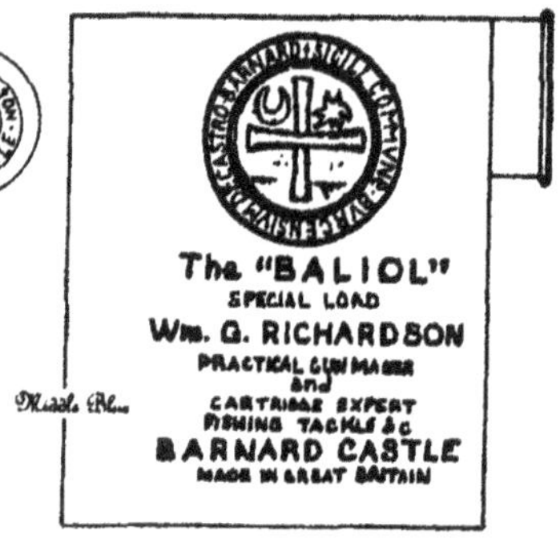

DATA
Gauge; 12.
Length; 64 mm.
Head; 8 mm.
Tube; Wound Middle blue paper.
Printing; Dark blue.
Base; Brass.
Cap; Copper.
Closure; Rolled turn-over.
Wad; White card, print black.
Business; Gunmakers.
Circa; 1930's.

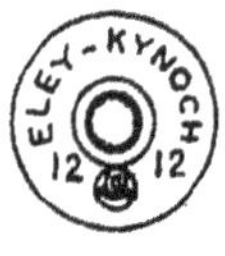

The "BALIOL"
SPECIAL LOAD
Wm. G. RICHARDSON
PRACTICLE GUNMAKER
and
CARTRIDGE EXPERT
FISHING TACKLE & C
BARNARD CASTLE
MADE IN GREAT BRITAIN

Drawn, 25/8/08.
© DN.3-0143.

WILLIAM GEORGE RICHARDSON: Benjamin Bank, Barnard Castle, County Durham, England.

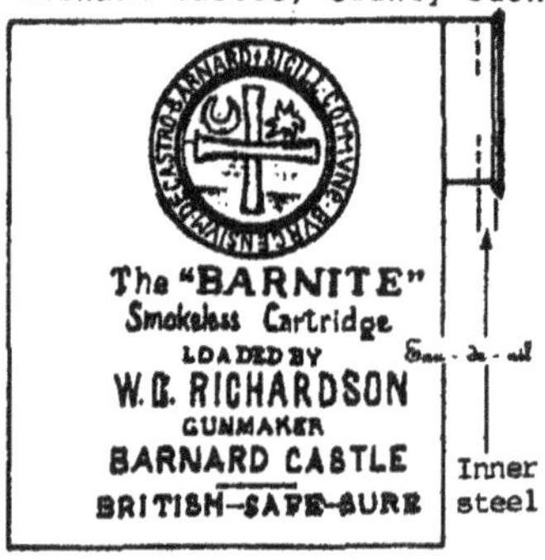

DATA
Gauge; 12.
Length; 64 mm.
Head; 8 mm.
Tube; Wound eau-de-nil paper.
Print; Navy blue.
Base; Reinforced brass.
Wad; White card, print black.
Business; Gunmaker.

The "BARNITE"
Smokeless Cartridge
LOADED BY
W.G.RICHARDSON
GUNMAKER
BARNARD CASTLE
BRITISH-SAFE-SURE

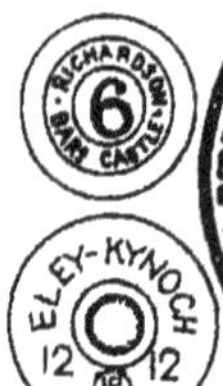

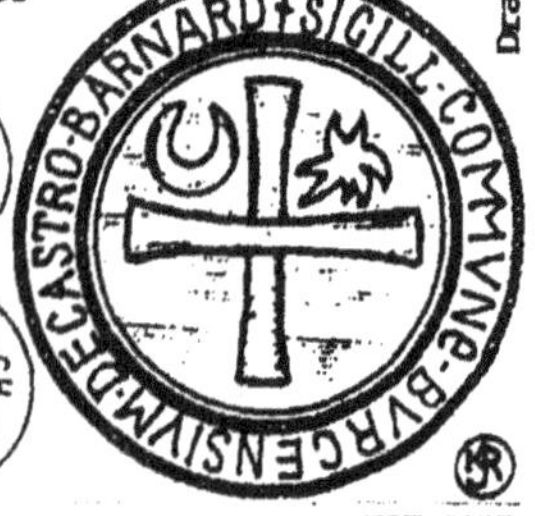

Drawn, 10/4/08.

© DN.3-0145.

WILLIAM G. RICHARDSON, LTD:
Barnard Castle, County Durham,
England.

THE "BARNOID"
Wm. G. RICHARDSON
PRACTICLE GUN MAKER
AND
CARTRIDGE EXPERT
FISHING TACKLE & C.

BARNARD CASTLE

Made in Great Britain

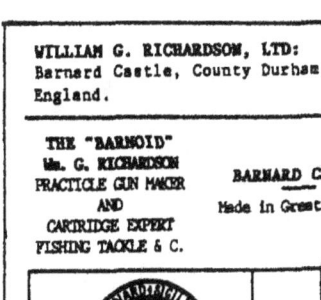

THE "BARNOID"
WM. G. RICHARDSON
PRACTICLE GUN MAKER
AND
CARTRIDGE EXPERT
FISHING TACKLE & C.
BARNARD CASTLE
Made in Great Britain

DATA
Gauge; 12.
Length; 64 mm.
Head; 16 mm.
Tube; Wound dark green paper.
Colour; Forest Green.
Print; Black or navy blue.
Base; Reinforced brass.
Closure; Rolled turn-over.
Wad; Orange card, print black.
Business; Gunmaker.
Circa; 1930's.

© DN.2-0144. Re-drawn; 30th June 2000

JOHN RIGBY & COMPANY: 32 King Street,
St. James's, London S.W.1., England.

DATA
Gauge; 12.
Length; 64 mm.
Head; 8 mm.
Tube; Wound pink paper.
Print; Black.
Base; Brass. May have had steel reinforcing.
Cap; Non-corrosive.
Closure; Rolled turn-over.
Wad; Dark blue card, print black.
Business; Gun and rifle makers.
Circa; Post World War Two.

JOHN RIGBY & CO.
32 KING STREET
ST.JAMES'S
LONDON.S.W.1

© DN.3-2805. Drawn, 21/3/08.

JOHN RIGBY & CO (GUNMAKERS), LTD: 43 Sackville
Street, London W.1., England.

JOHN RIGBY & CO.
(Gunmakers) Ltd.
43. SACKVILLE STREET,
LONDON. W.1
WATER-RESISTING
Made in Great Britain

Not examined for internal metals.

DATA
Gauge; 12.
Length; 64 mm.
Head; 16 mm.
Tube; Wound blue paper.
Colour; Middle blue.
Print; Black.
Base; Brass.
Cap; Copper.
Closure; Rolled turn-over.
Wad; White card, print black.
Business; Gun and rifle makers.
Circa; 1930's.

JOHN RIGBY & CO.
(Gunmakers) Ltd.
43 SACKVILLE STREET,
LONDON. W.1
WATER-RESISTING
Made in Great Britain

© DN.3-1375. Drawn, 9/4/08.

JOHN RIGBY & COMPANY:
72 St. James's Street, London, S.W., England.

Paper   7 mm

Brass   58 mm

KYNOCH EJECTOR

DATA
Gauge; 12.
Length; 65 mm.
Head; 58 mm including brass extension.
Tube; Wound brown paper.
Print; Nil.
Base including extended sleeve; Brass.
Closure; Rolled turn-over.
Wad; Deep orange, print purple.
Case; Kynoch & Co.
Business; Gun and rifle makers.

© DN.2-0767. Updated; December 1997.

C. RIGGS & COMPANY LIMITED:
107 Bishopsgate, London, E.C., England.

DATA
Gauge; 12.
Length; 64 mm.
Head; 8 mm.
Tube; Wound paper.
Colour; Light tan.
Print; Black.
Base; Brass.
Closure; Rolled turn-over.
Wad; Light pink, print black.
Case; Messrs Eley Brothers.

Ye
Bishop's Gate
Sports house
THE "GATE"
C. RIGGS & CO.,LTD.
107. BISHOPSGATE
LONDON. E.C.

Drawing made from a set of photographs.

© DN.2-2017. October 1997.

A. E. RINGWOOD:
Banbury, Oxfordshire, England.

THE
DREADNOUGHT
CARTRIDGE
A. E. RINGWOOD
GUNMAKER
BANBURY
MADE IN GREAT BRITAIN

DATA
Gauge; 12.
Length; 64 mm.
Head; 8 mm.
Tubes; Wound coloured papers.
Colours; Eau-de-nil with navy blue print, or grey-green with black.
Base; Reinforced brass.
Closure; Rolled turn-over.
Wad; White card, print red.
Business; Gunmaker.

THE
DREADNOUGHT
CARTRIDGE
A. E. RINGWOOD
GUNMAKER
BANBURY
MADE IN GREAT BRITAIN

© DN.2-0079. Re-drawn; 22nd June 2000

PLATE 325 [RIC – RIN]

A.E. RINGWOOD:
Banbury, Oxfordshire, England.

" I D E A L "
A.E.RINGWOOD
GUNMAKER
BANBURY

DATA

Gauge; 12.
Length; 64 mm.
Head; 8 mm.
Tube; Wound brown paper.
Colour; Greenish-grey.
Print; Black.
Base; Brass.
Closure; Rolled turn-over.
Wad; Not known.
Business; Gunmaker.
Case; Made in Belgium.

© DN.2-2153. 14th Apr 1992

A. E. RINGWOOD:
Banbury, Oxfordshire, England.

DATA

Gauge; 12.
Length; 64.5 mm.
Head; 8 mm.
Tube; Wound brown paper.
Colour; Dark red.
PANTONE® 1797.
Print; Black.
Base; Brass.
Closure; Rolled turn-over.
Wad; Yellow, print nil.
Business; Gunmaker.

"IDEAL"

© DN.2-1477. Updated; May 1995

A. E. RINGWOOD:
Banbury, Oxfordshire, England.

DATA

Gauge; 12.
Length; 64 mm.
Head; 14 mm.
Tube; Wound brown paper.
Colour; Dark crimson.
Print; Black.
Base; Brass.
Closure; Rolled turn-over.
Wad; White card, shot size in black.
Business; Gunmaker.

© DN.2-1478. Updated May 1995

AUGUSTUS J. ROBERTS:
55 Broad Street, Ludlow, Shropshire, England.

Drawn from a set of photographs

"THE ROBERTS"
SPECIAL SMOKELESS
BRITISH HAND LOADED
AUGUSTUS J. ROBERTS

IRONMONGER
55 BROAD ST.
LUDLOW
PHONE 160
FOREIGN MADE CASE

DATA

Gauge; 12.
Length, 64 mm.
Head; 7 mm.
Tube; Wound paper.
Colour; Crimson red.
Print; Black.
Base; Brass.
Closure; Rolled turn-over.
Wad; White card, print black.
Business; Ironmonger.
Case; Foreign made.

© DN.2-2025. October 1998

H. P. ROBERTS:
Ottery St. Mary, Devonshire, England.

THE
"OTTER VALE"
NITRO CARTRIDGE
H. P. ROBERTS
OTTERY ST. MARY

DATA

Gauge; 12.
Length; 64 mm.
Head; 8 mm.
Tube; Wound cream-white paper.
Colour; Cream-white.
Print; Black.
Base; Brass.
Closure; Rolled turn-over.
Wad; Primrose yellow, print black.
Business: Ironmonger.
Circa; 1930's.

© DN.2-0177. Re-drawn; 10th Jan 2000.

ALEXANDER ROBERTSON & SON:
Wick, Caithness, Scotland.

REGISTERED EB TRADE MARK
ELEY
GAS-TIGHT
CARTRIDGE CASE
Made in Great Britain
LOADED BY
ALEXR ROBERTSON & SON
IRONMONGERS
WICK

DATA

Gauge; 12.
Length; 64 mm.
Head; 16 mm.
Tube; Wound indian red paper.
Colour; Eley's indian red.
Print; Black.
Base; Reinforced brass.
Closure; Rolled turn-over.
Wad; Not known.
Business; Ironmongers.
Case; Eley Bros, Ltd. London.

© DN.2-1341. Re-drawn; 16th Apr 2001

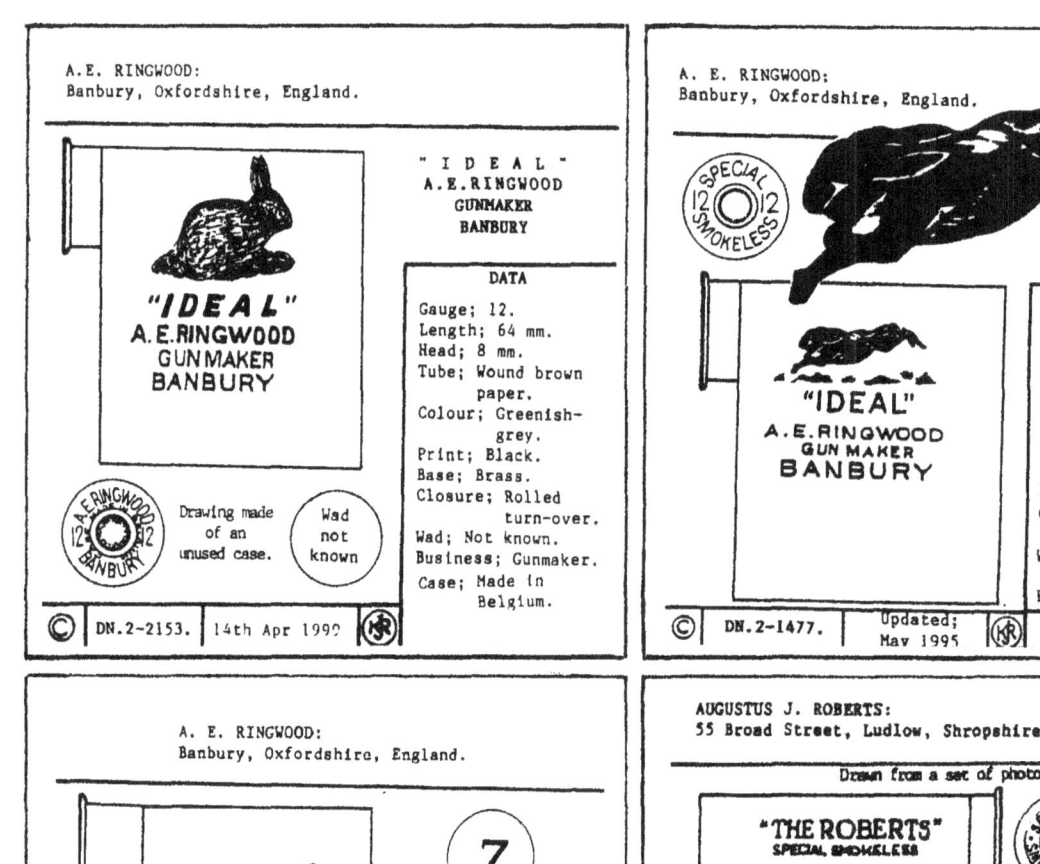

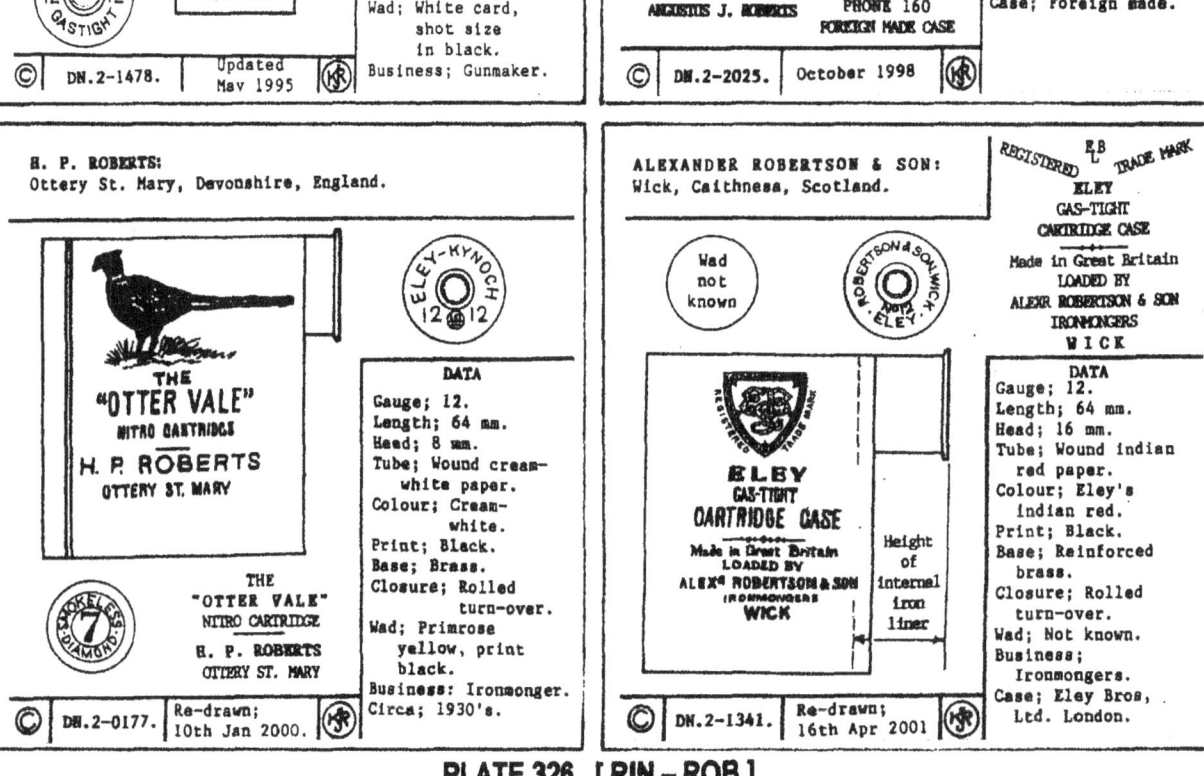

PLATE 326 [RIN – ROB]

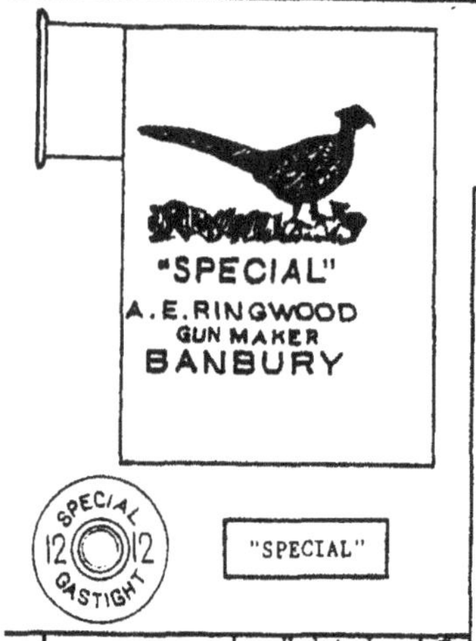

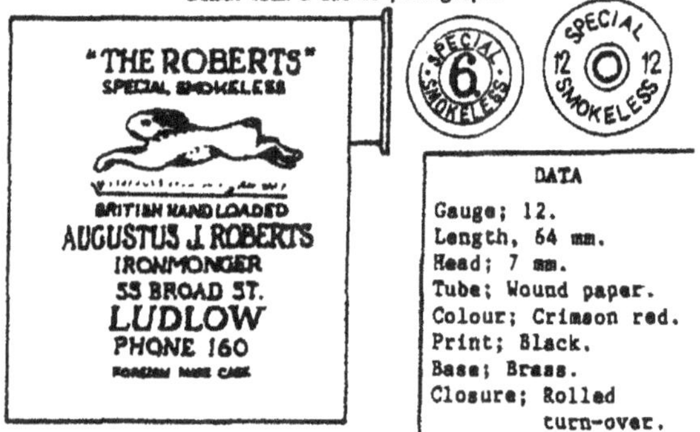

ROBIN HOOD AMMUNITION COMPANY:
Swanton, Vermont, North-East, United States of America.

DATA
Gauge; 12.
Length; 66 mm.
Head; 9 mm.
Tube; Wound pink paper.
Colour; Pink.
Print; Nil.
Base; Brass.
Closure; Rolled turn-over.
Wad; White card, print black.
Business; Gunpowder and ammunition manufacturers.

DN.2-1155. Re-drawn; 2nd Dec 2000.

H. ROBINSON & COMPANY:
Bridgnorth, Shropshire, England.

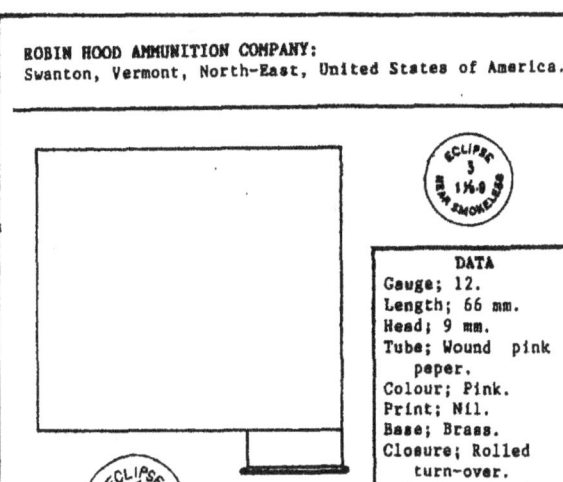

DATA
Gauge; 12.
Length; 65 mm.
Head; 7 mm.
Tube; Wound paper.
Colour; Maroon.
Print; Silver.
Base; Brass.
Closure; Rolled turn-over.
Wad; White card, print black.
Case; Foreign, possibly German.
Business; Ironmongers, gunsmiths and cycle makers.

"THE CASTLE"
SMOKELESS CARTRIDGE

DN.2-1356. Updated; March 1995.

ROBERT ROBINSON (GUNMAKERS) LIMITED:
7 Queen Street, Kingston upon Hull, Yorkshire (Humberside), England.

THE "HUMBER"
CARTRIDGE
LOADED BY
R. ROBINSON
(GUNMAKERS) LTD.
7 QUEEN STREET
HULL
MADE IN GREAT BRITAIN

DATA
Gauge; 12.
Length; 64 mm.
Head; 8 mm.
Tube; Wound off-white paper.
Colour; Cream-white.
Print; Black.
Base; Brass.
Closure; Rolled turn-over.
Wad; Yellow card, print black.
Wetproof; Clear lacquered.
Business; Gunmakers.
Circa; 1930's.

DN.2-0506. Re-drawn 28th Jan 1999.

ROBERT ROBINSON (GUNMAKERS) LIMITED:
7 Queen Street, Kingston upon Hull, Yorkshire (Humberside), England.

THE "HUMBER"
CARTRIDGE
LOADED BY
R. ROBINSON
(GUNMAKERS) LTD
HULL. Yorks
MADE IN GREAT BRITAIN

DATA
Gauge; 12.
Length; 64 mm.
Head; 8 mm.
Tube; Wound pink paper.
Colour; Pink.
Print; Black.
Base; Brass.
Closure; Rolled turn-over.
Wad; Light yellow, print black.
Business; Gunmakers.
Case; Eley-Kynoch I.C.I.
Circa; 1930's.

DN.2-0505. Re-drawn 28th Jan 1999.

ROBERT ROBINSON:
7 Queen Street, Kingston upon Hull, South Yorkshire (Humberside), England.

THE
"Magnet"
SMOKELESS CARTRIDGE
LOADED BY
ROBINSON
GUNMAKER
7 QUEEN STREET
HULL
"hq"

DATA
Gauge; 12.
Length; 64 mm.
Head; 8 mm.
Tube; Wound greyish-green paper.
Colour; Greyish-green.
Print; Black.
Base; Brass.
Closure; Rolled turn-over.
Wad; Emerald green, print black.
Business; Gunmaker.
Case; Nobel Explosives Co.

DN.2-0673. Re-drawn; 25th Feb 2000.

R. B. RODDA & CO: 2 Wellesley Place, Calcutta, India. Also in, Stafford Street, Birmingham, Warwickshire (West Midlands), England.

DATA
Gauge; 20.
Length; 64 mm.
Head; 7 mm.
Tube; Wound buff paper.
Print; Black.
Base; Reinforced brass.
Cap; Copper.
Wetproof; Clear lacquered.
Closure; Rolled turn-over.
Wad; White card, shot size purple.
Business; Gunmakers.
Circa; 1930's.

R.B. RODDA & CO.
"THE WELLESLEY"
CALCUTTA & BIRMINGHAM

DN.3-0445. Drawn, 25/3/08.

PLATE 327 [ROB - ROD]

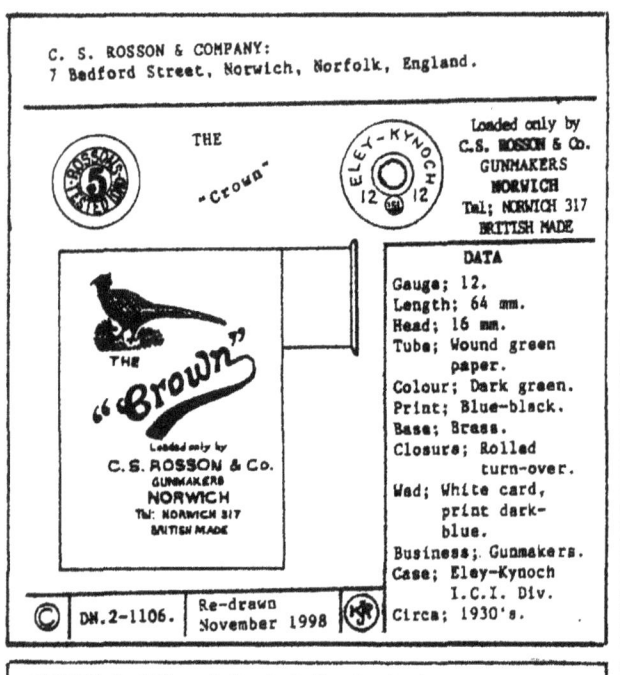
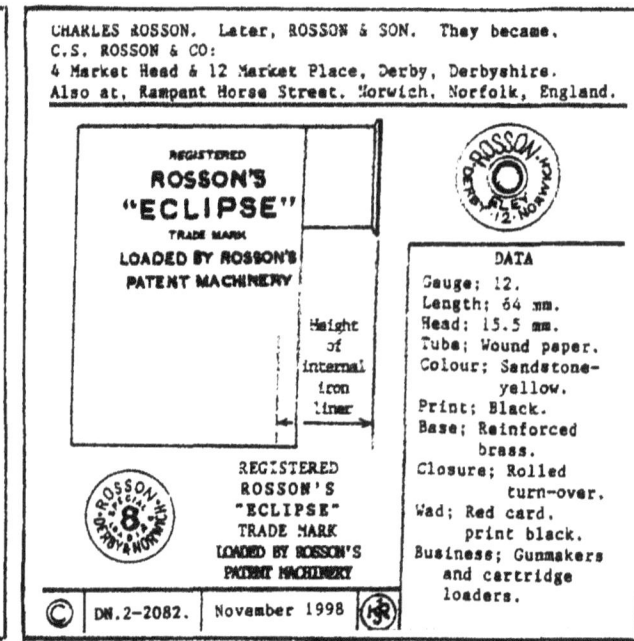
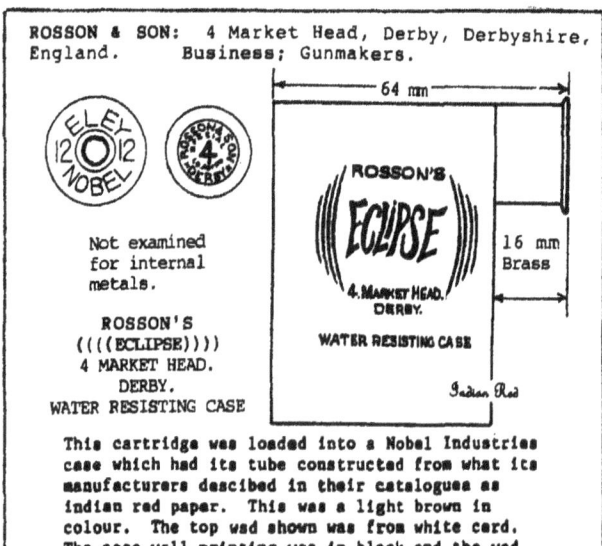
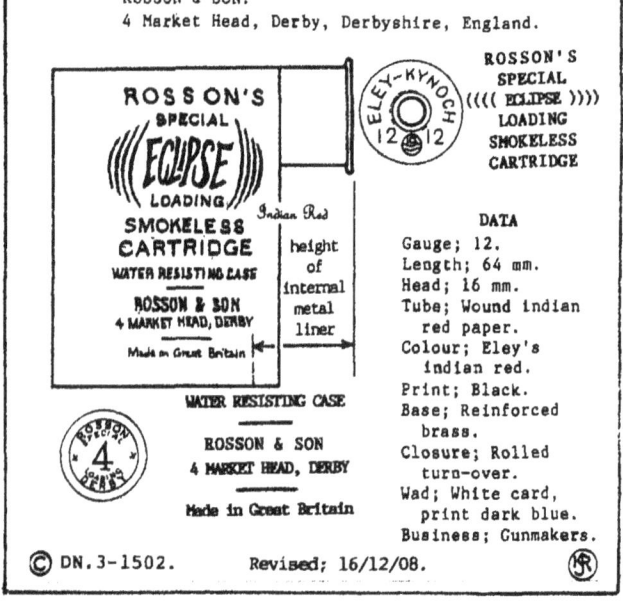
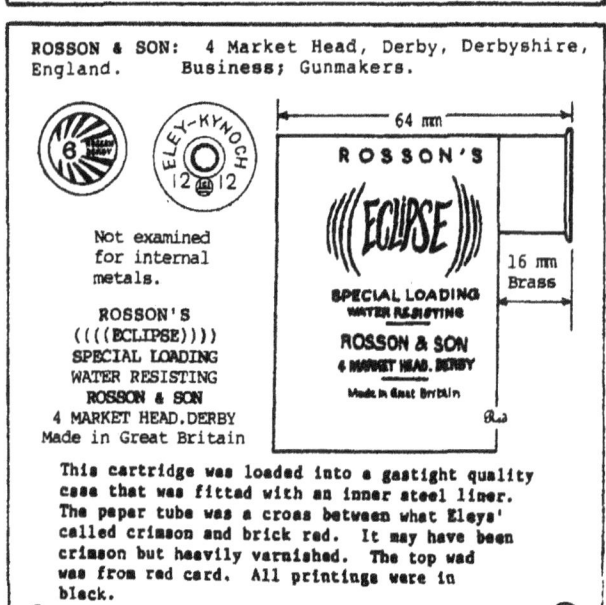
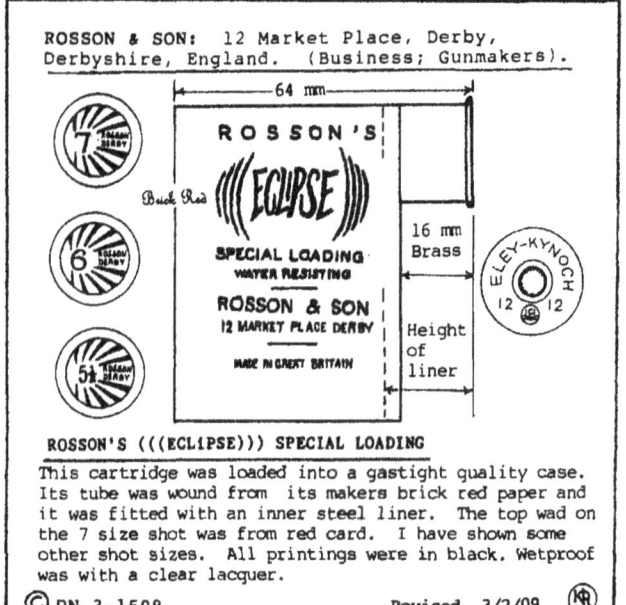

PLATE 328 [ROS – ROS]

CHARLES ROSSON & SON:
4 Market Head, Derby, Derbyshire, England.

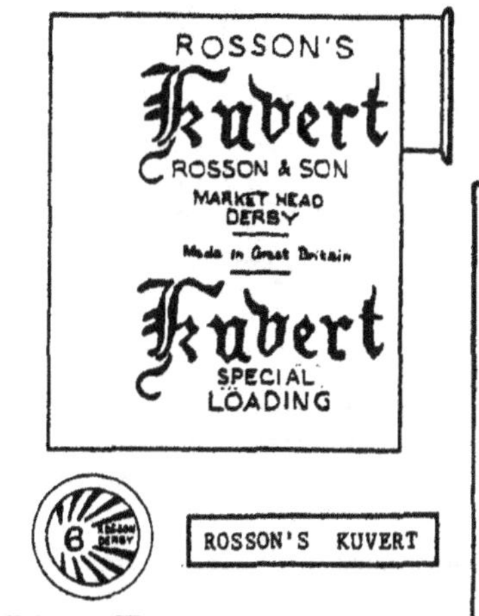

DATA
Gauge; 12.
Length; 64 mm.
Head; 8 mm.
Tube; Wound red paper.
Colour; E-K's crimson PANTONE® 193 C.
Print; Black.
Base; Brass.
Closure; Rolled turn-over.
Wad; Crimson red, print black.
Wetproof; Lacquered.
Circa; 1930's.
Business; Gunmakers.

© | DN.2-1830. | May 1995 | KR

C.S ROSSON & COMPANY:
13 Rampant Horse Street, Norwich.
Also, 7 Bedford Street, Norwich,
Norfolk, East Anglia, England.

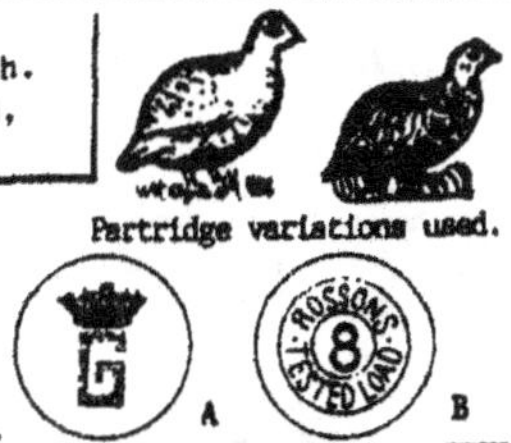

Partridge variations used.

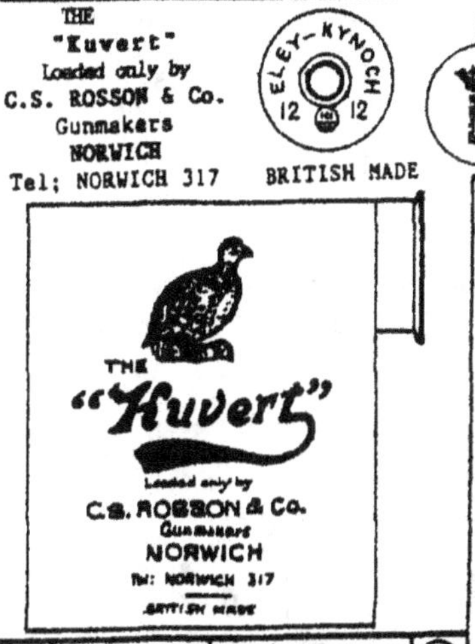

DATA
Gauge; 12.
Length; 64 mm.
Head; 8 mm.
Tube; Wound orange or red paper.
Printings; Black.
Base; Brass.
Closure; Rolled turn-over.
Wads shown;
A. White card, print black or blue. (May have been the Duke of Gloucester).
B. Deep yellow, print black.
Business: Gunmakers.

© | DN.2-0864. | Re-drawn 15th Jan 1999 | KR

C. S. ROSSON & CO, LTD:
Rampant Horse Street, Norwich, Norfolk, England.

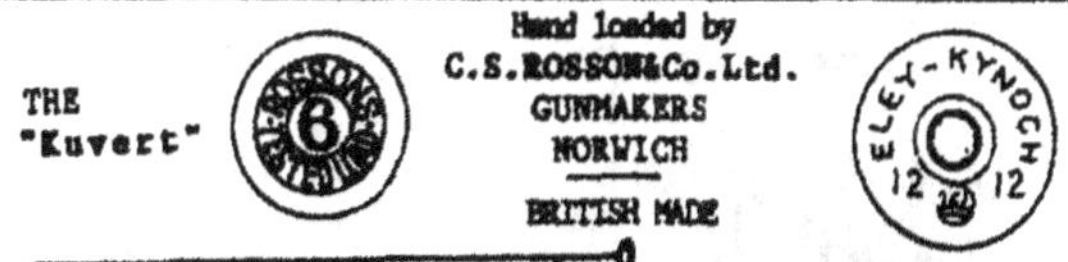

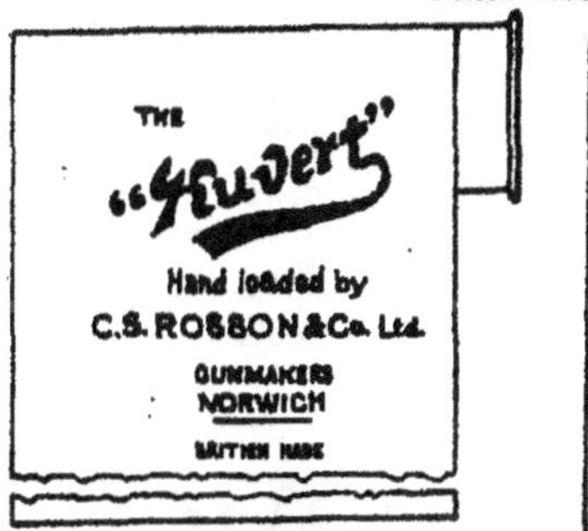

The wording, 'Hand loaded by' was deleted on later cartridges.

DATA
Gauge; 12.
Length; 64 mm.
Head; 8 mm.
Tube; Wound pink paper.
Colour; Pink.
Print; Black.
Base; Reinforced brass.
Closure; Rolled turn-over.
Wad; Green card, print black.
Business; Gunmakers.
Circa 1930's.

© | DN.2-0192. | Re-drawn 9th Feb 2000. | KR

ROSSON & SONS:
4 Market Head. Also, 12 Market Place, Derby, Derbyshire.
Also at, Rampant Horse Street, Norwich, Norfolk, England.

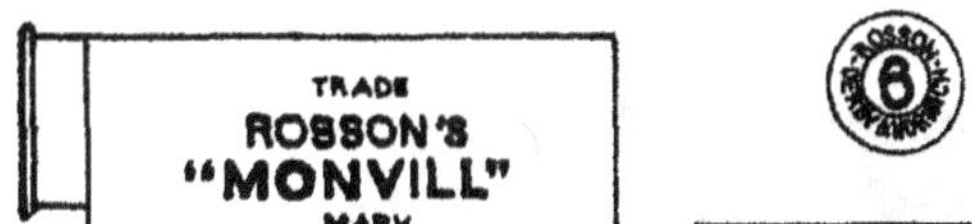

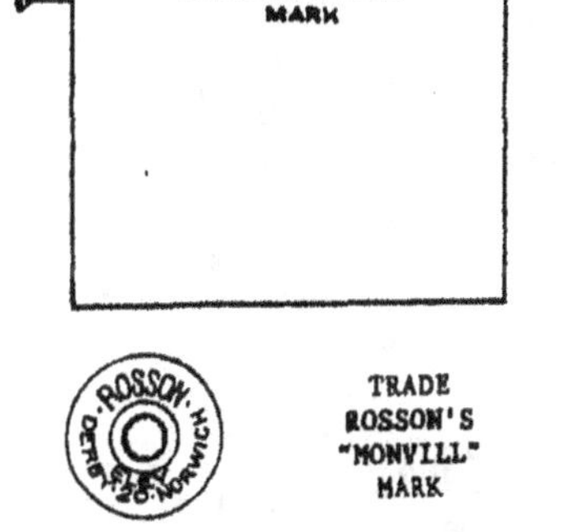

DATA
Gauge; 20.
Length; 64 mm.
Head; 7 mm.
Tube; Wound paper.
Colour; Crimson.
Print; Black.
Base; Brass.
Closure; Rolled turn-over.
Wad; White card, print dark blue.
Wetproof; Wax impregnated.
Business; Gunmakers.
Case; Eley Bros, Ltd. London.

© | DN.2-1505. | Re-drawn; 29th Nov 2000 | KR

CHARLES ROSSON & SON:
4 Market Head. Also at, 12 Market Place, Derby,
Derbyshire, England.

DATA
Gauge; 20.
Length; 64 mm.
Head; 14 mm.
Tube; Wound paper.
Colour; Dark green.
Print; Black.
Base; Brass.
Closure; Rolled turn-over.
Wad; Brown card, print black.
Business; Gunmakers.
Case; Nobel Industries, Ltd.
Circa; 1920's.

© | DN.2-1506. | Re-drawn; 17th Feb 2000. | KR

C. S. ROSSON & COMPANY:
Rampant Horse Street, Norwich, Norfolk, England.

Gauge; 16.
Length; 64 mm.
Head; 15 mm.
Tube; Wound blue paper.
Colour; Dark blue.
Print; Darker blue or black.
Base; Brass.
Closure; Rolled turn-over.
Wad; White card, print blue.
Wetproof; Lacquered.
Circa; 1930's.
Business; Gunmakers.

© | DN.2-0566. | Updated; March 1995 | KR

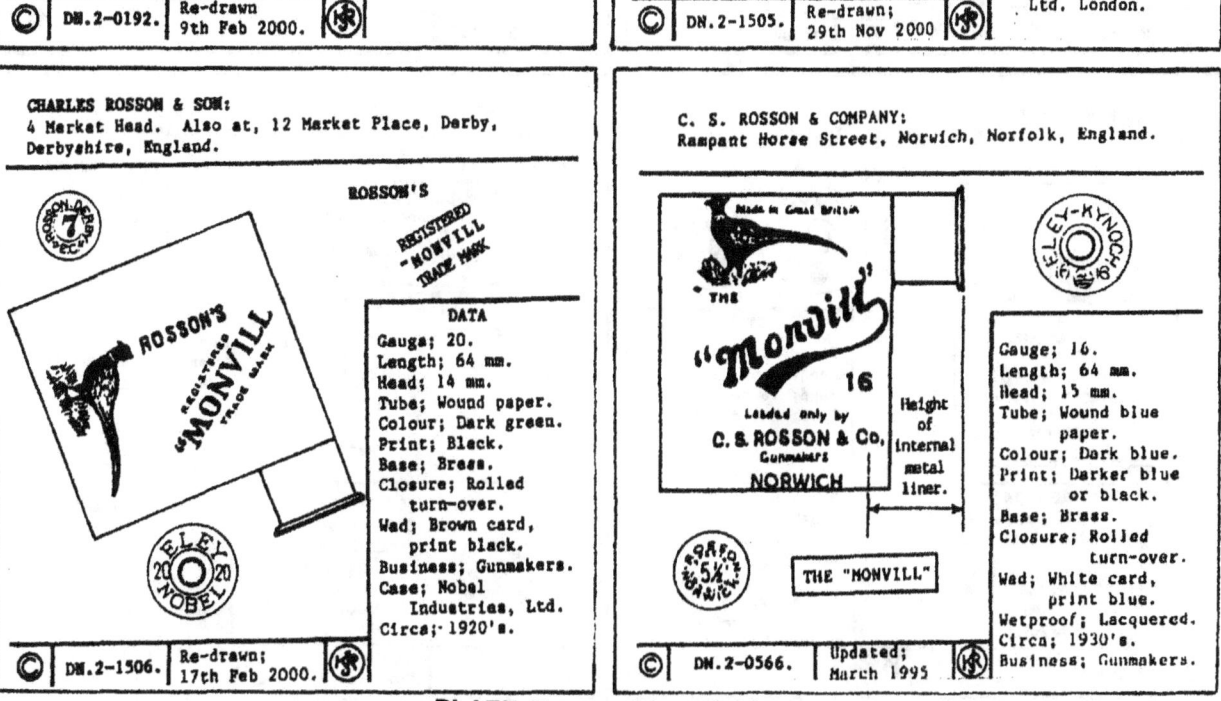

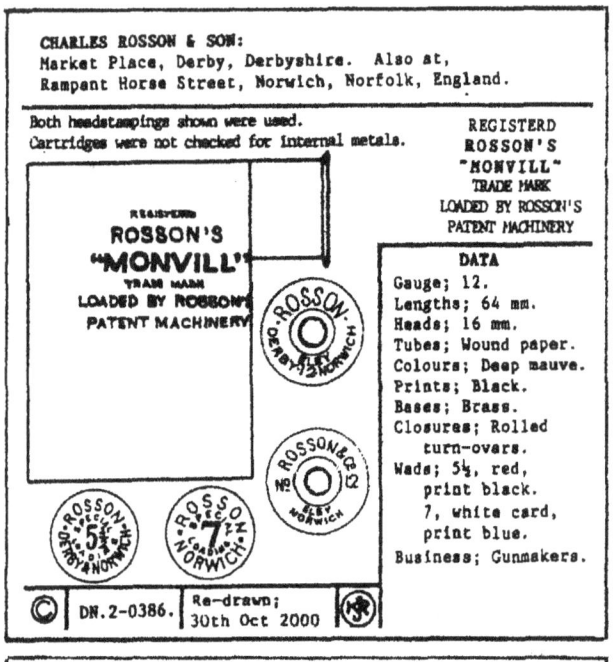
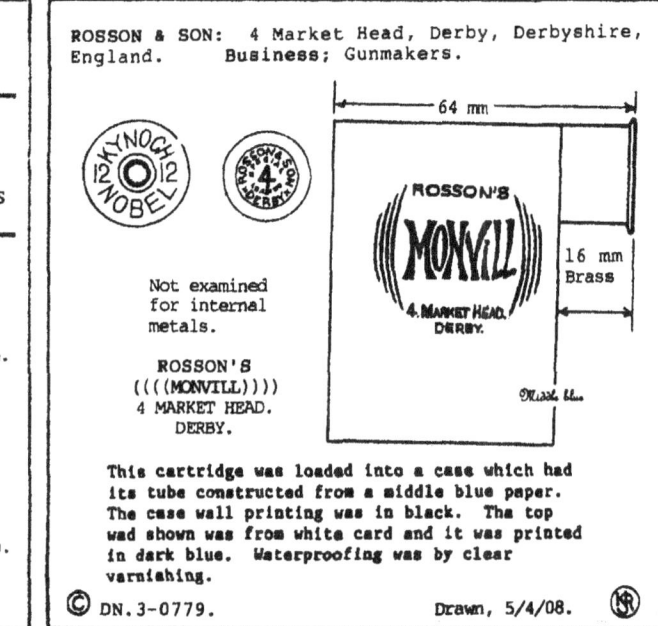
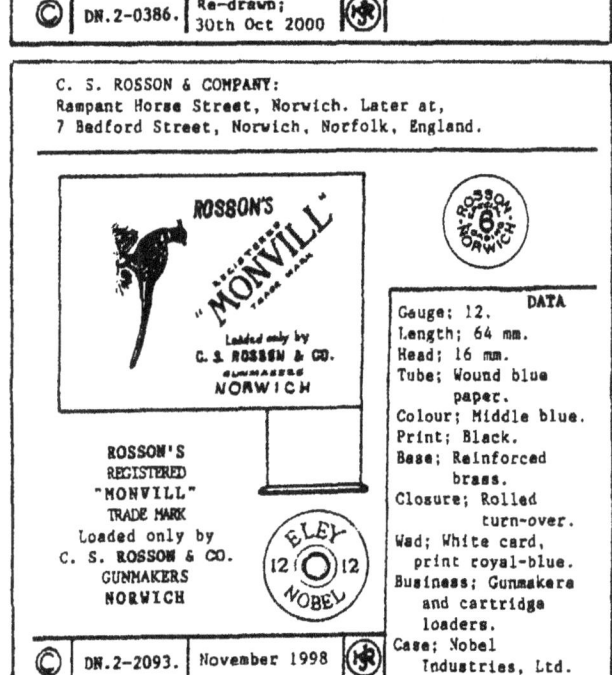
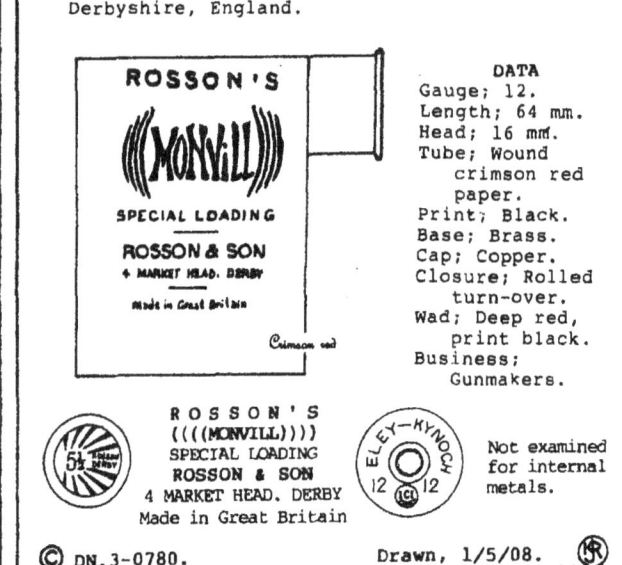
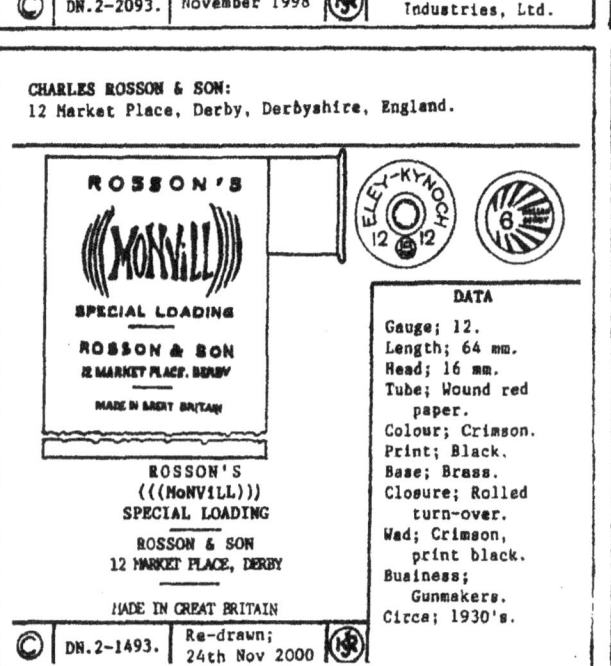

PLATE 330 [ROS - ROS]

CHARLES ROSSON & SON: 4 Market Head, Derby, Derbyshire, England.

DATA
Gauge; 12.
Length; 64 mm.
Head; 8 mm.
Tube; Wound paper.
Colour; Burnt orange.
Print; Black.
Base; Brass.
Cap; Copper.
Closure; Rolled turn-over.
Wad; Dull white card, print black.
Business; Gunmakers.
Case by; Nobel Industries, Ltd.

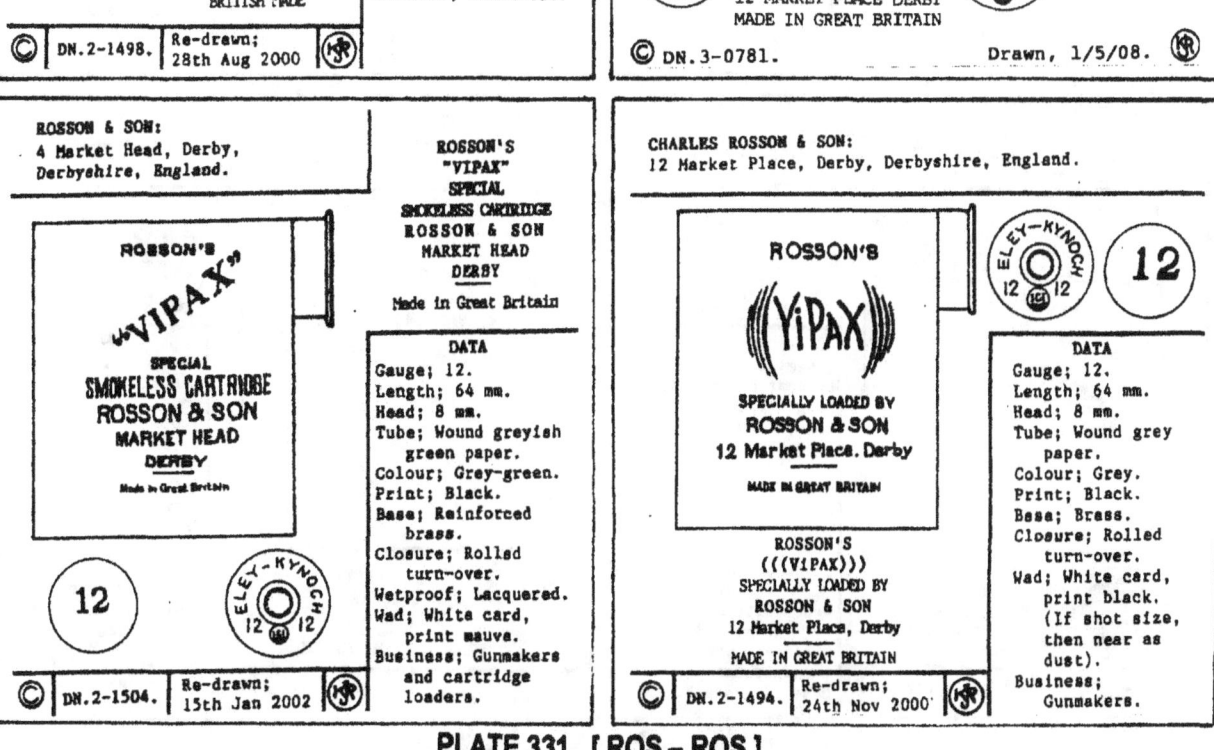

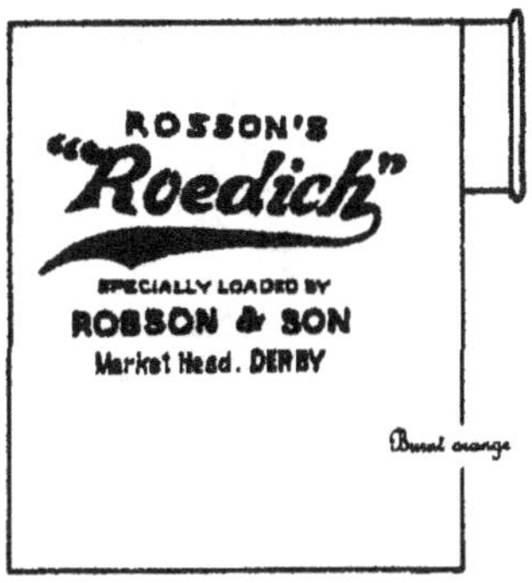

Not examined for internal metals.

ROSSON'S
"Roedich"
SPECIALLY LOADED BY
ROSSON & SON
Market Head. DERBY

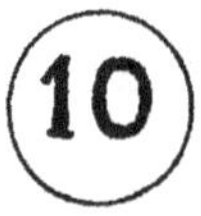

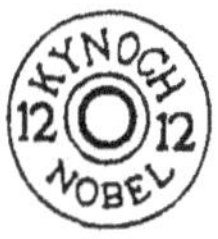

©DN.3-1503. Drawn, 7/7/08.

C. S. ROSSON & CO: Rampant Horse Street, Later at, 7 Bedford Street, Norwich, Norfolk, England.

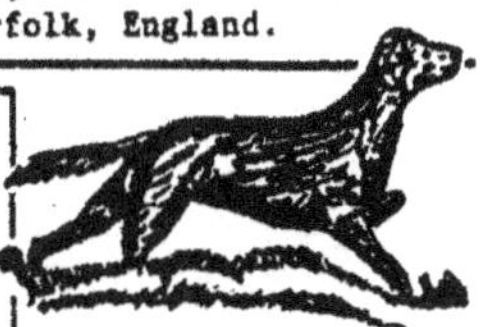

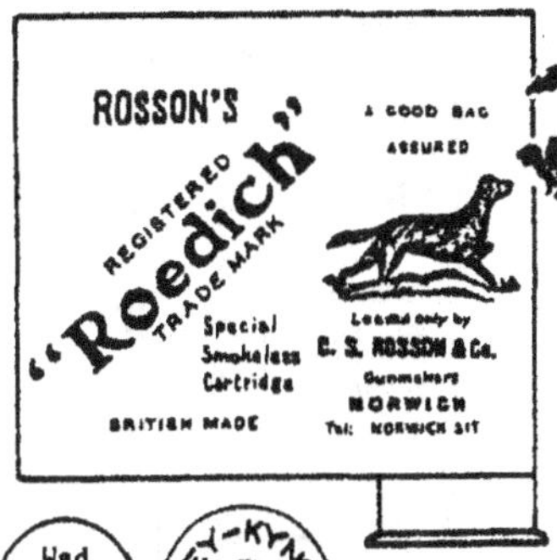

DATA
Gauge; 12.
Length; 64 mm.
Head; 8 mm.
Tube; Wound paper.
Colour; Grey 3.
Print; Black.
Base; Brass.
Closure; Rolled turn-over.
Wad; Not known.
Business; Gunmakers.

Wad not known

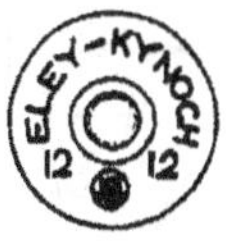

This drawing was made from a used case.

ROSSON'S "ROEDICH"

© DN.2-0344. Updated; December 1994

C. S. ROSSON & CO, LTD: 13 Rampant Horse Street, Norwich, Norfolk, England.

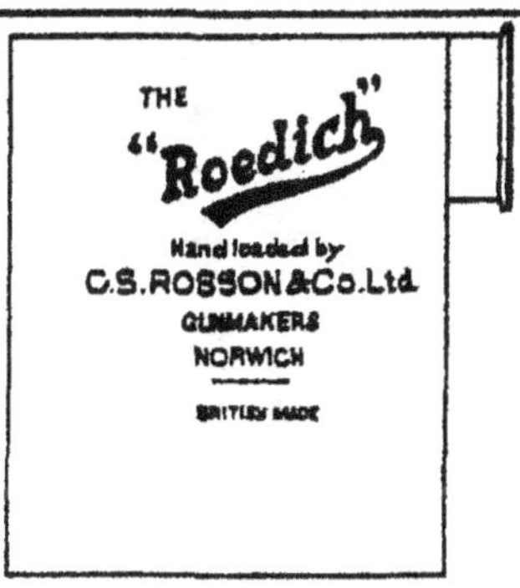

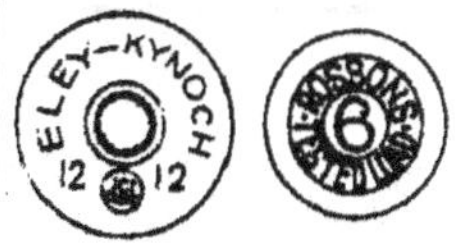

DATA
Gauge; 12.
Length; 64 mm.
Head; 8 mm.
Tube; Wound orange paper.
Colour; Orange.
Print; Black.
Base; Reinforced brass.
Closure; Rolled turn-over.
Wad; Dark red, print black.
Business; Gunmakers.

THE "Roedich"

Hand loaded by
C.S.ROSSON & Co,Ltd.
GUNMAKERS
NORWICH
BRITISH MADE

© DN.2-1498. Re-drawn; 28th Aug 2000

CHARLES ROSSON & SON: 12 Market Place, Derby, Derbyshire, England.

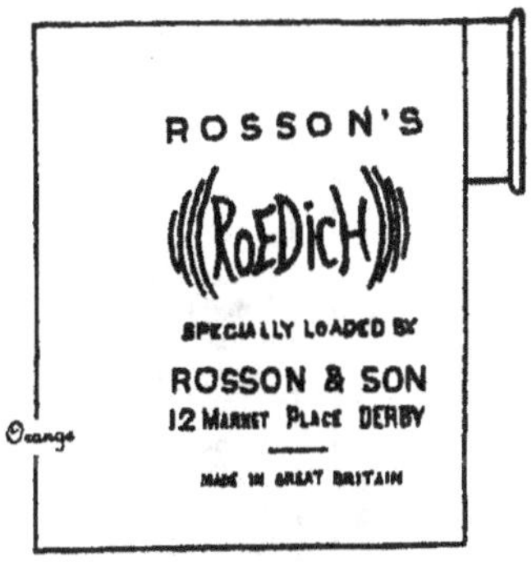

DATA
Gauge; 12.
Length; 64 mm.
Head; 8 mm.
Tube; Wound deep orange paper.
Print; Black.
Base; Brass.
Cap; Copper.
Closure; Rolled turn-over.
Wad; Lighter shade of orange, print black.
Business; Gunmakers.

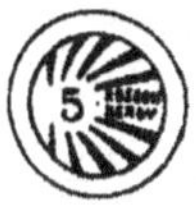

ROSSON'S
(((ROEDICH)))
SPECIALLY LOADED BY
ROSSON & SON
12 MARKET PLACE DERBY
MADE IN GREAT BRITAIN

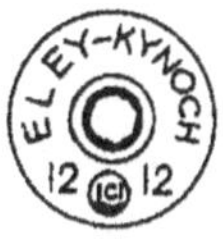

Not examined for internal metals.

© DN.3-0781. Drawn, 1/5/08.

ROSSON & SON: 4 Market Head, Derby, Derbyshire, England.

ROSSON'S
"VIPAX"
SPECIAL
SMOKELESS CARTRIDGE
ROSSON & SON
MARKET HEAD
DERBY
Made in Great Britain

DATA
Gauge; 12.
Length; 64 mm.
Head; 8 mm.
Tube; Wound greyish green paper.
Colour; Grey-green.
Print; Black.
Base; Reinforced brass.
Closure; Rolled turn-over.
Wetproof; Lacquered.
Wad; White card, print mauve.
Business; Gunmakers and cartridge loaders.

© DN.2-1504. Re-drawn; 15th Jan 2002

CHARLES ROSSON & SON: 12 Market Place, Derby, Derbyshire, England.

DATA
Gauge; 12.
Length; 64 mm.
Head; 8 mm.
Tube; Wound grey paper.
Colour; Grey.
Print; Black.
Base; Brass.
Closure; Rolled turn-over.
Wad; White card, print black. (If shot size, then near as dust).
Business; Gunmakers.

ROSSON'S
(((VIPAX)))
SPECIALLY LOADED BY
ROSSON & SON
12 Market Place, Derby
MADE IN GREAT BRITAIN

© DN.2-1494. Re-drawn; 24th Nov 2000

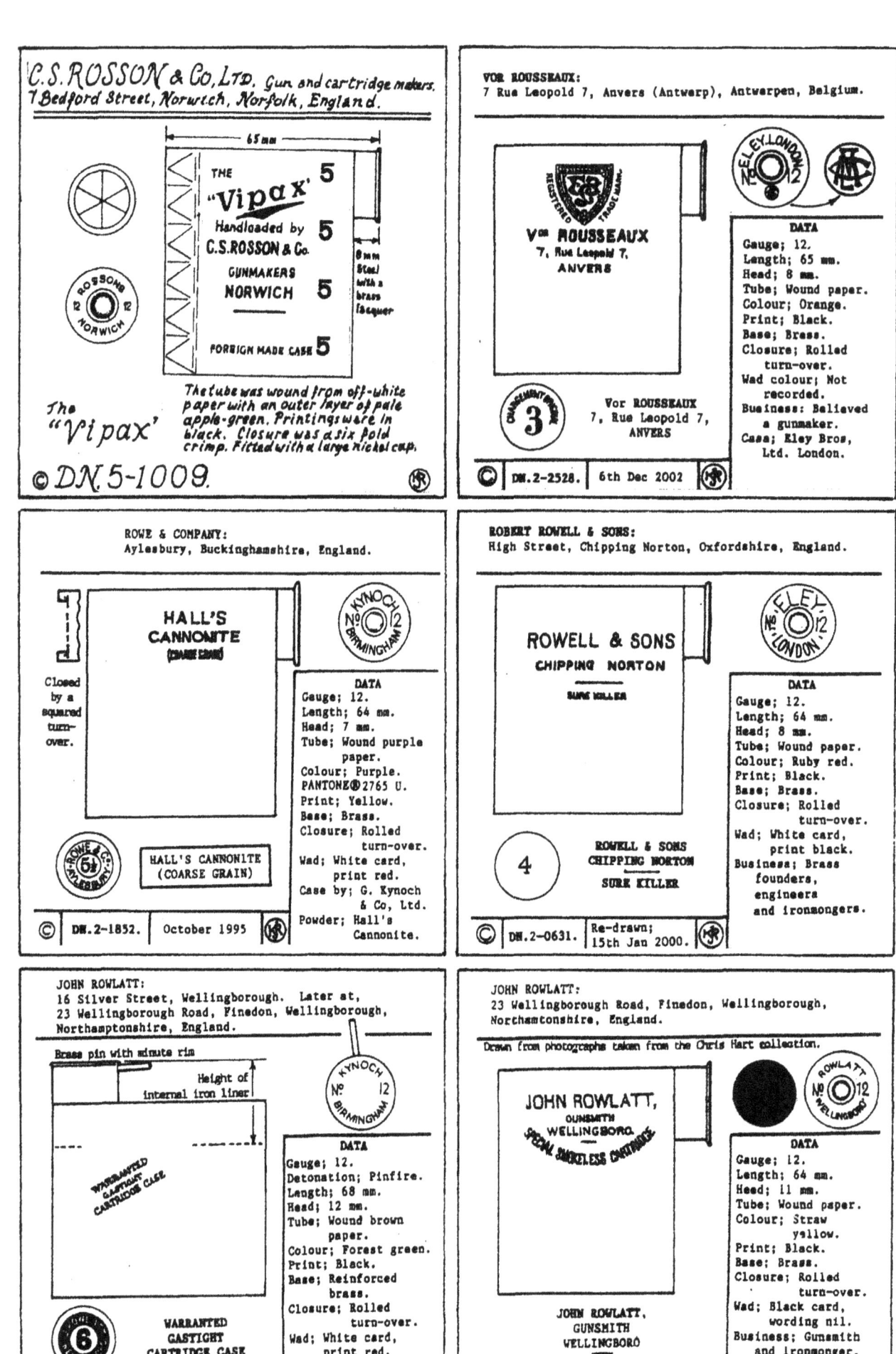
PLATE 332 [ROS - POW]

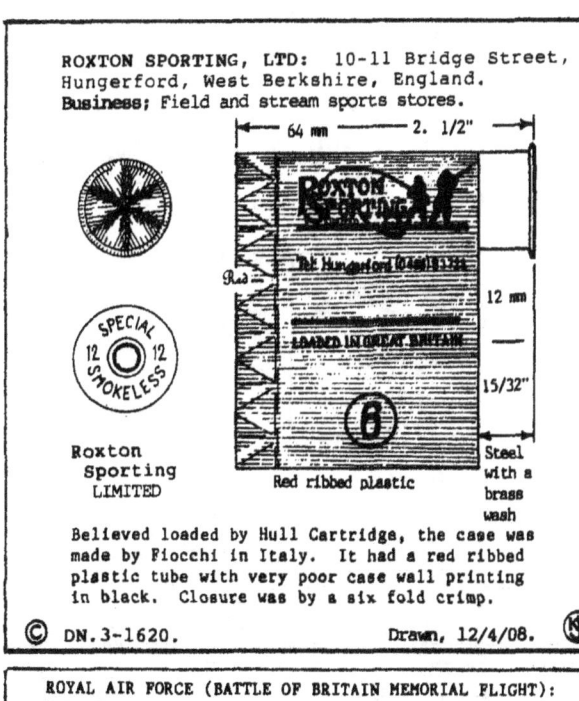
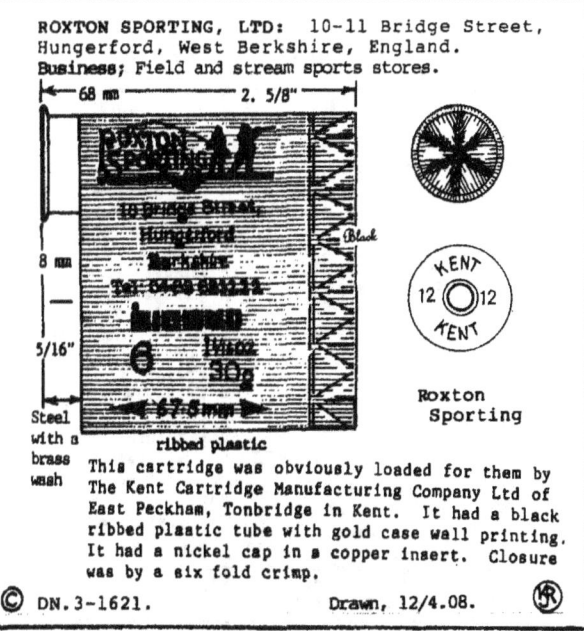
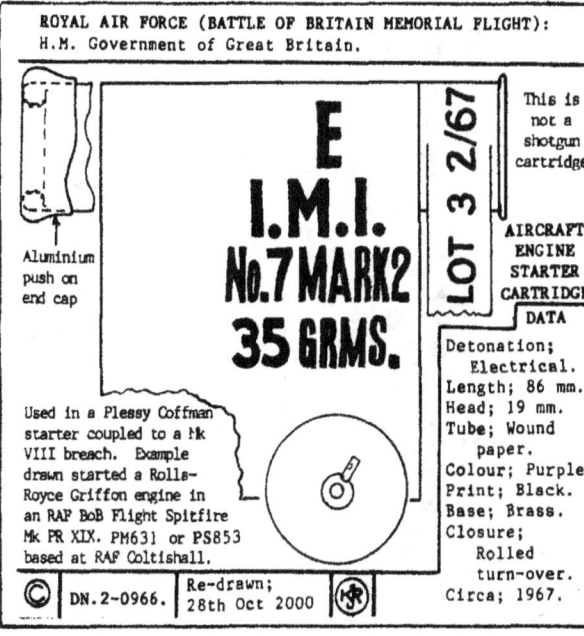
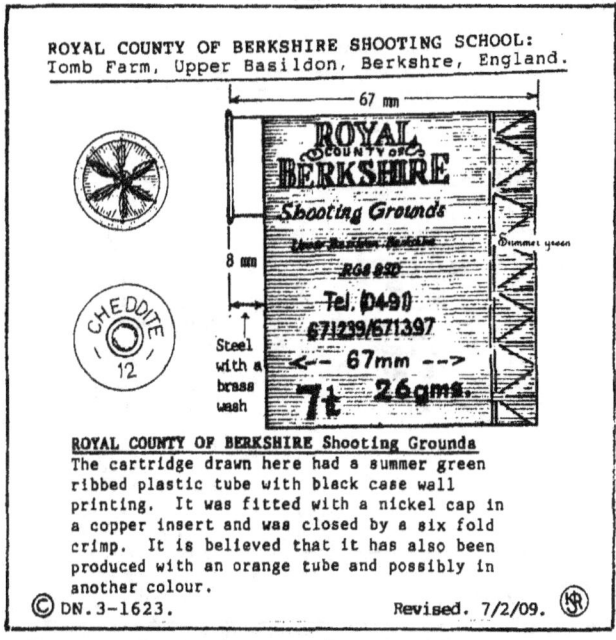
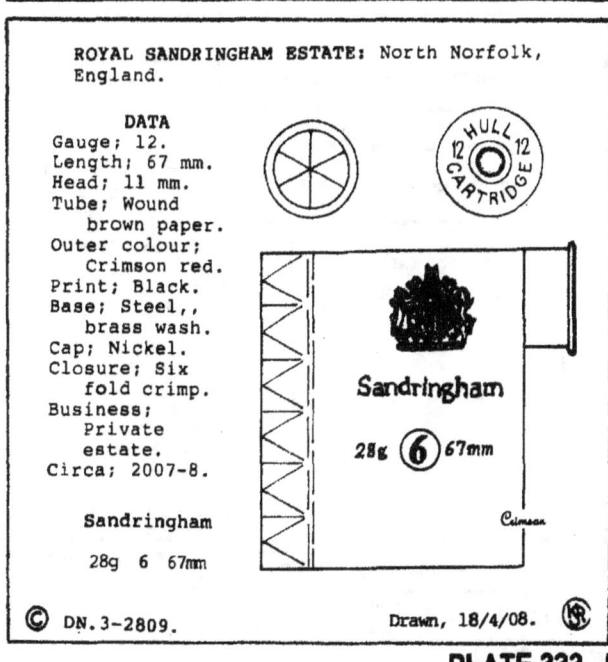
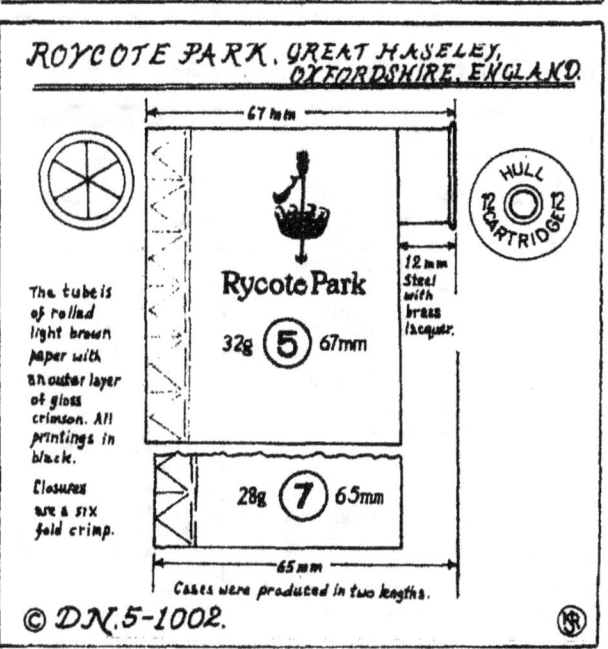

PLATE 333 [ROX – ROY]

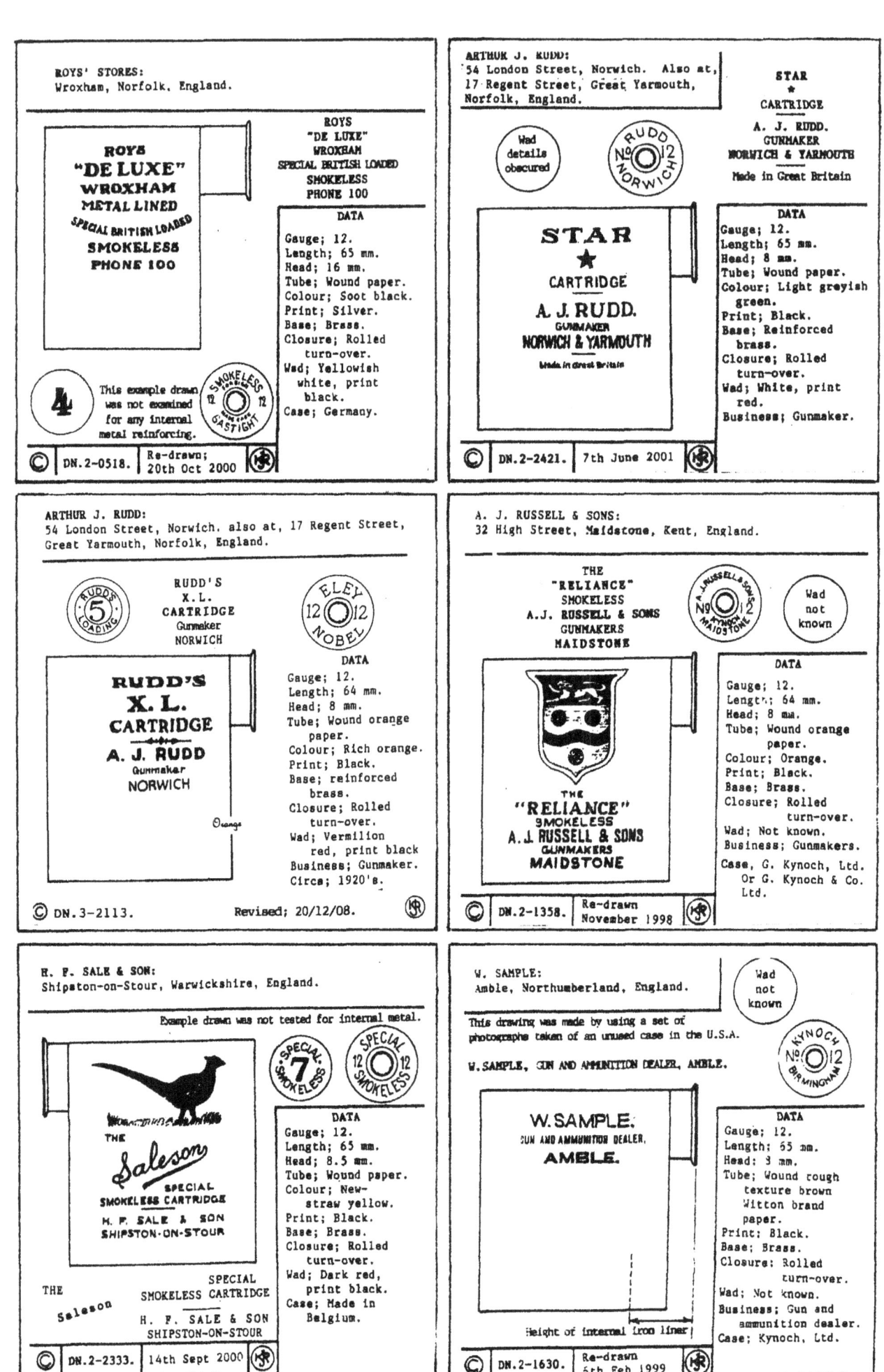

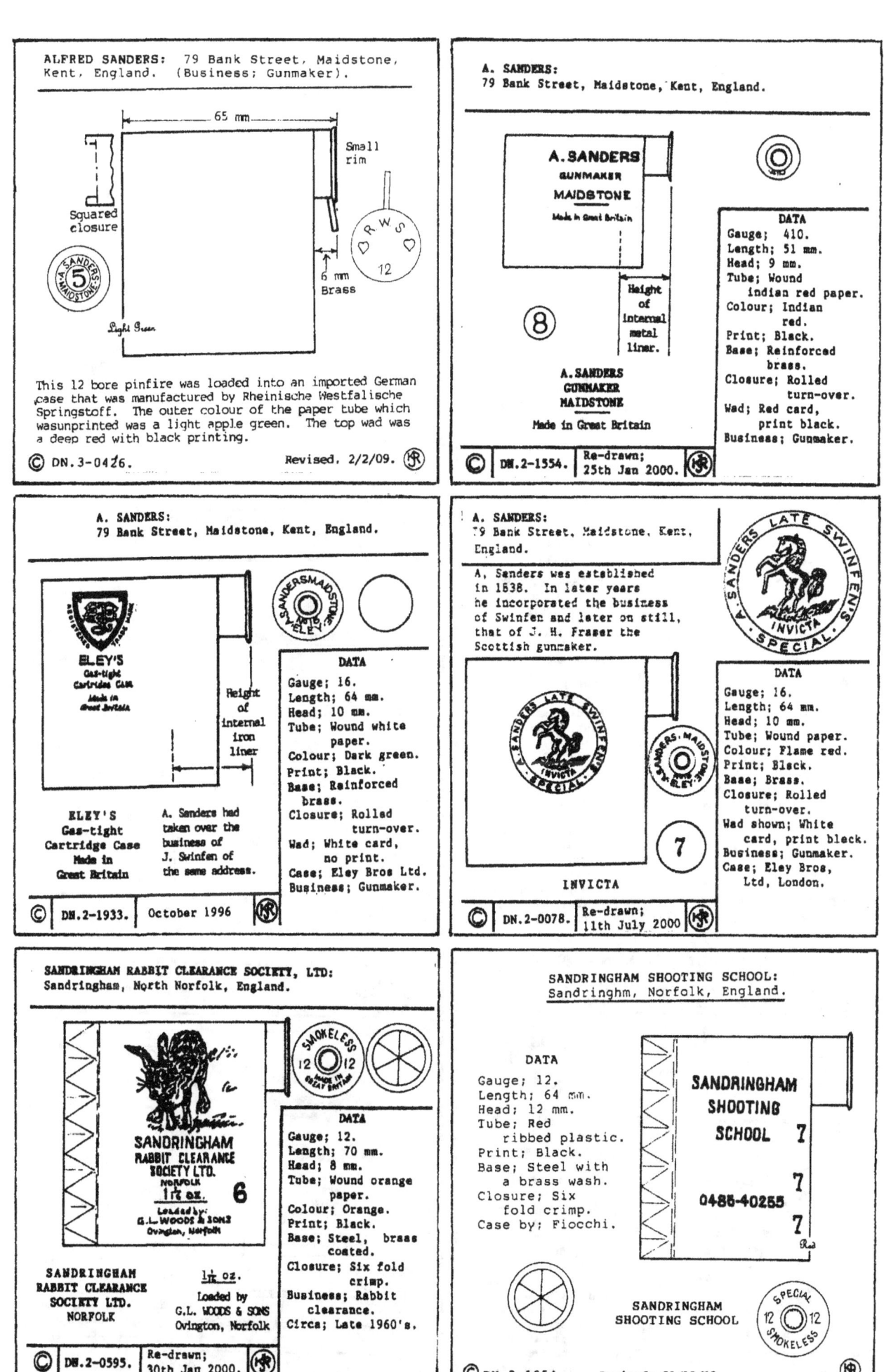

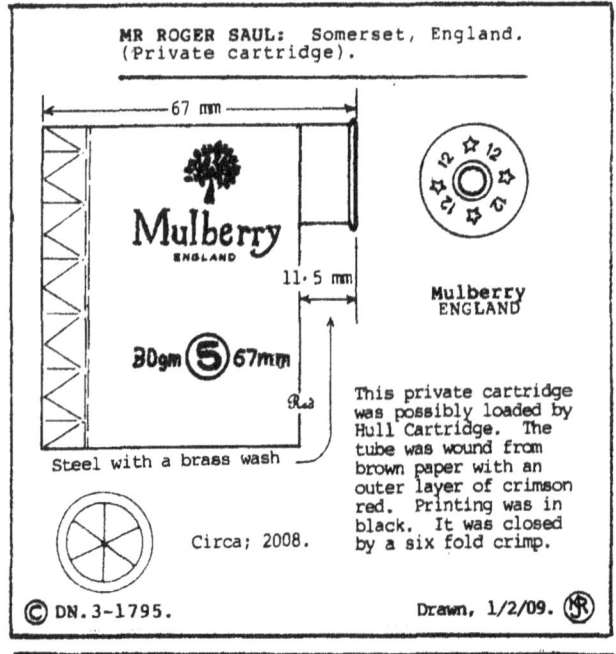
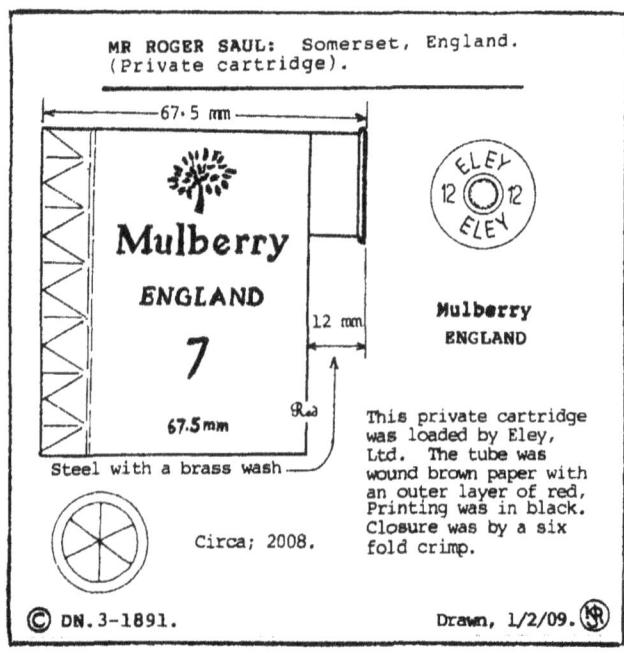
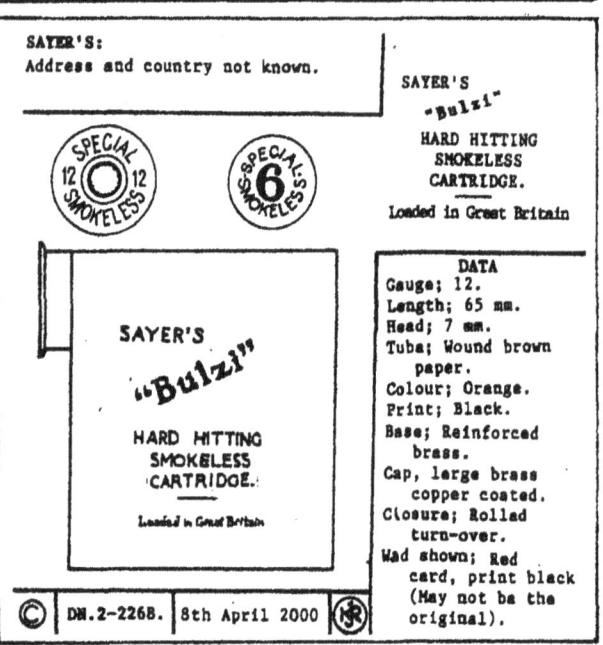
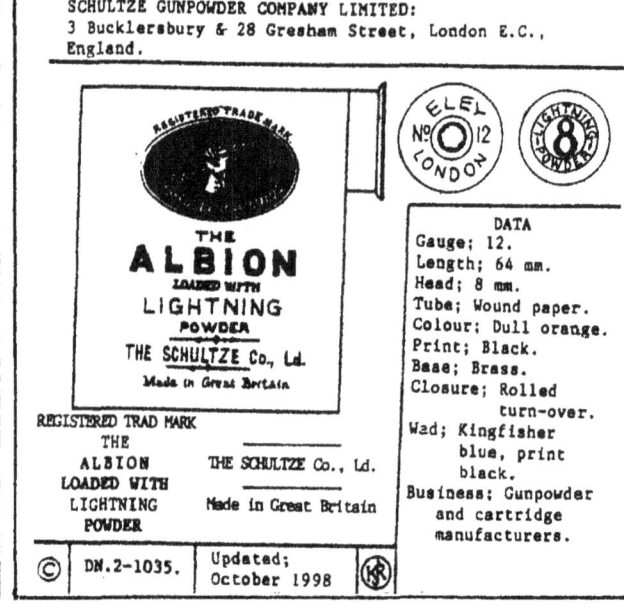
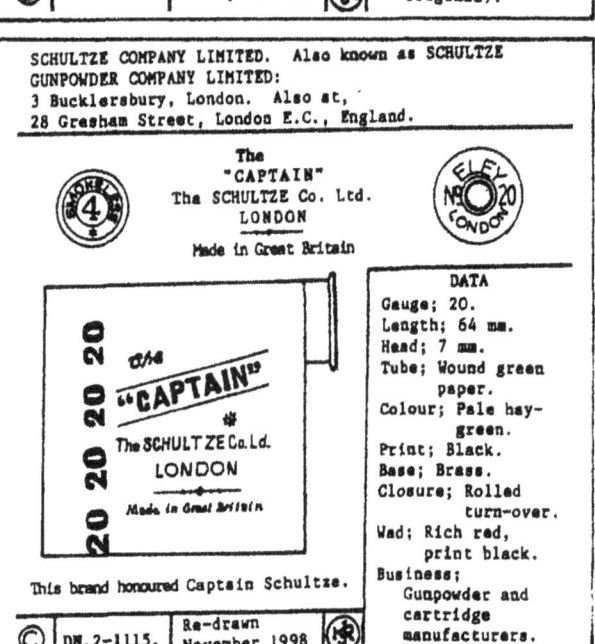
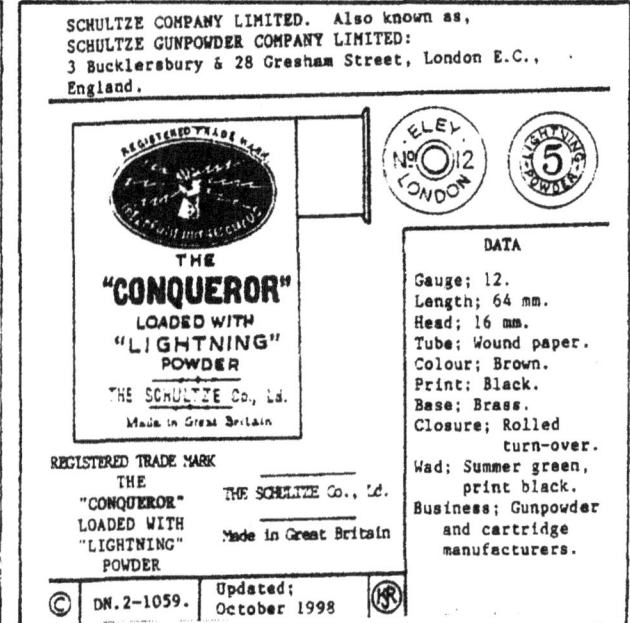

PLATE 336 [SAU – SCH]

SCHULTZE GUNPOWDER CO, LTD: 3 Bucklersbury.
Also at, 28 & 32 Gresham Street, London E.C.,
England.

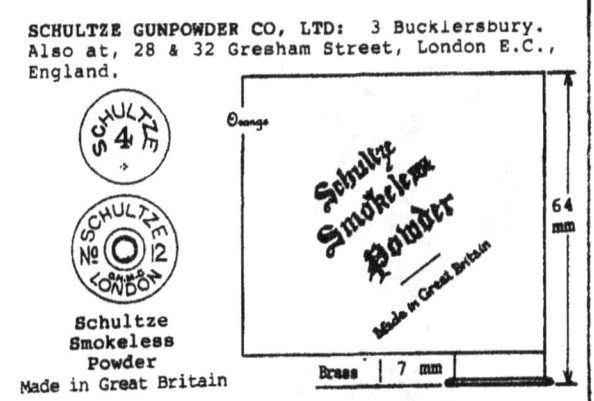

Schultze
Smokeless
Powder
Made in Great Britain

The details for this drawing was sent to me by
Doug Culver along with a set of photographs.
I take this cartridge to have been produced by
the Schultze Company. The orange tubed case had
black case wall printing and looked like a product from Cogswell & Harrison. I do not know and
I make a guess. Perhaps C.H.M.C on the head
stood for, Cogswell & Harrison Manufacturing
Company. The top wad was from cream yellow
card and was printed in black.

Wound
paper
tube

Drawn,
4/4/08.

DN.3-1561.

THE SCHULTZE GUNPOWDER COMPANY LIMITED:
32 Gresham Street, London, E.C., England.

WESTMINSTER
SCHULTZE
POWDER
Made in Great Britain

WESTMINSTER

DATA
Gauge; 16.
Length; 64 mm.
Head; 14 mm.
Tube; Wound amethyst
        paper.
Colour; Amethyst.
Print; Black.
Base; Brass.
Closure; Rolled
          turn-over.
Wad; Deep buff,
      print black.
Case; Eley Bros Ltd.
Business; Gunpowder
           and cartridge
           manufacturers.

© DN.2-1339. Updated; February 1995

THE SCHULTZE GUNPOWDER COMPANY LIMITED:
32 Gresham Street, London, E.C., England.

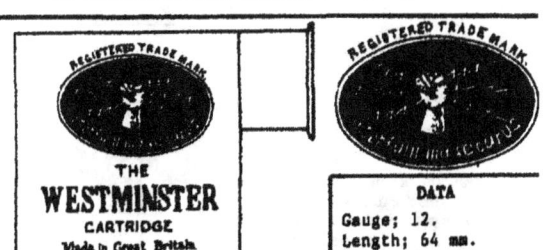

THE
WESTMINSTER
CARTRIDGE
Made in Great Britain
THE
Schultze Gunpowder Co. Ltd.

 Wad not known

DATA
Gauge; 12.
Length; 64 mm.
Head; 15 mm.
Tube; Wound tan
        paper.
Colour; Tan-brown.
Print; Black.
Base; Brass.
Closure; Rolled
          turn-over.
Wad; Not known.
Case; Eley Bros Ltd.
Business; Gunpowder
           and cartridge
           manufacturers.

© DN.2-1338. Updated; February 1995

SCHULTZE GUNPOWDER COMPANY, LIMITED:
28 Gresham Street, London E.C.;2.,
England.

REGISTERED TRADE MARK
Inter fulmina securus
THE
YEOMAN
SMOKELESS
CARTRIDGE
Made in Great Britain
THE
Schultze Gunpowder Co. Ltd.

THE
YEOMAN
SMOKELESS
CARTRIDGE
Made in Great Britain
THE
Schultze Gunpowder Co. Ltd.

DATA
Gauge; 12.
Length; 64 mm.
Head; 9 mm.
Tube; Wound white
        paper.
Colour; Off-white.
Print; Black.
Base; Brass.
Closure; Rolled
          turn-over.
Wad; Buff card,
      print black.
Business; Gunpowder
           manufacturers.
Case; Eley Bros,
       Ltd. London.

© DN.2-0222. Re-drawn; 3rd Dec 2000

JOHN A. SCOTCHER & SON:
4 The Traverse, Bury St. Edmunds, Suffolk, England.

The business of Scotcher & Son was taken over by Henry Hodgson in 1913.
This example was not inspected for internal metal reinforcing.

SCOTCHER'S
"INVINCIBLE"
SMOKELESS CARTRIDGE

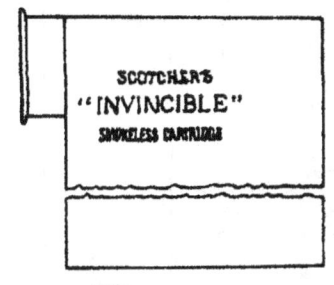

DATA
Gauge; 12.
Length; 64 mm.
Head; 10 mm.
Tube; Wound paper.
Colour; Brownish
         burnt-orange.
Print; Black.
Base; Brass.
Closure; Rolled
          turn-over.
Wad; Ruby red,
      print black.
Business;
  Gunmakers.

© DN.2-2351. 23rd Sept 2000

SELLIER & BELLOT:
Formerly, ZUNDHUTCHEN und PATRONENFABRIK:
Schoenbeck, Magdeburg, Eastern Germany.

Beste gasdichte
Patronenhülse
mit unfehlbarer Zündung.
Aus bestem Material
hergestellt und vorzüglich
gearbeitet.

DATA
Gauge; 12.
Length; 65 mm.
Head; 8 mm.
Tube; Wound orange
        paper.
Colour; Orange;
Print; Black.
Base; Reinforced
       brass.
Closure; Rolled
          turn-over.
Wad; White card,
      print black.
Cap; Large copper.
Business;
  Ammunition
  manufacturers.

© DN.2-1992. June 1997.

PLATE 337 [SCH - SEL]

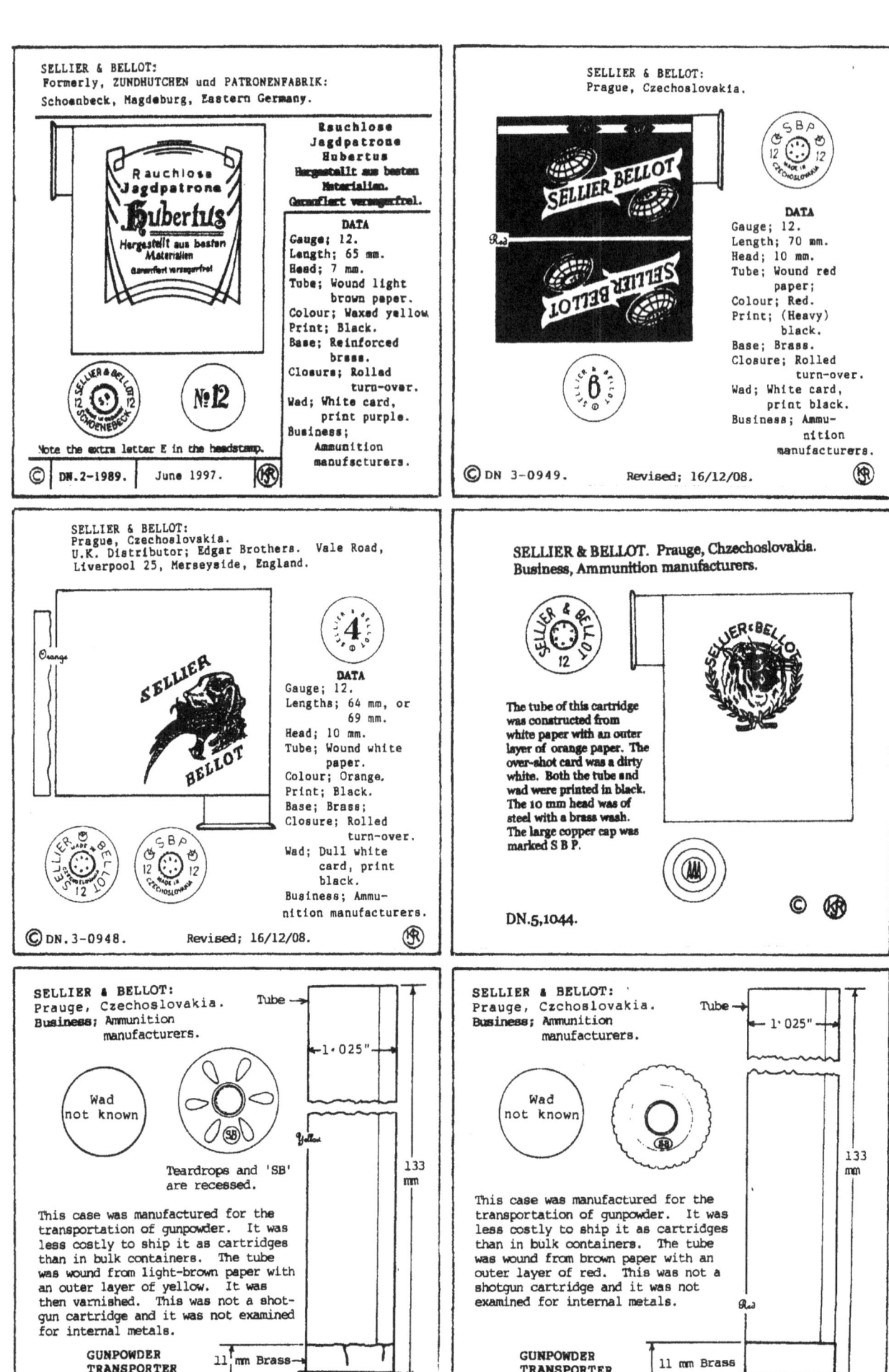

PLATE 338 [SEL – SEL]

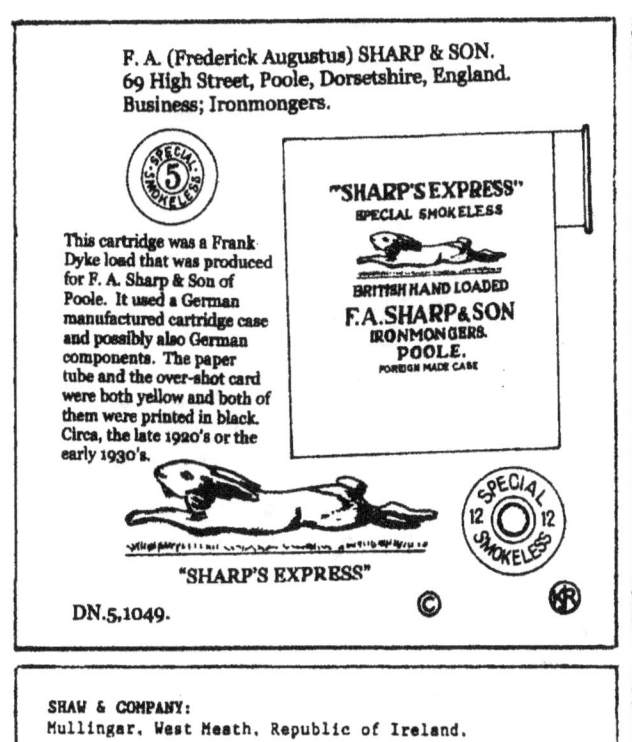

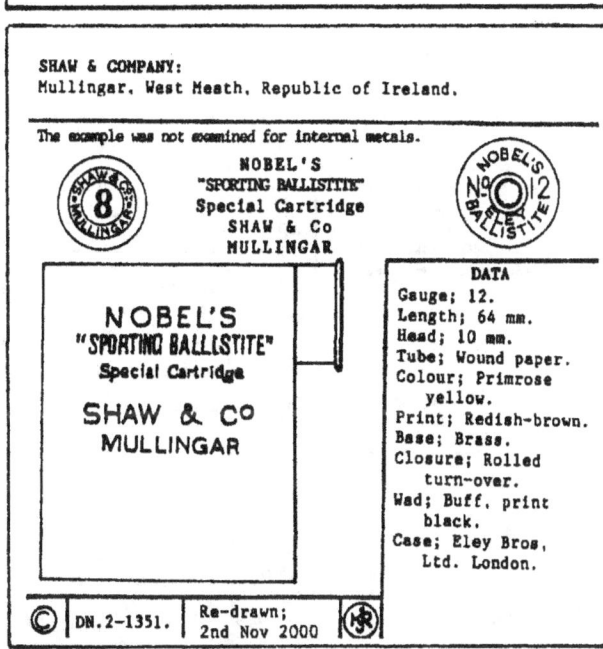
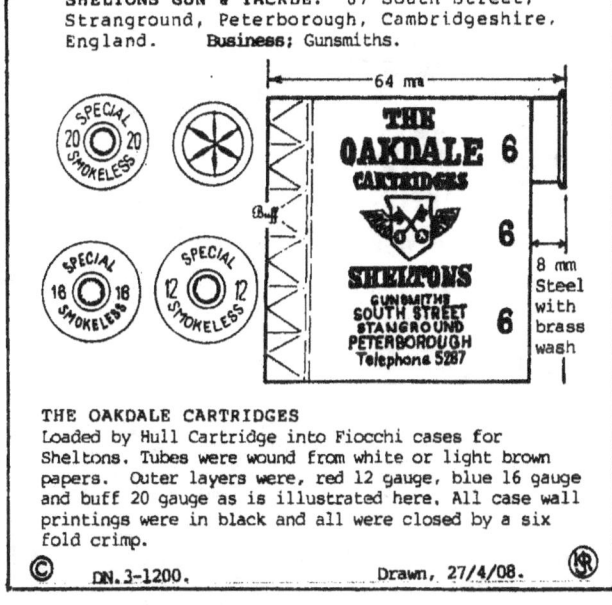
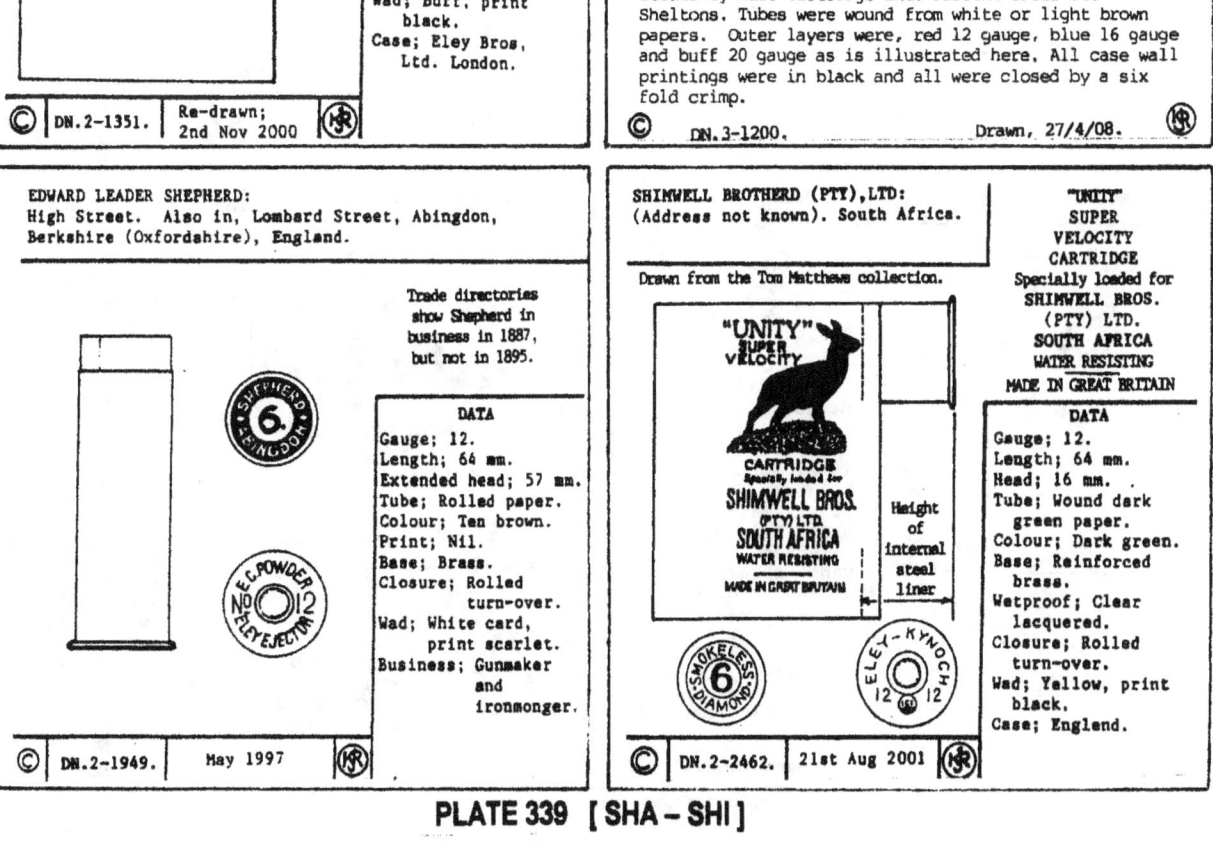

PLATE 339 [SHA – SHI]

SHUFFREYS LIMITED:
Walsall, Staffordshire (West Midlands), England.

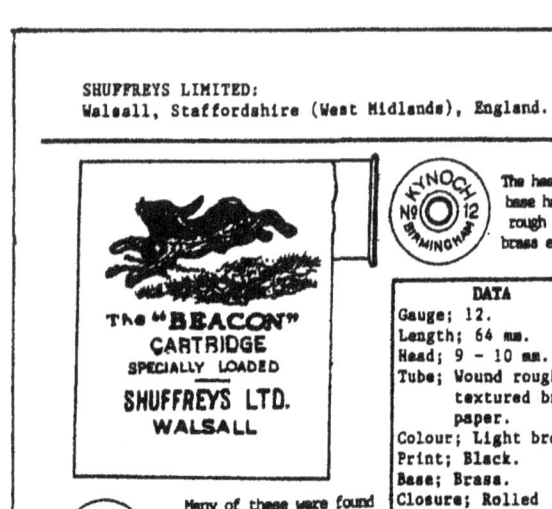

The head or base had a rough top brass edge.

DATA
Gauge; 12.
Length; 64 mm.
Head; 9 - 10 mm.
Tube; Wound rough textured brown paper.
Colour; Light brown.
Print; Black.
Base; Brass.
Closure; Rolled turn-over.
Wad; Light brown card, print nil.
Business; Not known.
Case; G. Kynoch, Ltd.
Circa; Not known.

Many of these were found under a shops flooring.

THE "BEACON"

© DN.2-0129.   Updated; April 1995

MICK SIMMONS, LIMITED:
720 George Street, Sydney, New South Wales, Australia.

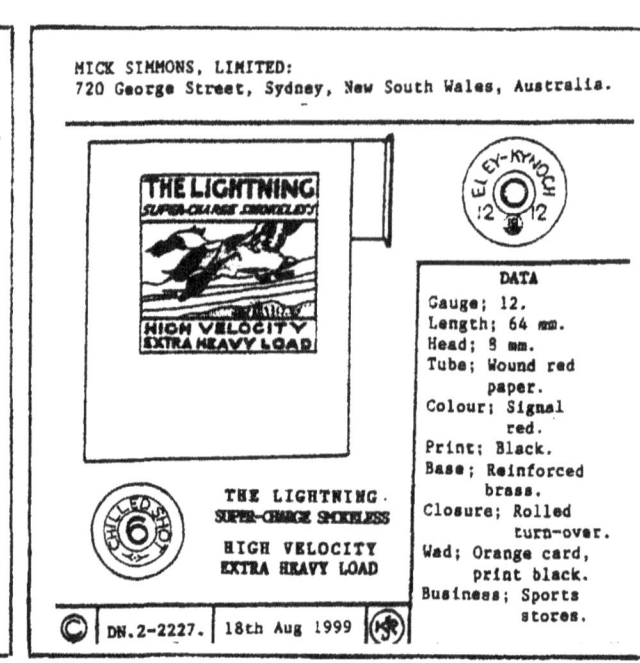

THE LIGHTNING
SUPER-CHARGE SMOKELESS
HIGH VELOCITY
EXTRA HEAVY LOAD

DATA
Gauge; 12.
Length; 64 mm.
Head; 9 mm.
Tube; Wound red paper.
Colour; Signal red.
Print; Black.
Base; Reinforced brass.
Closure; Rolled turn-over.
Wad; Orange card, print black.
Business; Sports stores.

© DN.2-2227.   18th Aug 1999

SIX MILE BOTTOM, Private shoot:
Private Shoot, Near Newmarket, Suffolk, England.

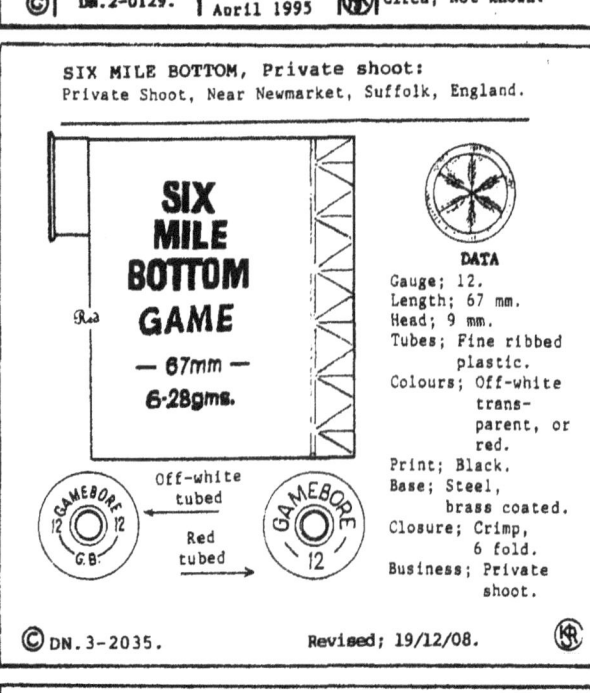

DATA
Gauge; 12.
Length; 67 mm.
Head; 9 mm.
Tubes; Fine ribbed plastic.
Colours; Off-white transparent, or red.
Print; Black.
Base; Steel, brass coated.
Closure; Crimp, 6 fold.
Business; Private shoot.

Off-white tubed / Red tubed

© DN.3-2035.   Revised; 19/12/08.

SKINNER & COMPANY:
62 Derby Street, Leek. Were also at,
Haywood Street, Leek, Staffordshire, England.

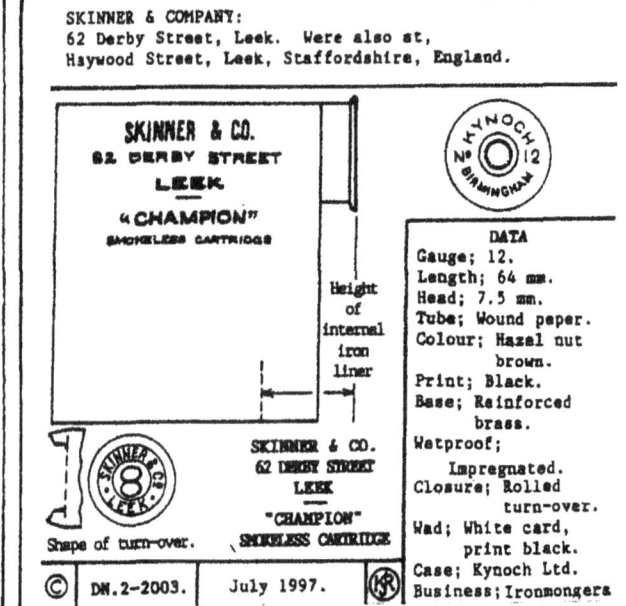

Height of internal iron liner

Shape of turn-over.

SKINNER & CO.
62 DERBY STREET
LEEK
"CHAMPION"
SMOKELESS CARTRIDGE

DATA
Gauge; 12.
Length; 64 mm.
Head; 7.5 mm.
Tube; Wound paper.
Colour; Hazel nut brown.
Print; Black.
Base; Reinforced brass.
Watproof; Impregnated.
Closure; Rolled turn-over.
Wad; White card, print black.
Case; Kynoch Ltd.
Business; Ironmongers

© DN.2-2003.   July 1997.

SLINGSBY BROTHERS: 10 High Street, Boston,
Lincolnshire, England.

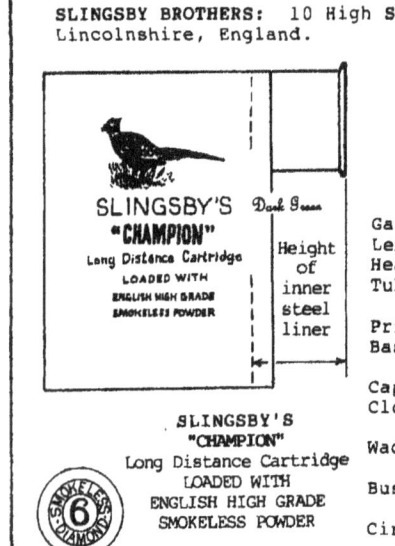
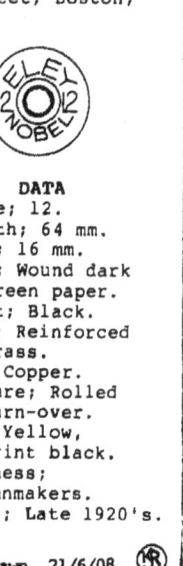

Dark Green

Height of inner steel liner

SLINGSBY'S
"CHAMPION"
Long Distance Cartridge
LOADED WITH
ENGLISH HIGH GRADE
SMOKELESS POWDER

DATA
Gauge; 12.
Length; 64 mm.
Head; 16 mm.
Tube; Wound dark green paper.
Print; Black.
Base; Reinforced brass.
Cap; Copper.
Closure; Rolled turn-over.
Wad; Yellow, print black.
Business; Gunmakers.
Circa; Late 1920's.

© DN.3-2829.   Drawn, 21/6/08.

SLINGSBY BROTHERS: 10 High Street, Boston,
Lincolnshire, England.

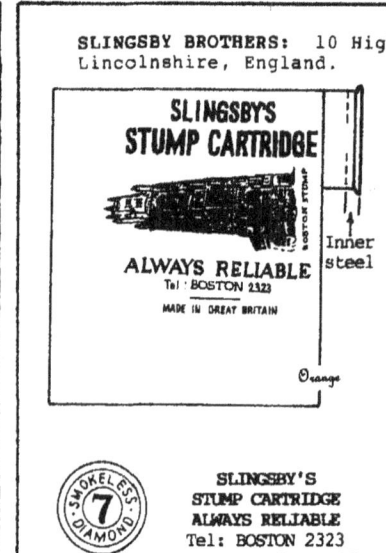
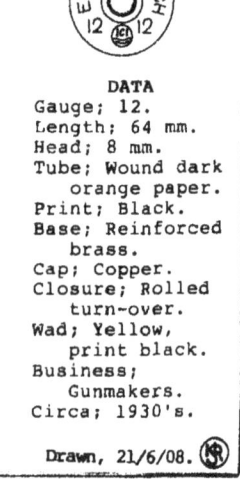

Inner steel
Orange

SLINGSBY'S
STUMP CARTRIDGE
ALWAYS RELIABLE
Tel: BOSTON 2323
MADE IN GREAT BRITAIN

DATA
Gauge; 12.
Length; 64 mm.
Head; 8 mm.
Tube; Wound dark orange paper.
Print; Black.
Base; Reinforced brass.
Cap; Copper.
Closure; Rolled turn-over.
Wad; Yellow, print black.
Business; Gunmakers.
Circa; 1930's.

© DN.3-2828.   Drawn, 21/6/08.

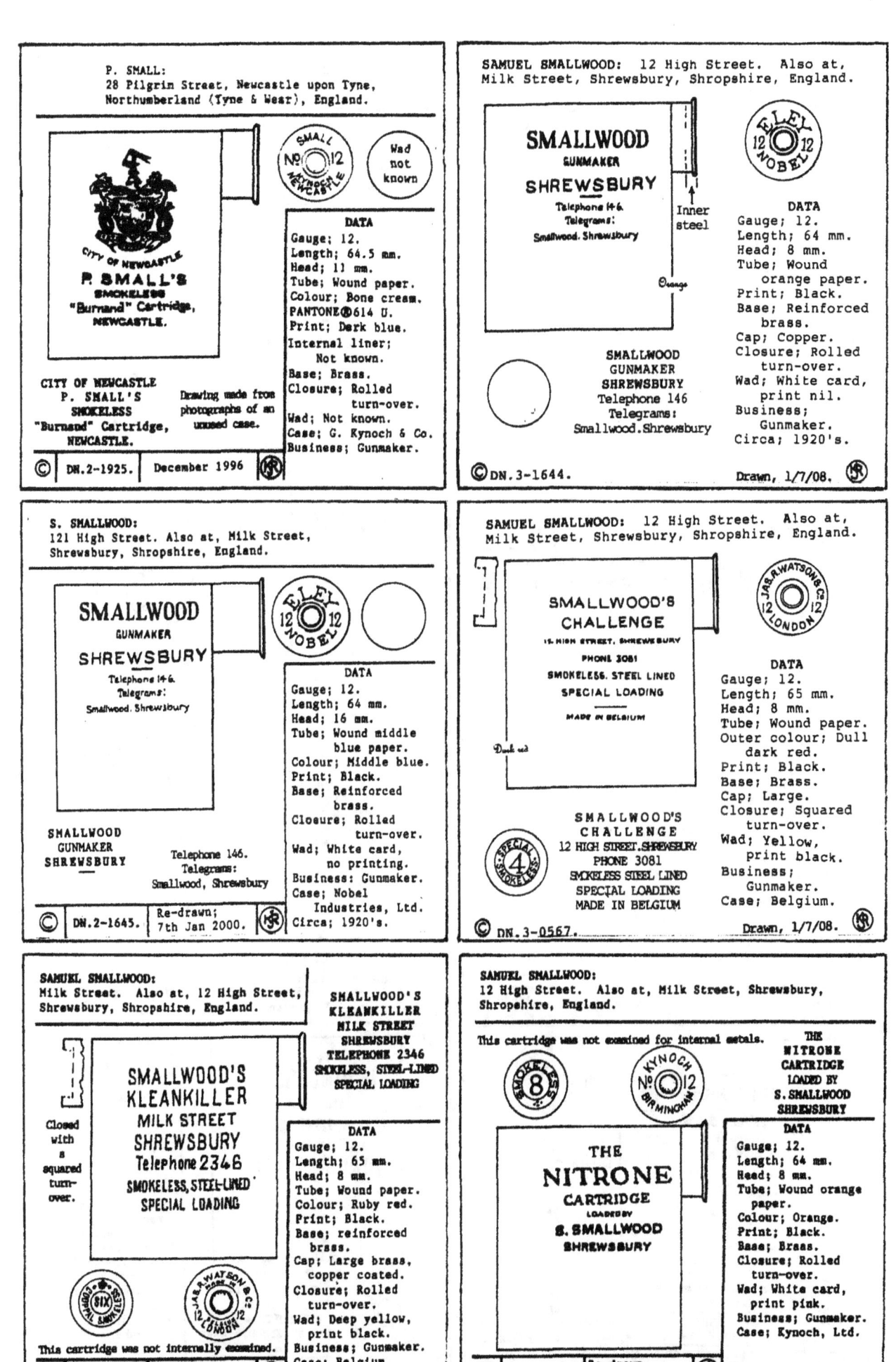
PLATE 341 [SMA - SMA]

ALFRED FISHER SMITH:
High Street, Hailsham. Also at, High Street, Heathfield, Sussex, England.

"YELLOW BOY"
SPECIAL SMOKELESS
—
A. F. SMITH
HAILSHAM
AND
HEATHFIELD

DATA
Gauge; 12.
Length; 65 mm.
Head; 8 mm.
Tube; Wound paper.
Colour; Yellow.
Print; Black.
Base; Brass.
Cap; Large copper.
Closure; Rolled turn-over.
Wad; Dull redish brown, print black.
Business; Ironmonger.

DN.2-1152. Re-drawn; 30th Nov 2000

CHAS SMITH & SONS, LTD:
47 Market Place, Newark, Nottinghamshire, England.

"THE CASTLE"
CHAS. SMITH & SON
GUNMAKERS
NEWARK
TELEPHONE NEWARK 228
FOREIGN MADE CASE
LOADED IN ENGLAND

DATA
Gauge; 12.
Length; 64 mm.
Head; 8 mm.
Tube; Wound paper.
Colour; Brownish orange.
Print; Black.
Base; Brass.
Closure; Rolled turn-over.
Wad; Summer green, print black.
Business; Gunmakers.
Case; Foreign.

Note printings, Son on case wall and Sons on top wad.

DN.2-0174. Re-drawn; 18th Dec 2000

CHAS SMITH & SONS: 47 Market Place, Newark, Nottinghamshire, England.

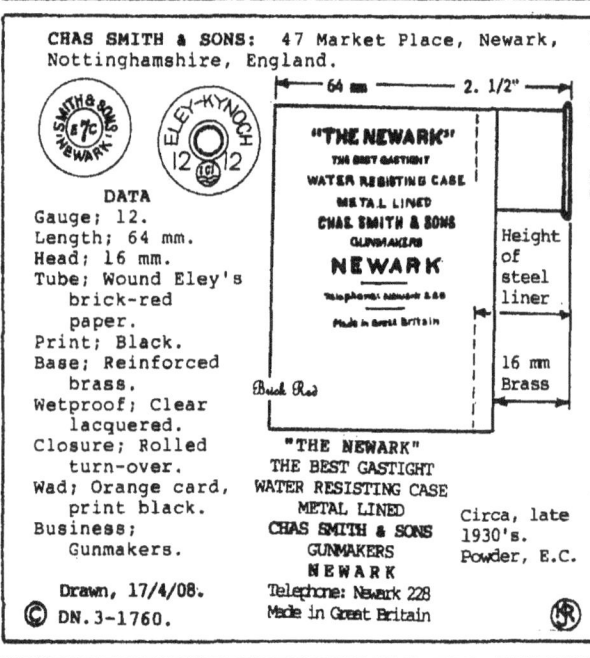

DATA
Gauge; 12.
Length; 64 mm.
Head; 16 mm.
Tube; Wound Eley's brick-red paper.
Print; Black.
Base; Reinforced brass.
Wetproof; Clear lacquered.
Closure; Rolled turn-over.
Wad; Orange card, print black.
Business; Gunmakers.

"THE NEWARK"
THE BEST GASTIGHT
WATER RESISTING CASE
METAL LINED
CHAS SMITH & SONS
GUNMAKERS
NEWARK
Telephone: Newark 228
Made in Great Britain

Circa, late 1930's.
Powder, E.C.

Drawn, 17/4/08.
DN.3-1760.

CHAS SMITH & SONS: 47 Market Place, Newark, Nottinghamshire, England.

THE
"UNIVERSAL"
CHAS SMITH & SONS
GUNMAKERS
NEWARK
Telephone No. 11X1
Telegrams: "Shooting Newark"

Orange

DATA
Gauge; 12.
Length; 64 mm.
Head; 9 mm.
Tube; Wound paper.
Colour; Orange.
Print; Black.
Base; Brass.
Cap; Copper.
Closure; Rolled turn-over.
Wad; Orange, print black.
Case by; Kynoch & Co.
Business; Gunmakers.

THE
"UNIVERSAL"
CHAS SMITH & SONS
GUNMAKERS
NEWARK
Telephone No. 11X1
Telegrams:"Shooting Newark"

Not examined for internal metals.

Shot size inked in by pen.

DN.3-1343. Drawn, 26/3/08.

CHAS SMITH & SONS:
47 Market Place, Newark, Nottinghamshire, England.

THE
"UNIVERSAL"
CHAS. SMITH & SONS
GUNMAKERS
NEWARK
Telephone: Newark 228
MADE IN GREAT BRITAIN

Made in Great Britain

Both versions of 'Made in Great Britain' have been used.

THE
"UNIVERSAL"

DATA
Gauge; 12.
Length; 64 mm.
Head; 8 mm.
Tube; Wound orange paper.
Colour; Orange 3.
Print; Black.
Base; Brass.
Closure; Rolled turn-over.
Wad; Yellow card, print black.
Wetproof; Lacquered.
Case; Eley-Kynoch.
Circa; 1930's.
Business; Gunmakers.

DN.2-1373. Updated; February 1995

C. H. SMITH & SONS:
123 Steelhouse Lane, Birmingham, Warwickshire (West Midlands), England.

THE
"INVINCIBLE"
LOADED BY
C.H. SMITH & SONS
123 STEELHOUSE LANE
BIRMINGHAM

DATA
Gauge; 12.
Length; 65 mm.
Head; 7 mm.
Tube; Wound paper.
Colour; Dark blood red.
Print; Black.
Base; Brass.
Closure; Rolled turn-over.
Wad; Orange, print black.
Business; Gunmakers.

THE
"INVINCIBLE"
LOADED BY
C.H. SMITH & SONS
123 STEELHOUSE LANE
BIRMINGHAM

DN.2-1336. Re-drawn; 27th June 2001

PLATE 342 [SMI – SMI]

C. H. SMITH & SONS:
123 Steelhouse Lane, Birmingham, Warwickshire (West Midlands), England.

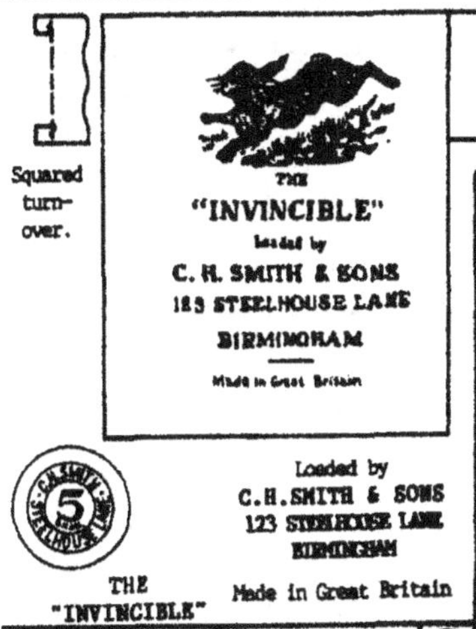

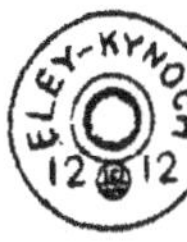

DATA
Gauge; 12.
Length; 64 mm.
Head; 8 mm.
Tube; Wound eau-de-nil paper.
Colour; Eau-de-nil.
Print; Navy blue.
Base; Reinforced brass.
Closure; Rolled turn-over.
Wad; Dark orange, print black.
Business; Gunmakers.
Circa; 1930's.

© DN.2-1342. Re-drawn; 17th Feb 2000.

STEVE SMITH:
42 High Friar Street. Also at, 37 Nelson Street, Newcastle-under-Lyme, Staffordshire, England.

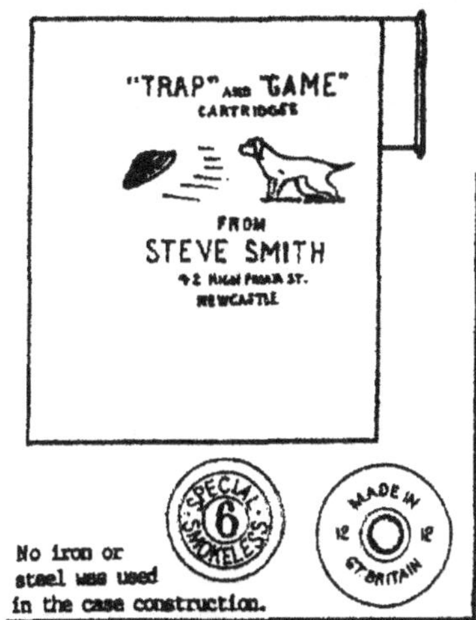

"TRAP" AND "GAME" CARTRIDGES FROM STEVE SMITH 42 HIGH FRIAR ST. NEWCASTLE

No iron or steel was used in the case construction.

DATA
Gauge; 12.
Length; 64 mm.
Head; 8 mm.
Tube; Wound orange paper.
Colour; Orange.
Print; Black.
Wetproof; Lacquered.
Base; Brass.
Closure; Rolled turn-over.
Wad; Dark green, print black.
Business; Gunsmith.
Case; Greenwood & Batley, Ltd.
Circa; Post W.W.2.

© DN.2-0503 Re-drawn; 19th March 2001

SMITH MIDGLEY & COMPANY:
Bradford, Yorkshire, England.

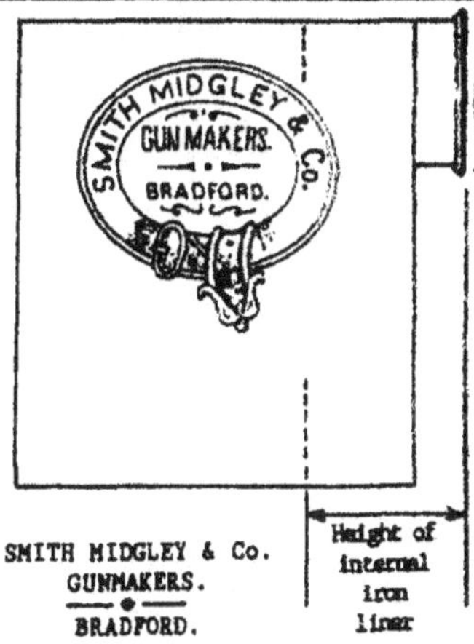

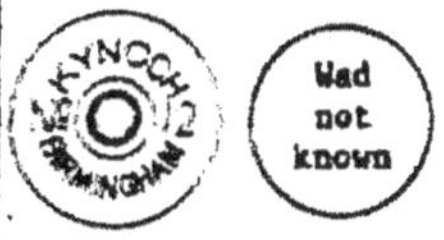

DATA
Gauge; 12.
Length; 66 mm.
Head; 8 mm.
Tube; Wound brown paper.
Colour; Middle blue.
Print; Black.
Base; Reinforced brass.
Closure; Rolled turn-over.
Wad; Not known.
Business; Gunmakers.
Case; Kynoch, Ltd.

© DN.2-1631. Re-drawn; 27th March 2001

SMITHS GORE CHARTERED SURVEYORS:
Fielden House, 12 Little Cottage Street, London. S.W.1.

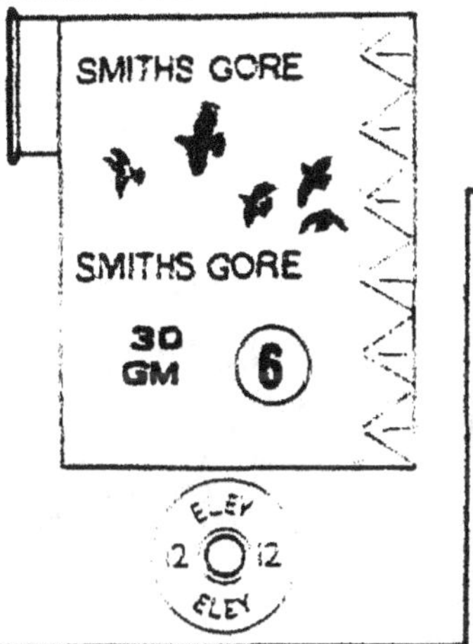

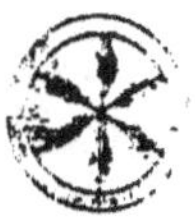

DATA
Gauge: 12.
Length; 66.5 mm.
Head: 8 mm.
Tube: Fine ribbed plastic.
Colour; Red 2.5.
Print; Black.
Base; Steel, nickel coated.
Closure; Crimp, 6 fold.
Business. Chartered surveyors.

© DN.2-0009. November 1994

THE SMOKELESS POWDER & AMMUNITION COMPANY LIMITED:
28 Gresham Street, London E.C., England.

This drawing was made from a used case.

DATA
Gauge: 12.
Length: 70 mm.
Head: 9 mm.
Tube: Wound brown paper.
Colour: Maroon.
Print: Nil.
Base: Reinforced brass.
Closure; Rolled turn-over.
Wad: Not known.
Business; Gunpowder and ammunition manufacturers.
Circa; 1900.

© DN.2-2115. December 1998

THE SMOKELESS POWDER AND AMMUNITION COMPANY LIMITED:
28 Gresham Street, London E.C., England.

The Smokeless Powder Company was formed in 1887 to market its S.S. gunpowder. Its addresses were, Dashwood House, New Broad Street, London E.C. with mills at, Barwick, Hertfordshire. A decade later in 1898 this firm was terminated. At the same time, a new firm came into being. It was The Smokeless Powder & Ammunition Company, Limited. Its address was as at the heading of this drawing. It is worth noting the logo similarities of The Smokeless Powder Company to those of The Explosives Company E.C. and that of The New Explosives Company, Limited.

Logo of, THE SMOKELESS POWDER COMPANY, LIMITED.

DATA
Gauge: 12.
Length: 64 mm.
Head: 9 mm.
Tube: Wound brown paper.
Colour: Light brown.
Print: Nil.
Base: Brass.
Closure: Rolled turn-over.
Wad: Not known.
Business; Gunpowder and ammunition manufacturers.

© DN.2-1268. Re-drawn December 1998

This drawing was made from a used case.

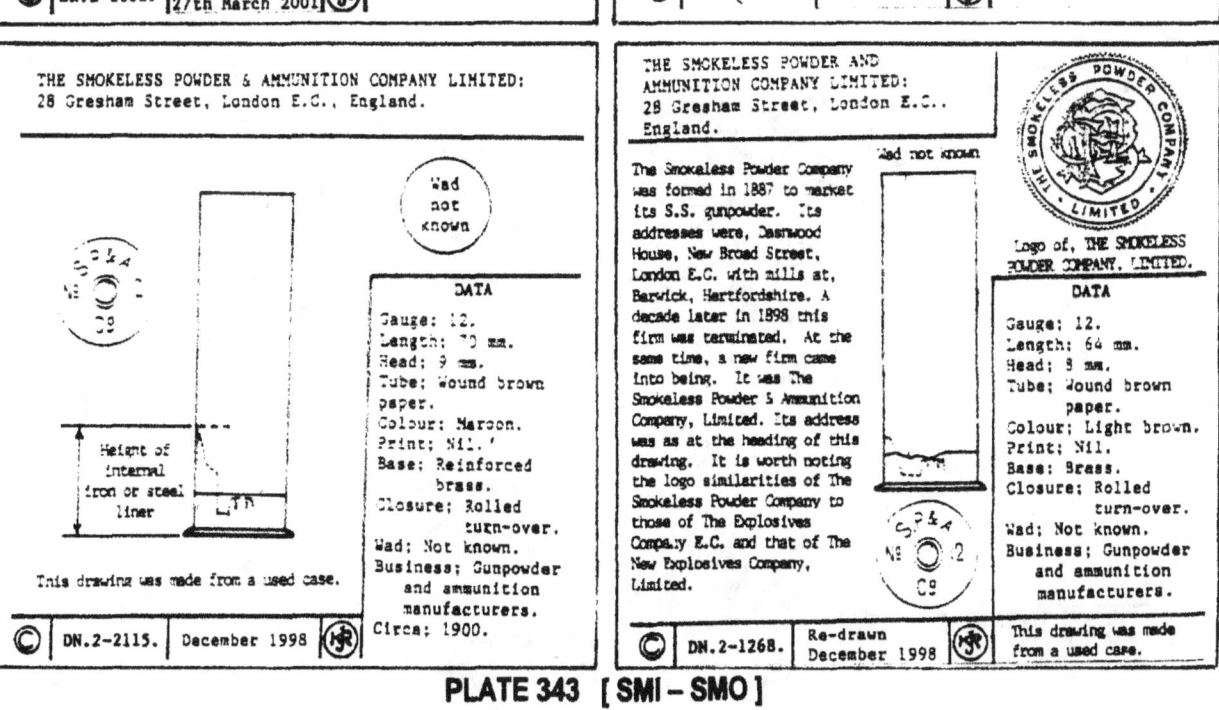

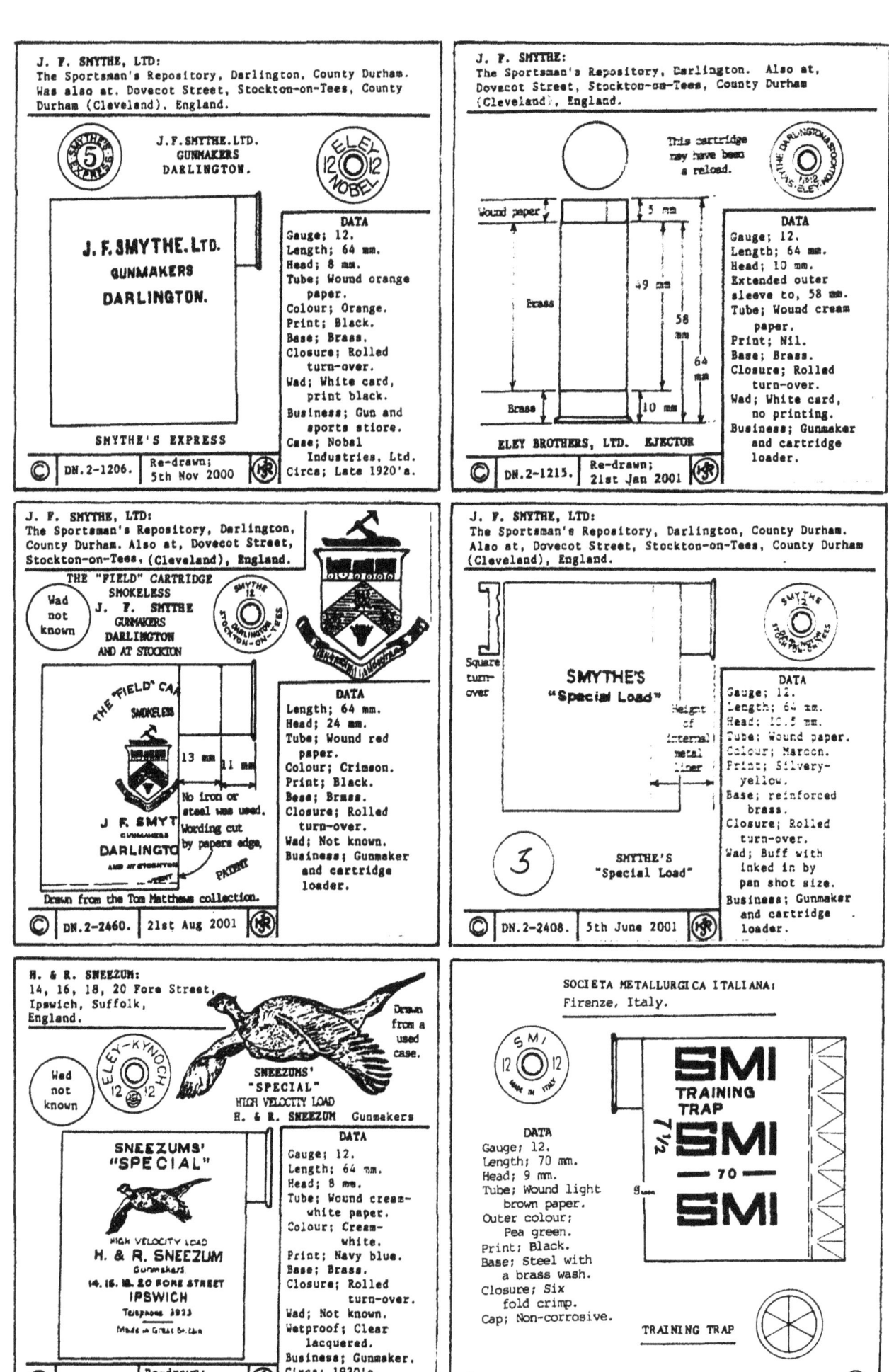

PLATE 344 [SMY – SOC]

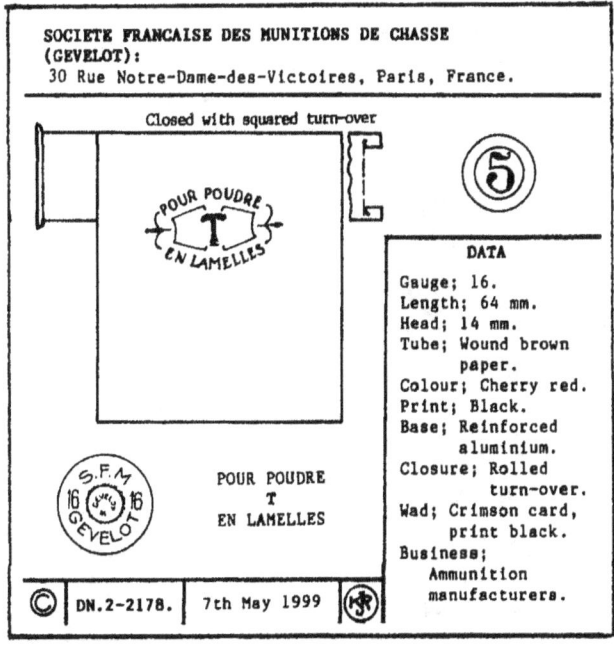
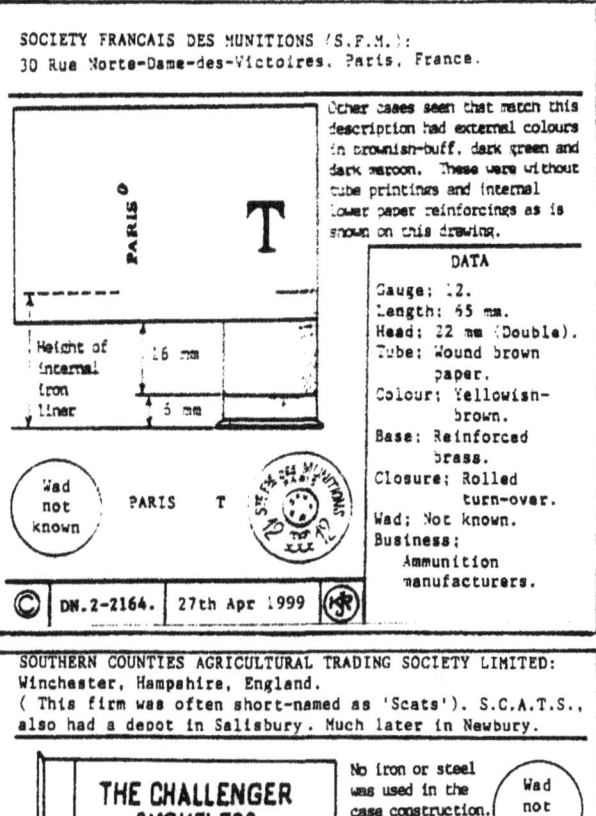
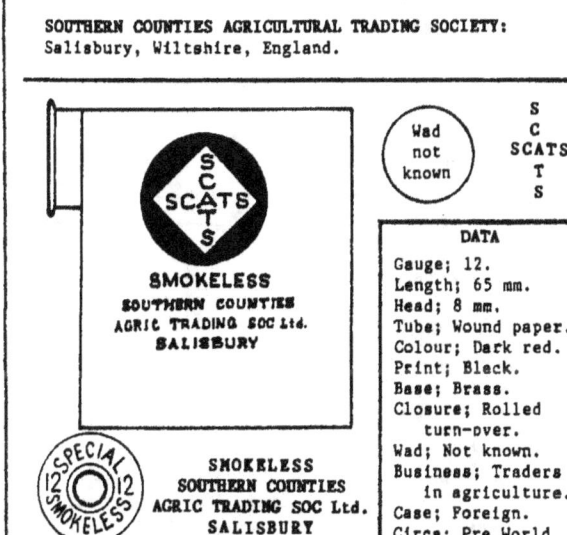
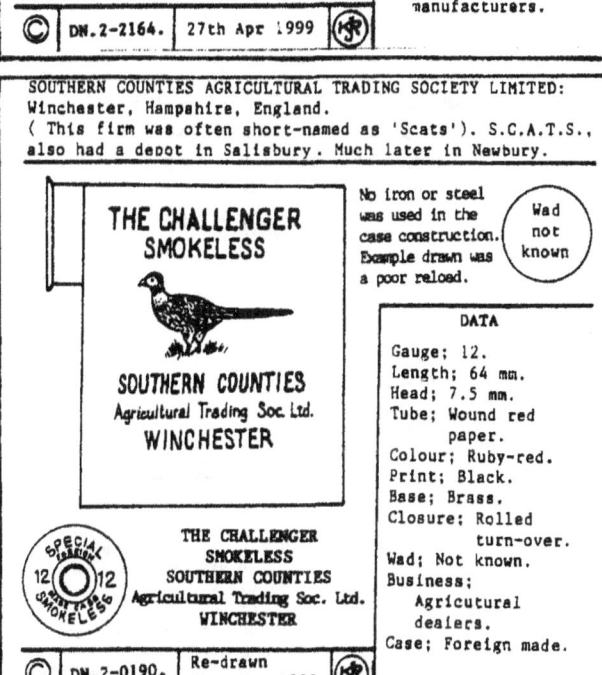
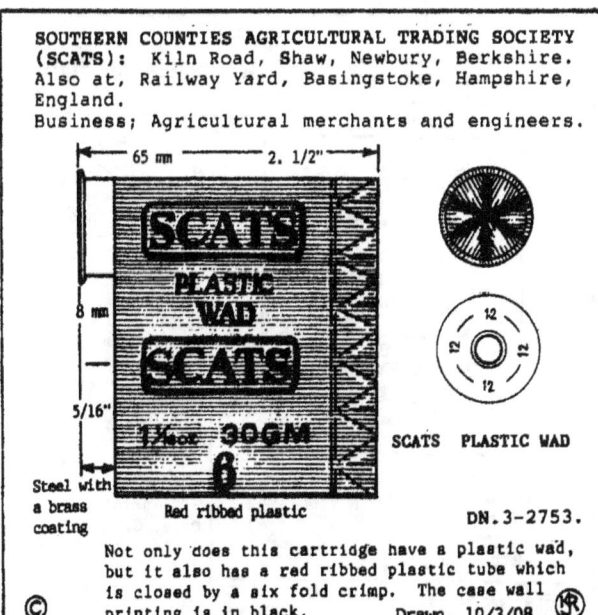
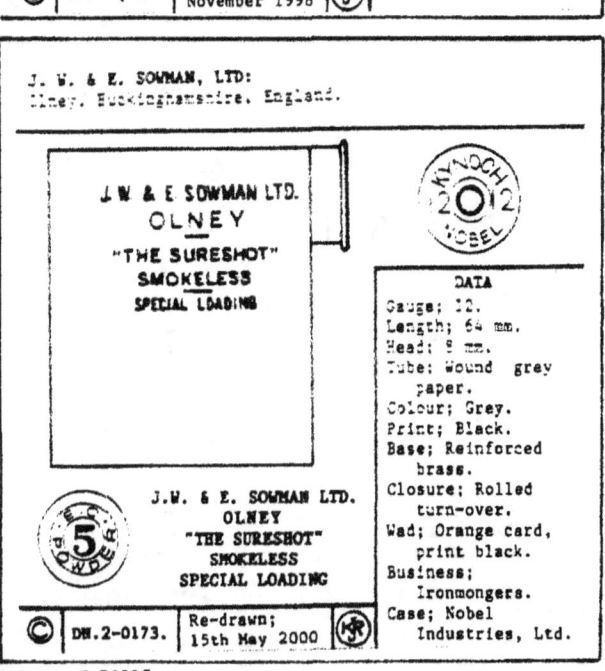

PLATE 345 [SOC - SOW]

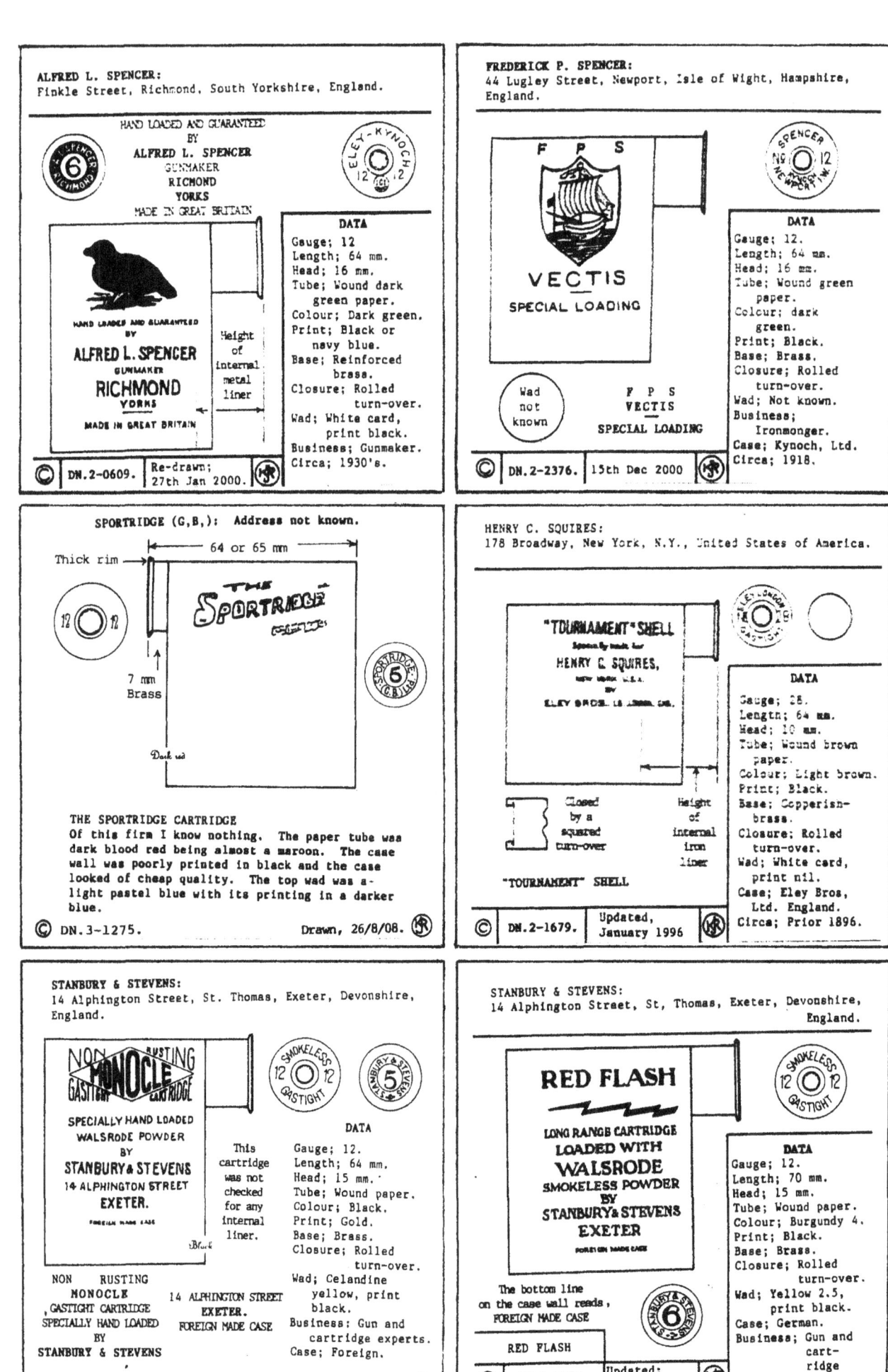

PLATE 346 [SPE – STA]

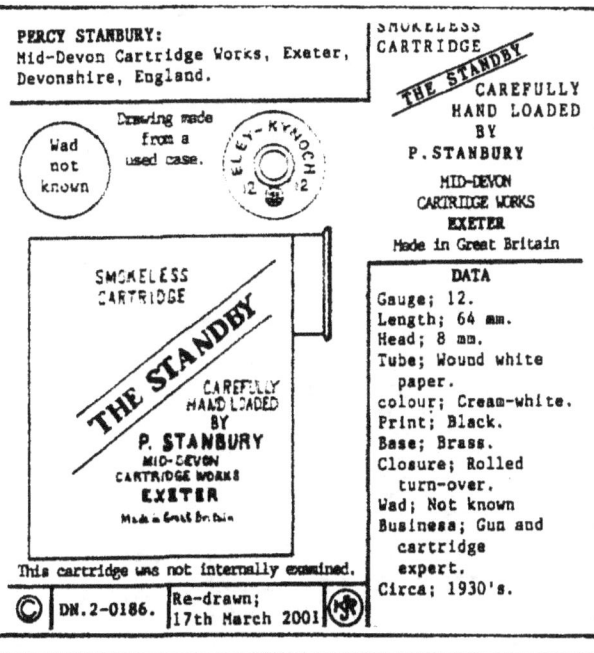
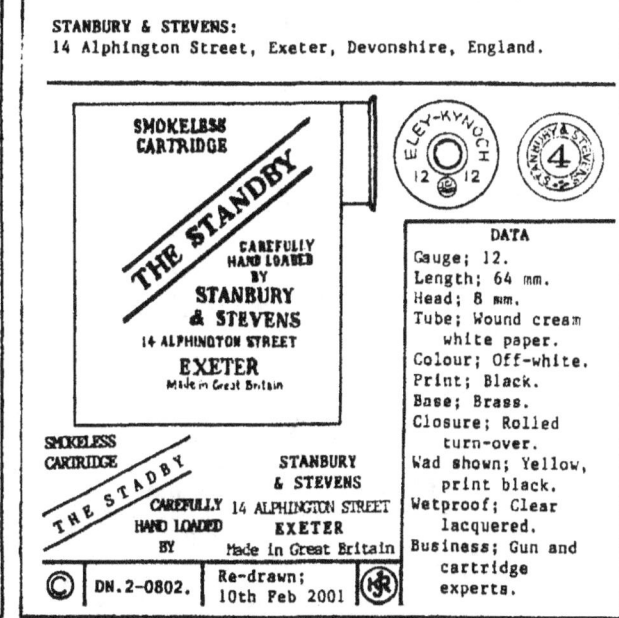
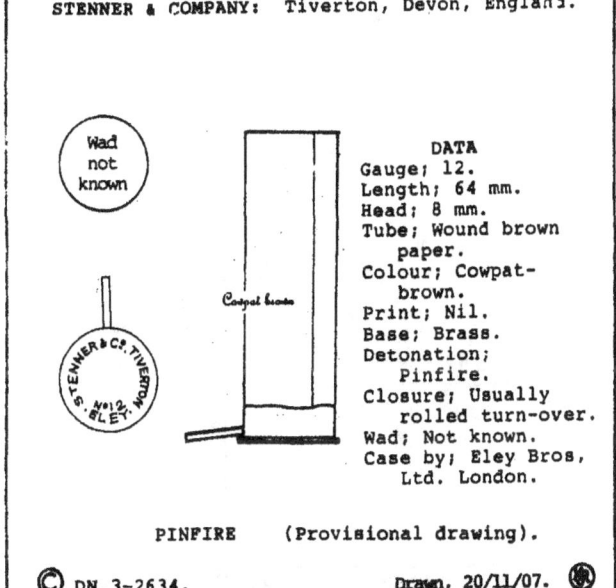
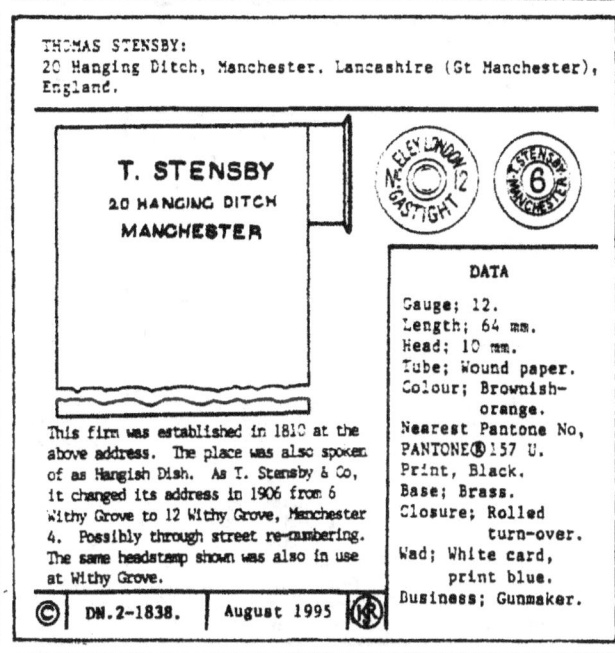
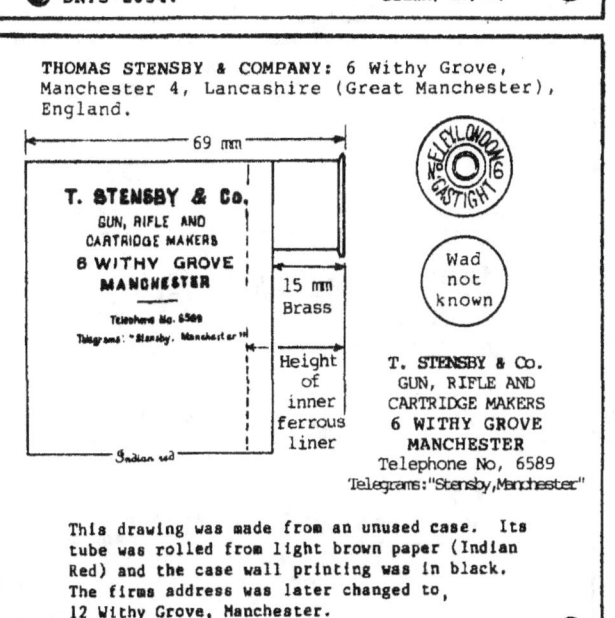
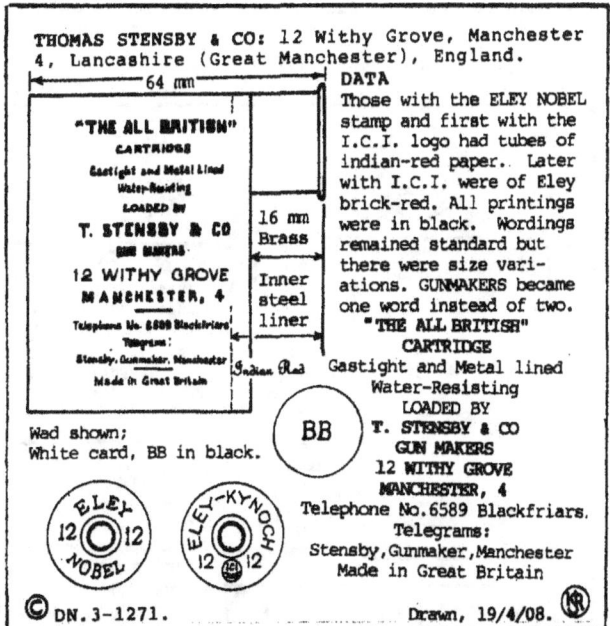

PLATE 347 [STA – STE]

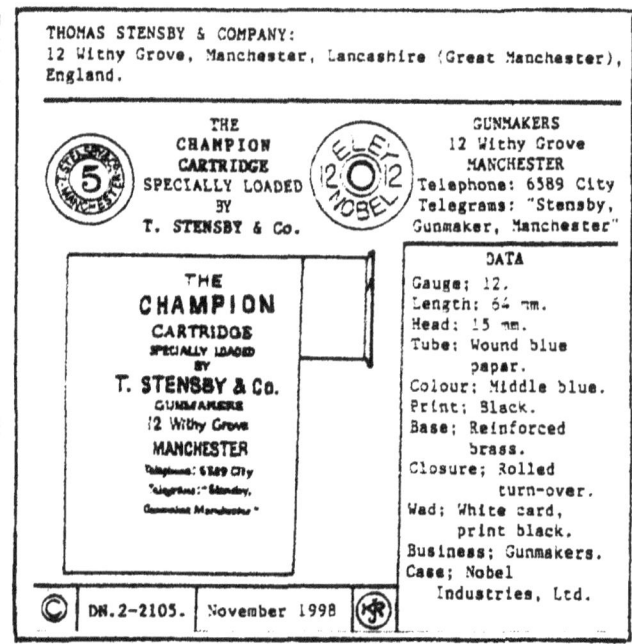
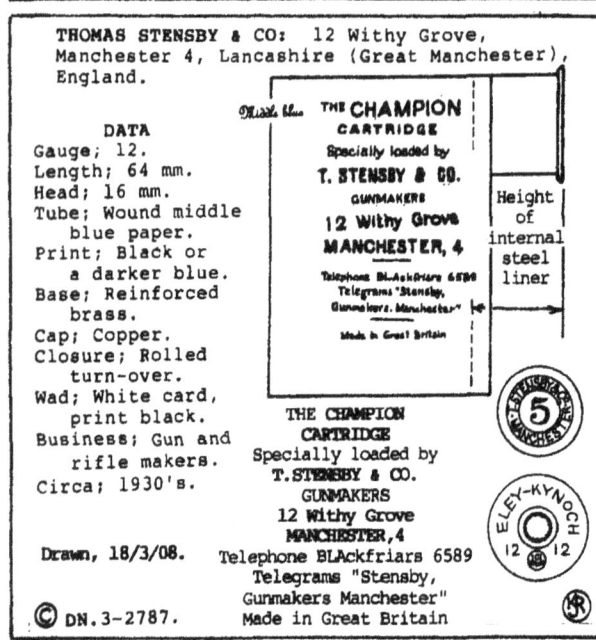
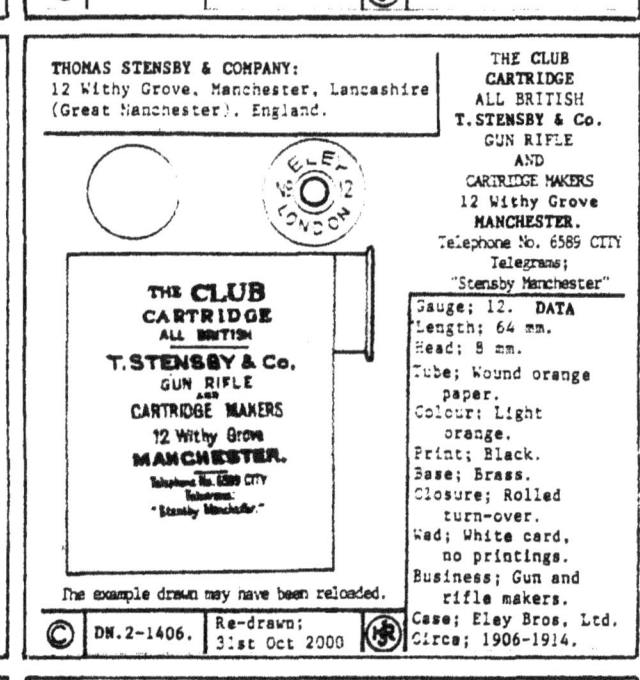
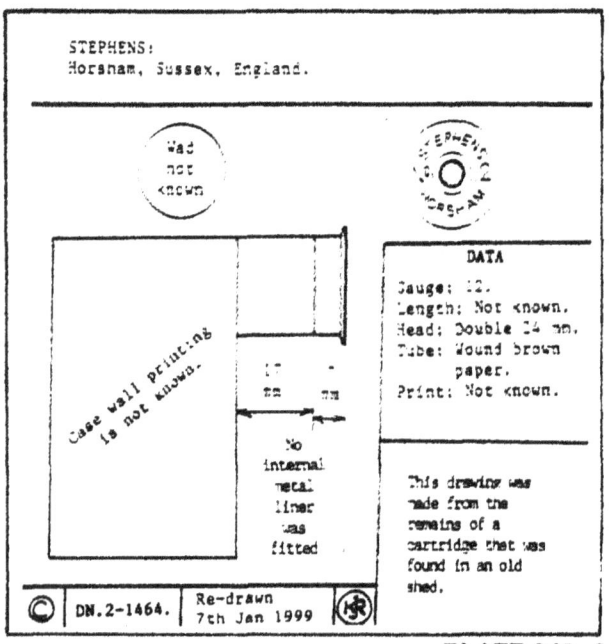
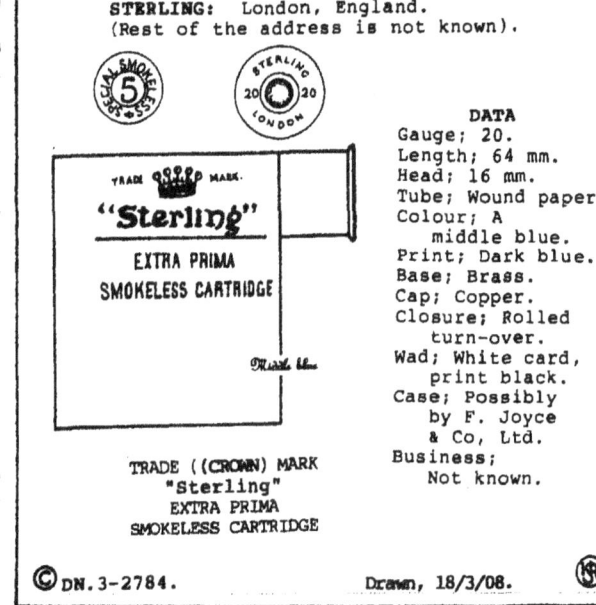

PLATE 348 [STE – STE]

CHARLES J. STIRK & SON:
Grahamstown, Cape Province, Union of South Africa (Republic of South Africa).

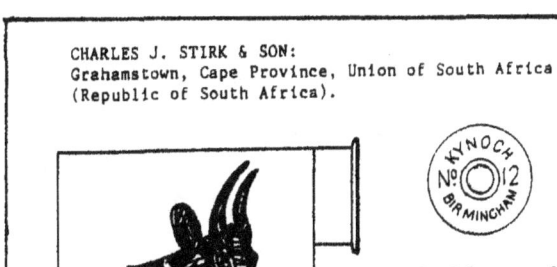

Updated from an early drawing of a sample case.

DATA
Gauge; 12.
Length; 64 mm.
Head; 10 mm.
Tube; Wound paper.
Colour; Salmon pink.
Print; Dark blue.
Base; Brass.
Closure; Rolled turn-over.
Wad; Not known.
Case by; Kynoch.

© DN.3-1902. Updated; November 2008.

A. J. STOCKER (C. & E. STOCKER):
Chulmleigh, Devonshire, England.

DATA
Gauge; 12.
Length; 64 mm.
Head; 8 mm.
Tube; Wound greyish green paper.
Colour; Greyish apple green.
Print; Black.
Base; Brass.
Closure; Rolled turn-over.
Wad; White card, print vermilion red.
Business; Ironmongers.
Circa; 1930's.

© DN.2-0384. Re-drawn; 26th Feb 2000.

A. J. STOCKER (C. & E. STOCKER):
Chulmleigh, Devonshire, England.

STOCKER'S SPECIAL LOAD MADE IN ENGLAND

DATA
Gauge; 12.
Length; 65 mm.
Head; 8 mm.
Tube; Wound red paper.
Colour; Deep red.
Print; Black.
Base; Reinforced brass.
Closure; Rolled turn-over.
Wad; Buttercup yellow, print black.
Business; Ironmongers.
Loading; Trant.

© DN.2-0385. Re-drawn; 19th Feb 2000.

THE STOCKTON SHOOT.
Stockton, Wylye Valley, Salisbury, Wiltshire, England.

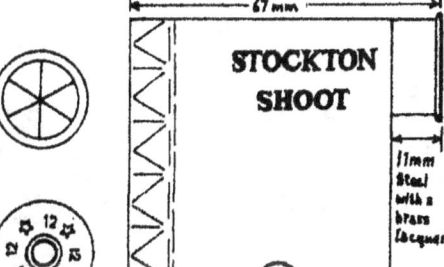

The tube was wound from brown paper with an outer layer of gloss crimson red. Printings were in black. Closure was a six fold crimp.

© DN.5-1008.

JOHN STREET & SONS:
Castle Street, Christchurch, Hampshire (Dorset).
Also at, 95 Christchurch Road, Boscombe, Bournemouth, Hampshire (Dorset), England.

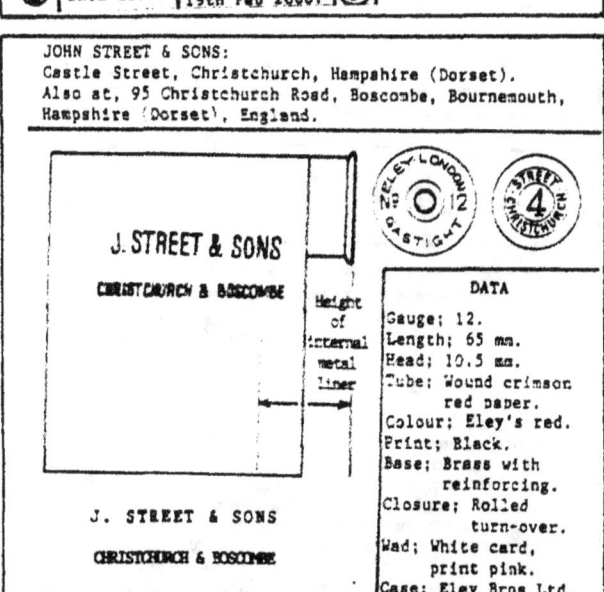

DATA
Gauge; 12.
Length; 65 mm.
Head; 10.5 mm.
Tube; Wound crimson red paper.
Colour; Eley's red.
Print; Black.
Base; Brass with reinforcing.
Closure; Rolled turn-over.
Wad; White card, print pink.
Case; Eley Bros Ltd.
Business; Ironmongers.

© DN.2-0770. Updated, April 1996

J. STRONG & SON:
65 Castle Street, Also,
88 Warwick Road, Carlisle,
Cumberland (Cumbria), England.

DATA
Gauge; 12.
Length; 64 mm.
Head; 9 mm.
Tube; Wound orange paper.
Colour; Orange.
Print; Black.
Base; Brass.
Closure; Rolled turn-over.
Wad; Yellow card, print black.
Business; Gun and ammunition dealers.
Circa; 1930's.

© DN.2-0504. Re-drawn; 12th Jan 2000.

STUCHBERY'S STORES (P. & S. THOMPSON, LTD).
63, 65, 67 High Street, Maidenhead, Berkshire, England.

DATA
Gauge; 12.
Length; 64 mm.
Head; 8 mm.
Tube; Wound orange paper.
Colour; Dull orange.
Print; Black.
Base; Brass.
Closure; Rolled turn-over.
Wad; Not known.
Business; Grocery, provisions and ironmongery.
Case; Eley Bros, Ltd. London.

DN.2-2369. Re-drawn; 19th Nov 2000

STUDLEY:
Uffculme, Devonshire, England.

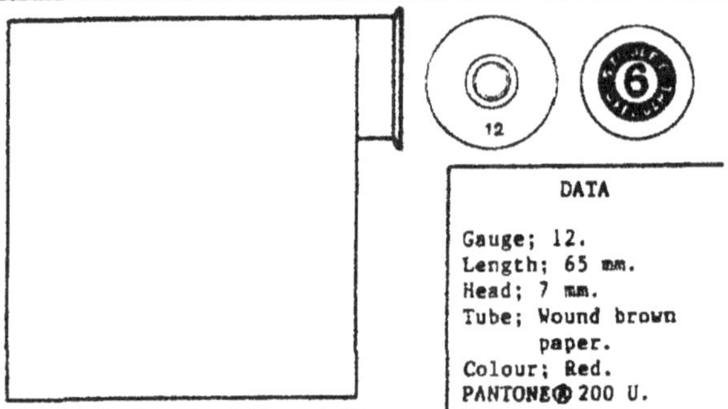

I found both the wad and the cartridge case at Uffculme. Both were very old and so I decided to join the two components together for entry into my own collection. No iron or steel was used in the construction of the unprinted and unvarnished case. I would place them as being back in the 1880's.

DATA
Gauge; 12.
Length; 65 mm.
Head; 7 mm.
Tube; Wound brown paper.
Colour; Red. PANTONE® 200 U.
Print; Nil.
Base; Brass.
Closure; Rolled turn-over.
Wad; White card, print a similar red to case.

DN.2-1046. Updated, March 1996

STYPE ESTATE:
Stype. Near Hungerford. Wiltshire-Berkshire Border, England.

Stype Estate

DATA
Gauge; 12.
Length; 65 mm.
Head; 3 mm.
Tube; Wound paper.
Colour; Orange.
Print; Black.
Base; Steel with brass coating.
Closure; Six fold crimp.
Business; Private country estate.
Circa; 1960's-1970's.

DN.2-0592. Re-drawn 30th Jan 1999

SUPER CARTRIDGE COMPANY PTY. LTD:
151 Raleigh Road, Maribynong, Melbourne, Victoria, Australia.

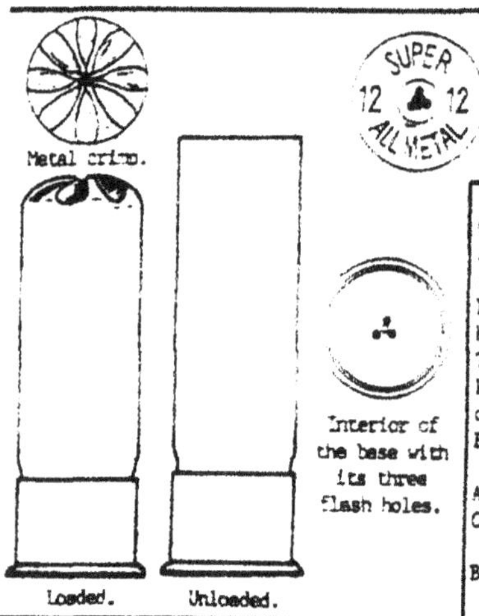

The headstamp shows the cap chamber with its central anvil minus the percussion cap.

Metal crimp. Loaded. Unloaded. Interior of the base with its three flash holes.

DATA
Gauge; 12.
All aluminium two piece case.
Length; 68.5 mm.
Head; 15 mm.
Tube; Aluminium.
Print on example drawn; Nil.
Base; Treated aluminium.
Anvil; Conical.
Closure; Eight fold crown crimp.
Business; Ammunition manufacturers.

DN.2-0584. Updated, March 1996. ALL METAL TWO PIECE

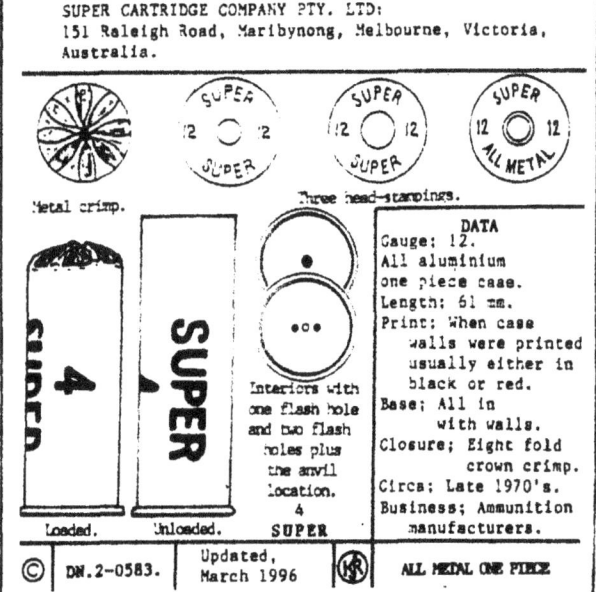

SUPER CARTRIDGE COMPANY PTY. LTD:
151 Raleigh Road, Maribynong, Melbourne, Victoria, Australia.

Metal crimp. Three head-stampings. Loaded. Unloaded. Interiors with one flash hole and two flash holes plus the anvil location.

DATA
Gauge; 12.
All aluminium one piece case.
Length; 61 mm.
Print; When case walls were printed usually either in black or red.
Base; All in with walls.
Closure; Eight fold crown crimp.
Circa; Late 1970's.
Business; Ammunition manufacturers.

DN.2-0583. Updated, March 1996. ALL METAL ONE PIECE

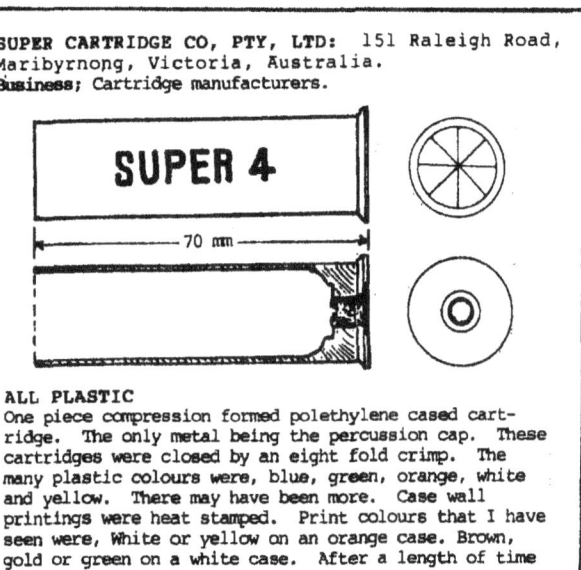

SUPER CARTRIDGE CO, PTY, LTD:
151 Raleigh Road, Maribyrnong, Victoria, Australia.
Business; Cartridge manufacturers.

SUPER 4 — 70 mm —

ALL PLASTIC
One piece compression formed polethylene cased cartridge. The only metal being the percussion cap. These cartridges were closed by an eight fold crimp. The many plastic colours were, blue, green, orange, white and yellow. There may have been more. Case wall printings were heat stamped. Print colours that I have seen were, White or yellow on an orange case. Brown, gold or green on a white case. After a length of time these cases developed a tendency to curve.

DN.3-0585. Drawn, 20/4/08.

PLATE 350 [STU – SUP]

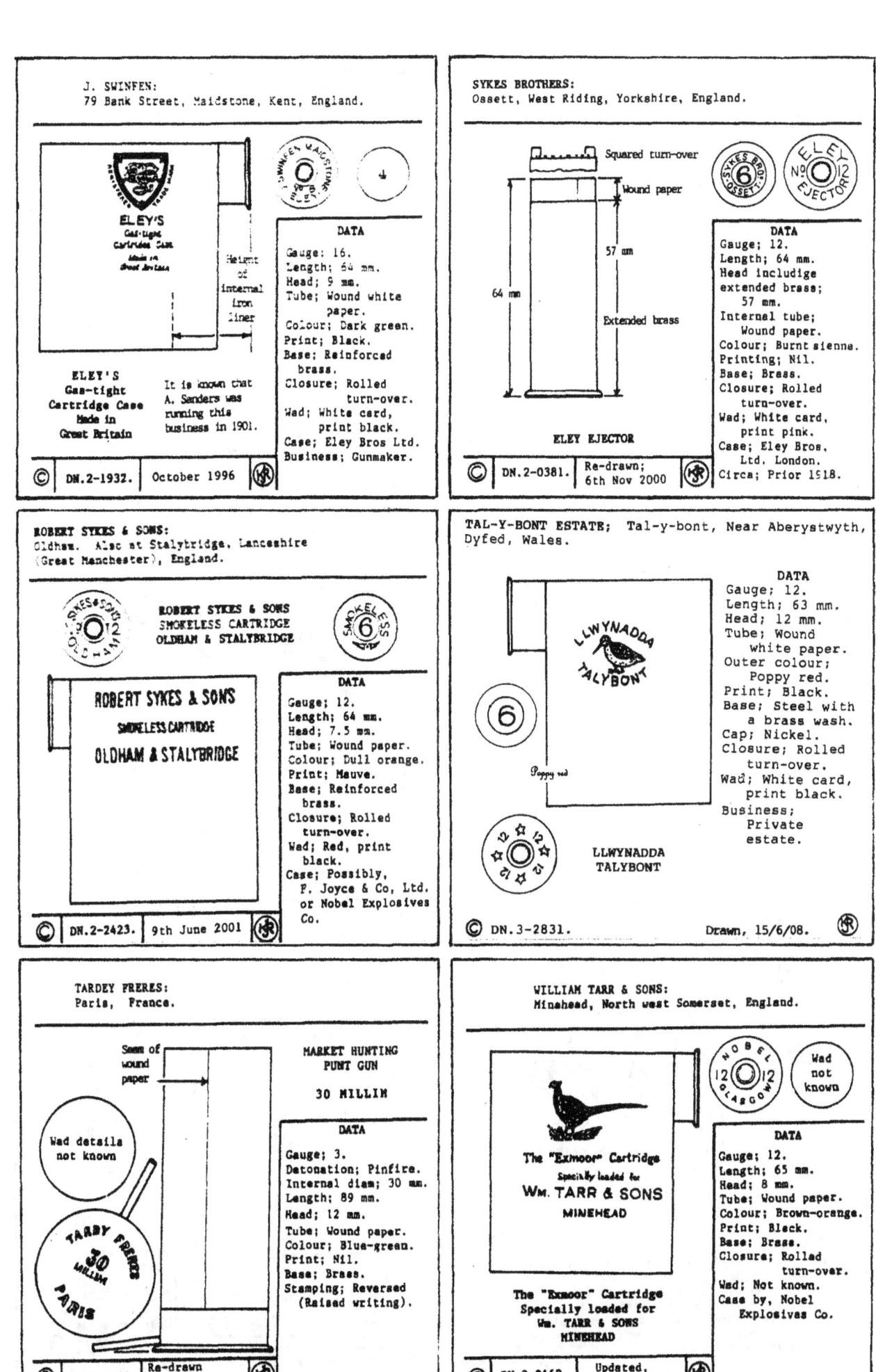

PLATE 351 [SWI - TAR]

ALBERT TAYLOR:
49 Bartholomew Street, Newbury, Berkshire, England.

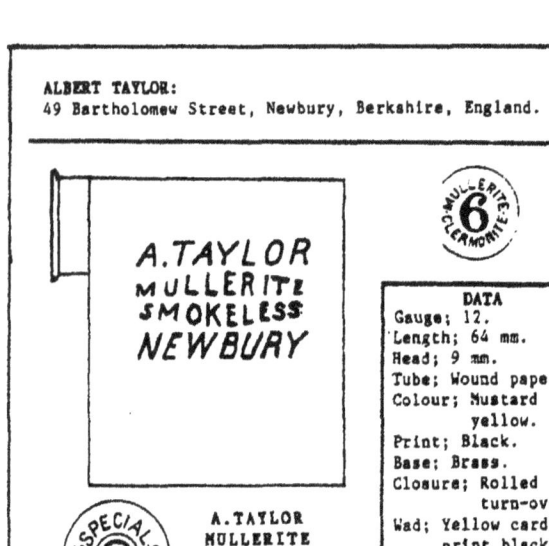

DATA
Gauge; 12.
Length; 64 mm.
Head; 9 mm.
Tube; Wound paper.
Colour; Mustard yellow.
Print; Black.
Base; Brass.
Closure; Rolled turn-over.
Wad; Yellow card, print black.
Business; Barber, gunsmith and field sports.
Loading: Mullerite Cartridge Works.

© DN.2-0189. Re-drawn; 17th Jan 2000.

JOHN T. TAYLOR & SON:
90 High Street, Bromsgrove, Worcestershire (Hereford & Worcester), England.

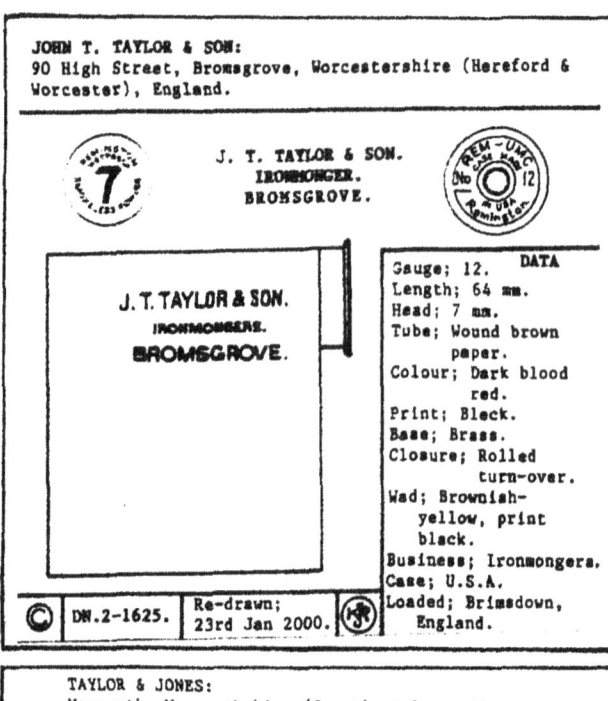

DATA
Gauge; 12.
Length; 64 mm.
Head; 7 mm.
Tube; Wound brown paper.
Colour; Dark blood red.
Print; Black.
Base; Brass.
Closure; Rolled turn-over.
Wad; Brownish-yellow, print black.
Business; Ironmongers.
Case; U.S.A.
Loaded; Brimsdown, England.

© DN.2-1625. Re-drawn; 23rd Jan 2000.

S. R. TAYLOR & SONS, LIMITED:
Penzance. Cornwall. Also at. St. Ives. Cornwall. England.
The overshot wad shown is; BRICHET:
Nantes, Pays De La Loire, France.

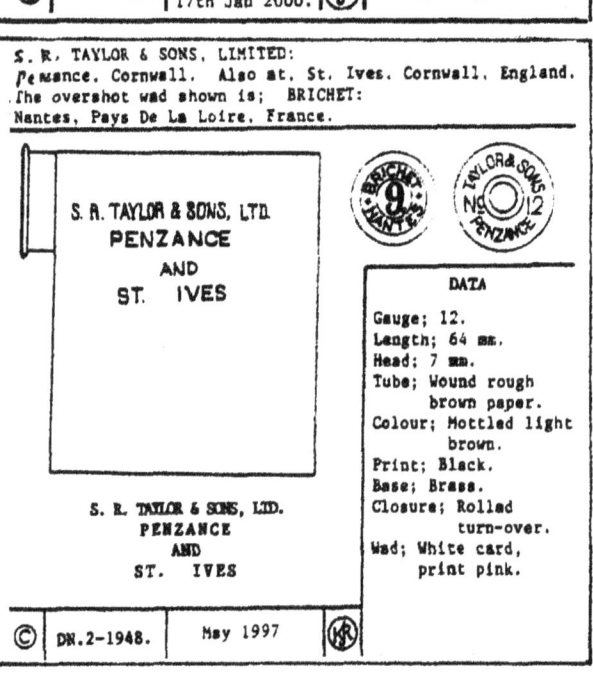

DATA
Gauge; 12.
Length; 64 mm.
Head; 7 mm.
Tube; Wound rough brown paper.
Colour; Mottled light brown.
Print; Black.
Base; Brass.
Closure; Rolled turn-over.
Wad; White card, print pink.

© DN.2-1948. May 1997

TAYLOR & JONES:
Monmouth, Monmouthshire (Gwent), Wales. Also at, Ross-on-Wye, Herefordshire (Hereford & Worcester), England.

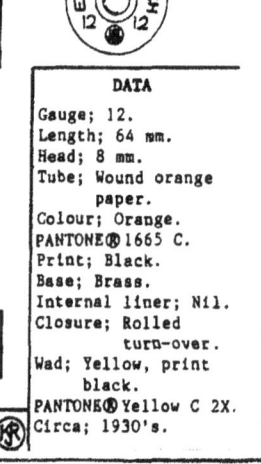

DATA
Gauge; 12.
Length; 64 mm.
Head; 8 mm.
Tube; Wound orange paper.
Colour; Orange.
PANTONE® 1665 C.
Print; Black.
Base; Brass.
Internal liner; Nil.
Closure; Rolled turn-over.
Wad; Yellow, print black.
PANTONE® Yellow C 2X.
Circa; 1930's.

© DN.2-0709. Updated, November 1995

TEIFI VALLEY SHOOTING SUPPLIES:
Llechryd, Cardigan, Dyfed, Wales.

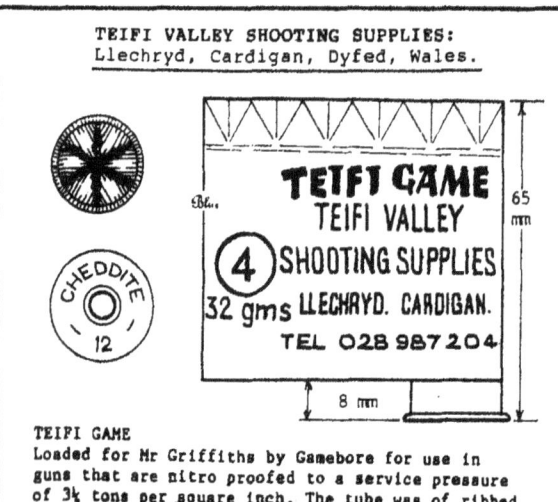

TEIFI GAME
Loaded for Mr Griffiths by Gamebore for use in guns that are nitro proofed to a service pressure of 3¼ tons per square inch. The tube was of ribbed mariner blue plastic and the head was from steel with a brass coating. The primer cap was nickel. Case wall printing being in black and the closure by a six fold star crimp.

© DN.3-1053. Revised; 27/12/08.

TEIKOKU E' YAKKYOSEIZA:
Tokyo, Japan.

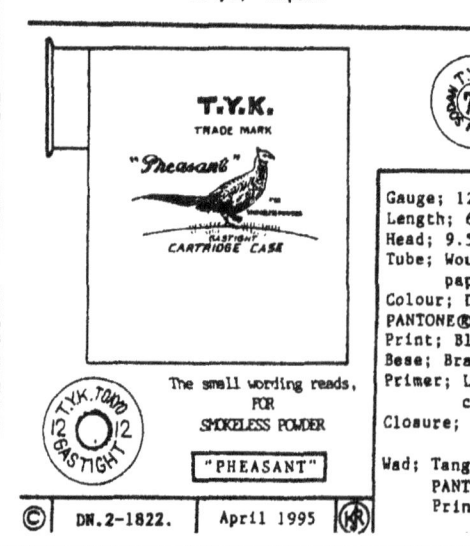

The small wording reads,
FOR
SMOKELESS POWDER
"PHEASANT"

DATA
Gauge; 12.
Length; 65 mm.
Head; 9.5 mm.
Tube; Wound white paper.
Colour; Dark green.
PANTONE® 343 C.
Print; Black.
Base; Brass.
Primer; Large copper.
Closure; Rolled turn-over.
Wad; Tangerine.
PANTONE® 1375.
Print black.

© DN.2-1822. April 1995

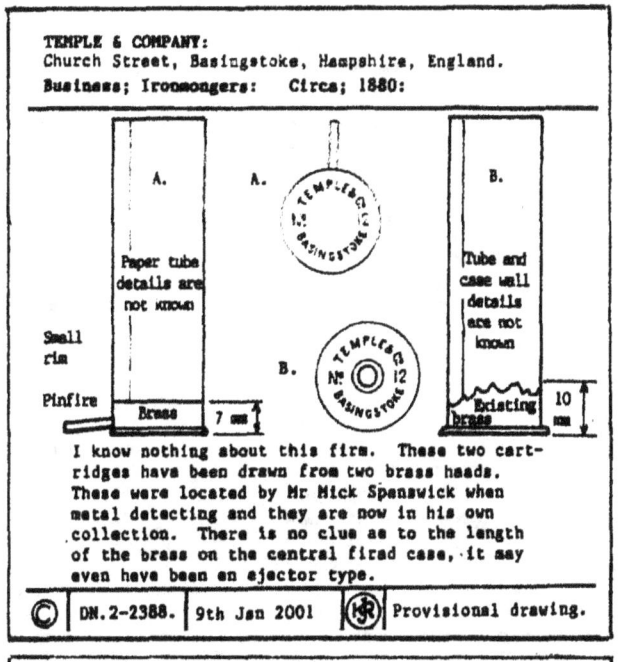

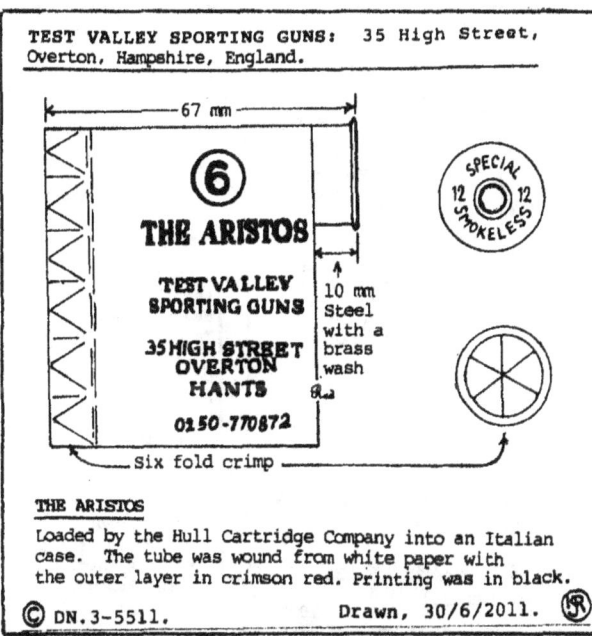

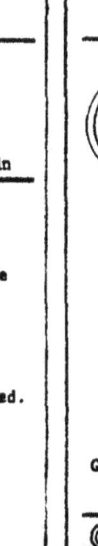
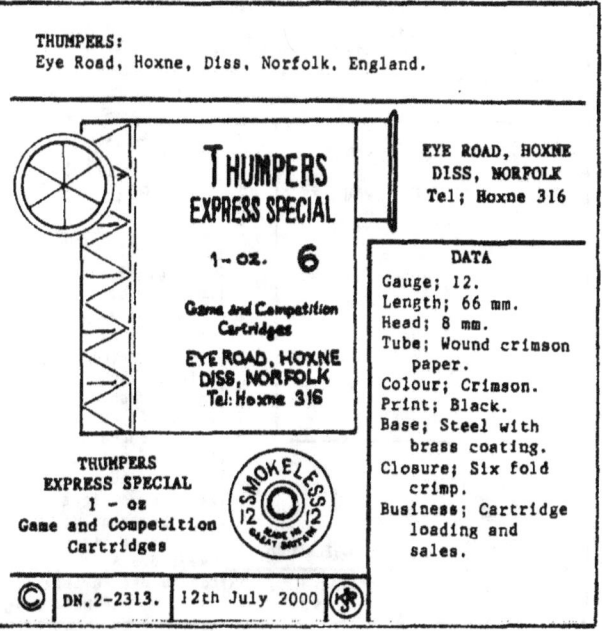

PLATE 353 [TEM – THU]

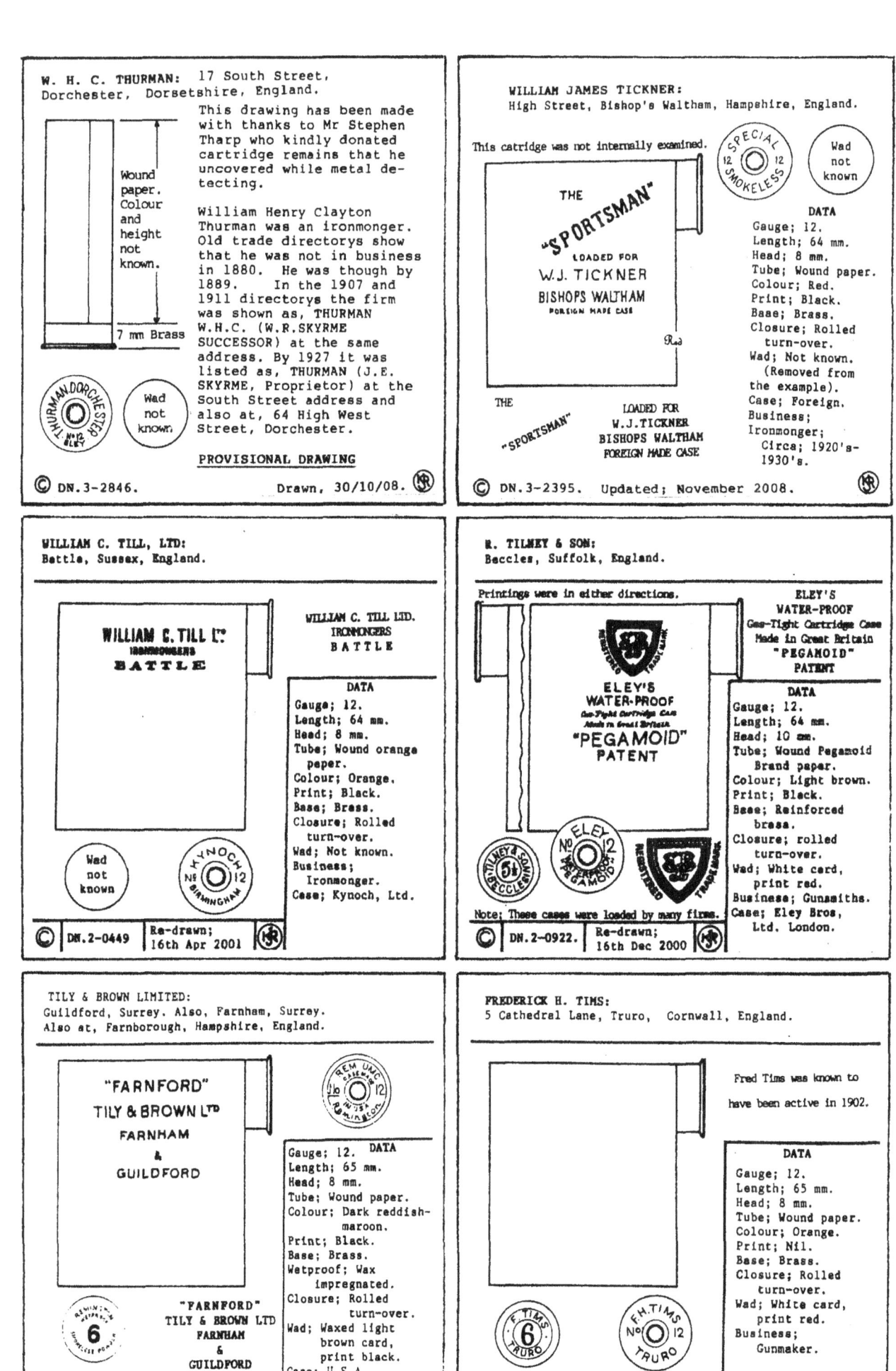

JOHN TINNING:
Longtown, Cumberland (Cumbria). Also at,
Newcastle-upon-Tyne, Northumberland (Tyne & Wear),
England.

JOHN TINNING,
LONGTOWN,
AND
NEWCASTLETON N.B.

Height of internal metal liner

Wad not known

JOHN TINNING,
LONGTOWN,
AND
NEWCASTLE N.B.

DATA
Gauge; 12.
Length; 64 mm.
Head; 8 mm.
Tube; Wound brown paper.
Colour; Cream-yellow.
Print; Blue-black.
Base; Reinforced brass.
Closure; Rolled turn-over.
Wad; Not known.
Case; Kynoch, Ltd.

© DN.2-0185. Re-drawn; 26th Feb 2001.

JOHN TISDALL:
8 South Street, Chichester. Also in,
Arundel, Sussex, England.

Drawing of a cartridge seen in the U.S.A.

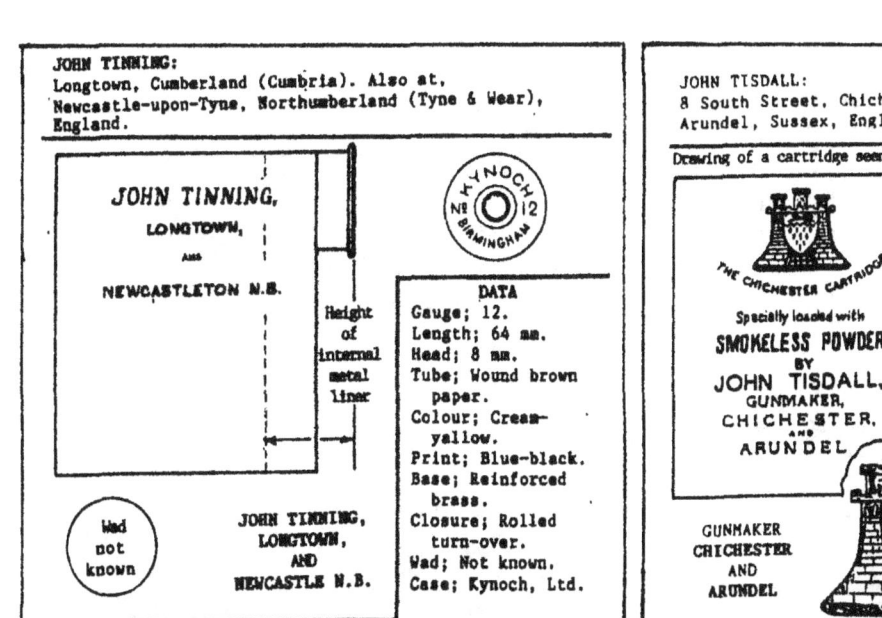

THE CHICHESTER CARTRIDGE
Specially Loaded with
SMOKELESS POWDER
BY
JOHN TISDALL.

DATA
Gauge; 12.
Length; 64 mm.
Head; 10 mm.
Tube; Wound paper.
Colour; Burgundy.
Print; Golden yellow.
Base; Brass.
Closure; Rolled turn-over.
Wad; White card, no printing.
Business; Gunmaker.

© DN.2-1547. Re-drawn 27th Jan 1999.

JOHN TISDALL:
Chichester & Arundel, Sussex, England.

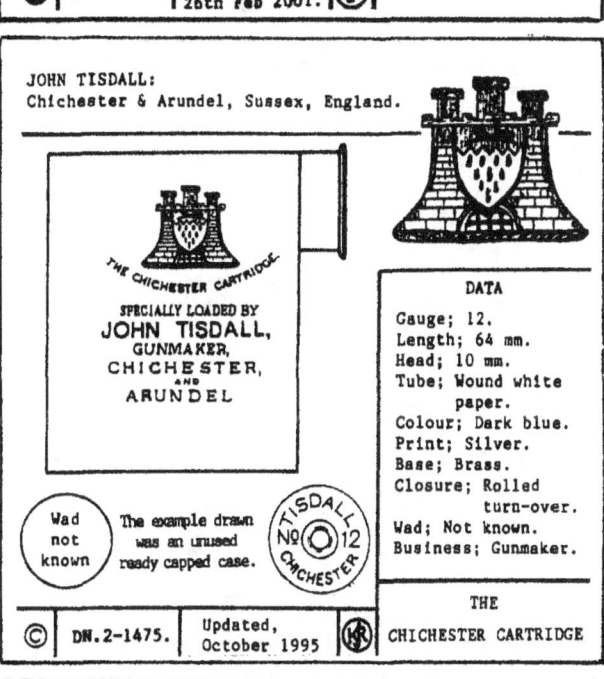

Wad not known. The example drawn was an unused ready capped case.

DATA
Gauge; 12.
Length; 64 mm.
Head; 10 mm.
Tube; Wound white paper.
Colour; Dark blue.
Print; Silver.
Base; Brass.
Closure; Rolled turn-over.
Wad; Not known.
Business; Gunmaker.

THE CHICHESTER CARTRIDGE

© DN.2-1475. Updated, October 1995

W. H. TISDALL, LTD:
Wellington & Christchurch, New-Zealand.

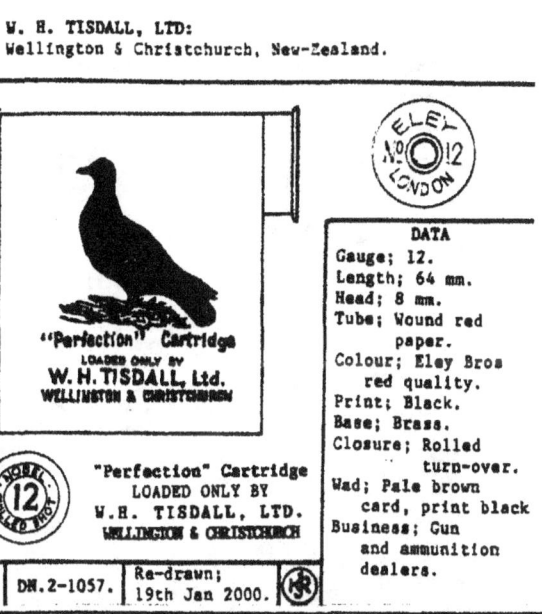

"Perfection" Cartridge
LOADED ONLY BY
W.H. TISDALL, LTD.
WELLINGTON & CHRISTCHURCH

DATA
Gauge; 12.
Length; 64 mm.
Head; 8 mm.
Tube; Wound red paper.
Colour; Eley Bros red quality.
Print; Black.
Base; Brass.
Closure; Rolled turn-over.
Wad; Pale brown card, print black.
Business; Gun and ammunition dealers.

© DN.2-1057. Re-drawn; 19th Jan 2000.

W. H. TISDALL LIMITED:
Auckland, Hamilton & Wellington, North Island.
Also at, Christchurch, South Island, New Zealand.

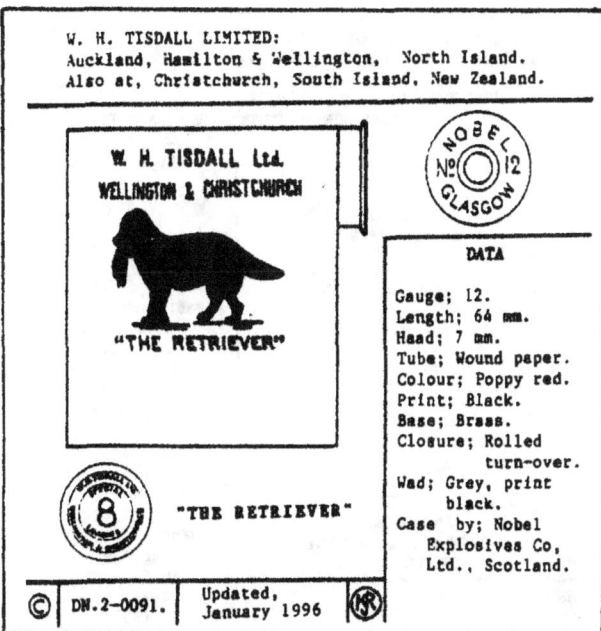

"THE RETRIEVER"

DATA
Gauge; 12.
Length; 64 mm.
Head; 7 mm.
Tube; Wound paper.
Colour; Poppy red.
Print; Black.
Base; Brass.
Closure; Rolled turn-over.
Wad; Grey, print black.
Case by; Nobel Explosives Co, Ltd., Scotland.

© DN.2-0091. Updated, January 1996

W. H. TISDALL, LIMITED:
Auckland, Wellington, Christchurch & Hamilton,
New Zealand.

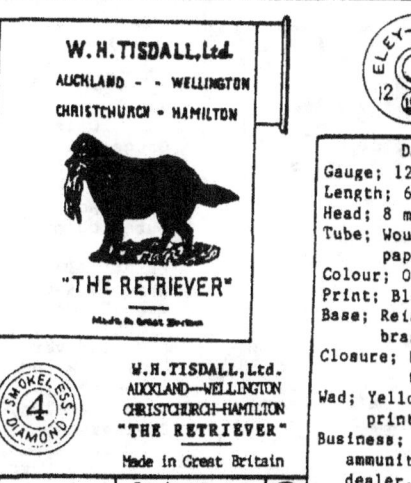

W.H. TISDALL, Ltd.
AUCKLAND—WELLINGTON
CHRISTCHURCH-HAMILTON
"THE RETRIEVER"
Made in Great Britain

DATA
Gauge; 12.
Length; 64 mm.
Head; 8 mm.
Tube; Wound orange paper.
Colour; Orange.
Print; Black.
Base; Reinforced brass.
Closure; Rolled turn-over.
Wad; Yellow card, print black.
Business; Gun and ammunition dealer.
Circa; 1930's.

© DN.2-1060. Re-drawn 17th Jan 1999.

TRENT GUN & CARTRIDGE WORKS: Wellholme Road, Grimsby, Lincolnshire (Humberside), England.

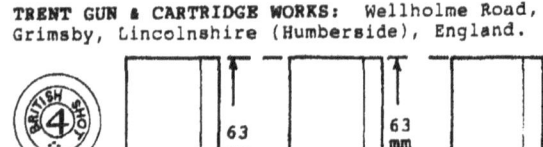
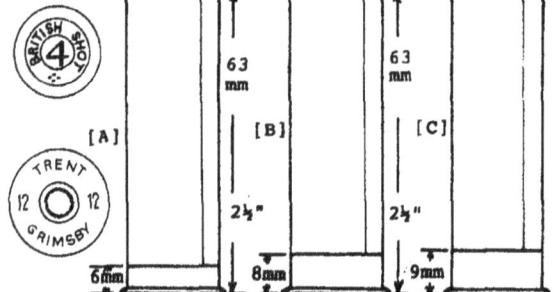

These unprinted cartridges each with a length of 63 mm had their tubes wound from coloured papers. Cartridge A has been seen in orange with both brass and steel heads. It has also been seen in maroon with a steel head. Cartridge B has been seen in maroon with a brass head. Cartridge C has been seen in a pale buff-brown with a brass head. Although I have called some steel, their composition I am not sure of, but they have shown rust marks. The wad shown was cut from brown card with black printing.

© DN.3-2797. Drawn, 20/3/08.

TRENT GUN & CARTRIDGES LTD: (SHOT TOWER GRIMSBY). Wellholme Road, Grimsby, Lincolnshire (Humberside), England.

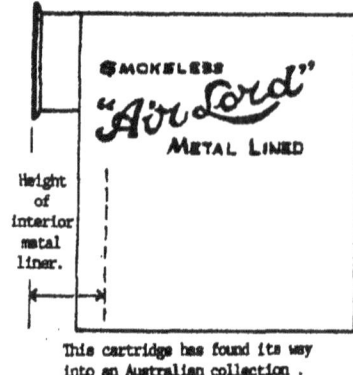

SMOKELESS "AIR LORD"

This cartridge has found its way into an Australian collection. It was loaded by Trent of Grimsby but it is not known for whom.

DATA
Gauge; 12.
Length; 70 mm.
Head; 10 mm.
Tube; Wound paper.
Colour; Brownish-orange.
PANTONE® 158 C.
Print; Black.
Base; Brass.
Closure; Rolled turn-over.
Wad; Red, print black.
PANTONE® 186 C.
Business; cartridge manufacturers.

© DN.2-1845. September 1995

TRENT GUNS & CARTRIDGES LTD: Shot Tower, Grimsby, Lincolnshire, England.

TRENT BEST SMOKELESS FOREIGN MADE Loaded in England WITH BRITISH SHOT

DATA
Gauge; 16.
Length; 64 mm.
Head; 7.5 mm.
Tube; Wound paper.
Colour; Dark red 4.
Print; Black.
Base; Brass.
Closure; Rolled turn-over.
Wad; Dark red 4.5 card, print black.
Business; Manufacturing merchants.

Drawn from a loaded cartridge.

© DN.2-0507. Updated; December 1994

TRENT GUN & CARTRIDGE WORKS: Wellholme Road, Grimsby, Lincolnshire (Humberside), England.

DATA
Gauge; 16.
Length; 65 mm.
Head; 8 mm.
Tube; Wound paper.
Outer colour; Ruby red.
Print; Black.
Base; Brass.
Cap; Large copper.
Closure; Rolled turn-over.
Wad; Dark red, print black.
Case; Foreign.
Business; Cartridge manufacturers.

TRENT BEST SMOKELESS 'FOREIGN MADE' Loaded in England WITH BRITISH SHOT.

Trents' were in business from around 1928 up until April 1953 when they were forced into liquidation.

This cartridge was not examined for internal metals.

© DN.3-2794. Drawn, 20/3/08.

TRENT GUN & CARTRIDGE WORKS: Wellholme Road, Grimsby, Lincolnshire (Humberside), England.

TRENT BEST SMOKELESS FOREIGN MADE LOADED IN ENGLAND

DATA
Gauge; 12.
Length; 65 mm.
Head; 9 mm.
Tube; Wound paper.
Outer colour; Ruby red.
Print; Black.
Base; Brass.
Cap; Large copper.
Closure; Rolled turn-over.
Wad; Dark red, print black.
Case; Foreign.
Business; Cartridge manufacturers.

This cartridge was not examined for internal metals.

© DN.3-2795. Drawn, 20/3/08.

TRENT GUNS & CARTRIDGES LIMITED: Shot Tower, Grimsby, Lincolnshire, England.

WAD; TRENT GUNS & CARTRIDGES LTD. GRIMSBY.
STAMPING; TRENT TRENT-GRIMSBY FOREIGN MADE LOADED IN ENGLAND

TRENT BEST SMOKELESS LOADED IN ENGLAND FOREIGN MADE

DATA
Gauge; 12.
Length; 64 mm.
Head; 8 mm.
Tube; Wound brown paper.
Colour; Dark crimson.
Print; Black.
Base; Reinforced brass.
Closure; Rolled turn-over.
Wad; Bright red, print black.
Business; Cartridge manufacturers and merchants.
Circa; 1930's.

© DN.2-2012. July 1997.

TRENT GUN & CARTRIDGE WORKS:
Wellholme Road, Grimsbury, Lincolnshire (Humberside),
England.

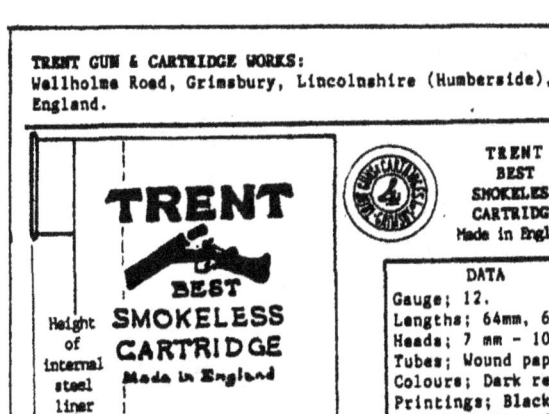

TRENT
BEST
SMOKELESS
CARTRIDGE
Made in England

All three stampings were used.
Should have said, Loaded in England.

DATA
Gauge; 12.
Lengths; 64mm, 65 mm.
Heads; 7 mm - 10 mm.
Tubes; Wound paper.
Colours; Dark red.
Printings; Black.
Bases; Brass, often
  with internal
  metal liners.
Closures; Rolled
  turn-overs.
Wad shown; Dark
  red, print black.
Business;
  Cartridge
  manufacturers.

© DN.2-0195.   Re-drawn; 5th May 2001

TRENT GUN & CARTRIDGES LTD:
Wellholme Road, Grimsby, Lincolnshire (Humberside),
England.

COSMO
BRITISH POWDER
SMOKELESS
CARTRIDGE
(MADE IN ENGLAND)

It is quite possible
that this brand was
intended for an over-
seas market.

DATA
Gauge; 12.
Length; 65 mm.
Head; 9 mm.
Tube; Wound paper.
Colour; Greenish-
  grey.
Print; Black.
Base; Brass.
Closure; Rolled
  turn-over.
Wad; Dark red card,
  print black.
Business; Gun and
  cartridge manu-
  facturers.

© DN.2-1655.   Updated; December 1994   COSMO

TRENT GUN & CARTRIDGE WORKS:
Wellholme Road, Grimsby, Lincolnshire (Humberside),
England.

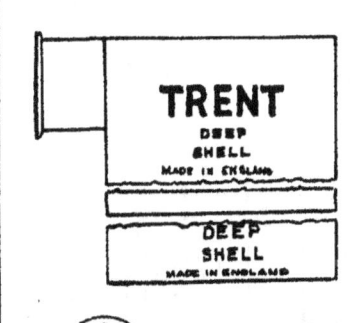

TRENT
DEEP
SHELL
MADE IN ENGLAND

DEEP
SHELL
MADE IN ENGLAND

TRENT
DEEP
SHELL
MADE IN ENGLAND

DATA
Gauge; 12.
Length; 65 mm.
Head; 16 mm.
Tube; Wound red
  paper.
Colour; dark blood
  red.
Print; Black.
Base; Reinforced
  brass or
  steel with
  brass wash.
Closure; Rolled
  turn-over.
Wad; Dark red,
  print black.
Circa; 1930's.

© DN.2-0312.   Re-drawn; 6th Jan 2001

TRENT GUN & CARTRIDGE WORKS: Wellholme Road,
Grimsby, Lincolnshire (Humberside), England.

TRENT
SUPER
RANGE
HEAVY LOAD
BRITISH LOADED

Dark red

TRENT
SUPER
RANGE
HEAVY LOAD
BRITISH LOADED

DATA
Gauge; 12.
Length; 65 mm.
Head; 16 mm.
Tube; Wound paper.
Outer colour; Dark
  brownish-red.
Print; Black.
Base; Brass.
Cap; Large copper.
Closure; Rolled
  turn-over.
Wad; Dark red,
  print black.
Business;
  Cartridge
  manufacturers.

This cartridge was
not examined for
internal metals.

© DN.3-2796.   Drawn, 20/3/08.

TROISDORF:
Troisdorf, Near Koln, West Germany.

Top of round

DATA
Gauge; 12.
Length; 65 mm.
Head; 9 mm.
Tube; Wound paper.
Outer colour;
  Light purple.
Print; Black.
Base; Brass.
Cap Large copper.
Closure; Rolled
  turn-over.
Load; Lead slug.

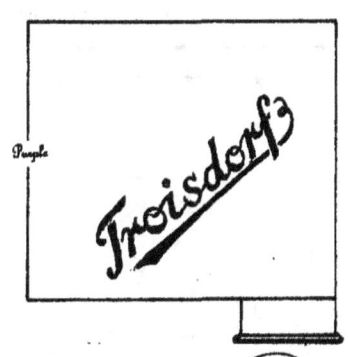

Purple

Troisdorf

The example was not tested for internal construction.

© DN.3-2585.   Drawn, 10/10/07.

S. TROUGHTON:
24 Caunce Street, Blackpool,
Lancashire, England.

S.TROUGHTON
PRACTICAL GUNMAKER
24 CAUNCE STREET
BLACKPOOL

S. TROUGHTON
PRACTICAL GUNMAKER
24 CAUNCE STREET
BLACKPOOL

DATA
Gauge; 12.
Length; 64 mm.
Head; 8 mm.
Tube; Wound red
  paper.
Colour; Crimson red.
Print; Black.
Base; Brass.
Closure; Rolled
  turn-over.
Wad; Dull red,
  print black.
Business; Gunmaker.
Case; Kynoch Ltd,
  Birmingham.

© DN.2-2431.   20th June 2001

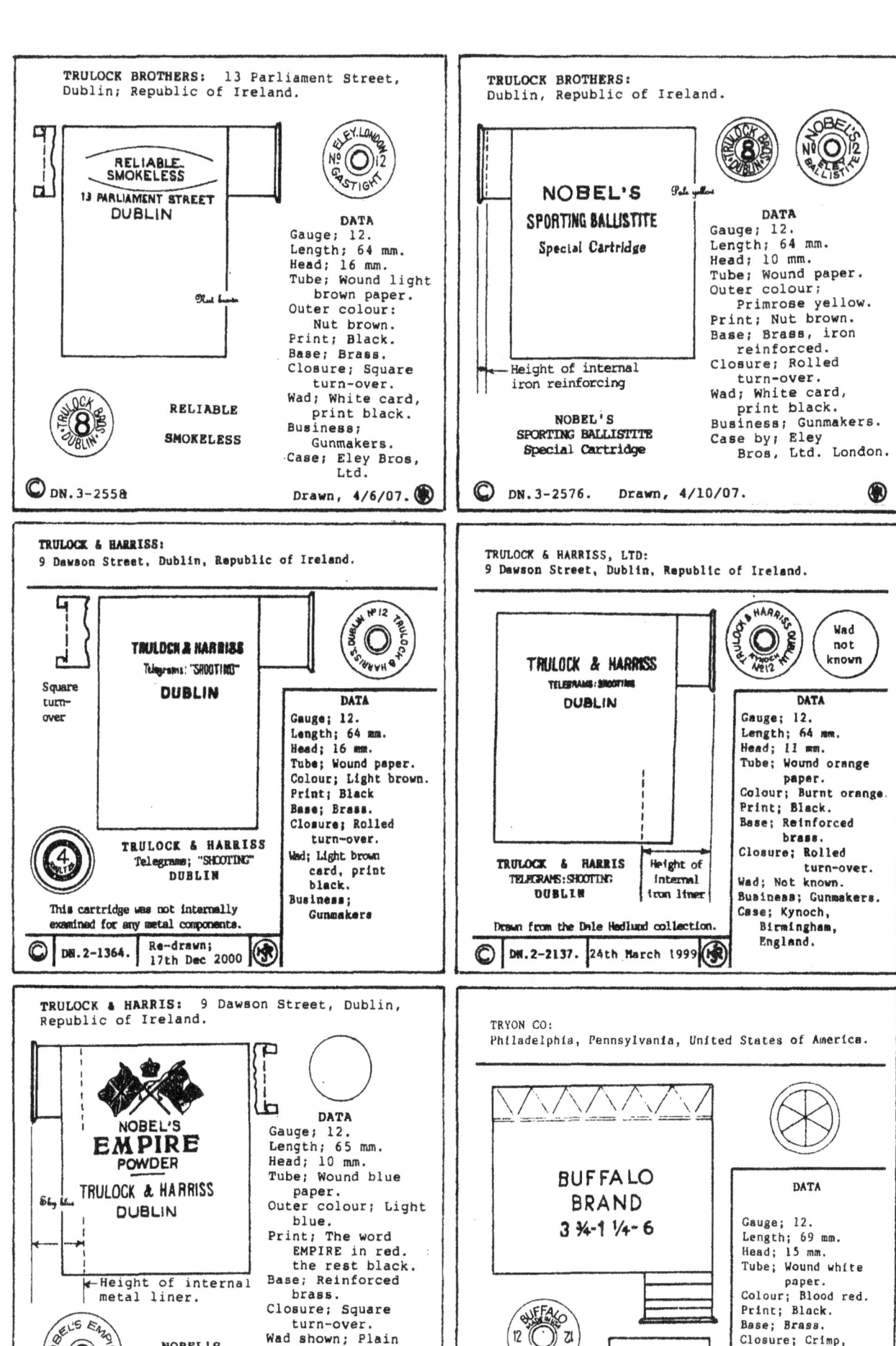

ANDREW TUCKER, LTD:
58 Portsmouth Road; Cobham, Surrey, England.

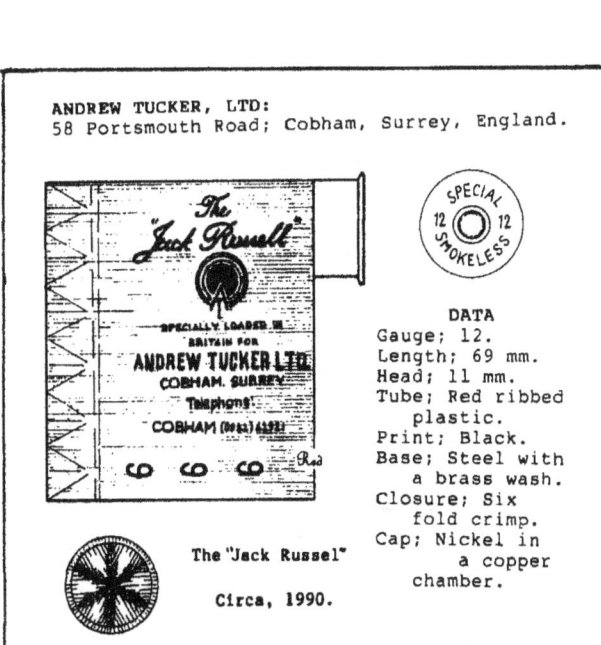

DATA
Gauge; 12.
Length; 69 mm.
Head; 11 mm.
Tube; Red ribbed plastic.
Print; Black.
Base; Steel with a brass wash.
Closure; Six fold crimp.
Cap; Nickel in a copper chamber.

The "Jack Russel"
Circa, 1990.

© DN.3-1162.   Revised; 20/12/08.

THE TULCHAN ESTATE:
Grantown-on-Spey, Morayshire, PH26 3PW, Scotland.

Some numbers may be incorrect due to poor case printings. Having cases printed is a waste of time if they are unreadable.

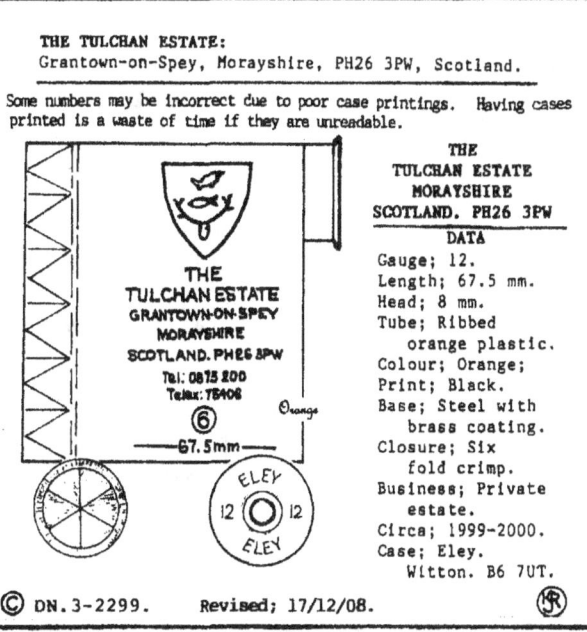

THE TULCHAN ESTATE
MORAYSHIRE
SCOTLAND. PH26 3PW

DATA
Gauge; 12.
Length; 67.5 mm.
Head; 8 mm.
Tube; Ribbed orange plastic.
Colour; Orange;
Print; Black.
Base; Steel with brass coating.
Closure; Six fold crimp.
Business; Private estate.
Circa; 1999-2000.
Case; Eley.
  Witton. B6 7UT.

© DN.3-2299.   Revised; 17/12/08.

ARTHUR TURNER. Later as, ARTHUR TURNER (SHEFFIELD) LTD:
5 West Bar, Sheffield, Yorkshire, England.

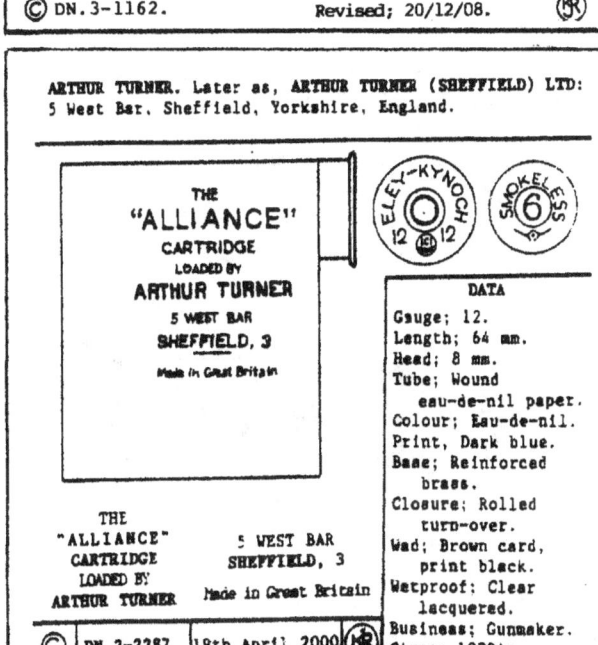

DATA
Gauge; 12.
Length; 64 mm.
Head; 8 mm.
Tube; Wound eau-de-nil paper.
Colour; Eau-de-nil.
Print; Dark blue.
Base; Reinforced brass.
Closure; Rolled turn-over.
Wad; Brown card, print black.
Wetproof; Clear lacquered.
Business; Gunmaker.
Circa; 1930's.

THE "ALLIANCE" CARTRIDGE
LOADED BY
ARTHUR TURNER
5 WEST BAR
SHEFFIELD, 3
Made in Great Britain

© DN.2-2287. 19th April 2000

ARTHUR TURNER: 5 West Bar, Sheffield, Yorkshire, England.

DATA
Gauge; 12.
Length; 64 mm.
Head; 8 mm.
Tube; Wound spring green paper.
Print; Black.
Base; Reinforced brass.
Cap; Copper.
Closure; Rolled turn-over.
Wad; Light green, print black.
Business; Gunmakers.
Circa; 1930's.

THE WIZARD
REGISTERED TRADE MARK
Loaded by
ARTHUR TURNER
LATE
MALEHAM & CO.
5 WEST BAR
SHEFFIELD, 3
MADE IN GREAT BRITAIN

© DN.3-2786. Drawn, 18/3/08.

ARTHUR TURNER (SHEFFIELD) LTD: 33-35 West Bar, Sheffield, Yorkshire, England.

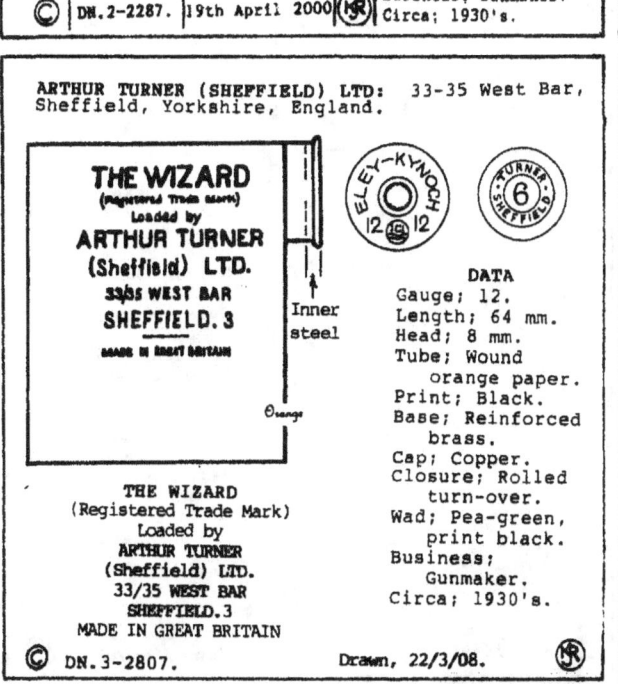

DATA
Gauge; 12.
Length; 64 mm.
Head; 8 mm.
Tube; Wound orange paper.
Print; Black.
Base; Reinforced brass.
Cap; Copper.
Closure; Rolled turn-over.
Wad; Pea-green, print black.
Business; Gunmaker.
Circa; 1930's.

THE WIZARD
(Registered Trade Mark)
Loaded by
ARTHUR TURNER
(Sheffield) LTD.
33/35 WEST BAR
SHEFFIELD.3
MADE IN GREAT BRITAIN

© DN.3-2807.   Drawn, 22/3/08.

HENRY A. TURNER, LTD:
142 High Street. Also, Bath Road, Marlborough, Wiltshire, England.

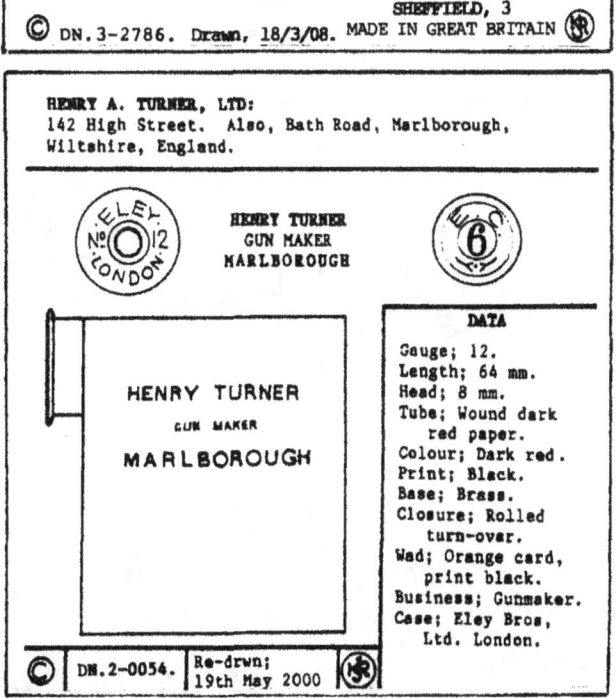

DATA
Gauge; 12.
Length; 64 mm.
Head; 8 mm.
Tube; Wound dark red paper.
Colour; Dark red.
Print; Black.
Base; Brass.
Closure; Rolled turn-over.
Wad; Orange card, print black.
Business; Gunmaker.
Case; Eley Bros, Ltd. London.

© DN.2-0054. Re-drwn; 19th May 2000

PLATE 359 [TUC - TUR]

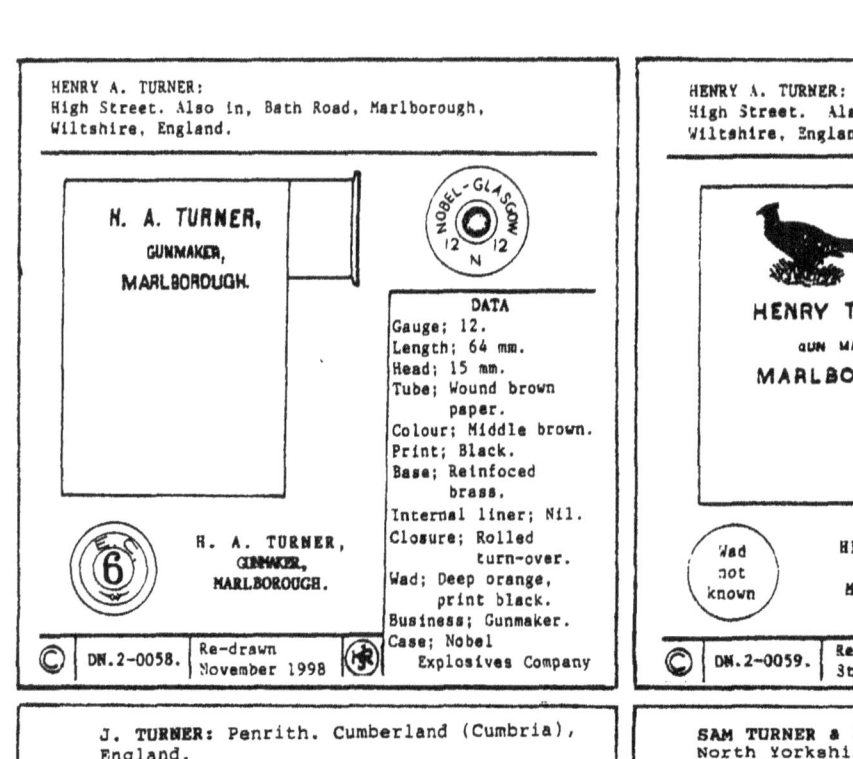
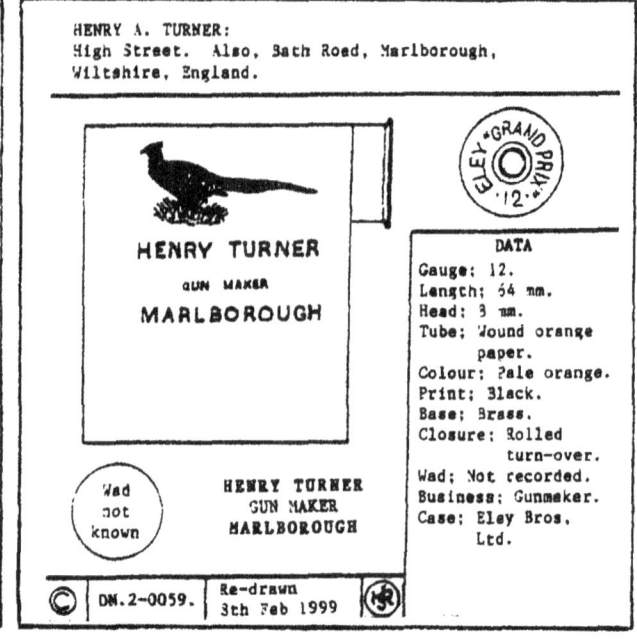
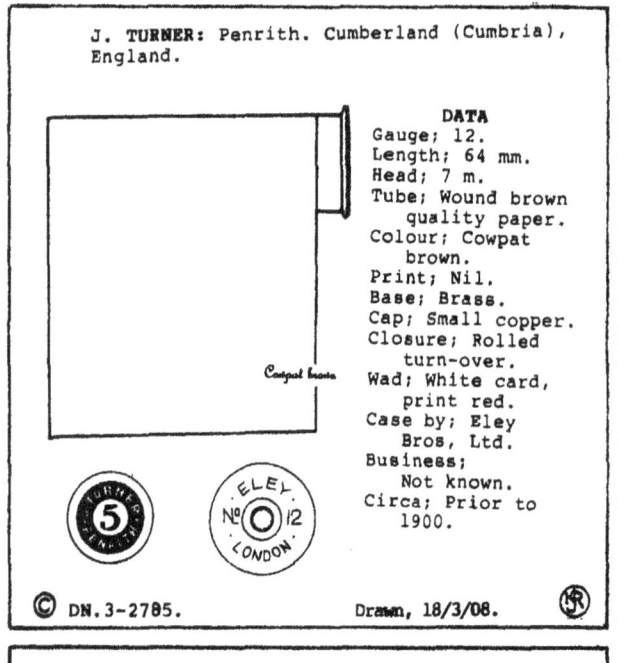
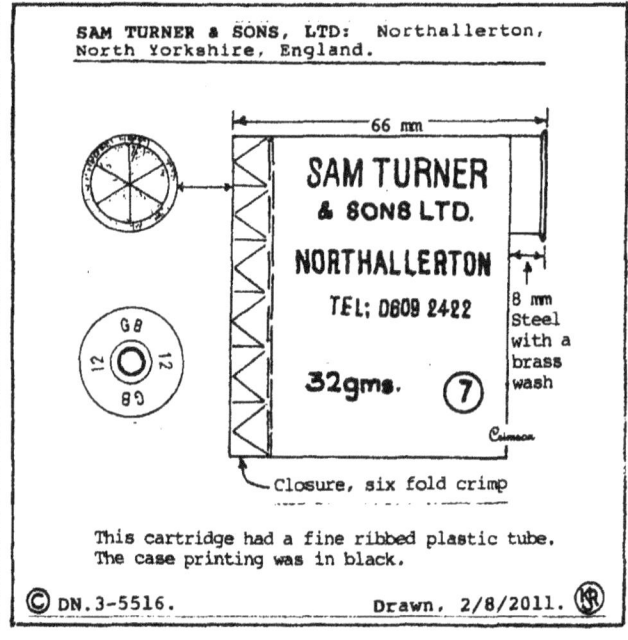
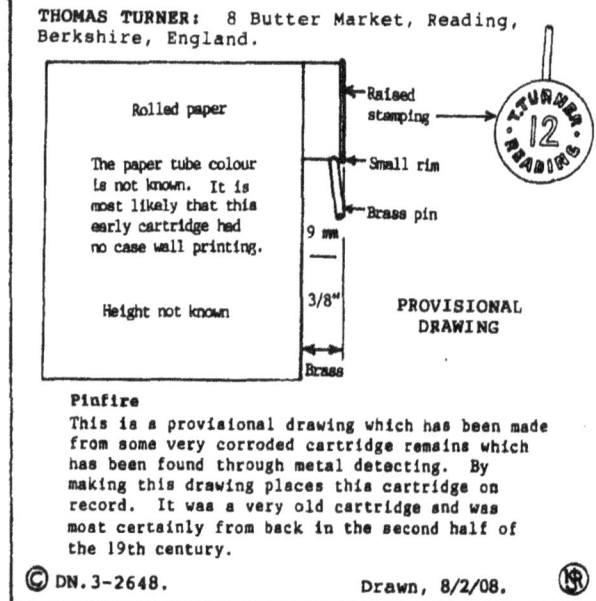
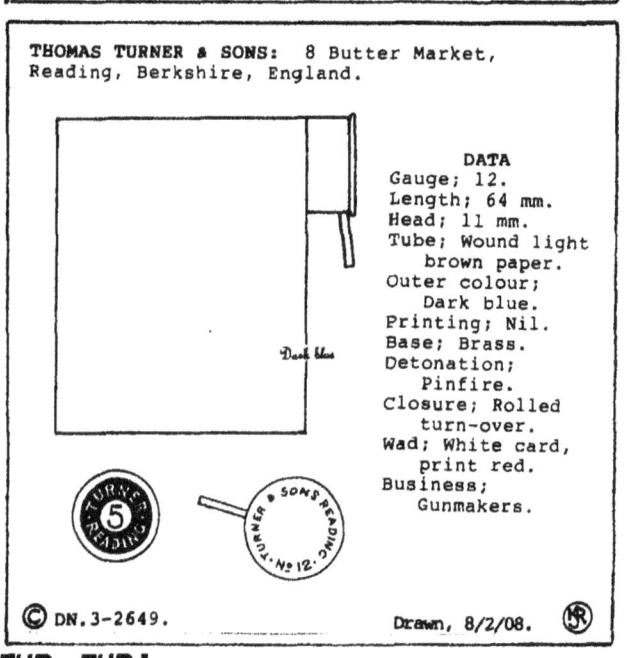

PLATE 360 [TUR – TUR]

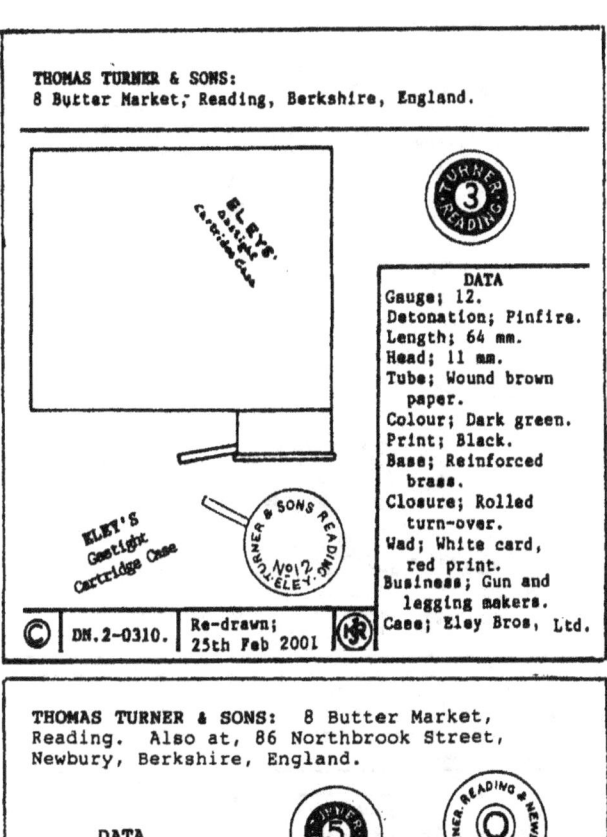
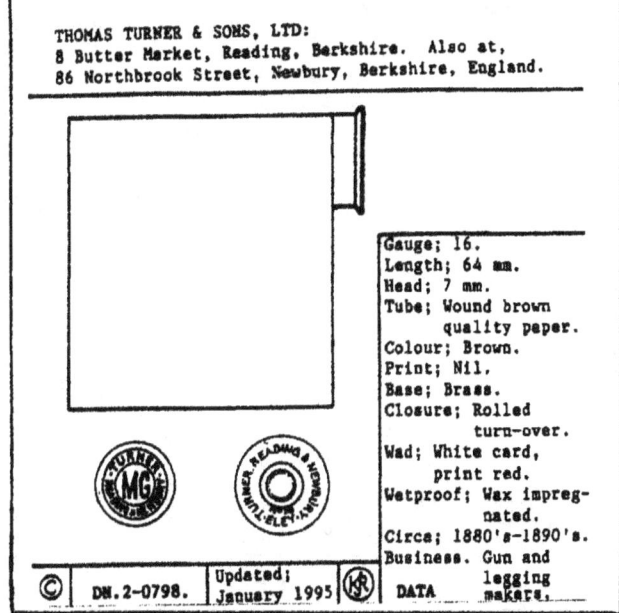
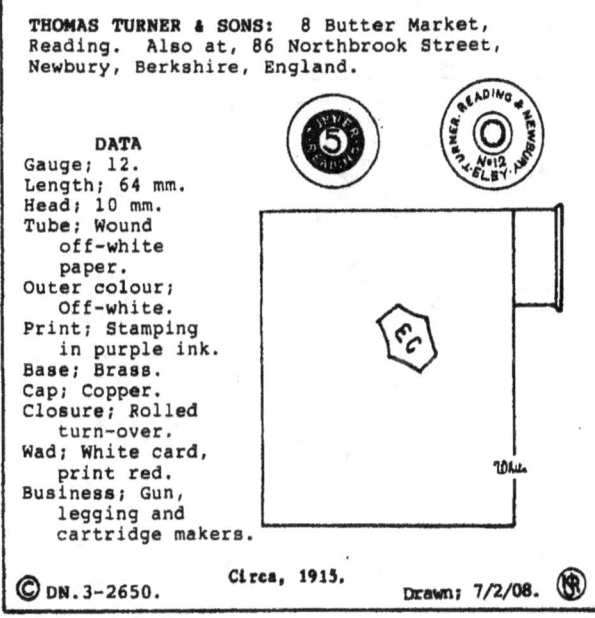
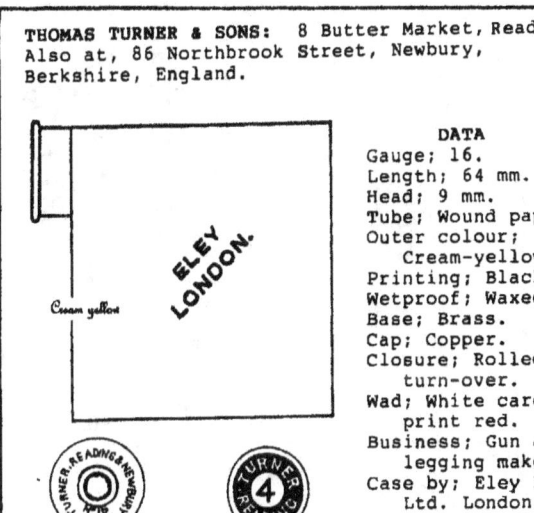
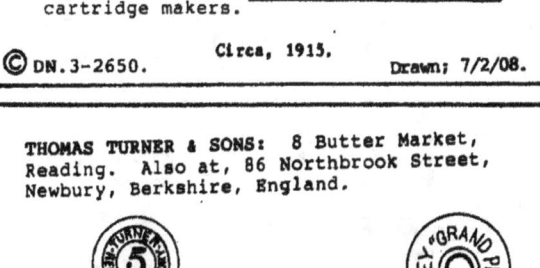
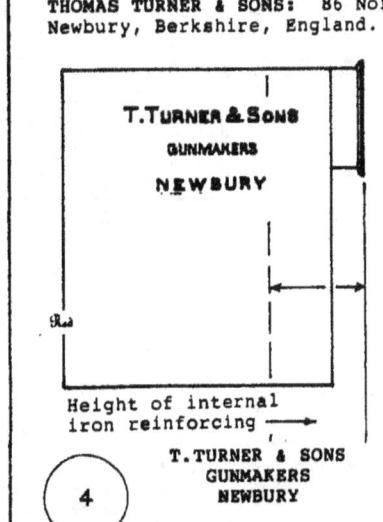
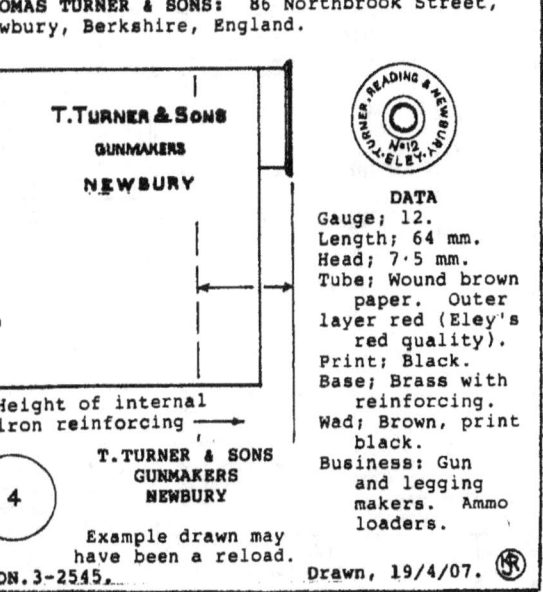
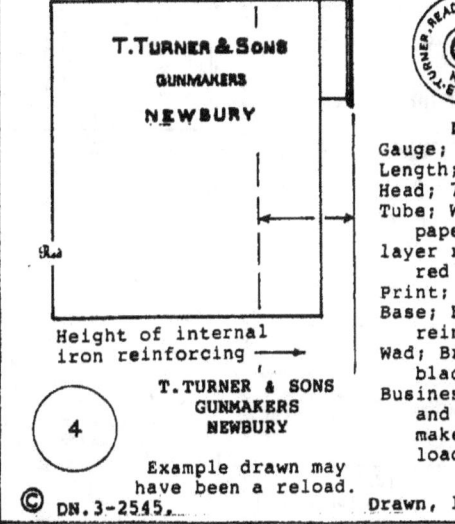

PLATE 361 [TUR–TUR]

THOMAS TURNER & SONS, LTD:
8 Butter Market, Reading. Also at, 86 Northbrook Street, Newbury, Berkshire, England.

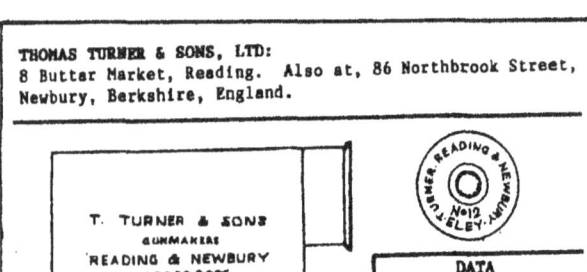

DATA
Gauge; 12.
Length; 64 mm.
Head; 10 mm.
Tube; Wound paper.
Colour; Pale yellow.
Print; Black.
Base; Brass.
Closure; Rolled turn-over.
Wad; White card, print red.
Business; Gun and legging makers.
Case; Eley Bros, Ltd. London.

DN.2-0051. Re-drawn; 17th Dec 2000.

---

8 Butter Market, Reading, Berkshire. Also, High Street, Hungerford, Berks. Also, 86 Northbrook St, Newbury, Berks. Also, 35 Wote St, Basingstoke, Hampshire, England.

Business; Gun and legging makers.

The Old Common Seal of Reading.

This old seal has been illustrated on many of Thos Turner & Sons Ltd cartridges.

Left, the basic geometry from which the old seal was drawn.

Right, The Reading Coat of Arms.

THOS TURNER & SONS LTD

THE CREST AS ON TURNER'S CARTRIDGES

This crest is the Old Common Seal of Reading. Note that this has five male heads while the Borough Coat of Arms has five female heads.

The wording on the Borough Arms is, A Deo et Regina. 'From God and the Queen'.

DN.2-0080. Updated; January 1995

THOMAS TURNER & SONS:
8 Butter Market, Reading. Also at, 86 Northbrook Street, Newbury, Berkshire, England.

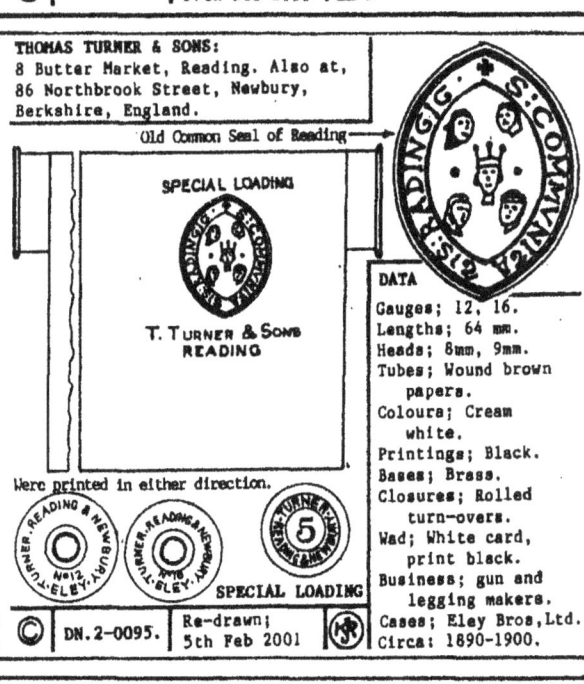

Old Common Seal of Reading

Were printed in either direction.

DATA
Gauges; 12, 16.
Lengths; 64 mm.
Heads; 8mm, 9mm.
Tubes; Wound brown papers.
Colours; Cream white.
Printings; Black.
Bases; Brass.
Closures; Rolled turn-overs.
Wad; White card, print black.
Business; gun and legging makers.
Cases; Eley Bros, Ltd.
Circa; 1890-1900.

DN.2-0095. Re-drawn; 5th Feb 2001

THOMAS TURNER & SONS, LTD:
8 Butter Market, Reading & 86 Northbrook Street, Newbury, Berkshire. Also at, 35 Wote Street, Basingstoke, Hampshire, England.

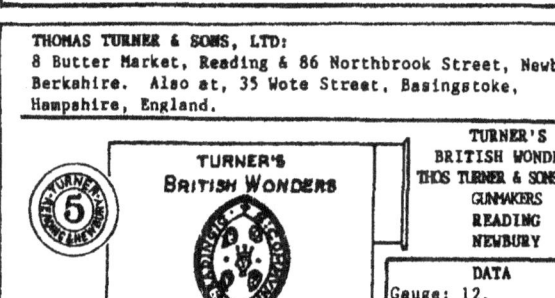

Circa, 1930's.

MADE IN GREAT BRITAIN
AND BASINGSTOKE Made in Great Britain
The crest is The Old Common Seal of Reading.

TURNER'S BRITISH WONDERS
THOS TURNER & SONS Ltd.
GUNMAKERS
READING
NEWBURY

DATA
Gauge; 12.
Lengths; 64 mm.
Heads; 8 mm.
Tubes; Wound coloured papers.
Coloured; Varied. Near white, eau-de-nil to greyish green.
Prints; Black and navy blue on eau-de-nil.
Bases; Reinforced brass.
Closures; Rolled.
Wad; Yellow, print black.
Business; Gunmakers.

DN.2-0088. Re-drawn; 23rd Nov 2000

THOMAS TURNER & SONS LIMITED:
86 Northbrook Street, Newbury, Berkshire (Royal Berkshire), England.

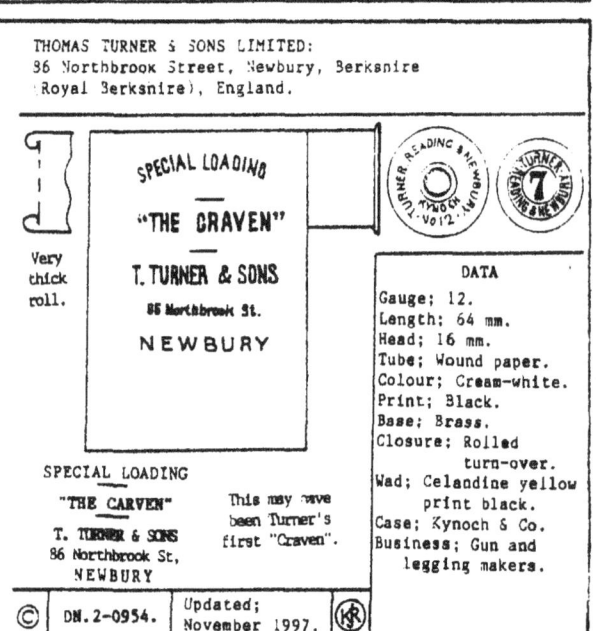

Very thick roll.

SPECIAL LOADING
"THE CARVEN"
T. TURNER & SONS
86 Northbrook St.
NEWBURY

This may have been Turner's first "Craven".

DATA
Gauge; 12.
Length; 64 mm.
Head; 16 mm.
Tube; Wound paper.
Colour; Cream-white.
Print; Black.
Base; Brass.
Closure; Rolled turn-over.
Wad; Celandine yellow print black.
Case; Kynoch & Co.
Business; Gun and legging makers.

DN.2-0954. Updated; November 1997.

THOMAS TURNER & SONS LIMITED:
8 Butter Market, Reading & 86 Northbrook Street, Newbury, Berkshire. Also at; 35 Wote Street, Basingstoke, Hampshire, England.

"THE CRAVEN"
SPECIAL LOADING
Dark blue

THOS. TURNER & SONS Ltd.
GUNMAKERS
READING
NEWBURY
AND
BASINGSTOKE
MADE IN GREAT BRITAIN
or
Made in Great Britain

"THE CRAVEN"
SPECIAL LOADING
THOS. TURNER & SONS Ltd.
GUNMAKERS
READING
NEWBURY

Height of internal metal liner

DATA
Gauge; 16.
Length; 63.5 mm.
Head; 15 mm.
Tube; Wound dark blue paper.
Colour; Mariner blue.
Prints; Black or darker navy blue.
Base; Reinforced brass.
Closure; Rolled turn-over.
Wad shown; White card, red printing.
Circa; 1930's.
Business; Gun and legging makers.

DN.3-2014.

PLATE 362 [TUR - TUR]

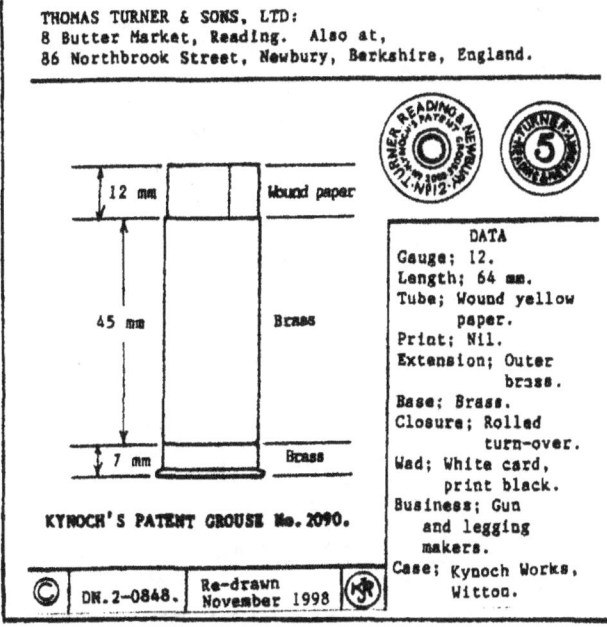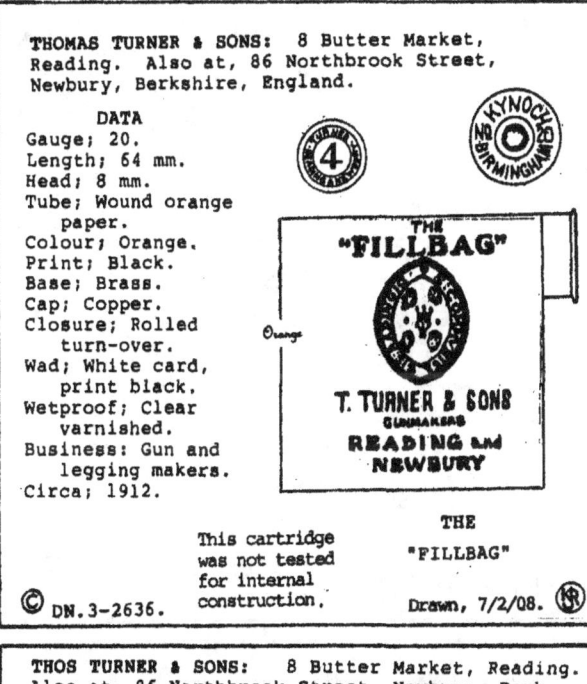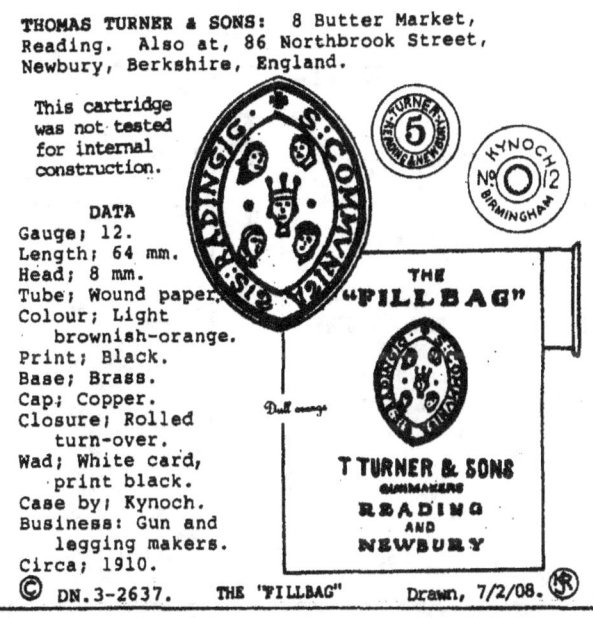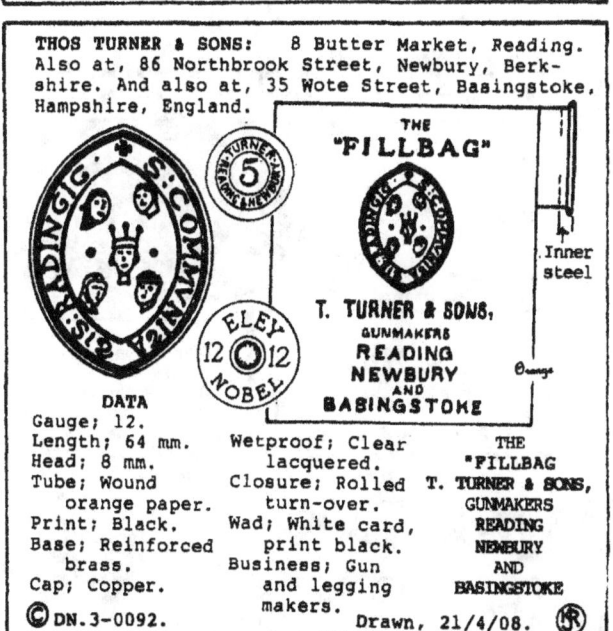

PLATE 363 [TUR - TUR]

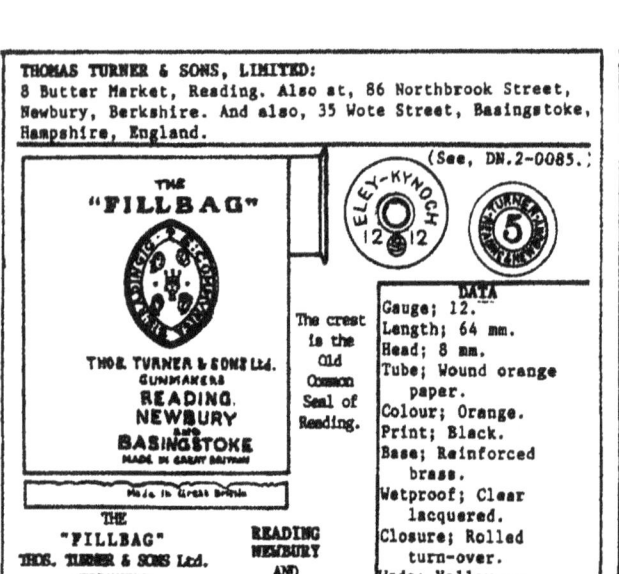

THOMAS TURNER & SONS, LIMITED:
8 Butter Market, Reading. Also at, 86 Northbrook Street, Newbury, Berkshire. And also, 35 Wote Street, Basingstoke, Hampshire, England.

(See, DN.2-0085.)

The crest is the Old Common Seal of Reading.

DATA
Gauge; 12.
Length; 64 mm.
Head; 8 mm.
Tube; Wound orange paper.
Colour; Orange.
Print; Black.
Base; Reinforced brass.
Wetproof; Clear lacquered.
Closure; Rolled turn-over.
Wads; Yellow or white, print black.
Business; Gun and legging makers.
Circa; 1930's.

DN.2-2303. Re-drawn; 23rd June 2000

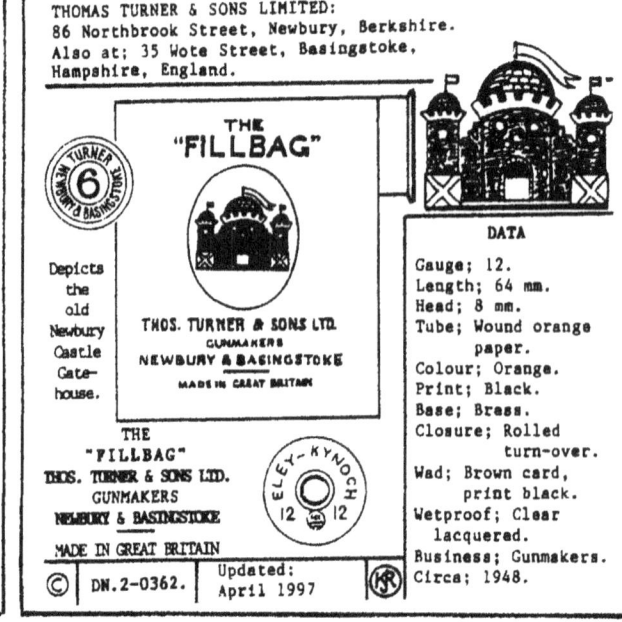

THOMAS TURNER & SONS LIMITED:
86 Northbrook Street, Newbury, Berkshire. Also at; 35 Wote Street, Basingstoke, Hampshire, England.

Depicts the old Newbury Castle Gatehouse.

DATA
Gauge; 12.
Length; 64 mm.
Head; 8 mm.
Tube; Wound orange paper.
Colour; Orange.
Print; Black.
Base; Brass.
Closure; Rolled turn-over.
Wad; Brown card, print black.
Wetproof; Clear lacquered.
Business; Gunmakers.
Circa; 1948.

DN.2-0362. Updated; April 1997

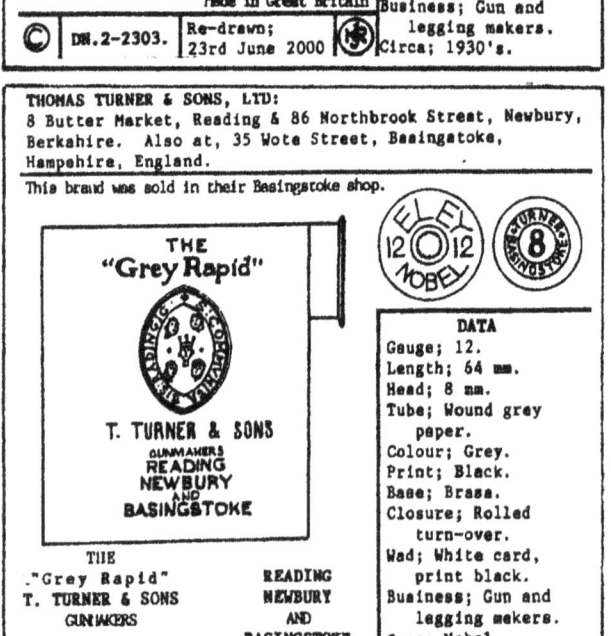

THOMAS TURNER & SONS, LTD:
8 Butter Market, Reading & 86 Northbrook Street, Newbury, Berkshire. Also at, 35 Wote Street, Basingstoke, Hampshire, England.

This brand was sold in their Basingstoke shop.

DATA
Gauge; 12.
Length; 64 mm.
Head; 8 mm.
Tube; Wound grey paper.
Colour; Grey.
Print; Black.
Base; Brass.
Closure; Rolled turn-over.
Wad; White card, print black.
Business; Gun and legging makers.
Case; Nobel Industries, Ltd.
Circa; 1925.

DN.2-0093. Re-drawn; 21st Nov 2000

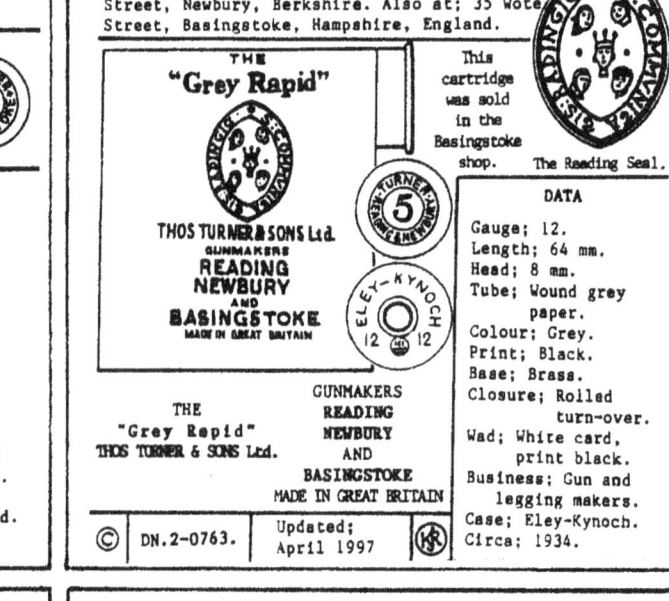

THOMAS TURNER & SONS, LIMITED:
8 Butter Market, Reading. Also; 86 Northbrook Street, Newbury. Also at; 35 Wote Street, Basingstoke, Hampshire, England.

This cartridge was sold in the Basingstoke shop. The Reading Seal.

DATA
Gauge; 12.
Length; 64 mm.
Head; 8 mm.
Tube; Wound grey paper.
Colour; Grey.
Print; Black.
Base; Brass.
Closure; Rolled turn-over.
Wad; White card, print black.
Business; Gun and legging makers.
Case; Eley-Kynoch.
Circa; 1934.

DN.2-0763. Updated; April 1997

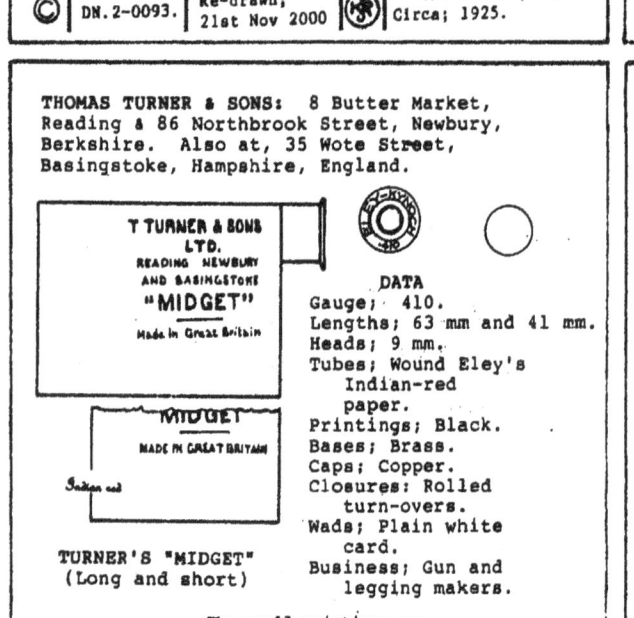

THOMAS TURNER & SONS: 8 Butter Market, Reading & 86 Northbrook Street, Newbury, Berkshire. Also at, 35 Wote Street, Basingstoke, Hampshire, England.

TURNER'S "MIDGET"
(Long and short)

DATA
Gauge; 410.
Lengths; 63 mm and 41 mm.
Heads; 9 mm.
Tubes; Wound Eley's Indian-red paper.
Printings; Black.
Bases; Brass.
Caps; Copper.
Closures; Rolled turn-overs.
Wads; Plain white card.
Business; Gun and legging makers.

Drawn, 3/2/08.
DN.3-2646. The small printings are, READING NEWBURY AND BASINGSTOKE. Made in Great Britain.

THOS TURNER & SONS LTD:
8 Butter Market, Reading, Berkshire. Also at, 86 Northbrook Street, Newbury, Berkshire, England.

Pictured is Newbury's old Castle Gate House.

DATA
Gauge; 20.
Length; 64 mm.
Head; 7 mm.
Tube; Wound paper.
Colour; Cream-yellow.
Print; Black.
Base; Brass.
Closure; Rolled turn-over.
Wad; White card, print black.
Business; Gun and legging makers.
Circa; 1905.

DN.2-0799. Updated; January 1995

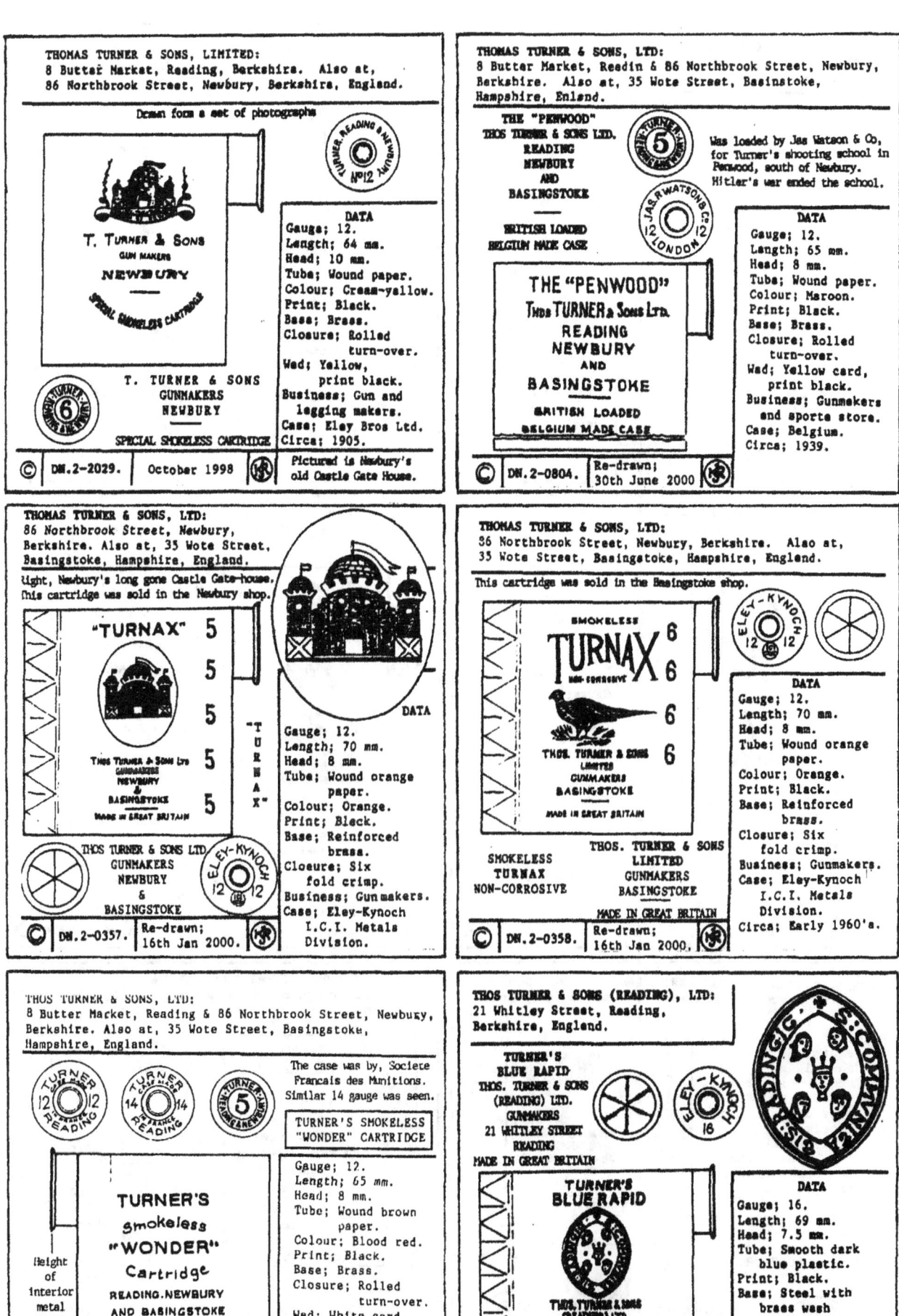

PLATE 365 [TUR - TUR]

THOMAS TURNER (GUNMAKER) READING:
208 Gosbrook Road, Caversham, Reading, Berkshire, England.

DATA
Gauge; 20.
Length; 67.5 mm.
Head; 8 mm.
Tube; Wound paper.
Colour; Creamed-buff.
Print; Black.
Base; Steel with a brass wash.
Closure; Six fold crimp.
Wetproof; Clear lacquered.
Business; Gunmakers.
Circa; 2001.

THOMAS TURNER'S HORNET
6
— 67.5 mm —

© DN.2-2517. 1st Aug 2002

THOMAS TURNER (GUNMAKER):
208 Gosbrook Road, Caversham, Reading, Berkshire, England.

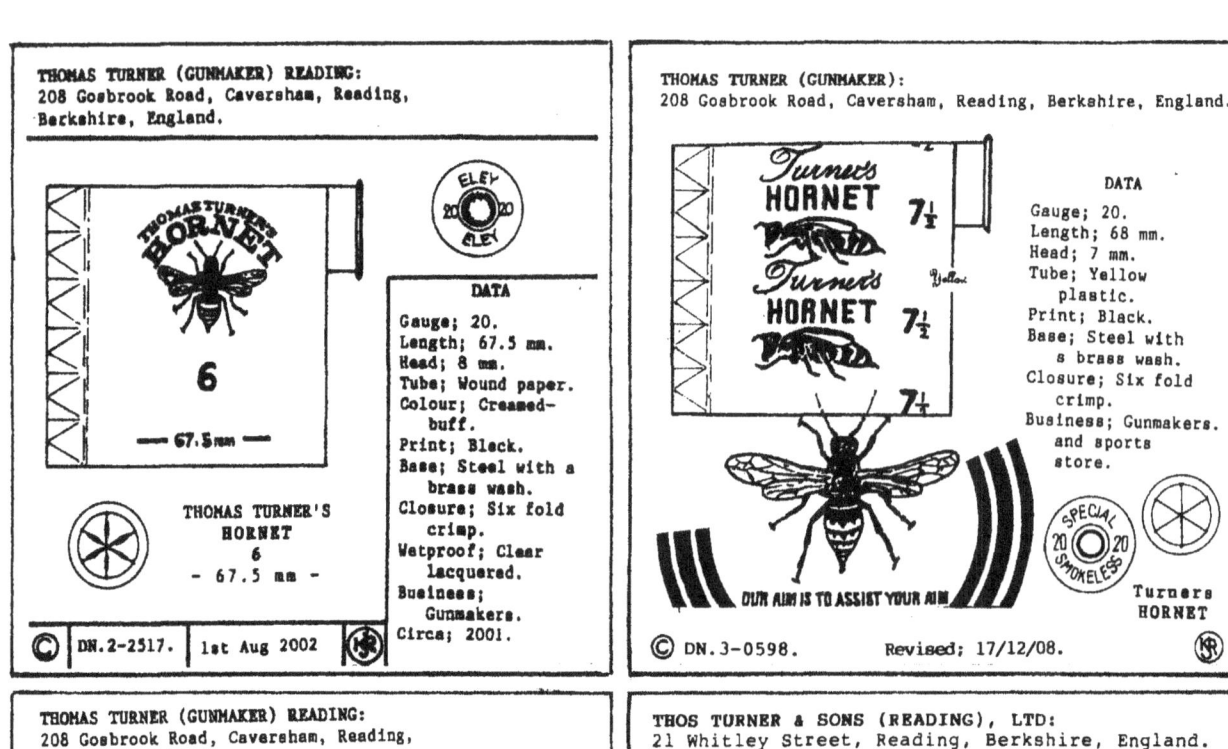

DATA
Gauge; 20.
Length; 68 mm.
Head; 7 mm.
Tube; Yellow plastic.
Print; Black.
Base; Steel with a brass wash.
Closure; Six fold crimp.
Business; Gunmakers. and sports store.

Turners HORNET

© DN.3-0598. Revised; 17/12/08.

THOMAS TURNER (GUNMAKER) READING:
208 Gosbrook Road, Caversham, Reading, Berkshire, England.

DATA
Gauge; 20.
Length; 67.5 mm.
Head; 16 mm.
Tube; Wound paper.
Colour; Creamed-buff.
Print; Black.
Base; Steel with a brass wash.
Closure; Six fold crimp.
Wetproof; Clear lacquered.
Business; Gunmakers.
Circa; 2004.

THOMAS TURNER'S HORNET
7
— 67.5 mm —

© DN.3-2572. Drawn, 6/8/07.

THOS TURNER & SONS (READING), LTD:
21 Whitley Street, Reading, Berkshire, England.

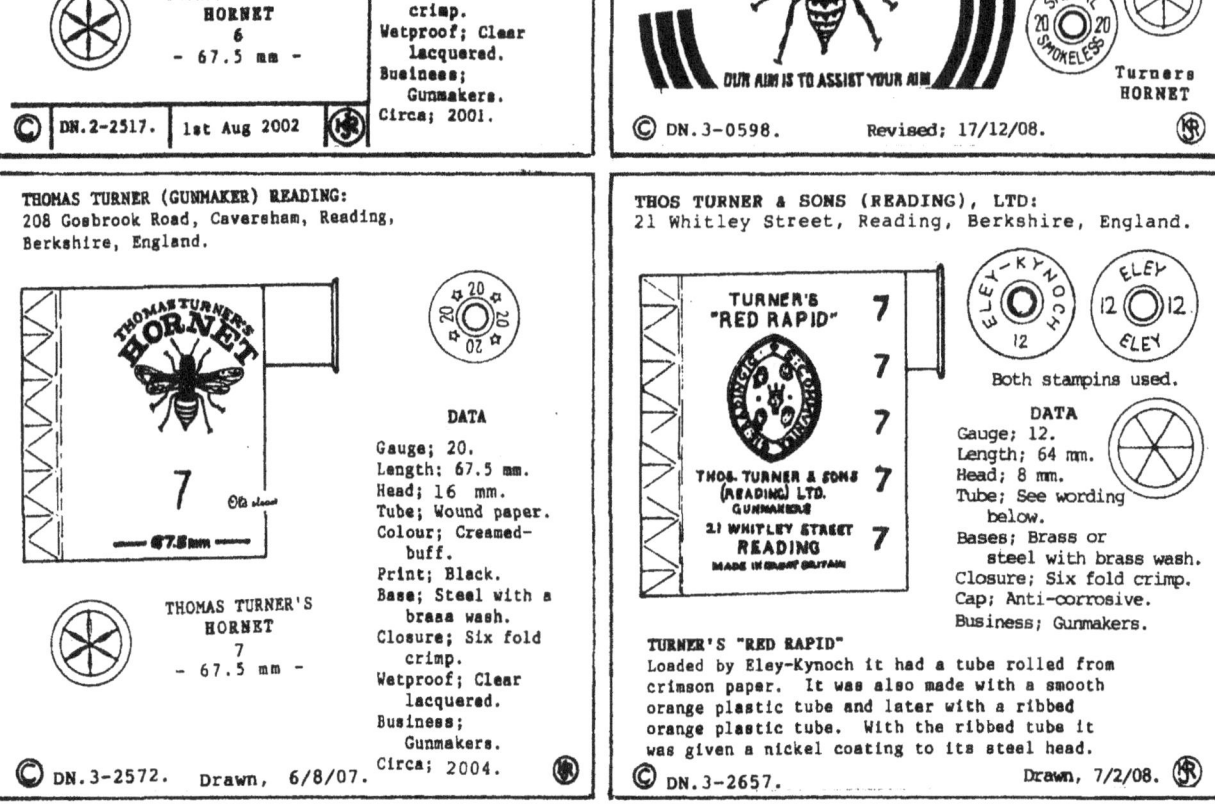

Both stampins used.

DATA
Gauge; 12.
Length; 64 mm.
Head; 8 mm.
Tube; See wording below.
Bases; Brass or steel with brass wash.
Closure; Six fold crimp.
Cap; Anti-corrosive.
Business; Gunmakers.

TURNER'S "RED RAPID"
Loaded by Eley-Kynoch it had a tube rolled from crimson paper. It was also made with a smooth orange plastic tube and later with a ribbed orange plastic tube. With the ribbed tube it was given a nickel coating to its steel head.

© DN.3-2657. Drawn, 7/2/08.

THOMAS TURNER (GUNMAKER) READING: 208 Gosbrook Road, Caversham, Reading, Berkshire, England.

DATA
Gauge; 12.
Length; 67.5 mm.
Head; 12 mm.
Tube; Wound brown paper.
Outer Colour; Light crimson.
Print; Black.
Base; Steel with a brass wash.
Cap; Nickel.
Closure; Six fold crimp.
Business; Gunmakers.
Circa; 2007-08.

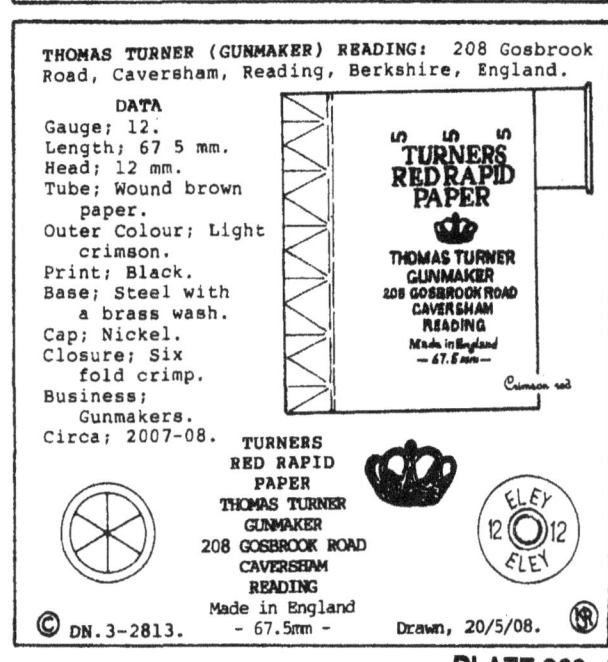

TURNERS
RED RAPID
PAPER
THOMAS TURNER
GUNMAKER
208 GOSBROOK ROAD
CAVERSHAM
READING
Made in England
— 67.5mm —

© DN.3-2813. Drawn, 20/5/08.

THOMAS TURNER (GUNMAKER) READING:
208 Gosbrook Road, Caversham, Reading, Berkshire, England.

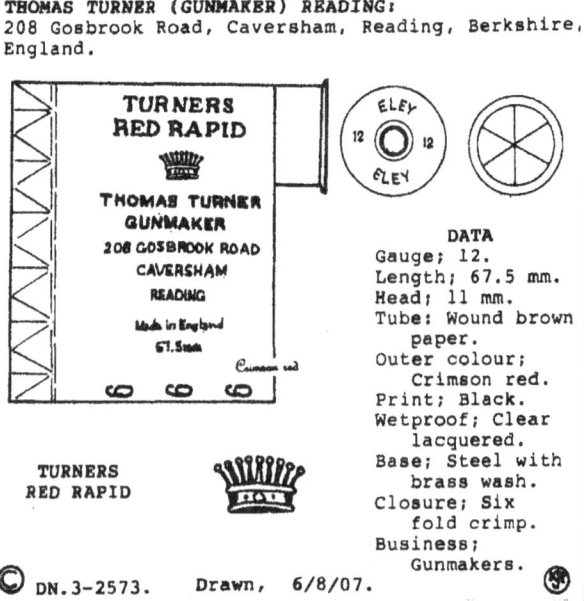

TURNERS
RED RAPID

DATA
Gauge; 12.
Length; 67.5 mm.
Head; 11 mm.
Tube; Wound brown paper.
Outer colour; Crimson red.
Print; Black.
Wetproof; Clear lacquered.
Base; Steel with brass wash.
Closure; Six fold crimp.
Business; Gunmakers.

© DN.3-2573. Drawn, 6/8/07.

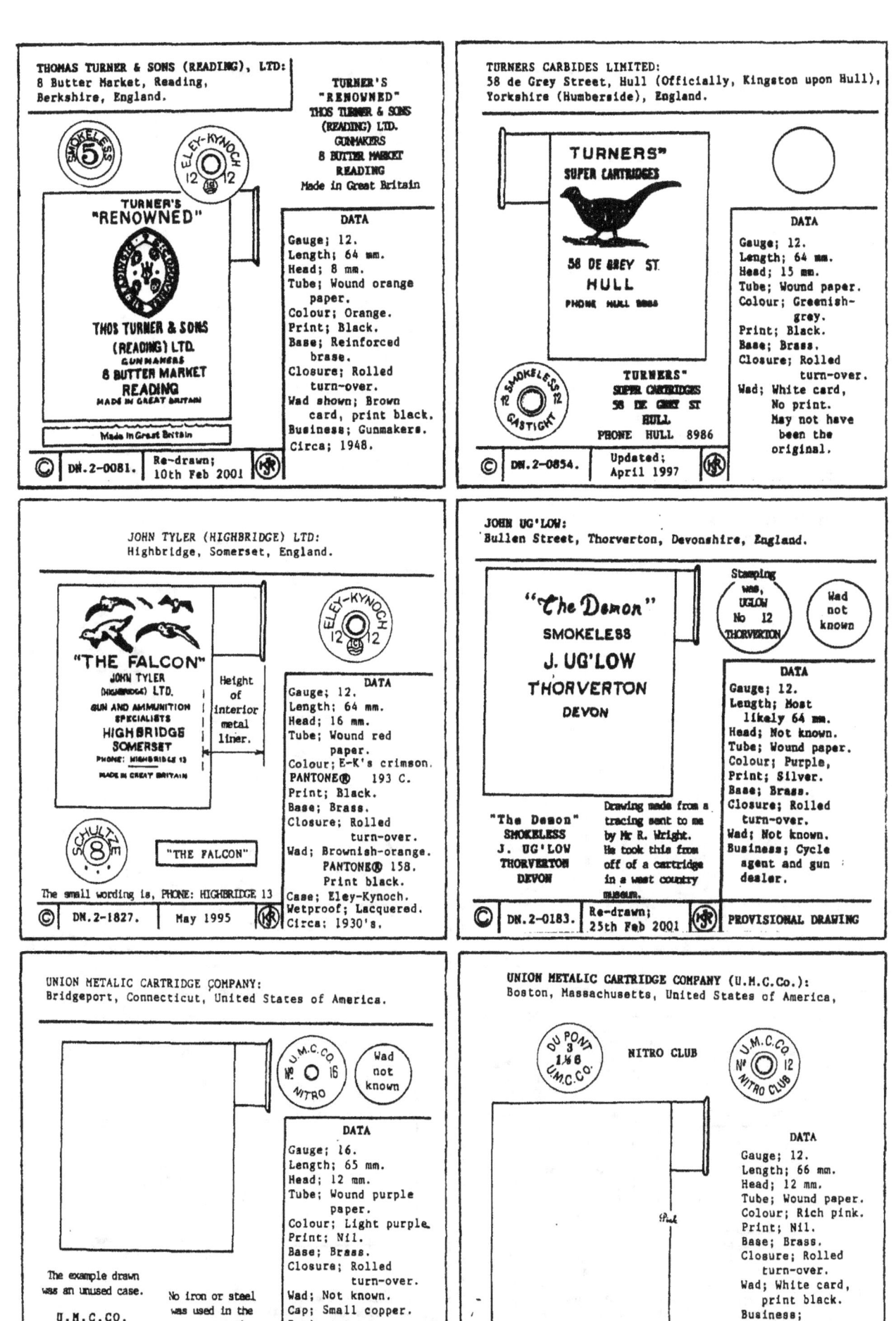

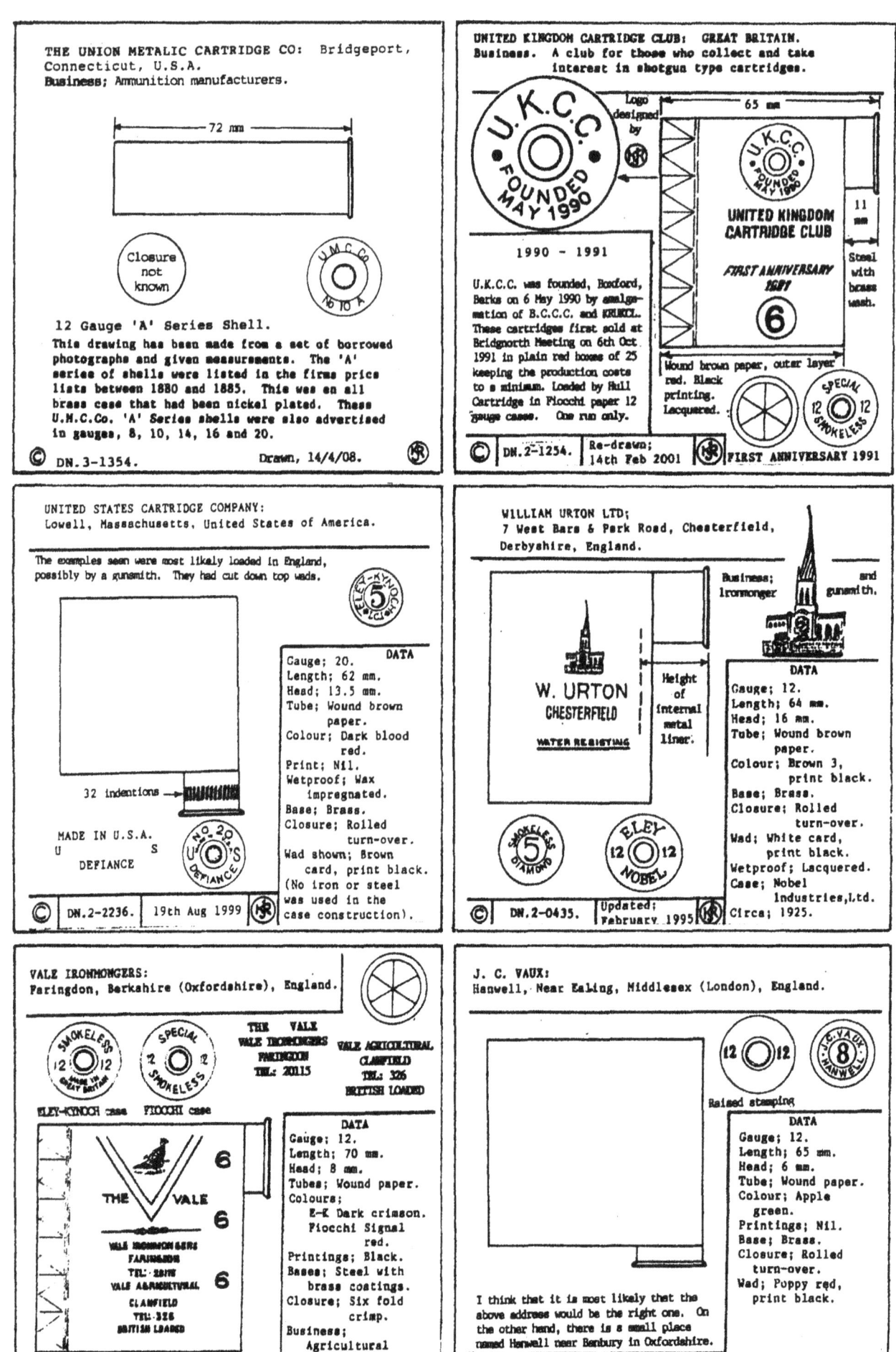

PLATE 368 [UNI – VAU]

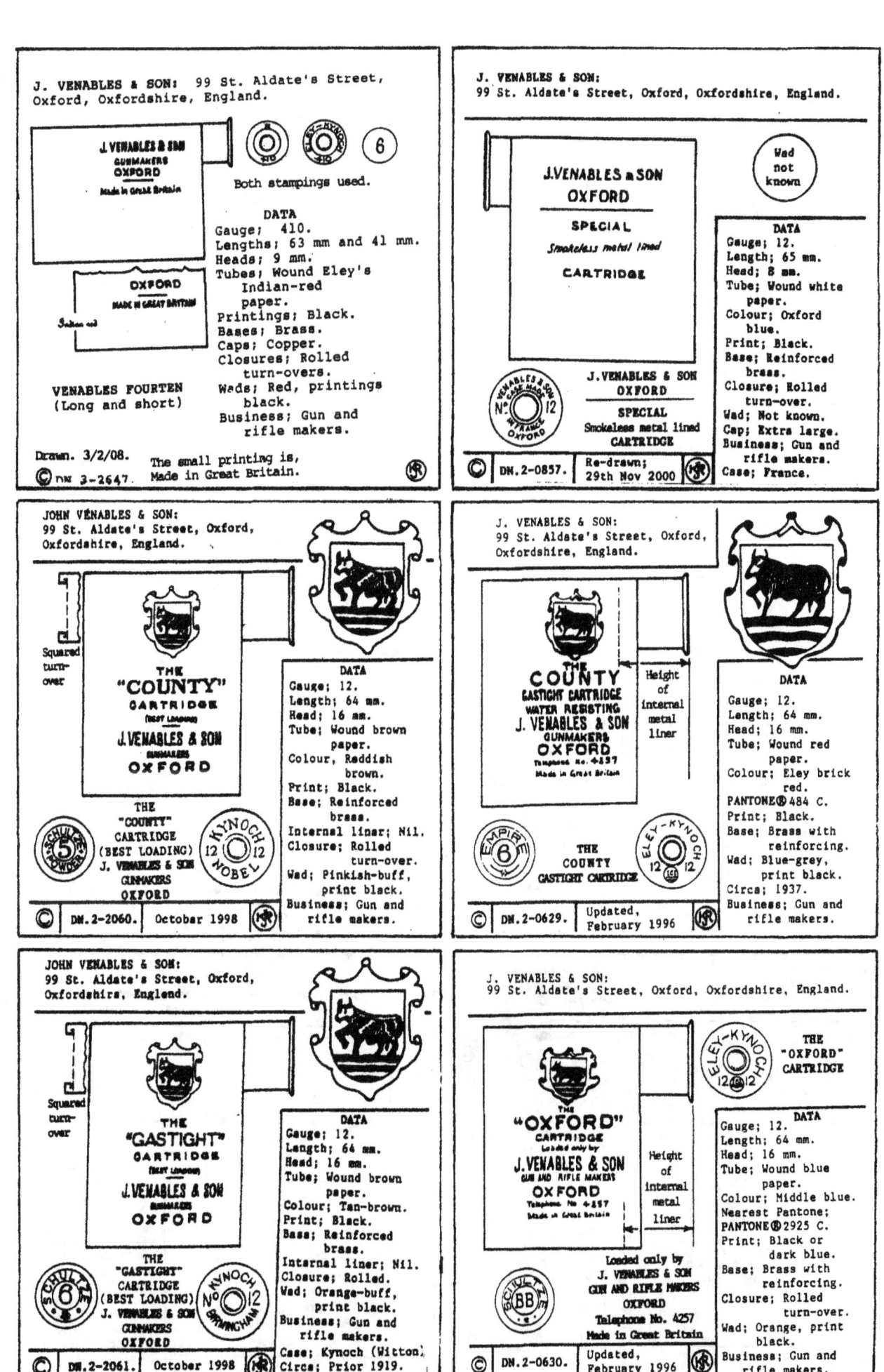

PLATE 369 [VEN - VEN]

VODAFONE LIMITED:
The Courtyard, 2-4 London Road, Newbury, Berkshire, England.

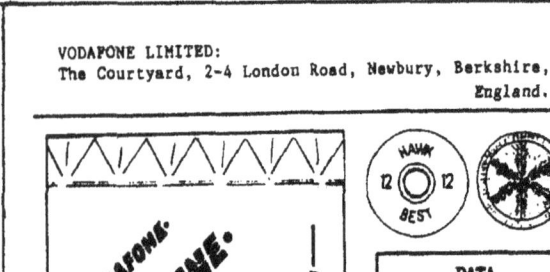

Kindly supplied by Racal Vodafone for a clay shoot at Farnborough Downs Farm, West Berkshire in September 1990. £12,000 was raised for MacMillan Cancer Care Fund. Sponsored by The Town and Country Estate Agents, John D. Wood & Co.

DATA
Gauge; 12.
Length; 67.5 mm.
Head; 8 mm.
Tube; Fine ribbed plastic.
Colour; red 2.5.
Print; Black.
Base; Steel, brass coated.
Closure; Crimp, 6 fold.
Business; Mobile phones.

© DN.2-1048. Updated; December 1994.

FREDERICK VON DREYES:
Sommerda, Prussia (Erfurt, East Germany).

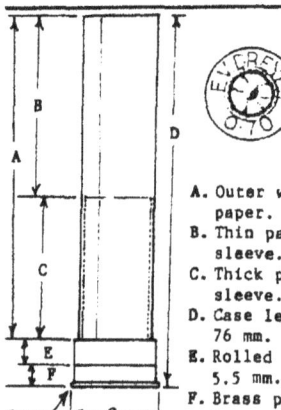

It is possible that this round held a conical bullet in a papier machie sleeve. What looks like a centre cap was a rubber disk which was pierced by the gun needle. This black rubber is drawn in the condition as seen on the example. The headstamping was not clear and a job to see.

A. Outer white paper. 66 mm.
B. Thin paper sleeve. 37 mm.
C. Thick paper sleeve. 29 mm.
D. Case length 76 mm.
E. Rolled card 5.5 mm.
F. Brass pressing 4.5 mm.
G. Approx 19 mm diam.

Brass small rim

DATA
Needle-fire.
Gauge; 0.70".
Case length; 76 mm.
Head; 10 mm.
Tube; Wound paper with thin upper region.
Colour; Snow white.
Print; Nil.
Base; Brass and brown card with rubber.
Closure; Not known.
Bussiness; Gun and cartridge maker. Also inventor.
Circa; 1845-1855.

© DN.2-2016. October 1997.

H. J. WADDON:
Wedmore; Somerset, England.

Height of internal metal liner.

This drawing has been made of an unused ready primed case.

DATA
Gauge; 12.
Length; 65 mm.
Head; 15 mm.
Tube; Wound yellow paper.
Colour; Rich straw yellow.
Print; Black.
Base; Brass.
Closure; Rolled turn-over.
Wad; Not known.
Primer; Large copper cap.

© DN.2-0203. Updated; February 1995.

R. H. WAGSTAFF & COMPANY:
Winchester Street, Basingstoke, Hampshire, England.

"A 1"
WAGSTAFF & Co
AMMUNITION DEALERS
BASINGSTOKE

Drawing made from a used case.

DATA
Gauge; 12.
Length; 64 mm.
Head; 8 mm.
Tube; Wound paper.
Colour; Orange.
Print; Black.
Base; Brass.
Closure; Rolled turn-over.
Wad; Not known.
Business; Ironmongers and ammunition dealers.
Case; Made in Germany.

© DN.2-0855. Re-drawn December 1998.

D. WALES:
16 Regent Street.
Great Yarmouth, Norfolk, England.

D. WALES GUN MAKER GT. YARMOUTH

D.WALES
GUN MAKER
GT. YARMOUTH

DATA
Gauge; 12.
Length; 64 mm.
Head; 10 mm.
Tube; Wound paper.
Colour; Orange.
Print; Black.
Base; Brass.
Closure; Rolled turn-over.
Wad; Buff card, print black.
Case; Eley Bros Ltd.
Business; Gunmaker.

© DN.2-1347. Updated; November 1997.

JAMES B. WALKER:
63 Newgate Street. Newcastle-upon-Tyne, Northumberland (Tyne & Wear), England.

THE
"NEWGATE"
JAMES B. WALKER
Gun and Fishing Tackle Dealer
63 NEWGATE STREET
NEWCASTLE-ON-TYNE
PHONE: 23607
Made in Great Britain

The small print reads as follows;
Gun and Fishing Tackle Dealer
PHONE: 23607
Made in Great Britain
THE "NEWGATE"

DATA
Gauge; 12.
Length; 64 mm.
Head; 8 mm.
Tube; Wound brown paper.
Colour; Bone brown.
Nearest Pantone No,
PANTONE® 465 C.
Print; Dark blue.
Base; Brass with reinforcing.
Wad; White card, print pink.
Wetproof; Lacquered.
Circa; 1930's.

© DN.2-1909. August 1996.

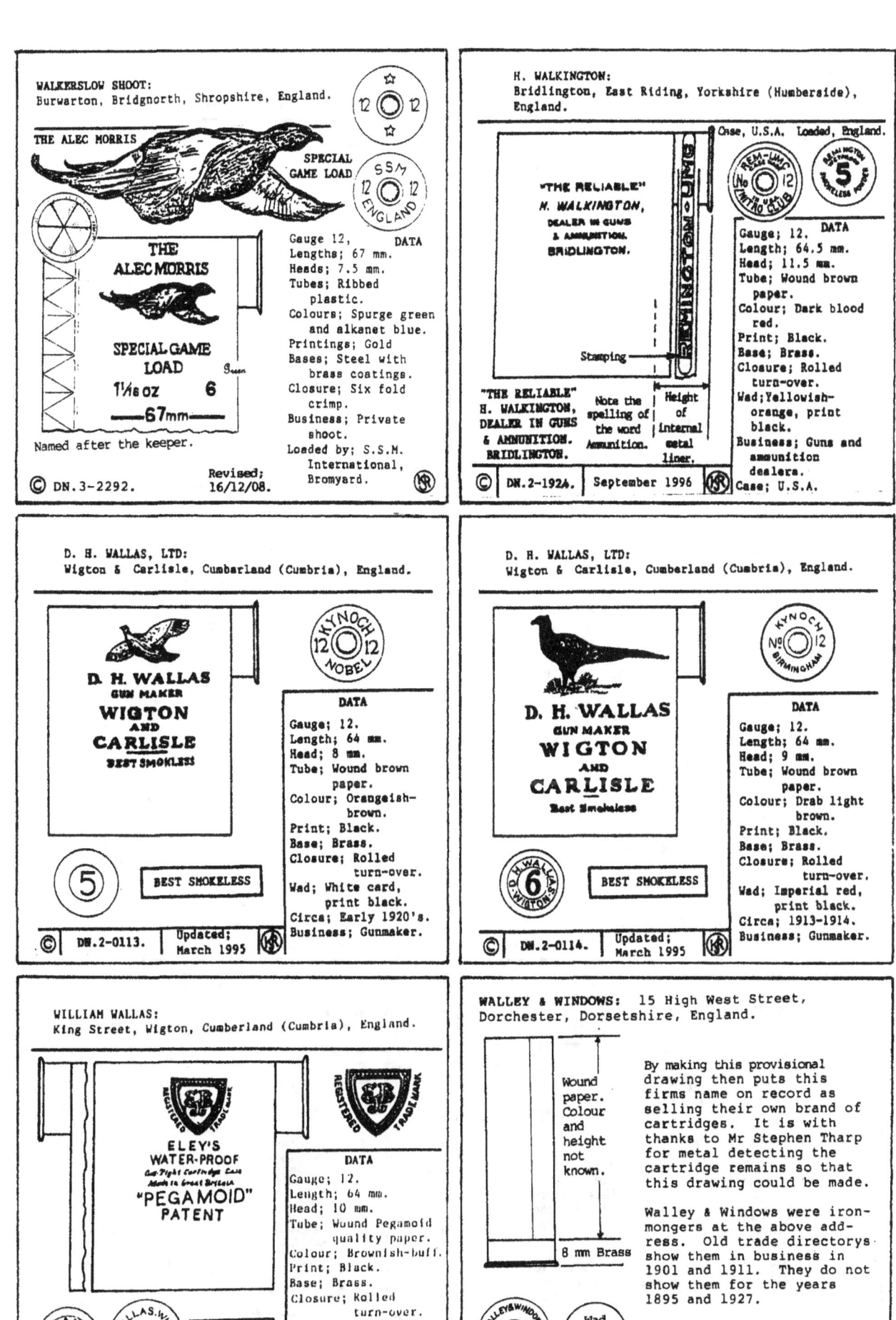

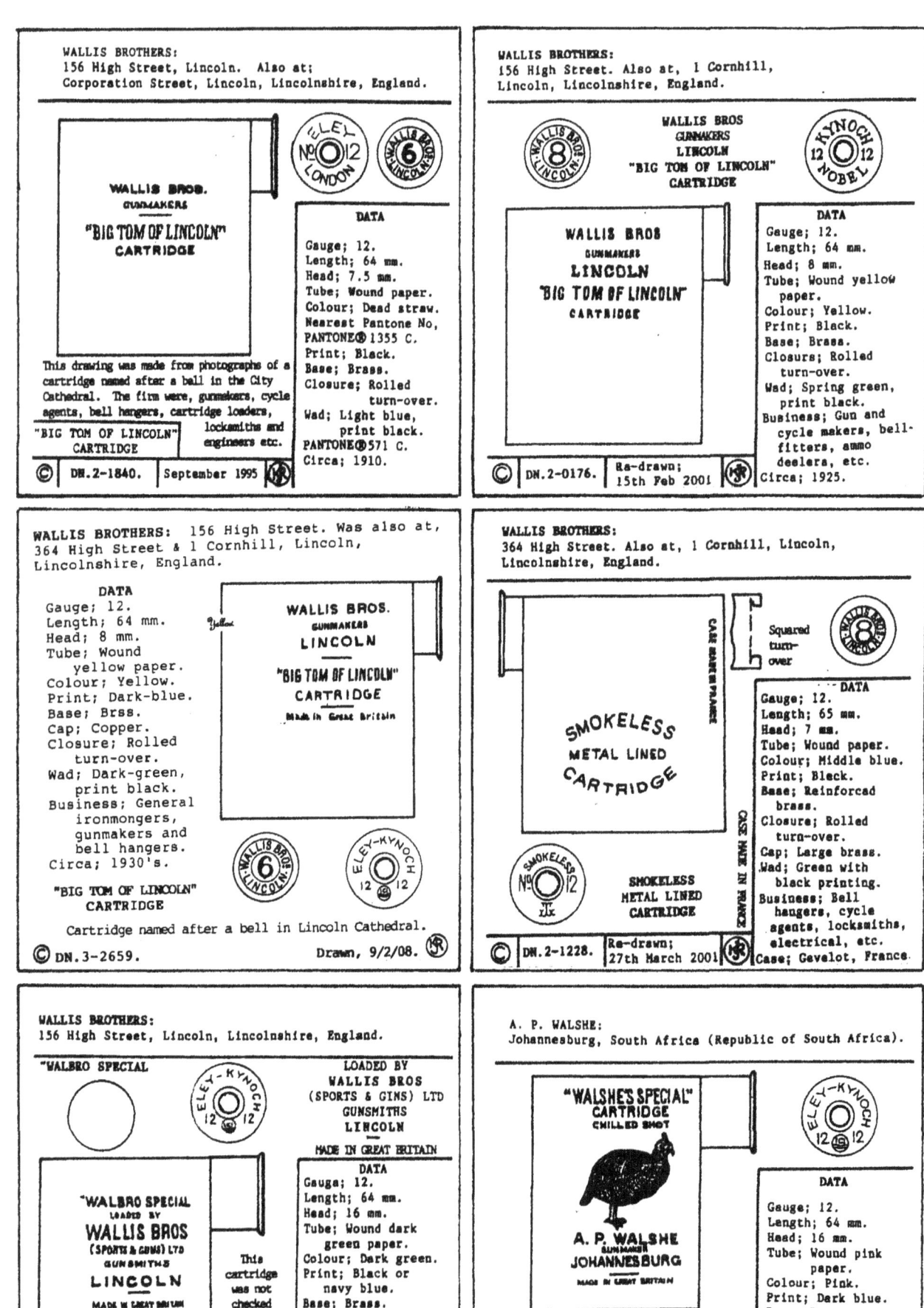

PLATE 372 [WAL – WAL]

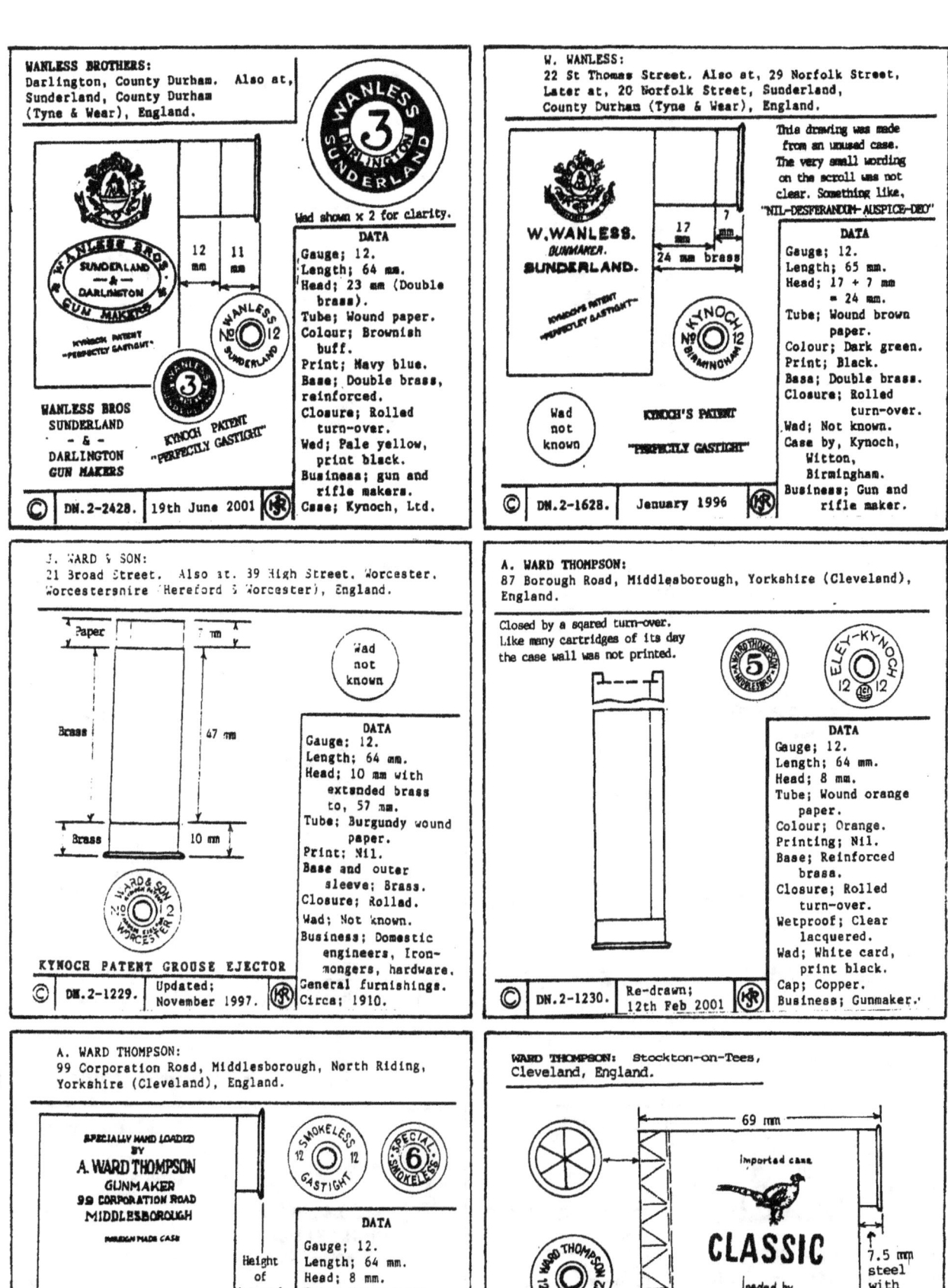

PLATE 373 [WAN – WAR]

A. WARD THOMPSON: 5-6 Albert Road, Stockton-on-Tees, Cleveland, England.

DATA
Gauge; 12.
Length; 70 mm.
Head; 8 mm.
Tube; Black thick ribbed plastic.
Print; Gold.
Base; Steel with brass wash.
Cap; Non corrosive.
Closure; Six fold crimp.
Business; Gunshop.

Imported case
C L A S S I C
loaded by
WARD THOMPSON
STOCKTON ON TEES
Tel 67060
Non-Corrosive

© DN.3-2844. Drawn, 10/9/08.

A. WARD THOMPSON: 5-6 Albert Road, Stockton-on-Tees, Cleveland, England.

 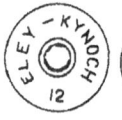 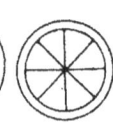

DATA
Gauge; 12.
Length; 70 mm.
Head; 8 mm.
Tube; Wound paper.
Outer colour; Orange.
Print; Black.
Base; Brass or steel with a brass wash.
Cap; Non-corrosive.
Closure; Eight fold crimp.
Business; Gun shop.

Oakleaf
precision loaded by
A.WARD THOMPSON
STOCKTON-ON-TEES
Tel. 67060
MADE IN GREAT BRITAIN

© DN.3-1066. Drawn, 28/4/08.

WARD THOMPSON BROTHERS:
87 Borough Road, Middlesborough, North Riding, Yorkshire (Cleveland), England.

WARD THOMPSON BROS.
GUNSMITHS
87 BOROUGH ROAD
MIDDLESBROUGH
Phone: 3206
MADE IN GREAT BRITAIN

WARD THOMPSON BROS.
GUNSMITHS
87 BOROUGH ROAD
MIDDLESBROUGH
Phone; 3206
MADE IN GREAT BRITAIN

DATA
Gauge; 12.
Length; 64.5 mm.
Head; 8 mm.
Tube; Wound orange paper.
Colour; Orange.
Print; Black.
Base; Brass with reinforcing.
Closure; Rolled turn-over.
Wad shown; Brown card, print black.
Wetproof; Lacquered.
Business; Gunsmiths.
Circa; 1930's.

© DN.2-1920. August 1996

EDWIN WARING:
High Street, Leamington Spa, Warwickshire, England.

SPECIALLY LOADED FOR
EDWIN WARING
Ironmonger and Gunsmith
HIGH STREET
LEAMINGTON
Telephone 555
MADE IN GREAT BRITAIN

SPECIALLY LOADED FOR
EDWIN WARING
Ironmonger and Gunsmith
HIGH STREET
LEAMINGTON
Telephone 555
MADE IN GREAT BRITAIN

DATA
Gauge; 12.
Length; 64 mm.
Head; 8 mm.
Tube; Wound orange paper.
Colour; Orange.
Print; Black.
Base; Reinforced brass.
Closure; Rolled turn-over.
Wad; Yellow. print black.
Wetproof; Clear lacquered.
Business; Gunsmith and ironmonger.

© DN.2-1329. Re-drawn; 17th Oct 2000

HENRY P. WARNER & SON:
11 Bank Street, Newton Abbot, Devonshire, England.

GENERAL SERVICE
CARTRIDGE
H.P. WARNER & SON
NEWTON ABBOT

DATA
Gauge; 12.
Length; 64 mm.
Head; 8 mm.
Tube; Wound paper.
Colour; Dark blue.
Print; Black.
Wetproof; Clear lacquered.
Base; Brass.
Cap; Large copper.
Closure; Rolled turn-over.
Wad; Imperial red, print black.
Business; Ironmongers.
Loading; Mullerite.

GENERAL SERVICE
CARTRIDGE
H.P. WARNER & SON
NEWTON ABBOT

Cartridge was not internally examined.

© DN.2-0179. Re-drawn; 15th Feb 2001

HENRY P. WARNER & SON:
11 Bank Street, Newton Abbot, Devonshire, England.

HIGH VELOCITY
SPECIAL
SMOKELESS CARTRIDGE
H.P. WARNER & SON
NEWTON ABBOT

HIGH VELOCITY
SPECIAL
SMOKELESS CARTRIDGE
H.P. WARNER & SON
NEWTON ABBOT

DATA
Gauge; 12.
Length; 64 mm.
Head; 8 mm.
Tube; Wound yellow paper.
Colour; Mustard yellow.
Print; Black.
Base; Brass.
Closure; Rolled turn-over.
Wad; Yellow card, print black.
Business; Ironmongers.
Loading; Mullerite Cartridge Works.

© DN.2-0180. Re-drawn; 18th Feb 2000.

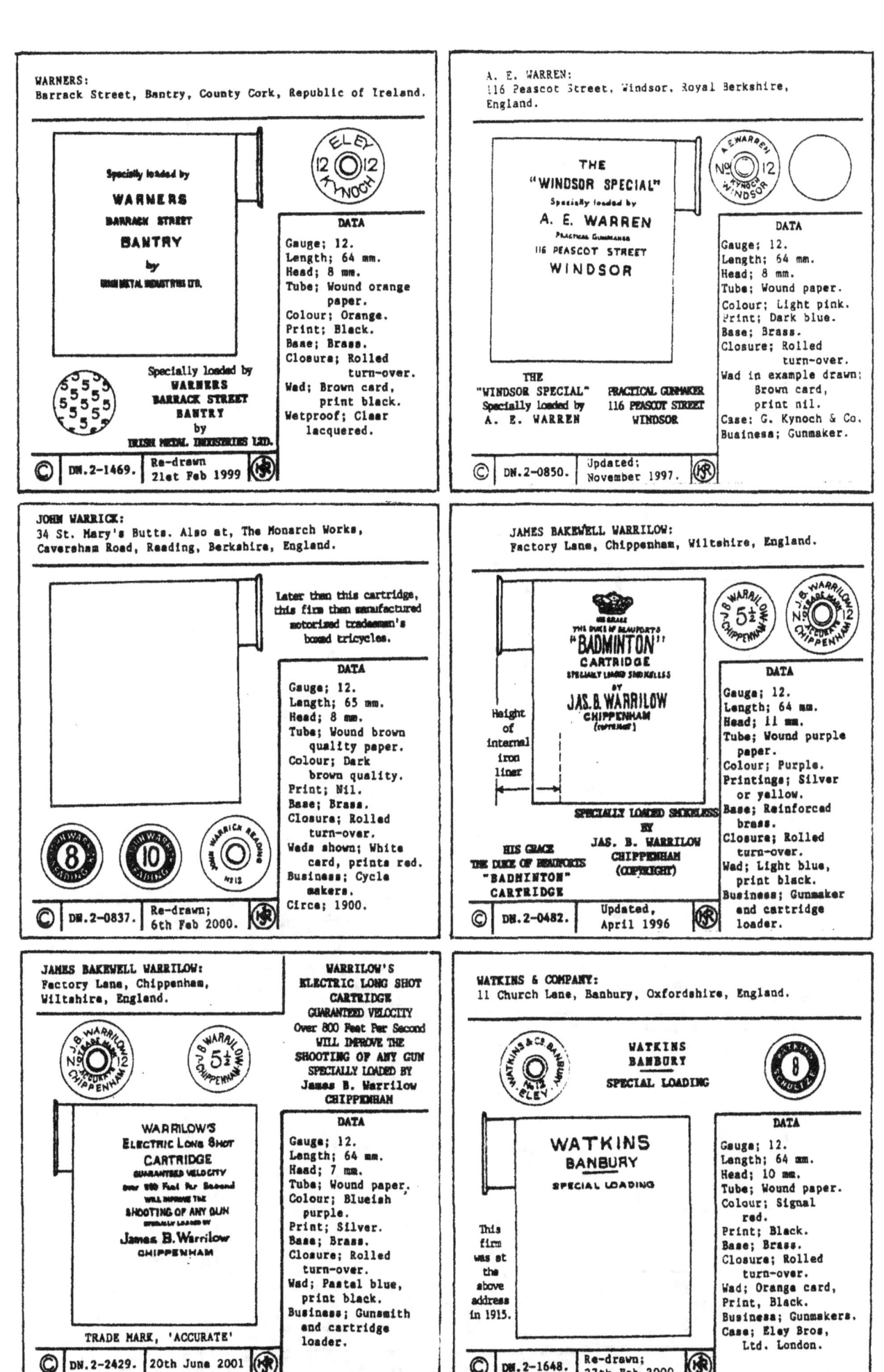
PLATE 375 [WAR – WAT]

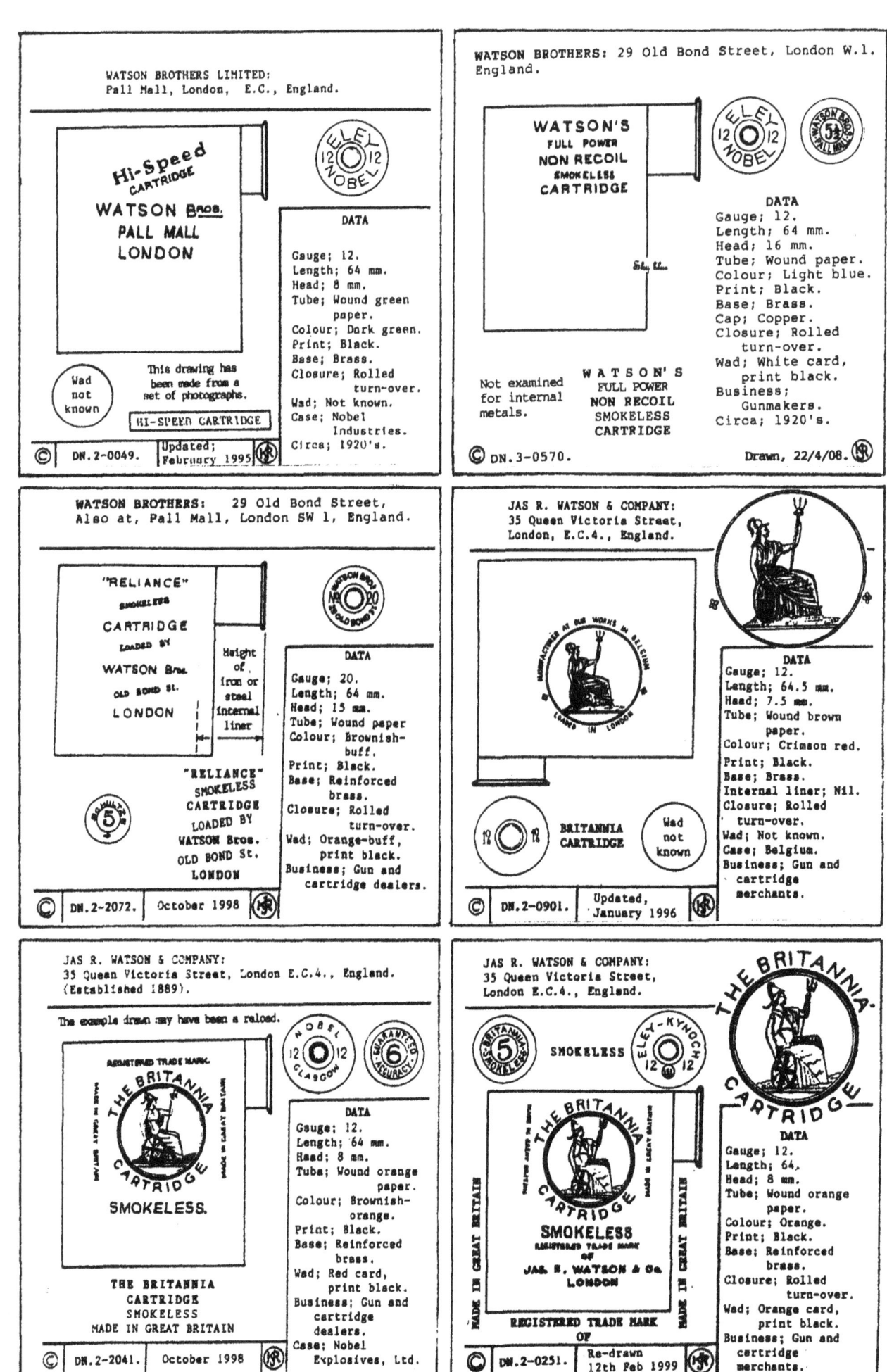

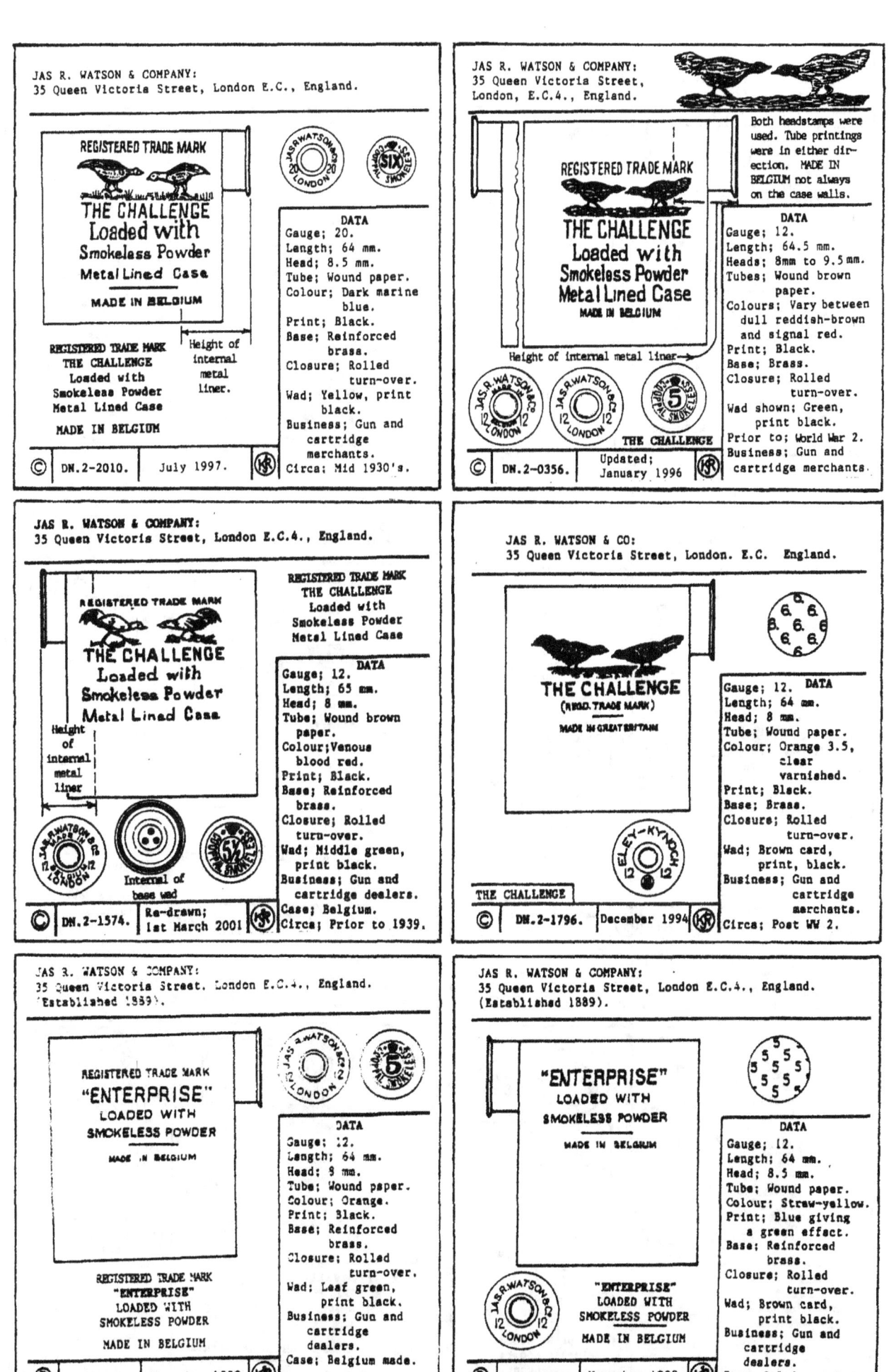

JAS R. WATSON & COMPANY:
35 Queen Victoria Street, London E.C.4, England.
(Established 1889).

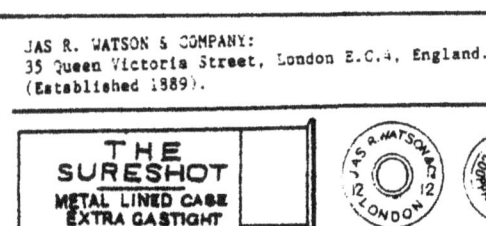

THE
SURESHOT
METAL LINED CASE
EXTRA GASTIGHT
LOADED WITH
COOPPAL
EXCELSIOR
(Leaflet Type)
SMOKELESS
AND
WATERPROOF
SPORTING POWDER
MADE IN BELGIUM

Height of internal iron or steel liner

THE SURESHOT
METAL LINED CASE
EXTRA GASTIGHT

COOPPAL EXCELSIOR
(Leaflet Type)
SMOKELESS AND
WATERPROOF
SPORTING POWDER

DATA
Gauge; 12.
Length; 64 mm.
Head; 16 mm.
Tube; Wound paper.
Colour; Crimson red.
Print; Black.
Base; Reinforced brass.
Closure; Rolled turn-over.
Wad; Deep green, print black.
Business; Gun and cartridge dealers.
Case; Possibly, F.N. Belgium.

© DN.2-2055. October 1998

JAS R. WATSON & COMPANY:
35 Queen Victoria Street, London E.C.4., England.
(Established 1889).

"THE WARRIOR"
BRITISH LOADED
SMOKELESS CARTRIDGE
REINFORCED CASE
COOPPAL SMOKELESS POWDER
BELGIAN MADE CASE

"THE WARRIOR"
BRITISH LOADED
SMOKELESS CARTRIDGE
REINFORCED CASE
COOPPAL SMOKELESS POWDER
BELGIUM MADE CASE

DATA
Gauge; 12.
Length; 64 mm.
Head; 7 mm.
Tube; Wound paper.
Colour; Rose-maroon.
Print; Black.
Base; Reinforced brass.
Closure; Rolled turn-over.
Wad; Buttercup yellow, print black.
Business; Gun and cartridge dealers.
Case; Possibly, F.N. Belgium.

© DN.2-2064. October 1998

JAS R. WATSON & COMPANY:
35 Queen Victoria Street, London E.C.4., England.
(Established 1889).

THE WETTEREN
COOPPAL EXCELSIOR
(LEAFLET TYPE)
SMOKELESS
AND
WATERPROOF

THE WETTEREN
COOPPAL EXCELSIOR
(LEAFLET TYPE)
SMOKELESS
AND
WATERPROOF

This drawing was made from a set. This drawing was made from a set of photographs.

DATA
Gauge; 12.
Length; 64 mm.
Head; 15 mm.
Tube; Wound brown paper.
Colour; Milk chocolate brown.
Print; Gold.
Base; Brass.
Closure; Rolled turn-over.
Wad; Yellow card, print black.
Business; Gun and cartridge dealers.
Case; Belgium.

© DN.2-2314. 15th July 2000

WATSON BRACEWELL:
Peebles, Peebles-shire (Borders), Scotland.

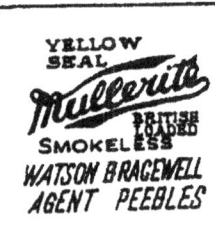

YELLOW
SEAL
Mullerite
SMOKELESS
BRITISH LOADED
WATSON BRACEWELL
AGENT PEEBLES

Shot size had been cossed out

YELLOW   SMOKELESS
SEAL   WATSON BRACEWELL
Mullerite   AGENT PEEBLES
BRITISH
LOADED

DATA
Gauge; 12.
Length; 65 mm.
Head; 8 mm.
Tube; Wound yellow paper.
Colour; Mustard yellow.
Print; Black.
Base; Brass.
Closure; Rolled turn-over.
Wad; Light yellow, print black.
Loaded by; Mullerita Cartridge Works, Birmingham.

© DN.2-1455. Re-drawn 4th Jan 1999

J. WEBBER & SONS:
Exeter. Also at, Torquay, Devonshire, England.

WEBBER'S
"ISCA"
Specially Loaded with
Highest Grade Powder
FOR
J. WEBBER & SONS
EXETER & TORQUAY
Made in Great Britain

Height of internal metal liner.

WEBBER'S   FOR
"ISCA"   J.WEBBER & SONS
Specially Loaded with   EXETER & TORQUAY
High Grade Powder
Made in Great Britain

DATA
Gauge; 12.
Length; 64 mm.
Head; 16 mm.
Tube; Wound green paper.
Colour; Dark green.
Print; Black or dark blue.
Base; Brass with reinforcing.
Closure; Rolled turn-over.
Wad; Yellow card, print black.
Business; Sports depot.
Circa; 1930's.

© DN.2-0728. Updated; April 1997

WEBBERS:
New Street, Honiton, Devonshire, England.

Both stampings have been seen.

"THE OTTERVALE"
SPECIAL SMOKELESS

BRITISH LOADED
WEBBERS
NEW ST, HONITON
PHONE: 73
FOREIGN MADE CASE

"THE OTTERVALE"   WEBBERS
SPECIAL SMOKELESS   NEW ST, HONITON
BRITISH LOADED   PHONE: 73
                       FOREIGN MADE CASE

Drawn from a set of coloured photographs.

DATA
Gauge; 12.
Length; 65 mm.
Head; 7 mm.
Tube; Wound white paper.
Colour; Red plum.
Print; Silver.
Base; Brass.
Closure; Rolled turn-over.
Wad; Yellow card, print black.
Case; Foreign, possibly German.

© DN.2-2246. 3rd Jan 2000.

WEBBER & SAUNDERS: Tiverton, Devonshire, England.

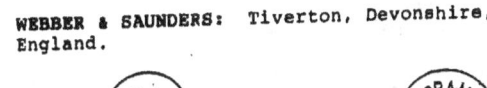

Wad not known

SURE SHOT
Webber & Saunders
TIVERTON

Pale green

SURE SHOT

ELEY GRAND PRIX 12

DATA
Gauge; 12.
Length; 64 mm.
Head; 8 mm.
Tube; Wound pale green paper.
Print; Black.
Base; Brass.
Cap; Copper.
Closure; Rolled turn-over.
Wad; Not known.
Business; Ironmongers.

© DN.3-2645. Drawn, 3/2/08.

G. R. WEBSTER:
30A Wide Bargate, Boston, Lincolnshire, England.

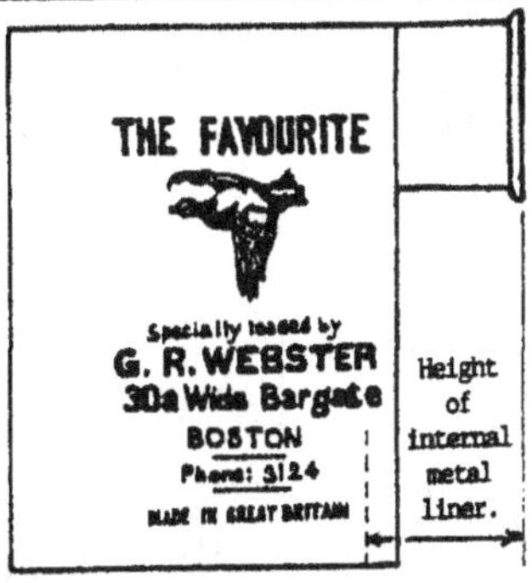

THE FAVOURITE
Specially loaded by
G. R. WEBSTER
30a Wide Bargate
BOSTON
Phone: 3124
MADE IN GREAT BRITAIN

Height of internal metal liner.

THE FAVOURITE
Specially loaded by
G. R. WEBSTER

30a Wide Bargate
BOSTON
Phone: 3124

MADE IN GREAT BRITAIN

DATA
Gauge; 12.
Length; 64 mm.
Head; 16 mm.
Tube; Wound green paper.
Colour; Spring green.
Print; Black.
Base; Brass with reinforcing.
Closure; Rolled turn-over.
Wad; Yellow card, print black.
Case; Eley-Kynoch.
Circa; 1930's.

© DN.2-0729. Updated; April 1997

G. R. WEBSTER:
30A Wide Bargate, Boston, Lincolnshire, England.

THE FIELD
Specially loaded by
G. R. WEBSTER
30a Wide Bargate
BOSTON
Phone: 3124
MADE IN GREAT BRITAIN

THE FIELD
Specially loaded by
G. R. WEBSTER

30a Wide Bargate
BOSTON
Phone; 3124

MADE IN GREAT BRITAIN

DATA
Gauge; 12.
Length; 64 mm.
Head; 8 mm.
Tube; Wound green paper.
Colour; Greyish pale green.
Print; Black.
Base; Reinforced brass.
Closure; Rolled turn-over.
Wad; White card, print pink.
Business; Gun shop.
Circa; 1930's.

© DN.2-2310. 30th June 2000

G. R. WEBSTER:
30A Wide Bargate, Boston, Lincolnshire, England.

THE SNIPE
Specially loaded by
G. R. WEBSTER
30A Wide Bargate
BOSTON
Phone: 3124
MADE IN GREAT BRITAIN

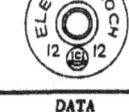

This drawing has been made from a set of six photographs.

THE SNIPE

DATA
Gauge; 12.
Length; 64 mm.
Head; 8 mm.
Tube; Wound orange paper.
Colour; Reddish orange.
PANTONE® 179 C.
Print; Black.
Base; Brass.
Wetproof; Lacquered.
Closure; Rolled turn-over.
Wad; Yellow, print black.
Circa; 1930's.

© DN.2-1823. May 1995

F. WEEKS:
101 High Street, Lymington, Hampshire, England.

FOREIGN MADE CASE
F. WEEKS
101 HIGH ST.
LYMINGTON

F. WEEKS
101 HIGH ST.
LYMINGTON

DATA
Gauge; 12.
Length; 64 mm.
Head; 7 mm.
Tube; Wound paper.
Colour; Dark red.
Print; Black.
Base; Brass.
Closure; Rolled turn-over.
Wad; White card, print red.
Business; Ironmonger.
Case; Possibly Germany.

© DN.2-1463. Re-drawn 7th Jan 1999

W. A. WELCH:
90-92 Southampton Road, Eastleigh. Also at,
2e High Street, Eastleigh, Hampshire, England.

 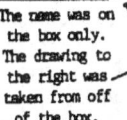

The name was on the box only. The drawing to the right was taken from off of the box.

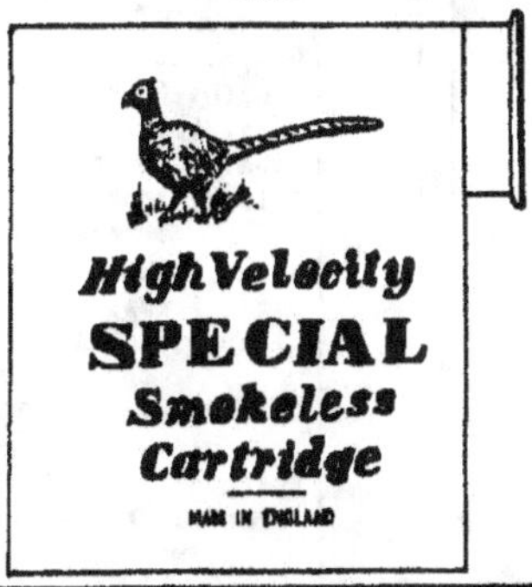

High Velocity
SPECIAL
Smokeless
Cartridge
MADE IN ENGLAND

DATA
Gauge; 12.
Length; 64 mm.
Head; 8 mm.
Tube; Wound paper.
Colour; Pink.
PANTONE® 197 U.
Print; Black.
Base; Brass.
Wad; White card, print red.
Business; Saddler and pathletic outfitter.
Loaded by;
PATSTONE & COX,
25 High Street,
Southampton.

© DN.2-0818. Updated, October 1995

PLATE 379 [WEB - WEL]

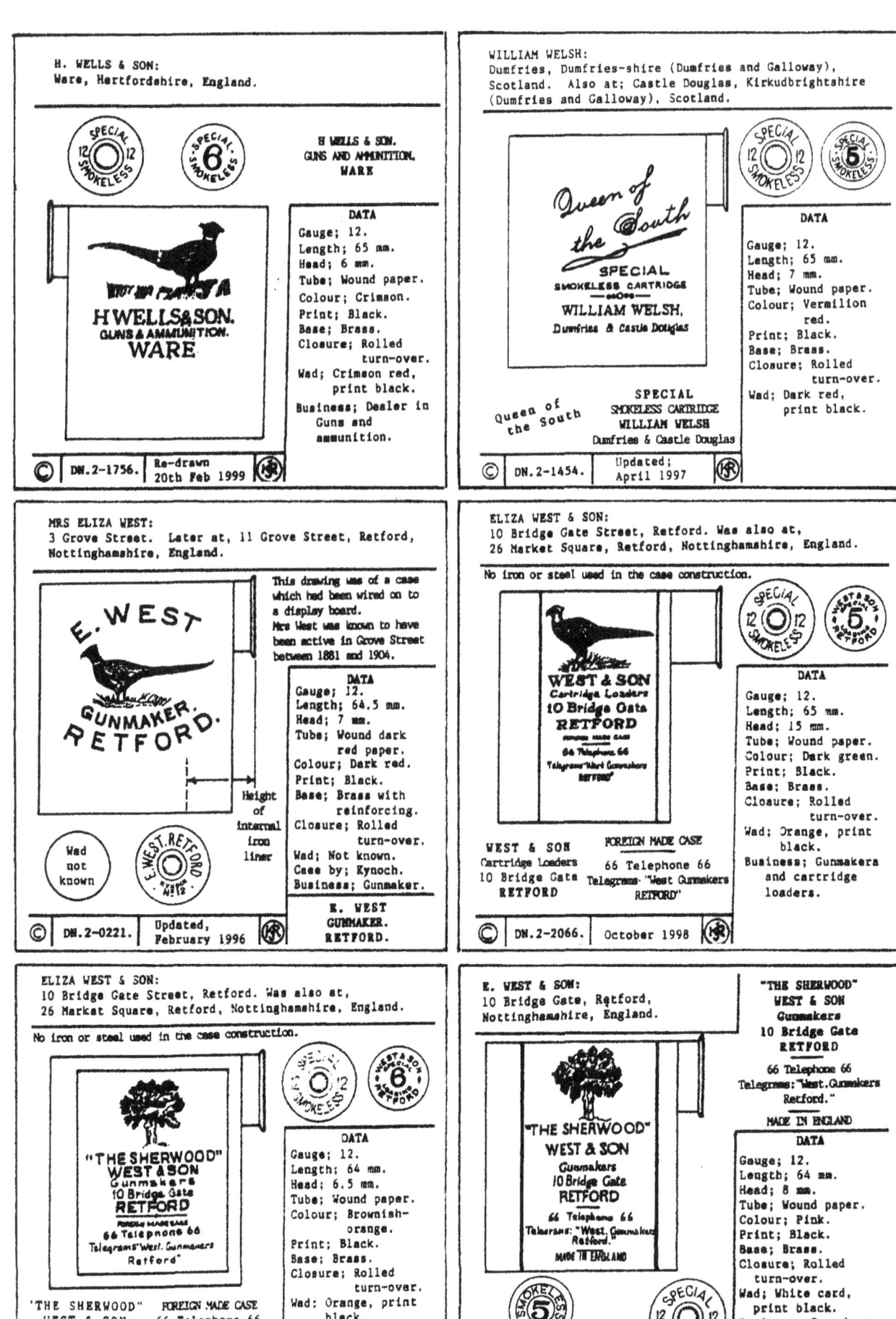

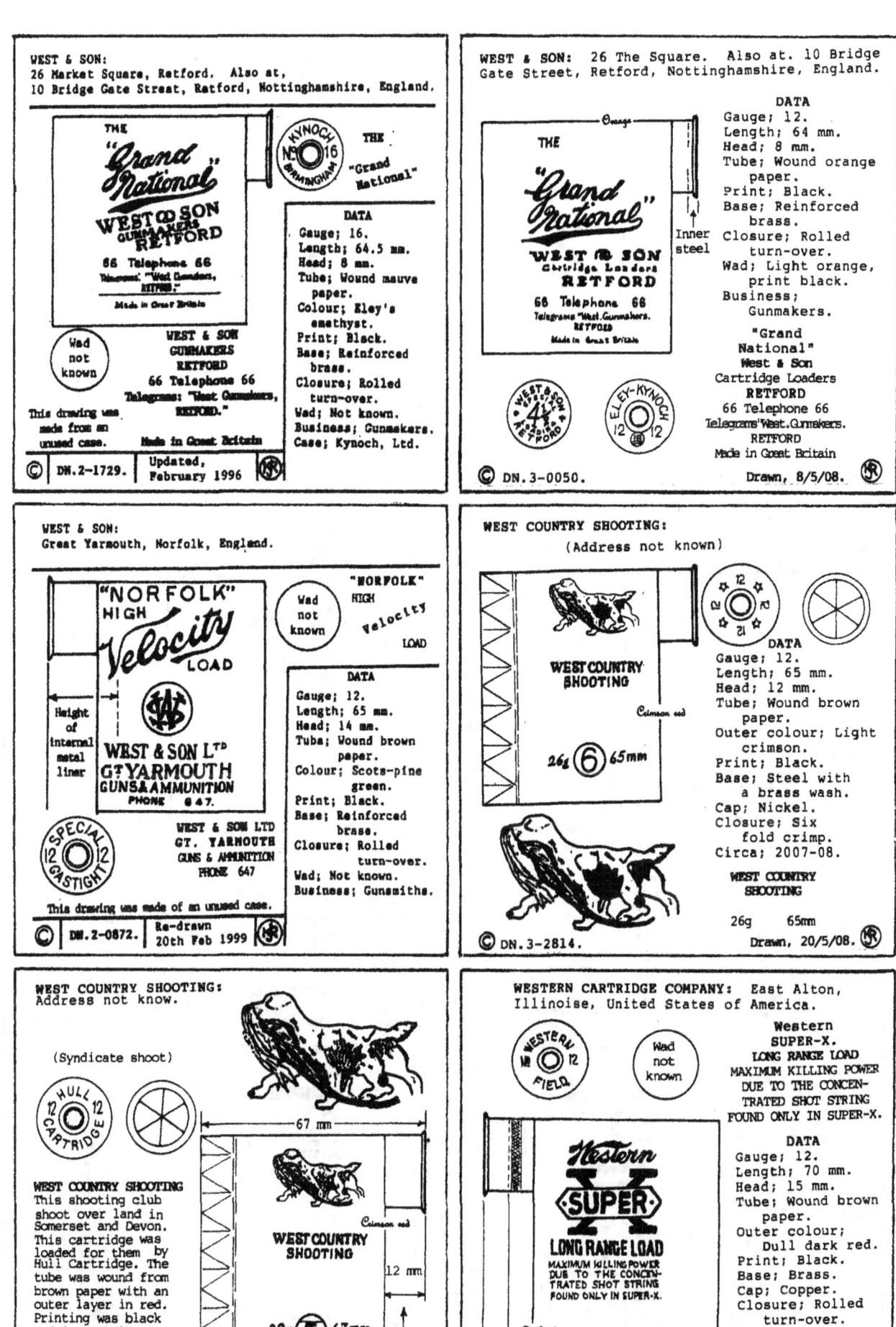

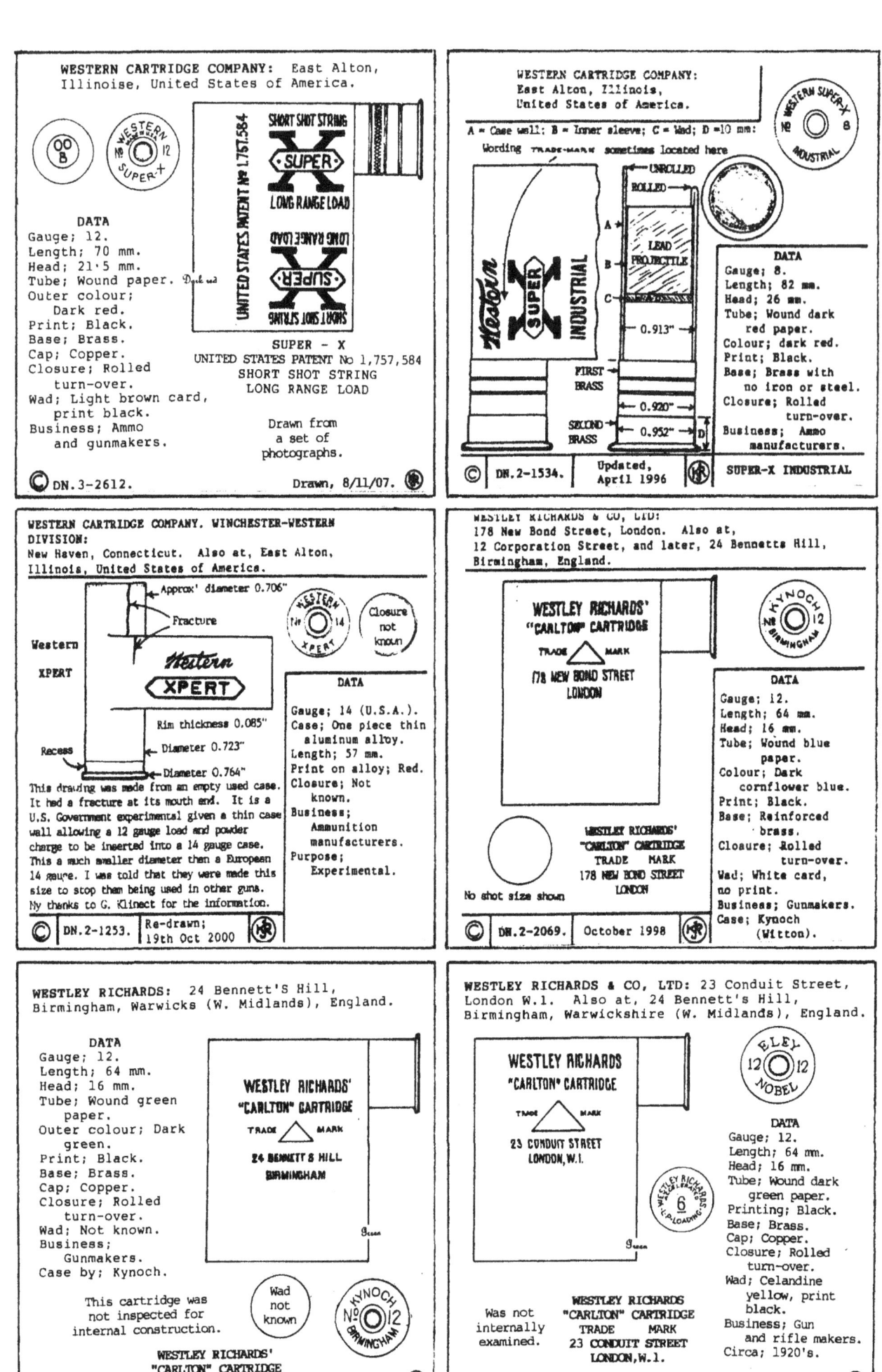

PLATE 382 [WES-WES]

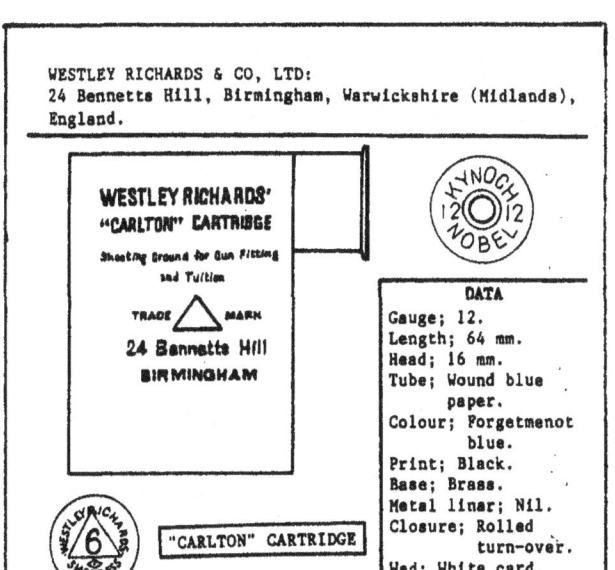
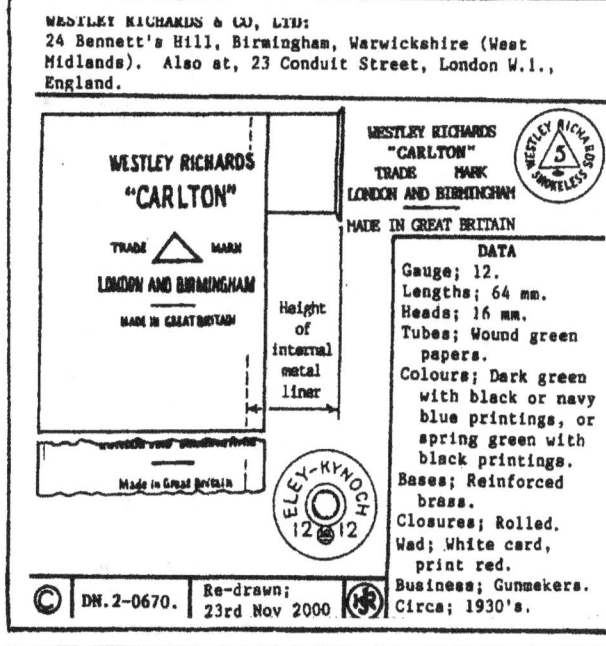
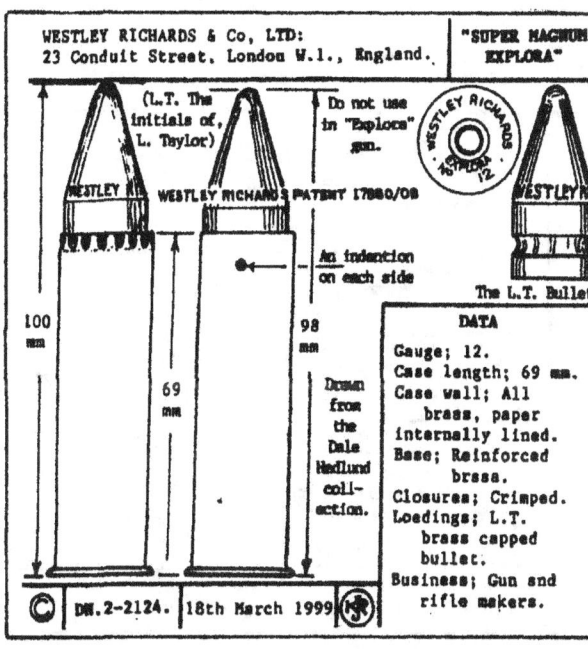
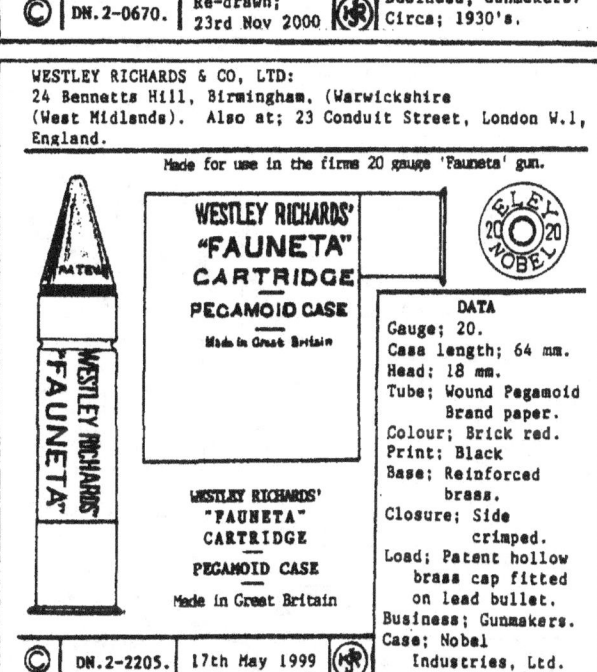
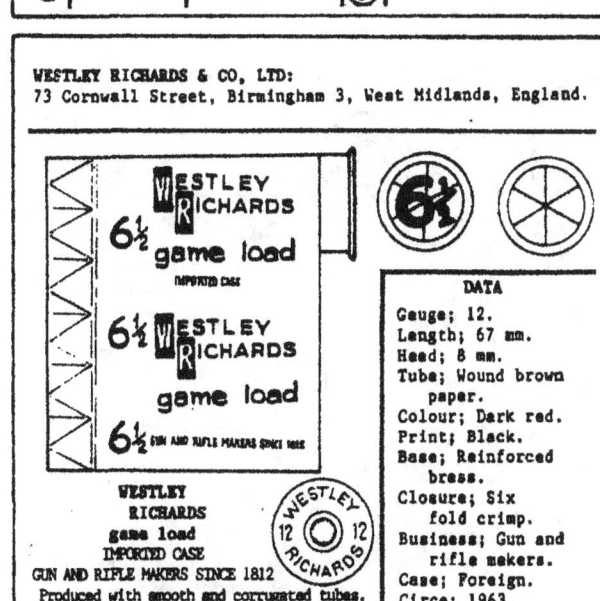
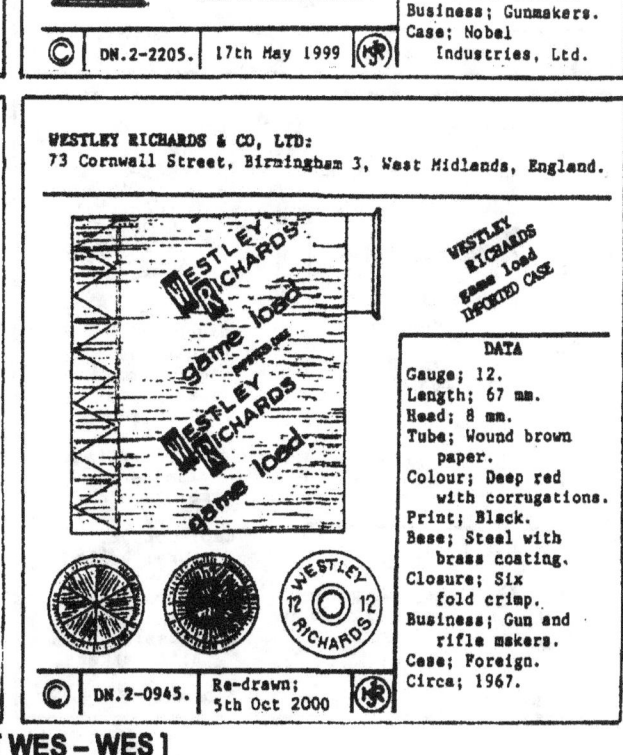

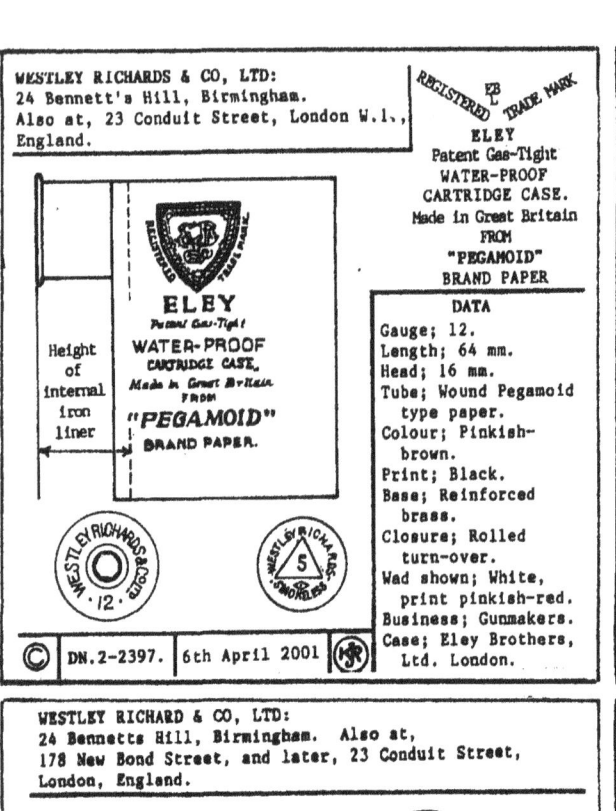
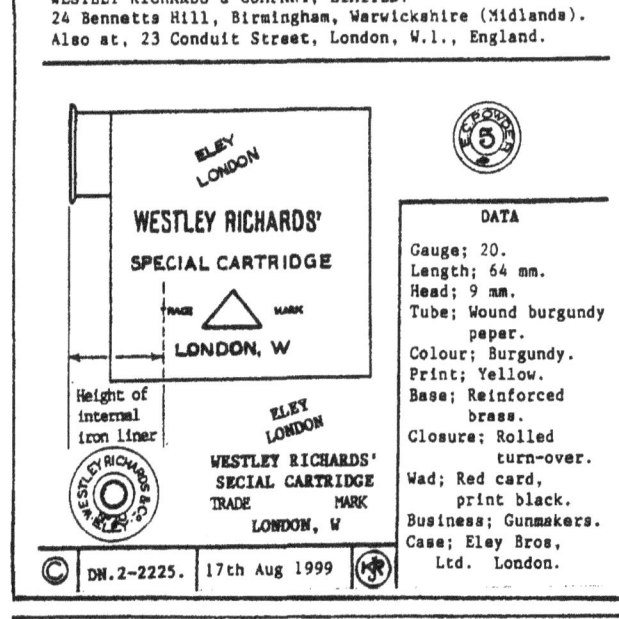
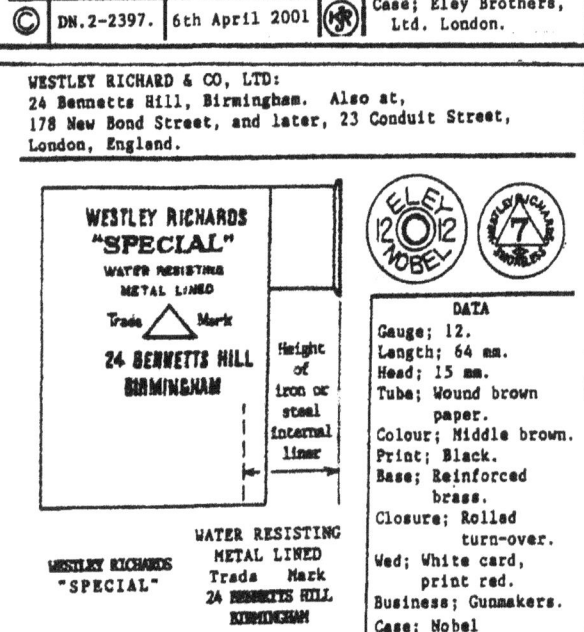
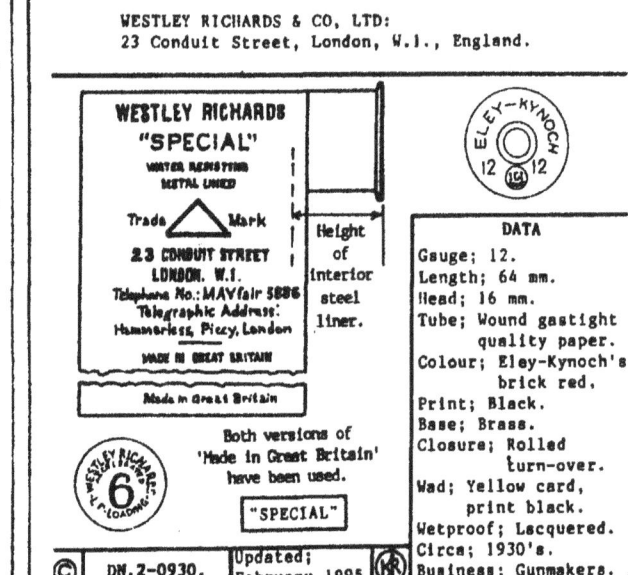
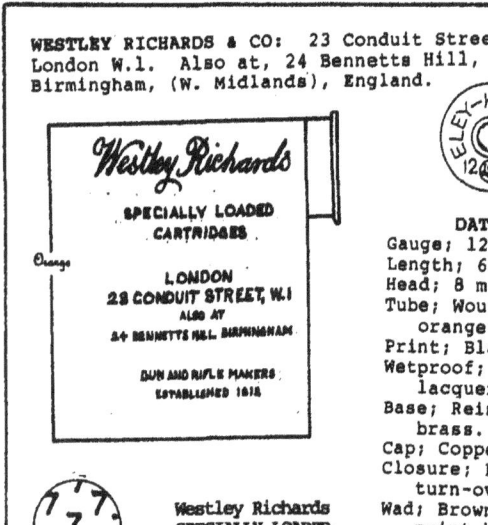
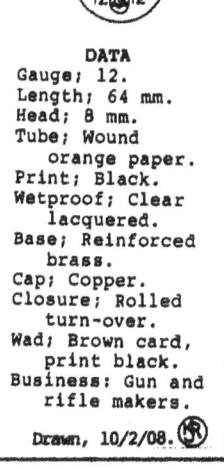
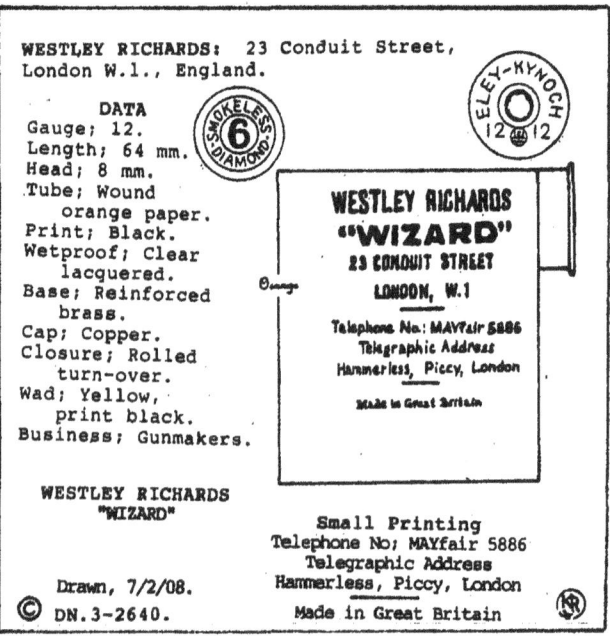

PLATE 384 [WES – WES]

WESTLEY RICHARDS & CO, LTD: 23 Conduit Street, London W.1. Also at, 24 Bennett's Hill, Birmingham, Warwickshire (W. Midlands), England.

"The WIZARD"
used at the Gun fitting and Shooting Grounds of
WESTLEY RICHARDS
LONDON   BIRMINGHAM
23 Conduit Street 24 Bennetts Hill
MADE IN GREAT BRITAIN

DATA
Gauge; 12.
Length; 64 mm.
Head; 8 mm.
Tube; Wound orange paper.
Print; Black.
Base; Reinforced brass.
Cap; Copper.
Closure; Rolled turn-over.
Wad; Yellow, print black.
Business; Gun and rifle makers.
Circa; 1930's.

© DN.3-0932.   Drawn, 24/8/08.

WESTLEY RICHARDS & CO, LTD: 24 Bennett's Hill, Warwickshire (West Midlands), England.

THE WIZARD CARTRIDGE
USED AT THE GUN FITTING & SHOOTING GROUNDS OF
WESTLEY RICHARDS
BIRMINGHAM
MADE IN GREAT BRITAIN

DATA
Gauge; 12.
Length; 64 mm.
Head; 8 mm.
Tube; Wound orange paper.
Base; Reinforced brass.
Printing; Black.
Wetproof; Clear lacquered.
Closure; Rolled turn-over.
Wad; Yellow card, print black.
Business; Gun and rifle makers.
Circa; 1930's.

© DN.3-0924.   Drawn, 24/8/08.

WEST LONDON SHOOTING SCHOOL: Perivale, Ealing, London West, England.

"EMPIRE"
West London Shooting School.
PERIVALE,
EALING, W.

"EMPIRE"
West London Shooting School.
PERIVALE,
EALING, W.

Drawing made by using a se of photographs.

DATA
Gauge; 12.
Length; 64 mm.
Head; 7 mm.
Tube; Wound paper.
Colour; Purple.
Print; Yellow.
Base; Brass.
Clousure; Rolled turn-over.
Wad; Blue-grey, print black.
Case; Nobel Explosives Co Ltd.
Business; Shooting School.

© DN.2-2024.   November 1997.

C. & A. WESTON: The Colonade, Brighton, Sessex, England.

C. & A. WESTON'S "BRIGHTON" CARTRIDGE
BRIGHTON
MADE IN GREAT BRITAIN

C. & A. WESTON'S "BRIGHTON" CARTRIDGE
BRIGHTON
MADE IN GREAT BRITAIN

DATA
Gauge; 12.
Length; 64 mm.
Head; 16 mm.
Tube; Wound crimson paper.
Colour; Crimson red.
Print; Black.
Base; Reinforced brass.
Closure; Rolled turn-over.
Wad; Yellow, print black.
Wetproof; Clear lacquered.
Business; Gunmakers.
Circa; 1930's.

© DN.2-0750.   Re-drawn; 11th Feb. 2001

CHARLES & HERBERT WESTON: 7 New Road, Brighton, Sussex, England.

DATA
Gauge; 12.
Length; 64 mm.
Head; 9 mm.
Tube; Wound rough textured paper.
Colour; Dark brown.
Nearest Pantone;
PANTONE® 464 U.
Print; Nil.
Base; Brass.
Wad; White card, print blue.
PANTONE® 288 U.
Case by; Eley Bros.
Business; Gunmakers.

This case had no iron nor steel in its construction whatsoever.

© DN.2-1868.   November 1995

CHARLES & HERBERT WESTON: 7 New Road, Brighton. Also, The High Street, Hailsham, Sussex, England.

GASTIGHT & METAL-LINED
C. & H. WESTON'S "BRIGHTON" CARTRIDGE

Closed by a squared turn-over.

GASTIGHT & METAL-LINED
C. & H WESTON'S "BRIGHTON" CARTRIDGE

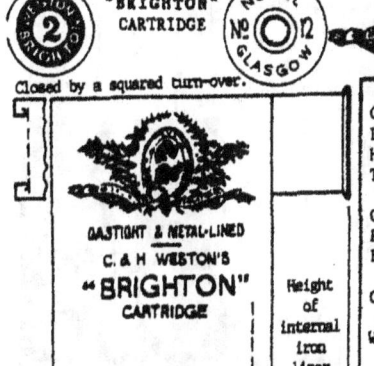

DATA
Gauge; 12.
Length; 64 mm.
Head; 16 mm.
Tube; Wound brown paper.
Colour; Middle brown.
Print; Black.
Base; Reinforced brass.
Closure; Rolled turn-over.
Wad; White card, print dark blue.
Business; Gunmakers.
Case; Nobel Explosives Co, Ltd.

© DN.2-2087.   November 1998

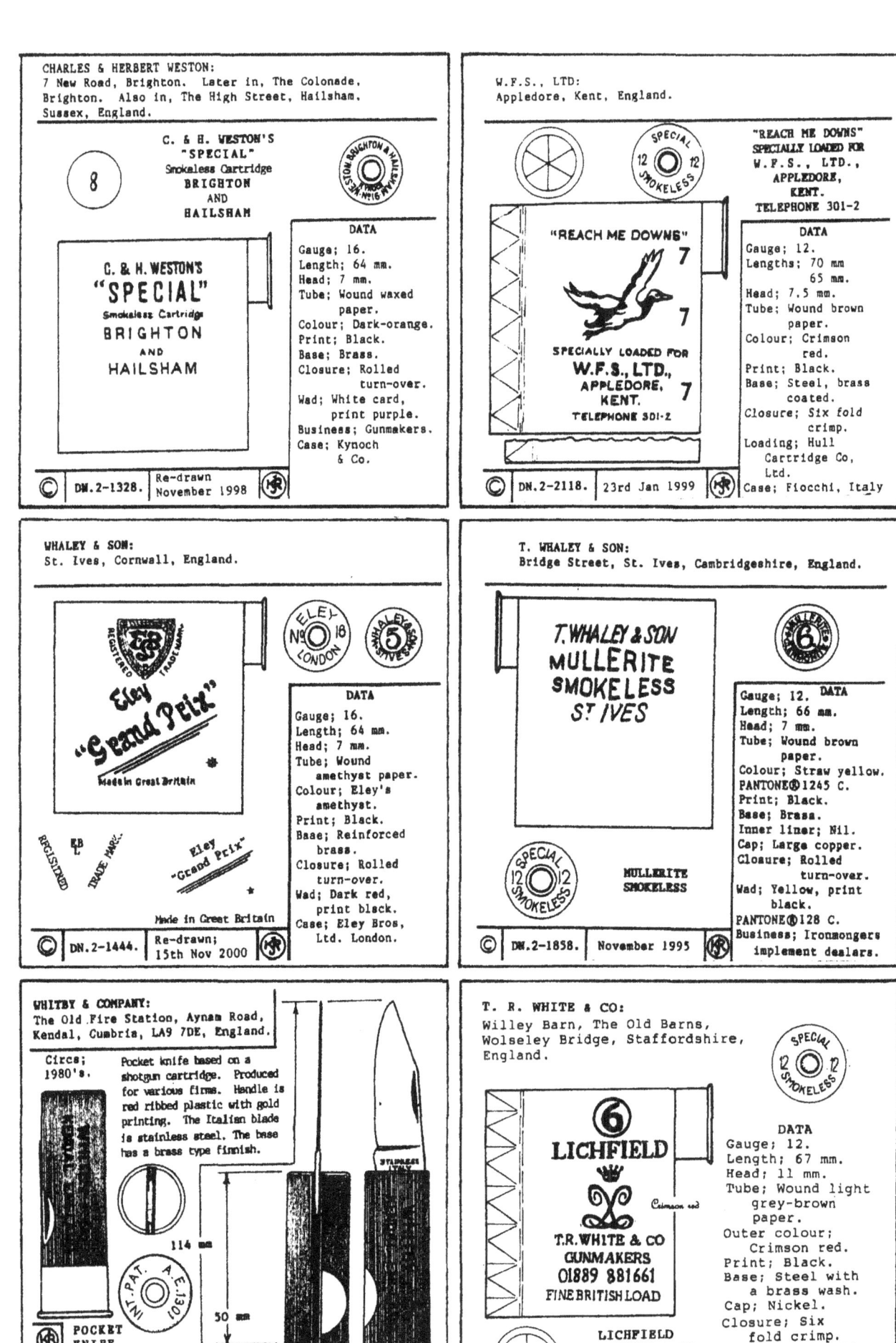

PLATE 386 [WES – WHI]

J. E. WHITEHOUSE & SON:
High Street, Oakham, Rutland (Leicestershire), England.

"The Quorn"

DATA
Gauge; 12.
Length; 64 mm.
Head; 8 mm.
Tube; Wound orange paper.
Print, Black.
Base; reinforced brass.
Closure; Rolled turn-over.
Wad; Yellow, print black.
Wetproof; Clear lacquered.
Business; Gunmakers.

This cartridge was marketed when John Edward Whitehouse had introduced his son into the family business. The firm was later to become, J. E. Whitehouse & Sons. This cartridge was named after the Leicestershire village and hall, also the local hunt.

© DN.2-1330. Re-drawn; 28th Nov 2000

JOHN EDWARD WHITEHOUSE & SONS:
High Street, Oakham, Rutland (Leicestershire).
Also in, Melton Mowbray, Leicestershire, England.

J. E. WHITEHOUSE & SONS
GOOD
LUCK
"RUTLAND"
SMOKELESS CARTRIDGE

OAKHAM
AND
MELTON MOWBRAY
BEST GASTIGHT
METAL LINED

DATA
Gauge; 12.
Length; 64 mm.
Head; 16 mm.
Tube; Wound light brown paper.
Colour; Light brown.
Print; Black.
Base; Reinforced brass.
Closure; Rolled turn-over.
Wad; White card, print black.
Business; Gunmakers.
Case; Nobel Industries, Ltd.
Circa; 1920's.

© DN.2-0672. Re-drawn; 30th Nov 2000

JOHN EDWARD WHITEHOUSE & SONS: High Street, Oakham, Rutland (Leicestershire), England.

Drawn, 2/2/08.

DATA
Gauge; 12.
Length; 64 mm.
Head; 16 mm.
Tube; Wound Eley's Gastight brick-red paper.
Print; Black.
Wetproof; Clear lacquered.
Base; Reinforced brass.
Cap; Copper.
Closure; Rolled turn-over.
Wad; White card, inked in shot size.
Business; Gunmakers.

"RUTLAND"
SMOKELESS CARTRIDGE

© DN.3-2642.

FRANK SIDNEY WHITEMAN:
20-21 Market Place, Wallingford, Berkshire (Oxfordshire), England.

Mr Whiteman was known active in Wallingford between 1928 and 1939, perhaps longer. Later the telephone number 76 was changed to 3276.

"THE FORDIAN"
SPECIAL SMOKELESS
BRITISH HAND LOADED

F. S. WHITEMAN
IRONMONGER & GUNSMITH
WALLINGFORD
PHONE 76

DATA
Gauge; 12.
Length; 64 mm.
Head; 8 mm.
Tube; Wound paper.
Colour; Maroon.
Print; Gold.
Base; Brass.
Closure; Rolle4d turn-over.
Wad; Primrose-yellow, print black.
Business; Gunsmith and ironmonger.
Case; Germany.

© DN.2-2122. Re-drawn 28th Feb 1999

WHITEMAN BROTHERS LIMITED:
18 Silver Street, Worcester. Also at, The Tything, Worcester, Worcestershire (Hereford & Worcester), England.

THE "RAPID"
CARTRIDGE

Specially loaded by
WHITEMAN BROS. LTD.
SILVER STREET
WORCESTER
Telephone 124
Entirely British Made

DATA
Gauge; 12.
Length; 64 mm.
Head; 8 mm.
Tube; Wound crimson red paper.
Colour; Crimspon red.
Print; Black.
Wetproof; Clear lacquered.
Base; Brass with reinforcing.
Closure; Rolled turn-over.
Wad; White card, print black.
Circa; 1930's.
Business; Ironmongers.

© DN.2-0481. Updated, April 1996

WILDER:
Birmingham, Warwickshire (West Midlands), England.

Purchaser;
H.M. Government of Gt Britain:
War Office, Westminster, London, England.
Circa: 1916-1918.

Cartridge Case by; Eley Bros, Ltd. 254 Gray's Inn Road, London W.C. England.

DATA
Gauge; ?.
Case length; 216 mm.
Round length; 248 mm.
Head; 14 mm.
Outer tube; Wound brown quality paper.
Colour; old brown.
Print; Purple.
Base; Brass.
Inner tube; White, print black.

© DN.2-1996. July 1997.

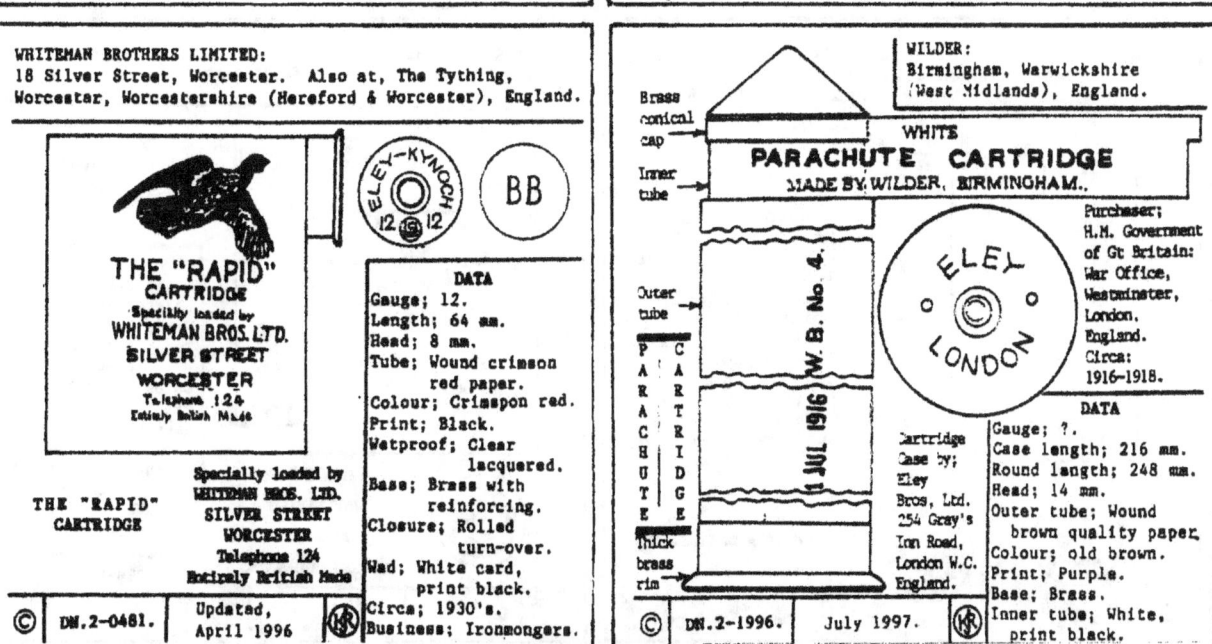

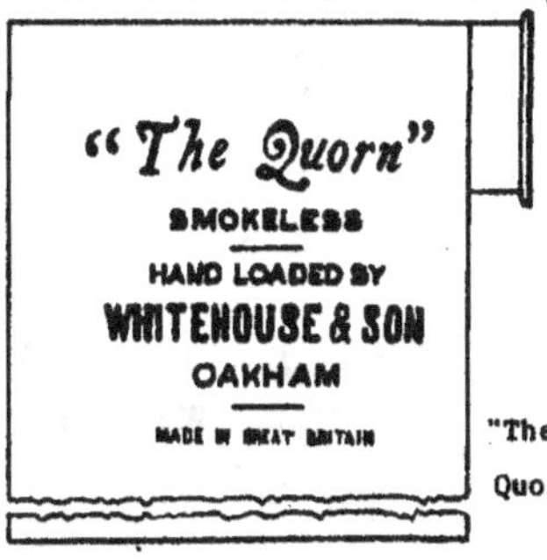

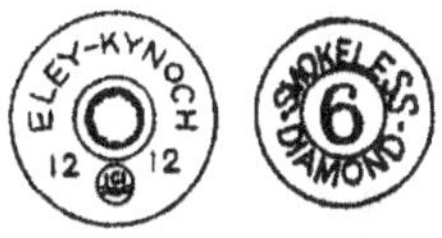

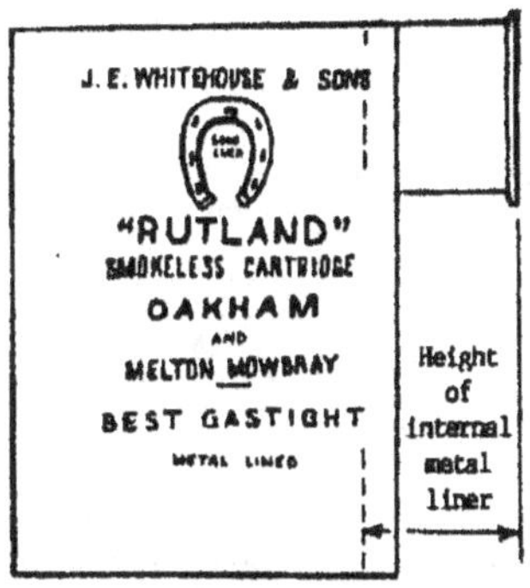

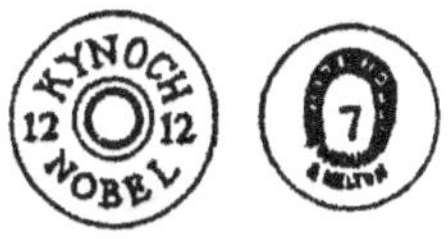

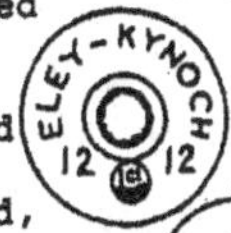

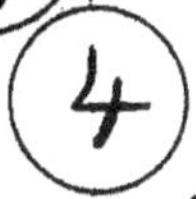

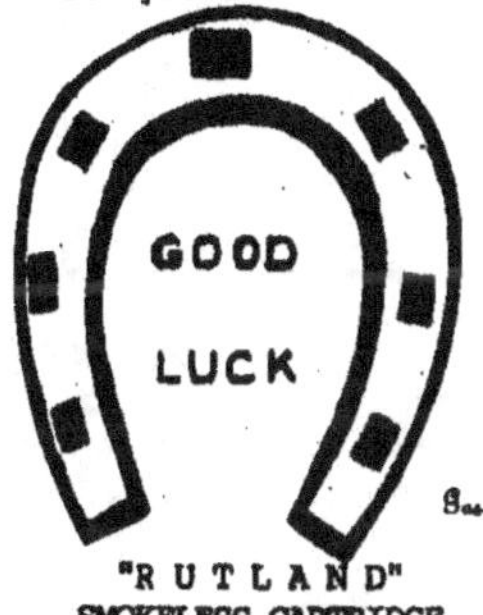

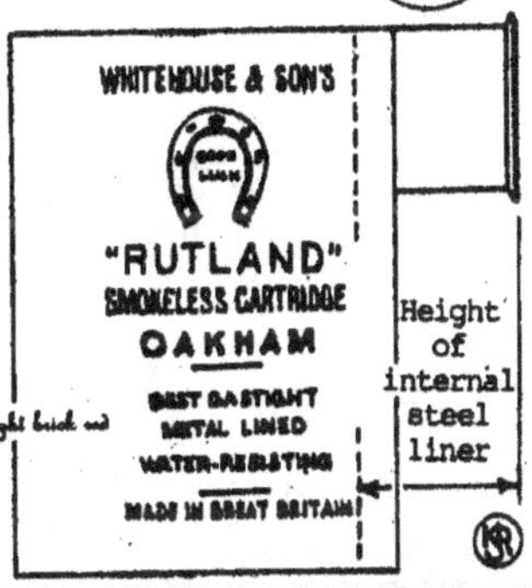

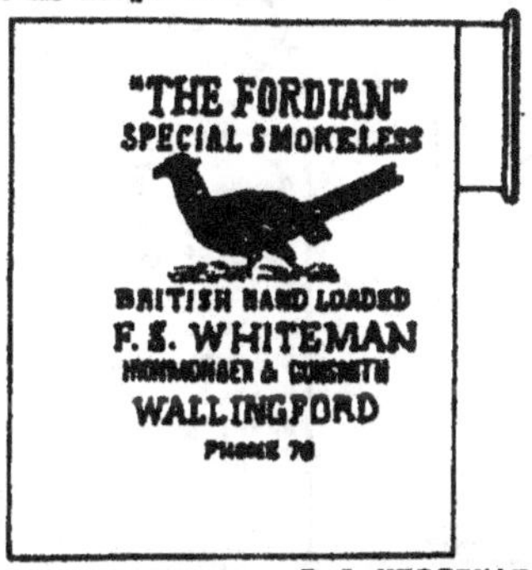

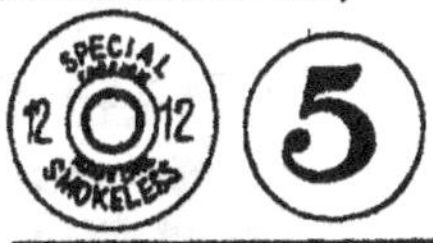

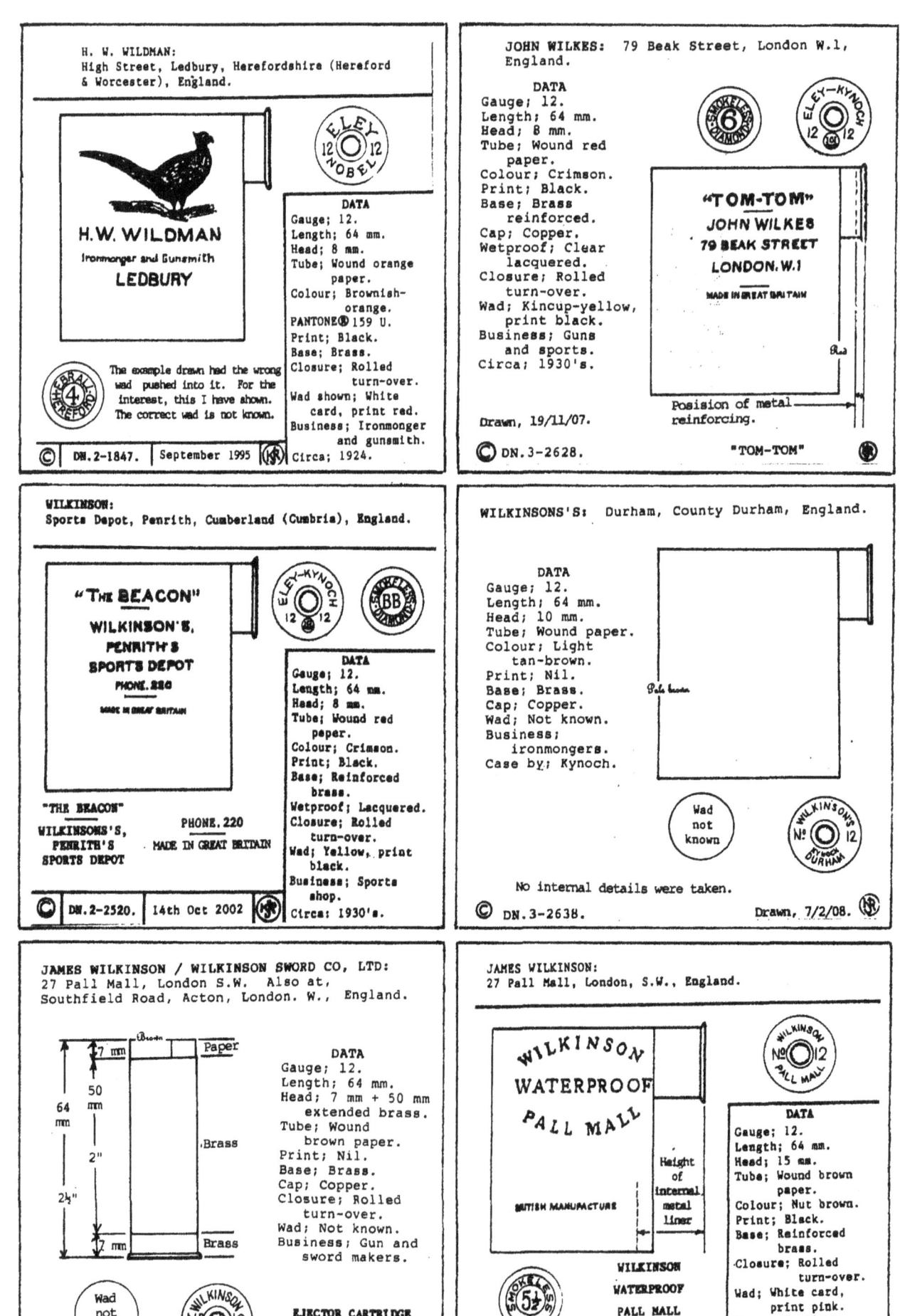

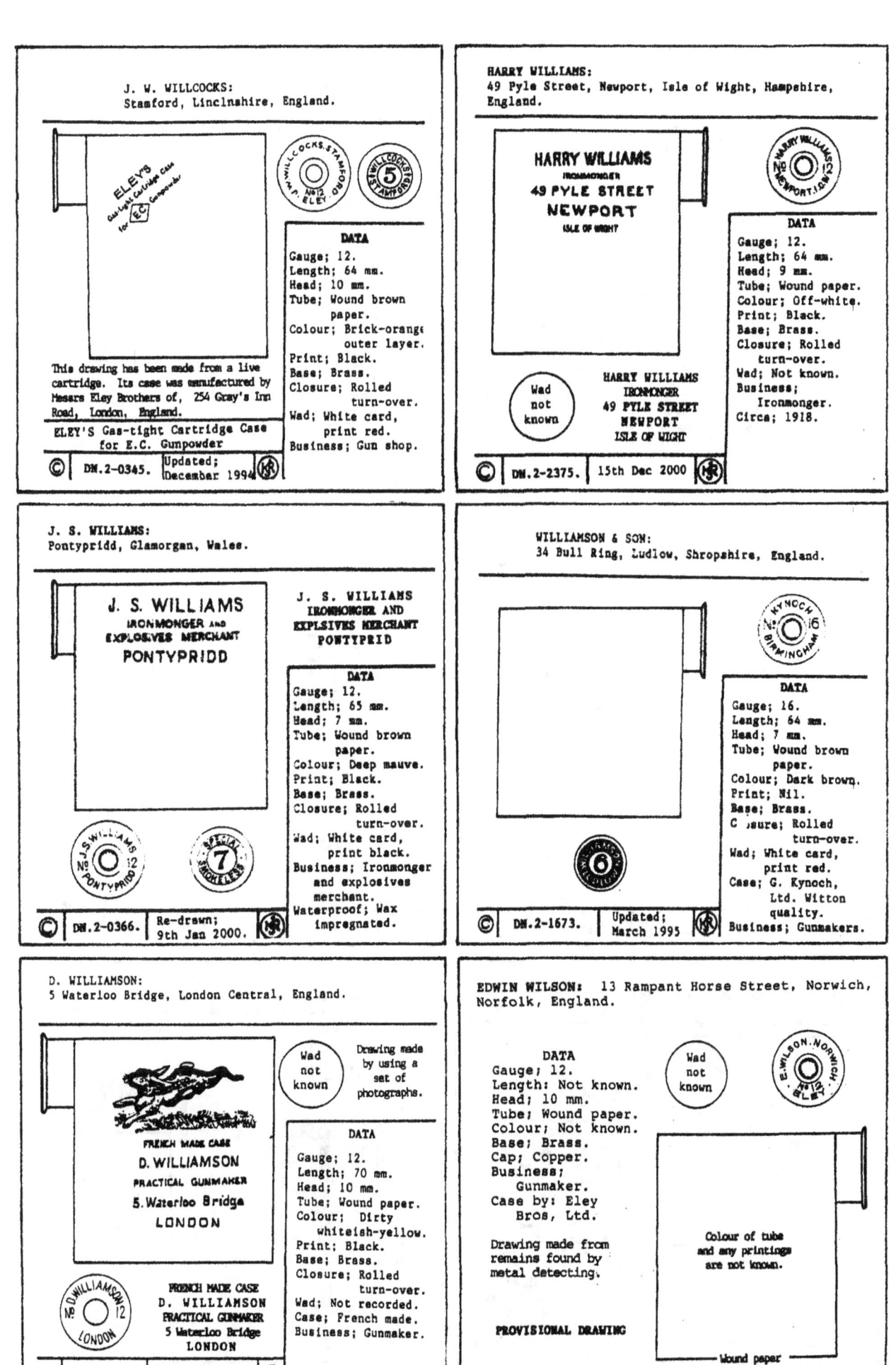

PLATE 389 [WIL-WIL]

GEOFFREY WILSON:
Skipton, North Yorkshire, England.

WILKILL SMOKELESS CARTRIDGE

GEOFFREY WILSON,
Practical Gunmaker,
15, BELMONT BRIDGE
SKIPTON, YORKS
Anti Corrosive foreign Cap & Case
LOADED IN GREAT BRITAIN

Headstamp: SMOKELESS GASTIGHT 12

DATA
Gauge; 12.
Length; 65 mm.
Head; 8.5 mm.
Tube; Wound brown paper.
Colour; Dark blue.
Print; Black.
Wetproof; Clear lacquered.
Base; Reinforced brass.
Cap; Brass with a copper coating.
Wad; Deep red, print black.
Business; Gunmaker.
Case; Foreign.

DN.2-2260. 30th March 2000

J. WILSON & SONS:
169, 171 South Street, St. Andrews, Fife-shire, Scotland.

Specially loaded for
J. WILSON & SONS
IRONMONGERS
169, 171 South Street
St. ANDREWS
"HIGH VELOCITY"

Headstamp: ELEY No 12 LONDON

Originally loaded by The New Explosives Co, Ltd.

DATA
Gauge; 12.
Length; 64 mm.
Head; 8 mm.
Tube; Wound orange paper.
Colour; Redish orange.
Print; Black.
Base; Reinforced brass.
Closure; Rolled turn-over.
Wad; Not known.
Business; ironmongers.
Case; Eley Bros, Ltd. London.

DN.2-2340. 17th Sept 2000

JAMES WILSON:
47 Goodramgate, York, Yorkshire, England.

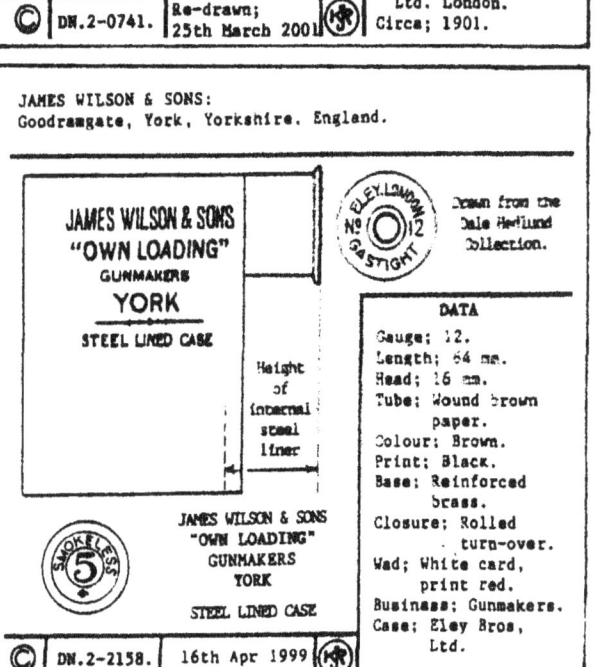

DATA
Gauge; 16.
Length; 65 mm.
Head; 10 mm with an extended brass sleeve to 57 mm.
Tube; Wound brown paper.
Print; Nil.
Base; Brass.
Closure; Rolled turn-over.
Wad; White card, print scarlet.
Business; Gunmaker.
Case; Eley Bros, Ltd. London.
Circa; 1901.

DN.2-0741. Re-drawn; 25th March 2001

JAMES WILSON & SONS:
47 Goodramgate, York, Yorkshire, England.

JAMES WILSON & SONS
"OWN LOADING"
GUNMAKERS
YORK
STEEL LINED CASE

Headstamp: ELEY No 12 LONDON

Drawn from the Dale Hedlund collection.

DATA
Gauge; 12.
Length; 64 mm.
Head; 8 mm.
Tube; Wound orange paper.
Colour; Orange.
Print; Black.
Base; Reinforced brass.
Closure; Rolled turn-over.
Wad; White card, print red.
Business; Gunmakers.
Case; Eley Bros, Ltd.

DN.2-2159. 16th Apr 1999

JAMES WILSON & SONS:
Goodramgate, York, Yorkshire, England.

JAMES WILSON & SONS
"OWN LOADING"
GUNMAKERS
YORK
STEEL LINED CASE

Headstamp: ELEY LONDON No 12 GASTIGHT

Drawn from the Dale Hedlund collection.

DATA
Gauge; 12.
Length; 64 mm.
Head; 16 mm.
Tube; Wound brown paper.
Colour; Brown.
Print; Black.
Base; Reinforced brass.
Closure; Rolled turn-over.
Wad; White card, print red.
Business; Gunmakers.
Case; Eley Bros, Ltd.

DN.2-2158. 16th Apr 1999

WILTSHIRE ROD & GUN:
23 High Street, Swindon, Wiltshire. England.

WILTSHIRE ROD & GUN
23 HIGH STREET,
SWINDON,
WILTSHIRE.
TEL: 0793 47455   30gms. (6)

Headstamp: GB 12 12 GB

DATA
Gauge; 12.
Length; 68.5 mm.
Head; 7 mm.
Tube; Medium ribbed plastic.
Colour; Red 3.5.
Print; Black.
Base; Steel, brass coated.
Closure; Crimp, 6 fold.
Business; Field sports store.

DN.2-0016. November 1994

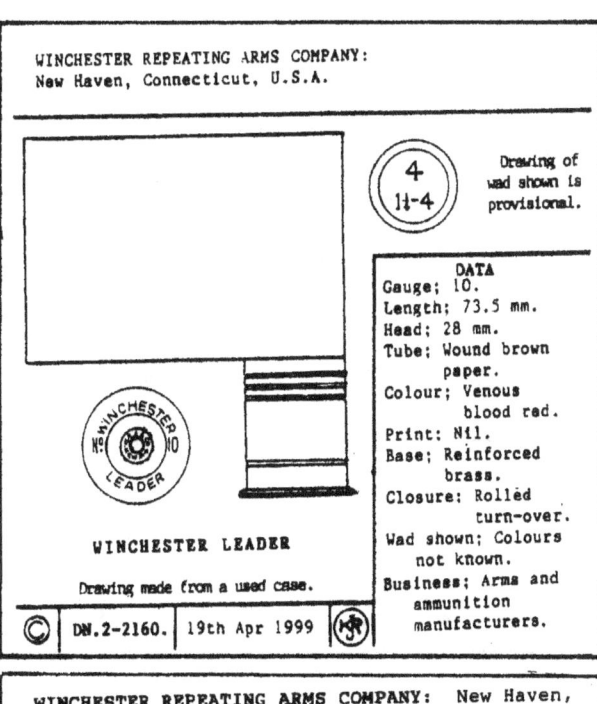
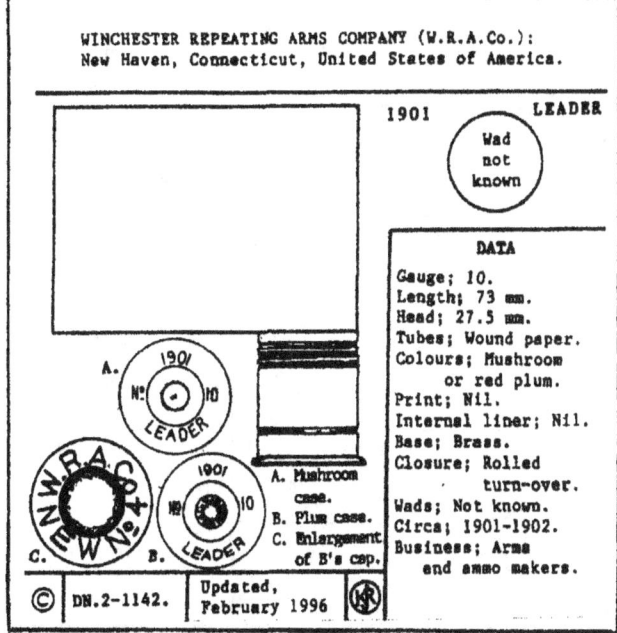
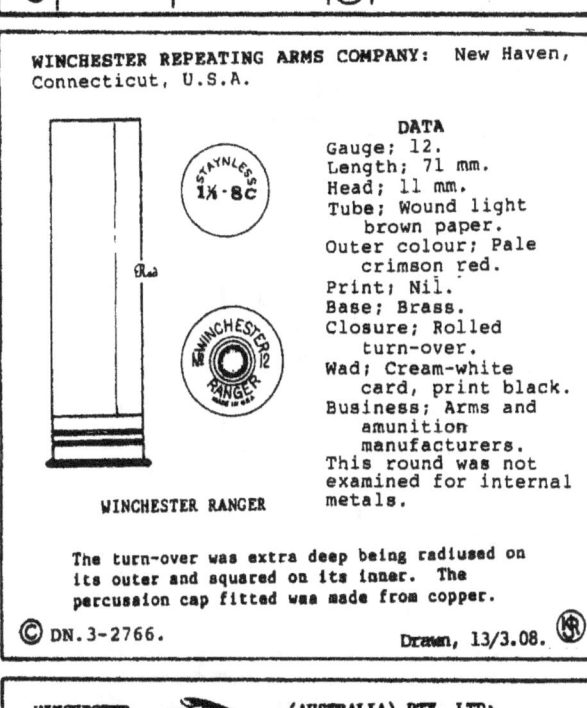
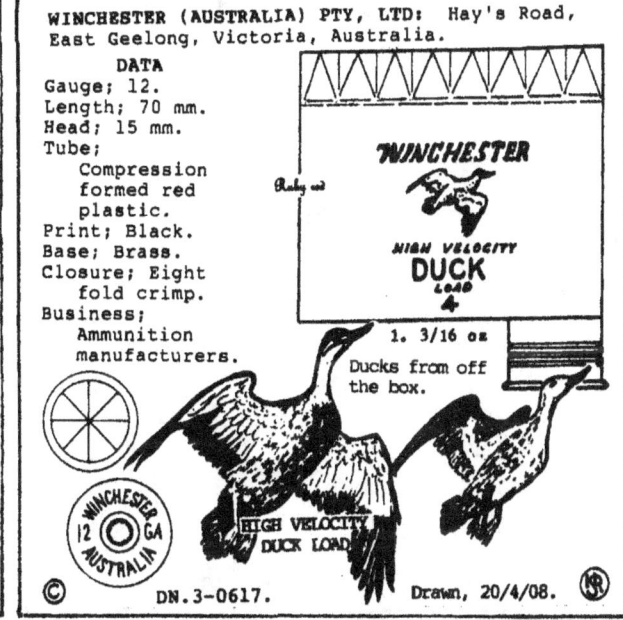

PLATE 391 [WIN – WIN]

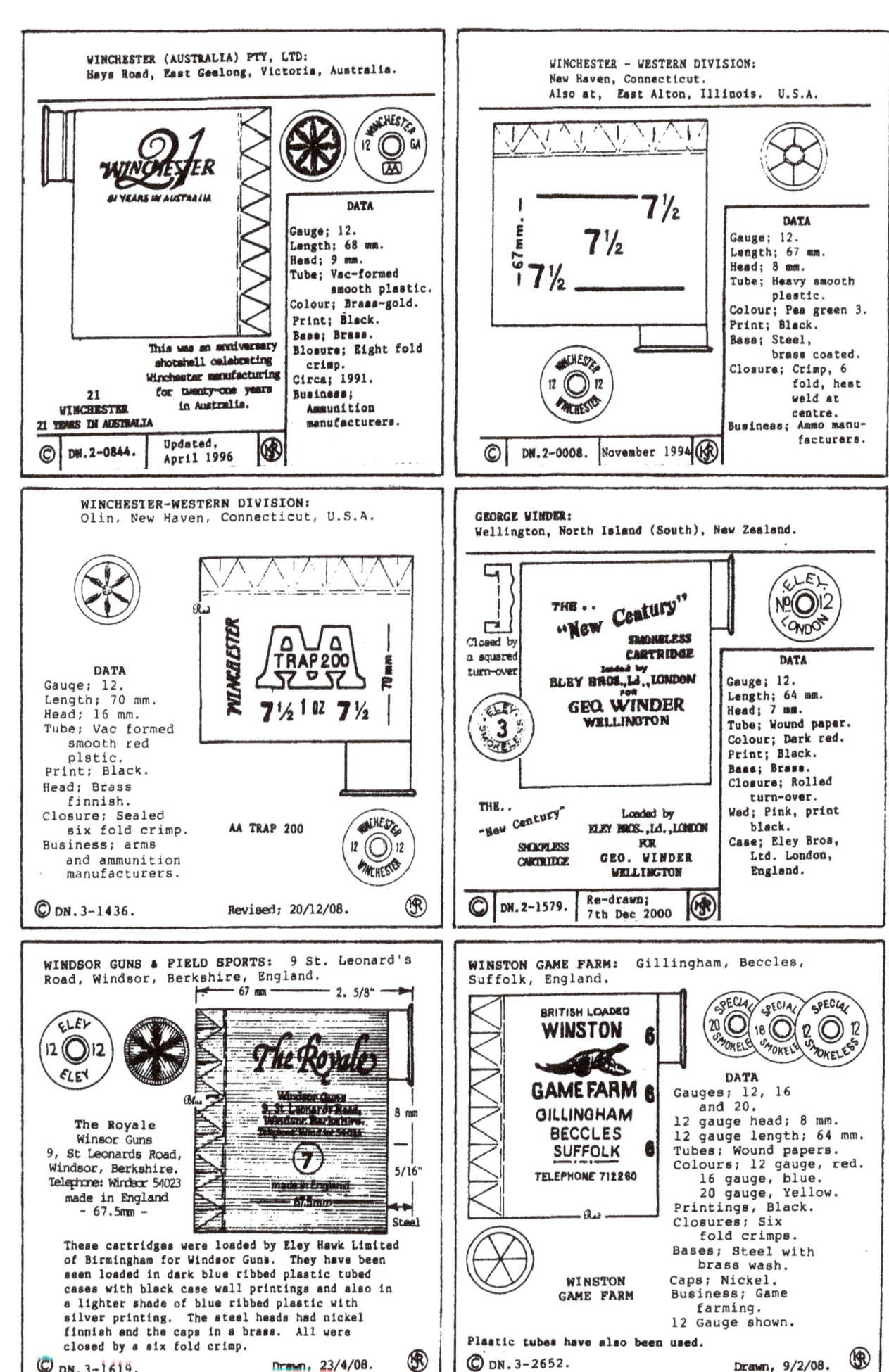

RICHARD WISE:
10 The Bull Ring, Kidderminster, Worcestershire (Hereford & Worcester), England.

THE "LIGHTNING" CARTRIDGE
SPECIALLY LOADED
———
RICHARD WISE
IRONMONGER
KIDDERMINSTER
———
Made in Great Britain

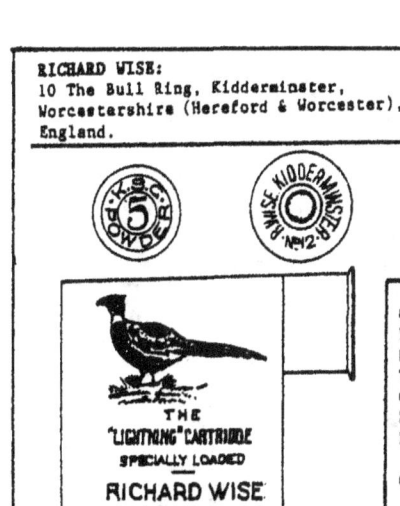

DATA
Gauge; 12.
Length; 64 mm.
Head; 15.5 mm.
Tube; Wound paper.
Colour; Crimson.
Print; Black.
Base; Reinforced brass.
Closure; Rolled turn-over.
Wad; Red card, print black.
Business; Ironmonger.
Case; Possibly by G. Kynoch, Ltd.
Circa; 1900-1920.

© DN.2-2278.   14th April 2000

WOBURN ABBEY ESTATE: Woburn Park, Bedfordshire, England.

DATA
Gauge; 12.
Length; 70 mm.
Head; 8 mm.
Tube; Wound white paper.
Outer colour; Red.
Print; Black.
Closure; Six fold crimp.
Base; Brass, or steel with a brass wash.
Cap; Nickel.
Business; Private estate.

WOBURN ABBEY

© DN.3-2653.   Drawn, 9/2/08.

WOBURN RABBIT CLEARANCE SOCIETY, LTD:
Woburn, Bedfordshire, England.

WOBURN
RABBIT CLEARANCE
SOCIETY LTD.
BEDFORDSHIRE
1 1/16 oz   SHOT
Loaded by:
G.L.WOODS & SONS
Ovington, Norfolk.

DATA
Gauge; 12.
Length; 70 mm.
Head; 8 mm.
Tube; Wound brown paper.
Colour; Orange.
Print; Black.
Base; Reinforced brass.
Waterproof; Clear lacquered.
Closure; Six fold crimp.
Circa; 1950-1960.

© DN.2-2396.   2nd April 2001

WOLFF & CO (GESELLSCHAFT):
Walsrode, Luneberg (Niedersachsen), Western Germany.

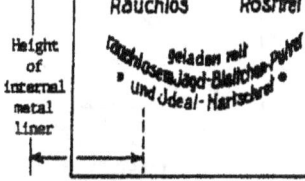

Height of internal metal liner

Extra Gasdicht
"Cymax Standard"
Rauchlos   Rostfrei

geladen mit
rauchlosem Jagd-Blättchen-Pulver
und Ideal-Hartschrot

DATA
Gauge; 12.
Length; 64.5 mm.
Head; 8 mm.
Tube; Wound paper.
Colour; Light red.
Print; Black.
Base; Reinforced brass.
Closure; Rolled turn-over.
Wad; White card, print black.
Cap; Sinoxid
Business; Ammunition and powder manufacturers.

© DN.2-1988.   June 1997.

WOLFF & CO (GESELLSCHAFT):
Walsrode, Luneberg (Niedersachsen), Western Germany.

Wad; WOLFF & Co WALSRODE 3 mm .5

ROSTFREI
RAUCHLOS
Birkhann-Marke

DATA
Gauge; 16.
Length; 65 mm.
Head; 8 mm.
Tube; Wound brown paper.
Colour; Poppy red.
Print; Black.
Base; Steel.
Closure; Rolled turn-over.
Wad; Vermilion red, print black.
Business; Powder and ammunition manufacturers.

© DN.2-1995.   June 1997.

WOLFF & CO (GESELLSCHAFT):
Walsrode, Luneburg (Niedersachsen), Western Germany.

Wolf-Marke
rauchlos n rostfrei

Wolff & Co.
Walsrode

Wolf-Marke   ENGLISH TRANSLATION
Rauchlos n rostfrei   Trade Mark.
Wolff & Co.   Smokeless and
Walsrode   free from rust.

DATA
Gauge; 12.
Length; 64 mm.
Head; 6.5 mm.
Tube; Wound paper.
Colour; Pale yellow.
Print; Black.
Base; Reinforced brass.
Closure; Rolled turn-over.
Wad; White card, print black.
Business; Ammunition and powder manufacturers.

© DN.2-1986.   June 1997.

PLATE 393 [WIS - WOL]

ARTHUR WOOD (NEWPORT I.W.)
114 Pyle Street, Newport, Isle of Wight,
Hampshire, England.

"DEMON" WETPROOF ARTHUR WOOD, NEWPORT.

Wad not known

DATA
Gauge; 12.
Length; 64 mm.
Head; 8 mm.
Tube; Wound brown paper.
Colour; Dark red.
Print; Black.
Base; Brass.
Closure; Rolled turn-over.
Wad; Not known.
Business; Gunsmith and ironmonger.

"DEMON" WETPROOF ARTHUR WOOD, NEWPORT.

Case made Case made in the U.S.A. and loaded in England.

© DN.2-1651.   Updated; April 1997

ARTHUR WOOD (NEWPORT, ISLE OF WIGHT) LIMITED:
114 Pyle Street, Newport, Isle of Wight,
Hampshire, England.

ARTHUR WOOD 114. PYLE ST. NEWPORT I.O.W. SPECIAL SMOKELESS BRITISH LOADED FOREIGN MADE CASE

DATA
Gauge; 12.
Length; 64 mm.
Head; 8 mm.
Tube; Wound paper.
Colour; Maroon.
Print; Gold.
Base; Brass.
Closure; Rolled turn-over.
Wad; Mustard yellow, print black.
Business; Ironmonger.
Case; Germany.
Circa; 1905.
Note; By 1911 the firm had become, Wood & Horspool.

ARTHUR WOOD 114, PYLE ST. NEWPORT I.O.W.   SPECIAL SMOKELESS BRITISH LOADED FOREIGN MADE CASE

© DN.2-0732.   Re-drawn 3rd Jan 1999

F. WOOD:
Believed to have been; Salisbury, England.

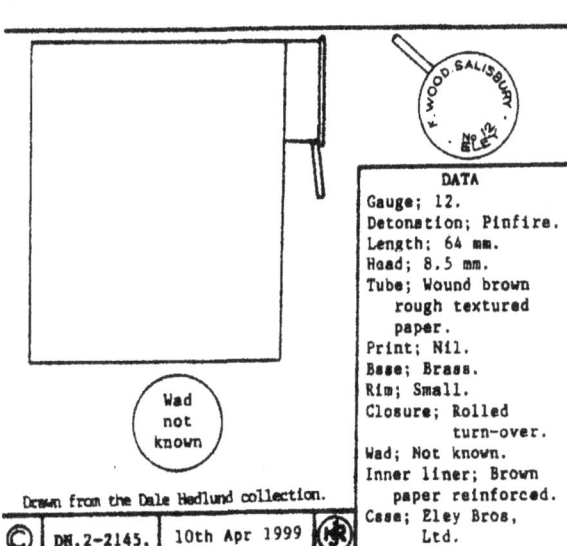

Wad not known

DATA
Gauge; 12.
Detonation; Pinfire.
Length; 64 mm.
Head; 8.5 mm.
Tube; Wound brown rough textured paper.
Print; Nil.
Base; Brass.
Rim; Small.
Closure; Rolled turn-over.
Wad; Not known.
Inner liner; Brown paper reinforced.
Case; Eley Bros, Ltd.

Drawn from the Dale Hedlund collection.

© DN.2-2145.   10th Apr 1999

J. L. WOOD:
35 St. Mary's Street, Stamford, Lincolnshire, England.

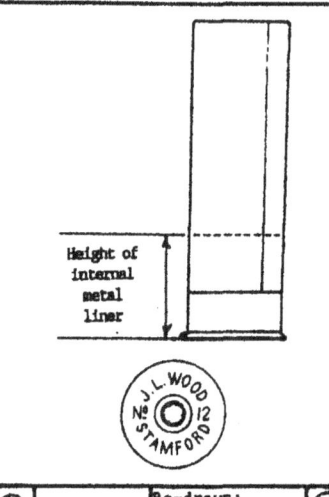

Wad not known

Height of internal metal liner

DATA
Gauge; 12.
Length; 65 mm.
Head; 10 mm.
Tube; Wound white paper.
Colour; Dark navy blue.
Print; Nil.
Base; Reinforced brass.
Closure; Rolled turn-over.
Wad; Not known.
Business; Gunmaker.
Case; Most likely foreign.

© DN.2-0731.   Re-drawn; 31st March 2001

WOOD & HORSPOOL:
114 Pyle Street, Newport, Isle of Wight, Hampshire, England.

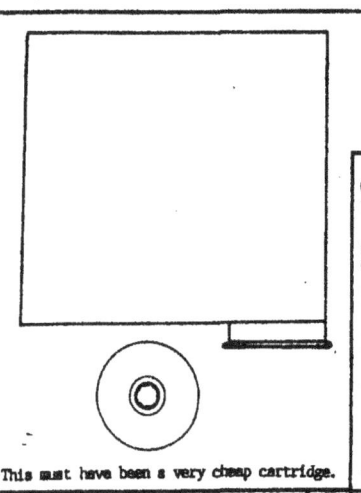

DATA
Gauge; 12.
Length; Approx' 64 mm.
Head; Approx' 5 mm.
Tube; Wound paper.
Colour; Green.
Print; Nil.
Base; Brass.
Closure; Rolled turn-over.
Wad colours; Not recorded.
Business; Ironmongers.
Circa; 1911.

This must have been a very cheap cartridge.

© DN.2-2374.   18th Dec 2000   Provisional drawing

R. J. WOODROW:
Brandon, Norfolk, East Anglia, England.

THE CHAMPION SMOKELESS CARTRIDGE R. J. Woodrow, IRONMONGER. TELEPHONE No. 2 BRANDON NORFOLK.

DATA
Gauge; 12.
Length; 65 mm.
Head; 8 mm.
Tube; Wound paper.
Colour; Vermilion red.
Print; Black.
Base; Brass.
Closure; Rolled turn-over.
Wad; Dark red, print black.
Business; Ironmonger.

THE CHAMPION SMOKELESS CARTRIDGE R. J. Woodrow,   IRONMONGER. TELEPHONE No. 2 BRANDON NORFOLK.

© DN.2-1453.   Updated; April 1997

R. J. WOODROW: Brandon, Suffolk, England.

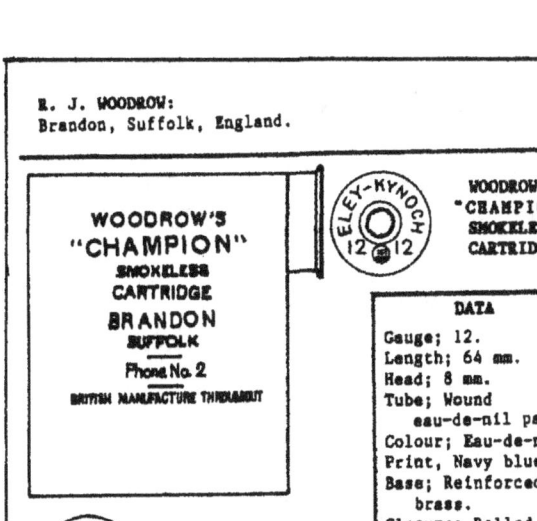

DATA
Gauge; 12.
Length; 64 mm.
Head; 8 mm.
Tube; Wound eau-de-nil paper.
Colour; Eau-de-nil.
Print, Navy blue.
Base; Reinforced brass.
Closure; Rolled turn-over.
Wad; White card, print pink.
Business; Ironmonger.
Circa: 1930's.

© DN.2-2295.   15th May 2000

EDMUND WOODS: 36 Bow Street, London, England.

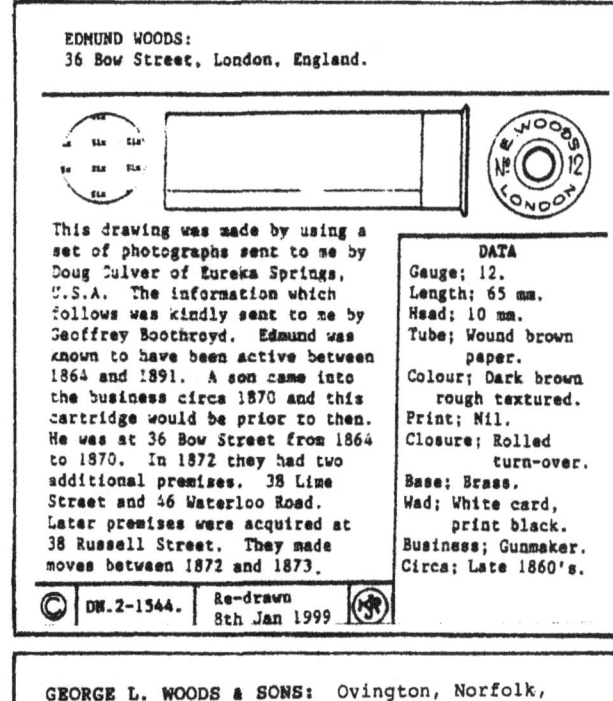

This drawing was made by using a set of photographs sent to me by Doug Culver of Eureka Springs, U.S.A. The information which follows was kindly sent to me by Geoffrey Boothroyd. Edmund was known to have been active between 1864 and 1891. A son came into the business circa 1870 and this cartridge would be prior to then. He was at 36 Bow Street from 1864 to 1870. In 1872 they had two additional premises. 38 Lime Street and 46 Waterloo Road. Later premises were acquired at 38 Russell Street. They made moves between 1872 and 1873.

DATA
Gauge; 12.
Length; 65 mm.
Head; 10 mm.
Tube; Wound brown paper.
Colour; Dark brown rough textured.
Print; Nil.
Closure; Rolled turn-over.
Base; Brass.
Wad; White card, print black.
Business; Gunmaker.
Circa; Late 1860's.

© DN.2-1544.   Re-drawn 8th Jan 1999

GEORGE L. WOODS: Ovington, Norfolk, England.

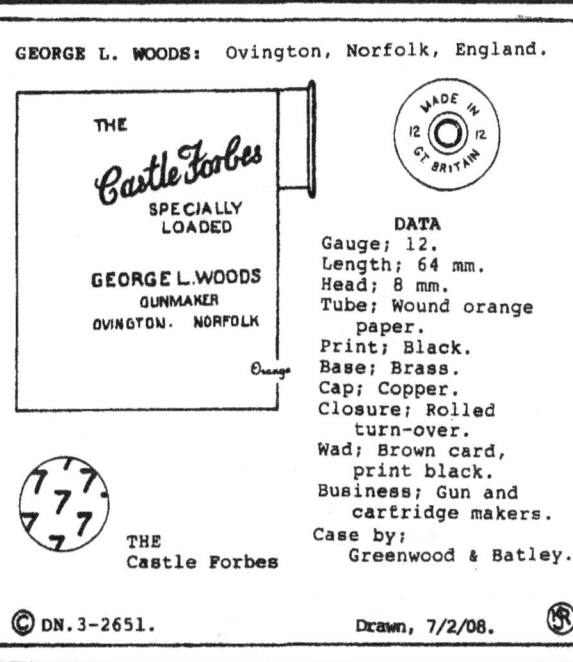

DATA
Gauge; 12.
Length; 64 mm.
Head; 8 mm.
Tube; Wound orange paper.
Print; Black.
Base; Brass.
Cap; Copper.
Closure; Rolled turn-over.
Wad; Brown card, print black.
Business; Gun and cartridge makers.
Case by; Greenwood & Batley.

© DN.3-2651.   Drawn, 7/2/08.

GEORGE L. WOODS & SONS: Ovington, Norfolk, England.

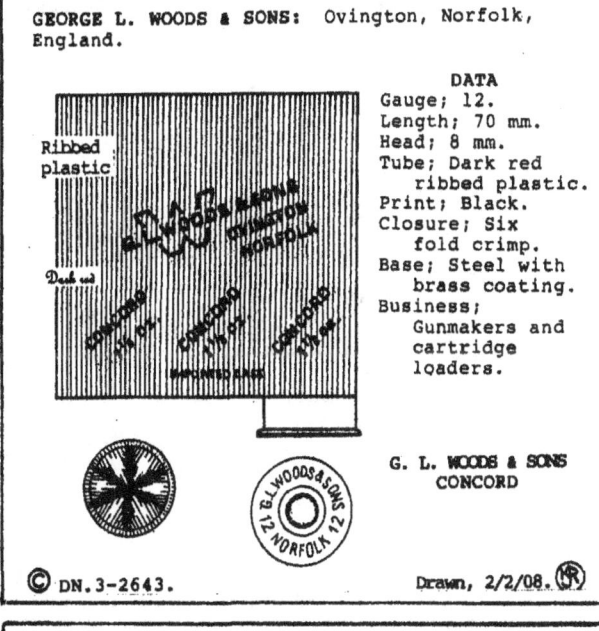

DATA
Gauge; 12.
Length; 70 mm.
Head; 8 mm.
Tube; Dark red ribbed plastic.
Print; Black.
Closure; Six fold crimp.
Base; Steel with brass coating.
Business; Gunmakers and cartridge loaders.

© DN.3-2643.   Drawn, 2/2/08.

G. L. WOODS & SONS: Ovigton, Norfolk, England.

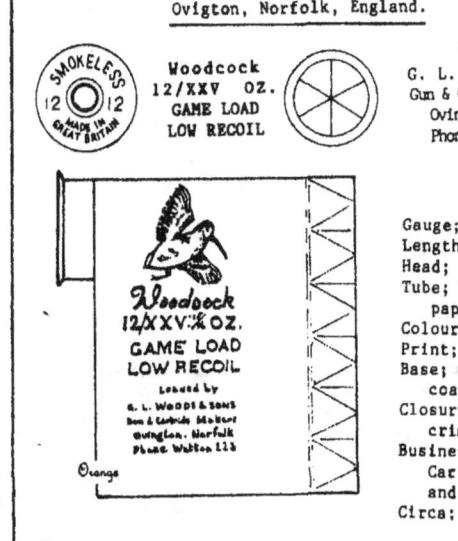

DATA
Gauge; 12.
Length; 65 mm.
Head; 8 mm.
Tube; Wound orange paper.
Colour; Orange.
Print; Black.
Base; Steel, brass coated.
Closure; Six fold crimp.
Business; Cartridge loaders and gunsmiths.
Circa: 1960's.

© DN.3-0590.   Revised; 16/12/08.

GEORGE L. WOODS & SONS: Ovington, Norfolk, England.

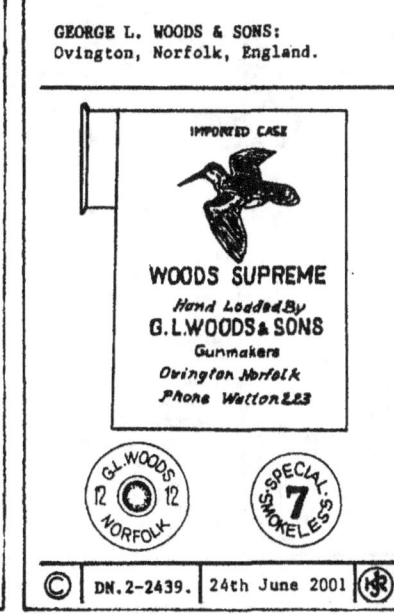

DATA
Gauge; 12.
Length; 57 mm.
Head; 8 mm.
Tube; Wound white paper.
Colour; Flame red.
Print; Silver.
Base; Brass.
Closure; Rolled turn-over.
Wad; Red, print black.
Business Gunmakers and cartridge loaders.
Case; Fiocchi, Italy.

© DN.2-2439.   24th June 2001

PLATE 395 [WOO - WOO]

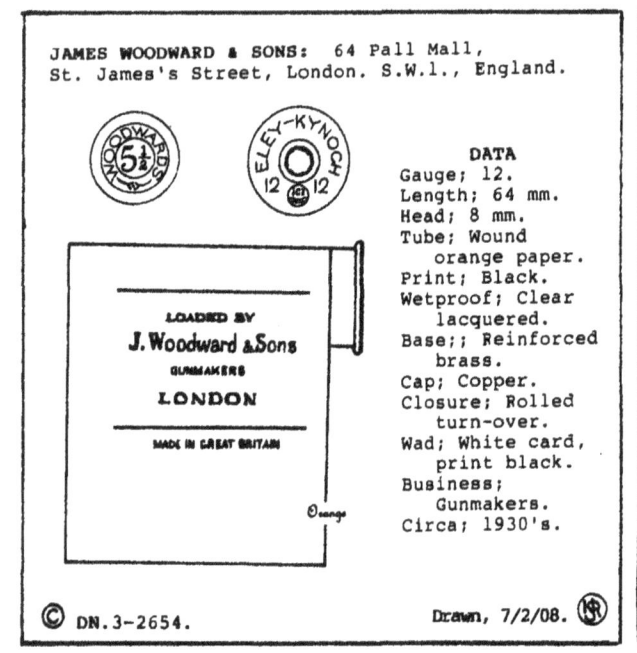

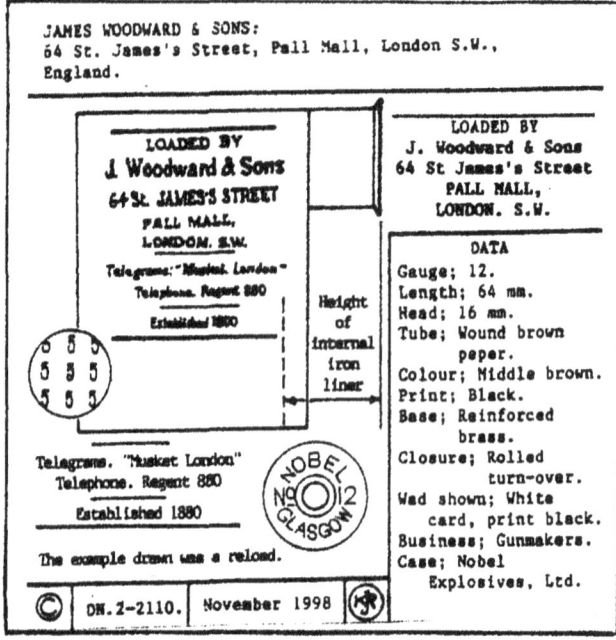

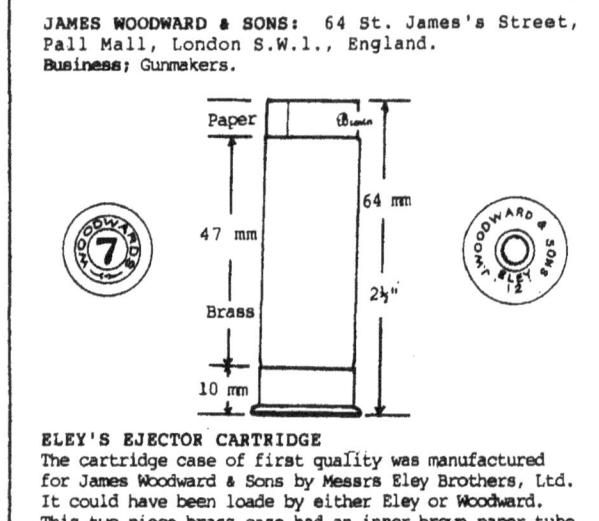

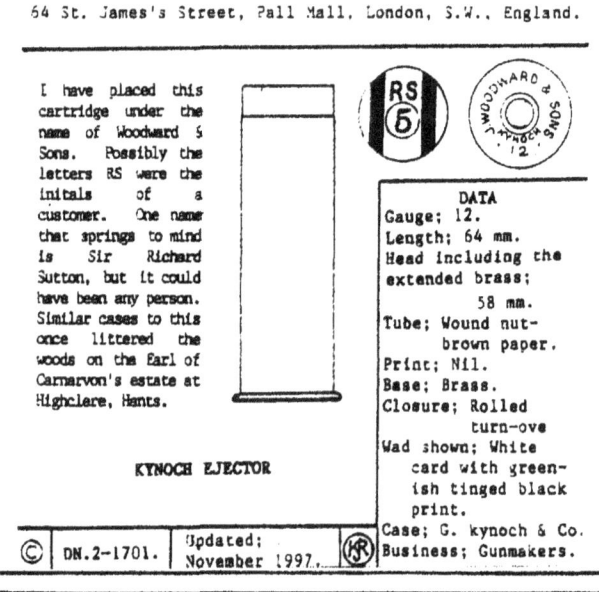

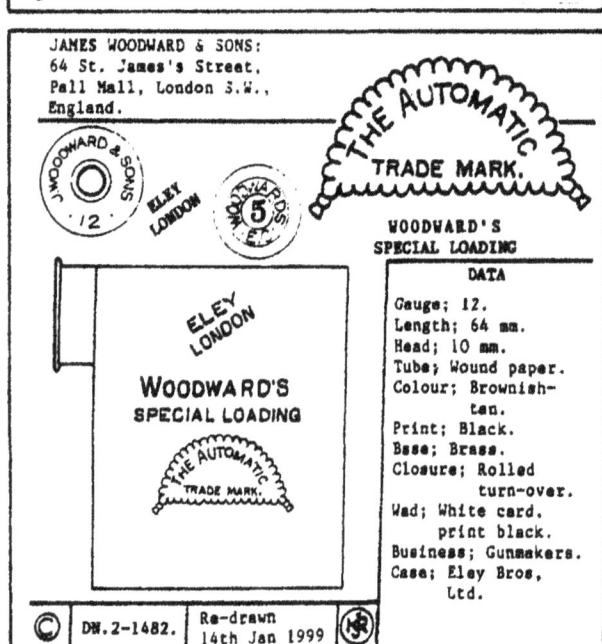

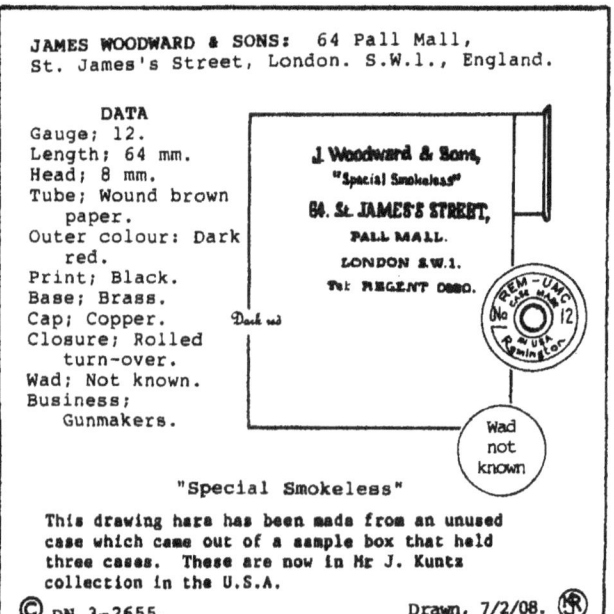

PLATE 396 [WOO - WOO]

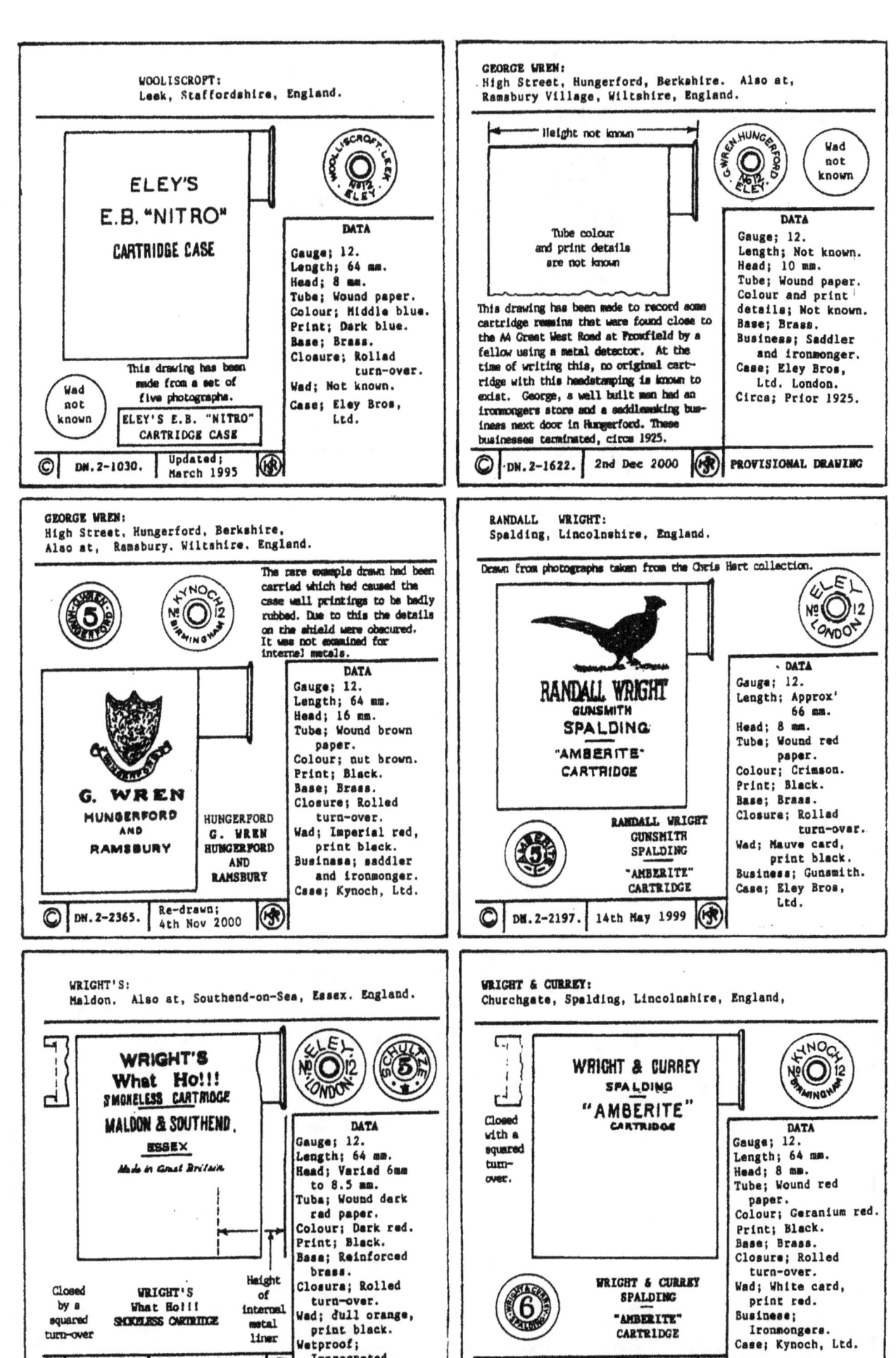

PLATE 397 [WOO - WRI]

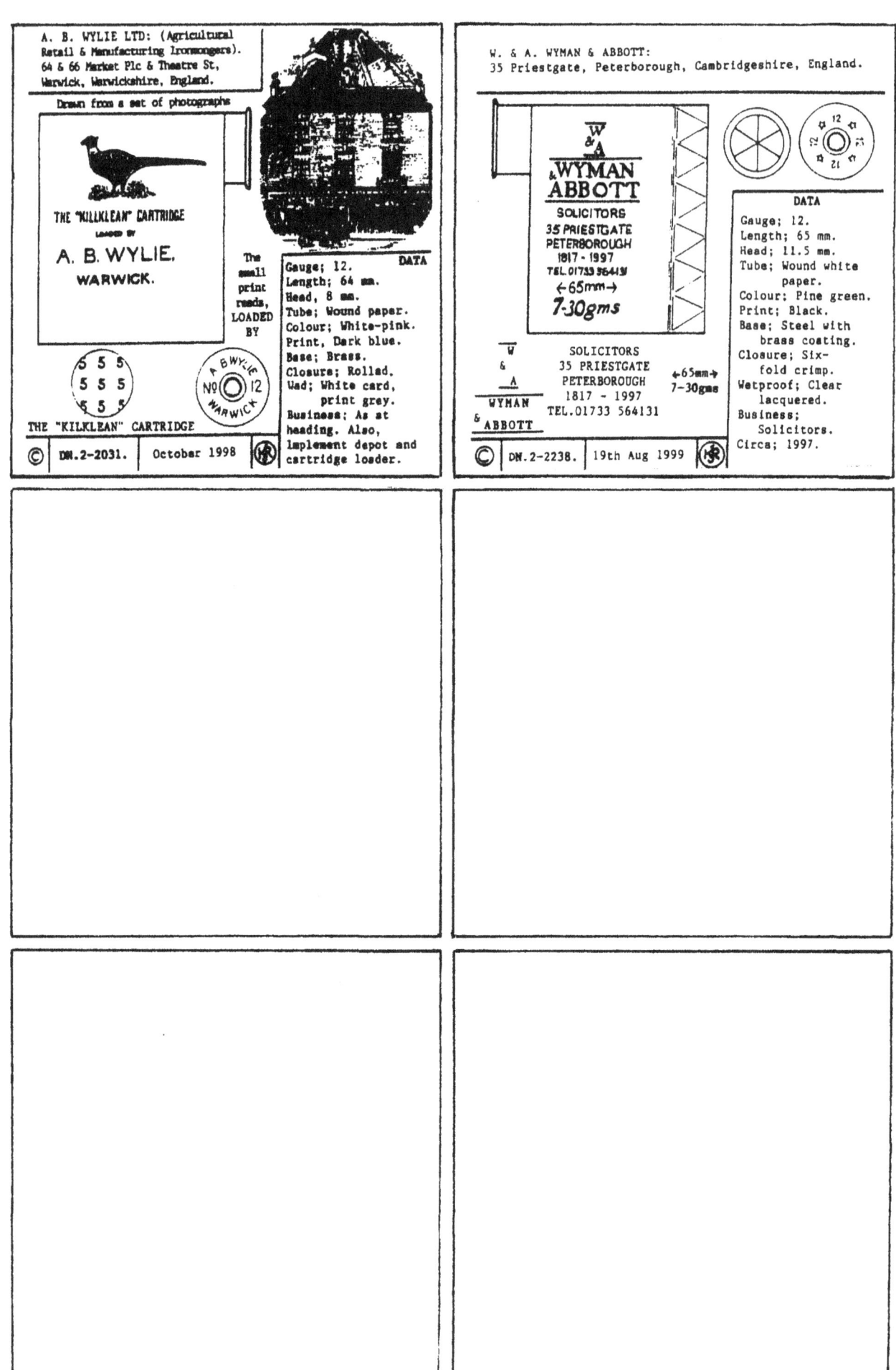

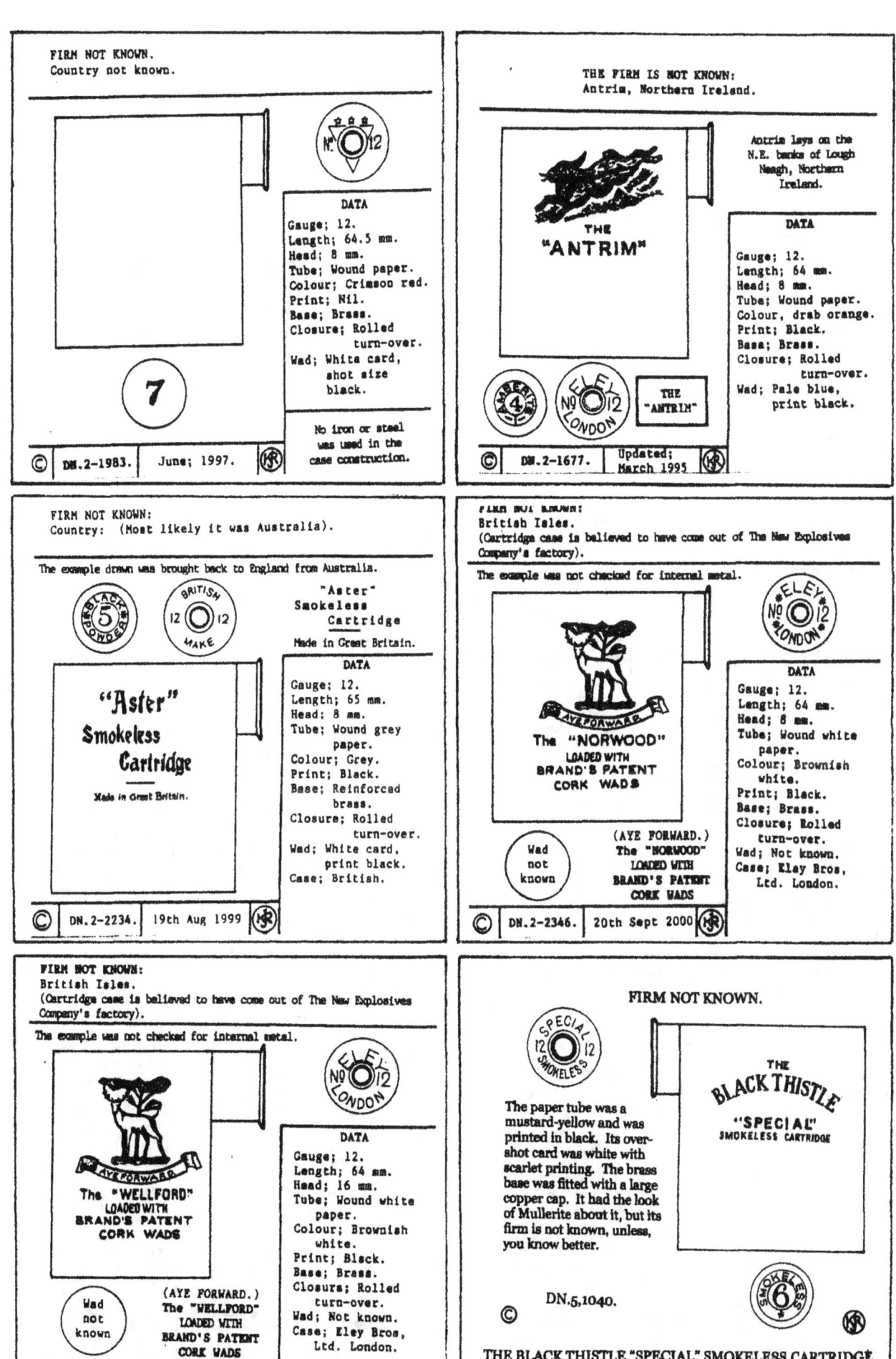

PLATE 399 Not known

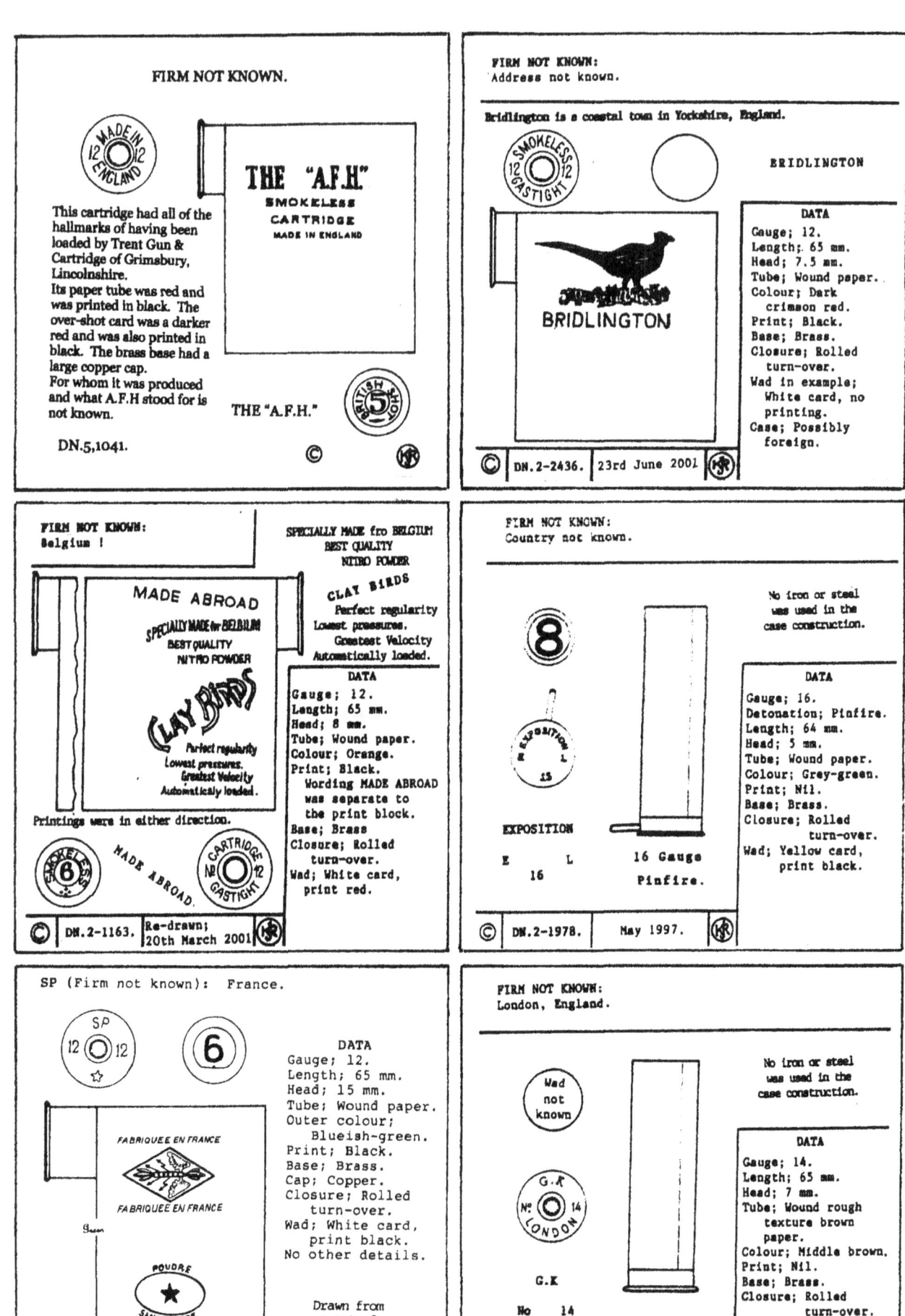

PLATE 400 Not known

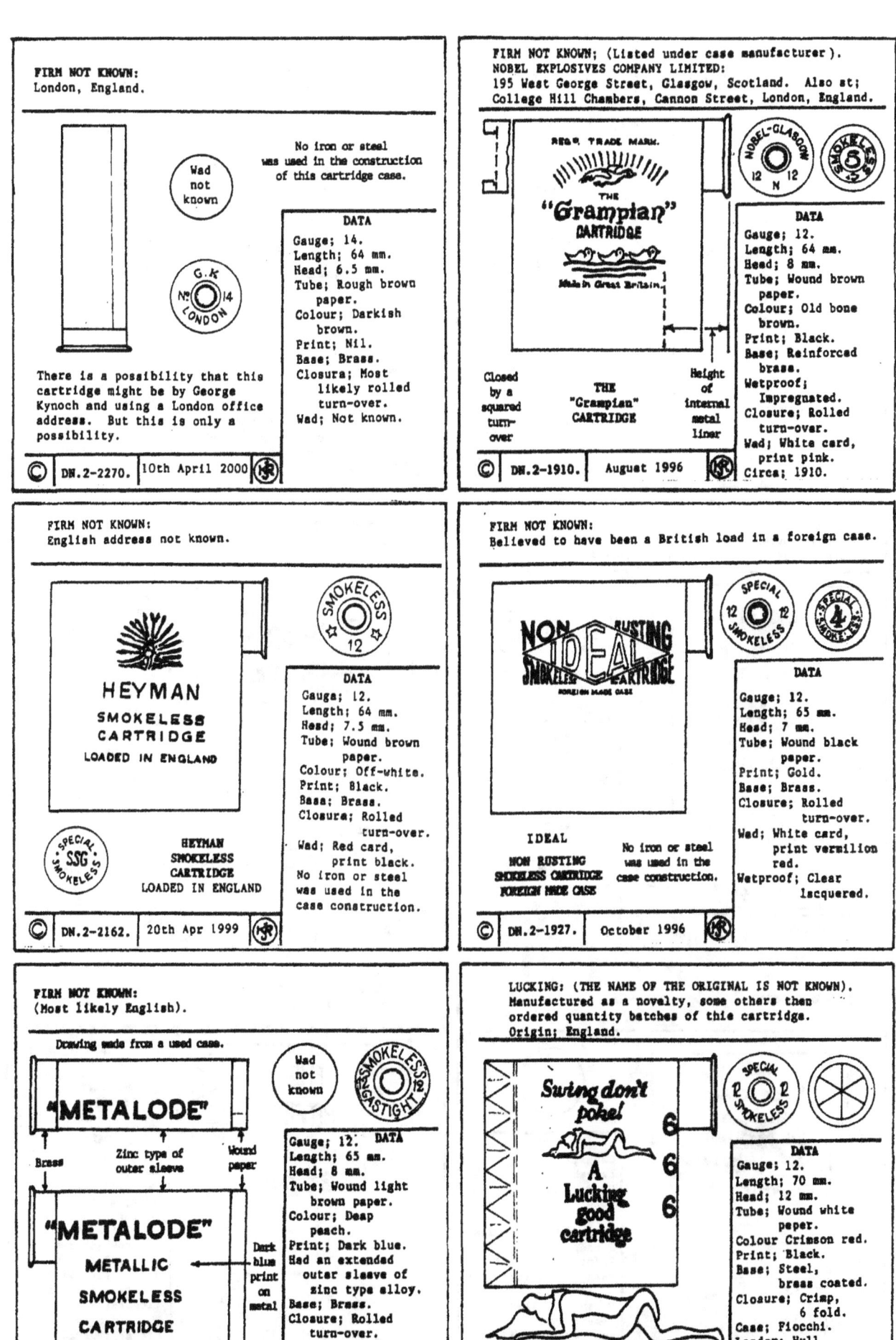

PLATE 401 Not known

LUX.
The firm, country and address is not known.

This drawing was made from a used case.

DATA
Gauge; 12.
Length; 65 mm.
Head; 5 mm.
Tube; Wound brown paper.
Colour; Brown.
Print; Nil.
Base; Brass.
Closure; Rolled turn-over.
Wad; Not known.

No iron or steel was used in the case construction.

© DN.3-2276.   Revised; 17/12/08.

THE FIRMS NAME IS UNKNOWN:
Most possibly, somewhere in England.

ENGLISH "PIONEER" CARTRIDGE
LOADED WITH ENGLISH SMOKELESS POWDER
MADE AND LOADED IN ENGLAND

DATA
Gauge; 12.
Length; 64 mm.
Head; 8 mm.
Tube; Wound dark green paper.
PANTONE® 336 C.
Print; Black.
Base; Brass with reinforcing.
Closure; Rolled turn-over.
Wad; Blue-grey, card, print black.

© DN.2-1047.   Updated, March 1996

FIRM NOT KNOWN:
Case constructed by; NOBEL'S EXPLOSIVES COMPANY, LIMITED: Kingsway House, Kingsway, London, England.

"RINGER" SMOKELESS CARTRIDGE
IMPROVED SHELL
Made in Great Britain

The origin of this case is still a mystery, but it was definitely manufactured by Nobel's Explosive Co, Ltd. Many unused cases have since come to light.

"RINGER" SMOKELESS CARTRIDGE

DATA
Gauge; 12.
Length; 65 mm.
Head; 8 mm.
Tube; Wound tan paper.
Colour; Orange-tan.
Print; Black.
Base; Brass.
Closure; Rolled turn-over.
Wad; Not known.
Business; Explosives and cartridge makers.

© DN.2-0339.   Updated; March 1995

FIRM NOT KNOWN:
(Possibly British).

"SPECIAL" SMOKELESS CARTRIDGE

Height of internal metal liner.

"SPECIAL" SMOKELESS CARTRIDGE

DATA
Gauge; 16.
Length; 65 mm.
Head; 8 mm.
Tube; Wound brown paper.
Colour; Dark crimson red.
Print; Black.
Base; Reinforced brass.
Closure; Rolled turn-over.
Wad; Not known.
Business; Not Known.
Case; Possibly foreign.

© DN.2-2252.   21st Jan 2000.

FIRM NOT KNOWN:

SPECIAL
SMOKELESS

SPECIAL
(Rabbit)
SMOKELESS

DATA
Gauge; 12.
Length; 60 mm.
Head; 7 mm.
Tube; Wound crimson paper.
Colour; Dull crimson red.
Print; Black.
Base; Reinforced brass.
Closure; Rolled turn-over.
Wad; White card, no printings. (Blank load).

© DN.2-2418.   7th June 2001

FIRM OR OWNERS NAME NOT KNOWN:
Country possibly England.

THE "SPITFIRE"
←67mm→
5-28gms

THE "SPITFIRE"
←67 mm→
5-28gms

DATA
Gauge; 12.
Length; 67 mm.
Head; 15.5 mm.
Tube; Wound brown paper.
Colour; Light brownish red.
Print; Black.
Base; Steel with brass coating.
Closure; Six fold crimp.
Circa; 1999-2000.

Shot size not known

© DN.2-2289.   19th April 2000

PLATE 402 Not known

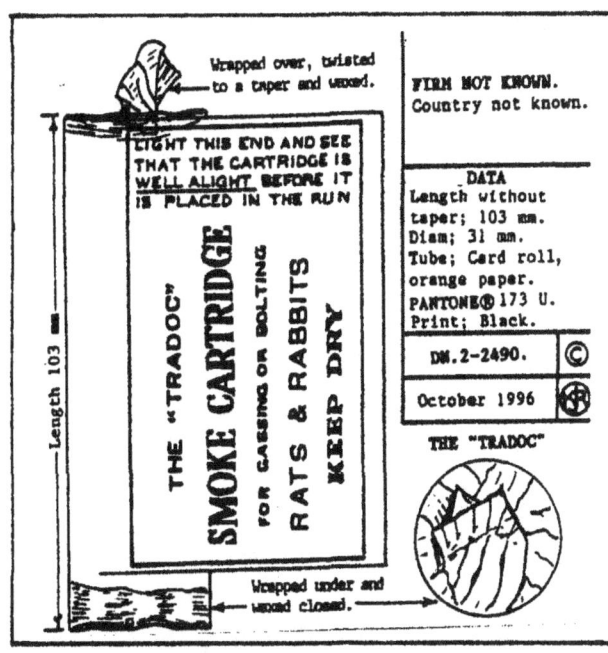
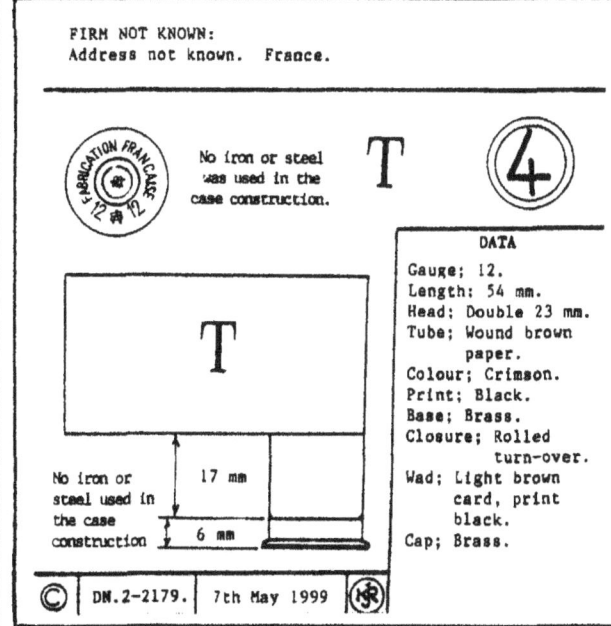

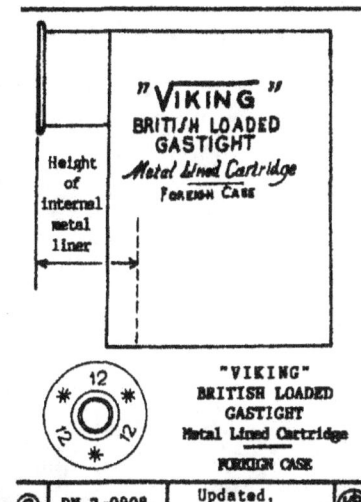

PLATE 403 Not known

INDEX to the Illustrated Firms, etc.

All numbers shown are of the plates unless stated otherwise.

ACCLES ARMS, AMMUNITION & MANUFACTURING. 1.
.ADAMS, HENRY R. 1.
ADAMS, J. H. & SONS. 1.
ADKIN, HENRY & SON. 1, 2.
ADLER, MARK. 2.
ADSETT, T. & SON. 3.
AGNEW & SON. [Exeter] 3.
AGNEW, J. [Colchester] 3.
AGRICULTURAL EXRECUTIVE COMMITTEE. 3.
AKRILL, H. ESAU. 4.
ALCOCK & PIERCE, PTY, LTD. 4.
ANDERSONS, LTD, 5.
ALDRIDGE, E. 5.
ALEXANDER W. F. & ALEXANDER BROS. 5, 6.
ALEXANDER & DUNCAN, LTD. 6.
ALLAN, ARTHUR, LTD. 6.
ALLWELL & PHIPPS. 6.
ALTHAM & SON. 7.
AMERICAN AMMUNITION CO. 7.
AMMUNITION (NOBEL) PTY, LTD. 7.
ANDERSON, F. A. [East Grinstead]. 7.
ANDERSON, JOHN & SON. [Malton] 8.
ANGLIA CARTRIDGE CO. 8.
ANNE, THOMAS WILLIAM. 8.
ARGYLE-HOUSE, D. G. 8.
ARMSTRONG (SPORTING GUN) 8, 9.
ARMY & NAVY CO-OP SOC LTD. 9, 10, 11
ARMY & NAVY STORES LTD 11.12,13
ARNOLD, S. R. 12.
ATKIN, HENRY, LTD. 12, 13.
ATKIN GRANT & LANG. 13.
ATKINS, JOHN. (DUMUNWAY), LTD. 13.
ATKINSON, T. & SON. [Kendal] 13, 14.
ATKINSON, WILLIAM & SON. [Lancaster]. 14.
ATKINSONS. [Swansea]. 14.
AUSTIN, T. C. 15.
AUSTRALIAN CLAY TARGET ASSOCIATION. 15,
AUSTRALIAN CARTRIDGE ENTERPRISE, LTD. 15.
AVERILL & SON. 15.

BACON & CURTIS, LTD. 16.
BAGNALL & KIRKWOOD. 16.
BAIKAL. 16.
BAILEY, CHARLES A. [U.S.A.] 17.
BAILEY, W. R. [Congresbury] 17.
BAKER, F. T. [London} 17
BAKER, J. C. [Worcester] 17.
BAKER, JOSEPH & SON. [Fakenham] 17, 18.
BAKER, J. T. [Darlington] 18

BAKER, W.E. [Tavistock] 18.
BALES, FRANK A. [Ipswich] 18.
BALES, G. W. [Ipswich] 18.
BALLS BROS. 19.
BAMFORD, J. C, LTD. (JCB). 19.
BANFIELD, J. G. & SONS, LTD. 19.
BAPTY & CO. 19.
BARFORD, H. W. & CO, LTD. 19.
BARHAM, C. H. 19, 20.
BARKE, P. W. 20.
BARKER BROS. [Grantham] 20.
BARKERS. [Huddersfield] 20.
BARNES, A. [Ulverston] 20.
BARNES, GEORGE JAS. [Calne] 21.
BARNES, W. [Ashbourne] 21.
BARNET & LEVET. 21.
BARNITTS, LTD. 21.
BARNWELL, H. & SONS. 21.
BARTRAM, GEORGE. 22.
BASCHIERI & PELLAGRI. S.P.A. 22.
BASSETT, G. J. 22.
BATE, GEORGE (GUNMAKERS), LTD. [Birmingham] 23.
BATES, A. [Canterbury] 22.
BATES, A. T. [Canterbury] 23.
BATES, GEORGE. [Eastbourne] 23.
BAYS & CO. 23.
BEARE, H. & S. 23.
BEESLEY, FREDERICK. 24.
BEAULIEU MANOR ESTATE. 24, 259.
BENIGNO, A. 24.
BENNETT, G. W. 24.
BENTLEY, JOSEPH. 24.
BISSET, G. & G. 25.
BLACK, J. 25.
BLACKADDER, C. G. 25.
BLAKE, JAMES. 25.
BLAND, THOMAS & SONS. 25, 26.
BLANTON. RICHARD. 26.
BOLE. H. W. 27.
BOMBRNINI PARODI DELFINO (B.P.D.). 27.
BOND. G. E. & SON. 27, 28.
BONETT, P.A. 28.
BONNEMAIN-RAVENEU. 28.
BONNER-WILLIAMS. 28.
BOREHAM, J. S. 28.
BOSS & CO. 28, 29, 30, 31, 32.
BOSWELL, CHARLES. 32.
BOWERBANKS. 32.
BRACKENBURY, GEORGE & SONS,LTD. 33.
BOYNE ESTATE. 33.
BRADDELL, JOSEPH & SON, LTD. 33.
BRAUN & BLOEM. 33.
BRAXTED PARK ESTATE. 34.
B.A.S.C. 34.

BRITT, WILLIAM & SON. 34.
BROCK'S EXPLOSIVES, LTD. 34.
BROOKER. 34.
BROWN, J. [Morpeth] 34, 35
BROWN, E. J. & CO. [Rotherham] 35.
B.S.A. GUNS, UK, LTD. 35.
BUCHHOLZ DIANA PULVERFABRIKEN 35.
BUCK & CO. [London]. 35.
BUCK, F. [Wincanton] 36.
BUCKHOLT PARK. 36.
BUCKLAND, J. & SONS. 36.
BUCKMASTER & WOOD. 36.
BUDGEN, J. & CO. 36.
BUGLER, J. U, LTD. 36.
BULL MORE, GEORGE G. 37.
BULPIN, A. C. 37.
BUNTING, W. 37.
BURGESS, FREDERICK H, LTD. 37.
BURROW, JAMES. 37, 38.
BUSSEMS & PARKING, LTD. 38.
BUSSEY, GEORGE G. & CO. 38.

CALEDONIAN CARTRIDGE CO, LTD. 38, 39.
CALIBERS G. & L. 39, 40.
CAMBER, N. B, LTD. 40.
CAMBRIDGE & CO. 41.
CAMPBELL, R. & SONS. 40.
CANADIAN INDUSTRIES, LTD. 41.
CAPELL, RICHARD LOVAT. 41.
CAREY (GUNMAKERS), LTD. 41.
CARNARVON, EARL OF. 42.
CARR BROS. [Huddersfield]. 42.
CARR & CO. [Nottingham] 42.
CARSWELL, W. C, LTD. 42, 43.
CARTER, W. & SONS. 43.
CARTOUCHERIE FRANCAISE. 43.
CARTRIDGE, THE. [Warwick] 43.
CARTRIDGE SYNDICATE. 44.
CARTUCHOS DEPOTIVOS DE MEXICO. 44.
CARVER (WOLVERHAMPTON), LTD. 44.
CASE, C. A. 45.
CAWDRON, HERBERT. 45.
CAWOOD GUN CO. 45.
CHAMBERLAIN, ARTHUR J. [Salisbury] 45, 46, 47.
CHAMBERLAIN, EDWARD. [Andover] 47, 48.
CHAMBERS, J. & SON. [Dunstable] 49.
CHAMBERS, SEPTIMUS. [Cardiff] 49.
CHAPLIN, B. E. 49.
CHEREAU, ISAAC. 50.
CHITTY, R. S. 50.
CHUBBS OF EDGWARE (GUNMAKERS), LTD. 50.
CHURCHILL, EDWIN J, LTD. 50, 51, 52, 53.
CLARK & BUTCHER, LTD. 55.
CLARKE, CHAS. [Salisbury] 53.
CLARKE, FRANK. [Thetford] 53.
CLARKE, HENRY & SONS. [Leicester] 54, 55.
CLARKE & DYKE. [Salisbury] 55, 56.
CLATWORTHY COOKE & CO, LTD. 56.

CLAYTON & SON. [Huntingdon] 56.
CLAYTON, R. & D. [Bury St Edmunds] 56.
CLIMIE, R. & SON. 56.
CLINTON CARTRIDGE CO. 56.
CLOUGH, R. H. [Hartlepool] 57.
CLOUGH, THOMAS & SON. [King's Lyn] 57.
CLUB CARTRIDGE CO, LTD. 57.
COCK, J. H. & CO. 57.
COGSCHULTZE AMMUNITION & POWDER CO. 57, 161.
COGSWELL & HARRISON, LTD. 57, 58, 59, 60, 61, 111.
COHEN, S. & SONS. 62.
COLE, F. J. [Cirencester] 62.
COLE, FRANK & SON. [Devizes] 62.
COLLATH WILHELM. 63.
COLLIS, J, LTD. 63.
COLONIAL AMMUNITION CO, LTD. 63, 64.
COLTMAN & CO. 64, 65.
COMMONWEALTH CARTRIDGE CO. 65.
CONWAY, ROY. 65.
CONYERS, ARTHUR. [Blandford] 65, 66, 67.
CONYERS, H. & SONS. [Gt Driffield] 67.
COOKE, J. E. 67.
COONEY, GEORGE. 68.
CORDEN, SIDNEY LANCELOT. 68.
CORDES, H. G. 68.
CORDING, J. C. & CO, LTD. 69.
CORNISH, JOHN. 69.
CORNWALL CARTRIDGE WORKS. 69, 70.
CORPORATION OF LONDON. 70.
COTON, WALTER. 70, 71.
COTSWOLD GAME FARM SERVICES, LTD. 71.
COULSON'S. 71, 72.
COUNTRY GENTLEMEN'S ASSOCIATION. 71, 72.
COUNTRYSIDE ALIANCE. 72.
COX & CLARKE. [Southampton] 72.
COX, W. & SON. [Southampton] 72, 73.
COZENS & SHAW, LTD. 73.
CREIGHTON, G. 73.
CROCKART, D. B. [Perth] 74.
CROCKART, D. & CO. [Stirling] 73.
CROCKART, JAS & SON. [Blairgowrie] 74.
CROSS BROS, LTD. [Cardiff] 74.
CROSS, S. B. [Birkenhead] 74.
CROWE RONNIE, LTD. 74.
CRUDGINGTON, I. M, LTD. 75.
CURTIS'S & HARVEY'S, LTD. 75, 76, 77.

DAINTITH, THOMAS. 77.
DANSK PATRON INDUSTRI (D.P.I.). 77.
DARLOW & CO. [Norwich] 78.
DARLOW, WALTER, LTD. [Norwich] 78.
DAVIDSON, JAMES A. 78, 79.
DAVIE, FRANCIS. 79.
DAVIES HOWARD. A. [Winchester] 79.
DAVIES, PETER J. [Heathfield] 79.
DAVIES, T. [Llandyssul] 80.

DAVIS, ALFRED. 80.
DAW, GEORGE H. [London] 80.
DAW & CO. [Calcutta] 80.
DAWSON, F. 80.
DE LAMBERT, A. 80.
DELORME, A. 81.
DENNIS, ARTHUR. 81.
DEREHAM GUN & TACKLE. 81.
DESBOROUGH & SON. 81.
DEVON & SOMERSET STORES, LTD. 81.
DICKINS, JOHN T. 81, 82.
DICKSON, JOHN & SON, LTD. 82, 83, 84.
DINWOODIE & NICHOLSON. 84.
DISTIN, E. & SON. 84.
DIXON & CO. 84.
DOBSON & ROSSON. 84.
DODD, D. D. [Shipdham] 84.
DODD, G. [Birmingham] 85.
DONALDSON, W. G. 85.
DOSSUL A. HAJI & SONS. 85.
DOTT THOMPSON, R. 85.
DOUGALL, JOHN D. 85, 86.
DOUILLES A BROUCHE SOC. 86.
DOUILLES EN ACTER ARMCO. 86.
DOWNING. 86.
DRETSE & COLLINSBUSCH. 87.
DREYES, FREDERICK VON. 87.
DRUM SPORTS, LTD. 87.
DUMOND. 87.
DUNCALFE, A. H, LTD. 87.
DUNCAN, C. V,. & CO. [Hull] 87.
DUNCAN, STANLEY & SONS. [Hull] 88.
DUNMORE SHOOTING CENTRE. 88.
DUNNELL, T. M. 88.
DYER & ROBSON. 88.
DYKE, FRANK & CO, LTD. 88, 89, 90.
DYMOND, MARTIN. 251.

EARLE, G. A. [Bridgnorth] 90.
EARLE, REYNOLS RICHARD. [Hungerford] 90.
EBRALL, R. H. [Hereford] 91.
EBRALL BROS. [Shrewsbury] 91.
E. C. POWDER CO, LTD. 91.
EDINBURGH GUNMAKERS. 91.
EDNIE & KININMONTH. 91, 92.
EDWARDS, AUBREY & CO, LTD. [Swansea] 92.
EDWARDS, LTD. [Newport] 92.
EDWARDS, C. G. & SON. [Plymouth] 92, 93.
EDWARDS, BAYS & RYE. [Swindon] 93.
EDWARDS & MELHUISH. [Birmingham] 93.
EICHEL. 93.
ELAHEE BUKSH & CO. 94.
ELDERKINS & SON. 94.
ELEY BROS, LTD. [London] 80, 82, 84, 86, 94-109, 115, 140, 146, 149, 169, 173, 178, 225, 281-286, 294, 295, 312, 319, 326, 354, 371, 384, 389, Page VI.
ELEY BROS (CANADA), LTD. 107, 108.
ELEY, LTD & ELEY HAWK, LTD. 108, 109.

ELEY I.M.I. AMMUNITION DIVISION. 109.
ELLICOTT. [Cardiff] 110.
ELLICOTT, WILLIAM. [Launceston] 110.
ELLIOTT. 110.
ELTON STORES. 110, 111.
ELVEDEN ESTATE. 111.
ELVEDEN ESTATE GUN CLUB. 111.
EMSLIE, DAVID. 111.
ENTWISTLE, S. 111.
ERRE. 111.
EVANS, C. A. [Burford] 112.
EVANS, THOMAS J. [Welshpool] 112.
EVANS, WILLIAM, LTD. [London] 112, 113, 114.
EVILL, ALAN & CO. 114.
EXPLOSIFS DE CLERMONT MULLER & CIE. 114.
EXPLOSIVES TRADES, LTD. (E.T.L.). 114, 115.

FABRIQUE NATIONALE D'ARMES. 115.
FALKE. 115.
FARMER, RICHARD. 115.
FARM HEALTH, LTD. 115.
FARRELL, G. F. & SONS. 116.
FARRELLY, BRYAN & SONS. 116.
FINCH, B. & SONS. 116.
FIOCCHI USA/LMCS. 116.
FIRLE SHOOT. 116.

FIRMS NOT KNOWN. 93, 111, 115, 253, 399-403.

F.I.T.A.S.C. 10th CHAMPIONSHIPS (AUSTRALIA). 116, 117.
FITCHEW, A. T. 117.
FLETCHER, C. [Leeds] 117.
FLETCHER, ELIZABETH. [Gloucester] 117.
FLETCHERS (SPORTS), LTD. [Gloucester] 117.
FLINT, H. & A. 118.
FLOBERT. 118.
FODEN, G. 118.
FORD, WILLIAM. 118, 119.
FOREST OF BERE ESTATE. 119.
FORREST & SONS. 119.
FOSTER, A. J. 119, 120.
FOX, CECIL. [Canterbury] 120.
FOX, ISAAC. [Canterbury] 120.
FRANCIS, CHARLES & SON. [Peterborough] 121.
FRANCIS & DEAN. [Stamford] 121.
FRASER, JOHN. [Edinburgh] 122.
FRASER, NORMAN, LTD. [Churchdown] 122.
FRENCH, W. H. & SON. 122.
FREENEY'S. 122.
FERES, REY. 122.
FROST, E. [.Exeter] 122.
FROST, EDWARD. [Bridlington] 123.
FRY, JOHN. 123.

FUSSELL'S, LTD. 123.

GALBRAITH, W. 123.
GALE, EDWARD & SON. 123, 124.
GALLOYN & SONS, LTD. 124, 125.
GAMAGE, A. W, LTD. 125.
GAMBLE, JOHN G. 126.
GAMEBORE CARTRIDGE CO. 126.
GARDEN, WILLIAM. 127.
GARDINER, T. M. 127.
GARDNER, WILLIAM. 127.
GARNETT, M. & SON. 127.
GARRETT, FRANK. 127, 128.
GATES OF BALDOCK. 128'
GATES TRACTORS. [Saffron Walden] 128.
GAUPILLAT. 128.
GEORGE, FREDERICK WILLIAM.
 [High Wycombe] 128.
GEORGE, W. J. [Dover] 129.
GEVELOT. [Paris] 129.
GEVELOT & CO. [London] 129.
GIBBS, GEORGE. 129, 130.
GILBERT, A. C. & SON, LTD. 131.
GILMAN, J.& SON, LTD. 131
GIULIO FIOCCHI LECCO. 131.
GLIDDON, J. & SONS. 131.
GLOBEMASTER ARMS & AMMUNITION. 132.
GODFREY, W. & SONS. 132.
GOLDEN, WILLIAM. 132.
GOLDING, C. E. 132.
GORDON CARTRIDGE CO. [Sydney] 132.
GORDON, FRANK R. [Wigton] 132.
GOW, JOHN R. & SONS. 133.
GOWER, OLIVER J, LTD. 133.
GRAHAM, G. P. [Cockermouth] 133.
GRAHAM, JOHN & CO, LTD. [Inverness]
 133, 134.
GRANT, STEPHEN & SON. [London] 134.
GRANT & LANG. [London] 134, 135.
GRAY, D. & CO. [Inverness] 135.
GRAY, DON (GUNS). [Chatham] 135.
GRAY, REGINALD. [Doncaster] 135.
GREEN, EDWINSON C. & SONS. 135, 136.
GREENER, WILLIAM W. 136-139.
GREENFIELD. [Storington] 140.
GREENFIELD, H. S. & SON. [Canterbury] 140.
GREENFIELD OF SALISBURY, LTD. 139, 140.
GREENWOOD & BATLEY. 141'
GREGSON. 140.
GRENFELL & ACCLES. 140.
GRIMES, S. J. 141.
GUINARD, A. 141.
GUN COUNTER, THE. 141.
GUNNERSIDE SHOOT. 141, 142.

HADDON, J. B. 142.
HAERENS KRUDTVAERK. 142.
HAFIZ GHOUSE & CO. 142.
HALL, C. & CO. [Knaresborough] 142.
HALL, FRANK. [Chesterfield] 143.

HALL, HUGH. [Wetherby] 143.
HALL, J. [Wigton] 143.
HALL, JOHN & SON. [London] 143,144.
HALLIDAY, B. & CO, LTD. 144.
HAMMANT'S. 145.
HAMMOND BROS. 145.
HAMPSHIRE ARMS CO. 145.
HANCOCK, W. T. 146.
HAND BROS. 146.
HANDY, G. J. & CO, LTD. 146.
HANSON, L. 146.
HARDING, J. 146.
HARDY BROS (ALNWICK), LTD.
 146-148..
HARDY, J. C. [Holbeach] 148.
HARKON, JOSEPH & SON. 148.
HARPER, PERCY J. 148.
HARPUR BROS. 148.
HARRIS, GEORGE & A. [Uttoxeter] 148.
HARRIS SCARFE, LTD. [Adelaide] 149.
HARRISON & HUSSEY, LTD. 149.
HARRODS STORES. 149, 150.
HART, E. F. [Clare] 150.
HART, FRED W. [Scarborough] 150.
HARTHAM PARK ESTATE. 150.
HARTLEY'S SPORTS STORE. 151.
HARVEY, A. B. & SON, LTD. [Falmouth] 151.
HARVEY SHAW SUCCESSORS. [Melbourne]
 151, 152.
HASHIM S. HASHIM. 152.
HAWKES BROS. [Geelong] 152
HAWKES & SONS, LTD. [Taunton] 152.
HAWKE, G. & SON. [St Austell] 153.
HAYGARTH, COLIN H. 153.
HAYMAN, HENRY ROBERT. 153.
HAYNES, WILLIAM. 153.
HAYWARD, S. E. & CO, LTD. 154.
HAZEL, R. 154.
HEAL, W. E, LTD. 154.
HEATHMAN, T., LTD. 154.
HELLIS, CHARLES & SONS, LTD.
 [London] 7, 154-158.
HELLIS-ROSSON, LTD. [Norwich] 158, 159.
HEMING, W. 159.
HENDERSON. 159.
HENRITE EXPLOSIVES. 159, 237.
HEPPLESTONE, T. 160.
HERCULES ARMAMENT CO, LTD. 160.
HERRING, W. 160.
HESFORD, C. M. & CO, LTD. 160.
HESKETH ESTATE. 160.
HEYER, CHARLES A. & CO. 161.
HEYWOOD & HODGE. 161.
HIBBARD W. G, SPENCER F. F. &
 BARTLETT, A. L. 161.
HIGGINS, HARRY. 161.
HIGHAM, E. & G. [Liverpool] 161.
HIGHAM, GEORGE G. [Oswestry] 162.
HIGHCLERE CASTLE ESTATE. 42, 162, 163.
HILL, ARTHUR & SON. 163.

HILLSDON, RUSSELL. 163.
HINGSTON-SMITH ARMS CO, LTD. 164.
HINTON, GEORGE & SONS, LTD. 164.
HIRTENBERG. 164.
H. M. GOVERNMENT OF GREAT BRITAIN.
 3, 165-167.
HOBSON, J. 167.
HOCKNELL, A. S. 167.
HODGSON, A. A. [Louth] 168.
HODGSON, HENRY. [Bury St Edmunds] 168.
HODGSON, R. C. [Ripon] 168.
HODGSON, R. T. [Harrogate] 168.
HODGSON, WILLIAM. [Ripon] 168, 169.
HOFFUNG, S. & Co, Ltd. 169.
HOLKHAM ESTATE. 169.
HOLLAND, C. R. [Cirencester] 169.
HOLLAND & HOLLAND, LTD. [London]
 170-172.
HOLLIS, ISAAC. 173, 197.
HOLTOM. 173.
HOME. 173.
HOOKE, T. J. & SON. 173.
HOOTON & JONES. 173, 174.
HOPKINS, H. G. & SONS. [Sandbach] 174.
HOPKINS, J. J, LTD. [Leighton Buzzard] 174.
HOPPING, ERNEST ALFRED. 174.
HORDERNS, ANTHONY. 174.
HORI, K. K. & CO,INC. 174.
HORRELL & SON. 175.
HORTON, W. 175.
HORSLEY, THOMAS & SONS, LTD. 175.
HOULLIER BLANCHARD PIDAULT SUCC.
 175.
HOWARD BROS. 176.
HOWE, WILLIAM & SONS. 176.
HOWES & SONS. 176.
HULL, T. L. & CO. [Shaftesbury] 177.
HULL CARTRIDGE CO, LTD [Hull] 176, 177.
HUNGERFORD PARK ESTATE. 177.
HUNTER & SON. 177.
HURLSTONE, WILLIAM. 177.
HUSSEY, H. J. Ltd. 178.
HUTCHINSON. 178.

ILCHESTER ESTATES. 178.
ILSLEY. 178.
IMPERIAL CHEMICAL INDUSTRIES, I.C.I.
 METALS, ELEY-KYNOCH, LTD. 128, 165,
 179-191, 229, 231, 242, 243, 303,353.
IMPERIAL CHEMICAL INDUSTRIES OF
 AUSTRALIA & NEW ZEALAND. 191-194.
IMPERIAL METAL INDUSTRIES (KYNOCH),
 LTD. [Birmingham] 194, 195.
IMPERIAL METAL INDUSTRIES (I.M.I.)
 AUSTRALIA. 195.
INGRAM, CHARLES. 197.
IRISH METAL INDUSTRIES, LTD. 196, 197.

JACKSON, ALFRED. [Abergavenny] 198.
JACKSON, WILLIAM & SON. [Gainsboro] 198.

JAKTKLUBB. 198.
JAMES & CO. [Hungerford] 198,199.
JAMES, M. & SONS. [Newcastle Emlyn] 199.
JAMES & TATTON. [London] 199.
JARRY, P. 199.
JEFFERY, A. R. & H. V, LTD. [Plymouth]
 199, 200.
JEFFERY, CHARLES & SONS. [Dorchester]
 200.
JEFFERY, SAMUEL RICHARD. [Guildford]
 200, 201.
JEFFERY, WILLIAM & SON. [Plymouth]
 201,202.JEFFERY, W. J. & CO, LTD.
 [London] 202-204.
JEWSON, ALFRED J. 205.
JOBSON, G. 205.
JOHNSON, ROBERT BRINDLY. [March] 205.
JOHNSON, THOMAS & SON. [Swaffham] 206.
JOHNSON & REID. [Darlington] 206.
JOHNSON & WRIGHT, LTD. [Northampton]
 206.
JONES, H. [Wrexham] 207.
JONES & SON. [Malmesbury] 206.
JONES, ROBERT. [Liverpool] 207.
JONES, WILLIAM PALMER (GUNS), LTD.
 [Birmingham] 207.
JOYCE, FREDERICK & CO. 78, 208-210.
JULIAN, H. & SONS, LTD. 210.

KAVANAGH, WILLIAM & SON. 211, Page VII.
KEEGAN, L. 211, Page VII.
KEMPTON, H. 212.
KENT, ALFRED & SON. [Wantage] 212, 213.
KENT, JOHN. [Wantage] 213.
KENT CARTRIDGE MANUFACTURING CO.
 [Tonbridge] 213.
KENYON & TROTT. 213.
KERR, CHARLES. 213.
KILLEEN, JOHN J. 214.
KINGDON, T. M. & CO, LTD. 214.
KINGSTONE LISLE SHOOT. 214.
KIRK, JAMES. 214.
KIRKEE FACTORY. 215.
KITHER. 215.
KNIGHT, J. H. [Wells] 215.
KNIGHT, PETER. [Nottingham] 215, 216.
KOLN-ROTTWEILER AG. 216.
KRIDER, JOHN. 216.
KRUCKL. 216.
KYNOCH, GEORGE & CO, LTD. 35, 42, 81,
 130, 132, 146, 159, 216-223, 258, 259,
 281-284, 288, Page VI.

LACE. 223, Page VI.
LACEY, J. & H. 223.
LADY'S WOOD SHOOTING SCHOOL, LTD.
 223.
LAKER, E. 223.
LAMBERT, S. A. (GUNSMITH). [Guestling] 223.
LAMBERT, T. LTD. [York] 224.

LANE BROS. [Faringdon] 224.
LANE, CHARLES E. [Peterchurch] 224.
LANE, CHARLES L. [Bridgewater] 224.
LANE, FRANK & CO. [Faringdon] 225.
LANCASTER, CHARLES & CO, LTD. 225, 226, Page VI.
LANG, JOSEPH H. Later, SON, LTD. 226, 227.
LANGDON, JOHN. 227.
LANGLEY, JAMES JOHN. [Luton] 227, 228.
LANGLEY & LEWIS. [Luton] 228.
LAW, THOMAS. Also, THOMAS (JUNIOR). 228.
LAWN & ALDER. 228, 229.
LAYCOCK, J. F. 229.
LEACH, R. 229.
LEATHAM. 229.
LEECH, WILLIAM & SONS. 229, 230.
LEGGETT, HERBERT E. 230.
LEMON, JOHN & SON, LTD. 230.
LEONARD, CHARLES. 230.
LEON BEAUX & CO. 231.
LEWIS. [Wells] 231.
LEWIS, AUBREY. [Luton] 231.
LEWIS, EDWIN GEORGE. [Basingstoke] 232.
LIBERTY CARTRIDGE CO. 232.
LIDDELL & SONS. 232.
LILAND WING SHOOTING. 232.
LIMMEX & CO. 232.
LINCOLN JEFFRIES. 233.
LINDARS, PETER (GUNS). 233.
LININGTON, JAMES H. 233.
LINSLEY BROS. 233, 234.
LISLE, ROBERT. 234.
LITTLE, H. C. & SON. [Yeovil] 235.
LITTLE HAMPDEN ESTATE. [High Wycombe] 235.
LIVERSIDGE, CHARLES FREDERICK. 235.
LLOYD & SONS. 235, 236.
LOCH, C. H. 236.
LOCKE, WALTER & CO, LTD. 236.
LONDON SPORTING PARK. 237.
LOVERIDGE & CO. 237.
LOWER HOPE ESTATE. 237.
LUCK'S EXPLOSIVES, LTD. 237.
LYAVALE, LTD. 238.
LYON & LYON, LTD. 238, 239.

McCALL, WILLIAM & SONS, LTD. 239.
McCALL, WILLIAM & CO. 239.
McCOLL & FRASER. 240.
McEWAN, JAMES & CO. 240.
McGALDIN. 240.
McKAY-BROWN, DAVID. 240.
McMORRAN, W. 240.
McSORLEY, JOHN. 242.
MACKENZIE & DUNCAN. 240.
MACNAUGHTON, JAMES & SONS. 241.
MACPHERSON, JOHN. 241, 242.
MAG-NIS. 242.
MAHILLON, H. 242, 243.
MALCOMSON, J. 243.

MALEHAM, CHARLES HENRY. 243.
MALLINSONS. 244.
MALLOCH, PETER D. 244.
MANBY, ALLAN. [Southwood] 245.
MANBY, F. & BROS. [Skipton] 245.
MANOR OF CADLAND ESTATE. 245.
MANTON & CO, LTD. 245, 246.
MANUFACTURE FRANCAISE D'ARMES. 246.
MARATOS, GEORGE. [Alexandria] 247.
MARATOS, N. & SON. [Port Said] 247.
MARK, STEWART J. 247.
MARLBOROUGH GUN SHOP. 247, 248.
MARSHALL, SONS & CO. [Gainsborough] 248.
MARSHALL & PEARSON. [Fort William] 248.
MARTIN, A. H. [Abergavenny] 249.
MARTIN, ALEX, LTD. [Glasgow] 249, 250.
MARTIN, ROY. [Dunham-on-Trent] 250.
MARTIN DYMOND. [Callington] 251.
MARTIGNONI. 251.
MARSDEN, T. & SONS, LTD. 251.
MARY ARM. 251.
MASON, J. F. 252.
MATHER, J. & CO. 252.
MAWBY, W. & SON. 252.
MAWER & SAUNDERS. 252.
MEMBURY ESTATE. 252.
MEGGINSON, B. 252.
MELBOURNE SPORTS DEPOT. 253.
MELLARD, W. 253.
METCALF, G. F. [Burton-on-Trent] 253.
METCALFE, R. [Richmond] 253.
METCALFE, W. [Richmond] 253.
METROLE. 253.
MICHIE, G. M. 254.
MIDLAND GUN CO. 254-256.
MILBURN, W. & SON. 257.
MILLS BROS. 258.
MODERN ARMS CO, LTD. 258.
MOGG, B.D. & SON. 258.
MONARCH GUN WORKS. 258.
MONK, HENRY W. 258, 259.
MONTAGU, LORD. 24, 259.
MOODY, CHARLES. [Romsey] 259.
MOODY, W. F. [Romsey] 259.
MOOR, THOMAS HENRY. [South Molton] 260.
MOOR END GAME FARM. [Whitby] 260.
MOORE & GREY. [London] 260.
MORGAN, FREDRICK T. 260.
MORREYS. 260.
MORRIS, H. M. [Burgess Hill] 261.
MORRIS, P. & SON. [Hereford] 261.
MORROW & CO. 261.
MORTIMER & SON. 261, 262.
MOULTON & BENNETT. 262.
MUES, JACK. 262.
MUNITIONSWERKE. 263.
MULLERITE CARTRIDGE WORKS. 20, 24, 37, 87, 153, 263-266, 374.
MULTI-SPORTS. 266.
MUNTHE-BRUN. 266.

MURRAY, T. W. & CO, LTD. 266.

NAUGHTON, T. & SONS. 266, 267.
NAYLOR, C, LTD. 267.
NEEDHAM, J. V. 267.
NELSON, FRAMNCIS. 267.
NESTOR, A. 267, 268.
NETTLEBED SHOOT. 268.
NEWBURY TOOLS, LTD. 268.
NEW EXPLOSIVES CO, LTD. 268-271.
NEWLAND & STIDOLPH, LTD. 271.
NEWNHAM, GEORGE. [Landport] 271.
NEWNHAM & CO. [Landport] 272.
NEW NORMAL AMMUNITION CO. 272.
NEWTON, T. 272.
NEW ZEALAND CARTRIDGE CLUB. 273.
NICKERSON, DAVID (TATHWELL), LTD. 273.
NIGHTINGALE, A. P. & SON, LTD. 273.
NITRO NOBEL. 273.
NITROKOL POWDER CO. 273.
NOBBS, SYDNEY A. 274.
NOBEL EXPLOSIVES CO, LTD. 82, 252, 274-280, 283, 289, 303, 339.
NOBEL INDUSTRIES, LTD (N.I.). 281-291.
NOBEL INDUSTRIES (AUSTRALIA), LTD. 291.
NORMAL POWDER CO. 291, 292.
NORMAN, B. & SONS. 292.
NORTON, C. W. [Newtown] 292.
NORTON ESTATES. [Craven Arms] 293.
NOTT, J. E. & CO. 293.

OAKES & CO. [Madras] 293, 294.
OAKES BROS, LTD. [Newbury] 293.
ODELL, JAMES. 294.
OLBYS, LTD. 294.
OLYMPIC TARGET CO. 294.
ORBEA. 294.
O'RIORDAN & FORREST. 294.
ORMSBY GAME SERVICES. 295.
ORR, P. & SONS, LTD. 295.
OSBORN, JOSEPH PHILLIPS. [Daventry] 296.
OSBORNE, CHARLES & CO. [Birmingham] 295, 296.

PACHMAYR GUN WORKS. 296.
PACKINGTON SHOOTING GROUND. 296.
PAGE WOOD & CO. [Bath] 296.
PAGE WOOD, A. [Bristol] 296.
PAGE-WOOD, THOMAS, LTD. [Bristol] 297, 298.
PALMER, SON & CO. [Barnet] 299.
PALMER, G. [Sittingbourne] 299.
PALMER, W. & H. E. [Rochester] 299.
PAPE, WILLIAM ROCHESTER. 299, 300.
PARAGON GUN SPECIALISTS. 300.
PARKER, HUGH. 301.
PARKINSON, TOM. 301'
PARSON, C. [Nuneaton] 301.
PARSON'S, SHERWIN & CO, LTD. [Nuneaton] 301, 302.

PATSTONE, JOHN & SON. [Southampton] 302.
PATSTONE & COX. [Southampton] 303.
PAXTON, S. & CO. 303.
PEACE, JOSEPH, LTD. 303.
PEARSON & CO. 303.
PELLIER-JOHNSON, CAPTAIN E. 303
PENNY & SON. 304.
PERROTTS, S. 304.
PHILLIPS BROS. [Marlborough] 304.
PHILLIPS & POWIS. [Reading] 304.
PIGNAUD. 304.
PINDER, CHARLES & CO. [Basingstoke] 304.
PINDER, J. E. [Salisbury] 305.
PITT, HERBERT B. 305.
PLUMBERS, LTD. 305'
PNEUMATIC CARTRIDGE CO, LTD. 305-307.
POLISH STATE AMMUNITION. 307.
POLLARD, HERBERT E. & CO. 307, 308.
POND & SON. 308.
PORTER, S. E. & CO. 308.
POSTANS, J. M. 308.
POTTER, R. C. [High Wycombe] 309.
POTTER & CO. [High Wycombe] 309.
POTTER, R. & E. [Thame] 309.
POUDERIES REUNIES DE BELGIQUE (P.R.B.). 309, 310.
POWELL, T. & CO. [Salisbury] 310.
POWELL, WILLIAM & SON, LTD. [Birmingham] 310, 311.
POWELL, W. J. [Leiston] 312.
PRATT, ALBERT. 312.
PRENTICE, THOMAS & CO. 312.
PRESTON & DISTRICT FARMERS TRADING SOCIETY, LTD. 312.
PRESTWICH & SON. 312.
PROGRESIVE CARTRIDGE CO. 312.
PUGH, C. F. 313.
PULLAN, HENRY. 313.
PULVERFABRIK POWDER FACTORY. 313.
PUNTER, ARTHUR F. 313, 314.
PURCEL, C. 314.
PURDEY, JAMES. [London] 314.
PURDEY, JAMES & SONS, LTD. [London] 314-316.
PURDEY, R. S. [Thirsk] 316.
PURVIS & CO. 316.

QATAR, H.M. THE RULER OF. 317.

RADCLIFFE, K. D. 317.
R.A.F. LAKENHEATH ROD & GUN CLUB. 318.
RAINE BROS. 318.
RAKER. 318.
RAMSBOTTOM, R. 318.
RANDELL, F, LTD. 318.
RANSTON ESTATE. 318.
RAUFOSS AMMUNISJONS FABRIKKER. 319.
RAY, M. 319
REILLY, E. M. & CO. 319.

XIX

REMINGTON U.M.C. CO. 127, 319.
REMINGTON (ENGLAND). 320-322.
REYNOLDS, E. G. E. [Saxmundham] 322.
REYNOLDS, J. [Cullompton] 322.
RHEINISCHE WESTFALISCHE SPRINGSTOFF. 332.
RICHARDS, C. C. [Wiveliscombe] 323.
RICHARDS, WILLIAM (LIVERPOOL), LTD. 323.
RICHARDS, W. [Preston] 324.
RICHARDSON, A. & SONS. [Halesworth] 324.
RICHARDSON, G. M. [Dumfries] 324.
RICHARDSON, WILLIAM GEORGE. [Barnard Castle] 324, 325.
RIGBY, JOHN & CO. 325.
RIGGS, C. & CO, LTD. 325.
RINGWOOD, A. E. 325, 326.
ROBERTS, AUGUSUS J. [Banbury] 326.
ROBERTS, H. P. [Ottery St Mary] 326.
ROBERTSON, ALEXANDER & SON. 326.
ROBIN HOOD AMMUNITION CO. 327.
ROBINSON, ROBERT (GUNMAKERS), LTD. 327.
RODDA, R. B. & CO. 327.
ROSSON, CHARLES & SON. [Derby] 328, 329, 331.
ROSSON, C. S. & CO. [Norwich] 329-332.
ROUSSEAUX. 322.
ROWE & CO. 332.
ROWELL, ROBERT & SONS. 332.
ROWLATT, JOHN. 332.
ROXTON SPORTING, LTD. 333.
ROYAL AIR FORCE B. B. M. F. 333.
ROYAL COUNTY OF BERKSHIRE SHOOTING SCHOOL. 333.
ROYAL SANDRINGHAM ESTATE. 333.
ROYCOTE PARK. 333.
ROY'S STORES. 334.
RUDD, ARTHUR J. 334.
RUSSELL, A. J. & SONS. 334.

SALE, H. F. & SON. 334
SAMPLE, W. 334.
SANDERS, ALFRED. 335, Page VII.
SANDRINGHAM RABBIT CLEARANCE SOCIETY, LTD. 335.
SANDRINGHAM SHOOTING SCHOOL. 335.
SAUL, ROGER. 336.
SAYER'S. 336.
SCHULTZE POWDER CO, LTD. 86, 290, 336, 337.
SCOTCHER, JOHN A. & SON. 337, Page VII.
SELLIER & BELLOT. 337, 338.
SHARP, FREDERICK AUGUSTUS. [Poole] 339.
SHARPE, J. S. [Aberdeen] 339.
SHAW & CO. 339.
SHELTONS GUN & TACKLE. 339.
SHEPHERD, EDWARD LEADER. 339.
SHIMWELL BROS (PTY), LTD. 339.

SHUFFREYS, LTD. 340.
SIMMONS, MICK, LTD. 340.
SIX MILE BOTTOM SHOOT. 340.
SKINNER & CO. 340.
SLINGSBY BROS. 340, Page VII.
SMALL, P. 341.
SMALLWOOD, SAMUEL. 341.
SMITH, ALFRED FISHER. [Hailsham] 342.
SMITH, CHARLES & SONS, LTD. [Newark] 342.
SMITH, C. H. & SONS. [Birmingham] 343.
SMITH, STEVE. [Newcastle-under-Lyme] 343.
SMITH MIDGLEY & CO. [Bradford] 343.
SMITH GORE CHARTERED SURVEYORS. 343.
SMOKELESS POWDER & AMMUNITION CO, LTD. (S.P.& A.). 343.
SMYTHE, J. F, LTD. 344.
SNEEZUM, H. & R. 344.
SOCIETA METALLUR ITALIANA. (S.M.I.). 344.
SOCIETY FRANCAIS DES MUNITIONS. (S.F.M.). 345.
SOUTHERN COUNTIES AGRICULTURAL TRADING SOCIETY. (SCATS). 345.
SOWMAN, J. W. & E, LTD. 345.
SPENCER, ALFRED L. [Richmond] 346.
SPENCER, FREDERICK P. [Newort IoW] 346.
SPORTRIDGE (G.B.). 346.
SQUIRES, HENRY C. 346.
STANBURY, PERCY. [Exeter] 347.
STANBURY & STEVENS. [Exeter] 346, 347.
STENNER & CO. 347.
STENSBY, THOMAS & CO. 347, 348.
STEPHENS. 348.
STERLING. 348.
STIRK, CHARLES J. & SON. 349.
STOCKER, A. J. & C. & E. 349.
STOCKTON SHOOT. 349.
STREET, JOHN & SON. 349.
STRONG, J. & SON. 349.
STUCHBERY'S STORES. 350.
STUDLEY. 350.
STYPE ESTATE. 350.
SUPER CARTRIDGE CO PTY, LTD. 350.
SWINFEN, J. 351.
SYKES BROS. [Ossett] 351.
SYKES, ROBERT & SONS. [Stalybridge] 351.

TAL-Y-BONT ESTATE. 351.
TARDEY FERRES. 351.
TARR, WILLIAM & SONS. 351.
TAYLOR, ALBERT. [Newbury] 352.
TAYLOR, JOHN T. & SON. [Bromsgrove] 352.
TAYLOR, S. R. & SONS, LTD. [Penzance] 352.
TAYLOR & JONES. [Monmouth] 352.
TEIFI VALLEY SHOOTING SUPPLIES. 352.
TEIKOKU E' YAKKYOSEIZA. 352.
TEMPLE & CO. 353.
TERLING PLACE. 353.
TEST VALLEY SPORTING GUNS. 353.
THACKER & CO. 353.
THRIPLAND, R, & SON. 353

THUMPERS. 353.
THURMAN, W. H. C. 354.
TICKNER, WILLIAM JAMES. 354.
TILL, WILLIAM C, LTD. 354.
TILNEY, R. & SON. 354.
TILY & BROWN, LTD. 354.
TIMS, FREDERICK H. 354.
TINNING, JOHN. 355.
TISDALL, JOHN. [Chichester] 355.
TISDALL, W. H, LTD. [Wellington NZ] 355.
TRENT GUN & CARARTIDGE WORKS. 165, 356, 357.
TROISDORF. 357.
TROUGHTON, S. 357.
TRULOCK BROS. [Dublin] 358.
TRULOCK & HARRISS. [Dublin] 358.
TRYON & CO. 358.
TUCKER, ANDREW, LTD. 359.
TULCHAN ESTATE. 359.
TURNER, ARTHUR (SHEFFIELD), LTD. 359.
TURNER, HENRY A, LTD. [Marlborough] 359, 360.
TURNER, J. [Penrith] 360.
TURNER, SAM & SONS, LTD. [Northallerton] 360.
TURNER, THOMAS & SONS. [Reading] 360-365.
TURNER, THOS & SONS (READING GUNMAKERS), LTD. 365-367.
TURNERS CARBIDES, LTD. [Hull] 367.
TYLER, JOHN (HIGHBRIDGE), LTD. 367.

UG'LOW, JOHN. 367.
UNION METALIC CARTRIDGE CO. 367, 368.
UNITED KINGDOM CARTRIDGE CLUB. (U.K.C.C.). 368.
UNITED STATES CARTRIDGE CO. 19, 368.
URTON, WILLIAM, LTD. 368.

VALE IRONMONGERS. 368.
VAUX, J. C. 368.
VENABLES, JOHN & SON. 369.
VODAFONE, LTD. 370.
VON DREYES, FREDERICK. 370.

WADDON, H. J. 370.
WAGSTAFF, R. H. & CO. 370.
WALES, D. 370.
WALKER, JAMES B. 370.
WALKERSLOW SHOOT. 371.
WALKINGTON, H. 371.
WALLAS, D. H, LTD. [Wigton] 371.
WALLAS, WILLIAM. [Wigton] 371.
WALLEY & WINDOWS. 371.
WALLIS BROS. 372.
WALSHE, A. P. 372.
WANLESS BROS. [Sunderland] 373.
WANLESS, W. [Sunderland] 373.
WARD, J. & SON. [Worcester] 373.
WARD THOMPSON. A. [Middlesboro] 373.

WARD THOMPSON. [Stockton-on-Tees] 373, 374.
WARD THOMPSON BROS. [Middlesborough] 374.
WARING, EDWIN. 374.
WARNER, HENRY F. & SON. [Newton Abbot] 374.
WARNERS. [Bantry] 375.
WARREN, A. E. 375.
WARRICK, JOHN. 375.
WARRILOW, JAMES BAKEWELL. 375.
WATKINS & CO. 375.
WATSON BROS, LTD. [London] 376.
WATSON, JAS R. & CO. [London] 252, 376-378.
WATSON BRACEWELL. [Peebles] 378.
WEBBER, J. & SONS. [Exeter] 378.
WEBBER & SAUNDERS. [Tiverton] 379.
WEBBERS. [Honiton] 378.
WEBSTER, G. R. 379.
WEEKS, F. 379.
WELCH, W. A. 379.
WELLS, H. & SON. 380.
WELSH, WILLIAM. 380.
WEST & SON. [Gt Yarmouth] 381.
WEST, E. & SON. [Retford] 380, 381.
WEST COUNTRY SHOOTING. 381.
WESTERN CARTRIDGE CO. 381, 382.
WESTLEY RICHARDS. 382-385.
WEST LONDON SHOOTING SCHOOL. 385.
WESTON, C. & A. [Brighton] 385.
WESTON, CHARLES & HERBERT. [Brighton] 385, 386.
W.F.S, LTD. 386.
WHALEY, T. & SON. 386.
WHITBY & CO. 386.
WHITE, T. R. & CO. 386.
WHITEHOUSE, JOHN EDWARD & SONS. 387.
WHITEMAN, FRANK SIDNEY [Wallingford] 387.
WHITEMAN BROS, LTD. [Worcester] 387.
WILDER. 387.
WILDMAN, H. W. 388.
WILKES, JOHN. 388.
WILKINSON. [Durham] 388.
WILKINSON. [Penrith] 388.
WILKINSON, JAMES (SWORD) Co, Ltd. [London] 388.
WILLCOCKS, J. W. 389.
WILLIAMS, HARRY. [Newport IoW] 389.
WILLIAMS J. S. [Pontypridd] 389.
WILLIAMSON & SON. [Ludlow] 389'
WILLIAMSON, D. [London] 389.
WILSON, EDWIN. [Norwich] 389.
WILSON, GEOFFREY. [Skipton] 390.
WILSON, J. & SONS. [St Andrews] 390.
WILSON, JAMES & SONS. [York] 390.
WILTSHIRE ROD & GUN. 390.
WINCHESTER REPEATING ARMS CO. (W.R.A.Co) 391

WINCHESTER (AUSTRALIA) PTY, LTD.
  391, 392.
WINCHESTER-WESTERN DIVISION. 392.
WINDER, GEORGE. 392.
WINDSOR GUNS & FIELD SPORTS. 392.
WINSTON GAME FARM. 392.
WISE, RICHARD. 393.
WOBURN ABBEY ESTATE. 393.
WOBURN RABBIT CLEARANCE SOCIETY,
  LTD. 393.
WOLFF & CO. 393.
WOOD, ARTHUR (NEWPORT I.W.), LTD. 394.
WOOD, F. [Salisbury] 394.
WOOD, J.L. [Stamford] 394.
WOOD & HORSPOOL. [Newport IoW] 394.
WOODROW, R. J. 394, 395.
WOODS, EDMUND. [London] 395.
WOODS, GEORGE L. [Ovington] 395.
WOODWARD, JAMES & SONS. 396.
WOOLISCROFT. 397.
WREN, GEORGE. 397.
WRIGHT, RANDELL. [Spalding] 397.
WRIGHT & CURREY. [Spalding] 397.
WRIGHTS. [Maldon] 397.
WYLIE, A. B, LTD. 398.
WYMAN & ABBOTT. 398.

www.ingramcontent.com/pod-product-compliance
Lightning Source LLC
Chambersburg PA
CBHW080849010526
44115CB00015B/2771